Fodor's

ESSENTIAL FRANCE

Welcome to France

Famed artists, writers, gourmands, and bon vivants have all been put under France's intoxicating spell. And travelers can still relish the same enchanting attractions, from Matisse's coastal villages to Hemingway's Parisian cafés to Marie-Antoinette's pastoral escape inside Versailles. France is a gastronomic wonderland, an artistic mecca, and a historical pop-up book. Vineyards blanket the wine regions, cathedrals crown the cities, and sandy beaches drape the coastline. With all these riches, you may start plotting your return visit before you even return home.

TOP REASONS TO GO

★ **Marvelous Food:** From the humble café to haute cuisine, the French know how to eat.

★ **Fairy-Tale Castles and Châteaux:** The elegance and majesty of France's past endure.

★ **Shopping:** Parisian luxuries, famed street markets, and handicrafts all beckon.

★ **Wineries and Vineyards:** White to red, you can sip your way across the countryside.

★ **Awesome Art:** From the grand, sprawling Louvre to the intimate Atelier Cézanne.

★ **Charming Villages:** Countryside hamlets with pretty cottages are plentiful.

Contents

EXPERIENCE
FRANCE

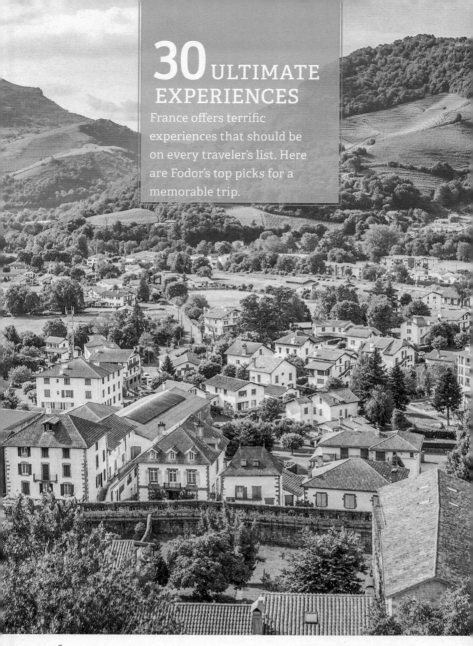

30 ULTIMATE EXPERIENCES

France offers terrific experiences that should be on every traveler's list. Here are Fodor's top picks for a memorable trip.

1 | Hiking the Pyrenees

Spanning the border of France and Spain, a hike in the Pyrenees Mountains can take you through towns like St-Jean-Pied-de-Port and to the Vignemale, the highest summit in southern France. *(Ch. 17)*

2 Skiing the French Alps

The Alps stand tall over the eastern side of the country, a land of snow-covered slopes, cozy cities, and high-fashion ski resorts. *(Ch. 11)*

3 Grand Cathedrals

For centuries, France was a proudly Christian nation, a legacy that can be seen in its many exquisitely designed cathedrals, like ones in Amiens and Chartres. *(Ch. 4, 8)*

4 World War II History in Normandy

When Allied troops landed on the beaches of Normandy on D-Day, the region became forever linked with World War II. A 25-mile historic trail takes you to Utah and Omaha beaches, and more. *(Ch. 6)*

5 The Lavender Route

Join the lavender-happy crowds from June to mid-July and travel the Route de la Lavande, a 560-mile blue-purple swath that produces a third of the world's lavender. *(Ch. 12)*

6 The Camargue

Take an unforgettable *promenade équestre* (horseback tour) of the Parc Régional de Camargue, an amazing nature park in Provence home to bulls and birds, including 50,000 flamingos. *(Ch. 12)*

7 Toulouse

The modern gateway to the south of France, Toulouse's brick-paved streets, rosy roofs, and redbrick mansions give the city its nickname: "La Ville Rose" (the Pink City). *(Ch. 16)*

8 Versailles

The famous château was home to Louis XIV and Marie Antoinette and remains the grandest palace in France, from its Hall of Mirrors to the landscaped gardens. *(Ch. 4)*

9 Carcassonne

Protected by a double ring of ramparts and 53 towers, this perfectly preserved fortified city is considered to be one of the most romantic medieval settings in France. *(Ch. 16)*

10 La Cité du Vin, Bordeaux

Before you visit the St-Émilion wine route, one of the world's best, head to the city of Bordeaux and La Cité du Vin, a museum dedicated to the history of wine making in the region. *(Ch. 18)*

11 German Culture in Alsace

As you head down Alsace's Wine Road, picturesque Hansel and Gretel villages pop up every few miles, and each has *winstubs* (wine bistros) serving up delicious German cuisine. *(Ch. 9)*

12 Champagne

The Route du Champagne leads fans of the famous bubbly to the prestigious champagne houses (and their caves) of Épernay and Reims (including Ruinart and Taittinger). *(Ch. 8)*

13 Basque Culture

An independent community in northern Spain and southern France located near the Pyrenees Mountains, the Basque are defined by their food, drink, and sports, including jai alai. *(Ch. 17)*

14 French Cafés

Still the center of social life for many French locals, neighborhood cafés offer great food and coffee, and even better people-watching. *(Ch. 3-19)*

15 Mont-St-Michel

Climb to the top and get a breathtaking view of this fabled Benedictine abbey, whose fortified medieval village is the crowning glory of the Normandy coastline. *(Ch. 6)*

16 Paris

From the Louvre to the Eiffel Tower, the City of Lights is considered by many to be the crowning jewel of France and perhaps the best city in the entire world. *(Ch. 3)*

17 The Lascaux Caves

Within the Dordogne region, the impressive Lascaux Caves are filled with Paleolithic drawings, etchings, and carvings that give a glimpse of France's first inhabitants. *(Ch. 19)*

18 Cycling in the Loire Valley

A 500-mile bike path, La Loire à Velo is a UNESCO World Heritage Site that travels through the Loire Valley's vine-covered slopes and emblematic villages. *(Ch. 5)*

19 Joan of Arc History

A patron saint of France, the celebrated folk hero Joan of Arc is still beloved throughout the country. From her seige in Orléans to her death in Rouen, you can retrace her journey to sainthood. *(Ch. 5, 6)*

20 Dining in Lyon

Forget Paris, Lyon is the world's true gastronomic capital, thanks to its galaxy of multistar superchefs and cozy *bouchons* (taverns). *(Ch. 11)*

21 Chateâux

From the humblest feudal ruin to Château d'Usse (the inspiration for *Sleeping Beauty*), the grand castles of France evoke the history of Europe as no museum can. *(Ch. 5)*

22 Shopping

France is a shopper's paradise, from haute couture in glamorous cities like Paris and Cannes to traditional street markets and *marches couvert* (covered markets) in smaller towns. *(Ch. 3, 12, 13)*

23 Carnaval in Nice

Started in 1924, Carnaval de Nice is now the third largest Carnaval celebration in the world. A million masqueraders descend upon the city for the Flower Battle parade. *(Ch. 13)*

24 Snorkeling in Corsica

The Mediterranean's fourth largest island and the birthplace of Napoléon, Corsica offers white sand beaches, clear waters, and a preserved marine environment. *(Ch. 15)*

25 Wineries in Burgundy

Burgundy produces some of the most expensive wines on the planet, with small family-owned producers making up the region's 100 different appellations from 74,000 acres of vineyards. *(Ch. 10)*

26 Artists in Provence

Use Aix-en-Provence, Arles, or Antibes as a base for touring the Modern Art Road, filled with villages and museums immortalized by the likes of Cézanne, Van Gogh, and Picasso. *(Ch. 4, 12, 13)*

27 Seafood in Brittany

Bounded on two of its three sides by water, Brittany is blessed with an abundance of fresh seafood. Cancale oysters are a must. *(Ch. 7)*

28 Provence Villages

Set your clock back 50 years, you've arrived in Provence. Everything here is about food, rosé, and visiting gravity-defying medieval perched villages like Les-Baux-de-Provence and Gordes. *(Ch. 12)*

29 French Riviera Beaches

The surprisingly rocky beaches of the Riviera might be the most affordable way to live like Scott and Zelda Fitzgerald once did in this ritzy part of the country. *(Ch. 13)*

30 Christmas Markets in Strasbourg

Strasbourg's Christmas markets date back to 1570, with a total of 11 markets in the city's Petit France district, the first city center to be named a UNESCO Heritage Site. *(Ch. 9)*

WHAT'S WHERE

1 Paris. A quayside vista that takes in the Seine, a passing boat, Notre-Dame, the Eiffel Tower, and mansard roofs all in one generous sweep is enough to convince you that Paris is indeed the most beautiful city on Earth.

2 Side Trips from Paris. Appearing like all France in miniature, the Ile-de-France region is the nation's heartland. Here Louis XIV built vainglorious Versailles, Chartres brings the faithful to their knees, and Monet's Giverny enchants all.

3 The Loire Valley. Chenonceaux, Chambord, and Saumur—the parade of royal and near-royal châteaux magnificently captures France's golden age of monarchy in an idyllic region threaded by the Loire River.

4 Normandy. Sculpted with cliff-lined coasts, Normandy has been home to saints and sculptors, painters and poets, with a dramatic past marked by Mont-St-Michel's majestic abbey, Rouen's towering cathedral, and the D-Day beaches.

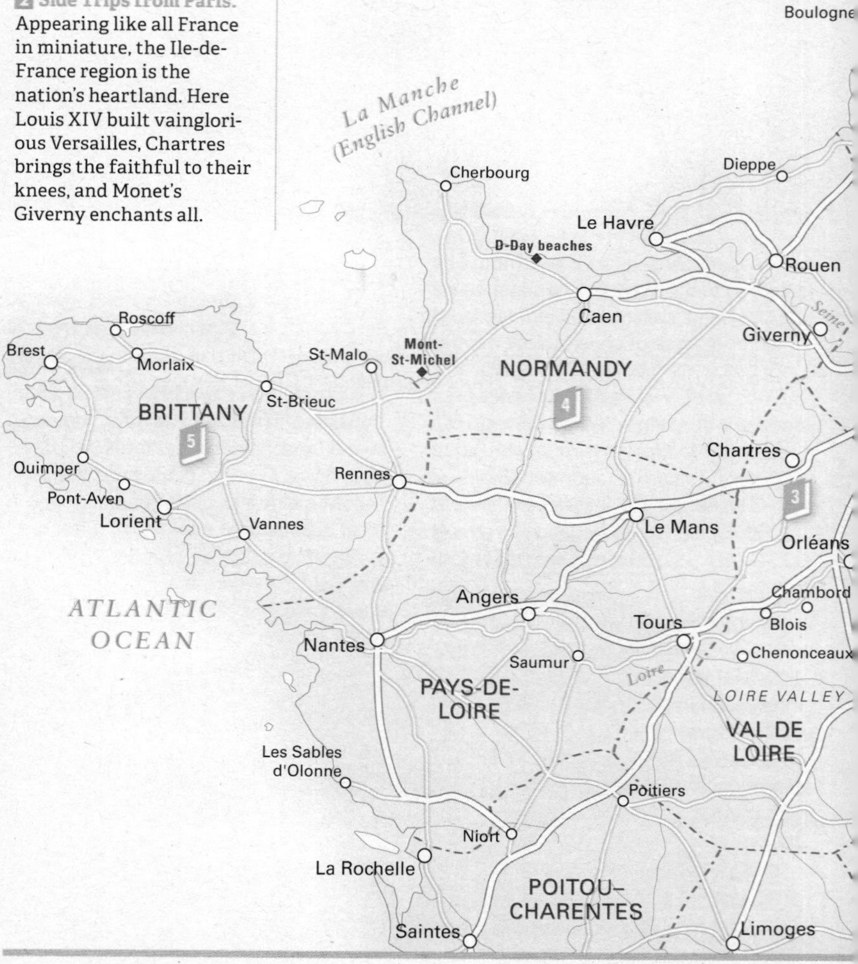

Boulogne

La Manche
(English Channel)

Cherbourg
Dieppe
Le Havre
D-Day beaches
Rouen
Caen
Giverny
Roscoff
Brest
Morlaix
St-Malo
Mont-St-Michel
NORMANDY
St-Brieuc
BRITTANY
5
Chartres
Quimper
Rennes
3
Pont-Aven
Lorient
Vannes
Le Mans
Orléans
ATLANTIC
OCEAN
Angers
Chambord
Nantes
Tours
Blois
Saumur
Chenonceaux
PAYS-DE-LOIRE
Loire
LOIRE VALLEY
VAL DE LOIRE
Les Sables d'Olonne
Poitiers
Niort
La Rochelle
POITOU–CHARENTES
Saintes
Limoges

Seine

5 Brittany. A long arm of rocky land stretching into the Atlantic, Brittany is a place unto itself, with its own language, customs, and time-defying towns, such as Gauguin's Pont-Aven and the pirate haven of St-Malo.

6 Champagne Country. The capital of bubbly is Reims, set near four great Gothic cathedrals and the beginning of the scenic Route de Champagne.

7 Alsace-Lorraine. Although this region bordered by the Rhine often looks German and sounds German, its main sights—18th-century Nancy, medieval Strasbourg, and the lovely Route du Vin—remain proudly French.

8 Burgundy. Hallowed ground for wine lovers, Burgundy hardly needs to be beautiful—but it is. Around the gastronomic hub of Dijon, the region is famed for its verdant vineyards and Romanesque churches.

9 Lyon and the Alps. Local chefs rival their Parisian counterparts in treasure-filled Lyon, the heart of a diverse region where you can ski Mont Blanc or take a heady trip along the Beaujolais Wine Road.

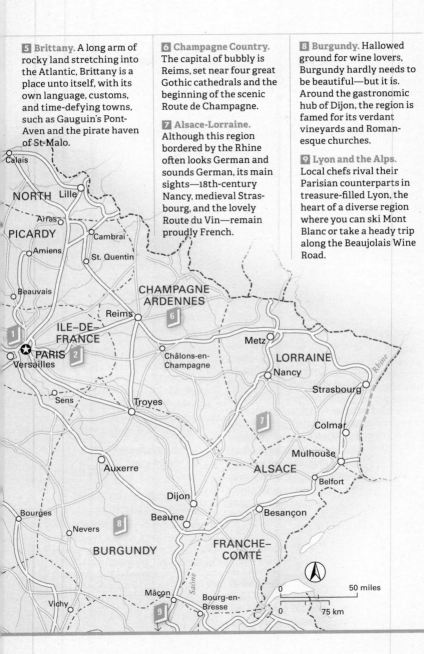

0   50 miles
0   75 km

WHAT'S WHERE

10 Provence. Famed for its Lavender Route, the honey-gold hill towns of the Luberon, and vibrant cities like Aix and Marseilles, this region was dazzlingly abstracted into vivid daubs of paint by Van Gogh and Cézanne.

11 French Riviera. From glamorous St-Tropez to sophisticated Nice, this sprawl of pebble beaches and zillion-dollar houses has always captivated sun lovers and socialites.

12 Monaco. Take the high-rises of Hong Kong, add the Cinderella feel of Disneyland, and mix in the fabulously wealthy, and there you have Monaco—all 473 acres of a princely playground.

13 Corsica. Corsica's gifts of artistic and archaeological treasures, crystalline waters, granite peaks, lush vineyards, and pine forests add up to one of France's most unspoiled sanctuaries.

14 Toulouse and the Languedoc. Rose-hue Toulouse, fairy-tale Carcassone, and the Matisse-beloved Vermillion Coast are among southwest France's most colorful sights.

15 Basque Country, Gascony, and the Hautes-Pyrénées. Whether you head for Bay of Biscay resorts like Biarritz, coastal villages such as St-Jean-de-Luz, or the Pyrenean peaks, this region will cast a spell.

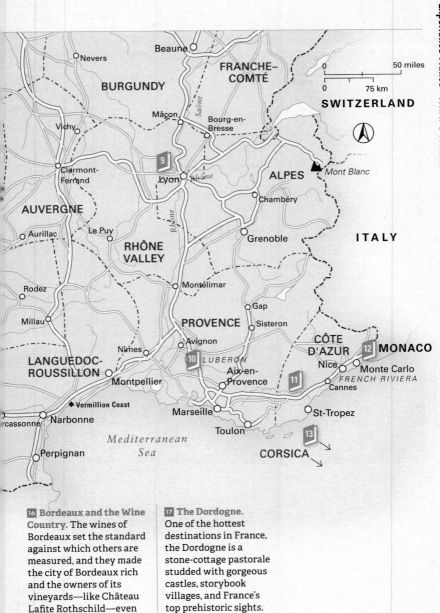

Beaune

Nevers

BURGUNDY

FRANCHE–COMTÉ

0   50 miles

0   75 km

SWITZERLAND

Mâcon

Saône

Bourg-en-Bresse

Vichy

9

Clermont-Ferrand

Lyon

Rhône

ALPES

Mont Blanc

AUVERGNE

Chambéry

Aurillac

Le Puy

RHÔNE VALLEY

Rhône

Grenoble

ITALY

Rodez

Montélimar

Millau

Gap

PROVENCE

Sisteron

Nîmes

Avignon

LANGUEDOC-ROUSSILLON

10   LUBERON

Aix-en-Provence

Montpellier

CÔTE D'AZUR

12   MONACO

Nice

Monte Carlo

FRENCH RIVIERA

11

Cannes

◆ Vermillion Coast

Marseille

St-Tropez

rcassonne   Narbonne

Mediterranean Sea

Toulon

13

Perpignan

CORSICA

16 Bordeaux and the Wine Country. The wines of Bordeaux set the standard against which others are measured, and they made the city of Bordeaux rich and the owners of its vineyards—like Château Lafite Rothschild—even richer.

17 The Dordogne. One of the hottest destinations in France, the Dordogne is a stone-cottage pastorale studded with gorgeous castles, storybook villages, and France's top prehistoric sights.

What to Eat in France

CRÊPES AND GALETTES
The crêpe and its heartier sibling, the galette, can be found in crêperies all over the country. The darker galette is made with tender buckwheat, and is best paired with savory fillings. The golden *sucré crêpe* is made with a lighter batter, and best with sweeter fillings.

FRENCH PASTRIES
For many, the only way to start a morning in France is with a buttery, flaky croissant. Other typical breakfast *viennoiseries* include the *pain au chocolate,* the custardy *pain aux raisins,* brioche with sugar or chocolate chips, and the *chouquette,* a small unfilled puff with sugar crystals.

CASSOULET
This bean stew first appeared in southwest France and became known for its simple ingredients of white beans with pork, sausage, duck confit, and gizzards. The history of cassoulet dates back to the Languedoc region and the 1355 siege of Castelnaudary by the Black Prince, Edward the Prince of Wales.

BOUILLABAISSE
Originating from the fishing port of Marseille, bouillabaisse is made in two parts. First, a broth of small fish, tomatoes, onion, garlic, fennel, olive oil, and saffron (and possibly parsley and potatoes) is made and served with croutons and a garlicky bread-crumb sauce called *rouille*. Next, four to six larger fish are added to the soup and served as a second course.

CANCALE OYSTERS
After the Roman invasion some 2,000 years ago, France and its 2,000 miles of coastline became the first European country to practice *l'ostréiculture* (oyster farming) on a large scale. In particular, Cancale's oyster beds benefit from some of the world's highest tides and strongest currents, which keep the oysters rich in oxygen and plankton, and result in a large, firm yet tender specimen.

CHEESE
There are more than 1,200 varieties of cheese here, 45 of which have a Protected Designation of Origin (AOP) certification. Orange or white, firm or creamy, cheese is recognizable by appearance and texture, and each variety should be eaten according to the season. Don't miss tangy chévre goat cheese from the Loire Valley; opulently creamy Camembert from Normandy; earthy (and not for the faint of heart) Époisses from Burgundy; nutty Munster from Alsace; and gooey Brie from the Ile de France.

Bouillabaisse

COQ AU VIN
This dish gets its name from King Henri IV's promise of a chicken in every peasant's pot. With this winter-warming chicken stew, an entire chicken is braised slowly in red wine from Burgundy, where the dish was first created. It's typically served with *gratin dauphinois* or polenta to soak up the juices.

NOUVELLE CUISINE
Hands down the most influential culinary innovation of the later 20th century, nouvelle cuisine was pioneered by Lyon native son chef Paul Bocuse. A lighter, healthier fare, this new cuisine favors simpler recipes, the freshest possible ingredients, and quick cooking times to highlight the natural flavors of vegetables and meat. While chef Bocuse sadly passed away in early 2018, his culinary genius lives on through several high-end restaurants throughout the country. But for a taste of the original, head to his eponymous restaurant in Lyon, which is widely considered one of the greatest restaurants in the world.

PÉRIGORD TRUFFLES
The winter black truffle of Périgord in the Dordgogne, known as the Black Diamond, is prized for its pungent smell and flavor; it costs on average $1,200 per pound. The price is partly driven by its scarcity, but also due to the specific soil it needs to grow on the roots of oak trees in the Périgord, as well as in a handful of other regions in France.

BŒUF BOURGUIGNON
This was once considered a peasant's meal: one large piece of chewy meat cooked slowly over two days to tenderize and absorb flavor. Burgundy is the birthplace of this beloved beef stew, and no place on Earth makes it better.

What to Drink in France

CALVADOS APPLE BRANDY

Normandy makes its mark in the spirits world with the apple-based Calvados, a fragrant oak-aged brandy. At 40% alcohol, Calvados can be consumed neat, on the rocks, or as the Automne en Normandie, a cocktail that combines apples with Calvados, lemon, and honey.

CHOCOLATE CHAUD

While chocolate was first introduced in France in 1615 for the marriage of Louis XIII and Anne of Austria, it was Louis XV who popularized its consumption as a beverage. He would make hot chocolate for himself in his private apartments, and around the same time, chocolate-making machines appeared in Paris.

KIR

This rosy and refreshing aperitif, combining an inexpensive white wine called Aligote with a dose of creme de cassis (blackcurrant liqueur), was first served by its namesake Canon Felix Kir during World War II. Typically, Kir is four parts dry white wine and one part crème de cassis.

BURGUNDY AND BORDEAUX RED WINES

Bordeaux produces four times as much vin as Burgundy and its wines are typically a blend of a variety of grapes, including Cabernet Sauvignon, Merlot, Malbec, Cab Franc, and Petit Verdot. Meanwhile Burgundy wine, known for its distinctive sloping bottle, uses the single varietal terroir, like Pinot Noir and Chardonnay, and has a more acidic or mineral taste than the polished Bordeaux.

CAFÉ AU LAIT

Coffee culture is pretty serious business in France, and it involves sitting or standing—not walking or driving. Most French drink un petit café (an espresso), but if that's too strong, order a diluted version: un café allongé (or un café serré if you need a jolt). A café crème is made with steamed milk, and you can sprinkle a little chocolate to make a cappuccino. A noisette is an espresso-size café crème. Lastly, an "American" is a larger cup of diluted espresso.

CHOUCHEN

Brittany's answer to mead, chouchen arrived with the Druids when they crossed the English Channel in 500 BC to reach the westernmost point of continental France. Today, the sweet aperitif is less potent (still, 14% alcohol), with honey fermented in water with freshly pressed apple juice to kick-start fermentation. This delicious drink is traditionally served cold as an aperitif to highlight its

Cafe au Lait

refreshing qualities and its soft, earthy flavor.

LOIRE AND ALSACE WHITE WINES

As the second driest region in France, Alsace in the northeast produces three varieties of whites: a dry versatile Riesling, a goes-with-anything Pinot Gris, and the aromatic Gewürztraminer, a sweeter wine best paired with cheese, foie gras, and spicy or sweet-and-sour food. The Loire Valley in the northwest has three sections, each producing different grape varieties for light-bodied white wines.

PASTIS

What could be more Provençal than sitting at Les Deux Garçons in Aix-en-Provence sipping a pastis? The French put back on average two liters a day of the chalky-light amber, anise-flavored spirit, which is served on ice with a carafe of cold water on the side. Ricard (now Ricard Pernod) was the first to produce the silky beverage. Enjoy one before or after your dinner.

PROVENÇAL ROSÉ WINE

Provence is the world's largest rosé producer, using Grenache, Cinsault, Mourvedre, and Syrah grapes, which help create that distinguished pale-orange-tinted pink color. Approximately one in five bottles of rosé sold stateside now comes from Chateau d'Esclans, the French wine house behind high-end Whispering Angel. While in Provence, you'll find plenty of more affordable options to sample.

CHAMPAGNE

Typically made with Chardonnay (white grape), Pinot Noir, or Pinot Meunier (black grapes), some of the world's most expensive bottles of sparkling wine are produced in France's Champagne region.

What to Buy in France

PERFUME

In the town of Grasse, you'll find the perfume capital of the world, thanks to Jean de Galimard who first invented fashionable perfumed gloves to cover the nauseating smell of tanners. Two-hundred-and-fifty years later, the $49.4 billion global perfume market is booming like never before.

CALISSON

The Calissons d'Aix, a candied fruit treat topped with ground almond and sugar icing, was first served in 1473 at the second wedding of King René. In the 16th century, as almond trees started to grow around the Aix-en-Provence region, production of the diamond-shape morsel took off. Today, you can find the candy in plenty of stores throughout Provence.

CHANTILLY LACE

It's all in the detail, and in 1830, some 4,000 people were employed in the Chantilly area north of Paris to make traditional handmade bobbin lace, which remains en vogue to this day. From Kate Middleton's wedding dress to the red carpet at the Cannes Film Festival, the delicately woven textile features intricate black (sometimes white) floral motifs often outlined in a *cordonnet* (a heavier but untwisted matte silk or linen thread).

DIJON MUSTARD

The capital of the Burgundy wine region, Dijon has been recognized for its mustard making since King Philip VI first used the pale yellow condiment in 1336. Made from white wine and mustard seed, which is grown as a cover crop beneath the rows of grapevines to provide them with nutrients, these mustards accompany many dishes. The most famous brand, the Grey-Poupon label was created in 1866 by Maurice Grey, who built a machine that made it faster to produce mustard, and Auguste Poupon, another mustard maker who acted as financial backer.

HERBS DE PROVENCE

Along with the usual suspects of thyme, rosemary, and bay leaf, other herbs that can be in this rock star of spice blends are oregano, basil, tarragon, marjoram, savory, sage, fennel, and dill, all grown in the southeast of France. The omnipresent Herbes de Provence became popular thanks to Julia Child, who included a recipe for Poulet Saute aux Herbes de Provence in her iconic cookbook *Mastering the Art of French Cooking*. However, there is no guarantee that your herbs are really from Provence because the name doesn't have Protected Geographical Status, so your best bet is to buy direct from a local Provençal market.

LAVENDER PRODUCTS

Driving through the lavender fields of Provence should be on everyone's bucket list. During the summer bloom, you'll see endless rows of vibrant purple lavandin, or French lavender, a hybrid created in 1920 for the French perfume industry. The less fragrant lavandin produces almost five times more essential oil than true lavender, with 1 ton producing 25 to 40 liters. That's plenty to scent the pretty soaps and candles that

visitors shop for, along with the creams and aromatic sprays that can act as disinfectants or help with sunburned lips, dry skin, insect bites, and nausea.

POTTERY
From the moment Picasso met Suzanne and Georges Ramié in 1946 at their ceramics factory in Vallauris in Provence, the pottery industry in France would never be the same. Picasso produced 633 original pieces over 23 years, and the Madoura workshop still attracts art enthusiasts eager to see his clay masterpieces. With the bonus of clay-rich soil and hot sun, many villages in the region continue to pay tribute to the country's earthen cookery history, especially in Provence, where you find the emblematic sunshine-yellow-color water jugs and two-part olive bowls.

PROVENÇAL FABRIC AND PLACE MATS
Known as *les indiennes*, these colorful cottons date back to the 16th century when they were first imported from India to Marseille. The material was so popular with the high bourgeoisie that in 1686, French textile manufacturers in Lyon were so worried about going out of business, they ordered an import ban. This led to Armenian craftsmen coming to France to create similar patterns that you still see today on everything from tablecloths and napkins to clothing and ceramics.

SALTED CARAMELS
A beloved French treat, the buttery and chewy caramel takes rich to a new level. Wanting to make a name for himself in the world of confectionary, Henry Le Roux came up with the salted-butter caramel. In addition to the classic, there are seasonal flavors,

from black sesame to piña colada. The big-name stores are the chains of Maisons Le Roux in Paris and Pâtisserie Bechard in Aix-en-Provence, but handcrafted salted caramels can be found at most chocolate shops, too.

WINE
Bordeaux or Burgundy, Sauternes or Sancerre, Romanée or Côte du Rhône, all throughout the country, the great wine regions of France attract hordes of travelers with just one thing on their minds: wine. But the fact is, you can buy the bottles of the most fabled regions anywhere, so why not nab a bottle to bring home from one of the lesser-known local crus from, say, the lovely vineyards in the Loire Valley, Bergerac, or Languedoc.

Best Museums in France

THE LOUVRE, PARIS

The Louvre holds the title as the world's most visited art museum. The building originally served as a palace to French kings until Louis XIV built Versailles in 1682. Its most famous residents are the "holy trinity" for art lovers: the *Mona Lisa*, *Winged Victory*, and *Venus de Milo*.

CAMP DES MILLES MEMORIAL, AIX-EN-PROVENCE

This extraordinary memorial to the Holocaust is actually located in Les Milles, a 10-minute bus ride from Aix-en-Provence. During World War II, the town was originally a camp meant to intern artists and intellectuals. In 1993 it became a permanent memorial, as well as a center to study intolerance and genocide.

COLLECTION LAMBERT, AVIGNON

Avignon is a city rich in French history and its Collection Lambert does an excellent job at linking the old with the contemporary. Housed in two 18th-century mansions in the center of Avignon, the works are by some of the most talented artists in the postwar and early 21st century, including Basquiat and Sol LeWitt.

CENTRE POMPIDOU, PARIS

If you've ever visited Paris, the Centre Pompidou is immediately recognizable from a distance by its unique architecture. The original idea was for the center to be a multicultural complex that would bring together different forms of art and literature. Today, it holds the city's most impressive collection of modern and contemporary art.

MEMORIAL DE CAEN, NORMANDY

Any student of modern history knows the important role that the city of Caen played in the D-Day invasion. Originally conceived as a museum to examine the causes and course of World War II, today the Memorial de Caen is dedicated to the history of violence and intensive outstanding conflicts of the 20th century.

MUSÉE D'ORSAY, PARIS

Originally built as a railway station in 1900 for the World's Fair, the d'Orsay is home to mainly French art from 1848 to 1914. This is your main stop for French Impressionists and Postimpressionists, including heavy hitters Monet, Degas, Cezanne, and Van Gogh.

MATISSE MUSEUM, NICE

Famed artist Henri Matisse settled in the seaside city of Nice in 1917, and remained there until his death in 1954. This museum in a 17th-century villa showcases his artwork, much of which was donated to the city by the artist himself before he died.

MUSÉE DE L'ECOLE DE NANCY, NANCY

In 1901, the Art Nouveau movement was born in the northeastern French city of Nancy. Embracing all decorative arts from painting to jewelry, the Musée de l'Ecole opened in 1964 and highlights the region's contributions to the movement, including architecture and furniture.

FONDATION MAEGHT, ST-PAUL-DE-VENCE

A popular tourist spot on the French Riviera, St-Paul-de-Vence is home to many small contemporary art galleries. One of the most impressive is the privately founded Fondation Maeght, home to works by some of the most important 20th-century artists, including Kandinsky and Miró.

LA CITÉ DU VIN, BORDEAUX

Part museum, part wine-tasting experience, and part cultural center, La Cité du Vin provides an interactive experience exploring Bordeaux's (and arguably France's) most famous export. Exhibits include a history of wine making in the area and a look into how wine barrels are made.

Best Small Towns and Villages in France

CHINON, THE LOIRE VALLEY

The town of Chinon was once the center of French life in the Middle Ages. Also the site of a former royal residence during the Middle Ages and the Renaissance, the cobblestone streets have been trodden by the likes of Joan of Arc, the Knights Templar, and Richard the Lionheart.

ÉZE, FRENCH RIVIERA

This medieval village has been wonderfully preserved. Take the shuttle or climb the steep Nieztsche Path (90 minutes) to make it to this perched town. It's worth the sweat for the panoramic views, especially from the Exotic Botanical Garden, with its sculptures and a neoclassical 18th-century church.

BAYEUX, NORMANDY

The town of 13,600 has a long history dating back to the Roman Empire, when it was a part of the Roman coastal defense, and stretching all the way to World War II and its strategic part in the D-Day invasion. Thanks to heavy fighting in Caen, Bayeux was almost untouched during Operation Overlord.

CLUNY, BURGUNDY

Located in the central part of France, Cluny was founded in 910 around a Benedictine abbey, which naturally remains one of the town's main tourist attractions. Use Cluny as a home base to visit the surrounding 16 medieval fortresses and castles of the Renaissance, Baroque, and Classicism periods, some of which serve as hotels, wineries, or museums today.

CORDES SUR CIEL, MIDI-PYRENEES

Situated on a small mountain, this town became an important defensive position for local inhabitants during the Middle Ages, with its walls and rocky heights not only protecting the townspeople but the local architecture, too. This same architecture offers present-day visitors some of the best examples of 13th- and 14th-century Gothic architecture in the country.

L'ISLE SUR LA SORGUE, VAUCLUSE, PROVENCE

After Paris, this exquisite island city is France's largest antiques center and has the third largest *brocante* (vintage market) in Europe. The biannual Grand Déballage ("Great Unpacking") is held for four days around Easter and in mid-August, and attracts bargain hunters from across Europe. The Sunday antiques/vintage market, which supposedly dates back to 1596, is the best in France. And there's the delightful bonus of a waterwheel setting along

the Sorgue River, which, in the 12th century, served as a natural protective moat.

RIQUEWIHR, ALSACE
Located close to the German border, Riquewihr is remarkably one of the few towns in the area unscathed by World War II. Largely considered one of the most beautiful towns in France, it's filled with medieval fortifications. You can visit the Thieves' Tower in the former prison or Monkey Mountain, a wildlife refuge for Barbary macaques monkeys. Located on the Alsace Wine Route, the town also has several wineries and many restaurants.

TRÉBEURDEN, BRITTANY
This tiny town of 3,800 boasts a stunning beach facing the English Channel, and thanks to its location on the northwestern coast of France, your chances of getting sunburn are slim. Another jewel of the area is the 18-mile Côte de Granite Rose, a unique rose-color pink-sand and granite seashore that wraps around Trébeurden.

TROYES, CHAMPAGNE
Located in the northeast-ern part of France, Troyes is the city of a thousand colors, due to its preserved multicolor timber-frame houses from the Middle Ages and the Renaissance. In addition to its rainbow of facades, Troyes is home to 10 notable historic churches, one of the highest per capita in France.

ROUSSILLON, PROVENCE
Located in the Luberon, the russet-red town of Roussillon is located in the heart of one of the biggest ocher deposits in the world. Commercially, the town is now part of France's largest wine-producing region, the Languedoc-Roussillon.

Best Churches and Cathedrals in France

BASILIQUE DU SACRÉ-CŒUR, PARIS

Every year, some 10 million tourists climb the 222 stairs or take the funicular up to Montmartre to visit the Sacred Heart of Paris. When it rains, the calcite has a bleaching effect that gives the exterior its famous chalky white appearance. It also has one of the largest mosaics in the world.

CATHÉDRALE ST-ETIENNE, BURGUNDY

Completed in 1176, Cathédrale St-Etienne once held more political power than Paris when it served as the capital of several different regions in France. The treasury contains a fragment of the true cross that was presented by Charlemagne, as well as the vestments of Thomas Becket.

AMIENS CATHEDRAL, CHAMPAGNE

When construction began on the Cathédrale Notre-Dame d'Amiens in 1220, the medieval builders were attempting to reach God's front doorstep, and so the internal dimensions were maximized to support the height of the cathedral.

CHAPELLE DU ROSAIRE, VENCE, FRENCH RIVIERA

Built between 1948 and 1951 and located 4 miles from the town of Vence, artist Henri Matisse called this chapel his *chef-d'œuvre* (masterpiece). It's the large stained-glass windows—with their blue, green, and yellow reflections across the white marble floors—that draw the most admiration.

STRASBOURG CATHEDRAL, STRASBOURG

Since 90 AD, the modern-day Strasbourg Cathedral has been the site of several different churches, which explains its Romanesque-style vestiges. Also known as the Cathédrale Notre-Dame, it was world's tallest medieval structure until 1874 and still is considered among the finest examples of late medieval architecture.

ABBAYE DU MONT-ST-MICHEL, NORMANDY
One of the most visited monuments in France, this UNESCO World Heritage Site is located a half-mile off the coast of Normandy on a rocky tidal island, which means you can only access Pont-Passerelle by foot, horse carriage, or shuttle bus during low tide.

BASILIQUE ST-SERNIN, TOULOUSE
The largest Romanesque church in France has been an important stop along the pilgrimage route to Santiago de Compostela for centuries; today, the Basilique St-Sernin is also a UNESCO World Heritage Site.

REIMS CATHEDRAL, CHAMPAGNE
Reims Cathedral (another cathedral officially known as Cathédrale Notre-Dame de Reims) was built on the site of several older churches and dates back to the Roman-Gallo era. Since 987 AD, with the exception of only one, all French kings were crowned in Reims.

CHARTRES CATHEDRAL, CHARTRES
Located 50 miles outside of Paris, the Chartres Cathedral, also known as Cathédrale Notre-Dame, is a UNESCO World Heritage Site, courtesy of its well-preserved original stained glass that dates back to the 13th century. True believers come to view the Sancta Camisa, said to be the tunic worn by the Virgin Mary at Christ's birth.

ROUEN CATHEDRAL, NORMANDY
One of the most impressive Gothic churches ever built, Rouen Cathedral (officially called the Cathédrale Notre-Dame) summarizes the evolution of Gothic art, starting with its construction in the 12th century on the foundations of a 4th-century basilica.

An Art Lover's Guide to France

CÉZANNE'S AIX-EN-PROVENCE

Follow in Paul Cézanne's footsteps through elegant, arts-loving Aix-en-Provence, up to the artist's favorite muse, the incomparable Mont Ste-Victoire, and then on to check out the Caumont Centre d'Art. The 2-mile Route de Cézanne is listed as a Historic Monument, the only road in France with such a distinction. It connects the artist's place of birth and death, Aix-en-Provence, to the village of Tholonet, and provides a glimpse of the life of the father of modern painting. In 1906, a letter to his son described how he was enjoying a three-hour aperitif with his friend, the novelist Emile Zola, at Les Deux Garçons (53 cours Mirabeau). You can still visit the studio where he lived from 1902 to his death in 1906, and walk to nearby Chemin de la Marguerite on the Lauves Hill facing Cezanne's obsession, Ste-Victoire. The city has transformed this lookout into the Land of Painters with reproductions of the artist's work.

COLOMBE D'OR INN, ST-PAUL-DE-VENCE

In the early 1920s, word got out that the owners of the beautiful Colombe d'Or Inn located in St-Paul-de-Vence would accept paintings and sketches in lieu of payment. Before you could paint a stroke, little-known artists were heading to dine and sleep here. The fact that those painters turned out to be Picasso, Matisse, and Braque means that La Colombe d'Or today is one of France's most unique "museums"—where you dine under a Picasso or on a terrace beside a ceramic Léger mural and dodge a Calder mobile while heading up to your room. In 2015, it won the category for best art experience in a hotel by Leading Culture Destinations—known as "the Oscars" in the museum world. Frankly, if you don't stay or dine here, you simply haven't been to the French Riviera.

MATISSE'S NICE

Walk to the east end of the flower market in Old Nice and you'll come face-to-face with an imposing yellow stone facade. From 1921 to 1938, Henri Matisse lived on the third and then fourth floor at Place Charles Félix. But there's no plaque that bears his name, only a broken shutter of his workshop serves as a commemoration. The crumbling building's future remains uncertain, but for many Niçois it's a part of the city's heritage. The Musée Matisse, located across from the former Regina Hotel where he lived until his death in 1954, exhibits one of the world's largest collections from the artist (for a glimpse at what he considered his own masterpiece, you'll have to head to the Chapelle du Rosaire in Vence). In 1917, he moved into his first studio at 105 quai des Etas-Unis on the Promenade. In the port of Nice you'll find the Club Nautique, where Matisse would paddle his own canoe nearly every morning.

MONET'S GIVERNY

In 1883, Claude Monet settled 45 miles northwest of Paris in Giverny, and remained there until his death in 1926. He transformed an abandoned domaine and 8-acre garden into a floral masterpiece, which inspired some of his greatest works. The Clos Normand Garden in the front of the house is filled with various blossoms from long-stemmed hollyhocks and daisies to ornamental trees and fruit trees. A Japanese-inspired water garden on the other side of the railroad line led to one of his most famous paintings: the Nymphéas water lilies (he was so particular about these water lilies that a full-time gardener was responsible to remove any dead leaves "to ensure the perfect beauty of the pond"). The house itself is equally intriguing with its Japanese engravings, blue kitchen, yellow dining room, and countless paintings that adorn the walls. There are many walking and hiking paths in the surrounding area, loaded with wildflowers, or for an adventure, follow the old railroad path to Vernon.

MUSEE TOULOUSE-LAUTREC

Artist Henri de Toulouse-Lautrec was a Postimpressionist artist best known for his artwork and images depicting late-19th-century Paris. His most famous works include the posters for Moulin Rouge. While the artist is inextricably tied to Paris, this charming museum in his hometown provides a stark contrast to the tumultuous life the artist lived. Situated in a former bishop's residence, it was the idea of Lautrec's mother after several Parisian museums rejected the donation of his work after he died. In addition to the numerous posters, portraits of local farmers, doctors, and his family are displayed with English explanations.

PARCOURS ESTUAIRE

This artistic trail joins St-Nazaire in western France with Nantes via 37 miles of the Loire estuary. A permanent open-air collection spread over 12 communes that can be accessed on foot, by bike, car, or boat, the collection of 30 pieces of art occupies settings that range from fragile nature reserves to gigantic industrial buildings. Explore the engineering masterpiece in Nantes, Les Machines de l'Île, which features the Carrousel des Mondes Marins (a massive carrousel with moving marine creatures) inspired by locally born writer Jules Verne.

PICASSO'S ANTIBES

In May 2019, Paul Signac's painting *Antibes, Soir* (Antibes, Night) sold for $7.67 million at a Sotheby's auction. The Chateau Grimaldi featured in the 1903 tableau is now the Picasso Museum, the first in the world to be dedicated to the cofounder of the Cubist movement. For two months in the fall of 1946, Pablo Picasso lived in the Musée Grimaldi,

as it was called then, and produced 44 drawings and 23 paintings, including *Joie de Vivre,* all of which he left to the city. Impressionist artist Claude Monet also spent a short but productive period in Antibes, producing 33 paintings from February to May 1888. Take a stroll along the Cap d'Antibes and you'll come across plaques of his work painted from that same spot.

VAN GOGH'S PROVENCE

Everyone knows Vincent van Gogh chopped off his ear when tempers flared with Paul Gauguin, but do you know where? It happened in Arles, in the south of France, where he produced 300 paintings and drawings from February 1888 to May 1889. After the ear incident, he moved to St-Remy-de-Provence, about 16 miles away, for psychiatric treatment at the St-Paul de Mausole. He continued to paint, and the surrounding Alpilles Mountains and village became instrumental in his most famous works. On May 16, 1890, he left, "cured," for Auvers-sur-Oise, but two months afterward, on July 27, he shot himself in the chest in a field. He died two days later.

Download the free Van Gogh Foundation's walking tour map and follow the 10 spots that mark the artist's easel, including the bridge where he painted the *Staircase of the Trinquetaille Bridge,* the Rhône River embankment for his *Starry Night over the Rhône,* and Place Lamartine where his *Yellow House* was located on Rue Mireille. For another highlight, stand at the northeastern corner of the Place du Forum, on the very spot where the artist painted *Le Café La Nuit.*

France Today

For more than 20 years, France has held the torch of being the most visited country in the world, racking up nearly 87 million tourists in 2018. The iconic Louvre in Paris is not only the most visited museum on the planet, but received more than 10 million visitors for the first time in 2018, a 25% surge over the previous year. These figures are somewhat bittersweet: a reminder to the French of how only a few years ago tourists shunned the country following a spate of fatal terrorist attacks in Paris and Nice in 2015 and 2016.

Sure, security remains reinforced at major locations throughout the country. Machine-gun-toting soldiers patrolling the seaside Promenade des Anglais in Nice have become commonplace. And yes, as Europe continues to cope with the influx of migrants arriving in Greece and Italy who then try to make their way westward, border controls have been tightened in France; these days, armed police onboard French trains is business as usual. In many places, you'll see the triangular sign reading "Vigipirate" (France's antiterrorism system), which means this extra vigilance can cause delays at the border or at major tourist attractions, for residents and tourists alike.

Yet France, which has the largest Muslim and Jewish populations in Europe, placed higher than the United States in the Global Finance 2019 ranking of safest countries in the world—an index based on war and peace, personal security, and natural disaster risk (France came in at 36 while the U.S. was listed at 65).

THE YELLOW VESTS

The country's joy in its tourism resurgence was a bit fleeting. By December 2018, videos of violent clashes in Paris between the police and French protestors wearing high-visibility yellow vests headlined across the globe, and hotel reservations were cancelled. The Gilets Jaunes movement, a grassroots protest rising from rural parts of France against a proposed hike on diesel tax, began on November 17.

Up to that point, the price at the pumps had already increased 20% in a year to an average of $1.68 per liter. In an effort to tackle climate change, President Emmanuel Macron had planned to again raise the diesel tax effective January 1, 2019. The president eventually backed down, but even in April, the yellow vests were continuing their fight for social justice on weekends, albeit on a smaller scale in major cities, picking up disgruntled students, teachers, and workers along the way. In an attempt to contain the handful of violent protestors and looters who joined in, the government imposed bans in some places, slapping demonstrators with a fine of €135—the same charge drivers face if they don't carry the mandatory fluorescent safety vest (which must have a European Union label) and warning triangle in their car.

POLITICS

The Fifth Republic, France's current political constitution founded in 1958, was largely driven by President Charles de Gaulle who led the French Resistance against Nazi Germany in WWII. This semi-presidential system has a head of state (the president) elected for a five-year term in two rounds of national voting. The president appoints a prime minister, and they work together to form a government.

Until recently, France had two major political parties, but with issues like immigration, terrorism, high unemployment, and income inequality dividing the country, popularity for the far-right National Front has surged. The party made it twice to the second round of the Presidential vote: once in 2002 and again in the 2017 presidential elections. In the end, the election of independent centrist Emmanuel Macron was a victory "for community harmony over anti-immigration, for centrism over populism."

Fast-forward two years and Macron's approval rating has plummeted to 26%. The leader of La République En Marche party, once descibed as charismatic but now seen as arrogant, has fallen out of grace with pretty much everyone—pensioners, the middle classes, and young voters—except the rich, who have benefited the most from Macronism.

FEMINISM

At a time when the world was tagging #MeToo and #TimesUp, French actress Catherine Deneuve, along with a hundred other prominent French women, wrote an open letter countering the movement saying, "rape is a crime, but trying to seduce someone, even persistently or crack-handedly, is not, nor is being gentlemanly a macho attack."

Whether this is the overall sentiment of most women in France is still up for debate, but President Macron has stated publicly that his country was "sick with sexism," and now catcalling and whistling, or any form of sexual harassment in public places, will be met with a €90 fine.

Then in March, the Académie Française, the authority on the French language, made a long-overdue concession by allowing the feminization of all professions. There's no one set of rules, but the feminine equivalent of job titles, functions, and professions will mean the letter "e" can be added to the end of the word (a female teacher will become a professeure) but in some cases, the feminine article "une" will be used instead.

So what took France so long? A deep ambivalence on the part of both men and women regarding gender roles certainly plays a part, as does entrenched inequality, with men still earning wages an average of 15.4% higher than women, which means that as of 3:35 pm, November 6, women in France effectively work the rest of the year for free.

TAXES

The French have long reconciled themselves to higher taxes in the interest of a fundamental French value, *égalité,* reaping the benefits in the form of one of the world's best health-care systems, low-cost education, universal childcare, and a plethora of other social safety nets. According to Trading Economics API, France's personal income tax rate is 45% (its peak was 59.60% in 1996), but Solidaires Finances Publiques says tax evasion cost the country €80 billion to €100 billion in 2017. To fight tax fraud, the government has a introduced a pay-as-you-earn income tax, which means you are taxed at source, and introduced a measure that allows authorities greater freedom to view the social media accounts of French citizens to look for any discrepancies in their lifestyle that would indicate higher than reported income.

The government is also targeting 30 companies with a proposed GAFA tax (an acronym for the four tech giants: Google, Apple, Facebook, and Amazon), which would create a 3% tax on digital advertising, the sale of personal data, and other revenue from any technology company that annually earns more than €25 million in France and €750 million worldwide. France estimates it will take in at least €500 million if passed.

The History of France

France has long been the standard-bearer of Western civilization—without it, neither English liberalism nor the American Constitution would exist today. It has given us Notre-Dame, Loire châteaux, Versailles, Stendhal, Chardin, Monet, Renoir, and the most beautiful city in the world, Paris. So it is no surprise that France unfolds like a gigantic historical pop-up book. To help you understand the country's masterful mélange of old and new, here's a quick overview of La Belle France's stirring historical pageant.

ANCIENT FRANCE

France's own "Stonehenge"—the megalithic stone complexes at Carnac in Brittany (circa 3500 BC)—were created by the Celts, who inhabited most of northwest Europe during the last millennia BC. In the 1st century BC, Julius Caesar conquered Gaul, and the classical civilizations of the Mediterranean soon made artistic inroads. The Greek trading colonies at Marseille eventually gave way to the Roman Empire, and those ancient Roman aesthetics left a lasting impression; it is no accident that the most famous modern example of a Roman triumphal arch—the **Arc de Triomphe**—was built in Paris.

What to See: France possesses examples of ancient Roman architecture that even Italy cannot match. Provence, whose name comes from the Latin, had been one of the most popular places to holiday for the ancient Romans. The result is that you can find the best-preserved Roman arena in Nîmes (along with the **Maison Carrée**), the best-preserved Roman theater at Orange, and the best-preserved Roman bridge aqueduct, the **Pont du Gard.**

THE MIDDLE AGES: FROM ROMANESQUE TO GOTHIC

By the 7th century AD, Christianity was well established throughout France. Its interaction with an inherited classical

Timeline: 58 BC–1572 AD

58–51 BC: Caesar's conquest of Gaul

800 AD: Charlemagne made Holy Roman Emperor

1066: William of Normandy invades England with victory at the Battle of Hastings

12th–13th century: Cathedrals of Notre-Dame and Chartres are built

1431: Joan of Arc burned; from lowest point, French nation revived

1572: St. Bartholomew Massacre of Protestants

tradition produced the first great indigenous French culture, created by the Germanic tribes who expelled the Romans from French soil. These tribes, called the Franks, gave their name to the new nation. Various French provinces began to unite as part of Charlemagne's new Holy Roman Empire and, as a central core of European Catholicism, France now gave rise to great monastic centers—Tours, Auxerre, Reims, and Chartres—that were also cultural powerhouses. After the Crusades, more settled conditions led to the flowering of the Romanesque style developed by reformist monastic orders like the Benedictines at Cluny. This then gave way to the Gothic, which led to the construction of many cathedrals—perhaps the greatest architectural achievement created in France—during the biggest building spree of the Middle Ages. Under the Capetian kings, French government became more centralized. The most notable king was Louis IX (1226–70), known as St-Louis, who left important monuments in the Gothic style, which lasted some 400 years and gained currency throughout Europe.

What to See: The Romanesque style sprang out of the forms of classical art left by the Romans; its top artistic landmarks adorn Burgundy: the giant transept of **Cluny,** the sculptures of Gislebertus at Autun's **Cathèdrale St-Lazare,** and the amazing tympanum of the **Basilique Ste-Madeleine at Vézelay.** Another top Romanesque artwork is in Normandy: the **Bayeux Tapestry** on view in Bayeux. The desire to span greater area with stone and to admit more light led to the development of the new Gothic style. This became famed for its use of the pointed arch and the rib vault, resulting in an essentially skeletal structure containing large areas of glass. First fully developed at **Notre-Dame,** Paris (from 1163), **Chartres** (from 1200), **Reims** (from 1211), and **Amiens** (from 1220), the Gothic cathedral contains distinctive Gothic forms: delicate filigree-like rose windows of stained glass, tall lancet windows, elaborately sculpted portals, and flying buttresses. King Louis IX commissioned Paris's **Sainte-Chapelle** chapel in the 1240s and it remains the most beautiful artistic creation of the Middle Ages.

THE RENAISSANCE

French nationalism came to the fore once the tensions and wars fomented by the Houses of Anjou and Capet climaxed in the Hundred Years' War (1328–1453). During this time, Joan of Arc helped drive English rulers from France, with the Valois line of kings taking the throne. From the late 15th century into the 16th, the golden light of the Italian Renaissance dawned over France. This was due, in large measure, to King François I (accession 1515), who returned from wars in Italy with many Italian artists and craftsmen, among them Leonardo da Vinci (who lived in Amboise from 1507). With decades of peace, fortresses soon became châteaux and the palaces of the Loire Valley came into being. The

Timeline: 1580–1793

1580–87: Montaigne's *Essays*

1678: Louis XIV adds the Hall of Mirrors to Versailles

18th century: Zenith of French enlightenment and influence, thanks to Molière, Racine, Voltaire, Diderot, and Rousseau

1789–92: The French Revolution

1793: Queen Marie-Antoinette is guillotined on Paris's Place de la Concorde

grandest of these, Fontainebleau and Chambord, reflected the growing centralization of the French court and were greatly influenced by the new Italian styles.

What to See: An earnest desire to rival and outdo Italy in cultural pursuits dominated French culture during the 15th and 16th centuries. For the decoration of the new **Palace of Fontainebleau** (from 1528) artists like Cellini, Primaticcio, and Rosso used rich colors, elongated forms, and a concentration on allegory and eroticism to help cement the Mannerist style. Gothic and vernacular forms of architecture were now rejected in favor of classical models, as could be seen in the châteaux in the Loire Valley such as **Blois** (from 1498), **Chambord** (from 1519,) where design elements were created by da Vinci, and **Chenonceau,** which was commissioned by the king's mother, Catherine de' Medici. The rebuilding of Paris's **Louvre,** begun in 1546, marked the final assimilation of Italian classical architecture into France.

ROYAL ABSOLUTISM AND THE BAROQUE STYLE

Rising out of the conflicts between Catholics and Protestants (thousands of Huguenots were murdered in the St. Bartholomew's Day massacre of 1572), King Henry IV became the first Bourbon king and promoted religious tolerance with the Edict of Nantes (1598). By the 17th century architecture still had an Italianate flavor, as seen in the Roman Baroque forms adorning Parisian churches. The new Baroque architectural taste for large-scale town planning gave rise to the many squares that formed focal points within cities. King Louis XIV, the Sun King, came to the throne in 1643, but he chose to rule from a new power base he built outside Paris. Versailles soon became a symbol of the absolutist court of the Sun King and the new insatiable national taste for glory. But with Louis XIV, XV, and XVI going for broke, a reaction against extravagance and for logic and empirical reason took over. Before long, writers like Jean-Jacques Rousseau argued for social and political reform—the need for revolution.

What to See: To create a more carefully ordered aristocratic bureaucracy, courtiers were commanded to leave their family châteaux and take up residence in the massive new **Versailles Palace.** A golden age for art began. The palaces of the **Louvre** (1545–1878) and **Versailles** (1661–1756) bear witness to this in their sheer scale. But by the early 18th century, France was on the verge of bankruptcy. In turn, the court turned away from the over-the-top splendor of Versailles and Paris's **Luxembourg Palace** to retreat to smaller, more domestic houses in Paris. Bombastic Baroque gave way to the rococo style, as the charming, feminine paintings of Watteau, Boucher, and Fragonard provided cultural diversions for an aristocracy withdrawn from the stage

Timeline: 1799–1863

1799–1804: Napoléon rules as First Consul of the Consulate

1805–12: Napoléon conquers large parts of Europe but is defeated in Russia

1815: Napoléon loses battle at Waterloo to England's Duke of Wellington

1848–70: The Second Empire, ruled by Emperor Napoléon III, with colonial expansion into Indochina, Syria, and Mexico

1863: Impressionists show at the Salon des Refusés in Paris

of power politics. Find their masterpieces at the Louvre and other museums.

REVOLUTION AND ROMANTICISM

The end of Bourbon rule came with the execution of Louis XVI and Marie-Antoinette. The French Revolution ushered in the First Republic (1792–1804). After a backlash to the Terror (1793–94), in which hundreds were guillotined, Napoléon Bonaparte rose to power from the ashes of the Revolutionary Directoire. With him a new intellectual force and aesthetic mode came to the fore: Romanticism. This new style focused on inner emotions and the self, leading to the withdrawal of the artists from politics, growing industrialization, and urbanization into a more subjective world. Napoléon's First Empire (1804–14) conquered most of Europe, but after the disastrous Russian invasion the Bourbon dynasty was restored with the rule of Charles X and Louis-Philippe. The latter, known as the Citizen King, abdicated in 1848 and made way for the Second Republic and the return of Napoleonic forces with Napoléon III's Second Empire (1852–70).

What to See: As often happens, art is one step ahead of history. The design of Paris's **Panthéon** by Soufflot, Gabriel's refined **Petit Trianon** at Versailles (1762), and the paintings of Greuze (1725–1805) and David (1745–1825), on view at the Louvre, display a conceit for moral order in great contrast to the flippancies of Fragonard. A renewed taste for classicism was seen in the Empire style promulgated by Napoléon; see the emperor's Paris come alive at the Left Bank's charming **Cour du Commerce St-André** and his shrine, **Les Invalides.** But the rigidly formal neoclassical style soon gave way to Romanticism, whose touchstones are immediacy of technique, emotionalism, and the ability to convey the uncertainties of the human condition. Go to Paris's **Musée Delacroix** to get an up-close look at this expressive, emotive master of Romanticism.

THE MODERN AGE BEGINS

Napoléon III's Second Empire led to the vast aggrandizement of France on the world stage, with colonies set up across the globe, a booming economy, and the capital city of Paris remade into Europe's showplace thanks to Baron Haussmann. After the Prussians invaded, France was defeated and culture was shattered and reformed. Romanticism became Realism, often carrying strong social overtones, as seen in the works of Courbet. The closer reexamination of reality by the Barbizon School of landscape painters led to Impressionism, whose masters approached their subjects with a fresh eye, using clear, bright colors to create atmospheric effects and naturalistic observation. By 1870 French rule was reinstated with the Third Republic, which lasted until 1940.

What to See: Thanks to Haussmann, Paris became the City of Light, with new large boulevards opening up the dark urban

Timeline: 1870–1969

1870: Franco-Prussian War; France defeated, but Flaubert's and Baudelaire's writings soar

1871: Alsace-Lorraine ceded to Germany

1940: France surrenders to Germany during World War II; Paris falls

1958: General de Gaulle elected president

1969: Student riots in Paris; government is subsequently stabilized through presidents including Georges Pompidou, François Mitterrand, and Nicolas Sarkozy

city, an outlook culminating in the **Eiffel Tower,** built for the Paris Exposition of 1889. Taking modern life as their subject matter, great Impressionist masters like Monet (1840–1926), Renoir (1841–1919), and Degas (1834–1917) proceeded to break down visual perceptions in terms of light and color, culminating in the late series of *Water Lilies* (from 1916), painted at **Monet's Giverny estate.** Along with masterpieces by Degas, Gauguin, Van Gogh, and Cézanne, the most famous Impressionist and Postimpressionist paintings can be seen at Paris's famed **Musée d'Orsay.** These artists began the myth of the Parisian bohemian artist, the disaffected idealist kicking at the shins of tradition, and they forged the path then boldly trod by the greatest artist of the 20th century, Picasso, whose works can be seen at Paris's **Musée Picasso** and **Centre Pompidou.**

What to Watch and Read Before You Go

AMÉLIE

Nominated for five Academy Awards, this 2001 French romantic comedy is perhaps the country's best-known cinematic export to many Americans. The film tells the story of a shy waitress, played by Audrey Tautou, who decides to make the lives of those around her better while trying to cope with her own isolation. The movie spotlights the colorful Montmartre neighborhood where Amélie lives; the Cafe de 2 Moulins where Amélie works is a real place, but don't expect any of the waitresses there to change your life.

A MOVEABLE FEAST BY ERNEST HEMINGWAY

This memoir first appeared in 1964, three years after the author committed suicide. The series of vignettes set in Paris in the early 1920s is so perfect that many consider it one of the best books about Paris ever written. With specific addresses of cafés, bars, and places he lived, you can retrace the journey of one of the most celebrated American writers of all time.

A YEAR IN PROVENCE BY PETER MAYLE

For many years, the south of France was a mecca for British expats. Half cautionary tale and half amusing memoir, *A Year in Provence* gives great insight into how wonderful and frustrating living in France can be. Mayle's book gives credence to the divide that still exists between the French and the British.

BEAUTY AND THE BEAST

The 1991 Disney animated classic is so well-known for its book-smart heroine, beautiful music, and timeless love story, that many people forget it was originally adapted from a French fairy tale by Jeanne-Marie Leprince de Beaumont and that it very much takes place in France. From characters like Gaston and Lumiére to songs like "Belle," this film gives a fictionalized but fun take on French provincial life.

BONJOUR TRISTESSE BY FRANÇOISE SAGAN

While these days most teenagers might aspire to go viral, back in the day young writers like Françoise Sagan dreamt of literary accolades. Her first novel, published in 1954 when she was just 18, became an overnight sensation. The plot revolves around a bored young girl and her equally bored philandering father who both find themselves bereft of meaning and love while spending the summer on the French Riviera. Spoiler alert: there is no happy ending.

CHOCOLAT

While most people know the French are serious about wine and cheese, a lesser-known fact is they are equally as serious about their chocolate. Each town, city, and region has its own rival chocolatiers, and the real winners are chocolate fans. In this 2000 film, Juliette Binoche arrives in a small fictional French village with her young daughter and sets up a chocolate shop that ends up influencing the lives of the townsfolk in very different ways. Johnny Depp plays a lovable Romani who encourages the locals to taste Binoche's chocolate.

THE 400 BLOWS

Considered by many to be best the best film to come out of the French New Wave genre, Francois Truffaut's *The 400 Blows* tells the story of a rebellious young man in Paris who struggles to find his place in the world. The movie was filmed on location in Paris and Honfleur.

LA VIE EN ROSE

It's hard to think of any other unofficial anthem for Paris other than "La Vie en Rose." The opening notes from the accordion are as emblematic of the city as a beret and a baguette. In 2007, Olivier

Dahan wrote and directed this stunning biopic on the iconic singer who made the song famous, Edith Piaf. Piaf's life was far from rose-tinted: she grew up a street urchin in Paris, lived through the Nazi occupation, and her love life was as heartbreaking as her eventual death. Marion Cotillard won an Oscar for her performance in the title role.

LES MISÉRABLES BY VICTOR HUGO

Victor Hugo's novel is considered one of the greatest novels of the 19th century, a love story that has been adapted to stage, television, and film. Forget reality TV, the storyline includes lies, theft, pregnancy, justice, and lots of secrets. Set against the backdrop of the June Rebellion of 1832, this is the story of Jean Valjean, who agrees to care for a factory worker's daughter while being hunted down by a policeman named Javert. It was adapted into a stage musical in 1980 and then a 2012 film starring Russell Crowe, Hugh Jackman, and Anne Hathaway.

THE MANDARINS BY SIMONE DE BEAUVOIR

Lifelong Parisian Simone de Beauvoir remains one of France's most celebrated literary women, thanks to her contributions to the world of feminism and existentialism. Her writings encompassed a variety of formats and topics, the most famous of which is *The Second Sex,* a book dedicated to her analysis of female oppression; today, it's still considered to be one of the Bibles of feminism. But it's her 1954 novel *The Mandarins* that gives readers the best sense of the Paris she inhabited. This coming-of-age tale is largely based on de Beauvoir's own life, and fittingly focuses on a group of intellectuals in Paris from the end of World War II to the early 1950s, exploring their relationships, thoughts, and realizations.

MARIE ANTOINETTE

The 2006 film from Sofia Coppola focusing on the life of notorious French queen Marie Antoinette is not quite historically accurate nor did it get rave reviews, but it's still a fun, colorful, and highly stylized look into the wife of King Louis XVI. Kirsten Dunst plays Marie, who comes to France as a teenager, marries the future king, and begins a life of pomp, indulgence, and luxury in the halls of Versailles until her reign is brought to an abrupt end by the French Revolution. Filming actually took place at the real Versailles, a fact alone that makes the movie worth a watch.

MARSEILLE

While the south of France is famous for scenic sea views, long hot summers, and endless rosé with every meal, it can also have a darker side. The Netflix television series *Marseille* explores the politics and culture of France's second largest city. The series stars Gerard Depardieu as the city's mayor of 20 years, who enters a war of succession with his political rival. It gives great insight into how local politics work, as well as showing you a part of France that is definitely not on the tourist map. Although not based on any actual people, the shifting cultural tensions depicted in the region are definitely real.

MY LIFE IN FRANCE BY JULIA CHILD

Perhaps the most famous (or at least most beloved) of all French chefs, Julia Child was one of the first French chefs to make French cuisine accessible to the wider public, particularly Americans. Her 2006 autobiography, written during the last eight months of her life and published after her August 2004 death, is a moving look into her life, from her childhood in Paris to her time living and cooking in Marseille and Provence. It's a love letter to cooking, her beloved husband, and, of course, France itself. For an extra bonus, pick up her much-celebrated cookbook, *Mastering the Art of French Cooking.*

THE NIGHTINGALE BY KRISTIN HANNAH

This 2015 novel is based on the true story of Andrée de Jongh, a Belgian woman who helped Allied pilots escape Nazi-occupied France during World War II. Vianne and her younger sister Isabel are estranged from one another and their father when war breaks out in 1939. Isabel eagerly joins the Resistance and becomes so good at getting downed Allied pilots to neutral Spain that she is hunted by the Nazis. Initially Vianne just wants to survive the war with her son, but as she watches Jewish families being rounded up, she also joins the Resistance.

SHANYTOWN KID BY AZOUZ BEGAG

Written in 1986 by Algerian-French writer Azouz Begag, this autobiography tells the story of a young Algerian boy growing up in a shantytown just outside Lyon. Algeria was a French colony from 1830 to 1962, and this book is a moving glimpse into how the fraught political relationship between the two countries affected actual people. It's also about cultural identity, and the dilemma many immigrants face between keeping their homeland culture and assimilating into a new country.

TENDER IS THE NIGHT BY F. SCOTT FITZGERALD

F. Scott Fitzgerald is the one who redefined the tourism industry for France in the early 20th century. In the 1920s, he was invited, along with his wife, Zelda Fitzgerald, to the French Riviera to spend time with some friends near Antibes, and his descriptions of the area changed the tourist season from winter to summer. Inspired by his lifestyle there, Fitzgerald wrote his fourth and final novel, which he considered his best work. Once you visit, you'll see why Fitzgerald's characters might view the area as a prescription for what ails them.

UNE VILLAGE FRANCAISE

Even if you just know the basics of World War II, you've probably wondered how anyone could've put up with Nazi rule. This is the French television series that answers that question, by looking at the German occupation of France within a small town along the occupation border. From its photography to the acting, the entire series is brilliant. Although not based on a real town, the series is incredibly historically accurate and you see good people in the helpless clutches of tyranny; some become reluctant heroes or martyrs and others become the most hated of all French words, *collaborateur.*

Chapter 2

TRAVEL SMART
FRANCE

Updated by
Nancy Heslin

★ **CAPITAL:**
Paris

👫 **POPULATION:**
67,120,000

💬 **LANGUAGE:**
French

$ **CURRENCY:**
Euro

☎ **COUNTRY CODE:**
33

⚠ **EMERGENCIES:**
112

🚗 **DRIVING:**
On the right

⚡ **ELECTRICITY:**
220v/50 cycles; electrical
plugs have two round prongs

🕐 **TIME:**
Six hours ahead of New York

🌐 **WEB RESOURCES:**
us.franceguide.com
www.paris.fr/english
www.parisinfo.com

PARIS

Bay of Biscay

FRANCE

What You Need to Know Before You Visit France

France is a big country, with several distinct regions, cultures, and landscapes, but no matter where you're going, here are a few tips that will help your trip go as smoothly as possible.

DON'T EXPECT TO SEE THE WHOLE COUNTRY IN ONE TRIP.

France is roughly the same size as Texas so it shouldn't be a surprise that you can't make the 550-mile drive from Paris to Cannes in two hours. Before you start planning your itinerary, it's helpful to learn the country's geography and make some decisions, because you can't expect to see the whole country in one trip. Luckily, it's definitely possible to visit several towns and cities, and even multiple regions, on the same trip. To the northwest lies historic Normandy, and, to the west, Brittany and some of the world's best oysters. Many visitors choose to visit these two regions, along with a trip to Paris.

In the south, between Italy and Spain, you have the iconic French Riviera beaches that stretch into Provence along the Mediterranean Sea; many tourists choose to take a trip that combines the two regions. The Pyrenees Mountains tower above the south while in the southeast the French Alps and Mont Blanc dominate; a trip that combines these mountain regions with Lyon is common. Even if you wanted to visit the wine regions it would be difficult, with Champagne in the northeast, the Loire Valley to the west, Burgundy in the east, Bordeaux to the southwest, Rhône in the southeast, and Languedoc and Provence both in the south. A trip that hits up every major wine region is quite ambitious; it's best to stick with one region and enjoy it as much as you can.

LEARN THE RULES FOR DINING OUT.

Table manners are important in France, but there are still more pressing issues to learn when it comes to eating out here. Most restaurants are open for lunch (from noon to 2) and dinner (starting 7:30 pm), but in the south lunches tend to linger. If dining at 6 pm is a must, brasseries and eateries in touristy areas tend to serve nonstop throughout the day. "Le Happy Hour" runs somewhere between 5 and 7 and leads to the nonnegotiable predinner apéro—drinks and snacks with friends—at 7. Second, forget the picky-eating culture at home; yes, that means abandoning your no wheat, no dairy, no fat diet, and no ordering off the menu. You can ask for dairy-free sauce, but regardless of what the server says, you'll most likely be served the same sauce from the same saucepan as everyone else. This can be a serious issue for those with severe food allergies; even if you're able to articulate your issue in French, not all places take allergies as seriously as they do in the United States. People with severe food allergies are better off preparing their meals at their lodging or eating at vegan or organic shops and bakeries; these eateries tend to be more up front with their ingredients, and their staff are more in tune with health concerns. Earn brownie points by ordering the plat du jour and break off an extra piece of bread to wipe the plate clean (but never butter your bread!).

And eat slowly—there are only two services for dinner so there's lots of time—and don't be embarrassed to order tap water (une carafe d'eau) instead of forking out for the bottled stuff. Also, and this is a biggie, don't do work or touch documents when you're eating a meal or you'll be the recipient of many gasps. To really blend in, make sure you order your tea or coffee after your dessert. Tipping is usually included and not an incentive to serve you better. Feel free to leave an extra 5%–10% if the service was excellent. But here's the biggest tip: dress nicely, and if you are with your kids, don't let them run wild.

LEARN TO SPEAK A LITTLE FRENCH, ESPECIALLY IN RURAL AREAS.

The French are big on ceremony, whether it's a kiss on each cheek when greeting someone (yes, even a stranger) or saying Mesdames, Messieurs (ladies and gentlemen) when they walk into a store. As a tourist, you'll be fine with the basics, especially in big cities. Stick with bonjour when you enter a shop or boulangerie. Say merci every time someone serves you a coffee or brings you change. The French will generally appreciate you trying, even if you can't keep the conversation going. But be prepared for some attitude, because no matter how nice you are or how much you try to speak French un peu, the French are notoriously surly, especially those you'll come across working in retail and restaurants (customer service does not exist in France). In more rural areas, you'll find fewer people who speak English, even in hotels. It can be helpful to bring along a vocab book or brush up on the most common phrases before you go.

UNDERSTAND THE MAGIC OF THE AUGUST HOLIDAY.

Even Paris is far from a 24/7 city, so planning your days in France beforehand can save you some aggravation upon finding things are closed. Museums are typically closed one day a week (usually Monday or Tuesday), but most stay open late at least one night each week, which is also the least crowded time to visit. Store hours are generally 9:30 or 10 am to 7 or 8 pm, Monday through Saturday, though the post office, banks, and smaller shops may close for several hours during the afternoon. In France, summertime (particularly August) is when many businesses shut down for their monthlong fermeture annuelle, or annual holiday, and escape to the country. This means that in the north (including Paris), museums, monuments, and attractions operate as usual, but will be much less crowded; certain restaurants and shops, however, might be closed entirely. And if you're traveling to the south during this time, be prepared for way more crowds than usual. If you haven't booked your reservations far in advance, you're most likely out of luck.

GET FAMILIAR WITH THE DIFFERENT TYPES OF FRENCH EATERIES.

The choice of restaurants in France is a feast in itself. Of course, at least once during your trip you'll want to include a luxurious meal at a great haute-cuisine restaurant. But to save your wallet, intimate, family-owned bistros serve classic French home-style dishes and wine, usually with different lunch and dinner menus. On the other hand, brasseries, named after the word brewery in French, are more casual and closer to a pub, serving beers with only a few wines, and the same dishes across the day like steak and frites, andouillette, and stews. At a café, you can grab a quick bite or lunch like a croissant, croque monsieur, or salad while a salon de thé is more formal, and serves quiches, salads, cakes, pastries, and a selection of tea. Crêperies serve, well, crêpes, but often salads and other quick lunch items as well. If you just want to eat on the go (although that's generally a no-no here) stop at a boulangerie (bread shop) or patisserie (bakery). Bars rarely sell food, but some wine bars offer a few plates at lunch or dinner.

RENTING A CAR CAN BE A GREAT IDEA.

Driving is the best option if you want to explore all those picturesque villages, but a few pointers go a long way. First, forget the SUV and rent a small car that's easy to maneuver and parallel park along tiny cobblestone streets. France's tolls on the autoroutes can add up quickly: Paris to Nice is nearly €160 one way. If you have the time, stick to the National (RN) or District (RD) roads. Generally, driving here isn't much different than driving in the States (yes, they drive on the same side of the road as us). But there's no turning right on a red light, a triangle with an X means to yield to the right at the next junction (that's the opposite in the United States), and when entering a roundabout, priority is to the left.

Getting Here

✈ Air Travel

Direct flying time to Paris is 7½ hours from New York, 8½ hours from Atlanta, 11 hours from Los Angeles, and 1½ hours from London. Flying time between Paris and Nice is also about 1½ hours.

AIRPORTS

There are two major gateway airports to France, both just outside the capital: Orly, 16 km (10 miles) south of Paris, and Charles de Gaulle, 26 km (16 miles) northeast of the city. Orly mostly handles flights to and from destinations within France and the rest of Europe, while Charles de Gaulle is France's leading international gateway. The smaller Beauvais Airport, 88 km (55 miles) north of Paris, is used by European budget airlines, most notably Ryanair. Many carriers have flights to Biarritz, Bordeaux, Lourdes, Lyon, Marseille, Nantes, Nice, Perpignan, and Toulouse. If you're going onward by rail, there is a TGV station at Charles de Gaulle's Terminal 2, where you can connect to trains heading all over the country.

GROUND TRANSPORTATION

From Charles de Gaulle (CDG), the fastest and least expensive way to get into Paris is on the RER-B line, the suburban express train, which runs daily from 5 am to 11 pm. The free CDGVal light-rail connects each terminal (except 2G) to the Roissypôle RER station in less than six minutes; for Terminal 2G, take the free N2 "navette" shuttle bus outside Terminal 2F. Trains to central Paris (Gare du Nord, Les Halles, St-Michel, Luxembourg) depart every 10–20 minutes. The fare (including métro connection) is €11.40, and the journey time is about 30 minutes.

The Air France shuttle service is a comfortable alternative, and you don't need to have flown the carrier to use it. The buses cost €19 if you pay on board or €31 if you buy your return ticket online; the approximate travel time is 75 minutes. Line 2 goes from CDG to Paris's Charles de Gaulle Étoile, Porte Maillot, and Eiffel Tower, from 5:30 am to 11:30 pm daily. Buses leave every 30 minutes. Line 4 goes to Montparnasse and the Gare de Lyon from 5:45 am to 10:45 pm. Buses run every 30 minutes. Passengers arriving in Terminal 1 should use Exit 32 on the Arrivals level; Terminals 2A , 2C, and 2D, Exit C10; Terminals 2E and 2F, Gate E8/F9. Terminal 2G, take the N2 shuttle to Terminal 2F, and then use Gate E8/F9. Bus terminal are at the arrivals level.

Another option is to take Roissybus, operated by the Paris Transit Authority (RATP), which runs between CDG and the Opéra every 15–20 minutes from 6 am to 12:30 am; the cost is €12.50, and you can pay on board. The trip takes about 45 minutes in regular traffic, about 90 minutes in rush-hour traffic.

Taxis are your least desirable mode of transportation into the city. If you're traveling at peak times, you may have to stand in a long line with many other disgruntled travelers. Journey times, and, as a consequence, prices, are unpredictable. At best, the trip takes 30 minutes, but it can take as long as 60 minutes during rush hour. There are fixed fares to the Right Bank (€55) and Left Bank (€50), but only with authorized taxi drivers from the designated areas outside the terminal, that have both an illuminated roof sign and a meter. Any driver that solicits customers near baggage carousels and airport exits is not official.

SuperShuttle Paris and Parishuttle are two van companies that serve both Charles de Gaulle and Orly airports. Prices are set, so it costs the same no matter how long the journey takes. To make a reservation, call or email your flight details several days in advance to the shuttle company and an air-conditioned van with a bilingual chauffeur will be waiting for you on arrival. Note that these shuttle vans pick up and drop off other passengers, which can add significant time to the journey. Always confirm your reservation.

From Orly, the most economical way to get into Paris is to take the RER-C or Orlyrail line. Catch the shuttle bus from the terminal to the Pont de Rungis train station. Trains to Paris leave every 15–20 minutes. Passengers arriving in South Terminal use Exit C, Gate 5; for West Terminal use Exit C, Gate 7 on the Arrivals level. The total fare is €6.35, and journey time is about 40 minutes. Another slightly faster option is to take the six-minute monorail service, Orlyval, which runs between the Antony RER-B station and Orly Airport every four–seven minutes from 6 am to 11:35 pm. Passengers arriving in the South Terminal should look for Exit K (between J and K); those arriving in the West Terminal, Exit A on the Arrivals level. The fare to central Paris is €12.10, including the RER transfer.

You can also take the Air France bus service from Orly to Montparnasse, Trocadéro, and Etoile; it runs every 20 minutes from 6:35 am to 11:55 pm. (You need not have flown on Air France to use this service.) The fare is €13 if you pay on board, €20 if you buy your return ticket online, and the trip takes 45–60 minutes, depending on traffic. Passengers arriving in Orly South need to look for Exit L; those arriving in Orly West, Exit D. The Paris Transit Authority's Orlybus is yet another option; buses leave every 10–15 minutes for the Denfert-Rochereau métro station in Montparnasse, and tickets cost €8.70. You can economize further by using RATP Bus No. 183, which shuttles you from the South Terminal to the Porte

de Choisy métro station (Line 7). It runs every 30 minutes from 6 am to 12:20 am (frequency may be reduced on Sunday and holidays); tickets cost €2, and the travel time is about 50 minutes.

There are several options for traveling between Paris's airports. The RER-B travels from CDG to Orly West, although you need to transfer at St-Michel-Notre Dame in Paris. Travel time is 60–80 minutes, and tickets cost €10.30. Air France Bus No. 3 also runs between the airports every 30 minutes for €22 one way; the trip takes 70 minutes. Taxis are available but expensive (€70–€90, depending on traffic).

❂ Boat Travel

A number of ferry routes link the United Kingdom and France, with fares depending on the length of the crossing and the number of passengers in your party. Ferries on the most popular route— Dover/Calais—cross the Channel in about 90 minutes. Driving distances from the French ports to Paris are as follows: from Calais, 290 km (180 miles); from Cherbourg, 358 km (222 miles); from Caen, 233 km (145 miles); from St-Malo, 404 km (250 miles). Trains also connect these ports with the capital. It's best to book directly through the ferry providers rather than from third-party websites offering cheap rates.

❂ Bus Travel

If you're traveling to or from another country, train service can be just as economical as bus travel, if not more so. The largest international bus operator is Eurolines France, whose main terminal is in the Parisian suburb of Bagnolet (a ½-hour métro ride from central Paris, at

Getting Here

the end of métro Line 3). Terminals are also located at Charles de Gaulle Airport, Porte de Clichy, and Porte de Charenton. Eurolines links scores of European destinations, with fares that vary greatly depending on where and when you travel. It will take you about 8½ hours to get from London to Paris, and a round-trip ticket will cost €34–€54. Other Eurolines routes to or from Paris include: Amsterdam (8½ hrs, €31); Barcelona (15 hrs, €61); and Berlin (14 hrs, €49). Economical passes are available—a 15-day version costs €225–€375, and a 30-day one costs €340–€490. These offer unlimited coach travel to all of Eurolines's European destinations.

France's excellent train service means that long-distance bus routes within France are rare; regional buses are found mainly where train service is spotty. The service can be unreliable in rural areas, and schedules can be incomprehensible for those who don't speak French. Your best bet is to contact local tourism offices.

🚗 Car Travel

Driving in France can be a leisurely experience. Autoroutes are well maintained, and there are ample service-oriented rest areas along major highways; smaller roads wind through scenic landscapes and quaint villages. An International Driver's Permit isn't required, but it can prove useful in emergencies—particularly when a foreign language is involved (check with your local Department of Motor Vehicles to obtain one at nominal cost). Drivers in France must be over 18 years old; however, there is no top age limit, provided your faculties are intact. Some road signs and driving laws in France differ from the United States; for example, a triangle with an X means to yield and you cannot

turn right at a red light. If you're driving from the United Kingdom to the Continent, you have a choice of ferry services or the Channel Tunnel (aka the Chunnel) via the Eurotunnel Shuttle. Reservations are essential at peak times.

ROAD CONDITIONS

Metropolitan France has a national road network (both national roads and non-toll motorways) of 11,800 km (7,332 miles). For the fastest route between two points, look for roads marked *autoroute* ("A"). A *péage* (toll) must be paid on most expressways: the rate varies but can be steep: you'll pay over €78 from Paris to Nice. The "N" (*route nationale*) roads—which are sometimes divided highways—and "D" (*route départementale*) roads are usually also wide and fast.

There are excellent links between Paris and most French cities, but poor ones between the provinces (the principal exceptions are A26 from Calais to Reims, A62 between Bordeaux and Toulouse, and A9/A8 the length of the Mediterranean coast).

Though routes are numbered, the French generally guide themselves from city to city and town to town by destination name. When reading a map, keep one eye on the next big city toward your destination as well as the next small town; most snap decisions will have to be based on town names, not road numbers. Even if you have GPS, look for signage pointing you in the right direction; this is especially useful in roundabouts, which can be rather confusing.

🚆 Train Travel

The French national train agency, the Sociète Nationale de Chemins de Fer, or SNCF, is fast, punctual, comfortable, and comprehensive (when it's not on strike).

Traveling across France, you have various options: local trains, overnight trains with sleeping accommodations, and the high-speed Trains à Grande Vitesse, known as the TGV.

TGVs are the best and the fastest domestic trains, averaging 255 kph (160 mph) on the Lyon–southeast line and 320 kph (200 mph) on the Lille and Bordeaux–southwest lines. The rail operator is now promising TGVs that will reach speeds of 350 kph (220 mph) by 2023. They operate between Paris and Lille/Calais, Paris and Brussels, Paris and Amsterdam, Paris and Lyon, Paris and Switzerland (TGV Lyria), Paris–Provence (Marseille and Nice), Paris and Angers–Nantes, and Paris–Avignon and Tours–Poitiers–Bordeaux. As with other main-line trains, a small supplement may be assessed at peak hours.

It's usually fast and easy to cross France without traveling overnight, especially on TGVs, which are generally affordable, efficient, and equipped with creature comforts, such as Wi-Fi. Be aware that capacity fills up quickly on weekends and holidays, so purchase tickets well in advance for these times. Otherwise, you can take a slow overnight train, which often costs more than a TGV, with the option of reclining in your assigned seat or bedding down in a *couchette* (bunk, six to a compartment in second class, four to a compartment in first, or private cabins), equipped with a complimentary bottle of water, wipes, earplugs, and tissues.

In Paris there are six international rail stations: Gare du Nord (northern France, northern Europe, and England via Calais or Boulogne); Gare St-Lazare (Normandy and England via Dieppe); Gare de l'Est (Strasbourg, Luxembourg, Basel, and central Europe); Gare de Lyon (Lyon, Marseille, Provence, Geneva, and Italy);

Gare d'Austerlitz (Loire Valley and central France, overnight to Nice and Spain); and Gare Montparnasse (southwest France and Spain).

BOOKING AND BUYING TICKETS

There are two classes of train service in France; first (*première*) or second (*deuxième*). First-class seats offer more legroom, plusher upholstery, private reading lamps, computer plugs on the TGV, and wireless connectivity, not to mention a hushed, no-cell-phone environment for those who want to sleep. The price can be nearly double, though there are often deals online.

It is best—and in many cases, essential—to prebook your train tickets. This requires making a reservation online, by phone, or in person at the train station. Rail Europe does an excellent job providing train tickets to those in the United States. It offers a service, and the higher prices reflect that. If you want to save money, however, book directly with the SNCF.

RAIL PASSES

There are two kinds of rail passes: those you must purchase at home (including the France Rail Pass and Eurail Pass) and those available in France from SNCF. If you plan to travel within France by train, consider purchasing a single-country Eurail France Pass, which provides unlimited travel for up to eight days over a one-month period. Prices range from $89 to $296.

France is also one of 31 countries in which you can use Eurail passes, which provide unlimited rail travel for a set amount of time. If you plan to rack up the miles, get a Global Pass; the Eurail Global Pass has replaced the multicountry pass and allows travel in 31 European countries, for 3, 5 or 7 days over a month, or 10 or 15 days over two months.

Getting Here

For continuous travel, chose between 15 or 22 days, or 1, 2, or 3 months. Second-class fares range from $250 to $1,034. Whichever pass you choose, remember that you must buy it before leaving for France.

When buying tickets directly from SNCF, check out its discount cards, valid for one year. There are multiple deals to be found, including for seniors, children, and people under age 28. If you don't benefit from any of these discount programs but plan on traveling at least 200 km (132 miles) round-trip and don't mind staying over on a Saturday night, look into the Carte Week-end Pass (€75); it gives you and your traveling companion 25% off your ticket prices.

BOARDING THE TRAIN

Get to the station at least an hour before departure to ensure you'll have time to buy your ticket and, in some cases, select your seat. If you're taking a TGV, your seat is reserved by car and seat number. Before boarding, you must punch your ticket (*composter le billet*) in one of the yellow machines at the entrance to the platforms (*quais*) or scan the ticket's QR code at the automatic gates (if these aren't working, you still need to validate your ticket before you board). If you board your train and don't have time to punch it, look for a conductor (*contrôleur*) as soon as possible and get him to sign it; if not, you risk a €20 fine. SNCF e-tickets and Eurail passes printed at home don't need validation. For passengers without any tickets, fines start at €50.

OTHER SERVICES

With an advance arrangement, SNCF will pick up and deliver your bags at a given time. For instance, if you're planning on spending a weekend in Nice, SNCF will collect your luggage at your hotel in Paris in the morning before checkout

and deliver it to your hotel in Nice, where it will be awaiting your arrival. The cost within France is €38 for the first bag (up to 25 kg), and €20 per additional bag, up to 10 max. Be advised that luggage service is only available Monday to Saturday mornings in mainland France, Germany, Luxembourg, and Switzerland (for travel outside of France, the service allows up to three bags of 25 kg; expect to pay €50/piece).

You can also book a driver to take you to or pick you up from the station. Rates are fixed, and pickup is guaranteed; even if your train is late, your driver (who carries a sign with your name) will wait for you at no extra cost. With prices starting at €10, it's much more economical than a taxi, and the same rate applies for up to four people per car (maximum four pieces of luggage). See ⊕ *www.idcab.sncf.com* for details.

TO AND FROM THE UNITED KINGDOM

When you factor in travel time to and from the airport, not to mention flight delays, taking the Channel Tunnel is the fastest and easiest way to travel between France and the United Kingdom. The high-speed Eurostar train from Paris's Gare du Nord to London's St. Pancras Station takes 2 hours 15 minutes. Eurostar prices vary widely—round-trip tickets range from €620 for first class to €98 for second class—but depending on when and where you travel and how far in advance you book, you should be able to find discounted rates; there are special ones available for early-bird purchasers, but don't expect fares to drop closer to your departure date (a £10 fee is added to any purchase by phone or in person). If you wish to drive most of the route, you can put your car on the train through Eurotunnel for the 35-minute Chunnel crossing between Calais and Folkestone.

Before You Go

🌐 Passport

All Canadian, U.K., and U.S. citizens—even infants—need only a valid passport to enter France for stays of up to 90 days.

🆚 Visa

No seperate visa is required from American citizens visiting France for less than 90 days.

✏️ Immunizations

No special vaccines or immunizations are currently required before traveling to France.

🇺🇸 U.S. Embassy/Consulate

The U.S. embassy in France is located in Paris, nearby the Champs-Élysées. There are also five U.S. consulates throughout the country, located in Bordeaux, Lyon, Marseilles, Rennes, and Strasbourg.

📅 When to Go

High Season: June through August is the most expensive and popular time to visit France. June and July in Paris are especially crowded; August, typically when a *canicule* (heat wave) brings the country to its knees for a few days, is quieter in Paris but is the busiest month in the south. Famously fickle weather means you never know what to expect in the north.

Low Season: Unless you are skiing, winter offers the least appealing weather, though it's the best time for airfares and hotel deals—and to escape the crowds.

Particularly in the south, the famous mistral winds make travel uncomfortable.

Value Season: September is lovely, with temperate weather, saner airfares, and cultural events. October has great weather, though temperatures drop by late November. Late April or May is a great time to visit, before the masses arrive but when cafés are abuzz. March and early April weather can be varied and wet.

➕ Safety

Practice caution like you would in any other European country, but be prepared for extra security. These days you'll see a triangular sign labeled "Vigipirate" (France's antiterrorism system), which means extra vigilance may cause delays at the border or at major tourist attractions, for residents and tourists alike.

France's big cities are generally safe, but you should always be streetwise and alert, especially in Marseille. Across the country, scarcely a week goes by without some kind of demonstration; the current *gilets jaunes* (yellow vests) are protesting against the economic policies of President Macron and although most are peaceful, it's best to avoid them. The CRS (French riot police) carefully guard all major public gatherings, directing traffic and preventing violence. However, they are armed and use tear gas when and if they see fit. With shields in tow, it can be pretty startling the first time you see them, just like witnessing armed police onboard French trains checking for illegal migrants, which is also happening at a more alarming frequency. During peak holidays, you'll also notice an increased number of security forces on the streets, hands on their machine guns.

Essentials

🛏 Lodging

According to industry statistics, there are around 18,424 hotels in France. These range from luxury properties (including some honest-to-goodness palaces) to budget lodgings. The quality of accommodations, particularly in older properties and even in luxury hotels, can vary greatly from room to room; if you don't like the room you're given, ask to see another.

Meal plans offered in addition to the room rate are generally only available with a minimum two- or three-night stay, and prices are often stated on hotel websites. Breakfast is not always included in the stated price, but luckily this is France and most hotels will be within walking distance of a café or bakery.

It's always a good idea to make online hotel reservations in Paris and other major tourist destinations as far in advance as possible, especially in late spring, summer, or early fall. If you wish to communicate further, email is the easiest way to proceed—the hotel staff are probably more likely to read English than to understand it spoken over the phone long-distance. Ask that the hotel provide written confirmation of your reservation and requests such as late check-ins (to prevent your room from being given away) or the location or the size of the room you want.

Many hotels in France are small, family-run establishments. Some are affiliated with hotel groups, such as Logis de France (⊕ www.logishotels.com), which can be relied on for comfort, character, and regional cuisine. Three prestigious international groups with numerous converted châteaux, manor houses, and boutique properties are Châteaux & Hotels Collection (⊕ www.chateauxhotels.com), Relais & Châteaux (⊕ www.relaischateaux.com), and Small Luxury

Hotels of the World (⊕ www.slh.com): check the websites for property listings. France also has numerous hotel chains. Examples in the upper price bracket are Novotel and Sofitel as well as InterContinental, Marriott, Hilton, Hyatt, Westin, and Sheraton. The Best Western, Holiday Inn, Campanile, Mercure, and Timhotel chains are more moderate. If you simply need a place to crash for one night (and aren't claustrophobic), the ubiquitous Ibis, Hotel Kyriad, and Formule1 brands fit the bill. Typically, chains offer a consistently acceptable standard of comfort (modern bathrooms, TVs, etc.) but tend to lack atmosphere. One notable exception is Best Western: its properties are independently owned and most try to maintain the local character.

Vacation rentals in France typically book from Saturday to Saturday. Always check on policies regarding pets and children, and specify if you want an enclosed garden for toddlers, a washing machine, a fireplace, a pool, and so on. If you plan to have overnight guests during your stay, let the owner know; there may be additional charges (insurance restrictions prohibit loading in guests beyond the specified capacity). Occasionally, further fees apply: these might include an end-of-stay cleaning, or even bed linen and towel rentals, because French vacationers tend to bring their own. Be sure to plan early: apartment and house rentals are quite popular, especially during the summer.

🍴 Dining

All establishments in France must post their menus outside, so take a look before you enter. Most restaurants have two basic types of menu: à la carte and fixed-price (un menu or prix-fixe). The prix-fixe menu is usually the best value, though choices are more limited. Many of these include three courses; however, it's increasingly common to see set menus with two—either a starter and main course (*entrée et plat*) or a main course and dessert (*plat et dessert*).

Many say that bistros served the world's first fast food. After the fall of Napoléon, the Russian soldiers who occupied Paris were known to bang on zinc-top café bars, crying "*Bistro!*" (Quickly!) in Russian. In the past, bistros were simple places with minimal decor and service. Nowadays many are upscale and trendy, but you can still find cozy, low-key establishments serving straightforward, frequently gutsy cooking.

Brasseries—ideal places for quick, one-dish meals—originated when Alsatians, fleeing German occupiers after the Franco-Prussian War, came to Paris and opened restaurants serving specialties from home. Pork-based dishes, choucroute (sauerkraut), and beer (*brasserie* also means "brewery") remain the mainstays here. The typical brasserie is convivial and keeps late hours. Some are open 24 hours a day, a good thing to know since many restaurants stop serving at 10 or 10:30 pm.

Like bistros and brasseries, cafés come in a variety of styles and sizes. Often informal neighborhood hangouts, cafés may also be veritable showplaces attracting chic, well-heeled crowds. At most cafés the regulars congregate at the bar, where coffee and drinks are cheaper than at tables. At noon tables are set, and a limited lunch menu is served. Sandwiches, usually with *jambon* (ham), *fromage* (cheese), or *mixte* (ham and cheese), are served throughout the day. Sometimes snacks are also for sale. Cafés are for lingering, for people-watching, and for daydreaming. If none of these options fit

the bill, head to the nearest *traiteur* (deli) for picnic fixings.

Breakfast is usually served from 7:30 am to 10 am, lunch from noon to 2 pm (later in the south), and dinner from 7:30 or 8 pm to 10 pm. Restaurants in Paris usually serve dinner until 10:30 pm. Many restaurants close on Sunday—head to the Latin Quarter, the Champs Élysées, or Montmartre for the greatest choice of eateries open then.

PAYING

By French law, prices must include tax and tip (*service compris* or *prix nets*), but pocket change left on the table to round up the bill in basic places, or an additional 5% in better restaurants, is always appreciated. (Don't expect the dangling generous tip to guarantee friendly service, though: customer service is practically nonexistent in France.) Beware of bills stamped *service not included* in English. The prices given in this book are per person for a main course at dinner, including tax (10%) and service; note that if a restaurant offers only prix-fixe meals, it is given a price category that reflects the full prix-fixe price.

📅 Holidays

With 11 national *jours feriés* (holidays) and at least five weeks of paid vacation, the French have their share of repose. In May there's a holiday nearly every week, so be prepared for stores, banks, and museums to shut their doors for days at a time. Be sure to call museums, restaurants, and hotels in advance to make sure they'll be open.

Holidays include the following days: January 1 (New Year's Day); Easter Sunday and Monday; May 1 (Labor Day); May 8 (V.E. Day); Ascension Day; Pentecost Monday; July 14 (Bastille Day); the Feast

Essentials

of the Assumption; November 1 (All Saints Day); November 11 (Armistice Day); and December 25 (Christmas Day).

Taxes

Taxes must be included in affixed prices in France. Prices in restaurants and hotels must by law include taxes and service charges. ■TIP➡ **If these appear as additional items on your bill, you should complain.** There is, however, one exception: don't be shocked to find the *taxe de séjour* (tourist tax) on your hotel tab when you check out. Running €0.20–€4 per person per day, it is applied to all types of lodging. Even if you prepaid your accommodation online through a third-party travel website, you'll still have to cough up the coins.

The standard rate of the V.A.T. (Value-Added Tax, known in France as T.V.A.) is now 20%, with luxury goods taxed at a higher rate (up to 33%) and restaurant food taxed at a lower one (10%). The V.A.T. for services (restaurants, theaters, etc.) is not refundable, but foreigners are often entitled to a V.A.T. refund on goods they buy. To be eligible for one, the item (or items) that you purchased must have been bought in a single day in a participating store (look for the "Tax-Free" sticker on the door) and must equal or exceed €175.01.

Tipping

The French have a clear idea of when they should be tipped. Bills in bars and restaurants include a service charge incorporated into the price, but it's customary to round out your bill with some small change unless you're dissatisfied. The amount varies: anywhere from €0.20, if you've merely bought a beer or coffee, to €1–€3 (or more) after a light meal—but leave 5%–10% in an expensive restaurant. Tip taxi drivers 5% and hair stylists 5%–10%. In some theaters and hotels, coat-check attendants may expect nothing (if there's a sign reading "*pourboire interdit*," or tips forbidden); otherwise give them €1. Washroom attendants usually get €0.50, though the sum is often posted.

If you stay in a hotel for more than two or three days, it's customary to leave something for the housekeeper (€1.50–€2 per day). In expensive hotels you may well use the services of a parking valet, doorman, bellhop, and concierge. All expect a tip. Expect to pay €2 (€1 in a moderately priced hotel) to the person who carries your bags or hails a taxi for you; if the concierge has been helpful, leave a tip of €5–€20 depending on the service; in hotels that provide room service, give €1–€2 to the server (this does not apply to breakfast served in your room).

Museum guides should get €1–€1.50 after a tour. For other kinds of tours, tip the guide or excursion leader 10% of the tour cost; it's standard practice to tip long-distance bus drivers about €2 after an excursion, too. Other tips will depend on how much you've used a person's services—common sense must guide you here.

◎ Visitor Information

All major cities and most small towns have tourism offices that can provide information on accommodation and sightseeing as well as maps.

Great Itineraries

Western France

Beginning in château country, head south and west, through Cognac country into wine country around Bordeaux. Then lose yourself in the Dordogne, a landscape of rolling hills peppered with medieval villages, fortresses, and prehistoric caves.

LOIRE VALLEY CHÂTEAUX

3 or 4 days. Base yourself at the crossroads of Blois, starting with its multi-era château. Then head for the huge château in Chambord. Amboise's château echoes with history, and the neighboring manor, Clos Lucé, was Leonardo da Vinci's final home—or instead of this "town" château, head west to the tiny village of Rigny-Ussé for the Sleeping Beauty castle of Ussé. Heading southeast, finish up at Chenonceau—the most magical one of all—then return to the transportation hub city of Tours.

BORDEAUX WINE COUNTRY

2 days. Pay homage to the great names of Médoc, north of the city of Bordeaux, though the hallowed villages of Margaux, St-Julien, Pauillac, and St-Estèphe aren't much to look at. East of Bordeaux, via the prettier Pomerol vineyards, the village of St-Émilion is everything you'd want a wine town to be, with ramparts and medieval streets.

DORDOGNE AND PÉRIGORD

2 or 3 days. Follow the famous Dordogne River east to the half-timber market town of Bergerac. Wind through the green, wooded countryside into the region where humans' earliest ancestors left their mark, in the caves in Les Eyzies-de-Tayac and the famous Grotte de Lascaux. Be sure to sample the region's culinary specialties: truffles, foie gras, and preserved duck. Then travel south to the stunning and sky-high pilgrimage village of Rocamadour.

BY PUBLIC TRANSPORTATION

It's easy to get to Blois and Chenonceaux by rail, but you'll need to take a bus to visit other Loire châteaux. Another option is a minivan tour, especially if you only have a few days to make the most of your surroundings. Forays farther into Bordeaux country and the Dordogne are difficult by train, involving complex and frequent changes (Limoges is a big railway hub). Further exploration requires a rental car or sometimes unreliable bus routes.

France from North to South

Zoom from Paris to the heart of historic Burgundy, its rolling green hills traced with hedgerows and etched with vineyards. From here, plunge into the arid beauty of Provence and toward the spectacular coastline of the French Riviera.

BURGUNDY WINE COUNTRY

2 to 3 days. Base yourself in the market town of Beaune and visit its famous hospices and surrounding vineyards. Make a day trip to the ancient hill town of Vézelay, with its incomparable basilica, stopping in Autun to explore Roman ruins and its celebrated Romanesque cathedral. For more vineyards, follow the Côte d'Or from Beaune to Dijon. Or make a beeline to Dijon, with its charming Vieille Ville and fine museums. From here it's a two-hour drive to Lyon, where you can feast on this city's famous earthy cuisine. Another three hours' push takes you deep into the heart of Provence.

ARLES AND PROVENCE

2 to 3 days. Arles is the atmospheric, sun-drenched southern town that inspired Van Gogh and Gauguin. Take a day trip into grand old Avignon, home to the 14th-century rebel popes, to view their imposing palace. And make a pilgrimage to the Pont du Gard, the famous

Great Itineraries

triple-tiered Roman aqueduct west of Avignon. From here, a 2½-hour drive will bring you to Antibes and the glittering Riviera.

ANTIBES AND THE FRENCH RIVIERA

2 to 3 days. This historic and atmospheric port town is well positioned for day trips. First, head east into Nice, with its exotic Vieille Ville and its bounty of modern art. There are ports to explore and walking paths in Villefranche and St-Jean-Cap-Ferrat, east of Nice. The next day, head west to glamorous Cannes; allow time for a hike along the Sentier du Littoral around the Cap d'Antibes, or spend an hour or two exploring its many sandy beaches.

BY PUBLIC TRANSPORTATION

The high-speed TGV travels from Paris through Burgundy and Lyon, then zips through the south to Marseille. From Paris, there is a direct TER service to Beaune, where you can take a connection to Autun (about 70 minutes). Vézelay can be reached via train by stopping at Sermizelles station and then taking the SNCF shuttle bus "Sermizelles-Vézelay." Rail connections are easy between Arles and Avignon; you'll need a bus to get to the Pont du Gard from Avignon. Antibes, Cannes, and Nice are easily reached by the scenic rail line, as are most of the resorts and ports along the coast. To squeeze the most daytime out of your trip, take a night train or a plane from Nice back to Paris.

Family-Friendly France

Make your way through Normandy and Brittany, with enough wonders and evocative topics to inspire any child to put down the iPhone games and gawk.

PARIS

2 days. Paris's major museums, like the Louvre, can be as engaging as they are educational—as long as you keep your visits short. Start out your Paris stay by giving your kids an idea of how the city was planned by climbing to the top of the Arc de Triomphe. From here work your way down the Champs-Élysées toward Place de la Concorde and continue walking down the Champs to the Jardin des Tuileries, where kids can sail boats on a small pond. Then taxi or hike over to the Louvre for an afternoon visit. Your reward? A famously thick hot chocolate at Angélina on Rue de Rivoli, across the street. The next morning, head to the Eiffel Tower for a bird's-eye view of the city. After you descend, ride on the Bateaux Bus or one of the Bateaux Mouches at Place de l'Alma, nearby. Then take the métro to the hunchback's hangout, Notre-Dame Cathedral. Finish up your Paris visit by walking several blocks over, through the center of the Ile de la Cité, to Paris's most storybook sight—the Saint-Chapelle, a fairy-tale, stained-glass chapel that looks like a stage set for Walt Disney's *Sleeping Beauty*. If you happen to be near Avenues Matignon and Gabriel on a Wednesday, Saturday, or Sunday afternoon, pop by for a traditional puppet show at the Marionnettes des Champs-Élysées (3, 4, or 5 pm).

VERSAILLES

1 day. Here's an opportunity for a history lesson: with its amazing Baroque extravagance, no other monument so succinctly

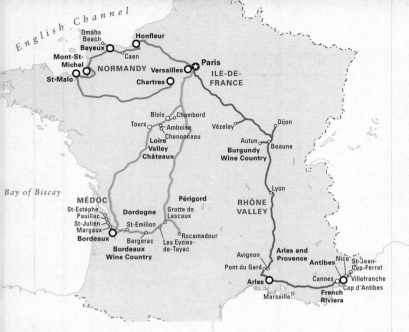

illustrates what inspired the rage of the French Revolution. Louis XIV's eye-popping château of Versailles pleases the secret monarch in most of us.

HONFLEUR

1 day. From this picture-book seaport lined with skinny half-timber row houses and salt-dampened cobblestones, the first French explorers set sail for Canada in the 15th century.

BAYEUX

2 days. William the Conqueror's extraordinary invasion of England in 1066 was launched from the shores of Normandy. The famous Bayeux tapestry, showcased in a state-of-the-art museum, spins the tale of the Battle of Hastings. From this home base you can introduce the family to the modern saga of 1944's Allied landings with a visit to the Museum of the Battle of Normandy, then make a pilgrimage to Omaha Beach.

MONT-ST-MICHEL

1 day. Rising majestically in a shroud of sea mist over vacillating tidal flats, this mystical peninsula is Gothic in every

sense of the word. Though its tiny, steep streets are crammed with visitors and tourist traps, no sight gives a stronger sense of the worldly power of medieval monasticism than Mont-St-Michel.

ST-MALO

1 day. Even in winter you'll want to brave the Channel winds to beachcomb the shores of this onetime pirate base. (Yes, kids, *pirates!*) In summer, of course, it's mobbed with sun seekers who stroll the old streets, restored to quaintness after World War II.

CHARTRES

1 day. Making a beeline on the autoroute back to Paris, stop in Chartres to view the loveliest of all of France's cathedrals.

BY PUBLIC TRANSPORTATION

Coordinating a sightseeing tour like this with a limited local train schedule isn't easy, and connections to Mont-St-Michel are especially complicated. Versailles, Chartres, and St-Malo are easy to reach, and Bayeux and Honfleur are doable, if inconvenient. But you'll spend a lot of vacation time waiting along train tracks.

Helpful French Phrases

BASICS

Yes/no	wee/nohn	Oui/non
Please	seel voo play	S'il vous plaît
Thank you	mair- **see**	Merci
You're welcome	deh ree- **ehn**	De rien
Excuse me, sorry	pahr- **don**	Pardon
Good morning/afternoon	bohn- **zhoor**	Bonjour
Good evening	bohn- **swahr**	Bonsoir
Good-bye	o ruh- **vwahr**	Au revoir
Mr. (Sir)	muh- **syuh**	Monsieur
Mrs. (Ma'am)	ma- **dam**	Madame
Miss	mad-mwa- **zel**	Mademoiselle
Pleased to meet you	ohn-shahn- **tay**	Enchanté(e)
How are you?	kuh-mahn-tahl-ay **voo**	Comment allez-vous?
Very well, thanks	tray bee-ehn, mair- **see**	Très bien, merci
And you?	ay voo?	Et vous?

NUMBERS

one	uhn	un
two	deuh	deux
three	twah	trois
four	**kaht**-ruh	quatre
five	sank	cinq
six	seess	six
seven	set	sept
eight	wheat	huit
nine	nuf	neuf
ten	deess	dix
eleven	ohnz	onze
twelve	dooz	douze
thirteen	trehz	treize
fourteen	kah- **torz**	quatorze
fifteen	kanz	quinze
sixteen	sez	seize
seventeen	deez- **set**	dix-sept
eighteen	deez- **wheat**	dix-huit
nineteen	deez- **nuf**	dix-neuf
twenty	vehn	vingt
twenty-one	vehnt-ay- **uhn**	vingt-et-un
thirty	trahnt	trente
forty	ka- **rahnt**	quarante
fifty	sang- **kahnt**	cinquante
sixty	swa- **sahnt**	soixante
seventy	swa-sahnt- **deess**	soixante-dix
eighty	kaht-ruh- **vehn**	quatre-vingts
ninety	kaht-ruh-vehn- **deess**	quatre-vingt-dix
one hundred	sahn	cent
one thousand	meel	mille

COLORS

black	nwahr	noir
blue	bleuh	bleu
brown	bruhn/mar- **rohn**	brun/marron
green	vair	vert
orange	o- **rahnj**	orange
pink	rose	rose
red	rouge	rouge
violet	vee-o- **let**	violette
white	blahnk	blanc
yellow	zhone	jaune

DAYS OF THE WEEK

Sunday	dee- **mahnsh**	dimanche
Monday	luhn- **dee**	lundi
Tuesday	mahr- **dee**	mardi
Wednesday	mair-kruh- **dee**	mercredi
Thursday	zhuh- **dee**	jeudi
Friday	vawn-druh- **dee**	vendredi
Saturday	sahm- **dee**	samedi

MONTHS

January	zhahn-vee- **ay**	janvier
February	feh-vree- **ay**	février
March	marce	mars
April	a- **vreel**	avril
May	meh	mai
June	zhwehn	juin
July	zhwee- **ay**	juillet
August	ah- **oo**	août
September	sep- **tahm**-bruh	septembre
October	awk- **to**-bruh	octobre
November	no- **vahm**-bruh	novembre
December	day- **sahm**-bruh	décembre

USEFUL PHRASES

Do you speak English?	par-lay **voo** ahn- **glay**	Parlez-vous anglais?
I don't speak …	zhuh nuh parl pah …	Je ne parle pas …
French	frahn- **say**	français
I don't understand	zhuh nuh kohm- **prahn** pah	Je ne comprends pas
I understand	zhuh kohm- **prahn**	Je comprends
I don't know	zhuh nuh say pah	Je ne sais pas
I'm American/British	zhuh sweez a-may-ree- **kehn** / ahn- **glay**	Je suis américain/anglais
What's your name?	ko-mahn vooz a-pell-ay- **voo**	Comment vous appelez-vous?
My name is …	zhuh ma- **pell** …	Je m'appelle …
What time is it?	kel air eh- **teel**	Quelle heure est-il?
How?	ko- **mahn**	Comment?
When?	kahn	Quand?
Yesterday	yair	Hier
Today	o-zhoor- **dwee**	Aujourd'hui

Tomorrow	duh- **mehn**	Demain
Tonight	suh **swahr**	Ce soir
What?	kwah	Quoi?
What is it?	kess-kuh- **say**	Qu'est-ce que c'est?
Why?	poor- **kwa**	Pourquoi?
Who?	kee	Qui?
Where is …	oo ay	Où est …
the train station?	la gar	la gare?
the subway station?	la sta- **syon** duh may- **tro**	la station de métro?
the bus stop?	la-ray duh booss	l'arrêt de bus?
the post office?	la post	la poste?
the bank?	la bahnk	la banque?
the … hotel?	lo- **tel**	l'hôtel …?
the store?	luh ma-ga- **zehn**	le magasin?
the cashier?	la kess	la caisse?
the … museum?	luh mew- **zay**	le musée …?
the hospital?	lo-pee- **tahl**	l'hôpital?
the elevator?	la-sahn- **seuhr**	l'ascenseur?
the telephone?	luh tay-lay- **phone**	le téléphone?
Where are the …	oo sohn lay	Où sont les …
restrooms?	twah- **let**	toilettes?
(men/women)	(**oh**-mm/ **fah**-mm)	(hommes/femmes)
Here/there	ee- **see** /la	Ici/là
Left/right	a goash/a draht	A gauche/à droite
Straight ahead	too drwah	Tout droit
Is it near/far?	say pray/lwehn	C'est près/loin?
I'd like …	zhuh voo- **dray**	Je voudrais …
a room	ewn **shahm**-bruh	une chambre
the key	la clay	la clé
a newspaper	uhn zhoor- **nahl**	un journal
a stamp	uhn **tam**-bruh	un timbre
I'd like to buy …	zhuh voo- **dray ahsh**-tay	Je voudrais acheter …
cigarettes	day see-ga- **ret**	des cigarettes
matches	days a-loo- **met**	des allumettes
soap	dew sah- **vohn**	du savon
city map	uhn plahn de **veel**	un plan de ville
road map	ewn cart roo-tee- **air**	une carte routière
magazine	ewn reh- **vu**	une revue
envelopes	dayz ahn-veh- **lope**	des enveloppes
writing paper	dew pa-pee- **ay** a **let**-ruh	du papier à lettres
postcard	ewn cart pos- **tal**	une carte postale
How much is it?	say comb-bee- **ehn**	C'est combien?
A little/a lot	uhn peuh/bo- **koo**	Un peu/beaucoup
More/less	plu/mwehn	Plus/moins
Enough/too (much)	a-say/tro	Assez/trop
I am ill/sick	zhuh swee ma- **lahd**	Je suis malade
Call a …	a-play uhn	Appelez un …
doctor	dohk- **tehr**	docteur
Help!	o suh- **koor**	Au secours!
Stop!	a-reh- **tay**	Arrêtez!
Fire!	o fuh	Au feu!
Caution!/Look out!	a-tahn-see- **ohn**	Attention!

DINING OUT

A bottle of …	ewn boo- **tay** duh	une bouteille de …
A cup of …	ewn tass duh	une tasse de …
A glass of …	uhn vair duh	un verre de …
Bill/check	la-dee-see- **ohn**	l'addition
Bread	dew panh	du pain
Breakfast	luh puh- **tee** day-zhuh- **nay**	le petit-déjeuner
Butter	dew burr	du beurre
Cheers!	ah **vo**-truh sahn- **tay**	A votre santé!
Cocktail/aperitif	uhn ah-pay-ree- **teef**	un apéritif
Dinner	luh dee- **nay**	le dîner
Dish of the day	luh plah dew **zhoor**	le plat du jour
Enjoy!	bohn a-pay- **tee**	Bon appétit!
Fixed-price menu	luh may- **new**	le menu
Fork	ewn four- **shet**	une fourchette
I am diabetic	zhuh swee dee-ah-bay- **teek**	Je suis diabétique
I am vegetarian	zhuh swee vay-zhay-ta-ree- **en**	Je suis végétarien(ne)
I cannot eat …	zhuh nuh puh pah mahn- **jay** deh	Je ne peux pas manger de …
I'd like to order	zhuh voo- **dray** ko-mahn- **day**	Je voudrais commander
Is service/the tip included?	ess kuh luh sair- **veess** ay comb- **pree**	Est-ce que le service est compris?
It's good/bad	say bohn/mo- **vay**	C'est bon/mauvais
It's hot/cold	say sho/frwah	C'est chaud/froid
Knife	uhn koo- **toe**	un couteau
Lunch	luh day-zhuh- **nay**	le déjeuner
Menu	la cart	la carte
Napkin	ewn sair-vee- **et**	une serviette
Pepper	dew **pwah**-vruh	du poivre
Plate	ewn a-see- **et**	une assiette
Please give me …	doe-nay- **mwah**	Donnez-moi …
Salt	dew sell	du sel
Spoon	ewn kwee- **air**	une cuillère
Sugar	dew **sook**-ruh	du sucre
Waiter!/Waitress!	muh- **syuh** / mad-mwa- **zel**	Monsieur!/Mademoiselle!
Wine list	la cart day vehn	la carte des vins

Contacts

✈ Air Travel

AIRPORTS Aeroport Beauvais. ⊠ *Rte. de l'aéroport Tillé, Beauvais* ☎ 08–92–68–20–66 *(€0.45 per min)* ⊕ *www.aeroportbeauvais.com.* **Charles de Gaulle/Roissy (***CDG***).** ☎ *3950 (€0.35 per min)* ⊕ *www.aeroportsdeparis.fr.* **Orly.** ☎ *3950 (€0.35 per min)* ⊕ *www.aeroportsdeparis.fr.*

GROUND TRANSPORTATION Air France Bus. ☎ *01–64–02–50–14* ⊕ *www.lebusdirect.com.* **Parishuttle.** ☎ *01–85–08–06–03* ⊕ *www.parishuttle.com.* **RATP.** ☎ *3424* ⊕ *www.ratp.fr.* **SuperShuttle.** ☎ *01–41–47–13–13* ⊕ *en.supershuttle.fr.*

⛴ Boat Travel

Brittany Ferries. ☎ *02–98–24–47–01* ⊕ *www.brittany-ferries.com.* **DFDS Seaways.** ☎ *02–32–14–68–50* ⊕ *www.dfdsseaways.co.uk.* **P&O European Ferries.** ☎ *03–66–74–03–25* ⊕ *www.poferries.com.*

🚌 Bus Travel

Eurolines. ☎ *08–92–89–12–00 (€0.35 per min), 01–41–86–24–21 outside France* ⊕ *www.eurolines.fr.*

🚢 Cruise Ship Travel

Abercrombie & Kent. ☎ *800/554–7016 in the U.S. and Canada* ⊕ *www.abercrombiekent.com.* **AmaWaterways.** ☎ *800/626–0126 in the U.S. and Canada* ⊕ *www.amawaterways.com.* **En-Bateau.** ☎ *04–67–13–19–62* ⊕ *www.en-bateau.com.* **European Waterways.** ☎ *800/394–8603 in the U.S., 877/574–3404 in Canada* ⊕ *www.europeanwaterways.com.* **French Country Waterways.** ☎ *800/222–1236 in the U.S. and Canada* ⊕ *www.fcwl.com.* **Viking River Cruises.** ☎ *800/304–9616 in the U.S. and Canada* ⊕ *www.vikingrivercruises.com.*

🛏 Lodging

Chambres Hôtes France. ⊕ *www.chambres-hotes.fr.* **Fédération Nationale des Gîtes de France.** ☎ *01–49–70–75–85* ⊕ *www.gites-de-france.com.* **VRBO.** ☎ *877/202–4291 in the U.S.* ⊕ *www.vrbo.com.*

🚆 Train Travel

Eurail. ☎ *6–405–793–58 WhatsApp messaging only* ⊕ *www.eurail.com.* **Eurostar.** ☎ *01–70–70–60–88, 343–218–6186 in the U.K.* ⊕ *www.eurostar.com.* **Eurotunnel.** ☎ *08–10–63–03–04 (€0.32 per min)* ⊕ *www.eurotunnel.com.* **Rail Europe.** ☎ *800/622–8600 in the U.S. and Canada* ⊕ *www.raileurope.com.* **SNCF.** ☎ *3635 (€0.40 per min)* ⊕ *www.sncf.com.* **TGV.** ☎ *3635 (€0.40 per min)* ⊕ *www.tgv.com.*

📍 Visitor Information

Centre des Monuments Nationaux. ⊕ *www.monuments-nationaux.fr.* **France Tourism.** ⊕ *us.france.fr.* **French Ministry of Culture.** ⊕ *www.culture.gouv.fr.*

Chapter 3

PARIS

Updated by
Jennifer Ladonne,
Linda Hervieux,
Nancy Heslin,
Virginia Power,
and Jack Vermee

👁 Sights	🍴 Restaurants	🛏 Hotels	🛍 Shopping	🍸 Nightlife
★★★★★	★★★★★	★★★★★	★★★★★	★★★★★

WELCOME TO PARIS

TOP REASONS TO GO

★ **Museum masterpieces:** There will always be something new to see at the Louvre—after all, the *Mona Lisa* is just one of 800,000 treasures.

★ **Culinary heaven:** From pastries and macarons to baguettes and crêpes, food in Paris is nothing short of sublime.

★ **Café society:** Whether you prefer a posh perch at Les Deux Magots or just the corner café, be sure to Hemingway an afternoon away over two café crèmes.

★ **Spend time on the Seine:** Take a leisurely stroll along the Rive Droite and the Rive Gauche, making sure to carve out time to visit the oldest part of Paris—Ile de la Cité and Ile St-Louis.

★ **Majestic churches:** Notre-Dame and Sacré-Coeur boldly mark the city's skyline and give a sense of its facinating history.

Paris is divided into 20 arrondissements (neighborhoods spiraling out from the center of the city. The number reveals the neighborhood's location, and its age: the 1st arrondissement at the city's heart is the oldest. The arrondissements in central Paris—the 1st to 8th—are the most visited. If you want to figure out what arrondissement something is in, check the zip code. The first three digits are always 750 for Paris, and the last two identify the arrondissement.

1 **Ile de la Cité and Ile St-Louis.** This is where you can find Notre-Dame and Sainte-Chapelle.

2 **Around the Eiffel Tower.** With the Champs de Mars, Invalides, and the Seine nearby, many lovely strolls give you striking views.

3 **Champs-Élysées.** The Champs-Élysées and Arc de Triomphe attract tourists, but there are also several excellent museums here.

4 **Around the Louvre.** The Faubourg St-Honoré, with its well-established shops and cafés, has always been chic and probably always will be.

5 **Les Grands Boulevards.** Use the Opéra Garnier as your landmark and set out to do some power shopping.

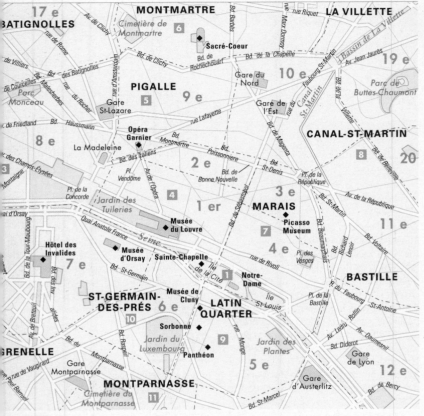

6 Montmartre. It feels
distinctly separate from
the rest of Paris, but
Montmartre is prime
tourist territory, with
Sacré-Coeur as its main
attraction.

7 The Marais. While
away the afternoon at the
Place des Vosges or shop to
your heart's content.

8 Eastern Paris. If it's new
and happening in Paris,
you'll find it out here.

9 The Latin Quarter.
Leave yourself time to
wander the Latin Quarter,
known for its vibrant
student life.

10 St-Germain-des-Prés.
The Musée d'Orsay is here,
but make sure to also
wander the Jardin du
Luxembourg.

11 Montparnasse. This
neighborhood is known
for its contemporary-art
scene.

12 Western Paris. The Bois
de Boulogne, a popular
park, is one great reason to
trek here.

If there's a problem with a trip to Paris, it's the embarrassment of riches that faces you. No matter which aspect of Paris you choose—touristy, historic, fashion-conscious, pretentious-bourgeois, thrifty, or the legendary bohemian, arty Paris of undying attraction—one thing is certain: you will carve out your own Paris, one that is vivid, exciting, ultimately unforgettable.

As world capitals go, Paris is surprisingly compact. The city is divided in two by the River Seine, with two islands (Ile de la Cité and Ile St-Louis) in the middle. Each bank of the Seine has its own personality; the Rive Droite (Right Bank), with its spacious boulevards and formal buildings, generally has a more genteel, dignified feel than the carefree and chic Rive Gauche (Left Bank), to the south. The east–west axis from Châtelet to the Arc de Triomphe, via rue de Rivoli and the Champs-Élysées, is the Right Bank's principal thoroughfare for sightseeing and shopping.

If this is your first trip, you may want to take a guided tour of the city—a good introduction that will help you get your bearings and provide you with a general impression before you return to explore the sights that particularly interest you. Each *quartier,* or neighborhood, has its own personality, which is best discovered by foot power. Ultimately, your route will be marked by your preferences, your curiosity, and your energy level. You can wander for hours without getting bored—though not, perhaps, without

getting lost. By the time you have seen only a few neighborhoods, drinking in the rich variety they have to offer, you should not only be culturally replete but downright exhausted—and hungry, too. Again, take your cue from Parisians and think out your next move in a sidewalk café.

Planner

When to Go

Although the City of Light is magical all year round, summer is the most popular (and priciest) time to go. It used to be that Paris was largely deserted in August when locals fled to the coast or countryside, leaving a wake of closed shops and restaurants. But today it remains very much alive throughout the summer, with outdoor music festivals, open-air movie screenings, and fun activities like those available at the popular Paris Plages, the "beaches" on the Right Bank of the Seine and along the upper Canal St-Martin. Nevertheless, the city is perhaps most appealing in late spring and early fall. June, when long, warm days translate into extended hours of sightseeing (the sun doesn't set until 10 pm), is particularly gorgeous. Ditto for September, which promises temperate weather, saner rates, and cultural events timed for the rentrée (or return), signifying the end of summer vacation. In the third weekend in September, scores of national buildings that are normally closed to the public open for visits during the annual Journées du Patrimoine (Patrimony Days). Winter can be dark and cold, but it's also the best time to find cheap airfares and hotel deals. Spring tends to remain damp and chilly into May, when prices start rising in synch with the mercury in local thermometers.

Saving Time and Money

Paris is one of the world's most visited cities—with the crowds to prove it—so it pays to be prepared. Buy tickets online when you can; most cultural centers, museums, and tour companies offer reduced ticket sales in advance, and the small service fee you'll pay will probably be worth the time saved waiting in line. Check out alternative entrances at popular sights, and check when rates are reduced, often during oncea- week evening openings. National museums are free the first Sunday of each month (this includes the Louvre, Musée d'Orsay, and Centre Pompidou). The Paris Museum Pass lets you bypass lines at major attractions; the two-, four-, and six-day passes cost €48, €62, and €74, respectively. The Paris Pass offers the perks of the Museum Pass plus a Travelcard for free unlimited travel across Central Paris on the métro, RER, and buses. Adult rates start at €131.

Getting Here and Around

Addresses in Paris are fairly straightforward: there's the number, the street name, and the zip code designating one of Paris's 20 *arrondissements* (districts); for instance, in Paris 75010, the last two digits ("10") indicate that the address is in the 10e arrondissement. The large 16e has two numbers assigned to it: 75016 and 75116.

The arrondissements are laid out in a spiral, beginning from the area around the Louvre (1er arrondissement), then moving clockwise through the Marais, the Latin Quarter, St-Germain, and then out from the city center to the outskirts to Ménilmontant/Père-Lachaise (20e arrondissement). Occasionally you may see an address with a number plus *bis*—for instance, 20 bis, rue Vavin. This indicates the next entrance or door down from 20 rue Vavin.

AIR TRAVEL

The major airports are Charles de Gaulle (CDG, also known as Roissy), 26 km (16 miles) northeast of Paris, and Orly (ORY), 16 km (10 miles) south of Paris. Both are easily accessible from the city. Whether you take a car or bus to travel from Paris to the airport on your departure, always allot an extra hour because of the often horrendous traffic tie-ups in the airports themselves (especially in peak seasons and at peak times). Free light-rail connections (Orlyval and CDGval) between major terminals are one option for avoiding some of the traffic mess, but you should still give yourself enough time to navigate through these busy airports.

BUS TRAVEL

With dedicated bus lanes now in place throughout the city—allowing buses and taxis to whiz past other traffic mired in tedious jams—taking the bus is an appealing option. Although nothing can beat the métro for speed, buses offer great city views, and the newer ones are equipped with air-conditioning—a real perk on those sweltering August days.

Paris buses are green and white; the route number and destination are marked in front, major stopping places along the sides. Glass-covered bus shelters contain timetables and route maps; note that buses must be hailed at these larger bus shelters, as they service multiple lines and routes. Smaller stops are designated simply by a pole bearing bus numbers.

When buying tickets, your best bet is a *carnet* of 10 tickets, available for €14.10 at any métro station, or a single ticket, which can be bought onboard for €1.80 (exact change appreciated).

CAR TRAVEL

Driving is not recommended within Paris. Parisian drivers are aggressive behind the wheel and it's often very difficult to park. Should you be driving into the city from elsewhere in Ile-de-France, the major ring road encircling the city is called the *périférique*, with the *périférique intérieur* going counterclockwise around the city, and the *périférique extérieur*, or the outside ring, going clockwise. Five lanes wide, the périférique is a highway from which *portes* (gates) connect Paris to the major highways of France. Highway names function on the same principle as the métro lines, with the final destination used as the route's name.

MÉTRO TRAVEL

Taking the métro is the most efficient way to get around Paris. Métro stations are recognizable either by a large yellow M within a circle or by the distinctive curly green Art Nouveau railings and archway bearing the full title (Métropolitain).

It's essential to know the name of the last station on the line you take, as this name appears on all signs. A connection (you can make as many as you like on one ticket) is called a *correspondance*. At junction stations, illuminated orange signs bearing the name of the line terminus appear over the correct corridors for each correspondance. Illuminated blue signs marked "*sortie*" indicate the station exit. Note that tickets are valid only inside the gates, or *limites*.

Access to métro platforms is through an automatic ticket barrier. Slide your ticket

in and pick it up as it pops out. Keep your ticket during your journey; you'll need it in case you run into any green-clad ticket inspectors, who will impose a hefty fine if you can't produce your ticket (they even accept credit cards!). Métro service starts at 5:30 am and continues the last trains reach their terminus at 1:15 am Sunday through Thursday, and until 2:15 am on Friday, Saturday, and some national holidays.. All métro tickets and passes are valid not only for the métro but also for all RER, tram, and bus travel within Paris. Métro tickets cost €1.90 each; a carnet (10 tickets for €14.90) is a better value.

TAXI TRAVEL

Taxi rates are based on location and time. Monday to Saturday, daytime rates (10 am–5 pm) within Paris are €1.06 per km (½ mile); nighttime rates (5 pm–midnight) are €1.27 per km. On Sunday, you'll pay €1.58 per km from midnight to 7 am and €1.30 from 7 am to midnight within Paris. Thanks to competition from ride-hailing services like Uber, the once unpredictable rates that official taxes charged to and from the airports into Paris are now fixed, and drivers are obligated to accept credit cards. Pay a flat €50 to and from Charles de Gaulle/Roissy for the Right Bank, €55 for the Left Bank; to and from Orly, pay €30 for Left Bank and €35 for Right Bank. There's a basic hire charge of €2.60 for all rides (excluding flat fares and taxis reserved in advance), and a minimum fare of €7. It's customary, but not obligatory, to tip up to 5%. Waiting time is charged at €35 per hour. The easiest way to get a taxi is to ask your hotel or a restaurant to call one for you or order one yourself with the handy app by Taxi G7, or find a taxi stand, which is marked by a square, dark-blue sign with a white "T" in the middle.

Uber and other ride-sharing services you order via an app on your smartphone have reshaped the transportation landscape in Paris, making rides easier to get and usually cheaper. Yet they remain controversial and extremely unpopular with traditional taxi drivers who resent the competition. Despite legal challenges, they have been allowed to operate with restrictions. The Uber app works worldwide, wherever the service is available, including to and from both CDG and Orly airports, though you'll need to ensure your smartphone works upon arrival in order to use it. Other options include Chauffeur Privé and Taxify. Download the apps to compare prices before you book.

Restaurants

Restaurants follow French mealtimes, serving lunch from noon to 2:30 pm and dinner from 7:30 or 8 pm. Some cafés serve food all day long. Always reserve a table for dinner, as top restaurants book up months in advance. When it comes to the check, you must ask for it (it's considered rude to bring it unbidden). In cafés you'll get a register receipt with your order. *Servis* (gratuity) is always included in the bill, but it's good form to leave something extra if you're satisfied with the service.

Brasseries often have nonstop service; some are open 24 hours. Assume a restaurant is open every day, unless otherwise indicated. Surprisingly, many prestigious restaurants close on weekends and sometimes Monday. July and August are the most common months for annual closings, although Paris in August is no longer the wasteland it once was.

Emblematic of the "bistronomy" movement is the proliferation of "gastrobistros"—often in far-flung or newly chic neighborhoods—helmed by established chefs fleeing the constraints of the star system or passionate young chefs unfettered by overblown expectations. Among the seasoned stars and exciting newcomers to the scene are Yannick Alléno, who left behind two Michelin stars at Le Meurice to open his locavore bistro Terroir Parisien at the Palais Brogniart and earned three stars at the storied Pavillon Ledoyen within his first year at the helm; David Toutain at the exceptional Restaurant David Toutain; Sylvestre Wahid at Brasserie Thoumieux; and Katsuaki Okiyama's Abri.

Hotels

If your Parisian fantasy involves romantic evenings in a historic grand-dame or a chic boutique hotel that pampers you in high style, here's some good news: you don't have to be wealthy to make your dreams come true. With 1,600 hotels, the City of Light gives visitors classy options in all price ranges, and a place with plenty of charm is practically a given, especially with the new generation of hotels popping up in the Right Bank (in neighborhoods like Pigalle, Ménilmontant, République, and Bastille) catering to style and affordability.

Unless stated in the review, hotels have elevators, and all guest rooms have TV, telephone, and a private bathroom. Recently, more and more hotels have standard air-conditioning, something that makes a summer stay much more bearable. Tubs don't always have shower curtains or showerheads. (How the French manage to scrub up without flooding the bathroom remains a cultural mystery.) If you book a budget hotel, be sure to confirm whether the bathroom is shared or not.

Restaurant and hotel reviews have been shortened. For full information, visit Fodors.com. Restaurant prices are the average cost of a main course at dinner or, if dinner is not served, at lunch. Hotel prices are the lowest cost of a standard double room in high season.

What It Costs in Euros

	$	$$	$$$	$$$$
RESTAURANTS				
	under €18	€18–€24	€25–€32	over €32
HOTELS				
	under €125	€125–€225	€226–€350	over €350

Nightlife

You haven't seen the City of Light until you've seen the city at night. Throngs pour into popular streets, filling the air with the melody of engaged conversation and clinking glasses. This is when locals let down their hair and reveal their true bonhomie, laughing and dancing, flirting and talking. Parisians love to savor life together: they dine out, drink endless espressos, offer innumerable toasts, and are often so reluctant to separate that they party all night.

Parisians go out weekends and weeknights, late and early. They tend to frequent the same places once they've found spots they like: it could be a wine bar, a corner café, a hip music club, or, more and more, a chic cocktail bar in an out-of-the-way neighborhood. A wise way to spend an evening is to pick an area in a neighborhood that interests you, then give yourself time to browse. Parisians also love to barhop, and the energy shifts throughout the evening, so be prepared to follow the crowds.

Performing Arts

The performing arts scene in Paris runs the gamut from highbrow to lowbrow, cheap (or even free) to break-the-bank expensive. Venues are indoors and outdoors, opulent or spartan, and dress codes vary accordingly. Regardless of the performance you choose, it's probably unlike anything you've seen before.

Parisians have an audacious sense of artistic adventure and a stunning eye for scene and staging. An added bonus in this city of classic beauty is that many of the venues themselves—from the opulent interiors of the Opéra Garnier and the Opéra Royal de Versailles to the Art Deco splendor of the Théâtre des ChampsÉlysées— are a feast for the eyes.

Detailed entertainment listings can be found online in English at ⊕ www.sortiraparis.com or in French from the weekly magazines *Pariscope* and *L'Officiel des Spectacles,* in the Wednesday entertainment insert Figaroscope in the *Figaro* newspaper (⊕ wevene.lefigaro.fr), and in the weekly *À Nous Paris,* distributed free in the métro. The webzine *Paris Voice* offers superb highlights in English. Most performing arts venues also have their own websites, and many include listings as well as other helpful information in English. The website of the Paris Tourist Office (⊕ www.parisinfo.com) has theater and music.

Shopping

In the most beautiful city in the world, it's no surprise to discover that the local greengrocer displays his tomatoes as artistically as Cartier does its rubies. Window-shopping is one of this city's greatest spectator sports; the French call it *lèche-vitrine* (literally, "licking the windows"), which is fitting because many of the displays look good enough to eat. Most stores, excepting department stores and flea markets, stay open until 6 or 7 pm, but many take a lunch break sometime between noon and 2 pm. Many shops traditionally close on Sunday.

Visitor Information

Paris is without question best explored on foot and, thanks to Baron Haussmann's mid-19th-century redesign, the City of Light is a compact wonder of wide boulevards, gracious parks, and leafy squares. Happily and conveniently, there are a half-dozen branches of the Paris tourist office located at key points in the capital.

CONTACTS Office du Tourisme de la Ville de Paris Pyramides ⊠ *25 rue des Pyramides, 1er, Louvre* ⊕ *www.parisinfo.com* Ⓜ *Pyramides.*

Île de la Cité and Île St-Louis

At the heart of Paris, linked to the banks of the Seine by a series of bridges, are two small islands: Île St-Louis and Île de la Cité. They're the perfect places to begin your visit, with postcard-worthy views all around. The Île de la Cité is anchored by mighty Notre-Dame, damaged by a recent fire but still standing; farther east, the atmospheric Île St-Louis is dotted with charming hotels, cozy restaurants, and small specialty shops.

◉ Sights

Ancien Cloître Quartier
NEIGHBORHOOD | Hidden in the shadows of Notre-Dame is an evocative, often-overlooked tangle of medieval streets. Through the years lucky folks, including Ludwig Bemelmans (who created the beloved *Madeleine* books) and the Aga Khan have called this area home, but back in the Middle Ages it was the domain of cathedral seminary students. One of them was the celebrated Peter Abélard (1079–1142)—philosopher, questioner of the faith, and renowned declaimer of love poems. Abélard boarded with Notre-Dame's clergyman, Fulbert, whose 17-year-old niece, Héloïse, was seduced by the compelling Abélard, 39 years her senior. She became pregnant, and the vengeful clergyman had Abélard castrated; amazingly, he survived and fled to a monastery, while Héloïse took refuge in a nunnery. The poetic, passionate letters between the two cemented their fame as thwarted lovers, and their story inspired a devoted following during the romantic 19th century. They still draw admirers to the Père-Lachaise Cemetery, where they're interred *ensemble.* The clergyman's house at 10 rue Chanoinesse was redone in 1849; a plaque at the back of the building at 9–11 quai aux Fleurs commemorates the lovers. ⊠ *Rue du Cloître-Notre-Dame north to Quai des Fleurs, Ile de la Cité* Ⓜ *Cité.*

★ Cathédrale Notre-Dame de Paris
RELIGIOUS SITE | Looming above Place du Parvis, this Gothic sanctuary is the symbolic heart of Paris and, for many, of France itself, now more than ever. A heartbreaking 2019 fire almost destroyed the entire cathedral, but luckily the majority of Notre-Dame's treasures survived intact. The roof was completely destroyed and the 300-foot spire collapsed, but after the fire was put out, the building was deemed structurally sound and most of its priceless relics and items survived, including the famed rose windows, the crown of thorns said to have been worn by Jesus Christ, the 800 year-old organ, and numerous pieces of classic artwork. Many of these items sustained some amount of damage, and thus restoration work for these and for the whole of the cathedral are expected to last several years. While visitors will not be able to visit inside for a while, the towers outside still stand as testaments to the power, history, and meaning of Notre-Dame. Napoléon was crowned here, and kings and queens exchanged marriage vows before its altar. Begun in 1163, completed in 1345, badly damaged during the Revolution, and restored in the 19th century by Eugène Viollet-le-Duc,

Ile de la Cité
and Ile St-Louis

KEY

1 *Exploring Sights*

1 *Restaurants*

1 *Hotels*

Sights ▼

1 Ancien Cloître
Quartier **F4**

2 Cathédrale Notre-Dame
de Paris **F5**

3 Conciergerie **D3**

4 Sainte-Chapelle **D3**

Restaurants ▼

1 Berthillon **H5**

2 Brasserie de l'Isle
Saint-Louis **G5**

Hotels ▼

1 Hôtel Saint-Louis
en l'Isle **G5**

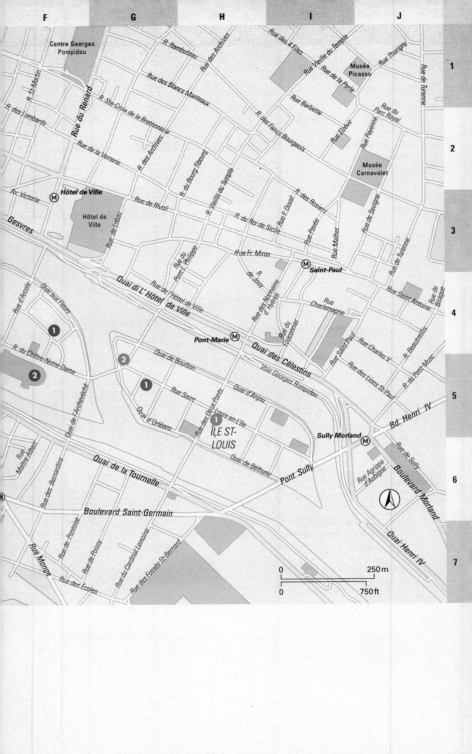

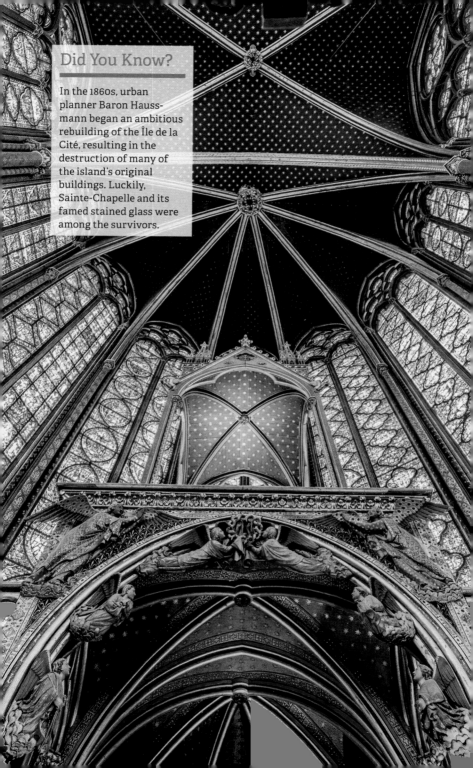

Notre-Dame may not be the country's oldest or largest cathedral, but in beauty and architectural harmony it has few peers. ✉ *6 parvis Notre-Dame–Place Jean-Paul II, Ile de la Cité* ☎ *01–42–34–56–10* ⊕ *www.notredameparis.fr* Ⓜ *Cité.*

Conciergerie

BUILDING | FAMILY | Most of the Ile de la Cité's medieval structures fell victim to wunderkind urban planner Baron Haussmann's ambitious rebuilding program of the 1860s. Among the rare survivors are the jewel-like Sainte-Chapelle, a vision of shimmering stained glass, and the Conciergerie, the cavernous former prison where Marie-Antoinette and other victims of the French Revolution spent their final days.

Constructed by Philip IV in the late 13th and early 14th centuries, the Conciergerie—which takes its name from the building's concierge or keeper—was part of the original palace of the kings of France before the royals moved into the Louvre around 1364. In 1391, it became a prison. During the French Revolution, Marie-Antoinette languished 76 days here awaiting her date with the guillotine. There is a re-creation of the doomed queen's sad little cell—plus others that are far smaller—complete with wax figures behind bars. In the chapel, stained glass, commissioned after the queen's death by her daughter, is emblazoned with the initials *M.A.* Outside you can see the small courtyard where women prisoners took meals and washed their clothes in the fountain (men enjoyed no similar respite). Well-done temporary exhibitions on the ground floor aim to please kids and adults alike; themes have included enchanted forests and Gothic castles. There are free guided tours (in French only) most days at 11 and 3. Download a free English guide from the website and/or rent a "Histopad" (€5), an "augmented reality" tablet that allows you to go back in time and view 30 reconstructions. ✉ *2 bd. du Palais, Ile de la Cité* ☎ *01–53–40–60–80* ⊕ *www. paris-conciergerie.fr* 🎫 *€9; €15 with joint ticket to Sainte-Chapelle* ☞ *Ticket window closes at 5:30* Ⓜ *Cité.*

★ Sainte-Chapelle

RELIGIOUS SITE | Built by the obsessively pious Louis IX (1214–70), this Gothic jewel is home to the oldest stained-glass windows in Paris. The chapel was constructed over three years, at phenomenal expense, to house the king's collection of relics acquired from the impoverished emperor of Constantinople. These included Christ's Crown of Thorns, fragments of the Cross, and drops of Christ's blood—though even in Louis's time these were considered of questionable authenticity.

The narrow spiral staircase by the entrance takes you to the upper chapel where the famed beauty of Sainte-Chapelle comes alive: 6,458 square feet of stained glass are delicately supported by painted stonework that seems to disappear in the colorful light streaming through the windows. Deep reds and blues dominate the background, noticeably different from later, lighter medieval styles such as those of Notre-Dame's rose windows.

The chapel is essentially an enormous magic lantern illuminating 1,130 biblical figures. Besides the dazzling glass, observe the detailed carvings on the columns and the statues of the apostles. The lower chapel is gloomy and plain, but take note of the low, vaulted ceiling decorated with fleurs-de-lis and cleverly arranged *L*s for "Louis." Audioguides (€3) are available, or you can download a free PDF guide from the website.

Sunset is the optimal time to see the rose window; however, to avoid waiting in killer lines, plan your visit for a weekday morning, the earlier the better. Come on a sunny day to appreciate the full effect of the light filtering through all that glorious stained glass. You can buy a joint ticket with the Conciergerie: lines are shorter if you purchase it there or online. The chapel makes a divine setting for classical concerts; check the schedule at www.classictic.com. ⊠ *4 bd. du Palais, Ile de la Cité* ☎ *01–53–40–60–80* ⊕ *www. sainte-chapelle.fr* ⊠ *€10; €15 with joint ticket to Conciergerie* ⤳ *Ticket window closes 30 mins before closing* Ⓜ *Cité.*

🍴 Restaurants

★ Berthillon
$ | FRENCH | Parisian ice cream is served at cafés all over town, but it's worth making a pilgrimage to the mecca of artisanal *crèmes glacées* to understand what all the fuss is about. The family-owned Berthillon shop features more than 30 flavors that change with the seasons, from mouth-puckering *cassis* (black currant) in summer to nutty *marron* (candied chestnut) in winter. **Known for:** delicious ice cream with natural ingredients; long lines; classic tea room atmosphere. ⓢ *Average main: €8* ⊠ *31 rue St-Louis-en-l'Ile, Île Saint-Louis* ☎ *01–43–54–31–61* ⊕ *www.berthillon.fr* ⊟ *No credit cards* ⊘ *Closed Mon. and Tues.* Ⓜ *Pont-Marie.*

Brasserie de l'Isle Saint-Louis
$$ | BRASSERIE | With its dream location on the tip of Île St-Louis overlooking the Seine and Notre-Dame, you'd think this charming brasserie, like so many before it, would have succumbed to its own success. Yet it remains exactly what a decent neighborhood brasserie should be, with an authentic decor, efficiently friendly service, and solid brasserie fare. **Known for:** fantastic views of Notre Dame; coveted outdoor terrace by the Seine; decent prices, considering the location. ⓢ *Average main: €24* ⊠ *55 quai de Bourbon, 4e, Île Saint-Louis* ☎ *01–43–54–02–59* ⊕ *www.labrasserie-isl.fr* ⊘ *Closed Wed.* Ⓜ *Pont Marie, Maubert-Mutualité, Sully-Morland.*

Hotels

Hôtel Saint-Louis en l'Isle
$$ | HOTEL | The location on the exceptionally charming Île St-Louis is the real draw of this five-story hotel, which retains many of its original 17th-century stone walls and wooden beams. **Pros:** romantic location; ancient architectural details; friendly staff. **Cons:** location is a bit far from the sights; métro stations are not so convenient; small rooms. ⓢ *Rooms from: €185* ⊠ *75 rue St-Louis-en-l'Ile, 4e, Île Saint-Louis* ☎ *01–46–34–04–80* ⊕ *www.saintlouisenlisle.com* ⇱ *20 rooms* ⦿ *No meals* Ⓜ *Pont Marie.*

Around the Eiffel Tower

One of Paris's most upscale neighborhoods, the posh 7e arrondissement (where nearly every block affords a view of La Tour Eiffel) is home to the French bourgeoisie and well-heeled expats. Commanding the southwestern end of Paris, the Eiffel Tower was considered an iron-latticed monstrosity when it opened in 1889. Today it is a beloved icon, especially at night when thousands of twinkling lights sparkle at the top of every hour.

👁 Sights

★ Eiffel Tower (*Tour Eiffel*)
BUILDING | FAMILY | The Eiffel Tower is to Paris what the Statue of Liberty is to New York and what Big Ben is to London: the ultimate civic emblem. French engineer Gustave Eiffel spent two years working to erect this iconic monument for the World Exhibition of 1889. Because its colossal bulk exudes such a feeling of permanence, it's hard to believe that the tower nearly became 7,000 tons of scrap when the concession expired in 1909. Only its potential use as a radio antenna saved the day. Though many prominent Parisians derided it at first, the tower gradually became part of the city's

Did You Know?

The Eiffel Tower did not begin life as the beloved icon it is today. Gustave Eiffel's iron creation for the 1889 World's Fair was greeted with disgust by Parisians, who dubbed it the Giant Asparagus.

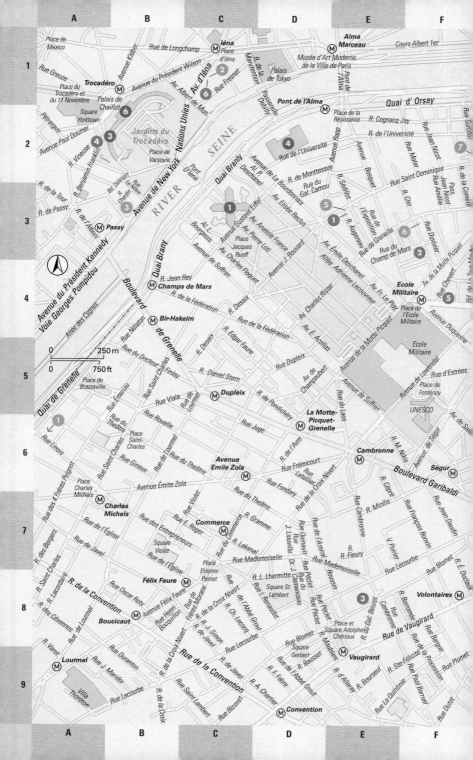

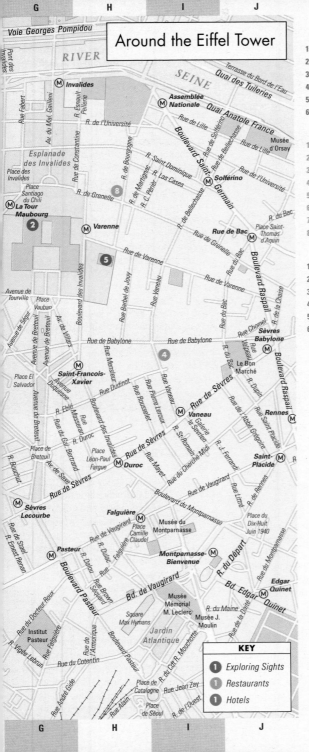

Around the Eiffel Tower

Sights ▼

Restaurants ▼

Hotels ▼

topography. Today it is most breathtaking at night, when every girder is highlighted in a glittering light show for five minutes every hour on the hour until 1 am.

More recent enhancements include a two-year, €30 million renovation of the first level that added a vertigo-inducing "transparent" floor 187 feet above the esplanade and a new miniturbine plant, four vertical-turbine windmills, and eco-friendly solar panels to minimize the tower's carbon footprint over time. You can stride up 704 steps as far as the second level, but only the elevator goes to the top. The view of the flat sweep of Paris at 1,000 feet is sublime—especially if you come in the late evening, after the crowds have dispersed. Beat the crushing lines by reserving your ticket online; you can also book a skip-the-line guided tour from one of many local companies (from €34). ⊠ *Quai Branly, Eiffel Tower* ☎ *08–92–70–12–39 €0.35 per min* ⊕ *www.toureiffel.paris* ⊠ *By elevator: from €16. By stairs: from €10* ⊗ *Closed last 2 wks in Jan. for annual maintenance* ⌛ *Stairs close at 6 pm in off-season (Oct.–June)* Ⓜ *Trocadéro, Bir-Hakeim, École Militaire; RER: Champ de Mars–Tour Eiffel.*

★ Hôtel des Invalides

HISTORIC SITE | The Baroque complex known as Les Invalides (pronounced "lehz-ahn-vah- *leed*") is the eternal home of Napoléon Bonaparte (1769–1821) or, more precisely, the little dictator's remains, which lie entombed under the towering golden dome. Louis XIV ordered the facility built in 1670 to house disabled soldiers (hence the name), and at one time 4,000 military men lived here. Today, a portion of it still serves as a veterans' residence and hospital. The Musée de l'Armée, containing an exhaustive collection of military artifacts from antique armor to weapons, is also here.

If you see only a single sight, make it the Église du Dome (one of Les Invalides' two churches) at the back of the complex. Napoléon's tomb was moved here in 1840 from the island of Saint Helena, where he died in forced exile. The emperor's body is protected by a series of no fewer than six coffins—one set inside the next, sort of like a Russian nesting doll—which are then encased in a sarcophagus of red quartzite. The bombastic tribute is ringed by statues symbolizing Napoléon's campaigns of conquest. To see more Napoléoniana, check out the collection in the Musée de l'Armée featuring his trademark gray frock coat and huge bicorne hat. Look for the figurines reenacting the famous coronation scene when Napoléon crowns his empress, Josephine. You can see a grander version of this scene by the painter David hanging in the Louvre. ■TIP→ **The best entrance to use is at the southern end, on Place Vauban (Avenue de Tourville); the ticket office is here, as is Napoléon's Tomb. There are automatic ticket machines at the main entrance on Place des Invalides.** ⊠ *Pl. des Invalides, Eiffel Tower* ☎ *01–44–42–38–77* ⊕ *www.musee-armee.fr* ⊠ *€12 with temporary exhibitions* ⌛ *Last admission 30 mins before closing* Ⓜ *La Tour–Maubourg, Varenne.*

Musée de l'Homme

MUSEUM | **FAMILY** | When President Jacques Chirac's legacy project (the Musée du Quai Branly, dedicated to the world's indigenous arts and cultures) pilfered half of this museum's pieces, few thought the rest of Paris's storied anthropology museum would survive, but luckily it has come roaring back to life. Focused now on "science and human societies," the Musée de l'Homme has 33,368 square feet of sparkling exhibition space in the west wing of the Palais de Chaillot, where it displays more than 700,000 prehistoric artifacts and art objects. And it now does so using the most modern of museum tricks—including interactive displays, 3-D projections, and educational games—to help visitors understand the history of the human species. While you're admiring the 25,000-year-old Venus of Lespugue or comparing the skull of Cro-Magnon man with that of René Descartes, don't forget to look out the window: the view from the upper floors across to the Eiffel Tower and southern Paris is spectacular. ✉ *Palais de Chaillot, 17 Pl. du Trocadéro, Eiffel Tower* ☎ *01–44–05–72–72* ⊕ *www.museedelhomme.fr* ✉ *€10 (€12 with temporary exhibitions)* ☞ *Closed Tues.* Ⓜ *Trocadéro.*

Musée du Quai Branly

MUSEUM | FAMILY | This eye-catching museum overlooking the Seine was built by star architect Jean Nouvel to house the state-owned collection of "non-Western" art, culled from the Musée National des Arts d'Afrique et d'Océanie and the Musée de l'Homme. Exhibits mix artifacts from antiquity to the modern age, such as funeral masks from Melanesia, Siberian shaman drums, Indonesian textiles, and African statuary. A corkscrew ramp leads from the lobby to a cavernous exhibition space, which is color coded to designate sections from Asia, Africa, and Oceania. The lighting is dim—sometimes too dim to read the information panels (which makes investing in the €5 audio guide a good idea).

Renowned for his bold modern designs, Nouvel has said he wanted the museum to follow no rules; however, many critics gave his vision a thumbs-down when it was unveiled in 2006. The exterior resembles a massive, rust-color rectangle suspended on stilts, with geometric shapes cantilevered to the facade facing the Seine and louvered panels on the opposite side. The colors (dark reds, oranges, and yellows) are meant to evoke the tribal art within. A "living wall" composed of some 150 species of exotic plants grows on the exterior, which is surrounded by a wild jungle garden with swampy patches—an impressive sight after dark when scores of cylindrical colored lights are illuminated. The trendy Les Ombres restaurant on the museum's

fifth floor (separate entrance) has prime views of the Tour Eiffel—and prices to match. The budget-conscious can enjoy the garden at Le Café Branly on the ground floor. ✉ *37 quai Branly, Eiffel Tower* ☎ *01–56–61–70–00* ⊕ *www.quaibranly.fr* ✉ *From €10 (free 1st Sun. of month)* 🕐 *Closed Mon.* ☞ *Ticket office closes 1 hr before museum* Ⓜ *Alma-Marceau.*

★ Musée Rodin

MUSEUM | FAMILY | Auguste Rodin (1840–1917) briefly made his home and studio in the Hôtel Biron, a grand 18th-century mansion that now houses this museum dedicated to his work. He died rich and famous, but many of the sculptures that earned him a place in art history were originally greeted with contempt by the general public, which was unprepared for his powerful brand of sexuality and raw physicality.

Most of Rodin's best-known sculptures are in the gardens. The front one is dominated by *The Gates of Hell* (circa 1880), illustrating stories from Dante's *Divine Comedy*. Rodin worked on the sculpture for more than 30 years, and it served as a "sketch pad" for many of his later works: you can see miniature versions of *The Kiss* (bottom right), *The Thinker* (top center), and *The Three Shades* (top center). The museum now showcases long-neglected models, plasters, and paintings, which offer insight into Rodin's creative process. Pieces by other artists from his personal collection, are on display as well—including paintings by van Gogh, Renoir, and Monet. There's also a room devoted to works by Camille Claudel (1864–1943), his student and longtime mistress, who was a remarkable sculptor in her own right. An English audio guide (€6) is available for the permanent collection and for temporary exhibitions. Tickets can be purchased online for priority access (€1 service fee). If you wish to linger, the lovely Café du Musée Rodin serves meals and snacks in the shade of the garden's linden trees. ✉ *77 rue de Varenne, Eiffel Tower*

☎ *01–44–18–61–10* 🌐 *www.musee-rodin.fr* 🎟 *€12 (free 1st Sun. of month)* 🕐 *Closed Mon.* [M] *Varenne.*

Palais de Chaillot

ARTS VENUE | FAMILY | This honey-colored Art Deco cultural center on Place du Trocadéro was built in the 1930s to replace a Moorish-style building constructed for the 1878 World's Fair. Its esplanade is a top draw for camera-toting visitors intent on snapping the perfect shot of the Eiffel Tower. In the building to the left is the Cité de l'Architecture et du Patrimoine—billed as the largest architectural museum in the world—and the Theâtre National de Chaillot, which occasionally stages plays in English. Also here is the Institut Français d'Architecture, an organization and school. The twin building to the right contains the Musée de l'Homme, a thoroughly modern anthropology museum. Sculptures and fountains adorn the garden leading to the Seine. ✉ *Pl. du Trocadéro, Eiffel Tower* [M] *Trocadéro.*

🍴 Restaurants

★ Comice

$$$$ | FRENCH | Don't let its off-the-beaten-path location keep you away from this elegant newcomer, which won a Michelin star before being open even a year. The husband-and-wife team—chef and sommelier respectively—are both veterans of top dining rooms in Paris, the United States, and Canada and create dishes and wine pairings of great sophistication and subtlety. **Known for:** exquisite presentation; beautiful decor; meticulous sourcing of all products and ingredients. [$] *Average main: €56* ✉ *31 av. de Versailles, 16e, Eiffel Tower* ☎ *01–42–15–55–70* 🌐 *www.comice.paris* 🕐 *Closed Sun., Mon., and late Apr.–early May* [M] *Mirabeau, Jasmin.*

★ La Table d'Aki

$$$$ | MODERN FRENCH | Set in a quiet, aristocratic *quartier* near the Musée Rodin, La Table d'Aki might just be the most perfect little-gem restaurant in all of Paris. Its simple elegance highlights the thrilling cuisine centered on the sea. **Known for:** romantic ambience; perfectly prepared fish; open kitchen serving just 16 diners at a time. [$] *Average main: €40* ✉ *49 rue Vaneau, 7e, Eiffel Tower* ☎ *01–45–44–43–48* 🕐 *Closed Sun., Mon., 2 wks in Feb., and Aug.* [M] *Saint-François-Xavier.*

★ L'Abeille

$$$$ | MODERN FRENCH | Everything here, from the dove-gray decor to the sparkling silver, speaks of quiet elegance—all the better to savor Christophe Moret's masterful cuisine. Choices include a "harlequin" of yellow, red, and white beets with a ginger-tinged yogurt and aloe vera emulsion; Breton langoustine in a cinnamon-perfumed gelée, with grapefruit pulp and a ginger-and-Tahitian-vanilla-infused mayonnaise; and lightly caramelized scallops in an ethereal cloud of white-chocolate foam. **Known for:** some of the best service in town (including a jar of honey as a parting gift); relaxed, intimate dining; elegant decor overlooking interior garden. [$] *Average main: €100* ✉ *Paris Shangri-La Hotel, 10 av. d'Iéna, 16e, Eiffel Tower* ☎ *01–53–67–19–90* 🌐 *www.shangri-la.com* 🕐 *Closed Sun. and Mon. No lunch Sat.–Wed.* [M] *Iéna.*

★ L'Astrance

$$$$ | MODERN FRENCH | Pascal Barbot rose to fame thanks to his restaurant's reasonable prices and casual atmosphere, but after the passage of several years, Astrance has become resolutely haute. His dishes often draw on Asian ingredients, as in grilled lamb with miso-lacquered eggplant and a palate-cleansing white sorbet spiked with chili pepper and lemongrass. **Known for:** set menus that change daily; space that seats only 25 lucky diners a night; extraordinary wine list. [$] *Average main: €120* ✉ *4 rue Beethoven, 16e, Eiffel Tower* ☎ *01–40–50–84–40* 🕐 *Closed Sat.–Mon., and Aug.* [M] *Passy.*

Le Café Constant

$ | **BISTRO** | Parisians are a nostalgic bunch, which explains the popularity of this down-to-earth venue, a relatively humble bistro with cream-color walls, red banquettes, and wooden tables. The menu reads like a French cookbook from the 1970s—who cooks veal cordon bleu these days?—but the dishes taste even better than before. **Known for:** excellent prices, especially at lunch; classic bistro fare with a gourmet twist; neighborhood favorite. $ *Average main: €17* ⊠ *139 rue St-Dominique, 7e, Eiffel Tower* ☎ *01–47–53–73–34* ⊕ *www.maisonconstant.com* Ⓜ *École Militaire; Métro or RER: Pont de l'Alma.*

Le Petit Cler

$ | **FRENCH** | With all the charm of a traditional Parisian *bistrot* and a menu of classics to match, this welcoming eatery is hands down Rue Cler's best for any meal of the day, any day of the week. Dishes like homemade foie gras, melt-in-your-mouth duck confit, and an excellent tarte tatin always satisfy, and daily specials, written on the giant mirror, always include fish and vegetarian options. **Known for:** charming ambience and sidewalk seating; all-day hours; quality market ingredients. $ *Average main: €14* ⊠ *29 rue Cler, 7e, Eiffel Tower* ☎ *01–45–50–17–50* ⊕ *www.lepetitcler. com* Ⓜ *La Tour-Maubourg, École Militaire.*

★ Restaurant David Toutain

$$$$ | **FRENCH FUSION** | Although chef David's Toutain's approach may be exasperatingly conceptual for some, others find his earthy, surprising, and inspired concoctions utterly thrilling. Each dish is a lesson in contrasts—of temperature, texture, and flavor—as well as a feat of composition: briny oysters, brussels sprouts, and foie gras in a warm potato consommé; creamy raw oysters with tart kiwi and yuzu; crispy pork chips alongside velvety smoked potato puree. **Known for:** equally wonderful choices for vegetarians and carnivores; epitome of "seasonal" cuisine; plenty of avant-garde thrills.

$ *Average main: €43* ⊠ *29 rue Surcouf, 7e, Eiffel Tower* ☎ *01–45–50–11–10* ⊕ *www.davidtoutain.com* ⊘ *Closed Sat. and Sun.* Ⓜ *Invalides, La Tour–Maubourg.*

★ Savarin la Table

$$$ | **FRENCH** | This cozy restaurant has a laid-back contemporary vibe that belies the immense sophistication of the dishes created by Mehdi Kebboul and Hliza Ayun, young chefs trained in some of Paris's leading kitchens. Here adventurous diners are treated to dishes of rare creativity, with delectable options such as rabbit cake with piquillo peppers, chard and octopus, or succulent duck ravioli. **Known for:** romantic dining upstairs; excellent quality-to-price value; wonderful desserts. $ *Average main: €26* ⊠ *34 rue de Bourgogne, 7e, Eiffel Tower* ☎ *09–86–59–19–67* ⊘ *Closed Sat. and Sun.* Ⓜ *Varenne, Solferino.*

Hotels

★ Hôtel de Londres Eiffel

$$ | **HOTEL** | Prices at this small, boutique hotel in an upscale neighborhood are fairly reasonable considering all you get—top-notch service, stylish homey decor, a lively neighborhood, and some spectacular views. **Pros:** excellent service; just steps from the Eiffel Tower; quaint setting. **Cons:** rooms on the small side; food not permitted in rooms; not super close to métro. $ *Rooms from: €225* ⊠ *1 rue Augereau, 7e, Eiffel Tower* ☎ *01–45–51–63–02* ⊕ *www.hotel-paris-londres-eiffel.com* ⊅ *30 rooms* ⦿ *No meals* Ⓜ *La Tour-Maubourg, École Militaire.*

Hôtel du Champ de Mars

$$ | **HOTEL** | Around the corner from picturesque Rue Cler, this charming, affordable hotel welcomes guests with a Provence-inspired lobby and huge picture windows overlooking a quiet street. **Pros:** good value; walking distance to Eiffel Tower, Les Invalides, and Rodin Museum; free Wi-Fi. **Cons:** small rooms compared to larger hotels; no air-conditioning; inconsistent service. $ *Rooms from:*

€150 ⌂ 7 rue du Champ de Mars, 7e, Eiffel Tower ☏ 01–45–51–52–30 ⊕ www.hotelduchampdemars.com ⤴ 25 rooms ⍰ No meals Ⓜ École Militaire.

★ Hotel Eiffel Blomet

$$ | HOTEL | FAMILY | Named for the cabaret a few doors down where Josephine Baker once sang, this handsome Art Deco hotel comes with a luxurious pool, hammam, and sauna. **Pros:** great pool, steam room, and sauna; chic rooms; good value. **Cons:** off-the-radar neighborhood; not that close to the Eiffel Tower; average breakfast. $ *Rooms from: €200* ⌂ 78 rue Blomet, 15e, Eiffel Tower ☏ 01–53–68–70–00 ⊕ www.hoteleiffel-blomet.com ⤴ 87 rooms ⍰ No meals Ⓜ Vaugirard, Volontaires.

Hôtel Eiffel Trocadéro

$$$ | HOTEL | A curious blend of Second Empire and rococo styling awaits guests in this hotel on a quiet corner just off Place Trocadéro. **Pros:** views of Eiffel Tower from upper floors; upscale residential district convenient to métro; organic breakfast buffet. **Cons:** no full-service restaurant; long walk to city center; basic rooms feel cramped. $ *Rooms from: €270* ⌂ 35 rue Benjamin-Franklin, 16e, Eiffel Tower ☏ 01–53–70–17–70 ⊕ www.hoteleiffeltrocadero.com ⤴ 17 rooms ⍰ No meals Ⓜ Trocadéro.

Hôtel Le Tourville

$$$ | HOTEL | This cozy, contemporary haven near the Eiffel Tower, Champs de Mars, and Invalides is a comfortable base for exploring Paris. **Pros:** convenient location near métro; friendly service; free Wi-Fi in all rooms. **Cons:** small standard rooms; air-conditioning only during summer months; no restaurant. $ *Rooms from: €280* ⌂ 16 av. de Tourville, 7e, Eiffel Tower ☏ 01–47–05–62–62 ⊕ www.paris-hotel-tourville.com ⤴ 30 rooms ⍰ No meals Ⓜ École Militaire.

★ Shangri-La Hotel Paris

$$$$ | HOTEL | Displaying French elegance at its best, this impressively restored 19th-century mansion gazing across the Seine at the Eiffel Tower was once the stately home of Prince Roland Bonaparte, grandnephew of the emperor himself, and his gilded private apartments have been transformed into La Suite Impériale. **Pros:** some of the best views in Paris; excellent dining; fabulous pool. **Cons:** astronomical rates; pool only open until 9 pm; expensive breakfast. $ *Rooms from: €1,100* ⌂ 10 av. Iéna, 16e, Eiffel Tower ☏ 01–53–67–19–98 ⊕ www.shangri-la.com ⤴ 101 rooms ⍰ No meals Ⓜ Iéna.

Champs-Élysées

Make no mistake: the Champs-Élysées, while ceding some of its elegance in recent times, remains the most famous avenue in Paris—and, perhaps, the world. Like New York's Times Square or London's Piccadilly Circus, it is a mecca for travelers and locals alike. Some Parisians complain that fast-food joints and chain stores have cheapened Avenue des Champs-Élysées, but others are more philosophical, noting that there is something here for everyone. If you can't afford lunch at Ladurée, there's always McDonald's (and the view from its second floor is terrific).

 ## Sights

★ Arc de Triomphe

MEMORIAL | Inspired by Rome's Arch of Titus, this colossal, 164-foot triumphal arch was ordered by Napoléon—who liked to consider himself the heir to Roman emperors—to celebrate his military successes. Unfortunately, Napoléon's strategic and architectural visions were not entirely on the same plane, and the Arc de Triomphe proved something of an embarrassment. Although the emperor wanted the monument completed in time for an 1810 parade in honor of his new bride, Marie-Louise, it was still only a few feet high, and a dummy arch of painted canvas was strung up to save face. Empires come and go, but Napoléon's had been gone for more than 20 years before the Arc was finally finished in 1836. A small museum halfway up recounts its history.

The Arc de Triomphe is notable for magnificent sculptures by François Rude, including *The Departure of the Volunteers in 1792,* better known as *La Marseillaise,* to the right of the arch when viewed from the Champs-Élysées. Names of Napoléon's generals are inscribed on the stone facades—the underlined names identify the hallowed figures who fell in battle.

The traffic circle around the Arc is named for Charles de Gaulle, but it's known to Parisians as L'Étoile, or "the Star"—a reference to the streets that fan out from it. Climb the stairs to the top of the arch and you can see the star effect of the 12 radiating avenues and the vista down the Champs-Élysées toward Place de la Concorde and the distant Musée du Louvre.

■TIP→ **France's Unknown Soldier is buried beneath the arch, and a commemorative flame is rekindled every evening at 6:30. That's the most atmospheric time to visit, but, to beat the crowds, come early in the morning or buy your ticket online.**

⚠ **Be wary of the traffic circle that surrounds the arch. It's infamous for accidents—including one several years ago that involved the French transport minister. Always use the underground passage from the northeast corner of the Avenue des Champs-Élysées.** ⊠ *Pl. Charles-de-Gaulle, Champs-Élysées* ☎ *01–55–37–73–77* ⊕ *www.paris-arc-de-triomphe.fr* ⌸ *€12* ☞ *Last admission 45 mins before closing* Ⓜ *Métro or RER: Charles-de-Gaulle–Étoile.*

Avenue des Champs-Élysées

NEIGHBORHOOD | FAMILY | Marcel Proust lovingly described the genteel elegance of the storied Champs-Élysées (pronounced "chahnz- *eleezay,*" with an "n" sound instead of "m," and no "p") during its Belle Époque heyday, when its cobblestones resounded with the clatter of horses and carriages. Today, despite unrelenting traffic and the intrusion of chain stores and fast-food franchises, the avenue still sparkles. There's always something happening here: stores are open late (and many are open on Sunday, a rarity in Paris); nightclubs remain top destinations; and cafés offer prime people-watching, though you'll pay for the privilege—after all, this is Europe's most expensive piece of real estate. Along the 2-km (1¼-mile) stretch, you can find marquee names in French luxury, like Cartier, Guerlain, and Louis Vuitton. Car manufacturers lure international visitors with space-age showrooms. Old stalwarts, meanwhile, are still going strong—including the Lido cabaret and Fouquet's, whose celebrity clientele extends back to James Joyce. The avenue is also the setting for the last leg of the Tour de France bicycle race (the third or fourth Sunday in July), as well as Bastille Day (July 14) and Armistice Day (November 11) ceremonies. The Champs-Élysées, which translates to "Elysian Fields" (the resting place of the blessed in Greek mythology), began life as a cow pasture and in 1666 was transformed into a park by the royal landscape architect André Le Nôtre. Traces of its green origins are visible toward the Concorde, where elegant 19th-century park pavilions house the historic restaurants Ledoyen and Laurent. ⊠ *Champs-Élysées* Ⓜ *Champs-Élysées–Clemenceau, Franklin-D.-Roosevelt, George V, Charles-de-Gaulle–Étoile.*

★ Grand Palais

ARTS VENUE | With its curved-glass roof and gorgeously restored Belle Époque ornamentation, you can't miss the Grand Palais whether you're approaching from the Seine or the Champs-Élysées. It forms an elegant duo with the Petit Palais across Avenue Winston Churchill: both stone buildings, adorned with mosaics and sculpted friezes, were built for the 1900 World's Fair, and, like the Eiffel Tower, were not intended to be permanent.

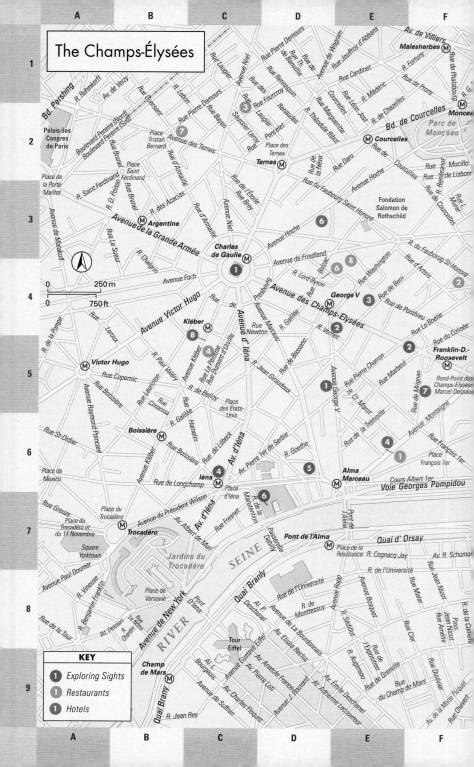

Sights ▼

1 Arc de Triomphe **C4**
2 Avenue des
  Champs-Élysées **E5**
3 Grand Palais. **G6**
4 Musée Guimet **C6**
5 Musée Yves Saint
  Laurent Paris............**D6**
6 Palais de Tokyo **D7**
7 Petit Palais, Musée des
  Beaux-Arts de la
  Ville de Paris **H6**

Restaurants ▼

1 Alain Ducasse au
  Plaza Athénée **E6**
2 L'Arôme **F4**
3 Le Petit Verdot du 17e...**C2**
4 LiLi........................**C5**
5 Mini Palais **G6**
6 Pierre Gagnaire.........**D4**
7 Rech.....................**B2**
8 Taillevent **E3**

Hotels ▼

1 Four Seasons Hôtel
  George V Paris..........**D5**
2 Hôtel Fouquet's
  Barrière...................**E4**
3 Hôtel Lancaster..........**E4**
4 Hôtel Plaza Athénée.....**E6**
5 La Réserve...............**G5**
6 Le Royal Monceau
  Raffles Paris.............**D3**
7 Marignan **F5**
8 The Peninsula
  Paris......................**C5**

The exquisite main exhibition space called Le Nef (or nave) hosts large-scale shows which focus on everything from jewelry to cars. The art-oriented shows staged here—including the annual FIAC, Paris's contemporary-art fair—are some of the hottest tickets in town. Previous must-sees included an Edward Hopper retrospective and *Picasso and the Masters*. To skip the long queue, booking an advance ticket online for an extra euro is strongly advised. ⊠ *Av. Winston Churchill, Champs-Élysées* ☎ *01–40–13–48–00* ⊕ *www.grandpalais.fr* ⊠ *Around €15 (exhibitions vary)* ⊘ *Closed Tues.* Ⓜ *Champs-Élysées–Clemenceau.*

★ Musée Guimet

MUSEUM | The outstanding Musée Guimet boasts the western world's biggest collection of Asian art, thanks to the 19th-century wanderings of Lyonnaise industrialist Émile Guimet. Exhibits, enriched by the state's vast holdings, are laid out geographically in airy, light-filled rooms. Just past the entry, you can find the largest assemblage of Khmer sculpture outside Cambodia. The second floor has statuary and masks from Nepal, ritual funerary art from Tibet, and jewelry and fabrics from India. Peek into the library rotunda, where Monsieur Guimet once entertained the city's notables under the gaze of eight caryatids atop Ionic columns; Mata Hari danced here in 1905. The much-heralded Chinese collection, made up of 20,000-odd objects, covers seven millennia, while the impressive Buddhist Pantheon features scores of Budhhas from China and Japan. Grab a free English-language audio-guide and brochure at the entrance. If you need a pick-me-up, stop at the Salon des Porcelaines café on the lower level for a ginger milk shake. And don't miss the Guimet's adjunct space just up the street at 19 avenue d'Iéna. ⊠ *6 pl. d'Iéna, Champs-Élysées* ☎ *01–56–52–54–33* ⊕ *www.guimet.fr* ⊠ *€8.50; €11.50 with temporary exhibition* ⊘ *Closed Tues.* Ⓜ *Iéna, Boissiére.*

Musée Yves Saint Laurent Paris

MUSEUM | As elegant and stylish as the master couturier's groundbreaking designs, this museum is housed in the very mansion where Yves Saint Laurent did his work and entertained celebrity clients. More than 50 prototypes—including such landmarks as the Mondrian dress, the original pantsuit, and the woman's tuxedo—are on display at any one time, as are dozens of design drawings and a glittering array of jewelry. Thanks to its huge windows, the light-bathed upstairs atelier, stuffed with books and fabrics, offers an intimate glimpse into YSL's world. Be sure not to miss the touching short film detailing the relationship between Saint Laurent and his longtime partner Pierre Bergé. All of the exhibits have detailed English labeling, and there is a free English guide available at reception. ⊠ *5 av. Marceau, Champs-Élysées* ☎ *01–44–31–64–00* ⊕ *www.museeyslparis.com* ⊠ *€10* ⊘ *Closed Mon.* ⎙ *Last entry 45 mins before closing* Ⓜ *Alma-Marceau.*

Palais de Tokyo

MUSEUM | The go-to address for some of the city's funkiest exhibitions, the Palais de Tokyo is a stripped-down venue that spotlights provocative, ambitious contemporary art. There is no permanent collection: instead, cutting-edge temporary shows are staged in a cavernous space reminiscent of a light-filled industrial loft. The programming extends to performance art, concerts, readings, and fashion shows. Night owls will appreciate the midnight closing. The museum's chic Les Grands Verres restaurant and cocktail bar—serving an avant-garde take on traditional French fare—is a haunt of hip locals, especially at lunch. But there's also a small café area at the restaurant entrance for a quick bite and glass of wine or cup of coffee if you don't feel like a sit-down meal. Visit the offbeat bookshop for souvenirs that are as edgy and subversive as the exhibits. ⊠ *13 av. du Président Wilson, Champs-Élysées*

☎ *01–81–97–35–88* 🌐 *www.palaisdetokyo.com* 🎫 *€12* 🕑 *Closed Tues.* [M] *Iéna.*

Petit Palais, Musée des Beaux-Arts de la Ville de Paris
MUSEUM | The "little" palace has a small, overlooked collection of excellent paintings, sculpture, and objets d'art, with works by Monet, Gauguin, and Courbet, among others. Temporary exhibitions, beefed up in recent years (and occasionally free), are particularly good. The building, like the Grand Palais across the street, is an architectural marvel of marble, glass, and gilt built for the 1900 World's Fair, with impressive entry doors and huge windows overlooking the river. Search directly above the main galleries for 16 plaster busts set into the wall representing famous artists. Outside, note two eye-catching sculptures: French World War I hero Georges Clemenceau faces the Champs-Élysées, while a resolute Winston Churchill faces the Seine. In warmer weather, head to the garden café with terrace seating. ✉ *Av. Winston Churchill, Champs-Élysées* ☎ *01–53–43–40–00* 🌐 *www.petitpalais.paris.fr* 🎫 *Free; €5–€15 for temporary exhibitions* 🕑 *Closed Mon.* [M] *Champs-Élysées–Clemenceau.*

🍴 Restaurants

★ Alain Ducasse au Plaza Athénée
$$$$ | MODERN FRENCH | Set within the Plaza Athénée hotel, Alain Ducasse's three-star Paris flagship totally redefines French haute cuisine. Arguably the world's most visible chef, Ducasse surprises here, devoting himself entirely to vegetables, grains, and fish and mixing the most luxe with the humblest ingredients to sublime effect. **Known for:** gorgeous, überopulent dining room; haute-vegetarian dining; consistent winner of three Michelin stars. [$] *Average main: €130* ✉ *Hôtel Plaza Athénée, 25 av. Montaigne, 8e, Champs-Élysées* ☎ *01–53–67–65–00* 🌐 *www.alain-ducasse.com* 🕑 *Closed weekends. No lunch Mon.–Wed.* 👔 *Jacket required* [M] *Alma-Marceau.*

L'Arôme
$$$$ | MODERN FRENCH | Eric Martins ran a popular bistro in the far reaches of the 15e arrondissement before opening this contemporary restaurant off the Champs-Élysées, and his background in haute cuisine makes this ambitious dining room an easy transition. The spot turns out seasonal dishes with a touch of finesse from the open kitchen. **Known for:** masterful wine pairings; Breton crab with avocado, Japanese rice, and tomato gelée with smoked pepper; pricey fixe-prix menus (no à la carte). [$] *Average main: €48* ✉ *3 rue St-Philippe du Roule, 8e, Champs-Élysées* ☎ *01–42–25–55–98* 🌐 *www.larome.fr* 🕑 *Closed Sat. and Sun., and Aug.* [M] *St-Philippe du Roule.*

Le Petit Verdot du 17e
$$ | BISTRO | Sandwich bars might be threatening the traditional two-hour lunch, but that doesn't stop this old-fashioned neighborhood bistro with its painted facade and wine-themed dining room from flourishing. Business executives loosen their neckties to feast on homemade pâté, plate-engulfing steak for two, or guinea hen with cabbage, along with one of 50 or so small-producer wines. **Known for:** small and authentic space; generous plates at great prices; legendary steak tartare. [$] *Average main: €19* ✉ *9 rue Fourcroy, 17e, Champs-Élysées* ☎ *01–42–27–47–42* 🕑 *Closed Sun. No lunch Sat.* [M] *Charles de Gaulle–Étoile.*

★ LiLi
$$$$ | CANTONESE | The operatically beautiful LiLi, in the Peninsula Hotel, places sophisticated Cantonese cuisine in its rightful place—the gastronomic center of the world. The menu features all the classics, raised to the status of haute cuisine: small plates of dim sum (seafood, vegetable, or pork dumplings) alongside more substantial fare like fried rice studded with market-fresh vegetables,

succulent Sichuan shrimp, and barbecued suckling pig. **Known for:** authentic Peking duck; gourmet dim sum; cocktails at the Bar Kléber. ⓢ *Average main: €36* ✉ *The Peninsula Paris, 19 rue Kléber, 16e, Champs-Élysées* ☎ *01–58–12–67–50* ⊕ *paris.peninsula.com* Ⓜ *Kléber, Charles de Gaulle–Étoile.*

Mini Palais

$$$ | **MODERN FRENCH** | Inside the Grand Palais, Mini Palais is a stylish dining room, but the menu is the real draw. The burger *de magret et foie gras,* a flavorful mélange of tender duckling breast and duck foie gras drizzled with truffled jus on a buttery brioche bun, underscores what's best about this place: a thoroughly modern cuisine with an old-fashioned extravagance. **Known for:** soaring outdoor terrace with views of the Petit Palais and Pont Alexandre III; late-night snacks; decent prices, considering the neighborhood. ⓢ *Average main: €25* ✉ *3 av. Winston Churchill, 8e, Champs-Élysées* ☎ *01–42–56–42–42* ⊕ *www.minipalais. com* Ⓜ *Champs-Élysées–Clemenceau.*

★ Pierre Gagnaire

$$$$ | **MODERN FRENCH** | If you want to venture to the frontier of contemporary cooking—and if money is no object—dinner here is a must. Chef Pierre Gagnaire's work is at once intellectual and poetic, often blending three or four unexpected tastes and textures in a single dish. Just taking in the menu requires concentration (ask the waiters for help), so complex are the multiline descriptions about each dish's six or seven ingredients. **Known for:** consistently ranked among the world's best (and most expensive) restaurants; combines French technical mastery with cutting-edge techniques; complicated menu descriptions. ⓢ *Average main: €150* ✉ *6 rue de Balzac, 8e, Champs-Élysées* ☎ *01–58–36–12–50* ⊕ *www.pierre-gagnaire.com* ⊗ *Closed Sat. and Sun., and Aug.* Ⓜ *Charles de Gaulle–Étoile.*

Rech

$$$$ | **SEAFOOD** | Having restored the historic Paris bistros Aux Lyonnais and Benoît to their former glory, star chef Alain Ducasse turned his piercing attention to this seafood brasserie founded in 1925. His wisdom lies in knowing what not to change: the original Art Deco chairs in the main-floor dining room; seafood shucker Malec, who has been a fixture on this chic stretch of sidewalk since 1982; and the supersized éclair that's drawn in locals for decades. **Known for:** most delicate line-caught sole sautéed in butter; luminous dining room that is a lovely setting at lunch or dinner; Mediterranean-inspired dishes. ⓢ *Average main: €35* ✉ *62 av. des Ternes, 17e, Champs-Élysées* ☎ *01–45–72–29–47* ⊕ *www.restaurant-rech.fr* ⊗ *Closed Sun. and Mon., and late July–late Aug.* Ⓜ *Ternes.*

★ Taillevent

$$$$ | **MODERN FRENCH** | Perhaps the most traditional of all Paris luxury restaurants, this grande dame basks in renewed freshness under brilliant chef David Bizet, who draws inspiration from the Basque country, Bordeaux, and Languedoc for his daily menu. Traditional dishes such as scallops meunière (with butter and lemon) are matched with contemporary choices like a splendid spelt risotto with truffles and frogs' legs or panfried duck liver with caramelized fruits and vegetables. **Known for:** one of the oldest names in Paris for fine French dining; discreet hangout for Paris politicians; 19th-century salon turned winter garden. ⓢ *Average main: €100* ✉ *15 rue Lamennais, 8e, Champs-Élysées* ☎ *01–44–95–15–01* ⊕ *www.taillevent.com* ⊗ *Closed Sat. and Sun., and Aug.* ⓘ *Jacket and tie* Ⓜ *Charles de Gaulle–Étoile.*

Hotels

★ Four Seasons Hôtel George V Paris

$$$$ | HOTEL | FAMILY | As poised and polished as the day it opened in 1928, this superb hotel's original plaster detailing and 17th-century tapestries have been restored, the bas-reliefs regilded, and the marble-floor mosaics rebuilt tile by tile, adding up to an opulence rarely equalled in the city. **Pros:** some of the best dining in the city; courtyard dining in summer; indoor swimming pool. **Cons:** several blocks from the nearest métro; definitely for the one percent; lacks the intimacy of smaller boutique hotels. [$] *Rooms from: €1100* ✉ *31 av. George V, 8e, Champs-Élysées* ☎ *01–49–52–70–00* 🌐 *www.fourseasons.com/paris* 🛏 *244 rooms* 🍴 *No meals* [M] *George V.*

Hôtel Fouquet's Barrière

$$$$ | HOTEL | Steps away from one of the world's most famous streets, this luxury hotel adjacent to the legendary Fouquet's Brasserie at the corner of the Champs-Élysées and Avenue George V is recognizable by its uniformed valets, parked sports cars, and elegant Haussmannian entryway. **Pros:** many rooms overlook the Champs-Élysées; very close to métro; beautiful spa and pool. **Cons:** expensive; bars can get overcrowded; corporate events give the place a business-hotel feel. [$] *Rooms from: €1000* ✉ *46 av. George V, 8e, Champs-Élysées* ☎ *01–40–69–60–00* 🌐 *www.lucienbarriere.com* 🛏 *114 rooms* 🍴 *No meals* [M] *George V.*

Hôtel Lancaster

$$$$ | HOTEL | Once a Spanish nobleman's town house, this luxurious retreat dating to 1889 dazzles with its elegant decor, lush courtyard, and acclaimed restaurant. **Pros:** steps away from the Champs-Élysées and five minutes from métro; excellent seasonal menus at La Table du Lancaster; peaceful street. **Cons:** size of rooms varies greatly; decor looks tired; no spa. [$] *Rooms from: €460* ✉ *7 rue de Berri, 8e, Champs-Élysées* ☎ *01–40–76–40–76* 🌐 *www.hotel-lancaster.fr* 🛏 *56 rooms* 🍴 *No meals* [M] *George V.*

★ Hôtel Plaza Athénée

$$$$ | HOTEL | FAMILY | Distinguished by the scarlet flowers cascading over its elegant facade, this glamorous landmark hotel sits on one of the most expensive avenues in Paris. **Pros:** Eiffel Tower views; great restaurant and bar; Dior Institute spa. **Cons:** attracts oligarchs; exorbitant prices; small fitness room. [$] *Rooms from: €1100* ✉ *25 av. Montaigne, 8e, Champs-Élysées* ☎ *01–53–67–66–65* 🌐 *www.dorchestercollection.com/en/paris/hotel-plaza-athenee* 🛏 *208 rooms* 🍴 *No meals* [M] *Alma-Marceau.*

★ La Réserve

$$$$ | HOTEL | Set in a splendid 19th-century mansion just steps from the presidential palace and the American Embassy, this aristocratic lodging vies for the most elegant small hotel in Paris. **Pros:** top-notch spa with pool; splendid views over the Champs-Élysées and Eiffel Tower; excellent dining. **Cons:** very expensive; can be snobby; out-of-the-way neighborhood. [$] *Rooms from: €1000* ✉ *42 av. Gabriel, 8e, Champs-Élysées* ☎ *01–58–36–60–60* 🌐 *www.lareserve-paris.com* 🛏 *40 rooms* 🍴 *No meals* [M] *Franklin-D.-Roosevelt.*

Le Royal Monceau Raffles Paris

$$$$ | HOTEL | FAMILY | The glamorous Royal Monceau Raffles offers tons of luxury, great dining, and an artsy atmosphere along with a hefty dose of cool. **Pros:** ethereal spa and fitness center; chic private apartments; nice terrace garden. **Cons:** hefty prices; away from the heart of Paris; fitness room is small. [$] *Rooms from: €850* ✉ *37 av. Hoche, 8e, Champs-Élysées* ☎ *01–42–99–88–00* 🌐 *www.leroyalmonceau.com* 🛏 *149 rooms* 🍴 *No meals* [M] *Charles-de-Gaulle-Étoile.*

Marignan

$$$$ | HOTEL | Set smack-dab in the middle of Paris's Golden Triangle, just off the Champs-Élysées, this sleek five-star hotel is a paragon of contemporary style that includes fine in-hotel dining and some breathtaking terrace views. **Pros:** stellar views from upper terraces; prices good for this standard of luxury; great location. **Cons:** a few rooms on the smaller side; not all rooms have great views; lack of outlets in bathrooms. $ *Rooms from: €420* ⊠ *12 rue de Marignan, 8e, Champs-Élysées* ☎ *01–40–76–34–56* ⊕ *www.hotel-marignan.com* ⇗ *50 rooms* ⊚ *No meals* Ⓜ *Franklin-D.-Roosevelt.*

★ The Peninsula Paris
$$$$ | HOTEL | FAMILY | After a €900 million renovation that restored the luster of this gem dating to 1908, the lavishly appointed Peninsula raises the bar for luxury hotels in Paris. **Pros:** world-class dining; fabulous spa and pool; amazing views from higher floors. **Cons:** price out of reach for most; not centrally located; stuffy neighborhood. $ *Rooms from: €850* ⊠ *19 av. Kléber, Champs-Élysées* ☎ *01–58–12–28–88* ⊕ *paris.peninsula.com* ⇗ *200 rooms* ⊚ *No meals* Ⓜ *Kléber, Etoile.*

 Nightlife

★ Crazy Horse
CABARET | This world-renowned cabaret has elevated the striptease to an art form. Founded in 1951, it's famous for gorgeous dancers and naughty routines characterized by lots of humor and very little clothing. What garments there are have been dazzlingly designed by the likes of Louboutin and Alaïa and shed by top divas (including Dita von Teese). Reserved seats for the show start at €85. ⊠ *12 av. George V, 8e, Champs-Élysées* ☎ *01–47–23–32–32* ⊕ *www.lecrazyhorseparis.com* Ⓜ *Alma–Marceau.*

★ Le Bar du Bristol
BARS/PUBS | Apparently not satisfied with its usual rich and powerful clientele, this tony spot is now vying for the impossibly hip, too. Along with enticing cocktails and rarified spirits, Le Bar promises exceptional wines and tapas. Weekdays from 7 pm to 9:30 pm, it also showcases

curated art videos on its behind-the-bar mirror screen. Chic Paris DJs heat up the scene between 9:30 pm and 2 am on Friday and Saturday. ⊠ *112 rue du Faubourg St-Honoré, 8e, Champs-Élysées* ☎ *01–53–43–43–00* ⊕ *www.lebristolparis.com* Ⓜ *Miromesnil.*

Lido
CABARET | The legendary Lido now adds a modern-day dose of awe-inspiring stage design to the cabaret's trademark style. The 100-minute productions—still featuring those beloved Bluebell Girls and 12 "Lido boys"—run at 9 pm and 11 pm, 365 days a year. Dinner for Two packages for the earlier show include the Soirée Etoile (€170), Soirée Champs-Élysées (€195), and the Soirée Triomphe (€300). If you're on a budget, €115 gets you a ticket plus half a bottle of bubbly. Yes, those prices are per person, but this is Paris nightlife as it's meant to be experienced. It's best to book your tickets in advance by phone, online, or on-site. ⊠ *116 bis, av. des Champs-Élysées, 8e, Champs-Élysées* ☎ *01–40–76–56–10* ⊕ *www.lido.fr* Ⓜ *George V.*

★ Saint James Club Paris
BARS/PUBS | Like a library room out of *Harry Potter,* the bar at the Saint James Club Paris—complete with 5,000 leather-bound volumes and a cozy fireplace—is studiously inviting. It's very French, and open to nonmembers only after 7 pm or during Sunday brunch. The owners are a venerable old Bordeaux family; accordingly, you'll find a respectable selection of champagnes and wines. ⊠ *5 pl du Chancelier Adenauer, 16e, Champs-Élysées* ☎ *01–44–05–81–81* ⊕ *www.saintjamesclub.com* Ⓜ *Porte Dauphine.*

Shopping

★ Balenciaga
CLOTHING | This venerable Paris house rose to fashion stardom under the brilliant Nicolas Ghesquière, whose architectural volumes and structural technique revolutionized the label. His

abrupt departure in 2012 opened the door for American wunderkind Alexander Wang's brief tenure. A frisson of delight rocked the fashion world when it was announced, in late 2015, that underdog designer Demna Gvasalia, previously of Margiela and the ultracool insider label Vetements, would take the helm. The risk paid off immediately—his rigorously experimental street-wear-influenced designs, which use 3-D printing technology, are edgy, innovative, and surprisingly elegant. ⊠ *10 av. George V, 8e, Champs-Élysées* ☎ *01–47–20–21–11* ⊕ *www.balenciaga.com* Ⓜ *Alma-Marceau.*

★ Bonpoint

CLOTHING | Outfit the prince or princess in your life at Bonpoint (yes, royalty *does* shop here). The prices are high, but the quality is exceptional, and the adorable miniduds couldn't be more stylish: picture a perfect hand-smocked Liberty-print dress, a velvety lambskin vest, or a double-breasted cashmere sweater for Little Lord Fauntleroy. The Avenue Raymond Poincaré boutique is one of more than a dozen citywide. ⊠ *64 av. Raymond Poincaré, 16e, Champs-Élysées* ☎ *01–47–27–60–81* ⊕ *www.bonpoint.com* Ⓜ *Trocadéro.*

★ Céline

CLOTHING | Reinvigorated by Michael Kors in the late 1990s, Céline got another much-needed jolt when Phoebe Philo arrived in 2008 and began dazzling the critics with her focused approach. Philo single-handedly redefined the codes of fashion for professional women, garnering a huge and fiercely loyal following for her streamlined, minimal designs, featuring flowing pants; long, unstructured jackets; and the Cabas bag. LVMH announced in January 2018 that she'd be succeeded by Hedi Slimane, who left Saint Laurent in 2016 after rocking (or rock 'n' rolling) the label to its core. As of this writing, it remains to be seen what he does with one of fashion's most beloved labels. ⊠ *53*

av. Montaigne, 8e, Champs-Élysées ☎ *01–40–70–07–03* ⊕ *www.celine.com* Ⓜ *Franklin-D.-Roosevelt.*

★ Chanel

CLOTHING | Elegant, modern looks with sex appeal and lasting value are Chanel's stock in trade. Although the spectacularly beautiful Avenue Montaigne flagship takes shoppers' breath away, the heart of this revered fashion house is still the boutique at 31 rue Cambon, where Chanel once perched high up on the mirrored staircase watching audience reactions to her collection debuts. Great investments include all of Coco's favorites: the perfectly tailored suit, a lean soigné dress, or a quilted bag with a gold chain. Handbags, jewelry, shoes, and accessories are all found at the fabulous 42 avenue Montaigne boutique, opposite the flagship store. ⊠ *51 av. Montaigne, 8e, Champs-Élysées* ☎ *01–44–50–73–00* ⊕ *www.chanel.com* Ⓜ *Franklin-D.-Roosevelt.*

★ Dior

CLOTHING | Following in John Galliano's outsized footsteps, Raf Simons did a brilliant job of redefining the label, but himself decamped in 2015, leaving the door open for Maria Grazia Chiuri, Dior's first female designer for a label that's traditionally defined the feminine. Chiuri proved herself quickly, starting with the runaway success of her "We Should All Be Feminists" T-shirt and gorgeous flower-strewn collections that she calls both "feminine and feminist." Now one of fashion's major darlings, Chiuri's collections are hotly anticipated each season and her Avenue Montaigne boutique is an absolute must while in Paris. ⊠ *30 av. Montaigne, 8e, Champs-Élysées* ☎ *01–40–73–73–73* ⊕ *www.dior.com* Ⓜ *Franklin-D.-Roosevelt.*

Guerlain

PERFUME/COSMETICS | This opulent address is a fitting home for Paris's first—and most famous—perfumer. Still the only Paris outlet for legendary perfumes like

Shalimar and L'Heure Bleue, it has added several new signature scents (including Myrrhe et Délires and Cuir Beluga). Personalized bottles in several sizes can be filled on demand, or, for a mere €30,000, a customized scent can be blended just for you. Sybarites will also appreciate Guerlain's makeup, scented candles, and redesigned spa featuring its much-adored skin-care line. There's an elegant gourmet restaurant for lunch or tea, too. ⊠ 68 av. des Champs-Élysées, 8e, Champs-Élysées ☎ 01–45–62–52–57 ⊕ www. guerlain.com Ⓜ Franklin-D.-Roosevelt.

★ Louis Vuitton

SHOES/LUGGAGE/LEATHER GOODS | Louis Vuitton has spawned a voracious fan base from Texas to Tokyo with its mix of classic leather goods and saucy revamped versions orchestrated by Marc Jacobs. His 2013 exit left tall boots to fill, but Nicholas Ghesquière—a daring designer who single-handedly resurrected the Balenciaga label—has done an admirable job. Melding his signature edgy modernism with vintage touches and colors, Ghesquière is taking the legendary luxe label to a glorious new level. ⊠ 101 av. des Champs-Élysées, 8e, Champs-Élysées ☎ 01–53–57–52–00 ⊕ www.louisvuitton.com Ⓜ George V.

Maison Ullens

CLOTHING | A glam Golden Triangle location, a Rem Koolhaas–designed boutique, sumptuous clothes—the Belgian label's first Paris outpost hits all the marks and then some. Founded in 2013, Maison Ullens puts the focus on luxe fabrics and skins in classic-chic designs with plenty of staying power. It has everything you need for après-ski or weekends on Capri. ⊠ 4 rue de Marignan, 8e, Champs-Élysées ☎ 01–47–20–23–56 ⊕ www.maisonullens.com Ⓜ Franklin-D.-Roosevelt.

Around the Louvre

The neighborhoods from the très chic Faubourg St-Honoré to trendy Les Halles are a study in contrasts, with the Louvre in the midst of the bustle. The posh Rue Faubourg St-Honoré, once the stomping ground of kings and queens, is now home to the French president and assorted foreign ambassadors. Beloved by fashionistas for three centuries, it is as popular today as it was when royal mistresses shopped here—which explains the plethora of high-end stores (almost every luxury brand is represented). Not surprisingly, ritzy restaurants and haute hotels are located here as well.

Sights

Église de la Madeleine

RELIGIOUS SITE | With its rows of uncompromising columns, this enormous neoclassical edifice in the center of Place de la Madeleine was consecrated as a church in 1842, nearly 78 years after construction began. Initially planned as a Baroque building, it was later razed and begun anew by an architect who had the Roman Pantheon in mind. Interrupted by the Revolution, the site was razed yet again when Napoléon decided to make it into a Greek temple dedicated to the glory of his army. Those plans changed when the army was defeated and the emperor deposed. Other ideas for the building included making it into a train station, a market, and a library. Finally, Louis XVIII decided to make it a church, which it still is today. Classical concerts are held here regularly, some of them free. ⊠ Pl. de la Madeleine, Louvre ☎ 01–44–51–69–00 ⊕ www.eglise-lamadeleine.com Ⓜ Madeleine.

★ Galerie Vivienne

STORE/MALL | Considered the grande dame of Paris's 19th-century passages couverts—the world's first shopping malls—this graceful covered arcade

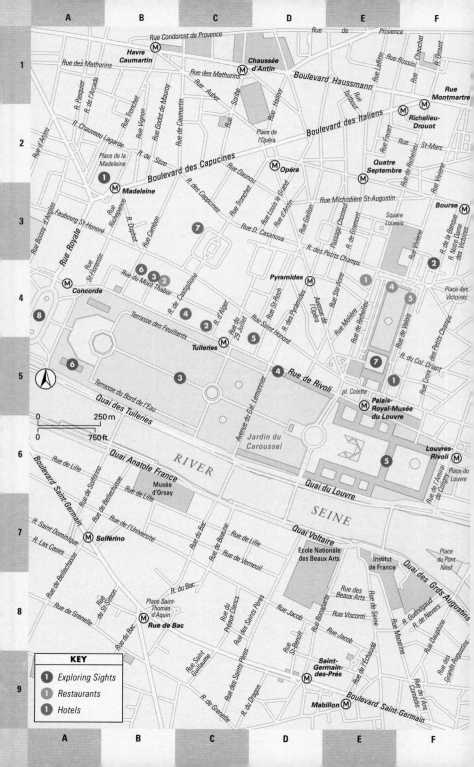

Around the Louvre

Sights ▼

1 Église de la
Madeleine **B2**

2 Galerie Vivienne **F4**

3 Jardin des Tuileries...... **C5**

4 Les Arts Décoratifs..... **D5**

5 The Louvre............... **E6**

6 Musée de
l'Orangerie.............. **A5**

7 Palais-Royal............. **E5**

8 Place de la
Concorde **A4**

9 Rue Montorgueil........ **H4**

Restaurants ▼

1 Juvéniles **E4**

2 L'Ardoise................ **B4**

3 La Régalade
Saint-Honoré........... **G6**

4 Le Grand Véfour.......... **E4**

5 Restaurant du
Palais-Royal............. **F4**

Hotels ▼

1 Grand Hotel du
Palais Royal **E5**

2 Hôtel Brighton........... **C4**

3 Hôtel du Continent...... **B4**

4 Hotel Le Meurice **C4**

5 Hôtel Le Pradey......... **D5**

6 Meliá Vendôme **B4**

7 The Ritz **C3**

evokes an age of gaslights and horse-drawn carriages. Once Parisians came to passages like this one to tread tiled floors instead of muddy streets and to see and be seen browsing boutiques under the glass-and-iron roofs. Today, the Galerie Vivienne still attracts unique retailers selling clothing, accessories, and housewares. La Marelle (No. 25) stocwks secondhand designer labels, and wine merchant Legrand Filles & Fils (1 rue de la Banque) is the place for an upscale wine tasting. The Place des Victoires, a few steps away, is one of Paris's most picturesque squares. In the center is a statue of an outsized Louis XIV (1643–1715), the Sun King, who appears almost as large as his horse. ⊠ *Main entrance at 4 rue des Petits-Champs, Louvre* Ⓜ *Palais-Royal–Louvre, Bourse.*

★ Jardin des Tuileries
CITY PARK | FAMILY | The quintessential French garden, with its verdant lawns, manicured rows of trees, and gravel paths, was designed by André Le Nôtre for Louis XIV. After the king moved his court to Versailles in 1682, the Tuileries became *the* place for stylish Parisians to stroll. (Ironically, the name derives from the decidedly unstylish factories, which once occupied this area: they produced *tuiles,* or roof tiles, fired in kilns called *tuileries.*) Monet and Renoir captured the garden with paint and brush, and it's no wonder the Impressionists loved it—the gray, austere light of Paris's famously overcast days make the green trees appear even greener.

The garden still serves as a setting for one of the city's loveliest walks. Laid out before you is a vista of must-see monuments, with the Louvre at one end and the Place de la Concorde at the other. The Eiffel Tower is on the Seine side, along with the Musée d'Orsay, reachable across a footbridge in the center of the garden. A good place to begin is at the Louvre end, at the Arc du Carrousel, a stone-and-marble arch ordered by Napoléon to showcase the bronze horses

he stole from St. Mark's Cathedral in Venice. The horses were eventually returned and replaced here with a statue of a *quadriga,* a four-horse chariot. On the Place de la Concorde end, twin buildings bookend the garden. On the Seine side, the former royal greenhouse is now the exceptional Musée de l'Orangerie, home to the largest display of Monet's lovely *Water Lilies* series, as well as a sizable collection of early-20th-century paintings. On the opposite end is the Jeu de Paume, which has some of the city's best photography exhibitions.

Note that the Tuileries is one of the best places in Paris to take kids if they're itching to run around. There's a carousel, trampolines, and, in summer, an amusement park. If you're hungry, look for carts serving gelato from Amorino or sandwiches from the chain bakery Paul at the eastern end near the Louvre. Within the gated part of the gardens are four cafés with terraces. Pavillon des Tuilleries near Place de la Concorde is a good place to stop for late-afternoon tea or an apéritif. ⊠ *Bordered by Quai des Tuileries, Pl. de la Concorde, Rue de Rivoli, and the Louvre, Louvre* ☎ *01–40–20–90–43* ⊠ *Free* Ⓜ *Tuileries or Concorde.*

★ The Louvre
MUSEUM | Simply put, the Louvre is the world's greatest art museum—and the largest, with 675,000 square feet of works from almost every civilization on earth. The *Mona Lisa* is, of course, a top draw, along with the *Venus de Milo* and *Winged Victory.* These and many more of the globe's most coveted treasures are displayed in three wings—the Richelieu, the Sully, and the Denon—which are arranged like a horseshoe. Nestled in the middle is I.M. Pei's *Pyramide,* the giant glass pyramid surrounded by a trio of smaller ones that opened in 1989 over the new entrance in the Cour Napoléon. To plot your course through the complex, grab a color-coded map at the information desk. For an excellent overview, book a 90-minute English-language tour

(€12, daily at 11 and 2); slick Nintendo 3DS multimedia guides (€5; pay for it when you buy your ticket), available at the entrance to each wing, offer a self-guided alternative.

Having been first a fortress and later a royal residence, the Louvre represents a saga that spans nine centuries. Its medieval roots are on display below-ground in the Sully wing, where vestiges of the foundation and moat remain. Elsewhere in this wing you can ogle the largest display of Egyptian antiques outside of Cairo, most notably the magnificent statue of Ramses II (salle 12). Upstairs is the armless *Venus de Milo,* a 2nd-century representation of Aphrodite (salle 7). Highlights of the wing's collection of French paintings from the 17th century onward include the *Turkish Bath* by Jean-August-Dominique Ingres (salle 60). American Cy Twombly's contemporary ceiling in salle 32 adds a 21st-century twist. In the Denon wing, climb the sweeping marble staircase (Escalier Daru) to see the sublime *Winged Victory of Samothrace,* carved in 305 BC. This wing is also home to the iconic, enigmatic *Mona Lisa* (salle 6); two other Da Vinci masterpieces hang in the adjacent Grand Galerie. The museum's latest architectural wonder is here as well—the 30,000-square-foot Arts of Islam exhibition space, which debuted in 2012. Topped with an undulating golden roof evoking a flowing veil, its two-level galleries contain one of the largest collections of art from the Islamic world. After admiring it, be sure to visit the Richelieu wing and the Cour Marly, with its quartet of horses carved for Louis XIV and Louis XV. On the ground floor, the centerpiece of the Near East Antiquities Collection is the Lamassu, carved 8th-century winged beasts (salle 4). The elaborately decorated Royal Apartments of Napoléon III are on the first floor. On the second floor, French and Northern School paintings include Vermeer's *The Lacemaker* (salle 38). Note that crowds

are thinner on Wednesday and Friday nights, when the museum is open late. Save queue time by purchasing online tickets for an additional fee; admission includes some temporary exhibitions and entry within 48 hours to the charming Musée Eugène-Delacroix. If you arrive without a ticket, you can buy one at the kiosks or automatic machines in a newly renovated space below the *Pyramide.* Avoid crowds by using the lesser-known entrance through the underground mall, Carrousel du Louvre. ✉ *Palais du Louvre, Louvre* ☎ *01–40–20–53–17 info* ⊕ *www. louvre.fr* ✉ *€15, includes 48-hr entry to Musée Eugène Delacroix (free 1st Sun. of month, Oct.–Mar., and free after 6 pm 1st Sat. of month)* ⊙ *Closed Tues.* Ⓜ *Palais-Royal–Louvre, Louvre-Rivoli.*

Musée de l'Orangerie

MUSEUM | In high season the lines can be long to see Claude Monet's huge, meditative *Water Lilies* (*Les Nymphéas*), displayed in two curved galleries designed in 1914 by the master himself. But they are well worth the wait. These works are the highlight of the Orangerie's small but excellent collection, which also features early-20th-century paintings by Renoir, Cézanne, and Matisse. Many hail from the private holdings of high-powered art dealer Paul Guillaume (1891–1934), among them Guillaume's portrait by Modigliani entitled *Novo Pilota* (*New Pilot*). Temporary exhibitions are typically quirky and well curated. Built in 1852 to shelter orange trees, the long rectangular building, a twin of the Jeu de Paume across the garden, includes a portion of the city's 16th-century wall (you can see remnants on the lower floor). A small café and gift shop are here, too. ✉ *Jardin des Tuileries at Pl. de la Concorde, Louvre* ☎ *01–44–77–80–07* ⊕ *www.musee-orangerie.fr* ✉ *€9; €16 joint ticket with Musée d'Orsay; €18.50 joint ticket with Giverny (open Mar.–Nov.)* ⊙ *Closed Tues.* Ⓜ *Concorde.*

Continued on page 114

MUSÉE DU LOUVRE

Try to wrap your mind around this: The Louvre has more than 37,000 pieces of art in its collection, representing nearly every civilization on earth, and more than 675,000 square feet of exhibition space. It's gone through countless cycles of construction and demolition, expansion and renovation, starting as a medieval fortress, then becoming a royal residence before opening its doors as the Museum Central des Arts at the end of the 18th century.

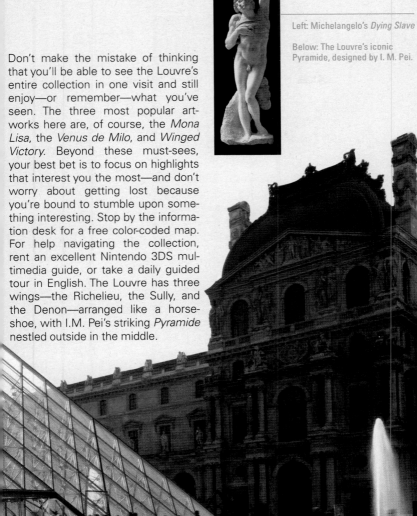

Don't make the mistake of thinking that you'll be able to see the Louvre's entire collection in one visit and still enjoy—or remember—what you've seen. The three most popular artworks here are, of course, the *Mona Lisa*, the *Venus de Milo*, and *Winged Victory*. Beyond these must-sees, your best bet is to focus on highlights that interest you the most—and don't worry about getting lost because you're bound to stumble upon something interesting. Stop by the information desk for a free color-coded map. For help navigating the collection, rent an excellent Nintendo 3DS multimedia guide, or take a daily guided tour in English. The Louvre has three wings—the Richelieu, the Sully, and the Denon—arranged like a horseshoe, with I.M. Pei's striking *Pyramide* nestled outside in the middle.

Left: Michelangelo's *Dying Slave*

Below: The Louvre's iconic Pyramide, designed by I. M. Pei.

RICHELIEU WING

COLLECTIONS
Near East Antiquities
French Painting
French Sculpture
Northern Schools
Decorative Arts

Below Ground & Ground Floor. Entering from the *Pyramide*, head upstairs to the sculpture courtyards, Cour Marly and Cour Puget. In Cour Marly you'll find the Marley Horses (see right). Salle 2 has fragments from Cluny, the powerful Romanesque abbey in Burgundy that dominated 11th-century French Catholicism. Salles 4–6 follows the evolution of French sculpture, and in Salles 7–10 you'll find funerary art. In Cour Puget, products from the Académie Royale, the art school of 18th-century France, fill Salles 25–33. Behind this is the Near East Antiquities Collection. Salle 3's centerpiece is the Codex of Hammurabi, an 18th-century BC black-diorite stela containing the world's oldest written code of laws. In Salle 4, you'll find Lamassu (see right).

First Floor. Head straight through Decorative Arts to see the magnificently restored Royal Apartments of Napoléon III *(see right)*.

Second Floor. Much of this floor is dedicated to French and Northern School paintings. At the entrance is a 14th-century painting of John the Good—the oldest-known individual portrait from the north of Italy. In Salle 4 hangs *The Madonna of Chancellor Rolin,* by the 15th-century Early Netherlandish master Jan van Eyck (late 14th century–1441). Peter Paul Rubens's (1577–1640) the *Disembarkation of Marie de' Medici at the Port of Marseille* is in Salle 18. In Salle 31 are several paintings by Rembrandt van Rijn (1606–69), including *Bathsheba*, his largest nude. The masterpiece of the Dutch collection is Vermeer's *The Lacemaker (see right)*.

TIPS

■ The 25 paintings by Rubens commisioned by Marie de Medici for the Luxembourg Palace in Salle 18 on the second floor each mark an event in the queen's life.

■ To see what's on the minds of the museum staff, check out the Painting of the Month in Salle 17, French section, on the 2nd floor.

■ Take a hot chocolate break in the Café Richelieu on the first floor, run by the upscale confiseur Angelina. There is an outdoor terrace in summer and a tempting lunch menu.

■ Save your ticket and duck out for lunch at one of the nearby cafés.

DON'T MISS

Lamassu

LAMASSU, 8TH CENTURY   SALLE 4

With their fierce beards and gentle eyes, these massive winged beasts are benevolent guardians straight from the dreamworld. Magical for children and adults, the strangely lifelike sculptures are located in the Near Eastern antiquities collection. The winged bull demigods are part of the Cour Khorsabad, a re-creation of the temple erected by Assyrian king Sargon II. ✥ *Richelieu, ground floor*

THE LACEMAKER, 1669–1671   SALLE 38

This is a small but justifiably famous gem of Dutch optical accuracy (and a must-see for fans of the movie and book, *Girl With a Pearl Earring*, to see how his style evolved over a 5-year period.) Here, Jan Vermeer (1632–75) painted the red thread in the foreground as a slightly blurred jumble, just as one would actually see it if focusing on the girl. The lacemaker's industriousness represents domestic virtue, but the personal focus of the painting is far more engaging than a simple morality tale. ✥ *Richelieu, second floor*

The Lacemaker

MARLY HORSES, 1699–1740   COUR MARLY

During the dramatic 1989 reorganization of the Louvre, two courtyards were elegantly glassed over to match the entrance pyramid. The dramatic glass-roofed Marly sculpture court houses several sculptures from Louis XIV's garden at Marly, including two magnificent winged horses by Antoine Coysevox. Later, the artist's nephew Guillaume Coustou created two accompanying earth-bound horse sculptures for Louis XV; their fame was such that, during the Revolution, these sculptures were moved to the Tuileries gardens for public viewing. Now the four original horses greet visitors to the Richelieu Wing, ready to gallop off into the museum; replicas stand guard in the Tuileries. ✥ *Richelieu, lower ground floor*

The Marly Horses

ROYAL APARTMENTS
OF NAPOLÉON III, 1860s   SALLE 87

These dozen reception rooms, hung with crystal chandeliers, elaborate mirrors, and imperial velour, are a gilt-covered reminder that the Louvre was a palace for centuries, regally designed to impress. En route, you'll pass decorative items like the solid-crystal Restoration dressing table (Salle 77) that prepare you for the eye-popping luxury of the Second Empire. ✥ *Richelieu, first floor*

Royal Apartments of Napoléon

SULLY WING

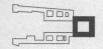

Below Ground & Ground Floor. Start your visit with a journey to the roots of the Louvre—literally. From the *Pyramide* entrance, tour the 13th-century foundations of the original fortress and the Medieval Moat. In Salle 12 you'll find towering Ramses II. Check out the mummies in Salles 14 and 15, along with rare examples of Egyptian funerary art.

Upstairs, the north galleries of the Sully continue the ancient Iranian collection begun in the Richelieu Wing. Salle 16 has the 2nd-century BC **Venus de Milo** *(see right)*, anchoring the Greek collection of Salles 7–17.

First Floor. The northern galleries of the first floor continue with the Decorative Arts collection including works from all over Europe, and connect with the Napoléon III apartments.

Second Floor. Sully picks up French painting in the 17th century where the Richelieu leaves off. The Académiciens are best exemplified by Nicolas Poussin (1594–1665, Salle 19), the first international painting star from France. The antithesis of this style was the candlelit modest work by outsider Georges de La Tour (Salle 28), as in his *Magdalene of Night Light.*

The Académie Royale defined the standards of painting through revolution, republic, and empire. Exoticism wafted in during the Napoleonic empire, as in the **Turkish Bath** (see right) painting of Jean-Auguste-Dominique Ingres (1780–1867). Fresh energy crackled into French painting in the 18th century. Antoine Watteau (1684–1721), was known for his theatrical scenes and *fêtes galantes,* portrayals of well-dressed figures in bucolic settings. In *Pilgrimage to the Island of Cythera* (Salle 36), he used delicate brushstrokes and soft tones to convey the court set, here depicted arriving on (or departing from) Cythera, the mythical isle of love.

TIPS

■ There is a little-known collection with Monet, Renoir, and Cezanne in Salle C on the second floor, the only Impressionist works in the Louvre.

■ There's a surprise in Salle 17 on the ground floor—the *Sleeping Hermaphrodite* by the entrance.

■ Be sure to look up as you make your way up Escalier Henri II. It took four years to complete this 16th-century vaulted ceiling.

■ Need a bathroom? There are some tucked between Salles 22 and 23 on the 1st floor. (And admire the colorful, 4,000-year-old Seated Scribe in Salle 22.)

■ For a breather, head to the bench in Salle 33 on the first floor and enjoy the sedate three-part ceiling by Georges Braque (1955) called *Les Oiseux* (The Birds).

DON'T MISS

RAMSES II, APPROX. 1200 BC   SALLE 12
The sphinx-guarded Egyptian Wing is the biggest display of Egyptian antiquities in the world after the Cairo museum—not surprising, considering that Egyptology as a Western concept was invented by a Frenchman, Champollion, founder of the Louvre's Egypt collection and translator of the hieroglyphics on the Rosetta Stone. This statue from the site of Tanis, presumed to be Ramses II, never fails to stop visitors' breath with its gleaming stone, beatific expression, and perfect proportions. ✛ *Sully, ground floor*

Ramses II

VENUS DE MILO, APPROX. 120 BC   SALLE 16
After countless photographs and bad reproductions, the original Aphrodite continues to dazzle. The armless statue, one of the most reproduced and recognizable works of art in the world, is actually as beautiful as they say. She was unearthed on the Greek island of Milos in the 19th century and sold for 6,000 francs to the French ambassador in Constantinople, who presented her to King Louis XVIII. ✛ *Sully, ground floor*

Venus de Milo

MEDIEVAL MOAT, 13TH CENTURY   MEDIEVAL LOUVRE
Wander around the perimeter of the solidly built original moat to reach the remarkable Salle Saint-Louis with its elegant columns and medieval artifacts. Keep an eye out for the parade helmet of Charles VI, which was dug up in 169 fragments and astonishingly reassembled. ✛ *Sully, lower ground floor*

Medieval Moat

THE *TURKISH BATH*, 1862   SALLE 60
Though Jean-August-Dominique Ingres' (1780–1867) long-limbed women hardly look Turkish, they are singularly elegant and his polished immaculate style was imitated by an entire generation of French painters. This painting is a prime example of Orientalism, where Western artists played out fantasies of the Orient in their work. Popular as a society portrait painter, Ingres returned repeatedly to langorous nudes—compare the women of the *Turkish Bath* with the slinky figure in his *La Grande Odalisque,* in the Denon Wing. ✛ *Sully, second floor*

The *Turkish Bath*

THE DENON WING

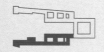

Below Ground & Ground Floor. The stunning Arts of Islam wing with 30,000 square feet of gallery space is built into the Cour Visconti and topped with an undulating glass roof meant to evoke a floating head scarf. Here you'll find Europe's largest collection of treasures from across the Islamic world, including the Ottoman Empire. On the lower level, don't miss the Baptistery of Saint Louis, a 14th-century sculpted golden basin. The galleries to the south and east of the *Pyramide* entrance display early Renaissance Italian sculpture, including a 15th-century *Madonna and Child* by Florentine Dontallo (1386–1466). Drift upstairs to the Italian sculptures on the ground level, where you'll find the exquisite Michelangelo's *Slaves* (1513–15) in Salle 4.

First Floor. Walk up the marble Escalier Daru to discover the sublime **Winged Victory of Samothrace** *(see right)*, cleaned in 2014. Then head to the stunning Galerie d'Apollon (Apollo Gallery). Built in 1661 but not finished until 1851, the hall was a model for Versailles's Hall of Mirrors.

Back out and into Paintings, you'll find four by Leonardo da Vinci (1452–1519). His enigmatic, androgynous St-John the Baptist hangs here, along with more overtly religious works such as the 1483 *Virgin of the Rocks*. Take a close look at the pretty portrait of La Belle Ferronnière, which Leonardo painted a decade before the **Mona Lisa** *(see right)*; it will give you something to compare with Mona when you finally get to meet her in the Salle des Etats, near Salles 5 and 6. Head across to Salle 75 for an artistic 180°: the gleaming pomp and circumstance of a new empire with the **Coronation of Napoléon** *(see right)* by French classicist Jacques-Louis David (1748–1825).

In Salle 77 is the graphic 1819 **The Raft of the Medusa,** *(see right)* by Théodore Géricault (1791–1824).

TIPS

■ Don't skip the coat check on the ground floor. Much of the museum is hot and stuffy.

■ Don't miss the glass case near *Winged Victory of Samothrace* on the first floor. It contains her two-fingered hand.

■ Need a bathroom? There are some tucked away at the end of the wing on the first floor near Salle 13.

DON'T MISS

MONA LISA, 1503   SALLE 7
The most famous painting in the world, *La Gioconda* (*La Joconde* in French) is tougher than she looks: the canvas was stolen from the Louvre by an Italian nationalist in 1911, recovered from a Florentine hotel, and survived an acid attack in 1956. She is believed to be the wife of Francesco del Giocondo, a Florentine millionaire, and was probably 24 when she sat for this painting; some historians believe the portrait was actually painted after her death. Either way, she has become immortal through da Vinci's ingenious "sfumato" technique, which combines glowing detail with soft, depth-filled brushwork.
⚜ *Denon, first floor*

Mona Lisa

THE RAFT OF THE MEDUSA, 1819   SALLE 77
Théodore Géricault was inspired by the grim news report that survivors of a wrecked French merchant ship were left adrift on a raft without supplies. Géricault interviewed survivors, visited the morgue to draw corpses, and turned his painting of the disaster into a strong indictment of authority, the first time an epic historical painting had taken on current events in this way. Note the desperate energy from the pyramid construction of bodies on the raft and the manipulation of greenish light.
⚜ *Denon, first floor*

The Raft of the Medusa

WINGED VICTORY OF SAMOTHRACE, 305 BC   STAIRS
Poised for flight at the top of the Escalier Daru, this exhilarating statue was found on a tiny Greek island in the northern Aegean. Depicted in the act of descending from Olympus, *Winged Victory*, or Nike, to the Ancient Greeks, was carved to commemorate the naval victory of Demetrius Poliorcetes over the Persians. ⚜ *Denon, first floor*

Winged Victory of Samothrace

CORONATION OF NAPOLÉON, 1805   SALLE 75
Classicist Jacques-Louis David (1748–1825) was the ultimate painter-survivor: he began his career under the protection of the King, became official designer of the Revolutionary government, endured two rounds of exile, and became one of the greatest of Napoléon's painters. Here, David avoided the politically fraught moment of December 2, 1804—when Napoléon snatched the crown from the hands of Pope Pius VII to place it upon his own head—choosing instead the romantic moment when the new emperor turned to crown Joséphine. ⚜ *Denon, first floor*

Detail from the Coronation of Napoléon

PLANNING YOUR VISIT

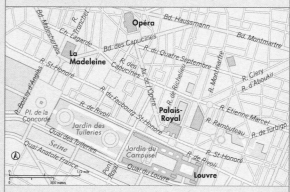

TOURS

There are 90-minute guided tours in English daily. The meeting point is at "Accueil des Groups" under the pyramid. There are also free thematic leaflets to self-guide through a particular trail—some designed especially for kids. The Louvre has a phenomenal program of courses and workshops (mostly in French); see website for details.

ACCESSIBILITY

Wheelchair visitors or those with strollers can skip the long entry line and use the marvelous cylinder lift inside the entrance pyramid.

WITH KIDS

Begin your tour in the Sully Wing at the Medieval moat, which leads enticingly to the sphinx-guarded entrance of the Egyptian Wing, a must for mummy enthusiasts. For a more in-depth visit, you can reserve private kid-centric family tours such as the Paris Muse Clues. Don't forget the Tuileries is right next door (with carnival rides in summer).

ENTRY TIPS

You can order your ticket online (€15 plus €2 fee) at ⊕ www. ticketlouvre.fr. Or save the fee and buy your ticket at the official Paris tourist office a short walk from the museum at 29 rue de Rivoli. See ⊕ www.en.parisinfo.com for more information.

Shorten your wait by avoiding the main entrance at the Pyramide and head for the entrance in the underground mall, Carrousel du Louvre. Automatic ticket machines are available. Note that crowds are thinner on Wednesday and Friday nights, when the museum is open late. Be sure to check the website for room closings; renovations are always taking place. Remember the Louvre is closed on Tuesday.

A WHIRLWIND TOUR

If you've come to Paris and feel you must go to the Louvre to see the Big Three—*Venus de Milo, Winged Victory*, and *Mona Lisa*—even though you'd rather be strolling along the Champs-Elysees, it can be done in an hour or less if you plan well. Start in Denon and head upstairs through Estruscan and Greek antiquities, walking down the long hall of sculptures until you see the *Winged Victory* in front of you. Take a right and head up the staircase through French painting to the *Mona Lisa*. Then go back down under the *Pyramide* to Sully to see the *Venus de Milo*.

⊠ Palais du Louvre, Louvre/Tuileries

☎ 01–40–20–53–17 (information)

⊕ www.louvre.fr

🕐 Mon., Thurs., and weekends 9–6; Wed., Fri., and first Sat. of the month, 9 am–9:30 pm; closed Tues.

Ⓜ Palais-Royal / Musée du Louvre

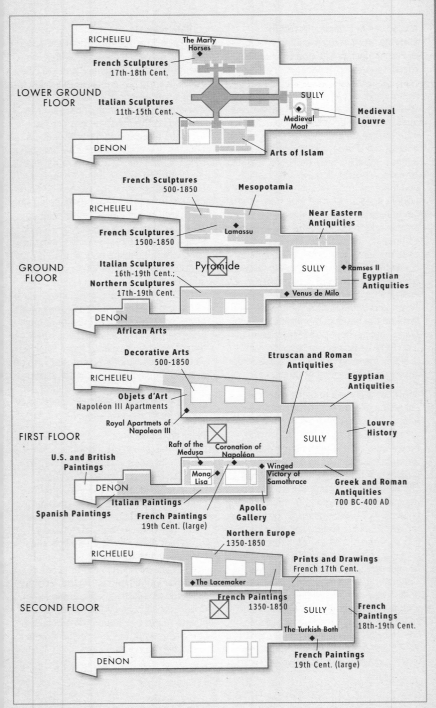

LOWER GROUND FLOOR

RICHELIEU

The Marly Horses

French Sculptures 17th-18th Cent.

Italian Sculptures 11th-15th Cent.

SULLY

Medieval Moat

Medieval Louvre

DENON

Arts of Islam

GROUND FLOOR

French Sculptures 500-1850

Mesopotamia

RICHELIEU

French Sculptures 1500-1850

Lamassu

Near Eastern Antiquities

Pyramide

SULLY

Ramses II

Egyptian Antiquities

Italian Sculptures 16th-19th Cent.; **Northern Sculptures** 17th-19th Cent.

Venus de Milo

DENON

African Arts

FIRST FLOOR

Decorative Arts 500-1850

Etruscan and Roman Antiquities

RICHELIEU

Egyptian Antiquities

Objets d'Art Napoléon III Apartments

Royal Apartmets of Napoleon III

Raft of the Medusa

Coronation of Napoléon

Louvre History

SULLY

U.S. and British Paintings

DENON

Mona Lisa

Winged Victory of Samothrace

Greek and Roman Antiquities 700 BC-400 AD

Spanish Paintings

Italian Paintings

French Paintings 19th Cent. (large)

Apollo Gallery

SECOND FLOOR

Northern Europe 1350-1850

RICHELIEU

Prints and Drawings French 17th Cent.

The Lacemaker

French Paintings 1350-1850

SULLY

French Paintings 18th-19th Cent.

The Turkish Bath

DENON

French Paintings 19th Cent. (large)

Musée des Arts Décoratifs (MAD)

MUSEUM | As the city's leading showcase of French design, Les Arts Décoratifs was rechristened the Musée des Arts Décoratifs—or MAD—in 2018 in an effort to better carve out a niche for itself in a city with many competitors for that title. Sharing a wing of the Musée du Louvre, but with a separate entrance and admission charge, MAD is actually three museums in one spread across nine floors. The stellar collection of decorative arts, fashion, and graphics includes altarpieces from the Middle Ages and furnishings from the Italian Renaissance to the present day. There are period rooms reflecting the ages, such as the early 1820s salon of the Duchesse de Berry (who actually lived in the building), plus several rooms reproduced from designer Jeanne Lanvin's 1920s apartment. Don't miss the gilt-and-green-velvet bed of the Parisian courtesan who inspired the boudoir in Émile Zola's novel *Nana*; you can hear Zola's description of it on the free English audio guide, which is highly recommended. The second-floor jewelry gallery is another must-see.

MAD is also home to an exceptional collection of textiles, advertising posters, films, and related objects that are shown in rotating exhibitions. Before leaving, take a break at the restaurant Le Loulou, where an outdoor terrace is an ideal spot for lunch or afternoon tea. Shoppers should browse through the on-site boutique as well. Stocked with an interesting collection of books, paper products, toys, tableware, accessories, and jewelry, it is one of the city's best museum shops. If you're combining a visit here with the Musée du Louvre, note that the two close on different days, so don't come on Monday or Tuesday. If you're pairing it with the exquisite Nissim de Camondo, joint tickets are available at a reduced cost. ⊠ *107 rue de Rivoli, Louvre* ☎ *01–44–55–57–50* ⊕ *madparis.fr* ⊡ *From €11* ⊘ *Closed Mon.* Ⓜ *Palais-Royal–Louvre.*

★ Palais-Royal

CITY PARK | The quietest, most romantic Parisian garden is enclosed within the former home of Cardinal Richelieu (1585–1642). It's the perfect place to while away an afternoon, cuddling with your sweetheart on a bench under the trees, soaking up the sunshine beside the fountain, or browsing the 400-year-old arcades that are now home to boutiques ranging from quirky (picture Anna Joliet's music boxes) to chic (think designs by Stella McCartney). One of the city's oldest restaurants is here, the haute-cuisine Le Grand Véfour, where brass plaques recall regulars like Napoléon and Victor Hugo. Built in 1629, the *palais* became royal when Richelieu bequeathed it to Louis XIII. Other famous residents include Jean Cocteau and Colette, who wrote of her pleasurable "country" view of the *province à Paris*. Today, the garden often plays host to giant-size temporary art installations sponsored by another tenant, the Ministry of Culture. The courtyard off Place Colette is outfitted with an eye-catching collection of squat black-and-white columns created in 1986 by artist Daniel Buren. ⊠ *Pl. du Palais-Royal, Louvre* Ⓜ *Palais-Royal–Louvre.*

Place de la Concorde

PLAZA | This square at the foot of the Champs-Élysées was originally named after Louis XV. It later became the Place de la Révolution, where crowds cheered as Louis XVI, Marie-Antoinette, and some 2,500 others lost their heads to the guillotine. Renamed Concorde in 1836, it got a new centerpiece: the 75-foot granite Obelisk of Luxor, a gift from Egypt quarried in the 8th century BC. Among the handsome 18th-century buildings facing the square is the Hôtel Crillon, which was originally built as a private home by Gabriel, the architect of Versailles's Petit Trianon. ⊠ *Rue Royale, Louvre* Ⓜ *Concorde.*

★ Rue Montorgueil

NEIGHBORHOOD | Rue Montorgueil was once the gritty oyster hub of Les Halles. Now lined with food shops and cafés, the cobbled street whose name translates to Mount Pride is the heart of one of the city's trendiest neighborhoods. History runs deep here. Monet captured the scene in 1878 when Montorgueil was ablaze with tricolor flags during the World's Fair (see it in the Musée d'Orsay). Honoré de Balzac and his 19th-century band of scribes frequented Au Rocher de Cancale at No. 78, whose famously crumbling facade has been painstakingly restored with gilt panache. Other addresses have been around for centuries: Stohrer at No. 51 has been baking elaborate pastries since 1730; and L'Escargot Montorgueil at No. 38, a favorite of Charlie Chaplin, is still graced by a giant golden snail. Relative newcomers include the luxury Nuxe spa at Nos. 32–34. Browse the boutiques on Rue Montmartre, which runs parallel, or shop for cookware at Julia Child's old haunt, E. Dehillerin, still in business at 18–20 rue Coquillière. Rue Tiquetonne is rife with bistros, and once-sleepy Rue St-Sauveur became a destination when the Experimental Cocktail Club (No. 37) moved in, joined by other trendy eating and drinking spots. Even Rue St-Denis, once a scruffy red-light district, is now a hipster fave with bar-restaurants like Le Pas Sage at the entrance of the lovely covered arcade, Passage du Grand Cerf. ⊠ *Rue Montorgueil, off Rue de Turbigo, Louvre* Ⓜ *Sentier, Les Halles.*

🍴 Restaurants

★ Juvéniles

$$ | **WINE BAR** | A favorite with the French and the expat crowd, Juvéniles is the ideal kind of neighborhood outpost that mixes great dining with an inspired wine list, all at affordable prices. The lunch menu might start with velvety foie gras *maison* (paired with a crisp Riesling), followed by slow-braised beef with a tangy tarragon-and-dill sauce *ravigote*. **Known for:** prix-fixe lunch that's an outstanding bargain; bottles of wine also available to take home; small space so reserve in advance. $ *Average main: €21* ⊠ *47 rue de Richelieu, 1er, Louvre* ☎ *01–42–97–46–49* ⊘ *Closed Sun. and Mon.* Ⓜ *Bourse, Pyramides.*

La Régalade Saint-Honoré

$$$ | **MODERN FRENCH** | **FAMILY** | After taking over the original La Régalade, chef Bruno Doucet kept some of what made the old restaurant so popular (country terrines, reasonably priced wines, convivial atmosphere). But he also had a few tricks under his toque, creating a successful haute-cuisine-meets-comfort-food destination with dishes like earthy morel mushrooms in a frothy cream for a starter, followed by the signature succulent caramelized pork belly over tender Puy lentils. **Known for:** grand-mère's creamy rice pudding for dessert; good-value prix-fixe menu for lunch and dinner; last-minute reservations sometimes possible. $ *Average main: €25* ⊠ *123 rue Saint-Honoré, 1er, Louvre* ☎ *01–42–21–92–40* Ⓜ *Louvre–Rivoli.*

L'Ardoise

$$$ | **BISTRO** | Despite the updated chic decor, this tiny, reliably good bistro has not sacrificed substance to style. This is first-rate dining, and the three-course dinner menu (you can also order à la carte, but it's less of a bargain) tempts with original dishes like mushroom-and-foie-gras ravioli with smoked duck; farmer's pork with porcini mushrooms; and red mullet with creole sauce. Just as enticing are the desserts, such as a superb *feuillantine au citron*—caramelized pastry leaves filled with lemon cream and lemon slices—and a boozy baba au rhum. **Known for:** good-value prix-fixe menus at lunch and dinner; ever-changing traditional fare with a contemporary twist; can be noisy. $ *Average main: €27* ⊠ *28 rue du Mont Thabor, 1er, Louvre* ☎ *01–42–96–28–18* ⊕ *www.lardoise-paris.com* ⊘ *No lunch Sun.* Ⓜ *Concorde.*

★ Le Grand Véfour

$$$$ | **MODERN FRENCH** | Originally built in 1784, Le Grand Véfour has welcomed everyone from Napoléon to Colette to Jean Cocteau under its mirrored ceiling, and is still a contender for the most beautiful restaurant in Paris today. The rich and fashionable continue to gather here to swoon over two-Michelin-star chef Guy Martin's unique blend of sophistication and rusticity. **Known for:** you can't beat it for romance; sumptuous historic decor with excellent updated cuisine; outstanding cheese trolley. $ *Average main: €130* ⊠ *17 rue de Beaujolais, 1er, Louvre* ☎ *01–42–96–56–27* ⊕ *www.grand-vefour. com* ⊗ *Closed Sat. and Sun., Aug., and Christmas holidays* Ⓜ *Palais-Royal.*

★ Restaurant du Palais-Royal

$$$$ | **BISTRO** | This stylish modern bistro serves stunning gastronomic cuisine to match its gorgeous location under the arcades of the Palais-Royal. Sole, scallops, and risotto—including a dramatic black-squid-ink-and-lobster version, or an all-green vegetarian one—are beautifully prepared, but the grilled suckling pig and roasted carrots is also popular with expense-account lunchers. **Known for:** peerless setting in the Palais Royal gardens; outdoor dining in the garden in warm weather; reservations needed well in advance. $ *Average main: €59* ⊠ *Jardins du Palais-Royal, 110 Galerie Valois, 1er, Louvre* ☎ *01–40–20–00–27* ⊕ *www. restaurantdupalaisroyal.com* ⊗ *Closed Sun. and Mon.* Ⓜ *Palais-Royal.*

Hotels

★ Grand Hotel du Palais Royal

$$$$ | **HOTEL** | Despite its splashy name, this gracious five-star hotel, housed in an 18th-century mansion just steps from the Palais Royal gardens, keeps a surprisingly relaxed profile, focusing less on flagrant luxury and more on the essentials that make a hotel truly grand—service, quality, comfort, refinement, and quiet. **Pros:** top-notch service; an island of quiet and calm

in a bustling neighborhood; great location steps from the Louvre and Palais Royal. **Cons:** not all rooms come with balconies; no pool; small fitness room. $ *Rooms from: €400* ⊠ *4 rue de Valois, 1er, Louvre* ☎ *01–42–96–15–35* ⊕ *www.grandhoteldu-palaisroyal.com* ⇄ *68 rooms* ⦿ *No meals* Ⓜ *Palais Royal–Musée du Louvre.*

Hôtel Brighton

$$ | **HOTEL** | **FAMILY** | A few of the city's most prestigious hotels face the Tuileries or Place de la Concorde, but the 19th-century Brighton occupies the same prime real estate and offers a privileged stay for a fraction of the price. **Pros:** convenient central location; friendly service; breakfast buffet (free for kids under 12). **Cons:** some areas in need of repair; variable quality in decor between rooms; no restaurant for lunch or dinner. $ *Rooms from: €220* ⊠ *218 rue de Rivoli, 1er, Louvre* ☎ *01–47–03–61–61* ⊕ *www. paris-hotel-brighton.com* ⇄ *62 rooms* ⦿ *No meals* Ⓜ *Tuileries.*

★ Hôtel du Continent

$$ | **HOTEL** | You'd be hard-pressed to find a budget hotel this stylish anywhere in Paris, let alone in an upscale neighborhood close to many of the city's top attractions. **Pros:** very friendly staff; all modern amenities; location, location, location. **Cons:** no lobby; tiny bathrooms; bold decor not for everyone. $ *Rooms from: €150* ⊠ *30 rue du Mont-Thabor, 1e, Louvre* ☎ *01–42–60–75–32* ⊕ *www. hotelcontinent.com* ⇄ *25 rooms* ⦿ *No meals* Ⓜ *Concord, Tuileries.*

★ Hôtel Le Meurice

$$$$ | **HOTEL** | **FAMILY** | Since 1835, the Meurice has welcomed royalty and celebrities from the Duchess of Windsor to Salvador Dalí—who both resided in the grande-dame establishment—and Paris's first palace hotel continues to please with service, style, and views. **Pros:** stunning art and architecture; views over the Tuileries gardens; central location convenient to métro and major sites. **Cons:** some amenities lacking like in-room coffee machine; front-desk service at times inattentive; incredibly expensive. $ *Rooms from: €900 ⊠ 228 rue de Rivoli, 1er, Louvre* ☎ *01–44–58–10–09* ⊕ *www.dorchestercollection.com* ⥵ *208 rooms* ⦿❘ *No meals* Ⓜ *Tuileries, Concorde.*

Hôtel Le Pradey

$$ | HOTEL | Offering Pierre Marcolini chocolates and Hermès and Nux toiletries, this compact boutique hotel near the Tuileries has a luxe feel. **Pros:** choice of copious breakfast buffet or quick coffee and croissant; designer touches throughout; kind staff. **Cons:** smaller rooms lack closet space; rooms vary greatly in style; few services. $ *Rooms from: €200 ⊠ 5 rue St-Roch, 1e, Louvre* ☎ *01–42–60–31–70* ⊕ *www.lepradey.com* ⥵ *28 rooms* ⦿❘ *No meals* Ⓜ *Tuileries.*

Meliá Vendôme

$$ | HOTEL | In a prestigious quarter a few minutes from the Jardin des Tuileries, Place de la Concorde, Opéra Garnier, and the Louvre, the Meliá Vendôme has handsome and spacious rooms in attractive contemporary tones that exude an understated elegance. **Pros:** outstanding location in the city center; near world-class shopping; elegant, immaculate rooms. **Cons:** expensive breakfast; no spa or pool; in-room cooling system unreliable. $ *Rooms from: €200 ⊠ 8 rue Cambon, 1e, Louvre* ☎ *01–44–77–54–00* ⊕ *www.melia.com/en/hotels/france/paris/melia-vendome-boutique-hotel/index.html* ⥵ *83 rooms* ⦿❘ *No meals* Ⓜ *Concorde, Madeleine.*

★ The Ritz

$$$$ | HOTEL | In novels, songs, and common parlance, there's not a word that evokes the romance and luxury of Paris better than the Ritz. **Pros:** spacious swimming pool; superlative selection of bars and restaurants; top-notch service. **Cons:** easy to get lost in the vast hotel; paparazzi magnet; astronomical prices. $ *Rooms from: €1000 ⊠ 15 pl. Vendôme, 1er, Louvre* ☎ *01–43–16–30–30* ⊕ *www.ritzparis.com* ⥵ *143 rooms* ⦿❘ *No meals* Ⓜ *Opéra.*

Nightlife

★ Ballroom du Beef Club

BARS/PUBS | Unmarked black door, basement setting, pressed-tin ceilings, atmospheric lighting—did someone say "speakeasy"? All this and luscious libations draw a sophisticated crowd that appreciates the extra touches that make this cocktail bar a standout. ⊠ *58 rue Jean-Jacques Rousseau, 1er, Louvre* ☎ *01–49–27–92–08* ⊕ *www.experimentalgroup.com* Ⓜ *Les Halles, Palais Royal–Musée du Louvre.*

Bar 8

BARS/PUBS | Ever since the monolithic marble bar at the Mandarin Oriental Hotel opened its doors, it has been the "in" game in town. There's an extensive champagne menu, and the terrace is especially busy during fashion weeks. ⊠ *251 rue Saint-Honoré, 1er, Louvre* ☎ *01–70–98–78–88* ⊕ *www.mandarinoriental.com* Ⓜ *Concorde, Tuileries.*

★ Experimental Cocktail Club

BARS/PUBS | Fashioned as a speakeasy on a tiny brick-paved street, the Experimental Cocktail Club seems like it should be lighted by gas lamps. The show is all about the *alcool*; colorful, innovative cocktails like the Lemon Drop are mixed with aplomb by friendly (and attractive) bartenders. By 11 pm it's packed with a diverse mix of locals, professionals, and fashionistas, who occasionally dress up like characters from a Toulouse-Lautrec painting on special costume nights. ⊠ *37 rue Saint-Sauveur, 2e, Louvre* ☎ *01–45–08–88–09* Ⓜ *Réamur–Sébastopol.*

The Hemingway Bar & the Ritz Bar

BARS/PUBS | Literature lovers, cocktail connoisseurs, and other drink-swilling devotees still flock to these two iconic bars within the Ritz Hotel. A $400 million renovation happily didn't alter the chill vibe or the wood-panelled, club chair decor in the tiny Hemingway Bar, where mixologist mainstays Colin Field and Roman Devaux will fix you a bespoke cocktail. Or try the Serendipity, their most popular drink, mixing champagne with Calvados and mint. Across the elegant corridor, the more spacious Ritz Bar offers a modern, "bistro-chic" ambience and live music. ⊠ *15 pl. Vendôme, 1er, Louvre* ⊕ *www.ritzparis.com* Ⓜ *Opéra.*

Kong

DANCE CLUBS | This club is glorious not only for its panoramic skyline views but also for its exquisite manga-inspired decor and kooky, disco-ball-and-kid-sumo-adorned bathrooms. On weekends, top-shelf DJs keep patrons dancing. ⊠ *1 rue du Pont Neuf, 1er, Louvre* ☎ *01–40–39–09–00* ⊕ *www.kong.fr* Ⓜ *Pont Neuf.*

🎭 Performing Arts

★ Comédie Française

THEATER | Founded in 1680, Comédie Française is the most hallowed institution in French theater. It specializes in splendid classical French plays by the likes of Racine, Molière, and Marivaux. Buy tickets at the box office, by telephone, or online. If the theater is sold out, the Salle Richelieu offers steeply discounted last-minute tickets an hour before the performance. ⊠ *Salle Richelieu, Pl. Colette, 1er, Louvre* ☎ *01–44–58–15–15* ⊕ *www.comedie-francaise.fr* Ⓜ *Palais-Royal–Musée du Louvre.*

Théâtre du Palais-Royal

THEATER | Located in the former residence of Cardinal Richelieu, this plush 716-seat, Italian-style theater is bedecked in gold and purple. It specializes in lighter fare, like comedies and theatrical productions aimed at the under-12 set. ⊠ *38 rue de Montpensier, 1er, Louvre* ☎ *01–42–97–59–76* ⊕ *theatrepalaisroyal. com* Ⓜ *Palais-Royal.*

🛍 Shopping

★ Chantal Thomass

CLOTHING | The legendary lingerie diva is back with a *Pillow Talk*–meets–Louis XIV–inspired boutique. This is French naughtiness at its best, striking the perfect balance between playful and seductive. Sheer silk negligees edged in Chantilly lace and lascivious bra-and-corset sets punctuate the signature line. ⊠ *211 rue St-Honoré, 1er, Louvre* ☎ *01–42–60–40–56* ⊕ *www.chantalthomass.fr* Ⓜ *Tuileries.*

Goyard

JEWELRY/ACCESSORIES | These colorful totes are the choice of royals, blue bloods, and the like (clients have included Sir Arthur Conan Doyle, Gregory Peck, and the Duke and Duchess of Windsor). Parisians swear by their durability and longevity; they're copious enough for a mile-long baguette, and durable enough for a magnum of Champagne. What's more, they easily transition into ultrachic beach or diaper bags. ⊠ *233 rue St-Honoré, 1er, Louvre* ☎ *01–42–60–57–04* ⊕ *www.goyard.com* Ⓜ *Tuileries.*

Hermès

JEWELRY/ACCESSORIES | The go-to for those who prefer their logo discreet yet still crave instant recognition, Hermès was established as a saddlery in 1837, then went on to create the eternally chic Kelly (named for Grace Kelly) and Birkin (named for Jane Birkin) handbags. The silk scarves are legendary for their rich colors and intricate designs, which change yearly. Other accessories are also extremely covetable: enamel bracelets, dashing silk-twill ties, and small leather goods. During semiannual sales, in January and July, prices are slashed by up to 50%, and the crowds line up for blocks. ⊠ *24 rue du Faubourg St-Honoré, 8e, Louvre* ☎ *01–40–17–46–00* ⊕ *www.hermes.com* Ⓜ *Concorde.*

Ladurée

FOOD/CANDY | Founded in 1862, Ladurée oozes period atmosphere—even at the big Champs-Élysées branch (No. 75)—but nothing beats the original tearoom on Rue Royale, with its pint-size tables and frescoed ceiling. Ladurée claims a familial link to the invention of the macaron and appropriately, there's a fabulous selection of these lighter-than-air cookies. Classic flavors include pistachio, salted caramel, and coffee; others, like violet–black currant, chestnut, and lime basil, are available seasonally. When you've worked your way through the macaron menu, try a cup of the famously rich hot chocolate with a flaky mille-feuille. Unfortunately, service has lagged at all three of the tearooms in recent years (including the charming upstairs room at 21 rue Bonaparte), and the crowded room feels ever more like an ersatz tourist destination than the historic tearoom that it is. Still, Ladurée's stylish boxes filled with sweet treats make memorable gifts. ⊠ *16 rue Royale, 8e, Louvre* ☎ *01–42–60–21–79* ⊕ *www.laduree.com* Ⓜ *Madeleine.*

Librairie Galignani

BOOKS/STATIONERY | Dating back to 1520s Venice, this venerable bookstore opened in Paris in 1801 and was the first to specialize in English-language books. Its present location, across from the Tuileries Garden on Rue de Rivoli, opened in 1856, and the wood bookshelves, creaking floors, and hushed interior provide the perfect atmosphere for perusing Paris's best collection of contemporary and classic greats in English and French, plus a huge selection of gorgeous art books. ⊠ *224 rue de Rivoli, 1er, Louvre* ☎ *01–42–60–76–07* ⊕ *www.galignani. com* Ⓜ *Tuileries.*

Maison Fabre

JEWELRY/ACCESSORIES | Until you've eased into an exquisite pair of gloves handcrafted by Fabre, you probably haven't experienced the sensation of having a second skin far superior to your own. Founded in 1924, this is one of Paris's historic *gantiers.* Styles range from classic to haute: picture elbow-length croc leather, coyote-fur mittens, and peccary driving gloves. ⊠ *128–129 Galerie de Valois, 1er, Louvre* ☎ *01–42–60–75–88* ⊕ *www.maisonfabre.com* Ⓜ *Palais-Royal–Louvre.*

Roger Vivier

SHOES/LUGGAGE/LEATHER GOODS | Known for decades for his Pilgrim-buckle shoes and inventive heels, Roger Vivier's name is being resurrected through the creativity of über-Parisienne Inès de la Fressange and the expertise of shoe designer Gherardo Felloni. The results are easily some of the best shoes in town: leather boots that mold to the calf perfectly, towering rhinestone-encrusted or feathered platforms for evening, and vertiginous crocodile pumps. ⊠ *29 rue du Faubourg St-Honoré, 8e, Louvre* ☎ *01–53–43–00–85* ⊕ *www.rogervivier.com* Ⓜ *Concorde.*

Les Grands Boulevards

In Belle Époque Paris, the Grands Boulevards were the place to see and be seen: in the cafés, at the opera, or in the ornate passages couverts (glass-roofed arcades that served as the world's first malls).

Sights

★ Au Printemps

STORE/MALL | Encompassing a trio of upscale department stores (Printemps Mode, Printemps Beauté-Maison-Enfant, and Printemps Homme), this vast, venerable retailer has been luring shoppers since 1865 and has lately upped its glamour quotient with a series of elegant store-wide restorations. Besides the clothes, shoes, housewares, and everything else, there are appealing dining options here. Two floors of the main building (Printemps Homme) have been completely renovated and are now home to Printemps du Goût, a celebration of French cuisine. If you are a do-it-yourself-er, you can find the best of French foodstuffs on the seventh floor. But if you want to eat in style while taking in spectacular views, either from inside via floor-to-ceiling windows or outside on the wraparound terrace, continue on to the eighth floor, where four noted chefs and food artisans—master cheesemaker

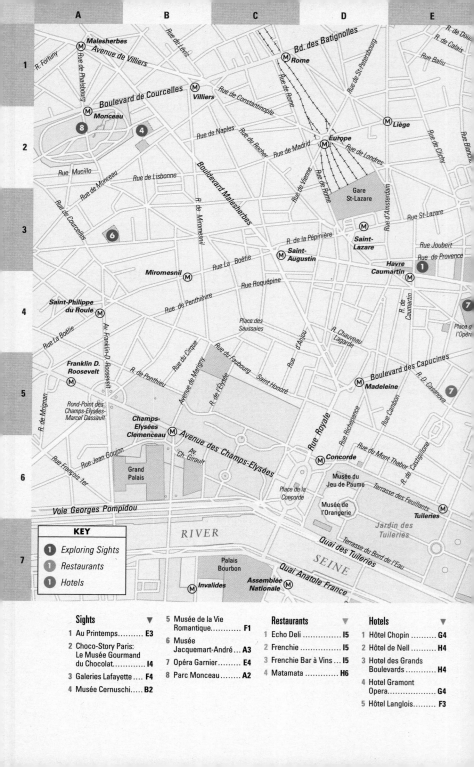

KEY

1 *Exploring Sights*

1 *Restaurants*

1 *Hotels*

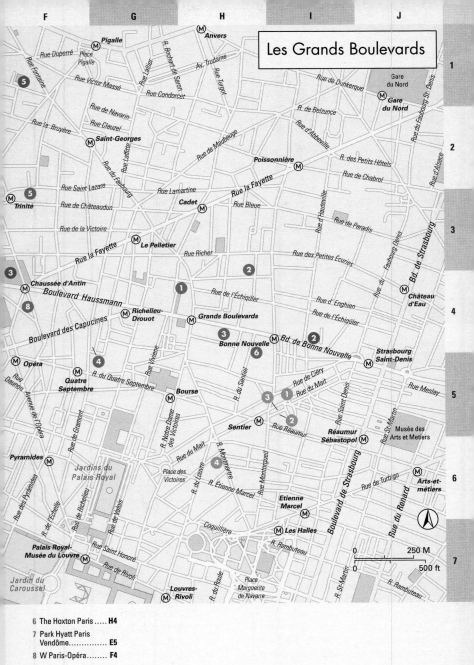

Les Grands Boulevards

	F	G	H	I	J

Pigalle
Anvers
Rue Duperré
Rue Fontaine
Place Pigalle
Rue Lallier
R. Bochart de Saron
Av. Trudaine
Rue Turgot
Rue de Dunkerque
Gare du Nord
Gare du Nord
Rue du Faubourg St-Denis
Rue Victor Massé
Rue Condorcet
R. de Belzunce
Rue d'Alsace
Rue de Navarin
Rue d'Abbeville
Rue Clauzel
Rue la Bruyère
Saint-Georges
R. des Petits Hôtels
Rue de Chabrol
Rue Lafitte
Rue de Maubeuge
Poissonnière
Rue Saint Lazare
Rue du Faubourg
Rue Lamartine
Trinité
Rue de Châteaudun
Cadet
Rue la Fayette
Rue Bleue
Rue de Hauteville
Rue de Paradis
Bd. de Strasbourg
Rue de la Victoire
Rue la Fayette
Le Pelletier
Rue Richer
Rue des Petites Écuries
Rue du Faubourg Denis
Chaussée d'Antin
Richelieu-Drouot
Rue de l'Échiquier
Rue d'Enghien
Rue d'Échiquier
Château d'Eau
Boulevard Haussmann
Grands Boulevards
Boulevard des Capucines
Rue Vivienne
Bonne Nouvelle
Bd. de Bonne Nouvelle
Strasbourg Saint-Denis
Opéra
Quatre Septembre
R. du Quatre Septembre
R. du Sentier
Rue de Cléry
Rue du Mail
Rue Saint Denis
Rue Meslay
Rue Daunou
Bourse
R. Notre Dame des Victoires
Sentier
Rue Réaumur
Réaumur Sébastopol
Rue St-Martin
Musée des Arts et Metiers
Avenue de l'Opéra
Rue de Gramont
Pyramides
Rue du Mail
R. du Louvre
R. Montmartre
Place des Victoires
R. Étienne Marcel
Rue Montorgueil
Boulevard de Strasbourg
Rue de Turbigo
Rue du Renard
Arts-et-métiers
Jardins du Palais Royal
Rue de Richelieu
Rue de Valois
Etienne Marcel
Rue des Pyramides
Rue de l'Échelle
Coquillière
Les Halles
R. Rambuteau
R. St-Martin
R. Rambuteau
Palais Royal-Musée du Louvre
Rue Saint Honoré
Rue de Rivoli
R. du Roule
Place Marguerite de Navarre
Jardin du Carousel
Louvres-Rivoli

0 — 250 M
0 — 500 ft

The interior of the Galeries Lafayette department store—especially the ceiling—almost outshines the fabulous merchandise.

Laurent Dubois, chef pâtissier Christophe Michalak, artisanal baker Gontran Cherrier, and master chef Akrame—oversee a gourmet cornucopia. You can also opt for a leisurely shopping break at La Brasserie Printemps, under the famous stained-glass cupola, or the magnificent terrace of restaurant Perruche, with 360-degree views over Paris. Shoppers will be pleased to know that Paris's grand department stores are now open Sunday. ⊠ *64 bd. Haussmann, 9e, Grands Boulevards* ☎ *01–42–82–50–00* ⊕ *www. printemps.com* Ⓜ *Havre–Caumartin, St-Lazare.*

Choco-Story Paris: Le Musée Gourmand du Chocolat

MUSEUM | FAMILY | Considering that a daily dose of chocolate is practically obligatory in Paris, it's hard to believe that this spot (opened in 2010) is the city's first museum dedicated to the sweet stuff. Exhibits on three floors tell the story of chocolate from the earliest traces of the "divine nectar" in Mayan and Aztec cultures, through to its introduction in Europe by the Spanish, who added milk

and sugar to the spicy dark brew and launched a Continental craze. There are detailed explanations in English, with many for the kids. While the production of chocolate is a major topic, there is also a respectable collection of some 1,000 chocolate-related artifacts, such as terra-cotta Mayan sipping vessels (they blew into straws to create foam) and delicate chocolate pots in fine porcelain that were favored by the French royal court. Frequent chocolate-making demonstrations finish with a free tasting. ⊠ *28 bd. de Bonne Nouvelle, 10e, Grands Boulevards* ☎ *01–42–29–68–60* ⊕ *www. museeduchocolat.fr* ⊠ *€11; €14 with a cup of hot chocolate* Ⓜ *Bonne-Nouvelle, Strasbourg, St-Denis.*

★ Galeries Lafayette

STORE/MALL | The stunning Byzantine glass *coupole* (dome) of the city's most famous department store is not to be missed. Amble to the center of the main store, amid the perfumes and cosmetics, and look up. If you're not in the mood for shopping, visit the (free) first-floor Galerie des Galeries, an art gallery devoted to fashion, applied arts, and design; or have lunch at one of the restaurants, including a rooftop bar and restaurant in the main store—it has some of the best panoramic views of the city. On your way down, the top floor of the main store is a good place to pick up interesting Parisian souvenirs. Across the street in Galeries Maison, the excellent Lafayette Gourmet food hall has one of the city's best selections of delicacies and several restaurants, including Maison de la Truffe. Try a classic madeleine filled with pistachio or lemon at patissière Yann Couvreur's popular teatime. The luxurious new Bar Kaspia, under the main building's famous coupole, serves caviar and all things from the sea. Don't miss the Bordeauxthèque on Galeries Maison's first floor, where €30,000 bottles of wine are on display. ⊠ 35–40 bd. Haussmann, 9e, Grands Boulevards ☎ 01–42–82–34–56 ⊕ www. galerieslafayette.com Ⓜ Chaussée d'Antin–La Fayette, Havre–Caumartin.

★ **Musée Cernuschi**

MUSEUM | Wealthy Milanese banker and patriot Enrico (Henri) Cernuschi fled to Paris in 1850 after the new Italian government collapsed, only to be arrested during the 1871 Paris Commune. He subsequently decided to wait out the unrest by traveling and collecting Asian art. Upon his return 18 months later, he had a special mansion built on the edge of Parc Monceau to house his treasures, notably a two-story bronze Buddha from Japan. Today, this well-appointed museum contains France's second-most-important collection of Asian art, after the Musée Guimet. Cernuschi had an eye not only for the bronze pieces he adored but also for Neolithic pottery (8000 BC), *mingqi* tomb figures (AD 300–900), and an impressive array of terra-cotta figures from various dynasties. A collection highlight is La Tigresse, a bronze wine vessel in the shape of a roaring feline (11th century BC) purchased after Cernuschi's death. Although the museum is free, there is a charge for

temporary exhibitions: previous shows have featured Japanese drawings, Iranian sculpture, and Imperial Chinese bronzes. ⊠ 7 av. Velasquez, 8e, Grands Boulevards ☎ 01–53–96–21–50 ⊕ www.cernuschi. paris.fr ☜ Free; €9 for temporary exhibitions ⊙ Closed Mon. Ⓜ Monceau.

Musée de la Vie Romantique

MUSEUM | A visit to the charming Museum of Romantic Life, dedicated to novelist George Sand (1804–76), will transport you to the countryside. Occupying a pretty 1830s mansion in a tree-lined courtyard, the small permanent collection features drawings by Delacroix and Ingres, among others, though Sand is the undisputed star. Displays include glass cases stuffed with her jewelry and even a mold of the hand of composer Frédéric Chopin—one of her many lovers. The museum, about a five-minute walk from the Musée National Gustave-Moreau, is in a picturesque neighborhood once called New Athens, a reflection of the architectural tastes of the writers and artists who lived there. There is usually an interesting temporary exhibit here, too. The garden café (open mid-March to mid-October) is a lovely spot for lunch or afternoon tea. ⊠ 16 rue Chaptal, 9e, Grands Boulevards ☎ 01–55–31–95–67 ⊕ www.museevieromantique.paris.fr ☜ Free; €5 temporary exhibits ⊙ Closed Mon. Ⓜ Blanche, Pigalle, St-Georges.

★ **Musée Jacquemart-André**

MUSEUM | Perhaps the city's best small museum, the opulent Musée Jacquemart-André is home to a huge collection of art and furnishings lovingly assembled in the late 19th century by banking heir Edouard André and his artist wife, Nélie Jacquemart. Their midlife marriage in 1881 raised eyebrows—he was a dashing bachelor and a Protestant, and she, no great beauty, hailed from a modest Catholic family. Still, theirs was a happy union fused by a common passion for art. For six months every year, the couple traveled, most often to Italy, where they hunted down works from the Renaissance, their preferred period. Their collection also includes French painters Fragonard, Jacques-Louis David, and François Boucher, plus Dutch masters Van Dyke and Rembrandt. The Belle Époque mansion itself is a major attraction. The elegant ballroom, equipped with collapsible walls operated by then-state-of-the-art hydraulics, could hold 1,000 guests. The winter garden was a wonder of its day, spilling into the *fumoir*, where André would share cigars with the *grands hommes* (important men) of the day. You can tour the separate bedrooms—his in dusty pink, hers in pale yellow. The former dining room, now an elegant café, features a ceiling by Tiepolo. Don't forget to pick up the free audio guide in English, and do inquire about the current temporary exhibition, which is usually top-notch. Plan on a Sunday visit and enjoy the popular brunch (€29.30) in the café from 11 am to 2:30 pm. Reservations are not accepted, so come early or late to avoid waiting in line. ⊠ *158 bd. Haussmann, 8e, Grands Boulevards* ☎ *01–45–62–11–59* ⊕ *www. musee-jacquemart-andre.com* 🔁 *From €14* Ⓜ *St-Philippe du Roule, Miromesnil.*

★ **Opéra Garnier**

ARTS VENUE | Haunt of the Phantom of the Opera and the real-life inspiration for Edgar Degas's dancer paintings, the gorgeous Opéra Garnier is one of two homes of the National Opera of Paris. The building, the Palais Garnier, was begun in 1860 by then-unknown architect Charles Garnier, who finished his masterwork 15 long years later, way over budget. Festooned with (real) gold leaf, colored marble, paintings, and sculpture from the top artists of the day, the opera house was about as subtle as Versailles and sparked controversy in post-Revolutionary France. The sweeping marble staircase, in particular, drew criticism from a public skeptical of its extravagance. But Garnier, determined to make a landmark that would last forever, spared no expense. The magnificent

grand foyer is one of the most exquisite salons in France. In its heyday, the cream of Paris society strolled all 59 yards of the vast hall at intermission, admiring themselves in the towering mirrors. To see the opera house, buy a ticket for an unguided visit, which allows access to most parts of the building, including a peek into the auditorium. There is also a small ballet museum with a few works by Degas and the tutu worn by prima ballerina Anna Pavlova when she danced her epic *Dying Swan* in 1905. To get to it, pass through the unfinished entrance built for Napoléon III and his carriage (construction was abruptly halted when the emperor abdicated in 1870). On the upper level, you can see a sample of the auditorium's original classical ceiling, which was later replaced with a modern version painted by a septuagenarian Marc Chagall. His trademark willowy figures encircling the dazzling crystal chandelier—today the world's third largest—shocked an unappreciative public upon its debut in 1964. Critics who fret that Chagall's masterpiece clashes with the fussy crimson-and-gilt decor can take some comfort in knowing that the original ceiling is preserved underneath, encased in a plastic dome.

The Opéra Garnier plays host to the Paris Ballet as well as a few operas each season (most are performed at the Opéra Bastille). If you're planning to see a performance, tickets cost €10–€230 and should be reserved as soon as they go on sale—typically a month ahead at the box office, earlier by phone or online; otherwise, try your luck last-minute. To learn about the building's history, and get a taste of aristocratic life during the Second Empire, take an entertaining English-language tour (daily at 11 and 2:30, €14) or rent an audio guide (€5) and proceed at your own pace. To complete the experience, dine at L'Opéra, the contemporary on-site restaurant run by chef Chihiro Yamazaki; or browse through the Palais Garnier gift shop for

The Grand Foyer proves that Paris's Opéra Garnier is the most opulent theater in the world.

ballet-inspired wares, fine Bernardaud porcelain depicting the famous Chagall ceiling, a jar of honey from the Opéra's own rooftop hives, and an exceptional selection of themed DVDs and books. ⊠ *Pl. de l'Opéra, 9e, Grands Boulevards* ☎ *08–92–89–90–90 (€0.35 per min), 01–71–25–24–23 from outside France* ⊕ *www.operadeparis.fr* ☒ *€11; €12 with temporary exhibition; €16 for tours* Ⓜ *Opéra.*

Parc Monceau
CITY PARK | FAMILY | This exquisitely landscaped park began in 1778 as the Duc de Chartres's private garden. Though some of the land was sold off under the Second Empire (creating the exclusive real estate that now borders the park), the refined atmosphere and some of the fanciful faux ruins have survived. Immaculately dressed children play under the watchful eye of their nannies, while lovers cuddle on the benches. In 1797 André Garnerin, the world's first-recorded parachutist, staged a landing in the park. The rotunda—known as the Chartres Pavilion—is surely the city's grandest public restroom: it started life as a tollhouse. ⊠ *Entrances on Bd. de Courcelles, Av. Velasquez, Av. Ruysdaël, and Av. van Dyck, Grands Boulevards* Ⓜ *Monceau.*

🍽 Restaurants

★ Echo Deli
$ | CONTEMPORARY | Parisians flock to the newly hip Sentier neighborhood for a taste of this chic coffee shop's fresh and imaginative California-style cuisine. Eggs are served in the most delicious ways: scrambled with cheese, scallions, and hot sauce; in a slow-cooked congee of wild mushrooms and whole brown rice; or with thick slices of multigrain bread, avocado, and anchovies. **Known for:** delicious Saturday and Sunday brunch; vegetarian, vegan, and gluten-free options; great coffee and other hot drinks. $ *Average main: €12* ⊠ *95 rue d'Aboukir, 2e, Grands Boulevards* ⊕ *www.echo-paris. com* 🕙 *Closed Mon. and Tues.* Ⓜ *Bonne Nouvelle, Strasbourg-Saint-Denis, Sentier.*

★ Frenchie

$$$$ | **BISTRO** | A brick-and-stone-walled bistro on a pedestrian street near Rue Montorgueil, Frenchie has quickly became one of the most packed bistros in town, with tables booked months in advance, despite two seatings each evening. This success is due to the good-value, five-course dinner menu (prix fixe only); boldly flavored dishes such as calamari gazpacho with squash blossoms, and melt-in-the-mouth braised lamb with roasted eggplant and spinach are excellent options. **Known for:** casual laid-back atmosphere that belies the ultrasophisticated dishes; extensive and original wine list; graciously accommodating to vegetarians. $ *Average main: €34* ⊠ *5 rue du Nil, 2e, Grands Boulevards* ☎ *01–40–39–96–19* ⊕ *www. frenchie-restaurant.com* ⊙ *Closed Sat. and Sun., 2 wks in Aug., and 10 days at Christmas. No lunch Mon.–Wed.* Ⓜ *Sentier.*

★ Frenchie Bar à Vins

$$ | **WINE BAR** | If this weren't one of Paris's outstanding wine bars, the wait and metal tractor seats might be a deterrent. Yet wine lovers would be hard-pressed to find a better venue for sampling a great list of French wines and inspired selections from Italy and Spain—every one of them sold by the bottle or glass—with superb tapas to match. **Known for:** choice selection of natural wines from France and Europe; rare expertise in natural, organic, and biodynamic wines; long waits unless you get there right when they open (7 pm). $ *Average main: €18* ⊠ *6 rue du Nil, 2e, Grands Boulevards* ☎ *No phone* ⊕ *www.frenchie-restaurant. com* ⊙ *Closed Sat. and Sun. No lunch* Ⓜ *Sentier.*

★ Matamata

$ | **CAFÉ** | This tiny gem of a coffee shop may not have the ambience of Paris's historic brasserie cafés, but it does have something you won't find in any brasserie in Paris—reliably excellent coffee served with care and enthusiasm. Additionally, a small menu of delicious homemade sweets and sandwiches and salads at lunchtime pretty much cover all your restoration needs in a warm and friendly atmosphere. **Known for:** consistently great coffee drinks of all kinds; quality beans sourced from around the world; friendly atmosphere. $ *Average main: €5* ⊠ *58 rue d'Argout, 2e, Grands Boulevards* ☎ *01–71–39–44–58* ⊕ *www.matamat-acoffee.com* Ⓜ *Sentier.*

Hotels

Hôtel Chopin

$$ | **HOTEL** | A unique mainstay of the district, the Chopin, set within the magnificent historic Passage Jouffroy, recalls its 1846 birth date with a creaky-floored lobby, aged woodwork, and its own homey charm. **Pros:** unique location; close to major métro station; great night-life district. **Cons:** thin walls; single rooms are very small; few amenities. $ *Rooms from: €140* ⊠ *10 bd. Montmartre, at 46 passage Jouffroy, 9e, Grands Boulevards* ☎ *01–47–70–58–10* ⊕ *hotelchopin-paris-opera.com* ⇌ *36 rooms* ⏐⊙⏐ *No meals* Ⓜ *Grands Boulevards.*

★ Hôtel de Nell

$$$$ | **HOTEL** | Tucked in a picturesque corner of a chic, up-and-coming neighborhood ripe for exploration, the serenely beautiful Hôtel de Nell offers contemporary luxury with clean lines and uncluttered spaces. **Pros:** great dining and bar on premises; interesting neighborhood to explore; beautiful rooms. **Cons:** area deserted at night; far from the major Paris attractions; no formal spa. $ *Rooms from: €385* ⊠ *9 rue du Conservatoire, 9e, Grands Boulevards* ☎ *01–44–83–83–60* ⊕ *www.charmandmore.com* ⇌ *33 rooms* ⏐⊙⏐ *No meals* Ⓜ *Bonne Nouvelle.*

★ Hotel des Grands Boulevards

$$ | **HOTEL** | Amid the hustle and bustle of the Grands Boulevards may not seem like the most serene or desirable place to lay your head, but this Revolution-era sanctuary tucked back in a vibrant up-and-coming neighborhood is an island of calm—and a very chic one at that. **Pros:** beautifully designed rooms; chic on-site cocktail bar and restaurant; lots of outdoor spaces and some fabulous private terraces. **Cons:** balconies can be noisy; not every room has a balcony; some rooms quite tiny. $ *Rooms from: €200* ✉ *17 bd. Poissonnière, 2e, Grands Boulevards* ☎ *01–85–73–33–33* ⊕ *www. grandsboulevardshotel.com* ⏎ *50 rooms* ❦ *No meals* Ⓜ *Bonne Nouvelle, Grands Boulevards.*

Hôtel Gramont Opéra

$$ | HOTEL | Near the Opéra Garnier and some of the city's best department stores, this family-owned boutique hotel has lots of little extras that make it a great value. **Pros:** good breakfast buffet with eggs made to order; personalized and professional service; connecting rooms for families. **Cons:** singles have no desk; small bathrooms; elevator doesn't go to top-floor rooms. $ *Rooms from: €190* ✉ *22 rue Gramont, 2e, Grands Boulevards* ☎ *01–42–96–85–90* ⊕ *www. hotel-gramont-opera.com* ⏎ *25 rooms* ❦ *No meals* Ⓜ *Quatre-Septembre.*

Hôtel Langlois

$$ | HOTEL | This darling hotel gained a reputation as one of the more atmospheric budget sleeps in the city, although rates have since crept up. **Pros:** excellent views from the top floor; close to department stores and Opéra Garnier; historic decor. **Cons:** noisy street; a bit out of the way; some sagging furniture and worn fabrics. $ *Rooms from: €162* ✉ *63 rue St-Lazare, 9e, Grands Boulevards* ☎ *01–48–74– 78–24* ⊕ *www.hotel-langlois.com* ⏎ *27 rooms* ❦ *No meals* Ⓜ *Trinité.*

★ The Hoxton Paris

$$$ | HOTEL | After wowing guests in London and Amsterdam, the Hoxton chain of trendsetting hotels applied its winning urban-chic formula to Paris—find a cool neighborhood, pare down, and tune in. **Pros:** cool neighborhood with lots to explore; historic mansion setting;

wonderful bar scene. **Cons:** off-the-radar-neighborhood is not for everyone; average dining; most affordable rooms are very no-frills. $ *Rooms from: €260* ✉ *30–32 rue du Sentier, 2e, Grands Boulevards* ☎ *01–85–65–75–00* ⊕ *www. thehoxton.com* ⏎ *172 rooms* ❦ *Free breakfast* Ⓜ *Grands Boulevards, Bonne Nouvelle.*

★ Park Hyatt Paris Vendôme

$$$$ | HOTEL | Understated luxury with a contemporary Zen vibe differentiates this Hyatt from its more classic neighbors between Place Vendôme and Opéra Garnier. **Pros:** stylish urban-chic design; the latest technology; only in-suite spas in Paris. **Cons:** as part of the Hyatt chain, it can feel anonymous; many corporate events held here; very expensive. $ *Rooms from: €850* ✉ *3–5 rue de la Paix, 2e, Grands Boulevards* ☎ *01–58– 71–12–34* ⊕ *www.hyatt.com/en-US/hotel/ france/park-hyatt-paris-vendome/parph* ⏎ *148 rooms* ❦ *No meals* Ⓜ *Concorde, Opéra.*

W Paris-Opéra

$$$$ | HOTEL | Located near Opéra Garnier, this 91-room hotel feels part Moulin Rouge, part art gallery, with cheeky and irreverent touches strewn throughout. **Pros:** coveted location in historic 19th-century building; excellent restaurant; cutting-edge rooms with comfortable beds. **Cons:** fee for Wi-Fi; rooms and public spaces feel claustrophobic; noisy neighborhood. $ *Rooms from: €550* ✉ *4 rue Meyerbeer, 9e, Grands Boulevards* ☎ *01–77–48–94–94* ⊕ *www.wpariso-pera.com* ⏎ *91 rooms* ❦ *No meals* Ⓜ *Chaussée d'Antin–La Fayette.*

 Nightlife

★ Bonhomie

BARS/PUBS | This newcomer to the Paris cocktail scene does a highly successful three in three—drinks, food, and ambience—a feat not to be taken lightly. What's more, the high-quality drinks include sourced coffees, yummy craft cocktails, and small-producer wines, basically anything your finicky heart desires. A menu of Mediterranean-inspired dishes is great for lunch, dinner, or sharing over cocktails or a glass of wine, and the café's late-morning and late-evening hours are a big plus in this neighborhood. ✉ *22 rue d'Enghien , 10e, Grands Boulevards* ☎ *09–83–88–82–51* ⊕ *www.bonhomie.paris* Ⓜ *Bonne Nouvelle, Château d'Eau.*

★ Experimental Cocktail Club

BARS/PUBS | The bar that launched the Paris cocktail scene a dozen years ago remains a Paris favorite among the cocktail cognoscenti, who know this shadowy raw brick and half-timbered watering hole will never disappoint. The cocktails change seasonally, but if nothing on the menu appeals, you can rely on the capable barmen and women to fix you right up with whatever you fancy. It has good bar snacks, too. ✉ *37 rue Saint-Sauveur, 2e, Grands Boulevards* ☎ *01–45–08–88–09* ⊕ *www.experimentalgroup.com/venue/experimental-cocktail-club* Ⓜ *Étienne Marcel, Strasbourg-Saint-Denis, Bonne Nouvelle.*

🎭 Performing Arts

★ Salle Cortot

MUSIC | This acoustic jewel was built in 1929 by Auguste Perret, who promised to construct "a concert hall that sounds like a Stradivarius." Tickets for jazz and classical concerts can only be bought from the box office 30 minutes beforehand; otherwise, go online to ⊕ *www.fnactickets.com* or ⊕ *www.concertclassic.com.* Free student recitals are offered at 12:30 on Tuesday and Thursday from October to April and on some Wednesday afternoons from January to May. ✉ *78 rue Cardinet, 17e, Batignolles* ☎ *01–47–63–47–48* ⊕ *www.sallecortot.com* Ⓜ *Malesherbes.*

🛍 Shopping

À la Mère de Famille

FOOD/CANDY | This enchanting shop dates from 1761 and is the oldest continuously open confectionary in Paris. Though it has gone the way of the chain, with multiple boutiques in Paris, À la Mère de Famille retains its authenticity and is well versed in French regional specialties as well as old-fashioned bonbons, chocolates, marzipan, ice creams, and more. ✉ *35 rue du Faubourg-Montmartre, 9e, Grands Boulevards* ☎ *01–47–70–83–69* ⊕ *www.lameredefamille.com* Ⓜ *Cadet.*

Charvet

CLOTHING | The Parisian equivalent of a Savile Row tailor, Charvet is a conservative, aristocratic institution. It's famed for made-to-measure shirts, exquisite ties, and accessories; for garbing John F. Kennedy, Charles de Gaulle, and the Duke of Windsor; and for its regal address. Although the exquisite silk ties, in hundreds of colors and patterns, and custom-made shirts for men are the biggest draw, refined pieces for women and girls, as well as adorable miniatures for boys, round out the collection. ✉ *28 pl. Vendôme, 1er, Grands Boulevards* ☎ *01–42–60–30–70* Ⓜ *Opéra.*

★ Rrraw

FOOD/CANDY | Just when Paris thought its already phenomenal chocolate scene couldn't get any better, chocolatier Frédéric Marr opened this chic chocolate factory and boutique. Now the words "healthy" and "chocolate" appear together in the organic, nondairy, vegan (and yes, tasty) chocolates made here from unheated raw beans in order to preserve all the nutrients, subtle flavors, and (minimal) natural sugars. There's no resisting the chic metal boxes filled with bite-size truffles perfumed with flavors like sesame-rose, hazelnut-vanilla, or honey-pollen, as well as *tablettes* (bars) and baking chocolate, a boon for vegan cooks. It's known for its vegan, gluten-free, organic, and low-sugar products, but it also has delicious hot chocolate. Plus, you can watch chocolate being made on the premises. ✉ *8 rue de Mulhouse, 2e, Grands Boulevards* ☎ *01–45–08–84–04* ⊕ *www.rrraw.fr* Ⓜ *Bonnes Nouvelle.*

★ Stohrer

FOOD/CANDY | This Paris institution opened in 1730, thanks to Louis XV's Polish bride, who couldn't bear to part with her pastry chef and thus brought Nicholas Stohrer along with her to Paris. Today it has all the to-die-for pastries that made the bakery's name, including the famous baba au rhum that originated here, as well as a tantalizing range of other sweets, breads, and savory prepared foods to go. ✉ *51 rue Montorgueil, 2e, Grands Boulevards* ☎ *01–42–33–38–20* ⊕ *stohrer.fr* Ⓜ *Étienne Marcel, Réaumur-Sébastopol.*

Montmartre

Montmartre has become almost too charming for its own good. Yes, it feels like a village (if you wander off the beaten path); yes, there are working artists here (though far fewer than there used to be); and yes, the best view of Paris is yours for free from the top of the hill (if there's no haze). That's why on any weekend day, year-round, you can find scores of visitors crowding these cobbled alleys, scaling the staircases that pass for streets, and queuing to see Sacré-Coeur, the "sculpted cloud," at the summit.

◉ Sights

★ Basilique du Sacré-Coeur

RELIGIOUS SITE | It's hard not to feel as though you're ascending to heaven when you visit Sacred Heart Basilica, the white castle in the sky, perched atop Montmartre. The French government commissioned it in 1873 to symbolize the return of self-confidence after the devastating years of the Commune and Franco-Prussian War, and architect Paul Abadie

employed elements from Romanesque and Byzantine styles when designing it—a mélange many critics dismissed as gaudy. Construction lasted until World War I, and the church was finally consecrated in 1919. Many people now come to Sacré-Coeur to admire the superlative view from the top of its 271-foot-high dome. But if you opt to skip the climb up the spiral staircase, the view from the front steps is still ample compensation for the trip.

Inside, expect another visual treat—namely the massive golden mosaic set high above the choir. Created in 1922 by Luc-Olivier Merson, *Christ in Majesty* depicts Christ with a golden heart and outstretched arms, surrounded by various figures, including the Virgin Mary and Joan of Arc. It remains one of the largest mosaics of its kind. In the basilica's 262-foot-high campanile hangs La Savoyarde, one of the world's heaviest bells, weighing about 19 tons.

The best time to visit Sacré-Coeur is early morning or early evening, and preferably not on a Sunday, when the crowds are thick. If you're coming to worship, there are daily Masses.

■ TIP➔ **To avoid the steps, take the funicular, which costs one métro ticket each way.** ✉ *Pl. du Parvis-du-Sacré-Coeur, Montmartre* ☎ *01–53–41–89–00* ⊕ *www. sacre-coeur-montmartre.com* 🎫 *Basilica free, dome €6* 🕑 *Crypt closed long-term* Ⓜ *Anvers, plus funicular; Jules Joffrin plus Montmartrobus.*

Bateau-Lavoir

HOUSE | The birthplace of Cubism isn't open to the public, but a display in the front window details this unimposing spot's rich history. Montmartre poet Max Jacob coined the name because the original structure here reminded him of the laundry boats that used to float in the Seine, and he joked that the warren of paint-splattered artists' studios needed a good hosing down (wishful thinking, because the building had only one water

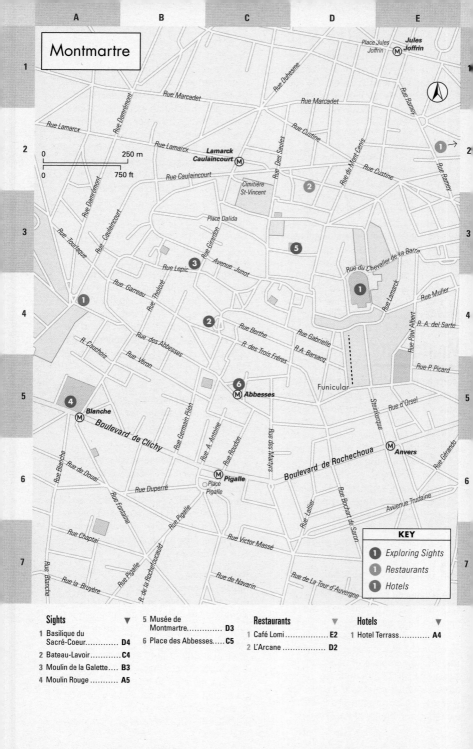

Montmartre

0 — 250 m
0 — 750 ft

Sights ▼

1 Basilique du
  Sacré-Coeur............ **D4**
2 Bateau-Lavoir............ **C4**
3 Moulin de la Galette.. **B3**
4 Moulin Rouge **A5**

5 Musée de
  Montmartre............. **D3**
6 Place des Abbesses..... **C5**

Restaurants ▼

1 Café Lomi **E2**
2 L'Arcane **D2**

Hotels ▼

1 Hotel Terrass............ **A4**

KEY

1 *Exploring Sights*

1 *Restaurants*

1 *Hotels*

tap). It was in the Bateau-Lavoir that, early in the 20th century, Pablo Picasso, Georges Braque, and Juan Gris made their first bold stabs at Cubism, and Picasso painted the groundbreaking *Les Demoiselles d'Avignon* in 1906–07. The experimental works of the artists weren't met with open arms, even in liberal Montmartre. All but the facade was rebuilt after a fire in 1970. Like the original building, though, the current incarnation houses artists and their studios. ⊠ *13 pl. Émile-Goudeau, Montmartre* Ⓜ *Abbesses*.

Moulin de la Galette

WINDMILL | Of the 14 windmills (*moulins*) that used to sit atop this hill, only two remain. They're known collectively as Moulin de la Galette, a name taken from the bread the owners once produced. The more storied of the two is Le Blute-Fin: in the late 1800s there was a dance hall on the site, famously captured by Renoir (you can see the painting in the Musée d'Orsay). A face-lift restored the windmill to its 19th-century glory; however, it is on private land and can't be visited. Down the street is the other moulin, Le Radet. ⊠ *Le Blute-Fin, at corner of Rue Lepic and Rue Girardot, Montmartre* Ⓜ *Abbesses*.

Moulin Rouge

ARTS VENUE | When this world-famous cabaret opened in 1889, aristocrats, professionals, and the working classes alike all flocked to ogle the scandalous performers (the cancan was considerably kinkier in Toulouse-Lautrec's day, when girls kicked off their knickers). There's not much to see from the outside except for tourist buses and sex shops; if you want to catch a show inside, ticket prices start at €87. Souvenir seekers should check out the Moulin Rouge gift shop (around the corner at 11 rue Lepic), which sells official merchandise, from jewelry to sculptures, by reputable French makers. ⊠ *82 bd. de Clichy, Montmartre* ☎ *01–53–09–82–82* ⊕ *www.moulinrouge. fr* Ⓜ *Blanche*.

Musée de Montmartre

MUSEUM | During its turn-of-the-20th-century heyday, this building—now home to Montmartre's historical museum—was occupied by painters, writers, and cabaret artists. Foremost among them was Pierre-Auguste Renoir, who painted *Le Moulin de la Galette* (an archetypal scene of sun-drenched revelers) while living here. Recapping the area's colorful past, the museum has a charming permanent collection, which includes many Toulouse-Lautrec posters and original Eric Satie scores. An ambitious renovation, completed in 2014, doubled its space by incorporating both the studio-apartment once shared by mother-and-son duo Suzanne Valadon and Maurice Utrillo (now fully restored) and the adjoining Demarne Hotel (which has been redesigned to house temporary exhibitions). The lovely surrounding gardens—named in honor of Renoir—have also been revitalized. An audio guide is included in the ticket price. ⊠ *12 rue Cortot, Montmartre* ☎ *01–49–25–89–39* ⊕ *www. museedemontmartre.fr* ⊠ *€9.50 (€12 with temporary exhibition; €4 gardens only)* Ⓜ *Lamarck–Caulaincourt*.

Place des Abbesses

PLAZA | This triangular square is typical of the countrified style that has made Montmartre famous. Now a hub for shopping and people-watching, the *place* is surrounded by hip boutiques, sidewalk cafés, and shabby-chic restaurants—a prime habitat for the young, neo-bohemian crowd and a sprinkling of expats. Trendy streets like Rue Houdon and Rue des Martyrs have attracted small designer shops, trendy secondhand clothing stores, and even a cupcake shop. Many retailers remain open on Sunday afternoon. ⊠ *Rue des Abbesses at Rue la Vieuville, Montmartre* Ⓜ *Abbesses*.

Residents of Montmartre often talk about "going down into Paris," and after climbing the many steps to get here you'll understand why.

Restaurants

Café Lomi
$ | CAFÉ | A trailblazer on the Paris gastro-coffee scene, Café Lomi first supplied expertly roasted single-origin coffees to the first wave of barista cafés and top restaurants. Now Lomi's industrial-chic loft is equal parts roaster, café, workshop, and pilgrimage stop for hard-core coffee lovers, serving a range of splendid brews along with a menu of warm and cold dishes and a hearty brunch on weekends. **Known for:** industrial-chic space; coffee roasted on the premises; consistently excellent brews. $ *Average main: €10* ✉ *3 ter rue Marcadet, 18e, Montmartre* ☎ *09–80–39–56–24* ⊕ *www. cafelomi.com* ◷ *Closed 3 wks in Aug.* Ⓜ *Marcadet-Poissonnière.*

★ L'Arcane
$$$$ | FRENCH | Once a well-guarded foodie secret, a Michelin star brought this cozy restaurant tucked behind the Sacré-Coeur richly deserved acclaim. Now the intimate 14-seat dining room is packed with diners enjoying impeccable contemporary French cuisine that's gorgeously presented and full of flavor. **Known for:** menus à l'aveugle (blind menus); location near the Sacré-Coeur; very friendly service. $ *Average main: €66* ✉ *9 rue Lamarck, 18e, Montmartre* ⊕ *www.restaurantlarcane.com* ◷ *Closed Sun. and Mon. No lunch Tues. Closed Aug., 1 week in mid-Apr., and last week of Dec.* Ⓜ *Lamarck-Cauliancourt.*

🛏 Hotels

★ Hotel Terrass
$$ | HOTEL | FAMILY | If you feel like being away from it all, but in a reasonably priced, fairly self-sufficient setting with a good on-site restaurant and a chic bar with stupendous views, this is the place. **Pros:** panoramic views of all Paris; awesome terrace bar; welcoming common areas with complimentary coffee. **Cons:** basic rooms are small; restaurant could be better; some street noise. $ *Rooms from: €141* ✉ *12–14 rue Joseph de Maistre, 18e, Montmartre* ☎ *01–46–06–72–85*

⊕ www.terrass-hotel.com ⇌ 92 rooms
🍴 No meals Ⓜ Blanche, Abbesses.

🎭 Nightlife

★ Au Lapin Agile

CABARET | An authentic survivor from the 19th century, Au Lapin Agile considers itself the doyen of cabarets. Founded in 1860, it inhabits the same modest house that was a favorite subject of painter Maurice Utrillo. It became the home-away-from-home for Braque, Modigliani, Apollinaire, and Picasso—who once paid for a meal with one of his paintings, then promptly exited and painted another that he named after this place. There are no topless dancers; this is a genuine French cabaret with songs, poetry, and humor (in French) in a publike setting. Entry is €28. ⊠ 22 rue des Saules, 18e, Montmartre ☎ 01–46–06–85–87 ⊕ www.au-lapin-ag-ile.com Ⓜ Lamarck–Caulaincourt.

Glass

BARS/PUBS | Masquerading as a dive in Pigalle's rapidly gentrifying red-light district, this dark, candlelighted space is actually a shrine to urban cool. Hipsters party to a DJ while knocking back sophisticated cocktails, artisanal beers, and frosty margaritas from the frozen-drinks machine. It might also be the only place in Paris to find a boilermaker (a beer and a shot). Gourmet hot dogs help fuel the late-night party scene. ⊠ 9 rue Frochot, 9e, Montmartre ☎ 06–25–16–72–17 ⊕ www.glassparis.com Ⓜ Pigalle.

★ Paname Brewing Company

BREWPUBS/BEER GARDENS | One of Paris's first and best microbreweries on the city's exploding brewery scene, Paname offers six masterful craft beers, plus limited-time specials, and a fabulous terrace on a plum spot facing the Canal de la Villette. ⊠ 41 bis, quai de la Loire, Montmartre ☎ 01–40–36–43–55 ⊕ www.panamebrewingcompany.com Ⓜ Crimée, Laumière, Ourcq.

🛍 Shopping

★ Marché aux Puces St-Ouen
(Clignancourt)

OUTDOOR/FLEA/GREEN MARKETS | This picturesque market on the city's northern boundary still lures crowds on weekends from 9 to 6 and Monday from 10 to 5, but its once-unbeatable prices are now a relic. Packed with antiques booths and brocante stalls, the century-old, miles-long labyrinth has been undergoing a mild renaissance lately: witness Habitat's "village vintage," a collection of ware-houses filled with mid-century-modern pieces at 77 rue des Rosiers, plus other buzzworthy shops and galleries (some of which keep weekend-only hours). Destination eateries—including Philippe Starck's popular Ma Cocotte and the chic MOB Hotel—also attract a hip Paris contingent. Arrive early to pick up the best loot, then linger over a meal or apéro. Be warned, though: if there's one place in Paris where you need to know how to bargain, this is it! If you're arriving by métro, walk under the overpass and take the first left at the Rue de Rosiers to reach the center of the market. Note that stands selling dodgy odds and ends (think designer knockoffs and questiona-ble gadgets) set up around the overpass. These blocks are crowded and gritty; be careful with your valuables here and throughout the marché. ⊠ 18e, Montmartre ⊕ www.marcheauxpuces-saintouen.com Ⓜ Porte de Clignancourt, Garibaldi, Mairie de Saint-Ouen.

The Marais

From swampy to swanky, the Marais has a fascinating history. The quartier has remade itself many times, and today retains several identities. It's the city's epicenter of cool with hip boutiques, designer hotels, and art galleries galore; the hub of Paris's gay community; and, though fading, the nucleus of Jewish life.

You could easily spend your entire visit to Paris in this neighborhood—there is that much to do.

Sights

★ Centre Pompidou

MUSEUM | FAMILY | Love it or hate it, the Pompidou is certainly a unique-looking building and inside, it holds some of the city's best contemporary art, from the 20th century to the present day. Most Parisians have warmed to the industrial, Lego-like exterior that caused a scandal when it opened in 1977. Named after French president Georges Pompidou (1911–74), it was designed by then-unknowns Renzo Piano and Richard Rogers. The architects' claim to fame was putting the building's guts on the outside and color-coding them: water pipes are green, air ducts are blue, electrics are yellow, and things like elevators and escalators are red.

The Musée National d'Art Moderne (Modern Art Museum, entrance on Level 4) occupies the top two levels. Level 5 is devoted to modern art from 1905 to 1960, including major works by Matisse, Modigliani, Marcel Duchamp, and Picasso; Level 4 is dedicated to contemporary art from the '60s on, including video installations. The Galerie d'Enfants (Children's Gallery) on the mezzanine level has interactive exhibits designed to keep the kids busy. Outside, next to the museum's sloping plaza—where throngs of teenagers hang out (and where there's free Wi-Fi)—is the Atelier Brancusi. This small, airy museum contains four rooms reconstituting Brancusi's Montparnasse studios with works from all periods of his career. On the opposite side, in Place Igor-Stravinsky, is the Stravinsky fountain, which has 16 gyrating mechanical figures in primary colors, including a giant pair of ruby red lips. On the opposite side of Rue Rambuteau, on the wall at the corner of Rue Clairvaux and Passage Brantôme, is the appealingly bizarre mechanical brass-and-steel clock, *Le Défenseur du Temps*.

The Pompidou's permanent collection takes up a relatively small amount of the space when you consider this massive building's other features: temporary exhibition galleries, with a special wing for design and architecture; a highly regarded free reference library (there's often a queue of university students on Rue Renard waiting to get in); and the basement, which includes two cinemas, a theater, a dance space, and a small, free exhibition space. On your way up the escalator, you'll have spectacular views of Paris, ranging from Tour Montparnasse, to the left, around to the hilltop Sacré-Coeur on the right. ✉ *Pl. Georges-Pompidou, Marais Quarter* ☎ *01–44–78–12–33* ⊕ *www.centrepompidou.fr* 🎟 *Center access free, Atelier Brancusi free, museum and exhibits €14 (free 1st Sun. of month)* ⊙ *Closed Tues.* Ⓜ *Rambuteau.*

★ Fondation Henri Cartier-Bresson

MUSEUM | Opened in 2003, this foundation, created by Cartier-Bression, Martine Franck, his photographer wife, and their daughter, recently moved to these sleek new premises in the upper reaches of the Marais, amping up this neighborhood's already exciting photography scene. Along with mounting highly regarded exhibitions of world-class photographers, the foundation acts as Cartier-Bresson and Franck's photographic archive and hosts talks and symposia. The beautiful space also houses an enhanced and enlarged bookstore. ✉ *79 rue des Archives, 3e, Marais Quarter* ☎ *01–40–61–50–50* ⊕ *www.henricartier-bresson.org* 🎟 *€9* ⊙ *Closed Mon.* Ⓜ *République, Filles du Calvaire, Rambuteau.*

Hôtel de Sully (*Hôtel de Béthune-Sully*)

GARDEN | This early Baroque gem, built in 1624, is one of the city's loveliest *hôtels particuliers*. Like much of the area, it fell into ruin until the 1950s, when it was rescued by the institute for French historic monuments (the Centre des Monuments

Paris's leading modern art museum, Centre Pompidou, is also a vast (and architecturally ambitious) arts center that presents films, theater, and dance performances.

Nationaux), which is based here. The recently renovated headquarters aren't open to the public; however, you are welcome to enjoy the equally lovely garden. Stroll through it, past the Orangerie, to find a small passage into nearby Place des Vosges: Sully's best buddy, King Henri IV, would have lived there had he not been assassinated in 1610. An on-site bookstore (with a 17th-century ceiling of exposed wooden beams) sells specialized English-language guides to Paris. ⊠ *62 rue St-Antoine, Marais Quarter* ☎ *01–44–61–20–00* ⊕ *www.hotel-de-sully.fr* ⊘ *Bookstore closed Mon.* Ⓜ *St-Paul.*

Maison de Victor Hugo

HOUSE | France's most famous scribe lived in this house on the southeast corner of Place des Vosges between 1832 and 1848. It's now a museum dedicated to the multitalented author. In Hugo's apartment on the second floor, you can see the tall desk, next to the short bed, where he began writing his masterwork *Les Misérables* (as always, standing up). There are manuscripts and early editions of the novel on display, as well as others

such as *Notre-Dame de Paris,* known to English readers as *The Hunchback of Notre-Dame.* You can see illustrations of Hugo's writings, including Bayard's rendering of the impish Cosette holding her giant broom (which has graced countless *Les Miz* T-shirts). The collection includes many of Hugo's own, sometimes macabre, ink drawings (he was a fine artist) and furniture from several of his homes. Particularly impressive is the room of carved and painted Chinese-style wooden panels that Hugo designed for the house of his mistress, Juliet Drouet, on the island of Guernsey, when he was exiled there for agitating against Napoléon III. Try to spot the intertwined Vs and Js (hint: look for the angel's trumpet in the left corner). The first floor is dedicated to temporary exhibitions that often have modern ties to Hugo's work. ⊠ *6 pl. des Vosges, Marais Quarter* ☎ *01–42–72–10–16* ⊕ *www.maisons-victorhugo.paris.fr* ⊠ *Free; from €6 for temporary exhibitions* ⊘ *Closed Mon.* Ⓜ *St-Paul, Bastille.*

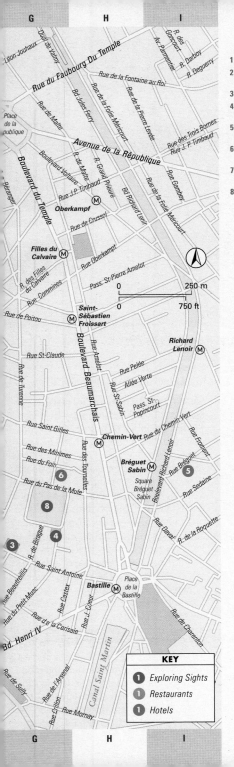

Sights ▼

1 Centre Pompidou **C5**
2 Fondation Henri Cartier-Bresson **E4**
3 Hôtel de Sully **G7**
4 Maison de Victor Hugo **G7**
5 Maison Européenne de la Photographie **E7**
6 Musée d'Art et d'Histoire du Judaïsme **D4**
7 Musée National Picasso-Paris **F5**
8 Place des Vosges **G7**

Restaurants ▼

1 Au Bourguignon du Marais **E7**
2 Breizh Café **F5**
3 L'As du Fallafel **E6**
4 Pain de Sucre **D5**

Hotels ▼

1 Hôtel Caron de Beaumarchais **E6**
2 Hôtel de la Bretonnerie **D6**
3 Hôtel Duo **C6**
4 Hôtel Jules & Jim **E3**
5 Maison Breguet **I6**
6 Pavillon de la Reine **G6**

KEY

1 *Exploring Sights*
1 *Restaurants*
1 *Hotels*

On a beautiful day, one of the best places to soak up the sun in the city is Place des Vosges.

★ **Maison Européenne de la Photographie**
(*Center for European Photography*)
MUSEUM | Much of the credit for the city's ascendancy as a hub of international photography goes to Maison Européenne de la Photographie (MEP) and its former director, Jean-Luc Monterosso, who also founded Paris's hugely successful Mois de la Photo festival (a biennial event held in April of odd-numbered years). MEP hosts up to four simultaneous exhibitions, changing about every three months. Shows feature an international crop of photographers and video artists. Works by superstar Annie Leibovitz or designer-photographer Karl Lagerfeld may overlap with a collection of self-portraits by an up-and-coming artist. MEP often stages retrospectives of the classics (by Doisneau, Cartier-Bresson, Man Ray, and others) from its vast private collection. Programs are available in English, and English-language tours are sometimes given; check the website for details. ⊠ *5/7 rue de Fourcy, Marais Quarter* ☎ *01–44–78–75–00* ⊕ *www.*

mep-fr.org ✉ *€10* ⊘ *Closed Mon. and Tues., between exhibitions* Ⓜ *St-Paul.*

Musée d'Art et d'Histoire du Judaïsme
MUSEUM | This excellent museum traces the tempestuous history of French and European Jews through art and history. Housed in the refined 17th-century Hôtel St-Aignan, exhibits have good explanatory texts in English, but the free English audio guide adds another layer of insight; guided tours in English are also available on request (€4 extra). Highlights include 13th-century tombstones excavated in Paris; a wooden model of a destroyed Eastern European synagogue; a roomful of early paintings by Marc Chagall; and Christian Boltanski's stark, two-part tribute to Shoah (Holocaust) victims in the form of plaques on an outer wall naming the (mainly Jewish) inhabitants of the Hôtel St-Aignan in 1939, and canvas hangings with the personal data of the 13 residents who were deported and died in concentration camps. The rear-facing windows offer a view of the Jardin Anne Frank. To visit it, use the entrance on Impasse Berthaud, off Rue Beaubourg,

just north of Rue Rambuteau. ⊠ *71 rue du Temple, Marais Quarter* ☎ *01–53–01–86–60* ⊕ *www.mahj.org* ⊠ *€10 with temporary exhibitions* ⊘ *Closed Mon.* Ⓜ *Rambuteau, Hôtel de Ville.*

★ Musée National Picasso-Paris

MUSEUM | Home to the world's largest public collection of Picasso's inimitable oeuvre, this spectacular museum covers almost 54,000 square feet in two buildings: the splendid 17th-century Hôtel Salé and a sprawling structure in the back garden dedicated to temporary exhibitions. Diego Giacometti's exclusively designed furnishings in the former are an added bonus. The collection of 200,000-plus paintings, sculptures, drawings, documents, and other archival materials (most of it donated to the City of Paris by Picasso or his family members) spans the artist's entire career. And while it doesn't include his most recognizable works, it does contain many of the pieces treasured most by Picasso himself. The first two floors cover Picasso's work from 1895 to 1972. The top floor illustrates his relationship to his favorite artists; landscapes, nudes, portraits, and still lifes taken from his private collection detail his "artistic dialogue" with Cézanne, Gauguin, Degas, Rousseau, Matisse, Braque, Renoir, Modigliani, Miró, and others. The basement centers around Picasso's workshops, with photographs, engravings, paintings, and sculptures that document or evoke key pieces created at the Bateau Lavoir, Château de Boisgeloup, Grands-Augustins, the Villa La Californie, and his farmhouse, Notre-Dame-de-Vie, in Mougins. With excellent temporary exhibitions and plenty of multimedia components and special activities that cater to kids, this is ideal for both children and adult art lovers alike. ■**TIP**→ **It's worth paying the extra €1 to buy tickets online well in advance of your planned visit. Also, try to avoid visiting on weekends, when the crowds are largest.** ⊠ *5 rue de Thorigny, Marais Quarter* ☎ *01–85–56–00–36* ⊕ *www.*

museepicassoparis.fr ⊠ *From €12.50* ⊘ *Closed Mon.* Ⓜ *St-Sébastien–Froissart.*

★ Place des Vosges

PLAZA | **FAMILY** | The oldest square in Paris and—dare we say it?—the most beautiful, Place des Vosges represents an early stab at urban planning. The precise proportions offer a placid symmetry, but things weren't always so calm here. Four centuries ago this was the site of the Palais des Tournelles, home to King Henry II and Queen Catherine de Medici. The couple staged regular jousting tournaments, and Henry was fatally lanced in the eye during one of them in 1559. Catherine fled to the Louvre, abandoning her palace and ordering it destroyed. In 1612 the square became Place Royale on the occasion of Louis XIII's engagement to Anne of Austria. Napoléon renamed it Place des Vosges to honor the northeast region of Vosges, the first in the country to pony up taxes to the Revolutionary government. At the base of the 36 redbrick-and-stone houses—nine on each side of the square—is an arcaded, covered walkway lined with art galleries, shops, and cafés. There's also an elementary school, a synagogue (whose barrel roof was designed by Gustav Eiffel), and several chic hotels. The formal, gated garden's perimeter is lined with chestnut trees; inside are a children's play area and a fountain. Aside from hanging out in the park, people come here to see the house of the man who once lived at No. 6—Victor Hugo, the author of *Les Misérables* and *Notre-Dame de Paris* (aka *The Hunchback of Notre-Dame*).

■**TIP**→ **One of the best things about this park is that you're actually allowed to sit— or snooze or snack—on the grass during spring and summer.** There is no better spot in the Marais for a picnic: you can pick up fixings at the nearby street market on Thursday and Sunday mornings (it's on Boulevard Richard Lenoir between Rues Amelot and St-Sabin). The most likely approach to Place des Vosges is from Rue de Francs-Bourgeois, the main shopping street. However, for a grander entrance walk along Rue St-Antoine until you get to Rue de Birague, which leads directly into the square. ✉ *Off Rue des Francs-Bourgeois, near Rue de Turenne, Marais Quarter* [M] *Bastille, St-Paul.*

🍴 Restaurants

Au Bourguignon du Marais

$$ | **BISTRO** | The handsome, contemporary look of this Marais bistro and wine bar is the perfect backdrop for traditional fare and excellent Burgundies served by the glass and bottle. Unusual for Paris, food is served nonstop from noon to 11 pm, and you can drop by just for a glass of wine in the afternoon. **Known for:** traditional bistro atmosphere; hearty Burgundian cuisine; sidewalk dining with nice views of the Marais. [$] *Average main: €22* ✉ *52 rue François-Miron, 3e, Marais Quarter* ☎ *01–48–87–15–40* [M] *St-Paul.*

★ **Breizh Café**

$ | **FRENCH** | **FAMILY** | Eating a crêpe in Paris might seem a bit clichéd, until you venture into this modern offshoot of a Breton crêperie. The plain, pale-wood decor is refreshing, but what really makes the difference are the ingredients—farmers' eggs, unpasteurized Gruyère, shiitake mushrooms, Valrhona chocolate, homemade caramel, and extraordinary butter from a Breton dairy farmer. **Known for:** some of the best crêpes in Paris; adventurous ingredients; Cancale oysters also on the menu. [$] *Average main: €12* ✉ *109 rue Vieille du Temple, 3e, Marais Quarter* ☎ *01–42–72–13–77* 🌐 *www.breizhcafe.com* 🕒 *Closed Mon., Tues., and Aug.* [M] *St-Sébastien–Froissart.*

★ **L'As du Fallafel**

$ | **MIDDLE EASTERN** | **FAMILY** | If you're looking for one of the cheapest and tastiest meals in Paris, look no further than the fantastic falafel stands on the pedestrian Rue de Rosiers. L'As (the Ace) is widely considered the best of the bunch, which accounts for the lunchtime line that extends down the street. **Known for:** the best, freshest, and most heaping falafel sandwich in town; fast take-out or seated service at lunch; shawarma sandwiches. [$] *Average main: €10* ✉ *34 rue des Rosiers, 4e, Marais Quarter* ☎ *01–48–87–63–60* 🕒 *Closed Sat. No dinner Fri.* [M] *St-Paul.*

★ **Pain de Sucre**

$ | **FRENCH** | A dazzling array of gourmet pastries here includes all the classics in imaginative and delicious flavor combinations. There are also impossibly moist individual cakes, Paris's best baba au rhum, sublime cookies, and the specialty *guimauve*, a flavored, melt-in-your-mouth marshmallow. **Known for:** some of Paris's best pastries; sublime gourmet sandwiches; take-out options for picnics. [$] *Average main: €7* ✉ *14 rue Rambuteau, 3e, Marais Quarter* ☎ *01–45–74–68–92* 🌐 *www.patisseriepaindesucre.com* [M] *Rambuteau.*

🛏 Hotels

★ **Hôtel Caron de Beaumarchais**

$$ | **HOTEL** | For that traditional French feeling, book a room at this intimate, affordable, romantic hotel—the theme is the work of former next-door-neighbor Pierre-Augustin Caron de Beaumarchais, a supplier of military aid to American revolutionaries and the playwright who penned *The Marriage of Figaro* and *The Barber of Seville*. **Pros:** cozy Parisian decor of yesteryear; breakfast in bed served until noon; excellent location within easy walking distance of major monuments. **Cons:** small rooms with few amenities; busy street of bars and cafés can be noisy; may feel old-fashioned for younger crowd. [$] *Rooms from: €180* ✉ *12 rue Vieille-du-Temple, 4e, Marais Quarter* ☎ *01–42–72–34–12* 🌐 *www.carondebeaumarchais.com* 🔑 *19 rooms* 🍴 *No meals* [M] *Hôtel de Ville.*

Hôtel de la Bretonnerie

$$ | **HOTEL** | In a 17th-century *hôtel particulier* (town house) on a side street in the Marais, this small hotel with exposed wooden beams and traditional styling sits

a few minutes from the Centre Pompidou and the numerous bars and cafés of Rue Vieille du Temple. **Pros:** typical Parisian character; moderate prices for the area; free Wi-Fi access. **Cons:** quality and size of the rooms vary greatly; no air-conditioning; rooms facing street can be noisy. [$] *Rooms from: €145* ✉ *22 rue Ste-Croix-de-la-Bretonnerie, 4e, Marais Quarter* ☎ *01–48–87–77–63* 🌐 *www.hotelparismaraisbretonnerie.com* 🛏 *29 rooms* 🍴 *No meals* [M] *Hôtel de Ville.*

Hôtel Duo

$$$ | HOTEL | For this hotel in the heart of the trendy Marais district, architect Jean-Philippe Nuel was commissioned to bring things up to date with bold colors and dramatic lighting; some rooms still have the original 16th-century beams but the overall feel is casual urban chic. **Pros:** central location near shops and cafés; walking distance to major monuments; good amenities. **Cons:** noisy neighborhood; service not always delivered with a smile; small standard rooms and bathrooms. [$] *Rooms from: €280* ✉ *11 rue du Temple, 4e, Marais Quarter* ☎ *01–42–72–72–22* 🌐 *www.duoparis.com* 🛏 *58 rooms* 🍴 *No meals* [M] *Hôtel de Ville.*

★ Hôtel Jules & Jim

$$$ | HOTEL | In the less-traveled corner of the trendy Marais district, this contemporary boutique hotel feels almost like an art gallery. **Pros:** bright and modern; stylish design; close to public transportation. **Cons:** the small "Jules" rooms are best for those traveling light or staying just one night; no restaurant; no in-room coffeemakers. [$] *Rooms from: €240* ✉ *11 rue des Gravilliers, 3e, Marais Quarter* ☎ *01–44–54–13–13* 🌐 *www.hoteljulesetjim.com* 🛏 *22 rooms, 1 duplex* 🍴 *No meals* [M] *Arts et Métiers.*

★ Maison Breguet

$$$ | HOTEL | This classy addition to the Parisian five-star scene is chic, well located, and full of lovely surprises—including a micro-pool, a lovely outdoor terrace (complete with an eight-person "maisonette"), and a superstylish restaurant and bar. **Pros:** walking distance to the Marais, Bastille, Canal St-Martin, and the hip 11th arrondissement; small but nice pool; great in-house restaurant, bar, and dining terrace. **Cons:** views aren't amazing; not a budget hotel; spa treatments in-room only. [$] *Rooms from: €280* ✉ *8 rue Breguet, 11e, Marais Quarter* ☎ *01–58–30–32–31* 🌐 *www.maisonbreguet.com* 🛏 *62 rooms* 🍴 *No meals* [M] *Bastille, Richard Lenoir.*

Pavillon de la Reine

$$$$ | HOTEL | Hidden off regal Place des Vosges behind a stunning garden courtyard, this enchanting château has gigantic beams, chunky stone pillars, and a weathered fireplace that speaks to its 1612 origins. **Pros:** historic character; quiet setting; free bicycles for guests. **Cons:** expensive for the area and the size of the rooms; the nearest métro is a few blocks away; no uniform theme for interior design. [$] *Rooms from: €460* ✉ *28 pl. des Vosges, 3e, Marais Quarter* ☎ *01–40–29–19–19* 🌐 *www.pavillon-de-la-reine.com* 🛏 *54 rooms* 🍴 *No meals* [M] *Bastille, St-Paul.*

🍸 Nightlife

★ Candelaria

BARS/PUBS | Steamy Candelaria is a taquería by day and a cocktail lounge by night. The tang of tequila hangs in the air at this hip hideaway, where deftly crafted drinks are poured for a contented crowd. ✉ *52 rue de Saintonge, 3e, Marais Quarter* ☎ *01–42–74–41–28* 🌐 *www.candelariaparis.com* [M] *Filles du Calvaire.*

🎟 Performing Arts

Théâtre de la Ville

DANCE | At *the* top spot for contemporary dance, you'll find French and international troupes choreographed by the world's best—like William Forsythe and Anne-Teresa de Keersmaeker's Rosas company. Concerts and theatrical performances

are also part of the season. Book early; shows sell out quickly. ⊠ *2 pl. du Châtelet, 4e, Marais Quarter* ☎ *01–42–74–22–77* ⊕ *www.theatredelaville-paris.com* Ⓜ *Châtelet.*

 ## Shopping

The Broken Arm

CLOTHING | Like the ready-made Duchamp "artwork" for which it is named, the Broken Arm projects a minimalist cool that puts the concept back in concept store. A hypercurated selection of A-list brands for men and women includes vivid separates from the likes of Martin Margiela, Raf Simons, and the sublime Christophe Lemaire. A choice selection of objects and accessories (books, hats, shoes, jewelry, and leather goods) elevates the everyday to art. ⊠ *12 rue Perrée, 3e, Marais Quarter* ☎ *01–44–61–53–60* ⊕ *www.the-broken-arm.com* Ⓜ *Temple.*

Comptoir de l'Image

BOOKS/STATIONERY | This is where designers John Galliano, Marc Jacobs, and Emanuel Ungaro stock up on old copies of *Vogue, Harper's Bazaar,* and *The Face.* You'll also find trendy magazines like *Dutch, Purple,* and *Spoon,* plus designer catalogs from the past and rare photo books. Don't go early: whimsical opening hours tend to start after lunch. ⊠ *44 rue de Sévigné, 3e, Marais Quarter* ☎ *01–42–72–03–92* Ⓜ *St-Paul.*

COS

CLOTHING | COS—which stands for Collection of Style—is the H&M group's answer to fashion sophisticates, who flock here in droves for high-concept, minimalist designs with serious attention to quality tailoring and fabrics at a reasonable price. Classic accessories and shoes look more expensive than they are. ⊠ *4 rue des Rosiers, 4e, Marais Quarter* ☎ *01–44–54–37–70* ⊕ *www.cosstores.com* Ⓜ *St-Paul.*

FrenchTrotters

CLOTHING | The flagship store features an understated collection of contemporary French-made clothes and accessories for men and women that emphasize quality fabrics, classic style, and cut over trendiness. You'll also find a handpicked collection of exclusive collaborations with cutting-edge French brands (like sleek leather-and-suede booties by Avril Gau for FrenchTrotters), as well as FrenchTrotters' namesake label and a limited selection of housewares for chic Parisian apartments. ⊠ *128 rue Vieille du Temple, Marais Quarter* ☎ *01–44–61–00–14* ⊕ *www.frenchtrotters.fr* Ⓜ *St-Sébastien–Froissart.*

L'Eclaireur

CLOTHING | This Rue de Sevigné boutique is Paris's touchstone for edgy, up-to-the-second styles. L'Eclaireur's knack for uncovering new talent and championing established visionaries is legendary—no surprise after 30 years in the business. Hard-to-find geniuses, like leather wizard Isaac Sellam and British prodigy Paul Harnden, cohabit with luxe labels such as Ann Demeulemeester, Haider Ackermann, and Gucci. ⊠ *40 rue de Sevigné, 3e, Marais Quarter* ☎ *01–48–87–10–22* ⊕ *leclaireur.com* Ⓜ *St-Paul.*

Mariage Frères

FOOD/CANDY | Mariage Frères, with its colonial *charme* and wooden counters, has 100-plus years of tea purveying behind it. Choose from more than 450 blends from 32 countries, not to mention teapots, teacups, books, and tea-flavor biscuits and candies. High tea and light lunches are served here and at several other Paris locations. ⊠ *30 rue du Bourg-Tibourg, 4e, Marais Quarter* ☎ *01–42–72–28–11* ⊕ *www.mariage-freres.com* Ⓜ *Hôtel de Ville.*

★ Merci

ANTIQUES/COLLECTIBLES | Paris's favorite concept store assembles top fashions for men and women, home furnishings (including those irresistible French bed and bath linens) vintage, jewelry, and housewares all plucked straight from top-tier French, European, and American designers. Every two months the store features a new design concept in the main entrance, with themes that range from Merci en Rose (featuring all things pink) to American Surf & Skate. The store's three cafés make lingering among Paris's fashion elite a pleasure. ⊠ *111 bd. Beaumarchais, 3e, Marais Quarter* ☎ *01–42–77–00–33* ⊕ *www.merci-merci. com* Ⓜ *St-Sebastien–Froissart.*

★ **WHITE bIRD**

JEWELRY/ACCESSORIES | Irresistible is the word for this scintillating collection of jewels by an assemblage of top-echelon international designers that range from the daintiest of diamond rings, bracelets, and necklaces, to brilliantly colored stones in edgy settings. This spare boutique, a stone's throw from concept store Merci, may be tiny, but it's had a big impact on fashion jewelry in Paris. If you're looking for a piece to be worn every day or a statement piece that goes from day to night, this is your place. Trunk shows and openings are held at WHITE bIRD's first and larger boutique at 38 rue du Mont Thabor just off the Rue Saint-Honoré. ⊠ *7 bd. des Filles du Calvaire, 3e, Marais Quarter* ☎ *01–40–24–27–17* ⊕ *www.whitebirdjewellery. com* Ⓜ *Filles du Calvaire.*

Eastern Paris

The Bastille used to be the star of this area, and a stop here—at the epicenter of the French Revolution—was a must. The small streets forking off Place de la Bastille still buzz at night, thanks to bars, music clubs, and the top-flight Opéra Bastille. But today the neighborhoods farther afield are the real draw, having evolved into some of Paris's top destinations. Canal St-Martin, once the down-and-out cousin on the northeastern border, is now trend-spotting central,

brimming with funky bars, cafés, art galleries, and boutiques. The scene is similar to the south, on Rues Oberkampf, St-Maur, and Jean-Pierre-Timbaud, where artists and small designers have set up shop, and where a substantial slice of the city's *bobo* (bourgeois-bohemian) contingent is buying up the no-longer-so-affordable apartments.

◉ Sights

★ **Atelier des Lumières**

SOUND/LIGHT SHOW | An abandoned iron foundry in the hip 11th arrondissement is the soaring backdrop for Culturespace's newest feast for the eyes and the senses, where visitors are invited to enter into the great masterpieces of 19th- and 20th-century painting (many found in famous Parisian museums). More than 100 video projectors cast vivid scenes of gorgeously colored artwork on the walls, ceilings, and floors, accompanied by a dynamic soundtrack for total immersion into a 30-minute explosion of color and sound. ⊠ *38–40 rue Saint-Maur, 11e, Père Lachaise* ☎ *01–80–98–46–00* ⊕ *www.atelier-lumieres.com/fr/votre-visite/horaires-et-acces* ⊡ *€14.50* Ⓜ *Voltaire, Rue Saint-Maur, Père Lachaise.*

★ **Canal St-Martin**

BODY OF WATER | This once-forgotten canal has morphed into one of the city's trendiest places to wander. A good time to come is Sunday afternoon, when the Quai de Valmy is closed to cars and some of the shops are open. Rent a bike at any of the many Vélib' stations, stroll along the banks, or go native and cuddle quai-side in the sunshine with someone special.

In 1802 Napoléon ordered the 4.3-km (2.7-mile) canal dug as a source of clean drinking water after cholera and other epidemics swept the city. When it finally opened 23 years later, it extended north from the Seine at Place de la Bastille to the Canal de l'Ourcq, near La Villette. Baron Haussmann later covered a 1.6-km

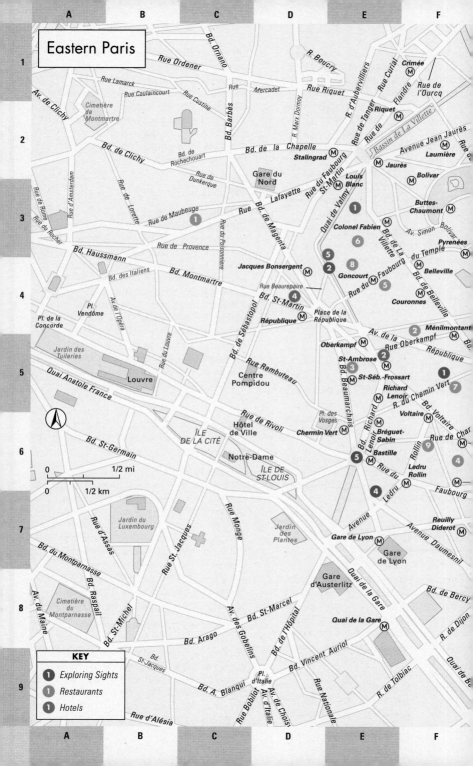

Eastern Paris

KEY

- 1 *Exploring Sights*
- 1 *Restaurants*
- 1 *Hotels*

Sights ▼

1 Atelier des Lumières **F5**
2 Canal St-Martin **E4**
3 Cimetière du
  Père-Lachaise **G5**
4 Coulée Verte
  René-Dumont
  Promenade Plantée **E7**
5 Place de la Bastille **E6**

Restaurants ▼

1 Abri **C3**
2 Astier **F4**
3 Au Passage **E5**
4 Le Bistrot Paul Bert...... **F6**
5 Le Dauphin **E4**
6 Le Galopin **E3**
7 Le Servan................. **F5**
8 Philou **E4**
9 Septime **F6**

Hotels ▼

1 Generator Paris **E3**
2 Hôtel Fabric **E5**
3 Hôtel Mama Shelter **H5**
4 Hôtel Taylor.............. **D4**
5 Le Citizen Hôtel **D3**

(1-mile) stretch of it, along today's Boulevard Richard Lenoir. It nearly became a highway in the 1970s, before the city's urban planners regained their senses. These days you can take a boat tour from end to end through the canal's nine locks: along the way, the bridges swing or lift open. The drawbridge with four giant pulleys at Rue de Crimée, near La Villette, was a technological marvel when it debuted in 1885. In recent years gentrification has transformed the once-dodgy canal, with artists taking over former industrial spaces and creating studios and galleries. The bar and restaurant scene is hipster central, and small designers have arrived, fleeing expensive rents in the Marais. To explore this evolving quartier, set out on foot. Start on the Quai de Valmy at Rue Faubourg du Temple (use the République métro stop). Here, at Square Frédéric Lemaître facing north, there is a good view of one of the locks (behind you the canal disappears underground). As you head north, detour onto side streets like Rue Beaurepaire, a fashionista destination with several "stock" (or surplus) shops for popular brands, some open on Sunday. Rues Lancry and Vinaigriers are lined with bars, restaurants, and small shops.

A swing bridge across the canal connects Lancry to the Rue de la Grange aux Belles, where you'll find the entrance to the massive Hôpital Saint-Louis, built in 1607 to accommodate plague victims and still a working hospital today. In front of you is the entrance to the chapel, which held its first Mass in July 1610, two months after the assassination of the hospital's patron, Henry IV. Stroll the grounds, flanked by the original brick-and-stone buildings with steeply sloping roofs. The peaceful courtyard garden is a neighborhood secret.

Back on Quai Valmy, browse more shops near the Rue des Récollets. Nearby is the Jardin Villemin, the 10e arrondissement's largest park (4½ acres) on the former site of another hospital. The nighttime scene, especially in summer, is hopping with twentysomethings spilling out of cafés and bars and onto the canal banks. If you've made it this far, reward yourself with a fresh taco or burrito at the tiny and authentically Mexican El Nopal taqueria at 3 rue Eugène Varlin. Farther up, just past Place Stalingrad, is the Rotonde de la Villette, a lively square with restaurants and twin MK2 cinemas on either side of the canal, plus a boat to ferry ticket holders across. Canauxrama (⊕ www.canauxrama.com) offers 2½-hour boat cruises through the locks (€18). Embarkation is at each end of the canal: at Bassin de la Villette or Port de l'Arsenal. ⊠ Canal St-Martin Ⓜ Jaurès (north end), République (south end), Gare de l'Est (middle).

★ Cimetière du Père-Lachaise

CEMETERY | Bring a red rose for "the Little Sparrow" Edith Piaf when you visit the cobblestone avenues and towering trees that make this 118-acre oasis of green perhaps the world's most famous cemetery. Named for Père François de la Chaise, Louis XIV's confessor, Père-Lachaise is more than just a who's who of celebrities. The Paris Commune's final battle took place here on May 28, 1871, when 147 rebels were lined up and shot against the Mur des Fédérés (Federalists' Wall) in the southeast corner. Aside from the sheer aesthetic beauty of the cemetery, the main attraction is what (or who, more accurately) is belowground.

Two of the biggest draws are Jim Morrison's grave (with its own guard to keep Doors fans under control) and the life-size bronze figure of French journalist Victor Noir, whose alleged fertility-enhancing power accounts for the patches rubbed smooth by hopeful hands. Other significant grave sites include those of 12th-century French philosopher Pierre Abélard and his lover Héloïse; French writers Colette, Honoré de Balzac, and Marcel Proust; American writers Richard Wright, Gertrude Stein, and Alice B. Toklas; Irish writer Oscar Wilde; French actress Sarah Bernhardt;

French composer Georges Bizet; Greek-American opera singer Maria Callas; Franco-Polish composer Frédéric Chopin; painters of various nationalities including Georges-Pierre Seurat, Camille Pissaro, Jean-Auguste-Dominique Ingres, Jacques-Louis David, Eugène Delacroix, Théodore Géricault, Amedeo Clemente Modigliani, and Max Ernst; French jazz violinist Stephane Grappelli; French civic planner Baron Haussmann; French playwright and actor Molière; and French singer Edith Piaf. (To visit the grave sites of a few other famous French men and women, head south to Cimetière du Montparnasse, north to Cimetière de Montmartre, or west to Passy Cemetery.)

■ TIP→ **Pinpoint grave sites on the website before you come, but buy a map anyway outside the entrances—you'll still get lost, but that's part of the fun.** One of the best days to visit is on All Saints' Day (November 1), when Parisians bring flowers to adorn the graves of loved ones or favorite celebrities. ⊠ *Entrances on Rue des Rondeaux, Bd. de Ménilmontant, and Rue de la Réunion, Eastern Paris* ☎ *01–55–25–82–10* ⊕ *www.pere-lachaise.com* 🖭 *Free* Ⓜ *Gambetta, Philippe-Auguste, Père-Lachaise.*

★ Coulée Verte René-Dumont/Promenade Plantée (*La Coulée Verte*)

GARDEN | Once a train line from the Paris suburbs to Bastille, this redbrick viaduct (often referred to as Le Viaduc des Arts) is now the green heart of the unpretentious 12e arrondissement. The rails have been transformed into a 4½-km (3-mile) walkway lined with trees, bamboo, and flower gardens, offering a bird's-eye view of the stately Haussmannian buildings along Avenue Daumesnil. Below, the *voûtes* (arcades) have been transformed by the city into artisan boutiques, many focused on decor and design. There are also temporary galleries showcasing art and photography. The Promenade, which gained fame as a setting in the 2004 film *Before Sunset,* was the inspiration for New York's High Line. It ends at the

Bastille. From there, you can continue your walk to the Bois de Vincennes. If you're hungry, grab a bite at L'Arrosoir, a cozy café under the viaduct at 75 avenue Daumesnil. ⊠ *1–129 av. Daumesnil, Bastille* ☎ *01–86–95–95–07* ⊕ *www.leviaducdesarts.com* Ⓜ *Bastille, Gare de Lyon.*

Place de la Bastille

HISTORIC SITE | Almost nothing remains of the infamous Bastille prison, destroyed more than 225 years ago, though tourists still ask bemused Parisians where to find it. Until the late 1980s, there was little more to see here than a busy traffic circle ringing the Colonne de Juillet (July Column), a memorial to the victims of later uprisings in 1830 and 1848. The opening of the Opéra Bastille in 1989 rejuvenated the area, however, drawing art galleries, bars, and restaurants to the narrow streets, notably along Rue de Lappe—once a haunt of Edith Piaf—and Rue de la Roquette.

Before it became a prison, the Bastille St-Antoine was a defensive fortress with eight immense towers and a wide moat. It was built by Charles V in the late 14th century and transformed into a prison during the reign of Louis XIII (1610–43). Famous occupants included Voltaire, the Marquis de Sade, and the Man in the Iron Mask. On July 14, 1789, it was stormed by an angry mob that dramatically freed all of the remaining prisoners (there were only seven), thereby launching the French Revolution. The roots of the revolt ran deep. Resentment toward Louis XVI and Marie-Antoinette had been building amid a severe financial crisis. There was a crippling bread shortage, and the free-spending monarch was blamed. When the king dismissed the popular finance minister, Jacques Necker, enraged Parisians took to the streets. They marched to Les Invalides, helping themselves to stocks of arms, then continued on to the Bastille. A few months later, what was left of the prison was razed—and 83 of its stones were carved into miniature Bastilles and sent to the provinces as a memento (you can see one of them in the Musée Carnavalet). The key to the prison was given to George Washington by Lafayette and has remained at Mount Vernon ever since. Today, nearly every major street demonstration in Paris—and there are many—passes through this square. ✉ *Bastille* [M] *Bastille.*

🍴 Restaurants

★ Abri

$$ | MODERN FRENCH | This tiny storefront restaurant's immense popularity has much to do with the fresh and imaginative food, the friendly servers, and great prices. The lauded Japanese chef works from a small open kitchen behind the zinc bar, putting forth skillfully prepared dishes like lemon-marinated mackerel topped with micro-thin slices of beet with honey vinaigrette, or succulent duck breast with vegetables au jus. **Known for:** daily changing menu of inventive French-Japanese cuisine; casual atmosphere and great prices; need to make reservations weeks in advance. [$] *Average main: €24* ✉ *92 rue du Faubourg-Poissonnière, 10e, Pigalle* ☎ *01–83–97–00–00* 🕒 *Closed Sun., Mon., 1 wk at Christmas, and Aug.* [M] *Poissonnière, Cadet.*

Astier

$$ | BISTRO | FAMILY | There are three good reasons to go to Astier: the generous cheese platter plunked on your table atop a help-yourself wicker tray, the exceptional wine cellar with bottles dating back to the 1970s, and the French bistro fare (even if portions seem to have diminished over the years). Dishes like marinated herring with warm potato salad, sausage with lentils, and baba au rhum are classics on the frequently changing set menu, which includes a selection of no less than 20 cheeses. **Known for:** same-day reservations possible; traditional atmosphere; excellent choice for authentic French cooking. [$] *Average main: €24* ✉ *44 rue Jean-Pierre Timbaud, 11e, République* ☎ *01–43–57–16–35* 🌐 *www.restaurant-astier.com* [M] *Parmentier.*

Au Passage

$ | WINE BAR | This *bistrot à vins* has the lived-in look of a longtime neighborhood hangout—which it was until two veterans of the raging Paris wine-bar scene reinvented the place, keeping the vintage, laid-back atmosphere and adding a serious foodie menu that's one of the best deals in town. A blackboard lists a selection of tapas, including several house-made pâtés, fresh tomato or beet salads, a superb seafood carpaccio, and artisanal charcuterie and cheeses. **Known for:** gastronomy on a budget; friendly, low-key vibe; roasted lamb haunch to share. [$] *Average main: €17* ✉ *1 bis, passage Saint-Sébastien, 11e, République* ☎ *01–43–55–07–52* 🌐 *www.restaurant-aupassage.fr* 🕒 *Closed Sun. No lunch* [M] *Saint-Ambroise, Saint-Sebastien–Froissart, Richard Lenoir.*

★ Le Bistrot Paul Bert

$$$ | BISTRO | The Paul Bert delivers everything you could want from a traditional Paris bistro (faded 1930s decor, thick steak with real frites, and good value), so it's no wonder its two dining rooms fill every night with a cosmopolitan crowd. The impressively stocked wine cellar helps, as does the heaping cheese cart, the laid-back yet efficient staff, and hearty dishes such as monkfish with white beans and duck with pears. **Known for:** excellent, and abundant, cheese trolley; delicious dessert soufflés; sidewalk seating in summer. [$] *Average main: €25* ✉ *18 rue Paul Bert, 11e* ☎ *01–43–72–24–01* 🕒 *Closed Sun. and Mon.* [M] *Rue des Boulets.*

Le Dauphin

$$ | WINE BAR | Avant-garde chef Inaki Aizpitarte transformed a dowdy café into a sleek, if chilly, all-marble watering hole for late-night cuisinistas. Honing his ever-iconoclastic take on tapas, the dishes served here are a great way to get an idea of what all the fuss is about.

Known for: late-night revelry; superb wines by the glass; tapas by a star chef. $ *Average main: €20* ✉ *131 av. Parmentier, 11e, Canal St-Martin* ☎ *01–55–28–78–88* ⊕ *www.restaurantledauphin. net* ⊙ *Closed Sun., Mon., and 1 wk at Christmas. No lunch Tues.* Ⓜ *Parmentier.*

★ Le Galopin
$$ | BISTRO | Across from a pretty square on the border of two up-and-coming neighborhoods, this light-drenched spot is one of Paris's standout gastrobistros. By adhering to a tried-and-true formula—meticulously sourced produce, natural wines, open kitchen—dishes here are small wonders of texture and flavor.
Known for: daily changing, market-fresh gastronomic menu; hip, laid-back atmosphere; veggie-centric dishes. $ *Average main: €22* ✉ *34 rue Sainte-Marthe, 10e, Canal St-Martin* ☎ *01–42–06–05–03* ⊕ *www.le-galopin.com* ⊙ *Closed Sat. and Sun. No lunch Mon.–Wed.* Ⓜ *Goncourt, Belleville, Colonel Fabien.*

★ Le Servan
$$ | MODERN FRENCH | Here an impressive but unfussy gastronomic menu features Asian-inflected dishes that express the food's far-flung influences. A starter of "zakouskis," several small dishes that may include deep-fried giblets, fresh radishes with anchovy butter, or herb-infused cockles, warms you up for a sublime entrée of whole lacquered quail, cod with spicy black-bean reduction, or crispy melt-in-your mouth pork on a bed of braised leeks. **Known for:** great-value lunch menu; accommodating to vegetarians; lovely, intimate setting. $ *Average main: €21* ✉ *32 rue Saint-Maur, 11e* ☎ *01–55–28–51–82* ⊙ *Closed Sat. and Sun. No lunch Mon.* Ⓜ *Voltaire, Rue Saint-Maur, Parmentier.*

Philou
$$ | BISTRO | On a quiet street between Canal St-Martin and the historic Hôpital Saint-Louis, grab a sidewalk table at this laid-back bistro two minutes from the canal. On a cool day, the red banquettes and Ingo Maurer chandelier cast a cozy glow, all the better to enjoy a hearty selection of dishes, like slices of foie gras served atop *crème de lentilles* and sprinkled with garlicky croutons, or a rosy beef entrecôte with roasted baby Yukon Gold potatoes and mushrooms *de Paris*.
Known for: view of Canal St-Martin; laid-back atmosphere; well-prepared takes on French classics. $ *Average main: €22* ✉ *12 av. Richerand, 10e, Canal St-Martin* ☎ *01–42–38–00–13* ⊕ *www.restophilou. com* ⊙ *Closed Sun. and Mon.* Ⓜ *Jacques Bonsergent.*

★ Septime
$$ | BISTRO | With amazing food and a convivial, unpretentious atmosphere, Septime has become one of the hottest tables in town. Seasonal ingredients, inventive pairings, and excellent natural wines bring in diners ready for exciting and sophisticated dishes like creamy gnochetti in an orange-rind-flecked Gouda sauce sprinkled with coriander flowers. **Known for:** exceptional Parisian bistro; one Michelin star; reservations needed far in advance. $ *Average main: €23* ✉ *80 rue de Charonne, 11e* ☎ *01–43–67–38–29* ⊕ *www.septime-charonne.fr* ⊙ *Closed Sat. and Sun. No lunch Mon.* Ⓜ *Ledru Rollin, Charonne.*

Hotels

Generator Paris
$ | HOTEL | FAMILY | It's impossible to find better lodging for 80 euros a night in Paris, especially one this close to edgy Belleville and Canal St-Martin, with panoramic views of the city and Sacré Coeur Basilica to boot. **Pros:** in-house nightclub and lots of lounging areas; private rooms available; close to great nightlife, restaurants, and the Parc du Buttes-Chaumont. **Cons:** shared rooms have only bunk beds; breakfast food can run out; beware if you're the antisocial type—it's very bustling and friendly. $ *Rooms from: €80* ✉ *9–11 Place du Colonel Fabien, 10e, Belleville* ☎ *01–70–98–84–00* ⊕ *www.*

generatorhostels.com ⇄ *199 rooms*
⎍〇⎍ *No meals* Ⓜ *Colonel Fabien, Jaurès.*

★ Hôtel Fabric

$$ | HOTEL | This urban-chic hotel tucked away on an old artisan street is fully in tune with the pulse of the lively Oberkampf neighborhood, close to fabulous nightlife, cocktail bars, restaurants, bakeries, and shopping (and the Marais and Canal St-Martin). **Pros:** all-you-can-eat breakfast for €17; lots of great sightseeing within walking distance; warm and helpful staff. **Cons:** rooms can be noisy; very popular so book well in advance; might be too party-focused for some. Ⓢ *Rooms from: €160* ✉ *31 rue de la Folie Méricourt, 11e, Oberkampf* ☏ *01–43–57–27–00* ⊕ *www.hotelfabric.com* ⇄ *33 rooms* ⎍〇⎍ *No meals* Ⓜ *Saint-Ambroise, Oberkampf.*

★ Hôtel Mama Shelter

$$ | HOTEL | Close to Père-Lachaise in the up-and-coming 20e arrondissement, this large hotel is an experiment in quirky postmodern countercultural cool, with a fun and funky interior designed by Philippe Starck. **Pros:** trendy design without designer prices; fun vibe with hip bar on-site; entertainment center in each room. **Cons:** 10-minute walk to métro; nearby club can be noisy; small rooms. Ⓢ *Rooms from: €159* ✉ *109 rue de Bagnolet, 20e, Belleville* ☏ *01–43–48–48–48* ⊕ *www.mamashelter.com* ⇄ *172 rooms* ⎍〇⎍ *No meals* Ⓜ *Gambetta.*

Hôtel Taylor

$$ | HOTEL | Tucked away on a tiny one-way street between République and Canal St-Martin, Hôtel Taylor offers large rooms (by Parisians standards) at affordable prices in the edgy 10e arrondissement. **Pros:** close to the métro; Wi-Fi available in rooms; larger than average rooms. **Cons:** bathrooms and some rooms need refurbishment; street can seem intimidating at night; open-plan bathrooms. Ⓢ *Rooms from: €152* ✉ *6 rue Taylor, 10e, Canal St-Martin* ☏ *01–42–40–11–01* ⊕ *www.*

paris-hotel-taylor.com ⇄ *54 rooms* ⎍〇⎍ *No meals* Ⓜ *République.*

★ Le Citizen Hôtel

$$ | HOTEL | Boasting direct views over the historic Canal St-Martin and a setting close to the Marais, Le Citizen features a minimalist-chic decor, high-tech touches like loaner iPads, and a cool eastern Paris vibe. **Pros:** trendy neighborhood; cool perks; friendly, attentive staff. **Cons:** smallest rooms are best for one person; noisy street; about 20 minutes by métro from the main attractions. Ⓢ *Rooms from: €199* ✉ *96 quai de Jemmapes, 10e, Canal St-Martin* ☏ *01–83–62–55–50* ⊕ *www.lecitizenhotel.com* ⇄ *12 rooms* ⎍〇⎍ *Free breakfast* Ⓜ *Jacques Bonsergent.*

Nightlife

★ Concrete

MUSIC CLUBS | On a barge moored in the Seine, superhip Concrete is one of Paris's preeminent hard-core dance venues and a trailblazer on the techno scene. The club goes full tilt until the wee hours on Friday and Saturday nights; it also opens on alternate Sundays, when you can party from 7 am to 2 am accompanied by live acts—heavy on the techno—and Paris's hottest DJs. ✉ *69 port de la Rapée, Bastille* ⊕ *www.concreteparis.fr* Ⓜ *Gare de Lyon, Gare d'Austerlitz.*

★ Le Lone Palm

BARS/PUBS | Knock back a few classic cocktails in a vintage 1950s atmosphere, where the booths and records are vinyl, the vibe is laid-back, and the prices go down as easy as the drinks. ✉ *21 rue Keller, 11e* ☏ *01–48–06–03–95* ⊕ *www.lonepalm.fr* Ⓜ *Voltaire, Bastille.*

Mama Shelter

BARS/PUBS | It's not just hotel guests who flock to the hotel's Island Bar, one of the hippest spots around Belleville. Local hipsters also appreciate the live music and DJ nights, foosball, and even the adjacent pizza bar. In summer, the fun extends to the bar's rooftop cocktail lounge, especially popular on weekend evenings. ✉ *109 rue de Bagnolet, 20e, Belleville* ☎ *01–43–48–48–48* ⊕ *www.mamashelter.com* Ⓜ *Alexandre Dumas*.

🎭 Performing Arts

Centre National de la Danse
DANCE | Occupying a former administrative center in the suburb of Pantin, this space is dedicated to supporting professional dancers by offering classes, rehearsal studios, and a multimedia dance library. A regular program of free and reasonably priced performances, expositions, screenings, and conferences is also open to the public from October to July. ✉ *1 rue Victor Hugo* ☎ *01–41–83–98–98* ⊕ *www.cnd.fr* Ⓜ *Hoche; RER: Pantin*.

Théâtre des Bouffes du Nord
THEATER | Welcome to the wonderfully atmospheric, slightly decrepit home of Peter Brook. The renowned British director regularly delights with his quirky experimental productions in French and, sometimes, English. ✉ *37 bis, bd. de la Chapelle, 10e, Stalingrad* ☎ *01–46–07–34–50* ⊕ *www.bouffesdunord.com* Ⓜ *La Chapelle*.

🛍 Shopping

★ Centre Commercial
CLOTHING | FAMILY | This store's A-list fashion credentials come with a big bonus—everything here is ethically and ecologically sourced. Peruse racks of men's and women's wear from handpicked European and U.S. labels; then head to the stellar shoe department to complete your look. Beneath glass skylights as clear as your conscience, you'll also find a fine selection of natural candles, leather goods, and jewelry. The kids' store just around the corner (*22 rue Yves Toudic*) is one of the city's best, with toys, decor, and color-coordinated togs that express

canal-side cool. ✉ *2 rue de Marseille, 10e, Canal St-Martin* ☎ *01–42–02–26–08* ⊕ *www.centrecommercial.cc* Ⓜ *Jacques Bonsergent*.

Isabel Marant
CLOTHING | This rising design star is a honeypot of bohemian rock-star style. Her separates skim the body without constricting: layered miniskirts, loose peekaboo sweaters ready to slip from a shoulder, and super fox-fur jackets in lurid colors. Look for the secondary line, Étoile, for a less expensive take. ✉ *16 rue de Charonne, 11e* ☎ *01–49–29–71–55* ⊕ *www.isabelmarant.com* Ⓜ *Ledru-Rollin*.

La Trésorerie
HOUSEHOLD ITEMS/FURNITURE | No place outfits chic Canal St-Martin lofts better than this soaring eco-friendly boutique. Housed in a historic treasury, it assembles the crème de la crème of French and European kitchen and dining ware, linens, bath products, small furnishings, hardware, lighting, paint, and more. Local hipsters come to La Trésorerie's bright, Scandinavian-style café for all things fresh, organic, and delicious. ✉ *11 rue du Château d'Eau, 10e, Canal St-Martin* ☎ *01–40–40–20–46* ⊕ *www.latresorerie.fr* Ⓜ *Jacques Bonsergent*.

★ Philippe Roucou
SHOES/LUGGAGE/LEATHER GOODS | By turns bold and dainty, these exquisitely constructed vintage-inspired bags are some of the yummiest in Paris. A python-and-calf tote is demure in storm gray: in ice blue it's a statement. Day bags in myriad shapes and sizes are always stylish; for evening, ingenious faceted clutches come in a range of colors and skins, with a sexy signature version chained to a python wristband. Other leather accessories (like iPad cases and wallets) and whimsical Polaroid-print silk scarves are also available. ✉ *30 rue de Charonne, 11e, Bastille* ☎ *01–49–29–97–35* ⊕ *www.philipperoucou.com* Ⓜ *Ledru-Rollin, Bastille*.

The Latin Quarter

The Quartier Latin is the heart of student Paris—and has been for more than 800 years. France's oldest university, La Sorbonne, was founded here in 1257, and the neighborhood takes its name from the fact that Latin was the common language of the students, who came from all over Europe. Today the area is full of cheap and cheerful cafés, bars, and shops.

Sights

★ **Jardin des Plantes** (*Botanical Gardens*)
GARDEN | FAMILY | Opened in 1640 and once known as the Jardin du Roi (King's Garden), this sprawling patch of greenery is a neighborhood gem. It's home to several gardens and various museums, all housed in 19th-century buildings that blend glass with ornate ironwork. The botanical and rose gardens are impressive, and plant lovers won't want to miss the towering greenhouses (*serre* in French)—they are filled with one of the world's most extensive collections of tropical and desert flora. If you have kids, take them to the excellent Grande Galerie de l'Évolution or one of the other natural history museums here: the Galerie de Paléontologie, replete with dinosaur and other skeletons, and the recently renovated Galerie de Minéralogie. If the kids prefer fauna, visit the Ménagerie, a small zoo founded in 1794 whose animals once fed Parisians during the 1870 Prussian siege. The star attractions are Nénette, the grande-dame orangutan from Borneo, and her swinging friends in the monkey and ape house.
■TIP➜ **If you need a break, there are three kiosk cafés in the Jardin.** ✉ *Entrances on Rue Geoffroy-St-Hilaire, Rue Cuvier, Rue de Buffon, and Quai St-Bernard, Latin Quarter* ☎ *01–40–79–56–01* ⊕ *www.jardindesplantes.net* 🎫 *Museums from €7, zoo €13, greenhouses €7, gardens free* ⊘ *Museums and greenhouses closed Tues.* Ⓜ *Gare d'Austerlitz, Jussieu; Place Monge, Censier–Daubenton for Grande Galerie de l'Évolution.*

★ **Musée de Cluny** (*Musée National du Moyen-Age [National Museum of the Middle Ages]*)
MUSEUM | Built on the ruins of Roman baths, the Hôtel de Cluny has been a museum since medievalist Alexandre Du Sommerard established his collection here in 1844. The ornate 15th-century mansion was created for the abbot of Cluny, leader of the mightiest monastery in France. Symbols of the abbot's power surround the building, from the crenellated walls that proclaimed his independence from the king, to the carved Burgundian grapes twining up the entrance that symbolize his valuable vineyards. The scallop shells (*coquilles St-Jacques*) covering the facade are a symbol of religious pilgrimage, another important source of income for the abbot; the well-traveled pilgrimage route to Spain once ran around the corner along Rue St-Jacques. The highlight of the museum's collection is the world-famous *La Dame à la Licorne* (*The Lady and the Unicorn*) tapestry series, woven in the 16th century, probably in Belgium, and now presented in refurbished surroundings. The vermillion tapestries (Room 13) are an allegorical representation of the five senses. In each, a unicorn and a lion surround an elegant young woman against an elaborate *millefleur* (literally, "1,000 flowers") background. The enigmatic sixth tapestry is thought to be either a tribute to a sixth sense, perhaps intelligence, or a renouncement of the other senses; "To my only desire" is inscribed at the top. The collection also includes the original sculpted heads of the *Kings of Israel and Judah* from Notre-Dame, decapitated during the Revolution and discovered in 1977 in the basement of a French bank. The *frigidarium* (Room 9) is a stunning reminder of the city's cold-water Roman baths; the soaring space, painstakingly renovated, houses temporary exhibits.

Also notable is the pocket-size chapel (Room 20) with its elaborate Gothic ceiling. Outside, in Place Paul Painlevé, is a charming medieval-style garden where you can see flora depicted in the unicorn tapestries. The English audio guide (€3) is highly recommended. For a different kind of auditory experience, check the event listings; concerts of medieval music are often staged Sunday afternoon and Monday at lunchtime (€7).

Note that extensive renovations, intended to vastly improve accessibility and transform the museum experience, are under way. They are slated to be complete sometime in 2020; in the interim, check the website for select exhibit closures. ⊠ *6 pl. Paul-Painlevé, Latin Quarter* ☎ *01–53–73–78–00* ⊕ *www.musee-moyenage.fr* ✉ *€5 (free 1st Sun. of month); €9 during temporary exhibitions* ☉ *Closed Tues.* Ⓜ *Cluny–La Sorbonne.*

Panthéon

RELIGIOUS SITE | Rome has St. Peter's, London has St. Paul's, and Paris has the Panthéon, whose enormous dome dominates the Left Bank. Built as the church of Ste-Geneviève, the patron saint of Paris, it was later converted to an all-star mausoleum for some of France's biggest names, including Voltaire, Zola, Dumas, Rousseau, and Hugo. Pierre and Marie Curie were reinterred here together in 1995, and feminist-politician Simone Veil became only the fifth woman in this illustrious group when she was entombed in 2018. Begun in 1764, the building was almost complete when the French Revolution erupted. By then, architect Jacques-German Soufflot had died—supposedly from worrying that the 220-foot-high dome would collapse. He needn't have fretted: the dome was so perfect that Foucault used it in his famous pendulum test to prove the Earth rotates on its axis. Today the crypt, nave, and dome still sparkle (the latter offering great views), and Foucault's pendulum still holds pride of place on the main floor, slowly swinging in its clockwise direction and reminding of us of earth's eternal spin. ⊠ *Pl. du Panthéon, Latin Quarter* ☎ *01–44–32–18–00* ⊕ *www.paris-pantheon.fr* ✉ *€9; €12 with dome access* ☉ *Dome closed Nov.–Mar.* Ⓜ *Cardinal Lemoine; RER: Luxembourg.*

★ Shakespeare & Company

STORE/MALL | The English-language bookstore Shakespeare & Company is one of Paris's most eccentric and lovable literary institutions. Founded by George Whitman, the maze of new and used books has offered a sense of community (and often a bed) to wandering writers since the 1950s. The store takes its name from Sylvia Beach's original Shakespeare & Co., which opened in 1919 at 12 rue d'Odéon, welcoming the likes of Ernest Hemingway, James Baldwin, and James Joyce. Beach famously bucked the system when she published Joyce's *Ulysses* in 1922, but her original store closed in 1941. After the war Whitman picked up the gauntlet, naming his own bookstore after its famous predecessor.

When Whitman passed away in 2011, heavy-hearted locals left candles and flowers in front of his iconic storefront. He is buried in the literati-laden Père-Lachaise cemetery; however, his legacy lives on through his daughter Sylvia, who runs the shop and welcomes a new generation of Paris dreamers. Walk up the almost impossibly narrow stairs to the second floor and you'll still see laptops and sleeping bags tucked between the aging volumes and under dusty daybeds; it's sort of like a hippie commune. A revolving cast of characters helps out in the shop or cooks meals for fellow residents. They're in good company; Henry Miller, Samuel Beckett, and William Burroughs are among the famous writers to benefit from the Whitman family hospitality.

Today, you can still count on a couple of characters lurking in the stacks, a sometimes spacey staff, the latest titles

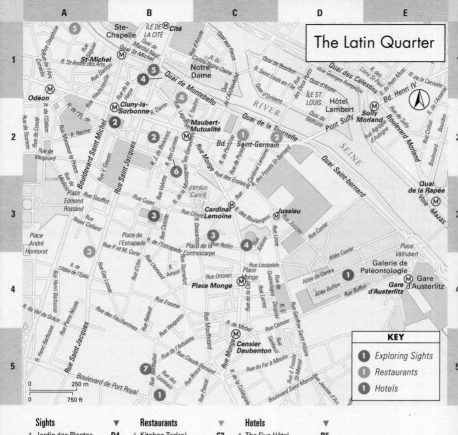

The Latin Quarter

KEY
1 *Exploring Sights*
1 *Restaurants*
1 *Hotels*

Sights ▼
1 Jardin des Plantes...... **D4**
2 Musée de Cluny......... **B2**
3 Panthéon **B3**
4 Shakespeare
& Company.............. **B1**

Restaurants ▼
1 Kitchen Ter(re) **C2**
2 La Tour d'Argent **D2**
3 Les Papilles **A4**
4 Sola **B1**
5 Ze Kitchen Galerie...... **A1**

Hotels ▼
1 The Five Hôtel **B5**
2 Hôtel Collège
de France................ **B2**
3 Hôtel des
Grandes Écoles......... **C3**
4 Hôtel Monge **C3**
5 Hôtel Notre Dame
Saint-Michel **B1**
6 Hôtel Saint-Jacques ... **B2**
7 Hotel Seven **B5**

from British presses, and hidden second-hand treasures in the odd corners and crannies. Check the website for readings and workshops throughout the week. ✉ *37 rue de la Bûcherie, Latin Quarter* ☎ *01–43–25–40–93* ⊕ *www.shakespeare-andcompany.com* Ⓜ *St-Michel.*

🍴 Restaurants

★ Kitchen Ter(re)

$$ | **FRENCH FUSION** | Michelin-starred chef William Ledeuil flexes his genius for France-meets-Asia flavors at this chic address—his third—a few blocks from the Île Saint-Louis and Notre Dame. Ledeuil is known and loved for his fearless pairings of bold and subtle flavors, like veal tartare pasta with crunchy peanuts and pungent bonito flakes or Thai beef soup with luscious Iberian ham, mushrooms, and sweet pear. **Known for:** Asian-inflected contemporary French cuisine; excellent value lunch menus; easy walk to many tourist sites. Ⓢ *Average main: €21* ✉ *26 bd. Saint-Germain, 5e, Latin Quarter* ☎ *01–42–39–47–48* ⊕ *www.zekitchengalerie.fr/kitchenterre* ⊗ *Closed Sun., Mon., and 2nd wk of Jan.* Ⓜ *Cardinal Lemoine, Maubert Mutualité.*

★ La Tour d'Argent

$$$$ | **MODERN FRENCH** | You can't deny the splendor of this legendary Michelin-starred restaurant's setting overlooking the Seine; if you don't want to break the bank on dinner, treat yourself to the three-course lunch menu for €105. This entitles you to succulent slices of one of the restaurant's numbered ducks (the great duck slaughter began in 1919 and is now well past the millionth mallard, as your certificate will attest). **Known for:** duck in all its glorious forms; one of the city's best wine lists; fabulous Seine-side setting with glorious views. Ⓢ *Average main: €115* ✉ *15–17 quai de la Tournelle, 5e, Latin Quarter* ☎ *01–43–54–23–31* ⊕ *www.tourdargent.com* ⊗ *Closed Sun., Mon., and Aug.* 🎩 *Jacket and tie* Ⓜ *Cardinal Lemoine.*

★ Les Papilles

$$$$ | **WINE BAR** | Part wineshop and épicerie, part restaurant, Les Papilles has a winning formula—pick any bottle off the well-stocked shelf and pay €7 corkage to drink it with your meal. You can also savor one of several superb wines by the glass at your table while enjoying the excellent set menu of dishes made with top-notch, seasonal ingredients. **Known for:** lively, authentic atmosphere; market menu that changes daily; excellent wines by the glass or bottle. Ⓢ *Average main: €38* ✉ *30 rue Gay-Lussac, 5e, Latin Quarter* ☎ *01–43–25–20–79* ⊕ *www.lespapillesparis.fr* ⊗ *Closed Sun., Mon., last wk of July, and 2 wks in Aug.* Ⓜ *Cluny–La Sorbonne.*

★ Sola

$$$$ | **ECLECTIC** | This foodie sanctuary is where dishes like miso-lacquered foie gras or sake-glazed suckling pig—perfectly crisp on the outside and melting inside—pair traditional Japanese and French ingredients to wondrous effect. The four-course set dinner menu (€98, with an option to add a pairing of five glasses of wine or sake), while not cheap, offers a choice of fish or meat and finishes with some stunning confections. **Known for:** beautiful atmosphere in a 17th-century building; contemporary French-Japanese cooking at its finest; traditional Japanese dining downstairs. Ⓢ *Average main: €98* ✉ *12 rue de l'Hôtel Colbert, 5e, Latin Quarter* ☎ *01–43–29–59–04* ⊕ *www.restaurant-sola.com* ⊗ *Closed Sun. and Mon.* Ⓜ *Maubert–Mutualité.*

★ Ze Kitchen Galerie

$$$$ | **MODERN FRENCH** | The name of this contemporary bistro might not be inspired, but the cooking shows creativity and a sense of fun. From a deliberately deconstructed menu featuring raw fish, soups, pastas, and grills, consider the pullet with a date, sesame, and yuzu condiment, or the scallops in a citrus, curcuma, and bergamot sauce. **Known for:** perfect location near the Seine;

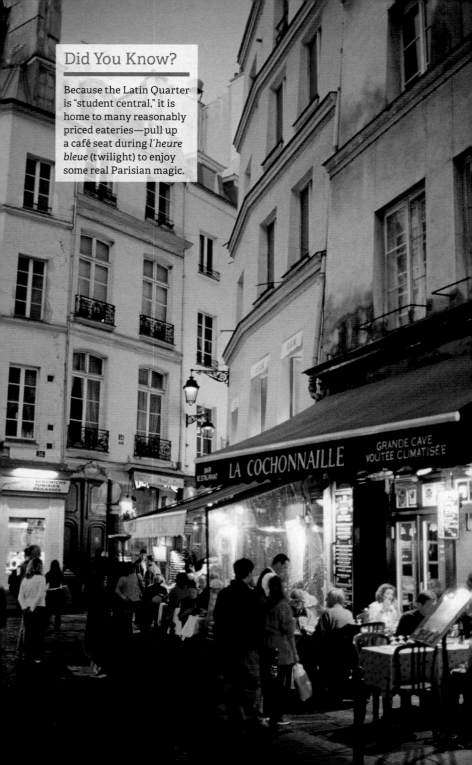

Did You Know?

Because the Latin Quarter is "student central," it is home to many reasonably priced eateries—pull up a café seat during *l'heure bleue* (twilight) to enjoy some real Parisian magic.

exquisitely presented French-Asian fusion dishes; locally sourced vegetables and spices. $ Average main: €41 ✉ 4 rue des Grands-Augustins, 6e, Latin Quarter ☎ 01–44–32–00–32 ⊕ www. zekitchengalerie.fr ✆ Closed weekends Ⓜ St-Michel.

 ## Hotels

The Five Hôtel

$ | HOTEL | Small is beautiful at this design hotel on a quiet street near the Rue Mouffetard market and the Latin Quarter. **Pros:** unique design; personalized welcome; quiet side street. **Cons:** most rooms are too small for excessive baggage; the nearest métro is a 10-minute walk; most rooms only have showers, not tubs. $ Rooms from: €95 ✉ 3 rue Flatters, 5e, Latin Quarter ☎ 01–43–31–74–21 ⊕ www.thefivehotel.com ✆ 25 rooms ⦿ No meals Ⓜ Gobelins.

Hôtel Collège de France

$ | HOTEL | Exposed stone walls, wooden beams, and medieval artwork echo the style of the Musée Cluny, two blocks from this charming, family-run hotel. **Pros:** walk to Rive Gauche sights; free Wi-Fi; ceiling fans. **Cons:** thin walls between rooms; no air-conditioning; old-fashioned bathrooms. $ Rooms from: €100 ✉ 7 rue Thénard, 5e, Latin Quarter ☎ 01–43–26–78–36 ⊕ www.hotel-collegedefrance. com ✆ 29 rooms ⦿ No meals Ⓜ Maubert–Mutualité, St-Michel, Cluny–La Sorbonne.

Hôtel des Grandes Écoles

$$ | HOTEL | Distributed among a trio of three-story buildings set back in a quiet cobbled courtyard, Madame Le Floch's rooms have a distinct grandmotherly vibe because of their flowery wallpaper and lace bedspreads, but they're spacious for this part of Paris. **Pros:** close to Latin Quarter nightlife spots; lovely courtyard; good value. **Cons:** uphill walk from the métro; walls are thin, meaning some internal noise; few amenities (and no television in room). $ Rooms from: €145 ✉ 75 rue du Cardinal Lemoine, 5e, Latin Quarter ☎ 01–43–26–79–23 ⊕ www. hotel-grandes-ecoles.com ✆ 51 rooms ⦿ No meals Ⓜ Cardinal Lemoine.

★ Hotel Monge

$$ | HOTEL | Chic, cozy, and welcoming, you couldn't land in a more charming—and reasonably priced—small boutique hotel in Paris. **Pros:** excellent neighborhood close to sights and legendary markets; great views from balconies; lovely spa. **Cons:** not all rooms have balconies; open-design showers; quiet neighborhood with few restaurants. $ Rooms from: €220 ✉ 55 rue Monge, 5e, Latin Quarter ☎ 01–43–54–55–55 ⊕ www. hotelmonge.com ✆ 30 rooms ⦿ No meals Ⓜ Jussieu, Cardinal Lemoine, Place Monge.

Hôtel Notre-Dame Saint-Michel

$$$ | HOTEL | If you love the quirky and eclectic fashions of Christian Lacroix and don't mind hauling your bags up some steps, this unique boutique hotel overlooking Notre-Dame may be for you. **Pros:** beautiful design by Christian Lacroix; stunning views of the cathedral and river; comfortable beds. **Cons:** stairs can be tricky with large bags; no minibar in rooms; some low ceilings. $ Rooms from: €280 ✉ 1 quai Saint-Michel, 5e, Latin Quarter ☎ 01–43–54–20–43 ⊕ www.hotelnotredameparis.com ✆ 26 rooms ⦿ No meals Ⓜ St-Michel.

Hôtel Saint-Jacques

$$ | HOTEL | Quaint is the word that springs to mind at this well-located Latin Quarter hotel, bedecked with faux-marble trompe-l'oeil, Renoiresque murals on walls and ceilings, and all those cozy details that remind you of a classic Parisian living room. **Pros:** unique Parisian decor; close to Latin Quarter sights; free Wi-Fi. **Cons:** busy street makes it noisy in summer; thin walls between rooms; decor needs some refurbishment. $ Rooms from: €180 ✉ 35 rue des Écoles, 5e, Latin Quarter ☎ 01–44–07–45–45 ⊕ www.

paris-hotel-stjacques.com ➥ *36 rooms* ⦿ *No meals* Ⓜ *Maubert–Mutualité.*

Hotel Seven

$$ | **HOTEL** | The "seven" may refer to the level of heaven you'll find at this wacky boutique hotel, but most likely it means the seven suites, where a team of designers and artists were let loose to riff on imaginative themes like Secret Agent, Sublime, and Nuit Chic. **Pros:** fun design elements; copious breakfast buffet; quiet location near Mouffetard market street. **Cons:** small closets; several blocks to closest métro; design detail can be a bit much. $ *Rooms from: €159* ✉ *20 rue Berthollet, 5e, Latin Quarter* ☎ *01–43–31–47–52* ⊕ *www.sevenhotelparis.com* ➥ *35 rooms* ⦿ *No meals* Ⓜ *Censier–Daubentin.*

St-Germain-des-Prés

If you had to choose the most classically Parisian neighborhood, this would be it. St-Germain-des-Prés has it all: genteel blocks lined with upscale art galleries, storied cafés, designer boutiques, atmospheric restaurants, and a fine selection of museums. Cast your eyes upward after dark and you may spy a frescoed ceiling in a tony apartment. These historic streets can get quite crowded, especially in summer, so mind your elbows and plunge in.

Sights

Carrefour de Buci

NEIGHBORHOOD | **FAMILY** | Just behind the neighborhood's namesake St-Germain church, this colorful crossroads (*carrefour* means "intersection") was once a notorious Rive Gauche landmark. During the French Revolution, the army enrolled its first volunteers here. It was also here that thousands of royalists and priests lost their heads during the 10-month wave of public executions known as the Reign of Terror. There's certainly nothing

sinister about the area today, though; brightly colored flowers are for sale alongside take-out ice cream and other gourmet treats. Devotees of the superb, traditional bakery Carton (6 rue de Buci) line up for fresh breads and pastries (try the *pain aux raisins, tuiles* cookies, and *tarte au citron*). ✉ *Intersection of Rues Mazarine, Dauphine, and de Buci, St-Germain-des-Prés* Ⓜ *Mabillon.*

Cour du Commerce St-André

HISTORIC SITE | Like an 18th-century engraving come to life, this charming street arcade is a remnant of *ancien* Paris with its uneven cobblestones, antique roofs, and old-world facades. Famed for its rabble-rousing inhabitants—journalist Jean-Paul Marat ran the Revolutionary newspaper *L'Ami du Peuple* at No. 8, and the agitator Georges Danton lived at No. 20—it is also home to Le Procope, Paris's oldest café. The passageway contains a turret from the 12th-century wall of Philippe-Auguste, which is visible through the windows of Un Dimanche à Paris, a chocolate shop and pastry atelier at No. 4. ✉ *Linking Bd. St-Germain and Rue St-André-des-Arts, St-Germain-des-Prés* Ⓜ *Odéon.*

★ Église St-Sulpice

RELIGIOUS SITE | Dubbed the Cathedral of the Rive Gauche, this enormous 17th-century Baroque church has entertained some unlikely christenings—among them those of the Marquis de Sade and Charles Baudelaire—as well as the nuptials of novelist Victor Hugo. More recently, the church played a supporting role in the best-selling novel *The Da Vinci Code,* and it now draws scores of tourists to its obelisk (part of a *gnomon,* a device used to determine exact time and the equinoxes, built in the 1730s). Other notable features include the exterior's asymmetrical towers and two magnificent Delacroix frescoes, which can be seen in a chapel to the right of the entrance. In the square just in front, view Visconti's magnificent 19th-century fountain—it's especially beautiful at

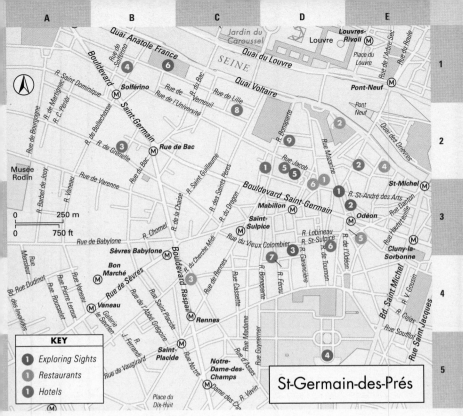

St-Germain-des-Prés

Sights ▼

1 Carrefour de Buci....... **D3**
2 Cour du Commerce
St-André.................. **E3**
3 Église St-Sulpice........ **D3**
4 Jardin du
Luxembourg............. **D5**
5 Musée Delacroix **D2**
6 Musée d'Orsay.......... **B1**

Restaurants ▼

1 Fish La Boissonnerie ... **D3**
2 Guy Savoy **D2**
3 Hélène Darroze **C4**
4 Lapérouse **E2**
5 Le Comptoir du Relais
Saint-Germain............ **E3**
6 Semilla **D3**

Hotels ▼

1 Hôtel Bel Ami **D2**
2 Hôtel d'Aubusson **E2**
3 Hôtel Duc de
Saint-Simon **B2**
4 Hotel Le Bellechasse .. **B1**
5 Hôtel Odéon
Saint-Germain........... **D2**
6 Hôtel Récamier **D3**
7 Hôtel Relais
Saint-Sulpice............ **D4**
8 L'Hôtel.....................**C2**
9 Relais Christine **D2**

The charming Luxembourg Gardens are the definition of a true Parisian park.

night. ✉ *Pl. St-Sulpice, 2 rue Palatine, St-Germain-des-Prés* ☎ *01–42–34–59–60* 🌐 *www.paris.catholique.fr/-saint-sulpice* Ⓜ *St-Sulpice, St-Germain-des-Pres, Mabillon.*

★ Jardin du Luxembourg

GARDEN | FAMILY | Everything that is charming, unique, and befuddling about Parisian parks can be found in the Luxembourg Gardens: cookie-cutter trees, ironed-and-pressed walkways, sculpted flower beds, and immaculate emerald lawns meant for admiring, not necessarily for lounging. The tree- and bench-lined paths are a marvelous reprieve from the bustle of the two neighborhoods it borders: the Quartier Latin and St-Germain-des-Prés. Beautifully austere during the winter months, the garden grows intoxicating as spring brings blooming beds of daffodils, tulips, and hyacinths, and the circular pool teems with wooden sailboats nudged along by children. The park's northern boundary is dominated by the Palais du Luxembourg, which houses the Sénat (Senate), one of two chambers that make up the Parliament. The

original inspiration for the gardens came from Marie de Medici, nostalgic for the Boboli Gardens of her native Florence; she is commemorated by the Fontaine de Medicis.

Les Marionettes du Théâtre du Luxembourg is a timeless attraction, where, on weekend mornings and afternoons along with Wednesday afternoons, you can catch classic *guignols* (marionette shows) for €6.60. The wide-eyed kids might be the real attraction—their expressions of utter surprise, despair, and glee have fascinated the likes of Henri Cartier-Bresson and François Truffaut. The park also has a merry-go-round, swings, and pony rides; the bandstand hosts free concerts on summer afternoons.

As you stroll the paths, you might be surprised by a familiar sight: one of the original (miniature) casts of the Statue of Liberty was installed in the gardens in 1906. Check out the rotating photography exhibits hanging on the perimeter fence near the entrance on Boulevard St-Michel and Rue de Vaugirard. If you want to burn off that breakfast *pain au chocolat*, there's a well-maintained trail around the perimeter that is frequented by gentrified joggers. Gendarmes regularly walk the grounds to ensure park rules are enforced; follow guidelines posted on entry gates. ⊠ *Bordered by Bd. St-Michel and Rues de Vaugirard, de Medicis, Guynemer, Auguste-Comte, and d'Assas, St-Germain-des-Prés* ⊕ *www.senat.fr/ visite/jardin* 🖘 *Free* ⊘ *Closed dusk–dawn* Ⓜ *Odéon; RER: B Luxembourg.*

Musée Delacroix

MUSEUM | The final home of artist Eugène Delacroix (1798–1863) contains only a small collection of his sketches and drawings. But you can check out the lovely studio he had built in the large garden at the back to work on frescoes he created for St-Sulpice Church, where they remain on display today. The museum also plays host to temporary exhibitions, such as Delacroix's experiments with photography. France's foremost Romantic painter had the good luck to live on Place Furstenberg, one of the smallest, most romantic squares in Paris; seeing it is reason enough to come. ⊠ *6 rue Furstenberg, St-Germain-des-Prés* ☎ *01–44–41–86–50* ⊕ *www.musee-dela-croix.fr* 🖘 *€7; €15 with admission to the Louvre within 48 hours* ⊘ *Closed Tues.* Ⓜ *St-Germain-des-Prés.*

★ Musée d'Orsay

MUSEUM | **FAMILY** | Opened in 1986, this gorgeously renovated Belle Époque train station displays a world-famous collection of Impressionist and Postimpressionist paintings on three floors. To visit the exhibits in a roughly chronological manner, start on the first floor, take the escalators to the top, and end on the second. If you came to see the biggest names here, head straight for the top floor and work your way down. English audio guides and free color-coded museum maps (both available just past the ticket booths) will help you plot your route.

Galleries off the main alley feature early works by Manet and Cézanne in addition to pieces by masters such as Delacroix and Ingres. The Pavillon Amont has Courbet's masterpieces *L'Enterrement à Ornans* and *Un Atelier du Peintre*. Hanging in Salle 14 is Édouard Manet's *Olympia*, a painting that pokes fun at the fashion for all things Greek and Roman (his nubile subject is a 19th-century courtesan, not a classical goddess). Impressionism gets going on the top floor, with iconic works by Degas, Pissarro, Sisley, and Renoir. Don't miss Monet's series on the cathedral at Rouen and, of course, samples of his water lilies. Other selections by these artists are housed in galleries on the ground floor. On the second floor, you'll find an exquisite collection of sculpture as well as Art Nouveau furniture and decorative objects. There are rare surviving works by Hector Guimard (designer of the swooping green Paris métro entrances), plus Lalique and Tiffany glassware. Postimpressionist galleries include work by van Gogh and Gauguin, while Neo-Impressionist galleries highlight Seurat and Signac.

■ TIP→ **To avoid the lines here, which are among the worst in Paris, book ahead online or buy a Museum Pass, then go directly to Entrance C. Otherwise, go early.** Thursday evening the museum is open until 9:45 pm and less crowded. Don't miss the views of Sacré-Coeur from the balcony—this is the Paris that inspired the Impressionists. The Musée d'Orsay is closed Monday, unlike the Pompidou and the Louvre, which are closed Tuesday. ⊠ *1 rue de la Légion d'Honneur, St-Germain-des-Prés* ☎ *01–40–49–48–14* ⊕ *www.musee-orsay.fr* 🖘 *€14* ⊘ *Closed Mon.* Ⓜ *Solférino; RER: Musée d'Orsay.*

🍴 Restaurants

★ Fish La Boissonerie

$$ | **BISTRO** | A perennial favorite, expats and locals prize this lively, unpretentious bistro for its friendly atmosphere, consistently good food, solid wine list, and English-speaking staff—a quartet sorely lacking in the neighborhood. Dishes like velvety black squid-ink risotto, roasted cod with tender braised fennel, and crispy pumpkin tempura always hit the spot, especially when followed by decadent molten chocolate cake, honey-roasted figs, or banana-bread pudding. **Known for:** convivial atmosphere; excellent selection of natural wines; good-value menu. [$] *Average main: €22* ✉ *69 rue de Seine, 6e, St-Germain-des-Prés* ☎ *01–43–54–34–69* [M] *St-Germain-des-Prés, Odéon.*

★ Guy Savoy

$$$$ | **MODERN FRENCH** | Within the beautifully restored La Monnaie (the old Paris Mint), you'll find star chef Guy Savoy's hallowed dining room. The market-fresh menu retains the master's classics—artichoke soup with black truffles—with some new dishes like oysters pot-au-feu and sweet, bitter, and peppery roasted duck *paletot* that reveal the magnitude of his talent. **Known for:** gorgeous setting overlooking the Seine; intimate, art-filled dining rooms; one of Paris's most highly rated dining experiences outside a palace hotel. [$] *Average main: €130* ✉ *18 rue Troyon, 17e, St-Germain-des-Prés* ☎ *01–43–80–40–61* 🌐 *www.guysavoy.com* 🕒 *Closed Sun. and Mon., and 1 wk at Christmas. No lunch Sat.* 👔 *Jacket required* [M] *Charles-de-Gaulle–Étoile.*

Hélène Darroze

$$$$ | **MODERN FRENCH** | The most celebrated female chef in Paris is now cooking at the Connaught in London, but her St-Germain dining room is still the setting for her sophisticated take on southwestern French food. Darroze's intriguingly modern touch comes through in such dishes as a sublime duck-foie-gras confit served with apricot pistachio sangria or pigeon stuffed with foie gras, wild strawberries, and mole. **Known for:** foie gras with wild strawberry and beetroot gelée; liquid chocolate cake; vegetarian and gluten-free options. [$] *Average main: €65* ✉ *4 rue d'Assas, 6e, St-Germain-des-Prés* ☎ *01–42–22–00–11* 🌐 *www.helenedarroze.com* 🕒 *Closed Sun. and Mon.* [M] *Sèvres-Babylone.*

Lapérouse

$$$$ | **BISTRO** | Émile Zola, George Sand, and Victor Hugo were regulars here, and the restaurant's mirrors still bear diamond scratches from the days when mistresses would double-check their jewels' value. It's hard not to fall in love with this storied 17th-century Seine-side town house with a warren of woodwork-graced salons, though the cuisine, a mix of traditional and modern, can be hit-or-miss. **Known for:** charming historic setting; location right on the Seine; high romance factor. [$] *Average main: €50* ✉ *51 quai des Grands Augustins, 6e, St-Germain-des-Prés* ☎ *01–43–26–68–04* 🌐 *www.laperouse.com* 🕒 *Closed Sun. No lunch* [M] *St-Michel.*

Le Comptoir du Relais Saint-Germain

$$$ | **BISTRO** | Run by legendary bistro chef Yves Camdeborde, this tiny Art Deco hotel restaurant is booked up well in advance for the single dinner sitting featuring five courses of haute-cuisine fare. On weekdays from noon to 6 pm and weekends until 10 pm, a brasserie menu is served; reservations are not accepted, resulting in long lines and brisk service. **Known for:** lively in the day, romantic at night; daily blackboard "menu du jour"; sidewalk dining. [$] *Average main: €25* ✉ *9 carrefour de l'Odéon, 6e, St-Germain-des-Prés* ☎ *01–44–27–07–97* 🌐 *www.hotel-paris-relais-saint-germain.com* [M] *Odéon.*

Semilla

$$$ | **BISTRO** | The duo behind the popular neighborhood bistro Fish and the excellent wineshop La Dernière Goutte have poured their significant expertise into this laid-back bistro in the heart of tony St-Germain-des-Prés. Its sophisticated cuisine, superb wines by the bottle or glass, and total lack of pretension have quickly made Semilla the toast of the

town. **Known for:** convivial dining room with a lively, appreciative crowd; great options for vegetarians; open kitchen with plenty of bistro classics. $ *Average main: €25* ✉ *54 rue de Seine, 6e, St-Germain-des-Prés* ☎ *01–43–54–34–50* ⊕ *www.semillaparis.com* Ⓜ *Odéon, St-Germain-des-Prés.*

Hotels

Hôtel Bel Ami

$$$$ | HOTEL | A short stroll from the famous Café de Flore, the Bel Ami hides its past as an 18th-century textile factory behind low-slung furnishings, computer stations, and flat-screen TVs. **Pros:** central St-Germain-des-Prés location; feels completely up-to-date; spacious fitness center and spa. **Cons:** some guests report loud noise between rooms; pretty pricey; books up quickly. $ *Rooms from: €420* ✉ *7–11 rue St-Benoît, 6e, St-Germain-des-Prés* ☎ *01–42–61–53–53* ⊕ *www. hotelbelami-paris.com* ➘ *108 rooms* ❑ *No meals* Ⓜ *St-Germain-des-Prés.*

Hôtel d'Aubusson

$$$$ | HOTEL | FAMILY | The showpiece at this 17th-century town house in the heart of St-Germain-des-Prés is the stunning front lobby, spanned by massive beams and a gigantic stone fireplace reminiscent of French aristocratic homes of yore. **Pros:** central location near shops and a market street; spacious rooms; on-site café and popular jazz club. **Cons:** some rooms lack character; street and bar can be noisy; very touristy. $ *Rooms from: €495* ✉ *33 rue Dauphine, 6e, St-Germain-des-Prés* ☎ *01–43–29–43–43* ⊕ *www. hoteldaubusson.com* ➘ *51 rooms* ❑ *No meals* Ⓜ *Odéon.*

Hôtel Duc de Saint-Simon

$$$ | HOTEL | For pure French flavor, including rooms decorated in floral chintz, head to this intimate hotel in a hidden location between Boulevard St-Germain and Rue du Bac. Four of the antiques-filled rooms have spacious terraces overlooking the courtyard. **Pros:** upscale neighborhood

close to St-Germain-des-Prés; historic character; friendly service. **Cons:** rooms in the annex are smaller and have no elevator; cramped bathrooms; no room service. $ *Rooms from: €295* ✉ *14 rue St-Simon, 7e, St-Germain-des-Prés* ☎ *01–44–39–20–20* ⊕ *www.hotelducde-saintsimon.com* ➘ *34 rooms* ❑ *No meals* Ⓜ *Rue du Bac.*

Hôtel Le Bellechasse

$$$ | HOTEL | If you like eclectic modern interior design, this tiny boutique hotel right around the corner from the popular Musée d'Orsay is a good choice for its access to the major sites. **Pros:** central location near top museums; one-of-a-kind style; helpful staff. **Cons:** steep rates; street-facing rooms can be noisy; open bathrooms lack privacy. $ *Rooms from: €350* ✉ *8 rue de Bellechasse, 7e, St-Germain-des-Prés* ☎ *01–45–50–22–31* ⊕ *www.lebellechasse.com* ➘ *33 rooms* ❑ *No meals* Ⓜ *Solferino.*

Hôtel Odéon Saint-Germain

$$$ | HOTEL | Exposed stone walls and original wooden beams give this 16th-century building typical Rive Gauche character, and designer Jacques Garcia's generous use of striped taffeta curtains, velvet upholstery, and plush carpeting imbues it with the distinct luxury of St-Germain-des-Prés. **Pros:** free Internet; luxuriously appointed rooms; in an upscale shopping district near Jardin Luxembourg. **Cons:** small rooms a challenge for those with extra-large suitcases; tiny elevator; prices high for room size and average service. $ *Rooms from: €250* ✉ *13 rue St-Sulpice, 6e, St-Germain-des-Prés* ☎ *01–43–25–70–11* ⊕ *www. hotelparisodeonsaintgermain.com* ➘ *27 rooms* ❑ *No meals* Ⓜ *Odéon.*

★ Hôtel Recamier

$$$ | HOTEL | This discreet boutique hotel in a quiet corner overlooking Eglise St-Sulpice is perfect if you're seeking a romantic and cozy hideaway in the sought-after St-Germain-des-Prés district. **Pros:** peaceful garden courtyard; free

Wi-Fi and computer station; well-appointed bathrooms. **Cons:** small closets and bathrooms; room service only until 11 pm; no fitness area, spa, or restaurant. [$] *Rooms from: €320* ✉ *3 bis, pl. St-Sulpice, 6e, St-Germain-des-Prés* ☎ *01–43–26–04–89* 🌐 *www.hotelrecamier.com* 🛏 *24 rooms* 🍴 *No meals* [M] *Mabillon.*

Hôtel Relais Saint-Sulpice

$$$ | **HOTEL** | Sandwiched between St-Sulpice and the Jardin du Luxembourg, this little hotel wins accolades for its location. **Pros:** chic location; close to two métro stations; bright breakfast room and courtyard. **Cons:** some smallish rooms; noise from the street on weekend evenings; poorly designed lighting. [$] *Rooms from: €260* ✉ *3 rue Garancière, 6e, St-Germain-des-Prés* ☎ *01–46–33–99–00* 🌐 *www.relais-saint-sulpice.com* 🛏 *26 rooms* 🍴 *No meals* [M] *St-Germain-des-Prés, St-Sulpice.*

★ L'Hôtel

$$$$ | **HOTEL** | There's something just a bit playful in the air at this sumptuously beautiful boutique hotel, thanks to its history as an 18th-century *pavillon d'amour* (inn for trysts) and as the place where Oscar Wilde died in 1900 (Room 16 to be exact). **Pros:** funky history; elegant bar and restaurant; romantic swimming pool in the basement. **Cons:** some rooms are on the small side; opulent decor not for everyone; only a few rooms have a terrace. [$] *Rooms from: €420* ✉ *13 rue des Beaux-Arts, 6e, St-Germain-des-Prés* ☎ *01–44–41–99–00* 🌐 *www.l-hotel.com* 🛏 *20 rooms* 🍴 *No meals* [M] *St-Germain-des-Prés.*

★ Relais Christine

$$$$ | **HOTEL** | You'll find discrete old-world service and tranquility at this venerable (some parts date to the 13th century), five-star hotel set back off a quiet street among its own flagstone courtyard and gardens. **Pros:** lovely spa; beautiful decor; historic character. **Cons:** some duplex rooms have stairs; only four rooms have garden access; small bathtubs. [$] *Rooms from: €440* ✉ *3 rue Christine, 6e, St-Germain-des-Prés* ☎ *01–40–51–60–80* 🌐 *www.relais-christine.com* 🛏 *46 rooms* 🍴 *No meals* [M] *Odéon.*

🍸 Nightlife

Bar du Marché

BARS/PUBS | Waiters wearing red overalls and revolutionary "Gavroche" hats serve drinks every day of the week at this local institution (they demonstrate particular zeal around happy hour). With bottles of wine at about €25, it draws a quintessential Rive Gauche mix of expats, fashion-house interns, and even some professional rugby players. Sit outside on the terrace and enjoy the prime corner location. ✉ *75 rue de Seine, 6e, St-Germain-des-Prés* ☎ *01–43–26–55–15* [M] *Mabillon, Odéon.*

Bar Josephine

PIANO BARS/LOUNGES | Within the newly renovated Hôtel Lutetia, Bar Josephine has been restored beyond its former glory. The vaulted Art Nouveau fresco ceiling, wrought-iron balcony, and colorful, carefully selected spirits—all lit by abundant natural light coming through the vast window facing Boulevard Raspail—has made this beautiful space the place to see and be seen. Enjoy one of star barman Nicola Battafarano's creative cocktails while you enjoy salad or sushi. The bar is open all day for food and drinks, and on Thursday, Friday, and Saturday evenings there is live piano music from 7:30 pm to 9:30 pm. ✉ *45 bd. Raspail, St-Germain-des-Prés* ☎ *01–49–54–46–00* 🌐 *www.hotellutetia.com* [M] *Sevres-Babylone.*

🛍 Shopping

★ Deyrolle

ANTIQUES/COLLECTIBLES | **FAMILY** | This fascinating 19th-century taxidermist has long been a stop for curiosity seekers. A 2008 fire destroyed what was left of the original shop, but it has been lavishly restored and remains a cabinet of curiosities par excellence. Create your own box of butterflies or metallic beetles from scores of bug-filled drawers or just enjoy the menagerie that includes stuffed zebras, monkeys, lions, bears, and more. Also in stock: collectible shells, corals, and crustaceans, plus a generous library of books and posters that once graced every French schoolroom. There is a line of cool wallpaper murals, too. ⊠ *46 rue du Bac, 7e, St-Germain-des-Prés* ☎ *01–42–22–30–07* ⊕ *www.deyrolle.com* Ⓜ *Rue du Bac.*

Henri Le Roux

FOOD/CANDY | The originator of the renowned *caramel au beurre salé,* Henri Le Roux pairs a Breton pedigree with Japanese flair. Brilliant confections result. You can also satisfy your sweet tooth in stores at 52 rue St-Dominique (*7e*) and 24 rue des Martyrs (*9e*). ⊠ *1 rue de Bourbon le Château, 6e, St-Germain-des-Prés* ☎ *01–82–28–49–80* ⊕ *www.chocolatleroux.com* Ⓜ *St-Germain-des-Prés.*

La Maison du Chocolat

FOOD/CANDY | This is chocolate's gold standard. The silky ganaches are renowned for subtlety and flavor. See the website for a full list of locations. ⊠ *19 rue de Sèvres, 6e, St-Germain-des-Prés* ☎ *01–45–44–20–40* ⊕ *www.lamaisonduchocolat.fr* Ⓜ *Sèvres-Babylone.*

★ Le Bon Marché

DEPARTMENT STORES | Founded in 1852, Le Bon Marché has emerged as the city's chicest department store. Long a hunting ground for linens and other home items, it has been undergoing a multimillion-euro face-lift that brings fashion to the fore. The fact that this department store isn't nearly as crowded as those near the Opéra is an added bonus. On the ground floor of the main building, look for makeup, perfume, and accessories; this is where celebs duck in for essentials while everyone pretends not to notice. On the floor above, you can do laps through labels chic (Givenchy, Stella McCartney, Lanvin) and überhip (Martin Margiela, Dries Van Noten). The next floor up is home to streetwise designers and edgy secondary lines, plus French favorites, including Athé by Vanessa Bruno and Isabel Marant's Étoile. Under the restored glass ceiling, the gleaming Le Soulier shoe department assembles the crème de la crème of European shoes. Meanwhile, the refurbished menswear department, Balthazar, has consumed the entire basement level. Across the street, the home store in the sister building is a great place to stock up on French linens, porcelain, cookware, and luggage, or just relax over tea or a gourmet lunch in the soaring atrium restaurant. Before leaving, be sure to visit the spectacular La Grande Épicerie and *cave* (wineshop); it's the haute couture of grocery stores. Artisanal jams, olive oils, and much more make great gifts, and the luscious pastries, fruit, and huge selection of prepared foods beg to be chosen for a snack. ⊠ *24 rue de Sèvres, 7e, St-Germain-des-Prés* ☎ *01–44–39–80–00* ⊕ *www.lebonmarche.com* Ⓜ *Sèvres-Babylone.*

Montparnasse

Once a warren of artists' studios and swinging cafés, part of Montparnasse was leveled in the 1960s to make way for a gritty train station and the Tour Montparnasse, Paris's only—and much maligned—skyscraper. Nevertheless, the neighborhood has maintained its reputation as a hub for its lively cafés and the kind of real-life vibe lost in some of the trendier sections of the city.

Sights

★ Les Catacombes

CEMETERY | This is just the thing for anyone with morbid interests: a descent through dark, clammy passages brings you to Paris's principal ossuary, which

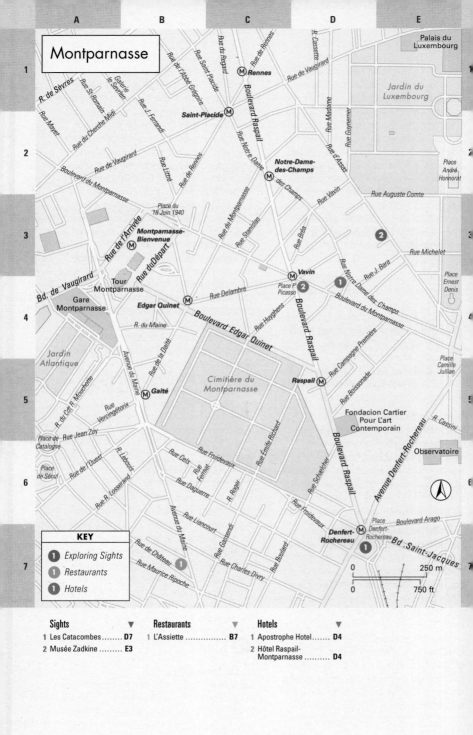

Montparnasse

also once served as a hideout maze for the French Resistance. Bones from the defunct Cimetière des Innocents were the first to arrive in 1786, when decomposing bodies started seeping into the cellars of the market at Les Halles, drawing swarms of ravenous rats. The legions of bones dumped here are stacked not by owner but by type—rows of skulls, packs of tibias, and piles of spinal disks, often rather artfully arranged. Among the nameless 6 million or so are the bones of Madame de Pompadour (1721–64), laid to rest with the riffraff after a lifetime spent as the mistress of Louis XV. Unfortunately, one of the most interesting aspects of the catacombs is one you probably won't see: *cataphiles,* mostly art students, have found alternate entrances into its 300 km (186 miles) of tunnels and here they make art, party, and purportedly raise hell. Arrive early as the line can get long and only 200 people can descend at a time. Audio guides are available for €5. Not recommended for claustrophobes or young children. ⊠ *1 av. du Colonel Henri Roi-Tanguy, Montparnasse* ☎ *01–43–22–47–63* ⊕ *www.catacombes.paris.fr* ⊠ *€13* ☉ *Closed Mon.* Ⓜ *Métro or RER: Denfert-Rochereau.*

★ Musée Zadkine

GARDEN | Sculptor Ossip Zadkine spent nearly four decades living in this bucolic retreat near the Jardin du Luxembourg, creating graceful, elongated figures known for their clean lines and simplified features. Zadkine, a Russian-Jewish émigré, moved to Paris in 1910 and fell into a circle of avant-garde artists. His early works, influenced by African, Greek, and Roman art, later took a Cubist turn, no doubt under the influence of his friend, the founder of the Cubist movement: Pablo Picasso. The museum displays a substantial portion of the 400 sculptures and 300 drawings bequeathed to the city by his wife, artist Valentine Prax. There are busts in bronze and stone reflecting the range of Zadkine's style, and an airy back room filled with lithe female nudes

in polished wood. The leafy garden is worth the trip alone: it contains a dozen statues nestled in the trees, including *The Destroyed City,* a memorial to the Dutch city of Rotterdam, destroyed by the Germans in 1940. ⊠ *100 bis, rue d'Assas, Montparnasse* ☎ *01–55–42–77–20* ⊕ *www.zadkine.paris.fr* ⊠ *Free; €7 during temporary exhibitions* ☉ *Closed Mon.* Ⓜ *Vavin, Notre-Dame-des-Champs; RER: Port Royal.*

🍴 Restaurants

★ L'Assiette

$$$ | BISTRO | David Rathgeber spent 12 years working for celebrity-chef Alain Ducasse before taking over this landmark restaurant, where he has created his own menu and welcomed a devoted clientele. Expect bourgeois classics with a subtle modern touch, perhaps white tuna steak with spinach, lemon, capers, and croutons, and crème caramel with salted butter—all executed with the precision you would expect of a Ducasse veteran. **Known for:** reliably excellent food; generous portions and good price-to-quality ratio; famous cassoulet. $ *Average main: €32* ⊠ *181 rue du Château, 14e, Montparnasse* ☎ *01–43–22–64–86* ⊕ *www. restaurant-lassiette.com* ☉ *Closed Mon., Tues., Aug., and 1 wk at Christmas* Ⓜ *Pernety, Mouton-Duvernet.*

🛏 Hotels

Apostrophe Hotel

$$ | HOTEL | Those enamored of the artistic and literary history of Paris's Left Bank will appreciate this whimsical family-run hotel between Montparnasse and Luxembourg Garden. **Pros:** friendly multilingual staff; quiet street in charming area; close to métro. **Cons:** limited closet space; little privacy with bathrooms opening up directly to rooms; no restaurant or bar. $ *Rooms from: €180* ⊠ *3 rue de Chevreuse, 6e, Montparnasse*

☎ *01–56–54–31–31* 🌐 *www.apostrophe-hotel.com* 🛏 *16 rooms* 🍴 *No meals* [M] *Vavin.*

★ **Hôtel Raspail-Montparnasse**

$ | **HOTEL** | **FAMILY** | Montparnasse was the art capital of the world in the '20s and '30s, and this hotel captures some of that spirit by naming its rooms after artists who lived in the neighborhood while also providing excellent service at hard-to-beat prices. **Pros:** some rooms have balconies and/or views of the Eiffel Tower; many markets and cafés nearby; friendly staff. **Cons:** traffic noise on first floor; some rooms small; not all rooms have Eiffel Tower views. [$] *Rooms from: €110* ✉ *203 bd. Raspail, 14e, Montparnasse* ☎ *01–43–20–62–86* 🌐 *www.hotelraspailmontparnasse.com* 🛏 *38 rooms* 🍴 *No meals* [M] *Vavin.*

🍸 Nightlife

La Closerie des Lilas

BARS/PUBS | La Closerie's swank "American-style" bar lets you drink in the swirling action of the adjacent restaurant and brasserie at a piano bar adorned with plaques honoring former habitués like Man Ray, Jean-Paul Sartre, Samuel Beckett, and Ernest Hemingway, who talks of "the Lilas" in *A Moveable Feast.* ✉ *171 bd. du Montparnasse, 6e, Montparnasse* ☎ *01–40–51–34–50* 🌐 *www.closeriedeslilas.fr* [M] *Montparnasse.*

Western Paris

Meet Paris at its most prim and proper. This genteel area is a study in smart urban planning, with classical architecture and newer construction cohabiting as easily as the haute bourgeoisie inhabitants mix with their expat neighbors. There's no shortage of celebrities seeking some peace and quiet here, but you're just as likely to find well-heeled families who decamped from the center of the city in search of a spacious apartment. Passy, once a separate village and home to American ambassadors Benjamin Franklin and Thomas Jefferson, was incorporated into the city in 1860 under Napoléon III.

👁 Sights

★ **Bois de Boulogne**

CITY PARK | **FAMILY** | When Parisians want to experience the great outdoors without going too far from home, they head to the Bois de Boulogne. Once a royal hunting ground, the Bois is like a vast tamed forest where romantic lakes and wooded paths are complemented by formal gardens and family-friendly amusements. On nice days, it's filled with cyclists, rowers, rollerbladers, joggers, and the like. Art lovers also flock here thanks to the Fondation Louis Vuitton, a stunning exhibition space dedicated to contemporary art.

The Parc de Bagatelle is a floral garden with irises, roses, tulips, water lilies, and roaming peacocks, while the Pré Catelan contains one of Paris's largest trees: a copper beech more than 200 years old. Romantic Le Pré Catelan restaurant (three Michelin stars), a Belle Époque classic with an elegant terrace, still draws diners and wedding parties. The Jardin Shakespeare inside the Pré Catelan has a sampling of the flowers, herbs, and trees mentioned in Shakespeare's plays, and it becomes an open-air theater for the Bard's works in spring. The Jardin d'Acclimatation is an amusement park that attracts hordes of preschoolers on summer Sundays. Boats or bikes can be rented for a few euros at Lac Inférieur. You can row or take a quick "ferry" to the island restaurant, Le Chalet des Iles. Two popular horse-racing tracks are also in the park: the Hippodrome de Longchamp and the Hippodrome d'Auteuil. Fans of the French Open can visit its home base, Stade Roland-Garros.

The main entrance to the Bois is off Avenue Foch near the Porte Dauphine

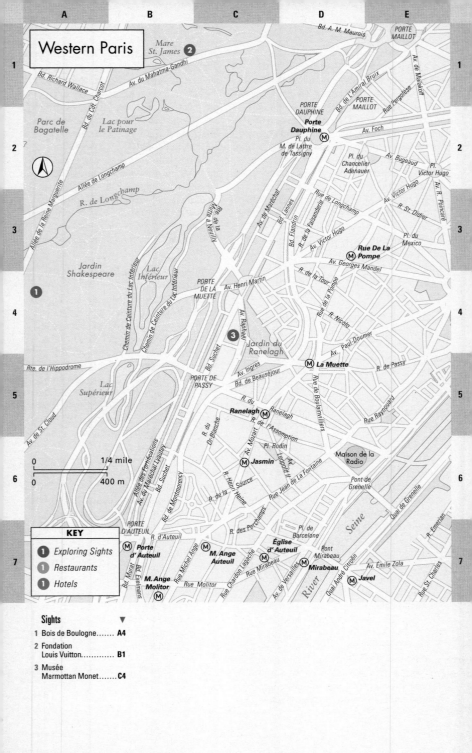

Western Paris

A | **B** | **C** | **D** | **E**

Mare St. James ②

Bd. A. M. Maurois

PORTE MAILLOT

1

Bd. Richard Wallace

Av. du Mahatma-Gandhi

Bd. du Cdt. Charcot

Av. de Malakoff

Bd. de l'Amiral Bruix

PORTE DAUPHINE

PORTE MAILLOT

Rue Pergolèse

Parc de Bagatelle

Lac pour le Patinage

Porte Dauphine Ⓜ

Pl. du M. de Lattre de Tassigny

Av. Foch

Av. Bugeaud

Pl. Victor Hugo

2

Allée de la Reine Marguerite

Allée de Longchamp

R. de Longchamp

Pl. du Chancelier Adenauer

Av. Victor Hugo

R. St. Didier

Av. R. Poincaré

Av. du Maréchal

Bd. Lannes

Bd. Flandrin

Rue de Longchamp

Pl. du Mexico

3

Jardin Shakespeare

Lac Inférieur

R. de la Faisanderie

Av. Victor Hugo

Rue De La Pompe Ⓜ

Av. Georges Mandel

Chemin de Ceinture du Lac Intérieur

Chemin de Ceinture du Lac Intérieur

PORTE DE LA MUETTE

Av. Henri Martin

R. de la Tour

R. de la Pompe

R. Nicolo

① Ⓜ

4

Rte. de l'Hippodrome

Bd. Suchet

Av. Raphaël

③

Jardin du Ranelagh

Av. Paul-Doumer

Av. Ingres

La Muette Ⓜ

R. de Passy

Lac Supérieur

PORTE DE PASSY

Bd. de Beauséjour

Rue de Boulainvilliers

Rue Raynouard

5

Av. de St. Cloud

R. du Ranelagh

Ranelagh Ⓜ

R. de l'Assomption

R. du Dr.-Blanche

Pl. Rodin

6

0 ___ 1/4 mile
0 ___ 400 m

Allée des Fortifications

Bd. Suchet

Av. Mozart

Jasmin Ⓜ

R. Henri Heine

R. de la Source

Rue Jean de La Fontaine

Av. Léopold II

Maison de la Radio

Pont de Grenelle

Seine

Quai de Grenelle

R. Emeriau

Bd. de Montmorency

Pl. de Barcelone

R. des Perchamps

Pl. de Barcelone

KEY

① *Exploring Sights*
① *Restaurants*
① *Hotels*

PORTE D'AUTEUIL

Bd. Murat

R. d'Auteuil

Porte d'Auteuil Ⓜ

Rue Michel Ange

M. Ange Auteuil Ⓜ

Rue Chardon Lagache

Église d'Auteuil

Rue Mirabeau

Pont Mirabeau

Mirabeau Ⓜ

Av. de Versailles

Quai André Citroën

Javel Ⓜ

Av. Emile Zola

River

R. St. Charles

M. Ange Molitor Ⓜ

Rue Molitor

Sights ▼

1 Bois de Boulogne....... **A4**

2 Fondation Louis Vuitton............. **B1**

3 Musée Marmottan Monet.......**C4**

métro stop on Line 2; it is best for accessing the Pré Catelan and Jardin Shakespeare, both located off the Route de la Grande-Cascade by the lake. For the Jardin d'Acclimatation and the Fondation Louis Vuitton, off Boulevard des Sablons, take Line 1 to Les Sablons or Porte Maillot, where you can walk or ride the Petit Train to the amusement park, which is next door to the foundation. The foundation also offers a €2-return-trip shuttle from Place de l'Étoile. The Parc de Bagatelle, off Route de Sèvres-à-Neuilly, can be accessed from either Porte Dauphine or Porte Maillot, though it's a bit of a hike. You'll want to leave the park by dusk, as the Bois—potentially dangerous after dark—turns into a distinctly "adult" playground. ⊠ *Western Paris* 🕾 *01–53–64–53–80 Parc de Bagatelle, 01–40–67–90–85 Jardin d'Acclimatation* ⊕ *www.jardindacclimatation.fr* 🖃 *Parc de Bagatelle €2.50 (€6 during exhibitions; free Dec.– Apr.); Jardin Shakespeare free; Jardin d'Acclimatation €5 entry, €3 per person for rides; Fondation Louis Vuitton €16* Ⓜ *Porte Dauphine for main entrance; Porte Maillot or Les Sablons for northern end; Porte d'Auteuil for southern end.*

★ **Fondation Louis Vuitton**

MUSEUM | Rising up out of the Bois de Boulogne like a magnificent ship sporting billowing crystal sails, Frank Gehry's contemporary-art museum and cultural center is the most captivating addition to the Parisian skyline since the unveiling of the Centre Pompidou in 1977. Commissioned by Bernard Arnault (chairman and CEO of luxury-goods conglomerate LVMH), the museum, which opened in 2014, houses Arnault's substantial private collection, including pieces by Pierre Huyghe, Gerhard Richter, Thomas Schütte, Ellsworth Kelly, Bertrand Lavier, Taryn Simon, Sarah Morris, and Christian Boltanski, among others. La Fondation Louis Vuitton also hosts extensive temporary exhibitions, like the mesmerizing light installations of Danish-Icelandic

artist Olafur Eliasson. Le Frank, the pricey on-site restaurant overseen by Michelin-starred chef Jean-Louis Nomicos, is noted for its sophisticated mix of French and international cuisine. The museum is a 12-minute walk from Les Sablons métro on Line 1; alternatively, you can catch the Fondation shuttle (€2 for a return ticket), which leaves every 10–15 minutes from Avenue de Friedland at Place de l'Étoile. ⊠ *8 av. du Mahatma Gandhi, Western Paris* 🕾 *01–40–69–96–00* ⊕ *www.fondationlouisvuitton. fr* 🖃 *€16, includes entrance to Jardin d'Acclimatation* ☞ *Closed Tues.* Ⓜ *Les Sablons.*

★ **Musée Marmottan Monet**

MUSEUM | This underrated museum boasts the largest collection of Monet's work anywhere. More than 100 pieces, donated by his son Michel, occupy a specially built basement gallery in an elegant 19th-century mansion, which was once the hunting lodge of the Duke de Valmy. Among them you can find such works as the *Cathédrale de Rouen* series (1892–96) and *Impression: Soleil Levant* (*Impression: Sunrise,* 1872), the painting that helped give the Impressionist movement its name. Other exhibits include letters exchanged by Impressionist painters Berthe Morisot and Mary Cassatt. Upstairs, the mansion still feels like a graciously decorated private home. Empire furnishings fill the salons overlooking the Jardin du Ranelagh on one side and the private yard on the other. There's also a captivating room of illuminated medieval manuscripts. To best understand the collection's context, pick up an English-language audio guide (€3) on your way in. ⊠ *2 rue Louis-Boilly, Western Paris* 🕾 *01–44–96–50–33* ⊕ *www.marmottan.fr* 🖃 *€12* ☉ *Closed Mon.* Ⓜ *La Muette.*

Chapter 4

SIDE TRIPS FROM PARIS

4

Updated by
Jennifer Ladonne

⊙ Sights	🍴 Restaurants	🛏 Hotels	🛍 Shopping	🍸 Nightlife
★★★★☆	★★★☆☆	★★★☆☆	★★☆☆☆	★☆☆☆☆

WELCOME TO SIDE TRIPS FROM PARIS

TOP REASONS TO GO

★ **Louis XIV's Versailles:** Famed as glorious testimony to the Sun King's megalomania, this is the world's most over-the-top palace and nature-tamed park.

★ **Gorgeous Chantilly:** Stately château and gardens, a stellar art collection, a fabulous forest, palatial stables…all within the same square mile.

★ **Van Gogh in Auvers:** The artist spent his last, manically productive three months here—you can see where he painted, where he got drunk, where he shot himself, and where he rests today.

★ **Chartres Cathedral:** A pinnacle of Gothic achievement, this recently restored 13th-century masterpiece has peerless stained glass and a hilltop silhouette visible for miles around.

★ **Monet's water lilies:** Come to Giverny to see his lily pond—a half-acre 3-D "Monet"—then peek around his charming home and stroll the time-warped streets to the exceptional Musée des Impressionnismes.

1 Versailles. A famed palace and beloved icon.

2 Rambouillet. An upscale town with a historic château.

3 Chartres. One of the most famous cathedrals in the country.

4 Giverny. Monet's inspiration for *Water Lilies*.

5 St-Germain-en-Laye. A suburb with a château inspired by *The Count of Monte Cristo*.

6 Rueil-Malmaison. Once home to Napoléon's wife, Joséphine.

7 Auvers-Sur-Oise. Where Van Gogh spent the last months of his life.

8 Chantilly. A popular Paris day trip.

9 Senlis. A medieval town offering a charming glimpse into the past.

10 Compiègne. Town history includes Joan of Arc and World War I.

11 Disneyland Paris. For the young and the young at heart.

12 Chateau de Vaux-le-Vicomte. Built to compete with Versailles.

13 Barbizon. A charming town that attracts artists.

14 Courances. A lavish château and water garden.

15 Fontainebleau. Another glorious competitor to Versailles.

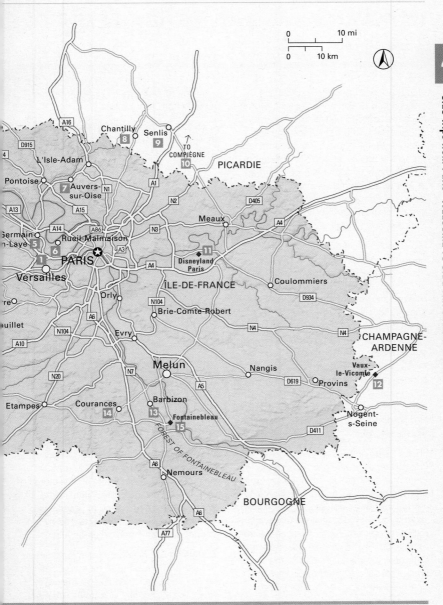

0   10 mi

0   10 km

A16

Chantilly **8**   Senlis **9**

L'Isle-Adam

TO
COMPIÈGNE **10**

PICARDIE

D915

Pontoise

Auvers-
sur-Oise **7**   N1

A1

A13   N2   D405

A15   N3   Meaux

Germain
n-Laye **5**   A14   A86   A4

Rueil-Malmaison   A3   Disneyland
Paris **11**

1   PARIS   A4   Coulommiers

Versailles **6**   ÎLE-DE-FRANCE   D934

Orly   N104   Brie-Comte-Robert   N4   N4   CHAMPAGNE-
ARDENNE

A6   Evry

uillet   N104   Melun   Nangis   Vaux-
le-Vicomte **12**

A10   N7   A5   Provins

N20   D619

Etampes   Courances **14**   Barbizon **13**   Nogent-
s-Seine

Fontainebleau **15**   D411

FOREST OF FONTAINEBLEAU

A6   Nemours

A6   BOURGOGNE

A77

Just what is it that makes the Île-de-France so attractive, so comfortingly familiar? Is it its proximity to the great city of Paris—or perhaps that it's so far removed?

Had there not been the world-class cultural hub of Paris nearby, would Monet have retreated to his Japanese gardens at Giverny? Or Paul Cézanne and Van Gogh to bucolic Auvers? Kings and courtiers to the game-rich forests of Rambouillet? Would Napoléon have truly settled at Malmaison and then abdicated at the palace of Fontainebleau? Would abbeys and cathedrals have sprung skyward in Chartres and Senlis?

If you had asked Louis XIV, he wouldn't have minced his words: the city of Paris—yawn—was simply *démodée*—out of fashion. In the 17th century the new power base was going to be Versailles, once a tiny village in the heart of the Île-de-France, now the site of a gigantic château from which the Sun King's rays could radiate, unfettered by rebellious rabble and European arrivistes. Of course, later heirs kept the lines open and restored the grandiose palace as the governmental hub it was meant to be—and commuted to Paris, well before the high-speed RER.

That, indeed, is the dream of most Parisians today: to have a foot in both worlds. Paris may be small as capital cities go, with slightly fewer than 2¼ million inhabitants, but the Île-de-France, the region around Paris, contains more than 12 million people—a sixth of France's entire population. That's why on closer inspection the once-rustic villages of the Île-de-France reveal cosseted gardens, stylishly gentrified cottages, and extraordinary

country restaurants no peasant farmer could afford to frequent.

The nation's heartland isn't really an *île* (island), of course. The green-forested buffer zone that enfolds Paris is only vaguely surrounded by the three rivers that meander through its periphery. But it nevertheless offers a rich and varied sampling of everything you expect from France—grand cathedrals, painters' villages, lavish palaces, plus the bubble gum–pink turrets of Disneyland Paris—all delightfully located within easy shooting distance of the capital.

MAJOR REGIONS

Western Île-de-France. If you want to dig into the past, the Île-de-France's richest frontier is the western half of the 60-km (35-mile) circle that rings Paris. The towns are charming and the sylvan woods are full of châteaux—including the world's grandest one, Château de Versailles. Haunt of Louis XIV, Madame de Pompadour, and Marie-Antoinette, it is a monument to splendidly wretched excess and once home to 20,000 courtiers and servants. More spiritual concerns are embodied in Chartres Cathedral, a soaring pinnacle of Gothic architecture. Nineteen kilometers (30 miles) north are landscapes of lasting impressions: Giverny and Auvers, immortalized by Monet and Van Gogh, respectively.

Eastern Île-de-France. By traveling an eastward arc through the remainder of the Île you can savor the icing on the cake. Begin with Chantilly, an opulent château noted for its royal stables, stunning gardens, and a top-notch art collection rivaled only by the Louvre's. Northward lie medieval Senlis, and heading east, you'll hit Disneyland Paris, where Mickey Mouse and his animated friends get a French makeover. Continuing south, two more magnificent châteaux—Vaux-le-Vicomte and Fontainebleau—were built for some of France's most pampered monarchs and ministers.

Planner

When to Go

Spring and fall are the optimal times to come. The Île's renowned gardens look their best in the former, and its extensive forests are particularly beautiful in the latter. From May through June or September through early October, you can still take advantage of memorable warm-weather offerings—such as a candlelight visit to Vaux-le-Vicomte or an evening of music, dancing, and fireworks at Versailles—without having to contend with the high summer heat or the crowds that pack places like Disneyland Paris or Monet's Giverny, especially on weekends.

Be aware when making your travel plans that some places are closed one or two days a week. The château of Versailles is closed Monday (the gardens remain open), and the château of Fontainebleau is closed Tuesday. In fact, as a rule, even well-touristed towns make their *fermeture hebdomadaire* (weekly closing) on Monday or Tuesday. At these times museums, shops, and markets may be shuttered—call ahead if in doubt. During the winter months, some spots shut completely (Vaux-le-Vicomte, for one, is closed from early November to mid-March, but reopens for the month of December for their festive Christmas celebrations). So it's always best to check websites or phone ahead before venturing out in the off-season.

Planning Your Time

A great advantage to exploring this region is that all its major monuments are within a half-day's drive from Paris, or less if you take the trains that run to many of the towns. The catch is that most of those rail lines connect Île communities with Paris—not, in general, with neighboring towns of the region. Thus, it may be easier to plan on "touring" the Île in a series of side trips from Paris, rather than expecting to travel through it in clockwise fashion (which, of course, can be easily done if you have a car).

Threading the western half of the Île, the first tour heads southwest from Paris to Versailles and Chartres, turns northwest along the Seine to Monet's Giverny, and returns to Paris after visiting Vincent van Gogh's Auvers. Exploring the eastern half of the Île, the second tour picks up east of the Oise Valley in glamorous Chantilly, then detours east to Senlis, and finishes up southward by heading to Disneyland Paris, Vaux-le-Vicomte, and Fontainebleau.

For a stimulating mix of pomp, nature, and spirituality, we suggest your three priorities should be Versailles, Giverny, and Chartres.

Experiencing Impressionism

Paris's Musée d'Orsay may have some of the most fabled Monet and Van Gogh paintings in the world, but the Île-de-France has something (almost) better—the actual landscapes that were rendered into masterpieces by the brushes of many great Impressionist and Postimpressionist artists. At Giverny, Claude Monet's house and garden are a moving visual link to his finest daubs—its famous lily-pond garden gave rise to his legendary *Water Lilies* series (some historians feel it was the other way around). Here, too, is the impressive Musée des Impressionnismes.

In Auvers-sur-Oise, Vincent van Gogh had a final burst of creativity before ending his life; the famous wheat field where he was attacked by crows and painted his last work is just outside town. Back then, they called him Fou-Roux (mad redhead) and derided his art; now the townspeople here love to pay tribute to the man who helped make their village famous. André Derain lived in Chambourcy, Camille Pissarro in Pontoise, and Alfred Sisley in Moret-sur-Loing: all were inspired by the silvery sunlight that tumbles over these hills and towns.

Earlier, Rousseau, Millet, and Corot paved the way for Impressionism with their penchant for outdoor landscape painting in the village of Barbizon, still surrounded by its romantic, quietly dramatic forest, as well as the untamed forest of Fontainebleau. A trip to any of these towns will provide lasting impressions.

Getting Here and Around

AIR TRAVEL

Proximity to Paris means that the Île-de-France is well served by both international and intracontinental flights. Charles de Gaulle Airport, commonly known as Roissy, is 26 km (16 miles) northeast of the capital; Orly Airport is 16 km (10 miles) south.

AIR TRAVEL INFORMATION Charles de Gaulle/Roissy and Orly Airports ☎ *3950 (€0.35 per min)* ⊕ *www.aeroportsdeparis. fr.*

BUS TRAVEL

Although many of the major sights have rail lines connecting them directly to Paris, the lesser destinations pose more of a problem and require taking a local bus run by the SNCF from the nearest

train station (*gare*). This will be the case if you're going onward to Senlis from the Chantilly Gare, to Fontainebleau and Barbizon from the Avon Gare, to Vaux-le-Vicomte from the Melun Gare, or to Giverny from the Vernon Gare.

CAR TRAVEL

A13 links Paris (from the Porte d'Auteuil) to Versailles. You can get to Chartres on A10 from Paris (Porte d'Orléans). For Fontainebleau take A6 from Paris (Porte d'Orléans). For a slower, more scenic route through the Forest of Sénart and the northern part of the Forest of Fontainebleau, take N6 from Paris (Porte de Charenton) via Melun. A4 runs from Paris (Porte de Bercy) to Disneyland. Although a comprehensive rail network ensures that most towns in the Île-de-France qualify as comfortable day trips from Paris, the only way to crisscross the region without returning to the capital is by car. There's no shortage of expressways or fast highways. However, you should be prepared for delays close to Paris, especially during the morning and evening rush hours.

TRAIN TRAVEL

Departing from Paris, it's easy to reach key locales in this region by rail because you can take advantage of the SNCF's main-line and Transilien networks, as well as RER routes, which are part of Paris's comprehensive RATP public transit system. Chartres and Chantilly, for example, are served by both main-line and Transilien trains; those bound for Chartres leave from Gare Montparnasse (50–70 minutes), while those going to Chantilly leave from Gare du Nord (25–30 minutes). Versailles is best accessed via the RER-C line, which gets you within a five-minute walk of the château (45 minutes); and the RER-A line deposits you 100 yards from the entrance to Disneyland (40 minutes). Note that the Parisian station you start from is typically determined by the direction you're heading in.

TRAIN INFORMATION RATP ⊕ *www.ratp. fr.* **SNCF** ☎ *3635* ⊕ *www.sncf.com.* **Transilien** ☎ *3658 (€0.25 per min)* ⊕ *www. transilien.com.*

Restaurants

The Île-de-France's fanciest restaurants can be just as pricey as their Parisian counterparts. Close to the Channel for fresh fish, lush Normandy for beef and dairy products, and the rich agricultural regions of Picardy and the Beauce, Île-de-France chefs have all the ingredients they could wish for, and shop for the freshest produce early each morning at the huge food market at Rungis, 18 km (10 miles) south of the capital. Traditional "local delicacies"—lamb stew, *pâté de Pantin* (pastry filled with meat), or pig's trotters—tend to be rare, although creamy Brie, made locally in Meaux and Coulommiers, remains a queen of the cheese board.

Hotels

In summer, hotel rooms are at a premium, and making reservations is essential; almost all accommodations in the swankier towns—Versailles, Rambouillet, and Fontainebleau—can be on the costly side. Take nothing for granted; picturesque Senlis, for instance, has only one hotel in its historic downtown area and its charming guesthouses fill up quickly.

Restaurant and hotel reviews have been shortened. For full information, visit Fodors.com.

What It Costs in Euros

	$	$$	$$$	$$$$
RESTAURANTS				
	under €16	€16–€24	€25–€32	over €32
HOTELS				
	under €125	€125–€225	€226–€350	over €350

Visitor Information

Special *forfait* tickets, combining travel and admission, are available for several regional tourist destinations (including Versailles, Fontainebleau, and Auvers-sur-Oise). For general information on the area, check the website of Espace du Tourisme d'Île-de-France (⊕ *www. visitparisregion.com*), or visit one of its kiosks; you'll find them at the Charles de Gaulle airport, Orly airport, Versailles, and Disneyland. Further information on Disneyland can be obtained from the Disneyland Paris reservations office.

Tours

Euroscope

BUS TOURS | You can sign on for half-day or full-day minibus trips from Paris to Versailles, Giverny, and Fontainebleau. Check the Euroscope website for all the options and prices. ✉ *46 rue de Provence, Paris* ☎ *01–56–03–56–81* ⊕ *www.euroscope.fr* ⌖ *From €110.*

★ Fat Tire Tours

BICYCLE TOURS | This company offers a wide range of tours in and around Paris by bicycle, Segway, or on foot. Tours are always led by cheerful, knowledgeable guides and some include refreshments or a picnic lunch. Skip-the-line tours are an excellent way to save time, especially at the Eiffel Tower and Versailles. Prices are reasonable and all tours can be booked online. ✉ *24 Rue Edgar Faure,*

Eiffel Tower ☎ *01–82–88–80–97* ⊕ *www. fattiretours.com* ✉ *From €80.*

My Daily Driver

DRIVING TOURS | There's nothing quite so luxurious as touring around Paris, or anywhere in the Île de France and beyond, with your own personal driver. This service offers personable, knowledgeable drivers who will tailor an itinerary to your personal needs and desires. You can even choose your conveyance from a fleet of luxury cars. ✉ *Paris* ☎ *01–86–90–22–70* ⊕ *www.mydailydriver.fr* ✉ *From €180.*

Pariscityvision

BUS TOURS | Guided coach excursions to Giverny, Versailles, Vaux le Vicomte, and Fontainebleau—plus multiple destination combinations—can be booked through Pariscityvision (€55–€220). Some are offered year-round, but most run April through October. Half- and full-day minibus excursions for up to eight people are also available (€75–€250). ✉ *2 rue des Pyramides, Paris* ☎ *01–44–55–60–00* ⊕ *www.pariscityvision.com.*

Versailles

16 km (10 miles) west of Paris.

It's hard to tell which is larger at Château de Versailles—the world-famous château that housed Louis XIV and 20,000 of his courtiers, or the mass of tour buses and visitors standing in front of it. The grandest palace in France remains one of the marvels of the world. But this edifice was not just home to the Sun King, it was also the new headquarters of the French government (from 1682 to 1789 and again from 1871 to 1879). To accompany the palace, a new city—in fact, a new capital—had to be built from scratch. Tough-thinking town planners took no prisoners, dreaming up vast mansions and avenues broader than the Champs-Élysées.

GETTING HERE AND AROUND

Versailles has three train stations, but its Rive Gauche gare—on the RER-C line from Paris, with trains departing from Austerlitz, St-Michel, Invalides, and Champ-de-Mars—provides the easiest access and puts you within a five-minute walk of the château (45 minutes, €3.55).

VISITOR INFORMATION Versailles Tourist Office ✉ *2 av. de Paris* ☎ *01–39–24–88–88* ⊕ *www.versailles-tourisme.com.*

 ## Sights

Avenue de Paris

NEIGHBORHOOD | Not far from the palace, a breadth of 120 yards makes Avenue de Paris wider than the Champs-Élysées, and its buildings are just as grand and even more historic. The avenue leads down to Place d'Armes, a vast sloping plaza usually filled with tour buses. Facing the château are the Trojan-size royal stables. Recently added bike lanes along the length of the avenue allow for a scenic cycling tour that leads to the historic neighborhoods that flank Versailles: the Quartier Saint-Louis to the south (to the left when facing the chateau) and the Quartier Notre-Dame to the north (to the right when facing the chateau). ✉ *Versailles.*

Cathédrale St-Louis

RELIGIOUS SITE | Not far from the Grandes Écuries stables, on a lovely square at the heart of the town's old center, the Cathédrale St-Louis (also known as the Cathédrale de Versailles) dates to the reign of Louis XV. Outside, the 18th-century seat of the Bishop of Versailles is notable for its dome and twin-tower facade; inside, the sanctuary is enriched with a fine organ and paintings. On Thursday and Saturday mornings, the square in front of the cathedral hosts a classic farmers' market. ✉ *Pl. Saint-Louis* ☎ *01–39–50–40–65* ⊕ *www.cathedrale-versailles.org.*

★ Château de Versailles

CASTLE/PALACE | A two-century spree of indulgence by the consecutive reigns of three French kings produced two of the world's most historic landmarks: gloriously, the Palace of Versailles and, momentously, the French Revolution. Less a monument than a world unto itself, Versailles is the king of palaces. The end result of countless francs, 40 years, and 36,000 laborers, it was Louis XIV's monument to himself—the Sun King. Construction of the sprawling palace and gardens, which Louis personally and meticulously oversaw, started in 1661 and took 40 years to complete. Today the château seems monstrously big, but it wasn't large enough for the army of 20,000 noblemen, servants, and hangers-on who moved in with Louis. A new city—a new capital, in fact—had to be constructed from scratch to accommodate them.

One of the palace highlights is the dazzling **Galerie des Glaces** (Hall of Mirrors). Lavish balls were once held here, as was a later event with much greater world impact: the signing of the Treaty of Versailles, which put an end to World War I on June 28, 1919. The **Grands Appartements** (State Apartments) are whipped into a lather of decoration, with painted ceilings, marble walls, parquet floors, and canopy beds topped with ostrich plumes. The **Petits Appartements** (Private Apartments), where the royal family and friends lived, are on a more human scale, lined with 18th-century gold and white rococo boiseries. The **Opéra Royal**, the first oval hall in France, was designed for Louis XV and inaugurated in 1770 for the marriage of 15-year-old Louis XVI to 14-year-old Austrian archduchess Marie-Antoinette. Considered the finest 18th-century opera house in Europe at the time (with acoustics to match), it is now a major venue for world-class performers. Completed in 1701 in the Louis XIV style, the **Appartements du Roi** (King's Apartments) comprise a suite of 15 rooms set in a "U" around the east facade's Marble Court. The **Chambre de la Reine** (Queen's Bed Chamber)—once among the world's most opulent—was updated for Marie-Antoinette in the chicest style of the late 18th century. The superb **Salon du Grand Couvert**, antechamber to the Queen's Apartments, is the place where Louis XIV took his supper every evening at 10 o'clock. The sumptuously painted walls and ceilings, tapestries, woodwork, and even the furniture have been returned to their original splendor, making this the only one of the queen's private rooms that can be seen exactly as it was first decorated in the 1670s. The park and gardens are a great place to stretch your legs while taking in details of André Le Nôtre's formal landscaping.

Versailles's royal getaways are as impressive in their own right as the main palace. A charmer with the ladies (as Louis's many royal mistresses would attest), the Sun King enjoyed a more relaxed atmosphere in which to conduct his dalliances away from the prying eyes of the court at the **Grand Trianon.** But Versailles's most famous getaway, the **Hameau de la Reine,** was added under the reign of Louis XVI at the request of his relentlessly scrutinized wife, Marie-Antoinette. Seeking to create a simpler "country" life away from the court's endless intrigues, between 1783 and 1787, the queen had her own rustic hamlet built in the image of a charming Normandy village, complete with a mill and dairy, roving livestock, and delightfully natural gardens. One of the most visited monuments in the world, Versailles is almost always teeming, especially in the summer; try to beat the crowds by arriving at 9 am, and buying your ticket online. ⊠ *Pl. d'Armes* ☎ *01–30–83–78–00* ⊕ *www.chateauversailles.fr* 🎫 *€18, all-attractions pass €20, Marie-Antoinette's Domain €12, park free (weekend fountain show €9.50, Apr.– Oct.)* ⊗ *Closed Mon.*

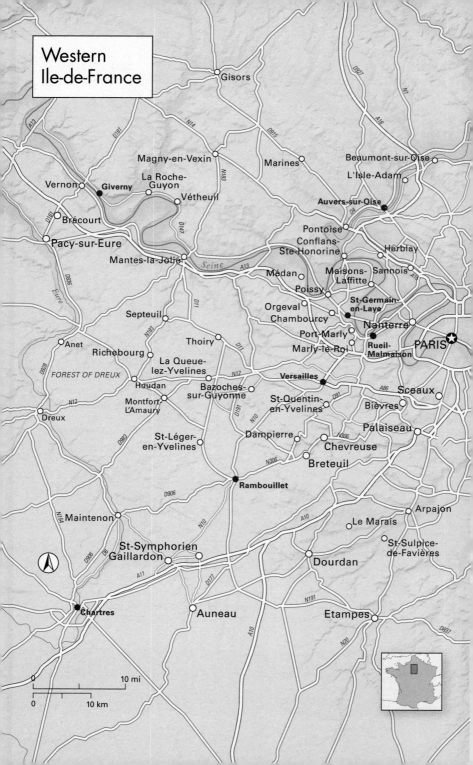

Western Ile-de-France

Gisors

Magny-en-Vexin

Marines

Beaumont-sur-Oise

L'Isle-Adam

Vernon • Giverny

La Roche-Guyon

Vétheuil

Auvers-sur-Oise

Brécourt

Pacy-sur-Eure

Pontoise

Conflans-Ste-Honorine

Hérblay

Mantes-la-Jolie

Seine

Médan

Maisons-Laffitte

Sannois

Poissy

Orgeval

Chambourcy

St-Germain-en-Laye

Septeuil

Thoiry

Port-Marly

Marly-le-Roi

Nanterre

PARIS

Rueil-Malmaison

Anet

Richebourg

La Queue-lez-Yvelines

Versailles

Sceaux

FOREST OF DREUX

Houdan

Bazoches-sur-Guyonne

St-Quentin-en-Yvelines

Bièvres

Montfort-L'Amaury

Dampierre

Palaiseau

Dreux

St-Léger-en-Yvelines

Chevreuse

Breteuil

Rambouillet

Maintenon

Arpajon

Le Marais

St-Sulpice-de-Favières

St-Symphorien Gaillardon

Dourdan

Chartres

Auneau

Etampes

0   10 mi

0   10 km

Musée Lambinet

MUSEUM | Around the back of Notre-Dame, on Boulevard de la Reine (note the regimented lines of trees), are the elegant Hôtel de Neyret and the Musée Lambinet, a sumptuous mansion from 1751, with collections of paintings, weapons, fans, and porcelain (including the Madame du Barry "Rose"). A tearoom—open Thursday, Saturday, and Sunday afternoons—provides an elegant way to refresh after an intensive round of sightseeing. ⊠ *54 bd. de la Reine* 🕾 *01–30–97–28–75* ⊕ *culture-lambinet. versailles.fr* 🖾 *€5* ⊘ *Closed Fri.*

Notre-Dame

RELIGIOUS SITE | If you have any energy left after exploring Louis XIV's palace and park, a tour of Versailles—a textbook 18th-century town—offers a telling contrast between the majestic and the domestic. From the front gate of Versailles's palace turn left onto Rue de l'Independence-Américaine and walk over to Rue Carnot past the stately Écuries de la Reine—once the queen's stables, now the regional law courts—to octagonal place Hoche. Down Rue Hoche to the left is the powerful Baroque facade of Notre-Dame, built from 1684 to 1686 by Jules Hardouin-Mansart as the parish church for Louis XIV's new town. ⊠ *Versailles* ⊕ *notredameversailles.org.*

Place du Marché-Notre-Dame

PLAZA | This lively square in the heart of the Notre-Dame neighborhood is home to the largest market in the region, far outstripping anything in Paris. Outdoors, stalls offer a veritable cornucopia of fresh fruits, vegetables, herbs, and spices; meanwhile, the four historic halls (dating to the reign of Louis XV and rebuilt in 1841) brim with every gourmet delight—foie gras, fine wines, seafood, game, prepared delicacies, cheese from every corner of France—providing a sensory experience that will overwhelm even the most jaded foodie. The open-air market runs three half days a week (Tuesday,

Friday, and Sunday 7–2), but the covered food halls are open every day except Monday, from early morning until 7:30 pm (closing is at 2 on Sunday). If you're in the mood for more shopping, the town's marvelous antiques district begins at the northwest corner of the market square and extends along the cobbled streets to the charming Passage de la Geôle. ⊠ *Versailles.*

★ Potager du Roi

GARDEN | The King's Potager—a 6-acre, split-level fruit-and-vegetable garden—was created in 1683 by Jean-Baptiste de La Quintinye. Many rare heirloom species are painstakingly cultivated here by a team of gardeners and students studying at the famous École Nationale Supérieure d'Horticulture. You can sample their wares (which are used in some of the finest Parisian restaurants) or pick up a bottle of fruit juice or jam made from the king's produce. Perfumed "Potager du Roi" candles, sold at the delightful boutique, make a nice souvenir. ⊠ *10 rue du Maréchal Joffre* 🕾 *01–39–24–62–62* ⊕ *www.potager-du-roi.fr* 🖾 *Weekends €7, weekdays €4.50* ⊘ *Closed Mon. year-round, weekends Jan.–Mar., and Sun. Nov.–Dec.*

Salle du Jeu de Paume

HISTORIC SITE | On June 20, 1789, members of the Third Estate—the commoner's section of the three-part Estates General, which included nobles (First Estate) and clergy (Second Estate)—found themselves locked out of their regular meeting place by palace guards, so they convened in this tennis court instead to discuss their demands. The resulting Tennis Court Oath stated that the sovereignty of the people did not reside with the king but with the people themselves. It became the first draft of the French Constitution (based closely on the American Declaration of Independence) and was a major first step in the Revolution and subsequent abolition of

Continued on page 190

VERSAILLES

By Robert I.C. Fisher

Louis XIV's Hall of Mirrors

A two-century spree of indulgence in the finest riches of the age by the consecutive reigns of three French kings produced two of the world's most historic artifacts: gloriously, the Palace of Versailles and, momentously, the French Revolution.

Less a monument than an entire world unto itself, Versailles is the king of palaces. The end result of 380 million francs, 36,000 laborers, and enough paintings, if laid end to end, to equal 7 miles of canvas, it was conceived as the ne plus ultra expression of monarchy by Louis XIV. As a child, the king had developed a hatred for Paris (where he had been imprisoned by a group of nobles known as the Frondeurs), so, when barely out of his teens, he cast his cantankerous royal eye in search of a new power base. Marshy, inhospitable Versailles was the stuff of his dreams. Down came dad's modest royal hunting lodge and up, up, and along went the minion-crushing, Baroque palace we see today.

Between 1661 and 1710, architects Louis Le Vau and Jules Hardouin Mansart designed everything his royal acquisitiveness could want, including a throne room devoted to Apollo, god of the sun (Louis was known as *le roi soleil*). Convinced that his might depended upon dominating French nobility, Louis XIV summoned thousands of grandees from their own far-flung châteaux to reside at his new seat of government. In doing so, however, he unwittingly triggered the downfall of the monarchy. Like an 18th-century Disneyland, Versailles kept its courtiers so richly entertained they all but forgot the murmurs of discontent brewing back home.

As Louis XV chillingly foretold, "After me, the deluge." The royal commune was therefore shocked—shocked!—by the appearance, on October 5, 1789, of a revolutionary mob from Paris ready to sack Versailles and imprison Louis XVI. So as you walk through this awesome monument to splendor and excess, give a thought to its historic companion: the French Revolution. A tour of Versailles's grand salons inextricably mixes pathos with glory.

CROWNING GLORIES: TOP SIGHTS OF VERSAILLES

Versailles from the outside

Seducing their court with their self-assured approach to 17th- and 18th-century art and decoration, a trinity of French kings made Versailles into the most vainglorious of châteaux.

Detail of the ceiling

Galerie des Glaces (Hall of Mirrors). Of all the rooms at Versailles, none matches the magnificence of the Galerie des Glaces (Hall of Mirrors). Begun by Mansart in 1678, this represents the acme of the Louis Quatorze (Louis-XIV) style. Measuring 240 feet long, 33 feet wide, and 40 feet high, it is ornamented with gilded candlesticks, crystal chandeliers, and a coved ceiling painted with Charles Le Brun's homage to Louis XIV's reign.

In Louis's day, the Galerie was laid with priceless carpets and filled with orange trees in silver pots. Nighttime galas were illuminated by 3,000 candles, their blaze doubled in the 17 gigantic mirrors that precisely echo the banner of windows along the west front. Lavish balls were once held here, and you can still get the full royal treatment at the Serenade Royale. This reenacts one of Louis XIV's grand soirées with dancers in period costumes. The 45-minute spectacle is held every Saturday from mid-June to late September at 6:30, 6:50, 7:10, 7:30, and 7:50 PM (✉€21-€42) ⊕ www.chateauversailles-spectacles.fr ☎01–30–83–78–98).

Hall of Mirrors

The Grands Appartements (State Apartments). Virtual stages for ceremonies of court ritual and etiquette, Louis XIV's first-floor state salons were designed in the Baroque style on a biceps-flexing scale meant to one-up the lavish Vaux-le-Vicomte château recently built for Nicolas Fouquet, the king's finance minister.

Inside the Apollo Chamber

Flanking the Hall of Mirrors and retaining most of their bombastic Italianate Baroque decoration, the Salon de la Guerre (Salon of War) and the Salon de la Paix (Salon of Peace) are ornately decorated with gilt stucco, painted ceilings, and marble sculpture. Perhaps the most extravagant is the Salon d'Apollon (Apollo Chamber), the former throne room.

Hall of Battles

Appartements du Roi (King's Apartments). Completed in 1701 in the Louis-XIV style, the king's state and private chambers comprise a suite of 15 rooms set in a "U" around the east facade's Marble Court. Dead center across the sprawling cobbled forecourt is Louis XIV's bedchamber—he would awake and rise (just as the sun did, from the east) attended by members of his court and the public. Holding the king's chemise when he dressed soon became a more definitive reflection of status than the possession of an entire province. Nearby is Louis XV's magnificent Cabinet Intérieur (Office of the King), shining with gold and white boiseries; in the center is the most famous piece of furniture at Versailles, Louis XV's roll-top desk, crafted by Oeben and Riesener in 1769.

Louis XIV

King's Apartments

Chambre de la Reine (Queen's Bedchamber). Probably the most opulent bedroom in the world, this was initially created for Marie Thérèse, first wife of Louis XIV, to be part of the Queen's Apartments. For Marie Antoinette, however, the entire room was glammed up with silk wall-hangings covered with Rococo motifs that reflect her love of flowers. Legend has it that the gardens directly beyond these windows were replanted daily so that the queen could enjoy a fresh assortment of blossoms each morning. The bed, decked out with white ostrich plumes *en panache*, was also redone for Louis XVI's queen. Nineteen royal children were born in this room.

VINTAGE BOURBON

Versailles was built by three great kings of the Bourbon dynasty. Louis XIV (1638–1715) began its construction in 1661. After ruling for 72 years, Louis Quatorze was succeeded by his great grandson, Louis XV (1710–74), who added the Royal Opera and the Petit Trianon to the palace. Louis XVI (1754–93) came to the throne in 1774 and was forced out of Versailles in 1789, along with Marie Antoinette, both guillotined three years later.

Queen's Bedchamber

Petits Appartements (Small Apartments). As styles of decor changed, Louis XIV's successors felt out of sync with their architectural inheritance. Louis XV exchanged the heavy red-and-gilt of Italianate Baroque for lighter, pastel-hued Rococo. On the top floor of the palace, on the right side of the central portion, are the apartments Louis XV commissioned to escape the wearisome pomp of the first-floor rooms. Here, Madame de Pompadour, mistress of Louis XV and famous patroness of the Rococo style, introduced grace notes of intimacy and refinement. In so doing, she transformed the daunting royal apartments into places to live rather than pose.

Parc de Versailles. Even Bourbon kings needed respite from Versailles's endless maze, hence the creation of one of Europe's largest parks. The sublime 250-acre grounds (☎ 01–30–83–77–88 for guided tour) is the masterpiece of André Le Nôtre, presiding genius of 17th-century classical French landscaping. Le Nôtre was famous for his "green geometries": ordered fantasies of clipped yew trees, multicolored flower beds (called parterres), and perspectival allées cleverly punctuated with statuary, laid out between 1661 and 1668. The spatial effect is best admired from inside the palace, views about which Le Nôtre said, "Flowers can only be walked on by the eyes."

Ultimately, at the royal command, rivers were diverted—to flow into more than 600 fountains—and entire forests were imported to ornament the park, which is centered around the mile-long Grand Canal. As for the great fountains; their operation costs a fortune in these democratic days, and so they perform only on weekends and some holidays (🕐 10-6) from April through mid-October and Tuesdays mid-May through mid-June; admission to the park during this time is €8. The park is open daily 7 am–8:30 pm in summer and 8-6 in winter.

LIGHTING UP THE SKY

The largest fountain at Versailles, the Bassin de Neptune, becomes a spectacle of rare grandeur during the Grandes Eaux Nocturnes, a light show to the strains of Baroque music, held Saturdays from mid-June through September at 8:30 pm, with fireworks at 11. Tickets start at €23 ⊕ www.chateauversailles-spectacles.fr ☎ 01–30–83–78–98.

Dauphin's Apartments

Bassin de Neptune

Chapel and Opéra Royal: In the north wing of the château are three showpieces of the palace. The solemn white-and-gold Chapelle was completed in 1710—the king and queen attended daily mass here seated in gilt boxes. The Opéra Royal (Opera House), entirely constructed of wood painted to look like marble, was designed by Jacques-Ange Gabriel for Louis XV in 1770. Connecting the two, the 17th-century Galeries have exhibits retracing the château's history.

Opéra Royal

VERSAILLES: FIRST FLOOR, GARDENS & ADJACENT PARK

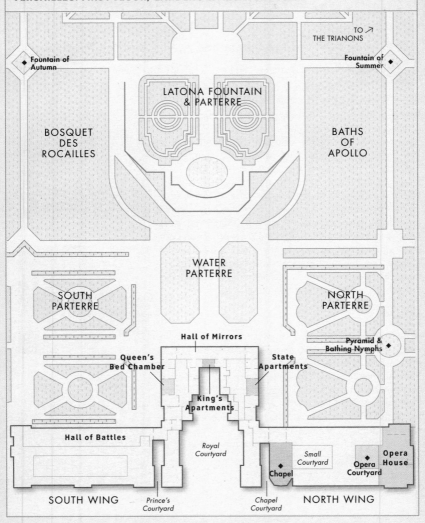

TO ↗
THE TRIANONS

◆ Fountain of
Autumn

Fountain of
Summer ◆

LATONA FOUNTAIN
& PARTERRE

BOSQUET
DES
ROCAILLES

BATHS
OF
APOLLO

WATER
PARTERRE

SOUTH
PARTERRE

NORTH
PARTERRE

Hall of Mirrors

Pyramid &
Bathing Nymphs ◆

Queen's
Bed Chamber

State
Apartments

King's
Apartments

Hall of Battles

Royal
Courtyard

Small
Courtyard

Opera
House

Opera
Courtyard ◆

◆ Chapel

SOUTH WING

Prince's
Courtyard

Chapel
Courtyard

NORTH WING

MARIE ANTOINETTE'S ROYAL LAIR

Was Marie Antoinette a luxury-mad butterfly flitting from ball to costume ball? Or was she a misunderstood queen who suffered a loveless marriage and became a prisoner of court etiquette at Versailles? Historians now believe the answer was the latter and point to her private retreats at Versailles as proof.

R.F.D. VERSAILLES?

Here, in the northwest part of the royal park, Marie Antoinette (1755–93) created a tiny universe of her own: her comparatively dainty mansion called Petit Trianon and its adjacent "farm," the relentlessly picturesque Hameau ("hamlet"). In a life that took her from royal cradle to throne of France to guillotine, her happiest days were spent at Trianon. For here she could live a life in the "simplest" possible way; here the queen could enter a salon and the game of cards would not stop; here women could wear simple gowns of muslin without a single jewel. Toinette only wanted to be queen of Trianon, not queen of France. And considering the horrible, chamber-pot-pungent, gossip-infested corridors of Versailles, you can almost understand why.

TEEN QUEEN

From the first, Maria-Antonia (her actual name) was ostracized as an outsider. Upon arriving in France in 1770—at a mere 14 years of age—she was married to the Dauphin, the future King Louis XVI. But shamed by her initial failure to deliver a royal heir, she grew to hate overcrowded Versailles and escaped to the Petit Trianon. Built between 1763 and 1768 by Jacques-Ange Gabriel for Madame de Pompadour, this bijou palace was a radical statement: a royal residence designed to be casual and unassuming. Toinette refashioned the Trianon's interior in the sober Neoclassical style.

Hameau

Queen's House

Temple of Love

Petit Trianon

"THE SIMPLE LIFE"

Just beyond Petit Trianon lay the storybook Hameau, a mock-Norman village inspired by the peasant-luxe, simple-life daydreams caught by Boucher on canvas and by Rousseau in literature. With its water mill, thatched-roof houses, pigeon loft, and vegetable plots, this make-believe farm village was run by Monsieur Valy-Busard, a farmer, and his wife, who often helped the queen—outfitted as a Dresden shepherdess with a Sèvres porcelain crook—tend her flock of perfumed sheep.

As if to destroy any last link with reality, the queen built nearby a jewel-box theater (open by appointment). Here she acted in little plays, sometimes essaying the role of a servant girl. Only the immediate royal family, about seven or so friends, and her personal servants were permitted entry; disastrously, the entire officialdom of Versailles society was shut out—a move that only served to infuriate courtiers. This is how fate and destiny close the circle. For it was here at Trianon that a page sent by Monsieur de Saint-Priest found Marie-Antoinette on October 5, 1789, to tell her that Paris was marching on an already half-deserted Versailles.

Was Marie Antoinette a political traitor to France whose execution was well merited? Or was she the ultimate fashion victim? For those who feel that this tragic queen spent—and shopped—her way into a revolution, a visit to her relatively modest Petit Trianon and Hameau should prove a revelation.

Marie Antoinette

LES BEAUX TRIANONS

A mile from the château, the Grand Trianon was created by Hardouin Mansart in 1687 as a retreat for Louis XIV; it was restored in the early 19th century, with Empire-style salons. It's a memorable spot often missed by foot-weary tourists exhausted by the château, but well worth the effort. A special treat is Marie Antoinette's hideaway nearby, the Petit Trianon, presumably restored to how she left it before being forced to Paris by an angry mob of soon-to-be revolutionaries.

the monarchy. The members are depicted in a monumental painting on the court's far wall. A fascinating guided visit in English is available through the Versailles tourist office. ✉ *Rue du Jeu de Paume, Quartier Saint-Louis* ☎ *01–30–83–78–00* 🎫 *Free.*

🍴 Restaurants

★ Gordon Ramsay au Trianon

$$$$ | **MODERN FRENCH** | Worldwide chef sensation Gordon Ramsay brings his conversation-worthy cuisine to this Versailles berth. Picture exemplary entrées like ravioli of langoustines and lobster cooked in a Riesling bisque with Petrossian caviar and lime consommé, or Périgord foie gras done "2 ways," roasted with a beetroot tart and pressed with green apple and Sauternes. **Known for:** stellar cuisine from a star chef; more casual Véranda outpost next-door; good option for French teatime. [$] *Average main: €80* ✉ *1 bd. de la Reine* ☎ *01–30–84–50–18* 🌐 *www.trianonpalace.fr/savourer/gastronomie/gordon-ramsay-au-trianon* 🕒 *Closed Sun., Mon., and late July–late-Aug.* 👔 *Jacket required.*

★ La Table du 11

$$$$ | **MODERN FRENCH** | With a Michelin star in his pocket, rising chef Jean-Baptiste Lavergne-Morazzani has answered the city's dire need for top-quality and well-priced dining at La Table du 11. A small menu features the freshest market dishes: maybe line-caught daurade with candied citrus, Argentine beef with roasted pumpkin and velvety buratina cheese, and a spectacular cheese plate for dessert. **Known for:** excellent traditional French cuisine; affordable prix-fixe menus; charming ambience. [$] *Average main: €44* ✉ *8 rue de la Chancellerie* ☎ *09–83–34–76–00* 🌐 *www.latabledu11.com* 🕒 *Closed Sun. and Mon.*

★ L'Angelique

$$$$ | **MODERN FRENCH** | Régis Douysset's refined yet unfussy French cuisine attracts the Versailles gourmet crowd. A seasonally changing menu offers a good balance of seafood and game: picture a delicate perch fillet with spaghetti *de mer* (in a shellfish bouillon) or venison shoulder with grilled turnips and a spätzle of girolle mushrooms. **Known for:** some of the best food in Versailles; historic 17th-century setting; swoon-worthy desserts. [$] *Average main: €39* ✉ *27 av. de Saint-Cloud* ☎ *01–30–84–98–85* 🌐 *www.langelique.fr* 🕒 *Closed Sun. and Mon., 1 wk at Christmas, 1 wk in Feb., and 2 wks in Aug.*

Le Sept

$$ | **FRENCH** | The 15-minute walk from the palace gates to this cozy, well-priced bistro is rewarded by an enticing daily menu of French classics all listed on a blackboard that's brought to your table. Dishes like homemade foie gras, roasted cod, and ham with parsley sauce are made with ingredients fresh from local suppliers. **Known for:** good-value prix-fixe menus; excellent natural wine list; gets busy, so reservations necessary. [$] *Average main: €18* ✉ *7 rue de Montreuil, Quartier Montreuil* ☎ *01–39–49–55–27* 🌐 *www.lesept-versailles.com/restaurant* 🕒 *Closed 1st 2 wks of Mar.*

★ Ore

$$$ | **FRENCH** | There's no doubt that dining in the world's most famous palace at a restaurant conceived by the world's most famous chef is an experience worth having. Although Alain Ducasse is not actually cooking here, you can enjoy a gourmet version of breakfast, lunch, or teatime in splendid surroundings with views of the palace from the first-floor restaurant's floor-to-celing windows. **Known for:** on-site Versailles dining (with some prix-fixe menus that include admission); elegant surroundings and linen-clad tables; serene atmosphere away from the crowds. [$] *Average main: €28* ✉ *Pl. d'Armes Château de Versailles, Quartier Saint-Louis* ☎ *01–30–84–12–96* 🌐 *www.ducasse-chateauversailles.com* 🕒 *Closed Mon.*

Hotels

Hôtel La Residence du Berry
$$ | **HOTEL** | On a quiet main street in the picturesque Saint-Louis district, this 18th-century hotel with wood-beam ceilings, antique engravings, and cozy rooms melds old-world charm with modern amenities. **Pros:** convenient yet quiet location; charming bar; reasonable prices. **Cons:** lovely breakfast not included in the price; some rooms need a spruce-up; no air-conditioning. [$] *Rooms from: €151* ✉ *14 rue Anjou* ☎ *01–39–49–07–07* 🌐 *www.hotel-berry.com* 🛏 *38 rooms* 🍴 *No meals.*

Le Cheval Rouge
$ | **HOTEL** | Built in 1676, this unpretentious option is in a corner of the market square, close to the château and strongly recommended if you plan to explore the town on foot. **Pros:** great setting in town center; good value for Versailles; original touches. **Cons:** bland public areas; some rooms need renovating; style dated. [$] *Rooms from: €94* ✉ *18 rue André-Chénier* ☎ *01–39–50–03–03* 🌐 *www.chevalrougeversailles.fr* 🛏 *40 rooms* 🍴 *No meals.*

Les Etangs de Corot
$$ | **HOTEL** | Enjoy the pleasures of both village and countryside at this charming hotel an easy 10-minute walk from Versailles. **Pros:** spacious, full-service spa; bucolic leafy setting on a lake; 15 minutes from Paris. **Cons:** restaurant service slow; some rooms overlook a busy road; decor varies widely. [$] *Rooms from: €200* ✉ *55 rue de Versailles* ☎ *01–41–15–37–00* 🌐 *www.etangs-corot.com* 🛏 *43 rooms* 🍴 *No meals.*

L'Orangerie White-Palacio
$$ | **B&B/INN** | Across a charming garden from the main house, this pretty cottage offers two quiet and comfortable suites with private bathrooms, a common kitchen, and full garden access for meals or relaxation. **Pros:** friendly, helpful host; very close to main sights; off-the-beaten tourist path. **Cons:** cold breakfast; handheld shower in bath; don't expect hotel-style services. [$] *Rooms from: €175* ✉ *37 av. de Paris, Quartier Saint-Louis* ☎ *09–53–61–07–57* 🌐 *www.l-orangerie-versailles.fr* 🛏 *2 rooms* 🍴 *Free Breakfast.*

Trianon Palace Versailles
$$$ | **HOTEL** | Like a modern-day Versailles, this deluxe turn-of-the-20th-century hotel is a creamy white creation of imposing size, filled with soaring rooms (including the historic Salle Clemenceau, site of the 1919 Versailles Peace Conference). **Pros:** palatial glamour; wonderful setting right by château park; Gordon Ramsay's on-site restaurant. **Cons:** lacks a personal touch; glamorous setting not for everyone; newer rooms not as glitzy. [$] *Rooms from: €320* ✉ *1 bd. de la Reine* ☎ *01–30–84–50–00* 🌐 *www.trianonpalace.fr* 🛏 *199 rooms* 🍴 *No meals.*

Performing Arts

Académie Equestre de Versailles
CIRCUSES | On most weekends (and on certain weekdays during school holidays), you can watch 28 elegant white horses and their expert riders perform balletic feats to music in a dazzling hour-long show directed by the great equine choreographer Bartabas. If you can't make the show, staged in the converted 17th-century *Manège* (riding school), opt for a tour of the aptly named Grandes Écuries (grand stables), which take place Sunday at 10:30 am. Located opposite the palace, the structure was built for Louis XIV's royal cavalry. ✉ *Av. Rockefeller* ☎ *01–39–02–62–75* 🌐 *www.bartabas.fr* 🎫 *Shows €25, stables visit €15.*

Centre de Musique Baroque
CONCERTS | An accomplished dancer, Louis XIV was also a great music lover who bankrolled the finest musicians and composers of the day—Lully, Charpentier, Rameau, Marais. So it's only fitting that France's foremost institute for

the study and performance of French Baroque music should be based at Versailles. An excellent program of concerts is presented in the château's Opéra Royal and chapel; the latter are free of charge. ☒ *Versailles* ☎ *01–39–20–78–10* ⊕ *www. cmbv.fr.*

Mois Molière

ARTS CENTERS | In June, Mois Molière (Molière Month) heralds a program of concerts, dramatic productions, and exhibits inspired by the famous playwright. ☒ *Pl. du Marché Notre-Dame* ☎ *01–30–21–51–39* ⊕ *www.moismoliere. com.*

★ Opéra Royal du Château de Versailles

DANCE | One of the most beautiful opera houses in Europe was built for 14-year-old Marie-Antoinette on the occasion of her marriage to Louis XVI, and entering this extravagantly gilded performance hall from the hewn-stone passageway can literally take your breath away. But the beauty is not just skin-deep—the intimate 700-seat venue is blessed with rich acoustics. Home to the Royal Opera, it hosts a world-class roster of orchestral and chamber concerts, as well as modern dance and ballet performances. For arts lovers, this spot alone will justify the quick trip from Paris. ☒ *Château de Versailles* ☎ *01–30–83–78–89* ⊕ *www. chateauversailles-spectacles.fr.*

Théâtre Montansier

DANCE | The calendar here features a full program of plays in French, music, dance, and children's entertainment. ☒ *13 rue des Réservoirs* ☎ *01–39–20–16–00* ⊕ *www.theatremontansier.com.*

 ## Shopping

Aux Colonnes

FOOD/CANDY | This charming, highly rated *confiserie* (candy shop) offers a cornucopia of chocolates and traditional French sweets. ☒ *14 rue Hoche* ⊕ *www.auxcolonnes.com* ☻ *Closed Mon.*

★ Costumes & Châteaux

SPECIALTY STORES | Anyone harboring a royal-for-a-day fantasy should head straight over to this charming costume boutique, where women, men, and kids can dress up in the high style of the Sun King's day. You can then have your picture taken or take the made-in-Versailles costume home as a memento. ☒ *1 pl. Saint Louis, Quartier Saint-Louis* ☎ *01–71–41–07–95* ⊕ *www.costumes-et-chateaux. com.*

Les Délices du Palais

FOOD/CANDY | Everyone heads here to pick up homemade pâté, cold cuts, cheese, salad, and other picnic essentials. ☒ *4 rue du Maréchal-Foch* ⊕ *www.charcuterie-lesdelicesdupalais.com.*

Rambouillet

32 km (20 miles) southwest of Versailles, 42 km (26 miles) southwest of Paris.

Haughty Rambouillet, once favored by kings and dukes, is now home to affluent gentry and, occasionally, the French president.

GETTING HERE AND AROUND
Frequent daily trains from Paris's Gare Montparnasse arrive at Gare de Rambouillet on Place Prud'homme (35 minutes, €8.45).

VISITOR INFORMATION Rambouillet Tourist Office ☒ *1 pl. de la Libération* ☎ *01–34–83–21–21* ⊕ *www.rambouillet-tourisme.fr.*

 ## Sights

Bergerie Nationale

FARM/RANCH | **FAMILY** | Located within Parc du Château, the Bergerie Nationale (National Sheepfold) is the site of a more serious agricultural venture: the famous Rambouillet Merinos raised here, prized for the quality and yield of their wool, are descendants of sheep imported from

Spain by Louis XVI in 1786. A museum alongside tells the tale and evokes shepherd life. Don't miss the wonderful boutique—it features products from the farm, including *fromage de brebis* (sheep's milk cheese), produce, potted pâtés, jams, honey, and, of course, wool. ✉ *Parc du Chateau* ☎ *01–61–08–68–70* 🌐 *www.bergerie-nationale.educagri.fr* 🎫 *€6* 🕓 *Closed Thurs., Fri., Mon., and Tues.*

Château de Rambouillet

CASTLE/PALACE | Surrounded by a magnificent 36,000-acre forest, this elegant château is a popular spot for biking and walking. Most of the structure dates to the early 18th century, but the brawny **Tour François-Ier** (François I Tower), named for the king who died here in 1547, was part of a fortified castle that earlier stood on this site. Highlights include the wood-paneled apartments, especially the **Boudoir de la Comtesse** (Countess's Dressing Room); the marble-sheathed **Salle de Marbre** (Marble Hall), dating to the Renaissance; and the **Salle de Bains de Napoléon** (Napoléon's Bathroom), adorned with Pompeii-style frescoes. Compared to the muscular forecourt, the château's lakeside facade is a scene of unsuspected serenity and, as flowers spill from its balconies, cheerful informality. Guided visits in English are available on the hour (10–5) by reservation. ✉ *Rambouillet* ☎ *01–34–83–00–25* 🌐 *www.chateau-rambouillet.fr* 🎫 *€9* 🕓 *Closed Tues.*

Parc du Château

NATIONAL/STATE PARK | An extensive park—complete with island-dotted lake—stretches behind the château. Within it is the **Laiterie de la Reine** (Queen's Dairy), built for Marie-Antoinette: inspired by the writings of Jean-Jacques Rousseau, she came here to escape from the pressures of court life, pretending to be a simple milkmaid. It has a small marble temple and grotto and, nearby, the shell-lined Chaumière des Coquillages (Shell Pavilion). ✉ *Rambouillet* 🌐 *www.chateau-rambouillet.fr* 🎫 *Included in château ticket.*

🍴 Restaurants

Auberge du Louvetier

$$ | **BISTRO** | With a roaring fire in winter and an outdoor terrace in summer, this quaint, country-style restaurant specializes in the fruits of the sea. Traditional dishes—like brioche-enrobed escargot with Roquefort sauce, plump seafood sausage, a hearty *soupe de poisson* (fish soup), and a heaping seafood platter—are served in a wood-beamed dining room. **Known for:** charming setting; homemade French specialties; friendly service. [$] *Average main: €23* ✉ *19 rue de l'Etang de la Tour* ☎ *01–34–85–61–00* 🌐 *aubergedulouvetier.com* 🕓 *Closed Mon. No lunch Sat. No dinner Sun.*

★ **Villa Marinette**

$$$ | **FRENCH** | Three km (2 miles) from Rambouillet near the small town of Gazeran, this ivy-clad 18th-century home is a romantic setting for an elegant gastronomic meal. Dishes like roasted cod in beef reduction with black-truffle risotto or filet of venison with parsnip mousse are made with the freshest ingredients—many from the kitchen garden—and can be followed by a copious cheese plate or tempting seasonal desserts. **Known for:** garden terrace; romantic and refined atmosphere; seasonal menu. [$] *Average main: €32* ✉ *20 av. du Général de Gaulle, Gazeran* 🌐 *www.villamarinette.fr* 🕓 *Closed Mon. and Tues. No dinner Sun.*

Chartres

39 km (24 miles) southwest of Rambouillet, 88 km (55 miles) southwest of Paris.

If Versailles is the climax of French secular architecture, Chartres is its religious apogee. All the descriptive prose and poetry that have been lavished on this supreme cathedral can only begin to suggest the glory of its 12th- and 13th-century statuary and stained glass, somehow suffused with burning mysticism and a strange sense of the numinous. Chartres is more than a church—it's a nondenominational spiritual experience. If you arrive in summer from Maintenon across the edge of the Beauce, the richest agrarian plain in France, you can see Chartres's spires rising up from oceans of wheat. The whole town, however, is worth a leisurely exploration. Ancient streets tumble down from the cathedral to the river, lined most weekends with *bouquinistes* selling old books and prints. The streets are especially busy each year on August 15, when pilgrims and tourists flock in for the Procession du Vœu de Louis XIII commemorating the French monarchy's vow to serve the Virgin Mary.

GETTING HERE AND AROUND

Both Transilien and main-line (Le Mans–bound) trains leave Paris's Gare Montparnasse for Chartres (50–70 minutes, €15.65). The train station on Place Pierre-Sémard puts you within walking distance of the cathedral.

VISITOR INFORMATION Chartres Tourist Office ✉ *8 rue de la Poissonnerie* ☎ *02–37–18–26–26* ⊕ *www.chartres-tourisme. com.*

 # Sights

★ **Cathédrale Notre-Dame** (*Chartres Cathedral*)

RELIGIOUS SITE | Worship on the site of the Cathédrale Notre-Dame, better known as Chartres Cathedral, goes back to before the Gallo-Roman period—the crypt contains a well that was the focus of druid ceremonies. In the late 9th century Charles II (aka "the Bald") presented Chartres with what was believed to be the tunic of the Virgin Mary, a precious relic that went on to attract hordes of pilgrims. The current cathedral, the sixth church on the spot, dates mainly to the 12th and 13th centuries and was erected after most of the previous building, dating to the 11th century, burned down in 1194. A well-chronicled outburst of religious fervor followed the discovery that the Virgin Mary's relic had miraculously survived unsinged. Motivated by this "miracle," princes and paupers, barons and bourgeoisie gave their money and their labor to build the new cathedral. Ladies of the manor came to help monks and peasants on the scaffolding in a tremendous resurgence of religious faith that followed the Second Crusade. Just 25 years were needed for Chartres Cathedral to rise again, and although it remained substantially unchanged for centuries, a recent 12-year, €20 million renovation restored the cathedral's famously gloomy interiors to their "original" creamy white, sparking a major controversy among those who embraced the original darker lighting. As spiritual as Chartres is, the cathedral also had its more earthbound uses. Look closely and you can see that the main nave floor has a subtle slant. It was designed to provide drainage because this part of the church was often used as a "hostel" by thousands of overnighting pilgrims in medieval times. Those who couldn't afford the entire pilgrimage could walk the cathedral's **labyrinth**, one of the most famous in the world; today it's open for visitors every Friday and for a month during Lent (on other days it is covered with chairs).

Though the windows no longer pop from the previously dark interiors, the gemlike richness of the stained glass, with the famous deep Chartres blue predominating, is still a thrilling experience. The **Royal Portal** is richly sculpted with scenes from the life of Christ—these sculpted figures are among the greatest created during the Middle Ages. The **rose window** above the main portal dates from the 13th century, and the three windows below it contain some of the finest examples of 12th-century stained-glass artistry

Did You Know?

Chartres's beautiful
Clocher Neuf (New Bell-
tower) was completed
in 1134, well before the
Clocher Vieux (Old
Bell-tower), on the right,
which was originally built
between 1145 and 1165,
then rebuilt following a
fire in the 16th century.

in France. The oldest window is arguably the most beautiful: **Notre-Dame de la Belle Verrière** (Our Lady of the Lovely Window), in the south choir.

Guided tours in English are offered at noon and 2:45, Monday through Saturday, Easter to mid-October, and a special tour of the cathedral crypt by candlelight is given every Friday at 10 pm (in French, book on the Chartres Tourism site, €18.50). For a bird's-eye view, book a tour of the towers. Guided tours of the **Crypte** start from the Maison de la Crypte opposite the south porch; tickets can be purchased at the gift store. ✉ *16 cloître Notre-Dame* ☎ *02–37–21–75–02* 🌐 *www.cathedrale-chartres.org* 🎫 *Crypt €4, tours €10.*

Chartres en Lumières

FESTIVAL | If you need an incentive to linger here until dusk, "Chartres en Lumières" (Chartres's festival of lights) provides it: 28 of the city's most revered monuments, including the glorious Notre-Dame Cathedral, are transformed into vivid light canvases. Thematically based on the history and purpose of each specific site, the animated projections are organized into a city walk that covers a wide swath of the Old Town's cobbled streets and bridges. The spectacle is free and occurs nightly from sunset to 1 am from mid-April through mid-October. A train tour of the illuminated city operates several times a night from May through September. ✉ *Chartres* 🌐 *www.chartresenlumieres.com.*

Galerie du Vitrail

MUSEUM | Since *vitrail* (stained glass) is the key to Chartres's fame, you may want to visit the Galerie du Vitrail, which specializes in the noble art. Pieces range from small plaques to entire windows, and there are books on the subject in English and French. ✉ *17 cloître Notre-Dame* ☎ *02–37–36–10–03 Closed Sun. and Mon. Oct.–Apr.* 🌐 *www.galerie-du-vitrail.com.*

Musée des Beaux-Arts (*Fine Arts Museum*)

MUSEUM | Just behind the famed cathedral, the town art museum is housed in a handsome 18th-century building that once served as the bishop's palace. Its varied collection includes Renaissance enamels, a portrait of Erasmus by Holbein, tapestries, armor, and some fine (mainly French) paintings from the 17th, 18th, and 19th centuries. There's also a room devoted to the forceful 20th-century landscapes of Maurice de Vlaminck, who lived in the region. ✉ *29 cloître Notre-Dame* ☎ *02–37–90–45–80* 🎫 *€5* 🕒 *Closed Mon. and Tues.*

★ St-Pierre

RELIGIOUS SITE | Like Chartres Cathedral, the church of St-Pierre, near the Eure River, is considered a masterpiece of Gothic architecture and its magnificent 13th- and 14th-century windows are from a medieval period not represented at the cathedral. The oldest stained glass here, portraying Old Testament worthies, is to the right of the choir and dates to the late 13th century. ✉ *Rue St-Pierre.*

🍴 Restaurants

★ Esprit Gourmand

$$ | FRENCH | FAMILY | On a picturesque street close to the cathedral, this quaint bistro is a lifesaver in a town sorely lacking in quality dining. The traditional French favorites it serves—like roast *poulet* with buttery potatoes, sautéed filet of dorade with grilled vegetables, and braised pork that's crisp on the outside and meltingly tender inside—are perennial crowd-pleasers. **Known for:** classic French bistro dishes; garden terrace for outdoor dining; small space, so reservations recommended. [$] *Average main: €18* ✉ *6 rue du Cheval-Blanc* ☎ *02–37–36–97–84* 🕒 *Closed Mon. and Tues. No dinner Sun.*

★ **La Table de Julie**

$ | **FRENCH** | This cozy bistro's namesake studied at the prestigious Ferrandi school and cut her teeth at Joël Robuchon in Paris before returning to her hometown to open her own "bistronomique" restaurant (meaning gastronomic bistro). The refined menu offers seasonal dishes made with ingredients from sustainable farms when possible, and all the wines are organic. **Known for:** cozy atmsophere and terrace; food that's a cut above most other local restaurants; close to the cathedral. [$] *Average main: €10* ✉ *7–11 rue Saint-Michel* ☎ *02–37–32–57–60* 🌐 *www.latabledejulie.fr* ⏲ *Closed Sun. and Mon.*

★ **Les Feuillantines**

$$ | **FRENCH** | The adventurous cuisine served at Les Feuillantines (one of Chartres's few gastronomic restaurants) rarely falters and very often soars. Try the superb house-made terrine with tangy cornichons to start, followed by duck risotto topped with caramelized shallots or beef ravioli perfumed with lemongrass and smoked tea. **Known for:** unique gastronomic dishes; outdoor garden; great prices. [$] *Average main: €21* ✉ *4 rue du Bourg* ☎ *02–37–30–22–21* 🌐 *www.restaurantlesfeuillantines.eatbu.com* ⏲ *Closed Sun. and Mon.*

Hotels

Best Western Le Grand Monarque

$$ | **HOTEL** | On Chartres's main square, not far from the cathedral, this converted coaching inn warmly evokes the 19th century; many guest rooms are outfitted with brick walls, attractive antiques, lush drapes, and modern bathrooms (the best are in a separate turn-of-the-20th-century building overlooking a garden, while the most atmospheric are tucked away in the attic). **Pros:** old-fashioned charm; spa and fitness center offering beauty treatments and massage; Michelin-starred restaurant on-site. **Cons:** best rooms are in an annex; uphill walk to cathedral; some decor is worn. [$] *Rooms from: €175* ✉ *22 pl. des Épars, Île de Nantes* ☎ *02–37–18–15–15* 🌐 *www.bw-grand-monarque.com* 🛏 *55 rooms* 🍴 *No meals.*

Giverny

70 km (44 miles) northwest of Paris.

The small village of Giverny (pronounced "jee-vair-knee"), just beyond the Epte River, which marks the boundary of the Île-de-France, has become a place of pilgrimage for art lovers. It was here that Claude Monet lived for 43 years, until his death at the age of 86 in 1926. Although his house is now prized by connoisseurs of 19th-century interior decoration, it's his garden, with its Japanese-inspired water-lily pond and bridge, that remains the high point for many—a 5-acre, three-dimensional Impressionist painting you can stroll around at leisure. Most make this a day trip, but Giverny has some lovely lodgings, so you could also overnight here.

GETTING HERE AND AROUND

Frequent main-line trains connect Paris's Gare St-Lazare with Vernon (50 minutes, €15.60); you can then cover the remaining 10 km (6 miles) to Giverny by taxi, bus, or bike (the last of these can be rented at the café opposite Vernon station). April through October, shuttle buses meet trains daily and whisk passengers to Giverny for €8.

Sights

★ **Maison et Jardin Claude Monet** (*Monet's House and Garden*)

GARDEN | After several years north of Paris, Monet moved downriver to Giverny in 1883. With its pretty pink walls and green shutters, the house has a warm feeling that's a welcome change after the stateliness of the French châteaux. Rooms have been restored to Monet's original designs: the kitchen with its blue

Entrancing views, like this one of a Japanese footbridge, are plentiful in Monet's Garden.

tiles, the buttercup-yellow dining room, and Monet's bedroom on the second floor. Reproductions of the painter's works, and some of the Japanese prints he avidly collected, crowd its walls. The garden *à la japonaise,* with flowers spilling out across the paths, contains the famous "tea-garden" bridge and water-lily pond. Looking across the pond, it's easy to conjure up the grizzled, bearded painter dabbing at his canvases—capturing changes in light and pioneering a breakdown in form that was to have a major influence on 20th-century art.

The garden—planted with nearly 100,000 annuals and even more perennials—is a place of wonder. No matter that about 500,000 visitors troop through each year; they seem to fade in the presence of beautiful roses, carnations, lady's slipper, tulips, irises, hollyhocks, poppies, daises, nasturtiums, larkspur, azaleas, and more. With that said, it still helps to visit midweek when crowds are thinner. If you want to pay your respects to the original gardener, Monet is buried in the family vault in Giverny's village church. ■TIP➜ **Although the gardens overall are most beautiful in spring, the water lilies bloom during the latter part of July and the first two weeks of August.** ⊠ *84 rue Claude Monet* ☎ *02–32–51–28–21* ⊕ *www. fondation-monet.com* ✉ *€9.50* ⊙ *Closed Nov.–late Mar.*

★ **Musée des Impressionnismes**

MUSEUM | After touring the painterly grounds of Monet's house, you may wish to see some real paintings at the Musée des Impressionnismes. Originally endowed by the late Chicago art patrons Daniel and Judith Terra, it featured a few works by the American Impressionists, including Willard Metcalf, Louis Ritter, Theodore Wendel, and John Leslie Breck, who flocked to Giverny to study at the hand of the master. But in recent years the museum has extended its scope with an exciting array of exhibitions that explore the origins, geographical diversity, and wide-ranging influences of Impressionism—in the process highlighting the importance of Giverny and the Seine Valley in the history of the movement. There's an on-site restaurant and *salon de thé* (tearoom) with a fine outdoor terrace, as well as a garden "quoting" some of Monet's plant compositions. Farther down the road, you can visit Giverny's landmark Hôtel Baudy, a restaurant that was once the preferred watering hole of many 19th-century artists. ✉ *99 rue Claude Monet* ☎ *02–32–51–94–65* 🌐 *www.mdig.fr* 🎟 *€7.50* ⏲ *Closed early Nov.–late Mar.*

🍴 Restaurants

★ Hôtel Baudy

$$ | **BRASSERIE** | Back in Monet's day, this pretty-in-pink villa was the favorite hotel of the American painters' colony. Today it remains one of the most charming spots in the Île-de-France (despite the tourists), althought the surroundings retain more historic charm than the simple cuisine (mainly salads large enough to count as a main course in their own right, or straightforward, if unremarkable, dishes like an omelet or *gigot d'agneau* [lamb and mutton]), but a decent three-course prix-fixe menu is available at lunch and dinner. **Known for:** lovely rose garden; crowd magnet; rustic atmosphere. [$] *Average main: €18* ✉ *81 rue Claude-Monet* ☎ *02–32–21–10–03* 🌐 *www.restaurantbaudy.com* ⏲ *Closed Nov.–Mar.*

★ Le Jardin des Plumes

$$$$ | **FRENCH** | Owner and chef Eric Guérin brings all his considerable expertise to bear in the beautiful dining room at this hotel restaurant, where the menu focuses on the bounty of the Norman seaside. A destination unto itself, the restaurant and hotel are favorites of Giverny visitors seeking a dining "experience," so be sure to reserve in advance for both lunch and dinner. **Known for:** seasonal local products; dining on the beautiful outdoor terrace; Michelin star. [$] *Average main: €33* ✉ *1 rue du Milieu* ☎ *02–32–54–26–35* 🌐 *www.jardindesplumes.fr/restaurant* ⏲ *Closed Mon. and Tues.*

🛏 Hotels

Le Clos Fleuri

$ | **B&B/INN** | Giverny's hotel shortage is offset by several stylish and affordable bed-and-breakfasts—this one, located just 600 yards from Monet's estate, is among the best. **Pros:** co-owner Danielle Fouche speaks fluent English thanks to years spent in Australia and will happily give advice about touring the area; colorful oasis in the heart of the village; each room has private patio. **Cons:** no air-conditioning; books up quickly; decor not for everyone. [$] *Rooms from: €110* ✉ *5 rue de la Dîme* ☎ *02–32–21–36–51* 🌐 *www.giverny-leclosfleuri.fr* ⏲ *Closed Oct.–Mar.* 🔑 *3 rooms* 🍽 *Free Breakfast.*

Le Jardin des Plumes

$$$ | **B&B/INN** | This Norman-style half-timbered inn with its lovely surrounding garden is a welcome addition to the oft-lamented Giverny lodging and dining scene. **Pros:** location, location, location; excellent restaurant; stylish rooms. **Cons:** dinner on the pricey side; extra cost for breakfast; can feel oddly deserted on Monday and Tuesday (when restaurant is closed). [$] *Rooms from: €230* ✉ *1 rue du Milieu* ☎ *02–32–54–26–35* 🌐 *www.lejardindesplumes.fr* ⏲ *Closed mid-Nov.–mid-Dec.* 🔑 *8 rooms* 🍽 *No meals.*

Les Jardins d'Epicure

$ | **HOTEL** | **FAMILY** | Set on 7 acres of picture-perfect parkland, this unique hotel occupies three charming 19th-century buildings: the picturesque stables, with "Gothic" brick trim, high-beamed ceilings, and the delightful Unicorn Suite; the Villa Florentine (once home to famed poet Paul Éluard) whose Chambre Marquise has no less than seven windows overlooking the park and stream; and the elegant Castel Napoléon III, with six separate guest rooms featuring period antiques and Oriental rugs. **Pros:** superb setting; wonderful restaurant; beautiful contemporary decor. **Cons:** a 20-minute drive from Giverny; restaurant closed

Monday and Tuesday. ⓢ *Rooms from: €120* ✉ *16 Grande Rue, 15 km (9 miles) northeast of Vernon on D86* ☎ *01–34–67–75–87* ⊕ *www.lesjardinsdepicure.com* ⇨ *20 rooms* ❍ *No meals.*

St-Germain-en-Laye

29 km (18 miles) southwest of L'Isle-Adam, 17 km (11 miles) west of Paris.

Encircled by forest and perched behind Le Nôtre's Grande Terrace overlooking the Seine, this idyllic town has lost little of its original cachet—despite the invasion of wealthy former Parisians who commute to work from here.

GETTING HERE AND AROUND
Being on the RER-A line, St-Germain-en-Laye's station handles frequent trains to and from Paris (€4.45).

VISITOR INFORMATION St-Germain-en-Laye Tourist Office ✉ *38 rue au Pain* ☎ *01–30–87–20–63* ⊕ *www.ot-saintgermainenlaye.fr.*

Sights

Château de Monte-Cristo (*Monte Cristo Castle*)
CASTLE/PALACE | If you're fond of the swashbuckling novels of Alexandre Dumas, you'll enjoy the Château de Monte-Cristo at Port-Marly on the southern fringe of St-Germain. Dumas built the château after the surging popularity of books like *The Count of Monte Cristo* made him rich in the 1840s. Construction costs and lavish partying meant he went broke just as quickly, and he skedaddled into a Belgian exile in 1849. You may find the fanciful exterior, where pilasters, cupolas, and stone carvings compete for attention, crosses the line from opulence to tastelessness, but—as in Dumas's fiction—swagger, not subtlety, is what counts. Dumas mementos aside, the highlight of the interior is the luxurious

Moorish Chamber, with spellbinding, interlacing plasterwork executed by Arab craftsmen (lent by the Bey of Tunis) and restored thanks to a donation from the late Moroccan king Hassan II. ✉ *1 av. du Président-Kennedy* ☎ *01–39–16–49–49 Closed Mon. year-round and weekdays Nov.–Mar.* ⊕ *www.chateau-monte-cristo.com* ✉ *€8.*

Château de St-Germain-en-Laye
CASTLE/PALACE | Next to the St-Germain RER train station, this stone-and-brick château, with its dry moat, intimidating circular towers, and La Grande Terrasse, is one of the most spectacular of all French garden set pieces. The château itself dates to the 16th and 17th centuries, but a royal palace has stood here since the early 12th century, when Louis VI—known as Le Gros (the Plump)—exploited St-Germain's defensive potential in his bid to pacify the Île-de-France. A hundred years later Louis IX (St. Louis) added the elegant **Sainte-Chapelle,** the château's oldest remaining section. Note the square-top, not pointed, side windows and the filled-in rose window on the back wall. Charles V (1364–80) built a powerful defensive keep in the mid-14th century, but from the 1540s François I and his successors transformed St-Germain into a palace with an appearance more domestic than warlike. Louis XIV was born here, and it was here that his father, Louis XIII, died. Until 1682, when the court moved to Versailles, it remained the country's foremost royal residence outside Paris, and several Molière plays were premiered in the main hall. Since 1867 the château has housed the impressive **Musée des Antiquités Nationales,** (Museum of National Antiquities), holding a trove of artifacts, figurines, brooches, and weapons, from the Stone Age to the 8th century. Behind the château is André Le Nôtre's **Grande Terrasse,** a terraced promenade lined by lime trees. Directly overlooking the Seine, it was completed in 1673 and has rarely been outdone

for grandeur or length. ✉ *Pl. Charles-de-Gaulle* ☎ *01–39–10–13–00* 🌐 *www.musee-archeologienationale.fr* 🎫 *€9* 🕐 *Closed Tues.*

Musée Maurice Denis (*Priory Museum*)
MUSEUM | This appealing museum in a historic priory is devoted to the work of artist Maurice Denis (1870–1943), his fellow Symbolists, and the Nabis—painters opposed to the naturalism of their 19th-century Impressionist contemporaries. Denis found the calm of the former Jesuit building, set above tiered gardens with statues and rosebushes, ideally suited to his spiritual themes, which he expressed in stained glass, ceramics, and frescoes as well as oils. ✉ *2 bis, rue Maurice-Denis* ☎ *01–39–73–77–87* 🌐 *www.musee-mauricedenis.fr* 🎫 *€4.50.*

🍴 Restaurants

★ **Lilla Krogen**
$$ | SWEDISH | In the center of town just a few minutes from the Musée Maurice Denis, this contemporary French-style bistro is popular for its bright decor and healthy Swedish-inflected recipes. Appetizers like toasts Skagen—tiny shrimps in homemade dilled mayonnaise on toast—and salmon gravlax or marinated herring are fresh, healthy, and delicious. **Known for:** freshest top-quality fish; healthy meals; warm and welcoming service. [$] *Average main: €20* ✉ *1 Place de Mareil* ☎ *09–81–89–89–56* 🌐 *www.lilla-krogen.com* 🕐 *No dinner Sun.*

🛏 Hotels

★ **Cazaudehore La Forestière**
$$ | HOTEL | St-Germain's most stylish hotel is a quintessential Île-de-France country retreat—surrounded by forest, it's rambling and solid, with shuttered windows and 18th-century-style furnishings. **Pros:** cozy, classy hotel; run by a third-generation hotelier; good restaurant. **Cons:** service can be indifferent; rooms lack air-conditioning; breakfast not included. [$] *Rooms from: €220* ✉ *1 av. du Président Kennedy* ☎ *01–30–61–64–64* 🌐 *www.cazaudehore.fr* 🛏 *30 rooms* 🍴 *No meals.*

🎭 Performing Arts

Fête des Loges (*Loges Festival*)
FESTIVALS | A giant fair and carnival is held in the Forest of St-Germain from late June to mid-August. Fans of cotton candy, roller coasters, and Ferris wheels turn up in droves every year. ✉ *Camp des Loges* 🌐 *www.fetedesloges.org.*

Rueil-Malmaison

8 km (5 miles) southeast of St-Germain-en-Laye, 8 km (5 miles) west of Paris.

Rueil-Malmaison is a slightly dreary western suburb of Paris, but the memory of Napoléon and Joséphine still haunts its neoclassical château.

GETTING HERE AND AROUND

From Paris, take RER-A (direction St-Germain-en-Laye) directly to Rueil-Malmaison (40 mins, €3.90).

VISITOR INFORMATION Rueil-Malmaison Tourist Office ✉ *33 rue Jean Le Coz* ☎ *01–47–32–35–75* 🌐 *www.rueil-tourisme.com/en.*

👁 Sights

★ **La Malmaison**
CASTLE/PALACE | Built in 1622, La Malmaison was bought by the future empress Joséphine in 1799 as a love nest for Napoléon and herself, three years after their marriage. Theirs is one of Europe's most dramatic love stories, replete with affairs, scandal, and hatred—the emperor's family often disparaged Joséphine, a name bestowed on her by Napoléon (her real name was Rose), as "the Creole." After the childless Joséphine was

divorced by the heir-hungry emperor in 1809, she retired to La Malmaison and died here on May 29, 1814. The château has 24 rooms furnished with exquisite tables, chairs, and sofas of the Napoleonic period; of special note are the library, game room, and dining room. The walls are adorned with works by artists of the day, such as Jacques-Louis David, Pierre-Paul Prud'hon, and Baron Gérard. Take time to admire the clothes and hats that belonged to Napoléon and Joséphine, particularly the empress's gowns. Their carriage can be seen in one of the garden pavilions; another contains a unique collection of snuffboxes donated by Prince George of Greece. The gardens are delightful, reflecting Joséphine's love of roses and exotic plants (her collection was one of the most important in France), and especially beautiful when the regimented rows of tulips are blooming in spring. ⊠ *15 av. du Château* ☎ *01–41–29–05–55* ⊕ *www.chateau-malmaison.fr* 🎫 *€6.50.*

Auvers-sur-Oise

74 km (46 miles) east of Giverny; 33 km (21 miles) northwest of Paris.

The tranquil Oise River valley retains much of the charm that attracted Camille Pissarro, Paul Cézanne, Camille Corot, Charles-François Daubigny, and Berthe Morisot to Auvers-sur-Oise in the second half of the 19th century. Despite this lofty company, though, it's the spirit of Vincent van Gogh—who spent the last months of his life painting no fewer than 70 works here—that haunts every nook and cranny of this pretty riverside village. On July 27, 1890, the tormented artist laid his easel against a haystack, walked behind the Château d'Auvers, shot himself, then stumbled to the Auberge Ravoux. He died on July 29. The next day, using a hearse from neighboring Méry (because the priest of Auvers refused to provide his for a suicide victim), Van

Gogh's body was borne up the hill to the village cemetery. His heartbroken brother Theo died the following year and, in 1914, was reburied alongside him in a simple ivy-covered grave. Today many visitors make a pilgrimage to town sites associated with Van Gogh (the tourist office has information). Short hikes outside the center will lead you to lovely rural landscapes, including the one that inspired Van Gogh's last painting, *Wheat Fields with Crows.*

GETTING HERE AND AROUND
Take the RER-C line from Paris (direction Pontoise) to St-Ouen l'Aumone, and then a second train (direction Creil) onward to Auvers; the total travel is 45–55 minutes, the total cost €6.35. There is no connecting public transportation from the area around Vernon.

VISITOR INFORMATION Auvers-sur-Oise Tourist Office ⊠ *38 rue du Général de Gaulle* ☎ *01–30–36–71–81* ⊕ *tourisme-auverssuroise.fr.*

 Sights

Maison-Atelier de Daubigny
MUSEUM | The landscape artist Charles-François Daubigny, a precursor of the Impressionists, lived in Auvers from 1861 until his death in 1878. You can visit his studio, the Maison-Atelier de Daubigny, and admire the mural and roof paintings by Daubigny and fellow artists Camille Corot and Honoré Daumier. ⊠ *61 rue Daubigny* ☎ *01–34–48–03–03* ⊕ *www.atelier-daubigny.com* 🎫 *€6* ☺ *Closed Nov.–late Mar. and Mon.–Wed.*

Maison de Van Gogh (*Van Gogh House*)
MUSEUM | Opposite the town hall, the Auberge Ravoux—where Van Gogh lived and died—is now the Maison de Van Gogh. The inn opened in 1876 and owes its name to Arthur Ravoux, the landlord from 1889 to 1891. He had seven lodgers in all, who paid 3.50 francs for room and board (that was cheaper than the other inns in Auvers, where 6 francs was the

going rate). A dingy staircase leads up to the tiny attic where Van Gogh stored some of modern art's most iconic paintings under his bed. A short film retraces the artist's time at Auvers, and there's a well-stocked souvenir shop. Stop for a drink or for lunch in the ground-floor restaurant. ✉ *8 rue de la Sansonne* ☎ *01–30–36–60–60* ⊕ *www.maisondevangogh.fr* 🎫 *€6* 🕑 *Closed Mon. and Tues.*

Maison du Dr. Gachet

MUSEUM | The former home of Van Gogh's closest friend in Auvers, Dr. Paul Gachet, is a local landmark. Documents and mementos evoke both Van Gogh's stay and Gachet's passion for the avant-garde art of his era. The good doctor was himself the subject of one of the artist's most famous portraits (and the world's second-most-expensive painting when it sold for $82 million in the late 1980s); the actual creation of it was reenacted in the 1956 biopic, *Lust for Life,* starring Kirk Douglas. Even this house was immortalized on canvas, courtesy of Cézanne. A friend and patron to many of the artists who settled in and visited Auvers in the 1880s, Gachet also contributed to their artistic education by teaching them about engraving processes. Don't overlook the garden—it provided the ivy that covers Van Gogh's grave in the cemetery across town. ✉ *78 rue du Dr-Gachet* ☎ *01–30–36–81–27* 🎫 *Free* 🕑 *Closed Mon. and Tues.*

Musée Daubigny

MUSEUM | You may want to visit the modest Musée Daubigny to admire the drawings, lithographs, and occasional oils by local 19th-century artists, some of which were collected by Daubigny himself. The museum is opposite the Maison de Van Gogh, above the tourist office, which shows a 15-minute film (in English on request) about life in Auvers, *From Daubigny to Van Gogh.* ✉ *Manoir des Colombières, Rue de la Sansonne* ☎ *01–30–36–80–20* ⊕ *www.museedaubigny.com* 🎫 *€5* 🕑 *Closed Mon.*

Voyage au Temps des Impressionnistes

(*Journey Through the Impressionist Era*)

MUSEUM | **FAMILY** | Set above split-level gardens, this 17th-century village château (also depicted by Van Gogh) now houses the Voyage au Temps des Impressionnistes. You'll receive a set of headphones (English available), with commentary that guides you past various tableaux illustrating life during the Impressionist years. Although there are no Impressionist originals—500 reproductions pop up on screens interspersed between the tableaux—this is one of France's most imaginative, enjoyable, and innovative museums. Some of the special effects, including talking mirrors, computerized cabaret dancing girls, and a simulated train ride past Impressionist landscapes, are worthy of Disney. The on-site Impressionist Café has three dining areas: the elegant 17th-century Orangerie, the Espaces Scénographiques, and a re-creation of a 19th-century *guinguette* (café–dance hall), where more casual fare is on the menu. ✉ *Rue de Léry* ☎ *01–34–48–48–48* ⊕ *www.chateau-auvers.fr* 🎫 *€15* 🕑 *Closed Mon.*

Restaurants

Auberge Ravoux

$$$ | **BISTRO** | For total Van Gogh immersion, have lunch—or dinner on Friday and Saturday—in the restaurant he patronized regularly more than 100 years ago, in the building where he actually died. A three-course prix-fixe menu is available, and saddle of lamb and homemade terrine are among Loran Gattufo's specialties. **Known for:** good traditional, regional dishes; historic backstory; rustic authenticity. 💲 *Average main: €26* ✉ *52 rue Général-de-Gaulle* ☎ *01–30–36–60–63* ⊕ *www.maisondevangogh.fr* 🕑 *Closed Mon. and Tues., and Dec.–Feb. No dinner Wed., Thurs., or Sun.*

Chantilly

37 km (23 miles) north of Paris.

Celebrated for lace, cream, and the most beautiful medieval manuscript in the world—*Les Très Riches Heures du Duc de Berry*—romantic Chantilly has a host of other attractions. Most notable among them are a faux Renaissance château with an eye-popping art collection second only to the Louvre's, a classy racecourse, and 18th-century stables that are called *grandes* for good reason.

GETTING HERE AND AROUND
Chantilly can be reached on both Transilien and main-line trains from Paris's Gare du Nord (25–30 minutes, €8.70).

VISITOR INFORMATION Chantilly Tourist Office ⊠ *73 rue du Connétable* ☎ *03–44–67–37–37* ⊕ *www.chantilly-tourisme.com.*

👁 Sights

★ Château de Chantilly
CASTLE/PALACE | Although its lavish exterior may be 19th-century Renaissance pastiche, the Château de Chantilly, sitting snugly behind an artificial lake, houses the outstanding **Musée Condé,** with illuminated medieval manuscripts, tapestries, furniture, and paintings. The most famous room, the **Santuario** (sanctuary), contains two celebrated works by Italian painter Raphael (1483–1520)—the *Three Graces* and the *Orleans Virgin*—plus an exquisite ensemble of 15th-century miniatures by the most illustrious French painter of his time, Jean Fouquet (1420–81). Farther on, in the **Cabinet des Livres** (library), is the world-famous Book of Hours whose title translates as *The Very Rich Hours of the Duc de Berry.* It was illuminated by the Brothers Limbourg with magical pictures of early-15th-century life as lived by one of Burgundy's richest lords; unfortunately, due to their fragility, painted facsimiles of the celebrated calendar illuminations

are on display, not the actual pages of the book. Other highlights of this unusual museum are the **Galerie de Psyché** (Psyche Gallery), with 16th-century stained glass and portrait drawings by Flemish artist Jean Clouet II; the **Chapelle,** with sculptures by Jean Goujon and Jacques Sarrazin; and the extensive collection of paintings by 19th-century French artists, headed by Jean-Auguste-Dominique Ingres. In addition, there are grand and smaller salons, all stuffed with palace furniture, family portraits, and Sèvres porcelains, making this a must for lovers of the decorative and applied arts. ⊠ *Domaine de Chantilly* ☎ *03–44–27–31–80* ⊕ *www.domainedechantilly.com* ⊠ *€17, includes Grandes Écuries and park* ⊘ *Closed Tues. Nov.–Mar.*

★ Grandes Écuries (*Grand Stables*)
MUSEUM | FAMILY | The grandest stables in France were built by Jean Aubert in 1719 to accommodate 240 horses and 500 hounds used for stag and boar hunting in the forests nearby. Now with 30 breeds of horses and ponies living here in straw-lined comfort, the palatial stables function as the **Musée Vivant du Cheval** (Living Horse Museum). Equine history is explored through an array of artifacts, prints, paintings, textiles, sculptures, equipment, and weaponry. Visitors can also enjoy the elaborate horse shows and dressage demonstrations year-round; check the website for dates and times. ⊠ *7 rue du Connétable* ☎ *03–44–27–31–80* ⊕ *www.domainedechantilly.com* ⊠ *Included in château ticket; horse shows €21.*

Hippodrome des Princes de Condé
SPORTS VENUE | Chantilly, France's equestrian epicenter, is home to the fabled Hippodrome racetrack. Established in 1834, it comes into its own each June with two of Europe's most prestigious events: the Prix du Jockey-Club (French Derby) on the first Sunday of the month, and the Prix de Diane for three-year-old fillies the Sunday after. On main race days, a free

shuttle bus runs between Chantilly's train station and the track. ✉ *Rte. de la Plaine-des-Aigles* ☎ *03–44–62–44–00* 🌐 *www.france-galop.com.*

Park

CITY PARK | Le Nôtre's park is based on that familiar French royal combination of formality and romantic eccentricity. The former is represented in the neatly planned parterres and a mighty, straight-banked canal; the latter comes to the fore in the waterfall and the Hameau, a mock-Norman village that inspired Marie-Antoinette's version at Versailles. You can explore on foot or on an electric train, and, in the warmer months, take a **rowboat** for a meander down the Grand Canal. ✉ *Chantilly* ☎ *03–44–27–31–80* 🌐 *www.domainedechantilly.com* 🎟 *€8 park only, €17 park and château* 🕓 *Closed Tues. Nov.–Mar.*

🍴 Restaurants

La Capitainerie

$$ | **FRENCH** | Housed in the stone-vaulted kitchens of the Château de Chantilly's legendary 17th-century chef Vorace Vatel, this quaint restaurant has an open-hearth fireplace big enough for whole lambs or oxen to sizzle on the spit. Reflect at leisure on your cultural peregrinations over mouthfuls of grilled turbot or roast quail, and don't forget to add a good dollop of homemade crème de Chantilly to your dessert. **Known for:** family-friendly vibe; quick dining; reasonable prices. [$] *Average main: €22* ✉ *Château de Chantilly* ☎ *03–44–57–15–89* 🌐 *www.domainedechantilly.com/fr/capitainerie* 🕓 *Closed Tues. Nov.–Mar. No dinner.*

🛏 Hotels

★ Auberge du Jeu de Paume

$$$ | **HOTEL** | Set within the Domaine de Chantilly, the largest princely estate in France, Auberge du Jeu de Paume combines its stunning setting with old-world elegance and modern comforts to create a deluxe country retreat. **Pros:** proximity to all the sights; sublime country setting; luxe amenities. **Cons:** dining room could be more intimate; some common areas feel corporate; garden-view rooms expensive. [$] *Rooms from: €350* ✉ *4 rue du Connétable* ☎ *03–44–65–50–00* 🌐 *www.aubergedujeudepaumechantilly.fr* 🛏 *92 rooms* 🍴 *No meals.*

Senlis

10 km (6 miles) east of Chantilly, 40 km (26 miles) north of Paris.

Senlis is an exceptionally well-preserved medieval town with a crooked maze of streets dominated by the svelte, soaring spire of its Gothic cathedral. For a glimpse into the more distant past, be sure to also inspect the superb Musée d'Art et d'Archéologie.

GETTING HERE AND AROUND

Take either the Transilien or main-line trains from Paris's Gare du Nord to Chantilly (25–30 minutes, €8.70), then a bus onward to Senlis.

VISITOR INFORMATION Senlis Tourist Office ✉ *Pl. du Parvis Notre-Dame* ☎ *03–44–53–06–40* 🌐 *www.senlis-tourisme.fr.*

👁 Sights

Cathédrale Notre-Dame

RELIGIOUS SITE | The breathtaking Cathédrale Notre-Dame, one of the country's oldest and narrowest cathedrals, dates to the second half of the 12th century. The superb spire—arguably the most elegant in France—was added around 1240, and the majestic transept, with its ornate rose windows, in the 16th century. ✉ *Pl. du Parvis.*

★ Musée d'Art et d'Archéologie

MUSEUM | The excellent Musée d'Art et d'Archéologie displays finds ranging from Gallo-Roman votive objects unearthed in the neighboring Halatte Forest to

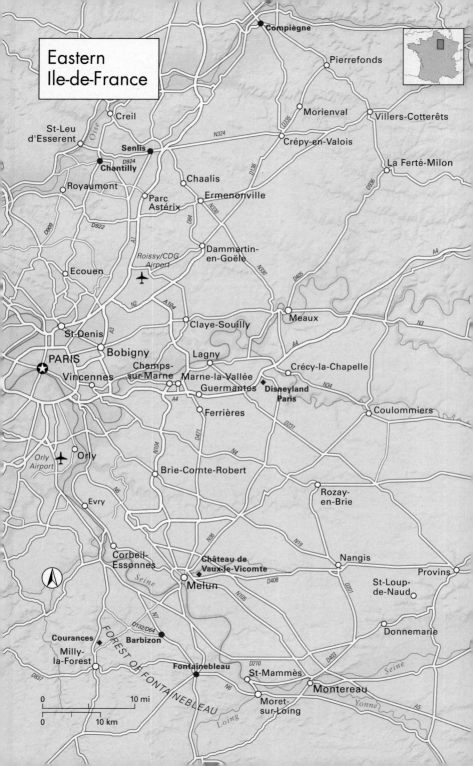

Eastern
Ile-de-France

Compiègne

Pierrefonds

St-Leu
d'Esserent

Creil

Morienval

Villers-Cotterêts

N324

Crépy-en-Valois

D335

Senlis

La Ferté-Milon

D936

Chantilly

D924

Royaumont

Chaalis

Ermenonville

D909

D922

Parc
Astérix

Dammartin-
en-Goële

N330

D405

Ecouen

Roissy/CDG
Airport

N2

A104

Meaux

N3

St-Denis

A3

Claye-Souilly

A4

Bobigny

Lagny

Crécy-la-Chapelle

PARIS

Vincennes

Champs-
sur-Marne

Marne-la-Vallée

Guermantes

Disneyland
Paris

N34

Coulommiers

Ferrières

D231

N104

D421

N4

Orly
Airport

Orly

Brie-Comte-Robert

N6

Rozay-
en-Brie

Evry

N19

Nangis

Provins

Corbeil-
Essonnes

Seine

Château de
Vaux-le-Vicomte

D408

D201

St-Loup-
de-Naud

Melun

N105

Donnemarie

N7

Courances

D132/D64

Barbizon

FOREST OF FONTAINEBLEAU

Milly-
la-Forest

D637

Fontainebleau

D210

St-Mammès

D403

Seine

N6

Montereau

Moret-
sur-Loing

Loing

Yonne

A5

0   10 mi

0   10 km

the building's own excavated foundations (visible in the basement); note the superb stone heads bathed in half light. Upstairs, paintings include works by Manet's teacher, Thomas Couture (who lived in Senlis) and charming naïve florals by the town's own Séraphine de Senlis. ✉ *Palais Épiscopal, Pl. du Parvis Notre-Dame* ☎ *03–44–24–86–72* 🌐 *www.musees-senlis.fr* 🎟 *€6* 🕒 *Closed Mon. and Tues.*

Parc Astérix

AMUSEMENT PARK/WATER PARK | FAMILY | A great alternative to Disneyland, and a wonderful day out for young and old, this Gallic theme park takes its cue from a French comic-book figure whose adventures are set during the Roman invasion of France 2,000 years ago. Among the 30 rides and six shows that attract thundering herds of families each year are a mock Gallo-Roman village, costumed druids, performing dolphins, splash-happy waterslides, and a giant roller coaster. ✉ *Senlis* ✣ *10 km (6 miles) south of Senlis via A1* ☎ *03–44–62–34–04* 🌐 *www.parcasterix.fr* 🎟 *€51* 🕒 *Closed early Jan.–early Apr.*

🍴 Restaurants

Le Scaramouche

$ | MODERN FRENCH | This well-priced bistro, in an enviable spot facing the cathedral, provides a pleasant setting in which to enjoy some good French classics thanks to a menu that covers all the bases: a warm casserole of escargots with parsley butter, hand-chopped steak tartare with crispy frites, buttery scallops with lentils and a garlicky mayonnaise, and an array of salads and desserts. On a warm day, diners can enjoy the outdoor terrace with excellent views of the cathedral. **Known for:** nice views of the cathedral; Italian specialties; attentive service. [$] *Average main: €15* ✉ *4 pl. Notre Dame* ☎ *03–44–53–01–26* 🌐 *www.le-scaramouche.fr* 🕒 *Closed Sun. and Mon.*

🛏 Hotels

L'Hostellerie de la Porte Bellon

$ | HOTEL | This old stone house, near the bus station and five minutes by foot from the cathedral, is the closest you can get to spending a night in the historic center of Senlis; prettiest is Room 14, which overlooks the garden and has sloping walls and exposed beams. **Pros:** only hotel close to historic town center; attractive old building; super quiet. **Cons:** modest facilities; some rooms need renovating; no minibar or coffeemaker in rooms. [$] *Rooms from: €89* ✉ *51 rue Bellon* ☎ *03–44–53–03–05* 🌐 *www.portebellon.fr* 🕒 *Closed 1st 2 wks of Jan.* 🔑 *18 rooms* 🍴 *No meals.*

Compiègne

32 km (20 miles) northeast of Senlis.

This bustling town of some 40,000 people sits at the northern limit of the Forêt de Compiègne (Compiègne Forest). The former royal hunting lodge here enjoyed its heyday in the mid-19th century under upstart emperor Napoléon III. But the town's history stretches further back—to Joan of Arc, who was captured in battle and held prisoner here, and to its 15th-century Hôtel de Ville (Town Hall), with its jubilant Flamboyant Gothic facade; and further forward—to the World War I armistice, signed in Compiègne Forest on November 11, 1918.

GETTING HERE AND AROUND

Frequent trains connect Compiègne with Paris's Gare du Nord (45 minutes, €15.40).

VISITOR INFORMATION Compiègne Tourist Office ✉ *28 pl. de l'Hôtel-de-Ville* ☎ *03–44–40–01–00* 🌐 *www.compiegne-tourisme.fr.*

Sights

★ Château de Compiègne

CASTLE/PALACE | FAMILY | The 18th-century Château de Compiègne, where the future Louis XVI first met Marie-Antoinette in 1770, was restored by Napoléon I and favored for wild weekends by his nephew Napoléon III. The first Napoléon's legacy is more keenly felt: his state apartments have been refurbished using the original designs for hangings and upholstery, and bright silks and damasks adorn every room. Much of the mahogany furniture gleams with ormolu, and the chairs sparkle with gold leaf. Napoléon III's furniture looks ponderous by comparison. Behind the palace is a gently rising 4-km (2½-mile) vista, inspired by the park at Schönbrunn, in Vienna, where Napoléon I's second wife, Empress Marie-Louise, grew up. Also here is the **Musée du Second Empire,** a collection of decorative arts from the Napoléon III era: its showstopper is Franz-Xaver Winterhalter's *Empress Eugénie Surrounded by Her Ladies in Waiting,* a famed homage to the over-the-top hedonism of the Napoléon Trois era. Make time for the **Musée de la Voiture** (Vehicle Museum) and its display of carriages, coaches, and old cars—including the *Jamais Contente* (*Never Satisfied*), the first car to reach 100 kph (62 mph). ✉ *Pl. du Général de Gaulle* ☎ *03–44–38–47–02* ⊕ *www.palais-decompiegne.fr* ✆ *€7.50* ☺ *Closed Tues.*

Musée de la Figurine Historique (*Toy Soldier Museum*)

MUSEUM | FAMILY | A collection of 85,000 miniature soldiers—fashioned of lead, cardboard, and other materials—depicting military uniforms through the ages is on display in the Musée de la Figurine Historique. ✉ *28 pl. de l'Hôtel de Ville* ☎ *03–44–20–26–04* ⊕ *www.musee-figurine.fr* ✆ *€4* ☺ *Closed Mon.*

Wagon de l'Armistice (*Armistice Railcar*)

MUSEUM | Off the road to Rethondes, the Wagon de l'Armistice is a replica of the one in which the World War I armistice was signed in 1918. In 1940 the Nazis turned the tables and made the French sign their own surrender in the same place, then tugged the original car off to Germany, where it was later destroyed. The replica is part of a small museum in a leafy clearing. ✉ *Carrefour de l'Armistice, 7 km (4 miles) east of Compiègne via N31 and D546* ☎ *03–44–85–14–18* ⊕ *www.musee-armistice-14-18.fr* ✆ *€7* ☺ *Closed Jan. and Feb.*

 Restaurants

★ Les Ferlempins

$$$ | FRENCH | Don't be fooled by the casual interior—this popular gastrobistro, helmed by two brothers passionate about food and wine, is where local foodies go for a special lunch or evening out. Products fresh from Compiègne's wonderful farmers' market are transformed into only a few sophisticated dishes each day that change with the season and are as beautiful to look at as they are delicious. **Known for:** ethically sourced products; English-speaking owners who love to talk about their food; excellent wine pairings. $ *Average main: €25* ✉ *13 Cours Guynemer* ☎ *03–44–83–53–31* ⊕ *www.lesferlempins.fr* ☺ *Closed Sun. and Mon.*

Hotels

Harlay

$ | HOTEL | A family-run hotel in a four-square stone building, the Harlay is conveniently situated by the bridge linking the train station and downtown; guest rooms are soberly decorated—the best overlook the River Oise and are sound-proofed with double glazing. **Pros:** close to the station; rooms are quiet; reasonable prices. **Cons:** bland interiors; smallish rooms; breakfast extra. $ *Rooms from: €84* ✉ *3 rue de Harlay* ☎ *03–44–23–01–50* ⊕ *www.hotel-compiegne.net* ⤴ *19 rooms* ⦿ *No meals.*

The Alice in Wonderland Labyrinth delights children—and intrigues guests of all ages—at Disneyland Paris.

Disneyland Paris

62 km (38 miles) south of Senlis; 38 km (24 miles) east of Paris.

Disneyland Paris is probably not what you've traveled to France for. But if you have a child in tow, the promise of a day with Mickey might get you through an afternoon at Versailles or Fontainebleau. If you're a dyed-in-the-wool Disney fan, you'll also want to make a beeline here to see how the park has been molded to suit European tastes (Disney's "Imagineers" call it their most lovingly detailed one, and it simultaneously feels both decidedly foreign and eerily familiar). And if you've never experienced this particular form of Disney showmanship before, you may want to put in an appearance simply to find out what all the fuss is about.

GETTING HERE AND AROUND

Take the RER-A from central Paris (stations at Étoile, Auber, Les Halles, Gare de Lyon, and Nation) to Marne-la-Vallée–Chessy—the gare there is 100 yards from the Disneyland entrance; trains operate every 10–30 minutes, depending on the time of day (40 minutes, €8). High-speed TGV train service (⊕ *www.tgv.com*) links Disneyland to Lille, Lyon, Brussels, and London (via Lille and the Channel Tunnel). Disneyland's hotel complex also offers a shuttle bus service connecting it with the Orly and Charles de Gaulle airports; in each case the trip takes about 45 minutes and tickets cost €23.

VISITOR INFORMATION Disneyland Paris Reservations Office ☎ *08–25–30–05–00, 1–60–30–60–53 from outside of France* ⊕ *www.disneylandparis.com.*

Sights

★ Disneyland Paris

AMUSEMENT PARK/WATER PARK | FAMILY | A slightly downsized version of its United States counterpart, Disneyland Paris is nevertheless a spectacular sight, created with an acute attention to detail. **Disneyland Park**, as the original theme park is styled, consists of five "lands": Main Street U.S.A., Frontierland,

Adventureland, Fantasyland, and Discoveryland. The central theme of each land is relentlessly echoed in every detail, from attractions to restaurant menus to souvenirs. In **Main Street U.S.A**, tots adore Alice's Curious Labyrinth, Peter Pan's Flight, and especially the whirling Mad Hatter's Teacups, while everyone loves the afternoon parades, with huge floats swarming with all of Disney's most beloved characters—just make sure to stake your place along Main Street in advance for a good spot.

Top attractions at **Frontierland** are the chilling Phantom Manor, haunted by holographic ghosts, and the thrilling runaway mine train of Big Thunder Mountain, a roller coaster that plunges wildly through floods and avalanches in a setting meant to evoke Utah's Monument Valley. Whiffs of Arabia, Africa, and the Caribbean give **Adventureland** its exotic cachet; the spicy meals and snacks served here rank among the best food in the park. Don't miss Pirates of the Caribbean, an exciting mise-en-scène populated by lifelike animatronic figures, or Indiana Jones and the Temple of Doom, a rapid-fire ride that re-creates some of this hapless hero's most exciting moments.

Fantasyland charms the youngest parkgoers with familiar cartoon characters from such classic Disney films as *Snow White, Pinocchio, Dumbo, Alice in Wonderland,* and *Peter Pan.* The focal point of Fantasyland, and indeed Disneyland Paris, is Le Château de la Belle au Bois Dormant (Sleeping Beauty's Castle), a 140-foot, bubble-gum-pink structure topped with 16 blue- and gold-tipped turrets. **Discoveryland** is a high-tech, futuristic eye-popper. Robots on roller skates welcome you on your way to Star Tours, a pitching, plunging, sense-confounding ride based on the *Star Wars* films; and another robot, the staggeringly realistic 9-Eye, hosts a simulated space journey in Le Visionarium.

The older the child, the more they will enjoy **Walt Disney Studios**, a cinematically driven area next to the Disneyland Park, where many of the newer Disney character–themed rides can be found. It's divided into four "production zones," giving visitors insight into different parts of the production process, including Animation Courtyard, where Disney artists demonstrate the various phases of character animation, and Production Courtyard, where you can go on a behind-the-scenes Studio Tram tour of location sites, movie props, studio interiors, and costumes, ending with a visit to Catastrophe Canyon in the heart of a film shoot. ✉ *Marne-la-Vallée* ☎ *08–25–30–05–00* 🌐 *www.disneylandparis.com* 🎟 *€99, 3-day Passport €185; includes admission to all individual attractions within Disneyland or Walt Disney Studios; tickets for Walt Disney Studios are also valid for admission to Disneyland during last 3 opening hrs of same day.*

Hotels

Newport Bay Club

$$$$ | **HOTEL** | Set at the far end of Disneyland Paris's lake, the nautical-themed Newport Bay Club is the biggest four-star hotel in France—with the largest capacity in Europe—so don't expect intimacy, but hallways are bright and spacious and rooms are quiet and light filled (especially those with lake views) and some offer balconies. **Pros:** three restaurant choices; easy walk to the park; nice views from lake-facing terraces. **Cons:** very expensive; no tea and coffee in rooms; expect a lot of other people. [$] *Rooms from: €400* ✉ *Av. Robert Schuman, Marne-la-Vallée* ☎ *08–25–30–05–00* 🌐 *www.disneylandparis.com/en-gb/hotels/disneys-newport-bay-club* 🛏 *1,093 rooms* 🍴 *No meals* [M] *RER A to Disneyland Paris.*

Sequoia Lodge

$$$ | **HOTEL** | Ranging from superluxe to just barely affordable, Disneyland Paris has 5,000 rooms throughout several

hotels, but your best bet on all counts may be the Sequoia Lodge—a grand re-creation of an American mountain lodge, just a few minutes' walk from the theme park. **Pros:** package deals include admission to theme park; cozy, secluded feel; great pools. **Cons:** restaurants a bit ho-hum; many rooms do not have lake views; prices can flutuate. $ *Rooms from: €300 ⊠ Marne-la-Vallée ☎ 08–25–30–05–00, 1–60–30–60–53 from outside of France ⊕ www.disneylandparis.com ☞ 1,020 rooms* ❍❏ *No meals.*

Nightlife

Disney Village

GATHERING PLACES | Nocturnal entertainment outside the park centers on Disney Village, a vast pleasure mall designed by American architect Frank Gehry. Homesick kids who've had enough croque monsieurs will be happy to hear that vintage American-style restaurants—a diner, a deli, and a steak house among them— dominate the food scene here. One highlight within Disney Village is **Buffalo Bill's Wild West Show**, a two-hour dinner extravaganza with a menu of sausage, spareribs, and chili. The entertainment component includes performances by a talented troupe of stunt riders, bronco busters, tribal dancers, and musicians; plus some 50 horses, a dozen buffalo, a bull, and an Annie Oakley–style sharpshooter, with a golden-maned "Buffalo Bill" as emcee. A re-creation of a show that dazzled Parisians 100 years ago, it's corny but great fun. Tickets for shows, which start nightly at 6:30 and 9:30, cost €65–€80. ⊠ *Marne-la-Vallée ☎ 01–60–45–71–00 ⊕ www.disneylandparis.com.*

Château de Vaux-le-Vicomte

48 km (30 miles) south of Disneyland Paris, 5 km (3 miles) northeast of Melun, 56 km (35 miles) southeast of Paris.

A manifesto for French 17th-century splendor, the Château de Vaux-le-Vicomte was built between 1656 and 1661 by finance minister Nicolas Fouquet. The construction program was monstrous. Entire villages were razed; 18,000 workmen were called in; and architect Louis Le Vau, painter Charles Le Brun, and landscape architect André Le Nôtre were recruited at vast expense to prove that Fouquet's taste was as refined as his business acumen. The housewarming party was so lavish it had star guest Louis XIV, testy at the best of times, spitting jealous curses. He hurled Fouquet in the slammer and set about building Versailles to prove just who was top banana. Poor Fouquet may be gone but his home, still privately owned, has survived to astonish and delight centuries of travelers.

GETTING HERE AND AROUND

Take a train from Paris's Gare de Lyon to Melun (25 minutes, €9.30), then a taxi for the 7-km (4-mile) trip to the château (about €20). April through mid-November, a special Châteaubus shuttle runs from the Melun train station (€7 round-trip).

Sights

★ Château de Vaux-le-Vicomte

CASTLE/PALACE | The high-roof Château de Vaux-le-Vicomte, partially surrounded by a moat, is set well back from the road behind iron railings topped with sculpted heads. A cobbled avenue stretches up to the entrance, and stone steps lead to the vestibule, which seems small given the noble scale of the exterior. Charles Le Brun's captivating decoration includes the ceiling of the **Chambre du Roi** (Royal Bedchamber), depicting *Time Bearing*

Louis XIV was so jealous of the splendor of Vaux-le-Vicomte that he promptly went out and built Versailles.

Truth Heavenward, framed by stuccowork by sculptors François Girardon and André Legendre. Along the frieze you can make out small squirrels, the Fouquet family's emblem—squirrels are known as *fouquets* in local dialect. But Le Brun's masterpiece is the ceiling in the **Salon des Muses** (Hall of Muses), a brilliant allegorical composition painted in glowing, sensuous colors that some feel even surpasses his work at Versailles. On the ground floor the impressive **Grand Salon** (Great Hall), with its unusual oval form and 16 caryatid pillars symbolizing the months and seasons, has harmony and style even though the ceiling decoration was never finished.

The state salons are redolent of *le style Louis Quatorze,* thanks to the grand state beds, Mazarin desks, and Baroque marble busts—gathered together by the current owners of the château, the Comte et Comtesse de Vogüé—that replace the original pieces, which Louis XIV trundled off as booty to Versailles. In the basement, where cool, dim rooms were once used to store food and wine and house the château's kitchens, you can find rotating exhibits about the château's past and life-size wax figures illustrating its history, including the notorious 19th-century murder-suicide of two erstwhile owners, the Duc and Duchess de Choiseul-Praslin.

Le Nôtre's carefully restored **gardens**, considered by many to be the designer's masterwork, are at their best when the fountains—which function via gravity, exactly as they did in the 17th century—are turned on (the second and last Saturdays of each month from April through October, 4–6 pm). The popular illuminated evenings, when the château is dazzlingly lighted by 2,000 candles, are held every Saturday from early May to early October. Open for dinner during this event only, the formal Les Charmilles restaurant serves a refined candlelit dinner outdoors, complete with crystal and white linens, on the lovely Parterre de Diane facing the château (reservations essential). There's also a delightful champagne bar with lounge chairs and music on these special evenings. At other times, L'Ecureuil (a more casual eatery) is a good choice for lunch or snacks and you are always welcome to bring along a picnic to enjoy in the extensive gardens. ✉ *Vaux-le-Vicomte* ☎ *01–64–14–41–90* 🌐 *www.vaux-le-vicomte.com* 🎫 *€16.90, candlelight château visits €19.90* ⏲ *Closed early Jan.–mid-Mar.*

🍴 Restaurants

La Table Saint Just

$$$$ | MODERN FRENCH | A pleasing mix of ancient and modern, this colorful, light-filled restaurant, with high-beamed ceilings and limestone walls hung with contemporary art and "candeliers," was once a farmstead on the grounds of the nearby Château de Vaux-le-Pénil. But Isabelle and Fabrice Vitu's warm welcome and Michelin-starred cuisine are the real draws; locals and Parisians alike appreciate the refined menu that includes surprising twists on French classics and plenty of delicacies from the sea. **Known for:** beautiful, intimate setting; excellent wine cellar; top-notch location near the chateau. [$] *Average main: €38* ✉ *11 rue de la Libération, 6 km (4 miles) southwest of Vaux-leVicomte, 13 km (8 miles) northwest of Barbizon, Vaux-le-Pénil* ☎ *01–64–52–09–09* 🌐 *www.restaurant-latablesaintjust.com* ⏲ *Closed Sun., Mon., and Aug.*

Barbizon

17 km (11 miles) southwest of Vaux-le-Vicomte, 52 km (33 miles) southeast of Paris.

On the western edge of the 62,000-acre Forest of Fontainebleau, the village of Barbizon retains its time-stained allure despite the intrusion of art galleries, souvenir shops, and busloads of tourists. The group of landscape painters known as the Barbizon School—Camille Corot, Jean-François Millet, Narcisse Diaz de la Peña, and Théodore Rousseau, among others—lived here from the 1830s on. They paved the way for the Impressionists by their willingness to accept nature on its own terms, rather than using it as an idealized base for carefully structured compositions. Sealed to one of the famous sandstone rocks in the forest—which starts, literally, at the far end of the main street—is a bronze medallion by sculptor Henri Chapu, paying homage to Millet and Rousseau. Threading the village is a Painters Trail (marked in yellow), which links main village landmarks to natural splendors such as the rocky waterfall once painted by Corot.

GETTING HERE AND AROUND

Take a Transilien train from Gare de Lyon to Melun (25 minutes, €8.70) or Avon (38 minutes, €8.90); you can pick up a taxi to Barbizon in either town (around €30).

VISITOR INFORMATION Barbizon Tourist Office ✉ *Pl. Marc Jacquet* ☎ *01–60–66–41–87* 🌐 *www.fontainebleau-tourisme.com.*

👁 Sights

Atelier Jean-François Millet (*Musée Millet*)

MUSEUM | Though there are no actual Millet works, the Atelier Jean-François Millet is cluttered with photographs and mementos evoking his career. It was here that the painter produced some of his most renowned pieces, including *The Gleaners.* ✉ *27 Grande rue* ☎ *01–60–66–21–55* 🌐 *www.musee-millet.com* 🎫 *€5* ⏲ *Closed Tues. year-round and Wed. Nov.–Mar.*

Musée Départemental des Peintres de Barbizon (*Barbizon School Museum*)

MUSEUM | Corot and company would often repair to the Auberge Ganne after painting to brush up on their social life; the inn is now the Musée de Peintres de Barbizon. Here you can find documents detailing village life in the 19th century, as well as a few original works. The Barbizon artists painted on every available surface, and even now you can see some of their creations on the upstairs walls. Two of the ground-floor rooms have been reconstituted as they were in Ganne's time—note the trompe-l'oeil paintings on the buffet doors. There's also a video about the Barbizon School. ✉ *92 Grande rue* ☎ *01–60–66–22–27* 🌐 *musee-peintres-barbizon.fr* 🎟 *€6* ⏲ *Closed Wed.*

🍴 Restaurants

Le Relais de Barbizon

$$$ | **FRENCH** | French country specialties and fish are served at this rustic restaurant with a big open fire and a large terrace shaded by lime and chestnut trees. The three-course weekday menu is a good value, but wine here is expensive and cannot be ordered by the *pichet* (pitcher). **Known for:** lovely leafy terrace; local favorite; top-quality French classic dishes. [$] *Average main: €25* ✉ *2 av. Charles de Gaulle* ☎ *01–60–66–40–28* 🌐 *www.lerelaisdebarbizon.fr* ⏲ *Closed Tues., Wed., part of Aug., and part of Dec.*

★ **L'Ermitage**

$$ | **FRENCH** | Beamed ceilings, tiled floors, and charming accents are just the beginning of a thoroughly enjoyable dining experience at this traditonal bistro in the heart of Barbizon. All the beloved French classics—*chevre chaud*, leeks vinaigrette, *entrecôte de boeuf, noix de St Jacques*, steak tartare—are served just as they're meant to be for lunch and dinner. **Known for:** lovely glassed-in terrace for all seasons; open seven days a week; excellent price-to-quality ratio. [$] *Average main: €18* ✉ *51 Grande rue* ☎ *01–64–81–96–96* 🌐 *www.lermitagesaintantoine.com.*

Courances

11 km (7 miles) west of Barbizon.

Set within one of the most lavish water gardens in Europe, the Château de Courances is a byword for beauty and style.

GETTING HERE AND AROUND

Take the train from Paris's Gare de Lyon to Fontainebleau-Avon, then a La Patache shuttle bus to Courances.

👁 Sights

★ **Château de Courances**

CASTLE/PALACE | Framed by majestic avenues of centuries-old plane trees, Château de Courances's style is Louis Treize, although its finishing touch—a horseshoe staircase (mirroring the one at nearby Fontainebleau)—was an opulent 19th-century statement made by Baron Samuel de Haber, a banker who bought the estate and whose daughter then married into the regal family of the de Behagués. Their descendants, the Marquises de Ganay, have made the house uniquely and famously *chez soi*, letting charming personal taste trump conventional *bon goût*, thanks to a delightful mixture of 19th-century knickknacks and grand antiques. Outside, the vast French Renaissance water gardens create stunning vistas of stonework, grand canals, and rushing cascades. The house can only be seen on a 40-minute tour. ✉ *13 rue de Chateau* ☎ *01–64–98–07–36* 🌐 *www.courances.net* 🎟 *€9.50, €7.50 park only* ⏲ *Park and château closed Nov.–Mar. and weekdays. Château closed July and Aug.*

Fontainebleau

9 km (6 miles) southeast of Barbizon, 61 km (38 miles) southeast of Paris.

Like Chambord in the Loire Valley or Compiègne to the north, Fontainebleau was a favorite spot for royal hunting parties long before the construction of one of France's grandest residences. Although not as celebrated as Versailles, this palace is almost as spectacular.

GETTING HERE AND AROUND

Fontainebleau—or rather, neighboring Avon—is a 38-minute train ride from Paris's Gare de Lyon (€8.90); from here, take one of the frequent shuttle buses to the château, 2 km (1½ miles) away (€4.20 round-trip).

VISITOR INFORMATION Fontainebleau Tourist Office ⊠ 4 bis Pl. de la République ☎ 01–60–74–99–99 ⊕ www.fontainebleau-tourisme.com.

 # Sights

★ Château de Fontainebleau

CASTLE/PALACE | The glorious Château de Fontainebleau was a pinnacle of elegance and grandeur more than 100 years before the rise of Versailles. The château began life in the 12th century as a royal residence and hunting lodge and still retains vestiges of its medieval past, though much of it dates to the 16th century. Additions made by various royal incumbents—including 30 kings of France—through the next 300 years add up to the fascinating and opulent edifice we see today. Fontainebleau was begun under the flamboyant Renaissance king François I, the French contemporary of England's Henry VIII, who hired Italian artists Il Rosso (a pupil of Michelangelo) and Primaticcio to embellish his château. In fact, they did much more: by introducing the pagan allegories and elegant lines of Mannerism to France, they revolutionized French decorative art. Their virtuoso frescoes and stuccowork can be admired in the **Galerie François-Ier** (Francis I Gallery) and in the jewel of the interior, the 100-foot-long **Salle de Bal** (Ballroom), with its luxuriant wood paneling and its gleaming parquet floor that reflects the patterns on the ceiling. Like the château as a whole, the room exudes a sense of elegance and style, but on a more intimate, human scale than at Versailles—this is Renaissance, not Baroque. **Napoléon's apartments** occupied the first floor. You can see a lock of his hair, his Légion d'Honneur medal, his imperial uniform, the hat he wore on his return from Elba in 1815, and one bed in which he definitely did spend a night (almost every town in France boasts a bed in which the emperor supposedly snoozed). Joséphine's **Salon Jaune** (Yellow Room) is one of the best examples of the Empire style—the austere neoclassical style promoted by the emperor. There's also a throne room—Napoléon spurned the one at Versailles, a palace he disliked, establishing his imperial seat in the former King's Bedchamber here—and the Queen's Boudoir, also known as the Room of the Six Maries (occupants included ill-fated Marie-Antoinette and Napoléon's second wife, Marie-Louise).

Although Louis XIV's architectural fancy was concentrated on Versailles, he commissioned Mansart to design new pavilions and had André Le Nôtre replant the gardens at Fontainebleau, where he and his court returned faithfully in fall for the hunting season. But it was Napoléon who spent lavishly to make a Versailles, as it were, out of Fontainebleau.

Created during the reign of Napoléon III for the Empress Eugénie, the exquisite **Théâtre Impérial** was "redisovered" in the early 2000s after being closed up in 1941. Though the theater's sumptuous golden upholstery, lighting, carpets, and gilded boiserie remained surprisingly intact, a restoration will be completed in 2020. Visitors can see this jewel on one of the château's marvelous tours. ⊠ Pl. du Général de Gaulle ☎ 01–60–71–50–70 ⊕ www.chateaudefontainebleau.fr ✉ Napoléon's Apartments and Museum €12; gardens free ⏱ Closed Tues.

Restaurants

★ Frédéric Cassel

$ | MODERN FRENCH | FAMILY | A mandatory stop for pastry and chocolate lovers alike, this master pâtissier excels in classic French confections with all the bells and whistles. Light as air and made with the best ingredients, Cassel's award-winning creations are as beautiful as they are scrumptious. **Known for:** to-die-for mille-feuille; chocolates, caramels, and other French specialty sweets that make great gifts; classic French tea salon. $ *Average main: €9 ⊠ 21 rue des Sablons* ☎ *01–60–71–00–64* ⊕ *www.frederic-cassel.com* ☾ *Closed Mon. No dinner.*

Les Prémices

$$$$ | MODERN FRENCH | Adjoining the property of the stately 17th-century Château de Bourron, in the heart of the Forest of Fontainebleau, this lovely restaurant is well worth the short trip out of town. Bright and airy, with an open terrace in warm weather, the elegant dining room shows meticulous attention to detail—from the crisp table linens to the stylish flower arrangements—all the better to highlight chef Dominique Maès's sophisticated French fare. **Known for:** excellent location; one of the town's few gastronomic tables; romantic atmosphere. $ *Average main: €40 ⊠ 12 bis rue Blaise de Montesquiou, 8 km (5 miles) south of Fontainebleau via D607, Bourron-Marlotte* ☎ *01–64–78–33–00* ⊕ *www.restaurant-les-premices.com* ☾ *Closed Mon., Tues., and late Dec.–early Jan. No dinner Sun.*

Hotels

Aigle Noir

$$ | HOTEL | This may be Fontainebleau's costliest hotel, but it does promise old-world elegance, graceful service, and oodles of atmosphere. **Pros:** period ambience; great location opposite château; emphasis on service. **Cons:** no restaurant; breakfast somewhat lackluster; some rooms could use a spruce-up. $ *Rooms from: €200 ⊠ 27 pl. Napoléon Bonaparte* ☎ *01–60–74–60–00* ⊕ *www.hotelaiglenoir.com* ⇌ *53 rooms* ⦿| *No meals.*

★ Hôtel de Londres

$$ | HOTEL | Established in 1850, the superbly located Londres has been run with pride by the same family for three generations, and guests are treated to a warm welcome by owners who go out of their way to make your stay pleasant. **Pros:** excellent value; château views from some rooms; two-minute walk to the Fontainebleau 18-hole golf course. **Cons:** not all rooms have air-conditioning; limited parking; breakfast not included in price. $ *Rooms from: €156 ⊠ 1 pl. du Général de Gaulle* ☎ *01–64–22–20–21* ⊕ *www.hoteldelondres.com* ☾ *Closed 1 wk in Aug. and Christmas–early Jan.* ⇌ *16 rooms* ⦿| *No meals.*

La Demeure du Parc

$$ | HOTEL | This beautiful design hotel and gourmet restaurant adds a welcome dose of chic to the Fontainebleau lodging and dining scene. **Pros:** quality in-hotel dining and bar; beautiful contemporary decor; set in the center of town close to chateau and all amenities. **Cons:** some rooms are very small; service is still working out kinks; restaurant closed three nights at dinnertime. $ *Rooms from: €170 ⊠ 36 rue Paul Séramy* ☎ *01–60–70–20–00* ⊕ *www.lademeureduparc.fr* ⇌ *27 rooms* ⦿| *No meals.*

Activities

Club Alpin Français

BICYCLING | The Forest of Fontainebleau is laced with hiking trails; the *Guide des Sentiers* (trail guide), available at the tourist office, has details. Bikes can be rented at **La Petite Reine** (⊠ *14 rue de la Paroisse*). The forest is also famed for its quirky rock formations, where many a novice alpinist first caught the climbing bug; for more information contact the Club Alpin Français. ⊠ *24 av. Laumière, Paris* ☎ *01–60–74–57–57* ⊕ *www.ffcam.fr.*

THE LOIRE VALLEY

Updated by
Jennifer Ladonne

👁 Sights   🍴 Restaurants   🛏 Hotels   🛍 Shopping   🍸 Nightlife

★★★★☆   ★★★☆☆   ★★★☆☆   ★★☆☆☆   ★☆☆☆☆

WELCOME TO THE LOIRE VALLEY

TOP REASONS TO GO

★ **Fairy-tale castles:** Play once-upon-a-time at Ussé—gleaming white against an emerald forest backdrop; it's so beautiful, it inspired Perrault's immortal tale.

★ **Chambord:** The world's most impressive rooftop, with a forest of chimneys to match the game-rich woodlands extending in all directions, marks the Loire's grandest château.

★ **Villandry Gardens:** The Renaissance reblooms in these geometric gardens that have been lovingly restored to floricultural magnificence.

★ **Romantic Chenonceau:** Half bridge, half pleasure palace, this epitome of picturesque France extends across the Cher River, so why not row a boat under its arches?

★ **Medieval Fontevraud:** The majestic abbey is the resting place of English kings—and a queen.

1 Tours. The region's central hub.

2 Loches. A medieval town with a famous citadel.

3 Montlouis-sur-Loire. A village with excellent white wines and one blissful hotel château.

4 Amboise. The location of a storied royal château and Leonardo da Vinci's last home.

5 Chenonceaux. Perhaps the most romantic of all France's châteaux.

6 Chaumont-sur-Loire. A château once belonging to Catherine de' Medici.

7 Cheverny. One of the area's more under-the-radar châteaux.

8 Chambord. The most show-stopping château in the region.

9 Orléans. An underrated city with important Joan of Arc history.

10 Meung-sur-Loire. A quiet village with literary history.

11 Blois. A charming town that makes a good base for the region.

12 Villandry. A château with the Loire Valley's most beautiful gardens.

13 Langeais. An often overlooked but wondrous château.

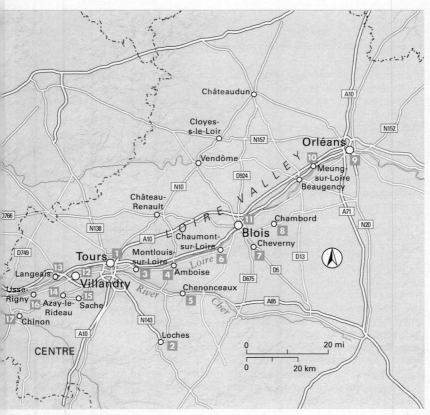

14 Azay-le-Rideau. A gorgeous fairy-tale castle.

15 Saché. Perhaps the Loire's prettiest village.

16 Ussé-Rigny. The château that was the inspiration for Sleeping Beauty.

17 Chinon. A once-upon-a-time town.

18 Fontevraud-L'Abbaye. A small village with the largest abbey in France.

19 Saumur. A romantic medieval town.

20 Angers. A lively city with an imposing château.

A fairy-tale realm par excellence, the Loire Valley is studded with storybook villages, time-burnished towns, and the famous châteaux de la Loire.

These postcard staples, like Chenonceau and Chambord, seem to be strung like pearls across a countryside so serene it could win the Nobel peace prize. With magic at every curve in the road, Cinderella's glass coach might be the optimal way to get around. If that is not available, buses and trains can carry you to the main towns of the three Loire provinces—Anjou (to the west), Orléans (to the east), and the heart of the region, Touraine.

For centuries, the Loire River (France's longest) was the region's principal means of transportation as well as an effective barrier against invading armies—and there were a lot of the latter. The valley was hotly disputed by France and England during the Middle Ages; it belonged to England (under the Anjou Plantagenet family) between 1154 and 1216 and again during the Hundred Years' War (1337–1453). So it's understandable that towering slopes would be fortified early on and that towns would arise at strategic bridgeheads.

But why did the Loire become so prized for its châteaux? With the wars of the 15th century fading, the Loire Valley, long known as "the Garden of France," became a showplace of new and fabulous châteaux d'agrément, or pleasure castles. In short order, there were boxwood gardens endlessly receding toward vanishing points, moats graced with swans, parades of delicate cone-top towers, frescoes, and fancywork ceilings. The glories of the Italian Renaissance, observed by the Valois while making war

on their neighbor, were brought to bear on these mega-monuments with all the elegance characteristic of antiquity.

By the time François I (the flamboyant contemporary of England's Henry VIII) took charge in 1515, extravagance knew no bounds: on a 13,000-acre forest estate, hunting parties at Chambord drew A-list crowds from the far reaches of Europe—and the availability of 430 rooms made weekend entertaining a snap. Queen Claudia hired only the most recherché Italian artisans: Chambord's famous double-helix staircase may, in fact, have been Leonardo da Vinci's design (he was a frequent houseguest when not in residence in a manor on the Amboise grounds). From massive kennels teeming with hunting hounds at Cheverny to luxurious stables at Chaumont-sur-Loire, from endless allées of pollarded lime trees at Villandry to the fanciful towers of Ussé—worthy of Sleeping Beauty herself—the Loire Valley became the power base and social center for the New France, allowing the monarchy to go all out in strutting its stuff.

All for good reason. In 1519 Charles V of Spain, at the age of 19, inherited the Holy Roman Empire, leaving François and his New France out in the cold. It was perhaps no coincidence that in 1519 François, in a grand stab at face-saving one-upmanship, commenced construction on his gigantic Chambord. Centuries later, even the Revolution and the efforts of latter-day socialists have not totally erased a lingering gentility in the people of the region, characterized by an air of refined assurance far removed from the shoulder-shrugging Gallic stereotypes. Here life proceeds at a pleasingly genteel pace, and—despite the delights of the 1,001 châteaux that await—you should, too.

GETTING ORIENTED

The Loire Valley, which pretty much splits France in two, has been heavily traveled through the ages—once by power-hungry armies and peaceful Santiago pilgrims, now by Bordeaux-bound TGV trains. Yet it retains a relaxing backwater feel that mirrors the river's languid, meandering flow. Tours is the main gateway to the region, not only for its central position but because the TGV links it with Paris in little more than an hour. Angers (at the west end of the valley) and Orléans (at the east end) are also well connected to the capital by train. Coming to the Loire by rail and renting a car on arrival in any one of these three cities will save you the hassle of Paris traffic, while still letting you enjoy the flexibility of a châteaux driving tour.

MAJOR REGIONS

The Eastern Loire Valley. East from Tours, strung like precious gems along the peaceful Loire, royal and near-royal châteaux are among the most celebrated sights in France. From magical Chenonceau—improbably suspended above the River Cher—to mighty Chambord, with its 440 rooms, to Amboise (where Leonardo da Vinci breathed his last breath), this architectural conveyor belt moves up along the southern bank to deposit you at Orléans, burnished to old-world splendor with its pedestrian-only *centre ville historique*. (It was here that Joan of Arc had her most rousing successes against the English.) Heading back to Tours on the northern bank, you'll discover the immense palace at Blois and some of the best hotels in the region.

Central and Western Loire Valley. Get your fairy-tale fix by castle-hopping among the most beautiful châteaux in France, from Villandry's fabled gardens to Ussé, which seems to levitate over the unicorn-haunted Forest of Chinon. From the Renaissance jewel of Azay-le-Rideau, continue west to Chinon for a dip in the Middle Ages along its Rue Haute St-Maurice—a pop-up illuminated manuscript. Continue time traveling at the 12th-century royal abbey of Fontevraud, resting place of Richard the Lionheart and Eleanor of Aquitaine. Then fast-forward to the 15th century at Saumur's storybook castle and Angers's brooding fortress.

Planner

When to Go

The Loire Valley divides France in two, both geographically and climatically: to the north is the moist, temperate climate of northern Europe; southward lies the drier climate of the Mediterranean. July and August are peak months for tourism, but the weather then can be hot and sultry, and the top attractions can be packed. Moreover, water levels in Europe's last great undammed river can drop, revealing unsightly sandbanks in midsummer. So the best time to arrive may be in the late spring, when the river still looks like a river and the châteaux gardens are beautifully blooming; or in the fall, when the crowds have thinned and the restaurant menus are showcasing the bounty of harvest and hunt. October is a particularly good off-season option—all is mist and mellow fruitfulness along the Loire and its tributaries.

On Sunday, when most shops are closed, try to avoid the main cities—Orléans, Tours, Angers.

Planning Your Time

More than a region in the usual sense, the Loire Valley is just that: a valley. Although most sites are close to the meandering river, it's a long way—225 km (140 miles)—between Orléans, on the eastern edge, and Angers to the west. If you have 10 days or so you can visit the majority of the destinations we cover. Otherwise, we suggest you divide the valley into three segments and choose the base(s) as time and taste dictate. To cover the eastern Loire (Chambord, Cheverny, Chaumont), base yourself in or near Blois; for the central Loire (Amboise, Chenonceaux, Villandry, Azay-le-Rideau), base yourself in or around Tours; and for the western Loire (Ussé, Chinon, Fontevraud, Angers), opt for pretty Saumur.

Getting Here and Around

The regional rail line along the riverbank will get you to the main destinations (Angers, Saumur, Tours, Blois, Orléans, plus 10 more towns); some other châteaux (Chenonceau, Azay, and Chinon among them) are served by branch lines. Occasionally, you may arrive at the rail station and need to take a taxi or bus to get to a site buried deep in the countryside. The bigger inconvenience with train travel is having to build your itinerary around rail routes and constraining timetables. That makes renting a car a particularly practical option. Given the flattish terrain here, hiring a bike may well appeal, too. Local shuttle and coach excursions are also available for day-trippers, especially during the tourist season, many of them departing from Tours.

BUS TRAVEL

Local bus services can provide a link between train stations and scenic areas off the river, making it possible to reach many villages and châteaux. However, routes are often geared to schoolchildren, meaning service is less frequent in summer and sometimes all but nonexistent on Sunday, so only consider the bus if you have no other options. Inquire at tourist offices about routes and timetables, as the bus companies rarely have information available in English. The leading operators are Les Rapides du Val de Loire, based in Orléans; Rémi, serving Chambord and Cheverny from Blois; Touraine Fil Vert and Fil Bleu, both of which serve the Touraine region, from Amboise in the east to Chinon in the west; and AnjouBus.

BUS INFORMATION AnjouBus ✉ *Esplanade de la gare SNCF, Angers* ☎ *08–20–16–00–49 (€0.34 per min)* ⊕ *aleop. paysdelaloire.fr/maine-et-loire.* **Fil Bleu** ✉ *9 rue Michelet, Tours* ☎ *02–47–66–70–70* ⊕ *www.filbleu.fr.* **Les Rapides du Val de Loire** ✉ *11 av. André Marie Ampère, Saint-Jean-de-Braye* ☎ *02–38–61–90–00* ⊕ *www.rvl-info.com.* **Rémi Centre-Val de Loire** ✉ *26 rue Charles Gille, Tours* ☎ *02–47–05–30–49* ⊕ *www.remi-centre-valdeloire.fr.*

CAR TRAVEL

The Loire Valley is an easy drive from Paris. A10 runs from the capital to Orléans—a distance of around 125 km (78 miles)—and on to Tours, with exits at Meung, Blois, and Amboise. After Tours, A10 veers south toward Poitiers and Bordeaux. A11 links Paris to Angers and Saumur via Le Mans. Slower but more scenic routes run from the Channel ports down through Normandy into the Loire region. Once here, driving is also the most time-efficient way to see the Loire châteaux—and you won't have to sacrifice scenic views; D952, which hugs the riverbank, is excellent for sightseeing. Just note that road signs can be few and far between once you get off the main road, and many a traveler has stories about a 15-minute trip lasting two hours. You can rent a car in Paris, in all the large towns in the region, or at train stations in Orléans, Blois, Tours, and Angers.

TRAIN TRAVEL

Train travel is quite helpful when touring the Loire Valley, as there is one line that goes up and down the river. Be aware, though, that not all destinations are served by rail, so a quick cab or bus ride from the nearest station might be needed to complete your trip.

Tours and Angers are both served by the superfast TGV (Trains à Grande Vitesse) from Paris's Gare Montparnasse, with a travel time of about 75 and 95 minutes, respectively. Loire Valley TGV trains from Charles de Gaulle Airport also go direct to Tours's suburban station in St-Pierre-des-Corps (just under 2 hrs) and to Angers (2 hrs 30 mins). Traditional express trains frequently depart from Paris's Gare d'Austerlitz for Orléans (1 hr) and Blois (1 hr 25 mins).

The main rail line follows the Loire from Orléans to Angers (2 hrs 5 mins); there are trains every few hours to Blois, Tours, and Saumur, as well as multiple daily ones to Onzain (for Chaumont), Amboise, and Langeais. Branch lines run from Tours to Chenonceaux (30 mins), Azay-le-Rideau (30 mins), and Chinon (50 mins).

Ask the SNCF for the brochure Les Châteaux de la Loire en Train for more detailed information. Helpful train-schedule brochures are available at most stations. Be aware that phone calls to the SNCF are charged €0.40 per minute.

TRAIN INFORMATION Gare SNCF Angers ✉ Pl. de la Gare, Angers ☎ 3635 (€0.40 per min). **Gare SNCF Orléans** ✉ Av. de Paris, Orléans ☎ 3635 (€0.40 per min). **Gare SNCF Tours** ✉ Pl. du Général Leclerc, Tours ☎ 3635 (€0.40 per min). **SNCF** ☎ 3635 (€0.40 per min) ⊕ www.voyages-sncf.com. **TGV** ☎ 3635 (€0.40 per min) ⊕ www.sncf.com.

Restaurants

Considering its resplendent châteaux, you might expect that the Loire Valley would feature restaurants fit for royals. Well, it does. The main destinations—Orléans, Tours, Saumur, Chinon, and Angers—all boast top-notch eateries, which take full advantage of the bounty found in the Garden of France. They offer regional cuisine and local wines in venues ranging from the intimate to the intimidating. Expect to pay less than you would in Paris or Lyon, and prepare to come away smiling.

Hotels

Even before the age of the railway, the Loire Valley drew vacationers from far afield, so there are hundreds of hotels of all types. At the higher end are sumptuous, stylishly converted châteaux, but even these are not as pricey as you might think. Note that most are in small villages, and that upscale hotels are in short supply in the major towns. At the lower end is a wide choice of gîtes, bed-and-breakfasts, and small, traditional inns, usually offering terrific value for the money. The Loire Valley is a popular destination, so make reservations well in advance—in July and August, they're essential (and we're talking weeks in advance, not days). Be aware that from November through Easter, many properties are closed.

Restaurant and hotel reviews have been shortened. For full information, visit Fodors.com. Restaurant prices are the average cost of a main course at dinner or, if dinner is not served, at lunch. Hotel prices are the lowest cost of a standard double room in high season.

What It Costs in Euros			
$	$$	$$$	$$$$
RESTAURANTS			
under €18	€18–€24	€25–€32	over €32
HOTELS			
under €106	€106–€145	€146–€215	over €215

Tours

Bus tours of the main châteaux leave daily in summer from Tours and other hubs: tourist offices have the latest times and prices.

Acco-Dispo Tours

EXCURSIONS | Travelers rave about Acco-Dispo van excursions, which usually include two or three top châteaux; half-day trips start at €25 and depart from Tours or Amboise. ✉ *18 rue des Vallees, Amboise* ☎ *06–82–00–64–51* ⊕ *www. accodispo-tours.com* ✉ *From €25.*

France Montgolfiéres

SPECIAL-INTEREST | A tranquil alternative to other tours, France Montgolfières offers balloon rides over the Château de Chenonceau that last one hour, and the experience as a whole takes about three hours. ☎ *03–80–97–38–61* ⊕ *www. franceballoons.com* ✉ *From €189.*

La Bélandre Croisières

BOAT TOURS | Depending on water levels, sightseeing by boat is a possibility. La Bélandre Crosières offers some unique outings; April through October, you can sail the Cher River on a traditional flat-bottom boat from the foot of Chenonceau. ✉ *Maison Eclusière de Chisseaux, Chisseaux* ☎ *02–47–23–98–64* ⊕ *www. labelandre.com* ✉ *From €10.*

Visitor Information

The Loire region has four area tourist offices. For Chinon and points east, contact the Comité Régional du Tourisme du Centre or L'Agence Départementale du Tourisme de Touraine. For Fontevraud and points west, contact the Comité Départemental du Tourisme de l'Anjou or the Comité Départemental du Tourisme des Pays de la Loire.

CONTACTS Comité Départemental du Tourisme de l'Anjou ✉ *Pl. Kennedy, Angers* ☎ *02–41–23–51–51* ⊕ *www.anjou-tourisme.com.* **Comité Départemental du Tourisme des Pays de la Loire** ⊕ *www. atlantic-loire-valley.com* . **Comité Régional du Tourisme du Centre** ✉ *37 av. de Paris, Orléans* ☎ *02–38–79–95–00* ⊕ *www. loirevalley-france.co.uk.* **L'Agence Départementale du Tourisme de Touraine** ✉ *30 rue de la Préfecture, Tours* ☎ *02–47–31–47–48* ⊕ *www.touraineloirevalley.com.*

Tours

240 km (150 miles) southwest of Paris.

Home to about 150,000 residents, Tours is the largest city and commercial center in its area. Vacationers concerned only with the quaint may be put off by the modern sprawl of factories, high-rise blocks, and overhead expressway junctions cluttering up the outskirts; however, Tours does have a lot to offer. Being a transportation hub, it's a practical base—trains run along the river in both directions, and the city is the starting point for many organized bus excursions. Moreover, Tours has a distinct energy, thanks to the university students who make up a fourth of its population and help to fill the many cafés, bars, and eateries in the pedestrian-only Vieille Ville. There's history here as well. Although much of the city was bombed in World War II, the attractive half-timber medieval quarter around Place Plumereau has

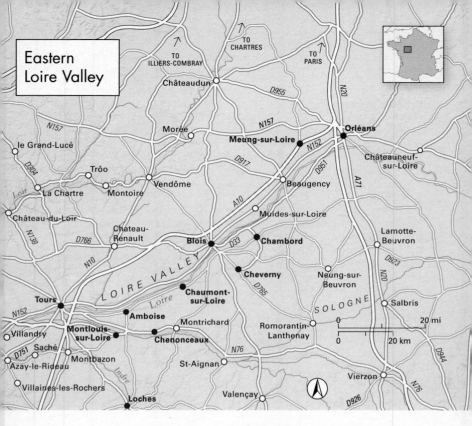

been smartly restored, and Tours's grand cathedral ranks among France's finest.

GETTING HERE AND AROUND

Tours is the Loire Valley rail hub. Eight direct TGVs from Paris's Gare Montparnasse arrive daily, covering 240 km (150 miles) in 75 minutes (€25–€65). A cheaper, slower alternative is the four-times-daily Intercities service from Gare d'Austerlitz, which takes around two hours but costs only €15–€28. Frequent trains also connect Tours to Langeais (20 mins, €5.70), Amboise (20 mins, €5.70), Chenonceaux (30 mins, €7), Azay-le-Rideau (30 mins, €5.90), Blois (35–45 mins, €11.20), Saumur (45 mins, €12.30), Chinon (50 mins, €9.90), Orléans (75 mins, €20.70), Angers (60–95 mins, €19), and other towns.

VISITOR INFORMATION Tours Tourist Office ⊠ *78–82 rue Bernard-Palissy* ☎ *02–47–70–37–37* ⊕ *www.tours-tourisme.fr.*

Sights

Basilique St-Martin

RELIGIOUS SITE | Only two sturdy towers—the Tour Charlemagne and the Tour de l'Horloge (Clock Tower)—remain of the great medieval abbey built over the tomb of St-Martin, the city's 4th-century bishop and patron saint (and credited as the founder of "modern" wine making in France). Most of the abbey, which once dominated the heart of Tours, was razed during the French Revolution. Today the site is occupied by the bombastic neo-Byzantine Basilique St-Martin, which was completed in 1924. There's a shrine to St-Martin in the crypt. ⊠ *Rue Descartes* ☎ *02–47–05–63–87* ⊕ *www. basiliquesaintmartin.fr.*

Cathédral St-Gatien

RELIGIOUS SITE | Built between 1239 and 1484, this noted cathedral, one of the greatest churches of the Loire Valley, reveals a mixture of architectural styles. The richly sculpted stonework of its majestic two-tower facade betrays the Renaissance influence on local château-trained craftsmen. The stained glass dates to the 13th century (if you have binoculars, bring them). Also take a look at both the little tomb with kneeling angels built in memory of Charles VIII and Anne of Brittany's two children, and the **Cloître de La Psalette** (Psalm Cloister), on the south side of the cathedral, where the canons of St-Gatien created some of the most beautiful illuminated manuscripts in medieval Europe. ⊠ *Rue Lavoisier* ☎ *02–47–47–05–19* ⊕ *www.la-psalette. monuments-nationaux.fr* 🖃 *Psalm Cloister €4.*

★ Château de Candé

CASTLE/PALACE | When King Edward VIII of England abdicated his throne in 1937 to marry the American divorcée Wallace Simpson, the couple chose to escape the international limelight and exchange their wedding vows at this elegant 16th-century château. Although it's decorated with period furnishings and features Art Deco bathrooms, all eyes are drawn to the mementos from the Duke and Duchess of Windsor's stay (including the famous Cecil Beaton photographs taken on their big day). Fashionistas will also appreciate the haute-couture wardrobe compiled by the stylish lady of the house, Fern Bedaux. Befitting the owners' flawless taste (if questionable politics, as the Bedauxs were known fascist sympathizers), the château is a particularly pretty example of late Gothic style. ⊠ *10 km (6 miles) southwest of Tours, Monts* ☎ *02– 47–34–03–70* ⊕ *www.domainecande.fr*

🖃 *€7* ⊙ *Closed early-Nov.–early-Apr., and Mon. and Tues. Sept.–June.*

Musée des Beaux-Arts (*Fine Arts Museum*)

MUSEUM | In what was once the archbishop's palace (built into an ancient Roman wall), this museum features an eclectic selection of furniture, sculpture, and wrought-iron work, plus art by Rubens, Rembrandt, Boucher, Degas, and Calder. A favorite is Fritz the Elephant, stuffed in 1902. ⊠ *18 pl. François-Sicard* ☎ *02–47– 05–68–82* ⊕ *www.mba.tours.fr* 🖃 *€6* ⊙ *Closed Tues.*

Musée du Compagnonnage (*Guild Museum*)

MUSEUM | Housed in the cloisters of the 13th-century church of St-Julien, this collection honors the *Compagnonnage,* a sort of apprenticeship-cum-trade-union system. On display you'll see virtuoso 19th-century works produced by candidates for guild membership, some of them eccentric (an Eiffel Tower made of slate, for instance, and a château constructed of varnished noodles). ⊠ *8 rue Nationale* ☎ *02–47–21–62–20* ⊕ *www. museecompagnonnage.fr* 🖃 *€6* ⊙ *Closed Tues. mid-Sept.-mid-June.*

★ Place Plumereau

NEIGHBORHOOD | North from the Basilique St-Martin to the river is **Le Vieux Tours.** This lovely medieval quarter—a warren of quaint streets, wood-beam houses, and grand mansions once owned by 15th-century merchants—has been gentrified with chic apartments and pedestrianized streets. It's centered on Place Plumereau, Tours's erstwhile *carroi aux chapeaux* (hat market). Local college students and tourists alike love to linger in its cafés, and the buildings rimming the square have become postcard staples. Numbers 1 through 7 form a magnificent series of half-timber houses; note the wood carvings of royal money-lenders on Nos. 11 and 12. At the top of the square a vaulted passageway leads to medieval **Place St-Pierre-le-Puellier.**

Running off Place Plumereau are other streets adorned with historic houses, notably Rue Briçonnet—at No. 16 is the **Maison de Tristan,** with a medieval staircase. ✉ *Bordered by Rues du Commerce, Briçonnet, de la Monnaie, and du Grand-Marché.*

🍴 Restaurants

★ Chez Gaster

$$ | **FRENCH** | Picturesque carved doors and medieval rafters set the scene for happy diners to feast on deeply satisfying French dishes updated to please modern palates. Chef Robin Pasquier, of Paris's legendary Akrame restaurant, serves a meat-centric menu that does not skimp on the fish or vegetables, all carefully sourced and prepared with a golden touch, with a stunning list of hand-picked wines to match. **Known for:** imaginative pairings; locally sourced meats and veggies; beautiful setting. [$] *Average main: €22* ✉ *27 rue Colbert* ☎ *02–47–05–79–63* 🌐 *chezgaster.fr* ⏲ *Closed Tues. and Wed.*

Le Petit Patrimoine

$ | **BISTRO** | Locals in the know reserve well in advance to get a table at this tiny restaurant in Vieux Tours, which specializes in traditional regional cuisine. Don't miss Balzac's much-loved Rillons de Tours, a glazed pork dish, and the delicious St-Maure goat cheese. **Known for:** serves Touraine specialties; popular with locals; excellent value fixed-price lunch menus (€13.50; €15.50). [$] *Average main: €15* ✉ *58 rue Colbert* ☎ *02–47–66–05–81* 🌐 *www.lepetitpatrimoine.fr* ⏲ *Closed Sun. and Mon.*

🛏 Hotels

Clarion Hotel Château Belmont

$$$ | **HOTEL** | **FAMILY** | A pleasant mix of the antique and the modern, this attractive lodging offers all the pleasures of a four-star hotel with the modern conveniences of a high-end chain. **Pros:** free parking; walking distance to Tours; nice spa with pool and sauna. **Cons:** tiny fitness room; not an actual château; restaurant not always on point. [$] *Rooms from: €200* ✉ *57 rue Groison, Monts* ☎ *02–47–46–65–00* 🌐 *www.chateaubelmont.com* 🔑 *65 rooms* 🍽 *No meals.*

Domaine de la Tortinière

$$$ | **RESORT** | This was reportedly one of Audrey Hepburn's favorites, and you can immediately see why: the neo-Gothic château, sitting atop a vast, sloping lawn, features a pair of fairy-tale towers, Louis Seize public salons, and soigné guest rooms—some in the turrets, others in the smartly converted stables and servants' quarters. **Pros:** gourmet restaurant; romantic setting; very clean rooms. **Cons:** some rooms on the small side; a bit off the beaten track; decor slightly outdated. [$] *Rooms from: €185* ✉ *10 rte. de Ballan-Miré, 12 km (7 miles) south of Tours, Veigné* ☎ *02–47–34–35–00* 🌐 *www.tortiniere.com* ⏲ *Closed mid-Dec.–Feb.* 🔑 *32 rooms* 🍽 *No meals.*

L'Adresse

$ | **HOTEL** | These functional guest rooms in the heart of Tours's Old Town, a block from half-timbered Place Plumereau and the open-air market, have a fresh look and a pleasant neutral palette; some have whitewashed wood-beam ceilings, while others have Juliet balconies. **Pros:** central location in Vieux Tours; flat-screen TVs; air-conditioning. **Cons:** student district can be very noisy at night; no parking; average breakfast. [$] *Rooms from: €90* ✉ *12 rue de la Rôtisserie* ☎ *02–47–20–85–76* 🌐 *www.hotel-ladresse.com* 🔑 *18 rooms* 🍽 *No meals.*

Les Hautes Roches

$$$$ | **HOTEL** | Far from their original role as monastic cells and even further from the Flintstone-influenced idea of cave dwellings, these luxe-troglodyte lodgings—with their limestone walls, Louis Treize seating, rich fabrics, carved fireplaces, gas lamps, finished marble steps, and riverside setting—exude a quiet luxury amid the soothing elements of

France's Most Famous Châteaux: A History

France's most famous châteaux range in style from medieval fortresses to Renaissance country homes, and they don't skip a beat in between. Today, travelers hop their way from the fairy-tale splendor of Ussé to the imposing dungeons at Angers to the graceful spaces of Chenonceau. But to truly appreciate these spectacular structures, it helps to review their evolution from warlike strongholds to Sleeping Beauty's home.

Origin in the Loire Valley

Loire and château are almost synonymous. There may be châteaux in every region of France, but nowhere are they so thickly clustered as they are in the Loire Valley. There are several reasons for this. By the early Middle Ages, prosperous towns had already evolved due to being strategically sited on the Loire River, and defensive fortresses—the first châteaux—were built by warlords to control certain key points along the route. And with good reason: the riches of this wildly fertile region drew many feuding lords; in the 12th century, the medieval Plantagenet kings of France and England had installed themselves here (at Chinon and Fontevraud, to be exact).

During this time, dukes and counts began to build châteaux, from which they could watch over the king's lands and also defend themselves from each others' invasions. Spare, cold, and uninviting (that being the point), their châteaux were fancy forts. The notion of defense extended to the decor:

massive high-back chairs protected the sitter from being stabbed in the back during dinner, and the credenza was a table used by a noble's official taster to test for poison in the food.

Influence of the Renaissance

These fortifications continued to come in handy during the Hundred Years' War, during which France and England quibbled over the French crown, for 116 years. When that war came to an end, in 1453, King François I went to Italy and came back with the Renaissance (he literally brought home Leonardo da Vinci). The king promptly built a 440-room "Xanadu" (Chambord) in the Italianate style.

By the 15th century, under the later medieval Valois kings, the Loire was effectively functioning as the country's capital, with new châteaux springing up apace, advertising their owners' power and riches. Many were built using a chalky local stone called *tuffeau* (tufa), whose softness and whiteness made it ideal for the sculpted details which were the pride of the new architectural style. The resulting Renaissance pleasure palaces were sumptuous both inside and out—Charles Perrault found the Château de Ussé to be so peaceful and alluring it inspired him to write "Sleeping Beauty" in 1697. A few years before, Louis XIV had started building his new seat of government. It wasn't long before it was "goodbye Loire Valley, hello Versailles."

Spend your first evening in the Loire Valley dining on gorgeous Place Plumereau, hub of the historic district of Tours, gateway to the region.

stone and water. **Pros:** unique troglodyte setting; river views; fabulous gourmet restaurant with terrace. **Cons:** apprentice-style service; busy road (hidden by shrubs) in front of hotel; steep outdoor stairs to access some rooms. [$] *Rooms from: €235* ✉ *86 quai de la Loire, 5 km (3 miles) east of Tours, Rochecorbon* ☎ *02–47–52–88–88* 🌐 *www.leshautes-roches.com* 🕒 *Closed mid-Feb.–Mar.* 🛏 *14 rooms* 🍴 *No meals.*

Loches

42 km (26 miles) southeast of Tours.

It is easy to see why Loches, set on a rocky spur overlooking the Indre Valley, became the 11th-century fief of Foulques Nerra, the warrior Count of Anjou.

GETTING HERE AND AROUND

More than a dozen daily buses and a few trains link Loches to Tours; all cost €9.60 and take 45–75 minutes, depending on time of day. Upon arrival, be sure to get a map of the town from the tourist office—nearly every street will lead you to medieval drawbridges, ancient houses, and towering ramparts.

VISITOR INFORMATION Loches Tourist Office ✉ *Pl. la Marne, Loches* ☎ *02–47–91–82–82* 🌐 *www.loches-touraine-cotesud.com.*

Sights

★ Cité Royale

CASTLE/PALACE | FAMILY | A "Cité Royale," Loche came to be adorned with a bevy of gorgeously picturesque medieval and Renaissance-era structures—none more imposing than its famous Citadelle, one of the most complete medieval fortifications extant, bristling with portcullises, posterns, keeps, and crenellated ramparts. Sections of these defensive walls are well preserved and function as part of the town.

By the 15th century Loches had become a pleasure dome. Charles VII and his famous amour, Agnés Sorel, set up shop in the town château, the **Logis Royal**, located on the north end of the citadel, and proceeded to set the style for much of courtly France with unmatched opulence, Italianate art, and the country's top painter, Jean Fouquet. Great hostess that she was, Agnés might have cottoned to the château's son-et-lumière show, presented during July and August and featuring a goodly chunk of Loches's population in chivalric tableaux.

Elsewhere in town are other historic sights (some with separate admissions): the **Donjon of Fouques Nerra**; the **Tour Ronde of Louis XI** (with its horrifying dungeons and their *fillettes,* or cages); a medieval-style garden; the massive Romanesque church of **Collegiale St-Ours** (on Rue Thomas-Pactius); a magnificent Renaissance-period **Hôtel de Ville,** built for François I; and the **Maison Lansyer,** beautifully set into the town ramparts and fitted out with 19th-century salons filled with the works of painter Emmanuel Lansyer (1835–93). There's also a lively night market during July and August. ✉ *Pl. Charles-VII, Loches* ☎ *02–47–59–01–32* 🌐 *citeroyaleloches.fr* 🎫 *Donjon and Logis Royal €11.*

Montlouis-sur-Loire

11 km (7 miles) east of Tours on south bank of the Loire.

Montlouis—like Vouvray, its sister town on the north side of the Loire—is noted for white wines, and you can learn all about the vintages produced here at the Cave Touristique on Place Courtemanche. Afterward, retreat to the Château de la Bourdaisière, Prince Louis-Albert de Broglie's suitably regal hotel on the eastern side of town (even day-trippers who can't spend a night can visit it on a guided tour).

GETTING HERE AND AROUND

Touraine Fil Vert's Line C bus runs from the Tours bus station to Montlouis-sur-Loire and the Château de la Bourdaisière (30 mins, €2.20); since the town is only 11 km (7 miles) from Tours, a taxi is a faster option.

VISITOR INFORMATION Montlouis-sur-Loire Tourist Office ✉ *4 pl. Abraham Courtemanche* ☎ *02–47–45–85–10* 🌐 *www.tourisme-montlouis-loire.fr.*

🛏 Hotels

★ Château de la Bourdaisière

$$$ | **HOTEL** | A 15th-century jewel of a castle, once the favored retreat of kings François I and Henri IV, is today the luxurious country setting for the Prince de Broglie's hotel—a magnificent place that magically distills all the grace, warmth, and élan of *la vie de châteaux* as no other. **Pros:** exquisite setting; secluded pool; beautiful extensive vegetable gardens. **Cons:** rooms lack air-conditioning; town is a bore; low beams in some stable rooms. [$] *Rooms from: €175* ✉ *25 rue de la Bourdaisière* ☎ *02–47–45–16–31* 🌐 *www.labourdaisiere.com* 🕒 *Closed mid-Nov.–Mar.* 🛏 *29 rooms* 🍴 *No meals.*

Amboise

13 km (8 miles) northeast of Montlouis, 24 km (15 miles) east of Tours.

It is hardly surprising that this hub town is considered a must-see on any Val de Loire itinerary. Crowned by a royal château that's soaked in history (and blood), Amboise also happens to be the site of Leonardo da Vinci's final home, the pretty Clos-Lucé. As if that wasn't enough, it has bustling markets plus an enviable selection of hotels and eateries. The caveat? On hot summer days, the plethora of tour buses turns this Renaissance town into a mass of carbon monoxide.

GETTING HERE AND AROUND

Amboise has frequent train connections with Tours (20 mins, €5.70), Blois (20 mins, €7.20), and many other towns on the main rail route, which follows the banks of the river. From Amboise's station, follow the signs across two bridges to the *centre ville* and Place Richelieu.

VISITOR INFORMATION Amboise Tourist Office ✉ *Quai du Général-de-Gaulle* ☎ *02–47–57–09–28* ⊕ *www.amboise-valdeloire.com.*

Sights

Château d'Amboise

CASTLE/PALACE | The Château d'Amboise became a royal palace in the 15th and 16th centuries. Charles VII stayed here, as did the unfortunate Charles VIII, best remembered for banging his head on a low doorway lintel (you will be shown it) and dying as a result. The gigantic **Tour des Minimes** drops down the side of the cliff, enclosing a massive circular ramp designed to lead horses and carriages up the steep hillside. François I, whose long nose appears in so many château paintings, based his court here, inviting Leonardo da Vinci as his guest. The castle was also the stage for the Amboise Conspiracy, an ill-fated Protestant plot against François II; you're shown where the corpses of the conspirators dangled from the castle walls. Partly due to the fact that most interior furnishings have been lost, most halls here are haunted and forlorn. The maze of underground passages are opened to the public for guided visits (April–September). While exploring the grounds, don't miss the little chapel of St-Hubert; built in the 1490s, this Flamboyant Gothic gem is fronted by a glorious tympanum, adorned with carvings, and graced by a tomb that's said to contain the remains of Leonardo. ✉ *Amboise* ☎ *02–47–57–00–98* ⊕ *www.chateau-amboise.com* ⫘ *€13.*

Clos Lucé

GARDEN | FAMILY | If you want to see where "the 20th century was born"—as the curators here like to proclaim—head to the Clos Lucé, about 600 yards up Rue Victor-Hugo from the château. Leonardo da Vinci (1452–1519) spent the last four years of his life in this handsome Renaissance manor, tinkering away at inventions, amusing his patron, King François I, and gazing out over a garden that was planted in the most fashionable Italian manner. The garden was completely restored in 2008 to contain plants and trees found in his sketches, as well as a dozen full-size renderings of machines he designed. The **Halle Interactive** contains working models of some of Leonardo's extraordinary inventions, all built by IBM engineers using the artist's detailed notebooks (by this time Leonardo had put away his paint box because of arthritis). Mechanisms on display include three-speed gearboxes, a military tank, a clockwork car, and a flying machine complete with designs for parachutes. Originally called Cloux, the property was given to Anne of Brittany by Charles VIII, who built a chapel for her that is still here. Some of the house's furnishings are authentically 16th century—indeed, thanks to the artist's presence, Clos Lucé was one of the first places where the Italian Renaissance made inroads in France: Leonardo's *Mona Lisa* and *Virgin of the Rocks,* both of which once graced the walls here, were bought by the king, who then moved them to the Louvre. ✉ *2 rue du Clos-Lucé* ☎ *02–47–57–00–73* ⊕ *www.vinci-closluce.com* ⫘ *€16.*

Hotels

Château de Noizay

$$$$ | HOTEL | Filled with the mystery of the past—this was once the fabled redoubt of the Protestant plotters in the 1559 Amboise Conspiracy—Château de Noizay is fitted out with Renaissance chimneys and salons, a parterre garden, and guest rooms so regal that you may feel like bowing or curtsying to the staff. **Pros:** historic ambience; excellent restaurant; romantic. **Cons:** some rooms have faded decor; high rates for the countryside; no elevator to second-floor rooms.

Eating and Drinking in the Loire Valley

The serene Loire imposes its placid personality throughout this fertile valley. The weather, too, is calm and cool, ideal for creating the Loire's diverse and memorable wines, from the elegant and refined Savennières to the mildly sweet, pretty-in-pink rosés of the Anjou. The culinary repertoire evokes a sense of the good life, with a nod to the royal legacy of châteaux living over centuries past. Many dishes are presented simply, and they couldn't be better: a perfect pike perch, called *sandre*, from the river, bathed in a silky beurre blanc; coq au vin prepared with a fruity red Sancerre; a tender fillet of beef in a Chinon red-wine reduction. It is the wines that highlight the Loire's gastronomic scene, and these alone justify a trip here.

Beurre Blanc

Made with a shallot, wine vinegar, and fish-stock reduction, and swirled with lots of butter, this iconic white sauce originated in the western Loire about a century ago in the kitchen of an aristocrat whose chef devised this variation on the classic béarnaise. Beurre blanc is the perfect accompaniment to the Loire's delicate shad and pike.

Chèvre

With your glass of Pouilly-Fumé, there are few things better than one of the region's tangy, herby, and assertive goat cheeses. Among the best, appellation controlled and farmhouse made: the squat, pyramid-shape Pouligny-St-Pierre; the creamy, cylindrical Ste-Maure de Touraine; and the piquant Crottins de Chavignol from Sancerre. Try a warmed and gooey Crottin atop a salad for a real treat.

Produce

The great kitchens of the royal households that set up throughout the Loire planned menus around the magnificent produce that thrives in this fecund region dubbed "the Garden of France." Local cooks still do. There are fat white asparagus in the spring; peas, red cherries, haricots verts, artichokes, and lettuces in the summer; followed by apples, pears, cabbages, and pumpkins in the fall.

Tarte Tatin

This luscious "upside-down" apple tart is sometimes claimed by Normandy, but originated, so legend has it, at the Hôtel tatin in the Loire Valley town of Beuvron-Lamotte south of Orléans. The best tarte Tatins are made with deeply caramelized apples cooked under a buttery puff pastry, then inverted and served while still warm.

White Wines (Reds, Too!)

The Loire region boasts not only dazzling châteaux, but also some of the best wines in France—this is an important region for white-wine lovers, thanks to great chenin blanc and sauvignon blanc grapes. Top white appellations to imbibe, starting at the eastern end of the Loire and moving west, include flinty Sancerres, slightly smoky Pouilly-Fumés, vigorous and complex Vouvrays, distinguished Savennières, sparkling Champagne-style Saumurs, and finally light, dry Muscadets, perfect with oysters on the half shell. In the realm of reds, try the raspberry-scented reds of Touraine, the heartier Chinons and Bourgueils, and the elegant rosés of the Anjou.

$ Rooms from: €235 ⊠ Promenade de Waulsort, 8 km (5 miles) west of Tours, Noizay ☎ 02–47–52–11–01 ⊕ www.chateaudenoizay.com ⊙ Closed mid-Jan.–mid-Mar. ⊷ 14 rooms ⦿ No meals.

★ Château de Perreux

$$$ | HOTEL | Though as magnificent a château as you'll find, the spacious and tasteful interiors are in a resolutely contemporary style that harmonizes with the manor's elegant bones. **Pros:** top-notch service; spacious rooms and bathrooms; quality restaurant on the premises. **Cons:** no bar, but drinks can be enjoyed in common rooms and outdoors; books up quickly in high season; those seeking old-fashioned charm may be disappointed. $ Rooms from: €162 ⊠ 36 rue de Pocé ☎ 02–47–57–27–47 ⊕ www.chateaudeperreux.fr ⊷ 11 rooms ⦿ Free Breakfast.

★ Château de Pray

$$$ | HOTEL | Like a Rolls-Royce Silver Cloud, this hotel keeps purring along, decade after decade, offering many delights: a romantic twin-tower château, a Loire River vista, tranquil guest rooms (four of the less expensive are in a charming "Pavillon Renaissance"), and an excellent restaurant. **Pros:** marvelous setting; superlative restaurant; open most of the year. **Cons:** service can be haughty; no bar; decor dated. $ Rooms from: €210 ⊠ Rue du Cèdre, 4 km (2 miles) east of Amboise, Chargé ☎ 02–47–57–23–67 ⊕ www.chateaudepray.fr ⊙ Closed Jan. and 2 wks in Nov. ⊷ 19 rooms ⦿ No meals.

★ Le Manoir Les Minimes

$$$ | HOTEL | Soigné as can be, this stylish 18th-century manoir is lucky enough to preside over a Loire riverbank under the shadow of Amboise's great cliff-side château, offering a calm oasis in a busy town center. **Pros:** historic style; flawlessly elegant; excellent service. **Cons:** overpriced breakfast; no outside food and drink allowed; some rooms have low beams. $ Rooms from: €149 ⊠ 34 quai Charles-Guinot ☎ 02–47–30–40–40 ⊕ www.manoirlesminimes.com ⊙ Closed last wk of Nov.–mid-Dec. and last wk of Jan.–mid-Feb. ⊷ 15 rooms ⦿ No meals.

Le Pavillon des Lys

$$ | HOTEL | An elegant yet laid-back atmosphere defines this stately 18th-century pavilion in the center of Amboise, where airy guest rooms may be done in classic 1930s or contemporary boutique-hotel style; some retain original architectural accents, like exposed beams or heavy wood moldings, and all have refurbished, retro-looking bathrooms. **Pros:** château views from the terrace; free parking; spacious rooms and baths. **Cons:** no on-site restaurant or bar; slightly dated decor; some rooms lack shower. $ Rooms from: €135 ⊠ 9 rue d'Orange ☎ 02–47–30–01–01 ⊕ www.pavillondeslys.com ⊷ 9 rooms ⦿ No meals.

Chenonceaux

12 km (8 miles) southeast of Amboise, 32 km (20 miles) east of Tours.

Achingly beautiful, the Château de Chenonceau has long been considered the "most romantic" of all the Loire châteaux, thanks in part to its showpiece—a breathtaking *galerie de bal* that spans the River Cher like a bridge.

GETTING HERE AND AROUND

Eleven trains run daily between Tours and Chenonceaux (30 mins, €7). The station is a minute's walk from the front gates of the château; across the tracks is the one-road town.

Sights

★ Château de Chenonceau

CASTLE/PALACE | Set in the village of Chenonceaux (spelled with an x) on the River Cher, this was the fabled retreat for the *dames de Chenonceau*, Diane de

Poitiers, Catherine de' Medici, and Mary, Queen of Scots. Spend at least half a day wandering through the château and grounds, and you will see that this monument has an undeniable feminine touch.

More pleasure palace than fortress, the château was built in 1520 by Thomas Bohier, a wealthy tax collector, for his wife, Catherine Briçonnet. When he went bankrupt, it passed to François I. Later, Henri II gave it to his mistress, Diane de Poitiers. After his death, Henri's not-so-understanding widow, Catherine de' Medici, expelled Diane to nearby Chaumont and took back the château. Before this time, Diane's five-arched bridge over the River Cher was simply meant as a grand ceremonial entryway leading to a gigantic château, a building never constructed. It was to Catherine, and her architect, Philibert de l'Orme, that historians owe the audacious plan to transform the bridge itself into the most unusual château in France. Two stories were constructed over the river, including an enormous gallery that runs from one end of the château to the other, a design inspired by Florence's covered Ponte Vecchio, commissioned by a Medici queen homesick for her native town.

July and August are the peak months at Chenonceau, but you can escape the madding crowds by exiting at the far end of the gallery to walk along the opposite bank (weekends only), rent a rowboat to spend an hour just drifting in the river (where Diane used to enjoy her morning dips), and enjoy the **Promenade Nocturne,** an evocative light show performed in the illuminated château gardens.

Before you go inside, pick up an English-language leaflet at the gate. Then walk around to the right of the main building to see the harmonious, delicate architecture beyond the formal garden—the southern part belonged to Diane de Poitiers, the northern was Catherine's—with the river gliding under the arches (providing superb "air-conditioning" to the rooms above). Inside the château are splendid ceilings, colossal fireplaces, scattered furnishings, and paintings by Rubens, del Sarto, and Correggio. As you tour the salons, be sure to pay your respects to former owner Madame Dupin, tellingly captured in Nattier's charming portrait: thanks to the affection she inspired among her proletarian neighbors, the château and its treasures survived the Revolution intact (her grave is enshrined near the northern embankment). The château's history is illustrated with wax figures in the **Musée des Cires** (Waxwork Museum) in one of the château's outbuildings. A cafeteria, tearoom, and the ambitious Orangerie restaurant handle the crowds' varied appetites. ✉ *Chenonceaux* ☎ *08–20–20–90–90 (€0.34 per min)* 🌐 *www.chenonceau.com* 🎫 *€15, includes Musée des Cires; night visit of gardens €6.*

🛏 Hotels

La Roseraie

$ | **HOTEL** | Set around a vast pool terrace and within walking distance of the château, these delightful guest rooms designed with florals, checks, and lace are overseen by charming (and English-speaking) hosts Sabine Müller and Thierry Bellanger. **Pros:** wonderful welcome; free Wi-Fi; verdant setting. **Cons:** some rooms in separate block; street noise in some rooms; decor not to all tastes. [$] *Rooms from: €75* ✉ *7 rue du Dr-Bretonneau* ☎ *02–47–23–90–09* 🌐 *www.hotel-chenonceau.com* 🕓 *Closed mid-Nov.–mid-Mar.* 🛏 *15 rooms* 🍴 *Free Breakfast.*

★ **Le Bon Laboureur**

$$$ | **HOTEL** | In 1882 this ivy-covered inn won Henry James's praise, and, thanks to four generations of the Jeudi family, the author might be even more impressed today—this remains one of the Loire's most wonderful auberges, with guest rooms enchantingly accented in toile de Jouy fabrics and Redouté

pink-and-blue pastels. **Pros:** charming decor; outstanding food; historic atmosphere. **Cons:** small bathrooms; some rooms overlook busy road; service can be indifferent. [$] *Rooms from: €171* ✉ *6 rue du Dr-Bretonneau* ☎ *02-47-23-90-02* 🌐 *www.bonlaboureur.com* 🕒 *Closed 1st wk of Jan.–mid-Feb.* 🛏 *27 rooms* 🍴 *No meals.*

Chaumont-sur-Loire

26 km (16 miles) northeast of Chenonceaux, 21 km (13 miles) southwest of Blois.

Once belonging to Catherine de' Medici, this dramatic hilltop château combines Gothic fortifications with Renaissance style. After touring the stunning interior, be sure to explore the grounds—they're especially gorgeous during the garden show, held annually from April to November.

GETTING HERE AND AROUND

Fifteen trains per day travel from Tours to Onzain Chaumont-sur-Loire, just across the river from the château (30 mins, €8.80); ones from Blois are even more frequent (10 mins, €3.70).

Sights

Château de Chaumont

CASTLE/PALACE | Although a favorite of Loire connoisseurs, the 16th-century Château de Chaumont is often overlooked by visitors who are content to ride the conveyor belt of big châteaux like Chambord and Chenonceau. It's their loss. Set on a dramatic bluff that towers over the river, Chaumont has always cast a spell—perhaps literally so. One of its fabled owners, Catherine de' Medici, occasionally came here with her court "astrologer," the notorious Ruggieri. In one of Chaumont's bell-tower rooms, the queen reputedly practiced sorcery. Whether or not Ruggieri still haunts the place (or Nostradamus, another on Catherine's guest list), there seem to be few castles as spirit-warm as this one.

Built by Charles II d'Amboise between 1465 and 1510, the château greets visitors with glorious, twin-tower *châtelets*—twin turrets that frame a double drawbridge. The castle became the residence of Henri II. After his death, his widow Catherine de' Medici took revenge on his mistress, the fabled beauty Diane de Poitiers, and forced her to exchange Chenonceau for Chaumont. Another "refugee" was the late-18th-century writer Madame de Staël. Exiled from Paris by Napoléon, she wrote *De l'Allemagne* (*On Germany*) here, a book that helped kick-start the Romantic movement in France. In the 19th century her descendants, the Prince and Princess de Broglie, set up regal shop, as you can still see from the stone-and-brick stables, where purebred horses (and one elephant) lived like royalty in velvet-lined stalls. The couple also renovated many rooms in the glamorous neo-Gothic style of the 1870s. Today the castle retains a sense of fantasy: witness the contemporary art installations displayed in different rooms or the latest horticultural innovations showcased during the **Festival International des Jardins,** held from April to November in the extensive park. The château is a stiff walk up a long path from the little village of Chaumont-sur-Loire, but cars and taxis can also drop you off at the top of the hill. ✉ *Chaumont-sur-Loire* ☎ *02-54-20-99-22* 🌐 *www.domaine-chaumont.fr* 🎟 *€18.*

Hotels

Domaine des Hauts-de-Loire

$$$$ | **HOTEL** | Turreted and vine covered, this 18th-century hunting lodge on a 200-acre property features an antiques-filled grand salon, a lovely pool, an adorable swan lake, and guest rooms that more often than not are simply beige and elegantly suave; those in the adjacent coach house can be considerably more

Did You Know?

Catherine de' Medici commissioned Chenon- ceau's river-spanning design because, homesick for her hometown, she wanted to pay homage to Florence's covered Ponte Vecchio.

spectacular—the best have exposed-brick walls and timbered cathedral ceilings. **Pros:** kingly service; luxurious style; superb dining. **Cons:** no château architecture; very pricey restaurant; rooms expensive. [$] *Rooms from: €315* ✉ *79 rue Gilbert Navard, Onzain* ☎ *02–54–20–72–57* 🌐 *www.domainehautsloire.com* ⏲ *Closed most of Dec.–mid-Feb.* 🛏 *36 rooms* 🍴 *Free Breakfast.*

Cheverny

24 km (15 miles) east of Chaumont, 14 km (9 miles) southeast of Blois.

Though not always included on the list of the upper-echelon Loire Valley superstars, the Château de Cheverny is a rare and beautiful example of early-17th-century classical architecture. Made from the pristine white stone of the nearby Cher Valley, its creamy color and graceful symmetry are utterly unique. The château's spectacular interiors, loaded with exceptional artworks and furnishings, is one of the most intact in the Loire, and its meticulously manicured park and gardens are a charming place to wander in any season.

GETTING HERE AND AROUND

TLC provides bus service from Blois (30 mins, €2); it also operates a twice-daily shuttle to Cheverny and Chambord, April through October (€6).

👁 Sights

Château de Cheverny

CASTLE/PALACE | Perhaps best remembered as Capitaine Haddock's mansion in the Tintin comic books, the Château de Cheverny is also iconic for its restrained 17th-century elegance. One of the last in the area to be erected, it was finished in 1634, at a time when the rich and famous had mostly stopped building in the Loire Valley. By then, the taste for quaintly shaped châteaux had given way to disciplined Classicism; so here a white, elegantly proportioned, horizontally coursed, single-block facade greets you across manicured lawns. To emphasize the strict symmetry of the plan, a ruler-straight drive leads to the front entrance. The Louis XIII interior with its stridently painted and gilded rooms, splendid furniture, and rich tapestries depicting the Labors of Hercules is one of the few still intact in the Loire region. Despite the priceless Delft vases and Persian embroideries, it feels lived in. That's because it's one of the rare Loire Valley houses still occupied by a noble family. You can visit a small Tintin exhibition called *Le Secret de Moulinsart* (admission extra), and are free to contemplate the antlers of 2,000 stags in the Trophy Room: hunting, called "venery" in the leaflets, continues vigorously here, with red coats, bugles, and all. In the château's kennels, hordes of hungry hounds lounge around dreaming of their next kill. Feeding times—*la soupe aux chiens*—are posted on a notice board (usually 11:30 am), and you are welcome to watch the "ceremony" (delicate sensibilities beware: the dogs line up like statues and are called, one by one, to wolf down their meal from the trainer). ✉ *Cheverny* ☎ *02–54–79–96–29* 🌐 *www.chateau-cheverny.fr* 🎟 *From €12.*

Chambord

13 km (21 miles) northeast of Chaumont-sur-Loire, 19 km (12 miles) east of Blois, 45 km (28 miles) southwest of Orléans.

The "Versailles" of the 16th century and the largest of the Loire châteaux, the Château de Chambord is the kind of place William Randolph Hearst might have built if he'd had the money. Variously dubbed "megalomaniacal" and "an enormous film-set extravaganza," this is one of the most extraordinary structures in Europe, set in the middle of a royal game forest, with just a cluster of buildings—barely a village—across the road.

GETTING HERE AND AROUND

There is surprisingly little public transportation to Chambord (a state-owned château, to boot). But TLC does make a twice-daily bus trip from Blois (35 mins, €2); April through October, it also runs a twice-daily shuttle that covers both Chambord and Cheverny (€6).

Sights

★ Château de Chambord

CASTLE/PALACE | FAMILY | As you travel the gigantic, tree-shaded roadways that converge on Chambord, you first spot the château's incredible towers—19th-century novelist Henry James said they were "more like the spires of a city than the salient points of a single building"—rising above the forest. When the entire palace breaks into view, it is an unforgettable sight.

With a 420-foot long facade, 440 rooms, 365 chimneys, and a wall that extends 32 km (20 miles) to enclose a 13,000-acre forest, the Château de Chambord is one of the greatest buildings in France. Under François I, building began in 1519, a job that took 12 years and required 1,800 workers. His original grandiose idea was to divert the Loire to form a moat, but someone (perhaps his adviser, Leonardo da Vinci, who some feel may have provided the inspiration behind the entire complex) persuaded him to make do with the River Cosson. François I used the château only for short stays; yet 12,000 horses were required to transport his luggage, servants, and entourage when he came. Later kings also used Chambord as an occasional retreat, and Louis XIV, the Sun King, had Molière perform here. In the 18th century Louis XV gave the château to the Maréchal de Saxe as a reward for his victory over the English and Dutch at Fontenoy (southern Belgium) in 1745. When not indulging in

wine, women, and song, the marshal planted himself on the roof to oversee the exercises of his personal regiment of 1,000 cavalry. Now, after long neglect—all the original furnishings vanished during the French Revolution—Chambord belongs to the state.

There's plenty to see inside. You can wander freely through the vast rooms, filled with exhibits (including a hunting museum)—not all concerned with Chambord, but interesting nonetheless—and lots of Ancien Régime furnishings. The enormous double-helix staircase (probably envisioned by Leonardo, who had a thing about spirals) looks like a single staircase, but an entire regiment could march up one spiral while a second came down the other, and never the twain would meet. The real high point here in more ways than one is the spectacular chimneyscape—the roof terrace whose forest of Italianate towers, turrets, cupolas, gables, and chimneys has been compared to everything from the minarets of Constantinople to a bizarre chessboard. During the year there's a packed calendar of activities on tap, from 90-minute tours of the park in a 4x4 vehicle (€18) to guided carriage tours (€11). A soaring three-story-tall hall has been fitted out to offer lunches and dinners. ⊠ *Chambord* ☎ *02–54–50–40–00* ⊕ *www.chambord. org/en* 🎫 *€13.*

Restaurants

La Maison d'à Côté

$$$$ | MODERN FRENCH | Just a five-minute drive from Chambord in a tiny village, two-Michelin-star La Maison à Côté serves French haute cuisine in an intimate yet contemporary dining room. Chef Christophe Hay insists on local whenever possible and his frequently changing menus, which vary with the seasons, include line-caught fish from the Loire, local Wagyu beef, and caviar de Sologne. **Known for:** gorgeous presentation; superb wine list featuring the local natural and biodynamic estates; gorgeous setting in a small village. $ *Average main: €36* ⊠ *25 rte. de Chambord, Montlivault* ☎ *02–54–20–62–30* ⊕ *www.lamaisondacote.fr* ☽ *Closed Tues., and Wed. Sept.–Apr.*

Hotels

★ Château de Colliers

$$$ | **B&B/INN** | Small enough to feel like a home, stuffed with lovely 18th-century decor, and replete with a beautiful river terrace, this overlooked treasure provides an unforgettable experience in the Loire. **Pros:** authentic antique furnishings; unique riverside setting; hospitable hosts. **Cons:** grounds and exterior a bit worse for wear; surrounding area fairly dull; must have a car to access. $ *Rooms from: €149* ⊠ *D951, 8 km (4 miles) northwest of Chambord, Muides-sur-Loire* ☎ *02–54–87–50–75* ⊕ *www.chateau-colliers.com* ☽ *Closed Sun.–Thurs. Dec.–Feb.* ⊋ *5 rooms* ⦿*| Free Breakfast.*

★ Château de Grotteaux

$$$$ | **B&B/INN** | We could not have dreamed up a more perfect assemblage of setting, building, and decor than this most delightful of bed-and-breakfasts set in the countryside in the golden triangle between Blois, Chambord, and Cheverny. **Pros:** stunning decor and grounds; superb breakfast included in price; superlative, and discreet, service. **Cons:** no restaurant on premises; children younger than 14 not permitted; no pets allowed. $ *Rooms from: €290* ⊠ *4 rue des Grotteaux* ☎ *02–54–52–01–43* ⊕ *www.chateau-grotteaux.com* ⊋ *5 rooms* ⦿*| Free Breakfast.*

Orléans

115 km (23 miles) northeast of Chambord, 112 km (70 miles) northeast of Tours, 125 km (78 miles) south of Paris.

Given that it's surrounded by locales renowned for their beauty, it's little

wonder that Orléans once suffered from an inferiority complex. A century ago ham-fisted urban planners razed many of its fine old buildings; then both German and Allied bombs helped finish the job during World War II. Today, though, Orléans is a thriving commercial city—and, thanks to a decade of sensitive urban renewal, its Vieille Ville (Old Town) has been gorgeously restored, thereby adding enormous charm to the streets between the Loire and the cathedral.

One thing that hasn't changed is the pride locals take in *la pucelle d'Orléans* (the Maid of Orleans)—otherwise known as Joan of Arc. She arrived in 1429 intent on rallying the troops and saving the kingdom from the English during a crucial episode in the Hundred Years' War. Admittedly, there's little left here from the saintly teen's time, but the city honors her through assorted statutes, museum exhibits, and an annual festival (Fêtes de Jeanne d'Arc).

GETTING HERE AND AROUND
Trains from Paris's Gare d'Austerlitz leave for Orléans every hour or so; the 137-km (78-mile) trip takes 60–95 minutes, with a change in suburban Les Aubrais sometimes required (€10–€21.40). Multiple direct trains per day also connect Orléans with Tours (75 mins, €20.70), Blois (25–45 mins, €11.50), and Angers (2 hrs 5 mins, €34.50). Once here, the civic tramway makes it easy to get from the rail station to the Vieille Ville and the banks of the Loire.

VISITOR INFORMATION Orléans Tourist Office ⊠ *2 pl. de l'Etape* ☎ *02–38–24–05–05* ⊕ *www.tourisme-orleansmetropole.com.*

Sights

Cathédrale Ste-Croix

RELIGIOUS SITE | A riot of pinnacles and gargoyles embellished with 18th-century wedding-cake towers, the Cathédrale Ste-Croix is both Gothic and pseudo-Gothic. After most of it was destroyed in the 16th century during the Wars of Religion, Henry IV and his successors rebuilt the cathedral. Novelist Marcel Proust (1871–1922) called it France's ugliest church, but most find it impressive. Inside are dramatic stained glass and 18th-century wood carvings, plus the modern **Chapelle de Jeanne d'Arc** (Joan of Arc Chapel), with a memorial honoring those who died in World War I. ✉ *Pl. Ste-Croix* 🌐 *www.orleans.catholique.fr.*

★ Hôtel Groslot

HOUSE | Just across the square from the cathedral is the Hôtel Groslot, a Renaissance-era extravaganza bristling with caryatids, strap work, and Flemish columns. Inside are regal salons redolent of the city's history (this used to be the Town Hall); they're done up in the most sumptuous 19th-century Gothic Troubadour style and perhaps haunted by King François II, who died here in 1560 by the side of his bride, Mary, Queen of Scots. ✉ *Pl. de l'Étape* ☎ *02–38–79–22–30* 🎟 *Free* 🕒 *Closed Sat., and Oct.–Apr.*

Maison de Jeanne d'Arc (*Joan of Arc House*)

HOUSE | During the 10-day Siege of Orléans in 1429, 17-year-old Joan of Arc stayed on the site of the Maison de Jeanne d'Arc. This faithful reconstruction of the house she knew contains exhibits about her life and costumes and weapons of her time. Several dioramas modeled by Lucien Harmey recount the main episodes in Joan's saintly saga, from the audience at Chinon to the coronation at Reims, her capture at Compiègne, and her burning at the stake at Rouen. ✉ *3 pl. du Général-de-Gaulle* ☎ *02–38–68–32–63* 🌐 *www.jeannedarc.com.fr* 🎟 *€6* 🕒 *Closed Mon.*

Musée des Beaux-Arts (*Fine Arts Museum*)

MUSEUM | Take the elevator to the top of this five-story building across from the cathedral, then make your way down to see works by such artists as Tintoretto, Velázquez, Watteau, Boucher, Rodin, and Gauguin. The museum's richest collection is its 17th-century French paintings, prints, and drawings, reputedly second only to the Louvre. ✉ *1 rue Fernand-Rabier* ☎ *02–38–79–21–55* 🎟 *€6, includes History and Archaeology Museum* 🕒 *Closed Mon.*

Musée Historique et Archéologique (*History and Archaeology Museum*)

MUSEUM | Housed in the **Hôtel Cabu,** a Renaissance mansion restored after World War II, this history and archaeology museum contains works of both "fine" and "popular" art connected with the town's past, including a remarkable collection of pagan bronzes depicting animals and dancers. These were hidden from zealous Christian missionaries in the 4th century and discovered in a sandpit near St-Benoît in 1861. One exhibit is dedicated to the life of Joan of Arc. ✉ *Sq. Abbé-Desnoyers* ☎ *02–38–79–25–60* 🎟 *€6, includes Fine Arts Museum* 🕒 *Closed Mon.*

🍴 Restaurants

★ De Sel et d'Ardoise

$ | FRENCH | With a chef fresh from one of Paris's top new-wave bistros, a chic interior, and a creative and changing menu, this gastrobistro is Orléans's best-kept secret. The finest ingredients—Challans duck, oysters just in from Brittany, and produce from the region's top producers—are in talented hands and add up to dishes of subtlety and sophistication. **Known for:** daily innovations; emphasis on vegetables; selective regional wine list. [$] *Average main: €17* ✉ *44 rue du Faubourg Bannier* ☎ *02–34–50–23–40* 🕒 *Closed Sun. and Mon.*

★ Les Becs à Vin

$ | WINE BAR | There's no forgetting that great wine is the theme at this cozy "bistro à vins," a local foodie favorite that's just the thing for an uncomplicated meal to go with your wine. Choose from the bottle-lined wall or get expert advice from the superfriendly staff. **Known for:** friendly atmosphere; great service; off the tourist radar. [$] *Average main: €12* ✉ *8 pl. du Châtelet* ☎ *09–65–16–64–09* 🌐 *www.becsavin.com.*

🛏 Hotels

Hôtel d'Orléans

$ | **HOTEL** | An excellent base for visiting Orléans, this small boutique hotel is set on a quiet street just minutes from the cathedral and plenty of cafés and restaurants. **Pros:** excellent location; good value; fun bar and lounge area. **Cons:** no free parking; some rooms have handheld showers; breakfast not included in price. [$] *Rooms from: €99* ✉ *6 rue Adolphe Crespin* ☎ *09–77–55–70–84* 🌐 *www.hotel-dorleans.com* 🔑 *19 rooms* 🍴 *No meals.*

Hôtel Escale Oceania Orleans

$ | **HOTEL** | **FAMILY** | If you're looking for basic comfort and good value, this hotel set in a handsome stone building opposite the Loire River is your best bet. **Pros:** helpful staff; free parking; pretty walk along the river into town. **Cons:** 15-minute walk from city center; no refrigerator in rooms; offers convenience, not luxury. [$] *Rooms from: €77* ✉ *16 quai St-Laurent* ☎ *02–38–54–47–65* 🌐 *www.oceaniahotels.co.uk* 🔑 *58 rooms* 🍴 *No meals.*

★ **L'Abeille**

$ | **HOTEL** | Conveniently located on the main shopping street in Orléans, this charming family-run hotel a block from the train/tram station welcomes guests in rooms with fresh floral wall coverings, parquet flooring, and immaculate tiled bathrooms (many as large as the rooms). **Pros:** easily accessible by train; spacious rooms; green philosophy. **Cons:** rooms facing street can be noisy; pricey city parking; breakfast not included in price. [$] *Rooms from: €94* ✉ *64 rue Alsace-Lorraine* ☎ *02–38–53–54–87* 🌐 *www.hoteldelabeille.com* 🔑 *25 rooms* 🍴 *No meals.*

🎫 Performing Arts

Fêtes de Jeanne d'Arc (*Joan of Arc Festival*)

FESTIVALS | Held in late April and early May, the venerable Fêtes de Jeanne d'Arc celebrates the heroic Maid of Orléans with a parade, religious procession, medieval fair, and reenactments of the famous siege of Orléans. ✉ *Orléans* 🌐 *www.fetesjeannedarc.com.*

Meung-sur-Loire

27 km (17 miles) southwest of Orléans.

This tiny, sleepy village's maze of medieval streets and charming half-timbered houses have a literary past. Described by Alexandre Dumas in *The Three Musketeers,* this is also where author Georges Simenon placed the summer house of his beloved Chief Inspector Maigret. Though off-the-beaten Loire path, the picturesque château, which spans many centuries of architecture, is as authentic as it gets and never fails to please visitors—who are blessedly less numerous than at the more frequented Loire châteaux.

GETTING HERE

Direct trains make the short hop from Orléans to Meung-sur-Loire 18 times per day (11 mins, €4.60); a dozen daily trains also arrive from Tours (1 hr, €17.20).

👁 Sights

Château de Meung

CASTLE/PALACE | From the middle of the 12th century until late in the 18th, this château served mainly as the country seat of the bishops of Orléans, although in 1429 Lord Salisbury used it as his headquarters during the Siege of Orléans. Château de Meung was sold after the French Revolution and stood derelict for years before private restoration began in the 1970s. It has

Bike Tour Options

With its nearly flat terrain, the Loire Valley seems custom-built for cycling, and the recently added Loire à Vélo signposted bike trails, extending 800 km (500 miles) from Orléans to the Atlantic Ocean, make it even easier to pedal between each town and village. The bigger communities all have bike rental agencies. One of the top choices is Loire Vélo Nature, which has more than a dozen outlets along the Loire, where you can rent bikes for independent exploration from €16 per day or €60 per week. The Anjou tourism offices in Angers and Saumur also rent out "Cyclopédia" GPS gadgets that attach to your bike and guide you through the paths and sights of the Anjou region. For stress-free cycling,

local bike tour companies such as Biking France and Loire à Vélo offer two- to six-day self-guided vacations costing as little as €150 per day per person, for which they arrange hotels, restaurants, itineraries, maps, baggage transfers, and bike hire. They even have electric bikes for those who prefer to glide *sans* effort.

CONTACTS Anjou Vélo ☎ *02–41–40–20–60 for Saumur Tourist Office* ⊕ *www.anjou-velo.com.* **Biking France** ✉ *2 rue Jean Moulin, Blois* ☎ *02–54–78–62–52* ⊕ *www.biking-france.com.* **Loire à Vélo** ✉ *37 av. de Paris, Orléans* ☎ *02–38–79–95–28* ⊕ *www.loireave-lo.fr.* **Loire Vélo Nature** ✉ *3 av. du 11 Novembre, Bréhémont* ☎ *06–03–89–23–14* ⊕ *www.lav.loirevelonature.com.*

since been furnished with a diverse collection of artifacts that range from age-old antiques to weaponry (the latter run the gamut from medieval crossbows to World War II submachine guns). The most unexpected parts of the hour-long tour are the underground dungeons, chapel, and torture chamber. ✉ *16 pl. du Martroi* ☎ *02–38–44–36–47* ⊕ *www.chateau-de-meung.com* 💶 *€9* 🕑 *Closed Mon., and Jan. and Feb., and weekdays in Mar., Apr., Nov., and Dec.*

Blois

54 km (34 miles) southwest of Orléans, 58 km (36 miles) northeast of Tours.

Perched on a steep hillside overlooking the Loire, the bustling big town of Blois is a convenient base, well served by train and highway. A signposted route leads you on a walking tour of the Vieille Ville (Old Town)—a romantic honeycomb of

twisting alleys, cobblestone streets, and half-timber houses. Its historic highlights include Place St-Louis, where you can find the Maison des Acrobats (note the timbers carved with *jongleurs,* or jugglers), Cathédrale St-Louis, and unexpected Renaissance galleries and staircases lurking in tucked-away courtyards; most visitors, however, are understandably distracted by Blois's superlative, era-bridging château.

GETTING HERE AND AROUND

Multiple direct trains per day leave Paris's Gare d'Austerlitz for Blois, making the 185-km (115-mile) trip in 1 hour 25 minutes (€10–€23.60). There are also dozens of daily trains from Tours (30–45 mins, €11.20) and Orléans (25–45 mins, €11.50), plus multiple direct ones from Angers (85 mins, €27.50).

VISITOR INFORMATION Blois Tourist Office ✉ *23 pl. du Château* ☎ *02–54–90–41–41* ⊕ *www.bloischambord.com.*

Sights

Château de Blois

CASTLE/PALACE | The massive Château de Blois spans several architectural periods and is among the valley's finest. Your ticket entitles you to a guided tour—given in English when there are enough visitors who don't understand French—but you're more than welcome to roam around on your own. Before entering, pause in the courtyard to admire examples of four centuries of architecture. On one side stand the 13th-century hall and tower, the latter offering a stunning view of the town and countryside. The Renaissance begins to flower in the Louis XII wing (built between 1498 and 1503), through which you enter, and comes to full bloom in the François I wing (1515–24). The masterpiece here is the openwork spiral staircase, painstakingly restored. The fourth side consists of the Classical Gaston d'Orléans wing (1635–38). Upstairs in the François I wing is a series of enormous rooms with tremendous fireplaces decorated with the gilded porcupine, emblem of Louis XII, the ermine of Anne of Brittany, and, of course, François I's salamander, breathing fire and surrounded by flickering flames. Many rooms have intricate ceilings and carved gilt paneling. In the council room, the Duke of Guise was murdered by order of Henri III in 1588. Every evening mid-April through mid-September, son-et-lumière shows are staged (audio guides are provided, but the earbuds will set you back €4). ✉ *Blois* ☎ *02–54–90–33–33* 🌐 *www.chateaudeblois.fr* 🎫 *From €12.*

Restaurants

★ Assa

$$$$ | **FRENCH FUSION** | While Blois is graced with several acclaimed restaurants, Assa is a relative newcomer to the scene and a total standout. The spare, serene dining room offers river views and Japanese-theme touches, which is your first clue of what's to come: masterfully prepared Asian-inflected dishes that are as beautiful as they are delicious. **Known for:** much lighter fare than traditional French; excellent price-to-quality ratio; beautiful views. [$] *Average main: €42* ✉ *189 quai Ulysse-Besnard* ☎ *02–54–78–09–01* 🌐 *www.assarestaurant.fr* 🕓 *Closed Mon. and Tues.*

Le Médicis

$$ | **FRENCH** | Decorated in a wacky Renaissance-meets-contemporary style with a coffered ceiling and white linens, this is the domain of highly acclaimed chef-owner Damien Garanger, who turns classic dishes into presentations—picture coquilles St-Jacques with bitter roquette, or thin slices of roast hare with a black currant sauce. The impressive wine list, a veritable primer in Loire wines, includes more than 250 choices. **Known for:** its ugly building; lengthy dining times; reasonable prices. [$] *Average main: €24* ✉ *2 allée François-Ier* ☎ *02–54–43–94–04* 🌐 *www.le-medicis.com* 🕓 *Closed Mon. No dinner Sun. Oct.–June.*

Hotels

Le Clos Pasquier

$$$ | **B&B/INN** | Time seems to have stood still at Claire and Laurent's snug 16th-century countryside manor set on the edge of the forest—an inviting place featuring heavy wooden beams, well-worn terra-cotta floor tiles, and welcoming stone fireplaces. **Pros:** spotless rooms; historic building; gourmet breakfast. **Cons:** no restaurant; away from urban amenities; check-in at 5 pm. [$] *Rooms from: €160* ✉ *10–12 impasse de l'Orée du Bois* ☎ *02–54–58–84–08* 🌐 *www.leclospasquier.fr* 🛏 *4 rooms* 🍴 *Free Breakfast.*

Did You Know?

Almost as famed as the vegetable gardens at the Château de Villandry are its gardens *à la française*, whose hedges are strikingly shaped into symbols, including hearts, fans, and daggers.

Villandry

18 km (11 miles) west of Tours.

The Château de Villandry is one of the best examples of Renaissance-era garden design in France.

GETTING HERE AND AROUND

Fil Bleu buses make frequent trips from Tours (30 mins, €2.70, round-trip).

Sights

★ Château de Villandry

CASTLE/PALACE | Green thumbs get weak in the knees at the mere mention of the Château de Villandry, a grand estate near the Cher River, thanks to its painstakingly relaid 16th-century **gardens,** now the finest example of Renaissance garden design in France. These were originally planted in 1906 by Dr. Joachim Carvallo and Anne Coleman, his American wife, whose passion resulted in three terraces planted in styles that combine the French monastic garden with Italianate models depicted in historic Du Cerceau etchings. Seen from Villandry's cliff-side walkway, the garden terraces look like flowered chessboards blown up to the *n*th power—a breathtaking sight.

Beyond the water garden and an ornamental garden depicting symbols of chivalric love is the famous *potager,* or vegetable garden, which stretches on for bed after bed—the pumpkins here are *les pièces de résistance.* Flower lovers will rejoice in the main *jardin à la française* (French-style garden): framed by a canal, it's a vast carpet of rare and colorful blooms planted *en broderie* ("like embroidery"), set into patterns by box hedges and paths. The aromatic and medicinal garden, its plots neatly labeled in three languages, is especially appealing. Below an avenue of 1,200 precisely pruned lime trees lies an ornamental lake that is home to swans: not a ripple is out of place. The château interior, still used

by the Carvallo family, was redecorated in the mid-18th century; of particular note are the painted and gilt Moorish ceiling from Toledo and one of the finest collections of 17th-century Spanish paintings in France.

The quietest time to visit is usually during the two-hour French lunch break, while the most photogenic time is during the **Nuits des Mille Feux** (Nights of a Thousand Lights, held the first weekends in July and August), when paths and pergolas are illuminated with myriad lanterns and a dance troupe offers a tableau vivant. There is a gardening weekend held in late September. ✉ *3 rue Principale* ☎ *02–47–50–02–09* ⊕ *www.chateauvillandry.com* 🎫 *From €7.*

Hotels

Le Haut des Lys

$ | **HOTEL** | **FAMILY** | Once a Catholic school, this ivy-clad 19th-century building—a 10-minute walk from the Château de Villandry—was completely restored in 2010 for its transformation into a charming boutique hotel. **Pros:** welcoming owners; pretty grounds; close to château and a quaint village. **Cons:** not all rooms air-conditioned; some rooms are much brighter than others; breakfast not included in price. $ *Rooms from: €103* ✉ *Les Barrières Blanches* ☎ *02–47–21–90–90* ⊕ *www.lehautdeslys.com* 🛏 *20 rooms* ❄ *No meals.*

Langeais

10 km (6 miles) west of Villandry.

Sometimes unjustly overlooked, the Château de Langeais—a castle in the true sense of the word—will particularly delight those who dream of knights in shining armor and the chivalric days of yore.

GETTING HERE AND AROUND

There are nine direct trains a day from Tours (20 mins, €5.70) and five from Saumur (25 mins, €8.30). Fil Vert provides a bus link with Chinon (40 mins, €2).

 ## Sights

Château de Langeais

CASTLE/PALACE | FAMILY | Built in the 1460s, bearing a massive portcullis and gate, and never altered, the Château de Langeais has an interior noted for its superb collection of medieval and Renaissance furnishings: its assorted fireplaces, tapestries, chests, and beds would make Guinevere and Lancelot feel right at home. Fifteen-minute waxworks and video shows tell the story of the secret dawn wedding of King Charles VIII with Anne of Brittany in the room where it took place in 1491. Outside, gardens nestle behind sturdy walls and battlements; kids will make a beeline for the playgrounds and tree house. The town itself has other sights, including a Renaissance church tower, but chances are you won't want to move from the delightful outdoor cafés that face the castle entrance. Do follow the road a bit to the right (when looking at the entrance) to discover the charming historic houses grouped around a waterfall and canal. ⊠ *Pl. Pierre de Brosse, Langeais* ☎ *02–47–96–72–60* ⊕ *www.chateau-de-langeais.com* 🎟 *€11.*

Azay-le-Rideau

11 km (7 miles) south of Villandry, 27 km (17 miles) southwest of Tours.

A largish town surrounding a sylvan dell on the banks of the River Indre, pleasant Azay-le-Rideau is famed for its white-wall Renaissance pleasure palace, called "a faceted diamond set in the Indre Valley" by Honoré de Balzac.

GETTING HERE AND AROUND

Azay-le-Rideau is on the main rail line between Tours (30 mins, €5.90) and Chinon (20 mins, €5.30). The Fil Bleu bus network also provides regular service from Tours train station (35 mins, €2.70).

 ## Sights

Château d'Azay-le-Rideau

CASTLE/PALACE | The 16th-century Château d'Azay-le-Rideau was created as a literal fairy-tale castle. When it was constructed, the nouveau-riche treasurer Gilles Berthelot decided he wanted to add tall corner turrets, a moat, and machicolations to conjure up the distant seigneurial past when knighthood was in flower and two families, the Azays and the Ridels, ruled this terrain. It was never a serious fortress—it certainly offered no protection to its builder when a financial scandal forced him to flee France shortly after the château's completion in 1529. For centuries the château passed from one private owner to another until it was finally bought by the state in 1905. Though the interior contains an interesting blend of furniture and artwork (one room is an homage to the Marquis de Biencourt who, in the early 20th century, led the way in renovating château interiors in sumptuous fashion—sadly, many of his elegant furnishings were later sold), you may wish to spend most of your time exploring the enchanting gardens, complete with a moatlike lake. ⊠ *Azay-le-Rideau* ☎ *02–47–45–68–60* ⊕ *www.azay-le-rideau.fr* 🎟 *€11.*

Hotels

Hotel de Biencourt

$ | B&B/INN | Charmingly set on the pedestrian street that leads to Azay's château gates, this shuttered town house has a delightful courtyard-garden that hides an authentic 19th-century schoolhouse, now converted into lodgings cozily furnished in traditional country style (complete with the stray blackboard and school desk). **Pros:** families welcome; free Wi-Fi; organic breakfast. **Cons:** no private parking; thin walls; no on-site restaurant. $ *Rooms from: €86* ⊠ *7 rue Balzac* ☎ *02–47–45–20–75* ⊕ *www. hotelbiencourt.fr* ✆ *Closed mid-Nov.–Mar.* ⤳ *17 rooms* ⦿ *No meals.*

Le Grand Monarque

$ | **HOTEL** | Home to one of France's most beauteous châteaux, Azay should rightly have a hotel that befits the town jewel and this landmark—a three-minute walk from the château gates—nicely fits the bill. **Pros:** fine restaurant with large wine list; town-center setting; free Wi-Fi. **Cons:** some rooms need redecorating; rooms lack character; restaurant serves dinner only and closes early (last service 8:30). $ *Rooms from: €105* ⊠ *1 rue du Château* ☎ *02–47–45–40–08* ⊕ *www.legrand-monarque.com* ✆ *Closed late Dec.–mid-Feb.* ⤳ *25 rooms* ⦿ *No meals.*

 ## Activities

J.C. Leprovost Cycles

BICYCLING | Rent bikes from J.C. Leprovost to ride along the Indre; the area around Azay-le-Rideau is among the most tranquil and scenic in Touraine. ⊠ *13 rue Carnot* ☎ *02–47–45–40–94.*

Saché

7 km (4½ miles) east of Azay-le-Rideau.

A crook in the road, a Gothic church, the centuries-old Auberge du XIIe Siècle, an Alexander Calder stabile (the great American sculptor created a modern atelier nearby), and the country retreat of novelist Honoré de Balzac (1799–1850)—these few but choice elements all add up to Saché, one of the prettiest (and most undiscovered) nooks in the Val de Loire. If you're heading into the town from the east, you're first welcomed by the Pont-de-Ruan—a dream sequence of a flower-bedecked bridge, water mill, and lake that is so picturesque it will practically click your camera for you.

GETTING HERE AND AROUND
No trains serve Saché, but you can ride as far as the Azay-de-Rideau rail station and cover the remaining 7 km (4½ miles) by cab. Alternatively, you can hop Fil Vert's Line 1 bus from Tours (75 mins, €2).

 ## Sights

★ Château de Saché

CASTLE/PALACE | In the center of town, the Château de Saché houses the **Musée Balzac.** If you've never read any of Balzac's "Comédies Humaine," you might find little of interest in it; but if you have, you can return to such novels as *Cousine Bette* and *Eugénie Grandet* with fresh enthusiasm and understanding. Much of the landscape around here, and some of the people back then, found immortality by being fictionalized in many a Balzac novel. Surrounded by 6 acres of gardens, the present château, built between the 16th and the 18th century, is more of a comfortable country house than a fortress. Born in Tours, Balzac came here—to stay with his friends, the Margonnes—during the 1830s, both to write such works as *Le Père Goriot* and to escape his creditors. The château's themed exhibits range from photographs and original manuscripts to the coffee service Balzac used (the caffeine helped to keep him writing up to 16 hours a day). A few period rooms impress with 19th-century charm, including a lavish emerald-green salon and the author's own writing room. Be sure to study some of the corrected book proofs on display. Balzac had to pay for corrections and additions beyond a certain limit. Painfully in debt, he made emendations filling all the margins of his proofs, causing dismay to his printers. Their legitimate bills for extra payment meant that some of his works, best sellers for nearly two

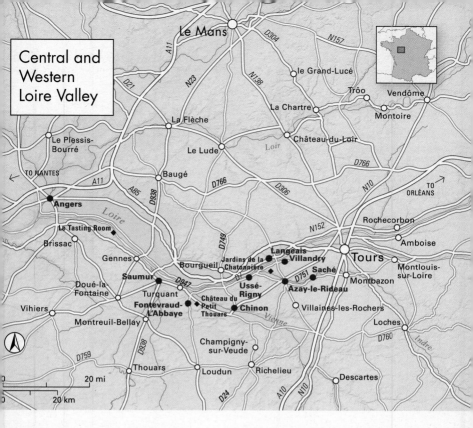

Central and Western Loire Valley

centuries, failed to bring him a centime. ✉ 2 rue de Château ☎ 02–47–26–86–50 ⊕ www.musee-balzac.fr 🎫 €6 ⊗ Closed Tues. Oct.–Mar.

🍴 Restaurants

★ Auberge du XIIe Siècle

$$$ | FRENCH | You half expect Balzac himself to come strolling in the door of this delightful half-timber auberge, so little has it changed since the 19th century, including its centuries-old dining room, now warmed by a fireplace, floral bouquets, and rich wood tables. Balzac's ample girth attested to his great love of food, and he would no doubt enjoy the sautéed lobster or the nouvelle spins on his classic *géline* chicken favorites served here today. **Known for:** lots of extras; charming outdoor terrace; sophisticated presentation. 💲 *Average main: €32* ✉ 1

rue du Château ☎ 02–47–26–88–77 ⊗ Closed Mon. No dinner Sun.; no lunch Tues.

Ussé-Rigny

14 km (9 miles) west of Azay-le-Rideau.

The Loire Valley is blessed with an abundance of eye-popping châteaux, but the fairest of them all is here. The Château d'Ussé, inspiration for Charles Perrault's (and Walt Disney's) "Sleeping Beauty," continues to cast a spell on visitors. There are no good lodging options in Ussé-Rigny, but Chinon makes a good base.

GETTING HERE AND AROUND

If don't have a car, the Château d'Ussé is a hard place to reach. Check with the tourism office in Chinon or Tours for daily shuttles or high-season bus excursions that take in two or three châteaux in a day.

Sights

★ Château d'Ussé

CASTLE/PALACE | FAMILY | The most beautiful castle in France is first glimpsed as you approach the Château d'Ussé, and an astonishing array of blue-slate roofs, dormer windows, delicate towers, and Gothic turrets greets you against the flank of the Forest of Chinon. Literature describes this château, overlooking the banks of the River Indre, as the original "Sleeping Beauty" castle; Charles Perrault, author of this beloved 17th-century tale, spent time here as a guest of the Count of Saumur, and legend has it that Ussé inspired him to write the famous story. Although parts of the castle are from the 1400s, most of it was completed two centuries later. By the 17th century, the region was so secure that one fortified wing of the castle was demolished to allow for grand vistas over the valley and the castle gardens, newly designed in the style Le Nôtre had made so fashionable at Versailles.

Only Disney could have outdone this white tufa marvel: the château is a flamboyant mix of Gothic and Renaissance styles—romantic and built for fun, not for fighting. Its history supports this playful image: it endured no bloodbaths—no political conquests or conflicts—while a tablet in the chapel indicates that even the French Revolution passed it by. Inside, a tour leads you through several sumptuous period salons, a 19th-century French fashion exhibit, and the Salle de Roi bedchamber built for a visit by King Louis XV (the red-silk, canopied four-poster bed is the stuff of dreams). At the end of the house tour, you can go up the fun spiral staircases to the *chemin de ronde* of the lofty towers; there are pleasant views of the Indre River from the battlements, and you can also find rooms filled with waxwork effigies detailing the fable of Sleeping Beauty herself. (Kids will love this.)

Before you leave, visit the exquisite Gothic-becomes-Renaissance chapel in the garden, built for Charles d'Espinay and his wife in 1523–35. Note the door decorated with pleasingly sinister skull-and-crossbones carvings. Just a few steps from the chapel are two towering cedars of Lebanon—a gift from the genius-poet of Romanticism, Viscount René de Chateaubriand, to the lady of the house, the Duchess of Duras. When her famous amour died in 1848, she stopped all the clocks in the house (à la "Sleeping Beauty") so as "never to hear struck the hours you will not come again." The castle then was inherited by her relations, the Comte and Comtesse de la Rochejaquelin, one of the most dashing couples of the 19th century. Today, Ussé belongs to their descendant, the Duc de Blacas, who is as soigné as his castle. If you do meet him, proffer thanks, as every night his family floodlights the entire château, a vision that is one of the Loire Valley's dreamiest sights. Long regarded as a symbol of *la vieille France*, Ussé can't be topped for fairy-tale splendor, so make this a must-do. ✉ *Rigny-Ussé, Rigny-Ussé* ☎ *02–47–95–54–05* ⊕ *www.chateaudusse.fr* 🎫 *€14* ⏱ *Closed mid-Nov.–mid-Feb.*

Chinon

13 km (8 miles) southwest of Rigny-Ussé, 44 km (28 miles) southwest of Tours.

Chinon—the birthplace of author François Rabelais (1494–1553)—is dominated by a 12th-century castle, perched imposingly above the River Vienne. But its leading photo op is the medieval heart of town. Rue Haute St-Maurice, in particular, stretches for more than 15 wondrous, time-warped blocks, and it's virtually

As an overnight guest, Charles Perrault was so seduced by the secluded beauty of Château d'Ussé that he was inspired to write "Sleeping Beauty."

impossible to stroll past the half-timber houses that line it without reaching for your camera. Little wonder that Jean Cocteau used Chinon's fairy-tale allure to effectively frame Josette Day when she appeared as Beauty in his classic 1949 film *La Belle et la Bête*.

GETTING HERE AND AROUND

Trains from Tours pull into Chinon eight times a day (50 mins, €9.90).

VISITOR INFORMATION Chinon Tourist Office ⊠ *1 rue Rabelais* ☎ *02–47–93–17–85* ⊕ *www.ville-chinon.com.*

 Sights

Forteresse de Chinon

CASTLE/PALACE | This vast fortress dates to the time of Henry II of England, who died within its 400-yard long walls in 1189; another historic event occurred in 1429, when Joan of Arc recognized the disguised dauphin (later Charles VII) here. Long years of neglect, however, eventually left the fortress little more than a ruin, completely open to the elements. The

good news is that sweeping restoration work has returned its majestic rooftop, ramparts, and towers to their former glory. A visitor center now welcomes guests a few steps from the glass elevator that provides direct access from the center of Chinon's Old Town. You can tour the **Logis Royal** (Royal Chambers), a section of which has been transformed into an interactive museum dedicated to Joan of Arc. For a bird's-eye look at the landscape, climb the **Tour Coudray** (Coudray Tower), where in 1307 leading members of the crusading Knights Templar were imprisoned before being taken to Paris, tried, and burned at the stake. The **Tour de l'Horloge** (Clock Tower), whose bell has sounded the hours since 1399, has a view over the ensemble of buildings; while the ramparts offer sensational ones over Chinon, the Vienne Valley, and (toward the back of the castle) the famous Le Clos de l'Echo vineyard. A *salon de thé* is open on the terrace from May through September. ⊠ *Chinon* ☎ *02–47–93–13–45* ⊕ *www.forteressechinon.fr* 🍴 *€9.*

Rue Haute St-Maurice
COMMERCIAL CENTER | Once you've visited the castle, recharge your camera batteries and head for the medieval heart of town, Rue Haute St-Maurice. Block after block of storybook half-timber houses make this street a virtual open-air museum that catapults you back to the days of Rabelais. It's also home to one actual museum—the **Musée d'Art et d'Histoire** at No. 44, which is devoted to the arts and crafts of Chinon and surrounding area from prehistory to the 19th century. ✉ *Chinon* 🎟 *Museum €3* 🕒 *Museum closed mid-Nov.–Mar., Tues. May–mid-Sept., and Mon.–Thurs. in Apr. and mid-Sept.–mid-Nov.*

🍴 Restaurants

Les Années Trente
$$$ | **FRENCH** | Located in the heart of medieval Chinon, at the foot of the royal fortress, this spot welcomes diners with a venerable 16th-century facade. A romantic Belle Époque interior continues the historic vibe, but the food—combining fish, game, and regional specialties—is prepared with a light, modern touch. **Known for:** its Michelin star; considered among Chinon's best; uses organic and local ingredients whenever possible. [$] *Average main: €29* ✉ *78 rue Haute St-Maurice* ☎ *02–47–93–37–18* 🌐 *www.lesannees30.com* 🕒 *Closed Tues. and Wed.*

🛏 Hotels

★ **Hôtel Diderot**
$ | **HOTEL** | With its ivy-covered stone, white shutters, mansard roof, dormer windows, and rococo spiral staircase, this hotel looks like an 18th-century François Boucher painting. **Pros:** parking in the courtyard or in a free lot nearby; cozy bar and breakfast room; accessible ground-floor rooms. **Cons:** somewhat worn decor; outdated bathrooms; bar closes at 8:30. [$] *Rooms from: €70* ✉ *4 rue de Buffon* ☎ *02–47–93–18–87* 🌐 *www.hoteldiderot.com* 🛏 *27 rooms* 🍴 *No meals.*

Fontevraud-l'Abbaye

20 km (12 miles) northwest of Chinon.

A refreshing break from the worldly grandeur of châteaux, the small village of Fontevraud is crowned with the largest abbey in France—a magnificent complex of Romanesque and Renaissance buildings that featured prominently in the history of both England and France.

GETTING HERE AND AROUND

Buses connect Saumur and Fontevraud four times per day (30 mins, €1.40). In high season, coach tours and shuttles travel from both Saumur and Chinon—check with town tourist offices for schedules and fares.

VISITOR INFORMATION **Fontevraud-l'Abbaye Tourist Office** ✉ *Pl. St-Michel* ☎ *02–41–51–79–45* 🌐 *www.ot-saumur.fr.*

👁 Sights

★ **Abbaye Royale de Fontevraud**
HISTORIC SITE | Founded in 1101, the Abbaye Royale de Fontevraud (Royal Abbey) had separate churches and living quarters for nuns, monks, lepers, "repentant" female sinners, and the sick. Between 1115 and the French Revolution in 1789, a succession of 39 abbesses—among them a granddaughter of William the Conqueror—directed operations. The great 12th-century **Église Abbatiale** (Abbey Church) contains the tombs of Henry II of England, his wife Eleanor of Aquitaine, and their son, Richard Cœur de Lion (the Lionheart). Although their bones were scattered during the Revolution, their effigies still lie *en couchant* in the middle of the echoey nave. Napoléon turned the abbey church into a prison, and so it remained until 1963, when historical restoration work began.

The **Salle Capitulaire** (Chapter House), adjacent to the church, with its collection of 16th-century religious wall paintings (prominent abbesses served as models), is unmistakably Renaissance; the paving stones bear the salamander emblem of François I. Next to the long refectory is the famously octagonal **Cuisine** (Kitchen), topped by 20 scaly stone chimneys led by the **Tour d'Evrault.** ✉ *Pl. des Plantagenêts* ☎ *02–41–51–73–52* 🌐 *www.fontevraud.fr* 🎟 *€11.*

Allée Sainte-Catherine

HISTORIC SITE | After touring the Abbaye Royale, head outside the gates of the complex a block to the north to discover one of the Loire Valley's most time-burnished streets, Allée Ste-Catherine. Bordered by the Fontevraud park, headed by a charming medieval church, and lined with a few scattered houses (which now contain the town tourist office, a gallery that sells medieval illuminated manuscript pages, and the lovely Licorne restaurant), this street still conjures up the 14th century. ✉ *Fontevraud-l'Abbaye.*

Château du Petit Thouars

CASTLE/PALACE | Try some local wines at the stunning, Renaissance-era Château du Petit Thouars, which enjoys an enchanting hilltop setting just off the Vienne River (between Chinon and Fontevraud). The descendents of Aristide du Petit Thouars, a French naval officer who fought in the American Revolution, have created a small museum illustrating the adventures of their family members that visitors can see after a *dégustation* of still and sparkling wines from their hillside vineyard. The historic château, alas, is still a private home, only to be enjoyed from the outside. ✉ *Rte. de la Chaussee, St-Germain-sur-Vienne* ☎ *02–47–95–96–40* 🌐 *www.chateaudptwines.com* 🎟 *Museum free. Tastings from €5* ⏲ *Closed Sun.*

🍴 Restaurants

La Licorne

$$$ | **FRENCH** | A hanging shop sign adorned with a painted unicorn beckons you to this pretty-as-a-picture 18th-century town-house restaurant on Fontevraud's idyllic Allée Ste-Catherine. Past a flowery garden and table-adorned terrace, tiny salons glow with happy folks feasting on classic French dishes: Loire salmon, boned quail, Triple Sec soufflé, and langoustine ravioli make most diners purr with contentment. **Known for:** close to the abbey; Michelin star; lovely terrace in warm weather. [$] *Average main: €32* ✉ *Allée Ste-Catherine* ☎ *02–41–51–72–49* 🌐 *www.lalicorne-restaurant-fontevraud.fr* 👔 *Jacket required.*

🛏 Hotels

Fontevraud L'Hôtel

$$$ | **HOTEL** | Set within the medieval splendor of Fontevraud, this series of outbuildings was once the abbey's lepers' hospice, but you'd never know it—a gorgeous, understated redesign has made it one of the more unusual hotels in the Loire Valley. **Pros:** serene historic setting; superb restaurant; dedicated to reducing environmental impact. **Cons:** rooms can be small; no minibar and minimal toiletries; don't expect charming period atmosphere. [$] *Rooms from: €172* ✉ *Abbaye Royale, 38 rue St-Jean de l'Habit* ☎ *02–46–46–10–10* 🌐 *www.fontevraud.fr* 🔑 *54 rooms* 🍽 *No meals.*

Saumur

15 km (9 miles) northwest of Fontevraud, 68 km (43 miles) west of Tours.

You'll find putting up with the locals' legendary *snobisme* well worth it once you get a gander at Saumur's *centre historique*, a camera-ready quarter studded with elegant 19th-century town houses and anchored by the vast 12th-century church of St-Pierre. Looming over it all is an equally photogenic riverside castle, the Château de Saumur. Architecture aside, this town (one of the largest along the Loire) is known for agriculture—in particular a flourishing mushroom industry, which produces 100,000 tons per year. The same cool tunnels in which the mushrooms grow provide an ideal storage place for the local *mousseux* (sparkling wines); many of the vineyards hereabouts are open for public tours.

GETTING HERE AND AROUND
More than a dozen daily direct trains link Saumur to Tours (45 mins, €12.30) and Angers (20–30 mins, €9.10).

VISITOR INFORMATION Saumur Tourist Office ✉ *8 bis quai Carnot* ☎ *02–41–40–20–60* ⊕ *www.ot-saumur.fr.*

◉ Sights

Cadre Noir de Saumur (*Riding School*)
COLLEGE | FAMILY | This prestigious national equestrian academy trains France's future riding stars. Unique in Europe, the Cadre Noir de Saumur has 400 horses, extensive stables, five Olympic-size riding rings, and miles of specially laid tracks. Try for a morning tour, which gives you a chance to admire the horses in training. A gala equestrian performance is put on for enthusiastic crowds during special weekends in April, May, July, September, and October; reservations are a must. ✉ *Av. de l'Ecole Nationale d'Equitation* ☎ *02–41–53–50–60* ⊕ *www.cadrenoir.fr* 🎫 *€8* ⊙ *Closed Sun.*

Château de Saumur
CASTLE/PALACE | If you arrive in the evening, the sight of the floodlighted 14th-century Château de Saumur will take your breath away. Look familiar? You've probably seen the elegant white edifice in reproductions of the famous *Très Riches Heures* (Book of Hours) painted for the Duc de Berry in 1416. Inside it's bright and cheerful, with a

gorgeous gateway and plentiful potted flowers. Owing to renovation of the castle walls, the **Musée des Arts Décoratifs** (Decorative Arts Museum) is now housed on the first floor, and exhibitions from the **Musée du Cheval** (Equestrian Museum) can be seen in the adjoining abbey; visitors can also access the gardens and panoramic terrace. In July and August, there are 30-minute medieval-style shows that include music, mime, and dance. From the cliffside promenade beyond the parking lot there's a thrilling vista of the castle on its bluff against the river backdrop. ✉ *Esplanade du Château* ☎ *02–41–40–24–40* ⊕ *www.chateau-saumur.fr* 🎫 *€7* ⊙ *Closed Mon. and Jan.–early-Feb.*

Le Tasting Room
WINERY/DISTILLERY | Based in an ancient farmhouse between Angers and Saumur, Le Tasting Room is a small company that showcases the Loire Valley's best wines through all-inclusive tastings and tours. Run by friendly British transplants Cathy and Nigel Henton, who have more than 25 years of experience in the wine industry, the fun, informative experiences provide you with an insider's perspective. You'll be picked up at Angers train station, given a primer on local wines, served a home-cooked meal, and then taken to see the neighboring vineyards. The Hentons can also recommend local accommodations or help plan your day trip from Paris. ✉ *37 chemin du Lavoir, Saint-Georges-des-Sept-Voies* ☎ *02–41–79–80–21* ⊕ *www.letastingroom.com* 🎫 *From €195.*

Les Caves Louis de Grenelle
WINERY/DISTILLERY | In the center of town and easily accessible on foot or by car, Les Caves Louis de Grenelle offer a fascinating 90-minute tour through the 15th-century quarry tunnels that today serve as aging cellars; a tasting of sparkling and still wines is included. ✉ *839 rue Marceau* ☎ *02–41–50–23–21* ⊕ *www.louisdegrenelle.fr* 🎫 *€3.*

Maison des Vins d'Anjou et de Saumur (*House of Wine*)

INFO CENTER | Saumur is the heart of one of the finest wine regions in France. To pay a call on some of the vineyards around the city, first stop into the Maison des Vins d'Anjou et de Saumur for the full scoop on hours and directions. ✉ *Quai Lucien-Gautier, next door to the Tourism Office* ☎ *02–41–38–45–83* 🌐 *www.vins-de-saumur.com* 🕒 *Closed Sun. and Mon. Oct.–Apr.*

Place St. Pierre

PLAZA | This atmospheric square is the focal point of the warren of streets that make up Saumur's *centre historique*. Fringed by half-timbered houses, many of which have been converted into shops and cafés, it's anchored by the grand Église St-Pierre (whose origins date back to the late 12th century) and serves as a popular destination for a refreshing summer *apéro*. ✉ *Saumur.*

Veuve Amiot

WINERY/DISTILLERY | This long-established producer of Saumur wines offers guided tours of its production facilities and cellars, followed by a wine-tasting session—all free of charge. ✉ *21 rue Jean-Ackerman, Saint-Hilaire-Saint-Florent* ☎ *02–41–83–14–14* 🌐 *www.veuveamiot.fr* 🕒 *Closed Sun. in Jan. and Feb.*

Hotels

Château le Prieuré

$$ | **HOTEL** | Feel royally pampered at this château a few miles from Saumur, where the highlight is the panorama of Loire River and valley majestically spread out before it. **Pros:** views from many rooms, bar, and restaurant; close to a charming village (Chênhutte); fine dining on the premises. **Cons:** not all rooms have views or terraces; opulent decor not to all tastes; larger rooms are pricey. [$] *Rooms from: €145* ✉ *Rue Comté de Castellane* ☎ *02–41–67–90–14* 🌐 *www.younancollection.com/en/chateau-le-prieure/hotel-loire.html* 🛏 *21 rooms* 🍴 *No meals.*

★ **Saint-Pierre**

$$ | **HOTEL** | At the very epicenter of historic Saumur, this little 15th- to 17th-century house is hidden beneath the medieval walls of the church of St-Pierre—look for its entrance on one of the pedestrian passages that circle the nave. **Pros:** central location; sophisticated decor; lovely courtyard and bar. **Cons:** no restaurant; some rooms face busy road; some rooms on the small side. [$] *Rooms from: €125* ✉ *Rue Haute-St-Pierre* ☎ *02–41–50–33–00* 🌐 *www.saintpierresaumur.com* 🛏 *15 rooms* 🍴 *No meals.*

Angers

45 km (28 miles) northwest of Saumur, 88 km (55 miles) northeast of Nantes.

The bustling city of Angers, on the banks of the Maine River just north of the Loire, has a fine Gothic cathedral, a tempting selection of art galleries, plus a network of pleasant, traffic-free streets lined with half-timber houses. Its focal point, though, is the imposing, tower-ringed Château d'Angers. After contemplating the massive, medieval Apocalypse Tapestry, which is beautifully displayed inside it, cap your day with a sip of Cointreau, the popular, locally made liqueur.

GETTING HERE AND AROUND

TGVs from Paris's Gare Montparnasse depart for Angers every hour or so; the 290-km (180-mile) trip takes 95 minutes (€36–€70). Multiple daily direct trains connect Angers to Saumur (20–30 mins, €9.10), Tours (60–95 mins, €19), Blois (85 mins, €27.50), and Orléans (2 hrs, 5 mins; €34.50). Angers's principal sights lie within a compact square formed by the three main boulevards and the Maine, all accessible via the city tramway.

VISITOR INFORMATION Angers Tourist Office ⊠ *7 pl. Kennedy* ☎ *02–41–23–50–00* ⊕ *www.anjou-loire-valley.co.uk.*

 ## Sights

Carré Cointreau

WINERY/DISTILLERY | To learn about the heartwarming liqueur made in Angers since 1849, head to the Carré Cointreau on the east side of the city. Guided tours of the distillery start with an introductory film, move past "Cointreau-versial" advertising posters, through the bottling plant and alembic room with its gleaming copper-pot stills, and end with a tasting. Bus No. 6 from the Angers train station gets you here in 17 minutes. ⊠ *2 bd. des Bretonnières, Saint-Barthélemy-d'Anjou* ☎ *02–41–31–50–50* ⊕ *www.cointreau. com/fr/fr/carre-cointreau* ⊠ *€10* ⊙ *Closed Sun. and Mon.*

Château d'Angers

CASTLE/PALACE | The banded black-and-white Château d'Angers, built by St-Louis (1228–38), glowers over the town from behind turreted moats, now laid out as gardens and overrun with flowers. As you explore the grounds, note the startling contrast between the thick defensive walls, guarded by a drawbridge and 17 massive round towers in a distinctive pattern, and the formal garden, with its delicate white-tufa chapel, erected in the 15th century. For a sweeping view of the city and surrounding countryside, climb one of the castle towers. A well-integrated modern gallery on the castle grounds contains the great **Tenture de l'Apocalypse** (Apocalypse Tapestry), woven in Paris in the 1380s for the Duke of Anjou. Measuring 16 feet high and 120 yards long, its many panels show a series of 70 horrifying and humorous scenes from the Book of Revelation. In one, mountains of fire fall from heaven while boats capsize and men struggle in the water; another features the Beast with Seven Heads. ⊠ *2 promenade du Bout-du-Monde*

☎ *02–41–86–48–77* ⊕ *www.chateau-angers.fr* ⊠ *€9, audio guide €3.*

Musée des Beaux-Arts (*Fine Arts Museum*)

MUSEUM | Set within the 15th-century Logis Barrault, the Musée des Beaux-Arts has an art collection spanning the 14th to the 21st century, as well as a section depicting the history of Angers through archaeological and artistic works from the Neolithic period to the present. The vast museum complex combines historic architecture with contemporary lighting and signage to optimize the experience. ⊠ *14 rue du Musée* ☎ *02–41–05–38–00* ⊕ *www.musees.angers.fr* ⊠ *From €4* ⊙ *Closed Mon. mid-Sept.–early-Apr.*

 ## Hotels

Best Western Hôtel d'Anjou

$$ | **HOTEL** | In business since 1846, the Anjou has vintage stained-glass windows in the Art Deco lobby and spacious guest rooms featuring high ceilings, double doors, and modern bathrooms. **Pros:** central location; stylish public areas; free Wi-Fi. **Cons:** sardine-size elevator; busy street outside; some rooms rather basic. Ⓢ *Rooms from: €130* ⊠ *1 bd. du Maréchal-Foch* ☎ *02–41–21–12–11* ⊕ *www.hoteldanjou.fr* ⟿ *53 rooms* ❌ *No meals.*

Mail

$ | **HOTEL** | A stately lime tree stands sentinel behind wrought-iron, wisteria-framed gates outside this 17th-century mansion with a surprisingly modern interior on a calm street between the Hôtel de Ville and the river. **Pros:** calm; good value; parking available. **Cons:** small rooms; no restaurant or bar; no elevator. Ⓢ *Rooms from: €90* ⊠ *8 rue des Ursules* ☎ *02–41–25–05–25* ⊕ *www.hoteldumail. fr* ⟿ *25 rooms* ❌ *No meals.*

Chapter 6

NORMANDY

Updated by
Diane Vadino

◉ Sights	🍴 Restaurants	🛏 Hotels	🛍 Shopping	🍸 Nightlife
★★★★★	★★★☆☆	★★★☆☆	★★★☆☆	★★☆☆☆

WELCOME TO NORMANDY

TOP REASONS TO GO

★ **Mont-St-Michel:** The spire-top silhouette of this mighty offshore mound, dubbed the Marvel of the Occident, is one of the greatest sights in Europe. Plan to arrive at high tide, when the water races across the endless sands.

★ **Bayeux:** Come not just for the splendor of the tapestry telling how William conquered England, but also for untouched medieval buildings and the beefy, bonnet-top cathedral.

★ **Honfleur:** From France's prettiest harbor, bobbing with boats and lined with beam-fronted houses, you can head to the ravishing wooden church of Ste-Catherine.

★ **Rouen:** Sanctified by the memory of Jeanne d'Arc, hallowed by its towering Gothic cathedral, and graced by a huge Renaissance clock, Rouen is the gateway to Normandy.

★ **D-Day beaches:** Contemplate the dramatic deeds of World War II by visiting Caen's Mémorial, then touring the beaches from rocky Omaha to pancake-flat Utah.

1 Rouen. The region's cultural and commercial capital.

2 Fécamp. A charming fishing town known for its seafood.

3 Étretat. A pretty town with white cliffs and white-sand beaches.

4 Le Havre. France's second-largest port, rebuilt after World War II.

5 Honfleur. A picturesque Flower Coast town.

6 Deauville-Trouville. A pair of Belle Époque resort towns.

7 Cean. The capital of Lower Normandy with medieval and World War II history.

8 Arromanches-les-Bains. A beach town with essential D-Day history.

9 Bayeux. Home to the famed Bayeaux Tapestry.

10 The D-Day Beaches. The five beaches where Allied forces landed during World War II.

11 St-Mère Église. The first French village to be liberated post-D-Day.

12 Granville. A seaside town with a casino and Monaco vibes.

13 Mont-St-Michel. One of France's most glorious, most visited churches.

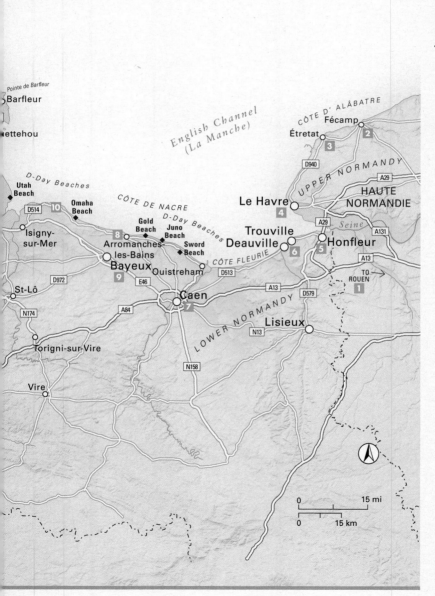

Pointe de Barfleur
Barfleur

ettehou

English Channel
(La Manche)

CÔTE D' ALÂBATRE

Fécamp
2

Étretat
3

D940

UPPER NORMANDY

A29

HAUTE
NORMANDIE

D-Day Beaches

Utah
Beach

D514

10

Omaha
Beach

CÔTE DE NACRE

Le Havre
4

Isigny-
sur-Mer

8

Gold
Beach

Juno
Beach

D-Day Beaches

Trouville
Deauville

A29

Seine

A131

Honfleur
5

Arromanches-
les-Bains

Bayeux

9

E46

Sword
Beach

Ouistreham

CÔTE FLEURIE

D513

6

A13

TO
ROUEN
1

St-Lô

D972

Caen

7

A13

D579

N174

A84

Lisieux

Torigni-sur-Vire

N13

LOWER NORMANDY

N158

Vire

0   15 mi

0   15 km

Normandy—shaped roughly like a jigsaw puzzle piece—sprawls across France's northwestern corner. Due to its geographic position, this region is blessed with a stunning natural beauty that once inspired Maupassant and Monet. Little wonder today's sightseers pack into colorful Rouen, seaside Honfleur, and magnificent Mont-St-Michel.

Happily, it is easy to escape all those travelers. Simply lose yourself along the spectacular cliff-lined coast or in the green spaces inland, where the closest thing to a crowd is a farmer with his herd of brown-and-white cows. Whatever road you turn down, the region is sure to enchant.

Say the name "Normandy," and which Channelside scenario comes to mind? Are you reminded of the dramatic silhouette of Mont-St-Michel looming above the tidal flats, its cobbles echoing with the footfalls of medieval scholars? Or do you think of iron-gray convoys massing silently at dawn, lowering tailgates to pour troops of young Allied infantrymen into the line of German machine-gun fire? At Omaha Beach you may marvel at the odds faced by the handful of soldiers who in June 1944 were able to rise above the waterfront carnage to capture the cliff-top battery, paving the way for the Allies' reconquest of Europe.

Perhaps you think of Joan of Arc—imprisoned by the English yet burned at the Rouen stake by the Church she believed in? In a modern church you may light a candle on the very spot where, in 1431, the Maiden Warrior died at the hands of panicky politicians and time-serving clerics: a dark deed that marked a turning point in the Hundred Years' War.

The destinies of England and Normandy have been intertwined ever since William, Duke of Normandy, insisted that King Edward the Confessor had promised him the succession to the English crown. When a royal council instead anointed the Anglo-Saxon Harold Godwinsson, the irate William stormed across the Channel with 7,000 well-equipped archers, well-mounted knights, and well-paid Frankish mercenaries. They landed at Pevensey Bay on September 28, 1066, and two weeks later, conquered at Hastings.

There followed nearly 400 years of Norman sovereignty in England. For generations England and Normandie (as the French spell it) blurred, merged, and diverged. Today you can still feel the strong flow of English culture over the Channel, from the Deauville horse races frequented by high-born ladies in gloves, to silver spoons mounded high with teatime cream; from the bowfront, slope-roof shops along the harbor at Honfleur to the black-and-white row houses of Rouen, which would seem just as much at home in the setting of *David Copperfield* as they are in *Madame Bovary*.

MAJOR REGIONS

Upper Normandy. Haute-Normandie is anchored by Rouen. Despite being battered in World War II, this alluring gateway city retains such an overwhelming number of churches, chapels, towers, fountains, and old cross-beam houses that many visitors take two full days to soak it all in. Heading some 60 km (35 miles) northwest to the Channel shore, the Côte d'Alabâtre (Alabaster Coast) beckons. Named for the white cliffs that stretch north, it includes the spectacular rock formations at Étretat that inspired Monet to pick up his paintbrush. Nearby Fécamp bridges the sacred and secular with its noted Benedictine abbey and distillery.

Lower Normandy. Basse-Normandie begins with the sandy Côte Fleurie (Flower Coast), announced by seaside Honfleur, an artist's paradise full of half-timber houses. Just south, Rothschilds by the Rolls arrive in season at the Belle Époque beach resort of Deauville. Modern, student-filled Caen is famed for two gigantic abbey churches begun by William the Conqueror, who is immortalized in nearby Bayeux's legendary tapestry. This town makes a great base for exploring somber D-Day sites along Utah and Omaha beaches; bus tours and moving memorials make a fitting prelude for a drive across Normandy's Cotentin Peninsula to Mont-St-Michel, whose tiny island is crowned by one of the most gorgeous Gothic abbeys in France.

Planner

When to Go

July and August are the busiest months but also the most activity filled: concerts are held every evening at Mont-St-Michel, and the region's most important equestrian events are held in Deauville, culminating with the Gold Cup Polo Championship and the Grand Prix race in late August. June 6, the anniversary of the Allied invasion, is the most popular time to visit the D-Day beaches. If you're trying to avoid crowds, come in late spring or early autumn, when it is still fairly temperate. May finds apple trees in full bloom and miles of waving flaxseed fields spotted with tiny sky-blue flowers. Some of Normandy's biggest events take place during these seasons: Rouen, for example, honors Joan of Arc at a festival named for her in late May, and Deauville hosts the American Film Festival in early September.

Planning Your Time

Normandy is a big region with lots to see. If you have 10 days or so you can do it justice; if not, you'll need to prioritize. In search of natural beauty? Head to the coastline north of Le Havre. Prefer sea and sand? Beat it to the beaches west of Trouville. Love little villages? Honfleur is one of France's most picturesque old fishing ports. Like city life? Pretty Rouen is for you. Are you a history buff? Base yourself in Caen to tour the D-Day beaches. Can't get enough of churches and cathedrals? You can go pretty much anywhere, but don't miss Bayeux, Rouen, or Mont-St-Michel. (The last is a bit isolated, so you might want to get there directly from Paris, or at the start or end of a Brittany tour.)

Getting Here and Around

High-speed rail service is very limited in Normandy—perhaps because it's so close to Paris or because it's not on a lucrative route to a neighboring country; depending on your destination, though, the regional rail network can be helpful. Rouen is the train hub for Upper Normandy, Caen for Lower Normandy. Unless you're driving, you'll ultimately need a bus to reach coastal locales like Honfleur and Mont-St-Michel. To visit the D-Day beaches, a guided minibus tour, leaving from Caen or Bayeux, is your best bet. For motorists, the A13 expressway is the gateway from Paris, running northwest to Rouen and then to Caen. From here the A84 takes you almost all the way to Mont-St-Michel, and the N13 brings you to Bayeux. If you're arriving from England or northern Europe, the A16/A28 from Calais to Rouen is a scenic (and near-empty) delight.

AIR TRAVEL

Air travelers will likely land at one of Paris's two major airports and proceed onward by bus, train, or car; however, Normandy does have its own regional facilities. These include Aéroport de Caen-Carpiquet, which receives regular flights from Air France (⊕ www.airfrance. com), budget carrier HOP! (⊕ www.hop. com), and Flybe (⊕ www.flybe.com); and Aéroport de Deauville-Normandie, which receives twice-weekly flights from London operated by Ryanair (⊕ www. ryanair.com). If your primary goal is to see Mont-St-Michel, Ryanair flies from London to the Breton town of Dinard (☎ 02–99–46–18–46 ⊕ www.dinard. aeroport.fr), putting you just 56 km (35 miles) west of the Mont.

AIRPORT INFORMATION Aéroport de Caen-Carpiquet ⊠ Rte. de Caumont, Carpiquet ☎ 02–31–71–20–10 ⊕ www. caen.aeroport.fr. **Aéroport de Deauville–Normandie** ⊠ 9 km (5½ miles) east of Deauville, Deauville ☎ 02–31–65–65–65 ⊕ www.deauville.aeroport.fr.

BUS TRAVEL

Bus Verts du Calvados covers the coast, connecting Caen with Honfleur, Bayeux, and other towns. Bus routes operated by Keolis and VTNI link many destinations, including Rouen, Fécamp, Étretat, Le Havre, Caen, Honfleur, Deauville, Trouville, and Arromanches. For Mont-St-Michel, catch buses from nearby Pontorson, or from St-Malo or Rennes in adjacent Brittany. Schedules are available at tourist offices and at the local gare routière (bus station).

BUS INFORMATION Bus Verts du Calvados ☎ 09–70–83–00–14 ⊕ www.busverts.fr. **Keolis Seine Maritime** ☎ 02–35–28–19–88 ⊕ www.keolis-seine-maritime.com. **VTNI** ⊕ www.vtni.fr.

CAR TRAVEL

From Paris, A13 slices its way to Rouen in 1½ hours (toll €15.20) before forking to Caen (an additional 87 mins, toll €9.20) or Le Havre (45 mins on A131, toll €8.50). N13 continues from Caen to Bayeux in another two hours. At Caen, the A84 forks off southwest toward Mont-St-Michel and Rennes. The Pont de Normandie, spanning the Seine between Le Havre and Honfleur, effectively unites Upper and Lower Normandy.

FERRY AND EUROTUNNEL TRAVEL

A number of companies sail between the United Kingdom and ports in Normandy. Brittany Ferries travels from Portsmouth to Le Havre, Caen, and Cherbourg year-round; its vessels run from Poole to Cherbourg as well. Daily ferries operated by DFDS Seaways connect Newhaven with Dieppe, and Dover with Calais or Dunkirk. The quickest crossing—a four-hour voyage between Newhaven and Dieppe—costs about €85 for a car and two passengers. If you'd rather travel under the Channel than on it, you can drive your car or motorcycle onto a

Eurotunnel Le Shuttle train at Folkestone for the 35-minute trip to Calais.

BOAT INFORMATION Brittany Ferries

☎ *02–98–24–47–01 in France, 0330–159–7000 in U.K.* ⊕ *www.brittanyferries.com.* **DFDS Seaways** ☎ *02–32–14–68–50 in France, 0871–574–7235 in U.K., 0208–127–8303 from U.S.* ⊕ *www.dfds.com.* **Eurotunnel Le Shuttle** ☎ *08–09–10–08–11 in France, 0844–335–3535 in U.K.* ⊕ *www.eurotunnel.com.*

TRAIN TRAVEL

Although there is no direct TGV service from Paris, separate SNCF rail lines originating at Gare St-Lazare head to Upper Normandy (Rouen and Le Havre) and Lower Normandy (Trouville-Deauville, Caen, and Bayeux, sometimes requiring a change in Lisieux). But unless you're content to stick to the major towns, visiting Normandy by train can be frustrating. You can occasionally reach smaller ones on snail-paced branch lines, but the irregular intricacies of what is said to be Europe's most complicated regional timetable may prove daunting. Other destinations, like Honfleur, Étretat, or Mont-St-Michel, invariably require a train-bus combination.

TRAIN INFORMATION Gare SNCF Rouen Rive Droite ⊠ *Pl. Bernard Tissot, Rouen* ☎ *3635* ⊕ *www.gares-sncf.com/fr/gare/frurd/rouen-rive-droite.* **SNCF** ☎ *3635 (€0.40 per min)* ⊕ *www.sncf.com.*

Tours

One of modern history's landmark events—the D-Day invasion of June 1944—was enacted on the beaches of Normandy. Omaha Beach and Utah Beach, as well as many sites on the Cotentin Peninsula, all bear witness to the furious fighting that once raged in this now-peaceful corner of France. Today, as seagulls sweep over the cliffs where American rangers scrambled desperately up ropes to silence murderous

German batteries, visitors wander through the blockhouses and peer into the bomb craters, the carnage of battle now a distant, if still horrifying, memory.

Unless you have a car, the D-Day beaches are best visited by bus. Public ones are relatively rare, but Bus No. 74 does go to Arromanches and Bus No. 70 heads to Omaha Beach and the American cemetery (summer only); both are operated by Bus Verts du Calvados and originate in Bayeux.

D-Day Tours

BUS TOURS | Guided, English-language excursions to the D-Day landing beaches are organized by the Mémorial de Caen, touring either the Anglo-American or Canadian landing beaches. With travel by a seven- or eight-seat minivan, you can select a 5½-hour tour of the beaches (€119) or include pick-up at Caen's railway station and lunch at the memorial's museum restaurant (€135). ⊠ *Esplanade General Eisenhower, Caen* ☎ *02–31–06–06–45* ⊕ *www.memorial-caen.fr.*

Normandy Sightseeing Tours

BUS TOURS | Bayeux-based outfitter Normandy Sightseeing Tours offers half- and full-day options. A half-dozen different itineraries focus on the experiences of the different armies involved; two visit Omaha Beach, while the others take in Gold Beach, the U.S. Army beaches, Sword Beach, Juno Beach, and the Canadian cemetery. ⊠ *5474 bd. Winston Churchill, Bayeux* ☎ *02–31–51–70–52* ⊕ *www.normandy-sightseeing-tours.com* 🚌 *From €65.*

Normandy Tours

BUS TOURS | The guides at Normandy Tours are basically walking encyclopedias of local war lore and can be flexible about focusing on what is interesting to you. Tours of Omaha Beach, German fortifications, Pointe du Hoc, and Gold Beach depart twice daily at 8 am and 1:15 pm, from Bayeux's Hôtel de la Gare. Four- to five-hour half-day tours in English are available year-round; full-day outings are offered as well. ✉ *Hôtel de la Gare, 26 pl. de la Gare, Bayeux* ☎ *02–31–92–10–70* 🌐 *www.normandy-landing-tours.com* 📧 *From €75.*

Restaurants

Most of Normandy's smaller restaurants and family-run eateries rely heavily on seasonal customers, so some close in winter. However, the region's proximity to Paris and its thriving casino culture ensure that the many Michelin-starred options remain open year-round. Local specialties differ from place to place. Rouen is famous for *canard à la rouennaise* (duck in blood sauce); Caen, for *tripes à la mode de Caen* (tripe cooked with carrots in a seasoned cider stock); Mont-St-Michel, for omelets Mère Poulard and *pré-salé* (salt-meadow lamb). Fish and seafood lovers can feast on oysters, lobster, shrimp, and sole *dieppoise* (poached in a sauce with cream and mussels) all along the coast.

Hotels

Accommodations to suit every taste can be found throughout Normandy, from basic bed-and-breakfasts to luxurious hotels—although there's a slimmer selection of the latter than you might expect in the region's two largest cities (Rouen and Caen). Even in popular resort towns like Deauville and Trouville it's possible to find delightful, inexpensive vacation spots. Spending the night on Mont-St-Michel is especially memorable, but be sure to reserve your room weeks in advance. Prices are ratcheted up in summer all along the coast, and you will need to book ahead, especially on weekends. In the beach resorts the season runs from the end of April to October, and many hotels are closed in winter. *Restaurant and hotel reviews have been shortened. For full information, visit Fodors.com.*

What It Costs in Euros

	$	$$	$$$	$$$$
RESTAURANTS				
	under €18	€18–€24	€25–€32	over €32
HOTELS				
	under €125	€125–€225	€226–€350	over €350

Visitor Information

The Normandy Regional Tourist Board's website is an invaluable source of information. For specifics about visiting Upper Normandy, contact Région Haute-Normandie; for Lower Normandy, contact Région Basse-Normandie. The numerous local tourist offices (listed under town names below) are also very useful.

CONTACTS Normandy Regional Tourist Board 🌐 *www.normandie-tourisme. fr .* **Région Basse-Normandie** ✉ *Abbaye-aux-Dames, Pl. Reine Mathilde, Caen* ☎ *02–31–06–98–98* 🌐 *www.normandie. fr.* **Région Haute-Normandie** ✉ *5 rue Robert Schuman, Rouen* ☎ *02–35–52–56–00* 🌐 *www.normandie.fr.*

Rouen

130 km (80 miles) northwest of Paris, 86 km (53 miles) east of Le Havre.

"O Rouen, art thou then to be my final abode!" was the agonized cry of Joan of Arc as the English dragged her out to be burned alive in the market square on May 30, 1431. The exact location of her pyre is marked by a concrete-and-metal cross in front of the modern Église Jeanne-d'Arc—and that eye-catching, flame-evoking church is just one of the many landmarks that makes this sizable port city so fascinating. Once the capital of the duchy of Normandy, it was hit hard during World War II, but a wealth of medieval half-timber houses

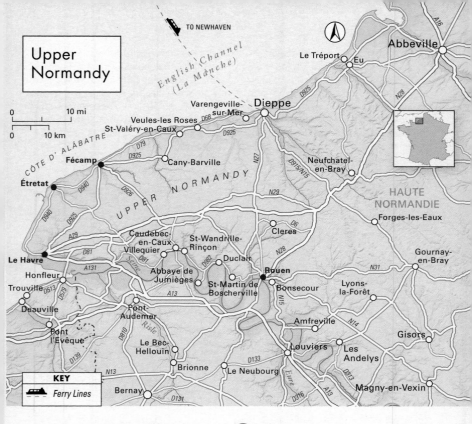

still line the tiny cobblestone streets of Vieux Rouen. The most famous of those streets—Rue du Gros-Horloge, between Place du Vieux-Marché (where Joan burned) and Cathédrale Notre-Dame—is suitably embellished halfway along with a massive and much photographed 14th-century *horloge* (clock). Of course, the glorious cathedral itself is nothing to scoff at: Claude Monet immortalized it in a memorable series of paintings.

GETTING HERE AND AROUND

Rouen-bound trains leave Paris's Gare St-Lazare every half hour or so (90 mins, €24.10); rail links are also available from Le Havre (55 mins, €16).

VISITOR INFORMATION Rouen Tourist Office ⊠ *25 pl. de la Cathédrale* ☎ *02–32–08–32–40* ⊕ *www.rouentourisme.com.*

⊙ Sights

Abbaye St-Ouen

RELIGIOUS SITE | Next to the imposing neo-classical City Hall, this stupendous example of high Gothic architecture is noted for its stained-glass windows, dating to the 14th to 16th centuries. They are the most spectacular grace notes of the spare interior, along with the 19th-century pipe organ, and are among the finest in France. ⊠ *Portail des Marmousets, Pl. du Général-de-Gaulle* ☎ *02–32–08–32–40* ⊕ *www.rouen.fr/abbatiale-saint-ouen* ⊙ *Closed Mon. and Fri.*

Cathédrale Notre-Dame (*Rouen Cathedral*)

RELIGIOUS SITE | Even in the so-called City of 100 Spires, the one crowning this cathedral stands out. Erected in 1876, it's the highest in France—a cast-iron tour de force rising 490 feet above the crossing.

The original 12th-century construction was replaced after a devastating fire in 1200; only the left-hand spire, the **Tour St-Romain** (St. Romanus Tower), survived the flames. Construction on the imposing 250-foot steeple on the right, known as the **Tour de Beurre** (Butter Tower), was begun in the 15th century and completed in the 17th, when a group of wealthy citizens donated large sums of money for the privilege of continuing to eat butter during Lent. Interior highlights include the 13th-century choir, with its pointed arcades; vibrant stained glass depicting the crucified Christ (restored after heavy damage during World War II); and massive stone columns topped by some intriguing carved faces. The first flight of the famous **Escalier de la Librairie** (Library Stairway), attributed to Guillaume Pontifs (also responsible for most of the 15th-century work seen in the cathedral), rises from a tiny balcony just to the left of the transept. ⊠ *Pl. de la Cathédrale, Saint-Maclou-de-Folleville* ☎ *02–35–71–51–23 for tour reservations* ⊕ *www.cathedrale-rouen.net* 🎫 *Tours €2.*

Église Ste-Jeanne-d'Arc (*Joan of Arc Church*)

RELIGIOUS SITE | Dedicated to Joan of Arc, this church was built in the 1970s on the spot where she was burned to death in 1431. The aesthetic merit of its odd cement-and-wood design is debatable—the shape of the roof is *supposed* to symbolize the flames of Joan's fire. Not all is new, however: the church showcases some remarkable 16th-century stained-glass windows taken from the former Église St-Vincent, bombed out in 1944. ⊠ *Pl. du Vieux-Marché, Le Vieux-Marché* ☎ *02–32–08–32–40.*

Église St-Maclou

RELIGIOUS SITE | A late-Gothic masterpiece, this church sits across Rue de la République behind the cathedral and bears testimony to the wild excesses of Flamboyant architecture. Take time to examine the central and left-hand portals of the main facade, covered with little bronze lion heads and pagan engravings. Inside, note the 16th-century organ, with its Renaissance wood carving, and the fine marble columns. Recent renovations revealed the beauty of the church's stone filigree. ⊠ *7 pl. Barthélémy, Saint-Maclou-de-Folleville* ☎ *02–32–08–32–40* ⊗ *Closed Tues.–Fri.*

Gros-Horloge

CLOCK | The name of the pedestrian Rue du Gros-Horloge, Rouen's most popular street, comes from the Gros-Horloge itself, a giant Renaissance clock. In 1527 the Rouennais had a splendid arch built especially for it, and today its golden face looks out over the street. You can see the clock's inner workings from the 15th-century belfry. Though the street is crammed with stores, a few old houses dating to the 16th century remain. Wander through the surrounding **Vieux Rouen** (Old Rouen), a warren of tiny streets lined with more than 700 half-timber houses, many artfully transformed into fashionable shops. ⊠ *Rue du Gros-Horloge, Le Vieux-Marché* ☎ *02–32–08–32–40* 🎫 *€7* ⊗ *Closed Mon.*

L'Historial Jeanne d'Arc (*Joan of Arc Museum*)

MUSEUM | This popular attraction tells the story of Joan of Arc in well-translated videos. As visitors tour the Archbishop's Palace, they follow in Joan's footsteps—she was condemned to death here in 1431 and pardoned posthumously in 1456 following a trial on the second floor. ⊠ *7 rue St-Romain, Gare* ☎ *02–35–52–48–00* ⊕ *www.historial-jeannedarc.fr* ⊗ *Closed Mon.*

Musée de la Céramique (*Ceramics Museum*)

MUSEUM | A superb array of local pottery and European porcelain can be admired at this museum, housed in an elegant mansion near the Musée des Beaux-Arts. ⊠ *1 rue Faucon, Gare* ☎ *02–35–07–31–74* ⊕ *www.museedelaceramique.fr.*

Did You Know?

Dating to the 14th century, the Gros-Horloge clock is the heart of Vieux Rouen, a warren of tiny streets lined with more than 700 half-timber houses, many gorgeously transformed into shops.

Musée des Antiquités

MUSEUM | Gallo-Roman glassware and mosaics, medieval tapestries and enamels, and Moorish ceramics vie for attention inside this extensive antiquities museum. Occupying a former 17th-century monastery, it also has a display devoted to natural history, which includes some skeletons dating to prehistoric times. ⊠ 198 rue Beauvoisine, Gare ☎ 02–76–30–39–50 ⊕ www.museede-santiquites.fr.

Musée des Beaux-Arts (Fine Arts Museum)

MUSEUM | One of Rouen's cultural mainstays, this museum is famed for its stellar collection of paintings and sculptures from the 16th to the 20th century, including works by native son Géricault as well as by David, Rubens, Caravaggio, Velasquez, Poussin, Delacroix, Degas, and Modigliani. Most popular of all, however, is the impressive Impressionist gallery, with Monet, Renoir, and Sisley, plus the Postimpressionist School of Rouen headed by Albert Lebourg and Gustave Loiseau. ⊠ Esplanade Marcel-Duchamp, Gare ☎ 02–35–71–28–40 ⊕ www.mba-rouen.fr ⊘ Closed Tues.

Musée Le Secq des Tournelles (Wrought Iron Museum)

MUSEUM | Not far from the Musée des Beaux-Arts, this museum claims to have the world's finest collection of wrought iron, with exhibits spanning the 4th through 19th centuries. The displays, imaginatively housed in a converted medieval church, include the professional instruments of surgeons, barbers, carpenters, clock makers, and gardeners. ⊠ Rue Jacques-Villon, Gare ☎ 02–35–88–42–92 ⊕ www.museelesecqdestour-nelles.fr ⊘ Closed Tues.

🍴 Restaurants

★ Gill Côté Bistro

$$$ | BISTRO | With two Michelin stars under his toque for his tony gastronomic Restaurant Gill, chef Gilles Tournadre jumped at the chance to open a bistro on Rouen's storied Place du Vieux-Marché. Sleek and modern, it specializes in updated bistro fare, offering a great value fixed-price menu. **Known for:** beloved French classics like magret de canard; local dishes like Rouen-style duck terrine; calling ahead for reservations recommended. $ Average main: €28 ⊠ 14 pl. du Vieux-Marché, Le Vieux-Marché ☎ 02–35–89–88–72 ⊕ www.gill-cote-bistro.fr.

★ La Couronne

$$$$ | MODERN FRENCH | Behind a half-timber facade filled with geraniums, the "oldest inn in France," dating to 1345, is crammed with stained leaded glass, sculpted wood beams, marble Norman chimneys, leather-upholstered chairs, and damask curtains. Fittingly, the star attractions on Vincent Taillefer's menu—lobster stew with Chablis wine, sheeps' feet, duck in blood sauce—make few modern concessions. **Known for:** adorably cozy, wood-lined Salon des Rôtisseurs, an antiquarian's delight; cool history; excellent value, prix-fixe dinner menu. $ Average main: €50 ⊠ 31 pl. du Vieux-Marché, Le Vieux-Marché ☎ 02–35–71–40–90 ⊕ www.lacouronne-rouen.co.uk.

Le 37

$$ | FRENCH | Chef Sylvain Nouin's focus at this sleek little eatery is contemporary bistro fare—and what his monthly changing menu lacks in size (it fits on a small blackboard) it more than makes up for in style. The two-course set menu features dishes like a veal tagine with a confit of dates and lemon, roasted quail with celery mousseline, or tête de veau (calf's head) with an herb vinaigrette; it's a steal at €21.80. **Known for:** excellent price-to-value ratio; solid wine list; shared ownership—and fine results—of Restaurant Gill, at a fraction of the price. $ Average main: €20 ⊠ 37 rue St-Etienne-des-Tonneliers,

Eating and Drinking in Normandy

Normandy's verdant landscape—a patchwork of pastures and orchards bordered by the sea—heralds a region of culinary delights. Apples feature in tarts, cakes, sauces, and *cidre bouché*, a sparkling cider sold in cork-top bottles. Brown-and-white cows—the famous *vaches normandes*—grazing beneath the apple blossoms each produce up to 7 gallons of milk a day, destined to become golden butter, thick crème fraîche, and prized cheeses. Coastal waters from Dieppe to Granville are equally generous, yielding sole, turbot, and oysters.

Apples

One fragrance evokes Normandy—the pungent, earthy smell of apples awaiting the press in autumn. Normandy is apple country, where apples with quaint varietal names, such as Windmill and Donkey Snout, are celebrated in the region's gastronomy, along the Route du Cidre, or at Vimoutier's Foire de la Pomme (Apple Festival) in October (where they vote for the Most Beautiful Apple).

Calvados

There are no wines in Normandy, but the region makes its mark in the spirits world with the apple-based Calvados, a fragrant oak-aged brandy. Like cognac, Calvados, which is distilled from cider, gets better and more expensive with age. Top producers, such as Dupont in Victot-Pontfol and Pierre Huet in Cambremer, sell Calvados from "Vieux" (aged a minimum of three years) to "X.O." or "Napoléon" (aged from 6 to 25 years). Many producers also offer Pommeau, an aperitif blending cider with a generous dose of Calvados.

Cheese

Camembert is king in the dairy realm of Normandy. Invented by a farmer's wife in the late 18th century, this tangy, opulently creamy cow's-milk cheese with a worldwide reputation hails from the Auge region. The best—Véritable Camembert de Normandie—with velvety white rinds and supple, sometimes oozy interiors, are produced on small farms, such as the esteemed Moulin de Carel. Other members of Normandy's (cheese) board are the savory, grassy Pont L'Évêque, the impressively pungent Livarot with rust-color rind, and the Pavé d'Auge, a robust cheese with a honey-hue center.

Omelets

There is no more famous omelet in the world than the puffy, pillowlike confection offered at La Mère Poulard in Mont-St-Michel. Whipped with a balloon whisk in a large copper bowl, then cooked in a long-handled skillet over a wood fire, the omelet is delicately browned and crusted on the outside, as soft and airy as a soufflé within. Order the omelet with ham and cheese as a main course, or sugared and flambéed as a divine dessert.

Oysters

On Normandy's Cotentin Peninsula, ports such as Blanville-sur-Mer, Granville, and particularly St-Vaast-La Hougue, are where oystermen haul in tons of plump, briny oysters distinguished by a subtle note of hazelnut. Enjoy a dozen on the half shell at the many traditional restaurants in this region, accompanied by a saucer of shallot vinegar and brown bread.

Le Vieux-Marché ☎ *02–35–70–56–65* 🌐 *www.le37.fr* 🕒 *Closed Sun., Mon., and 1st 3 wks of Aug.*

Les Nymphéas

$$$$ | **FRENCH** | At the end of a cobbled courtyard in the city's Old Town, this restaurant's half-timber building is a vintage charmer, and the elegant dining room is cozy and hushed. Regional flourishes dominate the menu, such as lobster served in a sweet Sauternes sauce, scallops with creamed cauliflower and quinoa risotto, or panfried beef tenderloin topped with foie gras. **Known for:** excellent prix-fixe dinner menus; traditional Norman cuisine; high-value lunch menu. [$] *Average main: €45* ✉ *7 rue Pie, Le Vieux-Marché* ☎ *09–74–56–46–19* 🌐 *www.lesnympheas-rouen.fr* 🕒 *Closed Mon. No dinner Sun.*

★ **Restaurant Gill**

$$$$ | **FRENCH** | On the quay at the heart of Rouen's gastronomic epicenter, Rouen's only Michelin two-star restaurant goes to great lengths to make sure you feel pampered from start to finish. With a reputation for culinary rigor, native son Gilles Tournadre is well versed in the splendors of the Norman woods, fields, and shore: oysters, crab, scallops, lobster, and several types of fish can be found on the menu every day, along with game like hare and piglet. **Known for:** pricey tasting menu that's worth the splurge; signature dishes like pigeon à la Rouennaise; dessert soufflé prepared with a silky old Norman Calvados. [$] *Average main: €45* ✉ *8-9 quai de la Bourse, Le Vieux-Marché* ☎ *02–35–71–16–14* 🌐 *www.gill.fr* 🕒 *Closed Sun., Mon., 2 wks in Apr., and 1st 3 wks in Aug.*

🛏 Hotels

Best Western–Hotel de Dieppe

$ | **HOTEL** | Established in 1880, the Dieppe remains up-to-date thanks to resolute management by five generations of the Guéret family who welcome guests to their fine restaurant and compact accommodations (Room 22 is the largest); all have modern color schemes, refurbished bathrooms, and flat-screen TVs. **Pros:** personal service; helpful, English-speaking owners; convenient to train station. **Cons:** slightly corporate; street noise gets through in spite of double-glazed windows; a bit away from city center. [$] *Rooms from: €85* ✉ *Pl. Bernard Tissot, Gare* ☎ *02–35–71–96–00* 🌐 *www.hotel-dieppe.fr* 🛏 *41 rooms* 🍴 *No meals.*

★ **Hotel de Bourgtheroulde-Autograph Collection**

$$ | **HOTEL** | One of Normandy's most magnificent *hôtels particuliers* (family mansions) is also Rouen's finest hotel. **Pros:** gorgeously Gothic decor; steps from the center of historic Rouen; great restaurant and well-equipped spa. **Cons:** minimalism is not for everyone; breakfast not included; rooms a bit on the small side. [$] *Rooms from: €180* ✉ *15 pl. de la Pucelle, Le Vieux-Marché* ☎ *02–35–14–50–50* 🌐 *www.hotelsparouen.com* 🛏 *78 rooms* 🍴 *No meals.*

Hôtel de la Cathédrale

$ | **HOTEL** | There are enough half-timber walls and beams here to fill a superluxe hotel, but the happy news is that this is a good budget option—even better, this 17th-century building is found on a narrow pedestrian street just behind Rouen's cathedral. **Pros:** storybook surroundings; can't-be-beat location; great value. **Cons:** some small rooms; no car access; can be difficult to find. [$] *Rooms from: €105* ✉ *12 rue St-Romain, Saint-Maclou-de-Folleville* ☎ *02–35–71–57–95* 🌐 *www.hotel-de-la-cathedrale.fr* 🛏 *26 rooms* 🍴 *Free Breakfast.*

Hotel Mercure Rouen Centre Cathedrale

$$ | **HOTEL** | In the jumble of streets near Rouen's cathedral—a navigational challenge if you arrive by car—this modern chain hotel has small, comfortable guest rooms decorated in breezy pastels; ask for one with a view of the cathedral.

Pros: functional design; central location; breakfast (included in the price) has a gluten-free option. **Cons:** interiors lack character; hard to find; parking area very small. *$ Rooms from: €130 ⊠ 7 rue de la Croix de Fer, Saint-Maclou-de-Folleville ☎ 02–35–52–69–52 ⊕ www.accorhotels.com/gb/hotel-1301-hotel-mercure-rouen-centre-cathedrale/index.shtml ⬦ 125 rooms ⦿I Free Breakfast.*

Le Vieux Carré

$ | **HOTEL** | In the heart of Old Rouen, this cute hotel has practical and comfortable rooms that, while recently refurbished, retain their taste for the exotic: picture lamps from Egypt, tables from Morocco, and 1940s English armoires. **Pros:** charming decor; central location; exceptional prices. **Cons:** small rooms; parking a bit of a walk away; breakfast not included. *$ Rooms from: €70 ⊠ 34 rue Ganterie, Gare ☎ 02–35–71–67–70 ⊕ www.hotel-vieux-carre.com ⬦ 13 rooms ⦿I No meals.*

Nightlife

Bar de la Crosse

BARS/PUBS | Enjoy an aperitif and a good chat with some outgoing Rouennais at this popular local haunt. Get there early as the packed terrace fills fast. *⊠ 53 rue de l'Hôpital, Saint-Maclou-de-Folleville ☎ 02–35–70–16–68.*

 Performing Arts

Théâtre des Arts

ARTS CENTERS | Operas, plays, and concerts are staged at the Théâtre des Arts. *⊠ 7 rue Dr-Rambert, Le Vieux-Marché ☎ 02–35–98–74–78 for box office ⊕ www.operaderouen.fr.*

Fécamp

71 km (44 miles) northwest of Rouen, 17 km (11 miles) northeast of Étretat via D940.

Founded in the 10th century as a fishing port (the name is a Germanic form of "fish"), Fécamp still relies on the sea for its sustenance. After taking in the sights, be sure to sample the catch of the day in one of its harborside eateries; you can cap the meal with a dram of Bénédictine, the town's own herbal liqueur.

GETTING HERE AND AROUND

Due to construction work, direct train service from Rouen is currently suspended. Otherwise, train service from Rouen will connect in Breaute (65 mins, €10.90); Keolis Seine Maritime's Bus No. 24 comes in from Le Havre via Étretat (90 mins, €2).

VISITOR INFORMATION Fécamp Tourist Office ⊠ *Quai Sadi Carnot ☎ 02–35–28–51–01 ⊕ www.fecamptourisme.com.*

Sights

Abbaye de La Trinité

RELIGIOUS SITE | The ancient cod-fishing port of Fécamp was once a major pilgrimage site, and this magnificent abbey church bears witness to its religious past. Founded by the Duke of Normandy in the 11th century, the Benedictine abbey became the home of the monastic order of the Précieux Sang de la Trinité (Precious Blood of the Trinity—referring to Christ's blood, which supposedly arrived here in the 7th century in a reliquary from the Holy Land). *⊠ Pl. des Ducs Richard.*

Palais de la Bénédictine (*Benedictine Palace*)

WINERY/DISTILLERY | Fécamp is also the home of Bénédictine liqueur. The Palais de la Bénédictine, across from the tourist office, is a florid building dating to 1892 that mixes neo-Gothic and Renaissance styles. Watery pastiche or taste-tingling architectural cocktail? Whether you're shaken or stirred, this remains one of Normandy's most popular attractions. Fans will want to take advantage of mixology workshops, special meals, or guided tours. There's also a shop selling Bénédictine products and souvenirs. ✉ *110 rue Alexandre-le-Grand* ☎ *02–35–10–26–10* 🌐 *www.benedictine.fr* 🎟 *From €12.*

🍴 Restaurants

La Marée

$$$ | SEAFOOD | Overlooking Fécamp's lively harbor, this popular seafood restaurant makes up in conviviality what it lacks in charm. Gigantic langoustine, plump crabs, and the renowned Fécamp herring are standouts; other good choices include the whole grilled sole and the salt cod poached in Normandy cream, a hearty local specialty. **Known for:** killer views of the harbor; substantial portions of the day's catch; wide variety of fresh seafood. [$] *Average main: €25* ✉ *77 quai Bérigny* ☎ *02–35–29–39–15* 🌐 *www.restaurant-maree-fecamp.fr* 🕑 *No dinner Thurs.*

Le Vicomté

$$ | FRENCH | Market-fresh ingredients grace a daily set menu at this friendly and inexpensive Fécamp favorite. On it, you might find grilled scallops or celeriac rémoulade to start, and a rich dogfish stew or guinea fowl in cider sauce for mains, all followed by cheese, a choice of homemade desserts, and coffee. **Known for:** exceptionally warm welcome; eclectic vintage design; cozy atmosphere. [$] *Average main: €23* ✉ *4 rue du Président-René-Coty* ☎ *02–35–28–47–63* 🕑 *Closed Sun., Wed., 1st wk of Apr., last 2 wks of Aug., and 2 wks at end of year.*

🛏 Hotels

Le Grand Pavois

$ | HOTEL | A fantastic base for exploring Fécamp, the Grand Pavois is directly across from the city's harbor—ask for a room with a view. **Pros:** free Wi-Fi; friendly staff; great views. **Cons:** back rooms overlook parking lot; breakfast not included; no tea or coffeemaker in rooms. [$] *Rooms from: €105* ✉ *15 quai de la Vicomté* ☎ *02–35–10–01–01* 🌐 *www.hotel-grand-pavois.com* 🛏 *35 rooms* 🍽 *No meals.*

Étretat

17 km (11 miles) southwest of Fécamp, 88 km (55 miles) northwest of Rouen.

Midway along Normandy's Alabaster Coast, Étretat might not at first seem worthy of a detour. However, its end-of-the-world location, its spectacular stone formations famously immortalized by the Impressionists, and the community itself—a Fisher-Price toy town lined with houses covered in picturesque 19th-century figural carvings—all add up to one of France's most unforgettable destinations. No matter there are no museums here—Étretat itself could be an exhibit.

GETTING HERE AND AROUND

Your best bet is to take Keolis Seine Maritime's Bus No. 24 from either Fécamp (30 mins, €2) or Le Havre (60 mins, €2).

VISITOR INFORMATION Étretat Tourist Office ✉ *Pl. Maurice Guillard* ☎ *02–35–27–05–21* 🌐 *www.etretat.net.*

👁 Sights

★ Falaises d'Étretat

NATURE SITE | This large village, with its promenade running the length of the pebble beach, is renowned for the magnificent tall rock formations that extend out into the sea. The Falaises d'Étretat are white cliffs that are as famous in France as Dover's are in England—and have been painted by many artists, Claude Monet chief among them.

A stunning white-sand beach and white-chalk rocks, such as the "Manneporte"—a limestone portal likened by author Guy de Maupassant to an elephant dipping its trunk into water—are major elements in the composition. Here Monet became a pictorial rock climber with the help of his famous "slotted box," built with compartments for six different canvases, allowing him to switch midstream from painting to painting, as weather patterns momentarily changed. With storms and sun alternating hour by hour, you'll quickly understand why they say, "Just wait: in Normandy we have great weather several times a day!"—it was yet another reason why the Impressionists, intent on capturing the ephemeral, so loved this town.

At low tide it's possible to walk through the huge archways formed by the rocks to neighboring beaches. The biggest arch is at the **Falaise d'Aval,** to the south, and for a breathtaking view of the whole bay be sure to climb the easy path up to the top. From here you can hike for miles across the Manneporte Hills, or play a round of golf on one of Europe's windiest and most scenic courses, overlooking **L'Aiguille** (The Needle), a 300-foot spike of rock jutting out of the sea just offshore. To the north towers the **Falaise d'Amont,** topped by the gloriously picturesque chapel of Notre-Dame de la Garde.

The plunging chalk cliffs of Étretat are so gorgeous and strange that they seem surreal at first—the hordes of camera-toting visitors, however, can bring you back to reality quickly. So plan on heading for the cliffs in early morning or early evening. ✉ Étretat ⊕ www.etretat.net.

Hotels

Domaine Saint Clair Le Donjon

$$ | **HOTEL** | From the look of this charming, ivy-covered, Anglo-Norman château—complete with storybook tower, private park, and lovely sea vistas—it is easy to understand why Monet, Proust, Offenbach, and other greats accepted invitations here. **Pros:** grand architecture; gorgeous setting; outdoor swimming pool. **Cons:** strident decoration in some rooms; restaurant expensive; quirky decor not for everyone. $ Rooms from: €150 ✉ Chemin de St-Clair ☎ 02–35–27–08–23 ⊕ www.hoteletretat.com ⇄ 27 rooms ¶ No meals.

Dormy House

$ | **HOTEL** | Ideally located halfway up the Étretat cliffs, this smart, modernish hotel is perched amid acres of manicured cliff-side parkland. **Pros:** grand views; excellent restaurant; beautiful location. **Cons:** small rooms; questionable value for fine but pricy breakfast; breakfast not included. $ Rooms from: €120 ✉ Rte. du Havre ☎ 02–35–27–07–88 ⊕ www.dormy-house.com ⇄ 63 rooms ¶ No meals.

Activities

Golf d'Étretat

GOLF | Don't miss the chance to play at Golf d'Étretat, where the stupendous 6,552-yard, par-72 course drapes across the cliff tops of the Falaise d'Aval. A restaurant offers seafood along with ocean views. ✉ Rte. du Havre ☎ 02–35–27–04–89 ⊕ www.golfetretat.com ♣. Low season, €55; high season, €75 ⊙ Closed Tues. Nov.–mid-Mar.

Le Havre

28 km (18 miles) southwest of Étretat, 86 km (53 miles) west of Rouen, 200 km (125 miles) northwest of Paris.

Considering it was bombarded 146 times during World War II, you might think there'd be little left to see in Le Havre—France's second-largest port (after Marseille). Think again. The rebuilt city, with its uncompromising recourse to reinforced concrete and open spaces, looks like no other city in the country, thanks in part to its share of some of France's most spectacular 20th-century edifices. The rational planning and audacious architecture of Auguste Perret (1874–1954) have earned the city UNESCO World Heritage status. His unforgettable **Église St-Joseph**—half rocket ship, half church—is alone worth the trip.

GETTING HERE AND AROUND

Direct trains from Paris's Gare St-Lazare arrive here 13 times a day (2 hrs 10 mins, €17). If you're coming from the United Kingdom, Brittany Ferries provides sea links between Portsmouth and Le Havre. Buses operated by Keolis Seine Maritime connect it to Fécamp and other communities in Upper Normandy; while Bus Verts routes go to Deauville, Honfleur, and Caen.

VISITOR INFORMATION Le Havre Tourist Office ✉ *186 bd. Clemenceau* ☎ *02–32–74–04–04* ⊕ *www.lehavretourisme.com.*

Sights

★ Auguste Perret Model Apartment

BUILDING | A fascinating relic of post–World War II Le Havre, the Auguste Perret Model Apartment is a testament to the city's postwar destruction—and to the determination of architects and city planners to create new homes for displaced residents. Sign up for a guided tour at the city's well-appointed Maison du Patrimoine; while the tour is in

French, even nonspeakers will find plenty to admire in the collection of midcentury furniture and utility-minded ceramics and artwork. The apartment makes an interesting counterpoint to Perret's nearby masterpiece, the Eglise St-Joseph. ✉ *Maison du Patrimoine, 181 rue de Paris* ☎ *02–35–22–31–22* ⊕ *www.lehavre. fr/annuaire/appartement-temoin-perret* 🎟 *€5* ⊙ *Closed Mon., Tues., and Thurs. Oct.–Mar.*

Église St-Joseph

RELIGIOUS SITE | Perhaps the most impressive Modernist church in France, the Église St-Joseph was designed by Auguste Perret in the 1950s. The 350-foot tower powers into the sky like a fat rocket, and the interior is just as thrilling. No frills here: the 270-foot octagonal lantern soars above the crossing, filled almost to the top with abstract stained glass that hurls colored light over the bare concrete walls. ✉ *130 bd. François-ler* ⊕ *www. lehavre.catholique.fr.*

★ Musée d'Art Moderne André-Malraux

MUSEUM | Occupying an innovative 1960s glass-and-metal building, the city's art museum has soaring plate-glass windows that bathe the interior in the famous sea light that drew scores of artists to Le Havre. Two local painters who gorgeously immortalized the Normandy coast are showcased here—Raoul Dufy (1877–1953), through a remarkable collection of his brightly colored oils, watercolors, and sketches; and Eugène Boudin (1824–98), a forerunner of Impressionism, whose compelling beach scenes and landscapes tellingly evoke the Normandy sea and skyline. ✉ *2 bd. Clemenceau* ☎ *02–35–19–62–62* ⊕ *www. muma-lehavre.fr* 🎟 *€7* ⊙ *Closed Mon.*

Hotels

Best Western–ART Hotel

$ | **HOTEL** | Designed by the famed architect Auguste Perret, and located by the soothing waters of the Bassin

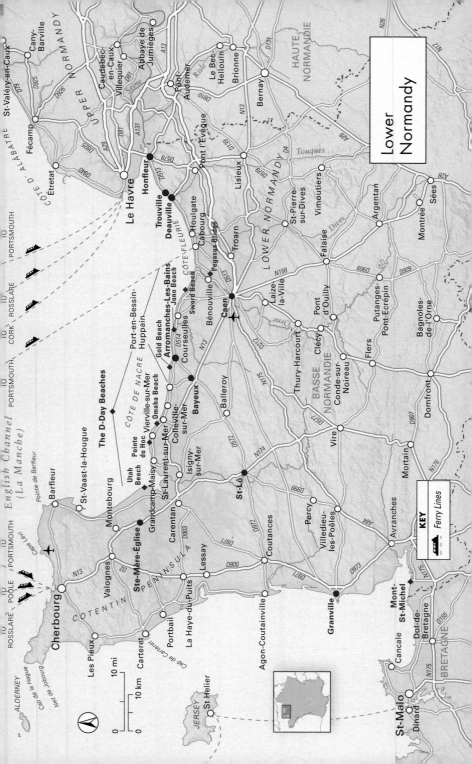

Lower Normandy

Normandy on Canvas

Long before Claude Monet created his Giverny lily pond by diverting the Epte River that marks the boundary with the Ile-de-France, artists had been scudding into Normandy for two watery reasons: the Seine and the sea. Just downstream from Vernon, where the Epte joins the Seine, Richard the Lionheart's ruined castle at Les Andelys was committed to canvas by Paul Signac and Félix Vallotton, while the soft-lighted, cliff-lined Seine Valley was Impressionistically reproduced by Albert Lebourg and Gustave Loiseau. Their pieces grace the Musée des Beaux-Arts in Rouen—where Camille Corot once studied, and whose mighty cathedral Monet painted until he was pink, purple, and blue in the face.

The Seine joins the sea at Le Havre, where Monet grew up. His mentor Eugène Boudin would boat across the estuary from Honfleur, where he hobnobbed with Gustave Courbet, Charles Daubigny, and Alfred Sisley at the Ferme St-Siméon. Le Havre in the 1860s was the base from which Monet and his pals Frédéric Bazille and Johan Barthold Jongkind explored the rugged coast up to Dieppe, often opening their easels beneath the cliffs of Étretat.

The railroad from Gare St-Lazare (also smokily evoked by Monet) put Dieppe within easy reach of Paris. Eugène Delacroix daubed seascapes here in 1852. Auguste Renoir visited Dieppe from 1878 to 1885; Paul Gauguin and Edgar Degas clinked glasses here in 1885; Camille Pissarro painted his way from Gisors to Dieppe in the 1890s. As the nearest port to Paris, Dieppe wowed the English, too. Walter Sickert moved in from 1898 to 1905, and other artists from the Camden Town Group he founded back in London often painted in Dieppe before World War I.

de Commerce, this hotel's light, airy rooms have contemporary furniture, and a few—like Room 63—have balconies and views of the port. **Pros:** modernist panache; nice bar on-site; central location. **Cons:** some street noise; smallest rooms are best value; breakfast not included. [$] *Rooms from: €69* ✉ *147 rue Louis-Brindeau* ☎ *02–35–22–69–44* 🌐 *www.art-hotel.fr* 🛏 *31 rooms, 4 apartments* 🍴 *No meals.*

Honfleur

35 km (22 miles) southwest of Étretat, 80 km (50 miles) west of Rouen.

Honfleur, the most picturesque of the Côte Fleurie's seaside towns, is a time-burnished place with a surplus of half-timber houses and cobbled streets that are lined with a solid selection of stylish boutiques. Much of its Renaissance architecture remains intact—especially around the 17th-century Vieux Bassin harbor, where the water is fronted on one side by two-story stone houses with low, sloping roofs and on the other by tall slate-topped houses with wooden facades. Maritime expeditions (including some of the first voyages to Canada) departed from here; later, Impressionists were inspired to capture it on canvas. But the town as a whole has become increasingly crowded since the impressive Pont de Normandie opened in 1995. Providing a direct link with Upper Normandy, the world's sixth-largest cable-stayed bridge is supported by two concrete pylons taller than the Eiffel Tower and designed to resist winds of 257 kph (160 mph).

Relentlessly picturesque Honfleur has been immortalized by many painters, most famously by J.M.W. Turner and Eugène Boudin.

GETTING HERE AND AROUND

With departures every few hours, Bus Verts's Line 20 can get you here from Deauville (37 mins, €2.10), Le Havre (35 mins, €4.20), and Caen (2 hrs, €4.20; or Line 39 1-hr express, €7.50). If you're driving, keep in mind that parking can be a problem—your best bet is the lot just beyond the Vieux-Bassin (Old Harbor) on the left as you approach from the land side.

VISITOR INFORMATION Honfleur Tourist Office ✉ *Quai Lepaulmier* ☎ *02–31–89–23–30* 🌐 *www.honfleur-tourism.co.uk.*

Sights

Musée Eugène Boudin

MUSEUM | This small museum, dedicated to the work of Honfleur-born Eugène Boudin, traces a career crucial to the development of Impressionism. His friendship with, and influence on, Claude Monet is visible in his masterful depiction of the region's skies and seaways. ✉ *Pl. Erik Satie, off Rue de l'Homme de Bois* 🌐 *www.musees-honfleur.fr* 🎫 *€8 July–Oct., €6 Nov.–June* ⏲ *Closed Tues.*

Ste-Catherine

RELIGIOUS SITE | Soak up the seafaring atmosphere by strolling around the old harbor and paying a visit to the ravishing wooden church of Ste-Catherine, which dominates a tumbling square. The sanctuary and ramshackle belfry across the way—note the many touches of marine engineering in their architecture—were built by townspeople to show their gratitude for the departure of the English at the end of the Hundred Years' War, in 1453. ✉ *Pl. Ste-Catherine* ☎ *02–31–89–23–30* 🌐 *www.calvados-tourisme.com/offre/eglise-sainte-catherine.*

Restaurants

Le Fleur de Sel

$$$ | **MODERN FRENCH** | A low-beamed 16th-century fisherman's house provides the cozy setting for chef Vincent's Guyon's locally influenced cuisine. Centered on the daily catch, the ambitious menu usually includes at least five different fish dishes—all presented with artistic panache—along with plenty of grilled meats, like salt-marsh lamb or duck. **Known for:** good value fixed-price menus; masterful desserts; informed cheese course. [$] *Average main: €26* ✉ *17 rue Haute* ☎ *02–31–89–01–92* 🌐 *www.lafleurdesel-honfleur.com* 🕑 *Closed Mon. and Tues., and Jan.*

★ SaQuaNa
$$$$ | MODERN FRENCH | Chef Alexandre Bourdas earned his second Michelin here after putting Honfleur on the gastronomic map with his first over a decade ago. From the ravishing dining room to the impeccable presentation, his restaurant is a study in getting it right down to the smallest detail, with surprising combinations like sea bream with nori and marinated sanshō or cabbage tempura with a truffle crust. **Known for:** elements of Bourdas's native Midi-Pyrénées cuisine; sweet masterpieces from pâtissier par excellence Justine Rethore; great wine list. [$] *Average main: €96* ✉ *22 pl. Hamelin* ☎ *02–31–89–40–80* 🌐 *saquana-alexandre-bourdas.com* 🕑 *Closed Mon.–Wed.*

🛏 Hotels

Ferme St-Siméon
$$$ | HOTEL | The story goes that this 19th-century manor house was the birthplace of Impressionism, and that its park inspired Monet and Sisley—neither of whom would have dismissed the welcoming mix of elegance and down-home Norman delights inside, where rich fabrics, grand paintings, and Louis XVI chairs are married with rustic antiques, ancient beams, and half-timber walls; the result casts a deliciously cozy spell. **Pros:** famed historic charm; great spa using local ingredients; delicious restaurants. **Cons:** expensive; decor not for everyone; breakfast not included. [$] *Rooms from: €330* ✉ *20 rte. Adolphe-Marais, on D513 to Trouville* ☎ *02–31–81–78–00* 🌐 *www.fermesaintsimeon.fr* 🛏 *34 rooms* 🍴 *No meals.*

L'Absinthe
$$ | HOTEL | A 16th-century presbytery with stone walls and beamed ceilings houses a charming little hotel and the acclaimed restaurant of the same name. **Pros:** enchanting building; superb restaurant; excellent views in some rooms. **Cons:** small rooms; gawky blend of old and modern furnishings; not all rooms have views. [$] *Rooms from: €140* ✉ *1 rue de Ville* ☎ *02–31–89–23–23* 🌐 *www.absinthe.fr* 🕑 *Closed mid-Nov.–mid-Dec.* 🛏 *9 rooms, 2 suites* 🍴 *Free Breakfast.*

Le Manoir des Impressionnistes
$$ | HOTEL | Set atop a small wooded hill 200 yards from the sea, this gorgeous half-timber, dormer-roof manor has a pretty green-and-white facade in the Anglo-Norman style, plus accommodations that promise sweeping views. **Pros:** exquisitely decorated and furnished; great views; stylish bathrooms. **Cons:** away from town center; no elevator; breakfast not included. [$] *Rooms from: €190* ✉ *23 rte. de Trouville* ☎ *02–31–81–63–00* 🌐 *www.manoirdesimpressionnistes.com* 🛏 *12 rooms* 🍴 *No meals.*

🎟 Performing Arts

Fête des Marins (*Marine Festival*)
FESTIVALS | The two-day Fête des Marins is held on Pentecost Sunday and Monday (50 days after Easter). On the first day all the boats in the harbor are decked out in flags and paper roses, and a priest bestows his blessing at high tide. The next day, model boats and local children head a musical procession to the small chapel of Notre-Dame de Grâce. ✉ *St. Catherine.*

Jazz aux Greniers (*Jazz Festival*)
FESTIVALS | There's a five-day jazz festival in mid-August, with performances in the streets and venues throughout the town center. ✉ *Honfleur* 🌐 *www.jazzauxgreniers.com.*

Deauville-Trouville

16 km (10 miles) southwest of Honfleur, 92 km (57 miles) west of Rouen.

Divided only by the River Touques, the twin beach towns of Deauville and Trouville are distinctly different in character. The latter, arguably France's oldest seaside resort, was discovered by artists and the upper crust in the days of Louis-Philippe; by the mid-1800s, it was the beach à la mode and painters like Eugène Boudin captured its beauty. Then the Duc de Mornay (half-brother of Napoléon III) and other aristocrats on the hunt for something more exclusive began building their villas along the deserted beach across the river. Thus was launched Deauville, a vigorous grande dame who started kicking up her heels in the Second Empire, kept swinging through the Belle Époque, and is still frequented by Rothschilds, princes, and movie stars. Few of them ever actually get in the water, though, because other attractions (including a gilt-edge casino and a fabled racecourse—to say nothing of the extravagant shops along Rue Eugène-Colas) prove so distracting. But perhaps Deauville is known best for its Promenade des Planches—a boardwalk extending along the seafront lined with deck chairs, bars, striped cabanas, elegant hotels, plus an array of lovely half-timber Norman villas and block after block of prewar apartment houses.

Overbuilding has diminished the charm of both towns, yet the two maintain their popularity. Deauville is sometimes jokingly referred to as Paris's 21st arrondissement; while Trouville is a more of a family resort, harboring few pretensions. Moreover, shuttling between them is still easy by means of a five-minute drive or boat crossing (€1.20).

GETTING HERE AND AROUND

Trains from Paris's Gare St-Lazare to Deauville-Trouville (the station between the two towns) occasionally require a change at Lisieux (2 hrs direct, €21). Bus Verts runs multiple buses per day to Deauville from Le Havre (1 hr, €4.20), Honfleur (37 mins, €2.10), and Caen (75 mins, €4.20).

VISITOR INFORMATION Deauville-Trouville Tourist Office ✉ *32 quai Fernand-Moureaux, Trouville-sur-Mer* ☎ *02–31–14–40–00* ⊕ *www.trouvillesur-mer.org.*

🍴 Restaurants

L'Essentiel

$$$ | FRENCH | A nice change from the grand, overly formal hotel dining rooms that dominate Deauville, the relaxed atmosphere and sensational, seasonal cuisine at this contemporary eatery have made it extremely popular. Chef Charles Thuillant, whose pedigree includes stints at two top Paris restaurants, focuses on lighter Asian-inspired dishes with European influences, like grilled duck with mushrooms and carrots or Wagyu beef with grilled vegetables. **Known for:** roomy terrace; excellent wines by the glass; bargain weekday lunch menu. $ *Average main: €32* ✉ *29 rue Mirabeau, Deauville* ☎ *02–31–87–22–11* ⊕ *www.lessentield-eauville.com* ⊙ *Closed Mon. and Tues. Sept.–June.*

🛏 Hotels

★ Hotel Barrière Le Normandy Deauville

$$$$ | HOTEL | This hotel—its facade a riot of pastel-green timbering, checkerboard walls, and Anglo-Norman balconies—has been a town landmark since it opened in 1912, and crowds still pack the place. **Pros:** grand interiors; luxurious amenities; Deauville's place to be seen. **Cons:** some elements of kitschy bombast; service can be patronizing; pretty pricey. $ *Rooms from: €370* ✉ *38 rue Jean-Mermoz,*

Deauville ☎ 02–31–98–66–22, 01–73–60–01–11 for reservations 🌐 www.hotelsbarriere.com 🛏 271 rooms 🍴 Free Breakfast.

Villa 81

$ | **HOTEL** | **FAMILY** | While this boutique hotel pours on the gloss, the nicer original features of the 1906 mansion—parquet floors, stained-glass windows, impossibly high ceilings—remain to complement the added postmodern touches (think faux-crocodile chairs, silver furniture, shrouded chandeliers, and ersatz-Baroque beds). **Pros:** flat-screen TVs; easy parking; free Wi-Fi. **Cons:** no restaurant; a walk to the beach; not the best soundproofing in rooms. [$] *Rooms from: €100* ✉ *81 av. de la République, Deauville* ☎ *02–31–14–15–16* 🌐 *www.lacloseriedeauville.com/en* 🛏 *13 rooms* 🍴 *Free Breakfast.*

🍸 Nightlife

Casino de Deauville

CASINOS | Formal attire is required at the Casino de Deauville. ✉ *2 rue Edmond-Blanc, Deauville* ☎ *02–31–14–31–14* 🌐 *www.lucienbarriere.com/fr/Casino/Deauville/accueil.html.*

Casino de Trouville

CASINOS | Trouville's casino is slightly less highbrow than Deauville's. ✉ *Pl. du Maréchal-Foch, Trouville-sur-Mer* ☎ *02–31–87–75–00* 🌐 *www.casinosbarriere.com/en/trouville.html.*

Le Chic

DANCE CLUBS | Open nightly from 11 pm to 6 am, Le Chic is *the* place to dance, according to many locals. ✉ *14 rue Désiré Le Hoc, Deauville* ☎ *02–31–88–30–91* 🌐 *www.lechicdeauville.fr.*

Le Seven

BARS/PUBS | Night owls enjoy Le Seven; it's open until dawn. ✉ *13 rue Albert-Fracasse, Deauville* ☎ *02–31–88–40–50* 🌐 *www.lesevendeauville.com.*

🎟 Performing Arts

American Film Festival

FESTIVALS | One of the biggest cultural events on the Norman calendar is the 10-day American Film Festival, held in Deauville in early September. ✉ *Centre International de Deauville, 1 av. Lucien Barrière, Deauville* ☎ *02–31–14–14–14* 🌐 *www.festival-deauville.com.*

🏃 Activities

Club Nautique de Trouville-Hennequeville

SAILING | Sailing boats large and small can be rented from the Club Nautique de Trouville-Hennequeville, with wind-surfing lessons available by the hour. ✉ *Digue des Roches Noires, Trouville-sur-Mer* ☎ *02–31–88–13–59* 🌐 *www.cnth.org.*

Hippodrome de Deauville–Clairefontaine

HORSE RACING/SHOW | Horse races and polo matches can be seen most summer afternoons at the Hippodrome de Deauville–Clairefontaine. ✉ *Rte. de Clairefontaine, Tourgeville* ☎ *02–31–14–69–00* 🌐 *www.hippodrome-deauville-clairefontaine.com.*

Hippodrome de Deauville—La Touques

HORSE RACING/SHOW | Deauville becomes Europe's horse capital in August, when breeders jet in from around the world for its yearling auctions and the races at its two attractive hippodromes. Afternoon horse races are held in the heart of Deauville at the Hippodrome de Deauville—La Touques. It hosts the Gold Cup Polo Championship (the final is held on the last Sunday of August), and the summer season closes with the course's signature event, the Grand Prix de Deauville. ✉ *45 av. Hocquart de Turtot, Deauville* ☎ *02–31–14–20–00* 🌐 *www.france-galop.com.*

Even in the 19th century, elegant Parisians flocked to Deauville to enjoy a promenade along its beautiful seafront boardwalk.

Caen

54 km (35 miles) southwest of Deauville-Trouville, 28 km (17 miles) southeast of Bayeux, 120 km (75 miles) west of Rouen.

Basically a modern commercial and administrative center with a vibrant student scene, Caen—the capital of Lower Normandy—is very different from the coastal resorts. Atmospheric castles and abbeys remain from the 11th-century glory days when William of Normandy ruled here before heading across the Channel to conquer England. During the two-month Battle of Caen in 1944, however, a fire raged for 11 days, devastating much of the town. The Caen Mémorial, an impressive museum devoted to World War II, is considered a must-see by travelers interested in 20th-century history; and many avail themselves of the excellent bus tours the museum sponsors to the nearby D-Day beaches.

GETTING HERE AND AROUND

Frequent daily trains arrive from Paris's Gare St-Lazare (2 hrs, €36.70); some continue to Bayeux (2 hrs, €40.30). Daily trains also link Caen to Rouen (90 mins, €28) and St-Lô (45 mins, €12). Bus Verts connects the city with Deauville (75 mins, €4.20), Le Havre (90 mins, €7.50, express Line 39), and Honfleur (1 hr, €12, express Line 39).

VISITOR INFORMATION Caen Tourist Office ⌧ *Pl. St-Pierre* ☎ *02–31–27–14–14* ⊕ *www.caenlamer-tourisme.fr.*

Sights

Abbaye aux Dames (*Ladies' Abbey*)
RELIGIOUS SITE | Founded in 1059 by William the Conqueror's wife, Matilda, the Abbaye aux Dames was rebuilt in the 18th century; it then served as a hospital and nursing home before being fully restored in the 1980s by the Regional Council, which promptly requisitioned it for office space. The abbey's elegant arcaded courtyard and ground-floor

reception rooms can, however, still be admired during free guided tours. You can also visit the squat **Église de la Trinité** (Trinity Church), a fine example of 11th-century Romanesque architecture, though its original spires were replaced by timid balustrades in the early 18th century. Note the intricate carvings on columns and arches in the chapel; the 11th-century crypt; and, in the choir, the marble slab commemorating Queen Matilda, who was buried here in 1083. ⊠ *Pl. de la Reine-Mathilde* ☎ *02–31–06–98–98 for tour reservations, 02–31–06–98–45* ⊕ *www.abbayes-normandie.com/abbaye/abbaye-aux-dames-caen* ⊠ *Free.*

★ **Abbaye aux Hommes** (*Men's Abbey*)
RELIGIOUS SITE | Caen's finest church, of cathedral proportions, is part of the Abbaye aux Hommes, built by William the Conqueror from local Caen stone (which was also used for England's Canterbury Cathedral, Westminster Abbey, and the Tower of London). The abbey was begun in Romanesque style in 1066 and expanded in the 18th century; its elegant buildings are now part of City Hall, and some rooms are brightened by the city's fine collection of paintings. Note the magnificent yet spare facade of the abbey church of **St-Étienne,** enhanced by two 11th-century towers topped by octagonal spires. Inside, what had been William the Conqueror's tomb was destroyed by 16th-century Huguenots during the Wars of Religion. However, the choir still stands; it was the first to be built in Norman Gothic style, and many subsequent choirs were modeled after it. To get the full historical scoop, sign up for one of the special tours: those in English are offered in July and August at 1:30 and 4 on weekdays. ⊠ *Esplanade Jean-Marie Louve* ☎ *02–31–30–42–81* ⊕ *caen.fr/decouvrir-patrimoine* ⊠ *From €3* ☉ *Closed weekends Jan.*

Château de Caen
CASTLE/PALACE | The ruins of William the Conqueror's fortress, built in 1060 and sensitively restored after the war, loom on a mound ahead of St-Étienne. The château gardens are a perfect spot for strolling, and the ramparts afford good views of the city. Inside, you'll discover two museums—the Musée des Beaux-Arts and the Musée de Normandie—plus the medieval church of **St-Georges,** which is used for exhibitions. ⊠ *Caen* ⊕ *www.musee-de-normandie.caen.fr/application-chateau* ☉ *Closed Mon. Jan.–June and Sept.–Dec.*

Église St-Pierre
RELIGIOUS SITE | Across the square, beneath a 240-foot spire, the late-Gothic church of St-Pierre is a riot of ornamental stonework. ⊠ *Pl. St-Pierre* ⊕ *www.sites.google.com/site/saintpierrecaen/home.*

Hôtel d'Escoville
HOUSE | A good place to begin exploring Caen is the Hôtel d'Escoville, a stately mansion in the city center built by wealthy merchant Nicolas Le Valois d'Escoville in the 1530s. The building was badly damaged during the war but has since been restored; the austere facade conceals an elaborate inner courtyard, reflecting the Italian influence on early Renaissance Norman architecture (there's no access to the interiors). The on-site city **tourist office** is an excellent resource. ⊠ *Pl. St-Pierre* ☎ *02–31–27–14–14 for tourist office* ⊕ *www.caen-tourisme.fr.*

★ **Mémorial de Caen**
MUSEUM | An imaginative museum erected in 1988 on the north side of the city, the Mémorial is a must-see if you're interested in World War II history. The stark, flat facade, with a narrow doorway symbolizing the Allies' breach in the Nazi's supposedly impregnable Atlantic Wall, opens onto an immense foyer with British Typhoon aircraft suspended overhead. The museum itself is down a spiral ramp, lined with photos and documents charting the Nazi's rise to power in the 1930s. The idea—hardly subtle but visually effective—is to suggest a

descent into the hell of war. The extensive displays range from wartime plastic jewelry to scale models of battleships, with scholarly sections on how the Nazis tracked down radios used by the French Resistance and on the development of the atomic bomb. A room commemorating the Holocaust, with flickering candles and twinkling overhead lights, sounds a jarring note. The D-Day landings are evoked by a tabletop map of the theater of war and by a spectacular split-screen presentation of the D-Day invasion from both the Allied and Nazi standpoints. Softening the effect of the modern structure are tranquil gardens, including a British one inaugurated by Prince Charles. Fittingly, the museum is located 10 minutes away from the Pegasus Bridge and 15 minutes from the D-Day beaches. ✉ *Esplanade Dwight-D.-Eisenhower* ☎ *02–31–06–06–45* 🌐 *www.memorial-caen.fr* 🎫 *€20* ⏲ *Closed Mon. in Nov. and Dec.*

Musée de Normandie (*Normandy Museum*)

MUSEUM | Set in a mansion built for the castle governor, this museum is dedicated to regional arts such as ceramics and sculpture. Some local archaeological finds are also on display. ✉ *Château de Caen, entrance by château gateway* ☎ *02–31–30–47–60* 🌐 *www.musee-de-normandie.caen.fr* 🎫 *From €4. Free 1st wk of every month* ⏲ *Closed Mon. Sept.–June.*

Musée des Beaux-Arts

MUSEUM | Within the castle's walls, the Musée des Beaux-Arts is a heavyweight among France's provincial fine arts museums. Its collection includes works by Monet, Poussin, Rubens, Brueghel, Tintoretto, and Veronese; there's also a wide range of 20th-century art on view. ✉ *Château de Caen, entrance by château gateway* ☎ *02–31–30–47–70* 🌐 *www.mba.caen.fr* 🎫 *From €4. Free 1st wk of every month* ⏲ *Closed Mon. Sept.–June.*

Pegasus Bridge

BRIDGE/TUNNEL | Early on June 6, 1944, the British 6th Airborne Division landed by glider and captured this bridge, which local residents later named for the division's emblem of Bellerophon astride his winged horse. This proved to be the first step toward liberating France from Nazi occupation, and the bridge itself became a symbol of the Allied invasion. To see it, take D514 north from Caen for 13 km (8 miles) and turn right at Bénouville. The original bridge—erected in 1935—has been replaced by a similar, slightly wider one, but the older span can be seen at the adjacent **Mémorial Pegasus** visitor center. **Café Gondrée,** by the bridge—the first building recaptured on French soil—is still standing and still serving; it also displays wartime memorabilia. A full-size replica Horsa glider is currently on view in the museum's park, with a fully refurbished cockpit. ✉ *Av. du Major Howard, Ranville* ☎ *02–31–78–19–44 for Mémorial Pegasus, 02–31–44–62–25 for Café Gondrée* 🌐 *musee.memorial-pegasus.com* 🎫 *Mémorial Pegasus €8.*

🍴 Restaurants

Le P'tit B

$$$ | **FRENCH** | On one of Caen's oldest streets near the castle, this half-timber 17th-century dining room—complete with stone walls, beam ceilings, and a large fireplace—showcases the regional cuisine of Stéphane Schiebold. Dishes like braised chuck with creamy polenta, or leek, mushroom, and quail ravioli are great options. **Known for:** good value, three-course menu; exceptional dessert options like pain perdu or apple tarte with rhubarb sorbet; location in the city's old quarter. [$] *Average main: €25* ✉ *15 rue de Vaugueux* ☎ *02–31–93–50–76* 🌐 *www.leptitb.fr.*

Le Verre à Soi

$$ | **WINE BAR** | Smack in the city center, overlooking the river, this convivial *cave à manger* has everything necessary for a satisfying, affordable dining experience. Opt for small plates of artisanal charcuterie and cheese, or go for a satisfying main course—like chicken breast served with cream and chorizo sauce or house-made foie gras with a confit of red onion. **Known for:** bargain prix-fixe lunch menus; friendly service; lively clientele. $ *Average main: €18* ✉ *23 quai Eugene Meslin* ☎ *02–31–83–08–77* ⊕ *le-verre-a-soi. business.site* ⊗ *Closed Sun. and Mon.*

Hotels

Best Western–Le Dauphin

$ | **HOTEL** | Despite being in the heart of the city, this hotel, in a restored 12th-century priory, is surprisingly quiet; some of the smallish guest rooms have exposed beams, those overlooking the street are soundproof, and the ones in back look out on the courtyard. **Pros:** quiet, historic building; spa and fitness center; great staff. **Cons:** breakfast not included; excellent but pricey restaurant; expensive and limited parking. $ *Rooms from: €90* ✉ *29 rue Gémare* ☎ *02–31–86–22–26* ⊕ *www. le-dauphin-normandie.com* ⤙ *37 rooms* ⦿ *No meals.*

Hotel Ivan Vautier

$ | **HOTEL** | A bastion of modern luxury, this quiet hotel is Caen's go-to spot for stylish lodging and dining. **Pros:** well maintained; fantastic on-site spa and gastronomic restaurant; good packages. **Cons:** not central location; no meals included in room price; rooms on the small side. $ *Rooms from: €120* ✉ *3 av. Henry Chéron* ☎ *02–31–73–32–71* ⊕ *www.ivanvautier.com* ⤙ *19 rooms* ⦿ *No meals.*

Shopping

Open Air Markets (*Farmers' Markets*)

OUTDOOR/FLEA/GREEN MARKETS | Farmers' markets (which often include clothing and household goods) run nearly every day, but the largest are held Friday morning on Place St-Sauveur and Sunday morning on Place Courtonne. In late April, around 100 collectors and dealers flock to Caen's bric-a-brac and antiques fair at the Parc des Expositions (entry €5). ✉ *Caen* ☎ *02–31–27–14–14* ⊕ *www. caenlamer-tourisme.fr.*

Arromanches-les-Bains

31 km (19 miles) northwest of Caen, 10 km (6 miles) northeast of Bayeux.

Now a tourist-friendly beach town, Arromanches played a pivotal role during the D-Day invasion. Vestiges of the great artificial ports called "mulberries" remain, and local attractions—including a landing-theme museum and a 360-degree movie theater—conjure up those desperate June days in 1944.

GETTING HERE AND AROUND
Bus Verts' Nos. 74 link Arromanches-le-Bains to Bayeux (30 mins, €2.10).

VISITOR INFORMATION Arromanches Tourist Office ✉ *2 rue Maréchal Joffre, Arromanches-les-Bains* ☎ *02–31–22–36–45* ⊕ *www.bayeux-bessin-tourisme.com.*

⊙ Sights

Arromanches 360

ARTS VENUE | This striking movie theater has a circular screen—actually nine curved screens synchronized to show a 19-minute film titled *Normandy's 100 Days,* which tells the story of the D-Day landings through previously unseen archival footage; the presentation comes courtesy of the team behind a popular French television series on the war, *Apocalypse.* The film is screened on the hour and half-hour. ✉ *Rue du Calvaire, Arromanches-les-Bains* ☎ *02–31–06–06–45* ⊕ *www.arromanches360.com* ⧉ *€7.*

Musée du Débarquement

MUSEUM | Little remains to mark the furious fighting waged hereabouts after D-Day. In the bay off Arromanches, however, some elements of the floating harbor are still visible. As you contemplate the seemingly insignificant hunks of concrete that form a broken offshore semicircle, try to imagine the extraordinary feat involved in towing them across the Channel from England. General Eisenhower said that victory would have been impossible without this prefabricated harbor, which was nicknamed "Winston." The Musée du Débarquement, on the seafront, has models, mock-ups, and photographs depicting the creation of this technical marvel. ✉ *Pl. du 6-Juin, Arromanches-les-Bains* ☎ *02–31–22–34–31* 🌐 *www.musee-arromanches.fr* 🎟 *€9.*

Hotels

Le Mulberry

$ | **HOTEL** | This little hotel, one block back from the seafront, is cheerfully run by Sophie and Christian Le Blanc. **Pros:** warm welcome; tasty home cooking and natural wines; central location. **Cons:** small, basic rooms; basic decor; breakfast not included. [$] *Rooms from: €90* ✉ *6 rue Maurice-Lithare, Arromanches-les-Bains* ☎ *02–31–22–36–05* 🌐 *www.lemulberry.fr* 🕒 *Closed Jan.–mid-Feb.* 🛏 *9 rooms* 🍴 *No meals.*

Bayeux

28 km (17 miles) northwest of Caen.

Bayeux makes a fine starting point for excursions to nearby World War II sites. Despite being close to scenes of such destruction, Bayeux itself was never bombed by either side (without factories or military bases, it served no strategic purpose); hence, its Norman Gothic cathedral and beautiful Old Town emerged intact. The highlight here for most visitors is the world's most celebrated piece of needlework: the Bayeux Tapestry, which vividly conjures up life circa 1066. For a different take on the past, plan to come for the boisterous Fêtes Médiévales, a market-cum-carnival held in the streets around the cathedral on the first weekend of July. A more conventional market is held every Saturday morning in the Place St-Patrice.

GETTING HERE AND AROUND

Bus Verts du Calvados's No. 30, originating at Caen's rail station, runs to Bayeux (€4.20) and other towns in the vicinity. Trains from Paris also arrive regularly (2 hrs, €40.30) via Caen (15 mins, €5).

VISITOR INFORMATION Bayeux Tourist Office ✉ *Pont St-Jean* ☎ *02–31–51–28–28* 🌐 *bayeux-bessin-tourisme.com.*

Sights

★ **Bayeux Tapestry**

MUSEUM | Essentially a 225-foot-long embroidered scroll stitched in 1067, the Bayeux Tapestry, known in French as the Tapisserie de la Reine Mathilde (Queen Matilda's Tapestry), depicts, in 58 comic strip–type scenes, the epic story of William of Normandy's conquest of England, narrating Will's trials and victory over his cousin Harold, culminating in the Battle of Hastings on October 14, 1066. The tapestry was probably commissioned from Saxon embroiderers by the count of Kent—who was also the bishop of Bayeux—to be displayed in his newly built Cathédrale Notre-Dame. Despite its age, the tapestry is in remarkably good condition; the extremely detailed, often homey scenes provide an unequaled record of the clothes, weapons, ships, and lifestyles of the day. It's showcased in the **Musée de la Tapisserie** (Tapestry Museum); free audio guides let you listen to an English commentary about the tapestry. ✉ *Centre Guillaume-le-Conquérant, 13 bis rue de Nesmond* ☎ *02–31–51–25–50* 🌐 *www.bayeuxmuseum.com* 🎟 *€10* 🕒 *Closed Jan.*

Cathédrale Notre-Dame

RELIGIOUS SITE | Bayeux's mightiest edifice, the Cathédrale Notre-Dame, is a harmonious mixture of Norman and Gothic architecture. Note the portal on the south side of the transept that depicts the assassination of English archbishop Thomas à Becket in Canterbury Cathedral in 1170, following his courageous opposition to King Henry II's attempts to control the church. Guided tours are offered at 10 am and 2:15 pm in July and August. ✉ *Rue du Bienvenu* ☎ *02–31–51–28–28* 🌐 *www.bayeux-bessin-tourisme.com/en/visiteguidee/the-cathedral-of-bayeux* 🎫 *Tour €5.*

Conservatoire de la Dentelle
MUSEUM | Handmade lace is a specialty of Bayeux. The best place to learn about it—and buy some to take home—is the Conservatoire de la Dentelle near the cathedral. ✉ *6 rue du Bienvenu* ☎ *02–31–92–73–80* 🌐 *dentelledebayeux.free.fr* 🎫 *Free* 🕒 *Closed Sun.*

Musée Baron-Gérard
MUSEUM | Housed in the Bishop's Palace beneath the cathedral, the Musée Baron-Gérard (also known as the Musée d'Art et d'Histoire de Baron Gérard or MAHB) displays a fine collection of Bayeux porcelain and lace, plus ceramics from Rouen, vintage pharmaceutical jars, 16th- to 19th-century furniture, and paintings by local artists. Note the magnificent plane tree out front—dubbed the Tree of Liberty, it was planted in 1797. ✉ *37 rue du Bienvenu* ☎ *02–31–92–14–21* 🌐 *www.bayeuxmuseum.com/mahb.html* 🎫 *€8* 🕒 *Closed Jan.*

Musée de la Bataille de Normandie (*Battle of Normandy Museum*)
MUSEUM | Exhibits at the Musée de la Bataille de Normandie trace the story of the struggle from June 6 to August 29, 1944. Located near the moving British War Cemetery, it contains some impressive war paraphernalia. ✉ *Bd. du Général-Fabian-Ware* ☎ *02–31–51–25–50* 🌐 *www.bayeuxmuseum.com/en/memorial-museum-battle-of-normandy* 🎫 *€8.*

🛏 Hotels

Château d'Audrieu
$$$ | **HOTEL** | With princely opulence, overstuffed chairs, wall sconces, and antiques, this family-owned château and its elegant 18th-century facade fulfill the Hollywood notion of a palatial property. **Pros:** grandiose building (including a treehouse suite); magnificent gardens; great restaurant. **Cons:** out-of-the-way location; restaurant is expensive; breakfast not included. [$] *Rooms from: €302* ✉ *Off D82, 13 km (8 miles) southeast of Bayeux, Audrieu* ☎ *02–31–80–21–52* 🌐 *www.chateaudaudrieu.com* 🕒 *Closed Nov.–Mar.* 🛏 *30 rooms* 🍴 *No meals.*

Grand Hôtel du Luxembourg
$ | **HOTEL** | Don't be misled by the name—the small guest rooms here are more bland than grand, but they do have updated comforts and all but two face a courtyard garden. **Pros:** quiet; central location; nice restaurant. **Cons:** unattractive lobby; some rooms are on the dark side; rooms on the small side. [$] *Rooms from: €110* ✉ *25 rue des Bouchers* ☎ *02–31–92–00–04* 🌐 *www.hotel-luxembourg-bayeux.com* 🕒 *Closed mid-Jan.–Feb.* 🛏 *28 rooms* 🍴 *No meals.*

The D-Day Beaches

History set its sights along the coasts of Normandy at 6:30 am on June 6, 1944, as the 135,000 men and 20,000 vehicles of the Allied forces made land in their first incursion in Europe in World War II. The entire operation on this "Longest Day" was called Operation Overlord—the code name for the invasion of Normandy. Five beachheads (dubbed Utah, Omaha, Gold, Juno, and Sword) were established along the coast to either side of Arromanches. Preparations started in mid-1943, and British shipyards worked furiously through the following winter and spring building two artificial harbors (called "mulberries"), boats, and landing equipment. The British and Canadian troops that landed on Sword, Juno, and Gold on June 6, 1944, quickly pushed inland and joined with parachute regiments previously dropped behind German lines, before encountering fierce resistance at Caen, which did not fall until July 9.

GETTING HERE AND AROUND

Since public buses from Bayeux are infrequent, it's best to take a guided bus tour or drive yourself on a DIY excursion through the area.

⊙ Sights

Musee du Débarquement Utah Beach

BEACH—SIGHT | In La Madeleine, inspect the sleek Musee du Débarquement Utah Beach (Utah Beach D-Day Museum)—a stunning facility, located right on the beachhead, where exhibits include vintage aircraft and a W5 Utah scale model detailing the German defenses. Continue north to the **Dunes de Varreville**, where you'll find a monument to French hero General Leclerc, who landed here. Offshore you can see the fortified **Iles St-Marcouf.** Carry on to Quinéville, at the far end of Utah Beach, to visit the **World War II Museum** at 18 avenue de la Plage (☎ 02–33–95–95–95 ⊕ www. worldwar2-museum.com); open daily from April to August, this small museum evokes life during the German Occupation (€7). ⊠ Plage de La Madeleine, Sainte-Marie-du-Mont ☎ 02–33–71–53–35 ⊕ www.utah-beach.com ⊠ €8.

★ Omaha Beach

BEACH—SIGHT | You won't be disappointed by the rugged terrain and windswept sand of Omaha Beach, 16 km (10 miles) northwest of Bayeux. Here you can find the **Monument du Débarquement** (Monument to the Normandy Landings) and the **Musée-Mémorial d'Omaha Beach,** a large shedlike structure packed with tanks, dioramas, and archival photographs that stand silent witness to "Bloody Omaha." Nearby, in Vierville-sur-Mer, is the **U.S. National Guard Monument.** Throughout June 6, Allied forces battled a hailstorm of German bullets and bombs, but by the end of the day they had taken the Omaha Beach sector—suffering grievous losses in the process. In Colleville-sur-Mer, overlooking Omaha Beach, is the hilltop **American Cemetery and Memorial,** designed by landscape architect Markley Stevenson; you can look out to sea across the landing beach from a platform on its north side. ⊠ Les Moulins, Av. de la Libération, Saint-Laurent-sur-Mer ☎ 02–31–21–97–44 ⊕ www.musee-memorial-omaha.com ⊠ €7 ⊗ Closed late Nov.–early Feb.

Pointe du Hoc Ranger Monument

BEACH—SIGHT | The most spectacular scenery along the coast is at the Pointe du Hoc, 13 km (8 miles) west of St-Laurent. Wildly undulating grassland leads past ruined blockhouses to a cliff-top observatory and a German machine-gun post whose intimidating mass of reinforced concrete merits chilly exploration. Despite Spielberg's cinematic genius, it remains hard to imagine just how Colonel Rudder and his 225 Rangers—only 90 survived—managed to scale the jagged cliffs with rope ladders and capture the German defenses in one of the most heroic and dramatic episodes of the war. A granite memorial pillar now stands on top of a concrete bunker, but the site otherwise remains as the Rangers left it—look down through the barbed wire at the jutting cliffs the troops ascended and see the huge craters left by exploded shells. The American Battle Monuments Commission, which maintains the site, provides a self-guided tour that passes ammunition bunkers, a hospital bunker, antiaircraft positions, and other sites. ⊠ Cricqueville-en-Bessin ☎ 02–31–51–62–00 ⊠ Free.

Utah Beach

BEACH—SIGHT | Head east on D67 from Ste-Mère to Utah Beach, which, being sheltered from the Atlantic winds by the Cotentin Peninsula and surveyed by lowly sand dunes rather than rocky cliffs, proved easier to attack than Omaha. Allied troops stormed the beach at dawn, and just a few hours later had managed to conquer the German defenses, heading inland to join up with the airborne troops. ✉ *Utah Beach, Sainte-Marie-du-Mont.*

Hotels

Hotel du Casino

$ | **HOTEL** | You can't get closer to the action than this—this handsome, triangular-gabled stone hotel looks directly onto Omaha Beach. **Pros:** calm atmosphere; right by the beach; delicious seafood restaurant. **Cons:** small bathrooms; slow service in restaurant; rooms could use an update. [$] *Rooms from: €100* ✉ *Rue de la Percée, Vierville-sur-Mer* ☎ *02–31–22–41–02* 🌐 *www.omaha-beach-hotel.biz* 🕒 *Closed mid-Nov.–Mar.* 🛏 *12 rooms* 🍴 *Free Breakfast.*

La Chenevière

$$$$ | **HOTEL** | Occupying an elegant 18th-century mansion that's topped by an impressive mansard roof and surrounded by cheerful gardens, this is a true oasis of peace—although located only a few miles inland from World War II sites like Omaha Beach, it feels light-years away. **Pros:** magnificent architecture; luxurious rooms; excellent restaurant. **Cons:** three different buildings; expensive; breakfast not included. [$] *Rooms from: €350* ✉ *Les Escures-Commes, off D6, Port-en-Bessin-Huppain* ☎ *02–31–51–25–25* 🌐 *www.lacheneviere.com* 🕒 *Closed Dec.–Mar.* 🛏 *27 rooms* 🍴 *No meals.*

Ste-Mère Église

59 km (22 miles) northwest of Bayeux.

Ste-Mère's symbolic importance as the first French village to be liberated from the Nazis is commemorated by the Borne 0 (Zero) outside the town hall—a large dome milestone marking the start of the Voie de la Liberté (Freedom Way), charting the Allies' progress across France. The main reason to visit, especially if you're here for the D-Day Beaches, is the fascinating Musée Airborne.

GETTING HERE AND AROUND

The nearest train station is in neighboring Carentan. Otherwise, the town is a short drive from the D-Day Beaches or Bayeux.

Sights

Musée Airborne (*Airborne Museum*)

MUSEUM | Constructed behind the town church in 1964 in the form of an open parachute, this fascinating museum houses documents, maps, mementos, and one of the Waco CG4A gliders used to drop troops. ✉ *14 rue Eisenhower, Sainte-Mère-Église* ☎ *02–33–41–41–35* 🌐 *www.musee-airborne.com* 🎟 *€10.*

Sainte-Mère Église

HISTORIC SITE | At 2:30 am on June 6, 1944, the 82nd Airborne Division was dropped over Ste-Mère, heralding the start of D-Day operations. After securing their position, U.S. forces pushed north, then west, cutting off the Cotentin Peninsula on June 18 and taking Cherbourg on June 26. German defenses proved fiercer farther south, and St-Lô was not liberated until July 19. ✉ *Sainte-Mère-Église* ☎ *02–33–21–00–33 for tourist office* 🌐 *www.ot-baieducotentin.fr.*

St-Lô

36 km (22 miles) southwest of Bayeux.

St-Lô, perched dramatically on a rocky spur above the Vire Valley, was a key communications center that suffered so badly in World War II it became known as the "capital of ruins." The medieval Église Notre-Dame bears mournful witness to those dark days: its imposing, spire-top west front was never rebuilt, merely shored up with a wall of greenish stone. Reconstruction elsewhere, though, was wholesale. Some of it was spectacular, like the slender, spiral-staircase tower outside the Mairie (Town Hall); the circular theater; or the openwork belfry of the church of Ste-Croix. The town was freed by American troops, and its rebuilding was financed with U.S. support, notably from the city of Baltimore. The Hôpital Mémorial France–États-Unis (France–United States Memorial Hospital), designed by Paul Nelson and featuring a giant mosaic by Fernand Léger, was named to honor those links.

GETTING HERE AND AROUND
Several trains daily come from Caen (50 mins, €14.10). Another 11 per day, departing from Gare St-Lazare, connect St-Lô and the capital; the trip requires a change in either Caen or Lison (3 hrs, €46).

VISITOR INFORMATION St-Lô Tourist Office ⊠ *Plage Verte, 60 rue de la Poterne* ☎ *02–14–29–00–17* ⊕ *www.ot-saintloag-glo.fr.*

Sights

Haras National (*National Stud*)
FARM/RANCH | St-Lô, the capital of the Manche *département* (province), also considers itself France's horse capital. Hundreds of breeders are based in its environs, and this stud farm was established here in 1886. It's open for unguided visits year-round. ⊠ *Rue du Maréchal*

Juin ☎ *02–14–29–00–17 for tourist office* ⊕ *www.haras-nationaux.fr.*

Musée des Beaux-Arts et d'Histoire
MUSEUM | St-Lô has the perfect French provincial art museum. Its halls are airy, seldom busy, and not too big, yet full of varied exhibits—including an unexpected masterpiece: *Gombault et Macée,* a set of nine silk-and-wool tapestries woven in Bruges around 1600 relating a tale about a shepherd couple, exquisitely showcased in a special circular room. Other highlights include brash modern tapestries by Jean Lurçat; paintings by Corot, Boudin, and Géricault; and court miniatures by Daniel Saint. Photographs, models, and documents evoke St-Lô's wartime devastation, as does a Fernand Léger watercolor, given to the museum by his wife in memory of his work on the town's postwar reconstruction ⊠ *Centre Culturel, Pl. du Champ-de-Mars* ☎ *02–33–72–52–55* ⊕ *www.musees-normandie.fr/musees-normandie/musee-des-beaux-arts-de-saint-lo* ☑ *€5* ☉ *Closed Mon.*

Granville

107 km (67 miles) southwest of Caen.

Proud locals like to call Granville the "Monaco of the North" for its seawater therapy center and casino, but gambling aside, Granville still has a down-to-earth feel. Granite houses cluster around the church in the Vieille Ville, and the harbor below is full of working boats. From the ramparts there are fine views of the English Channel; catamarans breeze over to Jersey and the Îles Chausey daily in summer. Drive a few miles down the coast to find sandy beaches and a view of distant Mont-St-Michel. The **Grand Pardon de la Mer et des Corporations,** a religious festival devoted to the sea, is celebrated in Granville on the last Sunday of July with a military parade, regatta, and platefuls of shellfish. The town's

Christian Dior museum, housed in the designer's childhood home, honors this famous native son.

GETTING HERE AND AROUND

Thirteen trains daily leave Paris-Montparnasse for Granville (3 hrs, €47.50); regular bus service also links it to St-Lô (€2.30).

VISITOR INFORMATION Granville Tourist Office ⊠ *4 cours Jonville, adjoining City Hall* ☎ *02–33–91–30–03* ⊕ *www. ville-granville.fr.*

Sights

Musée Dior

HOUSE | If you've ever imagined your home strewn with haute-couture creations, this place will, perhaps, give you a clearer picture. Christian Dior's childhood abode is now a museum dedicated to the fashion designer; the house would prove to be a source of inspiration throughout his career, as he recalled "the nostalgia of stormy nights, of the foghorn, of the Norman drizzle." A number of his garments are on display, and special exhibitions focus on themes like Dior creations worn by movie stars on- and off-screen. The beautiful "artist's" garden, created by Dior's mother Madeleine, overlooks the sea. On select Wednesdays, the museum offers themed workshops to children and adults. ⊠ *Villa "Les Rhumbs," 1 rue d'Estouteville* ☎ *02–33–61–48–21* ⊕ *www.musee-dior-granville.com* 🔑 *Museum €8; garden free* 🕒 *Closed Mon.*

Mont-St-Michel

61 km (39 miles) southwest of St-Lô, 123 km (77 miles) southwest of Caen, 67 km (42 miles) north of Rennes, 325 km (202 miles) west of Paris.

Mont-St-Michel is the third-most-visited sight in France, after the Eiffel Tower and the Louvre. This beached mass of granite, rising some 400 feet, was begun in

709 and is crowned with the "Marvel," or great monastery, which was built during the 13th century.

GETTING HERE AND AROUND

There are two routes to Mont-St-Michel, depending on whether you arrive from Caen or from Paris. From Caen you can take either an early-morning or an afternoon train to Pontorson, the nearest rail station (2 hrs, €28.80), and then hop a cab or bus for the 15-minute drive to the foot of the abbey (both leave from in front of the station). From Paris, take the TGV from Gare Montparnasse and connect by bus; the total journey costs €68, with restricted, nonrefundable fares as low as €27. There are several early-morning choices that allow you a full day on the Mont, including one train leaving at 7:40 am and arriving at 10:55 am, and another leaving at 8:14 am and arriving at 11:25 am.

Paris City Vision (⊕ *www.pariscityvision. com*) also runs full-day bus excursions from the capital to Mont-St-Michel for €169, meals and admissions included. But this is definitely not for the faint of heart—buses leave Paris at 7:15 am and return around 9:15 pm.

VISITOR INFORMATION Mont-St-Michel Tourist Office ⊠ *Corps de Garde, Bd. de l'Avancée, Le Mont-Saint-Michel* ☎ *02–33–60–14–30* ⊕ *www.ot-mont-saintmichel.com.*

Sights

Abbaye du Mont-St-Michel

RELIGIOUS SITE | A magnetic beacon to millions of travelers each year, this "wonder of the Western World"—a 264-foot mound of rock topped by a history-shrouded abbey—remains the crowning glory of medieval France. Wrought by nature and centuries of tireless human toil, the sea-surrounded mass of granite adorned with the soul-lifting silhouette of the Abbaye du Mont-St-Michel may well be your most lasting image of Normandy.

The abbey is perched on a 264-foot-high rock a few hundred yards off the coast: it's surrounded by water during the year's highest tides and by desolate sand flats the rest of the time. Be warned: tides in the bay are dangerously unpredictable. The sea can rise up to 45 feet at high tide and rushes in at incredible speed—more than a few ill-prepared tourists over the years have drowned. Also, be warned that there are patches of dangerous quicksand.

Legend has it that the Archangel Michael appeared in 709 to Aubert, Bishop of Avranches, inspiring him to build an oratory on what was then called Mont Tombe. The rock and its shrine were soon the objects of pilgrimages. The original church was completed in 1144, but additional buildings were added in the 13th century to accommodate monks as well as the hordes of pilgrims who flocked here even during the Hundred Years' War, when the region was in English hands. During the period when much of western France was subjected to English rule, the abbey remained a symbol, both physical and emotional, of French independence. Because of its legendary origins and the sheer exploit of its centuries-long construction, the abbey became known as the "Merveille de l'Occident" (Wonder of the Western World).

Year-round, free 75 minute-long guided tours in English and French (frequency depending on season) can take you through the impressive Romanesque and Gothic abbey and the spectacular **Église Abbatiale,** the abbey church, which crowns the rock, as well as the **Merveille,** a 13th-century, three-story collection of rooms and passageways. The tourism office also offers a list of local experts available for tours on its website. La Merveille was built by King Philippe Auguste around and on top of the monastery; on its second floor is the Mont's grandest chamber, the **Salle des Chevaliers.** Another longer tour, which

also includes the celebrated **Escalier de Dentelle** (Lace Staircase), and the pre-Roman, exquisitely evocative **Notre-Dame-sous-Terre** has a higher ticket price and is only given in French. Invest in at least one tour while you are here—some of them get you on top of or into things you can't see alone. If you choose to proceed independently, stop halfway up Grande-Rue at the medieval parish church of St-Pierre to admire the richly carved side chapel with its dramatic statue of St-Michael slaying the dragon.

Give yourself at least half a day here, and follow your nose. The mount is full of nooks, crannies, little gardens, and echoing views from the ramparts. It's worth lingering to see the Mont spectacularly illuminated, nightly from dusk to midnight. ⊠ *Le Mont-Saint-Michel* ☎ *02–33–89–80–00* ⊕ *www.mont-saint-michel. monuments-nationaux.fr* ⊠ *From €9.*

Archéoscope

MUSEUM | Explore the myths and legends of the Mont through a sound-and-light show at the Archéoscope. Some exhibits use wax figures fitted out in the most glamorous costumes of the 15th century. ⊠ *Grande-Rue, Le Mont-Saint-Michel* ☎ *02–33–89–01–85* ⊕ *www.lemont-saintmichel.info* ⊠ *From €9* ⊙ *Closed mid-Nov.–Jan., except for 2 wks of end-of-year holidays.*

The Logis Tiphaine

MUSEUM | Bertrand Duguesclin built this home for his wife Tiphaine in 1365. The former was a general fierce in his allegiance to the cause of French independence; the latter was a famed astrologer. Now a museum, the logis traces the intriguing couple's marital life through rooms filled with period furnishings and interesting artifacts—including a medieval chastity belt, armor, and astrological tools. ⊠ *Grande-Rue, Le Mont-Saint-Michel* ☎ *02–33–89–02–02* ⊕ *www.lemontsaintmichel.info* ⊠ *From*

Continued on page 296

MONT-ST-MICHEL

A magnetic beacon to millions
of travelers each year, this
"Wonder of the Western World"
—a 264-foot mound of rock
topped by a history-shrouded
abbey—remains the crowning
glory of medieval France.

by Jennifer Ladonne

Wrought by nature and centuries of tireless human toil, this mass of granite surmounted by the soul-lifting silhouette of the **Abbaye du Mont-St-Michel** is Normandy's most enduring image. Its fame stems not just from the majesty of its geographical situation but even more from its impressive history. Perched on the border between Normandy and Brittany, the medieval Mont (or Mount) was a political football between English conquerors and French kings for centuries. Mont-St-Michel was designed to be as much a fortress as it was a shrine, so it looks as tough as it is beautiful.

Legend has it that the Archangel Michael appeared in 709 to Aubert, Bishop of Avranches, inspiring him to build an oratory on what was then called Mont Tombe. The original church was completed in 1144, but further buildings were added in the 13th century to accommodate the hordes of pilgrims—known as *miquelots*—who flocked here even during the Hundred Years' War (1337–1453), when the region was in English hands.

Out of the French rulers' desire to protect Brittany from subjugation by the Normans (whose leader, William the Conqueror, had assumed the English throne in 1066) came the clever strategy of what we would call propaganda. Because of St. Michel's legendary role as dragon slayer and leader of the Heavenly Army, the French lords transformed him, and the Mont, into a major rallying force. During this period the abbey remained a symbol, both physical and emotional, of French independence.

By 1203, King Philippe-Auguste of France had succeeded in wresting the Mont back from the Normans and to shore up French popularity in Normandy he provided funds to restore the abbey. The resulting, greatly expanded, three-level Gothic abbey (1203–1228) became known as *La Merveille* (The Marvel).

During the French Revolution, the abbey was converted into a prison, but shortly after Victor Hugo (of *Hunchback of Notre Dame* fame) declaimed "A toad in a reliquary! When will we understand in France the sanctity of monuments?," the prison was converted into a museum in 1874 and, fittingly, Emmanuel Frémiet's great gilt statute of St. Michael was added to the spire in 1897.

Only at high tide is the Mont transformed into an island.

CLIMB EVERY MONT

Mont-St-Michel is the result of more than 500 years of construction, from 1017 to 1521, and traces the history of French medieval architecture, from earliest Romanesque to its last flowering, Flamboyant Gothic.

HOW TO TOUR THE MONT

There are two basic options for touring the abbey of Mont-St-Michel: guided tours and exploring on your own (which you can do with the aid of an excellent audioguide tour in English). Realistically, a visit to Mont-St-Michel's abbey and village needs a half a day, but an entire day is needed if you do several of the museums, go on one of the abbey's guided tours, and fit in a walk on the surrounding expanses of sand.

General admission to the abbey includes an optional 75-minute guided tour in English, offered twice a day and night in high season. The English-language tour takes you throughout the spectacular **Église Abbatiale**, the abbey church that crowns the rock, as well as the **Merveille,** a 13th-century, three-story collection of rooms and passageways built by King Philippe-Auguste. The French tour also includes the celebrated **Escalier de Dentelle** (Lace Staircase) and other highlights. Invest in at least one tour while you are here—each of them gets you on top of or into things you can't see alone.

If you do go it alone, stop halfway up Grande-Rue at the church of St-Pierre to admire its richly carved side chapel with its dramatic statue of St. Michael slaying the dragon. The famous **Grand Degré** staircase leads to the abbey entrance, from which a wider flight of steps climbs to the **Saut Gautier Terrace** outside the sober, dignified church. After visiting the arcaded cloisters alongside, you can wander at leisure, and probably get lost, among the maze of vaulted halls.

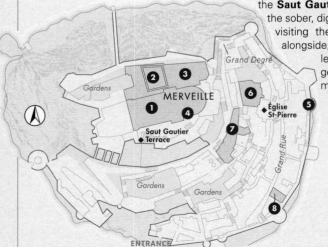

(above) Watchtower at Mont-Saint-Michel

DON'T MISS

1 Église Abbatiale (above). Crowning the mount, the Abbey Church is in two different styles. The main nave and transepts (1020–1135) were built in the Norman Romanesque style; after the collapse of the original chancel in 1421, it was rebuilt in Flamboyant Gothic with seven Rayonnant-style chapels.

2 La Cloitre de l'Abbatiale (above). The main cloister was the only part of the abbey complex open to "heaven"—the sky. Its southern gallery contains the lavabos (washing stands) of the monks. Look for the column capitals beautifully chiseled with flower and vine motifs.

3 Salle des Chevaliers (above). Part of the triple-tiered "La Merveille"—the complex of state chambers, refectory, and cloister that surrounds the main church—the Knights' Hall was originally a scriptorium for copying manuscripts. It was the only heated room on the Mont.

4 Escalier de Dentelle Set atop one of the "flying buttresses" (top right) of the main church, the famous perforated Lace Staircase is a bravura Gothic showpiece of carved stone. It leads to a parapet—adorned with stone gargoyles—390 feet above the sea.

MUSEUMS

Scattered through the Mont are four mini-museums. The most popular is the **5 Archéoscope** whose sound-and-light show, *L'Eau et La Lumiere* (Water and Light), offers the best introduction to the Mont. Some exhibits use wax figures garbed in the most elegant 15th-century–style clothes. **6 The Logis Tiphaine** is the home that Bertrand Duguesclin, a general fierce in his allegiance to the cause of French independence, built for his wife Tiphaine in 1365. **7 The Musée Historique** traces the 1,000-year history of the Mont in one of its former prisons. **8 The Musée Maritime** explores the science of the Mont's tidal bay and has a vast collection of model ships.

INFORMATION

☎ 02–33–60–14–30.
⊕ www.ot-montsaintmichel.com
🎫 From € 9.

€9 ⏲ Closed mid-Nov.–Jan., except for 2 wks of end-of-year holidays.

Musée de la Mer et de l'Ecologie (*Musée Maritime*)

MUSEUM | This museum explores the science of the Mont's tidal bay and has a vast collection of model ships. ✉ *Grande-Rue, Le Mont-Saint-Michel* ☎ *02–33–60–85–12* 🌐 *www.lemontsaintmichel.info* 🎫 *From €9* ⏲ *Closed mid-Nov.–Jan., except for 2 wks of end-of-year holidays.*

Musée Historique

MUSEUM | Inside a former prison, the Musée Historique traces the 1,000-year history of the Mont. ✉ *Grande-Rue, Le Mont-Saint-Michel* ☎ *02–33–60–07–01* 🌐 *www.ot-montsaintmichel.com* 🎫 *From €9* ⏲ *Closed mid-Nov.–Jan., except for 2 wks of end-of-year holidays.*

🍴 Restaurants

La Sirène

$ | FRENCH | Tunnel through a street-level gift shop to find this cheerful, second-floor crêperie, notable for its friendly service and local ingredients. It's a top choice for lunch if you're traveling with kids. **Known for:** family-friendly atmosphere; fantastic traditional Norman cider; classic crêpes. [$] *Average main: €12* ✉ *Grande-Rue, Le Mont-Saint-Michel* ☎ *02–33–60–08–60.*

Le Pré Sale

$$$ | FRENCH | While not on the Mont itself, Le Pré Sale makes up for this with a tasty menu of Normandy favorites, including a preparation of salt-marsh lamb, presented roasted or grilled, filleted or as a chop. Three set menus also call attention to nonlamb dishes, like locally sourced oysters, steak with Camembert sauce, and a rich gourmet salad with duck, ham, and foie gras. **Known for:** classic Normandy dishes; nontouristy option in the area; friendly atmosphere. [$] *Average main: €25* ✉ *Rte. du Mont-St-Michel, BP 8, Le Mont-Saint-Michel* ☎ *02–33–60–24–17* 🌐 *www.restaurantlepresale-montsaintmichel.com.*

🛏 Hotels

★ **Auberge St-Pierre**

$$$ | HOTEL | This inn is a popular spot due to the fact that it's in a half-timber 15th-century building adjacent to the ramparts and has its own garden restaurant (half-board rates are available). **Pros:** great location; good dining options; historic decor. **Cons:** not all rooms have views; no elevator; rooms on the small side. [$] *Rooms from: €230* ✉ *Grande-Rue, Le Mont-Saint-Michel* ☎ *02–33–60–14–03* 🌐 *www.auberge-saint-pierre.fr* 🔑 *21 rooms* 🍽 *Free Breakfast.*

La Mère Poulard

$$$ | HOTEL | Mont-St-Michel's most famous hostelry can be tough to book: after all, its historic restaurant is the birthplace of Mère Poulard's legendary soufflélike omelet. **Pros:** right at the entrance to the abbey; the best hotel dining in town; full of history. **Cons:** breakfast is extra; some rooms are small; restaurant fills up fast, especially in summer, so reserve ahead. [$] *Rooms from: €240* ✉ *Grande-Rue, Le Mont-Saint-Michel* ☎ *02–33–89–68–68* 🌐 *www.merepoulard.com* 🔑 *27 rooms* 🍽 *No meals.*

Les Terrasses Poulard

$$ | HOTEL | Run by the same folks who own the noted Mère Poulard hotel, this charming ensemble of buildings is clustered around a small garden in the middle of the Mont. **Pros:** lots of space in rooms; great setting; great views. **Cons:** a long way to the parking lot; steps to climb; breakfast not included. [$] *Rooms from: €125* ✉ *Grande-Rue, Le Mont-Saint-Michel* ☎ *02–33–89–02–02* 🌐 *www.lemontsaintmichel.info* 🔑 *29 rooms* 🍽 *No meals.*

Chapter 7

BRITTANY

7

Updated by
Jennifer Ladonne

👁 **Sights**
★★★☆☆

🍴 **Restaurants**
★★★★☆

🛏 **Hotels**
★★★☆☆

👜 **Shopping**
★★★☆☆

🍸 **Nightlife**
★☆☆☆☆

WELCOME TO BRITTANY

TOP REASONS TO GO

★ **The Granite Coast:** Experience the extreme drama of the Granite Coast, with its crazy-shape outcrops, or the rippling waters of the Bay of Morbihan, snuggling in the Gulf Stream behind the angry Atlantic.

★ **The Wild Isle:** Venture down the untamed Quiberon Peninsula and catch a boat to rugged, unspoiled Belle-Ile-en-Mer, Brittany's wildest island.

★ **Gauguin's Pont-Aven:** A city made for artists, Pont-Aven and its colorful folkloric ways helped ignite the painter's interest in Tahiti.

★ **St-Malo and Dinard:** A ferry ride across the Rance River links two delightfully contrasting towns: romantic, once pirate-ridden St-Malo and genteel, Edwardian Dinard.

★ **Ancient wonders:** Contemplate the solemn majesty of row upon row of ancient menhirs at Carnac, the "French Stonehenge."

Bretons like to say they are Celtic, not Gallic, and other French people sometimes feel they are in a foreign land when they visit this jagged triangle perched on the northwest tip of mainland Europe. Two sides of the triangle are defined by the sea. Brittany's northern coast faces the English Channel; its western coast defies the Atlantic Ocean. The north of Brittany tends to be wilder than the south, or Basse Bretagne, where the countryside becomes softer as it descends toward Nantes and the Loire. But wherever you go, the "Côtes d'Armor" (Lands of the Sea) are never too far away.

1 Vitré. A perfectly preserved medieval town.

2 Rennes. The lively capital of Brittany.

3 Combourg. The hometown of Romantic writer Chateaubriand.

4 Dinan. Another beautifully preserved medieval town.

5 Cancale. A charming fishing village famed for its oysters.

6 St-Malo. A historic sailing town once popular with pirates.

7 Dinard. Once a Belle Époque resort for aristocrats that still retains its elegance.

8 Trébeurden. A popular vacation town on the Côtes d'Armor.

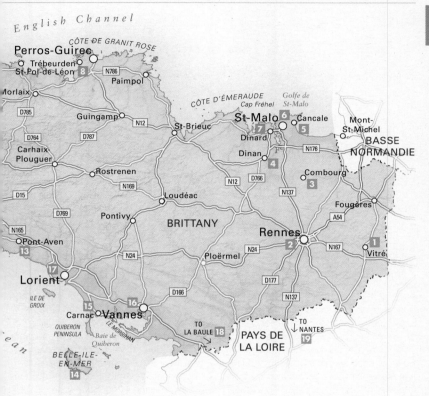

English Channel

CÔTE DE GRANIT ROSE

Perros-Guirec
Trébeurden
St-Pol-de-Léon **8**
Paimpol
N786

Morlaix
D785
Guingamp
N12
St-Brieuc
CÔTE D'ÉMERAUDE   Golfe de
Cap Fréhel   St-Malo
St-Malo **6** Cancale
7 **5**
Dinard   Mont-
St-Michel
D764
D787
Carhaix-
Plouguer
Rostrenen
D15
D769
Pontivy
N169
Loudéac
Dinan
4
Combourg
3
N176
BASSE
NORMANDIE
N12
D766
N137
Fougères
A54
BRITTANY
Rennes
2
N167
Vitré **1**
N165
Pont-Aven
13
N24
Ploërmel
N24
D177
17
Lorient
ILE DE
GROIX
15   **16**
Carnac Vannes
D166
N137
QUIBERON
PENINSULA   Baie de
Quiberon
TO
LA BAULE **18**
TO
NANTES
19
BELLE-ILE-
EN-MER
14
PAYS DE
LA LOIRE

9 **Ste-Anne-la-Palud.** A seaside village that holds an annual Breton event called the village pardon.

10 **Douarnenez.** A charming fishing town.

11 **Quimper.** The birthplace of Quimperware, the celebrated French hand-painted pottery.

12 **Concarneau.** An industrial yet picturesque town.

13 **Pont-Aven.** Once an artists' colony that attracted the likes of Paul Gauguin.

14 **Belle-Ile-en-Mer.** A beautiful island still mostly undiscovered by tourists.

15 **Carnac.** Home to beaches and ancient stone monuments.

16 **Vannes.** One of the region's few towns to be spared any damage during World War II.

17 **Lorient.** A fishing port with important World War II history.

18 **La Baule.** A 19th-century resort town.

19 **Nantes.** A historic Breton city.

Wherever you wander in Brittany—along jagged coastal cliffs, through cobbled seaport streets, into time-burnished cider pubs—you'll hear the primal pulse of Celtic music. Made up of bagpipes, drums, and the thin, haunting filigree of a tin whistle, these folkloric tunes tell you that you are in the land of the Bretons, where Celtic bloodlines run as deep as a druid's roots into the rocky, sea-swept soil.

France's most fiercely and determinedly ethnic people, Bretons delight in celebrating their ancient culture—circle dancing at street fairs, the women donning starched lace-bonnet *coiffes,* and the men in striped fishermen's shirts at the least sign of a regional celebration. They name their children Erwan and Edwige, carry sacred statues in ceremonial religious processions called pardons and pray in hobbit-scale stone churches decked with elfin, moonface gargoyles. Scattered over the mossy hillsides stand Stonehenge-like dolmens and menhirs (prehistoric standing stones), eerie testimony to a primordial culture that predated and has long outlived Frankish France.

Similarities in character, situation, or culture to certain islands across the Channel are by no means coincidental. Indeed, the Celts that migrated to this westernmost outcrop of the French landmass spent much of the Iron Age on the British Isles, where they introduced the indigenes to innovations like the potter's wheel, the rotary millstone, and the compass. This first influx of Continental culture to Great Britain was greeted with typically mixed feelings, and by the late 5th century AD the Saxon hordes had sent these Celtic "Brits" packing southward, to the peninsula that became Brittany. So completely did they dominate their new, Cornwall-like peninsula (appropriately named Finistère, from *finis terrae,* or "land's end") that when in 496 they allied themselves with Clovis, the king of the Franks, he felt as if he'd just claimed a little bit of England.

Needless to say, the cultural exchange flowed both ways over the Channel. From their days on the British Isles the Bretons brought a folklore that shares with England the bittersweet legend of Tristan and Iseult, and that weaves mystical tales of the Cornwall—Cornouaille—of King Arthur and Merlin. They brought a language that still renders village names unpronounceable: Aber-Wrac'h, Tronoën, Locmariaquer, Pouldreuzic, Kerhornaouen. They brought a way of life with them, too: half-timber seaside cider bars, their blackened-oak tables softened with prim bits of lace; stone cottages fringed with clumps of hollyhock, hydrangea, and foxglove; bearded fishermen in yellow oilskins heaving the day's catch into weather-beaten boats as terns and seagulls wheel in their wake. It's a way of life that feels deliciously exotic to the Frenchman and—like the ancient drone of the bagpipes—comfortably, delightfully, even innately familiar to the Anglo-Saxon.

MAJOR REGIONS

Northeast Brittany and the Channel Coast. The northern half of Brittany is demarcated by its 240-km (150-mile) Channel Coast, which stretches from Cancale, just west of Normandy's Mont-St-Michel, to Morlaix. This can be loosely divided into two parts: the Côte d'Emeraude (Emerald Coast), with cliffs punctuated by golden, curving beaches; and the Côte de Granit Rose (Pink Granite Coast), including the astonishing area around Trébeurden, where Brittany's granite takes amazing forms that glow an otherworldly pink. On the road heading there are the gateway city of Rennes; the oyster mecca of Cancale; and the great port of St-Malo, where stone ramparts conjure up the days of marauding corsairs.

The Atlantic Coast. Bypassing the lobster-claw of Brittany's Finistère ("Land's End"), this westernmost region tempts with folkloric treasures like Ste-Anne-la-Palud (famed for its *pardon* festival); Quimper, noted for its signature ceramics; and cheerful riverside villages like Pont-Aven, which Gauguin immortalized in many paintings. Here, the 320-km (200-mile) Atlantic coast zigzags southeast, its frenzied, cliff-bashing surf alternating with sprawling beaches and busy harbors. Belle-Ile is a jewel off the Morbihan coast, another beautiful stretch of shoreline. Enjoy its away-from-it-all atmosphere, because the bustling city of Nantes lies just to the southeast.

Planner

When to Go

The tourist season is short in Brittany: late June through early September. Long, damp winters keep visitors away, and many hotels are closed until Easter. Brittany is particularly crowded in July and August, when most French people are on vacation, so why not opt for crowd-free June or September? Some say early October, with autumnal colors and crisp evenings, is even better and truly makes for an invigorating visit. But if you want to sample local folklore, late summer is the most festive time to come.

Planning Your Time

If you have just a few days here, choose your coast: Channel or Atlantic. Cliffs and beaches, culture and history—both shorelines offer all these and more. St-Malo makes a good base if you're Channel bound. Dinard, the elegant Belle Époque resort once favored by British aristocrats, is nearby; and the lively, student-filled city of Rennes offers an urban respite.

Pretty Vannes is a good base for exploring the Atlantic coast. Highlights hereabouts include lively Quimper, with its fine cathedral and coveted pottery; the painters' village of Pont-Aven, made famous by Gauguin; the prehistoric menhirs of Carnac; the rugged island of Belle-Ile-en-Mer; and the picturesque Bay of Morbihan. The third side of the Brittany triangle is its verdant, unhurried hinterland—charming, but forget it unless you're here for a month.

Did You Know?

Elaborate half-timber houses (called *colombage* in French) are everywhere in Brittany, relics of the medieval days when this region, along with Normandy, was colonized by the English.

Festivals and Pardons

It has been said that there are as many Breton saints as there are stones in the ground. One of the great attractions of Brittany, therefore, remains its many festivals, *pardons* (religious processions), and folklore events. Banners and saintly statues are borne in colorful parades, accompanied by hymns, and the events are often capped by a feast. In February, the great Pardon de Terre-Neuve takes place at St-Malo. Nantes prepares for Easter with a pre-Lenten carnival procession, and then follows up in June with a ceremonial Feux de St-Jean (bonfire honoring St. John). July sees Quimper's Celtic Festival de Cornouaille, while August brings Pont-Aven's Festival of the Golden Gorse and a big pardon in Ste-Anne-la-Palud. Another pardon held in Le Folgoët during September is one of the most extraordinary, with flocks of bishops, Bretons in traditional costumes, and devout pilgrims.

Getting Here and Around

In just over two hours the TGV train from Paris can whisk you to Rennes, the hub of Brittany. Once in the region, you'll find that the rail network can take you onward to many popular places. You'll need to combine a train ride with a short bus jaunt, though, to reach others; and a car will be required if you want to see some of the most sublime (and secluded) landscapes. If you're driving from Paris, it's best to approach Brittany via the A11 expressway.

AIR TRAVEL
The closest major airports are Paris's Charles de Gaulle (Roissy) and Orly; however, Brittany does have several regional airports. The Aéroport Nantes Atlantique and the Aéroport Rennes Bretagne are both served by big players like Air France (⊕ *www.airfrance.com*), as well as assorted low-cost airlines—including

Flybe (⊕ *www.flybe.com*) and HOP! (⊕ *www.hop.fr*)—which provide air links to other European cities, sometimes on a seasonal basis. The Aéroport de Dinard-Pleurtuit-St-Malo, meanwhile, has four weekly connections to London (Stansted) operated by Ryanair (⊕ *www.ryanair.com*).

AIRPORT INFORMATION Aéroport de Dinard-Pleurtuit-Saint-Malo ✉ *RD64, 5 km (3 miles) south of town, Dinard* ☎ *02–99–46–18–46* ⊕ *www.dinard.aeroport.fr.* **Aéroport Nantes Atlantique** ✉ *D85, 8 km (5 miles) southwest of city center, Bouguenais* ☎ *08–92–56–88–00 (€0.34 per min)* ⊕ *www.nantes-aeroport.fr.* **Aéroport Rennes Bretagne** ✉ *D177, 6 kms (4 miles) southwest of city center, Rennes* ☎ *02–99–29–60–00* ⊕ *www.rennes.aeroport.fr.*

BOAT TRAVEL
Brittany Ferries is the leading company for maritime transportation between this region and the United Kingdom. It offers daily overnight crossings from Portsmouth to St-Malo in high season (11 hrs; from €190 for a car and two passengers). Vessels also make the crossing from Plymouth to Roscoff, on Brittany's westernmost tip, up to two times daily: daytime trips take six hours, nighttime ones take nine (from €240 for a car and two passengers).

BOAT INFORMATION Brittany Ferries ☎ *03–30–15–97–00–00* ⊕ *www.brittany-ferries.com.*

BUS TRAVEL
Brittany is serviced by a bewildering number of bus companies. Generally speaking, routes in each part of it are coordinated through an umbrella organization: for travel in the Ille-et-Vilaine region around Rennes, Illenoo is a good bet; for the Morbihan region around Vannes use CTM or Keolis Atlantique; for Finistère and coastal towns near Quimper, arrange your trip through CAT; and for the Côtes d'Armor region

around St-Malo, check out Tibus or Keolis Emeraude.

BUS INFORMATION CAT ☎ *02–98–44– 60–60* ⊕ *www.cat29.fr.* **CTM** ☎ *02–97– 01–22–01 for Vannes* ⊕ *www.lactm. com.* **Illenoo** ☎ *08–10–35–10–35* ⊕ *www. illenoo-services.fr.* **Keolis Atlantique** ☎ *02– 97–47–29–64* ⊕ *www.keolis-atlantique. com.* **Keolis Emeraude** ☎ *02–99–19–70–70* ⊕ *www.keolis-emeraude.com.* **Tibus** ☎ *08–10–22–22–22* ⊕ *www.tibus.fr.*

CAR TRAVEL

Rennes, the gateway to Brittany, is 347 km (215 miles) west of Paris. It can be reached in about three hours via Le Mans using A11 then A81 (A11 continues southwest from Le Mans to Nantes). Rennes is also linked by good roads to Quimper (N24/N165), Vannes (N24/ N166), and several other key locales. A car is pretty much essential if you want to see out-of-the-way places; when planning a coastal road trip, just remember to allocate plenty of time—winding roads make for slow (albeit scenic) driving.

TRAIN TRAVEL

High-speed TGVs from Paris's Gare Montparnasse travel multiple times a day to Rennes (2 hrs 10 mins), Nantes (2 hrs 15 mins), Vannes (3 hrs 20 mins), La Baule (3 hrs 15 mins), Lorient (3 hrs 50 mins), and Quimper (4 hrs 30 mins). The region as a whole is nicely threaded by train lines, making most Breton towns accessible by rail; however, some communities—like Cancale and Carnac—can be reached by car or bus only.

TRAIN INFORMATION SNCF ☎ *3635 (€0.34 per min)* ⊕ *www.voyages-sncf. com.* **TGV** ⊕ *www.sncf.com.*

Restaurants

Crêpes, galettes, and seafood, seafood, seafood are the star attractions at restaurants throughout Brittany. From the fresh oyster stands along the seafront

in Cancale to the finer restaurants of St-Malo and Rennes, you will find ample opportunity to indulge in these delicious offerings—all of which can be washed down by a bottle of locally produced *cidre* (cider). Other regional specialties include the Breton version of pot-au-feu (called *kig ha farz*), featuring tender pork or beef surrounded by buckwheat dumplings, and the legendary *kouign amann,* a divine butter cake.

Hotels

Aside from the usual selection of hotels in the main cities (Rennes and Nantes), Brittany has plenty of small and appealing family-run accommodations that cater to seasonal visitors. Note that many close for one or more months between October and March. Booking ahead is strongly advised for the Easter period. This is also the case for midsummer, when prices are routinely ratcheted up by 30%–50%. Dinard, on the English Channel, and La Baule, on the Atlantic, are the area's two most expensive resorts.

Restaurant and hotel reviews have been shortened. For full information, visit Fodors.com. Restaurant prices are the average cost of a main course at dinner or, if dinner is not served, at lunch. Hotel prices are the lowest cost of a standard double room in high season

What It Costs in Euros			
$	$$	$$$	$$$$
RESTAURANTS			
under €18	€18–€24	€25–€32	over €32
HOTELS			
under €125	€125–€225	€226–€350	over €350

Visitor Information

Different Breton regions have their own tourist offices, as do many individual communities; however, your single best source for trip-planning information in English is the Brittany Tourism website.

CONTACTS Brittany Tourism ⊕ *www.brittanytourism.com* . **Comité Départemental du Tourisme de Loire-Atlantique** ✉ *11 rue du Château de l'Eraudière, Nantes* ☎ *02–51–72–95–30* ⊕ *www.tourisme-loireatlantique.com.* **Côtes-d'Armor Tourisme** ✉ *7 rue St-Benoît, St-Brieuc* ☎ *02–96–58–06–58* ⊕ *www.cotesdarmor.com.* **Finistère Tourisme** ✉ *4 rue du 19 mars 1962, Quimper* ☎ *02–98–76–25–64* ⊕ *www.finisteretourisme.com.* **Maison de la Bretagne** ✉ *8 rue de l'Arrivée, Paris* ☎ *01–53–63–11–50* ⊕ *www.bretagne.bzh.*

Speaking Breton

Most place names in Brittany are in the Breton language; the popular term *plou* means "parish"—this is where the French got the word *plouc,* meaning "hick." Other common geographical names are *coat* (forest), *mor* (sea), *aber* or *aven* (estuary), *ster* (river), and *enez* (island). *Ty* and *ti,* like the French *chez,* mean "at the house of." Traditional Breton folkways are an integral part of France's cultural patrimony—and a priceless boost to tourism—so preserving the Breton language is a goal shared by many.

Vitré

42 km (26 miles) east of Rennes.

There's still a feel of the Middle Ages about the formidable castle, tightly packed half-timber houses, remaining ramparts, and dark alleyways of Vitré (pronounced "vee- *tray*"). Built high above the Vilaine Valley, the small medieval walled town that spreads out from the castle's gates is the best preserved in Brittany and utterly beguiling.

GETTING HERE AND AROUND
Several trains traveling from Paris through Rennes stop daily in Vitré. The trip from Rennes takes 30 minutes (€8.60).

VISITOR INFORMATION Vitré Tourist Office ✉ *Pl. Général de Gaulle* ☎ *02–99–75–04–46* ⊕ *www.bretagne-vitre.com.*

Sights

Château de Vitré

CASTLE/PALACE | Rebuilt in the 14th and 15th centuries to protect Brittany from invasion, the fairy-tale, 11th-century Château de Vitré—shaped in an imposing triangle with fat, round towers—proved to be one of the province's most successful fortresses: during the Hundred Years' War (1337–1453) the English repeatedly failed to take it, even when they occupied the rest of the town. It's a splendid sight, especially from the vantage point of Rue de Fougères across the river valley below. Time, not foreigners, came closest to ravaging the castle, which has been heavily though tastefully restored during the past century.

The **Hôtel de Ville** (town hall), however, is an unfortunate 1913 accretion to the castle courtyard. Visit the wing to the left of the entrance, beginning with the **Tour St-Laurent** and its museum, which contains 15th- and 16th-century sculptures, Aubusson tapestries, and engravings. Continue along the walls via the **Tour de l'Argenterie**—which contains a macabre collection of stuffed frogs and reptiles preserved in glass jars—to the **Tour de l'Oratoire** (Oratory Tower). ✉ *Pl. du Château* ☎ *02–99–75–04–54* ⊕ *www.bretagne-vitre.com* ⤳ *€6* ⊘ *Closed Tues. Oct.–Mar.*

Notre-Dame

RELIGIOUS SITE | The church of Notre-Dame, with its fine, pinnacled south front, was built in the 15th and 16th centuries. This is a good starting point to visit the 10 or so other picturesque historical sites, from medieval postern gateways to the 14th-century St-Nicolas hospital chapel (now a museum of religious art) within town; other jewels, such as Madame de Sévigné's Château-Musée des Roches-Sévigné, are set in the nearby countryside. Inquire at the tourist office for details. ✉ *Pl. Notre-Dame.*

Tour de la Bridole
BUILDING | Fragments of the town's medieval ramparts include the 15th-century Tour de la Bridole, five blocks up from Vitré's castle. ✉ *Rue de la Bridole, near Pl. de la République.*

🛏 Hotels

Le Petit Billot
$ | **HOTEL** | This small family-run hotel has been brought into the 21st century with a streamlined modern look; you'll find that the guest rooms may not be spacious, but they are contemporary, spic-and-span, and a steal at the price. **Pros:** in the heart of town; great value; lovely hosts. **Cons:** rooms are small; most bathrooms have only showers, not tubs; only one room for people with disabilities. [$] *Rooms from: €90* ✉ *5 bis, pl. du Général-Leclerc* ☎ *02–99–75–02–10* 🌐 *www.hotel-vitre.com* 🛏 *20 rooms* 🍴 *No meals.*

Rennes

347 km (215 miles) west of Paris, 107 km (66 miles) north of Nantes.

Rennes (pronounced "wren") is the capital of and traditional gateway to this region. It's also one of Brittany's liveliest cities, thanks to the 40,000-odd students who set a youthful tone during the school year. Place Ste-Anne, where bars and cafés are housed in medieval buildings with character to spare, is particularly packed. Although summer seems to happen elsewhere for most Rennais, it is still a pleasant time for visitors. United with the Kingdom of France in 1532, Rennes has long been the political center of Brittany, and its stature is reflected in grand public edifices—many of them erected after fire swept through the city in 1720. The remaining cobbled streets and 15th-century half-timber houses form an interesting contrast to the classical feel of the cathedral and Jacques Gabriel's disciplined 18th-century granite buildings, broad avenues, and spacious squares.

GETTING HERE AND AROUND

The TGV *Atlantique* arrives from Paris's Gare Montparnasse 22 times daily (2 hrs 10 mins, €30–€50). Rennes's train station (a 20-minute walk from the heart of the city) can also be reached from Nantes (1 hr 30 mins, €28) and St-Malo (55 mins, €16). Buses from Nantes (2 hrs, €2), St-Malo (2 hrs, €5.90), and Mont-St-Michel (70 mins, €12) pull into the *gare routière* next door, though it's not the safest place to hang out. Within the city, buses and subways operated by STAR (🌐 *www.metro-rennes-metropole.fr*) will get you anywhere you want to go. If you'd prefer to cycle, try the Vélo STAR rental scheme (🌐 *www.levelostar.fr*); you'll pay €1 for an hour of pedaling.

VISITOR INFORMATION Rennes Tourist Office ✉ *1 rue St-Malo* ☎ *02–99–67–11–11* 🌐 *www.tourisme-rennes.com.*

👁 Sights

Cathédrale St-Pierre
RELIGIOUS SITE | A late-18th-century building in Classical style that took 57 years to construct, the Cathédrale St-Pierre looms above Rue de la Monnaie at the west end of the Vieille Ville (Old Town), bordered by the Rance River. Stop in to admire its richly decorated interior and outstanding 16th-century Flemish altarpiece. ✉ *Carrefour de la Cathédrale* 🌐 *www.tourisme-rennes.com.*

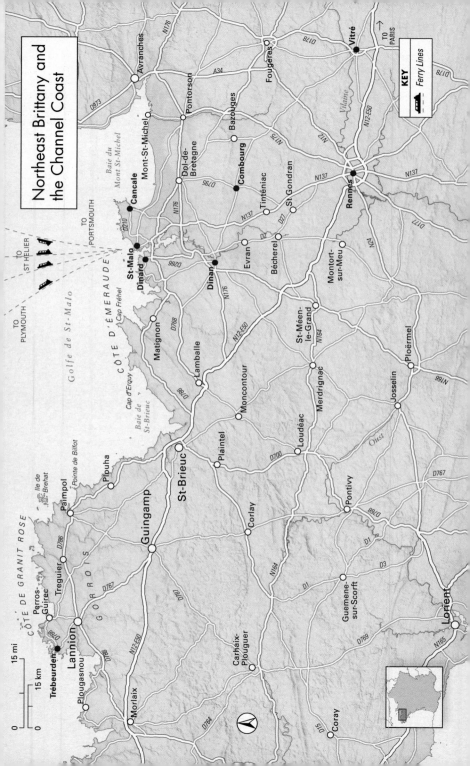

Northeast Brittany and the Channel Coast

KEY

Ferry Lines

TO ST HELIER

TO PORTSMOUTH

TO PLYMOUTH

TO PARIS

Golfe de St-Malo

CÔTE D'ÉMERAUDE

Baie du Mont St-Michel

CÔTE DE GRANIT ROSE

Baie de St-Brieuc

GOËLLO

Cap Fréhel

Cap d'Erquy

Pointe de Bihit

Île de Bréhat

Pointe de Bréhat

Vilaine

Oust

Avranches

Mont-St-Michel

Pontorson

Fougères

Vitré

Bazouges

Combourg

Dol-de-Bretagne

Cancale

St-Malo

Dinard

Dinan

Tinténiac

St-Gondran

Évran

Bécherel

Rennes

Montort-sur-Meu

Matignon

Lamballe

St-Méen-le-Grand

Moncontour

Merdrignac

Josselin

Ploërmel

Plaintel

Loudéac

St-Brieuc

Pontivy

Guingamp

Corlay

Paimpol

Pleubian

Tréguier

Perros-Guirec

Lannion

Trébeurden

Plougasnou

Morlaix

Carhaix-Plouguer

Guémené-sur-Scorff

Lorient

Coray

N176

N178

A34

D973

N176

D795

D210

D2

D27

N137

N137

N137

N12-E50

D778

D778

D177

N12-E50

N24

N12-E50

N137

N176

N176

D768

D766

D768

D700

D767

D766

D767

D786

D767

D766

N164

N164

D1

D1

D3

D767

D768

D769

D764

D787

N12-E50

N165

N166

D15

D992

D992

15 mi

15 km

0

0

Musée de Bretagne (*Museum of Brittany*)
MUSEUM | Designed by superstar architect Christian de Portzamparc, this museum occupies a vast three-part space that it shares with the Rennes municipal library and Espaces des Sciences. Portzamparc's layout harmonizes nicely with the organization of the museum's extensive ethnographic and archaeological collection, which depicts the everyday life of Bretons from prehistoric times to the present. There's also a space devoted to the famous Dreyfus Affair; Alfred Dreyfus, an army captain who was wrongly accused of espionage and whose case was championed by Émile Zola, was tried a second time in Rennes in 1899. ✉ *10 cours des Allies* ☎ *02–23–40–66–00* 🌐 *www.musee-bretagne.fr* 🎟 *From €6* 🕒 *Closed Mon.*

Musée des Beaux-Arts (*Fine Arts Museum*)
MUSEUM | Containing works by Georges de La Tour, Jean-Baptiste Chardin, Camille Corot, Paul Gauguin, and Maurice Utrillo, to name a few, this museum is particularly strong on French 17th-century paintings and drawings, and has an interesting collection of works by modern French artists. ✉ *20 quai Émile Zola* ☎ *02–23–62–17–45* 🌐 *www.mbar.org* 🎟 *€6 (free 1st Sun. of each month)* 🕒 *Closed Mon.*

Parc du Thabor
GARDEN | Make sure you stroll through this lovely park, east of the Palais des Musées. It's a large, formal French garden with regimented rows of trees, shrubs, and flowers, plus a notable view of the church of **Notre-Dame-en-St-Melaine.** ✉ *Pl. St-Melaine.*

Parlement de Bretagne
GOVERNMENT BUILDING | Originally the palatial home of the Breton Parliament and now of the Rennes law courts, the Parlement de Bretagne was designed in 1618 by Salomon de Brosse, architect of the Luxembourg Palace in Paris. It was the most important building in Rennes to escape the 1720 flames; however, in 1994, following a massive demonstration by Breton fishermen demanding state subsidies, another disastrous fire broke out that left it a charred shell. Fortunately, much of the artwork—though damaged—was saved by firefighters, who arrived at the scene after the building was already engulfed in flames. It was a case of the alarm that cried "fire" once too often; a faulty bell, which rang regularly for no reason, had led the man on duty to ignore the signal. It has been completely restored. Call the tourist office (☎ *02–99–67–11–11*) to book a 90-minute guided tour. ✉ *Rue Nationale* 🌐 *www.tourisme-rennes.com* 🎟 *€8, by guided tour only (reservation required)* 🕒 *Closed Tues., Thurs., and Fri.*

🍴 Restaurants

Le Galopin
$ | **FRENCH** | Everybody loves an authentic French brasserie, but very few of these establishments strive to maintain a quality worthy of their traditional cachet; happily, Le Galopin is one of them. The vintage murals, wood panelling, and plush banquettes are the perfect backdrop for all those traditional French favorites: a heaping plate of oysters, followed by steak or fish tartare, Breton lobster, grilled gambas shrimp, or marinated Wagyu beef. **Known for:** excellent prices, especially for fixed-price menus; copious servings; Breton sablée for dessert. [$] *Average main: €16* ✉ *21 av. Jean Janvier* ☎ *02–99–31–55–96* 🌐 *www.legalopin.fr* 🕒 *Closed Sun. No lunch Sat.*

★ **Racines**
$$$ | **MODERN FRENCH** | On full view from her open kitchen, chef Virginie Giboire is cool and precise as she prepares a sophisticated market cuisine that earned her a Michelin star, one of the few restaurants in Rennes to garner that distinction. Everyone nowadays is doing seasonal and local, but Giboire, who trained at Paris's prestigious Ferrandi

One delightful lunch on a Rennes square and all your troubles will melt away.

school and with superstar Thierry Marx, wields a traditional mastery in dishes that carry her unique signature: mixing wild-crafted herbs and seasonal ingredients in dishes like John Dory with spring asparagus, wild garlic, and roasted buckwheat. **Known for:** casual-elegant decor; refined dishes; excellent wine list. $ *Average main: €25* ✉ *12 rue de l'Arsenal* ☎ *02–99–65–64–21* ⊕ *www.racines-restaurant.fr* ⊗ *Closed Sun. and Mon. No lunch Sat.*

Hotels

Garden
$ | HOTEL | With all rooms overlooking a stone-lined, treillage-bedecked garden, this budget hotel likes to welcome visitors to "silent nights"—and cheerful ones, too, thanks to the guest rooms, which are plainly but pleasingly decorated. **Pros:** pretty architecture; central and handy for sights; superfriendly service. **Cons:** smallish rooms; difficult parking; basic amenities. $ *Rooms from: €75* ✉ *3 rue Jean-Marie Duhamel*

☎ *02–99–65–45–06* ⊕ *www.hotel-garden. fr* ⇆ *25 rooms* ⎮◎⎮ *No meals.*

Le Château du Pin
$ | B&B/INN | FAMILY | Bright, welcoming, and blissfully quiet, there's plenty to love about this B&B set in an 18th-century mansion on a lovely 22-acre wooded property a 20-minute drive from Rennes. **Pros:** beautiful grounds; welcoming hosts; in the pretty countryside. **Cons:** rooms are up a set of winding stairs; some rooms a bit outdated; not near nightlife. $ *Rooms from: €98* ✉ *Départementale 125* ☎ *02–99–09–34–05* ⊕ *www. chateau-pin.fr* ⇆ *6 rooms* ⎮◎⎮ *No meals* ▭ *No credit cards.*

Nightlife

Top spots for nightlife are on the streets around Place Ste-Anne.

Serum
BARS/PUBS | A cut above the usual Rennes pub, this sleek cocktail bar with an outdoor terrace may be friendly and laid-back, but it takes its drinks seriously.

Delicious concoctions mix Breton ingredients, like Plougastel strawberries, chouchen (a Breton mead), and infusions of local herbs. At happy hour, from 6 pm to 8 pm, all cocktails are €6. Mocktails are happily offered, too. ⊠ *20 rue du Pré Botté* ☎ *09–66–95–70–21* ⊕ *www.serum-bar.fr.*

Performing Arts

Les Tombées de la Nuit

FESTIVALS | During the first three weekends in July, Les Tombées de la Nuit (or "Nightfalls" Festival) features Celtic music, dance, and theater performances staged in the streets and in churches around town. ⊠ *Rennes* ☎ *02–99–32–56–56* ⊕ *www.lestombeesdelanuit.com.*

Les Trans Musicales

FESTIVALS | The famous annual international rock-and-roll festival, Les Trans Musicales, happens the first half of December in bars around town and at the Théâtre National de Bretagne. ⊠ *Rennes* ☎ *02–99–31–12–10* ⊕ *www.lestrans.com.*

Opéra de Rennes

CONCERTS | FAMILY | Brittany's top classical music venue is the Opéra de Rennes. ⊠ *Pl. de la Mairie* ☎ *02–23–62–28–28 ticket office* ⊕ *www.opera-rennes.com.*

Théâtre National de Bretagne

ARTS CENTERS | FAMILY | A range of performances are staged at the Théâtre National de Bretagne. ⊠ *1 rue St-Hélier* ☎ *02–99–31–55–33* ⊕ *www.t-n-b.fr.*

Combourg

40 km (25 miles) north of Rennes.

The pretty lakeside village of Combourg is dominated by Château de Combourg, the boyhood home of Romantic writer Viscount René de Chateaubriand (1768–1848).

GETTING HERE AND AROUND
A dozen daily trains (30 mins, €9.20) make the trip from Rennes. Bus service is also available through Illenoo.

Sights

Château de Combourg (*Cat's Tower*)

CASTLE/PALACE | Chateaubriand, an icon of the Romantic Era, grew up in the thick-walled, four-tower Château de Combourg. Topped with "witches' cap" towers that the poet likened to Gothic crowns, it dates mainly from the 14th and 15th centuries. Quartered in the tower called "La Tour du Chat" along with roosting birds and the ghost of the wooden-legged Comte de Combourg, young René succumbed to the château's moody spell and, in turn, became a leading light of Romanticism. His novel *Atala and René,* about a tragic love affair between a French soldier and a Native American maiden, was an international sensation in the mid-19th century, while his multivolume *History of Christianity* was required reading for half of Europe. The château grounds—ponds, woods, and cattle-strewn meadowland—are suitably mournful and can seem positively desolate when viewed under leaden skies. Its melancholy is best captured in Chateaubriand's famous *Mémoires d'outre-tombe* (*Memories from Beyond the Tomb*). Inside you can view neo-Gothic salons, the Chateaubriand archives, and the writer's severe bedroom up in the "Cat's Tower." ⊠ *Rue des Princes* ☎ *02–99–73–22–95* ⊕ *www.chateau-combourg.com* ⌨ *From €4* ☉ *Closed Sat. Sept.–June.*

Hotels

Château de La Ballue

$$$ | HOTEL | Nineteenth-century writers Alfred de Musset, Honoré de Balzac, and Victor Hugo were all once guests at this quintessential Normand château, famed for sophisticated gardens that feature

witty sculptures, leafy groves, impressive columns of yew, a fernery, a labyrinth, and a Temple of Diana. **Pros:** exceptional taste; a superb example of the "art de vivre"; cool history. **Cons:** isolated; expensive breakfast; ornate decor not for everyone. [$] *Rooms from: €230* ✉ *18 km (11 miles) east of Combourg, Bazouges-la-Pérouse* ☎ *02–99–97–47–86* 🌐 *www.la-ballue.com* 🛏 *5 rooms* 🍴 *No meals.*

Dinan

35 km (20 miles) west of Combourg.

During the frequent wars that devastated other cities in the Middle Ages, the merchants who ruled Dinan got rich selling stuff to whichever camp had the upper hand, well aware that loyalty to any side—be it the French, the English, or the Breton—would eventually lead to the destruction of their homes. The strategy worked: today Dinan is one of the best-preserved medieval towns in Brittany. Although there's no escaping the crowds here in summer, in the off-season or early morning Dinan feels like a time-warped medieval playground.

Along Place des Merciers, Rue de l'Apport, and Rue de la Poissonnerie, take note of the splendid gabled wooden houses. Rue du Jerzual, which leads to Dinan's harbor, is divided halfway down by the town walls and the massive Porte du Jerzual gateway; it's lined with 15th- and 16th-century warehouses that have been converted into restaurants, boutiques, and crafts shops. In summer, you can take a boat trip down the Rance River to St-Malo (€34 round-trip ☎ *08–25–13–81–00*), or head upstream to the medieval abbey of St-Magloire, and learn how Napoléon canalized the Rance to enable French boats to cut across to the Atlantic, thereby avoiding English warships in the Channel (€13.50 round-trip 🌐 *www.vedettejamaniv.com)*. Above the harbor, near Porte St-Malo, is the leafy Promenade des Grands Fossés, the best-preserved section of the town walls, which leads to the castle.

GETTING HERE AND AROUND

If you come to Dinan by train, you'll arrive in the Art Deco gare on Place du 11-Novembre-1918. Trains from Rennes take just over an hour and require a change at Dol-de-Bretagne (€16.10). Tibus buses transfer from the train stations in St-Malo (55 mins, €2) and Dinard (45 mins, €2). Illenoo buses also connect Dinan to Rennes (75 mins, €4.90) several times a day.

VISITOR INFORMATION Dinan Tourist Office ✉ *9 rue du Château* ☎ *02–96–87–69–76* 🌐 *www.dinan-capfrehel.com*.

Sights

Basilique St-Sauveur

RELIGIOUS SITE | Embracing a range of architectural styles, Basilique St-Sauveur has a Romanesque south front, a Flamboyant Gothic facade, and Renaissance side chapels. The old trees in the **Jardin Anglais** (English Garden) behind the church provide a nice frame; more spectacular views can be found at the bottom of the garden, which looks down the plummeting Rance Valley to the river below. ✉ *Pl. St-Sauveur* ☎ *02–96–39–06–67.*

Château

CASTLE/PALACE | The stolidly built, fortress-like Château, at the end of the Promenade des Petits Fossés, has a two-story tower and a 100-foot, 14th-century donjon (keep) containing a museum with varied displays of medieval effigies and statues, Breton furniture, and locally made lace *coiffes* (head coverings). ✉ *Porte de Guichet* ☎ *02–96–39–45–20* 🌐 *www.mairie-dinan.com* 🎟 *€7* 🕒 *Closed Jan. and Feb.*

Tour de l'Horloge (*Clock Tower*)

VIEWPOINT | For a superb view of town, climb to the top of this medieval tower.

✉ *Passage de la Tour de l'Horloge* ☎ *02–96–87–58–72* ⊕ *www.dinan-capfrehel.com* ✉ *€4* ⊗ *Closed Oct.–Apr.*

Hotels

Arvor

$ | **HOTEL** | The cobbled streets of the Vie-ille Ville are visible from this comfortable 18th-century hotel directly across from the town theater. **Pros:** reasonably priced; pleasant views from most rooms; lots of local character. **Cons:** smallish bathrooms; old fashioned decor; good but limited breakfast. **$** *Rooms from: €110* ✉ *5 rue Auguste-Pavie* ☎ *02–96–39–21–22* ⊕ *www.hotelarvordinan.com* ⊗ *Closed Jan.* ⤳ *24 rooms* ❖ *No meals.*

Le Logis du Jerzual

$ | **B&B/INN** | Up a storybook-perfect street lined with ancient half-timber houses, this fetching *maison d'hôte* dates to the 15th century and has been brought up-to-date in the best way, retaining much of its substantial character and charm. **Pros:** warm welcome; great prices; short walk into town and port. **Cons:** smallish rooms; steep climb up a cobblestone street; not state-of-the-art. **$** *Rooms from: €110* ✉ *25–27 rue du Petit-fort* ☎ *02–96–85–46–54* ⊕ *www.logis-du-jerzual.com* ⤳ *5 rooms* ❖ *Free Breakfast.*

⬤ Shopping

One of the leading craft havens in France, Dinan has attracted many wood-carvers, jewelers, leather workers, glass specialists, and silk painters, who have set up shop in the medieval houses that line the cobbled, sloping **Rue de Jerzual.** Other delightful studios and artisan boutiques can be found on the nearby **Rue de l'Apport, Place des Merciers,** and **Place des Cordeliers.**

Cancale

86 km (54 miles) northwest of Rennes.

Nothing says Brittany like seafood and nothing says seafood like this fishing village, one of the most picturesque in the region. Renowned for its offshore *bancs d'huîtres* (oyster beds), Cancale has countless quayside eateries where you can get a dozen preshucked oysters, sit on a wall facing the sea, and slurp down these magnificent mollusks. At the Château Richeux's bistro, Le Coquillage (a nearby culinary mecca), you can enjoy them as part of a full-on seafood feast. If your interest is more academic, learn how oysters are "farmed" at the Musée de la Ferme Marine.

GETTING HERE AND AROUND
Trains from Rennes (50 mins, €14.10) travel to La Gouesnière, and from there you can proceed by bus to Cancale; buses from St-Malo also make the 30-minute trip multiple times per day (€1.35).

VISITOR INFORMATION Cancale Tourist Office ✉ *44 rue du Port* ☎ *02–99–89–63–72* ⊕ *www.saint-malo-tourisme.com.*

◉ Sights

Musée de la Ferme Marine (*Sea Farm Museum*)

MUSEUM | Just south of town, this museum explains everything you ever wanted to know about farming oysters and has a display of 1,500 different types of shells. ✉ *L'Aurore* ☎ *02–99–89–69–99* ⊕ *www.ferme-marine.com* ✉ *€8* ⊗ *Closed Nov.–mid-Feb, and weekends mid-Sept.–Oct.*

Restaurants

★ Breizh Café

$ | **FRENCH** | **FAMILY** | Not all crêpes are created equal, and you'll taste the difference at Bertrand Larcher's original Cancale flagship (his Paris outpost is the city's go-to crêperie). Traditional crispy

Eating and Drinking in Brittany

Bounded on two of its three sides by water, Brittany is blessed with an abundance of fresh seafood. Aquatic delights, not surprisingly, dominate Breton cuisine, but crêpes, lamb, and butter also play starring roles. Maritime headliners include coquilles St-Jacques (scallops); langoustines, which are something between a large shrimp and a lobster; and oysters, prized for their balance of briny and sweet. Perhaps the most famous regional seafood dishes are *homard à l'armoricaine* (lobster with cream) and *cotriade* (fish soup with potatoes, onions, garlic, and butter).

Beyond the sea, the lamb that hails from farms on the little island of Ouessant is well known. Called *pré-salé*, or "salt meadow," lambs feed on sea-salted grass, which tenderizes their meat while their hearts are still pumping. Try the regional *ragoût de mouton* and you can taste the difference.

Chouchen

Chouchen, Brittany's classic meadlike beverage made from honey, dates back to Celtic times, when it was considered an aphrodisiac and an *elixir d'immortalité*. This delicious drink is traditionally served cold as an aperitif to highlight its refreshing qualities and its soft, earthy flavor.

Crêpes

Brittany's most illustrious contribution to French cuisine is the crêpe and its heartier sibling the galette. What's the difference between the two? The darker galette is made with tender buckwheat called *blé noir* or *blé sarrasin*, and has a deeper flavor that's best paired with savory fillings—like lobster, mushrooms, or the traditional ham and cheese. A crêpe is wafer thin and made with a lighter batter. It is typically served with sweet fillings like strawberries and cream, apples in brandy, or chocolate.

Le Beurre

Temperate Brittany's lush grazing lands make for exceptional milk products and, like wine, they are discussed in terms of *élévages* (maturity) and *terroir* (origin). Butter your roll at a four-star Paris restaurant and you're likely getting a taste of Brittany's finest—*le beurre Bordier*. Jean-Yves Bordier, headquartered in St-Malo's Vieille Ville, sets the gold standard for butter, and his luscious sweet-cream version is exported daily to top restaurants throughout France. Other flavors include a pungent purple-and-green-flecked algae butter (best slathered on sourdough bread and eaten with oysters), and the *beurre fleur de sel de Guérande*, laced with crunchy grains of the prized gray salt hand-harvested in the salt marshes of Guérande, near La Baule.

Produce

Together, the four regions of Brittany make up France's highest-yielding farmland. Among the more prosaic crops grown here two stand out: the large, fleshy camus artichoke and the plump Plougastel strawberry. Come spring, the markets of Brittany (and Paris, for that matter) are teeming with enthusiastic cooks just itching to get their hands on the first produce of the season. The juicy Plougastel strawberries only appear for a few weeks in June, while artichoke season runs into the fall.

buckwheat galettes are given a modern gourmet twist with the best locally sourced ingredients—organic eggs and vegetables, artisanal cheeses, local oysters and seafood, free-range meats, smoked or seaweed butter from the St-Malo–based dairy superstar Jean-Yves Bordier—and the tender white-flour dessert crêpes are to die for. **Known for:** a cut above the usual crêpe; laid-back setting good for families; nice cider list. $ *Average main: €14* ✉ *7 quai Thomas* ☎ *02–99–89–61–76* ⊕ *www.breizhcafe. com.*

★ La Table Breizh Café

$$$$ | FRENCH FUSION | Although an odd couple at first glance, the marriage of two seafood-centric cuisines—Japanese and Breton—actually makes perfect sense, especially once you've experienced the miracles of flavor that hail from the kitchen of Michelin-starred chef Raphaël-Fumio Kudaka. Imaginative, locally sourced dishes find just the right balance between French gourmandise and Japanese delicacy: lobster dumplings with pine nuts, crisp pork belly, morel, and shiitake mushrooms in a yuzu broth; langoustine, scallop, and foie gras tempura in a bonito-kombu broth; and for dessert, a luscious orange-crème mousseline, with blood-orange gelée and Brittany saffron coulis served over a melt-in-your-mouth Wasabon biscuit. **Known for:** Michelin star quality; sublime seafood; expensive for this region. $ *Average main: €35* ✉ *7 quai Thomas* ☎ *02–99–89–56–46* ⊕ *www.breizhcafe. com* ⏱ *Closed Tues. and Wed.*

Hotels

★ Château Richeux

$$$ | HOTEL | Retired superstar-chef Olivier Roellinger and his wife, Jane, still preside over their family's luxurious hotel empire, which includes the beautiful, castellated, 1920s waterfront Château Richeux.

Pros: famous cuisine; grounds designed specifically for those seeking quiet; beautiful sea views. **Cons:** isolated for those seeking crowds; breakfast is expensive; must have a car. $ *Rooms from: €240* ✉ *Le Point du Jour, Saint-Méloir-des-Ondes* ☎ *02–99–89–64–76* ⊕ *www. maisons-de-bricourt.com* ⏱ *Closed mid-Jan.–Feb.* ⇥ *13 rooms* ⅋ *No meals.*

Shopping

Grain de Vanille

FOOD/CANDY | Sublime tastes of Brittany—salted butter caramels, fruity sorbets, rare honeys, and heirloom breads—are sold in upper Cancale at the Roellingers' Grain de Vanille. Tables beckon, so why not sit a spell and enjoy a cup of Mariage Frères tea and—Brittany in a bite—some cinnamon-orange-flavored *malouine* cookies? ✉ *12 pl. de la Victoire* ☎ *02–23–15–12–70* ⊕ *www.maisons-de-bricourt. com.*

Les Entrepôts Épices-Roellinger

FOOD/CANDY | Monsieur Roellinger's newest addition to his culinary empire, Les Entrepôts Épices-Roellinger is dedicated to the exotic spices he personally searches the world to find. In addition to individual spices, it stocks exotic peppers, fleur de sel, choice vanillas, and the acclaimed owner's signature spice blends—such as Poudre Curry Corsaire (for mussels and shellfish) and Poudre du Vent (for squab or cream sauces). There's now a branch in St-Malo and another in Paris. ✉ *1 rue Duguesclin* ☎ *02–23–15–13–91* ⊕ *www. maisons-de-bricourt.com.*

St-Malo

23 km (14 miles) west of Cancale.

Thrust out into the sea and bound to the mainland only by tenuous man-made causeways, romantic St-Malo has built a reputation as a breeding ground for phenomenal sailors. Many were fishermen, but others—most notably Jacques Cartier, who claimed Canada for Francis I in 1534—were New World explorers. Still others were corsairs, "sea dogs" paid by the French crown to harass the Limeys across the Channel: legends like Robert Surcouf and Duguay-Trouin helped make St-Malo rich through their pillaging, in the process earning it the nickname "the pirates' city." The St-Malo you see today isn't quite the one they called home because a weeklong fire in 1944, kindled by retreating Nazis, wiped out nearly all of the old buildings. Restoration work was more painstaking than brilliant, but the narrow streets and granite houses of the Vieille Ville were satisfactorily re-created, enabling St-Malo to regain its role as a busy fishing port, seaside resort, and tourist destination. The ramparts that help define this city figuratively and literally are authentic, and the flames also spared houses along Rue de Pelicot in the Vieille Ville. Battalions of tourists invade this quaint part of town in summer, so arrive off-season if you want to avoid crowds.

GETTING HERE AND AROUND
The rail station (a 15-minute walk from the Old Town walls) receives more than 15 daily trains from Rennes (55 mins, €16). Buses based at the gare routière, immediately outside the walls, link St-Malo to Dinard (30 mins, €2.60), Cancale (30 mins, €1.25), Dinan (55 mins, €2), Rennes (2 hrs, €5.90), and Mont-St-Michel in Normandy (75 mins, €11.40). April through October, ferries operated by the Compagnie Corsaire (⊕ www.compagniecorsaire.com) also carry passengers to Dinard (10 mins, €7.90 return).

VISITOR INFORMATION St-Malo Tourist Office ⊠ Esplanade St-Vincent ☎ 08–25–13–52–00 (€0.15 per min) ⊕ www.saint-malo-tourisme.com.

Sights

Cathédrale St-Vincent (*Saint-Malo Cathedral*)
RELIGIOUS SITE | Originally founded in the 12th century, the Cathédrale St-Vincent represents an eclectic range of architectural styles. Inside you can pay homage to Jacques Cartier—who set sail from St-Malo in 1534 on a voyage during which he would discover the St. Lawrence River and claim what is now Québec in his king's name—at his tomb. ⊠ 12 rue Saint-Benoist ☎ 02–99–40–82–31.

Château (*Town History Museum*)
CASTLE/PALACE | At the edge of the ramparts sits a 15th-century château, its keep and watchtowers commanding an impressive view of the harbor and coastline. It contains the **Musée d'Histoire de la Ville,** devoted to great figures who have touched local history (like the founder of French Canada, Jacques Cartier, and Châteaubriand, the "Father of Romanticism"); plus the **Galerie Quic-en-Grogne,** a tower museum that uses waxworks to conjure up various episodes from St-Malo's past. ⊠ Hôtel de Ville, Quai St-Vincent ☎ 02–99–40–71–57 ⊕ www.ville-saint-malo.fr ⊡ €6 ⊗ Closed Mon. Oct.–Dec.

Fort National
MILITARY SITE | Lying offshore and accessible by causeway at low tide only, the "Bastille of Brittany" is a massive fortress with a dungeon constructed in 1689 by military-engineering genius Sébastien de Vauban. Thirty-five-minute tours commence at the drawbridge (English text available). ⊠ St-Malo ☎ 06–72–46–66–26 ⊕ www.fortnational.com ⊡ €5 ⊗ Closed Oct.–mid-Apr.

Ile du Grand Bé
ISLAND | Five hundred yards offshore is the Ile du Grand Bé, a small island housing the somber military tomb of the great Romantic writer Viscount René de Chateaubriand, who was born in St-Malo. The islet can be reached by a causeway

at low tide only. ✉ *St-Malo* 🌐 *www.st-malo.com* 🎫 *€5.*

Ramparts

MILITARY SITE | St-Malo's imposing stone ramparts have withstood the pounding of the Atlantic since the 12th century. They were considerably enlarged and modified in the 18th century, and now extend from the château for almost 2 km (1 mile) around the Vieille Ville—known as *intra-muros* (within walls). The views from them are stupendous, especially at high tide. Look for the statues of celebrated explorer Jacques Cartier and swashbuckling corsair Robert Surcouf; the latter, a hero of many daring 18th-century raids on the British navy, eternally wags an angry finger over the waves at England. ✉ *St-Malo.*

🍴 Restaurants

Ar Iniz

$ | **FRENCH** | **FAMILY** | When in St-Malo, what could be more fitting than a seafood meal overlooking the ocean? When dining at this gently priced, fish-centric restaurant and bar set in a seaside hotel, opt for copious plates of langoustine, shrimps, oysters, and *bulots* (sea snails), or choose a fixed-price menu that highlights what the kitchen does best: fresh fish and lots of veggies. **Known for:** friendly atmosphere; exceptionally priced fixed menus; terrace with views over the water. [$] *Average main: €16* ✉ *8 blvd. Hébert* ☎ *02–99–56–01–19* 🌐 *www.ariniz.com.*

Le Saint-Placide

$$$$ | **MODERN FRENCH** | This sleek, modern dining room has managed to garner serious accolades—not to mention a Michelin star—in a town where culinary talent is in no short supply. Chef Luc Mobihan's cuisine brilliantly blends flavors to draw out the intrinsic qualities of local meat and seafood without overpowering it. **Known for:** exquisite presentation of fresh local seafood; langoustine ravioli with coriander and Parmesan; three prix-fixe menus to choose from. [$] *Average main: €39* ✉ *6 pl. du Poncel* ☎ *02–99–81–70–73* 🌐 *www.st-placide.com* 🕓 *Closed Mon., Tues., and 3rd wk of Feb.*

🛏 Hotels

Beaufort

$ | **HOTEL** | A gracious welcome and infinite sea views greet you at this beachfront hotel, handsomely accented with a terra-cotta facade and stylish mansard roof. **Pros:** lovely facade facing the sea; walking distance to good restaurants and shops; beautiful decor. **Cons:** rooms are on the small side and not all face the water; not all rooms have balconies; fresh but unimaginative breakfast selection. [$] *Rooms from: €120* ✉ *25 Chaussée du Sillon* ☎ *02–99–40–99–99* 🌐 *www.hotel-beaufort.com* 🛏 *22 rooms* 🍴 *No meals.*

Château Hôtel du Colombier

$$ | **HOTEL** | This graceful 18th-century château (just 10 minutes from St-Malo and an hour from Mont-St-Michel) makes visitors feel like they're staying in a manor. **Pros:** plenty of outdoor activities; great restaurant; just a mile from the beach. **Cons:** not actually in town; handheld showers; needs freshening up. [$] *Rooms from: €179* ✉ *Lieu Dit le Colombier, Petit Paramé* ☎ *02–23–52–02–28* 🌐 *www.saintmalo-hotelcolombier.com* 🛏 *16 rooms* 🍴 *No meals.*

🍸 Nightlife

La Belle Époque

BARS/PUBS | A popular hangout for all ages, La Belle Époque rages until the wee hours. ✉ *11 rue de Dinan* ☎ *02–99–40–82–23.*

Performing Arts

Festival de Musique Sacrée

FESTIVALS | July and August bring a two-month-long religious music festival, the Festival de Musique Sacrée. ✉ St-Malo ☎ 06–08–31–99–93 ⊕ www.festivalde-musiquesacree-stmalo.com.

Folklores du Monde

FESTIVALS | The city hosts a weeklong festival of world folk music and dance in July. ✉ St-Malo ☎ 02–99–40–42–50 ⊕ www.folkloresdumonde.bzh.

Théâtre Chateaubriand

THEATER | In summer, assorted performances are staged at the Théâtre Chateaubriand. ✉ 6 rue du Grout-de-St-Georges ☎ 02–99–40–18–30 ⊕ www.theatresaintmalo.com.

Dinard

13 km (8 miles) west of St-Malo.

The most elegant resort town on this stretch of the Brittany coast, Dinard enjoys a picture-book perch on the Rance Estuary opposite the walled town of St-Malo. Toward the end of the 19th century, when sea air became a fashionable "cure," the English aristocracy arrived en masse. As a result, what started out as a small fishing port soon became a seaside mecca with lavish Belle Époque villas (more than 400 still dot the town and shoreline), grand hotels, and a bustling casino. Although a number of modern establishments punctuate the landscape, Dinard still retains something of an Edwardian tone. The town's natural beauty remains intact, too: make the most it by strolling along the narrow promenade or heading down to the Pointe de la Vicomté, at Dinard's southern tip, where the cliffs offer panoramic views across the Baie du Prieuré and Rance Estuary.

GETTING HERE AND AROUND
April through October, a ferry operated by Compagnie Corsaire (⊕ www.compagnie-corsaire.com) links St-Malo and Dinard (10 mins, €7.90 round-trip); the towns are 30 minutes apart by bus (€2.50).

VISITOR INFORMATION Dinard Tourist Office ✉ 2 bd. Féart ☎ 08–21–23–55–00 (€0.12 per min) ⊕ www.dinardemeraude-tourisme.com.

◉ Sights

Promenade du Clair de Lune

PROMENADE | Hugging the seacoast on its way toward the English Channel, the Promenade du Clair de Lune passes in front of the small jetty used by boats crossing to St-Malo. In Dinard, the road weaves along the shore and is adorned with luxuriant palm trees and mimosa blooms, which, from July to the end of September, are illuminated at dusk by spotlights; strollers are serenaded with recorded music. The promenade really hits its stride as it rounds the **Pointe du Moulinet** and heads toward the sandy **Plage du Prieuré,** named after a priory that once stood here. River meets sea in a foaming mass of rock-pounding surf: use caution as you walk along the slippery path to the calm shelter of the **Plage de l'Écluse,** an inviting sandy beach bordered by the casino and numerous stylish hotels. The coastal path picks up on the west side of Plage de l'Écluse, ringing the Pointe de la Malouine and the Pointe des Étêtés before arriving at the **Plage de St-Énogat.** ✉ Dinard.

 Restaurants

Didier Méril

$$$ | MODERN FRENCH | Nudging right up to the beach in Dinard's historic center, this chic Michenlin-starred restaurant has both gourmet fare and fabulous water views. Chef Méril takes his inspiration from the local bounty: fresh-from-the-sea

dishes, such as salty-sweet Cancale oysters, fricassee de langoustines, and *trilogie de poisson noble* with lobster coulis vie with Breton specialties, like deboned squab dressed in foie gras. **Known for:** impressive wine list; lovely views of the bay; excellent seafood. [$] *Average main: €31* ✉ *1 pl. du Général de Gaulle* ☎ *02–99–46–95–74* 🌐 *www.restaurant-didier-meril.com.*

Hotels

Manoir de Rigourdaine

$ | B&B/INN | Between Dinard and St-Malo on the beautiful Rance Estuary, Patrick Van Valenberg's renovated country estate provides exceptional comfort inside and great views outside, courtesy of its promontory perch. **Pros:** wonderful views; great ambience and friendly service; above-average breakfast. **Cons:** no restaurant, but host will cook for you; car essential; decor could be nicer. [$] *Rooms from: €105* ✉ *Plouër-sur-Rance* ☎ *02–96–86–89–96* 🌐 *www.hotel-rigourdaine.fr* 🕒 *Closed Nov.–Mar.* 🛏 *19 rooms* 🍴 *No meals.*

Royal Emeraude Hotel Dinard

$$ | HOTEL | Enter into Dinard's seafaring past at this beguiling seafront hotel, each of whose four floors offers an Art Deco–inspired theme that conjures the building's elegant Belle Époque roots. **Pros:** good continental breakfast; excellent location; nice fitness room and spa. **Cons:** rooms on the small side; some views better than others; parking expensive. [$] *Rooms from: €137* ✉ *1 bd. Albert 1er* ☎ *02–99–46–19–19* 🌐 *www.hotelemeraudeplage.com* 🛏 *44 rooms* 🍴 *No meals.*

Villa Reine-Hortense

$$ | HOTEL | All the Napoléon III glamour of 19th-century-resort France is yours when you stay at this *folie*—a villa built by the Russian Prince Vlassov in homage to his "queen," Hortense de Beauharnais (daughter of Napoléon's beloved Joséphine and mother to Emperor Napoléon III). **Pros:** high-style paradise; intimate; quirky. **Cons:** a little over-the-top; a bit of a walk to the beach; no elevator. [$] *Rooms from: €185* ✉ *19 rue de la Malouine* ☎ *02–99–46–54–31* 🌐 *www.villa-reine-hortense.com* 🕒 *Closed Oct.–early Apr.* 🛏 *8 rooms* 🍴 *No meals.*

Nightlife

Casino

CASINOS | The main nightlife activity in town is at the casino. ✉ *4 bd. du Président-Wilson* ☎ *02–99–16–30–30* 🌐 *www.casinosbarriere.com.*

Activities

Wishbone Club

WINDSURFING | For windsurfing, wander over to the Wishbone Club. ✉ *Plage de l'Écluse* ☎ *02–99–88–15–20* 🌐 *www.wishbone-club-dinard.com.*

Yacht Club

BOATING | Boats can be rented from the Yacht Club. ✉ *Promenade du Clair de Lune* ☎ *02–99–46–14–32* 🌐 *www.yacht-club-dinard.fr.*

Trébeurden

157 km (97 miles) west of Dinard.

Trébeurden is one of the highlights of the Côtes d'Armor. A pleasant fishing village that's popular with summer vacationers, it offers access to the rosy cliffs of the Corniche Bretonne. Look at the profile of dramatic rocks off the coast near Trégastel and Perros-Guirec and use your imagination to see La Tête de Mort (Death's Head), La Tortoise, Le Sentinel, and Le Chapeau de Wellington (Wellington's Hat). The coastal scene changes with the sunlight and with the ebb and flow of tides strong enough to leave formerly floating boats stranded on the dry sea floor.

A Belle Époque beauty, Dinard adds a big dollop of 19th-century elegance to the natural splendor of the Breton coast.

GETTING HERE AND AROUND

Buses from Lannion, a town 12 km (7 miles) inland, travel to Trébeurden several times a day, with stops in Perros-Guirec, Trestraou beach, and neighboring Ploumanac'h (45 mins, €2).

VISITOR INFORMATION Trébeurden Tourist Office ⊠ *Pl. de Crec'h hery* ☎ *02–96–23–51–64* ⊕ *www.bretagne-cotedegranitrose.com.*

Sights

Cité des Télécoms

MUSEUM | FAMILY | Five kilometers (3 miles) east of Trébeurden is the Parc du Radôme, site of the giant white radar dome, whose 340-ton antenna captured the first live TV satellite transmission from the United States to France in July 1962. Today the sphere houses the Cité des Télécoms, retracing the history of telecommunications back to the first telegraph in 1792, and featuring interactive exhibits on telecom's newest innovations. A spectacular sound-and-light show involves multicolor lasers and more than 200 video projectors. The site also includes one of Europe's largest **planetariums** and a children's discovery park, Le Jardin des Sciences. ⊠ *Pleumeur-Bodou* ☎ *02–96–46–63–80* ⊕ *www.cite-tele-coms.com* ⊠ *€9* ⊙ *Closed Dec.–Mar.*

Sentier des Douaniers

BEACH—SIGHT | FAMILY | The famous seaside footpath, the Sentier des Douaniers starts up at the west end of the Trestraou beach in the resort town of **Perros-Guirec,** 3 km (2 miles) east of Trébeurden; from there this beautifully manicured, fence-lined, and gorgeously scenic path provides a two-hour walk eastward, through fern forests, past cliffs and pink granite boulders to the pretty beach at Ploumanac'h. If you keep an eye out, you might even spot one of the mythical, 900-year-old Korrigans—native sprites with pointed ears, beards, and hooves, who come out at night from seaside grottoes to dance around fires. From Perros-Guirec you can take a boat trip out to the Sept Iles, a group of seven islets that are bird sanctuaries. On a hillside perch above **Ploumanac'h** is the village of La Clarté, home to the little Chapelle Notre-Dame de la Clarté, built of local pink granite and decorated with 14 stations of the cross painted by the master of the Pont-Aven school, Maurice Denis. During the **Pardon of la Clarté** (August 15), a bishop preaches an outdoor Mass for the Virgin Mary, village girls wear Trégor costumes, and the statue of the Virgin Mary wears a gold crown (she wears a fake one for the rest of the year). On Ploumanac'h's pleasant beach, Plage de la Bastille, you'll find the Oratoire de St-Guirec, a rose-granite chapel lodged in the sand with other rocks; facing the beach is the neo-medieval, 19th-century **Château de Costaeres,** where Henryk Sienkiewicz wrote *Quo Vadis.* Unfortunately, the magical castle-by-the-sea—whose image graces many postcards—is private property (you can, however, rent it for €15,000 per week.) ⊠ *Trébeurden* ⊕ *www.perros-guirec.fr.*

 Hotels

Manoir de Lan Kerellec

$$$ | HOTEL | The beauty of the coastline is embraced by this Relais & Châteaux hotel, where guest rooms are far more than just comfortable; long and cruise-liner-low, the renovated 19th-century Breton manor house has been outfitted with dramatic windows—plate-glass, round, panoramic—so as to frame stirring vistas of the endless sea and the cliffs of the Côte de Granit Rose (all rooms have sea views and some have terraces). **Pros:** great views; comfy rooms; warm welcome at this family-owned hotel. **Cons:** restaurant closed for lunch Monday through Thursday; balcony rooms more expensive; restaurant usually requires advance reservations. $ *Rooms from: €289* ⊠ *11 allée Centrale* ☎ *02–96–15–00–00* ⊕ *www.lankerellec.com* ⊗ *Closed Nov.–mid-Mar.* ➾ *19 rooms* ⏪ *Free Breakfast.*

Ste-Anne-la-Palud

136 km (82 miles) southwest of Trébeurden.

One of the biggest draws on the Breton events calendar is the celebration of a religious festival known as a village pardon, replete with banners, saintly statues, a procession, women in folk costume, a feast, and hundreds of attendees. Each year, the seaside village of Ste-Anne-la-Palud hosts one of the finest and most authentic on the last Sunday in August.

GETTING HERE AND AROUND
More than a dozen trains daily go from Vannes to Quimper (1 hr 20 mins, €21.90); from there, catch a bus onward to Ste-Anne-la-Palud (30 mins, €2).

 Hotels

Hôtel de la Plage

$$$ | HOTEL | Nestled in a cove on a quiet strip of sandy beach on the Bay of Douarnenez, this mansion, with its sturdy round tower, is a remote retreat perfect for long, restorative walks; some of the comfortably furnished guest rooms face the water, as does the glass-front restaurant, where reservations are essential. **Pros:** waterfront setting; lots to see nearby; top-ranking restaurant. **Cons:** very expensive; rather formal; snobby appeal. $ *Rooms from: €247* ⊠ *Sainte-Anne la Palud* ☎ *02–98–92–50–12* ⊕ *www.plage.com* ⊗ *Closed Nov.–Mar.* ➾ *28 rooms* ⏪ *Free Breakfast.*

Douarnenez

14 km (8 miles) south of Ste-Anne-la-Palud.

Douarnenez is a quaint old fishing town with quayside paths and zigzagging narrow streets. Boats come in from the Atlantic to unload their catches

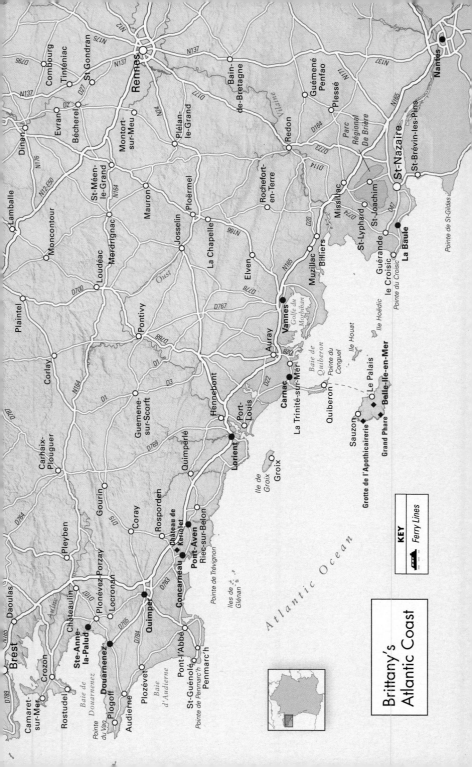

of mackerel, sardines, and tuna. Just offshore is the Ile Tristan, which is accessible on foot at low tide (by guided tour only, €6), and across the Port-Rhu channel is Tréboul, a seaside resort town favored by French families.

GETTING HERE AND AROUND

Douarnenez is served by buses from Quimper (30 mins, €2).

VISITOR INFORMATION Douarnenez Tourist Office ✉ *1 rue du Dr. Mével* ☎ *02–98–92–13–35* 🌐 *www.douarnenez-tourisme.com.*

Sights

Port-Musée (*Port Museum*)
MUSEUM | FAMILY | The unique Port-Musée combines maritime-theme museum displays with open-air exhibits. Along the wharves you can visit the workshops of boatbuilders, sailmakers, and other old-time craftspeople, then go aboard the historic trawlers, lobster boats, and barges anchored beside them. On the first weekend in May you can even sail on an antique fishing boat. ✉ *Pl. de l'Enfer* ☎ *02–98–92–65–20* 🌐 *www.port-musee.org* 🎟 *€8 (€6 Quai museum only, Feb. and Mar.)* 🕐 *Closed Nov.–Jan., and Mon. Apr.–June, Sept., and Oct.*

Hotels

Manoir de Moëllien
$ | HOTEL | Surrounded by extensive forested grounds, this textbook 17th-century granite manor, landmarked by a sturdy tower and filled with precious antiques, offers enviable lodgings; guest rooms vary greatly in size, but most have terraces overlooking the peaceful country garden. **Pros:** charming grounds; historic atmosphere; wonderful base for touring the area. **Cons:** out of the way; restaurant service can be offhand; rooms quite simply decorated considering the grandeur. [$] *Rooms from: €98* ✉ *12 km (7 miles) northeast of Douarnenez, Plonévez-Porzay* ☎ *02–98–92–50–40* 🌐 *www.manoirmoellien.fr* 🕐 *Closed mid-Oct.–mid-Mar.* 🛏 *18 rooms* 🍴 *No meals.*

Ty Mad
$ | HOTEL | This landmark hotel—frequented by artists and writers such as Picasso and Breton native Max Jacob in the 1920s—has been completely refitted with cool, light, modern furnishings that blend perfectly with its cove and beach setting. **Pros:** delightful seaside setting; stylish modern interior; fabulous prices. **Cons:** rooms are small and modestly equipped; breakfast not included in all bookings; small parking area. [$] *Rooms from: €122* ✉ *Plage St-Jean* ☎ *02–98–74–00–53* 🌐 *www.hoteltymad.com* 🕐 *Closed mid-Nov.–mid-Mar.* 🛏 *15 rooms* 🍴 *No meals.*

Quimper

22 km (14 miles) southeast of Douarnenez.

Quimper (pronounced "cam-pair") owes its strange name to its site at the confluence (*kemper* in Breton) of the Odet and Steir Rivers. A traditional crowd-puller, its twisting streets and tottering medieval houses supply rich postcard material; lovers of decorative arts, however, head here because this is the home of Quimperware, one of the more famous variants of French hand-painted pottery. After learning about the prized collectibles at the Musée de la Faïence, you can stroll through the Vieille Ville, ogle its immense 15th-century cathedral, then wander the surrounding shop-lined streets. Keep your camera handy—the ancient capital of the Cornouaille province is very photogenic.

GETTING HERE AND AROUND

The TGV travels here direct from Paris's Gare Montparnasse five times per day (4 hrs 30 mins, €30–€67). Multiple daily trains also connect Quimper with Lorient (40 mins, €13.10), Vannes (1 hr 15 mins,

€21.40), and Nantes (2 hrs 40 mins, €38.90). Frequent buses run to Concarneau (40 mins, €2).

VISITOR INFORMATION Quimper Tourist Office ✉ *Pl. de la Résistance* ☎ *02–98–53–04–05* 🌐 *www.quimper-tourisme.bzh.*

Sights

Cathédrale St-Corentin
RELIGIOUS SITE | Brittany's second-largest cathedral (surpassed size-wise only by the one in Dol-de-Bretagne) is a masterpiece of Gothic architecture enlivened by luminous 15th-century stained glass. Legendary King Gradlon is represented on horseback just below the base of the spires, which are harmonious mid-19th-century additions to the medieval ensemble. The church interior remains very much in use by fervent Quimperois, giving the candlelit vaults a meditative air. Behind the cathedral is the stately **Jardin de l'Évêché** (Bishop's Garden). ✉ *Pl. St-Corentin* ⏲ *Closed Sun.*

Musée de la Faïence (*Earthenware Museum*)
MUSEUM | In the mid-18th century Quimper sprang to nationwide attention as a pottery manufacturing center. Normands, whose distinctive Rouennaise faïence was already famous, imported the techniques. But the Quimpérois customized them by replacing the pottery's usual blue-and-white patterns with brighter Breton scenes depicting local life. Today's colorful designs, based on floral arrangements and marine fauna, are still often hand-painted. To understand Quimper's pottery-making past—and see more than 500 examples of *style Quimper*—take one of the guided tours at the Musée de la Faïence. ✉ *14 rue Jean-Baptiste-Bousquet* ☎ *02–98–90–12–72* 🌐 *www.musee-faience-quimper.com* 🎫 *€7, includes access to the Faïencerie Henriot-Quimper workshops* ⏲ *Closed Sun., and Oct.–mid-Apr.*

Ancient Evenings

During the second half of July, Quimper hosts the Celtic-theme **Festival de Cornouaille** (☎ *02–98–55–53–53* 🌐 *www.festival-cornouaille.com*). More than 250 artists, dancers, and musicians fill streets already packed with the 4,000 people who come each year to enjoy the exuberant six-day street fair.

Musée Départemental Breton (*Brittany Regional Museum*)
MUSEUM | Local furniture, ceramics, and folklore top the bill at the Musée Départemental Breton. ✉ *1 rue du Roi-Gradlon* ☎ *02–98–95–21–60* 🌐 *musee-breton.finistere.fr* 🎫 *€5* ⏲ *Closed Mon. Oct.–mid-June.*

Musée des Beaux-Arts (*Fine Arts Museum*)
MUSEUM | More than 400 works by such masters as Rubens, Corot, and Picasso mingle with pretty landscapes from the local Gauguin-inspired Pont-Aven school in the Musée des Beaux-Arts, next to the cathedral. Of particular note is a fascinating series of paintings depicting traditional life in Breton villages. ✉ *40 pl. St-Corentin* ☎ *02–98–95–45–20* 🌐 *www.mbaq.fr* 🎫 *€5* ⏲ *Closed Tues. Sept.–June.*

Restaurants

★ **Allium**
$$$ | **MODERN FRENCH** | When you've had your fill of crêpes, head over to this outstanding gastronomic dining room, beautifully set in its own kitchen garden, where each dish is a small work of art. With a wonderful backstory (the restaurant opened with the help of a crowd-funding campaign), flawless

Quimper hosts many parades, but the largest is reserved for the six-day Celtic extravaganza known as the Festival de Cornouaille.

presentation, and seasonal organic cuisine that incorporates local (from its own garden) and wild whenever possible, it's no mystery why a Michelin star was earned in 2019. **Known for:** marvelous tasting menus, including a nine-course one that can last 2½ hours; outdoor dining spaces; bright, contemporary decor. $ *Average main: €30 ⊠ 88 bd. de Créac'h Gwen ☎ 02–98–10–11–48 ⊕ www.restaurant-allium.fr ♥ Closed Sun. and Mon.*

Au Vieux Quimper

$ | **FRENCH** | **FAMILY** | In a town where the crêpe is king, Au Vieux Quimper promises an authentic dining experience in a charming rustic setting. Savory buckwheat galettes are exactly as they should be: nicely crisped on the edges and generously filled with quality versions of the classic egg and ham, seafood, or cheese and plenty of other combos. **Known for:** best crêpes in a town full of them; great prices; local artisanal ciders. $ *Average main: €13 ⊠ 20 rue Verdelet*

☎ *02–98–95–31–34 ⊕ www.creperieau-vieuxquimper.fr ♥ Closed Sun. and Mon.*

Hotels

★ Gindo Hotel & Spa

$ | **HOTEL** | Set in a beautifully refurbished historic grange near Quimper's old town, this resolutely contemporary hotel offers everything you'll need for a delightful stay and then some. **Pros:** views across the river in some rooms; beautiful outdoor terrace and garden; excellent spa with hammam and Jacuzzi. **Cons:** not all rooms air-conditioned; no minibar; 10-minute walk from city center. $ *Rooms from: €108 ⊠ 1 rue du Chanoine Moreau ☎ 02–30–99–75–35 ⊕ www.hotel-ginkgo. com ⇥ 20 rooms ⦿ No meals.*

Hôtel Gradlon

$ | **HOTEL** | This authentically Breton *hôtel particulier* has a mild (bordering on nondescript) facade that thoroughly disguises the charms that lie within. **Pros:** good breakfast; quiet rooms; pretty inner courtyard. **Cons:** no restaurant; no elevator; no air-conditioning. $ *Rooms from: €91* ✉ *30 rue de Brest* ☎ *02–98–95–04–39* ⊕ *www.hotel-gradlon.fr* ⇨ *20 rooms* ⎟⊙⎟ *No meals.*

🛍 Shopping

Rue du Parc

SHOPPING NEIGHBORHOODS | The streets around the cathedral, especially Rue du Parc, are full of shops selling woolen goods (notably thick marine sweaters). Also keep an eye out for such typical Breton products as woven and embroidered cloth, brass and wood objects, puppets, dolls, and locally designed jewelry. When it comes to distinctive Breton folk costumes, Quimper is the best place to look. ✉ *Quimper.*

Concarneau

22 km (14 miles) southeast of Quimper.

Concarneau may be an industrial town known for sardine packaging, but its 17th-century Vauban-designed Ville Close ranks among the most picturesque sites in Brittany.

GETTING HERE AND AROUND
Buses run here multiple times per day from Quimper (40 mins, €2) and Pont-Aven (45 mins, €2).

VISITOR INFORMATION Concarneau Tourist Office ✉ *Quai d'Aiguillon* ☎ *02–98–97–01–44* ⊕ *www.tourismeconcarneau.fr.*

👁 Sights

★ Château de Keriolet

CASTLE/PALACE | The village of Beuzec-Conq, just outside Concarneau, is home to the Château de Keriolet—a fairy-tale, neo-Gothic extravaganza dating to the 19th century that Walt Disney would have adored. Replete with gargoyles, storybook towers, and Flamboyant

Gothic–style windows, this showpiece was constructed by the Comtesse de Chauveau, born Zenaide Narishkine Youssoupov, an imperial Russian princess who was niece to Czar Nicholas II (and related to Prince Youssoupov, famed assassin of Rasputin). Take one of the four daily guided tours through the Arms Room, folkloric kitchen, and grand salons. ✉ *2 km (1 mile) southeast of Concarneau, Beuzec-Conq* ☎ *02–98–97–36–50* ⊕ *www.chateaudekeriolet.com* ⛁ *€7* ⊙ *Closed Oct.–May.*

★ Ville Close

MILITARY SITE | Sitting in the middle of Concarneau's harbor, topped by a cupola–clock tower, and entered by way of a quaint drawbridge, the fortress-islet of the Ville Close is a particularly photogenic relic of medieval days. Its fortifications were further strengthened by the English under John de Montfort during the Breton War of Succession (1341–64). Three hundred years later Sébastien de Vauban remodeled the ramparts into what you see today: a kilometer-long (half-mile) expanse, with splendid views across the two harbors on either side. The Fête des Filets Bleus (Blue Net Festival), a week-long folk celebration in which costumed Bretons whirl and dance to the wail of bagpipes, is held here in the middle of August. It is also home to the Musée de la Pêche (Maritime Museum). ✉ *Ramparts* ☎ *02–98–97–10–20 for museum* ⊕ *www.musee-peche.fr* ⛁ *Museum €5* ⊙ *Closed Mon. and Jan.*

🛏 Hotels

Les Sables Blancs

$$ | **HOTEL** | One of the fine-white-sand beaches that distinguish the Morbihan coast serves as the perfect backdrop for this spare, modern hotel, which calls to mind a cruise ship. **Pros:** miles of paths on the cliffs overlooking the water make for lovely walks; open year-round; on-site restaurant. **Cons:** crashing of waves can

disturb light sleepers; spotty service; some rooms on the small side. $ *Rooms from: €215* ✉ *45 rue des Sables Blancs* ☎ *02–98–50–10–12* ⊕ *www.hotel-les-sables-blancs.com* ⤸ *20 rooms* ⦿| *No meals.*

Pont-Aven

37 km (23 miles) east of Quimper.

This lovely village sits astride the Aven River as it descends from the Montagnes Noires to the sea, turning the town's mills along the way (there were once 14; now just a handful remain). A former artists' colony, Pont-Aven is where Paul Gauguin lived before he headed off to the South Seas—and where he left dewy, sunlit Impressionism behind for a stronger, more linear style. After exploring the town, you can seek inspiration (as so many painters did) in the Bois d'Amour or cool off on a boat trip down the estuary.

GETTING HERE AND AROUND

There are no direct trains, but you can ride the rails to nearby Quimperlé and transfer to a bus for the 20-minute drive into town (€2). Buses also arrive from Quimper (70 mins, €4) and Concarneau (45 mins, €2) several times a day. The last buses leave early in the evening, and service is limited on Sunday.

VISITOR INFORMATION Pont-Aven Tourist Office ✉ *3 rue des Meunières* ☎ *02–98–06–04–70* ⊕ *www.pontaven.com.*

⊙ Sights

Bois d'Amour

FOREST | One glance at these leafy, light-dappled woods, a bit north of Pont-Aven's town center, will make you realize why artists continue to come here. Past some meadows, just outside the Bois d'Amour, you can find Gauguin's inspiration for his famous painting *The Yellow Christ*—a wooden crucifix in the secluded **Chapelle de Trémalo**: it's privately

owned but usually open from 10 to 5 (until 6 in summer). ✉ *330 feet from town center, along opposite bank of river.*

Moulin du Grand Poulguin

ARTS VENUE | Now housing a restaurant, this pretty mill was built in the early 1600s. It's a delightful place to dine and enjoy live music on a terrace directly beside the flowing waters of the Aven River, in view of the footbridge. ✉ *2 quai Théodore Botrel* ☎ *02–98–06–02–67* ⊕ *www.moulin-pontaven.com.*

Musée des Beaux-Arts

MUSEUM | The town's art museum captures some of the history of the Pont-Aven School, whose adherents painted Breton landscapes in a bold yet dreamy style called Synthétisme. In addition to works by "member" artists—Paul Gauguin, Paul Sérusier, Maurice Denis, and Émile Bernard among them—the Musée de Beaux-Arts has a photography exhibit documenting the Pont-Aven School. ✉ *Pl. de l'Hôtel-de-Ville* ☎ *02–98–06–14–43* ⊕ *www.museepontaven.fr* ⌂ *From €5* ⊙ *Closed Mon. Sept.-June.*

Restaurants

La Taupinière

$$$ | **MODERN FRENCH** | At an airy roadside cottage with an attractive garden, Guy Guilloux turns out a range of Breton specialties. Since the chef places a special emphasis on seafood, options might include a galette stuffed with spider crab, a langoustine flan, or a *brochette de coquilles St-Jacques* that's been grilled on the large hearth in his open kitchen. **Known for:** seafood specialties; pretty setting; vegetarian-friendly. $ *Average main: €30* ✉ *Croissant St-André, 3 km (2 miles) west on Rte. de Concarneau* ☎ *02–98–06–03–12* ⊕ *www.la-taupiniere. fr* ⊙ *Closed Mon., Tues., and 3 wks in Oct. No dinner Sun.*

Gauguin and the Pont-Aven School

Surrounded by some of Brittany's most beautiful countryside, Pont-Aven was a natural to become a "cité des artistes" in the heady days of Impressionism and Postimpressionism. It was actually the introduction of the railroad in the 19th century that put travel to Brittany in vogue, and it was here that Gauguin and other like-minded artists founded the noted Pont-Aven School. Inspired by the vibrant light, vivid colors, and lovely vistas to be found here, they created Synthétisme, a painting style characterized by broad patches of pure color and strong symbolism, in revolt against the dominant Impressionist school back in Paris. Gauguin arrived in the summer of 1886, happy to find a place "where you can live on nothing" (Paris's stock market had crashed and cost Gauguin his job). At Madame Gloanec's boardinghouse, he welcomed a circle of painters to join him in his artistic quest for monumental simplicity and striking color.

Today Pont-Aven seems content to rest on its laurels. Although it's labeled a "city of artists," the galleries that line its streets display paintings that lack the unifying theme and common creative energy of the earlier works of art.

🛏 Hotels

La Chaumière Roz-Aven

$ | HOTEL | Partly built into a rock face on a bank of the Aven, this efficiently run hotel is a perfect blend of antique and modern—offering simple, clean rooms with 18th- and 19th-century-style touches. **Pros:** families welcome; rooms tastefully modernized; easy walk to town's sights. **Cons:** small rooms; rooms in annex lack character; no elevator. $ *Rooms from: €80* ⊠ *11 quai Théodore-Botrel* ☎ *02–98–06–13–06* ⊕ *www.hotelpontaven.com* ⊘ *Closed Jan.* ⇆ *14 rooms* ⦿*No meals.*

Les Mimosas

$ | HOTEL | Centrally located and with its own authentic charm, Les Mimosas offers everything guests need for a pleasant stay. **Pros:** friendly service; good seafood restaurant; good value. **Cons:** handheld showers; books up quickly in tourist season; old-fashioned decor. $ *Rooms from: €69* ⊠ *22 sq. Théodore Botrel* ☎ *02–98–06–00–30* ⊕ *www.lesmimosas-pontaven.com* ⇆ *10 rooms* ⦿*No meals.*

Belle-Ile-en-Mer

45 mins by boat from Quiberon, 78 km (52 miles) southeast of Pont-Aven.

Covering 84 square km (32 square miles), Belle-Ile is the largest of Brittany's islands; and, as its name implies, it is beautiful. Being less commercialized than its mainland counterpart, Quiberon (a spa town with pearl-like beaches on the eastern side of the Quiberon Peninsula), Belle-Ile maintains a natural appeal. Monet created several famous paintings on the island, and the pristine terrain may tempt you to set up an easel yourself.

GETTING HERE AND AROUND

Ferries, which run hourly in July and August, connect Belle-Ile's Le Palais with Quiberon's Gare Maritime (45 mins, from €35 round-trip). Because of the cost and inconvenience involved in taking a vehicle over, it's best to make the crossing as a foot passenger; you can then rent a car or (if you don't mind hilly terrain) a bike on arrival.

VISITOR INFORMATION Belle-Ile-en-Mer Tourist Office ✉ *Le Palais, Quai Bonnelle* ☎ *02–97–31–81–93* 🌐 *www.belle-ile.com.*

Sights

Citadelle Vauban

MILITARY SITE | Your first stop on Belle-Ile will most likely be Le Palais, the island's largest community. As you enter the port, it's impossible to miss the star-shape Citadelle Vauban, named for the famous military engineer who, in the early 1700s, oversaw a redesign of the original fort here (which dated back to the 11th century). Stroll the grounds, savor the views, and then bone up on local lore at the on-site Musée de la Citadelle Vauban. ✉ *Le Palais, Le Palais* 🌐 *www.citadelle-vauban.com* 🎟 *€11* 🕒 *Closed Jan.*

Grand Phare (*Great Lighthouse*)

LIGHTHOUSE | Built in 1835, the Grand Phare at Port Goulphar rises 275 feet above sea level and has one of the most powerful beacons in Europe, visible from 120 km (75 miles) across the Atlantic. If the keeper is available and you are feeling well rested, you may be able to climb to the top. ✉ *Belle-Ile-en-Mer.*

Grotte de l'Apothicairerie

CAVE | A huge ocean grotto, the Grotte de l'Apothicairerie derives its name from the local cormorants' nests that used to reside on it; it's also said to resemble apothecary bottles. ✉ *Belle-Ile-en-Mer.*

Sauzon

MARINA | Northwest of Le Palais, you'll discover the prettiest fishing harbor on the island; from here you can see across to the Quiberon Peninsula, with its dramatic coastal cliffs and sea-lashed coves. ✉ *Belle-Ile-en-Mer.*

Hotels

Castel Clara

$$$ | **RESORT** | Perched on a cliff overlooking the surf and the narrow Anse de Goulphar Bay, this 1970s-era hotel was François Mitterrand's address when he vacationed on Belle-Ile and it still retains presidential glamour, with its renowned spa, saltwater pool, and spectacular views. **Pros:** good facilities; spectacular setting; wonderful for beach walks. **Cons:** expensive; hard to get to; service can be indifferent. [$] *Rooms from: €295* ✉ *Port-Goulphar, Bangor* ☎ *02–97–31–84–21* 🌐 *www.castel-clara.com* 🕒 *Closed mid-Nov.–mid-Dec.* 🛏 *63 rooms* 🍴 *No meals.*

★ **La Désirade**

$$ | **HOTEL** | **FAMILY** | Close to both a small village and the untamed coastline, this peaceful family-run resort—complete with a wonderful restaurant and spa—has more than earned its consistently high accolades for comfort, charm, and top-notch service. **Pros:** perfect for families; excellent buffet breakfast; exquisite setting on the beach. **Cons:** breakfast is expensive; not close to restaurants or nightlife; best to book far ahead. [$] *Rooms from: €194* ✉ *Petit Cosquet* ☎ *02–97–31–70–70* 🌐 *www.hotel-la-desirade.com* 🛏 *32 rooms* 🍴 *No meals.*

Activities

Roue Libre

BICYCLING | The ideal way to get around to the island's 90 spectacular beaches is by bike. The best place to rent two-wheelers (and cars—this is also the island's Avis outlet) is at Roue Libre in Le Palais. ✉ *6 quai Jacques Le Blanc, Le Palais* ☎ *02–97–31–49–81* 🌐 *www.velobelleile.fr.*

Carnac

19 km (12 miles) northeast of Quiberon.

At the north end of Quiberon Bay, Carnac is known for its expansive beaches and its ancient stone monuments: "standing stones," called menhirs, that were erected by Brittany's pre-Celtic people 6,500 years ago.

GETTING HERE AND AROUND
Catch a bus from Quiberon (35 mins, €2) or take advantage of the SNCF's rail-road combination, which involves a train from Vannes to Auray followed by a bus to Carnac (1 hr 15 mins, €8.50).

VISITOR INFORMATION Carnac Tourist Office ⊠ *74 av. des Druides* ☎ *02–97–52–13–52* ⊕ *www.ot-carnac.fr.*

Sights

Menhirs
ARCHAEOLOGICAL SITE | Dating to around 4500 BC, Carnac's menhirs remain as mysterious in origin as their English contemporaries at Stonehenge, although religious beliefs and astronomy were doubtless an influence. The 2,395 monuments that make up the three *alignements*—Kermario, Kerlescan, and Ménec—form the largest megalithic site in the world, and are positioned with astounding astronomical accuracy in semicircles and parallel lines over about a kilometer (half a mile). The site, just north of the town, is fenced off for protection, and you can examine the menhirs up close only from October through March; in summer you must join a €7 guided tour (some are in English). This visitor center explains the menhirs' history and significance, plus it offers an excellent selection of interesting books in all languages, as well as DVDs and regional gifts. ⊠ *D196* ☎ *02–97–52–29–81 for Maison des Mégalithes* ⊕ *www.carnac. monuments-nationaux.fr.*

Tumulus de St-Michel
ARCHAEOLOGICAL SITE | Carnac also has smaller-scale dolmen ensembles and three *tumuli* (mounds or barrows), including the 390-foot-long, 38-foot-high Tumulus de St-Michel, topped by a small chapel with views of the rock-strewn countryside. ⊠ *Carnac.*

Hotels

★ Château de Locguénolé
$$ | HOTEL | According to legend, St-Guénolé (for whom the 19th-century château was named) took refuge on this spot while fleeing the devil, and it remains a grand retreat—after all, it's part of a sweeping 250-acre estate with lush garden and stunning water views. **Pros:** peace and quiet reign; lovely setting; large bathrooms are all in marble. **Cons:** out of the way (but worth the detour); rooms could use some sprucing up; not much to do except relax. Ⓢ *Rooms from: €194* ⊠ *Rte. de Port-Louis, 25 km (16 miles) south of Carnac, Kervignac* ☎ *02–97–76–76–76* ⊕ *www.chateau-de-locgue-nole.com* ⊗ *Closed Jan.–mid-Feb.* ⤶ *22 rooms* ⊙ *No meals.*

Hôtel Tumulus
$$ | HOTEL | Dramatic views over Carnac and Quiberon Bay, coupled with a prime location just beneath the famous Tumulus de St-Michel, have been big draws for this modest, family-run hotel from its inception in the 1930s. **Pros:** close to Carnac's menhirs; beautiful setting; good dining on premises. **Cons:** some rooms on the small side; some with less-than-pristine carpets; elevator does not go to top floor. Ⓢ *Rooms from: €185* ⊠ *Chemin de Tumulus* ☎ *02–97–52–08–21* ⊕ *www. hotel-tumulus.com* ⊗ *Closed mid-Nov.–mid-Feb.* ⤶ *29 rooms* ⊙ *No meals.*

One of France's prettiest islands, Belle-Ile-en-Mer casts an especially magical spell at sunset.

Vannes

35 km (20 miles) east of Carnac, 108 km (67 miles) southwest of Rennes.

Scene of the declaration of unity between France and Brittany in 1532, Vannes is one of the few towns in the region to have been spared damage during World War II. That makes its Vielle Ville (Old Town), where many of the prettiest sights are concentrated, particularly appealing. The ramparts crumble evocatively under ivy blankets, and each gateway has a character all its own. Visit the 16th-century cathedral; browse the antiques shops in the pedestrian streets around pretty Place Henri-IV; and then take a boat trip around the scenic Golfe du Morbihan.

GETTING HERE AND AROUND

Direct TGVs from Paris's Gare Montparnasse leave for Vannes six times daily (3 hrs 20 mins, €30–€65). Ten trains daily (many with a change at Redon) link Vannes to Nantes (1 hr 30 mins, €23.40); frequent trains also link it to Lorient (35 mins, €10.60) and Quimper (1 hr 15 mins, €21.20). Buses to Quiberon (2 hrs, €2) and Nantes (1 hr 45 mins, €12) are available as well.

VISITOR INFORMATION Vannes Tourist Office ⊠ *Quai Tabarly* ☎ *02–97–47–24–34* ⊕ *www.golfedumorbihan.bzh.*

👁 Sights

Cathédrale St-Pierre

RELIGIOUS SITE | A panoply of medieval art, St-Pierre boasts a 1537 Renaissance chapel, a Flamboyant Gothic transept portal, and a treasury. ⊠ *22 rue des Chanoines* ☎ *02–97–47–10–88* ⊕ *www.cathedrale-vannes.cef.fr.*

🍴 Restaurants

★ Le Roscanvec

$$$$ | MODERN FRENCH | On a pedestrian street in the charming old city, this modern gastronomic restaurant ditches stuffiness in favor of a relaxed, contemporary approach to food. What it doesn't dispense with is seriousness in the kitchen: chef Thierry Seychelles seeks out top-quality ingredients from a wealth of local suppliers for his seasonal, meticulously presented cuisine. **Known for:** gorgeous setting; reasonable prices; wonderful food like monkfish served with French caviar. $ *Average main: €45* ✉ *17 rue des Halles* ☎ *02–97–47–15–96* ⊕ *www.roscanvec.com* ⌚ *Closed Mon., and Tues. Sept.–June, last wk of June–1st wk of July, and mid-Jan.–early Feb. No dinner Sun.*

🛏 Hotels

Domaine de Rochevilaine

$$$ | **RESORT** | At the tip of the magical Pen Lan Peninsula, this luxurious collection of 15th- and 16th-century Breton stone buildings resembles a tiny village—albeit one surrounded by terraced gardens that promise grand vistas of the Baie de Vilaine (Vilaine Bay). **Pros:** stylish interiors; ocean views; superb spa facilities. **Cons:** decor not up-to-date; tons of steps from one house to another; staff can be indifferent. $ *Rooms from: €301* ✉ *Pointe de Pen-Lan, 30 km (19 miles) southeast of Vannes, Billiers* ☎ *02–97–41–61–61* ⊕ *www.domainerochevilaine.com* ⇆ *37 rooms* ⦿| *No meals.*

Kyriad

$ | **HOTEL** | In an old but thoroughly modernized building, this hotel attracts a varied foreign clientele, drawn by homey guest rooms that are clean, bright, and simple with budget prices. **Pros:** not far from sights; friendly, efficient staff; good prices. **Cons:** some rooms on the small side; some a bit noisy; don't expect charm. $ *Rooms from: €77* ✉ *8 pl. de la Libération* ☎ *02–97–63–27–36* ⊕ *www.kyriad-vannes.fr* ⇆ *33 rooms* ⦿| *No meals.*

Villa Kerasy Hotel & Spa

$ | **HOTEL** | **FAMILY** | The theme "voyage into Indian Brittany" may seem a little wacky, but why not—more colonial than exotic, this small hotel nonetheless gets points for taking a theme and running with it. **Pros:** delightful staff and service; good spa; fun decor. **Cons:** close to the railway means noise; breakfast not always included in price; breakfast service can be slow. $ *Rooms from: €90* ✉ *20 av. Favrel et Lincy* ☎ *02–97–68–36–83* ⊕ *www.villakerasy.com* ⇆ *15 rooms* ⦿| *No meals.*

Lorient

50 km (30 miles) west of Vannes.

France's most exotically named town was founded by Jean-Baptiste Colbert in 1666 as a base for the Compagnie des Indes, which sent ships from here to the Orient in search of spices. Now a major fishing port, Lorient was smashed into semi-oblivion during World War II (a massive submarine base—Base de Sous-Marins Keroman—attests to its wartime importance); however, you can still see a handful of Art Deco mansions, explore the mile-long quay, and enjoy nearby beaches. Lorient is at its liveliest during the Festival Interceltique in August.

GETTING HERE AND AROUND

Direct TGVs from Paris's Gare Montparnasse leave for Lorient five times per day (3 hrs 50 mins, €65–€97). Trains also run frequently from Nantes (2 hrs, €30.30), Vannes (35 mins, €10.60), and Quimper (40 mins, €12.90). For trips by bus or boat to any of the surrounding towns, contact the Compagnie des Transports de la Région Lorientaise (⊕ *www.ctrl.fr*).

VISITOR INFORMATION Lorient Tourist Office ✉ *Quai de Rohan, Lorient* ☎ *02–97–84–78–00* ⊕ *www.lorient-bretagnesudtourisme.fr.*

Brittany's version of Stonehenge, this stone menhir at Carnac is just one of the area's impressive megalithic sights.

Sights

Base de Sous-Marins Keroman

MILITARY SITE | Built by the Nazis during World War II, this submarine base is the world's largest 20th-century fort. Thirty submarines could be comfortably housed in the squat concrete bunker—and its 27-foot-thick roof withstood intensive Allied bombing virtually intact. Ninety-minute tours begin at noon and 3 pm daily in summer and during school vacations; they run at the same time on Sunday year-round. Call to find out when tours in English are scheduled. ⊠ Port de Keroman, Lorient ☎ 02–97–02–23–29 ⊕ www.la-flore.fr/fr ☒ €8 ⊙ Closed last 3 wks of Jan. and 1st wk Feb.

Festival Interceltique

FESTIVAL | FAMILY | Held in the first half of August, this festival focuses on Celtic culture—music, drama, poetry, dance—and fellow Celts from Cornwall, Wales, Ireland, Scotland, Galicia, and other Western European locales pour in to celebrate. ⊠ Lorient ☎ 02–97–21–24–29 ⊕ www.festival-interceltique.bzh.

Larmor-Plage

BEACH—SIGHT | There's a good beach, Larmor-Plage, 5 km (3 miles) south of Lorient. You can also take a ferry to the rocky yet utterly charming Ile de Groix or cross the bay to Port-Louis to see its 17th-century fort and ramparts. ⊠ D29, Lorient.

La Baule

72 km (45 miles) southeast of Vannes.

La Baule is a popular resort town that once rivaled Biarritz. Today it leans toward the tacky rather than the sophisticated, but you still can't beat its breathtaking 5-km (3-mile) beach or the lovely, long seafront promenade lined with hotels. Like Dinard, La Baule is a 19th-century creation, founded in 1879 to make the most of the sandy strands that extend around the broad, sheltered bay between Pornichet and Le Pouliguen. A pine forest helps keep shifting dunes in place. All in all, this can offer an idyllic stay for those who like the idea of a day at the beach and an evening at the casino.

GETTING HERE AND AROUND

Three TGVs per day arrive direct from Paris (3 hrs 15 mins, €59–€102); six more make the trip with a transfer in Nantes. Direct trains from Nantes run almost hourly (55 mins, €15.10).

VISITOR INFORMATION La Baule Tourist Office ✉ *8 pl. de la Victoire, La Baule-Escoublac* ☎ *02–40–24–34–44* 🌐 *www.labaule.fr.*

🍴 Restaurants

★ Carpe Diem

$$$ | MODERN FRENCH | Five minutes by car from La Baule and a few steps from the Église d'Escoublac, this bright, modern dining room overlooking a pretty garden is an absolute favorite among locals. The gastronomic dishes consist of the freshest seasonal ingredients and don't shy away from the kinds of imaginative pairings that could go wrong but rarely do. **Known for:** convivial dining room; vegetarian-friendly; affordable multicourse prix-fixe menus. [$] *Average main: €28* ✉ *29 av. Jean Boutroux* ☎ *02–40–24–13–14* 🌐 *www.le-carpediem.fr* ⏲ *No dinner Tues., Wed., and Sun.*

🛏 Hotels

Concorde

$ | HOTEL | This bright-blue-shuttered, white-walled establishment ranks among the least expensive "good" hotels in pricey La Baule. **Pros:** just a short block from the beach; some rooms flaunt sea views; good value. **Cons:** no restaurant; lengthy annual closure; no tea kettle or coffeemaker in room. [$] *Rooms from: €98* ✉ *1 bis, av. de la Concorde, La Baule-Escoublac* ☎ *02–40–60–23–09* 🌐 *www.hotel-la-concorde.com* ⏲ *Closed Oct.–Mar.* 🔑 *47 rooms* 🍴 *No meals.*

★ La Palmeraie

$$ | HOTEL | For a touch of the Riviera in Brittany (never mind the half-timbered houses visible from your balcony), this light-drenched boutique hotel is just the ticket. **Pros:** great prices; close to the beach; top-notch breakfast and delicious brunch. **Cons:** no hotel parking; breakfast not included in price; books up quickly due to popularity. [$] *Rooms from: €200* ✉ *7 av. des Cormorans* ☎ *02–51–10–58–51* 🌐 *www.lapalmeraie-labaule.fr* 🔑 *9 rooms* 🍴 *No meals.*

🍸 Nightlife

Casino

CASINOS | Occasionally you see high stakes on the tables at La Baule's casino. ✉ *24 esplanade Lucien Barrière, La Baule-Escoublac* ☎ *02–40–11–48–28* 🌐 *www.lucienbarriere.com.*

Nantes

72 km (45 miles) east of La Baule, 108 km (67 miles) south of Rennes.

The writer Stendhal remarked of 19th-century Nantes, "I hadn't taken 20 steps before I recognized a great city." Since then, the river that flowed around the upper-crust Ile Feydeau neighborhood has been filled in and replaced with a rushing torrent of cars on the major highways that now cut through the heart of town. Still, Nantes is more than the sum of its traffic jams, and even the bureaucratic severance of the city from Brittany—it's now the capital of the Pays de la Loire region—has not robbed it of its historic Breton character. Stay a spell to discover its many sights, among them an evocative 15th-century château and a cathedral from the same period that seems to float heavenward. Across the broad boulevard, Cours des 50-Otages, sits the 19th-century city.

GETTING HERE AND AROUND

Frequent Nantes-bound TGVs depart from Paris's Gare Montparnasse (2 hrs 15 minutes, €65–€91). The city is also well served by trains from La Baule (55 mins, €15.30), Vannes (1 hr 30 mins, €23.40), Rennes (1 hr 30 mins, €26.30), Lorient (2 hrs, €30.30), and Quimper (2 hrs 40 mins, €38.90). Nantes's train station, on Boulevard Stalingrad, is a 10-minute walk from the Vieille Ville. Regional bus service to nearby towns is available. Civic trams and buses operated by TAN (⊕ www.tan.fr) provide efficient public transit within the city.

VISITOR INFORMATION Nantes Tourist Office ⊠ 9 rue des États ☎ 08–92–46–40–44 ⊕ www.nantes-tourisme.com.

 Sights

Cathédrale St-Pierre–St-Paul

RELIGIOUS SITE | One of France's last Gothic cathedrals, this was begun in 1434—well after most other medieval cathedrals had been completed. The facade is ponderous and austere, in contrast to the light, wide, limestone interior, whose vaults rise higher (120 feet) than those of Notre-Dame in Paris. ⊠ Pl. St-Pierre ☎ 02–40–47–84–64 ⊕ www.cathedrale-nantes.fr.

Château des Ducs de Bretagne

CASTLE/PALACE | Built by the dukes of Brittany, who had no doubt that Nantes belonged in their domain, this moated 15th-century château looks well preserved, despite having lost an entire tower during a gunpowder explosion in 1800. François II, the duke responsible for building most of the massive structure, led a hedonistic life here, surrounded by ministers, chamberlains, and an army of servants. Numerous monarchs later stayed in the castle, where in 1598 Henri IV signed the famous Edict of Nantes advocating religious tolerance. ⊠ 4 pl. Marc-Elder ☎ 08–11–46–46–44 ⊕ www.

chateaunantes.fr ⊑ €8 ⊘ Closed Mon. Sept.–June.

★ Grand Eléphant et Galerie de les Machines de l'île

MUSEUM | Had Jules Verne (a son of Nantes) and Leonardo da Vinci somehow got together when they were both in a particularly whimsical frame of mind, they may well have established this unique and engaging workshop-gallery. Their spirit certainly lives on in the imaginative, artistic, and mechanically brilliant creations that are built and displayed here. The Grand Eléphant gets most attention—hardly surprising, since the 50-ton giant, just short of 40 feet high, regularly "ambles" along the quay carrying 49 passengers. Inside the gallery are works in many shapes and sizes—some of them interactive—and you can watch more being made in the workshop on weekdays. The eye-popping Carrousel des Mondes Marins (Marine Worlds Carousel) is located just outside the gallery on the banks of the Loire. ⊠ Les Chantiers, Bd. Léon Bureau, Île de Nantes ☎ 08–10–12–12–25 ⊕ www.lesmachines-nantes.fr ⊑ Gallery €9, elephant ride €9, carousel €9.

Musée des Beaux-Arts (Museum of Fine Arts)

MUSEUM | Designed by Clément-Marie Josso, this noted museum was opened in 1900. Inside, skylights cast their glow over a fine array of paintings, from the Renaissance period onward, including works by Jacopo Tintoretto, Georges de La Tour, Jean-Auguste-Dominique Ingres, and Gustave Courbet. To go from the sublime to the ridiculous, look for the famous late-19th-century painting of a gorilla running amok with a maiden. The main palais is currently closed for renovations, but the Chapelle de l'Oratoire (on Place de l'Oratoire) hosts temporary exhibitions of the permanent collection in the interim. ⊠ 10 rue Georges-Clemenceau ☎ 02–51–17–45–00 for museum, 02–51–17–45–00 ⊕ www.

museedesbeauxarts.nantes.fr 🎫 *€8 (free Thurs. after 6 pm and 1st Sun. of month Sept.–June)* 🕒 *Closed Tues.*

Passage Pommeraye
STORE/MALL | Erected in 1843, this is an elegant shopping gallery in the 19th-century part of town. ✉ *Rue Crébillon* 🌐 *www.passagepommeraye.fr.*

🍴 Restaurants

★ La Poissonnerie et Pas Que
$$ | **SEAFOOD** | Don't be fooled by the streamlined contemporary atmosphere and laid-back vibe, this is one of Nantes's best—and friendliest—seafood restaurants, specializing in the finest delicacies from the Breton coastline. Finistère native chef Manuel Le Gouil has the sea in his bones, and it shows in these sophisticated, beautifully presented dishes (there are also meat and poultry options if you prefer) and tasty desserts. **Known for:** excellent-value fixed-price menus; freshest seafood around; super-friendly service. [$] *Average main: €20* ✉ *4 rue Léon Maître* ☎ *02–40–47–79–50* 🌐 *www.lapoissonnerie.fr* 🕒 *Closed Sun., Mon., and 2 wks in May, Oct., and Jan. No lunch Sat.*

★ Les Chants d'Avril
$ | **BISTRO** | It may not be the fanciest restaurant in Nantes or the most central, but Les Chants d'Avril is where the locals go for affordable "bistronomic" fare. Murals, dark-wood paneling, and leather banquettes lend a warm, traditional look; the attention to market-driven ingredients and interesting wines, however, puts it on par with the best modern *bistrôts à vin.* **Known for:** amazingly priced modern bistro cuisine; fresh seasonal ingredients; lively atmosphere. [$] *Average main: €16* ✉ *2 rue Laënnec* ☎ *02–40–89–34–76* 🌐 *www.leschantsdavril.fr* 🕒 *Closed weekends.*

★ Lulu Rouget
$$$ | **FRENCH** | Market-fresh cuisine, industrial-chic decor with elegant touches of velvet and polished wood, and an adventurous wine list all help make this Michelin-starred bistro a standout on Nantes's culinary roadmap. Well-crafted dishes forego French fussiness in favor of innovative combinations like scallops with tamarind and roasted-red-pepper puree, seared monkfish with wild *l'ail d'ours* (French garlic) pesto, or succulent spring veal accompanied by tiny roasted veggies. **Known for:** excellent multicourse chef's menu; Michelin star; top-notch service. [$] *Average main: €26* ✉ *4 pl. Albert Camus* ☎ *20–40–47–47–98* 🌐 *www.lulurouget.fr/notre-travail* 🕒 *Closed Sun. and Mon.*

★ Pickles
$$ | **FRENCH** | At the hottest gastro-bistro in Nantes, Dominic Quirke, a young English chef, who worked in some of Paris's top kitchens before striking out on his own, combines a sophisticated menu featuring the best of the local producers with a stellar list of natural wines. Locals know a great thing when they taste it, and that's why they come here for Nantes veal with tartare of Breton langoustine, Sologne lamb with grilled polenta, beet pickles and glacéed vegetables, and roast sea bass with fennel risotto and capers with creamed zucchini. **Known for:** innovative, unpretentious ambience; fresh, quality ingredients; ultrapopular among foodies. [$] *Average main: €22* ✉ *2 rue du Marais* ☎ *02–51–84–11–89* 🌐 *pickles-restaurant.com* 🕒 *Closed Sun. and Mon. No lunch Sat.; no dinner Tues.*

🛏 Hotels

★ Hôtel Okko Château
$ | **HOTEL** | A centrally located budget hotel just a short walk from the château, Hôtel Okko Château is ultramodern without sacrificing warmth, comfort, or

amenities. **Pros:** excellent all-you-can-eat breakfasts included in price; lots of little extras; great value. **Cons:** garage often full; small rooms; very popular, so can be crowded. [$] *Rooms from: €109* ✉ *15 rue de Strasbourg* ☎ *02–52–20–00–70* 🌐 *www.okkohotels.com* 🛏 *80 rooms* 🍴 *Free Breakfast* 💳 *No credit cards.*

Nightlife

Le Lieu Unique
PIANO BARS/LOUNGES | This is the place to go for an impressive selection of cutting-edge cultural and leisure events, including music, dance, art exhibitions, and creative "happenings." The contemporary space includes a bar, restaurant, boutique, and, yes, a hammam, too. ✉ *2 quai Ferdinand-Favre* ☎ *02–40–12–14–34* 🌐 *www.lelieuunique.com.*

Performing Arts

Théâtre Graslin
CONCERTS | Nantes's principal concert hall was built in 1788, ravaged by fire in 1796, and rebuilt by the grace of Emperor Napoléon I in 1811. Today it's home to the acclaimed Angers Nantes Opéra. ✉ *1 rue Molière* ☎ *02–40–69–77–18* 🌐 *www.angers-nantes-opera.com.*

Univers
CONCERTS | An informal "speakeasy," Univers has live jazz concerts the first and third Wednesday of the month—and 60 brands of whiskey every day. ✉ *16 rue Jean-Jacques-Rousseau* ☎ *02–40–73–49–55* 🌐 *www.luniverscafe.com.*

Shopping

The main commercial quarter of Nantes stretches from Place Royale to Place Graslin. Legendary shopping street Rue Crébillon spawned the expression *crebillonner,* referring to an avid shopaholic. Don't miss the Passage Rommeraye, a lovely covered arcade that's crammed with boutiques, and boutique-lined Rue de la Fosse and Rue d'Orléons are nearby. Antiques lovers should not miss the shops lining Rue Jean-Jaurès or Rue Voltaire. But for the best bargains, head on over to the Place Viarme for the weekly Saturday morning flea market.

Activities

Bateaux Nantais
TOUR—SPORTS | **FAMILY** | Take a 90-minute cruise along the pretty Erdre River, past a string of gardens and châteaux, on the Bateaux Nantais. There are also four-course lunch and dinner cruises that last about 2½ hours (€65–€91). ✉ *Quai de la Motte Rouge* ☎ *02–40–14–51–14* 🌐 *www.bateaux-nantais.fr* 🎟 *€14.*

Chapter 8

CHAMPAGNE COUNTRY

8

Updated by
Lyn Parry

👁 Sights	🍴 Restaurants	🛏 Hotels	🛍 Shopping	🍸 Nightlife
★★★★☆	★★☆☆☆	★★★☆☆	★★☆☆☆	★☆☆☆☆

WELCOME TO CHAMPAGNE COUNTRY

TOP REASONS TO GO

★ **Champagne (obviously!):** Sample some bubbly, see the vineyards, and visit the cavernous chalk cellars where bottles are stored by the million.

★ **Gothic architecture:** No fewer than 10 Gothic cathedrals dot the region—don't miss the biggest (Amiens) or the tallest (neighboring Beauvais).

★ **Laon:** With its cathedral towers patrolling the hilly horizon, the "Crowned Mountain" has a site whose grandeur rivals Mont-St-Michel.

★ **Reims:** Beyond being a center for Champagne production, regal Reims is also home to France's great coronation cathedral.

★ **Hiking:** Hiking on one of Champagne's fabulous, forested *sentiers de Grandes Randonnées* can be an intoxicating outdoor activity.

1 Reims. The largest city in Champagne.

2 L'Epine. A small village with a beautiful church.

3 Châlons-en-Champagne. The administrative capital of the region.

4 Épernay. The center of the region's Champagne production.

5 Château-Thierry. The birthplace of Jean de La Fontaine.

6 Laon. A fantastic hilltop setting with a stunning cathedral.

7 Soissons. Once a major medieval city and now home to a magnificent cathedral.

8 Amiens. Home to the region's largest cathedral.

9 Beauvais. Home to the region's tallest cathedral.

10 Lille. The biggest city in northern France, currently undergoing an urban renovation.

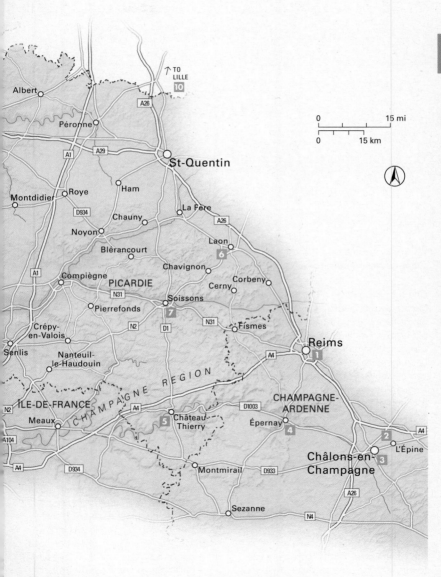

Albert

Péronne

St-Quentin

Montdidier
Roye
Ham

D934
Chauny
La Fère

Noyon
A26

Bléranancourt
Laon
6

Compiègne
Chavignon
Corbeny

PICARDIE
Cerny

N31
Pierrefonds
Soissons
7

Crépy-
en-Valois
N2
D1
N31
Fismes

Senlis
Nanteuil-
le-Haudouin
A4
Reims
1

CHAMPAGNE REGION

ÎLE-DE-FRANCE
CHAMPAGNE-
ARDENNE

N2
A4
D1003

Meaux
Château-
Thierry
5
Épernay
4
A4

A104
L'Épine
2

A4
D934
Montmirail
D933
Châlons-en-
Champagne
3

Sezanne
N4
A26

TO
LILLE
10

A26

A1
A29

A1

0   15 mi
0   15 km

Few drinks in the world have such a pull on the imagination as Champagne, yet surprisingly few tourists visit the pretty vineyards south of Reims. Perhaps it's because the Champagne region is seen as a bit of a backwater, halfway between Paris and Luxembourg. The arrival of the TGV line serving eastern France and Germany, and the UNESCO World Heritage status awarded to the vineyards, cellars, and sales houses in 2015 have both helped to change this perception and encourage tourism.

Champagne, a place-name that has become a universal synonym for joy and festivity, actually began as a word of humble meaning. Like *campagna,* its Italian counterpart, it's derived from the Latin *campus,* or "open field." In French *campus* became *champ,* with the old language extending this to *champaign,* for "battlefield," and *champaine,* for "district of plains." The gentle vine-covered slopes of the hillsides rising from vast chalky plains here have been the center of Champagne production for more than two centuries, stocking the cellars of its many conquerors (Napoléon, Czar Nicholas I, the Duke of Wellington) as well as those of contemporary case-toting bubblyphiles.

Meanwhile, great cathedrals testify to the wealth this region enjoyed thanks to its prime location between Paris and northern Europe. The flying buttresses and heaven-seeking spires of these sanctuaries remind us that medieval stoneworkers sought to raise radically new Gothic arches to improbable heights, running for cover if their ambitious efforts failed. Most have stood the test of time, though you might want to hover near the exits at Beauvais, the tallest cathedral in France—its height still makes some engineers nervous.

The region's crossroads status also exacted a heavy toll, and it paid heavily for its role as a battleground for the bickering British, German, and French. From pre-Roman times to the armistice of 1945, some of Europe's costliest wars were fought on northern French soil. World War I and World War II were especially unkind: epic cemeteries cover the plains of Picardy, and you can still see bullet-pocked buildings in Amiens. These days, happily, the vineyards of

Champagne attract tourists interested in less sobering events.

GETTING ORIENTED

As you head toward Reims, the landscape loosens and undulates, and the hills tantalize with vineyards that—thanks to *la méthode champenoise*—produce the world's antidote to gloom. Each year, millions of bottles of bubbly mature in hundreds of kilometers of chalk tunnels carved under the streets of Reims and Épernay, both of which fight for the title "The Champagne City." Long before a drink put it on the map, though, this area of northern France was marked by marvelous architecture, and it contains many of France's greatest medieval cathedrals.

Here, in the wake of regal Reims, lie four more of the most superlative: Amiens, the largest; Beauvais, the tallest; Laon, with the most towers and fantastic hilltop setting; and Soissons, beloved by Rodin. Add in those at St-Omer, St-Quentin, and Châlons-en-Champagne, along with the Flamboyant Gothic masterpieces in St-Riquier and L'Épine, and aficionados of medieval architecture may wish to explore the region more extensively, following the development of Gothic architecture from its debut at Noyon to its flamboyant finale at Abbeville, where, according to the 19th-century English essayist John Ruskin, Gothic "lay down and died."

MAJOR REGIONS

Champagne. An uplifting landscape tumbles about Reims and Épernay, perhaps because its inhabitants treat themselves to a regular infusion of the local, world-prized elixir. But unlike the great vineyards of Bordeaux and Burgundy, there are few country châteaux to go with the fabled names of this region—Mumm, Taittinger, Pommery, and Veuve-Clicquot. Most of the glory is to be found in *caves* (wine cellars), not to mention the fascinating guided tours offered by the most famous producers. The local obsession with Champagne is especially evident in Reims, the region's hub, which is home to the great Champagne houses and site of one of the most historically important cathedrals in France. Once you've paid tribute to the 34 VIPs who have been crowned here and toured some Champagne cellars to bone up on the backstory behind this noble beverage, you can head south. Smack-dab in the middle of the 280 square kilometers (108 square miles) that make up the entire Champagne-producing area, Épernay lives and dies for the bubbly brew. Continue on the Route du Champagne to other wine villages.

The Cathedral Cities. To the west of Champagne lies a region where the popping of Champagne corks is only a distant murmur, and not just because Reims is 160 km (100 miles) away. Here you'll find some of the most gargantuan Gothic hulks of architectural harmony—namely the cathedrals of Beauvais, Amiens, Laon, and Soissons. Beauvais is positively dizzying from within (it features the highest choir in France, and you nearly keel over craning your neck back to see it); Amiens, the largest church in the land, is fantastically ornate in places; while Laon is notable for its majestic towers; and Soissons shows Gothic at its most restrained.

Planner

When to Go

Of course, the optimal time to visit vineyards is around the fall harvest, when the weather is usually at its best. Summer also has its advantages. Compared to many other regions of France, Champagne remains relatively uncrowded in July and August; and the coolness of the chalk cellars makes it a pleasure to tour the Champagne houses then (note that many close after the busy winter holidays for the first few months of the year, as do some of the smaller hotels and restaurants). Spring is generally unpredictable weather-wise, but on the dry and sunny days it can be idyllic. Whatever you plan to do, be sure to come between May and October; the ubiquitous vineyards are a dismal, leafless sight the rest of the year.

Making the Most of Your Time

Threading the triangle between Reims, Épernay, and Château-Thierry are the famous Routes Touristique du Champagne (Champagne Roads), which divvy up the region into four fabulous itineraries. These follow the main four côtes of the Champagne vineyards. Northwest of Reims (use the Tinqueux exit) is the Massif de St-Thierry—a vineyard-rich region once hallowed by kings. Heading south of Reims to Épernay, veer west along the Vallée de la Marne through the Hauteurs d'Épernay, traveling west on the right bank of the river and east on the left. To the east of Épernay lies the most beautiful stretch of Champagne Country: the Montagne de Reims. To the south of Épernay is the Côte de Blancs, the "cradle of Chardonnay." More than 80 producers of Champagne are scattered along these roads, and you can guarantee a better reception if you call the ones you'd like to visit in advance.

The two main centers to the Champagne Wine Road are Reims and Épernay, which are about 64 km (40 miles) apart if you work your way through the wine villages that dot the slopes of the Montagne de Reims. Start in Reims, with its host of major Champagne houses, then go south on D951 and east on D26 through pretty Rilly-la-Montagne, Mailly-Champagne, and Verzy, where you can visit local producers Étienne and Anne-Laure Lefevre at 30 rue de Villers (☎ 03–26–97–96–99 ⊕ www.champagne-etienne-lefevre.com). Continue

south to Ambonnay, then track back west to Bouzy, Ay, and Hautvillers—where Dom Pérignon is buried in the village church—before crossing the Marne River to Épernay, whose Avenue de Champagne is home to several producers.

From Épernay, travel south along the Côte de Blanc to Vertus, 19 km (12 miles) away, where Pierre and Sophie Larmandier will sell and tell you all about their biodynamic Champagne at 19 avenue du General-de-Gaulle (☎ 03–26–52–13–24 ⊕ www.larmandier.fr). If you're heading back to Paris, take D1 from Épernay west along the banks of the Marne to Château-Thierry 50 km (30 miles) away. The steep-climbing vineyards hugging the river are the most scenic in Champagne. For maps of the four Routes Touristiques du Champagne, stop at the Marne Regional Tourist Office in Châlons-en-Champagne or the tourist offices in Reims or Épernay.

Getting Here and Around

Reims remains the natural hub—especially now that it's just 50 minutes from Paris by TGV. It's easy to get to major towns in the region by rail; as always in France, intercity buses are less frequent than trains, and much slower. If you're driving, Reims is linked to Laon by the A26 expressway and to Châlons-en-Champagne by the A4 expressway arriving from Paris. The west, Amiens and Beauvais, are connected by the A16. Épernay, south of Reims, can be reached from Reims by the twisting wine road or quicker D951. Only Soissons, 32 km (20 miles) southwest of Laon, is a bit off the beaten track.

AIR TRAVEL

If you're coming from the United States or most other locales, count on arriving at Paris's Charles de Gaulle or Orly airport. The former offers easy access to the northbound A16 and A1 for Beauvais and Amiens, and the eastbound A4 for

Reims. If coming from within the Europe, consider the direct flights into Beauvais operated by several budget carriers.

AIRPORT INFORMATION Aéroport de Beauvais-Tillé ☎ 08-92-68-20-66 (€0.45 per min) ⊕ www.aeroportbeauvais.com.

BUS TRAVEL

As train travel is so much more efficient and dependable, relying on bus service outside Paris isn't recommended. There are more than a dozen different bus operators in the Champagne and Picardy regions, but few of them have websites, reliable schedules, or any personnel who speak English; it's best to contact the local tourism office if you're looking into bus options. In Picardy the main bus hub is at the Gare Routière in Amiens, next to the train station. In the Champagne region, the main hub is Châlons-en-Champagne, with routes from Reims to Troyes, Épernay to Châlons, and Reims to Laon. In Reims, municipal buses depart from the train station.

CAR TRAVEL

The A4 heads east from Paris to Reims; allow 90 minutes to two hours, depending on traffic. The A16 leads from L'Isle-Adam, north of Paris, up to Beauvais and Amiens.

If you're arriving by car via the Channel Tunnel, you'll disembark at Coquelles, near Calais, and join A16 not far from its junction with A26, which heads to Reims (2 hrs 30 mins).

TRAIN TRAVEL

Most sites can be reached by regular service, except for the Champagne vineyards, which require a car. There are frequent daily trains from Paris (Gare du Nord) to Beauvais (1 hr 15 mins), Amiens (1 hr 20 mins), Soissons (1 hr 5 mins), and Laon (1 hr 40 mins). The super-express TGV service covers the 170 km (105 miles) from Paris (Gare de l'Est) to Reims in 50 minutes. Trains departing from Gare de l'Est regularly travel to Châlons as well, making the 174-km

(108-mile) trip in 1 hour 30 minutes—1 hour 3 minutes if you take the TGV. From the same station you can travel to Épernay (1 hr 15 mins) or to Château-Thierry (46 mins). Within the Champagne region, trains also connect Reims and Épernay (30 mins).

TRAIN INFORMATION Gare SNCF Reims ✉ Bd. Joffre, Reims. **SNCF** ☎ 3635 (€0.40 per min) ⊕ www.oui.sncf.com. **TGV** ⊕ www.sncf.com.

Restaurants

This region is less dependent on tourism than many in France, and most restaurants are open year-round. However, in the largest cities, Reims and Amiens, many do close for two to three weeks in July and August.

Smoked ham, pigs' feet, gingerbread, and Champagne-based mustard are specialties of the Reims area, along with sautéed chicken, kidneys, stuffed trout, pike, and snails. One particularly hearty dish is *potée champenoise,* consisting of smoked ham, bacon, sausage, and cabbage. Rabbit (often cooked with prunes) is common, while boar and venison are specialties in fall and winter, when vegetable soups are high on the menu. In Picardy, the popular *ficelle picarde* is a pancake stuffed with cheese, mushrooms, and ham.

Apart from Champagne, the region's *hydromel* (mead, made from honey) and Ratafia, a sweet aperitif made from grape juice and brandy, are worth sampling.

Hotels

The Champagne Region has a mix of old, rambling hotels, often simple rather than pretentious. In addition, there are a handful of stylish hostelries catering to those with more discerning tastes, including a large contingent of staffers who work in the Champagne industry. Be warned, though, that few of the destinations mentioned in this chapter have much in the way of upscale choice. Many of the region's most character-filled establishments are in the countryside and require a car to reach. *Restaurant and hotel reviews have been shortened. For full information, visit Fodors.com.*

What It Costs in Euros			
$	$$	$$$	$$$$
RESTAURANTS			
under €18	€18–€24	€25–€32	over €32
HOTELS			
under €106	€106–€145	€146–€215	over €215

Visitor Information

The regional tourist offices are goldmines of information. Reims, Amiens, and many smaller locales also operate their own helpful tourist offices; these are listed in this chapter under the destination's names. If traveling extensively by public transportation, you can load up on brochures, maps, and such upon arrival at the ticket counter or help desk of larger train and bus stations.

CONTACTS Marne Regional Tourist Office ✉ *13 bis, rue Carnot, Châlons-en-Champagne* ☎ *03–26–68–37–52* ⊕ *www.tourisme-en-champagne.com.* **Picardy Regional Tourist Office** ✉ *3 rue Vincent Auriol, Amiens* ☎ *03–22–22–33–66* ⊕ *www.picardietourisme.com.*

Reims

161 km (100 miles) northeast of Paris.

Behind a facade of austerity, Champagne's largest city remains one of France's richest tourist sites, thanks especially to the fact that it sparkles with some of the biggest names in Champagne production. This thriving industry has conferred wealth and sometimes an arrogant reserve on the region's inhabitants. The maze of Champagne cellars constitutes a leading attraction here. Several of these producers organize visits to their cellars, combining video presentations with guided tours of their cavernous, hewn-chalk underground warehouses. The city's tourist office will provide you with a complete list of Champagne cellars. While there, you can also get information on other standout sights. Although many of Reims's historic buildings were flattened in World War I and replaced by drab, modern architecture, those that do remain are of royal magnitude. Topping the list is the magnificent cathedral, in which the kings of France were crowned until 1825. *Note that Reim's museum of fine arts, the Musée des Beaux-Arts, is temporarily closed until 2023.*

GETTING HERE AND AROUND

You can make it to Reims in 50 minutes on the TGV express from Gare de l'Est: trains depart nine times daily and cost €35–€61. Several SNCF trains per day connect Reims to Épernay (30 mins, €7.30), and there is also regular daily train service to Châlons-en-Champagne (50 mins, €11.90) and Laon (50 mins, €10.40). Les Courriers de L'Aube runs seven daily buses to Reims from Châlons-en-Champagne (Line 140; 1 hr, €10).

VISITOR INFORMATION Reims Tourist Office ✉ *6 rue Rockefeller* ☎ *03–26–77–45–00* ⊕ *www.reims-tourisme.com.*

Sights

Basilique St-Remi
RELIGIOUS SITE | This 11th-century Romanesque-Gothic basilica honors the 5th-century saint who gave his name to the city and baptized Clovis (the first king of France) in 498. The interior seems to stretch into the endless distance, an impression created by its relative murk

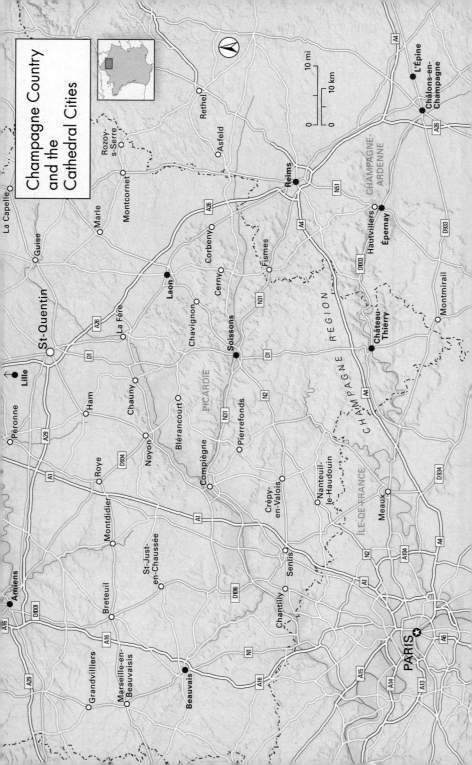

Champagne Country
and the
Cathedral Cities

Drinking Champagne in Champagne Country

Dom Pierre Pérignon, a monk and cellar master at Hautvilliers, is credited with inventing Champagne. The secret of the production lies in combining the still wines of the region and storing the beverage in bottles where it undergoes a second fermentation process that creates fizz and therefore Champagne. Today, the world's most famous sparkling wine comes from the very same vineyards, along the towering Marne Valley between Épernay and the Château-Thierry and on the slopes of the Montagne de Reims between Épernay and Reims.

Tasting Tours

When you take a Champagne tasting tour, you won't be at the vineyards—it's all done inside the various houses, miles away from where the grapes are grown. Champagne firms—Veuve-Clicquot, Mumm, Pommery, Taittinger, and others—regularly give travelers tours of their chalky, mazelike *caves* (cellars).

The quality of the tours can be inconsistent, ranging from hilarious to despairingly tedious, but most visitors will say that a glass of Champagne at the end makes even the most mediocre tour worth it. On the tours, you'll discover that Champagne today is not made so differently from the way the Dom himself did it three centuries ago.

Bubbly Basics

Three types of grape are used to make Champagne: Pinot Noir, Chardonnay, and Pinot Meunier. The two Pinots, which account for 75% of production,

are black grapes with white juice. Rosé Champagne is made either by Pinot Noir juice in contact with the grape skins just long enough to turn it pink, or by mixing local red wine with Champagne prior to bottling.

Vintage Versus Nonvintage

Vintage Champagne is named for a specific year, on the premise that the grapes harvested in that year were of extraordinary quality to produce a Champagne by themselves without being blended with wine from other years. Cuvées de Prestige are the finest and most expensive Champagnes that a firm has to offer.

What You'll Pay

Champagne relentlessly markets itself as a luxury product—the sippable equivalent of perfume and haute couture—so it's no surprise that two of the Champagne brands, Krug and Dom Pérignon, are owned by a luxury goods conglomerate (Louis Vuitton Moët Hennessy). Sure, at small local producers or in giant French hypermarkets, you can find a bottle of nonvintage bubbly for €20. But it's more likely to be closer to €40, and if you fancy something special—say a bottle of vintage Dom Pérignon Rosé—be prepared to fork over €350. One of the pricest Blanc de Noirs is Bollinger's Vieilles Vignes, tagged at around €650. At the very top of the line is Krug's single-vineyard Clos du Mesnil, with the stellar 2000 vintage retailing at around €1,220. Just 12,624 bottles were ever produced of this golden elixir.

Tally up the 34 kings who were crowned at Notre-Dame de Reims, one of the largest and greatest of French cathedrals.

and lowness. The airy four-story Gothic choir contains some fine stained glass from the 12th century. The holy phial used in the crowning of monarchs was formerly kept alongside the basilica in the Abbaye Royale; today that building houses an interesting museum that highlights the history of the abbey, the Gallo-Roman history of the town, and the military history of the region. ⊠ *Pl. Chanoine Ladame* ☎ *03–26–85–06–69* ⊕ *stremi-reims. cef.fr* ✉ *Museum €5.*

★ Cathédrale Notre-Dame de Reims

RELIGIOUS SITE | Recently restored for its 800th birthday, this magnificent Gothic cathedral provided the setting for the coronations of French kings. The great historical saga began with Clovis, king of the Franks, who was baptized in an early structure on this site at the end of the 5th century; Joan of Arc led her recalcitrant Dauphin here to be crowned King Charles VII; Charles X's coronation, in 1825, was the last. The east-end windows have stained glass by Marc Chagall and Imi Knoebel. Admire the vista toward the west end, with an interplay of narrow pointed arches. The glory of Reims's cathedral is its facade: it's so skillfully proportioned that initially you have little idea of its monumental size. Above the north (left) door hovers the Laughing Angel, a delightful statue whose famous smile threatens to melt into an acid-rain scowl now that pollution has succeeded war as the ravager of the building's fabric. With the exception of the 15th-century towers, most of the original building went up in the 100 years after 1211. You can climb to the top of the towers and peek inside the breathtaking timber-and-concrete roof (reconstructed in the 1920s with Rockefeller money) for €8. A stroll around the outside reinforces the impression of harmony, discipline, and decorative richness. The east end presents an idyllic sight across well-tended lawns. ⊠ *Pl. du Cardinal-Luçon* ☎ *03–26–47–81–79* ⊕ *www.cathedrale-reims. monuments-nationaux.fr* ✉ *Free, towers €8* ☉ *Towers closed Nov.–mid-Mar.; weekdays mid-Mar.–early May, Sept., and Oct.; and Mon. early May–Aug.*

Cryptoportique

ARCHAEOLOGICAL SITE | A Gallo-Roman underground gallery and crypt, now a semi-subterranean venue for municipal expositions, was initially constructed around AD 200 beneath the forum of Reims's predecessor, the Roman town of Durocortorum. ✉ *Pl. du Forum* ☎ *03–26–77–77–76* 🎫 *Free* ⏱ *Closed Oct.–Apr.*

Le Vergeur Museum

MUSEUM | One of the best examples of late medieval and early Renaissance architecture in Reims was built during the 13th century. Originally overlooking the historic linen-and-wheat market in the center of town, this noble town house changed hands between aristocrats and Champagne traders before being acquired in 1910 by Hugues Kraft—a man whose sole passion was preserving the city's historic buildings. It was completely restored after the WWI bombings and today houses an impressive collection of historical prints, paintings, and furnishings from the region, as well as an original, complete series of 15th-century Albert Dürer prints of the "Apocalypse" and "Large Passion." There are guided tours of the collection Tuesday through Sunday 2–5. ✉ *36 pl. du Forum* ☎ *03–26–47–20–75* ⊕ *www.museelevergeur.com* 🎫 *€5* ⏱ *Closed Mon.*

Mumm

WINERY/DISTILLERY | Mumm is now the third-largest Champagne producer in the world, and the distinctive Cordon Rouge label with its red slash is proudly held up at every Formula 1 winner's podium. These may not be the most spectacular cellars in the region, but it's a practical option if you don't have much time; you can walk here from the cathedral and the train station. Mumm was confiscated by the French state in World War I because it had always remained under German ownership. Later the state sold it to Dubonnet, and today Pernod Ricard is the proud owner. The 1½-hour visit starts with a short film and then takes you on

a journey into the cavernous cellars. A guide leads the way (English tours need to be reserved in advance online) explaining the Champagne-making process step by step. There is also a small museum showcasing ancient tools, machines, and barrels. The tour ends with your choice of three dégustations: a glass of Cordon Rouge (€23), a guided blind tasting of one cuvée (€29), or a Grand Cru tasting of two special cuvées (€42). ✉ *29 rue du Champ-de-Mars* ☎ *03–26–49–59–70* ⊕ *www.mumm.com* 🎫 *From €23* ⏱ *Closed Mon. and Tues. Nov. and Dec., and Sun.—Tues. Jan. and Feb.*

Musée de la Reddition (*Museum of the Surrender*)

MUSEUM | Also known as the Salle du 8-Mai-1945 or the "little red school house," this museum is a well-preserved map-covered room used by General Eisenhower as Allied headquarters at the end of World War II. It was here that General Alfred Jodl signed the German surrender at 2:41 am on May 7, 1945. Fighting officially ceased at midnight the next day. The museum also presents a collection of local photos, documents, uniforms, and artifacts recounting the fighting, occupation, and liberation of Reims. Guided tours begin with a short film in English and French. ✉ *12 rue Franklin-Roosevelt* ☎ *03–26–47–84–19* 🎫 *€5* ⏱ *Closed Tues.*

Palais du Tau

CASTLE/PALACE | Formerly the Archbishop's Palace, this UNESCO World Heritage List museum has an impressive display of tapestries and coronation robes of 32 French kings, as well as several statues rescued from the cathedral facade. The second-floor views of the cathedral, which stands alongside it, are terrific. ✉ *2 pl. du Cardinal-Luçon* ☎ *03–26–47–81–79* ⊕ *www.palais-tau.monuments-nationaux. fr* 🎫 *€8* ⏱ *Closed Mon.*

Pommery

WINERY/DISTILLERY | This turreted wedding-cake extravaganza on the city outskirts was designed by Jeanne-Alexandrine Pommery (1819–1890), a formidable Champagne widow. The 11 miles of cellars (about a hundred feet underground) are reached by a grandiose 116-step staircase. The visit continues with one-hour guided tours of the cellars, which date to Gallo-Roman times. Along the path, contemporary artwork and installations sit next to the stacks of bubbly. The tour ends with a sommelier-guided tasting of either one or two cuvées. Reserve ahead of time for guided tours in English. Be sure to also visit the Art Nouveau Villa Demoiselle across the street (owned by Pommery). ✉ *5 pl. du General-Gouraud* ☎ *03–26–61–62–56* 🌐 *www.visite-vrankenpommery.fr* 🎫 *From €22.*

★ Ruinart

WINERY/DISTILLERY | Founded back in 1729, just a year after Louis XV's decision to allow wine to be transported by bottle (previously it could only be moved by cask), Ruinart effectively kick-started the Champagne industry. Nicolas Ruinart established the high-end Champagne house in Reims, realizing the dreams of his uncle Dom Thierry Ruinart, who was a close friend of Dom Pérignon himself. Four of its huge, church-size chalk galleries (24 in all, over three levels) are listed as historic monuments. The two-hour guided tour starts with a view of the high-tech production line behind a glass wall, and then takes you through the warren of chalk-hewn caves stacked with Champagne bottles undergoing various stages of maturation. This is the costliest visit in the area; if you're willing to shell out €70, you can taste a cuvée premium and a vintage cuvée prestige Champagne, either a Blanc de Blancs or a rosé, in the stylish tasting room. Visits need to be reserved online, at least two weeks in advance. ✉ *4 rue des Crayères* ☎ *03–26–77–51–53* 🌐 *www.ruinart.com* 🎫 *From €70* 🕒 *Closed Sun. and Mon., and mid-Dec.–mid-Mar.*

★ Taittinger

WINERY/DISTILLERY | Cavernous chalk cellars, first used by monks for wine storage, house 15 million bottles and partly occupy the crypt of the 13th-century abbey that used to stand on this spot. You can see a model of the abbey and its elegant church, both demolished during the French Revolution. The one-hour guided tour starts with a short film, then continues with a walk through the 4th-century Gallo-Roman cellars and 13th-century vaults of St-Nicaise Abbey, and ends in a huge cave where locals were once sheltered from the Germans. The visit is topped off with a tasting. There are four categories of tastings; the top-end choice, L'Instant de Grâce (€60), includes three Champagnes, including Taittinger's finest cuvée, the Comtes de Champagne Blanc de Blancs. Tours in English happen just about every hour—check online for times. No appointment is necessary. ✉ *9 pl. St-Nicaise* ☎ *03–26–85–45–35* 🌐 *www.taittinger.com* 🎫 *From €19* 🕒 *Closed weekends mid-Nov.–mid-Mar.*

🍴 Restaurants

Anna–S. La Table Amoureuse

$$$ | **MODERN FRENCH** | About a five-minute walk from Reims's cathedral, this small one-room eatery features creative, contemporary French cuisine in charming pastel-tone surroundings. **Known for:** pretty desserts; excellent wine choices; fine food. [$] *Average main: €25* ✉ *6 rue Gambetta* ☎ *03–26–89–12–12* 🌐 *www.annas-latableamoureuse.com* 🕒 *Closed Mon. No dinner Sun. and Wed.*

Brasserie Excelsior

$$$ | **BRASSERIE** | This authentic brasserie has polished wood floors, Art Nouveau glass windows, and mirrored walls. The food is sophisticated, dependable, and includes seafood platters, and the service is sleek. **Known for:** good fixed-price menus that change weekly; summer dining on the outdoor terrace; signature dishes such as roast monkfish with cèpe

mushrooms and authentic desserts made with the classic biscuits Rose de Reims. $ *Average main: €25* ✉ *96 pl. Drouet d'Erlon* ☎ *03–26–91–40–50* ⊕ *www.brasserie-excelsior-reims.fr.*

Café du Palais
$$ | **BISTRO** | The walls at this 1930s restaurant are crammed with gilt-edged mirrors, golden cherubs, and old paintings, while crystal chandeliers hang from the ceiling, which itself is topped by a magnificent Art Deco glass roof signed by Jacques Simon. The café is popular among locals, so reserve a table in advance (request one inside as the terrace looks out over a tramline). **Known for:** classic bistro-style dishes such as duck confit with sautéed potatoes; extensive wine list includes a good selection of Champagnes and Coteaux Champenois wines; lively ambience. $ *Average main: €23* ✉ *14 pl. Myron T-Herrick* ☎ *03–26–47–52–54* ⊕ *www.cafedupalais.fr* ⊘ *Closed Sun. and Mon. No dinner Tues.–Fri.*

Le Bocal
$$ | **SEAFOOD** | Freshness is guaranteed at this tiny treasure, hidden at the back of a fishmonger's shop across from the old food court (Les Halles du Boulingrin). Everything is just off the boat, but most diners automatically go with the catch of the day; tables are in demand, so reserve ahead. **Known for:** cooked oysters; outdoor terrace; great choice of champagnes. $ *Average main: €20* ✉ *27 rue de Mars* ☎ *03–26–47–02–51* ⊕ *www.restaurantlebocal.fr* ⊘ *Closed Sun. and Mon.*

Le Millénaire
$$$$ | **MODERN FRENCH** | This traditional town house just off Place Royale, a few feet from the cathedral, has an updated Art Deco feel with plush beige carpets and sleek, chic chairs. Chef Laurent Laplaige finds an outlet for his decorative artistry with colorful food presented on elegant white plates. **Known for:** good value fixed-price menus; dazzling desserts;

plancha-grilled fish and steak. $ *Average main: €50* ✉ *4 rue Bertin* ☎ *03–26–08–26–62* ⊕ *www.lemillenaire.com* ⊘ *Closed Sun. No lunch Sat.*

Hotels

Château Les Crayères
$$$$ | **HOTEL** | In a grand park with towering trees planted by Champagne legend Madame Pommery, this celebrated hotel remains the showplace of Reims—a stylish, late-19th-century château featuring guest rooms bedecked with antiques, boiseries, and couture fabrics, plus the finest Champenoise restaurant of them all, Le Parc. **Pros:** hotel and two restaurants in same luxurious setting; innovative food and Champagne pairings; glorious salons are gilt trimmed and bouquet laden. **Cons:** outside the center of town; pretty expensive; no pool or spa. $ *Rooms from: €430* ✉ *64 bd. Henry-Vasnier* ☎ *03–26–24–90–00* ⊕ *www.lescrayeres.com* ⊘ *Closed 3 wks late Dec.–early Jan.* ⌁ *20 rooms* ⦿ *No meals.*

Grand Hôtel Continental
$$ | **HOTEL** | Centrally located on the main pedestrian street, this hotel was originally a private 19th-century mansion, and the lobby still exudes old-world charm with worn leather couches, low-level lighting, and a grand staircase. **Pros:** central location; air-conditioning; good amenities such as Nespresso coffee machines. **Cons:** some rooms lack charm; only the suites have tubs; no on-site parking. $ *Rooms from: €140* ✉ *93 pl. Drouet d'Erlon* ☎ *03–26–40–39–35* ⊕ *www.continental-hotel.fr* ⊘ *Closed 2 wks late Dec.–early Jan.* ⌁ *50 rooms* ⦿ *No meals.*

Hôtel Azur
$ | **HOTEL** | At this comfortable, friendly spot on a residential street in the center of Reims, rooms are simply furnished and decorated in cheerful primary colors with modern white tile bathrooms. **Pros:**

good value; near train station and 10-minute walk to cathedral; secure parking. **Cons:** few rooms have bathtubs; limited reception hours; no elevator. [$] *Rooms from: €75* ✉ *9 rue des Ecrevées* ☎ *03–26–47–43–39* 🌐 *www.hotel-azur-reims.com* 🕒 *Closed 2 wks late Dec.–early Jan.* 🛏 *19 rooms* 🍴 *No meals.*

La Paix

$$$ | HOTEL | An antidote to historical overload, this contemporary, eight-story Best Western–branded property is 10 minutes on foot from the cathedral and has modern furnishings and dramatic artwork. **Pros:** central location; private parking; indoor pool and fitness center. **Cons:** often hosts corporate groups; not all rooms have bathtubs; some rooms are on the small side. [$] *Rooms from: €180* ✉ *9 rue Buirette* ☎ *03–26–40–04–08* 🌐 *www.bestwestern-lapaix-reims.com* 🛏 *165 rooms* 🍴 *No meals.*

L'Épine

56 km (35 miles) southeast of Reims, 7 km (4½ miles) east of Châlons.

Legend has it that in the Middle Ages some shepherds herding their flock down from pasture found a statue of the Virgin in a burning thorn bush (*épine*). Their discovery triggered the building of a church—Basilique de Notre-Dame de l'Épine—which today looms over this otherwise uninspiring village.

GETTING HERE AND AROUND

Lying east of Châlons, L'Épine is best reached by car. If you don't have your own, expect to pay about €20 for cab fare from Châlons.

Sights

Basilique de Notre-Dame de l'Épine

RELIGIOUS SITE | Tiny L'Épine is dominated by its twin-tower church, the Flamboyant Gothic Basilique de Notre-Dame de l'Épine. Decorated with a multitude of leering gargoyles, the facade is a magnificent creation of intricate patterns and spires. The interior, conversely, exudes elegance and restraint; note the sculptures depicting the Entombment of Christ and the stone rood screen, carved in the late 15th century. ✉ *Rue de l'Église* ☎ *03–26–66–96–98* 🎫 *Free.*

Châlons-en-Champagne

7 km (4½ miles) west of L'Épine, 34 km (21 miles) southeast of Épernay.

The administrative capital of the Marne and the Champagne region is famous for its Blanc de Blancs vineyards. The town center, crisscrossed with canals and streams, is a charming mix of half-timber houses and riverside gardens; and several major churches bear eloquent testimony to Châlons's medieval importance.

GETTING HERE AND AROUND

Trains from Paris (Gare de l'Est) leave for Châlons every 2 hours or so (€29.80); the 174-km (108-mile) trip takes around 1 hour 30 minutes. There's also limited TGV service from Paris: one train in the afternoon, one in the evening (1 hr 5 mins, €57.50). Eighteen direct trains a day arrive here from Reims (40 mins, €11.90), and Les Courriers de L'Aube (☎ *03–25–71–28–42* 🌐 *www.courriersdelaube.fr*) runs regular buses from the same city (1 hr, €10). A great way to explore the town itself is by boat; tours are organized by the tourist office.

VISITOR INFORMATION Châlons-en-Champagne Tourist Office ✉ *3 quai des Arts* ☎ *03–26–65–17–89* 🌐 *www.chalons-tourisme.com.*

Sights

Cathédrale St-Étienne

RELIGIOUS SITE | The 13th-century Cathédrale St-Étienne is a harmonious structure with large nave windows and tidy flying buttresses; the exterior effect

Hiking the Champagne Region

There's nothing like getting out into Mother Nature to send the spirits soaring and, as it turns out, the region of Champagne is custom-made for easy and scenic hiking. Just south of Reims rises the Montagne de Reims, a vast forested plateau on whose slopes grow the Pinot Noir and Pinot Meunier grapes used to make Champagne. Several *sentiers de Grandes Randonnées* (long hiking trails; also known as GRs) run across the top of the plateau, burrowing through dense forest and looping around the edges. For example, the GR141 and the GR14 form a loop more than 50 km (30 miles) long around the plateau's eastern half, passing by several train stations en route. You can access some of these hiking trails from the Rilly-la-Montagne, Avenay, and Ay stops on the Reims–Épernay rail line.

If you're a serious hiker, make for the Ardennes region, which lies just to the northeast of Champagne.

is marred only by the bulky 17th-century Baroque west front. ⊠ *Rue de la Marne* ☎ *03–26–65–35–65*.

Notre-Dame-en-Vaux

RELIGIOUS SITE | With its twin spires, Romanesque nave, and early Gothic choir and vaults, the church of Notre-Dame-en-Vaux is one of the most imposing in Champagne. The small museum beside the excavated cloister contains outstanding medieval statuary. ⊠ *Rue Nicolas-Durand* ☎ *03–26–69–99–61* ⊡ *Museum €4* ☉ *Museum closed Tues.*

 **Restaurants**

Les Caudalies

$$$ | **FRENCH** | **FAMILY** | This elegant, semiformal restaurant has a pair of stylish Art Deco dining rooms: one with mosaic floors, sleek contemporary table settings, and a glass ceiling; the other with wood paneling and parquet floors. The menu focuses on creative takes on traditional French dishes. **Known for:** daring desserts; pretty walled terrace for summer dining; good wine list showcasing champagnes. $ *Average main: €28*

⊠ *2 rue de L'Abbé Lambert* ☎ *03–26–65–07–87* ⊕ *www.restaurant-chalons.com* ☉ *Closed Sun., late Dec.–early Jan., 2 wks in Feb., and 2 wks late Aug. No dinner Tues. and Thurs.*

 Hotels

Hôtel d'Angleterre

$$$ | **HOTEL** | Guests at this stylish spot in central Châlons can enjoy well-appointed rooms (think modern furniture, marble bathrooms, and either wood floors or plush carpets) along with outstanding dining options. **Pros:** on-site parking; two eateries; excellent buffet breakfast. **Cons:** the hotel and restaurants are all closed Sunday; the walls between the rooms are thin; no wellness amenities. $ *Rooms from: €150* ⊠ *19 pl. Monseigneur-Tissier* ☎ *03–26–68–21–51* ⊕ *www.hotel-dangleterre.fr* ☉ *Closed late July–mid-Aug., late Dec.–early Jan., and 2 wks in Feb. No rooms Sun. night* ⇪ *25 rooms* ⦶ *No meals.*

Épernay

28 km (18 miles) south of Reims, 35 km (24 miles) west of Châlons-en-Champagne, 50 km (31 miles) east of Château-Thierry.

Although Reims loudly proclaims itself to be the last word in Champagne production, Épernay—on the south bank of the Marne—is really the center of the bubbly drink's spirit. It was here in 1741 that the first full-blown Champagne house, Moët (now Moët et Chandon), took the lifetime passion of Dom Pérignon and turned it into an industry. Unfortunately, no relation exists between the fabulous wealth of Épernay's illustrious wine houses and the drab, dreary appearance of the town as a whole. Most Champagne firms—Moët et Chandon (20 av. de Champagne), Mercier (68–70 av. de Champagne), and De Castellane (57 rue de Verdun)—are spaced out along the long, straight Avenue de Champagne, and although their names may provoke sighs of wonder, their facades are either functional or overly dressy.

GETTING HERE AND AROUND

Trains from Paris (Gare de l'Est) leave for Épernay every hour or so (€25.30); the 145-km (90-mile) trip takes 1 hour 14 minutes. Several trains daily also link Épernay to Reims (35 mins, €7.30) and Châlons (15 mins, €7.10).

VISITOR INFORMATION Épernay Tourist Office ⊠ *7 av. Champagne* ☎ *03–26–53–33–00* ⊕ *www.ot-epernay.fr.*

◉ Sights

★ Castellane

WINERY/DISTILLERY | Unlike most of the Champagne tours, at Castellane you get a chance to see the bottling, corking, and labeling plant. During the 45-minute guided tour of the underground chalk cellars, every step of the Champagne-making process is carefully explained. The visit culminates with a glass of Castellane Brut. Above the cellars, there's a museum with an intriguing display of old tools, bottles, labels, and posters. A climb to the top of the iconic 200-foot tower rewards you with a great view over Épernay and the surrounding Marne vineyards. ⊠ *57 rue de Verdun* ☎ *03–26–51–19–11* ⊕ *www.castellane.com* ⊠ *€14, includes museum* ⊙ *Closed Jan. and Feb.*

Hautvillers

WINERY/DISTILLERY | To understand how the region's still wine became sparkling Champagne, head across the Marne to Hautvillers. Here Dom Pérignon (1638–1715)—a blind monk who was reputedly blessed with exceptional taste buds and a heightened sense of smell—invented Champagne as everyone knows it by using corks for stoppers and blending wines from different vineyards. Legend has it that upon his first sip he cried out, "Come quickly, I am drinking the stars." Dom Pérignon's simple tomb, in a damp, dreary Benedictine abbey church (now owned by Moët et Chandon), is a forlorn memorial to the man behind one of the world's most exalted libations. ⊠ *Épernay.*

Mercier

WINERY/DISTILLERY | A tour here will take you for a 20-minute ride on a laser-guided electric train with commentary provided by an audio guide. Admire the giant 200,000-bottle oak barrel it took 24 oxen three weeks to cart to the Exposition Universelle in Paris in 1889, and the decorative wall sculptures by Gustave Navlet. A panoramic elevator down to (and up from) the cellars is a welcome plus. A chilled glass of bubbly awaits at the end of the tour. There is a choice of three different tastings, and one of the options includes a Blanc de Noirs (made using only black-skinned grapes). ⊠ *68–70 av. de Champagne* ☎ *03–26–51–22–22*

🌐 *www.champagnemercier.com* 🎫 *From €18* 🕒 *Closed mid-Dec.–Jan. and Tues. and Wed. mid-Feb.–mid-Mar. and mid-Nov.–mid-Dec.*

★ Moët & Chandon

WINERY/DISTILLERY | Founded by Charles Moët in 1743, the world's largest Champagne producer is a must-see if you're in the region. Foreign royalty from Czar Alexandre I and Emperor Napoléon I to Queen Elizabeth II have visited these prestigious chalk-cellar galleries, which run for a mind-blowing 17 miles. During the one-hour tour, which takes place on foot, a savvy guide explains in detail the Champagne-making process. There are three sommelier-guided tasting choices, with the high-end option including a glass of Grand Vintage and Grand Vintage Rosé. Reserve a visit online. ✉ *20 av. de Champagne* ☎ *03–26–51–20–20* 🌐 *www.moet.com* 🎫 *From €25* 🕒 *Closed Jan., weekends Feb.–late Mar., and Mon. and Tues. mid-Nov.–Dec.*

🍴 Restaurants

La Cave à Champagne

$$ | **FRENCH** | This convivial little restaurant in the center of Épernay serves authentic regional dishes with a refined twist at reasonable prices. Chef Bernard Ocio executes a perfect marriage of flavors by highlighting the local wines; classics include grilled oysters with Champagne butter and rump steak with a Pinot Noir sauce. **Known for:** the quintessential potée à la chamepenoise (a simmered meat and vegetable stew); fills up quickly on weekends (thus reservations are essential); the dessert menu showcases old favorites like profiteroles and crème brûlée. [$] *Average main: €22* ✉ *16 rue Gambetta* ☎ *03–26–55–50–70* 🌐 *www.la-cave-a-champagne.com* 🕒 *Closed Wed. No dinner Tues.*

🛏 Hotels

Hotel Jean Moët

$$$ | **HOTEL** | This small boutique hotel puts you in the center of town, only a few minutes away from the famed Avenue de Champagne. **Pros:** central location; helpful staff; good amenities such as bathrobes, Nespresso machines, and upscale toiletries. **Cons:** expensive street parking; low oak-beamed ceilings in the top floor rooms; the buffet breakfast is basic. [$] *Rooms from: €170* ✉ *7 rue Jean Moët* ☎ *03–26–32–19–22* 🌐 *www.hoteljeanmoet.com/en* 🛏 *12 rooms* 🍴 *No meals.*

La Briqueterie

$$$$ | **HOTEL** | Épernay is short on good hotels, so it's worth driving south to Vinay and staying at this luxurious manor, which has spacious accommodations, wonderful gardens, an indoor pool, plus a well-equipped spa. **Pros:** pool has garden view; spa includes sauna and hammam facilities; good restaurant. **Cons:** rooms can be small; corporate feel (it hosts frequent business seminars); some traffic noise. [$] *Rooms from: €270* ✉ *4 rte. de Sézanne, 6 km (4 miles) south of Épernay, Vinay* ☎ *03–26–59–99–99* 🌐 *www.labriqueterie.fr* 🕒 *Closed late Dec.–late Jan.* 🛏 *39 rooms* 🍴 *No meals.*

Château-Thierry

37 km (23 miles) east of Épernay.

Château-Thierry is best known as the birthplace of the French fabulist Jean de La Fontaine (1621–95). Built along the Marne River beneath the ruins of a hilltop castle that dates from the time of Joan of Arc, it's within sight of the American **Belleau Wood War Cemetery** (open daily 9–5), which commemorates the 2,300 American soldiers slain here in 1918.

Rumor has it that even the air is 30-proof in Champagne—discover whether this is true or not on the many hiking trails in the region.

GETTING HERE AND AROUND
Château-Thierry is easily reached by train from Paris; 10 direct ones depart daily from Gare de l'Est (46 mins, €16.90).

 ## Sights

Musée Jean de La Fontaine
HOUSE | Recently restored, the 16th-century mansion where La Fontaine was born and lived until 1676 is now a museum, furnished in the style of the 17th century. It contains La Fontaine's bust, portrait, and baptism certificate, plus editions of his fables magnificently illustrated by Jean-Baptiste Oudry (1755) and Gustave Doré (1868). ⊠ *12 rue Jean-de-La-Fontaine* ☎ *03–23–69–05–60* ⊕ *www.musee-jean-de-la-fontaine.fr* 🎟 *€4, audio guide €3* ⊙ *Closed Mon., and Sun. Nov.–Mar.*

Laon

66 km (41 miles) north of Château-Thierry, 52 km (32 miles) northwest of Reims.

Thanks to its awe-inducing hilltop site and the forest of towers sprouting from its ancient cathedral, lofty Laon basks in the title of the "Crowned Mountain." The medieval ramparts, virtually undisturbed by passing traffic, provide a ready-made itinerary for a tour of old Laon. Panoramic views, sturdy gateways, and intriguing glimpses of the cathedral lurk around every bend. There's even a funicular, which makes frequent trips (except on Sunday in winter) up and down the hillside between the station and the Vieille Ville (Old Town).

GETTING HERE AND AROUND
There are regular direct trains from Paris (Gare du Nord) to Laon; the 145-km (90-mile) journey takes 1 hour 40 minutes (€24.10). Eight direct trains depart daily

linking Reims to Laon (50 mins, €10.40), and nine direct trains arrive daily from Amiens (1 hr 30 mins, €19).

VISITOR INFORMATION Laon Tourist Office ✉ *Pl. du Parvis* ☎ *03–23–20–28–62* 🌐 *www.tourisme-paysdelaon.com.*

Sights

★ Cathédrale Notre-Dame

RELIGIOUS SITE | Constructed between 1150 and 1230, the Cathédrale Notre-Dame is a superb example of early Gothic. The light interior gives the impression of order and immense length, and the first flourishing of Gothic architecture is reflected in the harmony of the four-tier nave: from the bottom up, observe the wide arcades, the double windows of the tribune, the squat windows of the triforium, and, finally, the upper windows of the clerestory. Medieval stained glass includes the rose window dedicated to the liberal arts in the left transept, and the windows in the flat east end, an unusual feature for France although common in England. The majestic towers can be explored during guided visits; these depart from the tourist office, which occupies a 12th-century hospital on the cathedral square. Audio guides can be rented for €5. ✉ *Pl. du Parvis* 🎫 *Cathedral guided tours €6; towers €3.*

Musée d'Art et d'Archéologie

MUSEUM | Laon's art and archaeology museum has a collection of Mediterranean finds from the Bronze Age through the Gallo-Roman era that is second in importance only to that at the Louvre. Other highlights include fine 17th- and 18th-century paintings by celebrated local artists Mathieu Le Nain and Jean-Simon Berthélemy, as well as the chilling effigy of Guillaume de Harcigny, doctor to the insane Charles VI. The Chapelle des Templiers in the garden—a small, octagonal, 12th-century chapel topped by a shallow dome—houses fragments of the cathedral's gable. ✉ *32 rue Georges-Ermant* ☎ *03–23–22–87–00* 🌐 *www.laon.fr* 🎫 *€4* 🕒 *Closed Mon.*

Hotels

Bannière de France

$ | HOTEL | In business since 1685, this ancient hostelry is five minutes from the cathedral and welcomes visitors with its cozy accommodations and venerable dining room. **Pros:** comfy rooms; historic setting; good on-site restaurant. **Cons:** some rooms need modernizing; short on parking space; street-side rooms get some noise. [$] *Rooms from: €95* ✉ *11 rue Franklin-Roosevelt* ☎ *03–23–23–21–44* 🌐 *www.hoteldelabannieredefrance.com* 🕒 *Closed mid-Dec.–mid-Jan.* 🛏 *17 rooms* 🍴 *No meals.*

La Maison des 3 Rois

$$ | B&B/INN | FAMILY | Within walking distance of the cathedral, this centuries-old town house blends modern comforts with timbered ceilings, creaky stairs, and either wood or terra-cotta tile floors. **Pros:** centrally located; nice rooms with a fun style; friendly owner. **Cons:** steep staircase to attic rooms; breakfast is scanty, but acceptable; a parking spot on the street in front can be tricky to find. [$] *Rooms from: €120* ✉ *17 rue St-Martin* ☎ *03–23–20–74–24* 🌐 *www.lamaisondes3rois.com* 🛏 *5 rooms* 🍴 *Free Breakfast.*

Soissons

38 km (22 miles) southwest of Laon.

Although this was a major city in medieval times, the ravages of the French Revolution and World War I left little of it intact. Nowadays only the magnificent cathedral and the evocative ruins of its onetime abbey bear witness to Soissons's illustrious past.

GETTING HERE AND AROUND

Trains from Paris Gare du Nord take at least 65 minutes (€18.60), while those from Laon take about 30 (€7.70).

VISITOR INFORMATION Soissons Tourist Office ✉ *16 pl. Fernand-Marquigny* ☎ *03–23–53–17–37* ⊕ *www.tourisme-soissons.fr.*

👁 Sights

Cathédrale Saint-Gervais Saint-Protais
RELIGIOUS SITE | Rodin famously declared that "there are no hours in this cathedral, but rather eternity." The Gothic interior, with its pure lines and restrained ornamentation, creates a more harmonious impression than the asymmetrical, one-tower facade. The most remarkable feature, however, is the rounded four-story southern transept, an element more frequently found in the German Rhineland than in France. Rubens's *Adoration of the Shepherds* hangs on the other side of the transept. ✉ *Pl. Fernand-Marquigny* 🎫 *Tours €5* 🕐 *Towers closed mid-Sept.–mid-June.*

Musée de Soissons
MUSEUM | Partly housed in the medieval abbey of St-Léger, the town museum has a varied collection of local archaeological finds and paintings, with fine 19th-century works by Gustave Courbet and Eugène Boudin. ✉ *2 rue de la Congrégation* ☎ *03–23–59–91–20* ⊕ *www.ville-soissons.fr* 🎫 *€2* 🕐 *Closed Mon.*

St-Jean-des-Vignes
RELIGIOUS SITE | The twin-spire facade, arcaded cloister, and airy refectory are all that remain of this hilltop abbey church. Constructed between the 14th and 16th century, St-Jean-des-Vignes was largely dismantled just after the Revolution, and its fallen stones were used to restore the Cathédrale St-Gervais Saint-Potrais. Nevertheless, the church is still the most impressive sight in Soissons, the hollow of what was once its rose window peering out over the town like the eye of some giant Cyclops. ✉ *Cours St-Jean-des-Vignes* ⊕ *www.ville-soissons.fr* 🎫 *Free.*

🛏 Hotels

Château de Courcelles
$$$$ | HOTEL | Loaded with charm, this refined château by the Vesles River has a Louis XIV facade, and the classic exterior somehow harmonizes nicely with the sweeping brass main staircase attributed to Jean Cocteau. **Pros:** verdant setting; historic decor; welcoming to families. **Cons:** accommodations vary in size and grandeur; no elevator; uneven service. Ⓢ *Rooms from: €315* ✉ *8 rue du Château, 20 km (12 miles) east of Soissons via N31, Courcelles-sur-Vesles* ☎ *03–23–74–13–53* ⊕ *www.chateau-de-courcelles.fr* 🔄 *18 rooms* ⦿ *Free Breakfast.*

Amiens

112 km (70 miles) northwest of Soissons, 58 km (36 miles) north of Beauvais.

Although Amiens showcases some pretty brazen postwar reconstruction, epitomized by Auguste Perret's 340-foot Tour Perret (a soaring concrete stump by the train station), the city is well worth exploring. It has lovely Art Deco buildings in its traffic-free center, as well as elegant, older stone structures like the 18th-century Beffroi (Belfry) and neoclassical prefecture. Crowning the city is its great Gothic cathedral, which has survived the ages intact. Nearby is the waterfront quarter of St-Leu—with its small, colorful houses—rivaling the squares of Arras and streets of old Lille as the cutest city district north of Paris.

GETTING HERE AND AROUND
Trains from Paris (Gare du Nord) leave for Amiens every hour or so; the 129-km (80-mile) trip takes 1 hour 20 minutes and costs €22.80. There are 12 direct trains daily from Laon to Amiens (1 hr 30 mins, €19). Buses operated by Oise-mobilité (☎ *09–70–15–01–50* ⊕ *www.cabaro.fr*) run between Beauvais and Amiens throughout the day (Bus No. 42;

1 hr, €12.20). Note that the TGV Haute Picardie train station is a 50-minute bus ride away; from here trains go to all major destinations, including Charles de Gaulle airport.

VISITOR INFORMATION Amiens Tourist Office ⊠ *23 pl. Notre-Dame* ☎ *03–22–71–60–50* ⊕ *www.amiens-tourisme.com.*

◉ Sights

★ Cathédrale Notre-Dame d'Amiens
RELIGIOUS SITE | By far the largest church in France, the Cathédrale Notre-Dame d'Amiens could enclose Paris's Notre-Dame twice. It may lack the stained glass of Chartres or the sculpture of Reims, but for architectural harmony, engineering proficiency, and sheer size, it's incomparable. The soaring, asymmetrical facade has a notable Flamboyant Gothic rose window and is brought to life on summer evenings when a sophisticated 45-minute light show re-creates its original color scheme. Inside, there's no stylistic disunity to mar the perspective, creating an overwhelming sensation of pure space. Construction took place between 1220 and 1264, a remarkably short period in cathedral-building terms. One of the highlights of a visit here is hidden from the eye, at least until you lift up some of the 110 choir-stall seats and admire the humorous, skillful misericord seat carvings executed between 1508 and 1518 (access with guide only). Audio guides can be rented from the tourist office. ⊠ *Pl. Notre-Dame* ☎ *03–22–92–03–32 for cathedral, 03–22–71–60–50 for tours contact tourist office* ⊕ *www.cathedrale-amiens.fr* 🎫 *Tours €6; audio guides €5.*

Hortillonnages
GARDEN | Situated on the east side of town, the Hortillonnages are commercial water gardens—covering more than 700 acres—where vegetables have been cultivated since Roman times. Every Saturday the products grown here are sold at the water market in the St-Leu district. There's a 45-minute boat tour of these aquatic jewels. ⊠ *Boats leave from 54 bd. de Beauvillé* ☎ *03–22–92–12–18* ⊕ *www.hortillonnages-amiens.fr* 🎫 *€6* ☉ *Closed Nov.–Mar.*

Maison Jules-Verne
MUSEUM | Jules Verne (1828–1905) spent his last 35 years in Amiens, and his former home contains some 15,000 documents about his life as well as original furniture and a reconstruction of the writing studio where he created his science-fiction classics. If you're a true Jules Verne fan, you might also want to visit his final resting place in the **Cimetière de la Madeleine** (2 rue de la Poudrière), where he is melodramatically portrayed pushing up his tombstone as if enacting his own sci-fi resurrection. ⊠ *2 rue Charles-Dubois* ☎ *03–22–45–45–75* ⊕ *www.amiens.fr* 🎫 *€8* ☉ *Closed Tues. mid-Oct.–mid-Apr.*

Musée de Picardie
MUSEUM | Behind an opulent columned facade, the Musée de Picardie, built 1855–67, looks like a pompous offering from the Second Empire. Initial impressions are hardly challenged by the grand staircase lined with marouflaged murals by local-born Puvis de Chavannes, or the Grand Salon hung with huge canvases like Gérôme's 1855 *Siècle d'Auguste* and Maignan's 1892 *La Mort de Carpeaux*. One step beyond, though, and you're in a rotunda painted top to bottom in modern minimalist fashion by Sol LeWitt. The basement, notable for its masterly brick vaulting, is filled with subtly lighted archaeological finds and Egyptian artifacts. The ground floor houses 18th- and 19th-century paintings by artists such as Fragonard and Boucher. The museum is closed for major renovations until late 2019. ⊠ *48 rue de la République* ☎ *03–22–97–14–00* ⊕ *www.amiens.fr/Vivre-a-Amiens/Culture-Patrimoine/Etablissements-culturels/Musee-de-Picardie* 🎫 *€6* ☉ *Closed Mon.*

🍴 Restaurants

Les Marissons

$$$ | **MODERN FRENCH** | This picturesque waterside restaurant occupies an elegantly transformed boatbuilding shed in the scenic St-Leu section of Amiens. Order from the prix-fixe menus, which feature regional ingredients, to avoid pricey à la carte dining. **Known for:** specialties such as Amiens duck, and lamb raised at the Baie de Somme; the seasonal Picardy truffle menu; romantic dining on the waterfront terrace. [$] *Average main: €32* ✉ *Pont de la Dodone, 68 rue des Marissons* ☎ *03–22–92–96–66* 🌐 *www.les-marissons.fr* 🕓 *Closed Sun., and 3 wks in May. No lunch Wed. and Sat.*

🛏 Hotels

Marotte Hotel

$$$ | **HOTEL** | **FAMILY** | Built as a private mansion in the 19th century, this five-star boutique hotel has a dead-center location, an eco-friendly attitude, and plenty of style to spare. **Pros:** centrally located; gentle prices; large guest rooms. **Cons:** no restaurant; no air-conditioning (rooms in original building can get stuffy in hot weather); no 24-hour reception. [$] *Rooms from: €175* ✉ *3 rue Marotte* ☎ *03–60–12–50–00* 🌐 *www.hotel-marotte.com* 🔑 *12 rooms* 🍽 *No meals.*

🎟 Performing Arts

Théâtre de Marionnettes

PUPPET SHOWS | Come to Théâtre de Marionnettes for a rare glimpse at traditional Picardy puppetry—known locally as Chés Cabotans d'Amiens. Shows are performed in French, with plot synopses printed in English; they're usually held on Sunday afternoon at 3, September through mid-July, and Tuesday to Sunday at 6, from mid-July through August. Expect to pay €5–€10 for tickets. ✉ *31 rue Edouard-David* ☎ *03–22–22–30–90* 🌐 *www.ches-cabotans-damiens.com.*

Beauvais

56 km (35 miles) south of Amiens, 96 km (60 miles) west of Soissons.

Beauvais and its neighbor Amiens have been rivals since the 13th century, when they locked horns over who could build the bigger cathedral. Beauvais lost—gloriously.

GETTING HERE AND AROUND

Flights land at the Aéroport de Beauvais-Tillé; an airport bus (municipal line No. 12) stops in the town center and train station (20 mins, €4.50 for a 48-hour ticket). Trains from Paris (Gare du Nord) leave for Beauvais every 30 minutes; the 80-km (50-mile) trip takes 1 hour, 15 minutes and costs €14.50. Buses operated by the Oisemobilité (☎ *09–70–15–01–50* 🌐 *www.cabaro.fr*) offer frequent daily service between Amiens and Beauvais (Bus No. 42; 1 hr, €12.20).

VISITOR INFORMATION Beauvais Tourist Office ✉ *1 rue Beauregard* ☎ *03–44–15–30–30* 🌐 *www.visitbeauvais.fr.*

👁 Sights

★ **Cathédrale St-Pierre**

RELIGIOUS SITE | Soaring above the town center is the tallest cathedral in France: the Cathédrale St-Pierre. You may have an attack of vertigo just gazing up at its vaults, 153 feet above the ground. Despite its grandeur, the cathedral has a shaky past. The choir collapsed in 1284, shortly after completion, and was rebuilt with extra pillars. This engineering fiasco, paid for by the riches of Beauvais's wool industry, proved so costly that the transept was not attempted until the 16th century. It was worth the wait: an outstanding example of Flamboyant Gothic, with ornate rose windows flanked by pinnacles and turrets. However, a megalomaniacal 450-foot spire erected at the same time came crashing down after just four years, and

Beauvais's dream of having the largest church in Christendom vanished forever. Now the cathedral is starting to lean, and cracks have appeared in the choir vaults because of shifting water levels in the soil. No such problems bedevil the **Basse Oeuvre** (lower edifice; closed to the public), which juts out impertinently where the nave should have been; it has been there for 1,000 years. Fittingly donated to the cathedral by the canon Étienne Musique, the oldest surviving chiming clock in the world—a 1302 model with a 15th-century painted wooden face and most of its original clockwork—is built into the wall of the cathedral. Perhaps Auguste Vérité drew his inspiration from this humbler timepiece when, in 1868, he made a gift to his hometown of the gilded, templelike **astrological clock** (€5; displays at 10:30, 11:30, 2:30, 3:30, and 4:30 with additional displays at 12:30 and 1:30 from April to October), which features animated religious figurines representing the Last Judgment. ✉ *Rue St-Pierre* ☎ *03–44–48–11–60* 🌐 *www.cathedrale-beauvais.fr.*

Musée de l'Oise (*Regional Museum*)
MUSEUM | One of the few remaining testaments to Beauvais's glorious past, the old Bishop's Palace is now the Musée de l'Oise. Don't miss Thomas Couture's epic canvas depicting the French Revolution, the 14th-century frescoes of instrument-playing sirens on a section of the palace's vaults, or the 1st-century brass Guerrier Gaulois (Gallic Warrior). ✉ *1 rue du Musée* ☎ *03–44–10–40–50* 🌐 *mudo.oise.fr* 🎟 *Free* 🕒 *Closed Tues.*

🍴 Restaurants

Le Zinc Bleu
$$ | BRASSERIE | This lively brasserie opposite Beauvais Cathedral offers sturdy if unadventurous lunch fare (duck, steak, and the like) along with a wide variety of fresh seafood. There is a good selection of generous salads and warming soups, too. **Known for:** open all day; tables under a glass-capped veranda and an outside terrace; great view of the cathedral. [$] *Average main: €18* ✉ *61 rue St-Pierre* ☎ *03–44–45–18–30* 🕒 *No dinner.*

🛏 Hotels

Chenal Hotel
$ | HOTEL | This foursquare street-corner establishment—close to the train station, a 10-minute walk from the cathedral, and served by a shuttle bus from the airport—is perhaps the most convenient choice in central Beauvais. **Pros:** good value breakfast; convenient location; private parking. **Cons:** small rooms; lacks charm; street noise. [$] *Rooms from: €88* ✉ *63 bd. Général-de-Gaulle* ☎ *03–44–06–04–60* 🌐 *hotel-chenal-beauvais.fr* 🛏 *29 rooms* 🍴 *No meals.*

Hôtel de la Cathédrale
$ | HOTEL | FAMILY | There's a shortage of hotels in central Beauvais, but this small one is close to key sights and staff provide a friendly welcome behind its heavily tinted glass doors. **Pros:** hard-to-beat location; courtyard terrace at the rear; helpful staff. **Cons:** pricey city parking; bar doubles as the reception area; showers only, no tubs. [$] *Rooms from: €85* ✉ *11–13 rue Chambiges* ☎ *03–44–04–10–22* 🌐 *www.hoteldelacathedrale.fr* 🛏 *12 rooms* 🍴 *No meals.*

Lille

Born from the ancient marshes that gave its name (from the Latin "insula" for island), Lille is the 10th-largest city in France and sports a distinct Flemish flavor, thanks to its close proximity to Belgium. Devastated during the two World Wars, Lille suffered further setbacks from decline of regional coal, mining, and textile industries. But there's been a revival thanks to the opening of the Channel Tunnel and the arrival of the Eurostar train linking Lille with Paris (1 hour), London (1½ hours), and Brussels

(35 minutes). Extensive urban renovation added parks, shopping areas, art museums, restaurants, and a concert hall.

Sights

★ Opera de Lille

ARTS VENUE | When fire destroyed Lille's opera house in 1903, a new, grander edifice began to rise after more than 10 years of construction. Unfortunately, the outbreak of World War I set everything several steps back; after the war, more renovation was required, but the theater eventually opened in 1923. As impressive as the Belle Époque facade is on the outside, it's the sumptuous *grande salle* on the inside that truly dazzles, with its gilding, marble, chandeliers, and massive dome. The space suffers no dearth of activity today; the stage teams with operas, concerts, and dance performances. ⊠ *2 rue des Bons Enfants* ☎ *03–62–21–21–21* ⊕ *www.opera-lille.fr* ⊘ *Closed Sun. and Mon.*

★ Palais des Beaux Arts

MUSEUM | Restored in the 1990s as part of the revitalization of the city, this museum now ranks among the best in France. It takes special pride in its prized Flemish and Dutch collection, with works by Van Dyck, Rubens, and Brueghel. There are also equally impressive paintings, sculptures, and ceramics by Monet, Goya, and Delacroix. The prints and drawings room alone holds 30 pieces by Raphael. Originally established by decree by Napoléon Bonaparte in 1801, the museum moved into its current Belle Époque–style building in the late 19th century. ⊠ *Pl. de la Republique* ☎ *03–20–06–78–00* ⊕ *www. pba-lille.fr* 🎫 *€7* ⊘ *Closed Tues.*

 Restaurants

Aux Epherites

$$ | MODERN FRENCH | A significant amount of Lille's culinary praise is reserved for this lovely little restaurant just south of the Place de la Republique. Expect fresh, local, and eco-friendly ingredients cooked to near perfection and given inventive twists. **Known for:** weekly changing menu that keeps it simple with four starters, four mains, and four desserts; traditional bistro setting; good value multicourse tasting menu. $ *Average main: €18* ⊠ *17 rue Nicolas Leblanc* ☎ *09–81–31–55–24* ⊕ *www.auxepherites.com* ⊘ *Closed Sun. and Mon. No dinner Tues. and Wed.*

Crêperie Beaurepaire

$ | FRENCH | No trip to France is complete without eating at least one crêpe, and any visit to Lille should include a meal at this Old Town crêperie. Options range from savory cheese, bacon, and mushroom (with egg cracked on top) to the sweet options like chocolate drizzled with Grand Marnier or banana with rum and Chantilly cream. **Known for:** classic French crêpes; beautiful cozy setting; big crowds so prepare for a wait unless you book ahead. $ *Average main: €10* ⊠ *1 rue de St-Etienne* ☎ *03–20–54–60–54* ⊕ *www.creperiebeaurepaire.com* ⊘ *Closed Sun.*

Hotels

★ L'Hermitage Gantois Hotel

$$$ | HOTEL | Set in a redbrick, 15th-century hospital that is bisected by a quaint, white chapel, this upscale Marriott perfectly marries the architectural elements of this historical monument with contemporary needs of 21st-century guests. **Pros:** fascinating history; beautiful architecture and interior garden; hamman, spa, and heated pool. **Cons:** pricey add-ons like parking; 20-minute walk from the Old Town; some rooms can be on the small side. $ *Rooms from: €160* ⊠ *224 rue de Paris* ☎ *03/20–85–30–30* ⊕ *www.hotelhermitagegantois.com* 🛏 *72 rooms* ⫶◯⫶ *No meals.*

Chapter 9

ALSACE-LORRAINE

Updated by
Lyn Parry

👁 **Sights**
★★★☆☆

🍴 **Restaurants**
★★★☆☆

🛏 **Hotels**
★★★☆☆

🛍 **Shopping**
★★★☆☆

🍸 **Nightlife**
★★☆☆☆

WELCOME TO ALSACE-LORRAINE

TOP REASONS TO GO

★ **The Wine Road:** Ribeauvillé and Riquewihr, a pair of medieval villages filled with "Hansel and Gretel" houses and bottle-laden cellars, are at the heart of the Alsatian wine route.

★ **Colmar:** After two world wars Colmar rebuilt itself—today the mazelike cobblestone streets and Petite Venise waterways of its Vieille Ville are as atmospheric as ever.

★ **Architecture in Nancy:** Classic 18th-century elegance and fanciful Art Nouveau innovation are reminders of the medieval past in this city.

★ **Joan of Arc:** If you're a fan of Jeanne d'Arc, you've come to the right place; she was born right here in Domrémy-la-Pucelle.

★ **Strasbourg, Capital of Alsace:** The symbolic capital of Europe is a cosmopolitan French city rivaled only by Paris in its medieval allure, history, and haute cuisine.

1 **Nancy.** The home of Art Nouveau in the heart of Lorraine, once considered the Paris of eastern France.

2 **Vaucouleurs.** Where Joan of Arc convinced the governor to support her.

3 **Domrémy-la-Pucelle.** The birthplace of Joan of Arc.

4 **Épinal.** One of France's most famous printing centers since 1735.

5 **Strasbourg.** A German-inspired medieval city in the heart of Alsace.

6 **Obernai.** A market town that's often the start of the Route du Vin.

7 **Andlau.** An essential Alsace wine town.

8 **Dambach-la-Ville.** The largest wine-producing village on the Route du Vin.

9 **Sélestat.** A lively historic town.

10 **Haut-Koenigsbourg.** The home of a 12th-century German castle.

11 **Ribeauvillé.** A half-timber town with some of the region's best wine.

12 **Riquewihr.** A charming town filled with old-fashioned architecture and excellent wine.

13 **Colmar.** A small city with storybook, candy-colored buildings.

BELGIUM

Longuyon

D1916

Verdun

A4

D635

D964

Toul

N4

Vaucouleurs **2**

Domrémy-la-Pucelle

3

Grand

A31

Neufchâteau

CHAMPAGNE ARDENNE

LUXEMBOURG

A31
Thionville

Saarbrücken

GERMANY

Metz
A4

D674
D955

Bitche

LORRAINE
A4
ALSACE

Hagenau

Nancy
N4
Saverne
A35
1

Lunéville
N4
Strasbourg
A5

N59
Obernai
5
6
D1420
D1083

St Dié
Andlau
7

D657
Dambach-la-Ville
8

Épinal
10
Haut-Koenigsbourg
4
Route de Vin
Sélestat

N57
Ribeauvillé
11
9

12
Riquewihr
GERMANY

N57
Colmar
13

Freiburg

VOSGES

FRANCHE
COMTE
N66
D1083

A35

A36
Mulhouse

Basel

SWITZERLAND

0   20 mi

0   20 km

Only the Rhine separates Germany from Alsace-Lorraine, a region that often looks German and even sounds German. But its heart—just to prove how deceptive appearances can be—is passionately French. One has only to remember that Strasbourg was the birthplace of the Marseillaise national anthem to appreciate why Alsace and Lorraine remain among the most intensely French of all France's provinces.

No matter how forcefully the French tout its Frenchness, though, Alsace's German roots do run deep, as one look at its storybook medieval architecture reveals. Gabled half-timber houses, ornate wells and fountains, oriels (upstairs bay windows), storks' nests, and carved-wood balustrades—all calling to mind the Brothers Grimm—will satisfy a visitor's deepest craving for Old World Germanic atmosphere. Strasbourg, perhaps France's most fascinating city outside Paris, offers this and urban sophistication as well.

Lorraine, on the other hand, has suffered a decline in its northern industry, and the miseries of its small farmers have left much of it tarnished and neglected—or, as others might say, kept it unspoiled. Yet Lorraine's rich caches of verdure, its rolling countryside dotted with *mirabelle* (plum) orchards and crumbling-stucco villages, abbeys, fortresses, and historic cities, such as the Art Nouveau center Nancy, offer a truly French view of life in the north. Its borders flank Belgium, Luxembourg, and Germany's mellow Mosel (Moselle in French). Home of Baccarat and St-Louis crystal (thanks to limitless supplies of firewood from the Vosges Forest), the birthplace of Gregorian chant, Art Nouveau, and Joan of Arc, Lorraine-the-underdog has much of its own to contribute.

The question remains: who put the hyphen in Alsace-Lorraine? Alsace's strip of vine-covered hills squeezed between the Rhine and the Vosges Mountains started out being called Prima Germania by the Romans, and belonged to the fiercely Germanic Holy Roman Empire for more than 700 years. West of the Vosges, Lorraine served under French and Burgundian lords as well as the Holy Roman Empire, coming into its own under the powerful and influential dukes of Lorraine in the Middle Ages and Renaissance. Stanislas, the duke of Lorraine who transformed Nancy into a cosmopolitan Paris of the East, was Louis XV's father-in-law. Thus, Lorraine's culture evolved as decidedly less German than its neighbor to the southeast.

But then, in the late 19th century, Kaiser Wilhelm sliced off the Moselle chunk of Lorraine and sutured it, à la Dr. Frankenstein, to Alsace, claiming the unfortunate graft as German turf—a concession after France's 1871 surrender in the Franco-Prussian War. At that point the region was systematically Teutonized—architecturally, linguistically, culinarily—and the next two generations grew up culturally torn. Until 1918, that is, when France undid its defeat and reclaimed its turf. Until 1940, when Hitler snatched it back and reinstated German textbooks in the primary schools. Until 1945, when France once again triumphantly raised the *bleu-blanc-rouge* over Strasbourg. Today, the Alsace-Lorraine region remains both officially and proudly French.

MAJOR REGIONS

Lorraine. Lorraine is the land of Joan of Arc, one of France's patron saints and an iconic figure worldwide. Following the D64 highway, which winds between Contrexéville and Void, puts you on her home turf; almost unchanged since the Middle Ages, it's a landscape that Joan would probably find familiar today. Certainly the names of some local communities will be familiar to her fans. Domrémy was the place where she was born in 1411 or 1412; Neufchâteau, then a fortified town guarding the region, was where a teenage Joan and her fellow villagers sought refuge from the menacing English armies; and Vaucouleurs was where she went in 1428 to enlist the aid of the governor and prepare for a mission that would take her onward to the king—and to her destiny. The biggest city, Nancy, is located in the heart of Lorraine while Épinal is an important town for the history of printing and World War II American soliders.

Alsace. Tinged with a German flavor, Alsace is a never-ending procession of colorful towns and villages, many fitted out with spires, gabled houses, and storks' nests in chimney pots. The Rhine River forms the eastern boundary of both Alsace and France. But the best of Alsace is not found along the Rhine's industrial waterfront. Instead, it's in the Ill Valley at the base of the Vosges, southwest of cosmopolitan Strasbourg. Northwest is the beginning of the Route du Vin, the great Alsace Wine Road, which winds its way south through the Vosges foothills, fruitful vineyards, and medieval villages like Obernai, Anlau, Dambach-la-Ville, and Sélestat. Signs for the road help you keep your bearings on the twisting way south, and you'll find limitless opportunities to stop at wineries and sample the local wares. The Wine Road stretches 170 km (105 miles) between Thann and Marienheim, and is easily accessible from Strasbourg or Colmar. Many of the towns and villages have designated "vineyard trails" winding between towns (a bicycle will help you cover a lot of territory). Riquewihr and Ribeauvillé are connected by an especially picturesque route; along the way, stop at any "Dégustation" sign for a tasting. Pick up brochures on the Alsace Wine Road at any tourist office. The wine route conveniently heads south to Colmar, where the half-timber buildings of the *centre ville* seem cut out of a child's coloring book. The town's main treasure is Grünewald's unforgettable 16th-century Issenheim Altarpiece.

Planner

When to Go

Alsace is blessed with four distinct seasons and one of the lowest rainfalls in all of France—so anytime at all is the right time to visit. Snow in winter adds magic to the Christmas markets; spring brings forth the scent of burgeoning grape flowers as the world turns green with life; summer can be warm, drawing crowds;

autumn is nature's symphony of color—the leaves of tree and vine become a riot of golden yellows and oranges, as the bountiful grapes are harvested.

Planning Your Time

If an overall experience is what you're after, setting up headquarters in Strasbourg or Colmar will give you the best access to the greatest number of sites, either by public transport or car. If wine tasting and vineyards are your priority, setting up in either Riquewihr or Ribeauvillé will put you at the heart of the action. Remember that many of the region's towns and villages stage summer festivals—among them the spectacular pagan-inspired burning of the three pine trees in Thann (late June), the Flower Carnival in Sélestat (mid-August), and the wine fair in Colmar (first half of August). And although Lorraine is a lusterless place in winter, Strasbourg pays tribute to the Germanic tradition with a Christmas fair.

Getting Here and Around

Alsace is a small region and fairly well integrated with bus and train routes, making it possible to travel extensively by public transportation. Be sure to stock up on information (schedules, the best taxi-for-call companies, etc.) upon arriving at the ticket counter or help desk of the bigger train and bus stations in the area, such as Nancy, Strasbourg, and Colmar. In Alsace, trains are the way to go. In Lorraine you may need to take short bus jaunts to the smaller towns. If you're relying on trains, download the handy widgets from the TER website at ⊕ www.ter-sncf.com. A useful up-to-date website with details on buses and trams is ⊕ www.vialsace.eu. Unfortunately, schedules change rather frequently in Alsace-Lorraine.

AIR TRAVEL

Air France (⊕ www.airfrance.com) and assorted budget carriers serve Aéroport International Strasbourg, located 15 km (9½ miles) southwest of the city in Entzheim. Train service from the main-line station in Strasbourg runs to the airport every 15 minutes on weekdays, every half hour on weekends (€2.70).

AIRPORT INFORMATION Aéroport International Strasbourg ✉ 15 km (9½ miles) southwest of city, Rte. de Strasbourg, Entzheim ☎ 03–88–64–67–67 ⊕ www.strasbourg.aeroport.fr.

BUS TRAVEL

The two main bus companies are Transdev Grand Est, based in Nancy, and Compagnie des Transports Strasbourgeois, based in Strasbourg. Nancy, Strasbourg, and Colmar all have civic transit systems, too.

BUS INFORMATION Compagnie des Transports Strasbourgeois (CTS) ☎ 03–88–77–70–70 ⊕ www.cts-strasbourg.eu. **Transdev Grand Est** ☎ 03–55–68–20–00 ⊕ www.transdev-grandest.fr.

CAR TRAVEL

A4 heads east from Paris to Strasbourg, via Verdun, Metz, and Saverne. It's met by A26, descending from the English Channel, at Reims. A31 links Metz to Nancy, continuing south to Burgundy and Lyon. D1083/D83/A35 connects Strasbourg, Colmar, and Mulhouse. A36 continues to Belfort and Besançon. A4, linking Paris to Strasbourg, passes through Lorraine via Metz, linking Lorraine and Alsace. Picturesque secondary roads lead from Nancy through Joan of Arc country. Several scenic roads climb switchbacks over forested mountain passes through the Vosges, connecting Lorraine to Alsace. A quicker alternative is the tunnel under the Vosges at Ste-Marie-aux-Mines, linking Sélestat to Lunéville. Alsace's Route du Vin, winding from Marlenheim in the north all the way south to Thann, is the ultimate in scenic driving.

TRAIN TRAVEL

Fourteen direct high-speed TGVs and three InterCityExpress (ICE) trains per day leave Paris's Gare de l'Est for Strasbourg, making the journey in just under 2 hours; another 10 direct trains depart daily from the same station bound for Nancy, with a travel time of about 90 minutes. Three daily direct TGVs head to Colmar, arriving in 2 hours and 30 minutes, and two travel to Épinal in 2 hours, 20 minutes. A network of regional trains and buses links popular locales (like Ribeauvillé or Obernai), but you'll need a car to visit the smallest villages.

TRAIN INFORMATION Gare SNCF Colmar ✉ *9 pl. de la Gare, Colmar* ☎ *3635 (€0.40 per min).* **Gare SNCF Nancy** ✉ *3 pl. Thiers, Nancy* ☎ *3635 (€0.40 per min).* **Gare SNCF Strasbourg** ✉ *20 pl. de la Gare, Strasbourg* ☎ *3635 (€0.40 per min).* **SNCF** ☎ *3635 (€0.40 per min)* ⊕ *www.oui.sncf.* **TGV** ⊕ *www.sncf.com.*

Restaurants

Strasbourg and Nancy may be two of France's more expensive cities, but you wouldn't know it judging by all the down-to-earth eating spots with down-to-earth prices—most notably *winstubs,* which are cozier and more wine-oriented than the usual French brasserie. In Strasbourg and Nancy, as well as the villages along Alsace's wine road, you'll need to arrive early (soon after noon for lunch, before 8 for dinner) to be sure of a restaurant table in July and August. Out-of-season is a different matter throughout.

Hotels

Alsace-Lorraine is well served in terms of accommodations. From the picturesque village inns of the Route du Vin and the "Fermes Auberges" of the Vosges to four-star palaces or international-style hotels in the main cities of Nancy and Strasbourg, the range is vast. Since much of Alsace is in the "countryside," there's also a range of *gîtes,* self-catering cottages or houses that provide a base for longer stays (⊕ *www.gites-de-france.com*). *Restaurant and hotel reviews have been shortened. For full information, visit Fodors.com.*

What It Costs in Euros			
$	$$	$$$	$$$$
RESTAURANTS			
under €16	€16–€24	€25–€32	over €32
HOTELS			
under €125	€125–€225	€226–€350	over €350

Visitor Information

The Alsace-Lorraine region has three main area tourist offices, all of which can be contacted by telephone, mail, or email. For the Alsace area, contact Access Alsace. For Lorraine, contact the Comité Régional du Tourisme de Lorraine. For the city of Strasbourg and its environs, contact the Office de Tourisme de Strasbourg et Sa Region.

CONTACTS Agence d'Attractivité de L'Alsace ✉ *24 rue de Verdun, Colmar* ☎ *03–89–29–81–00* ⊕ *www.alsace.com.* **Comité Régional Grand Est** ✉ *1 pl. Adrien Zeller, Strasbourg* ☎ *03–88–15–68–67* ⊕ *www.grandest.fr.* **Office de Tourisme de Strasbourg et Sa Région** ✉ *17 pl. de la Cathédrale, Strasbourg* ☎ *03–88–52–28–28* ⊕ *www.otstrasbourg.fr.*

Nancy

For architectural variety, few French locales match this one in the heart of Lorraine, 300 km (190 miles) east of Paris. Medieval ornamentation, 18th-century grandeur, and Belle Époque fluidity rub shoulders in the city center, where the bustle of commerce mingles with stately elegance. Nancy's majesty derives from its long history as the domain of the powerful dukes of Lorraine, whose double-barred crosses figure prominently on local statues and buildings. Never having fallen under the rule of the Holy Roman Empire or the Germans, the city retains an eminently Gallic charm that's exemplified by harmoniously constructed squares and buildings. Vestiges of the 18th century, these have the quiet refinement associated with the best in French architecture.

Ironically, a Pole was responsible for most of them. Stanislas Leszczynski, the ex-king of Poland and father of Maria Leszczynska (who married Louis XV of France) was given the Duchy of Lorraine by his royal son-in-law on the understanding that it would revert to France when he died. Stanislas installed himself in Nancy and devoted himself to the glorious embellishment of the city. Today, Place Stanislas remains one of the loveliest and most perfectly proportioned squares in the world, and Place de la Carrière—reached through Stanislas's Arc de Triomphe and graced with elegant, homogeneous 18th-century houses—is a close rival for this honor.

GETTING HERE AND AROUND

Nancy, the jewel in Lorraine's tourism crown, has benefited greatly from the introduction of the TGV Est European service. Nine direct TGVs depart daily from Paris's Gare de l'Est, arriving about 90 minutes later. Two other trains take up to 90 minutes longer; and another six involve a change in Metz. One-way fares run from €52.20 to €91.80 depending on the train type, time of day, and how far in advance you book. Twelve direct trains depart daily for Strasbourg (€67.80), and roughly every 30 minutes one leaves for Metz (€65). Two dozen TER trains also travel to Épinal (€35.60). Once in Nancy, you'll find that the central core is manageable on foot, but it still helps

to get acquainted with Stan (☎ 03–83–30–08–08 ⊕ www.reseau-stan.com) and Ted (☎ 08–20–20–54–54 ⊕ www.ted.cg54.fr). The former, Nancy's public transit system, has convenient buses and trams; the latter is a 40-line bus service that covers the entire *département* for a €2.75 flat rate.

VISITOR INFORMATION Nancy Tourist Office ✉ 14 pl. Stanislas ☎ 03–83–35–22–41 ⊕ www.nancy-tourisme.fr.

Sights

Think "Art Nouveau," and many will conjure up the rich salons of Paris's Maxim's restaurant, the lavender-hue Prague posters of Alphonse Mucha, or the stained-glass dragonflies and opalescent vases that, to this day, remain the darlings of collectors like Barbra Streisand. All of that beauty was born, to a great extent, in 19th-century Nancy. Inspired and coordinated by the glass master Émile Gallé, the local movement was formalized in 1901 as L'École de Nancy—from here, it spread like wildfire through Europe, from Naples to Monte-Carlo to Prague. The ensuing flourish encompassed the floral *pâte de verre* (literally, "glass dough") works of Gallé and Antonin Daum; the Tiffany-esque stained-glass windows of Jacques Gruber; the fluidity of Louis Majorelle's furniture designs; and the sinuous architecture of Lucien Weissenburger, Émile André, and Eugène Vallin. Thanks to these artists, Nancy's downtown architecture gives the impression of a living garden suspended above the sidewalks. Concentrated northeast of the train station, the historic center of Nancy—rich in architectural treasures as well as museums—includes classical Place Stanislas and the shuttered, medieval Vieille Ville.

Avenue Foch

NEIGHBORHOOD | This busy boulevard lined with mansions was laid out for Nancy's affluent 19th- and early-20th-century

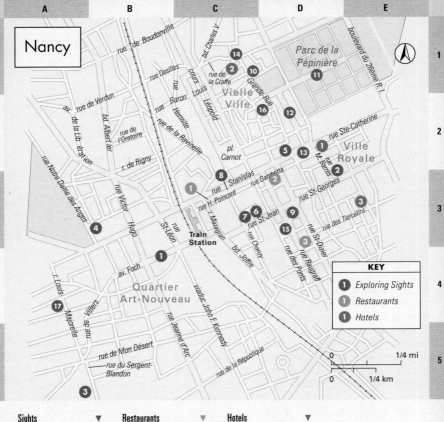

Nancy

KEY

- 1 *Exploring Sights*
- 1 *Restaurants*
- 1 *Hotels*

0 ——————————— 1/4 mi

0 ——————————— 1/4 km

Nancy 1900

History has a curious way of having similar events take place at the same time in different places. The creation of the Art Nouveau movement is one such event. Simultaneously emerging from the Pre-Raphaelite, High Victorian, and Arts and Crafts movements in England, it was also a synthesis of the Jugenstil (Youth style) movement in Germany; the Skonvirke movement in Denmark; the Mloda Polska (Young Poland) movement in Poland; Secessionism in Vienna, exemplified by the paintings of Gustav Klimt; and Modernisme in Spain, centered on Gaudí's outlandish architectural achievements in Barcelona. Its fluid, undulating, organic forms drawn from the natural world (picture seaweed, grasses, flowers, birds, and insects) also drew inspiration from Symbolism, Japanese woodcuts, and assorted other sources.

One of its founding centers was Nancy, which at the time was drawing the wealthy French bourgeoisie of Alsace, recently invaded by Germany, who refused to become German. Proud of their opulence, they had sublime houses built that were entirely furnished—from simple vases and wrought-iron beds to bathtubs in the shape of lily pads—in the pure Art Nouveau style.

Emile Gallé (1846–1904), the driving force behind Nancy's Art Nouveau movement, called on his fellow artists to follow examples in nature (as opposed to the Greek or Roman models then in favor) and aim for innovation. Working primarily in glass and inventing new, patented techniques, Gallé brought luxury craftsmanship to a whole range of everyday products, thus re-establishing the link between the ordinary and the exceptional. This was a major improvement on the bourgeois bad taste for mass-produced pieces of dubious quality that imitated styles of the past.

Everywhere stylized flowers suddenly became the preferred motif. The tree and its leaves, and plants with their flowers, were modified, folded, and curled to the artist's demand. Among the main Art Nouveau emblems figure lilies, irises, morning glories, bracken fern, poppies, peacocks, birds that feed on flowers, ivy, dragonflies, butterflies, and anything that evokes the immense poetry of the seasons. It reveals a world that is as fragile as it is precious.

By giving an artistic quality to manufactured objects, Gallé and the other creators of the École de Nancy accomplished a dream that had been growing since the romantic generation of Victorian England of making an alliance between art and industry. As a meeting point for the hopes and interests of artists, intellectuals, industrials, and merchants, the École de Nancy was a thoroughly global phenomenon. From Chicago to Turin, Munich to Brussels, and on to London, the industries of Nancy went on to conquer the world.

middle class. At No. 69, built in 1902 by Émile André, the occasional pinnacle suggests Gothic influence; André designed the neighboring No. 71 two years later. Number 41, built by Paul Charbonnier in 1905, bears ironwork by Louis Majorelle. ✉ *Quartier Art-Nouveau.*

Cathédrale

RELIGIOUS SITE | This vast, frigid edifice was built in the 1740s in a ponderous Baroque style, eased in part by the florid ironwork of Jean Lamour. The most notable interior feature is a murky 19th-century fresco in the dome. The **Trésor** (Treasury) contains minute 10th-century splendors carved of ivory and gold but is only open to the public on rare occasions. ✉ *Rue St-Georges, Ville Neuve.*

★ Musée de l'École de Nancy (*School of Nancy Museum*)

MUSEUM | France's only museum devoted to Art Nouveau is in an airy turn-of-the-last-century garden–town house built by Eugène Corbin, an early patron of the École de Nancy. Re-created rooms show off original works by local Art Nouveau glassmakers Emile Gallé, Antonin and Auguste Daum, Amalric Walter, and other artisans. Immerse yourself in the fanciful, highly stylized, curlicue style that crept into interiors and exteriors throughout Nancy in the early 20th century, then became a sensation around the world. ✉ *36 rue du Sergent-Blandan, Quartier Art-Nouveau* ☎ *03–83–40–14–86* ⊕ *www. ecole-de-nancy.com* 🎫 *€6* ⊗ *Closed Mon. and Tues.*

Musée des Arts et Traditions Populaires

(*Museum of Folk Arts and Traditions*) MUSEUM | Just up the street from the Palais Ducal, this quirky museum is in the **Couvent des Cordeliers** (Convent of the Franciscans, who were known as Cordeliers until the Revolution). Displays re-create how local people lived in preindustrial times, using a series of evocative rural interiors. Craftsmen's tools, colorful crockery, somber stone fireplaces, and dark waxed-oak furniture accent the tableaulike settings. The dukes of Lorraine are buried in the crypt of the adjoining **Église des Cordeliers**, a Flamboyant Gothic church; the detailed *gisant* (reclining statue) of Philippa de Gueldra, second wife of René II, is executed in limestone and serves as a moving example of Renaissance portraiture. The octagonal Ducal Chapel was begun in 1607 in the Renaissance style, modeled on the Medici Chapel in Florence. ⚠ **There are major restorations underway until 2022, and currently only the Église des Cordeliers is open to the public.** ✉ *64 Grande-Rue, Vieille Ville* ☎ *03–83–32–18–74* ⊕ *www. musee-lorrain.nancy.fr* ⊗ *Closed Mon.*

Musée des Beaux-Arts (*Fine Arts Museum*)

MUSEUM | In a splendid building that now spills over into a spectacular modern wing, a broad and varied collection of art treasures lives up to the noble white facade designed by Emmanuel Héré. The showpiece is Rubens's massive *Transfiguration,* and among the most striking works are the freeze-the-moment realist tableaux painted by native son Émile Friant at the turn of the 20th century. A sizable collection of Lipschitz sculptures includes portrait busts of Gertrude Stein, Jean Cocteau, and Coco Chanel. You'll also find 19th- and 20th-century paintings by Monet, Manet, Utrillo, and Modigliani; a Caravaggio *Annunciation*; and a wealth of other old masters from the Italian, Dutch, Flemish, and French schools; and impressive glassworks by Nancy native Antonin Daum. Audio guides in English are available at reception. ✉ *3 pl. Stanislas, Ville Royale* ☎ *03–83–85–30–01* ⊕ *mban.nancy.fr* 🎫 *€7* ⊗ *Closed Tues.*

No. 2 Rue Bénit

BUILDING | This elaborately worked metal exoskeleton, the first in Nancy (1901), exudes functional beauty. The floral decoration is reminiscent of the building's past as a seed supply store. Windows were worked by Jacques Gruber; the building was designed by Henry-Barthélemy

Gutton, while Victor Schertzer conceived the metal frame. ⊠ *2 rue Bénit, Quartier Art-Nouveau.*

No. 9 Rue Chanzy
BUILDING | Designed by architect Émile André, this lovely structure—now a bank—can be visited during business hours. You can still see the cabinetry of Louis Majorelle, the decor of Paul Charbonnier, and the stained-glass windows of Jacques Gruber. ⊠ *9 rue Chanzy, Quartier Art-Nouveau.*

No. 40 Rue Henri-Poincaré
BUILDING | The Lorraine thistle (a civic emblem) and brewing hops weave through this undulating exterior, designed by architects Émile Toussaint and Louis Marchal. Victor Schertzer conceived the metal structure in 1908, after the success of No. 2 rue Bénit. Gruber's windows are enhanced by the curving metalwork of Louis Majorelle. ⊠ *40 rue Henri-Poincaré, Quartier Art-Nouveau.*

Nos. 42–44 Rue St-Dizier
BUILDING | Furniture maker Eugène Vallin and architect Georges Biet left their mark on this graceful 1903 bank. ⊠ *42–44 rue St-Dizier, Quartier Art-Nouveau* ⊙ *Closed weekends.*

Palais Ducal (*Ducal Palace*)
CASTLE/PALACE | Built in the 13th century and completely restored in the 15th century and again after a fire at the end of the 19th century, this palace originally housed the Dukes of Lorraine, and today it is home to the Musée Lorrain. A major renovation project means the museum is closed to the public until 2023. Regardless, you can admire the palace's stunning architecture from the outside; one wing is a spectacular example of Flamboyant Gothic. ⊠ *64 Grande-Rue, Vieille Ville* ☎ *03–83–32–18–74* ⊕ *www.musee-lorrain.nancy.fr* ⊙ *Closed Mon.*

Parc de la Pépinière
NATIONAL/STATE PARK | **FAMILY** | This picturesque, landscaped city park has labeled ancient trees, a rose garden, playgrounds, a carousel, and a small zoo. ⊠ *Entrance off Pl. de la Carrière, Vieille Ville.*

Place de la Carrière
HISTORIC SITE | Lined with pollarded trees and handsome 18th-century mansions (another successful collaboration between King Stanislas and Emmanuel Héré), this UNESCO World Heritage Site's elegant rectangle leads from Place Stanislas to the colonnaded facade of the **Palais du Gouvernement** (Government Palace), former home of the governors of Lorraine. ⊠ *Vieille Ville.*

★ Place Stanislas
PLAZA | With its severe, gleaming-white Classical facades given a touch of rococo jollity by fanciful wrought gilt-iron railings, this perfectly proportioned square may remind you of Versailles. It is named for Stanislas Leszczynski, twice dethroned as king of Poland but offered the Duchy of Lorraine by Louis XV (his son-in-law) in 1736. Stanislas left a legacy of spectacular buildings, undertaken between 1751 and 1760 by architect Emmanuel Héré and ironwork genius Jean Lamour. The sculpture of Stanislas dominating the square went up in the 1830s. Framing the exit, and marking the divide between the Vieille Ville and the Ville Neuve (New Town), is the **Arc de Triomphe**, erected in the 1750s to honor Louis XV. The facade trumpets the gods of war and peace; Louis's portrait is here. ⊠ *Ville Royale.*

Porte de la Craffe
ARCHAEOLOGICAL SITE | A fairy-tale vision out of the late Middle Ages, this 14th- and 15th-century gate is all that remains of Nancy's medieval fortifications. With its twin turrets looming at one end of the Grande-Rue, the arch served as a prison through the Revolution. Above the main portal is the Lorraine Cross, comprising a thistle and cross. ⊠ *Vieille Ville.*

Rue Raugraff
NEIGHBORHOOD | Once there were two stores here—Vaxelaire and Pignot,

Place Stanislas—the crown jewel of the city—is a huge public square enclosed by gold-and-black gates and gorgeous neoclassical buildings.

both built in 1901. The facade is the last vestige of the work of Émile André and Eugène Vallin. ⊠ *13 rue Raugraff, Quartier Art-Nouveau.*

St-Epvre

RELIGIOUS SITE | A 275-foot spire towers over this splendid neo-Gothic church, completed in 1451 and rebuilt in the 1860s. Most of the 2,800 square yards of stained glass were created by the Geyling workshop in Vienna; the chandeliers were made in Liège, Belgium; many carvings are the work of Margraff of Munich; the heaviest of the eight bells was cast in Budapest; and the organ, though manufactured by Merklin of Paris, was inaugurated in 1869 by Austrian composer Anton Bruckner. ⊠ *Pl. St-Epvre, Vieille Ville.*

Villa Majorelle

HOUSE | In this villa, built in 1902 by Paris architect Henri Sauvage for Art Nouveau furniture designer Louis Majorelle, sinuous metal supports seem to sneak up on the unsuspecting balcony like swaying cobras. The two grand windows are by

Jacques Gruber: one lights the staircase (visible from the street) and the other is set in the dining room on the south side of the villa (peek around from the garden side). Guided tours of the interior are suspended until 2020 as major renovations take place. ⊠ *1 rue Louis-Majorelle, Quartier Art-Nouveau* ☎ *03–83–17–86–77* 🎟 *€6* ⊙ *Closed weekdays.*

🍴 Restaurants

Brasserie l'Excelsior

$$$ | BRASSERIE | Above all, you'll want to eat in this 1911 restaurant, part of the dependable Flo group, for its sensational Art Nouveau stained glass, mosaics, Daum lamps, and sinuous Majorelle furniture. But the food is stylish, too and the waiters exude Parisian chic. **Known for:** platters of shellfish and oysters; open all day every day; regional Alsatian desserts. $ *Average main: €27* ⊠ *50 rue Henri-Poincaré, Quartier Art-Nouveau* ☎ *03–83–35–24–57* ⊕ *www.brasserie-excelsior-nancy.fr.*

Le Capu

$$$ | FRENCH | Barely a stone's throw from Place Stanislas, this stylish landmark puts its best foot forward under chef Hervé Fourrière. The menu includes old favorites revisited and noteworthy desserts. **Known for:** excellent Sunday brunch buffet; variety of Toul wines; stylish dining room. $ *Average main: €28* ⊠ *31 rue Gambetta, Ville Royale* ☎ *03–83–35–26–98* ⊕ *www.lecapu.com* � *Closed Mon.*

Les Frères Marchand

$$ | BISTRO | If you were inspired by the rustic exhibits at the Musée des Arts et Traditions Populaires, cross the street and sink your teeth into authentic Lorraine cuisine in the form of mouthwatering choucroutes or pig's trotter with mustard sauce. Tables inside are tight, creating a bustling, canteenlike atmosphere, and the quality of the service seems to vary with the weather, but the hearty food is irreproachable. **Known for:** signature dishes include choucroute, flammenqueche, and calf's head; Sunday brunch buffet; great cheese selection. $ *Average main: €20* ⊠ *97 Grande-Rue, Vieille Ville* ☎ *03–83–32–85–94* ⊕ *www. restaurant-marchand.com.*

Hotels

Grand Hôtel de la Reine

$$ | HOTEL | Every bit as grand as Place Stanislas, on which it stands, this magnificent 18th-century building is officially classified as a historic monument with an interior that is just as regal: guest rooms are decorated in Louis XV style (the most luxurious overlook the square). **Pros:** sumptuous location; old-world atmosphere; dining on the terrace overlooking Place Stanislas. **Cons:** rooms get street noise; indifferent staff; some bedrooms can be small. $ *Rooms from: €125* ⊠ *2 pl. Stanislas, Ville Royale* ☎ *03–83–35–03–01* ⊕ *www.hoteldelareine.com* ☙ *51 rooms* ï◯ï *No meals.*

Hôtel de Guise

$ | HOTEL | Deep in the shuttered Vieille Ville, this quiet, convivial hotel occupies an 18th-century nobleman's mansion with a magnificent stone-floor entry and a delightful walled garden; some guest rooms are furnished with period pieces and charmingly incongruous floral patterns, while others have been redecorated in a sleek contemporary style. **Pros:** tidy rooms; central location; helpful staff. **Cons:** no air-conditioning; overheated, stuffy rooms; no on-site parking. $ *Rooms from: €90* ⊠ *18 rue de Guise, Vieille Ville* ☎ *03–83–32–24–68* ⊕ *www.hoteldeguise.com* ☙ *50 rooms* ï◯ï *No meals.*

Maison de Myon

$$ | B&B/INN | FAMILY | Tucked behind the cathedral, this 17th-century former canon's house combines cutting-edge style with period features to create a boutique B&B. **Pros:** central location; friendly owner; located on a quiet street with little traffic. **Cons:** no elevator; no on-site parking; lacks good choices for breakfast. $ *Rooms from: €140* ⊠ *7 rue Mably, Ville Neuve* ☎ *03–83–46–56–56* ⊕ *www.maisondemyon.com* ☙ *8 rooms* ï◯ï *Free Breakfast.*

Nightlife

Le Chat Noir

DANCE CLUBS | The "Black Cat" is a hit with thirtysomethings who enjoy retro-theme dance parties. ⊠ *63 rue Jeanne-d'Arc, Ville Neuve* ☎ *06–01–48–84–87* ⊕ *www.lechatnoir.fr.*

Les Caves du Roy

DANCE CLUBS | A young upscale crowd comes to dance at Les Caves du Roy. ⊠ *9 pl. Stanislas, Ville Royale* ☎ *07–89–59–74–76.*

 Performing Arts

Ballet de Lorraine
DANCE | Created in 1978 to assume the mission of a national ballet, it stages performances in the Opéra de Nancy on Place Stanislas. ⊠ *1 rue Ste-Catherine, Vieille Ville* ☎ *03–83–85–69–01* ⊕ *www.ballet-de-lorraine.eu.*

Opéra National de Lorraine
OPERA | The musical repertoire of this opera company ranges from ancient to contemporary. ⊠ *1 rue Ste-Catherine, Vieille Ville* ☎ *03–83–85–33–11* ⊕ *www.opera-national-lorraine.fr.*

Orchestre Symphonique et Lyrique
CONCERTS | Established in 1884, the Orchestre Symphonique et Lyrique organizes concerts from fall through spring. ⊠ *1 rue Ste-Catherine, Vieille Ville* ☎ *03–83–85–33–11* ⊕ *www.opera-national-lorraine.fr.*

Shopping

Daum Boutique
CERAMICS/GLASSWARE | This boutique sells deluxe crystal and examples of the city's traditional Art Nouveau *pâte de verre*, in which crushed glass is mixed with a binding material to form a decorative surface. ⊠ *14 pl. Stanislas, Vieille Ville* ☎ *03–83–32–21–65* ⊕ *www.daum.fr.*

Librairie Ancienne Dornier
BOOKS/STATIONERY | Located near the Musée des Arts et Traditions Populaires, Librairie Ancienne Dornier is an excellent bookstore that sells engravings as well as old and new books devoted to local history. ⊠ *74 Grande-Rue, Vieille Ville* ☎ *03–83–36–50–62.*

Vaucouleurs

73 km (41 miles) southwest of Nancy.

Above the modest main street in the market town of Vaucouleurs, you can see ruins of Robert de Baudricourt's medieval castle and the Porte de France. The barefoot Maid of Orléans, Joan of Arc, spent several months here, arriving on May 13, 1428, to ask Governor de Baudricourt for help. After wheedling an audience at the castle, she convinced him of the necessity of her mission, learning to ride and to wield a sword. Won over finally by her conviction and by popular sentiment, de Baudricourt offered to give her an escort to seek out the king. On February 23, 1429, clad in page's garb and with her hair cut short, Jeanne d'Arc rode out through the Porte de France, en route to Orléans.

GETTING HERE AND AROUND
Bus R410 runs from Nancy to Toul and takes around 35 minutes; from Toul, Bus R450 continues on to Vaucouleurs, but only on school days (€2.50 each leg).

Hotels

Hostellerie de l'Isle en Bray
$$ | B&B/INN | A night in the fine Renaissance-style Château de Montbras—where grand public salons are crammed with antiques and spacious guest rooms are graced with period furniture elegantly offset by modern fabrics—is ideal for anyone indulging in Joan of Arc–related medieval musings. **Pros:** romantic and secluded; marvelous museum atmosphere; decent prices with breakfast included. **Cons:** need a car; people who prefer modernity might not be impressed; no elevator. $ *Rooms from: €130* ⊠ *10 km (6 miles) south of Vaucouleurs, 3 rue des Erables* ☎ *03–29–90–49–90* ⊕ *www.chateau-montbras.com* ☉ *Closed winter* ⤴ *7 rooms* ⦿ *Free Breakfast.*

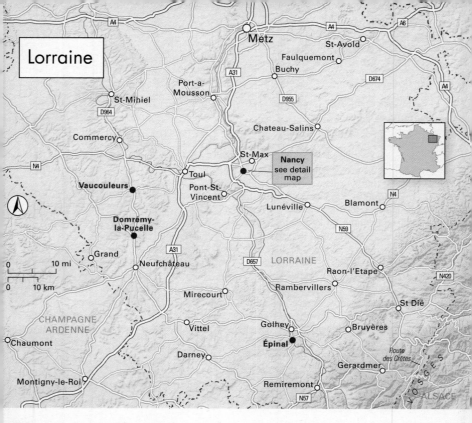

Domrémy-la-Pucelle

19 km (12 miles) south of Vaucouleurs.

Joan of Arc was born in a cottage here in either 1411 or 1412. You can see her birthplace, as well as the church where she was baptized, the actual statue of Ste-Marguerite before which she prayed, and the hillside where she tended sheep and first heard voices telling her to take up arms and save France from the English.

In the nearby forest of Bois-Chenu, perhaps an ancient sacred wood, Jeanne d'Arc gathered flowers. Near the village of Coussy, she danced with other children at country fairs attended by Pierre de Bourlémont, the local seigneur, and his wife Beatrice—the Château of Bourlémont may still be seen. Associated

with Coussey and Brixey are Saints Mihiel and Catherine, who, with the Archangel St-Michael, appeared before Joan. In the Chapel of Notre-Dame at Bermont, where Joan vowed to save France, are the statues that existed in her time.

GETTING HERE AND AROUND
If you don't have your own car, you can come by taxi from Vaucouleurs for about €40.

Sights

Basilique du Bois-Chenu (*Bois-Chenu Basilica*)
RELIGIOUS SITE | The ornate late-19th-century Basilique du Bois-Chenu, high up the hillside above Domrémy, boasts enormous painted and mosaic panels expounding on Joan's legend in glowing Pre-Raphaelite tones. Outside

lurk serene panoramic views over the emerald, gently rolling Meuse Valley. ⊠ *Domrémy-la-Pucelle.*

★ **Maison Natale de Jeanne d'Arc** (*Joan of Arc's Birthplace*)

HOUSE | The humble stone-and-stucco Maison Natale de Jeanne d'Arc—an irregular, slope-roof, two-story cottage—has been preserved with style and reverence, although there is little to see inside. The modern museum alongside, the **Centre Johannique,** shows a film (French with English subtitles), while mannequins in period costume recount the Hundred Years' War. After she heard mystical voices, Joan walked 19 km (12 miles) to Vaucouleurs. Dressed and mounted like a man, she later led her forces to lift the siege of Orléans, defeated the English, and escorted the unseated Charles VII to Reims, to be crowned king of France. Military missions after Orléans failed— including an attempt to retake Paris—and she was captured at Compiègne. The English turned her over to the Church, which sent her to be tried by the Inquisition for witchcraft and heresy. She was convicted and burned at the stake in Rouen. One of the latest theories is that Jeanne d'Arc was no mere "peasant" but was distantly connected to France's royal family—a controversial proposal that many historians discount. ⊠ *2 rue de la Basilique* ☎ *03–29–06–95–86* ⊕ *www. culture.vosges.fr* ◪ *€4* ⊘ *Closed Tues. Oct.–June.*

Épinal

74 km (44 miles) southeast of Dom- rémy-la-Pucelle, 72 km (45 miles) south of Nancy.

On the Moselle River at the feet of the Vosges, Épinal, a printing center since 1735, is famous throughout France for boldly colored prints, popular illustrations, and hand-colored stencils. Just 6½ km (4 miles) southwest of the city center is

the Épinal American War Cemetery (open daily 9–5), which contains 5,255 graves of American servicemen and women who died during World War II.

GETTING HERE AND AROUND

There are two direct TGVs from Paris's Gare de l'Est (2 hrs 20 mins; €72–€93); 19 TER trains also arrive daily from Nancy, making the trip in just under an hour (€14.60).

 Sights

Basilique St-Maurice

RELIGIOUS SITE | The small but bustling Vieille Ville is anchored by the lovely old Basilique St-Maurice, a low gray-stone sanctuary blending Romanesque and Gothic styles. Note its sturdy belfry and deep, ornate, 15th-century entry porch. ⊠ *Pl. St-Goëry* ☎ *03–29–82–58–36.*

Musée de l'Image

MUSEUM | FAMILY | This museum is next door to the town's most famous printing workshop, L'Imagerie d'Épinal. Begun in 1796, L'Imagerie has produced woodcuts, lithographs, and other forms of printed imagery that are displayed here, offering a beautiful—and often critical— pictorial history of France. ⊠ *42 quai de Dogneville* ☎ *03–29–81–48–30* ⊕ *www. museedelimage.fr* ◪ *€6.*

★ **Musée Départemental d'Art Ancien et Contemporain** (*Museum of Antiquities and Contemporary Art*)

MUSEUM | A renovated 17th-century hospital on an island in the center of Épinal is home to the spectacular Musée Départemental d'Art Ancien et Contemporain. The crowning jewel here is *Job Lectured by His Wife,* one of the greatest works of Georges de la Tour, the painter whose candlelight scenes constitute Lorraine's most memorable artistic legacy. Works of other old masters on view (including Rembrandt, Fragonard, and Boucher) were once part of the famous collection of the Princes of Salm. The museum also contains one of France's largest collections of contemporary art, as well as Gallo-Roman artifacts, rural tools, and local faïence. ✉ *1 pl. Lagarde* ☎ *03–29–82–20–33* ⊕ *www.museedepartemental. vosges.fr* 🎫 *€6* ⊗ *Closed Tues.*

🍴 Restaurants

Le Bistrot Gourmand

$$ | FRENCH | This restaurant on the backstreet of a shady square is run by a French-British wife-husband team. The setting is unassuming, with a menu that draws on seasonal produce with regional flourishes. **Known for:** homemade foie gras and panfried king prawns; outside seating on pretty square; good value fixed-price lunchtime menus. 💲 *Average main: €23* ✉ *5 rue du Chapitre* ☎ *03–29–34–20–77* ⊕ *www.le-bistrot-gourmand. zenchef.com* ⊗ *Closed Mon. No dinner Sun.*

Strasbourg

Although it's in the heart of Alsace, 490 km (304 miles) east of Paris, and draws appealingly on Alsatian *gemütlichkeit* (coziness), Strasbourg is a cosmopolitan French cultural center and the symbolic if unofficial capital of Europe. The Romans knew Strasbourg as Argentoratum before it came to be known as Strateburgum, or City of (Cross) Roads. After centuries as part of the Germanic Holy Roman Empire, it was united with France in 1681, but retained independence regarding legislation, education, and religion under the honorific title Free Royal City.

Against an irresistible backdrop of old half-timber houses, waterways, and the colossal single spire of its red-sandstone cathedral (which seems to insist imperiously that you pay homage to its majestic beauty), Strasbourg embodies Franco-German reconciliation and the wider idea of a united Europe. You'll discover an incongruously sophisticated mix of museums, charming neighborhoods like

La Petite France, elite schools (including that notorious hothouse for blooming politicos, the École Nationale d'Administration, or National Administration School), international think tanks, and the European Parliament. The *Strasbourgeoisie* have a lot to be proud of.

GETTING HERE AND AROUND

Strasbourg is two hours from Paris on any of the 19 daily direct TGVs (€90–€107). Frequent extraregional trains also link the city to Nancy, Metz, Lyon, and Geneva. Because Strasbourg's train station (20 pl. de la Gare) is the hub of the regional TER system, direct trains run at least every 30–60 minutes to Colmar (€13.20) and Sélestat (€9.40), too. Buses head to Obernai from the Gare Routière (☎ *03–88–23–43–23*) in Place des Halles. Within the city, you can take advantage of an extensive tram and bus network, operated by Companie des Transports Strasbourgeois (☎ *03–88–77–70–70* ⊕ *www.cts-strasbourg.eu*). Trams and buses depart from the train station, and the same tickets can be used on both. If you want to sightsee on foot, audioguide walking tours of Strasbourg's Vieille Ville and other attractions are available through the tourist office for €5.50 per headset (plus €100 deposit).

If you're driving, keep in mind that the configuration of downtown streets makes it difficult to approach the center via the autoroute exit marked Strasbourg Centre. Instead, hold out for the exit marked Place de l'Étoile and follow signs to Cathédrale/Centre Ville. At Place du Corbeau, veer left across the Ill, and go straight to the Place Gutenberg parking garage, a block from the cathedral.

VISITOR INFORMATION Strasbourg Tourist Office ✉ *17 pl. de la Cathédrale* ☎ *03–88–52–28–28* ⊕ *www.otstrasbourg.fr.*

TOURS

Batorama

TOUR—SIGHT | Strasbourg is a big town, but its center is easily explored on foot,

The Gothic grace of Strasbourg's cathedral in all its glory

or, more romantically, by boat. The company Batorama organizes 70-minute boat tours along the Ill. Tours depart four times a day in January and February, up to every 45 minutes in March, and from 15 minutes to every half hour from April through December; there are also nocturnal tours until 10:15 pm in July and August. Boats leave from behind the Palais Rohan. ⊠ *Strasbourg* ☎ *03–69–74–44–04* ⊕ *www.batorama.com* ✉ *From €14.*

👁 Sights

The best of Old Strasbourg is concentrated in a central area that extends from the cathedral to picturesque Petite France. Effectively an island within two arms of the River Ill, it's known for twisting backstreets, flower-lined courts, tempting shops, and inviting winstubs. If you've seen the center and have time to strike out in new directions, head across the Ill to view an architectural landmark unrelated to Strasbourg's famous medieval past: the Palais de l'Europe.

Barrage Vauban (*Vauban Dam*)
BUILDING | Just beyond the Ponts Couverts is the grass-roofed Vauban Dam, built by its namesake in 1682. Climb to the top for wide-angle views of the Ponts Couverts and, on the other side, the Museum of Modern and Contemporary Art. Then meander through its echoing galleries, where magnificent cathedral statuary lies scattered among pigeon droppings. ⊠ *Ponts Couverts* ✉ *Free.*

Cathédrale Notre-Dame
RELIGIOUS SITE | FAMILY | Dark pink, ornately carved Vosges sandstone masonry covers the facade of this most novel and Germanic of French cathedrals, a triumph of Gothic art begun in 1176. Not content with the outlines of the walls themselves, medieval builders lacily encased them with slender stone shafts. The off-center spire, finished in 1439, looks absurdly fragile as it tapers skyward some 466 feet; you can climb 330 steps to the base of the spire to take in sweeping views of the city, the Vosges Mountains, and the Black Forest.

The interior presents a stark contrast to the facade: it's older (mostly finished by 1275), and the nave's broad windows emphasize the horizontal rather than the vertical. Note Hans Hammer's ornately sculpted pulpit (1485) and the richly painted 14th- to 15th-century organ loft that rises from pillar to ceiling. The left side of the nave is flanked with richly colored Gothic windows honoring the early leaders of the Holy Roman Empire—Otto I and II, and Heinrich I and II. The choir is not ablaze with stained glass but framed by chunky Romanesque masonry. The elaborate 16th-century **Chapelle St-Laurent**, to the left of the choir, merits a visit; turn to the right to admire the Pilier des Anges (Angels' Pillar), an intricate column dating to 1230.

Just beyond the pillar, the Renaissance machinery of the 16th-century **Horloge Astronomique** whirs into action daily at 12:30 pm (but the line starts at the south door at 11:45 am) with macabre clockwork figures enacting the story of Christ's Passion. One of the highlights: when the apostles walk past, a likeness of Christ as a rooster crows three times. ✉ *Pl. de la Cathédrale* ⊕ *www.cathedrale-strasbourg.fr* 🎫 *Clock €3, spire platform €5.*

European Parliament
GOVERNMENT BUILDING | This sleek building testifies to the growing importance of the governing body of the European Union, which used to make do with rental offices in the Palais de l'Europe. Eurocrats continue to commute between Brussels, Luxembourg, and Strasbourg, hauling their staff and files with them. One week per month (August excepted), visitors can slip into the hemicycle and witness the tribune in debate, complete with simultaneous translation. Note: you must provide a *pièce d'identité* (ID) before entering. You don't have to reserve in advance, but spaces are limited so get there early. If you do get in, you also get to visit Le Parlementarium, which has high-tech interactive modules explaining how the European Union works. ✉ *Behind Palais de l'Europe* 🕾 *03–88–17–40–01* ⊕ *www.europarl.europa.eu* 🎫 *Free.*

L'Orangerie
GARDEN | Like a private backyard for the Eurocrats in the Palais de l'Europe, this delightful park is laden with flowers and punctuated by noble copper beeches. It contains a lake and, close by, a small reserve of rare birds, including flamingos and noisy local storks. ✉ *Av. de l'Europe.*

Musée Alsacien (*Alsatian Museum*)
MUSEUM | In this labyrinthine half-timber home, with layers of carved balconies sagging over a cobbled inner courtyard, local interiors have been faithfully reconstituted. The diverse activities of blacksmiths, clog makers, saddlers, and makers of artificial flowers are explained with the help of old-time craftsmen's tools and equipment. ✉ *23 quai St-Nicolas* 🕾 *03–88–52–50–01* ⊕ *www.musees.strasbourg.eu* 🎫 *€7* 🕒 *Closed Tues.*

Musée d'Art Moderne et Contemporain (*Modern and Contemporary Art Museum*)
MUSEUM | At the city's modern and contemporary art museum, Adrien Fainsilber's stunning 1998 building sometimes outshines the displays inside. The latter includes a fine collection of 20th-century fine art, graphic art, and photography. Downstairs there is a permanent collection of Impressionists and Modernists up to 1950 with some notable furniture by Spindler and Carabin; the mix of 20th-century artistic movements featured helps you compare and contrast modern pioneers like Monet and Gauguin with the New Realists. Drawings, watercolors, and paintings by Gustave Doré, a native of Alsace, are enshrined in a separate room. Upstairs there is a space dedicated to modern art exhibitions and installations. ✉ *1 pl. Hans-Jean Arp* 🕾 *03–68–98–51–55* ⊕ *www.musees.strasbourg.eu* 🎫 *€7* 🕒 *Closed Mon.*

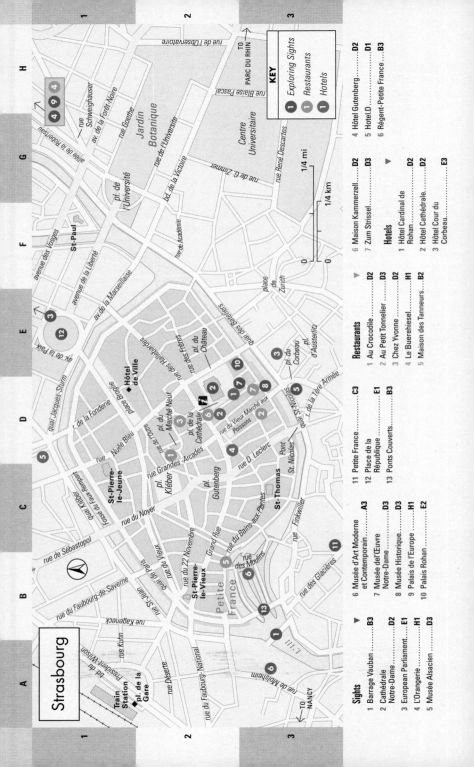

Strasbourg

Train Station ◆ pl. de la Gare

Sights ▶

1 Barrage Vauban B3
2 Cathédrale Notre-Dame D2
3 European Parliament E1
4 L'Orangerie H1
5 Musée Alsacien D3
6 Musée d'Art Moderne et Contemporain A3
7 Musée de l'Œuvre Notre-Dame E1
8 Musée Historique D3
9 Palais de l'Europe H1
10 Palais Rohan E2
11 Petite France C3
12 Place de la République E1
13 Ponts Couverts B3

Restaurants ▶

1 Au Crocodile D2
2 Au Petit Tonnelier D3
3 Chez Yvonne D2
4 Le Buerehiesel H1
5 Maison des Tanneurs B2
6 Maison Kammerzell D2
7 Zum Strissel D3

Hotels ▶

1 Hôtel Cardinal de Rohan D2
2 Hôtel Cathédrale D2
3 Hôtel Cour du Corbeau E3
4 Hôtel Gutenberg D2
5 Hôtel D. D1
6 Régent-Petite France B3

KEY

1 Exploring Sights
1 Restaurants
1 Hotels

0 ——— 1/4 km
0 ——— 1/4 mi

Musée de l'Œuvre Notre-Dame (*Cathedral Museum*)

MUSEUM | There's more to this museum than the usual assembly of dilapidated statues rescued from the cathedral before they fell off (you'll find *those* rotting in the Barrage Vauban). Sacred sculptures stand in churchlike settings, and secular exhibits are enhanced by the building's fine old architecture. Subjects include a wealth of Flemish and Upper Rhine paintings, stained glass, gold objects, and massive, heavily carved furniture. ⊠ *3 pl. du Château* ☎ *03–68–98–51–60* ⊕ *www.musees.strasbourg.eu* ▩ *€7* ♥ *Closed Mon.*

Musée Historique (*Local History Museum*)

MUSEUM | This museum, in a step-gabled slaughterhouse dating from 1588, contains a collection of maps, armor, arms, bells, uniforms, traditional outfits, printing paraphernalia, and two huge relief models of Strasbourg. The newer collection on the first floor covers civic history from the Napoleonic era to the present day. ⊠ *3 pl. de la Grande-Boucherie* ☎ *03–68–98–51–60* ⊕ *www.musees.strasbourg.eu* ▩ *€7* ♥ *Closed Mon.*

Palais de l'Europe

GOVERNMENT BUILDING | Designed by Paris architect Henri Bernard in 1977, this continental landmark is headquarters to the Council of Europe, founded in 1949 and independent of the European Union. A guided tour (1 hour, 15 minutes) introduces you to the intricacies of its workings and may allow you to eavesdrop on a session. Arrange your tour by telephone in advance (a minimum of 15 people must sign up before one will be conducted); appointments are fixed according to language demands and usually take place in the afternoon. Note that you must provide ID before entering. ⊠ *Av. de l'Europe* ☎ *03–88–41–20–29 for appointment* ▩ *Free* ♥ *Closed weekends.*

Palais Rohan (*Rohan Palace*)

MUSEUM | The exterior of this massive neoclassical palace (1732–42) by architect Robert de Cotte may be austere, but there's plenty of glamour inside. Decorator Robert le Lorrain's magnificent ground-floor rooms include the great Salon d'Assemblée (Assembly Room) and the book- and tapestry-lined Bibliothèque des Cardinaux (Cardinals' Library). The library leads to a series of less august rooms that house the **Musée des Arts Décoratifs** (Decorative Arts Museum) and its elaborate display of ceramics. This is a comprehensive presentation of works by Hannong, a porcelain manufacturer active in Strasbourg from 1721 to 1782; dinner services by other local kilns reveal the influence of Chinese porcelain. The **Musée des Beaux-Arts** (Fine Arts Museum), also in the château, includes masterworks of European painting from Giotto and Memling to El Greco, Rubens, and Goya. Downstairs, the **Musée Archéologique** (Archaeology Museum) displays regional finds, including gorgeous Merovingian treasures. ⊠ *2 pl. du Château* ☎ *03–68–98–51–60* ⊕ *www. musees.strasbourg.eu* ▩ *€7 each museum* ♥ *Closed Tues.*

★ **Petite France**

NEIGHBORHOOD | With gingerbread half-timber houses that seem to lean precariously over the canals of the Ill, plus old-fashioned shops and inviting little restaurants, "Little France" is the most magical neighborhood in Strasbourg. The district, just southwest of the center, is historically Alsatian in style and filled with Renaissance buildings that have survived plenty of wars. Wander up and down the tiny streets that connect Rue du Bain-aux-Plantes and Rue des Dentelles to Grande-Rue, and stroll the waterfront promenade. ⊠ *Strasbourg.*

Place de la République

HISTORIC SITE | The spacious layout and ponderous architecture of this monumental *cirque* (circle) have nothing in

Medieval buildings that look airlifted from Germany stunningly ornament Strasbourg's squares.

common with the Vieille Ville except for the local red sandstone. A different hand was at work here—that of occupying Germans, who erected the former Ministry (1902), the Academy of Music (1882–92), and the Palais du Rhin (1883–88). The handsome neo-Gothic church of St-Paul and the pseudo-Renaissance Palais de l'Université (University Palace), constructed between 1875 and 1885, also bear the German stamp. Heavy turn-of-the-20th-century houses, some reflecting the whimsical curves of the Art Nouveau style, frame Allée de la Robertsau, a tree-lined boulevard that would not look out of place in Berlin. ⊠ *Pl. de la République.*

Ponts Couverts (*Covered Bridges*)
BRIDGE/TUNNEL | These three bridges, distinguished by their four stone towers, were once covered with wooden shelters. Part of the 14th-century ramparts that framed Old Strasbourg, they span the Ill as it branches into a quartet of fingerlike canals. ⊠ *Strasbourg.*

🍴 Restaurants

Au Crocodile

$$$$ | FRENCH | At one of the temples of Alsatian-French haute cuisine, you get a real taste of old Alsace with a nouvelle spin. Founded in the early 1800s, its grand salon is still aglow with skylights, and a spectacular 19th-century mural showing the Strasbourgeoisie at a country fair continues to set the tasteful tone. **Known for:** extensive wine list; reasonably priced lunch menus Wednesday through Friday; top-notch regional cuisine. $ *Average main: €60* ⊠ *10 rue de l'Outre* ☎ *03–88–32–13–02* ⊕ *www.au-crocodile. com* ☉ *Closed Sun. and Mon.* ⸰ *Jacket and tie required.*

Au Petit Tonnelier

$$ | FRENCH | This modern restaurant on a touristy street offers up creative dishes with regional flourishes that are a hit with both locals and visitors. The small dining room is a discreet space decked out in black and white, with the owner's artwork adding dashes of color. **Known**

Eating and Drinking in Alsace

A visit to the proud region of Alsace promises sensory overload: gorgeous vistas, antique walled towns, satisfying meals—from farm-style to richly gastronomic—and, of course, superb wines. Predominantly white varietals, such as Riesling and Pinot Gris, complement the rich and varied old-school cooking. It's not for nouvelle-style or fusion dishes that you come to Alsace: tradition is king here, and copious is an understatement. Rustic regional fare includes hearty stews, custardy quiches, sauerkraut platters, and the thin-crusted onion tarts known as *flammekueche*.

Baeckeoffe

You can't get much heartier or homier than this baked casserole of pork, lamb, and beef marinated in white wine and slow cooked in a terra-cotta pot with potatoes, onions, garlic, and herbs. The name (pronounced "bake-eh oaf-eh") means "baker's oven" in the Germanic Alsatian dialect. It was so named because this was a dish traditionally assembled at home, then carried to the local baker to cook in his hot ovens.

Choucroute Garnie

Daunting in size, a heaping platter of choucroute garnie, laden with fermented sauerkraut, smoked bacon, ham, pork shoulder, sausages, and potatoes, is the signature dish of the region. You've never had sauerkraut like this, tender and delicate, dotted with juniper berries and often cooked with a splash of Riesling or Sylvaner white wine. Complement your choucroute with the region's own sweet white mustard.

Follow the Wines

Alsace is one of France's most important but lesser-known wine-producing regions, where vintners designate wines by grape varieties, not by town or château. Look for distinctive whites, like full-bodied Pinot Gris, citrusy Riesling, and spicy Gewürztraminer. In reds, Pinot Noir stands alone. Top producers include Hugel et Fils, De Ribeauvillé, and Zind-Humbrecht.

Kougelhopf

This tall, fluted, crown-shape cake, dusted with sugar and studded with raisins and almonds, beckons invitingly from every pastry-shop window in the region. The delicately sweet, yeast-based dough is kneaded and proofed, baked in a Bundt-style mold, and traditionally served, sometimes sprinkled with kirsch, at Sunday breakfast. Locals say it's even better on the second day, when it achieves a perfect, slightly dry texture.

Munster Cheese

This round, semisoft cow's-milk cheese with the orange rind, distinctive nutty aroma, and pungent flavor is Alsace's only claim to cheese fame, but it's a standout. The cheese, which is aged from five weeks to three months, originated in the Vosges valley town of Munster, just west of Colmar, and the best—farm produced—come from this area. Sample it with fresh cherries or pears, thin-sliced rye bread, and a glass of Gewürztraminer.

for: interesting twists on French classic dishes; standout desserts; weekly concerts in the basement. [$] *Average main: €20* ✉ *16 rue des Tonneliers* ☎ *03–88–32–53–54* 🌐 *www.aupetittonnelier.com* ⏲ *Closed Sun.*

Chez Yvonne

$$ | **FRENCH** | Behind red-checked curtains you can find artists, tourists, lovers, and heads of state sitting elbow-to-elbow in this classic winstub, founded in 1873. All come to savor steaming platters of local specialties. **Known for:** central location, near the cathedral; regional dishes like Munster cheese in puff pastry and seafood choucroute; chic Alsatian decor. [$] *Average main: €17* ✉ *10 rue du Sanglier* ☎ *03–88–32–84–15* 🌐 *www.restaurant-chez-yvonne.net.*

★ **Le Buerehiesel**

$$$$ | **MODERN FRENCH** | This lovely farmhouse, reconstructed in the Orangerie park, warrants a pilgrimage if you're willing to pay for the finest cooking in Alsace. Chef Eric Westermann focuses on the freshest of local-terroir specialties, supplemented by the best seafood from Brittany. **Known for:** standout seasonal desserts; glass and steel annex with great views of the park; truffle menu. [$] *Average main: €45* ✉ *4 parc de l'Orangerie* ☎ *03–88–45–56–65* 🌐 *www.buerehiesel.fr* ⏲ *Closed Sun. and Mon., 2 wks in Jan., and 2 wks in Aug.*

Maison des Tanneurs

$$ | **GERMAN** | This 16th-century half-timber landmark (one of oldest riverside buildings in Petite France) is draped with geranium-filled flower pots and perennially popular. Come for generous and delicious portions of choucroute garnie, as well as other regional favorites. **Known for:** historic setting; riverside terrace; French classics like foie gras and coq au Riesling. [$] *Average main: €24* ✉ *42 rue Bain aux Plantes* ☎ *03–88–32–79–70* ⏲ *Closed Sun., Mon., and 3 wks in early Jan.*

Maison Kammerzell

$$ | **FRENCH** | This restaurant occupies what must be the most familiar house in Strasbourg—a richly carved, 15th-century half-timber building adorned with sumptuous allegorical frescoes. Fight your way through the crowds on the terrace and ground floor to one of the atmospheric rooms above, with their gleaming wooden furniture, stained-glass windows, and unrivaled views of the cathedral. **Known for:** terrace tables on the cathedral square; choucroute with freshwater fish; historic setting. [$] *Average main: €24* ✉ *16 pl. de la Cathédrale* ☎ *03–88–32–42–14* 🌐 *www.maison-kammerzell.com.*

Zum Strissel

$$ | **BISTRO** | This rustic winstub near the cathedral has been in business since the 16th century. The charming decor provides a perfect backdrop for traditional Alsatian fare such as baeckeoffe and choucroute. **Known for:** extensive list of Alsatian wines; outdoor terrace; authentic Alsatian decor. [$] *Average main: €19* ✉ *5 pl. de la Grande-Boucherie* ☎ *03–88–32–14–73* 🌐 *www.strissel.fr.*

🛏 Hotels

Hôtel Cardinal de Rohan

$$ | **HOTEL** | Across from the cathedral on a picturesque pedestrian street, this modest little hotel with updated rooms has a welcoming air and a quirky sense of style. **Pros:** great location; air-conditioned; on-site restaurant. **Cons:** small standard rooms; some rooms get street noise; basic rooms are small. [$] *Rooms from: €140* ✉ *17 rue du Maroquin* ☎ *03–88–32–85–11* 🌐 *www.hotel-rohan.com* 🛏 *35 rooms* 🍴 *No meals.*

Hôtel Cathédrale

$ | **HOTEL** | Location and views, with windows framing the cathedral or 15th-century half-timber Maison Kammerzell, are what make these otherwise ordinary rooms so memorable. **Pros:** comfortable, clean accommodations; across from the cathedral; fun bar and lounge. **Cons:** some rooms are small; rooms with a cathedral view get some street noise (rooms that don't face the square are quieter); parking can be difficult to find. $ *Rooms from: €120* ✉ *13 pl. de la Cathédrale* ☎ *03–88–22–12–12* ⊕ *www. hotel-cathedrale.fr* ↗ *47 rooms* ❦❦ *No meals.*

Hôtel Cour du Corbeau
$$ | HOTEL | Opened as an inn in 1580 and magnificently restored to its former half-timber glory, the "courtyard of the crow" retains its Middle Ages facade while the interiors are another thing completely: luxe design, crystal chandeliers, period furniture, and colorful fabrics are the essence of modern style, sumptuousness, and comfort. **Pros:** dazzling and luxurious; great location a short walk from the cathedral; old-world charm. **Cons:** has a tea salon but no restaurant; pricey breakfast; the rooms around the courtyard can get noisy. $ *Rooms from: €150* ✉ *6–8 rue des Couples* ☎ *03–90–00–26–26* ⊕ *www.cour-corbeau.com* ↗ *57 rooms* ❦❦ *No meals.*

Hôtel Gutenberg
$ | HOTEL | In a 250-year-old mansion just off Place Gutenberg, this budget-rate urban hotel has colorful, modernized rooms with charming highlights from the past. **Pros:** excellent value; old-world style with modern amenities and design touches; picturesque location only a few blocks from the cathedral. **Cons:** some street noise; elevator doesn't reach the top floor; top floor rooms on the small side with low sloping ceilings. $ *Rooms from: €99* ✉ *31 rue des Serruriers* ☎ *03–88–32–17–15* ⊕ *www.hotel-gutenberg.com* ↗ *42 rooms* ❦❦ *No meals.*

Hotel.D
$ | HOTEL | At this design-focused hotel in a Vosges sandstone-built residence, cutting-edge style meets 19th-century elegance. **Pros:** quiet location; good-value buffet breakfast; helpful staff. **Cons:** more than 10-minute walk to the cathedral;

small bathrooms; elevator doesn't reach the top floor. $ *Rooms from: €120* ✉ *15 rue du Fossé des 13* ☎ *03–88–15–13–67* ⊕ *www.hoteld.fr* ↗ *37 rooms* ❦❦ *Free Breakfast.*

★ Régent-Petite France
$$$ | HOTEL | Surrounded by canals in the heart of the quaint La Petite France quarter, this centuries-old former ice factory—replete with noble pediment and mansard roofs—has been transformed into a boldly modern luxury hotel, where Philippe Starck–inspired sculptural furnishings contrast sharply with the half-timber houses and roaring river viewed from nearly every window. **Pros:** ideal location; great service; no skimping on the amenities—the beds and the bathrooms are divine. **Cons:** disappointing breakfast; restaurant closed Sunday and Monday; the rooms in the annex don't include free access to the spa. $ *Rooms from: €230* ✉ *5 rue des Moulins* ☎ *03–88–76–43–43* ⊕ *www. regent-petite-france.com* ↗ *55 rooms, 17 suites* ❦❦ *Free Breakfast.*

 # Nightlife

La Laiterie
BARS/PUBS | The Vieille Ville neighborhood east of the cathedral, along Rue des Frères, is the nightlife hangout for university students and twenty-somethings; among a clutch of heavily frequented bars is La Laiterie, a multiplex concert hall showcasing art, workshops, and music ranging from electronic to postrock and reggae. ✉ *16 rue Hohwald* ☎ *03–88–23–72–37* ⊕ *www.artefact.org.*

 # Performing Arts

Festival Musica (*Contemporary Music Festival*)
FESTIVALS | The annual Festival Musica is held in September and October. ✉ *Cité de la Musique et de la Danse, 1 pl. Dauphine* ☎ *03–88–23–46–46* ⊕ *www. festivalmusica.org.*

Jazzdor (Jazz Festival)

FESTIVALS | Strasbourg hosts its international jazz festival each November at venues both in and around the city. ✉ *25 rue des Frères* ☎ *03–88–36–30–48* ⊕ *www. jazzdor.com.*

Opéra National du Rhin

OPERA | A sizable repertoire makes the Opéra National du Rhin a popular—and accessible—choice. ✉ *19 pl. Broglie* ☎ *08–25–84–14–84* ⊕ *www.operanationaldurhin.eu.*

Orchestre Philharmonique

CONCERTS | Classical concerts are presented by the Orchestre Philharmonique. Performances are staged mainly at the Auditorium de la Cité de la Musique et de la Danse. ✉ *Palais des Congrès* ☎ *03–68–98–68–15* ⊕ *www.philharmonique-strasbourg.com.*

👜 Shopping

The lively city center is full of boutiques, including chocolate shops and delicatessens selling locally made foie gras. Look for warm paisley linens and rustic homespun fabrics, Alsatian pottery, and local wines. Forming the city's commercial heart are **Rue des Hallebardes,** next to the cathedral; **Rue des Grandes Arcades,** with its shopping mall; and **Place Kléber.** An **antiques market** takes place behind the cathedral on Rue du Vieil-Hôpital, Rue des Bouchers, and Place de la Grande Boucherie every Wednesday and Saturday morning. Strasbourg's fabled Christmas market, the oldest in France, is held every year from late November until New Year's Eve. Wander among the wooden chalets peddling pretty local crafts and Christmas baubles until you arrive at the Place Kléber, where you'll be dazzled by the giant Christmas tree.

Obernai

30 km (19 miles) southwest of Strasbourg.

Many visitors begin their trip down the Route du Vin at Obernai, a thriving, colorful Renaissance market town named for the patron saint of Alsace. Head to the central town enclosed by the ramparts to find some particularly photo-friendly sites, including a medieval belfry, Renaissance well, and late-19th-century church.

GETTING HERE AND AROUND

You can reach Obernai from Strasbourg by bus (50 mins, €2.50) or train (30–40 mins, €6.60). Trains also connect Obernai and Sélestat (25–40 mins, €5.50).

VISITOR INFORMATION Obernai Tourist Office ✉ *Pl. du Beffroi* ☎ *03–88–95–64–13* ⊕ *www.tourisme-obernai.fr.*

Sights

Kapelturm Beffroi (*Chapel Tower Belfry*)

BUILDING | Place du Marché, in the heart of town, is dominated by the 13th-century Kapelturm Beffroi. The stout, square structure is topped by a pointed steeple that's flanked at each corner by frilly openwork turrets. ✉ *Obernai.*

Puits à Six-Seaux (*Well of Six Buckets*)

BUILDING | An elaborate Renaissance well near the belfry, the Puits à Six-Seaux was constructed in 1579; its name recalls the six buckets suspended from its metal chains. ✉ *Obernai.*

St-Pierre–St-Paul

RELIGIOUS SITE | The twin spires of this parish church compete with the belfry for skyline preeminence. Like the rest of the sanctuary, they date to the 1860s, although the 1504 Holy Sepulchre altarpiece in the north transept is a survivor from the previous church. Other points of interest include the flower-bedecked **Place de l'Étoile** and the **Hôtel de Ville,** which is open to visitors the

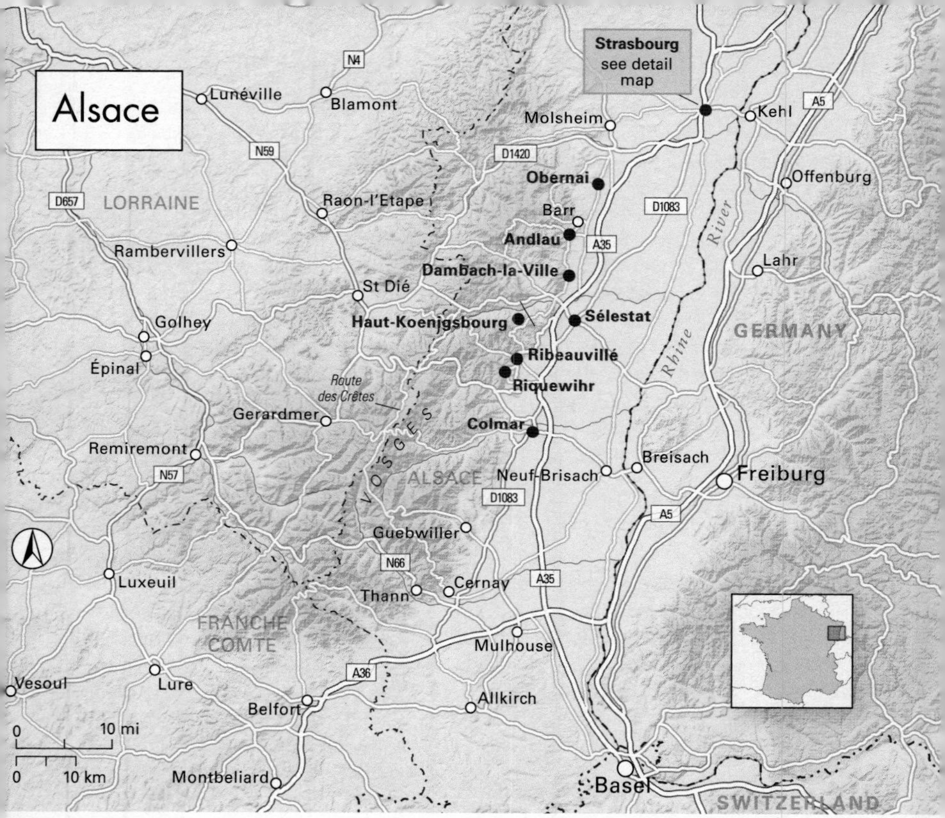

third weekend of September during Les Journées du Patrimoine (Heritage Days). ✉ *Obernai.*

Hotels

A La Cour d'Alsace

$$ | **HOTEL** | In a quiet location just a few steps from the Kapelturm Beffroi, this smart hotel balances old-fashioned coziness with up-to-date guest rooms that are both comfortable and stylish; some overlook the garden and ramparts. **Pros:** dead-center location; great restaurant; free on-site parking. **Cons:** pricey spa treatments; not all floors are serviced by an elevator; no indoor access from rooms to pool and spa—guests must cross the outdoor courtyard in their bathrobes. [$] *Rooms from: €155* ✉ *3 rue de Gail* ☎ *03–88–95–07–00* 🌐 *www.cour-alsace.com* 🕒 *Closed Christmas–late Jan.* 🛏 *53 rooms* 🍴 *Free Breakfast.*

Hôtel Le Gouverneur

$ | **HOTEL** | Behind the photogenic facade of this 17th-century half-timber house, you'll find comfy, clean-lined bedrooms set around a geranium-festooned interior courtyard; the quietest ones come with a view of the ramparts. **Pros:** good value; friendly staff; central location. **Cons:** small bathrooms; no air-conditioning; basic breakfast choices. [$] *Rooms from: €112* ✉ *13 rue de Sélestat* ☎ *03–88–95–63–72* 🌐 *www.hotellegouverneur.com* 🛏 *32 rooms* 🍴 *No meals.*

★ L'Ami Fritz

$ | **B&B/INN** | A few miles west of Obernai, this white-shuttered, flower-bedecked 18th-century house treats diners to fine meals and accommodates overnight guests in impeccable rooms with sleek contemporary furnishings (opt for one in the main building, not the adjacent annex). **Pros:** beautiful location; excellent restaurant; combines style, rustic warmth, and three generations of family tradition. **Cons:** a car is needed; uneven service; rooms in the annex are a walk from the main building where breakfast is served. [$] *Rooms from: €95* ✉ *8 rue des Châteaux, 5 km (3 miles) west of Obernai, Ottrott* ☎ *03–88–95–80–81* 🌐 *www.amifritz.com* 🕒 *Closed 2nd wk of July and 2 wks in mid-Jan.* 🛏 *42 rooms* 🍴 *No meals.*

Shopping

Dietrich

CERAMICS/GLASSWARE | Head to Dietrich for a varied selection of Beauvillé linens, locally handblown Alsatian wineglasses, and Obernai-pattern china. ✉ *74 rue du Général-Gouraud* ☎ *03–88–95–57–58* 🌐 *www.dietrich-obernai.fr.*

Andlau

13 km (8 miles) southwest of Obernai.

This small, yet important, wine town in the Andlau River valley is surrounded by the Vosges mountains. Its historic center has several noteworthy houses dating to the 15th through 18th centuries; however, Abbaye d'Andlau is the primary attraction.

GETTING HERE AND AROUND

By car, Andlau is 20 minutes from Obernai; if you don't have your own, expect to pay about €30 for cab fare.

Sights

Abbaye d'Andlau

RELIGIOUS SITE | Built in the 12th century, the Abbaye d'Andlau has the richest ensemble of Romanesque sculpture in Alsace. Sculpted vines wind their way around the doorway as a reminder of wine's time-honored importance to the local economy. A statue of a female bear, the abbey mascot—bears used to roam local forests and were bred at the abbey until the 16th century—can be seen in the north transept. Legend has it that Queen Richarde, spurned by her husband, Charles the Fat, founded the abbey in AD 887 when an angel enjoined her to construct a church on a site to be shown to her by a female bear. ✉ *Andlau.*

Hotels

Arnold

$ | **HOTEL** | Like Itterswiller—the cute wine village it overlooks—this yellow-walled, half-timber hillside hotel exudes charm, from the wood-beam lobby with its wrought-iron staircase right through to the "country deluxe" lodgings with views across the nearby vineyards. **Pros:** all-around excellence; good half-board meal plan; lovely views over the vineyards. **Cons:** no air-conditioning; additional charge for using the pool and fitness center; some bedrooms only have showers. [$] *Rooms from: €115* ✉ *98 rte. des Vins, 3 km (2 miles) south of Andlau, Itterswiller* ☎ *03–88–85–50–58* 🌐 *www.hotel-arnold.com* 🛏 *37 rooms* 🍴 *Free Breakfast.*

Dambach-la-Ville

8 km (5 miles) southeast of Andlau.

Dambach-la-Ville—the largest wine-producing village along the Alsace Wine Road—is protected by ramparts and three imposing 13th-century gateways. It's particularly rich in high-roof, half-timber houses from the 17th and 18th centuries, clustered mainly around Place du Marché (Market Square). Also on the square is the 16th-century Hôtel de Ville. As you walk the charming streets, notice the wrought-iron signs and rooftop oriels.

A Wine-Lover's Guide to Alsace

Threading south along the eastern foothills of the Vosges from Marienheim to Thann, the Alsatian Wine Road is home to delicious wines and beautiful vineyards. The 170-km (105-mile) Route du Vin passes through small towns, and footpaths interspersed throughout the region afford the opportunity to wander through the vineyards.

Buses from Colmar head out to the surrounding towns of Riquewihr, St-Hippolyte, Ribeauvillé, and Eguisheim; pick up brochures on the Wine Route from Colmar's tourist office. Although the route is hilly, bicycling is a great way to take in the countryside and avoid the parking hassle in the towns along this heavily traveled route.

Wine is an object of veneration in Alsace, and anyone traveling along the Route du Vin will want to become part of the cult. Just because Alsatian vintners use German grapes, don't expect their wines to taste like their counterparts across the Rhine.

German vintners aim for sweetness, creating wines that are best appreciated as an aperitif. Alsatian vintners, on the other hand, eschew sweetness in favor of strength, and their wines go wonderfully with knockdown, drag-out meals.

The main wines you need to know about are Gewurztraminer, Riesling, Muscat, Pinot Gris, and Sylvaner—all whites. The only red wine produced in the region is the light and delicious Pinot Noir. Gewurztraminer, which in Germany is an ultrasweet dessert wine, has a much cleaner, drier taste in Alsace, despite its fragrant bouquet. It's best served with the richest of Alsace dishes, such as goose.

Riesling is the premier wine of Alsace, balancing a hard structure with certain fruity roundness. With a grapey bouquet and clean finish, dry Muscat does best as an aperitif. Pinot Gris, also called Tokay, is probably the most full-bodied of Alsatian wines.

Sylvaner falls below those grapes in general acclaim, tending to be lighter and a bit dull. You can discover many of these wines as you drive along the Route du Vin.

GETTING HERE AND AROUND

Dambach-la Ville is about 45 minutes from Colmar by TER train (€6.90); you can also arrive from Strasbourg directly (€9.60) in under an hour, or Sélestat (€2.70) in 10 minutes.

Hotels

Le Vignoble

$ | **HOTEL** | Set in a beautifully restored 18th-century barn next to the village church, this unpretentious hotel offers real, rustic Alsatian charm; quiet, comfy guest rooms have functional dark-wood furnishings and, in some cases, balconies overlooking the street. **Pros:** Wine Road location; warm Alsatian welcome; good value. **Cons:** no air-conditioning; no restaurant; no on-site parking. [$] *Rooms from: €79* ✉ *1 rue de l'Eglise* ☎ *03–88–92–43–75* 🌐 *www.hotel-vignoble-alsace.fr* 🕒 *Closed Jan.–mid-Feb.* 🛏 *7 rooms* 🍴 *No meals.*

Alsace's Wine Road passes a parade of "Hansel and Gretel" villages, each more picturesque than the last.

Sélestat

9 km (5½ miles) southeast of Dambach, 47 km (29 miles) southwest of Strasbourg.

Sélestat, midway between Strasbourg and Colmar, is a lively, historic town with a Romanesque church and a library of medieval manuscripts. The fact that it has good transportation links is an added bonus. Head directly to the Vieille Ville and explore the quarter on foot.

GETTING HERE AND AROUND

TER trains depart Strasbourg every 30 minutes for Sélestat (€9.40). Frequent daily trains also connect the town to Colmar (€5.30), and buses run from here to Ribeauvillé (€2.80).

VISITOR INFORMATION Sélestat Tourist Office ⊠ *10 bd. Leclerc* ☎ *03–88–58–87–20* ⊕ *www.selestat-haut-koenigsbourg. com.*

Sights

Bibliothèque Humaniste (*Humanist Library*)

LIBRARY | Among the precious medieval and Renaissance manuscripts on display at the Bibliothèque Humaniste, founded in 1452 and installed in the former Halle aux Blés, are a 7th-century lectionary and a 12th-century Book of Miracles. There's also a town register from 1521, with the first-ever recorded reference to a Christmas tree. ⊠ *1 rue de la Bibliothèque* ☎ *03–88–58–07–20* ⊕ *www. bibliotheque-humaniste.fr* ⊡ *€6* ⊗ *Closed Mon.*

St-Foy

RELIGIOUS SITE | The church of St-Foy dates from between 1155 and 1190; its Romanesque facade remains largely intact (the spires were added in the 19th century), as does the 140-foot octagonal tower over the crossing. Sadly, the interior was mangled over the centuries, chiefly by the Jesuits, whose most inspired legacy is the Baroque pulpit of 1733 depicting the life of St-Francis Xavier. Note the Romanesque bas-relief next to the baptistery, originally the lid of a sarcophagus. ✉ *Pl. du Marché-Vert.*

🍴 Restaurants

La Vieille Tour

$$ | FRENCH | Named for the 13th-century stone tower that flanks it, La Vieille Tour gives classic dishes a contemporary spin. Chefs Nicolas and Samy Ruhlmann seek inspiration from locally sourced seasonal produce, and their love for it shows in the savory dishes and tantalizing desserts. **Known for:** excellent value fixed-price menus; traditional oak-beamed dining room complete with fireplace; signature dishes like choucroute, snails, and Tournedos Rossini. [$] *Average main: €24* ✉ *8 rue de la Jauge* ☎ *03–88–92–15–02* 🌐 *www.vieille-tour.fr* ⏲ *Closed Tues. and Wed.*

🛏 Hotels

Hôtel Vaillant

$$ | HOTEL | More promising than you'd expect from the bland 1970s exterior, this easy-to-find hotel near the train station has a distinct sense of style. **Pros:** air-conditioning, flat-screen TVs, and free Wi-Fi; warm welcome; on-site restaurant. **Cons:** 10-minute walk to historic center; there's a large car park in front of hotel, but there is a fee; walls a bit thin. [$] *Rooms from: €125* ✉ *Pl. de la République, 7 rue Ignace Spies* ☎ *03–88–92–09–46* 🌐 *www.hotel-vaillant.com* 🛏 *47 rooms* 🍴 *No meals.*

Haut-Koenigsbourg

11 km (7 miles) west of Sélestat.

One of the most popular spots in Alsace is the romantic, crag-top castle of Haut-Koenigsbourg, originally built as a fortress in the 12th century.

GETTING HERE AND AROUND

A shuttle bus provides round-trip transport (€5) from Sélestat to Orschwiller daily from June to September and on weekends from March to December; from there it's a short walk to Haut-Koenigsbourg.

👁 Sights

★ **Château du Haut-Koenigsbourg**

CASTLE/PALACE | FAMILY | The ruins of the Château du Haut-Koenigsbourg were presented by the town of Sélestat to German emperor Wilhelm II in 1901. The château looked just as a kaiser thought one should, and he restored it with some diligence and no lack of imagination—squaring the main tower's original circle, for instance. The site, panorama, drawbridge, and amply furnished imperial chambers may lack authenticity, but they are undeniably dramatic. ✉ *Orschwiller* ☎ *03–69–33–25–00* 🌐 *www.haut-koenigsbourg.fr* 🎟 *€9* ⏲ *Closed Mon. Nov.–Feb.*

Ribeauvillé

13 km (8 miles) south of Haut-Koenigsbourg, 16 km (10 miles) southwest of Sélestat.

The beautiful half-timber town of Ribeauvillé, surrounded by rolling vineyards and three imposing châteaux, produces some of the best wines in Alsace. (The Trimbach family has made Riesling and superb Gewürztraminer here since 1626.) Its narrow main street, crowded with winstubs, pottery shops, bakeries, and wine sellers, is bisected by the 13th-century **Tour des Bouchers,** or Butcher's Tower—a clock-belfry completed (gargoyles and all) in the 15th century.

GETTING HERE AND AROUND

Multiple daily buses let you reach Ribeauvillé via Colmar (€4.25) or Sélestat (€2.80).

VISITOR INFORMATION Ribeauvillé Tourist Office ✉ *1 Grande-Rue* ☎ *03–89–73–23–23* 🌐 *www.ribeauville-riquewihr.com.*

Sights

Place de l'Hôtel de Ville

HISTORIC SITE | Ignore the guides herding around French and German tour groups, and head straight for the Place de l'Hôtel de Ville. Its town hall contains a famous collection of silver-gilt 16th-century tankards and chalices; and the *place* itself is a pretty place to perch. It is particularly lively the first Sunday in September, when the town hosts a grand parade to celebrate the Fête des Ménétriers (Festival of the Minstrels)—a day when at least one fountain here spouts free Riesling. Headlined by medieval musicians, the party begins midafternoon. Entrance tickets cost €8, and the best street seats go for €18 (contact the tourist office for details). ✉ *Pl. de l'Hôtel de Ville* ☎ *No phone.*

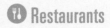

Restaurants

★ L'Auberge de L'Ill

$$$$ | **MODERN FRENCH** | Marlene Dietrich and Spanish opera star Montserrat Caballé are just two of the famous guests who have feasted at this culinary temple, where chef Marc Haeberlin marries traditional Alsatian cuisine with contemporary nuances. The kitchen's touch is incredibly light, so you'll have room left for the masterful desserts. **Known for:** lovely terrace overlooking pretty tree-lined garden; salmon soufflé and mousseline of frogs' legs; great wine list. [$] *Average main: €90* ✉ *2 rue de Collonges au Mont d'Or, 10 km (6 miles) east of Ribeauvillé, Illhaeusern* ☎ *03–89–71–89–00* 🌐 *www.auberge-de-l-ill.com* 🕒 *Closed Mon. and Tues., and Feb.*

Zum Pfifferhüs

$$$ | **GERMAN** | This is a true-blue winstub, with yellowed murals, glowing lighting, and wines available by the glass. The cooking is pure Alsace, with German-scale portions of choucroute, ham hocks, and fruit tarts. **Known for:** good value fixed-price menu; wine list showcasing local producers; genuine and friendly service. [$] *Average main: €25* ✉ *14 Grande-Rue* ☎ *03–89–73–62–28* 🕒 *Closed Wed.; Thurs. Nov.–July; mid-Feb.–mid-Mar.; and 1st 2 wks in July.*

Hotels

Hôtel de la Tour

$ | **HOTEL** | Guest rooms at this erstwhile family winery in the center of Ribeauvillé, with an ornate Renaissance fountain outside its front door, are modern, surprisingly spacious, and well positioned for experiencing the atmospheric town by night; those on the top floor have exposed timbers and wonderful views of ramshackle rooftops. **Pros:** family run; good amenities, including a sauna and Jacuzzi; central location. **Cons:** no air-conditioning; no on-site restaurant; rooms on the top floor are a bit small. [$] *Rooms from: €88* ✉ *1 rue de la Mairie* ☎ *03–89–73–72–73* 🌐 *www.hotel-la-tour.com* 🕒 *Closed Jan.–early Mar.* 🛏 *31 rooms* 🍴 *Free Breakfast.*

Hôtel des Berges

$$$$ | **B&B/INN** | Designed to evoke an Alsatian tobacco barn, replete with Havanese woods, this hotel has rooms named after famous cigars and a lovely country-luxe decor. **Pros:** romantic and opulent; close to excellent restaurant; spa, hamman, and Jacuzzi. **Cons:** pricey; no meals included; closed Monday and Tuesday. [$] *Rooms from: €360* ✉ *4 rue de Collonges au Mont d'Or, 10 km (6 miles) east of Ribeauvillé, Illhaeusern* ☎ *03–89–71–87–87* 🌐 *www.auberge-de-l-ill.com* 🕒 *Closed Mon., Tues., and Feb.* 🛏 *13 rooms* 🍴 *No meals.*

Seigneurs de Ribeaupierre

$$ | **B&B/INN** | On the edge of Ribeauvillé's old quarter, this gracious 18th-century half-timber inn offers a warm welcome;

a crackling fire greets you downstairs, while exposed timbers, sumptuous fabrics, and slick bathrooms await upstairs. **Pros:** tasteful and cozy; central location; generous breakfast included. **Cons:** stuffy in summer (no air-conditioning); no restaurant; bathrooms are old-fashioned. $ *Rooms from: €165* ✉ *11 rue du Château* ☎ *03–89–73–70–31* 🌐 *www.ribeaupierre.com* 🕒 *Closed Jan.–early Mar.* 🛏 *5 rooms* 🍴 *Free Breakfast.*

Riquewihr

5 km (3 miles) south of Ribeauvillé.

With its unique once-upon-a-timeliness, Riquewihr is the Wine Road's pièce de résistance and a living museum of old Alsace's quaint architecture. Its steep main street, ramparts, and winding back alleys have scarcely changed since the 16th century, and could easily serve as a film set. Merchants cater to the sizable influx of tourists with a plethora of kitschy souvenir shops; bypass them and instead peep into courtyards with massive winepresses, study the ornately decorated houses, stand in the narrow old courtyard that was once the Jewish quarter, or climb up the Dolder Belfry for a stunning view of the town. You would also do well to settle into a winstub to sample some of Riquewihr's famous wines. Just strolling down the heavenly streets will reward your eye with half-timber houses, storybook gables, and storks'-nest towers. The facades of certain houses dating to the late-Gothic period take center stage, including the Maison Kiener (1574), the Maison Preiss (1686), and the Maison Liebrich (1535), but the Tower of Thieves and the Postal Museum, ensconced in the château of the duke of Württemberg, are also fascinating.

GETTING HERE AND AROUND

Riquewihr can be reached by bus from Colmar or Sélestat. From Colmar it is a 45-minute journey by bus (No. 106; €4.25) from Monday through Saturday.

VISITOR INFORMATION Riquewihr Tourist Office ✉ *2 rue de la 1ère Armée* ☎ *03–89–73–23–23* 🌐 *www.ribeauville-riquewihr.com.*

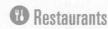

🍴 Restaurants

Au Tire-Bouchon

$$ | **FRENCH** | With its stone walls, wooden tables, and friendly waiters, "The Corkscrew" is the best place in town to sample Alsatian choucroute garnie. The menu also promises some seasonally changing innovations, plus a fine selection of Pinot Blanc and Riesling wines. **Known for:** house-produced wines; outdoor terrace; generous portions of authentic Alsace dishes. $ *Average main: €17* ✉ *29 rue du Général-de-Gaulle* ☎ *03–89–47–91–61* 🕒 *Closed Mon., mid-Jan.–early Feb., and 1st wk in Mar. No lunch Wed.; no dinner Sun.*

🛏 Hotels

Hôtel à l'Oriel

$ | **HOTEL** | Perfectly placed within the city's ramparts (so be prepared for crowds of visitors in the daytime), this quaint, half-timber, ocher-front hotel offers traditional Alsace decor. **Pros:** charming atmosphere; peaceful inner courtyard; no street noise at night. **Cons:** some guest rooms can only be reached by steep stairs; no air-conditioning; not all rooms have tubs. $ *Rooms from: €90* ✉ *3 rue des Ecuries Seigneuriales* ☎ *03–89–49–03–13* 🌐 *www.hotel-oriel.com* 🛏 *22 rooms* 🍴 *No meals.*

Hôtel de la Couronne

$ | **HOTEL** | Looking like an illustration out of the Brothers Grimm, this hotel is set in a 16th-century house with a central tower, steep mansard roof, country shutters,

and rusticated stone trim; inside, several guest rooms have grand timber beams and folkloric wall stencils, making this a truly charming base for touring a truly charming town. **Pros:** good location; on-site parking; old-world charm. **Cons:** no elevator; service can be inconsistent; bathrooms are small. ⓢ *Rooms from: €67* ✉ *5 rue de la Couronne* ☎ *03–89–49–03–03* ⊕ *www.hoteldelacouronne.com* ⌁ *41 rooms* ⓧ *Free Breakfast.*

Colmar

13 km (8 miles) southeast of Riquewihr, 71 km (44 miles) southwest of Strasbourg.

Forget that much of Colmar's architecture is modern (because of the destruction wrought by World Wars I and II): its Vieille Ville heart—an atmospheric maze of narrow streets lined with candy-color, half-timber Renaissance houses hanging over cobblestone lanes in a disarmingly ramshackle way—out-charms Strasbourg. Each shop-lined backstreet winds its way to the 15th-century customs house, the Ancienne Douane, and the square and canals that surround it.

GETTING HERE AND AROUND
Three daily direct TGVs run from Paris's Gare de l'Est to Colmar (€112), each taking 2 hours, 30 minutes. Sixteen semi-direct, TGV/TER combos depart from the same station; these require a change at Strasbourg, which typically adds from 10 minutes up to one hour to the total travel time. Nine other TER services run from Paris Gare de Lyon to Colmar, requiring a change at either Dijon or Mulhouse; the journey time varies from 3 hours 10 minutes to 3 hours 50 minutes (€93). More than a dozen daily trains will take you from Colmar to Sélestat (€5.30), and seven daily buses (the last at 7:15 pm) make the 45-minute trip to Ribeauvillé (€3.95). The LK Groupe (⊕ *www.l-k.fr*) has regular bus service

from the Gare SNCF to towns throughout the region. Within Colmar, TRACE buses (☎ *03–89–20–80–80* ⊕ *www.trace-colmar.fr*) provide efficient public transit.

VISITOR INFORMATION Colmar Tourist Office ✉ *Pl. Unterlinden* ☎ *03–89–20–68–92* ⊕ *www.tourisme-colmar.com.*

TOURS
Sweet Narcisse Boat Trips
BOAT TOURS | An enchanting way to explore Little Venice is by taking a cruise in a traditional flat-bottomed boat. Sweet Narcisse organizes 30-minute boat trips on the Lauch River with English commentary, leaving daily every 30 minutes from April to October, operating from 10 am to noon and from 1:30 pm until 6; afternoons only in November. Boats leave from the quay next to the St-Pierre Bridge. ✉ *10 rue de La Herse* ☎ *03–89–41–01–94* ⊕ *www.barques-colmar.fr* ⓧ *From €6.*

◉ Sights

Collégiale St-Martin
RELIGIOUS SITE | Built between 1235 and 1365, this collegiate church is essentially Gothic (the Renaissance bell tower was added in 1572 following a fire). There are some interesting medieval sculptures on the exterior; and the interior, which was heavily vandalized during the Revolution, includes an ambulatory, a rare feature in

Colmar's Wine Festival

During the first half of August, Colmar celebrates with its annual Foire Régionale des Vins d'Alsace, an Alsatian wine fair in the Parc des Expositions. Events include folk music, theater performances and, above all, the tasting and selling of wine.

Alsatian sanctuaries. ⊠ *22 pl. de la Cathe-drale* ☎ *03–89–20–68–92.*

Église des Dominicains (*Dominican Church*)

RELIGIOUS SITE | The Flemish-influenced *Madonna of the Rosebush* (1473), noted German artist Martin Schongauer's most celebrated painting, hangs in the Église des Dominicains. Stolen from St-Martin's in 1972 and later recovered, the work has almost certainly been reduced in size from its original state but retains enormous impact. The grace and intensity of the Virgin match that of the Christ Child; yet her slender fingers dent the child's soft flesh (and his fingers entwine her curls) with immediate intimacy. Schongauer's text for her crown is: *Me carpes genito tuo o santissima virgo* (Choose me also for your child, O holiest Virgin). ⊠ *Pl. des Dominicains* ☎ *03–89–24–46–57* 🖅 *From €2.*

La Petite Venise (*Little Venice*)

NEIGHBORHOOD | To find Colmar at its most charming, wander along the calm canals that wind through La Petite Venise, an area of bright Alsatian houses with colorful shutters and window boxes that's south of the center of town. Here, amid half-timber buildings bedecked with flowers and weeping willow trees that shed their tears into the eddies of the Lauch River, you have the sense of being in a tiny village. ⊠ *Colmar.*

Maison aux Arcades (*Arcades House*)

HOUSE | Up the street from the Ancienne Douane on the Grande-Rue, the Maison aux Arcades was built in 1609 in High Renaissance style with a series of arched porches (arcades) anchored by two octagonal towers. ⊠ *11 Grande-Rue.*

Maison Pfister

HOUSE | Built in 1537, the Maison Pfister is the most striking of Colmar's many old dwellings. Note the decorative frescoes and medallions, carved balcony, and ground-floor arcades. ⊠ *11 rue Mercière.*

Musée Bartholdi

MUSEUM | The Bartholdi Museum is the birthplace of Frédéric-Auguste Bartholdi (1834–1904), the sculptor who designed the Statue of Liberty. Exhibits of his work claim the ground floor; a reconstruction of the artist's Paris apartment is upstairs; and, in adjoining rooms, the creation of Lady Liberty is explored. ⊠ *30 rue des Marchands* ☎ *03–89–41–90–60* ⊕ *www.musee-bartholdi.fr* 🖅 *€7* ☙ *Closed Tues., Jan., and Feb.*

★ Musée d'Unterlinden

MUSEUM | The cultural highlight of Colmar is the Musée d'Unterlinden; once a Dominican convent and a hotbed of Rhenish mysticism, the building's star attraction is one of the greatest altarpieces of the 16th century, the *Retable d'Issenheim* (1512–16), by Matthias Grünewald, which is displayed in the convent's Gothic chapel. Originally painted for the convent at Issenheim, 22 km (14 miles) south of Colmar, the multipanel work is either the last gasp of medievalism or a breathtaking preview of modernism and all its neuroses. Replete with raw realism (note the chamber pots, boil-covered bellies, and dirty linen), Grünewald's altarpiece was believed to have miraculous healing powers over ergotism; widespread in the Middle Ages, this malady was produced by the ingestion of fungus-ridden grains and caused its victims—many of whom were being nursed at the Issenheim convent—to experience delusional, nearly hallucinogenic fantasies. Other treasures can be found around the enchanting 13th-century cloister, including arms and armor. Upstairs are fine regional furnishings and a collection of Rhine Valley paintings from the Renaissance, among them Martin Schongauer's opulent 1470 altarpiece painted for Jean d'Orlier. A copper-roofed wing has three floors dedicated to modern and contemporary art (including the *Guernica* tapestry by Jacqueline de La Baume-Dürbach), as well as space for temporary exhibitions.

✉ *1 rue Unterlinden* ☎ *03–89–20–15–50* 🌐 *www.musee-unterlinden.com* 🎟 *€13* ⏲ *Closed Tues.*

🍴 Restaurants

Au Koïfhus

$$ | **FRENCH** | Not to be confused with the shabby little Koïfhus winstub on Rue des Marchands, this popular landmark (the name means "customhouse") serves huge portions of regional standards, plus changing specialties like coq au vin with spaetzle, and choucroute "Colmarienne" with six different meats. Appreciative tourists and canny locals contribute to the lively atmosphere. **Known for:** shady terrace on the broad square; good value fixed-price menus; lots of crowds. [$] *Average main: €17* ✉ *2 pl. de l'Ancienne-Douane* ☎ *03–89–23–04–90* 🌐 *www.restaurant-koifhus-colmar.fr.*

L'Atelier du Peintre

$$$$ | **MODERN FRENCH** | This slick gastronomic restaurant in the historic center strikes a chord with in-the-know locals. Art-decked walls provide a fitting backdrop for the artful dishes prepared by chef-owner Loïc Lefebvre, who whips up dazzling creations while his partner Caroline Cordier ensures service at the "atelier" is top-notch. **Known for:** good wine selection; affordable three-course lunch menu; central location. [$] *Average main: €39* ✉ *1 rue Schongauer* ☎ *03–89–29–51–57* 🌐 *www.atelier-peintre.fr* ⏲ *Closed Sun. and Mon. No lunch Tues.*

Le Théâtre

$$ | **FRENCH** | Facing Colmar's theater, this bistro is popular with locals and well-informed tourists. The Baroque-style interior plays up the drama with theatrical candelabras, red velvet drapes, and an eclectic collection of old mirrors, clocks, and vintage posters while the menu offers creative takes on traditional French dishes. **Known for:** late hours; quality meat choices; reservations on weekends a must. [$] *Average main: €22* ✉ *1 rue des Bains* ☎ *03–89–29–29–29* 🌐 *www.restaurantletheatrecolmar.com* ⏲ *Closed Tues. and Wed.*

🛏 Hotels

James Boutique Hotel

$$ | **HOTEL** | Just a two-minute stroll from Petite Venise, this boutique makes an attractive base for exploring the city's sights. **Pros:** private parking; excellent buffet breakfast; modern comforts. **Cons:** rooms facing the street get some noise; standard rooms don't come with tubs; city's urban district lacks historical charm. [$] *Rooms from: €212* ✉ *15 rue St-Eloi* ☎ *03–89–21–93–70* 🌐 *www.james-hotel.com* 🔑 *30 rooms* 🍽 *No meals.*

Le Maréchal

$$ | **HOTEL** | Built in 1565 in the fortified walls that encircle the Vieille Ville, this romantic, riverside inn is made up of a series of Renaissance houses lavished with glossy rafters, rich brocades, four-poster beds, Jacuzzis, and other extravagant details. **Pros:** pretty location; good food; amiable staff. **Cons:** some rooms are small and unimpressive; parking is difficult to find; elevator doesn't reach all rooms. [$] *Rooms from: €150* ✉ *4 pl. des Six-Montagnes-Noires* ☎ *03–89–41–60–32* 🌐 *www.hotel-le-marechal.com* 🔑 *30 rooms* 🍽 *Free Breakfast.*

Rapp

$ | **HOTEL** | In the Vieille Ville, just off the Champ de Mars, this solid, modern hotel has business-class comforts, a professional and welcoming staff, and an extensive indoor pool complex, plus a good German-scale breakfast. **Pros:** good value; modern amenities, including pool and hamman; helpful staff. **Cons:** breakfast is extra; lacks historic character; the rooms are basic for this category of hotel. [$] *Rooms from: €115* ✉ *1–3–5 rue Weinemer* ☎ *03–89–41–62–10* 🌐 *www.rapp-hotel.com* 🔑 *39 rooms* 🍽 *No meals.*

Chapter 10

BURGUNDY

Updated by
Lyn Parry

👁 Sights	🍴 Restaurants	🛏 Hotels	💼 Shopping	🍸 Nightlife
★★★★☆	★★★★☆	★★★☆☆	★★★☆☆	★★☆☆☆

WELCOME TO BURGUNDY

TOP REASONS TO GO

★ **Burgundy wines:** They are among the world's best, so take the time to stroll through Clos de Vougeot and really get a feel for the "terroir."

★ **Dijon:** One of France's prettiest cities, with colorful banners and polished storefronts along narrow medieval streets, Dijon is perpetually being dolled up for a street fair.

★ **Romanesque history:** Burgundy is home to a knee-weakening concentration of Romanesque churches, and Vézelay's Basilique has the region's greatest 12th-century sculptures.

★ **Beaune:** The "Capital of Caves" is famed for its wine caves and its 15th-century Flemish-style Hospices.

★ **Cluny, "Light of the World":** Previously the center of a vast Christian empire and today a ruin, the sheer volume of this Romanesque abbey still impresses.

Burgundy, on the main route from Paris to both the Riviera and Switzerland/Italy, has always had fast train service, with Dijon serving as the region's Grand Central Terminal. This lively city makes the best hub, enabling travelers to discover Burgundy's many spokes, perhaps with the help of local bus stations (which often conveniently hook up with train stations).

1 Sens. A "floral city" filled with plenty of greenery and a great medieval cathedral.

2 Troyes. Technically the historic capital of Champagne, but closer geographically to the heart of Burgundy.

3 Auxerre. A fascinating town with a Flamboyant Gothic cathedral.

4 Chablis. A charming famed wine village.

5 Tanlay. A quiet village with a Renaissance-style château.

6 Ancy-le-Franc. Another château that perfectly captures the Italian Renaissance.

7 Montbard. A small riverside town that's home to Abbaye de Fontenay.

8 Vézelay. Home to one of the most beloved basilicas of the medieval Christian world.

9 Saulieu. A small town famed for food and Christmas trees.

10 Dijon. Burgundy's only big city and a gastronomic delight.

11 Clos de Vougeot. Home to one of Burgundy's most famous vineyards.

12 Nuits-St-Georges. A wine village that's been in operation since Roman times.

13 Beaune. The heart of Burgundy's wine region.

14 Château de Sully. A classic romantic château.

15 Autun. A town filled with ancient Roman ruins and medieval architecture.

16 Cluny. A village famous for its abbey that was once the center of medieval Christianity.

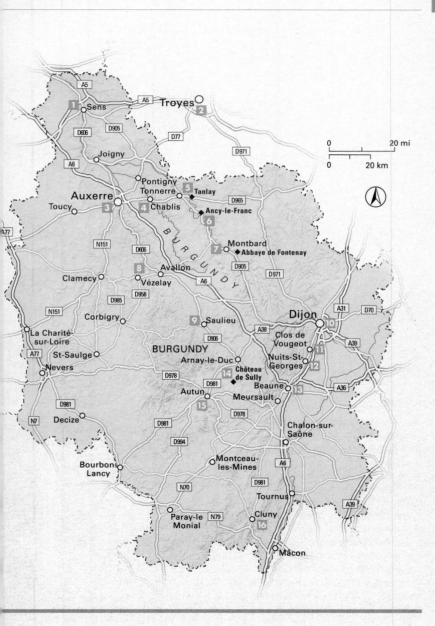

A5

A5 Troyes 2

1 Sens

D606 D905 D77

D971

Joigny

A6

0 ____ 20 mi
0 ____ 20 km

Pontigny 5 Tanlay
Tonnerre
Auxerre 3 4 Chablis D965

Toucy 6 Ancy-le-Franc

A77 B U R G U N D Y

N151 7 Montbard
♦ Abbaye de Fontenay
D606

8 Avallon D905 D971

Clamecy
Vézelay A6

D985 D958

N151

Corbigny A31 D70

9 Saulieu Dijon

La Charité- A38 Clos de 10
sur-Loire Vougeot
A39
D906 11
A77 St-Saulge BURGUNDY
Nuits-St-
Arnay-le-Duc Georges 12
Nevers 14 Château
de Sully 13 A36
D978 Beaune
D981
Autun Meursault
15
N7 Decize
D978
D981 Chalon-sur-
Saône
D994

Bourbon- Montceau-
Lancy les-Mines A6

N70 D981

Paray-le N79 Tournus A39
Monial Cluny
16

Mâcon

Producing a rarefied concentration of what many consider the world's greatest wines and harboring a sigh-worthy collection of magnificent Romanesque abbeys, Burgundy hardly needs to be beautiful—but it is. Its green-hedgerow countryside, medieval villages, and stellar vineyards deserve to be rolled on the palate and savored. Like glasses filled with Clos de Vougeot, the sights here— from the stately city of Dijon to the medieval sanctuaries of Sens, Auxerre, Vézelay, and Cluny—invite us to tarry and partake of their mellow splendor.

Although you may often fall under the influence of extraordinary wine during a sojourn in Burgundy—called Bourgogne by the French—the beauty surrounding you is no boozy illusion. Passed over by revolutions, left unscarred by world wars, and relatively inaccessible thanks to circuitous country roads, the region still reflects the lovely pastoral prosperity it enjoyed under the Capetian kings. Those were the glory days, when self-sufficient Burgundy held its own against the creeping spread of France and the mighty Holy Roman Empire. This grand period was characterized by the expanding role of the dukes of Bourgogne. Consider these Capetians, history-book celebrities all: there was Philippe le Hardi (the Bold), with his power-brokered marriage to Marguerite of Flanders. There was Jean sans Peur (the Fearless), who murdered Louis d'Orléans in a cloak-and-dagger affair in 1407 and was in turn murdered, in 1419. And then there was Philippe le Bon (the Good), who threw in with the English against Joan of Arc.

Yet the Capetians couldn't hold a candle to the great Abbaye de Cluny: founded in 910, it grew to such overweening ecclesiastical power that it dominated the European Church on a papal scale for some four centuries. It was Pope Urban II himself who dubbed it "la Lumière du Monde" (the Light of the World). But the stark geometry of Burgundy's Cistercian abbeys, such as Clairvaux and Cîteaux, stands in silent rebuke to Cluny's excess. The basilicas at Autun and Vézelay remain today in all their noble simplicity, yet manifest some of the finest Romanesque sculpture ever created; the tympanum at Autun rejects all time frames in its visionary daring.

It's almost unfair to the rest of France that all this history, all this art, all this natural beauty comes with delicious refreshments. As if to live up to the extraordinary quality of its Chablis, its Chassagne-Montrachet, its Nuits-St-Georges, its Gevrey-Chambertin, Burgundy flaunts some of the best food in the world. Once you taste a licensed and diploma'd *poulet de Bresse* (Bresse chicken) embellished by the poetry of one perfect glass of Burgundian Pinot Noir, you won't be surprised to see that food and drink entries will take up as much space in your travel diary as the sights you see.

MAJOR REGIONS

Burgundy Wine Country. South of Dijon, follow the Côte d'Or, one of the most famous wine routes. While the "Or" in Côte d'Or doesn't mean "gold" (it's an abbreviation of "Orient," an antiquated term for East), the area does represent a golden opportunity for wine lovers as it branches out over the countryside in four great vineyard *côtes* (slopes or hillsides). The northernmost, the Côte de Nuits, sometimes called the Champs-Élysées of Burgundy, is the land of the unparalleled Grand Cru reds from the Pinot Noir grape. The Côte de Beaune, just to the south, is known for both full-bodied reds and some of the best dry whites in the world. Even farther south is the Côte Chalonnaise. Although not as famous, it produces bottle after bottle of Chardonnay almost as rich as its northern neighbors. Finally, the Côte Mâconnaise, the largest of the four, brings its own quality whites to the market. There are hundreds of vintners in this region, many of them producing top wines from surprisingly small parcels of land. To connect these dots, consult the regional tourist offices for full information about noted wine routes. The 74-km (50-mile) Route des Grands Crus ranges from Dijon to Beaune and Santenay. You can extend this route southward by the Route Touristique des Grands Vins, which travels some 98 km (60 miles) in and around Chalon-sur-Saône. Wherever you go in this killer countryside, you'll find that small towns with big wine names draw many travelers to their cellars. At the Hospices take in the great Rogier van der Weyden *Last Judgment* and the intimate *cour d'honneur* (three-sided courtyard), the perfect postcard setting. Continuing south you'll find Autun, with renowned Roman ruins and the Romanesque landmark of Cluny, once the largest Christian church until St. Peter's was built in Rome.

Dijon. Burgundy's only real city, Dijon became the capital of the duchy of Burgundy in the 11th century, and acquired most of its important architectural and artistic treasures during the 14th and 15th centuries under four Burgundian dukes. The churches, the ducal palace, and one of the finest art museums in France are evidence of their patronage. Other treasures are culinary, including the world's best *bœuf bourguignonne.*

Northwest Burgundy. The northern part of Burgundy came under the sway of the medieval Paris-based Capetian kings, and the mighty Gothic cathedrals they built are still here, notably St-Étienne at Sens. Thirty-two kilometers (20 miles) to the east is Troyes, its charming half-timber houses adding to the appeal of a town overlooked by most bus tours. Southeast lies Auxerre, beloved for its steep, crooked streets and magnificent churches; the wine village of Chablis; and two great Renaissance châteaux, Tanlay and Ancy-le-Franc. Closer to Dijon are the great Cistercian abbey at Fontenay and the noted Romanesque basilica at Vézelay, with a delightful hilltop setting.

Did You Know?

Burgundy at its best is during harvest time; many head to such hallowed landmarks as the Château du Clos de Vougeot during mid-September so they can witness the famous *vendages* (grape harvests).

Planner

When to Go

Whenever it's gray and cloudy in Paris, chances are the sun is shining in Burgundy. Situated in the heart of France, Burgundy has warm, dry summers. May here is especially lovely, as are September and October, when the sun is still warm on the shimmering golden trees, and the grapes, now ready for harvesting, scent the air with anticipation. This is when the vines are colorful and the *caves* (cellars) are open for business. Many festivals also take place around this time. The climate in early spring and late fall isn't quite as idyllic, with a mixture of sun and scattered showers. The winter months vary from year to year, and although snow is not common, freezing temperatures mean the bare vines and trees are covered with a soft white hue. Layers of clothing are always advisable, so you're ready for cooler mornings and hotter afternoons. Waterproof outer layers are wise on longer day trips if the weather forecast is changeable.

Planning Your Time

France's prime preoccupations with food and wine are nowhere better celebrated than in Burgundy. Although it might sound glib, the best way to experience the region is to stay for as long as possible because there is so much to see and do here. If you want to go bike riding, the obvious place to set up is Beaune. If, on the other hand, you're an amateur medieval art historian or are interested in the lesser-known wines of Irancy, Chitry, and Tonnerre, base yourself at Auxerre or Vézelay in northern Burgundy. This will allow you to focus on these pursuits while also visiting vineyards, the cathedral of Sens, and (on a northward detour) the elegant, delightful town of Troyes. If you prefer the conveniences of modern cities but also want a taste of medieval Burgundy, then Dijon offers you the best of both worlds. Burgundy's capital has all the charm of another era and all the functionality of a major metropolis. It's the gateway to the Côte d'Or, as well as the perfect place to set off for exploring the back roads of Burgundy.

Getting Here and Around

Burgundy, whose northern perimeter begins 75 km (50 miles) from Paris, is one of the largest regions in France. It's sliced in half by the north–south A6, so it's generally quicker to move in this direction than from west to east or vice versa. But a vast network of secondary roads makes travel from city to city or even village to village both practical and picturesque.

BUS TRAVEL

Local bus services are typically reliable; where the private company Mobigo does not venture, the national SNCF network often does. One top choice is Mobigo's No. 113 bus through the Côte d'Or wine region, which links Dijon to Beaune (1 hr) via Vougeot (40 mins) and Nuits-St-Georges (47 mins), with a €1.50 fare per leg. Inquire at the local tourist office for timetables and ask your hotel concierge for further recommendations.

BUS INFORMATION Mobigo ⊠ *Gare Routière, Rue Perrières, Dijon* ☎ *03–80–11–29–29* ⊕ *www.viamobigo.fr.*

CAR TRAVEL

Although bus lines do service smaller towns, traveling through Burgundy by car allows you to explore its meandering country roads at leisure. A6 is the main route through the region; it heads southeast from Paris through Burgundy, past Sens, Auxerre, Chablis, Saulieu, and Beaune, continuing on to Lyon and the south. A38 links A6 to Dijon, 290 km (180 miles) from Paris; the trip takes around three hours. A31 heads down from Dijon to Beaune, a distance of 45 km (27 miles). D974 is a slower, more atmospheric option; but if it's scenery you want, D122 is the Route des Grands Crus, which reads like a wine list as it meanders through every wine village. The uncluttered A5 links Paris to Troyes, where the A31 segues south to Dijon.

TRAIN TRAVEL

Perhaps the most efficient way of arriving on Burgundy's doorstep is by rail. The TGV travels to Dijon from Paris's Gare de Lyon up to 16 times a day (1 hr 40 mins); there's also daily TGV service direct from Paris's Charles de Gaulle Airport to Dijon (1 hr 45 mins). Beaune is well served by trains arriving from Dijon, Lyon, and Paris; and Sens is on a main-line route from the capital (60–90 mins). The region has a local train route as well linking destinations such as Sens, Dijon, Beaune, and Chalon. If you want to get to smaller towns or to vineyards, take a bus or car.

TRAIN INFORMATION SNCF ☎ *3635 (€0.40 per min)* ⊕ *www.oui.sncf.* **TGV** ☎ *3635 (€0.40 per min)* ⊕ *www.sncf. com.*

Restaurants

Dijon ranks with Lyon as a gastronomic capital of France, and Burgundy's hearty traditions help explain why. It all began in the early 15th century when Jean, Duc de Berry, arrived here, built a string of castles, and proceeded to make food, wine, and art top priorities for his courtiers. Today, Parisian gourmands consider a three-hour drive a small price to pay for the cuisine of Burgundy's best restaurants, such as Le Pré aux Clercs and Stéphane Derbord in Dijon, and Relais Bernard Loiseau in Saulieu.

Dijon is not quite the wine–mustard capital of the world it used to be, but the happy fact remains that mustard finds its way into many regional specialties,

including the sauce that usually accompanies *andouillette,* a fabled sausage made with pork chitterlings (intestine). Other sausages—notably the *rosette du Morvan* and others served with a potato puree—are great favorites. Game, freshwater trout, coq au vin, *poulet au Meursault* (chicken in white-wine sauce), snails, and, of course, bœuf à la bourguignonne (incidentally, this dish is only called bœuf bourguignonne when you are *not* in Burgundy) also number among the region's specialties.

The queen of chickens is the poulet de Bresse, which hails from east of the Côte d'Or and can be as pricey as a bottle of fine wine. Ham is a big item, especially around Easter, when garlicky *jambon persillé*—ham boiled with pig's trotters and served cold in jellied white wine and parsley—often tops the menu. Also look for *saupiquet des Amognes*—a Morvan delight of hot braised ham served with a spicy cream sauce. As for desserts, *pain d'épices* (gingerbread) is the dessert staple of the region. And, like every other part of France, Burgundy has its own cheeses. The Abbaye de Cîteaux, birthplace of Cistercian monasticism, has produced its mild cheese for centuries. Chaource and hearty Époisses also melt in your mouth—as do Bleu de Bresse and Meursault.

Hotels

The vast range of lodging here includes everything from simple *gîtes d'étape* (bed-and-breakfasts) to four-star châteaux. But Burgundy is often overrun with tourists, especially in summer, so finding accommodations can be a problem. It's wise to make advance reservations—particularly if you're bound for wine country (from Dijon to Beaune). *Restaurant and hotel reviews have been shortened. For full information, visit Fodors.com.*

What It Costs in Euros			
$	$$	$$$	$$$$
RESTAURANTS			
under €16	€16–€24	€25–€32	over €32
HOTELS			
under €125	€126–€225	€226–€350	over €350

Visitor Information

Both the regional tourism board and the Dijon tourist office are invaluable sources of information. The numerous local tourist offices (listed under their respective towns) are also very helpful.

CONTACTS Comité Régional du Tourisme de Bourgogne-Franche-Comté ⊠ *5 av. Garibaldi, Dijon* ☎ *03–81–25–08–00* ⊕ *www.bourgognefranchecomte.com.* **Dijon Tourist Office** ⊠ *11 rue des Forges, Dijon* ☎ *08–92–70–05–58 (€0.35 per min)* ⊕ *www.destinationdijon.com.*

Sens

112 km (70 miles) southeast of Paris.

Pretty Sens enjoys a "four-leaf" ranking as a *ville fleurie,* or floral city—and you'll understand why when you see the Moulin à Tan (a gorgeous park with more than 35 acres of greenery), the excellently manicured Jean-Cousin square, and the municipal greenhouses. It finds full botanical expression on the second Sunday in September, when everything and everyone are festooned with flowers during the Fête de la St-Fiacre, a festival named after the patron saint of gardeners. But anytime during the year, the glorious Cathédrale St-Étienne makes a trip here worthwhile.

GETTING HERE AND AROUND

It makes sense for Sens to be your first stop in Burgundy, because it's only 90 minutes by car from Paris on the A6, a fast road that hugs the pretty Yonne Valley south of Fontainebleau. Traveling in and out of Sens is a breeze as it's on a major route with 26 direct TER trains (€20) leaving Paris's Gare de Bercy or Gare de Lyon station on weekdays with 21 trains on Saturday and 19 on Sunday. Regional trains also link Sens to Dijon, Beaune, and Chalon.

VISITOR INFORMATION Sens Tourist Office ⊠ *Pl. Jean-Jaurès* ☎ *03–86–65–19–49* ⊕ *www.tourisme-sens.com.*

Sights

★ **Cathédrale St-Étienne**
RELIGIOUS SITE | Historically linked more with Paris than Burgundy, Sens was the country's ecclesiastical center for centuries. Today it's still dominated by Cathédrale St-Étienne, once the French sanctuary for Thomas à Becket and a model for England's Canterbury Cathedral. You can see the 240-foot south tower from miles away. As you draw near, the pompous 19th-century buildings lining the town's narrow main street—notably the meringue-like Hôtel de Ville—can give you a false impression; in fact, the streets leading off it near the cathedral (notably Rue Abelard and Rue Jean-Cousin) are full of medieval half-timber houses. On Monday the cathedral square is crowded with merchants' stalls, and the beautiful late-19th-century market hall—a distant cousin of Baltard's former iron-and-glass Halles in Paris—hums with people buying meat and produce. A smaller market is held on Friday morning.

Begun around 1130, the cathedral once had two towers: one was topped in 1532 by an elegant though somewhat incongruous Renaissance campanile that contained two monster bells; the other was

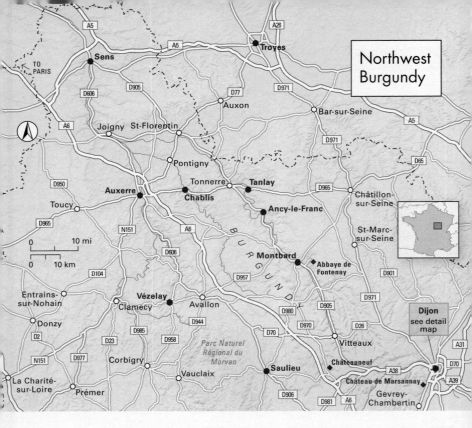

taken down in the 19th century. Note the trefoil arches decorating the exterior of the remaining tower. The gallery, with statues of former archbishops of Sens, is a 19th-century addition, but the statue of St. Stephen (aka St-Étienne) between the doors of the central portal, is thought to date to late in the 12th century. The vast, harmonious interior is justly renowned for its stained-glass windows: the oldest (circa 1200) are in the north transept and include the stories of the Good Samaritan and the Prodigal Son; those in the south transept were manufactured in 1500 in Troyes and include a much-admired Tree of Jesse. Stained-glass windows in the north of the chancel retrace the story of Thomas à Becket: Becket fled to Sens from England to escape the wrath of Henry II before returning to his cathedral in Canterbury, where he was murdered in 1170. Below the window—which shows him embarking on his journey in a boat, and also at the moment of his death—is a medieval statue of an archbishop said to have come from the site of Becket's home in Sens. Becket's *aube* (vestment) is displayed in the annex to the Palais Synodal. ⊠ *Pl. de la République* ☎ *03–86–65–06–57.*

Musées des Sens

MUSEUM | The roof of the 13th-century Palais Synodal, alongside Sens's cathedral, is notable for its yellow, green, and red diamond-tile motif—incongruously added in the mid-19th century by monument restorer Viollet-le-Duc. Six grand windows and the vaulted Synodal Hall are outstanding architectural features; the building now functions as an exhibition space. Annexed to the Palais is an ensemble of Renaissance buildings with a courtyard offering a fine view of the cathedral's Flamboyant Gothic south transept, constructed by master stonemason Martin Chambiges at the start of the 16th century (rose windows were his specialty, as you can appreciate here). Inside is a museum with archaeological finds from the Gallo-Roman period. The cathedral treasury, now on the museum's first floor, is one of the richest in France, comparable to that of Conques. It contains a collection of miters, ivories, the shrouds of St-Sivard and St-Loup, and sumptuous reliquaries. But the star of the collection is Thomas à Becket's restored brown-and-silver-edged linen robe which is displayed alongside his chasuble, stole, and sandals. ✉ *Pl. de la République* ☎ *03-86-64-46-22, 03-86-83-88-90 for museum info* 🌐 *www.musees-sens.fr* 🎫 *€6* 🕒 *Closed Tues.*

🍴 Restaurants

Au Crieur de Vin

$$$ | **BISTRO** | **FAMILY** | Tucked away in a backstreet, this bijou bistro is one of the top-rated spots in town (the place is always packed so be sure to book ahead). Excellent in terms of both value and quality, its menus include modern, market-driven dishes showcasing top-quality produce served with masterfully prepared sauces. **Known for:** creative dishes that attest to the chef's flair; good wine list focusing on local producers; relaxed, casual atmosphere. [$] *Average main: €28* ✉ *1 rue d'Alsace Lorraine* ☎ *03-86-65-92-80* 🌐 *www.restaurant-aucrieurdevin.fr* 🕒 *Closed Sun. and Mon. No lunch Tues.*

Clos des Jacobins

$$$$ | **MODERN FRENCH** | At this popular restaurant in the center of town, the balance between elegant and casual finds expression in the wide choice of dishes on offer. The upscale à la carte menu is replete with exceptional fish specialties, while fixed-price menus include more traditional Burgundian choices. **Known for:** location in the historic center of town; top value lunch menu includes wine and coffee; refined and contemporary setting. [$] *Average main: €37* ✉ *49 Grande-Rue* ☎ *09-74-56-06-44* 🌐 *www.restaurantlesjacobins.com* 🕒 *Closed Wed. No dinner Sun. and Tues.*

🛏 Hotels

Paris & Poste

$ | **HOTEL** | At this inn, which began life as a canon's house in 1776, guest rooms are clean, spacious, and well-appointed. **Pros:** unbeatable value; central location; great food. **Cons:** street-side rooms get some early morning noise; not all rooms have a bathtub; some rooms lack space. [$] *Rooms from: €100* ✉ *97 rue de la République* ☎ *03-86-65-17-43* 🌐 *www.hotel-paris-poste.fr* 🛏 *30 rooms* 🍴 *No meals.*

Troyes

64 km (40 miles) east of Sens, 150 km (95 miles) southeast of Paris.

The inhabitants of Troyes would be dismayed if you mistook them for Burgundians. After all, Troyes is the historic capital of the counts of Champagne, but we retain it here—closer to Burgundy's treasures—because it's some 80 km (50 miles) south of the heart of Champagne province. Troyes was also the home of the late-12th-century writer Chrétien (or Chrestien) de Troyes who, in seeking to please his patrons, Count Henry the Liberal and Marie de Champagne, penned the first Arthurian legends. Few, if any, other French town centers contain so much to see. In the Vauluisant and St-Jean districts, a web of enchanting pedestrian streets with timber-frame houses, magnificent churches, fine museums, and a wide choice of restaurants makes the Old Town (Vieux Troyes) especially appealing.

Home to a famous cathedral, Sens also has many streets leading to atmospheric half-timber houses.

Keep an eye out for the delightful architectural accents that make Troyes unique: *essentes,* geometric chestnut tiles that keep out humidity and are fire resistant; and sculpted *poteaux* (in Troyes they are called *montjoies*), carvings at the joint of corner structural beams. There's a lovely one of Adam and Eve next door to the Comtes de Champagne hotel. GPS-equipped audio guides (€6), available from the Troyes tourist office, will help history buffs make the most of a visit here. There's enough to keep shoppers content, too. Along with its neighbors Provins and Bar-sur-Aube, Troyes was one of Champagne's major fair towns in the Middle Ages. The wool trade gave way to cotton in the 18th century when Troyes became the heartland of hosiery; today Troyes draws millions of shoppers from all over Europe, who come to scour its outlet clothing stores for bargains.

GETTING HERE AND AROUND
With the first train at 6:42 am, and then around one every hour until 8:42 pm, you can get to Troyes in about 90 minutes

from Paris Gare de l'Est (€27.90). Sens to Troyes is a little harder; there are seven daily trains, but they involve changing in Paris, Laroche Migennes, or St-Florentin Vergigny. The journey takes just over three hours and costs €20.10–€41.50. Within Troyes, public transit is provided by TCAT buses (⊕ *www.tcat.fr*); single tickets cost €1.35.

VISITOR INFORMATION Troyes Tourist Office ✉ *16 rue Aristide Briand* ☏ *03–25–82–62–70* ⊕ *www.tourisme-troyes.com.*

Sights

Basilique St-Urbain
RELIGIOUS SITE | Started in 1261 by Pope Urban IV (a native son) and eventually consecrated in 1389, St-Urbain is one of the most remarkable churches in France—a perfect culmination of the Gothic quest to replace stone walls with stained glass. Its narrow porch frames a 13th-century Last Judgment tympanum, whose highly worked elements include a frieze of the dead rising out of their

coffins (witness the grimacing skeleton). Look for a carved crayfish on one of the statue's niches (a testament to the local river culture). Inside, a chapel on the south side houses the *Vièrge au Raisin* (*Virgin with Grapes*), clutching Jesus with one hand and a bunch of Champagne grapes in the other. ⊠ *Pl. Vernie* ☎ *03–25–73–37–13.*

Cathédrale St-Pierre St-Paul

RELIGIOUS SITE | Dominating the heart of Troyes, this remarkable cathedral is a prime example of the Flamboyant Gothic style—regarded as the last gasp of the Middle Ages. Note the incomplete single-tower west front, the small Renaissance campaniles on top of the tower, and the artistry of Martin Chambiges, who worked on Troyes's facade (with its characteristic large rose window and flamboyant flames) around the same time as he did the transept of Beauvais. At night the floodlighted features burst into dramatic relief. The cathedral's vast five-aisle interior, refreshingly light thanks to large windows and the near-whiteness of the local stone, dates mainly to the 13th century. It has fine examples of 13th-century stained glass in the choir, such as the Tree of Jesse (a popular regional theme), and richly colored 16th-century glass in the nave and west front rose window. ⊠ *Pl. St-Pierre* ☎ *03–25–76–98–18.*

Hôtel de Vauluisant

MUSEUM | FAMILY | This charmingly turreted 16th- to 17th-century mansion contains two museums: the **Musée d'Art Champenois** (Regional Art Museum) and the **Musée de la Bonneterie** (Textile-Hosiery Museum). The former traces the development of Troyes and southern Champagne, with a particularly rich selection of religious sculptures and paintings of the late-Gothic era; the latter outlines the history and manufacturing procedures of the town's 18th- to 19th-century textile industry. ⊠ *4 rue de Vauluisant* ☎ *03–25–43–43–20* ⊕ *www.*

musees-troyes.com ✉ *€3 (free Nov.– Mar.)* ⊘ *Closed Mon.*

Hôtel de Ville (*Town Hall*)

GOVERNMENT BUILDING | Place du Maréchal-Foch, the main square of Troyes, is flanked by cafés, shops, and this delightful town hall. The central facade has black marble columns and a niche with a helmeted Minerva, which replaced a statue of Louis XIV that was destroyed during the French Revolution. In summer the square is filled with people from morning to night. ⊠ *Pl. du Maréchal-Foch.*

Hôtel-Dieu (*Hospital*)

HOSPITAL—SIGHT | Across the Bassin de la Préfecture, an arm of the Seine, is this historic hospital, fronted by superb 18th-century wrought-iron gates topped with the blue-and-gold fleurs-de-lis emblems of the French monarchy. Around the corner is the entrance to the **Apothicairerie de l'Hôtel-Dieu**, a former medical laboratory and the only part of the Hôtel-Dieu open to visitors. Inside, time has been suspended: floral-painted boxes and ceramic jars containing medicinal plants line the antique shelves. Due to a major renovation project, the apothecary is closed until 2020. ⊠ *Quai des Comtes de Champagne* ☎ *03–25– 80–98–97* ⊕ *www.musees-troyes.com* ✉ *€3 (free Nov.–Mar.)* ⊘ *Closed Mon.*

Hôtel du Petit Louvre

BUILDING | This former coaching inn is a handsome example of 16th-century architecture. ⊠ *Pl. du Préau.*

Musée St-Loup

MUSEUM | The former 18th-century abbey of St-Loup, to the side of the cathedral, now houses a superlative collection of paintings from the 15th to the 19th century—including works by Peter Paul Rubens, Anthony Van Dyck, Antoine Watteau, François Boucher, and Jacques-Louis David. Other highlights include an impressive assortment of birds and meteorites; medieval statuary; and local archaeological finds, most

Eating and Drinking in Burgundy

While Burgundy's glittering wine trade imparts a sophisticated image to the region, Burgundy itself is basically prosperous farm country. Traditional cuisine here reflects the area's farm-centric soul, with lots of slow-cooked, wine-laced dishes.

Bœuf à la Bourguignonne

Burgundy is the birthplace of this beloved beef stew, aka bœuf bourguignonne, and no place on Earth makes it better. A bottle or two of hearty red wine cooked down in the sauce is one secret to its success; the other is the region's prime Charolais beef. The beef is braised with wine, onions, bacon, and mushrooms, turning tender as the sauce reduces and intensifies. Other wine-soaked specialties here include coq au vin and *œufs en meurette*—eggs poached in red wine.

Époisses Cheese

The greatest of Burgundian cheeses, the rich, earthy, cow's-milk Époisses is not for the faint of heart. This assertive—yes, even odorous—cheese with the russet-hue rind develops its character from a daily scrubbing with marc-de-Bourgogne brandy as it ripens, a process that inhibits mold but encourages the growth of a particular bacteria necessary for the development of its creamy interior and distinctive flavor. Go to the modest village of Époisses and buy your cheese from top producers Berthaut and Gaugry. But be sure to transport it in a tightly sealed container.

Escargots

Burgundy's plump snails, which are found in the vineyards, appear on menus throughout the region. The signature preparation is *à la Bourguignonne*—simmered in white wine, stuffed with a garlicky parsley-shallot butter, and baked until bubbling. The delicacy is served in portions of six or eight on ceramic escargot dishes called *escargotières*, accompanied by tongs and a little fork.

Kir

This rosy and refreshing aperitif, combining an inexpensive white wine called Aligoté with a dose of *crème de cassis* (black-currant liqueur), was dubbed a "Kir" during World War II when the Resistance hero and mayor of Dijon, Canon Félix Kir, began promoting the drink to boost local sales of cassis liqueur. Traditionally made, the Kir has four to five parts dry white wine to one part crème de cassis. In the Kir's aristocratic cousin, the Kir Royale, Champagne replaces the wine.

Mustard

Visit the 18th-century Maille mustard emporium at 32 rue de la Liberté to savor Dijon's world-famous mustards. Produced from stone-ground dried black or brown seeds macerated in *verjus* (the juice of unripe white grapes), these mustards accompany many dishes and heat up *lapin à la moutarde*, rabbit in mustard sauce. There is coarse-grain *moutarde à l'ancienne* or the classic, creamy, much hotter variety.

notably gold-mounted 5th-century jewelry and a bronze Gallo-Roman statue of Apollo. Major renovations are underway, so parts of the museum may be closed to the public until 2022. ✉ *1 rue Chrestien-de-Troyes* ☎ *03–25–42–20–09* 🌐 *www.musees-troyes.com* 🎟 *€6 (free Nov.–Mar.)* ⏲ *Closed Tues.*

Ste-Madeleine

RELIGIOUS SITE | The oldest church in Troyes, Ste-Madeleine is best known for its elaborate triple-arch stone rood screen separating the nave and the choir. Only a handful of other such screens still remain in France—most were dismantled during the French Revolution. This filigreed Flamboyant Gothic beauty was carved with panache by Jean Gailde between 1508 and 1517. The superbly tranquil Garden of the Innocents, established on the ancient "children's graveyard," symbolizes medieval spirituality. ✉ *Rue de la Madeleine* ☎ *03–25–73–82–90.*

🍴 Restaurants

Aux Crieurs de Vin

$$ | **FRENCH** | **FAMILY** | This popular bistro-cum-wineshop is often packed, and with good reason: modern dishes share the chalkboard menu with classic bistro choices like homemade terrine and andouillette. The wine selection is excellent; natural wines and Champagnes are a specialty. **Known for:** on-site wineshop where you can buy wine for your meal; lively atmosphere; excellent platters of cheese and cured meats. [$] *Average main: €17* ✉ *4 pl. Jean Jaurès* ☎ *03–25–40–01–01* ⏲ *Closed Sun. and Mon.*

🛏 Hotels

Brit Hotel Comtes de Champagne

$ | **HOTEL** | In Vieux Troyes's topsy-turvy 16th-century former mint, this bargain find has a quaint inner courtyard and pleasant, refurbished rooms with iron bedsteads. **Pros:** affordable, old-fashioned charm; central location; suites have kitchenettes. **Cons:** bathrooms are a bit plain and small; no air-conditioning; soundproofing could be improved. [$] *Rooms from: €79* ✉ *54–56 rue de la Monnaie* ☎ *03–25–73–11–70* 🌐 *hotel-troyes.brithotel.fr* 🔑 *45 rooms* 🍽 *No meals.*

★ **Le Champ des Oiseaux**

$$$ | **HOTEL** | Tin chandeliers, Nantes silk and calico hangings, antique scrollwork panels, and other traditional luxe touches make lodgings in this trio of vine-clad, pink-and-yellow 15th- and 16th-century houses especially alluring. **Pros:** quiet, comfortable rooms; genial service; first-class dining. **Cons:** parking costs extra; no elevator; rooms under the eaves have low-beamed ceilings. [$] *Rooms from: €250* ✉ *20 rue Linard-Gonthier* ☎ *03–25–80–58–50* 🌐 *www.champdesoiseaux.com* 🔑 *12 rooms* 🍽 *No meals.*

Relais St-Jean

$ | **HOTEL** | This half-timber hotel, in the pedestrian zone near the church of St-Jean, has rooms that are refreshingly done in a sleek modern style; their white-and-pastel-color walls contrast tastefully with the sophisticated, multihue furnishings. **Pros:** good-size rooms; friendly service; interesting bar. **Cons:** rooms sometimes feel overheated ; some street noise; not all rooms have a view. [$] *Rooms from: €101* ✉ *51 rue Paillot-de-Montabert* ☎ *03–25–73–89–90* 🌐 *www.hotel-relais-saint-jean.com* 🔑 *23 rooms* 🍽 *No meals.*

🛍 Shopping

If there's an ideal place for a shopping spree, it's Troyes. Many clothing manufacturers are just outside town, clustered together in three large suburban malls: **Marques Avenue,** in St-Julien-les-Villas (take D671 toward Dijon), and **Marques City** and **McArthur Glen,** in Pont-Ste-Marie (take D677 toward Châlons-en-Champagne). Ralph Lauren and Calvin Klein at McArthur Glen face off with Laura Ashley at Marques Avenue and Doc Martens at Marques City, to name a few of the shops. The malls are open weekdays 10–7, Saturday 9:30–7.

Auxerre

58 km (36 miles) southeast of Sens.

Auxerre is an evocative, architecturally interesting town with a trio of imposing churches perched above the Yonne River and an ample supply of antique hous- es. Yet it's an underappreciated place, perhaps because of its location, midway between Paris and Dijon. Fanning out from Auxerre's main square, Place des Cordeliers (just up from the cathe- dral), are a number of steep, crooked streets lined with half-timber and stone buildings. The best way to see them is to start from the riverside on Quai de la République, where you can find the tourist office (and pick up a handy local map); then continue along Quai de la Marine. The medieval arcaded gallery of the Ancien Evêché (Old Bishop's Palace), now an administrative building, is just visible on the hillside beside the tourist office. At 9 rue de la Marine (which leads off one of several riverside squares) are the two oldest houses in Auxerre, dating from the end of the 14th century. Contin- ue up the hill to Rue de l'Yonne, which leads into Rue Cochois. Here, at No. 23, is the higgledy-piggledy home and shop of a *maître verrier* (lead-glass maker). Closer to the center of town, the most beautiful of Auxerre's many poteaux (the carved tops of wooden corner posts) can be seen at 8 rue Joubert. The building dates to the late 15th century, and its Gothic tracery windows, acorns, and oak leaves are an open-air masterpiece.

GETTING HERE AND AROUND
Seven direct trains arrive daily from Paris's Gare de Bercy (€30). Thirteen daily trains link Auxerre to Montbard (€20), mostly via Laroche-Migennes, with Dijon (€30) being at the end of the line. Train service to Beaune, via Laroche Migennes, is also available (€35). If you're driving, Auxerre is served by several major arteries, including the A6 (Autoroute of the Sun) and the D606/D906.

VISITOR INFORMATION **Auxerre Tourist Office** ✉ *1 quai de la République* ☎ *03- 86–52–06–19* ⊕ *www.ot-auxerre.fr.*

 Sights

Abbaye de St-Germain
RELIGIOUS SITE | North of Place des Cordeliers is the former Abbaye de St-Germain, which stands parallel to the cathedral some 300 yards away. The church's earliest aboveground section is the 12th-century Romanesque bell tower, but the extensive underground crypt was inaugurated by Charles the Bald in 859 and contains its original Carolingi- an frescoes and Ionic capitals. It's the only monument of its kind in Europe—a layout retaining the plan of the long-gone church built above it—and was a place of pilgrimage until Huguenots burned the remains of its namesake, a Gallo-Roman governor and bishop of Auxerre, in the 16th century. ✉ *Pl. St-Germain* ☎ *03–86– 18–02–90* 🖅 *Crypt €7* ⊙ *Closed Tues.*

Cathédrale St-Étienne
RELIGIOUS SITE | The town's dominant fea- ture is the ascending line of three mag- nificent churches—St-Pierre, St-Étienne, and St-Germain—with Cathédrale St-Éti- enne, in the middle, rising majestically above the squat houses around it. The 13th-century choir, the oldest part of the edifice, contains its original stained glass, dominated by brilliant reds and blues. Beneath the choir, the frescoed 11th-cen- tury Romanesque crypt keeps company with the treasury, which has a panoply of medieval enamels, manuscripts, and miniatures, plus a rare depiction of Christ on horseback. A 75-minute son-et-lu- mière show focusing on Roman Gaul is

Continued on page 422

GRAPE EXPECTATIONS
A BURGUNDY WINE PRIMER

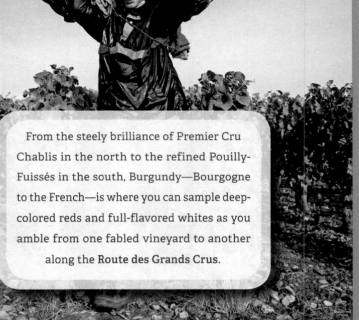

From the steely brilliance of Premier Cru Chablis in the north to the refined Pouilly-Fuissés in the south, Burgundy—Bourgogne to the French—is where you can sample deep-colored reds and full-flavored whites as you amble from one fabled vineyard to another along the **Route des Grands Crus**.

An oenophile's nirvana, Burgundy is accorded almost religious reverence, and with good reason: its famous chardonnays and pinot noirs, and the "second-tier" gamays and aligotés, were perfected in the Middle Ages by the great monasteries of the region.

The specific character of a Burgundy wine is often dependent on the individual grower or négociant's style. There are hundreds of vintners and merchants in this region, many of them producing top wines from surprisingly small parcels of land.

Get to know the *appellation d'Origine Protégée*, or AOP, wine classification system. In Burgundy, it specifies vineyard, region, and quality. The most expensive, top-tiered wines are called *monopole* and *grand cru*, followed by *premier cru*, *village*, and generic *Bourgogne*. Although there are 100 different AOP wines in the area, the thicket of labels and names is navigable once you learn how to read the road signs; and the payoff is tremendous, with palate-pleasing choices for all budgets.

By Christopher Mooney

GEOGRAPHY + CLIMATE = *TERROIR*

Soil, weather conditions, grapes, and savoir-faire are the basic building blocks of all great wines, but this is particularly true in Burgundy, where grapes of the same variety, grown a few feet apart, might have different names and personalities, as well as tremendously varying prices.

CHABLIS

Chablis' famous chardonnays are produced along both banks of the Serein River. The four appellations, in ascending order of excellence, are Petit Chablis AOP, Chablis AOP, Chablis Premier Cru AOP, and Chablis Grand Cru AOP. Flinty and slightly acidic, with citrus, pineapple, and green apple flavors and aromas, they age well (except the Petit Chablis, which are best drunk young) and are typically less intense than other burgundy whites, due to their colder northern climate.

CÔTE D'OR

The 30-mile long Côte d'Or contains two of the world's most gorgeous and distinguished wine regions: **Côte de Nuits** and **Côte de Beaune.**

The northern area, the **Côte de Nuits**, is sometimes called the "Champs-Elysées of Burgundy" as it is the site of Burgundy's top-rated grand cru wines. These Burgundian pinot noirs are ruby colored with red fruit and spice flavors. They tend to be richly textured with a full body. The wines develop savory, gamey notes with age, and are perfect matches for hearty Burgundian beef and game dishes. The best wines come from the grand cru appelations of Gevrey-Chambertin, Vougeot, Vosne-Romanée, and Nuits-St-Georges.

The **Côte de Beaune**, just to the south, is known for making the world's best dry whites, made from chardonnay. These wines are green-gold in color and aromatically complex. They typically have a buttery texture and are medium- to full-bodied. Search out wines from the appelations of Aloxe-Corton, Beaune, and Pommard, then head south for the storied Montrachets, which are the most expensive chardonnay wines in the world. Renowned reds are also made here, though are lighter and less concentrated than their counterparts from the Côte de Nuits.

CÔTE CHALONNAISE

Farther south is the Côte Chalonnaise. Although not as famous, it produces chardonnays almost as rich as its northern neighbors. Pinot noirs with *villages* appellations Rully, Givry, and Mercurey are well-structured, with body, bouquet, and a distinction very similar to Côte de Beaune reds. Montagny and Rully whites are dry, light, well balanced, and fruity—much ends up in sparkling Crémant de Bourgogne. Bourgogne Aligoté de Bouzeron are worth a stop, too. Named after its grape, it is the fresh and lively white wine traditionally mixed with Crème de Cassis to make a Kir, but is just as delicious on its own.

CÔTE MÂCONNAISE

Next is the Côte Mâconnaise, the largest of the four Côtes, which brings its own quality dry whites to the market, particularly the distinctive and refined Saint Vérans, Virés and the more famous Pouilly-Fuissés. With lightly oaked aromas of toast and hazelnuts, these are three of France's best wines for seafood. Macon *villages* light and fruity reds are drinkable but hardly worth a detour. The best are found between Hurigny and Viré and, like the whites, should be drunk young while they still have their freshness.

LABEL KNOW—HOW

1. SOCIÉTÉ CIVILE DU DOMAINE DE LA ROMANÉE-CONTI
PROPRIÉTAIRE A VOSNE-ROMANÉE (CÔTE-D'OR) FRANCE

2. **MONTRACHET**
APPELLATION MONTRACHET CONTROLÉE

3. 1.718 Bouteilles Récoltées

4. BOUTEILLE Nº 01201
ANNÉE 1995

LES ASSOCIÉS-GÉRANTS

5. Mise en bouteille au domaine

1. The name and address of the proprietor.
2. This wine was produced in the Montrachet region
3. Number of bottles made
4. Bottle number 1,201 and Vintage
5. 'Made and bottled on the estate'—a great signifier of quality

FOR THE VINE INSPIRED

If you're going to spend a fortune on a bottle of Romanée-Conti and want to know how to savor it, sign up for one of the wine classes offered by Beaune's Ecole des Vins de Bourgogne, sponsored by the Bureau Interprofessionel des Vins de Bourgogne. They offer several choices of classes, including a one-day outing with a tutored wine workshop and a wine-themed lunch followed by a cellar visit and tasting.

Presided over by Cathédrale St-Etienne, Auxerre is a medieval beauty filled with historic churches.

presented every evening from June to September. ✉ *Pl. St-Étienne* ☎ *03–86–52–31–68* 🌐 *www.cathedrale-auxerre.com* 🎟 *Crypt and treasury €4.*

🍴 Restaurants

Le Jardin Gourmand

$$$$ | **MODERN FRENCH** | This restaurant in a former manor house has a pretty garden (*jardin*) where you can dine on summer evenings, as well as an organic vegetable garden producing fresh herbs, gorgeous greens, and other foods that wind up on the table. The interior, accented by subtle-yellow panels and polished wood floors, is congenial and elegant, while the menu (which changes eight times a year) shows both flair and invention. **Known for:** discreet and friendly staff; the chef who draws inspiration from the finest seasonal ingredients; excellent wine list. [$] *Average main: €45* ✉ *56 bd. Vauban* ☎ *03–86–51–53–52* 🌐 *www.lejardingourmand.com* 🕒 *Closed Mon. and Tues., 1 wk in Mar., last 2 wks of June, 1 wk in Sept., last 2 wks of Nov. No dinner Sun.*

🛏 Hotels

Château de Ribourdin

$ | **B&B/INN** | Retired farmer Claude Brodard began building his *chambres d'hôte* (bed-and-breakfast) in an old stable, bucolically enshrined just south of Auxerre, more than 20 years ago, and the cozy, comfortable, reasonably priced rooms overlook his fields. **Pros:** tasteful rooms; beautiful location; great complimentary breakfast. **Cons:** can feel a little isolated; no credit cards; the decor may be too outdated for some. [$] *Rooms from: €95* ✉ *8 rte. de Ribourdin, 8 km (5 miles) southwest of Auxerre on D1, Chevannes* ☎ *03–86–41–23–16* 🌐 *www.chateauderibourdin.com* 💳 *No credit cards* 🛏 *5 rooms* 🍽 *Free Breakfast.*

Normandie

$ | **HOTEL** | Erected in the 19th century, this rather grand, vine-covered mansion is close to the center of Auxerre, just a short walk from the cathedral. **Pros:** free public parking opposite hotel; helpful staff; on-site billiards room, gym, and garage. **Cons:** not in town center; guest rooms lack charm; the rooms at the front look out onto the busy boulevard. [$] *Rooms from: €89* ✉ *41 bd. Vauban* ☎ *03–86–52–57–80* 🌐 *www.hotelnormandie.fr* 🛏 *47 rooms* 🍴 *No meals.*

Chablis

16 km (10 miles) east of Auxerre.

The pretty village of Chablis is poised amid the hillside vineyards that produce its famous white wine on the banks of the River Serein and protected by the massive, round, turreted towers of the Porte Noël gateway. Although in America "Chablis" has become a generic name for cheap white wine, it's not so in France: here it's a bone-dry, slightly acacia-tasting wine of tremendous character, with the Premier Cru and Grand Cru wines standing head to head with the best French whites. Prices in the local shops tend to be inflated, so your best bet is to buy directly from a vineyard; keep in mind that most are closed Sunday. The town's tourist office will provide information on nearby cellars where you can take tours, enjoy tastings, and learn all you need to know about the region's illustrious wine tradition.

GETTING HERE AND AROUND

Chablis is a 30-minute car ride from Auxerre; if you don't have your own transport, a cab ride costs around €45.

VISITOR INFORMATION Chablis Tourist Office ✉ *Rue du Maréchal de Lattre de Tassigny* ☎ *03–86–42–80–80* 🌐 *www.escale-chablis.fr.*

TOURS

Chablis Vititours

SPECIAL-INTEREST | Personalized wine-theme excursions for two to six people are offered by Chablis Vititours. Choose a half-day vineyards tour followed by a cellar visit and tasting opportunity, or a 90-minute outing that includes a glass of wine. Transportation is by air-conditioned minibus. ✉ *Chablis* ☎ *06–11–47–82–98* 🌐 *www.chablis-vititours.fr* 🎫 *From €25.*

Hotels

Hostellerie des Clos

$ | **HOTEL** | Rooms at this moderately priced inn are simply, yet smartly, decorated; most people, however, come for the cooking, which is some of the best in the region. **Pros:** rooms in the main building are large and well-appointed; stellar food; great location. **Cons:** older rooms are a bit small; bathrooms in lower-grade lodgings have showers only; guest rooms lack character. [$] *Rooms from: €115* ✉ *18 rue Jules-Rathier* ☎ *03–86–42–10–63* 🌐 *www.hostellerie-des-clos.fr* 🛏 *36 rooms* 🍴 *No meals.*

Hôtel du Vieux Moulin

$$ | **HOTEL** | Understated chic meets 18th-century authenticity at this boutique-style hotel in a converted water mill. **Pros:** central location; suites have two bathrooms; excellent buffet breakfast. **Cons:** some rooms lack tubs; poor soundproofing; reception staff are only around in the mornings so arrangements need to be made if you arrive later. [$] *Rooms from: €145* ✉ *18 rue des Moulins* ☎ *03–86–42–47–30* 🌐 *www.larochewines.com* 🛏 *7 rooms* 🍴 *No meals.*

Tanlay

26 km (16 miles) east of Chablis.

Built along the banks of the Canal de Bourgogne, Tanlay is a sleepy village that's best known for the Renaissance-style château that sits slap-bang in the center of it. A stopover for cruise boats, the tree-lined banks of the canal are also a pleasant place to stroll.

GETTING HERE AND AROUND

An hourly train service runs from Auxerre to Tonnerre; the journey time is just less than an hour (€10).

Sights

★ Château de Tanlay

CASTLE/PALACE | Unlike most aristocrats who heeded the royal summons to live at Versailles and fled the countryside, the Marquis and Marquise de Tanlay opted to live here among their village retainers. As a result, the Château de Tanlay, built around 1550, never fell into neglect and is a masterpiece of early French Baroque. Spectacularly adorned with rusticated obelisks, pagoda-like towers, the finest in French Classicist ornamentation, and a "grand canal," the château is centered around a typical cour d'honneur. Inside, the Hall of Caesars vestibule, framed by wrought-iron railings, leads to a wood-panel salon and dining room filled with period furniture. A graceful staircase climbs to the second floor, which has the showstopper: a gigantic gallery frescoed in Italianate trompe-l'oeil. A small room in the tower above was used as a secret meeting place by Huguenot Protestants during the 1562–98 Wars of Religion; note the cupola with its fresco of scantily clad 16th-century religious personalities. ⊠ Tanlay ☎ 03–86–75–70–61 ⊕ www. chateaudetanlay.fr ☜ €10 ⊙ Closed Tues. and mid-Nov.–early Apr.

Ancy-le-Franc

14 km (9 miles) southeast of Tanlay.

It may be strange to find a textbook example of the Italian Renaissance in Ancy-le-Franc, but in mid-16th-century France the court had taken up this import as the latest rage. So, quick to follow the fashion and gain kingly favor, the Comte de Tonnerre decided to create a family seat using all the artists François I (1515–47) had summoned from Italy to his court at Fontainebleau.

GETTING HERE AND AROUND
An hourly train service runs from Auxerre to Tonnerre; the journey time is just less than an hour (€10).

Sights

★ Château d'Ancy-le-Franc

CASTLE/PALACE | Built from Sebastiano Serlio's designs, with interior blandishments by Primaticcio, the Château d'Ancy-le-Franc is an important example of Italianism, less for its plain, heavy exterior than for its sumptuous rooms and apartments, many with carved or painted walls and ceilings plus original furnishings. Niccolò dell'Abate and other court artists created the magnificent Chambre des Arts (Art Gallery) and other rooms filled with murals depicting the signs of the zodiac, the Battle of Pharsala, and the motif of Diana in Her Bath (much favored by Diane de Poitiers, sister of the Comtesse de Tonnerre). Such grandeur won the approval of no less than the Sun King, Louis XIV, who once stayed in the Salon Bleu (Blue Room). The east wing of the ground floor, which housed Diane de Poitier's apartments, has recently been restored. Highlights here include Diane's bedroom with its 16th-century murals. ⊠ 18 pl. Clermont-Tonnerre ☎ 03–86–75–14–63 ⊕ www.chateau-ancy.com ☜ From €10 ⊙ Closed Mon. and mid-Nov.–Mar.

Montbard

45 km (28 miles) southeast of Tonnerre.

Attractions in this modest town on the banks of the Brenne River include an Ursuline convent that's been converted into a Musée des Beaux-Arts and the lovely Parc Buffon. The gardens of the latter were planted on the site of an ancient château by Georges-Louis Leclerc de Buffon (the Count of Buffon), an important scientist and naturalist who influenced Charles Darwin. Just outside town, the work of another man—St-Bernard—draws visitors to the 12th-century Abbaye de Fontenay.

GETTING HERE AND AROUND
Frequent daily TER trains run to Montbard direct from Dijon (€15), and TGV service from Paris's Gare de Lyon is offered four times a day (€47–€94). Abbaye de Fontenay—in Marmagne, a mere 6 km (3 miles) away—is easily reached by car; if you don't have your own, cab fare is about €15. Rental bikes are also available through the Montbard tourist office.

VISITOR INFORMATION Montbard Tourist Office ✉ *Pl. de la Gare, Montbard* ☎ *03–80–92–53–81* ⊕ *www.ot-montbard.fr.*

 ## Sights

★ Abbaye de Fontenay
RELIGIOUS SITE | The best-preserved of the Cistercian abbeys, the Abbaye de Fontenay was founded in 1118 by St-Bernard. The same Cistercian criteria applied to Fontenay as to Pontigny: no-frills architecture and an isolated site—the spot was especially remote, for it had been decreed that these monasteries could not be established anywhere near "cities, feudal manors, or villages." The monks were required to live a completely self-sufficient existence, with no contact whatsoever with the outside world. By the end of the 12th century the buildings were finished, and the abbey's community grew to some 300 monks. Under the protection of Pope Gregory IX and Hughes IV, duke of Burgundy, the monastery soon controlled huge land holdings, vineyards, and timberlands. It prospered until the 16th century, when religious wars and administrative mayhem hastened its decline. Dissolved during the French Revolution, the abbey was used as a paper factory until 1906. Fortunately, the historic buildings emerged unscathed. The abbey is surrounded by extensive, immaculately tended gardens dotted with the fountains that gave it its name. The church's solemn interior is lightened by windows in the facade and by a double row of three narrow windows, representing the Trinity, in the choir. A staircase in the south transept leads to the wooden-roof dormitory (spare a thought for the bleary-eyed monks, obliged to stagger down for services in the dead of night). The chapter house, flanked by a majestic arcade, and the scriptorium, where monks worked on their manuscripts, lead off from the adjoining cloisters. ✉ *6 km (3 miles) from Montbard TGV station, Marmagne* ☎ *03–80–92–15–00* ⊕ *www.abbayedefontenay.com* 💶 *€10.*

Vézelay

48 km (30 miles) west of Abbaye de Fontenay.

In the 11th and 12th centuries Vézelay was one of the most important places of pilgrimage in the Christian world. Today the hilltop village is picturesque and somewhat isolated. Its one main street, Rue St-Étienne, climbs steeply and stirringly to the summit and its medieval basilica, world famous for its Romanesque sculpture. In summer you have to leave your car at the bottom and walk up. Off-season you can drive up and look for parking in the square.

In addition to the artistic treasures of Basilique Ste-Madeleine, Vézelay has other Romanesque-era delights. Hiding below its narrow *ruelles* (small streets) are several medieval cellars that once sheltered pilgrims. Sections of several houses have arches and columns dating to the 12th and 13th centuries: don't miss the hostelry across from the tourist office and, next to it, the house where Louis VII, Eleanor of Aquitaine, and the king's religious supremo, Abbé Suger, stayed when they came to hear St-Bernard preach the Second Crusade in 1146.

GETTING HERE AND AROUND

To reach Vézelay, you can take a TER train to Sermizelles from Paris's Gare de Bercy (2 hrs 45 mins, €35); the remaining 10 km (6 miles) into town is covered by a shuttle bus twice daily (€5).

VISITOR INFORMATION Vézelay Tourist Office ⊠ *12 rue St-Étienne* ☏ *03–86–33–23–69* ⊕ *www.vezelaytourisme.com.*

Sights

★ Basilique Ste-Madeleine

RELIGIOUS SITE | In the 11th and 12th centuries, the celebrated Basilique Ste-Madeleine was one of the focal points of Christendom. Pilgrims poured in to see the relics of St-Mary Magdalene (in the crypt) before setting off on the great trek to the shrine of St-James at Santiago de Compostela, in northwest Spain. Several pivotal church declarations of the Middle Ages were made from here, including St-Bernard's preaching of the Second Crusade (which attracted a huge French following) and Thomas à Becket's excommunication of English king Henry II. By the mid-13th century the authenticity of St-Mary's relics was in doubt; others had been discovered in Provence. The basilica's decline continued until the French Revolution, when the basilica and adjoining monastery buildings were sold by the state. Only the basilica, cloister, and dormitory escaped demolition, and were falling into ruin when ace restorer Viollet-le-Duc, sent by his mentor Prosper Merimée, rode to the rescue in 1840 (he also restored the cathedrals of Laon and Amiens and Paris's Notre-Dame).

Today the UNESCO-listed basilica has recaptured much of its glory and is considered to be one of France's most prestigious Romanesque showcases. The exterior tympanum was redone by Viollet-le-Duc (have a look at the eroded original as you exit the cloister), but the narthex (circa 1150) is a Romanesque masterpiece. Note the interwoven zodiac signs and depictions of seasonal crafts along its rim, similar to those at both Troyes and Autun. The pilgrims' route around the building is indicated by the majestic flowers, which metamorphose into full-blown blooms, over the left-hand entrance on the right; an annual procession is still held on July 22. The basilica's exterior is best seen from the leafy terrace to the right of the facade. Opposite, a vast, verdant panorama encompasses vines, lush valleys, and rolling hills. In the foreground is the Flamboyant Gothic spire of St-Père-sous-Vézelay, a tiny village 3 km (2 miles) away. ⊠ *Pl. de la Basilique* ☏ *03–86–33–39–50* ⊕ *www.basiliquede-vezelay.org* 🍴 *Guided tour by donation (phone for reservations).*

Château de Bazoches

MILITARY SITE | The former home of Sébastien de Vauban is just outside Vézelay in the small town of Bazoches-du-Morvan. Built during the 12th century in the stolid form of a trapezium with four towers and a keep, it was bought by Vauban in 1675 with the money Louis XIV awarded him for devising the parallel trenches successfully used in the siege of Maastricht. He transformed Château de Bazoches into a fortress and created many of his military engineering designs here. Vauban is considered the "father of civil engineering," and his innovations influenced innumerable forts throughout France. His designs and furnishings of his day are on display. ⊠ *14 km (9 miles) south of Vézelay, Bazoches* ☏ *03–86–22–10–22* ⊕ *www.chateau-bazoches.com* 🍴 *€10* 🕑 *Closed late Nov.–early Feb.*

🍽 Restaurants

Le Bougainville

$$$ | **FRENCH** | One of the few affordable restaurants in this well-heeled town occupies an old house with a fireplace in the dining room and the requisite Burgundian color scheme of brown, yellow, and red. Philippe Guillemard presides in the kitchen, turning out regional favorites like hare stew, crayfish, escargot ragout in Chardonnay sauce, and venison with chestnuts. **Known for:** homemade dishes; friendly service; short walk away from the basilica. [$] *Average main: €30* ✉ *26 rue St-Étienne* ☎ *03–86–33–27–57* ⏲ *Closed Tues. and Wed., and mid-Nov.–mid-Feb.*

Hotels

Château de Vault de Lugny

$$$ | **HOTEL** | **FAMILY** | A bit off the beaten track, but only a short drive from Vézelay, this moated château with stellar period decor was built between the 13th and 16th centuries; its regal guest quarters are accented with high ceilings, wooden floors, open fireplaces, and toile de Jouy fabrics. **Pros:** old-style luxury; peaceful setting; great restaurant. **Cons:** car essential; pricey breakfast; closed in winter. [$] *Rooms from: €320* ✉ *11 rue du Château, 13 km (8 miles) northeast of Vézelay at Vault de Lugny* ☎ *03–86–34–07–86* 🌐 *www.lugny.fr* ⏲ *Closed Nov.–Apr.* 🛏 *14 rooms* 🍴 *No meals.*

La Cimentelle

$ | **B&B/INN** | Originally part of the Vassy cement works, this elegant 19th-century manor offers comfortable guest rooms decorated with family heirlooms; even the bathrooms are inviting (the Hippolyte Room, for instance, has an open-plan bathroom with a freestanding tub near the fireplace). **Pros:** idyllic setting; outdoor pool; good breakfast included. **Cons:** car is essential; no air-conditioning; far from urban conveniences. [$] *Rooms from: €96* ✉ *4 rue de la Cimentelle, 21 km (13 miles) northeast of Vézelay, Avallon* ☎ *03–86–31–04–85* 🌐 *www.lacimentelle.com* 🛏 *5 rooms* 🍴 *Free Breakfast.*

L'Hôtel de la Poste et du Lion d'Or

$$ | **HOTEL** | A terrace out front welcomes you to this rambling hotel, which features light, bright (if somewhat staid) rooms—most with private balconies. **Pros:** good-size rooms with balconies; great food; friendly staff. **Cons:** some rooms get street noise; parking is difficult; guest rooms lack a splash of color. [$] *Rooms from: €135* ✉ *Pl. du Champ-de-Foire* ☎ *03–73–53–03–20* 🌐 *www.hplv-vezelay.com* ⏲ *Closed Jan.–mid-Mar.* 🛏 *39 rooms* 🍴 *No meals.*

Les Glycines

$ | **HOTEL** | This typical Burgundy town house built in 1763 and now a hotel offers plenty of history and charm. **Pros:** a stone's throw from the basilica; friendly and helpful owner; thoroughly modern bathrooms. **Cons:** parking can be difficult to find; no air-conditioning; bell ringing may disturb some guests. [$] *Rooms from: €111* ✉ *33 rue St Pierre* ☎ *03–86–47–29–81* 🌐 *www.vezelay-laterrasse.com/lhotel-sy-les-glycines-a-vezelay* ⏲ *Closed Jan. and Feb.* 🛏 *13 rooms* 🍴 *No meals.*

Manoir de Val en Sel

$ | **B&B/INN** | Five classically decorated, color-coded rooms—all with private entrances and en suite bathrooms—are set in a picturesque 18th-century country residence and surround a spectacular walled flower garden that's hailed as one of the world's finest. **Pros:** gardens are a fragrant haven of calm; comfortable, spacious rooms; friendly owner. **Cons:** car essential; credit cards aren't accepted; basic bathrooms. [$] *Rooms from: €110* ✉ *1 Chemin de la Fontaine* ☎ *03–86–33–26–95* 🌐 *valensel.vezelay.free.fr* 💳 *No credit cards* ⏲ *Closed mid-Nov.–Apr.* 🛏 *5 rooms* 🍴 *Free Breakfast.*

Saulieu

48 km (30 miles) southeast of Vézelay.

Saulieu's reputation belies its size: it's renowned for good food (Rabelais, that roly-poly 16th-century man of letters, extolled its gargantuan hospitality) and for Christmas trees (a staggering million are packed and sent off from the area each year).

GETTING HERE AND AROUND

You can drive to Saulieu via the A6; otherwise, take a train to Montbard (a TGV stop), and then catch a bus into town (€1.50). Two buses also run from Beaune to Saulieu every day except Sunday, making the trip in two hours (€1.50).

 ## Sights

Basilique St-Andoche

RELIGIOUS SITE | The town's Basilique St-Andoche, one of Burgundy's finest Romanesque churches, is almost as old as that in Vézelay, though less imposing and much restored. Note the impressive Romanesque nave with 12th-century carved capitals. ⊠ *4 rue Savot* ☎ *03–80–64–07–03* ⊙ *Closed Mon. Oct.–June.*

Musée François-Pompon

MUSEUM | Beside the basilica, Musée François-Pompon is partly devoted to the work of animal-bronze sculptor Pompon (1855–1933), whose smooth, stylized creations seem contemporary but predate World War II. The museum also contains Gallo-Roman funeral stones, sacred art, and a room highlighting local gastronomic lore. ⊠ *3 pl. Dr. Roclore* ☎ *03–80–64–19–51* 💶 *€3* ⊙ *Closed Tues., Jan., and Feb.*

 ## Hotels

Hostellerie La Tour d'Auxois

$ | HOTEL | The retro, zinc-topped bar, stone floors, and log fire strike a perfect balance with the modern-day comforts of this handsome, family-run hotel that was once a convent. **Pros:** attractive budget option close to Relais Bernard Loiseau; the pool is a welcome amenity; suites have rustic charm. **Cons:** rooms facing the busy road can be noisy; decor looks a bit worn; some rooms are small. 💲 *Rooms from: €109* ⊠ *Sq. Alexandre Dumaine* ☎ *03–80–64–36–19* ⊕ *www.tourdauxois. com* ⊙ *Closed late Dec.–mid-Feb., Mon. Oct.–Apr., and Sun. Nov.–Mar.* 🛏 *29 rooms* ⊙ *No meals.*

★ Relais Bernard Loiseau

$$$ | HOTEL | At Relais Bernard Loiseau, lovely lodgings ooze rustic-chic with exposed beams, traditional red-clay tile floors, and elegantly understated furnishings. **Pros:** first-class facilities include a spa and pool; stellar food; spacious rooms. **Cons:** restaurant prices are stratospheric; restaurant closed midweek; some rooms face the busy road. 💲 *Rooms from: €265* ⊠ *2 rue d'Argentine, off D906* ☎ *03–80–90–53–53* ⊕ *www.bernard-loiseau.com* ⊙ *Closed late Jan.–Feb.* 🛏 *32 rooms* ⊙ *No meals.*

Dijon

38 km (23 miles) northeast of Châteauneuf, 315 km (195 miles) southeast of Paris.

You may never have been to Dijon but you've certainly tasted it. Many of the gastronomic specialties that originated here are known worldwide. They include snails (many now imported from the Czech Republic), mustard (although the handmade variety is becoming a lost art), and cassis (a black-currant liqueur often mixed with white wine—preferably Burgundy Aligoté—to make Kir, the popular aperitif). The city itself is also a feast for the eyes, with charming streets, chic shops, and an impressive array of medieval art. It has magnificent half-timber houses and *hôtels particuliers,* some rivaling those in Paris. There's also a striking trio of central churches, built one following the other for three distinct parishes— St-Bénigne, its facade distinguished by Gothic galleries; St-Philibert, Dijon's only Romanesque church (with Merovingian vestiges); and St-Jean, an asymmetrical building now used as a theater. On top of that, it has a tourist-friendly vibe; many travelers feel it is the perfect French community, possessing the charm of a village as well as the sophistication and liveliness you'd expect of a capital.

Dijon was a major player in the history of the region. Throughout the Middle Ages, Burgundy was a duchy that led a separate existence from the rest of France, culminating in the rule of the four "Grand Dukes of the West" between 1364 and 1477—Philippe le Hardi (the Bold), Jean sans Peur (the Fearless), Philippe le Bon (the Good), and the unfortunate Charles le Téméraire (the Foolhardy, whose defeat by French king Louis XI at Nancy spelled the end of Burgundian independence). A number of monuments date to this period, including the Palais des Ducs (Ducal Palace), now largely converted into an art museum. Luckily, Dijon's fame and fortune outlasted the dukes, and it flourished under French rule from the 17th century on. It has remained the largest city in Burgundy—and the only one with more than 150,000 inhabitants; moreover, its location, on the major European north–south trade route and within striking distance of the Swiss and German borders, has helped maintain its economic importance. Dijon continues to be a thriving cultural center as well.

GETTING HERE AND AROUND

As the administrative capital of Burgundy, Dijon has most everything a city should, including fast train service. Up to 16 TGVs come from Paris daily (90 mins, €67–€73); once here, the TER network can take you virtually anywhere within the region by rail, with frequent connections to Sens (€35), Beaune (€10), and Auxerre (€30). Right next to the Dijon Ville train station is the Gare Routière, from which the regional Mobigo bus company operates 32 routes that crisscross the Côte d'Or. For wine lovers, the No. 113 between Dijon and Beaune (€3 round-trip) has an itinerary that reads like an oenologist's wish list; the 12:30 pm bus will get you to the cellar of your choice in time for an early-afternoon tasting. Inside the city, Divia (⊕ www.divia.fr)—Dijon's public transit system—provides both regular bus and tram service (€1.40 for a one-hour pass) and a free minibus shuttle in the historic center.

VISITOR INFORMATION Dijon Tourist Office ⊠ 11 rue des Forges ☎ 08–92–70–05–58 (€0.35 per min) ⊕ www.destinationdijon.com.

The Original Grey Poupon

Dijon's legendary Maille shop at 32 rue de la Liberté (⊕ fr.maille.com), established in 1777, still sells mustard in painted ceramic pots at outrageous prices, along with a huge selection of oils, vinegars, and spices.

Sights

Cathédrale St-Bénigne
RELIGIOUS SITE | The chief glory of this comparatively austere cathedral is its atmospheric 11th-century crypt, in which a forest of pillars is surmounted by a rotunda. ⊠ Rue du Dr. Maret ⊕ www.cathedrale-dijon.fr ☜ Crypt €2.

Chartreuse de Champmol
BUILDING | All that remains of this former charter house—a half-hour walk or a 10-minute bus ride from Dijon's center and now surrounded by a psychiatric hospital—are the exuberant 15th-century church porch and the Puits de Moïse (Well of Moses), one of the greatest examples of late-medieval sculpture. The well was designed by Flemish master Claus Sluter, who also created several other masterpieces during the late 14th and early 15th centuries, including one of the tombs of the dukes of Burgundy. If you closely study Sluter's six large sculptures, you will discover the Middle Ages becoming the Renaissance right before your eyes. Representing Moses and five other prophets, they are set on

a hexagonal base in the center of a basin and remain the most compellingly realistic figures ever crafted by a medieval sculptor. ⊠ *Centre Hospitalier Spécialisé de la Chartreuse, Av. Albert 1er* ⊠ *Well of Moses €4.*

Château de Marsannay

WINERY/DISTILLERY | Situated a few kilometers south of Dijon at the beginning of the Route des Grands Crus, this domaine has vineyards that extend down to Vosne Romanée. It specializes in all three colors of Marsannay AOP (red, white, and rosé), but also produces Fixin, Gevrey-Chambertin, Vosne-Romanée, and Clos de Vougeot. Tours of its gleaming facilities (built in 1990 in traditional Burgundy style) include a visit to the cellars and three tasting options: six wines, including one Premier cru, for €13; eight wines for €18; and the high-end Prestige tasting (€29) which offers ten wines including a Grand Cru. ⊠ *2 rue des Vignes, Marsannay-la-Côte* ☎ *03–80–51–71–11* ⊕ *www.chateau-marsannay.com* ⊗ *Closed Jan., and Sun. mid-Nov.–Mar.*

Hôtel de Vogüé

BUILDING | This stately 17th-century Renaissance mansion has a characteristic red, yellow, and green Burgundian tile roof—a tradition whose disputed origins lie either with the Crusades and the adoption of Arabic tiles or with Philip the Bold's wife, Marguerite of Flanders. ⊠ *8 rue de la Chouette.*

Musée Archéologique (*Antiquities Museum*)

MUSEUM | This museum, in the former abbey buildings of the church of St-Bénigne, outlines the history of the region through archaeological finds. ⊠ *5 rue Dr. Maret* ☎ *03–80–48–83–70* ⊠ *Free* ⊗ *Closed Tues. yr-round and Mon., Thurs., and Fri. Nov.–Mar.*

Musée de la Vie Bourguignonne et d'Art Sacré (*Museum of Burgundian Traditions and Religious Art*)

MUSEUM | Housed in the former Cistercian convent, one museum here contains religious art and sculpture; the other has crafts and artifacts from Burgundy—including old storefronts saved from the streets of Dijon that have been reconstituted, in Hollywood-studio style, to form an imaginary street. ⊠ *17 rue Ste-Anne* ☎ *03–80–48–80–90* ⊠ *Free* ⊗ *Closed Tues.*

Musée Magnin

MUSEUM | In a 17th-century mansion, this museum showcases a private collection of original furnishings and paintings from the 16th to the 19th century. ⊠ *4 rue des Bons-Enfants* ☎ *03–80–67–11–10* ⊕ *www.musee-magnin.fr* ⊠ *€4 (free 1st Sun. of month)* ⊗ *Closed Mon.*

Muséum Jardin des Sciences de l'Arquebuse (*Natural History Museum*)

MUSEUM | The natural history museum in the **Pavillon de L'Arquebuse** focuses on current issues such as sustainable development. It is part of an impressive botanical garden, the **Jardin de l'Arquebuse**, which showcases local and exotic plant life. Strolling among the wide variety of trees and tropical flowers provides a pleasant break from sightseeing. ⊠ *1 av. Albert 1er* ☎ *03–80–48–82–00 for museum* ⊠ *Free* ⊗ *Museum closed Tues.*

Notre-Dame

RELIGIOUS SITE | One of the city's oldest churches, Notre-Dame stands out with spindlelike towers, delicate arches gracing its facade, and 13th-century stained glass. Note the windows in the north transept tracing the lives of five saints, as well as the 11th-century Byzantine linden-wood Black Virgin. Local tradition has it that stroking the small owl sculpted on the outside wall of the adjoining chapel with your left hand grants you a wish. ⊠ *Rue de la Préfecture* ☎ *03–45–34–27–61.*

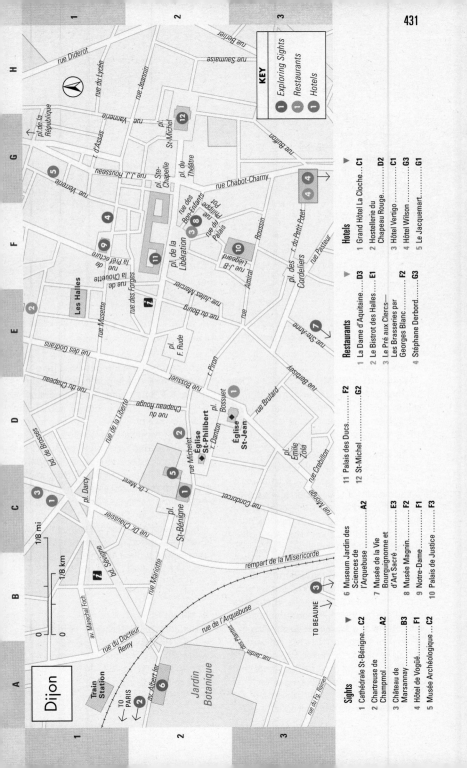

Dijon

KEY

- **1** Exploring Sights
- **1** Restaurants
- **1** Hotels

1/8 mi

1/8 km

Sights ▶

1 Cathédrale St-Bénigne... **C2**
2 Chartreuse de Champmol... **A2**
3 Château de Marsannay... **B3**
4 Hôtel de Vogüé... **F1**
5 Musée Archéologique... **C2**
6 Museum Jardin des Sciences de l'Arquebuse... **A2**
7 Musée de la Vie Bourguignonne et d'Art Sacré... **E3**
8 Musée Magnin... **F2**
9 Notre-Dame... **F1**
10 Palais de Justice... **F3**
11 Palais des Ducs... **F2**
12 St-Michel... **G2**

Restaurants ▶

1 La Dame d'Aquitaine... **D3**
2 Le Bistrot des Halles... **E1**
3 Le Pré aux Clercs—Les Brasseries par Georges Blanc... **F2**
4 Stéphane Derbord... **G3**

Hotels ▶

1 Grand Hôtel La Cloche... **C1**
2 Hostellerie du Chapeau Rouge... **D2**
3 Hôtel Vertigo... **C1**
4 Hôtel Wilson... **G3**
5 Le Jacquemart... **G1**

Train Station

TO PARIS

TO BEAUNE

Jardin Botanique

Les Halles

Église St-Philibert

Église St-Jean

Palais des Ducs' white-on-white exterior projects a regal elegance over the Cours de Flore.

Palais de Justice

GOVERNMENT BUILDING | The meeting place for the old regional Parliament of Burgundy serves as a reminder that Louis XI incorporated the province into France in the late 15th century. ⊠ *Rue du Palais*.

★ Palais des Ducs (*Ducal Palace*)

CASTLE/PALACE | The elegant, classical exterior of this former palace can best be admired from half-moon Place de la Libération and the cour d'honneur. The kitchens (circa 1450), with their six huge fireplaces and (for their time) state-of-the-art aeration funnel in the ceiling, catch the eye, as does the 15th-century Salle des Gardes (Guard Room), with its richly carved and colored tombs and late-14th-century altarpieces. The palace now houses one of France's major art museums, the **Musée des Beaux-Arts** (Fine Arts Museum). The magnificent tombs sculpted for dukes Philip the Bold and his son John the Fearless (note their dramatically moving mourners, hidden in shrouds) are just two highlights of a rich collection of medieval objects and Renaissance furniture gathered here as testimony to Marguerite of Flanders (Philip the Bold's wife). She brought to Burgundy not only her dowry, namely the rich province of Flanders, but also a host of distinguished artists—including Rogier van der Weyden, Jan van Eyck, and Claus Sluter. Their artistic legacy can be seen here, as well as at several of Burgundy's other museums and monuments. Among the paintings are works by Italian old masters and French 19th-century artists, such as Théodore Géricault and Gustave Courbet, plus their Impressionist successors, notably Édouard Manet and Claude Monet. ⊠ *Cours de Bar* ☎ *03–80–74–52–09* ⊕ *beaux-arts.dijon.fr* 🎫 *Free* ⊗ *Closed Tues.*

St-Michel

RELIGIOUS SITE | This church, with its chunky Renaissance facade, fast-forwards 300 years from Notre-Dame. ⊠ *Pl. St-Michel* ☎ *03–80–63–17–80* ⊕ *www.saint-michel-dijon.com*.

Restaurants

As a culinary capital of France, Dijon has many superb restaurants, with three areas popular for casual dining: Place Darcy (a square catering to all tastes and budgets), Place Émile-Zola, and the old market (Les Halles), along Rue Bannelier.

La Dame d'Aquitaine

$$$$ | MODERN FRENCH | In the handsome stone cellar of a sumptuous 17th-century mansion, La Dame d'Aquitaine has long been a gastronomic mainstay on the Dijonaise scene. The talented owners prepare dishes with modern spins on French classics such as oysters, foie gras, and wild boar (in season). **Known for:** fixed-price menu with add-ons that allow you to create your own menu; tournedos "Rossini" topped with warm foie gras; historic, romantic dining room. $ *Average main: €37* ✉ *23 pl. Bossuet* ☎ *03–80–30–45–65* ⊕ *www.ladamedaquitaine.fr* ☾ *Closed Sun. No lunch Mon.–Wed.*

Le Bistrot des Halles

$$ | BISTRO | This eatery facing Les Halles marketplace caters to trendy locals, who are tempted by imaginative bistro dishes and beautifully presented desserts. Pull up a seat on the sidewalk or dine inside, where glass-topped wine casks serve as tables. **Known for:** good choice of wines by the glass; wide-ranging menu with Mediterranean, Asian, and Burgundy options; beef burger with Époisse cheese, tartare of Charolais beef, and tatin-style French toast. $ *Average main: €17* ✉ *10 rue Bannelier* ☎ *03–80–35–45–07* ☾ *Closed Sun. and Mon.*

Le Pré aux Clercs—Les Brasseries par Georges Blanc

$$$ | FRENCH | A informal offshoot of Georges Blanc, this crowded brasserie is headed by chef Jean-Bruno Gosse, who is well-versed in preparing inspired versions of French classics. The wine list features the region's best producers, and there is a good choice of half bottles too. **Known for:** outdoor tables on the square;

chalkboard daily specials; fixed-price lunchtime and evening menus. $ *Average main: €25* ✉ *13 pl. de la Libération* ☎ *03–80–38–05–05* ⊕ *www.lepreaux-clercs.fr.*

Stéphane Derbord

$$$$ | FRENCH | The talented Stéphane Derbord, the city's rising gastronomic star, ensures that dining in the restaurant that bears his name is an elegantly refined affair. Tempting prix-fixe menus range from a three-course market-driven "surprise" lunch to a top-end dinner extravaganza where the dishes are served family-style. **Known for:** dazzling desserts, including classic Grand Marnier soufflé; sleek service that's more friendly than formal; good selection of menus, including a gourmet children's menu. $ *Average main: €45* ✉ *10 pl. Wilson* ☎ *03–80–67–74–64* ⊕ *www.restaurant-stephanederbord.fr* ☾ *Closed Sun. and Mon., and early Jan., last wk in Feb., and 1st 2 wks in Aug.*

Hotels

Grand Hôtel La Cloche

$$ | HOTEL | At this luxurious, 19th-century grand hotel, ask for one of the large, plush guest rooms overlooking the tiny, tranquil back garden and its reflecting pool. **Pros:** very comfortable beds; attentive staff; central location. **Cons:** bad soundproofing; some rooms lack space; uneven service. $ *Rooms from: €225* ✉ *14 pl. Darcy* ☎ *03–80–30–12–32* ⊕ *www.hotel-lacloche.fr* ⇥ *88 rooms* ⊠ *No meals.*

Hostellerie du Chapeau Rouge

$$ | HOTEL | Colorful, well-appointed rooms display charm and designer chic at the "Red Hat," where the pleasant surroundings are complemented by the fine fare at William Frachot's on-site restaurant. **Pros:** great fine dining restaurant; central location; wellness center with hammam, sauna, and (pricey) massages. **Cons:** breakfast is extra; staff

can be gruff; some rooms are small for the price. $ *Rooms from: €145* ✉ *5 rue Michelet* ☎ *03–80–50–88–88* ⊕ *www. chapeau-rouge.fr* ⤴ *29 rooms* ⦿ *No meals.*

Hôtel Vertigo

$$ | HOTEL | This city-center boutique hotel is located in a converted Haussmann building, where a young clientele is lured by guest rooms decorated in a brash black-and-white color scheme. **Pros:** most of the major sites are within walking distance; can rent electric bikes to explore the city; basement spa and pool. **Cons:** only one small elevator for all floors; breakfast room can fill up quickly on weekends; open-plan bathrooms don't allow for much privacy. $ *Rooms from: €145* ✉ *3 rue Devosge* ☎ *03–80–40–40–40* ⊕ *www.vertigohoteldijon.com* ⤴ *42 rooms* ⦿ *No meals.*

Hôtel Wilson

$ | HOTEL | This hotel's "bones" are 17th century, as it is a fetching timber-frame post house; inside, the guest rooms are accented with wooden beams and rustic furniture. **Pros:** central location; near Stéphane Derbord's noted restaurant; historic setting. **Cons:** some rooms are small and claustrophobic; rooms in front get street noise; no air-conditioning. $ *Rooms from: €90* ✉ *Pl. Wilson* ☎ *03–80–66–82–50* ⊕ *www.wilson-hotel. com* ⤴ *27 rooms* ⦿ *No meals.*

Le Jacquemart

$ | HOTEL | In an 18th-century building in Old Dijon surrounded by antiques shops, a steep staircase leads up to high-ceilinged guest rooms of variable comfort, decorated with rustic furniture. **Pros:** cheerful; good value; nice bathrooms. **Cons:** far from the train station; no elevator or air-conditioning; some rooms don't have private bathrooms. $ *Rooms from: €65* ✉ *32 rue Verrerie* ☎ *03–80–60–09–60* ⊕ *www.hotel-lejacquemart.fr* ⤴ *33 rooms* ⦿ *No meals.*

Nightlife

La Pharmacy

BARS/PUBS | Located in the center of town, this wine bar has a superb selection of Burgundy wine and champagne. Sip your favorite cru alongside a platter of charcuterie or cheese. ✉ *9 rue de la Chouette* ☎ *03–80–48–26–11.*

Le Chat Noir

DANCE CLUBS | The popular "Black Cat" disco draws a huge crowd of dedicated groovers. Styles are eclectic and prices are high: €25 for a vodka and orange. Expect to pay a €6–€15 cover charge. ✉ *20 av. Garibaldi* ☎ *03–80–73–39–57* ⊕ *www.lechatnoir.fr/dijon.*

Performing Arts

Bell-Ringing Festival

FESTIVALS | During the Pentecost Bell-Ringing Festival, St-Bénigne's bells chime and chime. ✉ *Rue du Dr. Maret.*

Festival International de Musiques et Danses Populaires (*Fêtes de la Vigne*)

FESTIVALS | The city stages the Festival International de Musiques et Danses Populaires at the end of August in even-number years. ✉ *Dijon* ⊕ *www. fetesdelavigne.org.*

International Gastronomy Fair

FESTIVALS | Dijon plays host to the International Gastronomy Fair the first two weeks in November. Each year a different country is invited to show off its produce and cuisine. ✉ *Dijon* ⊕ *www.foirededijon. com.*

🛍 Shopping

Dr. Wine

WINE/SPIRITS | This closet-size wine shop has a mind-boggling range of around 600 different wines, mainly from Burgundy. The knowledgeable staff are at hand to help you to pick out a bottle or two. There is also a Dr. Wine bar just around the corner that offers a nice selection of wines by the glass. ✉ *5 pl. Notre Dame* ☎ *03–80–53–35–16* ⊕ *www.drwine.fr.*

Les Halles
LOCAL SPECIALTIES | This 19th-century glass-and-metal-covered market was designed by Dijon-born Gustave Eiffel. It buzzes with locals every Tuesday, Thursday, Friday, and Saturday. On Saturday, it spills out onto the neighboring streets. Food is the highlight, including local Charolais beef, Bresse chicken, jambon persillé, and lots of regional cheeses. The outside stalls are piled high with clothes, hats, and handbags. ✉ *Rue Odebert.*

Mulot et Petitjean
FOOD/CANDY | Don't miss a visit to the venerable Mulot et Petitjean, the spice-cake specialists founded in 1796, on Place Bossuet. The shop is remarkable not only for its edible wares, but also for its historic, red-timber facade. ✉ *13 pl. Bossuet* ☎ *03–80–30–07–10* ⊕ *www.mulotpetitjean.fr.*

Clos de Vougeot

16 km (10 miles) south of Dijon.

The reason to come to Vougeot is to see its *grange viticole* (wine-making barn) surrounded by its famous vineyard—a symbolic spot for all Burgundy aficionados.

GETTING HERE AND AROUND
Mobigo's Bus No. 113 connects Dijon to Vougeot (40 mins, €1.50); from there it's about a 10-minute walk from the town center to the château.

Sights

Abbaye de Cîteaux
RELIGIOUS SITE | Robert de Molesmes founded the austere Cistercian order at this abbey near Clos de Vougeot in 1098, and the complex has housed monks ever since. Destroyed and rebuilt over the centuries, it is, understandably, a mix of styles and epochs: 13th-century cloisters, a 16th-century library, and a large, imposing 18th-century main building from an eclectic ensemble. From D996, follow signs pointing the way along a short country road that breaks off from the road to Château de Gilly, a four-star hotel. Call ahead for a guided tour. ✉ *St-Nicolas-lès-Cîteaux, off D996, Vougeot* ☎ *03–80–61–32–58* ⊕ *www.citeaux-abbaye.com* 🎫 *Tour €8* ⊙ *No tours Mon., Nov.–Apr., and Tues. in May, June, and Oct.*

★ Château du Clos de Vougeot
WINERY/DISTILLERY | Although it wasn't completed until the Renaissance, construction on Château du Clos de Vougeot was actually begun in the 12th century by Cistercian monks from neighboring Cîteaux who needed wine for Mass and wanted to make a diplomatic offering. It's best known as the seat of Burgundy's elite company of wine lovers, the Confrérie des Chevaliers du Tastevin, who gather here in November at the start of an annual three-day festival, Les Trois Glorieuses. You can admire the château's cellars, where ceremonies are held, and ogle the huge 13th-century grape presses, marvels of medieval engineering. There are regular photo exhibitions and concerts. A 45-minute guided tour (€10) leaves at 11:30 and 2:30 daily. ✉ *Clos de Vougeot* ☎ *03–80–62–86–09* ⊕ *www.closdevougeot.fr* 🎫 *€8.*

🍽 Restaurants

Restaurant Christian Quenel
$$$$ | **FRENCH** | **FAMILY** | On the main square of Flagey-Echézeaux, a stellar wine village lying a few kilometers southeast of Clos de Vougeot, this inconspicuous culinary haven fills up with locals out for a quiet, French-inspired terroir-driven meal. Expect creations such as langoustines with butternut squash and a beetroot dressing, or *joues de boeuf* (beef cheeks) with a Pinot Noir sauce. **Known for:** classic French cuisine; location on the church square in an authentic

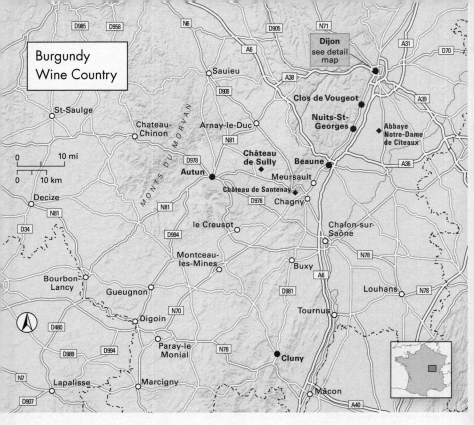

Burgundy
Wine Country

0   10 mi

0   10 km

MONTS DU MORVAN

---

wine village; vast selection of wines. $ *Average main: €40* ✉ *12 pl. de l'Eglise, 3½ km (2 miles) southeast of Clos de Vougeot* ☎ *03–80–62–88–10* ⏱ *Closed Wed. No dinner Sun.*

Hotels

Château de Gilly

$$ | **HOTEL** | Considered by some to be an obligatory stop on their tour of Burgundy's vineyards, this château retains glorious vestiges of bygone days: painted ceilings, a gigantic vaulted crypt-cellar (now the dining room), suits of armor, and (some) guest rooms with magnificent beamed ceilings and lovely views. **Pros:** great location for visiting the local wineries; good restaurant; wonderful grounds. **Cons:** pricey; lots of tourists; the bathrooms are classic, but not modern. $ *Rooms from: €199* ✉ *Gilly-lès-Cîteaux,*

Vougeot ☎ *03–80–62–89–98* ⏍ *www. grandesetapes.fr* ➴ *48 rooms* ⏍⏍ *No meals.*

Château de Saulon

$$ | **HOTEL** | The impeccably restored Château de Saulon blends late 18th-century authenticity with 21st-century comfort. **Pros:** fantastic restaurant; heated outdoor pool; quality buffet breakfast. **Cons:** frequently hosts wedding parties on the grounds; elevator doesn't reach the top floor; few rooms have tubs. $ *Rooms from: €169* ✉ *67 rue de Dijon, Saulon la Rue, Vougeot* ✛ *12 km (7½ miles) northeast of Clos de Vougeot* ☎ *03–80–79–25–25* ⏍ *www.chateau-saulon.com* ⏱ *Closed mid-Feb.–late Mar.* ➴ *32 rooms* ⏍⏍ *No meals.*

Nuits-St-Georges

21 km (13 miles) south of Dijon, 5 km (3 miles) south of Clos de Vougeot.

Wine has been made in Nuits-St-Georges since Roman times; its "dry, tonic, and generous qualities" were recommended to Louis XIV for medicinal use. But this is also the heart of currant country, where crops yield the wonderfully delicious ingredient known as cassis (the signature flavor in the famous Kir cocktail).

GETTING HERE AND AROUND
Mobigo's Bus No. 113 makes the trip from Dijon (47 mins, €1.50) and Beaune (26 mins, €1.50) to Nuits-St-Georges daily. TER train service is also available.

VISITOR INFORMATION Nuits-St-Georges Tourist Office ⌧ *3 rue Sonoys* ☎ *03–80–62–11–17* ⊕ *www.gevreynuitstourisme.com.*

Sights

Cassissium
WINERY/DISTILLERY | Inside the Cassissium's sparkling glass-and-steel building, the world of cassis is explored through films and interactive displays. A 90-minute tour of Védrenne's liqueur production ends (of course!) with a cassis tasting. ⌧ *8 passage Montgolfier* ☎ *03–80–62–49–70* ⊕ *www.cassissium.fr* 🏷 *€10* 🕐 *Closed Mon. and Sun. mid-Nov.–Mar.*

La Maison Jean-Claude Boisset–Les Ursulines.
WINERY/DISTILLERY | Within walking distance of the town center, this swanky winery is in an ancient convent dating from the 17th century. The Boisset family currently own the 108 acres of Domaine de la Vougeraie vineyards situated on the slopes of the Côtes de Nuits and Côte de Beaune. The vines are all cultivated using biodynamic methods. A cellar visit (€32, reservations only) starts with a short film explaining how the convent cellars were converted into today's winery; the guide then goes on to explain the concept of biodynamic wine production. The tour ends with a tasting of five wines: two white and three red. ⌧ *Chemin des Plateaux* ☎ *03–80–62–61–61* ⊕ *www.jeanclaudeboisset.com* 🕐 *Closed Sun. Oct.–Apr.*

 Restaurants

La Cabotte
$$$ | BISTRO | If you're tired of hearty Burgundian classics, just follow savvy locals to this stylish little restaurant on the town's main street. Its creative menus include market-inspired dishes. **Known for:** wine list that showcases Burgundy and Rhône wines; excellent value multicourse meals; small, intimate dining room. 💲 *Average main: €25* ⌧ *24 Grand Rue* ☎ *03–80–61–20–77* ⊕ *www.lacabotte.fr* 🕐 *Closed Sun. yr-round, Mon. May–Aug., and 2 wks in Feb.*

La Toute Petite Auberge
$$$ | BISTRO | Vosne-Romanée, the greatest wine village on the côte, also entices with one of the most charming restaurants in Burgundy. The menu changes four times a year and is replete with succulent local dishes (picture a generous mound of frogs' legs, farm-reared capon, andouillette from Chablis, coq au vin, and crème brûlée). **Known for:** reasonable prices; top-notch wine list; rustic-chic dining room. 💲 *Average main: €27* ⌧ *On RD 974, 2 km (1 mile) north of Nuits-St-Georges, Vosne-Romanée* ☎ *03–80–61–02–03* ⊕ *www.la-toute-petite-auberge.fr* 🕐 *Closed Wed. No dinner Tues.*

Hotels

La Gentilhommière
$ | HOTEL | FAMILY | Lush grounds, an outdoor pool complex, and a countryside location are the main lures at this peaceful property. **Pros:** peaceful setting; easy to park; cheery hosts. **Cons:** a car is essential; standard rooms get some noise from guests walking by; the guest

rooms aren't in the same building as the breakfast room. $ *Rooms from: €118* ✉ *13 Vallée de la Serrée, 3 km (2 miles) west of Nuits-St-Georges* ☎ *03–80–61–12–06* ⊕ *www.lagentilhommiere.fr* ⇛ *31 rooms* ⦿ *No meals.*

Le Richebourg

$$ | **HOTEL** | Just north of town, Le Richebourg looks so ordinary from the outside that you wouldn't give it a second glance as you drive by on the busy thoroughfare through Vosne-Romanée, but the good-size guest rooms inside are super stylish. **Pros:** centrally located for visiting area vineyards; some rooms on the garden side have a private terrace; indoor pool has views over the Burgundy countryside. **Cons:** rooms on road side can be noisy; service in the restaurant and bar is erratic; exterior is dull. $ *Rooms from: €189* ✉ *Ruelle du Pont, 2 km (1 mile) north of Nuits-St-Georges, Vosne-Romanée* ☎ *03–80–61–59–59* ⊕ *www.hotel-lerichebourg.com* ⇛ *24 rooms* ⦿ *No meals.*

 ## Performing Arts

Street Art on the Roc Festival - La Karrière

FESTIVALS | A disused stone quarry provides a magical backdrop to this open-air art and music festival. Rock, jazz, and classical music concerts, plays, cinema screenings, and art exhibitions take place every year over a week in late August. ✉ *RD 35, Villars-Fontaine* ✛ *3 km (2 miles) from Nuits St-Georges* ☎ *06–30–25–42–90* ⊕ *www.villart.fr.*

Beaune

19 km (12 miles) south of Nuits-St-Georges, 40 km (25 miles) south of Dijon, 315 km (197 miles) southeast of Paris.

Beaune is sometimes considered the wine capital of Burgundy because it is at the heart of the region's vineyards, with the Côte de Nuits to the north and the Côte de Beaune to the south. It's also a popular spot for festivals, with top draws including the International Festival of Baroque Opera in July, Jazz O'Verre in September, and the wine-themed Les Trois Glorieuses in November. That combination makes Beaune one of Burgundy's most visited communities. Despite the hordes, however, it remains a very attractive provincial town, teeming with art aboveground and wine barrels down below.

GETTING HERE AND AROUND

Seventeen TGVs leave Paris's Gare de Lyon daily for Beaune, with changes at Dijon, and there are five direct TER services from Paris Bercy. Travel times vary from 2 hours, 13 minutes to 4 hours, depending on transfers; fares range from €35 on the slower TER trains to €98.50 on the TGV. Beaune is 20 minutes from Dijon (€10) and gets plenty of train traffic from the through line to Lyon (€27.20). For those heading farther north, trains to Auxerre (€35), via Laroche Migennes, and a direct service to Sens (€35) are available. Mobigo buses, departing from the SNCF station, run to Dijon via Nuits-St-Georges (No. 113, the wine-lovers line), and to Saulieu (No. 72, no service Sun.).

VISITOR INFORMATION Beaune Tourist Office ✉ *Porte Marie de Bourgogne, 6 bd. Perpreuil* ☎ *03–80–26–21–30* ⊕ *www.beaune-tourisme.fr.*

 ## Sights

Bouchard Père et Fils Château de Beaune

WINERY/DISTILLERY | Bouchard is one of the major domaines and négociants in Beaune. Its unparalleled legacy of 50,000 bottles from the Côte de Beaune and Côte de Nuits appellations includes a unique collection of rare vintages dating back to the 19th century. The guided visit takes you through the 15th-century cellars and ends with a tasting of five red and three white wines.

Showing off its colorfully patterned roof tiles, medieval courtyard, and Rogier van der Weyden altarpiece, the Hôtel-Dieu is Beaune's most eye-popping edifice.

✉ *Caveau Bouchard Père & Fils, 15 rue du Château* ☎ *03–80–24–80–45* ⊕ *www. bouchard-pereetfils.com* 💶 *€49* 🕑 *No guided tours Sun. and Mon.*

Château de Meursault

WINERY/DISTILLERY | A miraculous Meursault has been produced at this elegant spot since the 7th century. Walk up the Allée des Maronniers through the vines to the château's cour d'honneur. Visits to cellars dating from the 14th and 16th centuries and an art gallery are part of the guided tour, which includes a sommelier-aided tasting of six wines (€24). More elaborate theme-based guided tours (€35) are available by appointment. ✉ *Château de Meursault, Rue du Moulin Foulot, Meursault* ☎ *03–80–26–22–75* ⊕ *www.chateau-meursault.com* 🕑 *Closed Dec., Jan., and Mon. and Tues. in Feb. and Mar.*

Château de Santenay

WINERY/DISTILLERY | Philippe le Hardi, the son of the king of France, was the illustrious owner of this majestic 9th- to 16th-century castle. The surrounding estate—one of the largest in Burgundy—has 237 acres of vines, and a visit to it culminates with a tasting of four wines. The award-wining St-Aubin "En Vesvau," matured and aged in wooden casks, is a must-try, as is the Château Philippe le Hardi AOP Aloxe-Corton "Les Brunettes et Planchots." The tour and wine tasting (€8) is organized three times a day at 10:30, 2, and 4 (reservations recommended). English is spoken. ✉ *1 rue du Château, Santenay* ☎ *03–80–20–61–87* ⊕ *www.chateau-de-santenay.com* 🕑 *Closed Dec.–Mar.*

Collégiale Notre-Dame

RELIGIOUS SITE | A series of tapestries relating the life of the Virgin hangs in Beaune's main church, the 12th-century Romanesque Collégiale Notre-Dame. They are on public display from Easter to mid-November. ✉ *Pl. du General Leclerc, just off Av. de la République* ☎ *03–80–24–77–95* 💶 *Guided tour for tapestries €3.*

⭐ **Hospices de Beaune** (*Hôtel-Dieu*)
MUSEUM | With its steep, gabled roof colorfully tiled in intricate patterns, the famed Hospices de Beaune is this city's top attraction—and one of Burgundy's most iconic sights. Better known to some as the Hôtel-Dieu, it was founded in 1443 as a hospital to provide free care for the poor after the Hundred Years' War. The interior looks medieval but was repainted by 19th-century restorer Ouradou (Viollet-le-Duc's son-in-law); it centers on the grand salle, more than 160 feet long, with the original furniture, a great wooden roof, and the super-picturesque **cour d'honneur**. The Hospices carried on its medical activities until 1971—its nurses still wearing their habitlike uniforms—and the hospital's history is retraced in the museum, whose wide-ranging collections contain some odd medical instruments from the 15th century. You can also see a collection of tapestries that belonged to the repentant founder of the Hospices, ducal chancellor Nicolas Rolin, who hoped charity would relieve him of his sins—one of which was collecting wives. Outstanding are both the tapestry he had made for Madame Rolin III, with its repeated motif of "my only star," and one relating the legend of St-Eloi and his miraculous restoration of a horse's leg.

But the showstopper at the Hôtel-Dieu is Rogier Van der Weyden's stirring, gigantic 15th-century masterpiece *The Last Judgment,* commissioned for the hospital's chapel by Rolin. The intense colors and mind-tripping imagery were meant to scare the illiterate patients into religious submission. Notice the touch of misogyny; more women are going to hell than to heaven, while Christ, the judge, remains completely unmoved. The Hospices own around 150 acres of the region's finest vineyards, much of it classified as Grand or Premier Cru. ⊠ *Pl. de la Halle, Rue de l'Hôtel-Dieu* ☎ *03–80–24–45–00* ⊕ *www. hospices-de-beaune.com* 💳 *€9.*

La Moutarderie Edmond Fallot
FACTORY | This family-run mustard factory is the only one in France that still uses stone millstones to grind up the mustard seeds. Choose between two guided tours: the "Découvertes" includes a visit to a small museum featuring ancient mustard-making tools and machines, and a chance to make your own mustard, and it finishes with a tasting; and the "Sensations Fortes" tour includes a guided visit to the factory in action. The sleek boutique stocks a wide range of mustards, with several available to taste. ⊠ *31 rue du Faubourg Bretonnière* ☎ *03–80–22–10–02* ⊕ *www.fallot.com* 💳 *€10* 🕒 *Closed Sun. Oct.–Apr.*

Marché aux Vins (*Wine Market*)
WINERY/DISTILLERY | The liquid highlight of many Burgundian vacations is a visit to the Marché aux Vins, where you can sample a tongue-tingling, mind-spinning array of regional wines in an atmospheric setting made up of barrel-strewn cellars and vaulted passages. Opt for nine wines which include four Premier Cru wines (€21) or the Grand Cru tasting (€29); no need to reserve in advance. Other Beaune tasting houses include Cordelier on Rue de l'Hôtel-Dieu and the Caves Patriarche on Rue du Collège. ⊠ *7 rue de l' Hôtel-Dieu* ☎ *03–80–25–08–20* ⊕ *www.marcheauxvins.com* 💳 *From €10* 🕒 *Closed late Jan.–early Feb.*

🍴 Restaurants

Le Carmin
$$$$ | FRENCH | In a dead-center location facing the market hall and within sight of the Hospices de Beaune, Le Carmin serves dishes that play on texture and visuals, the hallmarks of chef Christophe Quéant, who has already been crowned as one of Beaune's up-and-coming stars. The simply decorated and refined dining room provides the backdrop to creative market-driven dishes. **Known for:** exquisitely presented dishes; delicious desserts; great cheese plate. $ *Average*

Wine tastings abound in and around Beaune—check in with the tourist office to get a full list of vineyards and wine caves.

main: €50 ✉ 4 pl. Carnot ☎ 03–80–24–22–42 ⊕ www.restaurant-lecarmin.com ⊙ Closed Sun. and Mon., and 2 wks in late Feb.

★ Le P'tit Paradis

$$ | FRENCH | It's well worth squeezing into this tiny corner of paradise to experience the modern bistro fare of Beaune's most capable culinary couple. Burgundy staples such as Charolais beef with an Époisses cream sauce, and fricassee of snails with fresh herbs grace the heavenly menu. **Known for:** pretty terrace overlooking a medieval cobbled street; great selection of wine by the half bottle; innovative twist to regional dishes. $ *Average main: €20* ✉ *2 rue du Paradis* ☎ *03–80–24–91–00* ⊕ *www. restaurantleptitparadis.fr* ⊙ *Closed Sun. and Mon., and Aug., Dec., and Jan.*

L'Écusson

$$$$ | FRENCH | Don't be put off by its unprepossessing exterior: this friendly, oak-beam restaurant offers good-value prix-fixe menus. Chef-owner Thomas Campagnon's sure-footed culinary mastery is evident in his bold and passionate presentation of local produce dishes. **Known for:** courtyard terrace; Corton pigeon and Bresse chicken; extensive wine list. $ *Average main: €40* ✉ *2 rue du Lieutenant-Dupuis* ☎ *03–80–24–03–82* ⊕ *www.ecusson.fr* ⊙ *Closed Sun., Wed., and Feb.*

Loiseau des Vignes

$$$$ | FRENCH FUSION | Where else would you expect one of Burgundy's leading culinary establishments to open a wine bar? A massive range of 70 wines, all available by the glass, is the perfect accompaniment to a selection of Bernard Loiseau's famous regional dishes such as *œufs meurette Bernard Loiseau* (poached eggs in red-wine sauce) and a ballotine of Bresse chicken. **Known for:** wine-tasting menus; old-fashioned French favorites; courtyard terrace. $ *Average main: €60* ✉ *31 rue Maufoux* ☎ *03–80–24–12–06* ⊕ *www.bernard-loiseau.com* ⊙ *Closed Sun., Mon., and Feb.*

Hotels

Hostellerie de Levernois

$$$ | **HOTEL** | This idyllic Relais & Châteaux property—a gracious country manor, smartly run by Jean-Louis and Susanne Bottigliero—enchants on many levels, from its unique fleur-de-lys topiary and its superb restaurant to its wood-beamed cathedral guest rooms. **Pros:** lovely, spacious rooms; personable staff; amazing food. **Cons:** pricey; no elevator; out-of-town location. ⓢ *Rooms from: €250 ⊠ Rue du Golf, 3 km (2 miles) east of Beaune, Levernois* ☎ *03–80–24–73–58* ⊕ *www.levernois.com* ☉ *Closed Feb.– mid-Mar.* ⇆ *20 rooms* ⍥ *No meals.*

★ Hôtel Le Cep

$$$ | **HOTEL** | This stylish ensemble of buildings spanning the 14th to 16th centuries oozes history from every arcade of its Renaissance courtyard, and, even better, all guest rooms—named for different Burgundy wines—have been luxuriously modernized and decorated with individual panache; some have wood beams, others canopied or four-poster beds. **Pros:** luxurious rooms; wonderful spa; friendly staff. **Cons:** breakfast is extra; the basic rooms are small and best avoided if you have a lot of luggage; pricey. ⓢ *Rooms from: €300 ⊠ 27 rue Jean François Maufoux* ☎ *03–80–22–35–48* ⊕ *www. hotel-cep-beaune.com* ⇆ *65 rooms* ⍥ *No meals.*

La Cueillette

$$$ | **HOTEL** | Sitting pretty in the middle of manicured rows of Meursault vines, the Château de Cîteaux provides a stately setting for this hotel and spa. **Pros:** vineyard setting; luxurious spa and pool; gorgeous decor. **Cons:** few rooms have bathtubs; a car is essential; restaurant closed Sunday and Monday. ⓢ *Rooms from: €240 ⊠ Rue de Cîteaux, 9 km (5½ miles) southwest of Beaune, Meursault* ☎ *03–80–20–62–80* ⊕ *www.lacueillette. com* ⇆ *19 rooms* ⍥ *No meals.*

Performing Arts

International Festival of Baroque Opera

FESTIVALS | In July Beaune stages its annual, monthlong International Festival of Baroque Opera, which draws big stars of the music world. ⊠ *Beaune* ☎ *03–80–22–97–20* ⊕ *www.festivalbeaune.com.*

Les Trois Glorieuses

FESTIVALS | Beaune holds its famous wine festival—Les Trois Glorieuses—on the third weekend in November. It starts with a public tasting on Saturday, continues with an auction on Sunday, and closes with a tipsy lunch for the wine elite at Château de Meursault on Monday. ⊠ *Beaune.*

Château de Sully

16 km (10 miles) northeast of Autun, 75 km (47 miles) southwest of Dijon, 35 km (19 miles) west of Beaune.

This magnificent château is landmarked by four lantern-topped corner towers that loom over a romantic moat filled with the waters of the River Drée. Birthplace of Maurice de MacMahon, the Duc de Magenta, Château de Sully is still home to the present Duchesse de Magenta and her family.

GETTING HERE AND AROUND
Take a local TER train to Autun, and then hop a bus for the 50-minute ride to Château de Sully (see ⊕ *www.destineo.fr* for times and prices).

Sights

Château de Sully

CASTLE/PALACE | "The Fontainebleau of Burgundy" was how Madame de Sévigné described this turreted Renaissance château with its Italianate inner court. Originally constructed by the de Rabutin family and once owned by Gaspard de Saulx-Tavannes—an instigator of the 1572

St-Bartholomew's Day Massacre, during which mobs attacked Huguenots in and around Paris—the château was partly reconstructed in elegant Régence style in the 18th century. Maurice de MacMahon, Napoléon III's field marshal, was born here in 1808; he went on to serve as the president of France's Third Republic from 1873 to 1879. ☎ 03–85–82–09–86 ⊕ www.chateaudesully.com ✉ From €5.

Autun

48 km (30 miles) west of Beaune.

One of the most richly endowed *villes d'art* in Burgundy, Autun is a great draw for fans of both Gallo-Roman and Romanesque art. The name derives from Augustodonum—city of Augustus—and it was Augustus Caesar who called Autun "the sister and rival of Rome itself." You can still see traces of the Roman occupation, dating to an era when this place was much larger and more important than it is now, in its well-preserved archways (Porte St-André and Porte d'Arroux) and Théâtre Romain (once the largest theater in Gaul). Parts of the Roman walls surrounding the town also remain. In addition to ancient ruins, Autun is home to a magnificent medieval cathedral and one of the region's best museums—Musée Rolin.

GETTING HERE AND AROUND
Some TGVs stop at Le Creusot, between Chalon and Autun—from here, you can catch a bus for the 45-minute ride to Autun. Local train lines also link Autun to Auxerre and Dijon.

VISITOR INFORMATION Autun Tourist Office ✉ 13 rue Général Demetz ☎ 03–85–86–80–38 ⊕ www.autun-tourisme.com.

Summer Theater in Autun

On Friday and Saturday night from late July to early August, time rewinds in Autun as its ancient Roman theater brings the Celtic and Gallo-Roman periods to life in a Busby Berkeley–esque extravaganza featuring Celtic fairies, Roman gladiators, and chariot races. Check ⊕ www.autun-tourisme.com for all the details.

◉ Sights

Cathédrale St-Lazare
RELIGIOUS SITE | Autun's principal monument is the Cathédrale St-Lazare, a Romanesque cathedral in Gothic clothing. It was built between 1120 and 1146 to house the relics of St-Lazarus; the main tower, spire, and upper reaches of the chancel were added in the late 15th century. Lazarus's tricolor tomb was dismantled in 1766 by canons (vestiges of the exquisite workmanship can be seen in the neighboring Musée Rolin); and those same gentlemen did their best to transform the Romanesque-Gothic cathedral into a classical temple, adding pilasters and other ornaments willy-nilly. Fortunately, the lacy Flamboyant Gothic organ tribune and some of the best Romanesque stonework, including the inspired nave capitals and the tympanum above the main door, emerged unscathed. Jean-Auguste-Dominique Ingres's painting *The Martyrdom of St. Symphorien* has been relegated to the dingy north aisle of the nave, partly masked by the organ. The Last Judgment carved in stone above the main door was plastered over in the 18th century, which preserved not only the stylized Christ and elongated apostles but also the inscription "*Gislebertus hoc fecit*" (Gislebertus

did this); Christ's head, which had disappeared, was found by a local canon shortly after World War II. In summer, you can visit the cathedral's **Salle Capitulaire**, which houses Gislebertus's original capitals, distinguished by their relief carvings. ✉ *Pl. St-Louis* ☎ *03–85–52–12–37* 🌐 *www.art-roman.net/autun/autun.htm* 🎫 *Salle Capitulaire €2* 🕒 *Salle Capitulaire closed Sept.–June.*

Musée Rolin

MUSEUM | Built by Chancellor Nicolas Rolin, an important Burgundian administrator and famous art patron (he's immortalized in one of the Louvre's greatest paintings, Jan van Eyck's *Madonna and the Chancellor Rolin*), this museum across from the cathedral is noteworthy for its early Flemish paintings and sculpture. Among them is the magisterial *Nativity* painted by the Maître de Moulins in the 15th century, but the collection's star is a Gislebertus masterpiece, the *Temptation of Eve,* which originally topped one of the side doors of the cathedral. Try to imagine the missing elements of the scene: Adam on the left and the devil on the right. It is worth watching the 12-minute film describing the cathedral's tympanum sculptures before visiting the cathedral. ✉ *5 rue des Bancs* ☎ *03–85–52–21–60* 🎫 *€6* 🕒 *Closed Jan. and Tues.*

Théâtre Romain

ARCHAEOLOGICAL SITE | **FAMILY** | The ancient theater, sitting at the edge of Autun on the road to Chalon-sur-Saône, makes an atmospheric picnic spot. Select lunch fixings in town, and then settle in on the stepped seats, where as many as 15,000 Gallo-Roman spectators perched two millennia ago. On Friday and Saturday nights in the height of summer, a themed performance—the only one of its kind—is put on by locals wearing period costumes. Elsewhere on the outskirts of town are the remains of a Roman Temple of Janus. ✉ *Autun.*

Restaurants

Le Monde de Don Cabillaud

$$$ | **FRENCH** | **FAMILY** | This tiny restaurant, hidden down a cobbled street near the cathedral, has become a neighborhood staple. The chalkboard showcases a fish-focused menu which changes according to the catch of the day and the whims of the chef. **Known for:** simple grilled fish dishes in classic sauces; friendly service; two fixed-price menu options. [$] *Average main: €32* ✉ *4 rue des Bancs* ☎ *07–60–94–21–10* 🕒 *Closed Sun. and Mon.*

Le Chateaubriant

$$ | **FRENCH** | Regional dishes are the focus at this family-run eatery situated on a street behind the city's theater. The menu offers Burgundian staples like oeufs en meurette, snails with garlic butter, steak with Époisses cheese sauce, and chateaubriand for two. **Known for:** good selection of local wines; traditional cuisine; city center location. [$] *Average main: €20* ✉ *14 rue Jeannin* ☎ *03–85–52–21–58* 🌐 *www.lechateaubriant-autun.com* 🕒 *Closed Sun. and Mon.*

Hotels

Maison Sainte-Barbe

$ | **B&B/INN** | **FAMILY** | Slip past the cathedral to reach this 17th-century canon's residence that was turned into a cozy bed-and-breakfast. **Pros:** great location; affordable prices; friendly owners. **Cons:** street-side rooms can get some noise; no on-site parking; comfortable but time-worn. [$] *Rooms from: €89* ✉ *7 pl. Ste-Barbe* ☎ *03–85–86–24–77* 🌐 *www.maisonsaintebarbe.com* 🛏 *4 rooms* 🍴 *Free Breakfast.*

Moulin Renaudiots

$$ | **B&B/INN** | **FAMILY** | This converted paper mill in a tree-lined garden exudes rustic charm; its spacious guest rooms—some with views of the river, others looking out over the countryside—have a

The basilica of the Abbaye de Cluny was the world's largest church before St. Peter's in Rome took the title.

smart country-luxe decor. **Pros:** calm surroundings; restaurant serves meals in the garden in warmer months; great food. **Cons:** 10-minute drive from the center; no elevator; outdoor pool is unheated. $ *Rooms from: €165* ✉ *Chemin du Vieux Moulin* ☎ *03–85–86–97–10* 🌐 *www.moulinrenaudiots.com* 🕓 *Closed Jan.* 🛏 *5 rooms* 🍴 *Free Breakfast.*

Cluny

77 km (46 miles) southeast of Autun.

The village of Cluny is legendary for its medieval abbey, once the center of a vast Christian empire. Although most of the complex was destroyed in the French Revolution, a single, soaring transept of this church remains standing. It's one of the most magnificent sights of Romanesque architecture.

GETTING HERE AND AROUND

Eight TGVs make the journey from Paris's Gare de Lyon daily (€84.20), though all require a 20-minute bus liaison from Mâcon. Regular buses also link Cluny to Chalon-sur-Saône, where you can connect to Autun and Le Creusot TGV railway stations. Driving to Cluny is a delight, as the surrounding countryside of the Mâconnais is among the most beautiful in France, with rolling fields and picturesque villages.

VISITOR INFORMATION Cluny Tourist Office ✉ *6 rue Mercière* ☎ *03–85–59–05–34* 🌐 *www.cluny-tourisme.com.*

Sights

★ **Ancienne Abbaye**

RELIGIOUS SITE | Founded in the 10th century, the Ancienne Abbaye was the largest church in Europe until the 16th century, when Michelangelo built St. Peter's in Rome. Art historians have written themselves into knots tracing the fundamental influence of its architecture in the development of early Gothic style. Cluny's medieval abbots were as powerful as popes; in 1098 Pope Urban II (himself a Cluniac) assured the head of his old abbey that Cluny was the "light of the world." That assertion, of dubious religious validity, has not stood the test of time; after the Revolution the abbey was sold as national property and much of it used as a stone quarry. Today Cluny stands in ruins, a reminder of the vanity of human grandeur. What remains, however, suggests the size and gorgeous glory of the abbey at its zenith, and piecing it back together in your mind is part of the attraction.

In order to get a clear sense of what you're looking at, start at the Porte d'Honneur, the entrance to the abbey from the village, whose classical architecture is reflected in the pilasters and Corinthian columns of the Clocher de l'Eau-Bénite (a majestic bell tower), crowning the only remaining part of the abbey church, the south transept. Between the two is the reconstructed monumental staircase, which led to the portal of the abbey church, and the excavated column bases of the vast narthex. The entire nave is gone. On one side of the transept is a national horse-breeding center (*haras*) founded in 1806 by Napoléon and constructed with materials from the destroyed abbey; on the other is an elegant pavilion built as new monks' lodgings in the 18th century. The gardens in front of it once contained an ancient lime tree (destroyed by a 1982 storm) named after Abélard, the controversial philosopher who sought shelter here in 1142. Off to the right is the 13th-century *farinier* (flour store), with its fine oak-and-chestnut roof and collection of exquisite Romanesque capitals from the vanished choir. The **Musée d'Art et d'Archéologie,** in the Palais Jean de Bourbon, contains Europe's foremost Romanesque lapidary museum. Vestiges of both the abbey and the village constructed around it are conserved here, as well as part of the Bibliothèque des Moines (Monks' Library). ✉ *Pl. de l'abbaye* ☎ *03–85–59–12–79 for Abbaye, 03–85–59–15–93 for Palais de Bourbon* 🌐 *www.cluny-abbaye.fr* 🎫 *€10 abbey and museum (valid for 2 days).*

Hôtel des Monnaies (*Abbey Mint*)
HOUSE | The village of Cluny was built to serve the abbey's more practical needs, and several fine Romanesque houses around Rue d'Avril and Rue de la République—including the so-called Hôtel des Monnaies—are prime examples of the period's different architectural styles. ✉ *6 rue d'Avril.*

Tour des Fromages
MILITARY SITE | Parts of the town ramparts and the much-restored Tour des Fromages (Cheese Tower, now home to the tourist office) also remain intact. You can ascend the 11th-century defensive tower to take in stellar views. ✉ *6 rue Mercière* ☎ *03–85–59–05–34 for tourist office* 🎫 *From €3* 🕒 *Closed Sun. Oct.–Mar.*

Hotels

Hôtel de Bourgogne
$ | HOTEL | Time-burnished if not time-stained, this old-fashioned hotel was built in 1817 on a site where parts of the abbey once stood. **Pros:** historic setting; good value; helpful staff. **Cons:** no elevator; breakfast is extra but copious; bathrooms could do with upgrading. [$] *Rooms from: €102* ✉ *Pl. de l'Abbaye* ☎ *03–85–59–00–58* 🌐 *www.hotel-cluny.com* 🕒 *Closed Dec., Jan., and Tues. and Wed. in Feb.* 🛏 *16 rooms* 🍴 *No meals.*

Performing Arts

Grandes Heures de Cluny
FESTIVALS | The ruined abbey of Cluny forms the backdrop of the Grandes Heures de Cluny, a classical music festival held late July to mid-August. Free Burgundy wine tastings are offered after concerts. ✉ *Hotel des Monnaies, 6 rue d'Avril* ☎ *03–85–59–05–34 OdT tel number* 🌐 *www.grandesheuresdecluny.com.*

Chapter 11

LYON AND THE ALPS

Updated by
Jennifer Ladonne

◉ Sights	🍴 Restaurants	🛏 Hotels	🛍 Shopping	🍸 Nightlife
★★★☆☆	★★★★★	★★★★☆	★★★☆☆	★★☆☆☆

WELCOME TO LYON AND THE ALPS

TOP REASONS TO GO

★ **Old Lyon:** Lyon's Old Town passageways and 16th-century courtyards reveal a hidden trove of Renaissance architecture.

★ **Beaujolais wine:** The third Thursday of November is a party like no other in France, when celebrations in honor of the new Beaujolais wine go around the clock.

★ **Mont Blanc:** Whether you brave the vertiginous slopes at Chamonix or enjoy the gentler skiing of Megève, you'll be singing "Ain't No Mountain High Enough" once you see Mont Blanc, France's tallest peak.

★ **Grenoble's markets:** Sunday morning offers a chance to walk miles through half a dozen different markets selling everything from herbs to haberdashery.

★ **Epicureanism:** There is no possible way to cite Lyon–Rhône Alps without mentioning food. As the traditional gastronomic capital of France, the influence of the late great Paul Bocuse still resonates loud and clear in the city's robust foodie scene.

Lyon is a magnet for the surrounding region, including the vineyards of Beaujolais. South of Lyon is the quaint Rhône Valley. Along the southeastern border of France rises a mighty barrier of mountains that provides some of the most spectacular scenery in Europe: the French Alps, soaring to their climax in Western Europe's highest peak, Mont Blanc.

1 **Lyon.**

2 **Beaujolais Wine Route.**

3 **Bourg-en-Bresse.**

4 **Villars-les-Dombes.**

5 **Pérouges.**

6 **Vienne.**

7 **Tain l'Hermitage.**

8 **Tournon-sur-Rhône.**

9 **Valence.**

10 **Cliousclat.**

11 **Grenoble.**

12 **Chambéry.**

13 **Annecy.**

14 **Chamonix-Mont Blanc.**

15 **Megéve.**

16 **Val Thorens.**

17 **Méribel.**

18 **Courchevel.**

19 **Val d'Isére.**

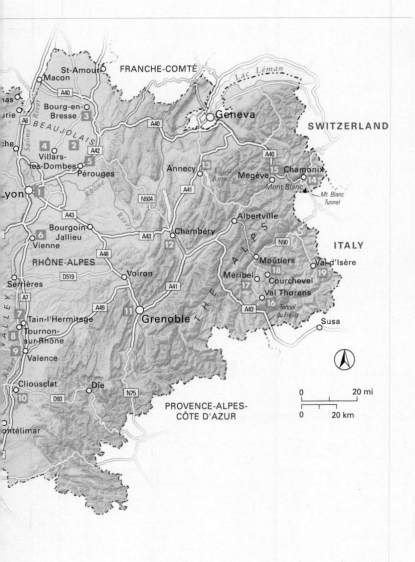

FRANCHE-COMTÉ

St-Amour

Macon

A40

Bourg-en-
Bresse 3

Villars-
les-Dombes 4 2

Pérouges 5

A42

BEAUJOLAIS

Saône River

A6

Rhône River

yon 1

A43

Bourgoin
Jallieu 6

Vienne

RHÔNE-ALPES

A43

N504

A41

Annecy 13

Chambéry

A48

D519

Voiron

A41

Serrières

A7

Tain-l'Hermitage 7

Tournon-
sur-Rhône 8

Valence 9

Cliousclat 10

D93

Die

N75

RHÔNE VALLEY

ntélimar

A49

Grenoble 11

PROVENCE-ALPES-
CÔTE D'AZUR

Lac Léman

Geneva

SWITZERLAND

Megève 15 Chamonix 14

Mont Blanc ▲ Mt. Blanc
Tunnel

Albertville

N90

Moûtiers

Méribel 18 Courchevel

Val Thorens 17

16 Tunnel
du Fréjus

A43

ITALY

Val-d'Isère 19

Susa

THE ALPS

0   20 mi
0   20 km

Lyon and the Alps are as alike as chocolate and broccoli. Lyon is fast, lively, and saturated with culture. In the bustling city—often called the gateway to the Alps—it's hard to believe that those pristine peaks are only an hour's train ride away. Likewise, when you're in a small Alpine village you could almost forget France has any large cities at all, because everything you imagined about the Alps—soaring snowcaps, jagged ridges, refreshing lakes—is true. Culturally, Lyon and the Alps could well be on different continents, but geographically they make for a great vacation combo.

Cheek by jowl, they share a patch of earth sculpted by the noble Rhône as it courses down from Switzerland, flowing out of Lake Geneva. And this soil, or as the French call it, the *terroir,* provides many tasty treasures, beginning with the region's saucy Beaujolais wines. Glinting purple against red-checked linens in a Lyonnais *bouchon,* pink-cheeked Beaujolais vintages flatter every item listed on those famous blackboard menus: a fat *boudin noir* bursting from its casing, a tangle of country greens in tangy mustard vinaigrette, or a taste of crackling roast chicken.

If you are what you eat, then Lyon itself is real and hearty, as straightforward and unabashedly simple as a *poulet de Bresse.* Yet the refinements of superlative opera, theater, and classical music also happily thrive in Lyon's gently patinated urban milieu, one strangely reminiscent of 1930s Paris—lace curtains in painted-over storefronts, elegant bourgeois town houses, deep-shaded parks, and low-slung bridges lacing back and forth over the broad, lazy Saône and Rhône rivers.

When you've had your fill of this, pack a picnic to tide you over and head for the hills—the Alps, to be exact. Here is a land of green-velvet slopes and icy mists, ranging from the modern urban hub of Grenoble and the crystalline lake of Annecy to the state-of-the-art ski resorts of Chamonix, Courchevel, and Megève. Let your grand finale be Mont Blanc: at 15,700 feet, it's Western Europe's highest peak.

MAJOR REGIONS

Beaujolais. Follow the Saône River north from Lyon to the area around Ville-franche and you will find the vineyards of Beaujolais, a moving pilgrimage for any wine lover. Diminutive villages with poetic names such as St-Amour, Fleurie, and Juliénas are surrounded by rolling hillsides bristling with grapevines. To the east lies Bourg-en-Bresse, famed for its church and its chickens. South toward the Rhône, the great river of southern France, is the well-preserved medieval village of Pérouges.

The Rhône Valley. Like predestined lovers, the Rhône joins the Saône to form a fluvial force rolling south to the Mediter-ranean. Their bounty includes hundreds of steep vineyards and small-town winemakers tempting you with samples. The ancient Roman ruins of Vienne and the Romanesque relics of Valence reflect the Rhône's importance as an early trade route. To the west is the rugged, rustic Ardèche *département*, where time seems to have slowed to a standstill in towns like Tournon-sur-Rhône and Cliouscat.

Grenoble and the Alps. Grenoble, in the Dauphiné, is the gateway to the Alps at the nexus of rivers and highways con-necting Marseille, Valence, Lyon, Geneva, and Turin. Literati will love its Stendahl sites and art-filled *musée*. To the east, rustic towns announce the Alps, none more idyllic than Annecy, thanks to its cerulean blue lake, covered lanes, and quiet canals. The region's natural Alpine splendors are showcased at Chamo-nix, Courchevel, Val Thorens, Megève, Méribel, and Val d'Isére, ski resorts that

buzz with life from December to April. In summer, the lake resorts, as well as the regions favored by hikers and climbers, come into their own.

Planner

When to Go

Lyon and the Rhône-Alpes are so diverse in altitude and climate that the weather will depend mostly on where you are, when you're there, and which way the wind blows. Tropical weather has been know to turn Lyon's late September Street Food Festival into a summer smash with delicious breezes off the Saône. As a rule, however, Lyon may be rainy and misty, but not especially cold. Conversely, Grenoble and the Alps can be bitter at any time of year, especially from December to April. The Beaujolais wine region is generally temperate, though a recent Beaujolais Nouveau festival (held on the third Thursday in November) saw frozen vines and revelers alike. South of Lyon along the Rhône the sun beats down on the vineyards in full summer, but the winds howl in winter.

Planning Your Time

Lyon, with its ample range of architec-ture, food, and culture, deserves several days—two at the very least. The wine country of the Beaujolais up the River Saône is another two-day visit, unless a drive-through directly to Bourg-en-Bresse is all that time constraints will allow. Medieval Pérouges is another good day's browse, with time left over for a late afternoon and evening drive into the Alps to Annecy, where the Vieille Ville (Old Town) is an eyeful by day or night.

The upscale mountain resorts of Megève or Courchevel are good places to settle in for a few days. Grenoble offers opportunities for perusing masterpieces in its superb museum or following the novelist Stendhal's footsteps through the old quarter.

How to Talk Wine

With the Beaujolais region to the north and the Côtes du Rhône to the south, there are hundreds of village wine *caves* (cellars). Do some advance research according to your tastes, or opt for those with signs reading "*Dégustation, vente en direct*" (sold directly from the property) or "*Vente au détail*" (sold by the bottle). Also look for the town's co-op *caveau,* which often represents some of the more sophisticated wine growers and where you can taste all the wine you want for free or just a few euros.

Getting Here and Around

Lyon is best explored on foot, along with the excellent tramway or subway connection to get you across town, or to the train station or airport, in a hurry. Boat tours around the Presqu'île open up another perspective on this riverside metropolis, while the city's Vélo'v bike rentals are a handy way to see the city. Consider taking advantage of the Lyon City Card, a one-, two-, or three-day pass (€22, €32, and €42, respectively) to museums, with discounts at boutiques, restaurants, and cultural events. Lyon is an important rail hub with three major stations. Trains from the Gare de la Part-Dieu connect easily with Villefranche-sur-Saône in the middle of the Beaujolais country, while the Gare de Perrache serves points south such as Valence and Vienne.

A car is probably the best way to get around the Beaujolais wine country and the rest of Rhône-Alpes, although bus routes, if infrequent, do usually extend to the far reaches of these regions.

AIR TRAVEL

The region's international gateway airport is Aéroport-Lyon-Saint-Exupéry, 26 km (16 miles) east of Lyon, in Satolas. There are domestic airports at Grenoble, Valence, Annecy, Chambéry, and Aix-les-Bains.

BUS TRAVEL

Buses from Lyon and Grenoble thoroughly and efficiently serve the region's smaller towns. Many ski centers, such as Chamonix, have shuttle buses connecting them with surrounding villages. As for Alpine villages, regional buses head out from the main train stations at Annecy, Chambéry, Megève, and Grenoble.

CAR TRAVEL

Regional roads are fast and well maintained, though smaller mountainous routes can be difficult to navigate and high passes may be closed in winter. A6 speeds south from Paris to Lyon—a distance of 463 km (287 miles). The Tunnel de Fourvière, which cuts through Lyon, is a classic hazard, and at peak times you may sit idling for hours. Lyon is 313 km (194 miles) north of Marseille on A7.

To make the 105-km (63-mile) trip southeast to Grenoble from Lyon, take A43 to A48. Coming from the south, take A7 to Valence and then swing east on A49 to A48 to Grenoble. From Grenoble to Megève and Chamonix through Annecy take A41–E712 to Annecy (direction Geneva), and then A40 (direction Montblanc-Chamonix). Turn off A40 at Sallanches for the 17-km (10½-mile) drive on the N212 to Megève.

TRAIN TRAVEL

High-speed TGV trains depart Paris's Gare de Lyon hourly and arrive in Lyon just two hours later. There are also two to eight TGVs daily between Paris's Charles de Gaulle Airport and Lyon. Two in-town train stations and a third at the airport (Lyon-Saint-Exupéry) make the city a major transportation hub. The Gare de la Part-Dieu (⊠ *Bd. Vivier-Merle*) is used for the TGV routes and links

Lyon with many other cities, including Bordeaux, Montpellier, and Marseilles, along with Grenoble. On the other side of town, the *centre-ville* station at Gare de Perrache (✉ *Cours de Verdun, Pl. Carnot* ☎ *04–72–56–95–30*) is the more crowded option and serves all the sights of the center ville—many trains stop at both stations. The TGV station at Aéroport-Lyon-Saint-Exupéry serves Avignon, Arles, Valence, Annecy, Aix-les-Bains, and Chambéry, as well as Paris. The TGV also has a less frequent service to Grenoble, where you can connect to local SNCF trains headed for villages in the Alps. For the Beaujolais Wine Country, most people travel to Villefranche-sur-Saône's station on Place de la Gare; trains run to smaller towns from here.

TRAIN CONTACTS SNCF ☎ *3635* ⊕ *www. sncf.com.*

Restaurants

The food you'll find in the Rhône-Alps region is some of France's best—after all, this is considered the birthplace of the country's traditional cuisine, while also being the engine room of tomorrow's latest trends and gourmet styles. In Lyon's countless bouchons, you'll find everything from *gras double* (tripe) to boudin noir to *paillasson* (fried hashed potatoes). If it's a light or vegetarian meal you're after, some of the newer wine bars or contemporary French restaurants are your best options.

Hotels

Hotels, inns, *gîtes d'étapes* (hikers' way stations), and *chambres d'hôte* (bed-and-breakfasts) run the gamut from grand luxe to spartanly rustic in this multifaceted region embracing ultraurban chic in Lyon as well as ski huts in the Alps. Lyon accommodations range from guest rooms with panoramic views high in the hilltop Fourvière or Croix Rousse

districts to chic hotels in Vieux Lyon and Presqu'île. The Alps, of course, are well furnished with top hotels, especially in Grenoble and the time-honored ski resorts such as Chamonix, Courchevel, and Megève. *Restaurant and hotel reviews have been shortened. For full information, visit Fodors.com.*

What It Costs in Euros			
$	$$	$$$	$$$$
RESTAURANTS			
under €18	€18–€24	€25–€32	over €32
HOTELS			
under €125	€125–€226	€226–€350	over €350

Tours

The Lyon tourist office organizes walking tours of the city in English.

Lyon City Boat
This company arranges daily boat trips—with or without a meal—from Lyon's Quai des Célestins along the Saône and Rhône rivers. ✉ *Quai des Célestins, Lyon* ☎ *04–78–42–96–81* ⊕ *www.lyoncityboat. com.*

Visitor Information

CONTACT Comité Départemental du Tourisme ✉ *142 bis av. Maréchal de Saxe, Lyon* ☎ *04–72–56–70–40* ⊕ *www.rhone-tourisme.com.*

Lyon

The city's setting at the confluence of the Saône and the Rhône is a spectacular riverine landscape overlooked from the heights to the west by the imposing Notre-Dame de Fourvière church and from the north by the hilltop neighborhood of La Croix Rousse. Meanwhile,

La Confluence Project at the southern tip of the Presqu'île (the land between the Saône and the Rhône) has reclaimed from the rivers nearly a square mile of center-city real estate that has become a neighborhood of thrilling architecture, with parks, shops, restaurants, and cultural sites. Another attraction is Lyon's extraordinary dining scene—the city has more good restaurants per square mile than any other European city except Paris.

GETTING HERE AND AROUND

To get between the Aéroport-Lyon-Saint-Exupéry and the city center take the Rhône Express (☎ 08–26–00–17–18 ⊕ www.rhonexpress.fr €15.90), a tramway that makes the 30-minute trip every quarter hour between 6 am and 9 pm, with various stops along the way—including the Lyon Part-Dieu train station. If you're coming by train, Lyon has three major stations so is easily reached by rail. To get here by car, take A6 south from Paris for 463 km (287 miles).

VISITOR INFORMATION Lyon Tourist Information ✉ Pl. Bellecour ☎ 04–72–77–69–69 ⊕ www.lyon-france.com.

 # Sights

Lyon's development owes much to its riverside location halfway between Paris and the Mediterranean, and within striking distance of Switzerland, Italy, and the Alps. The Lyonnais are proud that their city has been important for more than 2,000 years. Under the Romans, who called it Lugdunum (meaning "hill or fortress of Lug," the supreme deity of Celtic mythology), it became the second-largest city in their empire and was named the capital of Gaul around 43 BC. High up on the Fourvière Hill, the remains of the Roman theater and the Odéon, the Gallo-Roman music hall, are among the most spectacular Roman ruins in the world.

In the middle of the city is the Presqu'île (literally, "almost an island"), a fingerlike peninsula between the rivers where modern Lyon throbs with shops, restaurants, museums, theaters, and a postmodern Jean Nouvel–designed opera house. West of the Saône is Vieux Lyon (Old Lyon), with its peaceful Renaissance charm; above it is the old Roman district of Fourvière. To the north is the hilltop Croix Rousse district, where Lyon's silk weavers once operated their looms in lofts designed as workshop dwellings, while across the Rhône to the east are a mix of older residential areas, the famous Halles de Lyon market, and the ultramodern Part-Dieu business district with its landmark gratte-ciel (skyscraper) beyond.

Vieux Lyon—one of the richest groups of urban Renaissance dwellings in Europe—has narrow cobblestone streets, 15th- and 16th-century mansions, small museums, and a divine cathedral. When Lyon became an important silk-weaving town in the 15th century, Italian merchants and bankers built dozens of Renaissance-style town houses. Officially cataloged as national monuments, the courtyards and passageways are open to the public during the morning. The excellent Renaissance Quarter map of the traboules and courtyards of Vieux Lyon, available at the tourist office and in most hotel lobbies, offers some of the city's most gratifying exploring. Above Vieux Lyon, in hilly Fourvière, are the remains of two Roman theaters and the colorful Basilique de Notre-Dame, visible from all over the city.

Presqu'île, the peninsula flanked by the Saône and the Rhône, is Lyon's modern center, with fashionable shops, a trove of restaurants and museums, and squares graced by fountains and 19th-century buildings. This is the core of Lyon, and you'll be tempted to explore the entire stretch, from the southern point of the peninsula at La Confluence, up past the Gare de Perrache train station to Place

Bellecour, and all the way up to Place des Terreaux.

Basilique de Notre-Dame-de-Fourvière

RELIGIOUS SITE | The rather pompous late-19th-century basilica, at the top of the *ficelle* (funicular railway), is—for better or worse—the symbol of Lyon. Its mock-Byzantine architecture and hilltop site make it a close relative of Paris's Sacré-Coeur. Both were built to underline the might of the Roman Catholic Church after the Prussian defeat of France in 1870 gave rise to the birth of the anticlerical Third Republic. The excessive gilt, marble, and mosaics in the interior underscore the Church's wealth, although they masked its lack of political clout at that time. One of the few places in Lyon where you can't see the basilica is the adjacent terrace, whose panorama reveals the city—with the cathedral of St-Jean in the foreground and the glass towers of the reconstructed Part-Dieu business complex glistening behind. For a more sweeping view still, climb the 287 steps to the basilica observatory. ⊠ *8 pl. de Fourvière, Fourvière* ☎ *04–78–25–13–01* ⊕ *www.fourviere.org.*

Basilique de Saint-Martin d'Ainay

RELIGIOUS SITE | This fortified church dates back to a 10th-century Benedictine abbey and a 9th-century sanctuary before that. The millenary energy field is palpable around the hulking structure, especially near the rear of the apse where the stained-glass windows glow richly in the twilight. In 1844 it became one of the first buildings in France to be classified a national monument; its interior murals and frescoes, though, are disappointingly plain and austere compared to the quirky, rough exterior. ⊠ *Pl. de l'Abbaye d'Ainay, Presqu'île* ☎ *04–72–40–02–50* ✉ *Free.*

★ Berges du Rhône

PROMENADE | Lyon has spent the last 15 years spiffing up 3 miles of its Berges du Rhône waterfront via pedestrian-only walking paths and cycling routes that take you past water gardens, meadows,

Secret Passageways

Look for the quaint *traboules*, passageways under and through town houses dating to the Renaissance (in Vieux Lyon) and the 19th century (in La Croix Rousse). Originally designed as shortcuts for silk weavers delivering their wares, they were used by the French Resistance during World War II to elude German street patrols.

sunning decks, petanque pitches, and a slew of lively bars and cafés all enjoying fabulous views and cool breezes over the Rhône. Open year-round, this is a big summer hot spot for the Lyonnais, who flock here after work to jog, picnic, and simply bask in the warm weather. For a map of the Berges areas, stop in at the tourist office at Place Bellecoeur or have a look online. ⊠ *Berges du Rhône* ⊕ *www.en.lyon-france.com/Discover-Lyon/activities-and-relaxation/Parks-gardens-and-places-to-go-for-a-stroll/Banks-of-the-Rhone.*

Cathédrale St-Jean

RELIGIOUS SITE | Solid and determined—having withstood the sieges of time, revolution, and war—the cathedral's stumpy facade is stuck almost bashfully onto the nave. Although the mishmash inside has its moments—the fabulous 13th-century stained-glass windows in the choir and the varied window tracery and vaulting in the side chapels—the interior lacks drama and harmony. Still, it's an architectural history lesson. The cathedral dates to the 12th century, and the chancel is Romanesque, but construction on the whole continued over three centuries. The 14th-century astronomical clock, in the north transept, is a marvel of technology very much worth seeing. It chimes a hymn to St.

John on the hour at noon, 2, 3, and 4, as a screeching rooster and other automatons enact the Annunciation. ✉ *70 rue St-Jean, Vieux Lyon* ☎ *04–78–92–82–29* ⊕ *www.cathedrale-lyon.cef.fr.*

Centre d'Histoire de la Résistance et de la Déportation (*Museum of the History of the Resistance and the Deportation*)

MUSEUM | During World War II, Lyon played an important role in the Resistance movement against the German occupation of France. Displays include equipment, such as radios and printing presses, photographs, and exhibits re-creating the clandestine lives and heroic exploits of Resistance fighters. ✉ *14 av. Berthelot, Part-Dieu* ☎ *04–78–72–23–11* ⊕ *www.chrd.lyon.fr/chrd/sections/fr/pied/english_1* 💲 *From €8* ⊘ *Closed Mon. and Tues.*

Église Saint-Paul

RELIGIOUS SITE | The 12th-century church of St-Paul is noted for its octagonal lantern, its frieze of animal heads in the chancel, and its late-period Flamboyant Gothic chapel. ✉ *Pl. St-Paul, Vieux Lyon* ☎ *04–78–29–69–58.*

Hôtel Bullioud

HOUSE | This superb Renaissance mansion, close to the Hôtel Paterin, is noted for its courtyard, with an ingenious gallery built in 1536 by Philibert Delorme, one of France's earliest and most accomplished exponents of classical architecture. Delorme also worked on several spectacular châteaux in central France, including those at Fontainebleau and Chenonceaux. ✉ *8 rue Juiverie, off Pl. St-Paul, Vieux Lyon* 💲 *Free.*

Hôtel de Ville (*Town Hall*)

BUILDING | Architects Jules Hardouin-Mansart and Robert de Cotte redesigned the very impressive facade of the Town Hall after a 1674 fire. The rest of the building dates to the early 17th century. The tourist office organizes visits to the hall's salons. ✉ *Pl. des Terreaux, Presqu'île* ⊕ *www.en.lyon-france.com* 💲 *€12.*

Institut Lumière

MUSEUM | On the site where the Lumière brothers, Auguste and Louis, invented cinematography in their family home, this museum has daily showings of early film classics and contemporary movies as well as a permanent exhibit about the Lumières. ✉ *25 rue du Premier Film, Part-Dieu* ☎ *04–78–78–18–95* ⊕ *www.institut-lumiere.org* 💲 *€7* ⊘ *Closed Mon.*

Jardin Archéologique (*Archaeological Garden*)

ARCHAEOLOGICAL SITE | Inside this garden are the excavated ruins of two churches that succeeded one another. The foundations of the churches were unearthed during a time when apartment buildings—constructed here after churches had been destroyed during the Revolution—were being demolished. One arch forms part of the ornamentation in the garden. ✉ *Rue de la Bombarde, Vieux Lyon.*

Jardin des Chartreux

CITY PARK | One of several small, leafy parks in Lyon, this one is a peaceful place to take a break while admiring the splendid vistas of the river and Fourvière Hill. ✉ *Entrance on Quai St-Vincent, Presqu'île.*

Jardin des Plantes (*Botanical Garden*)

GARDEN | In these luxurious botanical gardens you'll find remnants of the once-huge Amphithéâtre des Trois Gaules (Three Gauls Amphitheater), built in AD 19. ✉ *Rue Lucien Sportisse, Vieux Lyon.*

Lugdunum Musée et Théâtres Romains (*Gallo-Roman Museum*)

MUSEUM | Since 1933, systematic excavations have unearthed vestiges of Lyon's opulent Roman precursor. The statues, mosaics, vases, coins, and tombstones are excellently displayed in this partially subterranean museum next to the Roman theaters. The large, bronze Table Claudienne is inscribed with part of Emperor Claudius's address to the Roman Senate in AD 48, conferring senatorial rights on the Roman citizens of Gaul. ⊠ *17 rue Clébert, Fourvière* ☎ *04–72–38–49–30* ⊕ *www.lugdunum. grandlyon.com* 🖼 *€4* ⊙ *Closed Mon.*

Maison des Canuts (*Silk Weavers' Museum*)
MUSEUM | FAMILY | Old-time Jacquard looms are still in action at this historic house in La Croix Rousse, and the weavers are happy to show children how the process works. The boutique is a great place to stock up on a colorful range of silk, wool, and linen scarves—all made in Lyon. ⊠ *10–12 rue d'Ivry, La Croix Rousse* ☎ *04–78–28–62–04* ⊕ *www.maisondes-canuts.com* 🖼 *€8* ⊙ *Closed Sun.*

Maison du Crible
HOUSE | This 17th-century mansion is one of Lyon's oldest. In the courtyard you can glimpse a charming garden and the original Tour Rose, an elegant pink tower. In those days, the higher the tower, the greater the prestige. This one was owned by a tax collector. ⊠ *16 rue du Bœuf, off Pl. du Petit-Collège, Vieux Lyon* 🖼 *Free.*

Musée des Beaux-Arts (*Fine Arts Museum*)
MUSEUM | In the elegant 17th-century Palais St-Pierre, formerly a Benedictine abbey, this museum houses one of France's largest art collections after that of the Louvre. Byzantine ivories, Etruscan statues, Egyptian artifacts, and top-notch sculptures (most notably Rodin's *Walker*) are all on display; however, paintings remain the highlight. Amid old master, Impressionist, and modern paintings are works by the tight-knit Lyon School, characterized by exquisitely rendered flowers and overbearing religious sentimentality. Note Louis Janmot's *Poem of the Soul*, immaculately painted visions that are by turns heavenly, hellish, and downright spooky. A newer trove of treasures includes works by Manet, Monet, Degas, Bacon, Braque, and Picasso. ⊠ *Palais St-Pierre, 20 pl. des Terreaux, Presqu'île* ☎ *04–72–10–17–40* ⊕ *www.mba-lyon.fr* 🖼 *From €8* ⊙ *Closed Tues.*

★ **Musée des Confluences** (*Confluence Museum*)
MUSEUM | This futuristic glass-and-stainless-steel museum—an architectural extravaganza designed by the Austrian firm Coop Himmelblau—attempts an ambitious and sweeping three-part overview of anthropology, ethnology, and the natural sciences. Dramatically set at the confluence of the Saône and Rhône rivers and meant to reflect both sky and water, the building was designed to harmonize with the landscape, and its soaring interior gracefully interacts with an assemblage of pedestrian walkways, boutiques, cafés, and restaurants below. One of Lyon's most engaging and fascinating museums, visitors can spend an hour or an afternoon exploring the superb permanent collection and a range of multifaceted exhibits on subjects as varied as the origins of the universe to the question of an afterlife. ■ TIP➔ **The museum bookshop is a pleasure to browse and there are several appealing contemporary in-museum restaurants for lunch, dinner, or a quick snack.** ⊠ *Centre d'Information, 86 quai Perrache, Presqu'île* ☎ *04–78–37–30–00* ⊕ *www.museedesconfluences.fr* 🖼 *€9* ⊙ *Closed Mon.*

Musée des Tissus et Musée des Arts Décoratifs (*Textile Arts Museum*)
MUSEUM | Two formerly separate museums have combined to create one of France's most extensive collections of decorative arts and the world's largest textile collection, which spans nearly 2,000 years. The fascinating history of Lyon's silk industry, so crucial to the city's fame and fortune, is set out from the Renaissance period to its 20th-century demise. Other highlights include Asian tapestries from as early as the 4th century, Turkish and Persian carpets from the 16th to the 18th century, and 18th-century Lyon silks, so lovingly depicted in many portraits of the time. The museum's fine collections of silverware, furniture, porcelain, tapestries, and other decorative objects are displayed in lovely

Sights ▼

1 Basilique de Notre-Dame-de-Fourvière **C6**
2 Basilique de St-Martin d'Ainay **E9**
3 Berges du Rhône **G9**
4 Cathédrale St-Jean **D7**
5 Centre d'Histoire de la Résistance et de la Déportation **H9**
6 Église Saint-Paul **D5**
7 Hôtel Bullioud **D7**
8 Hôtel de Ville **G4**
9 Institut Lumière **I9**
10 Jardin Archéologique .. **D7**
11 Jardin des Chartreux **C4**
12 Jardin des Plantes **E3**
13 Lugdunum Musée et Théâtres Romains **B7**
14 Maison des Canuts **F1**
15 Maison du Crible **D6**
16 Musée des Beaux-Arts **F5**
17 Musée des Confluences **F9**
18 Musée des Tissus et Musée des Arts Décoratifs **F9**
19 Musées Gadagne **E6**
20 Musée Urbain Tony Garnier **I9**
21 Opéra de Lyon **G4**
22 Place Bellecour **G9**
23 Place des Terreaux **F5**
24 Rue du Bœuf **D7**
25 Rue St-Jean **E6**
26 Théâtres Romains **B7**

Restaurants ▼

1 Au 14 Février **D7**
2 Brasserie Georges **E9**
3 Café des Fédérations **F5**
4 Café du Jura **G6**
5 Chez Hugon **G5**
6 Christian Têtedoie **C7**
7 Comptoir Abel **D9**
8 Daniel & Denise **D7**
9 La Bijouterie **E4**
10 La Boîte à Café **F3**
11 La Famille **E1**
12 La Mère Brazier **G3**
13 L'Ame Soeur **I7**
14 L'Auberge du Pont de Collonges **A3**
15 Le Garet **G5**
16 Le Kitchen Café **H9**
17 Le Neuvième Art **I5**
18 Le Passe Temps **I3**
19 Les Apothicaires **I4**
20 Les Lyonnais **D7**
21 L'Étage **F4**
22 M Restaurant **I3**
23 Ô Vins d'Anges **F1**
24 Prairial **F5**
25 Takao Takano **I3**

Hotels ▼

1 Dock Ouest **A3**
2 Hôtel Carlton Lyon **G7**
3 Hôtel des Artistes **F7**
4 La Cour des Loges **D6**
5 Mama Shelter **F9**
6 Okko Hotels Lyon Pont Lafayette **H5**
7 Phénix Hôtel **E5**
8 Villa Florentine **D6**
9 Villa Maïa **C7**

Lyon's economic and cultural success has always owed much to its location at the confluence of the Saône and the Rhône rivers.

rooms that re-create each period. ✉ *34 rue de la Charité, Presqu'île* ☎ *04–78–38–42–00* ⊕ *www.mtmad.fr* ✉ *€10* ⊘ *Closed Mon.*

Musée Urbain Tony Garnier (*Tony Garnier Urban Museum*)

MUSEUM | Built between 1920 and 1933, this project (also known as the Cité de la Création), was France's first attempt at low-income housing. Over the years, several tenants have contributed artwork in an effort to beautify the space. Most notably, 22 giant murals depicting the work of Tony Garnier, the turn-of-the-20th-century Lyon architect, were painted on the walls. Artists from around the world, with the support of UNESCO, have added their vision to the creation of the ideal housing project. ✉ *4 rue des Serpollières, Quartier des États-Unis* ⊹ *Take métro to Monplaisir-Lumière, then walk 10 mins south along Rue Antoine* ☎ *04–78–75–16–75* ⊕ *www.museeurbaintonygarnier.com* ✉ *€3* ⊘ *Closed Sun. and Mon.*

Musées Gadagne (*Lyon Historical Museum and Puppet Museum*)

MUSEUM | **FAMILY** | These two museums are housed in the city's largest ensemble of Renaissance buildings, the Hôtel de Gadagne, built between the 14th and 16th century. The **Musée d'Histoire de Lyon** traces the city's history from its pre-Roman days onward, displaying sculpture, furniture, pottery, paintings, and engravings. The **Musée des Marionnettes du Monde** focuses on the history of puppets, beginning with Guignol and Madelon—Lyon's Punch and Judy—created by Laurent Mourguet in 1795. It includes two hanging gardens, a café, and a shop. ✉ *1 pl. du Petit-Collège, Vieux Lyon* ☎ *04–78–42–03–61* ⊕ *www.gadagne.musees.lyon.fr* ✉ *€8 for both museums* ⊘ *Closed Mon. and Tues.*

Opéra de Lyon

ARTS VENUE | The barrel-vaulted Lyon Opera, a reincarnation of a moribund 1831 building, was designed by star French architect Jean Nouvel and built in the early 1990s. It incorporates a columned exterior, soaring glass vaulting, neoclassical public spaces, and an all-black interior. ⊠ *1 pl. de la Comédie, Presqu'île* ☎ *04–72–00–45–00* ⊕ *www. opera-lyon.com.*

Place Bellecour

PLAZA | Shady, imposing Place Bellecour is one of the largest squares in France, and is Lyon's fashionable center, midway between the Saône and the Rhône. Classical facades erected along its narrower sides in 1800 lend architectural interest. The large, bronze equestrian statue of Louis XIV, installed in 1828, is the work of local sculptor Jean Lemot. ⊠ *Pl. Bellecour, Presqu'île.*

Place des Terreaux

PLAZA | The four majestic horses rearing up from a monumental 19th-century fountain in the middle of this large square are an allegory of the River Saône by Frédéric-Auguste Bartholdi, who sculpted New York Harbor's Statue of Liberty. The 69 fountains embedded in the wide expanse of the square are illuminated by fiber-optic technology at night. The notable buildings on either side are the Hôtel de Ville and the Musée des Beaux-Arts. ⊠ *Pl. des Terreaux, Presqu'île.*

⭐ Rue du Bœuf

NEIGHBORHOOD | Like parallel Rue St-Jean, Rue du Bœuf has traboules, courtyards, spiral staircases, towers, and facades. The traboule at No. 31 hooks through and out onto Rue de la Bombarde. At No. 19 is the standout Maison de l'Outarde d'Or, so named for the great bustard, a gooselike game bird, depicted in the coat of arms over the door. The late-15th-century house and courtyard inside have spiral staircases in the towers, which were built as symbols of wealth and power. Number 20 conceals one of the rare open-shaft spiral staircases allowing for a view all the way up the core. The Hotel Tour Rose at No. 22 has, indeed, a beautiful *tour rose* (pink tower) in the inner courtyard. At the corner of Place Neuve St-Jean and Rue du Bœuf is the famous sign portraying the bull for which Rue du Bœuf is named, the work of the Renaissance Italy–trained French sculptor Jean de Bologne. ⊠ *Rue du Boeuf, Vieux Lyon.*

⭐ Rue St-Jean

NEIGHBORHOOD | Once Vieux Lyon's major thoroughfare, this street leads north from Place St-Jean to Place du Change, where money changers operated during medieval trade fairs. The elegant houses along it were built for illustrious Lyonnais bankers and Italian silk merchants during the French Renaissance. The traboule at No. 54 leads all the way through to Rue du Bœuf (No. 27). Beautiful Renaissance courtyards can be visited at No. 50, No. 52, and No. 42. At 27 rue St-Jean, an especially beautiful traboule winds through to 6 rue des Trois Maries. Number 28 has a pretty courtyard, as do No. 18 and No. 24. Maison Le Viste at No. 21 has a splendid facade. ⊠ *Rue St-Jean, Vieux Lyon.*

Théâtres Romains (*Roman Theaters*)

ARCHAEOLOGICAL SITE | Two ruined, semicircular, Roman-built theaters are tucked into the hillside, just down from the summit of Fourvière. The **Grand Théâtre,** the oldest Roman theater in France, was built in 15 BC to seat 10,000. The smaller **Odéon,** with its geometric flooring, was designed for music and poetry performances. ⊠ *Colline Fourvière, Fourvière* 🎫 *Free.*

Restaurants

Au 14 Février

$$$ | MODERN FRENCH | Cupid's arrows don't quite account for the rapturous reviews (and one Michelin star) garnered by Tsuyoshi Arai in his tiny chocolate box of a restaurant. The persnickety Lyonnais have fallen hard, waiting weeks to savor dishes that combine Japanese subtlety with rigorous French technique—like poached foie gras and creamy parsnip puree with caramelized carrot sauce,

Eating and Drinking in Lyon

No other city in France teases the taste buds like Lyon, birthplace of traditional French cuisine. Home to both the workingman's bouchons and many celebrity chefs, the capital of the Rhône-Alpes region has become the engine room for France's modern cooking canon.

Lyon owes much of its success as a gastronomic center to its auspicious location at the crossroads of several regional cuisines—the hearty cooking of the mountainous east; Auvergne's lambs to the west; Mediterranean tomato-vegetable-and-olive-oil-rich dishes to the south; and the luscious butters and cheeses of the north. Not to mention Rhône-Alpes' own natural riches: fish from local rivers, apricots and cherries from hillside orchards, and dairy and pork products from valley farms.

Charcuterie

One of Lyon's great contributions to France's gastronomic pantheon, charcuterie was a way to both preserve and use every part of a pig. Cured, brined, smoked, or potted, the meat appears as sausages, cured or air-dried ham, or rustic terrines of hearty paté. Although charcuterie is traditionally pork-based, it can also use beef, duck, or goose, mostly in the form of *rillettes*, a flavorful paté preserved in a silky layer of rendered fat. Previously in decline in France due to industrial versions and a loss of know-how, charcuterie is now being revived by artisans. Wandering the Sunday morning market serves as a great primer in Lyon charcuterie, with stand after stand selling sausages in every combination of meat, some made with herbs, nuts, or even cheese.

Nouvelle Cuisine

Hands down the most influential culinary innovation of the later 20th century, nouvelle cuisine was conceived in 1933 by Eugénie Brazier, France's first female chef to win three Michelin stars (her restaurant Mère Brazier is still a Lyon classic) and pioneered by Lyon native son chef Paul Bocuse. A lighter, healthier fare, this new cuisine favors simpler recipes, the freshest possible ingredients, and quick cooking times to highlight the natural flavors of vegetables and meat. Although it may seem something of a paradox coming from the capital of hearty dishes, savory sauces, and cured meats, nouvelle caught on like wildfire, sparking a worldwide revolution that paved the way for both the locavore and slow-food movements.

Quenelle de Brochet

Traditionally made with whitefish, especially the native pike from the Saône and Rhône rivers, the velvety quenelle remains a Lyon classic. Found in every neighborhood bouchon— each with its own special recipe—the dumplinglike fish cake is made with a flour-based white sauce mixed with cooked fish, then strained for a light and fluffy consistency. The mixture is shaped into ovals, briefly poached, and served with sauce mousseline (whisked egg, mustard, and lemon juice).

scallops rolled in sole and smoky bacon, verbena-infused lobster consommé with caviar, and salmon tartare in a gingery court bouillon with zucchini mousse. The cozy atmosphere only adds to its allure. **Known for:** gorgeous presentation; meticulous attention to details; beautiful dining room. $ *Average main: €32* ⊠ *6 rue Mourguet, 5e, Vieux Lyon* ☎ *04–78–92–91–39* ⊕ *www.au14fevrier.com* ⊗ *Closed Sun. and Mon. No lunch Tues.–Fri.*

Brasserie Georges

$$ | FRENCH | This inexpensive brasserie at the south end of Rue de la Charité is one of the city's largest and oldest, founded in 1836 and housed in a palatial building dating from 1925. Meals range from hearty veal stew or sauerkraut and sausage to more refined fare. **Known for:** eye-popping, Art Deco atmosphere; tradition Lyonnais food; beer brewed on premises. $ *Average main: €21* ⊠ *30 cours Verdun, Perrache* ☎ *04–72–56–54–54* ⊕ *www.brasseriegeorges.com.*

Café des Fédérations

$$ | FRENCH | FAMILY | For 80 years this sawdust-strewn café with homey red-check tablecloths has reigned as one of the city's leading bouchons, and although its glory days are long past, it's still a good bet for an authentic experience. For a taste of classic Lyon gastronomy in a historic setting, the deftly prepared local classics like boudin noir, *boudin blanc* (white-meat sausage), or *andouillettes* (veal and pork tripe sausage) are hard to beat. **Known for:** well-priced prix-fixe lunch menu; authentic atmosphere; great for families. $ *Average main: €18* ⊠ *8 rue du Major-Martin, Presqu'île* ☎ *04–78–28–26–00* ⊕ *www.restaurant-cafesfederations-lyon.com* ⊗ *Closed late Dec.–Jan. No dinner Sun.*

Café du Jura

$ | FRENCH | The *gateau de foies de volaille aux raviolis* (chicken-liver ravioli) is a masterpiece at this eatery founded in 1864. Game and steak dishes are robust, as is the *cassoulet des escargots* (stew of beans, mutton, and snails). **Known for:** top-notch Lyonnais charcuterie; authentic atmosphere; decent prices. $ *Average main: €16* ⊠ *25 rue Tupin, Presqu'île* ☎ *04–78–42–20–57* ⊕ *www.bouchonlejura.fr* ⊗ *Closed Sun. and Mon., and Aug.*

Chez Hugon

$$ | FRENCH | One of the city's best-known insider spots, this typical bouchon with the de rigueur red-check tablecloths sits behind the Musée des Beaux-Arts. Practically a club, it's crowded with regulars who trade quips with the owner while the kitchen prepares the best *tablier de sapeur* (tripe marinated in wine and fried in bread crumbs) in town. **Known for:** authentic Lyonnais cuisine; pricier than some bouchons; laid-back ambience. $ *Average main: €19* ⊠ *12 rue Pizay, Presqu'île* ☎ *04–78–28–10–94* ⊕ *www.bouchonlyonnais.fr* ⊗ *Closed weekends, and Aug.*

Christian Têtedoie

$$$$ | MODERN FRENCH | Star chef Christian Têtedoie's rocked the culinary world when, after 20 years, he shuttered his Michelin-starred gastronomic temple to open this soaring art-filled aerie perched atop Lyon's Fourvière hill. The minimalist design and immense bay windows offering staggering views of the city signaled a new direction in the great chef's approach, breaking free of classicism in favor of a more audacious menu: roasted foie gras with bitter orange, pineapple, and onion in a duck reduction; roast pigeon stuffed with garlic, cabbage, and chestnuts; or the chef's signature pressed *tête de veau* (calf's head) served with a half lobster *en cocotte* (casserole). **Known for:** stellar views; good-value prix-fixe menus at Le Phosphore wine bar downstairs; outdoor dining. $ *Average main: €40* ⊠ *Chemin Neuf, 1 rue de l'Antiquaille, Fourvière* ☎ *04–78–29–40–10* ⊕ *www.tetedoie.com* ⊗ *Closed Sun.*

★ Comptoir Abel

$$ | FRENCH | About 400 years old, this charming house is one of Lyon's most

The Bouchon Tradition 🍴

Lyon's iconic bouchons are casual bistrolike restaurants with a modest decor along the lines of tiled walls, wooden benches, and zinc counters. In the late 19th century, these informal eateries dished out hearty fare for working-class customers like pony express riders, stagecoach drivers, silk workers, and field laborers.

The term *bouchon* originated as a description for the bundles of straw that hung over the entrance of early bouchons, indicating the availability of food and drink for horses as well as humans. These friendly, family-run taverns were customarily run by female chefs, serving cuisine that relied heavily on humble pork and beef cuts, such as stomachs, brains, trotters, ears, cheeks, and livers.

Today, many restaurants call themselves bouchons that would not fit the traditional definition. For the real thing, look for a little plaque at the door showing Gnafron, a drunken marionette with red nose and wine glass in hand. He signifies that the establishment is part of the official bouchon association. These official bouchons are still a less pricey dining choice: in many establishments, €25 will buy an appetizer, main course, salad, and dessert or cheese plate.

frequently filmed and photographed taverns. Simple wooden tables in wood-panel dining rooms, quirky art on every wall, heavy-bottom *pot lyonnais* wine bottles—every detail is obviously pampered and lovingly produced. **Known for:** authentic Lyonnais specialties; unbeatable atmosphere; reasonable prices. [$] *Average main: €20* ✉ *25 rue Guynemer, Presqu'île* ☎ *04–78–37–46–18* 🌐 *www.cafecomptoirabel.fr* 🕓 *No dinner Sun.*

Daniel & Denise

$$ | **BISTRO** | Among other honors, chef Joseph Viola has distinguished himself by creating a world-champion *pâté en croûte* (foie gras in a pastry crust)—nothing to sneeze at, especially if you're at the helm of one of Lyon's better bouchons. Here you'll find a charming atmosphere, complete with checked tablecloths, lace curtains, and some of the city's most satisfying local specialties, including the quenelles *au brochet* (a tender, sausage-shape dumpling made from river pike). *Cervelle de veau* (calf brains) is another standout, and the faint of heart can't go wrong with the excellent boudin noir. **Known for:** pike quenelles and crayfish omelets; more contemporary atmosphere than other bouchons; good wine list. [$] *Average main: €18* ✉ *36 rue Tramassac, 5e, Vieux Lyon* ☎ *04–78–42–24–62* 🌐 *daniel-et-denise.fr* 🕓 *Closed Sun. and Mon.*

★ **La Bijouterie**

$$ | **FRENCH FUSION** | Set on a tiny street at the foot of the Croix Rousse neighborhood, this small, casual eatery has only six tables and a long communal table. Surely the best bargain in town, the €20 lunch menu (€26 with dessert) offers a choice of three Asian-inflected "bijoux" from a variety of 10 that include fish, meat, and vegetarian options, plus a bowl of soup and a bowl of rice. **Known for:** exquisite small dishes; resolutely locavore and vegetarian-friendly; reservations a must. [$] *Average main: €20* ✉ *16 rue Hippolyte Flandrin, La Croix Rousse* ☎ *04–78–08–14–03* 🌐 *www.labijouterierestaurant.fr* 🕓 *Closed Sun. and Mon.* [M] *Cordeliers.*

Lyon's Place des Terreaux is a true spectacle, thanks to 69 Daniel Buren fountains and Bartholdi's centerpiece watery marvel.

★ La Boite à Café

$ | CAFÉ | Watch the world go by on the street-side terrace at this small but lively café on a picturesque square at the foot of the hill leading to Croix Rousse. Low-key and casual, the focus here is squarely on the java—every kind of caffeinated beverage can be conjured up here, and coffee aficionados are reassured by the fact that the meticulously sourced beans are roasted on the premises. **Known for:** delicious desserts and pastries; one of Lyon's best coffee shops; friendly atmosphere great for hanging out. $ *Average main: €5* ⊠ *3 rue Abbé Rozier, Presqu'île* ☎ *04–27–01–48–71* ⊕ *www.cafemokxa.com.*

La Famille

$ | FRENCH | FAMILY | As the name would suggest, family photographs adorn the walls of this low-key bistro high on the Croix Rousse hillside. The simple cuisine tends toward traditional recipes and authentic Lyon fare made with organic and local ingredients. **Known for:** quality ingredients; excellent-value fixed-price menus at lunch and dinner; family-friendly atmosphere. $ *Average main: €17* ⊠ *18 rue Duviard, La Croix Rousse* ☎ *04–72–98–83–90* ⊕ *www.la-famille-croix-rousse.fr* ⊘ *Closed Sun. and Mon. No dinner Tues. and Wed.*

★ La Mère Brazier

$$$$ | FRENCH | This is a legendary location in Lyon—even more so now that Mathieu Viannay, one of the top names in the city's contemporary cuisine scene, has honored gastronomy pioneer Eugénie Brazier—the founder of nouvelle cuisine and the first woman to gain three Michelin stars in 1933—by opening a restaurant in her former space. A winner of the coveted Meilleur Ouvrier de France prize, Viannay continues to experiment with taste, textures, and ingredients in this carefully restored and recently remodeled traditional house. **Known for:** upscale authentic Lyon dining; pricey but worth it; Bresse chicken with black truffles under the skin. $ *Average main: €60* ⊠ *12 rue Royale, Presqu'île* ☎ *04–78–23–17–20*

🌐 *lamerebrazier.fr* 🕓 *Closed weekends, and Aug.*

★ L'Ame Soeur

$$ | MODERN FRENCH | Just behind the Palais de Justice, this little *néo-bistrot* (think comfortable vibe but contemporary design) has a €25 prix-fixe *formule* that is nothing short of superb in terms of both value and quality. Artisanal terrine of free-range duck, *rillettes de maquereau en salade de chou chinois* (mackerel fillets in Chinese cabbage salad), and fillet of rockfish with peppers are just some of the interesting morsels at this innovative, affordable address. **Known for:** excellent quality-to-price quotient; one of the best values in town; welcoming service. [$] *Average main: €18* ✉ *209 rue Duguesclin, Vieux Lyon* ☎ *04–78–42–47–78* 🌐 *www.restaurantlamesoeur.fr* 🕓 *Closed weekends. No dinner Mon.*

★ L'Auberge du Pont de Collonges

$$$$ | FRENCH | The late great Paul Bocuse—who kick-started nouvelle cuisine back in the 1970s and became a superstar in the process—may no longer be with us, but dishes like the legendary black-truffle soup in pastry crust he created in 1975 to honor President Giscard d'Estaing always will be. So will the frogs' leg soup with watercress; the green bean and artichoke salad with foie gras; and the "tripled" wood pigeon, consisting of a drumstick in puff pastry, a breast roasted and glazed in cognac, and a dark aromatic pâté of the innards. **Known for:** one of the best restaurants in Lyon with three Michelin stars; serves all Paul Bocuse's greatest recipes; extravagant €270 tasting menu. [$] *Average main: €65* ✉ *40 quai de la Plage, 10 km (6 miles) north of city center, Collonges-au-Mont-d'Or* ☎ *04–72–42–90–90* 🌐 *www.bocuse.fr* 👔 *Jacket required.*

★ Le Garet

$$ | FRENCH | From quenelles to the house favorite, andouillettes, this is the perfect primer in bouchon fare. Salade lyonnaise (frisée lettuce, pork lardons, croutons, and a poached egg, with a Dijon vinaigrette) is an institution at this famous dining room near the Hôtel de Ville. **Known for:** picturesque atmosphere; way above the average bouchon; historic setting. [$] *Average main: €20* ✉ *7 rue Garet, Presqu'île* ☎ *04–78–28–16–94* 🕓 *Closed weekends, and late July–late Aug.*

★ Le Kitchen Café

$ | FRENCH | Though delicious coffee, croissants, and pastries are on the all-day menu, Swedish chef Connie Zagora and her pastry chef husband, Laurent Ozan, dish up one of the more exciting gastronomic lunches in town in this luminous little café. A new concept that's catching hold in Paris and Lyon alike, the restaurant is open from 8 am to 6:30 pm, serving an all-day menu of sweet or savory breakfast foods (think broiled eggs with soy sauce, trout gravlax with dill cream, homemade granola, and *fromage frais*) and a range of homemade pastries. **Known for:** delicious all-day breakfasts; one of the best lunches in town; bright, friendly atmosphere. [$] *Average main: €12* ✉ *34 rue Chevreul* ☎ *06–03–36–42–75* 🌐 *www.lekitchencafe.com.*

★ Le Neuvième Art

$$$$ | MODERN FRENCH | Christophe Roure, who earned his chops with the likes of Bocuse and Gagnaire, now has two Michelin stars at this smashing restaurant. Considered one of Lyon's top tables, Roure's artistry extends to even the smallest details in dishes of exquisite refinement: Breton langoustine poached in saffron bouillon with tender violet artichokes; shellfish and shiitake ragout served with lemongrass-ginger hollandaise; pigeon and citrus-infused beets with a sauce of blackberry and bitter-orange marmalade. **Known for:** innovative dining; beautiful presentation; stunning desserts. [$] *Average main: €48* ✉ *173 rue Cuvier, Brotteaux* ☎ *04–72–74–12–74* 🌐 *www.leneuviemeart.com* 🕓 *Closed Sun. and Mon.*

★ Le Passe Temps

$$$$ | **MODERN FRENCH** | Korean chef Young-hoon Lee brings a pared-down aesthetic to both his stylishly spare dining room and a menu of exciting, imaginative dishes that has made this one of Lyon's most sought-after tables. The house Champagne-and-yuzu aperitif is a perfect send-off for a scintillating starter of pressed foie gras and smoked eel, followed by monkfish in a crayfish-and-shiitake bouillon or Wagyu beef with sweet onion puree and crispy hazelnut tuiles. **Known for:** one Michelin star; beautiful presentation; great wine list filled with small producers. $ *Average main: €45* ⊠ *52 rue Tronchet, 6e, Brotteaux* ☏ *04–72–82–90–14* ⊕ *www.lepassetemps-restaurant.com* ☾ *Closed Sun. and Mon.* Ⓜ *Masséna.*

★ Les Apothicaires

$$ | **FRENCH** | Chefs Tabata and Ludovic Mey made instant waves when they opened this stylish but casual dining room serving a "liberated and sincere" menu that plays with textures, temperatures, and flavor pairings. Options include crisp white beans paired with velvety smoked eel and cubes of bone marrow with sparks of lemon thyme; you can also enjoy the crunch of roasted chamomile flowers over tender squid, with tart-sweet meyer lemon and chamomile oil. **Known for:** stunning flavor pairings; minute attention to details; superb wine list. $ *Average main: €20* ⊠ *23 rue de Sèze, Brotteaux* ☏ *04–26–02–25–09* ⊕ *www.lesapothicairesrestaurant.com* Ⓜ *Foch.*

Les Lyonnais

$$ | **FRENCH** | Decorated with photographs of local celebrities, this popular bistro is particularly animated. Simple food—chicken simmered for hours in wine, meaty stews, and grilled fish—is served on bare wood tables. **Known for:** good price-to-quality ratio; very popular with locals; lighter bouchon fare. $ *Average main: €19* ⊠ *19 rue de la Bombarde, Vieux Lyon* ☏ *04–78–37–64–82* ⊕ *www.restaurant-lyonnais.com* ☾ *Closed Mon., and 1 wk at Christmas. No dinner Sun.*

★ L'Étage

$$$ | **FRENCH** | Hidden over Place des Terreaux, this semisecret upstairs dining room in a former silk-weaving loft prepares some of Lyon's finest and most daring cuisine. A place at the window (admittedly hard to come by), overlooking the facade of the Beaux Arts academy across the square, is a moment to remember—especially during December's Festival of Lights. **Known for:** tiny, elegant dining room; stunning cuisine; great value three-course lunch menu. $ *Average main: €25* ⊠ *4 pl. des Terreaux, 3rd fl., Presqu'île* ☏ *04–78–28–19–59* ⊕ *www.letage-restaurant.com* ☾ *Closed Sun. and Mon., and late July–late Aug.*

M Restaurant

$$ | **FRENCH** | Accomplished chef Julien Gautier struts his considerable stuff at this stylish upper-Brotteaux-district bistro east of the Rhône. Expect an inventive, market-driven cuisine, characterized by dishes like slow-cooked lamb with grilled eggplant, buffalo mozzarella, and pine nuts; jumbo shrimp in a broth of garlic and tarragon; or succulent Basque chicken with grilled chorizo and roasted red peppers to savor along with a fine selection of good-value wines by the bottle or glass. **Known for:** popular with young professional crowd; good-value lunch menu; stylish decor. $ *Average main: €20* ⊠ *47 av. Foch, Brotteaux* ☏ *04–78–89–55–19* ⊕ *www.mrestaurant.fr* ☾ *Closed weekends, and Aug.*

★ Ô Vins d'Anges

$$ | **WINE BAR** | He's an indefatigable champion of small-producer wines, and you'd have to be a stone not to be swept up in Sébastien Milleret's passion. A congenial atmosphere prevails at this wineshop and bar, and excellent small dishes—luscious burrata cheese served with fruity olive oil and capers, freshly shaved bresaola and lardo, or briny smoked eel—are complemented by reasonably priced wines by the glass. **Known for:** congenial wine tastings; great for discovery of new dishes; lovely neighborhood. $ *Average main: €20 ⊠ 2 pl. Bertone, La Croix Rousse ☎ 09–51–88–20–99 ⊕ www.ovinsdanges.fr/ ⊘ Closed Sun. and Mon., and 2 wks in Jan. No food Tues. and Wed.*

★ Prairial

$$$$ | MODERN FRENCH | Culinary innovation runs deep in this food-centric city, and Gaëton Gentil is among the new generation chefs shaking things up, with a fruit-and-vegetable-centered cuisine that's as subtle as it is surprising. Unexpected flavor combinations (grapefruit and marigold; chicken and lemon verbena) are refreshingly original and presented with an almost pictorial beauty. **Known for:** vegetarian fixed menu; cod with creamy sabayone, yellow squash, and a dusting of roasted lemon powder; small space so reservations are a must. $ *Average main: €36 ⊠ 11 rue Chavanne, Presqu'île ☎ 04–78–27–86–93 ⊕ www.prairial-restaurant.com ⊘ Closed Sun. and Mon.*

★ Takao Takano

$$$ | MODERN FRENCH | After barely a year on his own, Takao Takano's eponymous restaurant earned off-the-charts accolades and a coveted Michelin star (now two) for his imaginative cuisine. Takano honed his craft during eight years as sous chef to Nicholas Le Bec (now in Shanghai), but he brings his own aesthetic to the fore in a warm, pared-down space outside the city center. **Known for:** vibrant, superbly crafted cuisine; refined presentation; only the best ingredients. $ *Average main: €30 ⊠ 33 rue Malesherbes, 6e, Part-Dieu ☎ 04–82–31–43–39 ⊕ takaotakano.com ⊘ Closed Sun. and Mon.*

Hotels

Dock Ouest

$ | HOTEL | One of the newer hotels in the Paul Bocuse empire, Dock Ouest aims for a more youthful clientele that cares more about stylish comforts and budget prices than an out-of-the-way location. **Pros:** excellent value; couldn't be quieter; underground parking. **Cons:** 10-minute walk from the metro; out-of-the-way location; not service oriented. $ *Rooms from: €65 ⊠ 39 rue des Docks, 9e, Saint-Rambert ☎ 04–78–22–34–34 ⊕ www.dockouest.com ⇆ 42 rooms ¶◯ No meals.*

Hôtel Carlton Lyon

$$$ | HOTEL | As one of a handful of upscale hotels in the city, the centrally located Carlton overlooks the Place de la République, adding a much-needed frisson of international style to Lyon's lodging scene. **Pros:** top-notch service; centrally located near shopping and restaurants; nice cocktail lounge. **Cons:** some rooms are quite small; decor not to all tastes; some rooms need upgrading. $ *Rooms from: €336 ⊠ 4 rue Jussieu, Presqu'île ☎ 04–78–42–56–51 ⊕ www. sofitel.com/gb/hotel-2950-hotel-carlton-lyon-mgallery-collection/index.shtmll ⇆ 80 rooms ¶◯ No meals* Ⓜ *Cordeliers Bourse.*

Hôtel des Artistes

$$ | HOTEL | On an elegant square opposite the Théâtre des Célestins, this chic hotel has a sense of theatricality—logically enough because it has long been popular among stage and screen artists (many of whose photographs adorn the lobby walls). **Pros:** central location for Presqu'île; pretty view over square; modern and stylish decor. **Cons:** slightly cluttered spaces; a few clicks behind cutting-edge technology; breakfast is extra. $ *Rooms from: €129 ⊠ 8 rue Gaspard-André, Presqu'île ☎ 04–78–42–04–88 ⊕ www.hotel-des-artistes.fr ⇆ 45 rooms ¶◯ No meals.*

★ **La Cour des Loges**
$$$$ | **HOTEL** | King Juan Carlos of Spain, Céline Dion, and the Rolling Stones have all graced this former convent whose glowing fireplaces, Florentine crystal chandeliers, Baroque credenzas, and guest rooms swathed in antique Lyon silks now make monastic austerity a very distant memory. **Pros:** top Vieux Lyon location; friendly and meticulous service; extraordinary restaurant. **Cons:** hard on the budget; could stand some remodeling; bar is not as cozy as you would think. [$] *Rooms from: €370* ✉ *6 rue du Bœuf, Vieux Lyon* ☎ *04–72–77–44–44* 🌐 *www.courdesloges.com* 🛏 *60 rooms* 🍴 *No meals.*

Mama Shelter
$$ | **HOTEL** | "Mama loves you" is this Philippe Starck–designed hotel chain's motto, and, to prove it, guests are wrapped in the angular embrace of minimal, gadget-happy rooms that make up for their size with artsy touches and a general atmosphere of too-cool-for-school fun. **Pros:** lively bar scene; good prices; free Wi-Fi and movies. **Cons:** cramped rooms and bathrooms; superhero-heavy decor not for everyone; average service. [$] *Rooms from: €149* ✉ *13 rue Domer, Presqu'île* ☎ *04–78–02–58–00* 🌐 *www.mamashelter.com* 🛏 *156 rooms* 🍴 *No meals* [M] *Jean-Macé.*

★ **Okko Hotels Lyon Pont Lafayette**
$$ | **HOTEL** | A mix of old-world Lyon elegance and edgy urban style, this well-located hotel, housed in a gorgeous 18th-century mansion, has the double advantage of putting you at the center of the action with comfort and style to spare. **Pros:** views of the river and Notre Dame de Fourvière from some rooms; superb breakfasts; excellent value. **Cons:** no minibar in rooms; rooms on the small side; no adjoining family rooms. [$] *Rooms from: €130* ✉ *14 bis quai du Général Sarrail, Part-Dieu* ☎ *04–28–00–02–50* 🌐 *www.okkohotels.com* 🛏 *87 rooms* 🍴 *Free Breakfast* [M] *Cordeliers.*

Phénix Hôtel
$$ | **HOTEL** | This little hotel overlooking the River Saône has a winning combination of handy location, charming staff, tasteful rooms, and moderate prices. **Pros:** convenient to but not in the middle of Vieux Lyon; stylish but not stuffy; easy on the budget. **Cons:** interior rooms on the air shaft; a long walk to the middle of the Presqu'île; some rooms have low ceilings. [$] *Rooms from: €165* ✉ *7 quai Bondy, Vieux Lyon* ☎ *04–78–28–24–24* 🌐 *hotel-phenix-lyon.fr* 🛏 *36 rooms* 🍴 *No meals.*

★ **Villa Florentine**
$$$ | **HOTEL** | High above the Vieille Ville, this pristine hotel was once a 17th-century convent; glowing in its ocher-yellow exterior, it has vaulted ceilings, lovely terraces, and marvelous views, seen to best advantage from the Terrasses de Lyon restaurant. **Pros:** panoramic location above the Saône; wonderful restaurant; good access to Vieux Lyon. **Cons:** a hot climb up to the hotel in summer; tricky access by car; somewhat removed from the action. [$] *Rooms from: €295* ✉ *25–27 montée St-Barthélémy, Fourvière* ☎ *04–72–56–56–56* 🌐 *www.villaflorentine.com* 🛏 *28 rooms* 🍴 *No meals.*

★ **Villa Maïa**
$$$$ | **HOTEL** | With this chic boutique hotel, Lyon can finally boast the kind of bespoke contemporary luxury the city has long lacked, including all the standout touches: a beautiful day-lit swimming pool and small spa, a private garden, elegant marble baths, and flawless service. **Pros:** totally removed from the city bustle; unbelievable sunset views over Lyon; across the street from one of the city's top gastronomic restaurants and bar (Tetedoie). **Cons:** walk or cab ride from Lyon's main dining scene and nightlife; no in-house restaurant; expensive, especially the larger suites. [$] *Rooms from: €410* ✉ *8 rue Pierre Marion, Fourvière* ☎ *04–78–16–01–01* 🌐 *www.villa-maia.com* 🛏 *37 rooms* 🍴 *Free Breakfast* [M] *Fourvière.*

Did You Know?

Every year in early December, Lyon puts on the incredible Fête des Lumières (Festival of Lights), during which more than 70 light installations transform the city's streetscapes into thrilling works of art.

ⓨ Nightlife

Lyon is the region's liveliest arts center. Check the weekly *Lyon-Poche* (⊕ *www. lyonpoche.com*) for cultural events and goings-on at the dozens of discos, bars, and clubs.

Black Forest Society

BARS/PUBS | One of the pioneers of Lyon's cocktail bar explosion, this cozy Bavarian-theme hot spot, with a long bar and sidewalk tables, is a favorite among those in the know. Drinks are well made and well priced and there are plenty of mocktails and German beers, of course. Cheese and charcuterie boards stave off late-night hunger. ⊠ *29 rue de l'Arbre Sec* ☎ *06–66–17–00–14* Ⓜ *Hôtel de Ville - Louis Pradel.*

Hot Club

MUSIC CLUBS | Live jazz has been played in the stone basement of the Hot Club since 1948, so they are obviously getting it right. ⊠ *26 rue Lanterne, Presqu'île* ☎ *04–78–39–54–74* ⊕ *www.hotclubjazzlyon.com.*

La Cave des Voyageurs

WINE BARS—NIGHTLIFE | Just below the St-Paul train station, La Cave des Voyageurs is a cozy place to sample some carefully selected wines. ⊠ *7 pl. St-Paul, Vieux Lyon* ☎ *04–78–28–92–28* ⊕ *lacavedesvoyageurs.fr.*

★ Le Fantôme de l'Opéra

BARS/PUBS | A carefully staged scene of plush velvets, romantic lighting, vintage touches, and mood music on a phonograph create a delicious atmosphere and that's even before you get to the drinks. Inventive ambrosias with expressive names like Monkey Shoulder or Sex on the Beach are concocted from house-made syrups and fresh juices, and change monthly according to what's in season. There's also an impressive list of spirits and wines as well as small plates of cheese and charcuterie to keep you going through the night. ⊠ *19 rue Royale* ☎ *04–37–92–03–88* ⊕ *www.lefantomedelopera.fr.* Ⓜ *Hôtel de Ville, Louis Pradel.*

Le Marché Gare

MUSIC CLUBS | Live music from salsa to hip-hop rules at Le Marché Gare. ⊠ *34 rue Casimir Périer, Presqu'île* ☎ *04–72–77–50–25* ⊕ *www.marchegare.fr.*

★ Le Sucre

MUSIC CLUBS | Atop the La Sucrière arts center, set in a refurbished 1930s sugar factory in the up-and-coming Confluence neighborhood, Le Sucre is Lyon's most happening bar-nightclub for the more artsy crowd. Here you'll find DJ sets, offbeat performances, and an eclectic series of art shows and dance events all centered on the cutting-edge music scene. All special performances, and prices, are listed online; some are free, or you can buy a ticket in advance online or at the door for €2 more. You can go to the bar as a walk-in. ⊠ *50 quai Rambaud* ⊕ *www.le-sucre.eu.*

★ L'Officine

BARS/PUBS | Set in Lyon's hip Hôtel Dieu complex, L'Officine's elegant decor, featuring leather banquettes, plush velvet chairs, wood paneling, and mood lighting, conveys a luxe private club atmosphere. It's the perfect backdrop for a menu of sublime cocktails made by Lyon's star mixologists. An ample selection of whiskeys, bourbons, gins, wines, and champagnes attract aficionados, and the outdoor terrace is a delight in warm weather. Small gourmet plates mean you can get there early and sample for dinner, a good idea at this popular address. ⊠ *3 cour St-Henri Grand Hôtel-Dieu, Part-Dieu* ☎ *04–72–41–84–96* ⊕ *www.lofficinedugrandrefectoire.com.*

Smoking Dog

BARS/PUBS | For the hottest English pub in Lyon, the Smoking Dog is the place to head. You can't miss the bright red awning out front. ⊠ *16 rue Lainerie, Vieux Lyon* ☎ *04–78–28–38–27.*

★ Soda

BARS/PUBS | One of more than half a dozen cocktail meccas near Lyon's City Hall and just across the rivers, this one is a standout for its laid-back lounge atmosphere and tantalizing menu of virtuosic cocktail concoctions. There are delicious small plates, too. ⊠ *7 rue de la Martinière* ☎ *04–78–39–06–66* ⊕ *www.soda-bar.fr.*

 Performing Arts

Espace Gerson

CABARET | The café-theater Espace Gerson presents revues and assorted stand-up shows. ⊠ *1 pl. Gerson, Vieux Lyon* ☎ *04–78–27–96–99* ⊕ *www.espace-gerson.com.*

L'Accessoire Café-Théâtre

CAFES—NIGHTLIFE | Here you can eat and drink while watching a comedy show. ⊠ *26 rue de l'Annonciade, Presqu'île* ☎ *04–78–27–84–84* ⊕ *www.accessoire-cafe-theatre.com.*

Le Complexe du Rire

COMEDY CLUBS | Also known as the Minette Theatre, Le Complexe du Rire is a lively satirical café-theater above Place des Terreaux. ⊠ *7 rue des Capucins, Presqu'île* ☎ *04–78–27–23–59* ⊕ *www.complexedurire.com.*

Shopping

Lyon remains France's silk-and-textile capital, and all big-name designers have shops here. The 19th-century Passage de l'Argue (between Rue du Président Édouard-Herriot and Rue de la République in the center of town) is lined with traditional shops. The Carré d'Or district has more than 70 luxury ones between Place Bellecour and Cordeliers.

Food markets are held Tuesday to Sunday on Boulevard de la Croix-Rousse, at Les Halles on Cours Lafayette, on Quai Victor Augagneur, and on Quai St-Antoine. For antiques, wander down Rue Auguste-Comte. For secondhand books try the market along Quai de la Pêcherie near Place Bellecour, held every weekend 10–6.

Antic Wine

FOOD/CANDY | For great wines, tasting sessions, and up-to-the-minute information on local restaurants, don't miss the prize-winning "flying sommelier," Georges Dos Santos, at Antic Wine. ⊠ *18 rue du Bœuf, Vieux Lyon* ☎ *04–78–37–08–96* ⊕ *anticwine.e-monsite.com.*

Bernachon

FOOD/CANDY | Some say Bernachon is the best chocolaterie in France. It's a family business that proudly passes the torch from father to son. ⊠ *42 cours Franklin-Roosevelt, Brotteaux* ☎ *04–78–24–37–98* ⊕ *www.bernachon.com.*

Bouillet

FOOD/CANDY | With a stunning selection of artisanal chocolate, Bouillet is paradise for chocoholics. It also has stores at 14 rue des Archers and 3 rue d'Austerlitz. ⊠ *15 pl. de la Croix Rousse, La Croix Rousse* ☎ *04–78–28–90–89* ⊕ *www.chocolatier-bouillet.com.*

Cha Yuan

FOOD/CANDY | The best tea shop in Lyon, Cha Yuan stocks more than 300 varieties from all over the world. You can also buy candies, gourmet goodies, and everything you need to brew the perfect cup of tea. ⊠ *7–9 rue des Remparts d'Ainay, Presqu'île* ☎ *04–78–41–04–60* ⊕ *www.cha-yuan.com.*

Diogène

BOOKS/STATIONERY | Smelling of old leather and ancient paper, this shop sells rare and antique books. ⊠ *29 rue St-Jean, Vieux Lyon* ☎ *04–78–42–29–41* ⊕ *www.librairiediogene.fr.*

La Maison des Canuts

CLOTHING | In Lyon's old silk *quartier*, this boutique is replete with fine examples of locally made fabrics that you can wear or take home with you. ⊠ *10–12 rue d'Ivry,*

La Croix Rousse ☎ 04–78–28–62–04 ⊕ www.maisondescanuts.com.

L'Atelier de Soierie

TEXTILES/SEWING | Plan a trip here to see how silk prints are made, and perhaps take home a piece of Lyon. ⊠ *33 rue Romarin, Presqu'île* ☎ *04–72–07–97–83* ⊕ *www.atelierdesoierie.com.*

Les Halles de Lyon Paul Bocuse

FOOD/CANDY | Take a cue from super-star chef Paul Bocuse and shop at the market stalls of Lyon's most extensive and vibrant food market, named after its legendary chef. ⊠ *102 cours Lafayette, Part-Dieu* ☎ *04–78–62–39–33.*

Nicolas Fafiotte Couture

CLOTHING | This shop specializes in Fafiotte's high-end evening wear, and you need an appointment to visit. ⊠ *8 rue du Plat, Presqu'île* ☎ *04–72–41–84–79* ⊕ *www.nicolasfafiotte.com.*

Part-Dieu

SHOPPING CENTERS/MALLS | One of the biggest shopping centers in Europe is Part-Dieu, where you'll find more than 250 shops and boutiques. Galeries Lafayette, a major department store, brings Parisian flair to Lyon. ⊠ *Rue du Dr-Bouchut, Part-Dieu* ☎ *04–72–60–60–62* ⊕ *www.centrecommercial-partdieu.com.*

Pignol

FOOD/CANDY | This shop's pastries, meats, and wines are so good that it has expanded to become a mini-chain, with locations selling gourmet prepared foods at 8 place Bellecour, 48 rue Vendôme, and 42 rue de la République. The tearoom is at this address. ⊠ *17 rue Émile-Zola, Presqu'île* ☎ *04–78–92–43–92* ⊕ *www.pignol.fr.*

Printemps

DEPARTMENT STORES | This is the Lyon outpost of the famous Parisian department store specializing in fashions for men and women. ⊠ *42 rue de la République, Presqu'île* ☎ *04–72–41–29–29* ⊕ *www.printemps.com.*

Reynon

FOOD/CANDY | This is *the* place for char-cuterie. Look for the wonderful array of sausages hanging in the front window. ⊠ *13 rue des Archers, Presqu'île* ☎ *04–78–37–39–08* ⊕ *www.reynonlyon.com.*

★ Village des Créateurs

CRAFTS | In La Croix Rousse—once the heart of Lyon's silk trade and the traditional neighborhood for artists and craftspeople—this pleasant pedestrian street is a showplace for 70 talented young designers. Along with fashions for women (often using locally made silk), men, and children, you'll also find beautiful handmade ceramics, leather goods, and jewelry. ⊠ *Passage Thiaffait, 19 rue René Leynaud, La Croix Rousse* ☎ *04–78–27–37–21* ⊕ *www.villagedescreateurs.com.*

Voisin

FOOD/CANDY | For the famous chocolate *coussins* (pillows), check out Voisin. The confections have become so popular that there are now eight shops in Lyon, including one at 11 place Bellecour, right next to the main tourist office. ⊠ *28 rue de la République, Presqu'île* ☎ *04–78–42–46–24* ⊕ *www.chocolat-voisin.com.*

Beaujolais Wine Route

16 km (10 miles) north of Villefranche-sur-Saône, 49 km (30 miles) north of Lyon.

Not all Beaujolais wine is promoted as *vin nouveau* (new wine), despite the highly successful marketing campaign that has made Beaujolais Nouveau synonymous with French wine. Wine classed as "Beaujolais Villages" is higher in alcohol and produced from a clearly defined region northwest of Villefranche. Beaujolais is made from one single variety of grape: *gamay noir à jus blanc.* However, there are 12 different appellations: Beaujolais, Beaujolais Villages, Brouilly, Chénas, Chiroubles, Côte de Brouilly, Fleurie, Juliénas, Morgon, Moulin à Vent,

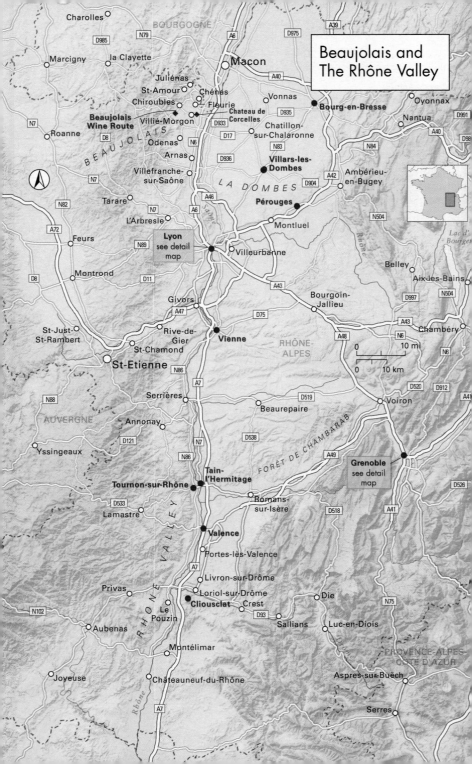

Beaujolais and
The Rhône Valley

Régnié, and St-Amour. The Beaujolais Route du Vin (Wine Road), a narrow strip 23 km (14 miles) long, is home to nine of these deluxe Beaujolais wines, also known as *grands crus.*

GETTING HERE AND AROUND

For the Beaujolais wine country, most people take the train to the station on Place de la Gare in Villefranche-sur-Saône, 31 km (19 miles) north of Lyon, where trains to smaller towns are available. SNCF trains link Lyon Part-Dieu with Villefranche-sur-Saône (26 mins, €7.80). Cars du Rhône (Line 18) connects Lyon with Villefranche-sur-Saône with multiple connections to surrounding towns.

VISITOR INFORMATION Beaujolais Tourist Office ✉ *96 rue de la Sous-Préfecture, Villefranche-sur-Mer* ☎ *04–74–07–27–40* 🌐 *www.destination-beaujolais.com.* **Cars du Rhône** ☎ *08–00–10–40–36* 🌐 *www.carsdurhone.fr.*

Sights

Château de Corcelles

WINERY/DISTILLERY | The 15th-century Château de Corcelles is noted for its Renaissance galleries, canopied courtyard well, and medieval carvings in its chapel. The guardroom is now an atmospheric boutique and tasting cellar, where you can buy and taste the estate wines. ✉ *D9, 3 km (2 miles) east of Villié-Morgon via D9, Corcelles-en-Beaujolais* ☎ *04–74–66–00–24* 🌐 *www.chateaudecorcelles.fr* 🎫 *€5* 🕑 *Closed Sun.*

Hotels

★ **Château de Bagnols**

$$$$ | HOTEL | A destination in itself, Lady Hamlyn's dazzlingly elegant castle-hotel is one of the glories of the Beaujolais, as anyone can tell with one glance at the *fantastique* Grand Salon. **Pros:** grandly elegant; panoramic views; unrivaled dining. **Cons:** a little like living in a museum; very expensive rates; breakfast not included. [$] *Rooms from: €425* ✉ *D38, 15 km (9 miles) southwest of Villefranche, Bagnols* ☎ *04–74–71–40–00* 🌐 *www.chateaudebagnols.com* 🛏 *27 suites* 🍴 *No meals.*

Bourg-en-Bresse

30 km (18 miles) east of St-Amour on N79, 81 km (49 miles) northeast of Lyon.

Cheerful, flower-festooned Bourg-en-Bresse is esteemed among gastronomes for its chickens—the striking-looking poulet de Bresse, with plump white bodies, bright blue feet, and red combs (adding up to France's *tricolore,* or national colors). The town's southeastern-most district, Brou, is its most interesting and the site of a singular church. This is a good place to stay before or after a trip along the Beaujolais Wine Road.

GETTING HERE AND AROUND

Ouibus connects Lyon-Saint-Exupéry airport with Bourg-en-Bresse three times daily (1 hr 25 mins, €7). SNCF trains link Lyon Perrache station with Bourg-en-Bresse (1 hr 22 mins, €12.90).

VISITOR INFORMATION Bourg-en-Bresse Tourist Office ✉ *2 rue Clavagry* ☎ *04–74–22–49–40* 🌐 *www.bourgenbresse-tourisme.fr.* **Ouibus** ☎ *01–71–53–01–80* 🌐 *www.fr.ouibus.com.*

Sights

Église de Brou

RELIGIOUS SITE | A marvel of the Flamboyant Gothic style, the Église de Brou is no longer in religious use. The church was built between 1513 and 1532 by Margaret of Austria in memory of her husband, Philibert le Beau, Duke of Savoy, and their finely sculpted tombs highlight the rich interior. Outside, a massive restoration of the roof has brought it back to its 16th-century state, with the same gorgeous, multicolor, intricate patterns found throughout Burgundy. The

For a true Beaujolais blowout book a stay at Lady Hamlyn's Château de Bagnols, where even Louis XIV would feel right at home.

museum in the nearby cloister stands out for its paintings: 16th- and 17th-century Flemish and Dutch artists keep company with 17th- and 18th-century French and Italian masters, 19th-century artists of the Lyon School, Gustave Doré, and contemporary local painters. ✉ *63 bd. de Brou* ☎ *04–74–22–83–83* 🌐 *www.monastere-de-brou.fr* 🎟 *€9.*

🍴 Restaurants

★ Georges Blanc

$$$$ | FRENCH | In the village of Vonnas, a simple 19th-century inn with 30 rooms full of antique country furniture doubles as one of the greatest gastronomic addresses in all of Gaul. Poulet de Bresse, truffles, and lobster are just some of the divine dishes featured on the legendary menu created by three-Michelin-star chef Monsieur Blanc, whose culinary DNA extends back to innkeepers from the French Revolution. **Known for:** stellar wine list; stately, over-the-top dining room; stiff prices. [$] *Average main: €100* ✉ *Pl. du Marché, 23 km (14 miles) from Bourg-en-Bresse, Vonnas* ☎ *04–74–50–90–90* 🌐 *www.georges-blanc.com* 🕓 *Closed Mon. and Tues., and Jan. No lunch Wed. and Thurs.*

L'Auberge Bressane

$$$$ | FRENCH | Overlooking the town's wonderful church, this modern, polished dining room is a good match for chef Jean-Pierre Vullin's cuisine. Frogs' legs and Bresse chicken with a wild-morel cream sauce are the specialties, but also consider the quenelles *de brochet* (poached-fish dumplings). Jean-Pierre wanders through the dining room ready for a chat while his staff provides excellent service. **Known for:** pretty views; warm atmosphere; local flavor. [$] *Average main: €38* ✉ *166 bd. de Brou* ☎ *04–74–22–22–68* 🌐 *www.aubergebressane.fr* 🕓 *Closed Tues.*

🛏 Hotels

Hôtel de France

$ | HOTEL | This centrally located budget hotel offers comfortable rooms equipped with the full range of modern amenities. **Pros:** convenient location for exploring the town; all amenities included; excellent restaurant next door. **Cons:** in the midst of the hustle and bustle; uninspired corporate decor; needs modernizing. $ *Rooms from: €100 ⊠ 19 pl. Bernard ☎ 04–74–23–30–24 ⊕ www.bestwestern-hotelde-france.com ⤳ 45 rooms ⦿⦿ No meals.*

Villars-les-Dombes

29 km (18 miles) south of Bourg-en-Bresse, 37 km (23 miles) northeast of Lyon.

Villars-les-Dombes is the unofficial capital of La Dombes, an area once covered by a glacier. When the ice retreated, it left a network of lakes and ponds that draws anglers and bird-watchers today.

Sights

Parc des Oiseaux

ZOO | The 56-acre Parc des Oiseaux, one of Europe's finest bird sanctuaries, is home sweet home to 400 species of birds from five continents. More than 400 aviaries house species from waders to birds of prey, and tropical birds in vivid hues fill the indoor birdhouse. Allow two hours for a visit. ⊠ D1083 ☎ 04–74–98–05–54 ⊕ www.parcdesoiseaux.com ⤳ €20 ⊗ *Closed mid-Nov.-mid-Mar.*

Pérouges

36 km (22 miles) northeast of Lyon.

With its medieval houses and narrow cobbled streets surrounded by ramparts, wonderfully preserved Pérouges is only 200 yards across. Handweavers first brought it prosperity; but the Industrial Revolution meant their downfall, and by the late 19th century the population had dwindled from 1,500 to 12. Now the government has restored the most

interesting houses, giving the town a new lease on life. A number of restaurants make Pérouges a good lunch stop.

GETTING HERE AND AROUND

Park your car by the main gateway, Porte d'En-Haut, alongside the 15th-century fortress-church. Rue du Prince, the town's main street, leads to the Maison des Princes de Savoie (Palace of the Princes of Savoy), the erstwhile home of the influential Savoie family that once controlled the eastern part of France.

Sights

Musée du Vieux Pérouges (*Old Pérouges Museum*)

MUSEUM | To one side of Place de la Halle, the Musée du Vieux Pérouges contains local artifacts and a reconstructed weaver's workshop. The medieval garden is noted for its array of rare medicinal plants. ⊠ Pl. du Tilleul ☎ 04–74–46–70–84 ⤳ €5 ⊗ *Closed Nov.–Mar.*

Vienne

27 km (17 miles) south of Lyon.

If you do nothing but head up to this town's famed Roman Theater and look out over the red-tile roofs of the Rhône Valley, you'll be happy you made the 20-minute trip from Lyon. Vienne is a historian's dream, and every street takes you to yet another ancient church, another austere Roman ruin, or another postcard-perfect view of crumbling walls and sloped roofs.

The Billet Intermusée (€8) admits you to all local monuments and museums within a 48-hour period. Even better, the Billet-Pass (€6) admits you to three museums and the Théâtre Roman. Both are available at the first site that you visit.

11

Lyon and the Alps VIENNE

GETTING HERE AND AROUND

SNCF trains link Lyon Perrache or Lyon Part-Dieu stations with Vienne (18–32 mins, €7.40). From Lyon-Saint-Exupéry, the best connection to Vienne is to take the shuttle to Lyon Part-Dieu and the train to Vienne.

VISITOR INFORMATION Vienne Tourist Office ⊠ *14 cours Brillier* ☎ *04–74–53–70–10* ⊕ *www.vienne-condrieu.com.*

 # Sights

Cité Gallo-Romaine de St-Romain-en-Gal (*Gallo-Roman City*)

ARCHAEOLOGICAL SITE | Across the Rhône from the town center is the excavated Cité Gallo-Romaine, covering several acres. Here you can find villas, houses, workshops, public baths, and roads, all built by the Romans. Views of the site can be had from the stunning glassed-in museum, which houses temporary exhibitions, mosaics excavated at the site, a boutique, and a pleasantly bright café. ⊠ *Rte. Départementale 502, Saint-Romain-en-Gal* ☎ *04–74–53–74–01* ⊕ *www.musees-gallo-romains.com* ☒ *From €6* ⊘ *Closed Mon.*

Roman gateway

ARCHAEOLOGICAL SITE | The last vestige of the city's sizable Roman baths is a Roman gateway decorated with delicate friezes. ⊠ *Rue Chantelouve.*

St-André-le-Bas

RELIGIOUS SITE | Rue des Orfèvres (off Rue de la Charité) is lined with Renaissance facades and distinguished by the church of St-André-le-Bas, once part of a powerful abbey, with beautifully restored 12th-century capitals and a 17th-century wood statue of St. Andrew. It's best to see the cloisters during the music festival held here and at the cathedral from June through August. ⊠ *Pl. du jeu de Paume* ☎ *04–74–85–18–49* ☒ *From €3* ⊘ *Closed Mon.*

St-Maurice

RELIGIOUS SITE | Although religious wars deprived the cathedral of St-Maurice of many of its statues, much of the original decoration is intact; the portals on the 15th-century facade are carved with Old Testament scenes. The cathedral was built between the 12th and 16th centuries, with later additions, such as the splendid 18th-century mausoleum to the right of the altar. A frieze of the zodiac adorns the entrance to the vaulted passage that once led to the cloisters but now opens onto Place St-Paul. ⊠ *Pl. St-Paul* ☎ *04–74–85–60–28.*

St-Pierre

RELIGIOUS SITE | Beside the Rhône is the church of St-Pierre—note the rectangular 12th-century Romanesque bell tower with its arcaded tiers. The lower church walls date from the 6th century, and there is a collection of Gallo-Roman architectural fragments on display. ⊠ *Quai Jean-Jaurès.*

Temple d'Auguste et de Livie (*Temple of Augustus and Livia*)

ARCHAEOLOGICAL SITE | The remains of the Temple d'Auguste et de Livie, accessible via Place St-Paul and Rue Clémentine, probably date in part from Vienne's earliest Roman settlements (1st century BC). The Corinthian columns were walled in during the 11th century, when the temple was used as a church; in 1833 Prosper Mérimée intervened to have the temple restored. ⊠ *Pl. du Palais.*

★ Théâtre Romain (*Roman Theater*)

ARCHAEOLOGICAL SITE | Measuring 143 yards across, the Théâtre Romain is one of the largest in Gaul. It held 13,000 spectators and is only slightly smaller than Rome's Theater of Marcellus. Rubble buried Vienne's theater until 1922; excavation has uncovered 46 rows of seats, some marble flooring, and the frieze on the stage. ⊠ *7 rue du Cirque* ☎ *04–74–85–39–23* ☒ *From €3* ⊘ *Closed Mon.*

One of the most important towns of Roman Gaul, Vienne is a historian's fantasyland famed for its ancient theater.

🍴 Restaurants

⭐ La Pyramide

$$$$ | FRENCH | Back when your grandmother's grandmother was making the grand tour, La Pyramide's Fernand Point had perfected haute cuisine for a generation and became the first superstar chef, teaching a regiment of students who glamorize French dining the world over. Many decades later, La Pyramide has dropped its museum status and now offers contemporary classics by acclaimed chef Patrick Henriroux, accompanied by a peerless selection of wines featuring local stars from the nearby Côte-Rôtie and Condrieu vineyards. **Known for:** good-value fixed-price menus; warm welcome; extensive wine list covering all regions of France. $ *Average main: €75* ✉ *14 bd. Fernand-Point* ☎ *04–74–53–01–96* ⊕ *www.lapyramide. com* ⌚ *Closed Tues., Wed., early Feb.– early Mar., and 1 wk in Aug.*

Le Bec Fin

$$ | FRENCH | With its understated yet elegant dining room and an inexpensive weekday menu, this unpretentious enclave opposite the cathedral is a good choice for lunch or dinner. Red meat, seafood, and both fresh- and saltwater fish are well prepared here. **Known for:** no-frills atmosphere; good for families; superb cheese board. $ *Average main: €21* ✉ *7 pl. St-Maurice* ☎ *04–74–85–76– 72* ⊕ *www.le-bec-fin-restaurant.com* ⌚ *Closed Mon., Tues., and 2 wks in Jan. No dinner Sun. and Wed.*

Tain-l'Hermitage

59 km (37 miles) south of Vienne.

As you approach Tain-l'Hermitage by car or train, you can't help but notice the steep vine-clad hills on either side of the Rhône sporting enormous placards with the names of the region's leading wine brands: Chapoutier, Jaboulet, Amadieu, etc. This is the heart of the Rhône Valley's great appellations—Côte-Rôtie, Condrieu, Saint-Joseph, Hermitage, Crozes-Hermitage—and within a few-minute's walk from the train station you'll find enough wine boutiques, tasting rooms, and dining to last you the weekend. Tain-l'Hermitage is also the world headquarters of Valrhona Chocolate, whose delightful museum and boutique provide a delicious afternoon of discovering and tasting the world's favorite sweet.

GETTING HERE AND AROUND

On the banks of the Rhône just across the river from Tournon-sur-Rhône, Tain-l'Hermitage is an easy one-hour train ride from Lyon Part Dieu train station, making it an excellent wine-and-chocolate-lover's day-trip from Lyon. Within two hours of dozens of other must-see places, it also makes a good base for the Rhône Valley.

Sights

★ Cave de Tain

WINERY/DISTILLERY | This cooperative of Rhône winemakers is a pioneer in sustainable wine making and boasts some of the region's most prestigious vintages. The cave offers a wide range of tastings in a friendly atmosphere, plus outdoor wine and food experiences, including cycling through the vineyards. The boutique also carries a mind-boggling selection of Rhône appellations. Friendly wine experts are on hand to guide you to the best vintages to taste and buy. ✉ *22 rte. de Larnage, Tain-l'Hermitage* ☎ *04–75–08–91–86* 🌐 *www.cavedetain.com.*

★ Cité du Chocolat Valrhona

FACTORY | One of the word's best gourmet chocolate makers, this is Valrhona's world headquarters. The museum's interactive exhibits for adults and kids immerse visitors in every step of the chocolate-making process, from beans to bars—with all the free samples you can eat. The on-site café uses chocolate in all of its dishes, both savory and sweet, and you can participate in a chocolate-making workshop (see more information online). After your visit stock up on the entire range of products at gentle prices at the boutique. ✉ *12 av. du Président Roosevelt, Tain-l'Hermitage* ☎ *04–75–09–27–27* 🌐 *www.citeduchocolat.com/en* 🕒 *Shop closed Sun.*

Maison Chapoutier

WINERY/DISTILLERY | One of the Rhône's great names and a leader in biodynamic winemaking, this is a stellar place for tasting and stocking up on all the best Chapoutier vintages from both sides of the river and around France. Tastings are free for parties of five or fewer and an extensive program of workshops, evenings, and events pairing wines with food, truffles, and chocolate (many in English) helps you explore the full range of these world-class wines. Chapoutier also offers full- or half-day tours of the vineyards on electric bikes, with backpack, water, helmet, and snacks provided. ✉ *18 av. Dr Paul Durand, Tain-l'Hermitage* ☎ *04–75–08–28–65* 🌐 *www.chapoutier.com/fr/.*

Restaurants

Bistrot Marius

$$$$ | **BRASSERIE** | This popular contemporary-elegant bistro in the heart of town specializes in fresh, seasonal Mediterranean-inflected cuisine. The beef is aged on the premises, and all dishes are paired with delicious Rhône and Provençal wines. **Known for:** prized beef; convivial atmosphere; excellent level of service. [$] *Average main: €35* ✉ *1 av. Dr Paul Durand, Tain-l'Hermitage* ☎ *04–75–08–65–00* 🌐 *www.chapoutier-gites.com.*

Hotels

Fac & Spera Hotel & Spa

$$ | **B&B/INN** | This contemporary hotel is set a few minutes from the train station, across from the Chapoutier boutique and tasting rooms and within easy walking distance of Cité du Chocolat Valrhona. **Pros:** beautiful pool and spa; in the heart of town; free parking. **Cons:** decor slightly boring; pricey for the region; some rooms get more light than others. [$] *Rooms from: €160* ✉ *1 av. Dr Paul Durand, Tain-l'Hermitage* ☎ *04–75–08–65–00* 🌐 *www.pavillon-ermitage.com* 🛏 *55 rooms* 🍴 *No meals.*

M. Chapoutier Gites

$$$ | B&B/INN | Six fully equipped luxury houses provide serenity and privacy in the middle of some of Chapoutier's most prestigious vineyards. **Pros:** elegant decor; great for families; awesome views. **Cons:** two-night minimum; some houses more secluded than others; car is needed. [$] *Rooms from: €300* ✉ *18 av. Dr Paul Durand, Tain-l'Hermitage* ☎ *04–75–08–92–61* 🌐 *www.chapoutier-gites.com* 🛏 *6 guesthouses* 🍴 *No meals.*

Tournon-sur-Rhône

3 km (2 miles) west of Tain l'Hermitage.

This small village located on the banks of the Rhône has several beautiful buildings dating back to the 15th century, as well as one of France's last remaining steam trains.

Sights

Château

CASTLE/PALACE | Tournon's hefty Château, dating to the 15th and 16th centuries, is the chief attraction. The castle's twin terraces have wonderful views of the Vieille Ville, the river, and—towering above Tain-l'Hermitage across the Rhône—the steep vineyards that produce Hermitage wine, one of the region's most refined, and costly, reds. In the Château is a museum of local history, the **Musée Rhodanien.** ✉ *14 pl. Auguste-Faure, Tournon-sur-Rhône* ☎ *04–75–08–10–30* 🌐 *www.chateaumusee-tournon.com* 🎫 *€4* ⏲ *Closed mid-Dec.–mid-Mar.*

Chemin de Fer du Vivarais

TRANSPORTATION SITE (AIRPORT/BUS/FERRY/TRAIN) | FAMILY | A ride on one of France's last steam trains, the Chemin de Fer du Vivarais, makes an adventurous two-hour, 33-km (21-mile) trip along the narrow, rocky Doux Gorges to Lamastre and back to Tournon. Check the website for a complete train schedule. ✉ *Departs from Tournon station, 21 av. Dr Paul Durand, Tournon-sur-Rhône* ☎ *04–75–06–07–00* 🌐 *trainardeche.fr* 🎫 *€23 round-trip.*

Restaurants

Le Tournesol

$$ | FRENCH | At Le Tournesol, a local favorite since it opened in 2001, you can expect friendly service, pleasant decor, and classic French cooking. The menu draws heavily from the area's many regional delights and seasonal veggies, which are showcased in dishes such as the Ardèche veal tartare with truffle oil, baby lettuces, and shaved Parmesan, or line-caught hake roasted with garlic and served with a turmeric-infused cauliflower puree. **Known for:** excellent wine list focusing on regional wines; friendly owners speak fluent English; charming atmosphere. [$] *Average main: €21* ✉ *44 av. Maréchal Foch, Tournon-sur-Rhône* ☎ *04–75–07–08–26* 🌐 *www.letournesol.net* ⏲ *Closed Tues. and Wed. No dinner Sun.*

Hotels

★ **Hotel de la Villeon**

$$ | HOTEL | A spectacular 17th-century building provides the elegant bones for this stunning hotel conveniently located in the heart of Tournon. **Pros:** close to both town and countryside; excellent breakfast; top-notch service. **Cons:** no parking; breakfast not included with price; guests cannot control air-conditioning in rooms. [$] *Rooms from: €195* ✉ *2* *rue Davity, Tournon-sur-Rhône ☎ 04–75–06–97–50 ⊕ www.hoteldelavilleon.com ⊷ 16 rooms ⦿ No meals.*

Valence

17 km (11 miles) south of Tournon, 92 km (57 miles) west of Grenoble, 127 km (79 miles) north of Avignon.

Considered the "doorway to the South," Valence, the capital of the Drôme département, harbors several ancient monuments that attest to its status as a major historical crossroads along the Rhône Valley corridor. While most people know Valence as home of the world-famous Anne-Sophie Pic—France's only female three-star chef—and her eponymous gastronomic restaurant and hotel, in the last few years, the city has quietly become the Rhône Valley's best-kept foodie secret. Besides boasting one of the region's most scenic farmers' markets, for five days every September the Valence en Gastronomie Festival highlights the culinary dynamism of this renowned wine region. A handful of Michelin-starred chefs and some charming old-fashioned bistros also qualify Valence as a worthy stop, not to mention its picturesque old town and museum.

GETTING HERE AND AROUND
SNCF trains link Lyon Part-Dieu station with Valence (1 hr 12 mins, €18.60). The high-speed TGV also connects Lyon Part-Dieu to Valence (39 mins, €30) with six or seven trains daily.

VISITOR INFORMATION Valence Tourist Office ✉ 11 bd. Bancel ☎ 04–75–44–90–40 ⊕ www.valence-romans-tourisme.com.

Sights

★ Musée de Valence
MUSEUM | The luminous Valence Museum offers plenty of art throughout the ages, from prehistory and Roman times to the present. Its fine collection of Roman artifacts includes several superb mosaic floors excavated in the area, as well as marbles and other objects. The painting collection includes notable works from the Dutch, Flemish, and European schools and the contemporary collection highlights the works of local artist André Lhote and French artist Sophie Calle. The museum's two outdoor terraces offer splendid views of Valence and the Rhône River. ✉ 4 rue Saint-Didier ☎ 04–75–79–20–80 ⊕ www.museedevalence.fr.

St-Apollinaire
RELIGIOUS SITE | Follow some steep-curbed alleyways, called *côtes,* from the banks of the Rhône into the Vieille Ville to discover, at its center, the imposing cathedral of St-Apollinaire. Although begun in the 12th century in the Romanesque style, it's not as old as it looks: parts of it were rebuilt in the 17th century, with the belfry rebuilt in the 19th. ✉ Pl. des Ormeaux ⊕ www.valence.fr.

★ Vieux Valence (Old Town)
HISTORIC SITE | Between the Place des Ormeaux next to the cathedral, and Rue Madier de Montjau and the Boulevards Maurice Clerc et Boulevard Bancel, the winding medieval streets of Valence's Old Town are a delight to explore. Along with its leafy squares, welcoming cafés, and gastronomic restaurants, there are several sites to spot. On the Grand Rue you can't miss the Renaissance confection Maison des Têtes (1452) and the Moorish-style Maison Mauresque (1858), at 1 rue Gaston Rey. Closer to the cathedral, an open square funerary chapel called the Pendentif (1545) was one of the first French edifices to be listed as a historic monument, in 1834. The Valence outdoor market, held on several different tree-shaded squares depending on the day (it's worth picking up a schedule at the tourist office or checking online), is particularly picturesque. The Marché Producteurs (local farmers' and organic market) is held from 5 pm to 8

pm every Tuesday under a historic *halle* on the Place Saint-Jean. The old town is the perfect spot to seek out the Valence specialty called the *Suisse,* a delicious buttery pastry, somewhere between a brioche and a cookie, that's perfumed with orange flower and flavored with orange rind and rum. ✉ *Vieux Valence* ⊕ *www.valence-romans-tourisme.com/en.*

Restaurants

André

$$$ | FRENCH | If famous chef Anne-Sophie Pic's gastronomic mothership is too much of a splurge (and a splurge it is), her gourmet bistro just two steps away will set you right up. Named for her grandfather, founder of the Pic empire, the menu riffs on all the French classics that built the Pic name. **Known for:** quiet, chic decor; excellent service; contemporary-classic recipes. $ *Average main: €26* ✉ *285 av. Victor Hugo* ☎ *04–75–44–53–86* ⊕ *www.anne-sophie-pic.com.*

Bistro des Clercs

$$ | FRENCH | Stepping through the door of this ravishing Belle Époque brasserie is a bit like traveling back in time, so beautifully preserved is its turn-of-the-century ambience, with classic globe lighting, tile floor, linen-bedecked wooden tables, and the expansive menu. The spell is only enhanced by a traditional menu of all the classics: delicious steak tartare, *moules frites* (mussels and fries), foie gras, and escargots, all washed down with a local Côtes du Rhône. **Known for:** gorgeous historical atmosphere; all the classic dishes; delightful desserts. $ *Average main: €19* ✉ *48 rue Grande* ☎ *04–75–55–55–15.*

★ Flaveurs

$$$$ | FRENCH | If you think the Pic empire has a lock on Valence gastronomy, think again: the extraordinary precision and refinement of Baptiste Poinot's cooking makes a foodie stopover in Valence an absolute must. Though the dining room

itself is a bit on the quirky side, there is nothing to quibble over when it comes to the gorgeous presentation and scintillating tastes in dishes like melt-in-your-mouth trout fillet with salsify puree and crunchy grains of roasted buckwheat all in a cloud of curried foam. **Known for:** exquisite presentation; off-the-charts innovation; exceptional cheese cart. $ *Average main: €38* ✉ *32 rue Grande* ☎ *04–75–56–08–40* ⊕ *www.flaveurs-restaurant.com* ⊘ *Closed Sun., Mon., and mid-Dec.–Jan.*

★ La Cachette

$$$$ | FRENCH | Set on the edge of Valence's Old Town, a few minutes from the Parc Jouvet, this hidden gem is one more reason to get thee to Valence. Chef Masashi Ijichi's Japanese roots and pedigreed French training (at the House of Pic) merge in a stunning cuisine that is virtuosic without being bombastic. **Known for:** virtuosic Japanese-inflected French cuisine; laid-back dining room; Michelin star. $ *Average main: €38* ✉ *16 rue des Cévennes* ☎ *04–75–55–24–13* ⊘ *Closed Sun. and Mon.*

🛏 Hotels

★ Maison Pic

$$$ | HOTEL | Celebrated as a culinary landmark for decades, the Maison Pic is also a feast for the eyes, with vaulted white salons, deep plush-velvet sofas, 18th-century billiard tables, gigantic Provençal armoires, lovely gardens, and an inviting swimming pool. **Pros:** paradise of pampering and repose; home to Valence's most famous restaurant; sports and leisure activities from golf and cycling to flying. **Cons:** on an unattractive street; pricey; not everyone loves the contemporary decor. $ *Rooms from: €340* ✉ *285 av. Victor Hugo* ☎ *04–75–44–15–32* ⊕ *www.anne-sophie-pic.com* ⊐ *15 rooms* ⦿ *No meals.*

Cliousclat

21 km (13 miles) south of Valence, 27 km (17 miles) north of Montélimar.

Less than 10 km (6 miles) off A7 and N7, the roads running south from Valence to Montélimar and on to Provence, is the delightful, tiny village of Cliousclat, built on a hillside, with room for just one narrow street running through it. A center for pottery since the 10th century, there is only a single manufacturer left, but it's worth a visit to see how this local craft developed. Cliousclat's charming atmosphere and its gorgeous views make it very appealing.

Sights

Poterie de Cliousclat

MUSEUM | Founded in 1903, this is the last original pottery in Cliouscat and a registered historic monument. You can learn about the manufacturing operations here and purchase some lovely pieces, both traditional and contemporary. ✉ *Le Village, Cliousclat* ☎ *04–75–43–60–39* 🌐 *www.poteriedecliou.com* 🎫 *€6.*

Restaurants

La Treille Muscate

$$$ | **FRENCH** | Between Lyon and Avignon there's no better place to dine and spend a night than at this old-style hotel, a symphony of muted 18th-century pastels, Provençal furnishings, and a decidedly rustic-luxe air. Though the decor feels slightly dated, the restaurant gets kudos from all the critics, and has a beautiful outdoor terrace, with views of the distant mountains, for warm-weather dining. **Known for:** honey-lacquered duck breast; quaint atmosphere; pretty outdoor terrace. [$] *Average main: €26* ✉ *Le Village, Cliousclat* ☎ *04–75–63–13–10* 🌐 *www.hotelrestaurant-latreillemuscate.com* 🕒 *Closed early Dec.–mid-Feb. No lunch Mon.*

Grenoble

104 km (65 miles) southeast of Lyon, 86 km (52 miles) northeast of Valence.

Capital of the Dauphiné region, Grenoble sits at the confluence of the Isère and Drac rivers and lies within three *massifs* (mountain ranges): La Chartreuse, Le Vercors, and Belledonne. This cosmopolitan city's skyscrapers bear witness to the fierce local desire to move ahead with the times, and it's not surprising to find one of France's most noted universities here. Grenoble's main claim to fame is as the birthplace of the great French novelist Henri Beyle (1783–1842), better known as Stendhal, author of *The Red and the Black* and *The Charterhouse of Parma.* The native Grenoblois, known for their down-home friendliness, are delighted—and generally surprised—if you know of him.

GETTING HERE AND AROUND

Paris's Gare de Lyon dispatches more than a dozen trains daily (either direct or via Lyon Part-Dieu) to Grenoble (3 hrs 3 mins, €96; or 3 hrs 40 mins, €114 via Lyon). Six TGV trains daily connect Lyon-Saint-Exupéry airport with Grenoble (1 hr 7 mins, €27). Ouibus buses connect Lyon-Saint-Exupéry with Grenoble every hour on the half hour (1 hr 5 mins, €17). Altibus connects Grenoble with 60 ski stations and towns throughout the Alps.

Grenoble's layout is maddening: your only hope lies in the big, illuminated maps posted throughout town or the free map from the tourist office. The heart of the city forms a crescent around a bend of the Isère, with the train station at the western end and the university all the way at the eastern tip. As it fans out from the river toward the south, the crescent seems to develop a more modern flavor. The hub of the city is Place Victor Hugo, with its flowers, fountains, and cafés, though most sights and nightlife are near

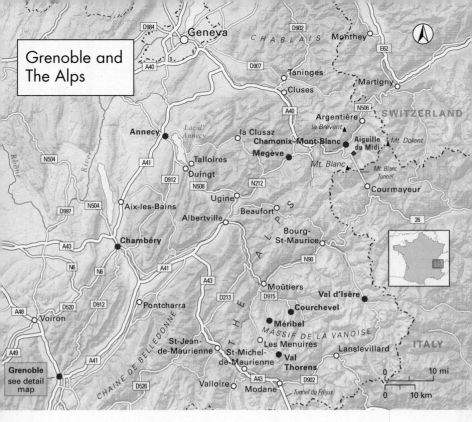

Grenoble and The Alps

the Isère in Place St-André, Place de Gordes, and Place Notre-Dame.

TRAVEL INFORMATION Altibus ☎ *08–20–32–03–68* ⊕ *www.altibus.com.* **Ouibus** ☎ *01–71–53–01–80* ⊕ *www.ouibus.fr.*

VISITOR INFORMATION Grenoble Tourist Office ✉ *14 rue de la République* ☎ *04–76–42–41–41* ⊕ *www.grenoble-tourisme.com.*

👁 Sights

Cathédrale Notre-Dame

RELIGIOUS SITE | Despite its 12th-century exterior, the 19th-century interior of the Cathédrale Notre-Dame is somewhat bland. But don't miss the adjoining bishop's house, now a museum on the history of Grenoble; the main treasure is a noted 4th-century baptistery. ✉ *Pl. Notre-Dame* 🎫 *Free.*

Centre National d'Art Contemporain

MUSEUM | Contemporary art enthusiasts should check out the Centre National d'Art Contemporain. Behind the train station in an out-of-the-way district, it's noted for its distinctive warehouse space and avant-garde collection. ✉ *155 cours Berriat* ☎ *04–76–21–95–84* ⊕ *www.magasin-cnac.org* 🎫 *€4* ⊙ *Closed Mon.*

La Bastille

VIEWPOINT | FAMILY | Starting at Quai St-Stéphane-Jay, this *téléphérique* (cable car) whisks you over the River Isère and up to the hilltop where there are splendid views and a good restaurant. Walk back down via the footpath through the Jardin Dauphinoise. ✉ *Quai Stéphane Jay* ☎ *04–76–44–89–65* ⊕ *www.bastille-grenoble.fr/english* 🎫 *€9 round-trip.*

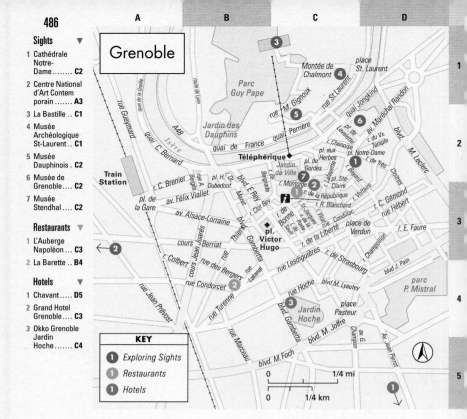

Grenoble

KEY

1 Exploring Sights

1 Restaurants

1 Hotels

Musée Archéologique St-Laurent

RELIGIOUS SITE | The church of St-Laurent, near the Musée Dauphinois, has a hauntingly ancient 6th-century crypt—one of the country's oldest Christian monuments—supported by a row of formidable marble pillars. A tour of the church traces the emergence of Christianity in the Dauphiné. ⊠ *2 pl. St-Laurent* ☎ *04–76–44–78–68* ⊕ *www.musee-archeologique-grenoble.fr* ⊡ *Free* ⊗ *Closed Tues.*

Musée Dauphinois

MUSEUM | On the north side of the River Isère is Rue Maurice-Gignoux, lined with gardens, cafés, mansions, and a 17th-century convent that contains the Musée Dauphinois, detailing the history of mountaineering and skiing. The Premiers Alpins section explores the evolution of the Alps and its inhabitants.

⊠ *30 rue Maurice-Gignoux* ☎ *04–57–58–89–01* ⊕ *www.musee-dauphinois.fr* ⊡ *Free.*

Musée de Grenoble

MUSEUM | Place de Lavalette—on the south side of the river, where most of Grenoble is concentrated—is where you'll find the Musée de Grenoble. Founded in 1796, it's one of France's oldest museums and was the first to concentrate on modern art (Picasso donated his *Femme Lisant* in 1921). An addition incorporates the medieval Tour de l'Isle (Island Tower), a Grenoble landmark. The collection includes 4,000 paintings and 5,500 drawings, among them works by Impressionists such as Renoir and Monet, and 20th-century masters like Matisse, Signac, Derain, Vlaminck, Magritte, Ernst, Miró, and Dubuffet. Artists from the Italian Renaissance and Flemish

School are also represented. ✉ *5 pl. de Lavalette* ☎ *04–76–63–44–44* ⊕ *www. museedegrenoble.fr* 🎫 *€8* ⏱ *Closed Tues.*

★ Musée Stendhal

MUSEUM | Established in Stendhal's grandfather's house, this museum is a fascinating testament to the eminent author. It's one of three local landmarks where his legacy can be explored—the others being his birthplace and the Bibliothèque Municipale, which houses his manuscripts. The English-language "Stendhal Itinerary," offered by the Grenoble Chamber of Commerce, recaps all the major sites associated with him. ✉ *20 Grande-Rue* ☎ *04–76–86–52–08* ⊕ *www. bm-grenoble.fr/1083-musee-stendhal. htm* 🎫 *€5 with audio guide.*

🍴 Restaurants

★ La Barette

$$ | **MODERN FRENCH** | You'll know this is a foodie favorite in town by its convivial atmosphere full of locals tucking into a menu of delicious gourmet classics savored with the city's finest handpicked selection of natural wines. Dishes like melt-in-your mouth roasted pork with pureed garlic-celery root and hearty rabbit stew paired with a Côte Rotie never fail to satisfy. **Known for:** well-priced menus; great food; natural wines, many by the glass. 💲 *Average main: €22* ✉ *6 pl. Championnet* ☎ *04–76–43–86–48* ⊕ *www.restaurant-la-baratte.fr* ⏱ *Closed Sun. and Mon. No dinner Tues. and Wed.*

L'Auberge Napoléon

$$$$ | **FRENCH** | Frédéric Caby's culinary haven in a meticulously restored town house—once inhabited by Napoléon Bonaparte himself—is where chef Agnès Chotin, one of France's top *cuisinières* (female chefs), puts together the best table in Grenoble. She specializes in dishes unique to the region, ranging from *daube de sanglier en aumônière croustillante* (wild boar stewed in port wine with

lemon crust) to *crème de potiron* (cream of squash soup). **Known for:** foie gras menu; regional cru chocolate dessert; historic setting. 💲 *Average main: €39* ✉ *7 rue Montorge* ☎ *04–76–87–53–64* ⊕ *www.auberge-napoleon.fr* ⏱ *Closed Sun., early May, and 2 wks in Aug. No lunch.*

🛏 Hotels

★ Chavant

$$ | **HOTEL** | It's worth the drive 8 km (5 miles) south of Grenoble to this ivy-covered mansion-hotel, where elegant, spacious guest rooms overlook the meadows and forests that lie beyond the lush garden and pool. **Pros:** lovely village with pretty views and walks; classic cuisine and outstanding wine cellar; tasteful rooms. **Cons:** not handy to central Grenoble; tricky driving directions; dining room not open every day. 💲 *Rooms from: €165* ✉ *2 rue Emile Chavant, Bresson* ⊹ *Leave Grenoble on Av. J. Perrot to Av. J. Jaurès, which becomes Rte. D269* ☎ *04–76–25–25–38* ⊕ *www.chavanthotel. com* 🛏 *6 rooms* ⏐◎⏐ *No meals.*

Grand Hotel Grenoble

$ | **HOTEL** | There's not much lacking in this handsome, centrally located hotel. **Pros:** valet parking; close to the area's best shopping and bars; some rooms with balconies. **Cons:** standard rooms can be on the small side; no coffeemakers in rooms; breakfast not included. 💲 *Rooms from: €109* ✉ *5 rue de la Republique* ☎ *04–76–51–22–59* ⊕ *www.grand-ho-tel-grenoble.com* 🛏 *57 rooms* ⏐◎⏐ *No meals.*

Okko Grenoble Jardin Hoche

$ | **HOTEL** | Close to the old town, restaurants, and shopping, this stylish four-star hotel is a new concept in urban budget hotels. **Pros:** good all-you-can-eat breakfast included in price; close to shopping, sights, and restaurants; lots of snacks and extras. **Cons:** bathrooms are small; free parking sometimes full;

Starting at Quai St-Stéphane-Jay, Grenoble's *téléphérique* (cable car) helps visitors cross the Isère and ascend to the Fort de la Bastille.

contemporary decor can seem cold. $ *Rooms from: €105* ✉ *3 rue Hoche* ☎ *04–85–19–00–10* ⊕ *www.okkohotels. com/en/hotels/okko-hotels-greno-ble-jardins-hoche* ⇥ *138 rooms* ❌ *Free Breakfast.*

Nightlife

Look for the monthly *Grenoble-Spectacles* for a list of events around town.

Barberousse
BARS/PUBS | Resembling a pirate ship, Barberousse is an always-popping rum mill. ✉ *3 rue Bayard* ☎ *04–76–51–14–53* ⊕ *www.barberousse.com.*

Performing Arts

★ Les Détours de Babel
FESTIVALS | For three weeks in late March and early April this "transcultural" music festival is prime time for 85 or more concerts of exceptional originality and cultural breadth held in venues through-out the city, from historic churches to state-of-the-art concert venues. ✉ *Grenoble* ⊕ *www.detoursdebabel.fr.*

Chambéry

58 km (36 miles) northwest of Grenoble, 52 km (32 miles) south of Annecy.

As for centuries—when it was the crossroads for merchants from Germany, Italy, and the Middle East—elegant old Chambéry remains the region's shopping hub. Townspeople congregate for coffee and people-watching on pedestrians-only Place St-Léger.

VISITOR INFORMATION **Chambéry Tourist Office** ✉ *5 bis pl. du Palais de Justice* ☎ *04–79–33–42–47* ⊕ *www.cham-bery-tourisme.com.*

◉ Sights

Château des Ducs de Savoie
CASTLE/PALACE | Chambéry's premier sight, the 14th-century Château des Ducs de Savoie, features one of Europe's

largest carillons. Its Gothic Ste-Chapelle has lovely stained glass and houses a replica of the Turin Shroud. At the moment, the château can be visited only by guided tour on weekends at 2:30 pm. The 90-minute tour includes a visit to Chambéry's historic center and ends at the château. Tours leave from 71 rue St-Réal in the *centre historique*. ✉ *Pl. du Château* ☎ *04–79–33–42–47* ⊕ *www. chambery-tourisme.com* 🎫 *€6* ⏱ *Closed Mon.*

Hotels

Château de Candie

$$ | **HOTEL** | If you wish to experience *la vie Savoyarde* in all its pastel-hued glory, head to this towering 14th-century manor on a hill east of Chambéry. **Pros:** glorious views over the neighboring Chartreuse monastery and village; interesting antiques abound; personal service from host. **Cons:** not right in town, so a car is required; won't appeal to minimalists; not much in the way of nightlife. 💲 *Rooms from: €170* ✉ *Rue du Bois de Candie, 6 km (4 miles) east of Chambéry, Chambéry-le-Vieux* ☎ *04–79–96–63–00* ⊕ *www.chateaudecandie.com* 🛏 *25 rooms* 🍴 *No meals.*

Annecy

137 km (85 miles) east of Lyon, 43 km (27 miles) southwest of Geneva.

Sparkling Annecy is on crystal clear Lac d'Annecy, surrounded by snow-tipped peaks. Though the canals, flower-decked bridges, and cobbled pedestrian streets are filled with shoppers and tourists on market days—Tuesday and Friday—the town is still tranquil.

Does it seem that the River Thiou flows backward, that is, out of the lake? You're right: it drains the lake, feeding the town's canals. Most of the Vieille Ville (Old Town) is now a pedestrian zone lined with half-timber houses. Here is where the best restaurants are, so you'll probably be back in the evening.

GETTING HERE AND AROUND

There's a direct TGV train connection from Lyon-Saint-Exupéry airport to Annecy (1 hr 55 mins, €41). The TGV connects Paris's Gare de Lyon to Annecy (3 hrs 42 mins, €104). Annecy Haute-Savoie Airport (⊕ *www.annecy.aeroport.fr*) receives flights from other French and some European destinations.

Transdev Crolard buses connect Lyon-Saint-Exupéry airport with Annecy (2 hrs, €36) and the main winter-sport stations in the Alps year-round. Tickets must be purchased online or at the airport or bus station.

VISITOR INFORMATION Annecy Tourist Office ✉ *Centre Bonlieu, 1 rue Jean-Jaurès* ☎ *04–50–45–00–33* ⊕ *www. lac-annecy.com.* **Trasdev Crolard** ☎ *04–50–51–08–51* ⊕ *www.transdevhautesavoie. com.*

Sights

The funky, asymmetrical, added-on, squished-in buildings of Annecy's Vieille Ville and the sheer limestone cliffs and jagged peaks of its mountain setting are impossibly picturesque. No matter that the paddleboat vendors try to outcharm each other for your business, you'll be tempted to stay here and dawdle awhile.

★ **Château de Menthon-Saint-Bernard**
CASTLE/PALACE | The exterior of the magnificent Château de Menthon-Saint-Bernard is the stuff of fairy tales (so much so that Walt Disney modeled his version of Sleeping Beauty's castle on it); the interior is even better. The castle's medieval rooms—many adorned with tapestries, Romanesque frescoes, Netherlandish sideboards, and heraldic motifs—have been lovingly restored by the owner, who can trace his ancestry directly back to Saint-Bernard himself. All in all, this is

Just one of the scenic delights of Annecy, the photogenic Palais de l'Isle (Island Palace)

one of the loveliest dips into the Middle Ages you can make in all of Europe. You can get a good view of the castle by turning onto the Thones road out of Veyrier. ✉ *Allée du Château* ☎ *04–50–60–12–05* 🌐 *www.chateau-de-menthon.com* 🎫 *€10* 🕒 *Closed Nov.–Mar.*

★ **Musée-Château d'Annecy**

MUSEUM | Crowning the city is one of France's most gorgeous castles, the medieval Musée-Château d'Annecy. High on a hill opposite the Palais and bristling with stolid towers, the complex is landmarked by the Tour Perrière, which dominates the lake, and the Tour St-Paul, Tour St-Pierre, and Tour de la Reine (the oldest, dating to the 12th century), which overlook the town. All provide storybook views over the town and countryside. Dwellings of several eras line the castle courtyard, one of which contains a small museum on Annecy history and how it was shaped by the Nemeurs and Savoie dynasties. ✉ *Pl. du Château* ☎ *04–50–33–87–30* 🌐 *www.musees.annecy.fr* 🎫 *From €6.*

Palais de l'Isle (*Island Palace*)

CASTLE/PALACE | Meander through the Vieille Ville, starting on the small island in the River Thiou, at the 12th-century Palais de l'Isle, once site of law courts and a prison, now a landmark. Like a stone ship, the small islet perches in midstream, surrounded by cobblestone quays, and is easily one of France's most photographed sites. ✉ *Annecy.*

🍴 Restaurants

★ **Auberge de Père Bise**

$$$$ | **FRENCH** | For those who've never dined in one of France's grand old restaurants, this would be a fine start. In a century-old chalet-inn in the tiny village of Talloires, on the incomparably beautiful Lac d'Annecy, from start to finish you'll be pampered in the old style. **Known for:** stunning lakeside setting; distinguished menu of French classics; legendary restaurant. [$] *Average main: €84* ✉ *303 rte. du Port* ☎ *04–50–60–72–01* 🌐 *www.perebise.com* 🕒 *Closed Tues., Wed., and mid-Dec.–mid-Feb.*

★ Le Bouillon

$$ | FRENCH | FAMILY | Set back near the river in Annecy's picturesque old town, this casual, laid-back restaurant is a place the locals would rather keep to themselves. From the first amuse bouche to dessert, diners can't wait to taste what's next from a cuisine anchored in French technique and enhanced with plenty of far-flung influences. **Known for:** great value French cuisine; charming atmosphere; reservations usually necessary. Ⓢ *Average main: €18* ✉ *9 rue de la Gare* ☎ *04–50–77–31–02* ⏱ *Closed Sun. and Mon.*

Hotels

L'Impérial Palace

$$$$ | HOTEL | Across the lake from the town center, Annecy's leading hotel has spacious, high-ceilinged guest rooms in subdued contemporary colors behind its Belle Époque exterior. **Pros:** beautiful location; splendid rooms; superior cuisine in La Voile. **Cons:** sluggish to haughty service; pricey; breakfasts expensive for what you get. Ⓢ *Rooms from: €350* ✉ *Allée de l'Impérial* ☎ *04–50–09–30–00* ⊕ *www.hotel-imperial-palace.com* ⇆ *99 rooms* ⦿ *No meals.*

★ Splendid Hotel

$$ | HOTEL | Just steps from crystalline Lac d'Annecy, overlooking a lovely canal running through Annecy's Old Town, this nicely renovated hotel has all the comfort and charm you could want plus the best location possible. **Pros:** hotel-subsidized parking nearby; some rooms have balconies; nice contemporary decor. **Cons:** some noise due to hardwood floors; not all rooms have showers; service varies. Ⓢ *Rooms from: €125* ✉ *4 quai Eustache Chappuis* ☎ *04–50–45–20–00* ⊕ *www.hotel-annecy-lac.fr* ⇆ *47 rooms* ⦿ *No meals.*

 Performing Arts

Annecy Festival

FESTIVALS | Started in the 1960s, this international animated film festival, one of the most respected in the industry, takes place for one week every June in and around the town of Annecy. The festival receives more than 2,500 entries annually from which 200 are short-listed to take part in the official selection. In addition to indoor screenings around town—the Musée-Château, La Turbine, the Parc Vignières-Pommaries—there's a free screening on the giant screen on the Pâquier lawn each evening. ✉ *18 av. du Trésum* ☎ *04–50–10–09–00* ⊕ *www. annecy.org.*

Chamonix-Mont-Blanc

94 km (58 miles) east of Annecy, 83 km (51 miles) southeast of Geneva.

Chamonix is the oldest and biggest of the French winter-sports resort towns and was the site of the first Winter Olympics, held in 1924. As a ski resort, however, it has its limitations. The ski areas are spread out, none is very large, and the lower slopes often suffer from poor snow conditions.

On the other hand, some runs are extremely memorable, such as the 20-km (12-mile) one through the Vallée Blanche or the off-trail area of Les Grands Montets. And the situation is getting better: many lifts have been added, improving access to the slopes as well as shortening lift lines. In summer it's a great place for hiking, climbing, and enjoying dazzling views. If you're heading to Italy via the Mont Blanc Tunnel, Chamonix will be your gateway.

GETTING HERE AND AROUND

TGV trains from Lyon-Saint-Exupéry airport take 1 hour 55 minutes (€35.20). There's also TGV service from Paris's Gare de Lyon (3 hrs 42 mins, €92).

The required train ride from St-Gervais-Les-Bains to Chamonix is in itself an incredible trip, up the steepest railway in Europe. You'll feel your body doing strange things to adjust to the pressure change.

Ouibus transfers passengers from Geneva to Chamonix (1 hr 10 mins, €29).

VISITOR INFORMATION Chamonix Tourist Office ✉ *85 pl. du Triangle de l'Amitié, Chamonix-Mont-Blanc* ☎ *04–50–53–00–24* 🌐 *www.chamonix.com.* **Ouibus** 🌐 *www.fr.ouibus.com.*

Sights

★ Aiguille du Midi

VIEWPOINT | This 12,619-foot granite peak is topped with a needle-like observation tower, terrace, and restaurants. The world's highest cable car soars 12,000 feet up, almost to the top (an elevator completes the journey to the summit), providing positively staggering views of 15,700-foot Mont Blanc, Europe's loftiest peak. Be prepared for a lengthy wait, both going up and coming down—and wear warm clothing. ✉ *100 pl. de l'aiguille du Midi, Chamonix-Mont-Blanc* 🌐 *www.montblancnaturalresort.com* 🎫 *Cable car €63 round-trip.*

★ Mer de Glace

NATURE SITE | Literally, the "sea of ice," the Mer de Glace glacier can be seen up close from the Train du Montenvers, a cogwheel mountain train that leaves from behind the main train station. At the top end of the track, you can mount yet another transportation device—a mini *téléphérique* (cable car) that suspends you over the glacier for five minutes. You can also venture into the *grotte de glace* (ice cave) and the Glacorium, an interactive space recounting the glacier's formation and history. The hike back down is an easy two-hour ramble. ✉ *Chamonix-Mont-Blanc* 🌐 *www.montblancnaturalresort.com* 🎫 *€34 round-trip.*

Musée Alpin

MUSEUM | Chamonix was little more than a quiet mountain village until a group of Englishmen "discovered" the spot in 1741 and sang its praises far and wide. The town became forever tied to mountaineering when Horace de Saussure offered a reward for the first Mont Blanc ascent in 1760. Learn who took home the prize at the town's Musée Alpin, which documents the history of mountaineering; exhibits include handmade skis, early sleds, boots, skates, and mementos from every area of Alpine climbing lore. ✉ *89 av. Michel Groz, Chamonix-Mont-Blanc* ☎ *04–50–53–25–93* 🌐 *www.chamonix.com/musee-alpin,49-187321,en.html* 🎫 *€6* 🕒 *Closed Tues. in Apr.*

Hotels

Auberge du Manoir

$$ | **HOTEL** | **FAMILY** | For the feel of an authentic family-run mountain lodge—complete with wood paneling, flower-festooned balconies with delicious mountain views, and a resident golden retriever, this a great choice. **Pros:** centrally located; good breakfast; great value. **Cons:** management can be inflexible; people with allergies beware—cats and dogs at the hotel; rooms on the smaller side. [$] *Rooms from: €170* ✉ *8 rte. du Bouchet, Chamonix-Mont-Blanc* ☎ *04–50–53–10–77* 🌐 *www.chalethotelchamonix.fr* 🛏 *18 rooms* 🍴 *No meals.*

Hameau Albert 1er

$$$$ | **HOTEL** | At one of Chamonix's most desirable hotels, most of the beautifully furnished guest rooms have private balconies, with many (such as Suite Martine) offering unsurpassed views of Mont Blanc. **Pros:** dazzling panoramas; superb cuisine; polished and cheerful service. **Cons:** hard to get a reservation in season; the actual location is less than pristine; snob appeal. [$] *Rooms from: €419* ✉ *119 impasse du Montenvers, Chamonix-Mont-Blanc* ☎ *04–50–53–05–09*

Even at the bottom of one of its ski runs, you'll feel on top of the world in stunning Chamonix.

🌐 *www.hameaualbert.fr* ⏲ *Closed 3 wks in Nov.* 🛏 *39 rooms* 🍴 *No meals.*

★ **Hôtel Mont-Blanc**

$$$$ | **RESORT** | In the center of town, this Belle Époque hotel has catered to an A-list clientele since it opened its doors in 1878. **Pros:** near shops and ski lifts; amazing cuisine; lovely pool and spa. **Cons:** staff could be more knowledgeable; some rooms on the cozy side; expensive, but not unreasonable for the area. [$] *Rooms from: €420* ✉ *62 allée du Majestic, Chamonix-Mont-Blanc* ☎ *04–50–53–05–64* 🌐 *www.hotelmontblancchamonix.com* 🛏 *40 rooms* 🍴 *No meals.*

Nightlife

Casino de Chamonix

CASINOS | Besides games of chance like roulette and blackjack, the Casino de Chamonix has a bar and restaurant. Entrance is free with a passport or driver's license. ✉ *Pl. de Saussure, Chamonix-Mont-Blanc* ☎ *04–50–53–07–65.*

Chambre Neuf

BARS/PUBS | Fabled landmark Chambre Neuf is a hot après-ski bar in the Hotel Gustavia. ✉ *Hotel Gustavia, 272 av. Michel Croz, Chamonix-Mont-Blanc* ☎ *04–50–53–00–31* 🌐 *www.hotelgustavia.eu.*

Megève

35 km (22 miles) west of Chamonix, 69 km (43 miles) southeast of Geneva.

The smartest of the Mont Blanc stations, idyllic Alpine Megève is not only a major ski resort but also a chic winter watering hole that draws royalty, celebrities, and fat wallets from all over the world. Because the slopes are comparatively easy, beginners and skiers of only modest ability will find Megève more to their liking than Chamonix: Megève, conveniently, also has one of France's largest ski schools. In summer the town is a popular spot for golfing and hiking.

GETTING HERE AND AROUND

Driving is by far the best way to get to Megève. From Grenoble to Megève the journey takes about 2½ hours whether via Annecy or Albertville. SNCF rail connections from Annecy to Megève (1 hr 17 mins, €14.80) are routed to Sallanches, 12 km (8 miles) away. Shuttle buses connect Sallanches and Megève (25 mins, €3.50).

VISITOR INFORMATION Megève Tourist Office ✉ *Rue Monseigneur Conseil* ☎ *04–50–21–27–28* 🌐 *www.megeve.com.*

🍴 Restaurants

★ Flocons de Sel

$$$$ | **FRENCH** | Emmanuel Renaut's Flocons de Sel ("flakes of salt"), located in Leutaz, brings new meaning to the world of haute cuisine—and, even with the drive out of town, it's an excellent Megève dining option. Though the 10-course tasting menu is very expensive, it offers a rare experience from one of France's great chefs based on simple but carefully selected ingredients—freshwater crayfish, scallops en croute with sea salt, and roast wood pigeon are just a few of the creatively prepared specialties. **Known for:** Michelin star; gorgeous rustic dining room; finest dining in around. [$] *Average main: €65* ✉ *1775 rte. du Leutaz, 4 km (2½ miles) southwest of Megève* ☎ *04–50–21–49–99* 🌐 *www.floconsdesel.com* 🕓 *Closed Tues., Wed., May, and Nov. No lunch Mon. and Thurs.*

★ Le 1920

$$$$ | **FRENCH** | Part of the beautiful Domaine du Mont d'Arbois, Le 1920 offers an ultrarefined menu of classics updated to reflect modern tastes and using only the freshest seasonal produce. It took chef Julian Gatillon, veteran of top restaurants in France and Switzerland, two short years to earn his first Michelin star and gain the restaurant an avid following. **Known for:** sumptuous decor; classic French cooking raised to new heights; full disclosure of where everything on the menu comes from. [$] *Average main: €65* ✉ *447 chemin de la Rocaille* ☎ *04–50–21–25–03* 🌐 *www.mont-darbois.fr.*

🛏 Hotels

★ Flocons de Sel

$$$$ | **HOTEL** | Set in several charming Swiss-style chalets, this opulent "country" lodging, beautifully set on a grassy hillside among pine stands and manicured lawns, is far and away nicer than most other hotels in Megève. **Pros:** beautiful scenery and views; impeccable service; superb restaurant and spa. **Cons:** incredibly expensive; might be too small and intimate for some; no air-conditioning. [$] *Rooms from: €520* ✉ *1775 rte. du Leutaz* ☎ *04–50–21–49–99* 🌐 *www.floconsdesel.com* 🕓 *Closed Nov. and mid-Apr.–May* 🔑 *9 rooms* 🍴 *No meals.*

Les Cîmes

$$ | **B&B/INN** | This small, homey hotel, run by an English couple, offers cozy rooms and a pleasant little restaurant where simple dishes like roast lamb and grilled fish are served. **Pros:** friendly and comfortable; young and lively crowd; central location. **Cons:** smallish common areas; on a busy street; can get noisy. [$] *Rooms from: €165* ✉ *341 av. Charles Feige* ☎ *06–31–04–74–18* 🌐 *www.hotellescimes.info* 🕓 *Closed mid-Apr.–early June* 🔑 *8 rooms* 🍴 *Free Breakfast.*

★ Les Fermes de Marie

$$$ | **HOTEL** | **FAMILY** | By bringing a number of chalets and hay houses down from the mountains and decorating rooms with old Savoie furniture (including shepherds' tables, sculptured chests, and credenzas), Jocelyne and Jean-Louis Sibuet have created a luxury hotel with a delightfully rustic feel for both winter and summer getaways. **Pros:** ultracomfortable quarters in authentic Alpine chalets; beautiful taste down to smallest detail; top Megève cuisine. **Cons:** somewhat

isolated within the town; shuttle or car necessary to reach ski lifts; service can vary when crowded. $ *Rooms from: €300* ⊠ *Chemin de Riante Colline* 🕾 *04–50–93–03–10* ⊕ *www.fermesde-marie.com* 🕙 *Closed mid-Apr.–late June* 🛏 *70 rooms* 🍽 *No meals.*

⊻ Nightlife

⭐ Jazz Club des Cinq Rues

MUSIC CLUBS | Hot both figuratively and literally (you'll probably end up stripping down to a T-shirt), this popular music bar near Plaza de l'Église packs in the après-ski party animals as soon as the sun is over the yardarm, which can be as early as 4 or 5 pm in December. ⊠ *19 passage des Cinq Rues* 🕾 *04–50–89–65–68.*

Val Thorens

131 km (81 miles) south of Chamonix, 153 km (95 miles) south of Geneva.

Skiing is this bustling resort town's raison d'être, so it's no surprise that lifts and gondolas fan out in every direction and that many of the trails pass over bridges and barrel through the main square. Just about anywhere in town you can strap on your skis and head downhill.

GETTING HERE AND AROUND

The best way to get to Val Thorens is by car. There are also shuttle buses that navigate the route from the airports in Lyon and Geneva.

VISITOR INFORMATION Val Thorens
Tourism Office ⊠ *Grand-Rue, Val Thorens* 🕾 *04–70–00–08–08* ⊕ *www.valthorens. com.*

👁 Sights

Val Thorens

RESORT—SIGHT | Europe's highest ski resort, Val Thorens has such a lofty position that you see nothing but snow-covered mountains in every direction. The landscape is so iconic that the three adjoining peaks that grace every bottle of Evian are found here. The season here lasts longer than at resorts down the mountain, often from mid-November to early May.

High-speed lifts of all types transport you up to 68 runs of various ski levels. More than 50 are best suited for intermediate-level skiers, but there is also a handful for beginners or experts. Val Thorens is connected to the Trois Vallées ski area, so you have access to more than 600 km (373 miles) of slopes in nearby Les Menuires and elsewhere.

It was first built in the 1970s, so Val Thorens isn't the loveliest resort in the French Alps. But it buzzes with energy day and night, thanks to a clientele of couples enjoying romantic getaways and groups of friends challenging the slopes and taking advantage of a wild après-ski scene. ⊠ *D117, Val Thorens* 🕾 *79–00–08–08* ⊕ *www.valthorens.com* 🚠 *From €55.*

🛏 Hotels

⭐ Hôtel Le Pashmina

$$$$ | HOTEL | FAMILY | Besides the thrill of hurtling down the world-renowned Val Thorens slopes, there's really no reason to leave this idyllic, family-friendly hotel, where everything you need or desire is at your fingertips. **Pros:** two acclaimed restaurants; set right on the slopes; family-friendly with activities for kids. **Cons:** expensive; a 10-minute walk to the village; some rooms don't have showers. $ *Rooms from: €450* ⊠ *Pl. du Slalom, Val Thorens* 🕾 *04–79–00–09–99* ⊕ *www. hotelpashmina.com* 🕙 *Closed early May–late Nov.* 🛏 *52 rooms* 🍽 *All-inclusive.*

🛍 Shopping

⭐ La Belle en Cuisse

FOOD/CANDY | Hams cured right on the premises hang from the ceiling at this small gourmet shop, where you can sample just about any kind of regional meat or cheese. Looking for a pot of foie gras, or perhaps a bottle of the locally made liquor called *génépi*? This is the place. ✉ *1 rue de Caron, Val Thorens* ☎ *04–79–00–04–30* 🌐 *www.la-belle-en-cuisse.fr.*

Activities

Intersports

SKIING/SNOWBOARDING | The staffers here are all expert skiers, so they really know their stuff. In minutes they'll set you up with a helmet, poles, skis, and boots (heated, of course). If you have a problem, there are many other locations in Val Thorens and around the region. ✉ *Pl. du Péclet, Val Thorens* ☎ *04–79–00–06–65* 🌐 *www.valthorens-intersport.com/en.*

Méribel

111 km (69 miles) south of Chamonix, 178 km (110 miles) south of Geneva.

No building can be taller than the surrounding trees in this mountainside village, so Méribel feels tucked away in the forest. All the architecture must be typical of the region, down to the types of wood used for the graceful balconies and the color of the slate lined up on the gently sloped roofs. The result is one of the most gorgeous resorts in the French Alps.

GETTING HERE AND AROUND

A car is the most convenient way to get to Méribel, although if you're not used to driving in snowy conditions you might consider a shuttle from the airport in Lyon and Geneva. During ski season there's also daily train service to Méribel.

VISITOR INFORMATION Méribel Tourism Office ✉ *Rte. du Centre, Méribel* ☎ *04–79–08–60–01* 🌐 *www.meribel.net.*

Sights

Méribel

RESORT—SIGHT | Méribel's first ski lift was built in 1938, and within a year construction had started on the accommodations that would turn this into a world-class ski resort. But because it sits inside Vanoise National Park, Méribel never experienced a period of rampant growth. Done up in the traditional Savoyard style, its rows of gorgeous chalets make Méribel feel like a village that's been here for centuries.

Back in 1992, the Winter Olympics were held in nearby Albertville. Méribel was the site for women's alpine skiing events, a testament to its world-class slopes. There are 150 km (93 miles) of ski trails, serviced by more than 50 lifts. There are some gentle green runs, but most of the slopes here are best for intermediate skiers. ✉ *D90, Méribel* ☎ *78–08–60–01* 🌐 *www.meribel.net* 🎫 *From €53.*

Restaurants

Le Bistrot de l'Orée

$$ | **BISTRO** | Done up in delectable shades of red and orange, hip Le Bistrot de l'Orée sits right across from the main slope that runs through the resort of Méribel. On the lower level of the Hôtel L'Orée du Bois, this eatery is truly a family affair: the grandson of the hotel's original owner runs the kitchen, turning out modern takes on classics like cream of eggplant soup and veal chops flavored with brandy. **Known for:** local specialties; family-friendly atmosphere; decent prices for the area. [$] *Average main: €23* ✉ *Hôtel L'Orée du Bois, Rte. du Belvédère, Méribel* ☎ *04–79–00–31–29* 🌐 *www.meribel-oree.com.*

Le Cèpe

$$$ | **FRENCH** | This place feels warm and welcoming even before you head through the front door, thanks to the rustic lanterns outside pointing the way. The wood-panel dining room is hushed, as most patrons seem like couples out for a romantic evening; good choice, as this is food you'll want to share: mushroom soup for a starter, perhaps, then crispy duck breast with roasted potatoes and a mushroom cream sauce. **Known for:** hearty traditional dishes with an emphasis on mushrooms; cozy atmosphere; nice terrace. $ *Average main: €26* ⊠ *Rte. D Plateau, Méribel* ☎ *04–79–22–46–08.*

Hotels

Le Savoy

$$$ | **HOTEL** | On the main drag running through Méribel, Le Savoy has a traditional stone-and-wood facade that leads to a rustic restaurant with wide-plank floors and rough-hewn beams that call to mind an old-time ski lodge. **Pros:** central location; refreshing design; staff who go the extra mile. **Cons:** Wi-Fi connection isn't consistent; some noise from other rooms; smallish bathrooms. $ *Rooms from: €350* ⊠ *Pl. du Centre, Méribel* ☎ *04–79–55–55–50* ⊕ *www.hotel-savoy-meribel.com* ⇄ *36 rooms* ⟊⟊ *Free Breakfast.*

Nightlife

L'Abreuvoir

BARS/PUBS | If you'd rather avoid elbow-to-elbow crowds at the slope-side bars, head to Le Poste de Secours. Dispensing with the chalet-chic decor that's so popular in the region's watering holes, it has a futuristic feel. In the purple haze, spherical lighting fixtures float like planets while clusters of podlike chairs sit low to the ground. This is the best place in town for classic cocktails, made by bartenders who know their stuff. ⊠ *Immeuble Les Gentianes, Méribel* ☎ *04–79–22–81–82.*

Shopping

Farto

FOOD/CANDY | To sample a sensational *tartiflette,* the Savoie casserole made

with potatoes, diced bits of salt pork, and locally produced Reblochon cheese, head to this tiny gourmet shop in Méribel Mottaret. It's made by hand in the spotless open kitchen, along with piles of *diots* (sausages) and other delicacies. ⊠ *Centre Commercial Mottaret, Méribel* ☎ *04–79–04–27–93.*

Courchevel

16 km (10 miles) south of Méribel, 114 km (95 miles) southeast of Geneva.

Don't be fooled by the quaint Swiss-chalet-style buildings and diminutive charm, as even the gondolas here are covered with ads for Chanel—your first clue that Courchevel caters to an upscale clientele. The gently curving streets are lined with top-of-the-line boutiques offering the latest scarves from Hermès or bags from Louis Vuitton. And visitors take their dining seriously. There are more Michelin-starred restaurants here than in any other ski resort.

GETTING HERE AND AROUND
Driving is the best way to get to Courchevel. You can also take a taxi from the train station in Méribel or shuttle buses from the airports in Lyon and Geneva.

VISITOR INFORMATION Courchevel Tourism Office ⊠ *Le Coeur de Courchevel, Courchevel* ☎ *04–79–08–00–29* ⊕ *www. courchevel.com.*

Sights

Courchevel

RESORT—SIGHT | It has a reputation as one of the most luxurious ski resorts in the French Alps, and Courchevel doesn't do much to dispel that notion. Ski shops glitter like designer boutiques, and ski valets place your skis and poles outside on the snow so you don't have to carry them.

But it turns out that Courchevel is also one of the area's most inviting towns.

The upscale ski resort of Courchevel offers charming ski runs and the most Michelin-starred restaurants in the region.

None of the locals seem stiff or snooty. The sommelier in the restaurant written up in all the food magazines is happy to give you a tour of the wine cellar, even when the dining room is crowded. Leave behind your voltage converter, and the front desk staff might just give you one for free.

And the skiing is amazing. There's a huge variety of slopes that cater to skiers of every skill level. It's heaven for intermediate skiers, and beginners will find plenty to keep them occupied (including one that has a great view of Courchevel's postage-stamp airport). The lifts are unusually speedy, keeping lines to a minimum. What's more, the scenery just doesn't get better than this in the French Alps. ✉ *D91A, Courchevel* ☎ *79–08–00–29* 🌐 *www.courchevel.com/winter/en* 🎟 *From €55.*

🍴 Restaurants

La Cave des Creux

$$$ | **FRENCH** | An amazing view of Mont Blanc is yours at the Cave des Creux, opened by a couple of ski instructors on top of what was once a shelter for shepherds and their flocks (you can still see some of the old cheese cellar and its equipment on the lower level). It's hard to resist the stone-trimmed dining room, where huge iron beams, industrial lighting, and a sleek fireplace give the place a modern feel. **Known for:** fabulous decor and setting, including a wraparound deck; menu of forward-thinking French classics; organic wine list. [$] *Average main: €32* ✉ *Courchevel 1850, Courchevel* ☎ *04–79–06–76–14* 🌐 *www.cavedescreux-courchevel.com* 🕓 *Closed May–Nov.*

L'Azimut

$$$$ | **FRENCH** | This is hardly a jacket-and-tie kind of place, as the clientele often come straight from the slopes. The laid-back atmosphere, congenial staff, and simple wood tables are among the joys of L'Azimut, where chef François Moureaux's cooking has earned the place a Michelin star. **Known for:** updated classics like panfried foie gras with passion-fruit foam; local cheese menu; friendly vibe. $ *Average main: €40* ✉ *Le Praz, Courchevel* ☎ *04–79–06–25–90* ⊕ *www.restaurantazimut.com* ⊗ *Closed May–Nov. No lunch Mon. and Wed.*

 Hotels

Hotel Annapurna

$$$$ | **HOTEL** | On the edge of the slopes, the ski-in, ski-out Hotel Annapurna could hardly have a better location if you plan on spending your days pounding the powder. **Pros:** set right on slopes; free shuttle service; exquisite decor. **Cons:** expensive; snotty atmosphere; large hotel for the area. $ *Rooms from: €720* ✉ *Rte. de l'Altiport, Courchevel* ☎ *04–79–08–04–60* ⊕ *www.annapurna-courchevel. com* ⇄ *69 rooms* ⦿ *Free Breakfast.*

★ Le Strato

$$$$ | **HOTEL** | Despite its undeniable sophistication, Le Strato manages to convey a delicious coziness that extends from the elegant dining room to the beautifully appointed guest rooms and pristine-white marble baths. **Pros:** superb views; fun programs for kids; cozy elegance. **Cons:** room lighting can be tricky but allows for subtlety; live bar entertainment sometimes amateurish; off-the-charts expensive. $ *Rooms from: €3430* ✉ *Rue de Bellecôte, Courchevel* ☎ *04–79–41–51–60* ⊕ *www.hotelstrato. com* ⊗ *Closed Apr.–mid-Dec.* ⇄ *25 rooms* ⦿ *Free Breakfast.*

Val d'Isère

153 km (95 miles) southeast of Chamonix, 220 km (136 miles) southeast of Geneva.

Men's downhill racing was held in Val d'Isère during the 1992 Winter Olympics, and since then it's been a must-see for skiers wanting to challenge the impossibly steep slope called Bellevarde. But it has an incredible array of slopes, including an impressive number of easy green slopes at the top of the mountain.

GETTING HERE AND AROUND

To get to Val d'Isère, a car or taxi is your best option from the train station in Méribel or the airports in Lyon and Geneva.

VISITOR INFORMATION Val d'Isère Tourism Office ✉ *Pl. Jacques Mouflier, Val d'Isère* ☎ *04–79–06–06–60* ⊕ *www. valdisere.com.*

 Sights

Val d'Isère

RESORT—SIGHT | One of the joys of Val d'Isère is that the easy slopes aren't concentrated at the bottom of the mountains. Beginners can take the gondola to the top and ski for hours at the upper altitudes. Val d'Isère and neighboring Tinges form the Espace Killy, a massive ski area with 154 runs of various ski levels extending for a total of 300 km (186 miles).

Wish the ski season didn't have to end? Val d'Isère's Pissaillas Glacier and Tignes's Grand Motte Glacier both offer summertime skiing. And there are plenty of other activities in both resorts during warmer weather. ✉ *D902, Val d'Isère* ☎ *79–06–06–60* ⊕ *www.valdisere.com/ en* 🎫 *€59 for 1-day Val d'Isère and Tigne pass.*

 Restaurants

★ L'Atelier d'Edmond

$$$$ | MODERN FRENCH | This chalet-style two-star Michelin restaurant is a one of your best option's for a spectacular postski lunch or a romantic gastronomic dinner that will impress even the pickiest gourmande. Chef Benoit Vidal is uncompromising when it comes to local ingredients and what he does with them is pure art. **Known for:** beautiful setting with views; some of the best food in town; meticulously sourced ingredients. *Average main: €65 ⊠ Rue du Fornet, Val d'Isère ☎ 04–79–00–00–82 ⊕ www. atelier-edmond.com ۞ Closed Sun. No lunch Mon. and Tues.*

Hotels

Avenue Lodge Hotel

$$$$ | RESORT | FAMILY | This five-star luxury boutique favorite caters to your every need and then some. **Pros:** ultra-attentive service; superb breakfasts; good ski boutique and services. **Cons:** lower-category rooms not enormous; some guests snooty; some rooms face a bar. *Rooms from: €689 ⊠ Av. Olympique, Val d'Isère ☎ 04–79–00–67–67 ⊕ www.hotelavenue-lodge.com ۞ Closed mid-Apr.–mid-Dec. ⮫ 54 rooms ۩ Free Breakfast.*

Chapter 12

PROVENCE

12

Updated by
Jennifer Ladonne

● Sights	🍴 Restaurants	🛏 Hotels	🛍 Shopping	🍸 Nightlife
★★★★★	★★★★☆	★★★★☆	★★★★☆	★★☆☆☆

WELCOME TO PROVENCE

TOP REASONS TO GO

★ **Vincent van Gogh's Arles:** Ever since the fiery Dutchman immortalized Arles in all its chromatic drama, this town has had a starring role in museums around the world.

★ **The Camargue:** The marshy landscapes of the Camargue will swamp you with their strange beauty, white horses, pink flamingoes, and black bulls.

★ **Lavender fields:** The Lavender Route stretches from the Abbaye de Sénanque (near Gordes) to a wide, blue-purple swath that ranges across the Drôme and the Vaucluse.

★ **Bouillabaisse in Marseille:** The version at Chez Fonfon will make your taste buds stand up and sing "La Marseillaise."

★ **Cézanne country:** Views of Mont Ste-Victoire, rising near the artist's hometown of Aix-en-Provence, may inspire you to pick up a brush.

1 Nîmes. A Roman town turned modern city.

2 Pont du Gard. A famed Roman bridge.

3 Arles. A town defined by Van Gogh.

4 Abbaye de Montmajour. Once Provence's spiritual center.

5 The Camargue. One of France's most remarkable terrains.

6 Les Baux-de-Provence. A lively tangle of medieval streets.

7 St-Rémy-de-Provence. Van Gogh's famous ritzy retreat.

8 Avignon. A dramatic monument to France's history.

9 L'Isle-sur-la-Sorgue. Home to one of the world's best antiques markets.

10 Gordes. A charming Provençal village.

11 Roussillon. A hilltop town known for its red cliffs.

12 Ménerbes. A beautiful Provençal village.

13 Aix-en-Provence. Provence's cultural capital.

14 Marseille. A vibrant port city.

15 Cassis. The prettiest coastal town in Provence.

16 Îles d'Hyrés. Once a haven for pirates.

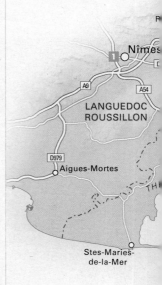

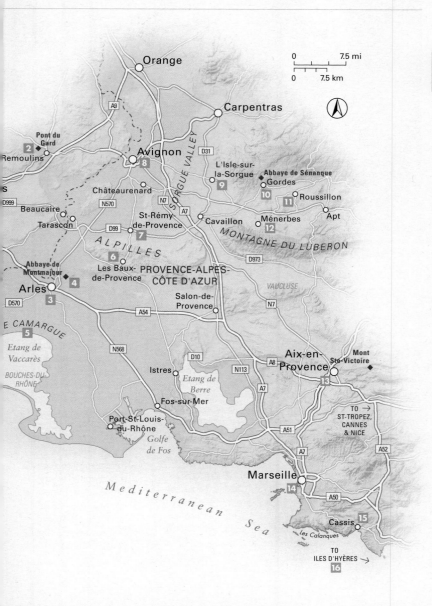

Orange

Carpentras

0   7.5 mi
0   7.5 km

Pont du Gard **2**

Remoulins

Avignon **8**

D31

Châteaurenard

L'Isle-sur-la-Sorgue **9**

Abbaye de Sénanque
Gordes **10**

Roussillon **11**

D999

Beaucaire

N570

St-Rémy-de-Provence **7**

N7

A7

Cavaillon

Ménerbes **12**

Apt

Tarascon

D99

MONTAGNE DU LUBERON

ALPILLES

6

Abbaye de Montmajour **4**

Les Baux-de-Provence

PROVENCE-ALPES-CÔTE D'AZUR

D973

VAUCLUSE

Arles

D570

3

Salon-de-Provence

N7

A54

E CAMARGUE **5**

Etang de Vaccarès

N568

D10

Istres

N113

Etang de Berre

A8

Aix-en-Provence **13**

Mont Ste-Victoire

BOUCHES-DU-RHÔNE

A7

Fos-sur-Mer

Port-St-Louis-du-Rhône

Golfe de Fos

A51

TO →
ST-TROPEZ,
CANNES
& NICE

A7

A52

Marseille

14

A50

Cassis **15**

Les Calanques

Mediterranean Sea

TO
ILES D'HYÈRES →
16

PROVENCE'S VILLAGE MARKETS

In Provence, forget about the supermarket and head to the marketplace—an integral part of French culture anywhere in France, but even more so in this region.

Provence is the equivalent of market heaven. Whether food, collectibles, antiques, or clothing, there is a (very often famous) street market in every Provençal town, each with an energy of its own and offering the best way to interact with the natives. So even though you may wonder if you should resist that tablecloth of pink-and-yellow Souleiado fabric, yield to the delight of puttering through a village market. Happily, they are a daily occurrence in Provence, passed from village to town—Sunday is for L'Isle-sur-la-Sorgue, Saturday for Arles, Wednesday for St-Rémy, and Tuesday, Thursday, and Saturday for Aix-en-Provence. Remember to pick the wheat from the chaff. Provence lovers back home will appreciate those sunflower coasters much more than Day-Glo versions of Van Gogh masterpieces.

FEATS OF CLAY

Top gifts include miniature figures called *santons*, or "little saints." When the French Revolution cracked down on Christmas reenactments, a crafty Marseillais decided to make terra-cotta figurines, which soon upstaged their human counterparts for good. Sold year-round, models include red-cheeked town drunks, lavender-cutters, and—wait, isn't that Gérard Depardieu and Carla Bruni Sarkozy?

AIX-EN-PROVENCE

Aix has some delightful street markets. Unlike some of the more traditional fare of other markets, Aix is more focused on food: you can find rare delicacies side by side with cured sausages bristling with Provençal spices; vats of olives, tapenade, and oils from the Pays d'Aix (Aix region); or bags of orange-spice shuttle-shape *navettes* (cookies). The food market takes place every day in Place Richelème.

ARLES AND THE CAMARGUE

Every Saturday morning, over 2 km (1 mile) along Boulevard des Lices hosts one of the richest and most varied markets in the area. Stands overflow with olives of every kind, fresh-pressed oils, herbs, cheeses, and all the generous bounty of Provence. You can also find the famous *boutis* (cotton throws), textured fabrics, and an endless array of tablecloths, children's clothes, and Arlesian costumes. On the first Wednesday of every month, Boulevard Emile Combes converts into an antiques and collectibles market.

AVIGNON AND THE VAUCLUSE

Avignon has a great mix of French chains and youthful clothing shops, and Les Halles food stalls are a sight to see. Every Wednesday morning, St-Rémy-de-Provence hosts one of the most popular markets in France. Place de la République and the narrow town streets abound with fresh produce, olives, tapenade by the vat, and a variety of other delicacies. In the Vaucluse area, you can find anything made from lavender.

MARSEILLE

The main shopping drag lies between La Canebière and the Préfecture, but Marseille offers up a large selection of shops, boutiques, and stores all over the city. There is an assortment of street markets, from the daily fish market in the old port to the stamp market every Sunday morning in Cours Julien (which is also home to the Wednesday organic market). Probably the most famous item you'll find is the Savon de Marseille (Marseille soap).

THE SORGUE VALLEY

The best place to go trolling for time-burnished treasure is the famed antiques market held in the lovely Isle-sur-la-Sorgue every weekend. Twice a year, around Easter and mid-August, in addition to the town's 250 art and antiques dealers, some 200 antiques merchants set up shop over four days for the Grand Déballage, or "Great Unpacking."

As you approach Provence there's a magical moment when you finally leave the north behind: cypresses and red-tile roofs appear; you hear the screech of cicadas and breathe the scent of wild thyme and lavender. Along the highway, oleanders bloom against a backdrop of austere, sun-filled landscapes, the very same that inspired the Postimpressionists.

Ever since Peter Mayle abandoned the London fog and described with sensual relish a life of unbuttoned collars and espadrilles in his best-selling *A Year in Provence,* the world has beaten a path here. Now Parisians and a slew of European and American expats are heard in the local marketplaces passing the word on the best free-range rabbit and the lowest price on a five-bedroom *mas* (a traditional Provençal farmhouse). This *bon-chic-bon-genre* city crowd languishes stylishly at Provence's country inns and restaurants. Ask them, and they'll agree: when Princess Caroline of Monaco moved to St-Rémy, Provence became the new Côte d'Azur.

But chichi Provence hasn't eclipsed idyllic Provence, except that now every farmer and crafts vendor has a smartphone. Still, it's possible to melt into a Monday-morning market crowd, where blue-aproned *paysannes* scoop fistfuls of mesclun into willow baskets, matron-connoisseurs paw through bins containing the first Cavaillon asparagus, and a knot of *pépés* in workers' blues take a pétanque break.

Relax, join them—and plan to stick around awhile. There are plenty of sights to see: great Roman ruins; the pristine Romanesque abbeys of Senanque and de Montmajour; weathered mas; the monolithic Papal Palace in old Avignon; the narrow streets in Arles immortalized on canvas by Van Gogh. Check out all these treasures but remember that highlights of any trip here are those hours spent dawdling at a sidewalk café, wandering aimlessly down narrow cobbled alleyways, and, after a three-hour lunch, taking a quick snooze in the cool shade of a 500-year-old plane tree. Allow yourself time to feel the rhythm of modern Provençal life, to listen to the pulsing *cigales,* smell the *parfum* of a tiny country path, and feel the jasmine-scented night air on your skin.

GETTING ORIENTED

What many visitors remember best about Provence is the light. The vibrant sun here bathes vineyards, olive groves, fields full of lavender, and tall stands of sunflowers with an intensity that captivated Cézanne and Van Gogh. Bordering the Mediterranean and flanked by the

Alps and the Rhône River, Provence attracts hordes of visitors. Fortunately, many of them are siphoned off to the resorts along the Riviera, which is part of Provence but whose jet-set image doesn't fit in with the tranquil charm of the rest of the region.

The southeastern portion of this part of Provence, on the edge of the Côte d'Azur, is dominated by two major towns: Aix-en-Provence, considered the main hub of Provence and the most cultural community in the region; and Marseille, a vibrant port city that combines seediness with fashion and metropolitan feistiness with classical grace. To fully experience the dramatic contrast between the azure Mediterranean Sea and the rocky, olive tree–filled hills, take a trip along the coast east of Marseille and make an excursion to the Iles d'Hyères and the charming town of Cassis.

MAJOR REGIONS

Nîmes, Arles, and the Camargue. Sitting on the banks of the Rhône River, with a Vieille Ville where time seems to have stood still since 1888—the year Vincent van Gogh immortalized the city in his paintings—Arles remains both a vibrant example of Provençal culture and the gateway to the Camargue, a wild and marshy region that extends south to the Mediterranean. Arles, in fact, once outshone Marseille as the major port of the area before sea gave way to sand. Today it competes with nearby Nîmes for the title of "Rome of France," thanks to its magnificent Roman theater and Arènes (amphitheater). A bus ride away, the Camargue is a vast watery plain formed by the sprawling Rhône delta and extending over 800 square km (309 square miles)—its landscape remains one of the most extraordinary in France, complete with cowboys, horseback rides, and exclusive mas (converted farmhouse) hotels.

The Alpilles. Whether approaching from the damp lowlands of Arles and the Camargue or the pebbled vineyards around Avignon, the countryside changes dramatically as you climb into the arid heights of the low mountain range called the Alpilles (pronounced "ahl- *pee*-yuh"). A rough-hewn, rocky landscape rises into nearly barren limestone hills, the fields silvered with ranks of twisted olive trees and alleys of gnarled *amandiers* (almond trees). It's the heart of Provence, appealing not only for the antiquities in St-Rémy and the feudal ruins in Les Baux, but also for its mellow pace when the day's touring is done.

Avignon and the Vaucluse. This area is the heart of Provençal delights. Anchored by the magnificent papal stronghold of Avignon, the Vaucluse spreads luxuriantly east of the Rhône. Its famous vineyards seduce connoisseurs, and its Roman ruins draw scholars and art lovers alike. Arid lowlands with orchards of olives, apricots, and almonds give way to a rich and wild mountain terrain around the formidable Mont Ventoux and flow into the primeval Luberon, made a household name by Peter Mayle. The hill villages around the Luberon are as lovely as any you'll find in the south of France. About 16 km (10 miles) east of Avignon is the Sorgue Valley, where everybody goes "flea"-ing in the famous antiques market at L'Isle-sur-la-Sorgue. Just east are the Luberon's hilltop villages (globalized by Peter Mayle), such as picture-perfect Gordes. South lies Roussillon, set like a ruby in its red cliffs.

Aix-en-Provence and the Mediterranean Coast. Café-sitting, people-watching, and boutique-shopping are a way of life in Aix-en-Provence. For a day, join the fashionable folk doing just that along the elegant 18th-century streets, then visit Cézanne's studio and nearby Mont Ste-Victoire, one of his favorite subjects. Head south to become a Calanques castaway before diving into Marseille, which ranks among France's most multicultural and vibrant cities.

12

Provence

Planner

When to Go

Spring and fall are the best months to experience the dazzling light, rugged rocky countryside, and fruited orchards and vineyards of Provence. Though the lavender fields show peak color in July, summertime here is beastly hot; worse, it's always crowded on the beaches and connecting roads. In winter (November through February, sometimes even into March) services catering to tourists can be closed, including certain hotels and restaurants. Much of the terrace life is driven indoors by rain and wind, but around Easter the plane trees begin to leaf out and the café tables begin to sprout once more.

Planning Your Time

The best place to start your trip is in Avignon. It's on a fast train link from Paris, but even if you arrive in record time, once you arrive it's all about slowing down. Amid all that magnificent architecture and art, enjoy the wonder and breathe deeply. Provence is about lazy afternoons and spending "just one more day," and Avignon is a good place to have a practice run. It's cosmopolitan enough to keep the most energetic visitor occupied, while old and wise enough to teach the value of time.

Getting Here and Around

Provence is home to one of France's largest airports (Aéroport de Marseille Provence), plus it has high-speed TGV train service from Paris. Departing from the Gare de Lyon, you can get to Nîmes, Aix-en-Provence, Marseille, or Avignon in three hours or less; you can even be whisked to Provence directly on arrival at Paris's Charles de Gaulle airport. Once in the region, well-organized public transport makes most towns accessible by train or bus. It's best to plan on combining the two—often smaller Provençal communities won't have their own train station, but rather a local bus connection to one in the nearest town over. Driving is also a good option, although negotiating the highways in Provence can be a scary experience. They're fast … regardless of the speed limit. Off the highway, however, on the national roads, or the district roads, driving can be the best and most relaxing way to get around.

AIR TRAVEL

Marseille has the fifth-busiest airport in France, the Aéroport de Marseille Provence in Marignane. Located about 20 km (12 miles) northwest of the city center, it receives flights from both major airlines—including Air France—and a broad range of budget carriers; airport shuttle buses regularly run to Marseille (€8.20) and Aix (€8.30). The smaller Aéroport de Nîmes-Alès-Camargue-Cévennes, 12 km (7½ miles) south of Nîmes, is served by Ryanair, which operates multiple weekly flights from Brussels, London, and Liverpool. A shuttle bus into Nîmes costs €6; if you're bound for Arles, cab fare for the 20-km (12-mile) trip is about €50 and takes about 20 minutes.

BUS TRAVEL

Buses, often working in tandem with trains, can get you almost anywhere you want to go. The official websites for individual communities (and even some attractions) typically include detailed bus-access information; a quick email or phone call will confirm it. Schedules and *trajets* (journeys) also can be found on the websites of the region's primary bus companies. Cartreize controls bus routes to and from the Bouches du Rhône; Lignes Express Régionales (LER) operates between main hubs like Marseille, Aix, Arles, and Avignon, with some routes servicing smaller villages; while buses around the Nîmes area are the domain of Edgard Transport.

CAR TRAVEL

The A6–A7 toll road from Paris, known as the Autoroute du Soleil—the Highway of the Sun—takes you straight to Provence, dividing at Orange, 659 km (412 miles) from the capital; the trip can be done in a fast six or so hours. After Orange, the A7 continues southeast to Marseille, on the coast; the A9 heads west to Nîmes, while the A8 carries on to Aix-en-Provence and then to the Côte d'Azur and Italy.

TRAIN TRAVEL

The Marseille-St-Charles station—serving all parts of France, including Paris, Strasbourg, and Bordeaux—is at the northern end of Marseille's city center. Regional trains to Aix-en-Provence (40 mins), Arles (1 hr), Nîmes (1 hr 20 mins), Avignon (1 hr 10 mins), and other destinations run from there as well. Avignon itself is a major rail crossroads and a springboard for the Vaucluse. From Paris, you can make it to Avignon in 2 hours 40 minutes aboard daily high-speed trains on the TGV *Méditerranée* line; these pull into a dedicated station a few miles southwest of the city. TGVs then connect with Nîmes (18 mins), Marseille (35 mins), and Nice (3 hrs). Many other locales within Provence can be reached by rail from Gare Avignon Centre, including Arles (20 mins) and Aix-en-Provence (100 mins with two connections).

Restaurants

You'll eat later in the south, rarely before 12:30 for lunch, usually around 8 for dinner. In summer, shops and museums may shut down, after their morning hours, from noon until 3 or even 4 pm, as much to accommodate lazy lunches as for the crowds taking sun on the beach.

But a late lunch works nicely with a late breakfast—and that's another southern luxury. As morning here is the coolest part of the day and the light is at its sweetest, hotels and cafés of every class take pains to make breakfast memorable and whenever possible serve it outdoors. Complete with tables in the garden with sunny-print cloths and a nosegay of flowers, accompanied by birdsong, it's one of the three loveliest meals of the day.

Hotels

Accommodations in Provence range from luxurious villas to elegantly converted mas to modest city-center hotels. Reservations are essential for much of the year. Provence is more about charming bed-and-breakfasts and lovely expensive hideaways than big hotels, so space is at a premium—especially in summer. Book as far in advance as possible for high season (return guests often reserve next year's stay at the end of the current year's visit); even in low season, you should call ahead because many hotels close for the winter. Assume that all hotel rooms have TV, telephones, Wi-Fi, and a private bath, unless otherwise noted. *Restaurant and hotel reviews have been shortened. For full information, visit Fodors.com.*

What It Costs in Euros			
$	$$	$$$	$$$$
RESTAURANTS			
under €18	€18–€24	€25–€32	over €32
HOTELS			
under €106	€106–€145	€146–€215	over €215

Nîmes

35 km (20 miles) north of Aigues-Mortes, 43 km (26 miles) south of Avignon, 121 km (74 miles) west of Marseille.

If you have come to the south to seek out Roman treasures, you need look no farther than Nîmes (pronounced "*neem*"), for the Arènes and Maison Carrée are among Continental Europe's best-preserved antiquities. But if you have come to seek out a more modern mythology—a lazy, graceful Provence—give Nîmes a wide berth: it's a feisty town in transition. Its medieval Old Town has none of the gentrified grace of those in Arles or St-Rémy. Yet its rumpled and rebellious ways trace directly back to its Roman incarnation, when its population swelled with soldiers, arrogant and newly victorious after their conquest of Egypt in 31 BC. A 24,000-seat coliseum, a thriving forum with a magnificent temple patterned after Rome's temple of Apollo, and a public water network fed by the Pont du Gard attest to its classical prosperity.

Nîmes has opted against becoming a lazy, atmospheric Provençal market town and has invested in progressive modern architecture. Smack-dab across from the Maison Carrée stands the city's contemporary answer to it: the modern-art museum, dubbed the Carrée d'Art (Art Square) after its ruthlessly modernist four-square form—a pillared, symmetrical glass reflection of its ancient twin. Other investments in contemporary art and architecture confirm Nîmes's commitment to modern ways. If you want to see everything—or a lot of things—in Nîmes, the Visite Ensemble ticket is a good value: it costs a mere €11.70, is valid for three days, and can be purchased at most local monuments and sites.

GETTING HERE AND AROUND

On the Paris–Avignon–Montpellier train line, Nîmes has a direct link to and from Paris (about a three-hour ride). The Nîmes *gare routière* (bus station) is just behind the train station. Edgard runs several buses to and from Arles (one daily, Monday through Saturday; two on Sunday); STD Gard has several buses (running Monday through Saturday) between Avignon and Nîmes and Uzès and Nîmes. Some Uzès buses stop at Remoulins for the Pont du Gard and a few continue on to St-Quentin-la-Poterie. Note that although all the sites in Nîmes are walkable, the useful Tango bus runs a good loop from the station and passes by many of the principal sites along the way for €1.30.

VISITOR INFORMATION Nîmes Tourist Office ⊠ *6 rue Auguste, Nîmes* ☎ *04–66–58–38–00* ⊕ *www.nimes-tourisme.com.*

Sights

★ Arènes

ARCHAEOLOGICAL SITE | The best-preserved Roman amphitheater in the world is a miniature of the Colosseum in Rome (note the small carvings of Romulus and Remus, the wrestling gladiators, on the exterior and the intricate bulls' heads etched into the stone over the entrance on the north side). More than 435 feet long and 330 feet wide, it had a seating capacity of 24,000 in its day. Bloody gladiator battles, criminals being thrown to animals, and theatrical wild-boar chases drew crowds to its bleachers. Nowadays the corrida transforms the arena (and all of Nîmes) into a sangria-flushed homage to Spain. Concerts are held here year-round, thanks to a high-tech glass-and-steel structure that covers the arena for winter use. ⊠ *Bd. des Arènes, Nîmes* ☎ *04–66–21–82–56, 04–66–02–80–80 for féria box office* ⊕ *www.arenes-nimes. com* ⊠ *From €10.*

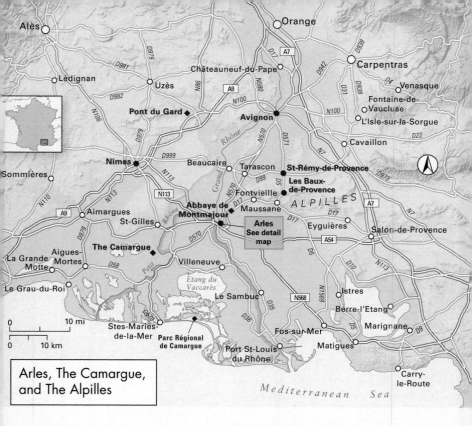

Arles, The Camargue,
and The Alpilles

Carrée d'Art

MUSEUM | Directly opposite the Maison Carrée and looking like an airport terminal, the glass-fronted Carrée d'Art was designed by British architect Sir Norman Foster as its neighbor's stark contemporary mirror. It literally reflects the Maison Carrée's creamy symmetry and figuratively answers it with a featherlight deconstructed colonnade. It contains a library, archives, and the **Musée d'Art Contemporain** (Contemporary Art Museum). The permanent collection falls into three categories: French painting and sculpture; English, American, and German works; and Mediterranean styles—all dating from 1960 onward. There are often temporary exhibits of new work, too. But as lovely as the museum is, the facade has suffered traffic pollution and could do with a bit of a cleanup. ✉ *Pl. de la Maison Carrée, Nîmes* ☎ *04–66–76–35–70* ⊕ *www.carreartmusee.com* ✉ *€5.*

Cathédrale Notre-Dame et St-Castor (*Nîmes Cathedral*)

RELIGIOUS SITE | Destroyed and rebuilt in several stages, Nîmes Cathedral was damaged by Protestants during the 16th-century Wars of Religion but still shows traces of its original construction in 1096. A remarkably preserved Romanesque frieze portrays Adam and Eve cowering in shame, the gory slaughter of Abel, and a flood-wearied Noah. Inside, look for the 4th-century sarcophagus (third chapel on the right) and a magnificent 17th-century chapel in the apse. ✉ *Pl. aux Herbes, Nîmes* ☎ *04–66–67–27–72* ✉ *Free.*

Jardins de la Fontaine (*Fountain Garden*)

GARDEN | The Jardins de la Fontaine, an elaborate formal garden, was landscaped on the site of the Roman baths in the 18th century, when the Source de Nemausus, a once-sacred spring, was channeled into pools and a canal. It's a shady haven of mature trees and graceful stonework, and a testimony to the taste of the Age of Reason. It makes for a lovely approach to the Temple de Diane and the Tour Magne. ⊠ *Corner of Quai de la Fontaine and Av. Jean-Jaurès, Nîmes* ☎ *04–66–58–38–00* 🔁 *Free.*

Maison Carrée (*Square House*)

ARCHAEOLOGICAL SITE | Lovely and forlorn in the middle of a busy downtown square, this exquisitely preserved temple strikes a timeless balance between symmetry and whimsy, purity of line and richness of decoration. Modeled on the Temple to Apollo in Rome, adorned with magnificent marble columns and elegant pediment, the Maison Carrée remains one of the most noble surviving structures of ancient Roman civilization anywhere. Built around 5 BC and dedicated to Gaius Caesar and his brother Lucius, the temple has survived subsequent use as a medieval meeting hall, an Augustine church, a storehouse for Revolutionary archives, and a horse shed. Temporary art and photo exhibitions are held here, and among a permanent display of photos and drawings of ongoing archaeological work is a splendid ancient Roman fresco of Cassandra (being dragged by her hair by a hunter) that was discovered in 1992 and carefully restored. There's even a fun 3-D projection of the heroes of Nîmes. ⊠ *Pl. de la Maison Carrée, Nîmes* ☎ *04–66–21–82–56* ⊕ *www.arenes-ni-mes.com* 🔁 *From €6.*

Musée Archéologique et d'Histoire Naturelle (*Museum of Archaeology and Natural History*)

MUSEUM | FAMILY | This old Jesuit college houses a wonderful collection of local archaeological finds, including sarcophagi, beautiful pieces of Roman glass, statues, busts, friezes, tools, coins, and pottery. Among the highlights are a rare pre-Roman statue called *The Warrior of Grezan* and the Marbacum Torso, which was dug up at the foot of the Tour Magne. ⊠ *13 bd. Amiral Courbet, Nîmes* ☎ *04–66–76–74–80* 🔁 *€5* 🕙 *Closed Mon.*

Musée des Beaux-Arts (*Fine Arts Museum*)

MUSEUM | The centerpiece of this early-20th-century building, stunningly refurbished by architect Jean-Michel Wilmotte, is a vast ancient mosaic depicting a marriage ceremony that provides intriguing insights into the lifestyle of Roman aristocrats. Also in the varied collection are seven paintings devoted to Cleopatra by 18th-century Nîmes-born painter Natoire Italian, plus some fine Flemish, Dutch, and French works (notably Rubens's *Portrait of a Monk* and Giambono's *The Mystic Marriage of St. Catherine*). ⊠ *23 rue de la Cite Foulc, Nîmes* ☎ *04–66–28–18–32* ⊕ *www. nimes.fr* 🔁 *€5* 🕙 *Closed Mon.*

Musée du Vieux Nîmes (*Museum of Old Nîmes*)

MUSEUM | Housed in the 17th-century bishop's palace opposite the cathedral, this museum shows off garments embroidered in the exotic and vibrant style for which Nîmes was once famous. Look for the 14th-century jacket made of blue *serge de Nîmes,* the famous fabric—now simply called denim—from which Levi Strauss first fashioned blue jeans. ⊠ *Pl. aux Herbes, Nîmes* ☎ *04–66–76–73–70* ⊕ *www.nimes.fr* 🔁 *€5* 🕙 *Closed Mon.*

Temple de Diane (*Temple of Diana*)

ARCHAEOLOGICAL SITE | This shattered Roman ruin dates to the 2nd century BC. The temple's function is unknown, though it's thought to have been part of a larger Roman complex that is still unexcavated. In the Middle Ages Benedictine nuns occupied the building before it was converted into a church. Destruction came during the Wars of Religion. ⊠ *Jardins de la Fontaine, Nîmes.*

Thanks to Provence's extraordinary light, Nîmes is one of the prettiest towns in France.

Tour Magne (*Magne Tower*)
ARCHAEOLOGICAL SITE | At the far end of the Jardins de la Fontaine are the remains of a tower the emperor Augustus had built on Gallic foundations; it was probably used as a lookout post. Despite losing 30 feet in height over the course of time, the tower still provides fine views of Nîmes for anyone energetic enough to climb the 140 steps. ✉ *Jardins de la Fontaine , Pl. Guillaume-Apollinaire, Nîmes* ☎ *04–66–21–82–56* 🎫 *From €4.*

🍴 Restaurants

★ Alexandre

$$$$ | **MODERN FRENCH** | Michelin-starred chef Michel Kayser adds a personal touch both to the gradual transformation of the restaurant's modern interior—the restoration of the dining room, a library sitting room—and to local specialties and seasonal menus. Marinated rabbit traditionally cooked with a mustard dressing followed by a rich bull steak with pan-roasted Cantal potatoes and black olives served with a celery, caper, and anchovy "chausson" pastry, all drizzled in Camargue sauce, may not leave room for dessert. **Known for:** top-notch tasting menus; lovely garden terrace; seasonal, regional products. [$] *Average main: €59* ✉ *2 rue Xavier Tronc, Rte. de l'Aeroport, Nîmes* ☎ *04–66–70–08–99* 🌐 *www.michelkayser.com* ⏰ *Closed Mon. and Tues. Sept.–June, Sun. and Mon. in July and Aug., 3 wks in mid-Feb., and 2 wks in late Aug. No dinner Sun.*

★ Bistrot Le République

$$ | **FRENCH** | This quintessential locals' hangout is packed for lunch pretty much all year-round thanks to that dishes that are deeply French and deeply satisfying. The traditional bistro decor—long bar, leatherette banquettes, large mirrors, and brass railings—has something to do with the appeal of this marvelous restaurant that's casual in every sense except when it comes to food and wine. **Known for:** exceptional service; unpretentious atmosphere; breakfast and lunch. [$] *Average main: €18* ✉ *3 rue de la République,*

Nîmes ☎ *04–66–64–26–17* 🕒 *Closed weekends. No dinner.*

★ **Skab**

$$$$ | **FRENCH** | Don't be put off by the name—a blend of the initials of owners Sébastien Kieffer and Alban Barbette—because this restaurant has an enchanting shaded garden terrace and a seasonal menu by chef Damien Sanchez that will not disappoint. Crispy Provençal lamb with seasonal vegetables makes for a great main dish, and for dessert there's poached apple sections on a crispy pastry with apple jelly, nougat, heavy cream, and gingerbread ice cream. **Known for:** outstanding wine list; pretty outdoor courtyard for dining; accommodate vegetarian and gluten-free diets. [$] *Average main: €50* ✉ *7 rue de la République, Nîmes* ☎ *04–66–21–94–30* 🌐 *www.restaurant-skab.fr* 🕒 *Closed Sun. and Mon., and last 2 wks in Apr.*

Hotels

Hôtel de l'Amphithéâtre

$ | **HOTEL** | This old private home has fortunately fallen into the hands of a loving and very hospitable owner, who has refinished 18th-century double doors and fitted rooms with restored-wood details, white-tiled bathrooms, and antique bedroom sets. **Pros:** ideally located; good value; friendly hosts. **Cons:** underground parking is a few blocks away; amenities are limited; no elevator. [$] *Rooms from: €90* ✉ *4 rue des Arènes, Nîmes* ☎ *04–66–67–28–51* 🌐 *www.hoteldelamphitheatre.com* 🛏 *14 rooms* 🍴 *No meals.*

★ **L'Imperator**

$$$$ | **HOTEL** | **FAMILY** | Reopened in summer 2019 after a several-year, top-to-toe renovation, this local grande dame near the Jardins de la Fontaine has emerged butterflylike as a gorgeous contemporary hotel, complete with a pool and gastronomic restaurant overseen by superstar chef Pierre Gagnaire. **Pros:** richly atmospheric; excellent location; gorgeous new interiors hotel-wide. **Cons:** pricey; some rooms have better views than others, be sure to ask; gets crowded in June around féria time. [$] *Rooms from: €320* ✉ *15 rue Gaston Boissier, off Quai de la Fontaine, Nîmes* ☎ *04–66–21–90–30* 🌐 *www.maison-albar-hotels-l-imperator.com* 🛏 *57 rooms, 8 private villas* 🍴 *No meals.*

Shopping

In Nîmes's Old Town there's the expected rash of chain stores but also fabulous interior-design boutiques and fabric shops selling the Provençal cottons that used to be produced here en masse (Les Indiennes de Nîmes, Les Olivades, Souleiado) as well as a concentration of antiques and collectibles shops, which also are found throughout the city's backstreets.

Les Halles

OUTDOOR/FLEA/GREEN MARKETS | This permanent covered market is at the heart of the city and puts on a mouthwatering show of olives, fresh fish, cheeses, and produce. ✉ *5 rue des Halles, Nîmes* ☎ *04–66–21–52–49* 🌐 *www.leshallesdenimes.com.*

Pont du Gard

24 km (15 miles) northeast of Nîmes.

No other ancient Roman sight in Provence rivals the Pont du Gard, a mighty, three-tiered aqueduct midway between Nîmes and Avignon—the highest bridge the Romans ever built. Erected some 2,000 years ago as part of a 48-km (30-mile) canal supplying water to Roman Nîmes, it is astonishingly well preserved. You can't walk across it anymore, but you can get close enough to see the amazing gigantic square blocks of stone (some weighing up to 6 tons) by traversing the 18th-century bridge built alongside it.

GETTING HERE AND AROUND

The best way to get to Pont du Gard is via Nîmes, which is on the direct TGV line from Paris and takes about three hours. The Nîmes bus station is right behind the train station, and Edgard runs several buses daily except Sunday between Nîmes and Pont du Gard (1 hour, €1.50 one way). If you are coming by car, take the A9 to Nîmes, exit 50; then take the D979, direction Uzès. Pont du Gard is 14 km (9 miles) southeast of Uzès on the D981.

Sights

★ Pont du Gard

ARCHAEOLOGICAL SITE | The ancient Roman aqueduct is shockingly noble in its symmetry. The rhythmic repetition of arches resonate with strength, a testimony to an engineering concept that was relatively new in the 1st century AD, when the structure was built under Emperor Claudius. And, unsullied by tourists or by the vendors of postcards and Popsicles that dominate the site later in the day, nature is just as resonant, with the river flowing through its rocky gorge unperturbed by the work of master engineering that straddles it.

You can approach the aqueduct from either side of the Gardon River. If you choose the south side (Rive Droite), the walk to the *pont* (bridge) is shorter and the views arguably better. Although the spectacular walkway along the top of the aqueduct is now off-limits, the sight of the bridge is still breathtaking. The nearby Espaces Culturels details the history of the bridge and includes an interactive area for kids. ✉ *400 rte. du Pont du Gard, Vers-Pont-du-Gard* ☎ *04–66–37–50–99* 🌐 *www.pontdugard.fr* 🎟 *€10, includes Espaces Culturels.*

Hotels

La Bégude Saint Pierre

$$$ | **HOTEL** | A mere 2 km (1 mile) from Pont du Gard, a 17th-century coach house on 30 acres of greenery has been lovingly converted into this boutique hotel and gourmet restaurant. **Pros:** practical location; friendly staff; lovely pool. **Cons:** street-facing rooms can be noisy; can be difficult to find; vintage atmosphere. [$] *Rooms from: €198* ✉ *295 chemin des Bégudes, Vers-Pont-du-Gard* ☎ *04–66–02–63–60* 🌐 *www.hotel-begude-saint-pierre.com* 🛏 *25 rooms* 🍴 *No meals.*

Arles

31 km (19 miles) east of Nîmes.

If you were obliged to choose just one city to visit in Provence, lovely little Arles would give Avignon and Aix a run for their money. It's too charming to become museumlike, yet has a wealth of classical antiquities and Romanesque stonework; quarried-stone edifices and shuttered town houses shading graceful Old Town streets and squares; and pageantry, festivals, and cutting-edge arts events. Its atmospheric restaurants and picturesque small hotels make it the ideal headquarters for forays into the Alpilles and the Camargue.

It wasn't always such a mellow site. A Greek colony since the 6th century BC, little Arles took a giant step forward when Julius Caesar defeated Marseille in the 1st century BC, transforming it into a formidable civilization—by some accounts, the Rome of the north. Fed by aqueducts, canals, and solid roads, it profited from all the Romans' modern conveniences: straight paved streets and sidewalks, sewers and latrines, thermal baths, a forum, a hippodrome, a theater, and an arena. It became an international crossroads by sea and land, and a market to the world. The emperor Constantine himself moved to Arles and brought with him Christianity.

Van Gogh wasn't the only artist enamored with Arles's legendary light as reflected off its creamy white stone. Both Gauguin and Picasso adored the ancient Arènes, still home to bullfights, and painted canvases here. Today, Arles is a heavy hitter on the international art scene, with the world-famous Les Rencontres de la Photographie, held every year from July 1 until the end of September. In 2020, the Luma Foundation—an arts center featuring exibitions and workshops around contemporary art, food, performance, and sustainability—will inhabit an astonishing silvery tower conceived by star architect Frank Gehry. Les Sud, the city's weeklong music festival featuring rock, jazz, experimental, and world music, kicks off in July.

The remains of this golden age are reason enough to visit Arles today. Yet its character nowadays is as gracious and low-key as it once was cutting-edge. If you plan to visit many of the monuments and museums in Arles, purchase a *visite générale* ticket for €16, which covers admission to all of them.

GETTING HERE AND AROUND

If you're arriving by plane, note that Arles is roughly 20 km (12 miles) from the Nîmes-Arles-Camargue airport. The easiest way from the landing strip to Arles is by taxi (about €35). Buses run between Nîmes and Arles 11 times daily on weekdays and four times on Saturday (not at all on Sunday). Four buses run weekdays between Arles and Stes-Maries-de-la-Mer, through Cartreize. The SNCF runs three buses Monday through Saturday from Avignon to Arles. Arles is along the main coastal train route, and you can take the TGV to Avignon from Paris and jump on the local connection to Arles. You can also reach Arles directly by train from Marseille. Once there, its monuments and pretty old neighborhoods are conveniently concentrated between the main artery Boulevard des Lices and the broad, meandering Rhône

VISITOR INFORMATION Arles Tourist Office ✉ *Bd. des Lices, Arles* ☎ *04–90–18–41–20* ⊕ *www.arlestourisme.com.*

 ## Sights

★ **Arènes** (*Arena*)

ARCHAEOLOGICAL SITE | Rivaled only by the even better-preserved version in Nîmes, the arena dominating old Arles was built in the 1st century AD to seat 21,000 people, with large tunnels through which wild beasts were forced to run into the center. Before being plundered in the Middle Ages, the structure had three stories of 60 arcades each; the four medieval towers are testimony to a transformation from classical sports arena to feudal fortification. Complete restoration of the arena began in 1825. Today it's primarily a venue for the traditional spectacle of the corridas, which take place annually during the *féria pascale,* or Easter festival. The less bloodthirsty local variant Course Carmarguaise (in which the bull is not killed) also takes place here. Festivities start with the Fête des Gardians on May 1, when the Queen of Arles is crowned, and culminate in early July with the award of the Cocarde d'Or (Golden Rosette) to the most successful *raseteur.* Tickets are usually available, but be sure to book ahead. ✉ *24 bis, Rond Point des Arènes, Arles* ☎ *04–90–18–41–20 for arena info, 08–91–70–03–70 for Courses Carmarguaise info* ⊕ *www.arlestourisme.com* 🎫 *€9, includes admission to Théâtre Antique.*

Cloître St-Trophime (*St. Trophime Cloister*)

RELIGIOUS SITE | This peaceful haven, one of the loveliest cloisters in Provence, is tucked discreetly behind St-Trophime, the notable Romanesque treasure. A sturdy walkway above the Gothic arches offers good views of the town. ✉ *Off Pl. de la*

Straddling the Gardon River and built during the rule of Emperor Claudius, the Pont du Gard was an aqueduct that brought water to nearby Nîmes.

République, Arles ☎ *04–90–18–41–20* ⊕ *www.arlestourisme.com* 💳 *€6.*

Cryptoportiques

ARCHAEOLOGICAL SITE | Entering through the elegant 17th-century City Hall, you can gain access to these ancient underground passages dating to 30–20 BC. The horseshoe of vaults and pillars buttressed the ancient forum from below ground. Used as a bomb shelter in World War II, the galleries still have a rather ominous atmosphere. Yet openings let in natural daylight and artworks of considerable merit have been unearthed here, adding to the mystery of the site's original function. ⊠ *Pl. de la République, Arles* ☎ *04–90–18–41–20* 💳 *€5.*

Église St-Trophime

RELIGIOUS SITE | Classed as a world treasure by UNESCO, this extraordinary Romanesque church alone would justify a visit to Arles. The side aisles date to the 11th century and the nave to the 12th; the church's austere symmetry and ancient artworks (including a stunning early Christian sarcophagus) are fascinating. But it's the church's superbly preserved Romanesque sculpture on the 12th-century **portal,** the renovated entry facade, that earns international respect. Particularly remarkable is the frieze of the Last Judgment, with souls being dragged off to Hell in chains or, on the contrary, being lovingly delivered into the hands of the saints. Christ is flanked by his chroniclers, the evangelists: the eagle (John), the bull (Luke), the angel (Matthew), and the lion (Mark). ⊠ *Pl. de la République, Arles* ⊕ *www.arlestourisme.com* 💳 *Free.*

★ Espace Van Gogh

GARDEN | A strikingly resonant site, this was the hospital to which the tortured artist repaired after cutting off his earlobe. Its courtyard has been impeccably restored and landscaped to match one of Van Gogh's paintings. The cloistered grounds have become something of a shrine for visitors, and there is a photo plaque comparing the renovation to some of the master's paintings, including *Le Jardin de la Maison de Santé.* The exhibition hall is open for temporary

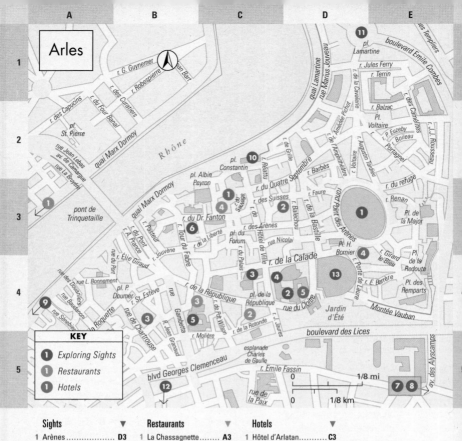

Arles

exhibitions; the garden is always on view. ✉ *Pl. Dr. Félix Rey, Arles* ☎ *04–90–18–41–20* ✆ *Free.*

Fondation Vincent Van Gogh

MUSEUM | Van Gogh's 15-month stay in Arles represents a climax in the artist's career. Enchanted with Arles's limpid light, vibrant landscape, and scenic monuments, Van Gogh experienced here what was to be his greatest blossoming in a decade as a painter. The Fondation Vincent Van Gogh, originally conceived in the mid-1980s in response to the 100th anniversary of the artist's arrival in Arles, pays homage to Van Gogh's legacy and monumental influence via an impressive range of artworks contributed by 90 contemporary artists. Opened in 2014 in the beautifully restored 15th-century Hôtel Léautaud de Donines, the Fondation houses a superb collection of contemporary art and provides a vital addition to Arles's cultural life with a revolving series of temporary art exhibitions, performance art, concerts, and other events. ✉ *35 rue du Docteur Fanton, Arles* ☎ *04–90–93–08–08* ⊕ *www.fondation-vincentvan-gogh-arles.org* ✆ *From €9.*

Les Alyscamps

CEMETERY | Although the romantically melancholic Roman cemetery lies 1 km (½ mile) southeast of the Vieille Ville, it's worth the hike—certainly Van Gogh thought so, as several of his famous canvases prove. This long necropolis amassed the remains of the dead from antiquity to the Middle Ages. Greek, Roman, and Christian tombs line the shady road that was once the main entry to Arles, the Aurelian Way. The finest of the stone coffins have been plundered over the centuries, thus no single work of surpassing beauty remains here (they're in the Musée Départmental Arles Antiques). Next to the ruins rise the Romanesque tower and ruined church of St-Honorat, where (legend has it) St-Trophime fell to his knees when God spoke to him. ✉ *Allée des Sarcophages, Arles*

☎ *04–90–49–38–20* ⊕ *www.arlestourisme.com* ✆ *€5.*

★ Luma Arles

MUSEUM | The Luma artistic center focuses on the pioneers of contemporary art and culture, bringing together sculpture, painting, dance, philosophy, literature, gastronomy, sustainability, and design. Luma's several spaces house a rotating series of cutting-edge exhibitions and workshops geared toward art lovers and the curious of all ages, and the new Frank Gehry building, a twisting silo sheathed in glittering silver scales, will open in 2020. ✉ *45 ch. des Minimes, Arles* ⊕ *www.luma-arles.org.*

Musée Départemental Arles Antiques
(*Museum of Ancient Arles*)

MUSEUM | Although it's a hike from the center, this state-of-the-art museum is a good place to set the tone and context for your exploration of Arles. You can learn all about the city in its Roman heyday, from the development of its monuments to details of daily life. The bold, modern triangular structure (designed by Henri Ciriani) lies on the site of an enormous Roman *cirque* (chariot-racing stadium), and the permanent collection includes jewelry, mosaics, town plans, and carved 4th-century sarcophagi. ■ TIP→ **One wing of the museum features a rare intact barge dating to AD 50 and a fascinating display illustrating how the boat was meticulously dredged from the nearby Rhône.** The quantity of these treasures gives an idea of the extent of Arles's importance. Seven superb floor mosaics can be viewed from an elevated platform, and you exit via a hall packed tight with magnificently detailed paleo-Christian sarcophagi. As you leave you will see the belt of St-Césaire, the last bishop of Arles, who died in AD 542 when the countryside was overwhelmed by the Franks and the Roman era met its end. Ask for an English-language guidebook. ✉ *Av. de la 1ère Division Française Libre, Presqu'île du Cirque Romain, Arles* ☎ *04–13–31–51–03*

Van Gogh immortalized the courtyard of this former hospital—now the Espace Van Gogh, a center devoted to his works—in several masterpieces.

🌐 *www.arlestourisme.com* 💶 *€8 (free 1st Sun. of month)* 🕐 *Closed Tues.*

Musée Réattu

MUSEUM | Three rooms of this museum, housed in a Knights of Malta priory dating to the 15th century, are dedicated to local painter Jacques Réattu. But the standouts are works by Dufy, Gauguin, and 57 drawings (and two paintings) done by Picasso in 1971—including one delightfully tongue-in-cheek depiction of noted muse and writer Lee Miller in full Arles dress. They were donated to Arles by Picasso himself, to thank the town for amusing him with bullfights. ✉ *10 rue Grand Prieuré, Arles* ☎ *04–90–49–37–58* 🌐 *www.museereattu.arles.fr* 💶 *€6 (free 1st Sun. of month)* 🕐 *Closed Mon.*

Place Lamartine

PLAZA | Stand on the site of Van Gogh's residence in Arles—the now-famous Maison Jaune (Yellow House), destroyed by bombs in 1944. The artist may have set up his easel on the Quais du Rhône, just off Place Lamartine, to capture the view that he transformed into his legendary

Starry Night. Eight other sites are included on the city's "Arles and Vincent van Gogh" tour (🌐 *www.arlestourisme.com*), including Place du Forum, the Trinquetaille bridge, Rue Mireille, the Summer Garden on Boulevard des Lices, and the road along the Arles à Bouc canal—each of which features in one canvas or another. ✉ *Arles.*

Pont Van Gogh (*Langlois Bridge*)

BRIDGE/TUNNEL | He immortalized many everyday objects and captured views still seen today, but Van Gogh's famous painting of the Langlois Bridge over the Canal d'Arles à Bouc—on the southern outskirts of Arles, about 3 km (2 miles) from the old city—seems to strike a particular chord among locals. Bombed in World War II, the bridge has been restored to its former glory. ✉ *Rte. de Port St-Louis, Arles.*

Théâtre Antique (*Ancient Theater*)

ARCHAEOLOGICAL SITE | Directly up Rue de la Calade from Place de la République, are these ruins of a theater built by the Romans under Augustus in the

1st century BC. It's here that the noted Venus of Arles statue, now in the Louvre, was dug up and identified. The theater was once an entertainment venue that held 10,000 people, and is now a pleasant, parklike retreat. Only two columns of the amphitheater's stage walls and one row of arches remain; the fine local stone was used to build early Christian churches. Only a few vestiges of the original stone benches are left, along with the two great Corinthian columns. Today the ruins are a stage for the Festival d'Arles, in July and August, and site of Les Recontres d'Arles (Photography Festival) from early July to mid-September. During these festivals, check for early closing hours. ⊠ *Rue de la Calade, Arles* ☎ *04–90–49–38–20* ⊕ *www.arlestourisme.com* ⊠ *€9, includes admission to Arènes.*

🍴 Restaurants

★ La Chassagnette

$$$$ | **FRENCH** | Reputedly the original registered "organic" restaurant in Provence, this sophisticated yet comfortable spot, 12 km (7½ miles) south of Arles at the entrance of the Camargue, is fetchingly designed and has a dining area that extends outdoors, where large family-style picnic tables await under a wooden-slate canopy overlooking the extensive gardens. Using ingredients that are grown right on the property, innovative master chef Armand Arnal serves only prix-fixe menus that are a refreshing, though not inexpensive, mix of modern and classic French country cuisine (dinner €69, €79, €85, €115; lunch €55). **Known for:** bucolic setting; outdoor dining; local, seasonal products. ⓢ *Average main: €37* ⊠ *Rte. du Sambuc, D36, Arles* ☎ *04–90–97–26–96* ⊕ *www. chassagnette.fr* ⊗ *Closed 2 wks in Nov. and Christmas–early Jan. No dinner Sun.–Wed.*

L'Atelier de Jean-Luc Rabanel

$$$$ | **MODERN FRENCH** | Jean-Luc Rabanel is the culinary success story of the region, famous for fresh garden-inspired cuisine that he features in this stylish restaurant and cooking school—one of the few organic eateries in France to merit two Michelin stars. Menus are prix-fixe only; the seven-dish tapas-style lunch (€65) is a treat not to be missed, and the "Emotion" dinner menu (€125) is unforgettable. **Known for:** dedicated to local and organic; veggie-centric; sophisticated presentation and pairings. ⓢ *Average main: €125* ⊠ *7 rue des Carmes, Arles* ☎ *04–90–91–07–69* ⊕ *www.rabanel.com* ⊗ *Closed Mon. and Tues.*

L'Autruche

$$ | **BISTRO** | This small contemporary bistro in central Arles provides cheerful, friendly service and innovative, affordable cuisine with modern leanings. The menu changes frequently, depending on what's available in the market, but sumptuous dishes that are typical of this inventive chef's repertoire include fillet of cod with golden turnips, pumpkin puree, and wild mushrooms sprinkled with fresh chervil; and creamy risotto with beef bouillon and cheese crisps sprinkled with hazelnuts. **Known for:** a welcome respite from typical tourist fare; highlights local products; sidewalk dining on quiet street. ⓢ *Average main: €22* ⊠ *5 rue Dulau, Arles* ☎ *04–90–49–73–63* ⊗ *Closed Sun. and Mon.*

★ Le Galoubet

$$ | **MODERN FRENCH** | Tucked away under a canopy of green, this cozy and popular-with-locals bistro with a spacious and pretty outdoor terrace serves contemporary French fare far above the usual. Relax in a vintage armchair over an appetizer of creamy burrata cheese with perfectly ripe heirloom tomatoes, or grilled sardines with arugula and olives, followed by succulent guinea fowl or steak smothered in fresh morels with golden frites on the side. **Known for:** seafood; terrific wines; friendly service. ⓢ *Average main: €18* ⊠ *18 rue du Dr. Fanton, Arles* ☎ *04–90–93–18–11.*

Van Gogh in Arles and St-Rémy

It was the light that drew Vincent van Gogh to Arles. For a man raised under the iron-gray skies of the Netherlands and the city lights of Paris, Provence's clean, clear sun was a revelation. In his last years he turned his frenzied efforts to capture the town's magic.

Arles, however, was not drawn to Van Gogh. Although it makes every effort today to make up for its misjudgment, Arles treated the artist badly during the time he passed here near the end of his life—a time when his creativity, productivity, and madness all reached a climax. It was 1888 when he settled in to work in Arles with an intensity and tempestuousness that first drew, then drove away, his companion Paul Gauguin, with whom he had dreamed of founding an artists' colony.

Frenziedly productive—he applied a pigment-loaded palette knife to some 200 canvases in that year alone—he nonetheless lived in intense isolation, counting his *sous*, and writing his visions in lengthy letters to his long-suffering, infinitely patient brother Theo. Often drinking heavily, occasionally whoring, Vincent alienated his neighbors, goading them to action. In 1889 the people of Arles circulated a petition to have him evicted, a shock that left him less and less able to cope with life and led to his eventual self-commitment to an asylum in nearby St-Rémy. The houses he lived in are no longer standing, though many of his subjects remain as he saw them. The paintings he daubed and splashed with such passion have been auctioned elsewhere.

Thus you have to go to Amsterdam or Moscow to view Van Gogh's work.

But with a little imagination, you can glean something of Van Gogh's Arles from a tour of the modern town. In fact, the city has provided helpful markers and a numbered itinerary to guide you between landmarks. You can stand on Place Lamartine, where his famous Maison Jaune stood until it was destroyed by World War II bombs. *Starry Night* may have been painted from the Quai du Rhône just off Place Lamartine, though another was completed at St-Rémy.

The Café La Nuit on Place Forum is an exact match for the terrace platform, scattered with tables and bathed in gaslight under the stars, from the painting *Terrasse de café le soir*; Gauguin and Van Gogh used to drink here. (Current owners have determinedly maintained the Fauve color scheme to keep the atmosphere.) Both the Arènes and Les Alyscamps were featured in paintings, and the hospital where he came after he broke down and cut off his earlobe is now a kind of shrine, its garden reconstructed exactly as it figured in *Le jardin de l'Hôtel-Dieu*.

About 25 km (15½ miles) away is St-Rémy-de-Provence, where Van Gogh retreated to the asylum St-Paul-de-Mausolée. Here he spent hours in silence, painting the cloisters. On his ventures into town, he painted the dappled lime trees at the intersection of Boulevard Mirabeau and Boulevard Gambetta. Between Arles and St-Rémy-de-Provence are the orchards whose spring blooms ignited his joyous explosions of yellow, green, and pink.

Hotels

★ Hôtel d'Arlatan

$$$$ | **HOTEL** | Once home to the counts of Arlatan, this ideally located 15th-century stone house stands on the site of a 4th-century basilica, and a glass floor reveals the excavated vestiges under the lobby. **Pros:** the best French hospitality; warm welcome from staff; tasty foods. **Cons:** heated pool is quite small; rooms range dramatically in price; mad color schemes may prove distracting to some. [$] *Rooms from: €299* ✉ *26 rue du Sauvage, Arles* ☎ *04–90–93–56–66* 🌐 *www.hotel-arlatan.fr* 🕐 *Closed Jan.* 🛏 *45 rooms* 🍴 *No meals.*

Hotel de la Muette

$$ | **HOTEL** | This prosaic Old Town option has 12th-century exposed stone walls, a 15th-century spiral staircase, and weathered wood everywhere. **Pros:** excellent value; convenient to all landmarks; generous buffet breakfast included in price. **Cons:** some rooms can be noisy, especially in summer; parking for only three cars; no elevator. [$] *Rooms from: €111* ✉ *15 rue des Suisses, Arles* ☎ *04–90–96–15–39* 🌐 *www.hotel-muette.com* 🕐 *Closed Jan. and Feb.* 🛏 *18 rooms* 🍴 *Free breakfast.*

Le Calendal

$$$ | **HOTEL** | In a prime location in Arles's Old Town just steps from the Théâtre Antique, this quaint hotel lacks nothing in the way of charm or service—a more welcoming staff could hardly be imagined. **Pros:** extremely central; some rooms have stunning views of the arena; discounted parking for guests. **Cons:** rooms can be dark; breakfasts plentiful but standard issue; strict no-food policy in rooms. [$] *Rooms from: €149* ✉ *5 rue Porte de Laure, Arles* ☎ *04–90–96–11–89* 🌐 *www.lecalendal.com* 🛏 *38 rooms* 🍴 *No meals.*

Le Cloître

$$ | **HOTEL** | Built as the private home for the provost of the Cloisters, this grand old medieval building has luckily fallen into the hands of a friendly, multilingual couple devoted to making the most of its historic details—with their own hands. **Pros:** lovely architecture enhanced by clever use of color; top-notch service from friendly owners; excellent location. **Cons:** no elevator; single rooms quite small; no safe or kettle in room (but available at front desk). [$] *Rooms from: €139* ✉ *18 rue du Cloître, Arles* ☎ *04–90–96–29–50* 🌐 *www.hotelducloitre.com* 🛏 *19 rooms* 🍴 *No meals.*

★ L'Hôtel Particulier

$$$$ | **HOTEL** | Once owned by the Baron de Chartrouse, this extraordinary 18th-century *hôtel particulier* is delightfully intimate and decorated in sophisticated yet charming style, with gold-framed mirrors, white-brocade chairs, marble writing desks, artfully hung curtains, and hand-painted wallpaper. **Pros:** combines historical style with high-tech conveniences; quiet and secluded; only a five-minute walk to town center. **Cons:** nonrefundable deposit required when booking; small swimming pool; expensive breakfast (€26). [$] *Rooms from: €389* ✉ *4 rue de la Monnaie, Arles* ☎ *04–90–52–51–40* 🌐 *www.hotel-particulier.com* 🕐 *Closed Jan.–mid-Mar.* 🛏 *18 rooms* 🍴 *No meals.*

Nightlife

To find out what's happening in and around Arles, check the free monthly *Journal Farandole* (🌐 *www.journal-farandole.com*) or *Arles Info* (🌐 *www.arles-agenda.fr*), which list films, plays, cabarets, and music events. Both can be picked up at the tourist office.

Patio de Camargue

BARS/PUBS | Although Arles seems like one big sidewalk café in warm weather, the best place to drink is at the hip bar-restaurant Patio de Camargue, with its great location on the banks of the Rhône. It serves terrific tapas, and you

One of the centers of Provençal folklore, Arles is host to a bevy of parades featuring locals dressed in regional costume.

can hear guitar music and watch traditional dance from Chico and Los Gypsies, led by a founding member of the Gypsy Kings. Reservations are a good idea in high season. ⊠ *49 ch. de Barriol, Arles* ☎ *04–90–49–51–76* ⊕ *www.patiodecamargue.com.*

🎭 Performing Arts

Association du Méjan
ARTS CENTERS | Founded in partnership with Actes Sud and housed in the beautiful Chapelle St-Martin du Méjan, this arts organization hosts a year-round program of classical and sacred music; a revolving series of exhibitions featuring painting, sculpture, and photography; and the superb Arles Jazz Festival, held every year in May. ⊠ *Pl. Nina Berberova, Arles* ☎ *04–90–49–56–78* ⊕ *www.lemejan. com.*

🛍 Shopping

Despite being chic and popular, Arles hasn't sprouted the rows of designer shops found in Aix-en-Provence and St-Rémy. Its stores remain small and eccentric and contain an overwhelming variety of Provençal goods.

Arles's colorful markets, with produce, regional products, clothes, fabrics, wallets, frying pans, and other miscellaneous items, take place every Saturday morning along **Boulevard des Lices,** which flows into Boulevard Clemenceau.

Christian Lacroix
CLOTHING | This shop has fabulous picks for women—exuberant scarves, accessories, and colorful sunglasses (Jackie O herself once bought a pair here), as well as a vibrant selection of scented candles, stationery, and glassware in a range of gorgeous jewel tones. There are also some vintage items. ⊠ *52 rue de la République, Arles* ☎ *04–90–96–11–16* ⊕ *www.christian-lacroix.com.*

★ La Botte Gardiane

SHOES/LUGGAGE/LEATHER GOODS | A family enterprise since 1957, this boot-making company earned the coveted status of *Entreprise du Patrimoine Vivant* (living heritage company) as the last shoemaker offering authentic boots for the famous Camargue cowboys, *les Gardians*. Aside from some chic cowboy-esque models, there are stylish and durable full-length fashion boots and booties, suede and leather chukka boots, supersoft espadrilles, and strappy sandals, all made from supple vegetable-tanned calf from the same tanner that supplies Hermès. ✉ *ZA Lallemande rte. nationale 113 296 vieille rte., Aigues-Mortes* ☎ *04–66–73–20–85* ⊕ *labottegardiane.com.*

Le Château du Bois

PERFUME/COSMETICS | This boutique specializes in a huge range of pure, plant-based cosmetics from Le Château du Bois, one of Provence's oldest and most venerable producers of fine lavender oil. The range includes face creams, hand and body lotions, toning gels, massage oil, bath milk, hydrosol, and much more, all made with the purest essential oils produced nearby. ✉ *42 rue de la République, Arles* ☎ *04–90–52–01–35* ⊕ *www.lavandeandco.fr.*

L'Occitane

LOCAL SPECIALTIES | Having put Provence on the worldwide fragrance map, the scents from this region flourish at this shop close to where it all began. The products here are still made in nearby Manosque using regional ingredients. Make sure to sniff Jasmine Immortelle Neroli, the newest women's fragrance, and Arlésienne, a floral tribute to the women of the South of France. ✉ *58 rue de la République, Arles* ☎ *04–90–96–93–62* ⊕ *www.loccitane.com.*

Abbaye de Montmajour

6 km (4 miles) north of Arles.

Once the spiritual center of the region and a major 12th-century pilgrimage site (it contained a small relic of the true cross), the haunting ruins of the Abbaye de Montmajour still dominate this romantic windswept landscape.

GETTING HERE AND AROUND

From Arles by car, take the D17 in the direction of Fontvieille and follow the signs to the Abbaye. Cartreize Bus No. 29 runs from Arles 10 times per day weekdays and twice per day on weekends (€2).

Sights

★ Abbaye de Montmajour

RELIGIOUS SITE | This magnificent Romanesque abbey looming over the marshlands north of Arles stands in partial ruin. Begun in the 10th century by a handful of Benedictine monks, the abbey grew according to an ambitious plan of church, crypt, and cloister and, under the management of worldly lay monks in the 17th century, became more sumptuous. When the Catholic church ejected those monks, they sacked the place, and what remained was eventually sold off as scrap. A 19th-century medieval revival spurred a partial restoration, but portions are still in ruins; what remains is a spare and beautiful piece of Romanesque architecture. The cloister rivals that of St-Trophime in Arles for its balance, elegance, and air of mystical peace: Van Gogh, drawn to its isolation, came often to the abbey to reflect, but the strong mistral winds kept him from painting there. The interior, renovated by contemporary architect Rudy Ricciotti, is used for world-class contemporary art exhibitions. ✉ *D17* ☎ *04–90–54–64–17* ⊕ *www.abbaye-montmajour.fr* 🎫 *€6* ◷ *Closed Mon. Oct.–Mar.*

The Camargue

15 km (9 miles) south of Arles.

For 1,500 square km (580 square miles), the vast alluvial delta of the Rhône River known as the Camargue stretches to the horizon, an austere marshland unrelievedly flat, scoured by the mistral, swarmed over by mosquitoes. Between the endless flow of sediment from the Rhône and the erosive force of the sea, its shape is constantly changing. Yet its harsh landscape harbors a concentration of exotic wildlife unique in Europe, and its isolation has given birth to an ascetic and ancient way of life that transcends national stereotype. It is a strange region, one worth discovering slowly, either on foot or on horseback—especially as its wildest reaches are inaccessible by car. If people find the Camargue interesting, birds find it irresistible. Its protected marshes lure some 400 species, including more than 160 in migration—little egrets, gray herons, spoonbills, bitterns, cormorants, redshanks, and grebes, and the famous flamingos. All this nature surrounds a few far-flung villages, rich in the region's odd history and all good launching points for forays into the marshlands.

GETTING HERE AND AROUND

The best way to explore the park is by car. Roads around and throughout the park have parking areas from which you can set out on foot. You can also explore by bicycle, boat, on horseback, or guided tour. Detailed information on trails and rentals can be found at the tourist offices of both Aigues-Mortes and Stes-Maries-de-la-Mer—the park's major points of entry—and through the Camargue's main Centre d'Information Parc Naturel Camargue at La Capelière (on the D36b road, 25 km [15½ miles] from Arles).

VISITOR INFORMATION Camargue Tourist Office ⊠ *1 pl. Frédéric Mistral, Saint-Gilles* ☎ *04–66–87–33–75* ⊕ *tourisme.saint-gilles.fr/en.*

 Sights

Parc Régional de Camargue

NATIONAL/STATE PARK | As you drive the few roads that crisscross the Camargue, you'll usually be within the boundaries of the Parc Régional de Camargue. Unlike state and national parks in the United States, this area is privately owned and utilized within rules imposed by the state. The principal owners, the famous *manadiers* (the Camargue equivalent of a small-scale rancher), with the help of their *gardians,* keep it for grazing their wide-horned bulls and their broad-bellied, white-dappled horses. It is thought that these beasts are the descendents of ancient, indigenous wild animals, and though they're positively bovine in their placidity today, they still bear the noble marks of their ancestors. The strong, heavy-tailed Camargue horse has been traced to the Paleolithic period (though some claim the Moors imported an Arab strain) and is prized for its stolid endurance and tough hooves. The curved-horned *taureau* (bull), if not indigenous, may have been imported by Attila the Hun.

When it's not participating in a bloodless bullfight (mounted players try to hook a ribbon from the base of its horns), a bull may well end up in the wine-rich regional stew called *gardianne de taureau.* Riding through the marshlands in leather pants and wide-rimmed black hats and wielding long prongs to prod their cattle, the gardians themselves are as fascinating as the wildlife. Their homes—tiny, whitewashed, cane-thatched huts with the north end raked and curved apselike against the vicious mistral—dot the countryside. The signature wrought-iron crosses at the gable invoke holy protection, and if God isn't watching over this treeless plain, they ground lightning. ⊕ *www.parc-camargue.fr.*

Hotels

★ Mas de Peint

$$$$ | HOTEL | Sitting on roughly 1,250 acres of Camargue ranch land, this exquisite 17th-century farmhouse may just offer the ultimate mas experience. **Pros:** isolated setting makes for a romantic getaway; staff offers a warm welcome; no detail is missed in service or style. **Cons:** make sure you confirm room with a shower; unheated pool chilly for some, refreshing for others; not much to do once sun goes down. $ *Rooms from: €330* ⊠ *D36, 20 km (12 miles) south of Arles, Le Sambuc* ☎ *04–90–97–20–62* ⊕ *www.masdepeint.com* ⊗ *Closed mid-Nov.–late Dec. and Jan.–late Mar.* ⤳ *13 rooms* ⦿ *No meals.*

Les Baux-de-Provence

18 km (11 miles) northeast of Arles.

When you first search the craggy hilltops for signs of Les Baux-de-Provence (that's "*boh*"), you may not quite be able to distinguish between bedrock and building, so naturally does the ragged skyline of towers and crenellation blend into the sawtooth jags of stone.

It was from this intimidating vantage point that the lords of Baux ruled throughout the 11th and 12th centuries over one of the largest fiefdoms in the south, commanding some 80 towns and villages. Their virtually unchallenged power led to the flourishing of a rich medieval culture: courtly love, troubadour songs, and knightly gallantry; but by the 13th century the lords of Baux had fallen from power, their stronghold destroyed.

Today Les Baux offers two faces to the world: the ghostly ruins of its fortress, once referred to as the *ville morte* ("dead town"), and its beautifully preserved Renaissance village. As dramatic in its perched isolation as Mont-St-Michel, in Brittany, and St-Paul-de-Vence, this tiny château-village ranks as one of the most visited tourist sites in France, yet has somehow escaped the usual tourist-trap tawdriness. Lovely 16th-century stone houses, even their window frames still intact, shelter elegant shops, cafés, and galleries that line its car-free main street, overwhelmed by day with the smell of lavender-scented souvenirs. But don't deprive yourself for fear of crowds: stay late in the day, after the tour buses leave; spend the night in one of its modest hotels (or at one of its two splendid domaine hotels); or come off-season, and you can experience its spectacular character—a tour-de-force blend of medieval color and astonishing natural beauty.

GETTING HERE AND AROUND

The easiest way to get to Les Baux is by car. Take the A7 until you reach Exit 25, then the D99 between Tarascon and Cavaillon. Les Baux is 8 km (5 miles) south of St-Rémy by the D5 and the D27. Otherwise, Cartreize runs a bus between Arles and Les Baux (summer only, €2.50). Local trains stop at Tarascon; from here in summer you can take a Cartrieze bus to St-Rémy and Les Baux (20 mins, €2).

VISITOR INFORMATION Les Baux-de-Provence Tourist Office ⊠ *Maison du Roy, Rue Porte Mage, Les Baux-de-Provence* ☎ *04–90–54–34–39* ⊕ *www.lesbauxde-provence.com.*

Sights

Carrières de Lumières

ARTS VENUE | This vast old bauxite quarry has 66-foot-high stone walls that make a dramatic setting for a multimedia show in which thousands of images are projected onto the walls. Exhibitions change periodically, but recent showings have showcased the life and work of Van Gogh and Picasso and the Spanish Masters. ⊠ *Petite rte. de Mailliane, D27, Les Baux-de-Provence* ☎ *04–90–54–47–37* ⊕ *www. carrieres-lumieres.com* 🎟 *From €13.*

Château des Baux

ARCHAEOLOGICAL SITE | **FAMILY** | High above the Val d'Enfer, the 17-acre cliff-top sprawl of ruins is contained under the Château des Baux umbrella. At the entrance, the Tour du Brau contains the **Musée d'Histoire des Baux,** a small collection of relics and models that shelters a permanent music-and-slide show called *Van Gogh, Gauguin, Cézanne au Pays de l'Olivier,* featuring artworks depicting olive orchards in their infinite variety. From April through September there are fascinating medieval exhibitions: people dressed up in authentic costumes, displays of medieval crafts, and even a few jousting tournaments with handsome knights carrying fluttering silk tokens of their beloved ladies. Fire the catapult or try the crossbow: it's up to medieval you. The exit gives access to the wide and varied grounds, where the tiny **Chapelle St-Blaise** and towers mingle with skeletal ruins. ⊠ *Rue du Trencat, Les Baux-de-Provence* ☎ 04–90–54–55–56 ⊕ *www.chateau-baux-provence.com* 🎟 *From €10.*

 ## Restaurants

★ Les Baux Jus

$ | **VEGETARIAN** | Who would have thought to find this caliber of 100% organic, raw, gluten-free, and vegan restaurant in the heart of Provence? Like foodie heaven to those with restricted diets, Les Baux Jus offers a tantalizing range of cold-pressed juices, salads, pastries, and smoothies—the food is so good that even carnivores will appreciate its innovation and freshness. **Known for:** vegan and gluten-free; 100% organic; friendly atmosphere. $ *Average main: €15* ⊠ *Passage de la Calade, Les Baux-de-Provence* ⊗ *Closed Tues.*

 ## Hotels

★ Baumanière Les Baux de Provence

$$$$ | **HOTEL** | Spread over five historic buildings just outside the village of Les Baux, guest rooms at this fabled hotel—sheltered by rocky cliffs and set amid formal landscaped terraces and gardens—are the last word in Provençal chic: breezy, private, and beautifully furnished. **Pros:** two of the great restaurants of Provence; full-service spa; three pools. **Cons:** get ready for some snob action; service hit-or-miss. $ *Rooms from: €275* ⊠ *Val d'Enfer, Les Baux-de-Provence* ☎ 04–90–54–33–07 ⊕ *www.baumaniere. com/en* ⊗ *Closed Mon. and Tues. early Jan.–early Mar. Restaurant closed Jan. and Feb., and Mon. and Tues. in Mar.* 🛏 *54 rooms* ⊘ *No meals.*

★ Domaine de Manville

$$$$ | **HOTEL** | With so much to recommend it—lovely decor, an idyllic setting, impeccable service, a spa, a golf course—the new Domaine de Manville is poised to outdo every luxury retreat in this exquisite corner of Provence. **Pros:** full-service spa; superb gastronomic restaurant; well-equipped golf center and boutique. **Cons:** expensive; not lacking in snob appeal; service can be lacking. $ *Rooms from: €500* ⊠ *Les Baux-de-Provence* ☎ 04–90–54–40–20 ⊕ *www. domainedemanville.fr* 🛏 *38 rooms* ⊘ *No meals.*

St-Rémy-de-Provence

8 km (5 miles) north of Les Baux.

There are other towns as pretty as St-Rémy-de-Provence, and still others in more dramatic or more picturesque settings; ruins can be found throughout the south, and so can authentic village life. Yet something felicitous has happened in this market town in the heart of the Alpilles—a steady infusion of style, of art, of imagination—all brought by people with a respect for local traditions and a love of Provençal ways. Here, more than anywhere, you can meditate quietly on antiquity, browse aromatic markets with basket in hand, peer down the very row of plane trees you remember from a Van Gogh, and also enjoy urbane galleries, cosmopolitan shops, and specialty food boutiques. An abundance of chic choices in restaurants, mas, and even châteaux awaits you; the almond and olive groves conceal dozens of stone-and-terra-cotta gîtes, many with pools. In short, St-Rémy has been gentrified through and through, and is now a sort of arid, southern Martha's Vineyard or, perhaps, "the Hamptons of Provence."

St-Rémy has always attracted the right sort of people. First established by an indigenous Celtic-Ligurian people who worshipped the god Glan, the village Glanum was adopted by the Greeks of Marseille in the 2nd and 3rd centuries BC, who brought in sophisticated building techniques. Rome moved in to help ward off Hannibal, and by the 1st century BC Caesar had taken full control. The Romans eventually fell, but the town that grew up next to their ruins came to be an important market town, and wealthy families built fine *hôtels* (mansions) in its center—among them the family De Sade (whose distant black-sheep relation held forth in the Lubéron at Lacoste). Another famous native son, the eccentric doctor, scholar, and astrologer Michel Nostradamus (1503–66), is credited by some as having predicted much of the modern age.

Perhaps the best known of St-Rémy's visitors was the ill-fated Vincent van Gogh. Shipped unceremoniously out of Arles at the height of his madness (and creativity), he had himself committed to the asylum St-Paul-de-Mausolé and wandered through the ruins of Glanum during the last year of his life.

GETTING HERE AND AROUND
Like Les Baux-de-Provence, the easiest way to get to St-Rémy is by car. Take the A7 until you reach Exit 25, then the D99 between Tarascon and Cavaillon, direction St-Rémy on the D5. Otherwise, in summer Cartreize runs an Arles–St-Rémy–Les Baux bus service (Monday–Saturday, €2.50). Local trains stop at nearby Tarascon, and from here you can take a Cartrieze bus to St-Rémy (20 mins, €2).

VISITOR INFORMATION St-Rémy Tourist Office ☒ *Pl. Jean-Jaurès, St-Rémy-de-Provence* ☎ *04–90–92–05–22* ⊕ *www.saintremy-de-provence.com.*

◉ Sights

Collégiale St-Martin
RELIGIOUS SITE | St-Rémy is wrapped by a lively commercial boulevard, lined with shops and cafés and anchored by its 19th-century church Collégiale St-Martin. Step inside—if the main door is locked, the side door is always open—to see the magnificent 5,000-pipe modern organ, one of the loveliest in Europe. Rebuilt to 18th-century specifications in the early 1980s, it has the flexibility to interpret new and old music with pure French panache; you can listen for free on weekends mid-April–September. ☒ *Pl. de la République, St-Rémy-de-Provence* 🎟 *Free.*

Glanum
ARCHAEOLOGICAL SITE | **FAMILY** | A slick visitor center prepares you for entry into the ancient village of Glanum, with scale models of the site in its various heydays. A good map and an English brochure guide you stone by stone through the maze of foundations, walls, towers, and columns that spread across a broad field; helpfully, Greek sites are denoted by numbers, Roman ones by letters. Glanum is across the street from Les Antiques and set back from the D5, and the only parking is in a dusty roadside lot on the D5 south of town (in the direction of Les Baux). Hours vary, so check ahead. ☒ *Rte. des Baux de Provence, off D5, direction Les Baux, St-Rémy-de-Provence* ☎ *04–90–92–23–79* ⊕ *www.site-glanum.fr* 🎟 *€8* ⊗ *Closed Mon. Oct.–Mar.*

Did You Know?

St-Rémy-de-Provence has more than its share of chic shops and restaurants; nevertheless, the town has succeeded in remaining true to its Provençal roots.

Les Antiques

ARCHAEOLOGICAL SITE | Two of the most miraculously preserved classical monuments in France are simply called Les Antiques. Dating to 30 BC, the **Mausolée** (mausoleum), a wedding-cake stack of arches and columns, lacks nothing but a finial on top, and is dedicated to a Julian, probably Caesar Augustus. A few yards away stands another marvel: the **Arc Triomphal,** dating to AD 20. A lovely spot for a stroll—and within easy walking distance from the city center—the site is open during the day and at night (when handsomely illuminated). ✉ *Av. Vincent Van Gogh, St-Rémy-de-Provence.*

Musée Estrine Présence Van Gogh

MUSEUM | The 18th-century Hôtel Estrine now houses this museum and has many reproductions of the artist's work, along with letters to his brother Theo and exhibitions of contemporary art, much of it inspired by Vincent. It also contains a permanent collection dedicated to the father of Cubism, Albert Gleizes, who lived in St-Rémy for the last 15 years of his life, and hosts temporary exhibitions. ✉ *Hôtel Estrine, 8 rue Lucien Estrine, St-Rémy-de-Provence* ☎ *04–90–92–34–72* 🌐 *www.musee-estrine.fr* 🎟 *€7* 🕒 *Closed Mon.*

St-Paul-de-Mausolé

HOSPITAL—SIGHT | This is the isolated asylum where Van Gogh spent the last year of his life (1889–90). Enter quietly: the hospital shelters psychiatric patients to this day, all of them women. You're free to walk up the beautifully manicured garden path to the church and its jewel-box Romanesque **cloister,** where the artist found womblike peace. ✉ *Chemin St-Paul, St-Rémy-de-Provence* ☎ *04–90–92–77–00* 🌐 *www.saintpauldemausole.fr* 🎟 *€6* 🕒 *Closed Jan.*

Vieille Ville

NEIGHBORHOOD | Within St-Rémy's fast-moving traffic loop, a labyrinth of narrow streets leads you away from the action and into the slow-moving inner sanctum of the Vieille Ville. Here trendy, high-end shops mingle pleasantly with local life, and the buildings, if gentrified, blend in unobtrusively. ✉ *St-Rémy-de-Provence.*

🍴 Restaurants

★ Chez Tata Simone

$ | FRENCH | FAMILY | Opened in 2018 and set in an 18th-century Provençal mas once owned by the *grandmère* of one of the owners , this countrified restaurant is a short drive outside the city but well worth the small effort. Sit inside at wooden tables or out under towering plane trees to enjoy delicious dishes made with locally sourced ingredients that mix classic recipes (yes, from Tata Simone) with a modern touch. **Known for:** country atmosphere; welcoming service; copious dishes. [$] *Average main: €16* ✉ *Chemin du Mas de Jacquet* ☎ *04–90–99–65–12.*

🛏 Hotels

★ Château des Alpilles

$$$$ | HOTEL | Reached via a lane of majestic plane trees and set on 8 acres of luxuriant parkland, cypress groves, and gardens, this gracious mas and château dates back to medieval times, and it's one of St-Rémy's dreamiest spots—and that's saying a lot in this château-saturated territory. **Pros:** service anticipates your every need; gorgeous Italian designer linens; spectacular grounds. **Cons:** outside the city center; not a lot to do after dark; if you prefer contemporary design it isn't for you. [$] *Rooms from: €350* ✉ *Rte. de Rougadou, St-Rémy-de-Provence* ☎ *04–90–92–03–33* 🌐 *www.chateaudesalpilles.com* 🕒 *Closed Jan.–mid-Mar.* 🛏 *21 rooms* 🍴 *No meals.*

★ Hotel de Tourrel

$$$$ | HOTEL | Rarely does a hotel aspire to, let alone achieve, such level of craft and elegance down to the finest details. **Pros:** St-Rémy's most beautiful hotel; gourmet dining and delicious breakfasts; at the center of town. **Cons:** not cheap;

breakfast not included in price; only nine rooms. $\boxed{\$}$ *Rooms from: €350* ✉ *5 rue Carnot, St-Rémy-de-Provence* ☎ *04–84–35–07–20* ⊕ *www.detourrel.com* 🛏 *9 rooms* ❄️ *No meals.*

🛍 Shopping

Every Wednesday morning St-Rémy hosts one of the most popular and picturesque markets in Provence, during which Place de la République and narrow Vieille Ville streets overflow with herbs and spices, olive oil by the vat, and tapenade by the scoop, as well as fabrics and *brocante* (collectibles). There's a smaller version Saturday morning.

Joël Durand Chocolatier

FOOD/CANDY | Known for his creamy ganaches, Joël Durand carries a range of gourmet chocolates, nut creams, toffee, and marmalades made in Provence from tree-ripened fruit. ✉ *3 bd. Victor Hugo, St-Rémy-de-Provence* ☎ *04–90–92–38–25* ⊕ *www.joeldurand-chocolatier.fr.*

★ Lilamand Confiseur

FOOD/CANDY | Much more than just a sweets shop, this historical *confiseur* dates back to 1866 and is in its fifth generation of family ownership on the same St-Rémy premises. Makers of the famous Provençal *calisson,* an almond-shape marzipan confection, as well as a gorgeous array of candied fruits— including everything from cherries and strawberries to kiwis, fennel, and even whole pumpkins—from a recipe credited to Nostradamus (a native son). There are also fruit syrups, jams, chocolates, and regional honey. A tour of the factory and a stop in the beautiful boutique make for a highly pleasurable hour or two. ✉ *5 av. Albert Schweitzer, St-Rémy-de-Provence* ☎ *04–90–92–11–08* ⊕ *www.confiserie-lilamand.com.*

Avignon

82 km (51 miles) northwest of Aix-en-Provence, 98 km (59 miles) northwest of Marseille, 229 km (140 miles) south of Lyon.

Of all the monuments in France—cathedrals, châteaux, fortresses—the ancient city of Avignon (pronounced "ah-veen-yonh") is one of the most dramatic. Wrapped in a crenellated wall punctuated by towers and Gothic slit windows, its historic center stands distinct from modern extensions, crowned by the Palais des Papes, a 14th-century fortress-castle that's nothing short of spectacular. Standing on the Place du Palais under the gaze of the gigantic Virgin that reigns from the cathedral tower, with the palace sprawling to one side, the bishops' Petit Palais to the other, and the long, low bridge of childhood-song fame stretching over the river ("Sur le pont d'Avignon / On y danse tous en rond …"), you can beam yourself briefly into the 14th century, so complete is the context, so evocative the setting.

Yet you'll soon be brought back to the present with a jolt by the skateboarders leaping over the smooth-paved square. Avignon is anything but a museum: it surges with modern ideas and energy, and thrives within its ramparts as it did in the heyday of the popes—like those radical church lords, sensual, cultivated, and cosmopolitan, with a taste for lay pleasures. For the French, Avignon is almost synonymous with its theater festival in July; thousands pack the city's hotels to bursting for the official festival and Le Festival OFF, the fringe festival with an incredible 1,300 performances each day. If your French isn't up to a radical take on Molière, look for English-language productions or try the circus and mime— there are plenty of shows for children, and street performers abound.

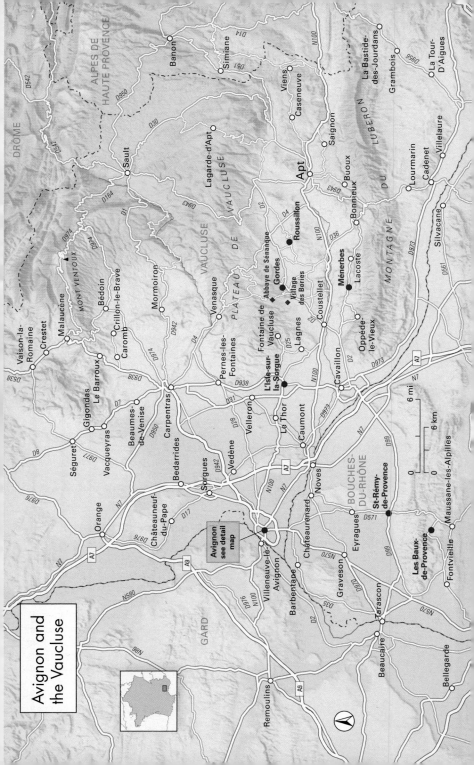

Avignon and the Vaucluse

DRÔME

ALPES DE HAUTE PROVENCE

Banon

Simiane

Viens

Caseneuve

La Bastide-des-Jourdans

Grambois

La Tour-D'Aigues

Sault

Lagarde-d'Apt

Saignon

Apt

Buoux

Villelaure

Bonnieux

Lourmarin

Cadenet

Silvacane

Roussillon

Ménerbes

Lacoste

MONTAGNE DU LUBERON

VAUCLUSE

Mormoiron

Venasque

Abbaye de Sénanque

Gordes

Village des Bories

Coustellet

Oppède-le-Vieux

Cavaillon

Crillon-le-Brave

Malaucène

Bédoin

Caromb

Fontaine de Vaucluse

Lagnes

Vaison-la-Romaine

Crestet

MONT VENTOUX

Pernes-les-Fontaines

L'Isle-sur-la-Sorgue

Le Barroux

Beaumes-de-Venise

Carpentras

Velleron

Le Thor

Caumont

Gigondas

Séguret

Vacqueyras

Bedarrides

Vedène

Sorgues

Orange

Châteauneuf-du-Pape

Avignon see detail map

Noves

Villeneuve-lès-Avignon

Barbentane

Châteaurenard

Eyragues

BOUCHES-DU-RHÔNE

St-Rémy-de-Provence

Maussane-les-Alpilles

Graveson

Fontvieille

Les Baux-de-Provence

GARD

Tarascon

Beaucaire

Bellegarde

Remoulins

6 mi

6 km

0

0

GETTING HERE AND AROUND

Avignon is a major rail crossroads and springboard for the Vaucluse and has plenty of car-rental agencies at the Gare Avignon TGV (best to reserve your car in advance). The quickest train link is the high-speed TGV *Méditerranée* line that connects Paris and Avignon (2 hrs 40 mins); Nice to Avignon on the TGV (3 hrs) costs €49. Keep in mind that the Gare Avignon TGV is a few miles southwest of the city (a train shuttle bus connects with the train station in town every 15 minutes from early morning to late at night). Other trains, such as the Avignon–Orange line (35 mins, €6.60) use the Gare Avignon Centre station; other lines go to Arles, Nîmes, Orange, Toulon, and Carcassonne. Next door you'll find the bus terminal; buses run to and from Avignon, Arles (1 hr, €7.30), Carpentras (45 mins, €2), Cavaillon (1 hr, €2), Nîmes (1½ hrs, €2), and farther afield to Orange, Isle/Sorgue, Marseille, Nice, and Cannes. The Avignon–Orange bus runs several times during the day and takes less than an hour (€2 one way). In addition, there are 27 city buses to get you around Avignon itself, run by TCRA.

VISITOR INFORMATION Avignon Tourist Office ⊠ *41 cours Jean-Jaurès, Avignon* ☎ *04–32–74–32–74* ⊕ *www.avignon-tourisme.com.*

Sights

Cathédrale Notre-Dame-des-Doms

RELIGIOUS SITE | Built in a pure Provençal Romanesque style in the 12th century, this cathedral was soon dwarfed by the extravagant palace that rose beside it. The 14th century saw the addition of a cupola, which promptly collapsed. As rebuilt in 1425, the cathedral is a marvel of stacked arches with a strong Byzantine flavor and is topped with a gargantuan Virgin Mary lantern—a 19th-century afterthought—whose glow can be seen for miles around. ⊠ *Pl. du Palais, Avignon*

☎ *04–90–80–12–21* ⊕ *www.metropole.diocese-avignon.fr.*

★ Collection Lambert

MUSEUM | Known for the breadth of its collection as well as the scope of its exhibitions, the Lambert—a must-see for contemporary art lovers—reopened in 2015 after a yearlong renovation that doubled its exhibition space. Housed in two elegant 17th-century mansions, this impressive assembly of contemporary artworks came out of the private collection of Paris art dealer Yvon Lambert, who founded the museum in 2000 in honor of Avignon's designation as European Capital of Culture. Comprising more than 1,200 pieces dating from the 1960s to the present, the Lambert Collection also hosts an influential series of three to four major exhibitions per year, cultural events, lectures, and arts eduction programs independently or in conjunction with other arts institutions worldwide. The foundation closes three months out of the year between new exhibitions, so be sure to check before going. The impressive bookshop carries dozens of original, limited-edition works by artists represented in the collection, including prints by Cy Twombly, Sol LeWitt, and Jenny Holzer, and the breezy courtyard café offers gourmet snacks, beverages, and light lunches under the shade of sleepy plane trees. ⊠ *5 rue Violette, Avignon* ☎ *04–90–16–56–20* ⊕ *www.collectionlambert.fr* 🎫 *€10.*

Les Halles

MARKET | By 6 every morning (except Monday), merchants and artisans have stacked their herbed cheeses and arranged their vine-ripened tomatoes with surgical precision in pyramids and designs that please the eye before they tease the salivary glands. This permanent covered market is as far from a farmers' market as you can get, each booth a designer boutique of *haute de gamme* (top-quality) goods, from jewel-like olives to silvery mackerel to racks of hanging hares worthy of a Flemish still life. Even if you don't have a kitchen to stock, consider enjoying a cup of coffee or a glass of (breakfast) wine while you take in the sights and smells. Tuck into a plate of freshly shucked oysters and a *pichet* of the crisp local white. On Saturdays from 11 to noon, September through July, you can watch a cooking demonstration, "La Petite Cuisine du Marché," by a well-known Provençal chef. ⊠ *Pl. Pie, Avignon* ☎ *04–90–27–15–15* ⊕ *www. avignon-leshalles.com.*

Musée Angladon

MUSEUM | This superb collection of major 18th- to 20th-century paintings and furnishings was assembled by the famous Parisian couturier Jacques Doucet (1853–1929), who counted many of the major painters and writers of his day among his close circle and purchased— or funded—some of the great works of the 20th century (he was the original owner of Picasso's *Demoiselles d'Avignon*). With an unerring eye, this great appreciator of the arts created a collection that he then housed in this mansion, which he purchased toward the end of his life; it includes works by Degas, Van Gogh, Manet, Cézanne, Modigliani, and Picasso, along with important drawings, sculpture, photography, and furniture. The museum also hosts temporary exhibitions. ⊠ *5 rue Laboureur, Avignon* ☎ *04–90–82–29–03* ⊕ *www.angladon. fr* ⊠ *€8* ⊗ *Closed Mon. Apr.–Oct., Mon. and Tues. Nov.–Mar., and Christmas–Jan.*

Musée Calvet

MUSEUM | Worth a visit for the beauty and balance of its architecture alone, this fine old museum contains a rich collection of antiquities and classically inspired works. Acquisitions include neoclassical and Romantic pieces and are almost entirely French, including works by Manet, Daumier, and David. There's also a good modern section, with works by Bonnard, Duffy, and Camille Claudet (note Claudet's piece depicting her brother Paul,

who incarcerated her in an insane asylum when her relationship with Rodin caused too much scandalous talk). The main building itself is a Palladian-style jewel in pale Gard stone dating to the 1740s; the garden is so lovely that it may distract you from the art. ⊠ *65 rue Joseph-Vernet, Avignon* ☎ *04–90–86–33–84* ⊕ *www. musee-calvet.org* ⊠ *From €6, permanent collections free* ⊗ *Closed Tues.*

Musée du Petit Palais

CASTLE/PALACE | This residence of bishops and cardinals before Pope Benedict XII built his majestic palace houses a large collection of old-master paintings, the majority of which are Italian works from the early Renaissance schools of Siena, Florence, and Venice—styles with which the Avignon popes would have been familiar. Later works here include Sandro Botticelli's *Virgin and Child,* and Venetian paintings by Vittore Carpaccio and Giovanni Bellini. The museum café and tearoom, with a picturesque outdoor terrace in the mansion's ancient courtyard, is a favorite spot for lunch, coffee, or teatime (open 10–7). ⊠ *Pl. du Palais, Avignon* ☎ *04–90–86–44–58* ⊕ *www.petit-palais. org* ⊠ *€6, permanent collections free.*

★ Palais des Papes

CASTLE/PALACE | This colossal palace creates a disconcertingly fortresslike impression, underlined by the austerity of its interior. Most of the original furnishings were returned to Rome with the papacy; others were lost during the French Revolution. Some imagination is required to picture the palace's medieval splendor, awash with color and with worldly clerics enjoying what the 14th-century Italian poet Petrarch called "licentious banquets." On close inspection, two different styles of building emerge at the palace: the severe **Palais Vieux** (Old Palace), built between 1334 and 1342 by Pope Benedict XII, a member of the Cistercian order, which frowned on frivolity, and the more decorative **Palais Nouveau** (New Palace), built in the following decade by the

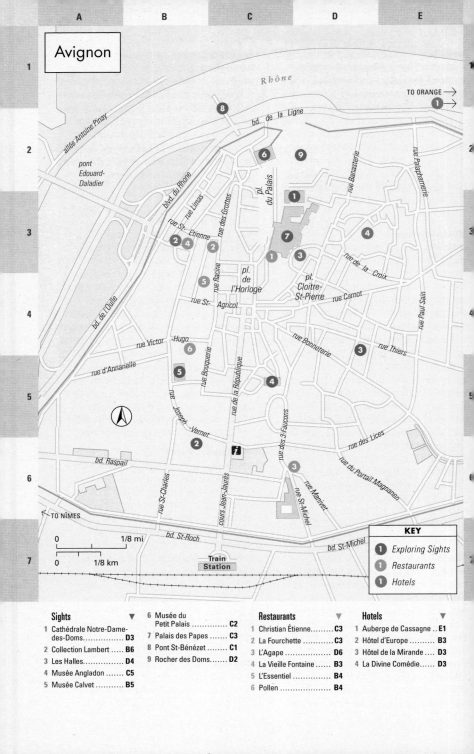

Avignon

Rhône

TO ORANGE →

bd. de la Ligne

pont Edouard-Daladier

allée Antoine Pinay

blvd. du Rhône

rue St-Étienne

rue des Limas

rue des Grottes

rue Banasterie

rue Palaphamerie

pl. du Palais

bd. de l'Oulle

rue Racine

pl. de l'Horloge

pl. Cloitre-St-Pierre

rue de la Croix

rue St-Agricol

rue Carnot

rue Paul Sain

rue Victor-Hugo

rue Bonneterie

rue d'Annanelle

rue Joseph-Vernet

rue le Bouquerie

rue de la République

rue Thiers

rue des 3-Faucons

rue des Lices

bd. Raspail

cours Jean-Jaurès

rue du Portail Magnanen

rue St-Charles

rue Manivet

rue St-Michel

← TO NÎMES

bd. St-Roch

bd. St-Michel

Train Station

| 0 | 1/8 mi |
| 0 | 1/8 km |

KEY

1 Exploring Sights
1 Restaurants
1 Hotels

---

artsy, lavish-living Pope Clement VI. The Great Court, entryway to the complex, links the two.

The main rooms of the Palais Vieux are the **Consistory** (Council Hall), decorated with some excellent 14th-century frescoes by Simone Martini; the **Chapelle St-Jean,** with original frescoes by Matteo Giovanetti; the **Grand Tinel,** or Salle des Festins (Feast Hall), with a majestic vaulted roof and a series of 18th-century Gobelin tapestries; the **Chapelle St-Martial,** with more Giovanetti frescoes; and the **Chambre du Cerf,** with a richly decorated ceiling, murals featuring a stag hunt, and a delightful view of Avignon. The principal attractions of the Palais Nouveau are the **Grande Audience,** a magnificent two-nave hall on the ground floor, and, upstairs, the **Chapelle Clémentine,** where the college of cardinals once gathered to elect the new pope. To get the most out of the experience, consider a €2 audio tour. ⊠ *6 rue Pente Rapide, Avignon* ☎ *04–32–74–32–74* ⊕ *www.palais-des-papes.com* ⌨ *€12.*

Pont St-Bénézet (*St. Bénézet Bridge*)
BRIDGE/TUNNEL | "*Sur le pont d'Avignon / On y danse, on y danse …*" Unlike the London Bridge, this other subject of a childhood song (and UNESCO World Heritage Site) stretches its arches only partway across the river. After generations of war and flooding, only half the *pont* (bridge) remained by the 17th century. Its first stones allegedly laid with the miraculous strength granted St-Bénezet in the 12th century, it once reached all the way to Villeneuve. It's a bit narrow for dancing "*tous en rond*" (round and round), though the traditional place for dance and play was under the arches. You can climb along its high platform for broad views of the Old Town ramparts. The ticket price includes an audio guide or tablet, and the latter (for which you'll need to show your passport or drivers' license) illustrates how the bridge appeared in medieval times. ⊠ *Port du Rhône, Avignon*

☎ *04–32–74–32–74* ⊕ *www.avignon-pont. com* ⌨ *€5.*

★ **Rocher des Doms** (*Rock of the Domes*)
GARDEN | Set on a bluff above town, this lush hilltop garden has grand Mediterranean pines, a man-made lake (complete with camera-ready swans), plus glorious views of the palace, the rooftops of Old Avignon, the Pont St-Bénézet, and formidable Villeneuve across the Rhône. On the horizon loom Mont Ventoux, the Luberon, and Les Alpilles. The garden has lots of history as well: often called the "cradle of Avignon," its rocky grottoes were among the first human habitations in the area. ⊠ *Montée du Moulin, off Pl. du Palais, Avignon* ☎ *04–32–74–32–74* ⊕ *www.avignon-et-provence.com/ sites-naturels/rocher-doms-avignon.*

🍴 Restaurants

★ **Christian Étienne**
$$$$ | **FRENCH** | The stellar period interior of this renovated 12th-century mansion makes for an impressive backdrop to innovative and delicious cuisine that has earned the chef a Michelin star. Try the pan-roasted veal medallion with dried

porcini blinis and thinly sliced mushrooms with chervil, or splurge for the whole lobster sautéed in olive oil, muscat grapes, and beurre blanc with verjuice. **Known for:** meticulous sourcing and presentation; romantic setting with views of Papal Palace; one of Avignon's top chefs. [$] *Average main: €35* ✉ *10 rue de Mons, Avignon* ☎ *04–90–86–16–50* 🕓 *Closed Wed. and Thurs.*

La Fourchette

$$ | **FRENCH** | **FAMILY** | The food here is delicious, plentiful, and satisfying, as the bevy of locals clamoring to get in proves. Service is friendly, and you can dig in to heaping portions of escalope of salmon, chicken cilantro à l'orange, or what just might be the best Provençal daube (served with macaroni gratin) in France. **Known for:** cozy and elegant atmosphere; family friendly; reasonable prices, especially for fixed-price menus. [$] *Average main: €21* ✉ *17 rue Racine, Avignon* ☎ *04–90–85–20–93* 🌐 *www.la-fourchette.net* 🕓 *Closed weekends, and 1st 3 wks in Aug.*

La Vieille Fontaine

$$$ | **FRENCH** | Summer evening meals around the old fountain and boxwood-filled oil jars in the courtyard of the Hôtel d'Europe would be wonderful with *filet de boeuf* alone, but combine this romantic backdrop with top-notch southern French cuisine and you have a special event. Give yourself over to one of the great restaurants of the Vaucluse, complete with fine regional wines and an army of urbane servers—and hope for moonlight. **Known for:** beautiful setting; outdoor dining; exquisite presentation. [$] *Average main: €30* ✉ *12 pl. Crillon, Avignon* ☎ *04–90–14–76–76* 🌐 *www.heurope.com* 🕓 *Closed Sun. and Mon.*

★ **L'Agape**

$$$$ | **MODERN FRENCH** | An Avignon hot spot, this contemporary gastropub in the heart of the city aspires to something more akin to haute cuisine. Chef Julien Gleize applies a light, playful touch to a modern gastronomy steeped in the French tradition. **Known for:** devoted to freshest local ingredients; superb price-to-quality ratio; excellent wine list. [$] *Average main: €33* ✉ *21 pl. des Corps-Saints, Avignon* ☎ *04–90–85–04–06* 🌐 *www.restaurant-agape-avignon.com* 🕓 *Closed Sun. and Mon.*

L'Essentiel

$$$$ | **FRENCH** | This chic hot spot, steps from the Palais des Papes, is part of the "bistronomy" movement, which focuses on top-notch cooking, a casual atmosphere, and reasonable prices. Trained by Joël Robuchon and Alain Ducasse, chef Evan Neumann makes his experience apparent in dishes of sublime subtlety that are small feats of flavor and beauty. **Known for:** quality ingredients highlighting seafood; beautiful dining room; fabulous €25 lunch menu. [$] *Average main: €36* ✉ *2 rue Petite Fusterie, Avignon* ☎ *04–90–85–87–12* 🌐 *www.restaurant-lessentiel.com* 🕓 *Closed Sun. and Mon., 2 wks in Nov., 2 wks in Feb., and 1 wk in Apr.*

★ **Pollen**

$$ | **FRENCH** | Opened in summer 2018, this luminous, casual dining room is already an absolute must on any foodie circuit. Chef Mathieu Desmarest's thoughtful approach to seasonal Provençal products and wild ingredients and exquisite attention to unusual flavor pairings make for a revelatory experience far beyond the usual gourmet cuisine. **Known for:** set on a charming street at the center of town; wild and sourced ingredients; casual setting for super-elegant dishes. [$] *Average main: €22* ✉ *3 bis rue Petite Calade* ☎ *04–86–34–93–74* 🌐 *pollen-restaurant.fr.*

🛏 Hotels

★ **Auberge de Cassagne**

$$$ | **HOTEL** | Once past the residential surroundings, an oasis of splendid gardens, indoor and outdoor pools, a full-service

Beautiful town squares form the hub of Avignon's historic center, as seen in this view from the roof of the famed Palais des Papes.

spa and fitness room, an excellent gastronomic restaurant, and an old-world welcome await. **Pros:** some rooms overlook gardens; exemplary service and fantastic restaurant; prices reasonable in most seasons. **Cons:** residential neighborhood doesn't appeal to everyone; 15-minute drive from Avignon; breakfast not included in room price. [$] *Rooms from: €202* ✉ *450 allée de Cassagne, Avignon* ☎ *09–75–18–85–28* 🌐 *www.aubergedecassagne.com* 🛏 *42 rooms* 🍴 *No meals.*

★ Hôtel de la Mirande

$$$$ | **HOTEL** | A romantic's dream of a hotel, this *petit palais* permits you to step into 18th-century Avignon—complete with painted coffered ceilings, sumptuous antiques, extraordinary handmade wall coverings, and beautiful Oriental rugs. **Pros:** a step back in time to a more gracious era; luxurious toiletries; beautiful courtyard garden. **Cons:** old-fashioned decor many not appeal to all; very pricey rooms and dining; breakfast not included in price. [$] *Rooms from: €485* ✉ *Pl. de la Mirande, Avignon* ☎ *04–90–14–20–20* 🌐 *www.la-mirande.fr* 🛏 *27 rooms* 🍴 *No meals.*

Hôtel d'Europe

$$$$ | **HOTEL** | This classic, vine-covered 16th-century home once hosted Emperor Maximilian (as well as Victor Hugo and Napoléon Bonaparte), and some of its guest rooms are emperor size. **Pros:** authentic historical setting; romantic hideaway; close to everything. **Cons:** least expensive rooms are small and slightly shabby; high season can mean noisy evenings, especially from nearby bars; service should be better. [$] *Rooms from: €380* ✉ *12 pl. Crillon, Avignon* ☎ *04–90–14–76–76* 🌐 *www.heurope.com* 🛏 *44 rooms* 🍴 *No meals.*

★ La Divine Comédie

$$$$ | **HOTEL** | Divine is the word for this extraordinary, newly opened property hidden away in the center of Avignon not far from the Palais des Papes. **Pros:** tranquil garden setting; Avignon's most beautiful interiors; delightful hosts. **Cons:** no restaurant; not ideal for young kids

(but they're welcome); you'll have to leave sometime. $ *Rooms from: €400* ✉ *16 Impasse Jean Pierre Gras* ☎ *06–77– 06–85–40* ⊕ *www.la-divine-comedie.com* ⥅ *5 rooms* ❄ *No meals.*

Shopping

Avignon has a cosmopolitan mix of French chains, hip clothing shops (it's a college town after all), and a few choice boutiques. Rue de la République is the main shopping artery, but the town's pedestrian area has a stretch of stores along Rue du Vieux Sextier, Rue des Fourbisseurs, and Rue des Marchands, where Hermès sits at the corner of Place de l'Horloge.

Les Délices du Luberon

FOOD/CANDY | For those with a taste for all things Provençal, this gourmet épicerie is a treasure trove of the many delicacies found in the best local markets, all neatly packaged and suitcase ready—if they make it that far. There's everything from olive oils, tapenades, herbs, sweet and savory preserves, bottled soups, fruit jams, honey, pastries, and lavender-based sweets and cosmetics to much more. ✉ *20 pl. du Change, Avignon* ☎ *04–90– 84–03–58* ⊕ *www.delices-du-luberon.fr.*

L'Isle-sur-la-Sorgue

26 km (16 miles) east of Avignon.

Crisscrossed with lazy canals and still alive with waterwheels that once drove its silk, wool, and paper mills, this charming valley town retains its gentle appeal—except on Sunday, when this easygoing old town transforms itself into a Marrakech of marketeers. That day it's "the most charming flea market in the world," its streets crammed with antiques and brocantes, and its cafés swelling with crowds of chic bargain browsers making a day of it. After London's Portobello district and the flea market at St-Ouen outside Paris, L'Isle-sur-la-Sorgue is reputedly Europe's third-largest antiques market. It ratchets up to high speed twice a year when the town hosts a big antiques show, usually four days around Easter and another in mid-August, nicknamed the Grand Déballage, or the Great Unpacking (⊕ *www. oti-delasorgue.fr*). Prices can be high and bargains are few, but remember that in many cases dealers expect to bargain.

GETTING HERE AND AROUND
It's a 40-minute bus ride (No. 6) from the Avignon center train station to Place Robert Vasse in Isle-sur-la-Sorgue. It's €2 one way or €1 if returning on the same day. By car the distance is 5 km (3 miles). The TER train line links Avignon and L'Isle-Fontaine train station in L'Isle-sur-la-Sorgue.

VISITOR INFORMATION L'Isle-sur-la-Sorgue Tourist Office ✉ *Pl. de la Liberté, L'Isle-sur-la-Sorgue* ☎ *04–90–38–04–78* ⊕ *www.oti-delasorgue.fr.*

Sights

Campredon Centre d'Art

HOUSE | One of the finest of L'Isle's mansions, the 18th-century Hôtel de Campredon has been restored and reinvented as a modern-art gallery, mounting three temporary exhibitions per year. ✉ *20 rue du Docteur Tallet, L'Isle-sur-la-Sorgue* ☎ *04–90–38–17–41* ⊕ *www.campredon-centredart.com* 🎫 *€6.*

Collégiale Notre-Dame-des-Anges

RELIGIOUS SITE | L'Isle's 17th-century church is extravagantly decorated with gilt, faux marble, and sentimental frescoes. The double-colonnade facade commands the center of the Vieille Ville. Visiting hours change frequently, so check with the tourist office. ✉ *L'Isle-sur-la-Sorgue* 🎫 *Free.*

🍴 Restaurants

★ Le 17 Place aux Vins

$ | **WINE BAR** | A *cave* (wine store) by day and happening wine and tapas bar by night, this is *the* place on the isle for sampling the best local wines and a charcuterie or artisanal cheese plate (or for a taste of the famous house-made foie gras paired with a local Beaume-de-Venise). Delighted to share their knowledge and crazy about wine, the charming staff will pour samples until you've found the perfect pairing. **Known for:** local favorite; menu of local specialties; extensive list of wines by the glass. [$] *Average main: €11* ✉ *17 pl. Rose Goudard, L'Isle-sur-la-Sorgue* 🌐 *www.17placeauxvins.fr* ⏲ *Closed Mon.*

🛏 Hotels

★ Château La Roque

$$ | **B&B/INN** | This historic château, about 8 miles (13 km) from Îsle-sur-la-Sorgue, in the heart of the Luberon, will make you feel to the manor born, as your gracious hosts assure the best possible experience, from your stately room to a superfresh breakfast and intimate gourmet dinner (reserve in advance). **Pros:** impeccable service; beautiful rooms and grounds; breakfast and parking included. **Cons:** must have a car; not for excitement seekers; hard to find (GPS is a big help). [$] *Rooms from: €144* ✉ *263 ch. du Château* ☎ *04–90–61–68–77* 🌐 *www.chateaularoque.com* 🔑 *5 rooms* 🍴 *Free Breakfast.*

★ Grand Hôtel Henri

$$ | **HOTEL** | The refurbished Grand Hotel Henri is the best thing to happen to the L'Îsle-sur-la-Sorgue lodging scene in a while, providing a much-needed dash of high style and panache to the local hotel scene. **Pros:** free parking; very reasonable prices; within easy walking distance to market and antique shops. **Cons:** no in-room coffee; lower-category rooms need more storage space; restaurant books up quickly. [$] *Rooms from: €115* ✉ *1 Cours René Char* ☎ *04–90–38–10–52* 🌐 *www.grandhotelhenri.com* 🔑 *17 rooms* 🍴 *No meals.*

★ La Prévôté

$$$ | **B&B/INN** | Five beautifully decorated and freshly painted rooms, each styled with exquisite taste in soft colors and Provence chic, offer an ideal respite after a long day of antiques shopping. **Pros:** price includes breakfast; wonderful dining room; antiques-bedecked interiors. **Cons:** a little tricky to find; parking may be difficult; design in some rooms a bit kitschy. [$] *Rooms from: €165* ✉ *4 bis rue Jean Jacques Rousseau, L'Isle-sur-la-Sorgue* ☎ *04–90–38–57–29* 🌐 *www.la-prevote.fr* ⏲ *Closed Tues. and Wed., and 2 wks late Nov. and 2 wks late Feb.* 🔑 *5 rooms* 🍴 *Free Breakfast.*

🛍 Shopping

Throughout the pretty backstreets of L'Isle's Vieille Ville (especially between Place de l'Église and Avenue de la Libération), there are boutiques spilling baskets full of tempting goods onto the sidewalk to lure you inside; most focus on home design and Provençal goods.

Passage du Pont

ANTIQUES/COLLECTIBLES | Of the dozens of antiques shops in L'Isle, this one conglomerate (also known as L'Ile aux Brocantes) concentrates some 40 dealers under the same roof. ✉ *7 av. des Quatre Otages, L'Isle-sur-la-Sorgue* ☎ *06–20–10–58–15.*

Un Jour

HOUSEHOLD ITEMS/FURNITURE | For more than 200 years, Brun de Vian-Tiran has been making wool blankets, cozy quilts, and other bed accessories. You can find its signature throws here among other home-style names like Nina Ricci, Cire Trudon, Yves Delorme, and Le Jacquard Français. ✉ *8 pl. Ferdinand Buisson, L'Isle-sur-la-Sorgue* ☎ *04–90–38–50–19* 🌐 *www.unjour-lingedemaison.fr.*

Xavier Nicod

ANTIQUES/COLLECTIBLES | Higher-end antiques are in plentiful supply at Xavier Nicod, which "pays tribute to eclecticism" in art and architecture. ✉ *9 av. des Quatre Otages, L'Isle-sur-la-Sorgue* ☎ *06–07–85–54–59* 🌐 *www.xaviernicod.com.*

Gordes

39 km (24 miles) east of Avignon.

This ancient stone village still rises like a glorious mirage above the valley in painterly hues of honey gold, and its cobbled streets—lined with boutiques, galleries, and real-estate offices—still wind steep and narrow to its Renaissance château, making this certainly one of the most beautiful towns in Provence.

GETTING HERE AND AROUND

There's no bus service to Gordes, so you'll need a car: a taxi ride from Avignon is about €75.

VISITOR INFORMATION Gordes Tourist Office ✉ *Le Château, Gordes* ☎ *04–90–72–02–75* 🌐 *www.gordes-village.com.*

👁 Sights

★ Abbaye de Sénanque

RELIGIOUS SITE | If you've fantasized about Provence's famed lavender fields, head to the wild valley some 4 km (2½ miles) north of Gordes (via D177), where this photogenic 12th-century Romanesque abbey seemingly floats above a redolent sea of lavender (in full bloom late June through August). Begun in 1150 and completed at the dawn of the 13th century, the **church** and adjoining **cloister** are without decoration but still touch the soul with their chaste beauty. Along with the abbeys of Le Thornet and Silvacane, this is one of a trio of "Three Sisters" built by the Cistercian Order in this area. Next door, the enormous vaulted **dormitory** contains an exhibition on Abbaye de Sénanque's construction, and the **refectory** shelters a display on the history of Cistercian abbeys. The few remaining monks here now preside over a cultural center presenting concerts and exhibitions. The bookshop has a huge collection of books about Provence (lots in English). ✉ *Gordes* ☎ *04–90–72–05–72* 🌐 *www.senanque.fr* 🎫 *€8.*

Village des Bories

ARCHAEOLOGICAL SITE | Just outside Gordes, on a lane heading north from D2, are signs for this village. The bizarre and fascinating little stone hovels called *bories* are found throughout this region of Provence, and in this village they are concentrated some 20 strong in an ancient community. Their origins are provocatively vague—built as shepherds' shelters with tight-fitting, mortarless stone in a hivelike form, they may date to the Celts, the Ligurians, or even the Iron Age—and they were inhabited or used for sheep through the 18th century. A photo exhibition shows other structures, similar to bories, in countries around the world. ✉ *Gordes* ☎ *04–90–72–03–48* 🌐 *levillagedesbories.com* 🎫 *€6.*

🍴 Restaurants

Les Cuisines du Château

$$ | **FRENCH** | This tiny (only 26 seats) but deluxe bistro across from the château may look like a tourist trap, but it has wonderful home cooking like roast Luberon lamb, beef with truffle sauce, and the like, and the service is friendly. The '30s-style bistro tables and architectural lines are a relief from Gordes's ubiquitous rustic-chic, and there is a revolving array of paintings by local artists, many of which are for sale. **Known for:** responsive to dietary requests; good value fixed-price dinner menu; accommodating service. [$] *Average main: €22* ✉ *Pl. Genty Pantaly, Gordes* ☎ *04–90–72–01–31* 🌐 *www.lescuisinesduchateau.com* 🕒 *Closed Mon. Mar.–June and Sept.–Nov., and Sat. yr-round. No dinner Sun. July and Aug.*

Continued on page 550

Van Gogh may have made the sunflower into the icon of Provence, but it is another flower —one that is unprepossessing, fragrant, and tiny—that draws thousands of travelers every year to Provence. They come to journey the famous "Route de la Lavande" (the Lavender Route), a wide blue-purple swath that connects over 2,000 producers across the south of France.

THE LAVENDER ROUTE

Once described as the "soul of Haute-Provence," lavender has colored Provence's plains since the days of the ancient Romans. Today it brings prosperity, as consumers are madly buying hundreds of beauty products that use lavender essence. Nostrils flared, they are following this route every summer. To help sate their lavender lust, the following pages present a detail-rich tour of the Lavender Route.

TOURING THE LAVENDER ROUTE

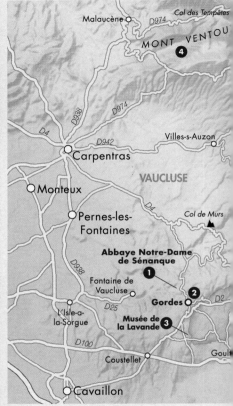

❶ Have your camera ready for the beautifully preserved Cistercian simplicity of the **Abbaye Notre-Dame de Sénanque**, a perfect foil for the famous waving fields of purple around it.

❷ No shrinking violet, the hilltop village of **Gordes** is famous for its luxe hotels, restaurants, and lavender-stocked shops.

❸ Get a fascinating A to Z tour—from harvesting to distilling to production—at the **Musée de la Lavande** near Coustellet.

❹ If you want to have a peak lavender experience—literally—detour 18 km (10 miles) to the northwest and take a spectacular day's drive up the winding road to the **summit of Mont Ventoux** (follow signs from Sault to see the lavender-filled valleys below).

❺ Even if you miss the biggest blow-out of the year, the Fête de la Lavande in **Sault** (usually on August 15), take in the charming *vieille ville* boutiques or the fabulous lavender fields that surround the hillside town.

❻ The awe-inspiring lavender fields around **Forcalquier** are one step away from perfection, and the Monday morning market is a treasure trove of local products.

❼ **Distillerie "Le Coulets"** on the outskirts of Apt has been a lavender farm for generations and offers free tours and products for sale at its boutique.

Provence is threaded by the "Routes de la Lavande" (the Lavender Routes), a wide blue-purple swath that connects over 2,000 producers across the Drôme, the plateau du Vaucluse, and the Alpes-de-Haute-Provence, but our itinerary is lined with some of the prettiest sights—and smells—of the region. Whether you're shopping for artisanal bottles of the stuff (as with wine, the finest lavender carries its own Appellation d'Origine Contrôlée), spending a session at a lavender spa, or simply wearing hip-deep purple as

Forcalquier Market

Purple haze

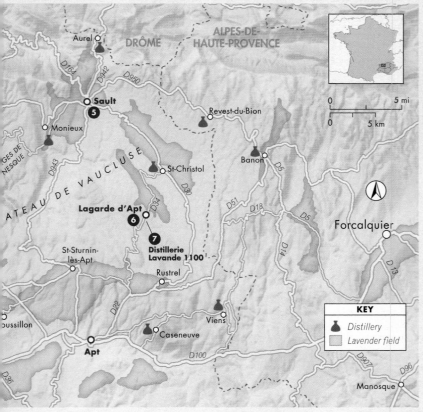

KEY

🏺 Distillery
▢ Lavender field

you walk the fields, the most essential aspect on this trip is savoring a magical world of blue, one we usually only encounter on picture postcards.

To join the lavender-happy crowds, you have to go in season, which (if you're lucky) runs from June to early August. Like Holland's May tulips, the lavender of Haute-Provence is in its true glory only once a year: the last two weeks of July, when the harvesting begins—but fields bloom throughout the summer months for the most part. Below, we wind through the most generous patches of lavender. Drive the colorful gambit southeastward (Coustellet, Gordes, Sault and Forcalquier), which will give you good visiting (and shopping) time in a number of the villages that are *fou de la lavande* (crazy for lavender).

Abbaye Notre-Dame de Sénanque

DAY 1

SÉNANQUE
A Picture-Perfect Abbey

An invisible Master of Ceremonies for the Lavender Route would surely send you first to the greatest spot for lavender worship in the world: the 12th-century Cistercian **Abbaye Notre-Dame de Sénanque**, which in July and August seems to float above a sea of lavender, a setting immortalized in a thousand travel posters. Happily, you'll find it via the D177 only 4 km (2½ miles) north of Gordes, among the most beautiful of Provence's celebrated perched villages.

An architecture student's dream of neat cubes, cylinders, and pyramids, its pure Romanesque form alone is worth contemplating in any context. But in this arid, rocky setting the gray stone building seems to have special resonance—ancient, organic, with a bit of the borie about it. Along with the abbeys of Le Thornet and Silvacane, this is one of the trio of "Three Sisters" built by the Cistercian order in this area. Sénanque's church is a model of symmetry and balance. Begun in 1150, it has no decoration but still touches the soul with its chaste beauty.

THE ESSENCE OF THE MATTER

Provence and lavender go hand in hand—but why? The flower is native to the Mediterranean, and grows so well because the pH balance in the soil is naturally perfect for it (pH 6–8). But lavender was really put on the map here when ancient Romans arrived to colonize Provence and used the flower to disinfect their baths and perfume their laundry (the word comes from Latin *lavare*, "to wash"). From a small grass-roots industry, lavender proliferated over the centuries until the first professional distillery opened in Provence in the 1880s to supply oils for southern French apothecaries. After World War I, production boomed to meet the demand of the perfumers of Grasse (the perfume center of the world). Once described as the "soul of Haute-Provence," lavender is now farmed in England, India, and the States, but the harvest in the South of France remains the world's largest.

The adjoining cloister, from the 12th century, is almost as pure, with barrel-vaulted galleries framing double rows of discreet, abstract pillars. Next door, the enormous vaulted dormitory and the refectory shelter a display on the history of Cistercian abbeys. The few remaining monks here now preside over a cultural center that presents concerts and exhibitions. The bookshop is one of the best in Provence, with a huge collection of Provençaliana (lots in English).

After spending the morning getting acquainted with the little purple flower at Sénanque, drive south along the D2 (or D177) back to **Gordes**, through a dry, rocky region mixed with deep valleys and far-reaching plains.

Wild lavender is already omnipresent, growing in large tracts as you reach the entrance of the small, unspoiled hilltop village, making for a patchwork landscape as finely drawn as a medieval illumination. A cluster of houses rises above the valley in painterly hues of honey gold, with cobbled streets winding up to the village's picturesque Renaissance château, making it one of the most beautiful towns in Provence.

Gordes has a great selection of hotels, restaurants, and B&Bs to choose from (see our listings under Gordes). Spend the

ON THE CALENDAR

If you plan to be at the Musée de la Lavande between July 1 and August 25 you can watch animations of workers swathing lavender with copper scythes.

early afternoon among tasteful shops that sell lovely Provençal crafts and produce, much of it lavender-based, and then after lunch, head out to Coustellet.

COUSTELLET
A Great Lavender Museum
Set 2 miles south of Gordes, Coustellet is noted for its **Musée de la Lavande** (take the D2 southeast to the outskirts of Coustellet). Owned by one of the original lavender families, who have cultivated and distilled the flower here for over five generations, this museum lies on the outskirts of more than 815 acres of prime lavender-cultivated land.

Not only can you visit the well-organized and interesting museum (note the impressive collection of scythes and distilling apparatus), you can buy up a storm in the boutique, which offers a great selection of lavender-based products at very reasonable prices.

There are four main species. True lavender (Lavandula angustifolia) produces the most subtle essential oil and is often used by perfume makers and laboratories. Spike lavender (Lavandula latifolia) has wide leaves and long floral stems with several flower spikes. Hybrid lavender (lavandin) is obtained from pollination of true lavender and spike lavender, making a hybrid that forms a highly developed large round cluster. French lavender (Lavendula stoechas) is wild lavender that grows throughout the region and is collected for the perfume industry. True lavender thrives in the chalky soils and hot, dry climate of higher altitudes of Provence. It was picked systematically until the end of the 19th century and used for most lavender-based products. But as the demand for this remarkable flower grew, so did the need for a larger production base. By the beginning of the 20th century, the demand for the flower was so great that producers planted fields of lavender at lower altitudes, creating the need for a tougher, more resistant plant: the hybrid lavandin.

In many towns, Provence's lavender harvest is celebrated with charming folkloric festivals.

DAY 2

LAGARDE D'APT
A Top Distillerie

On the second day of your lavender adventure, begin by enjoying the winding drive 25 km (15 miles) east to the town of **Apt**. Aside from its Provençal market, busy with all the finest food products of the Luberon and Haute Provence, Apt itself is unremarkable (even actively ugly from a distance) but is a perfect place from which to organize your visits to the lavender fields of Caseneuve, Viens, and Lagarde d'Apt.

Caseneuve (east exit from Apt onto the D900 and then northwest on the D35) and Viens (16 km/10 miles east from Apt on the D209) are small but charming places to stop for a quick bite along the magnificent drive through the rows upon rows of lavender, but if you have to choose between the three, go to the minuscule village of Lagarde d'Apt (12 km/7 miles east from Apt on the D209).

Or for a closer look, take the D22 (direction Rustrel) a few kilometres outside of Apt to **Distillerie "Les Coulets."** From mid-July to mid-August you can take a free tour of the distillery, visit the farm and browse the gift shop.

SAULT
The Biggest Festival

To enjoy a festive overnight, continue northwest from Lagarde d'Apt to the village of **Sault**, 15 km (9 miles) to the northeast. Beautifully perched on a rocky outcrop overlooking the valley that bears its name, Sault is one of the key stops along the Lavender Route.

There are any number of individual distilleries, producers, and fields to visit—to make the most of your visit, ask the Office du Tourisme (☎ *04-90-64-01-21* ⊕ *www.saultenprovence.com*) for a list of events. Make sure to pop into the Centre de Découverte de la Nature et du Patrimoine Cynégétique to see the exhibitions on the natural history of the region, including some on lavender. Aim to be in Sault for the not-to-be-missed **Fête de la Lavande**, a day-long festival entirely dedicated to lavender, the best in the region, and usually held around August 15.

Village folk dress in traditional Provençal garb and parade on bicycles, horses leap over barrels of fragrant bundles of hay, and local producers display their wares at the market—all of which culminates in a communal Provençal dinner served with lavender-based products.

DAY 3

FORCALQUIER
The Liveliest Market

On your third day, the drive from Sault over 53 km (33 miles) east to Forcalquier is truly spectacular.

As you approach the village in early July, you will see endless fields of *Lavandula vera* (true wild lavender) broken only by charming stone farmhouses or discreet distilleries.

The epicenter of Haute-Provence's lavender cultivation, **Forcalquier** boasts a lively Monday morning market with a large emphasis on lavender-based products, and it is a great departure point for walks, bike rides, horse rides, or drives into the lavender world that surrounds the town.

In the 12th century, Forcalquier was known as the capital city of Haute-Provence and was called the *Cité des Quatre Reines* (City of the Four Queens) because the four daughters (Eleanor of Aquitaine among them) of the ruler of this region, Raimond Béranger V, all married royals.

Relics of this former glory can be glimpsed in the Vieille Ville of Forcalquier, notably its Cathédrale Notre-Dame and the Couvent des Cordeliers.

MAKING SCENTS

BLOOMING

Lavender fields begin blooming in late June, depending on the area and the weather, with fields reaching their peak from the end of July to early August. The first two weeks of July are considered the best time to catch the fields in all their glory.

HARVESTING

Lavender is harvested from July to September, when the hot summer sun brings the essence up into the flower. Harvesting is becoming more and more automated; make an effort to visit some of the older fields with narrow rows—these are still picked by hand. Lavender is then dried for two to three days before being transported to the distillery.

DISTILLING

Distillation is done in a steam alembic, with the dry lavender steamed in a double boiler. Essential oils are extracted from the lavender by water vapor, which is then passed through the cooling coils of a retort.

Hotels

★ La Bastide de Gordes

$$$$ | **HOTEL** | Spectacularly perched on Gordes's hilltop, the 16th-century 10-level Bastide underwent a lengthy renovation in 2015 that restored its old-world charm and promptly earned the hotel Palace status. **Pros:** views are unmatched in the area; impeccable service; extensive programs for kids. **Cons:** hard to choose which restaurant to try; expensive; street-side rooms disappointing considering the views opposite. Ⓢ *Rooms from: €650* ✉ *Le Village, Rue de la Combe, Gordes* ☎ *04–90–72–12–12* ⊕ *www.bastide-de-gordes.com* ⊘ *Closed Jan. and Feb.* ⇌ *39 rooms* ⊚I *No meals.*

Roussillon

10 km (6 miles) east of Gordes.

In shades of deep rose and russet, this quintessential cluster of hilltop houses blends into the red-ocher cliffs from which its stone was quarried. The ensemble of buildings and jagged, hand-cut slopes is equally dramatic, and views from the top look out over a landscape of artfully eroded bluffs that Georgia O'Keeffe would have loved. Roussillon is definitely one of the finalists in Provence's beauty contest. Unlike neighboring hill villages, though, it offers little of real historic significance; the pleasure of a visit lies in the richly varied colors that change with the light of day, and in the views of the contrasting countryside, where dense-shadowed greenery sets off the red stone with Cézanne-esque severity. There are pleasant *placettes* (tiny squares) to linger in nonetheless, and a Renaissance fortress tower crowned with a clock in the 19th century; just past it, you can take in expansive panoramas of forest and ocher cliffs. Since the village can get overcrowded with tourists in summer, the best time to visit is in spring or early fall.

GETTING HERE AND AROUND

There is no direct bus service to Roussillon. The only way to get here is by car from the D4.

VISITOR INFORMATION Tourist Office
✉ *19 rue de la Poste, Roussillon* ☎ *04–90–05–60–25* ⊕ *otroussillon.pagesperso-orange.fr.*

 ## Sights

Sentier des Ocres (*Ocher Trail*)

TRAIL | This popular trail starts out from the town cemetery and allows you to wend your way through a magical, multicolor palette *de pierres* (of rocks) replete with eroded red cliffs and chestnut groves; the circuit takes about 45 minutes. Hours are complicated, so plan in advance. ✉ *Roussillon* ⊕ *otroussillon. pagesperso-orange.fr* 🎫 *From €3.*

Usine Mathieu de Roussillon (*Roussillon's Mathieu Ocher Works*)

MINE | The area's famous vein of natural ocher, which spreads some 25 km (16 miles) along the foot of the Vaucluse plateau, has been mined for centuries, beginning with the ancient Romans, who used it for their pottery. You can visit the old Usine Mathieu de Roussillon to learn more about ocher's extraction and its modern uses. Guided tours (50 mins) in English are on offer throughout the year. ✉ *D103, Roussillon* ☎ *04–90–05–66–69* ⊕ *www.okhra.com* 🎫 *From €7.*

Ménerbes

30 km (19 miles) southeast of Avignon.

This picturesque fortified town isn't designated one of the "plus beaux villages du France" for nothing. Perched high on a rocky precipice, Ménerbes's narrow streets, winding passageways, and limitless views have clinched its status as one of most visited villages of the region, along with its fellow most beautiful villages Gordes and Roussillon. Look for

Uniting natural and man-made beauty, ocher quarried from the surrounding painted-desert cliffs is applied directly to many roofs and facades in Roussillon.

the Maison Dora Maar, on the Rue du Portal Neuf—this lovely mansion with a stupendous view is where the artist and photographer lived after her years with Picasso (open only in July and August).

GETTING HERE AND AROUND
There is no direct bus service to Ménerbes. The only way to get here is by car.

👁 Sights

Musée du Tire-Bouchon (*Corkscrew museum*)
MUSEUM | Don't miss this quirky museum, which has an enormous collection of 1,200 corkscrews on display and interesting historical detail on various wine-related subjects. ⊠ *Domaine de la Citadelle, Rte. de Cavaillon, Ménerbes* ☎ *04–90–72–41–58* ⊕ *www.domaine-cit-adelle.com* 🎫 *€4.*

Place de l'Horloge (*Clock Square*)
PLAZA | A campanile tops the Hôtel de Ville on pretty Place de l'Horloge, where you can admire the delicate stonework on the arched portal and mullioned windows of a Renaissance house. Just past the tower on the right is an overlook taking in views toward Gordes, Roussillon, and Mont Ventoux. ⊠ *Ménerbes.*

🍴 Restaurants

Maison de la Truffe et du Vin (*La Cantine des Gourmets*)
$$$ | FRENCH | Set in a stately 17th-century mansion atop Ménerbes, the restaurant at the Maison de la Truffe et du Vin is where you can sample the region's most prized delicacy in an all-truffle lunch (€65). The Maison also hosts wine tastings of the best Provençal appellations, and the wine boutique is absolutely tops in the area and a great place to stock up (they ship). **Known for:** truffle tastings; excellent wines and wine boutique; views. $ *Average main: €30* ⊠ *Pl. de l'horloge* ☎ *04–90–72–38–37* ⊕ *www.vin-truffe-luberon.com* 🕙 *Closed Nov. and Sun.–Wed. Dec.–Mar.*

Hotels

★ **La Bastide de Marie**

$$$$ | HOTEL | This picturesque farmstead, set on its own 57-acre vineyard and updated to accommodate every luxe 21st-century need, is a close approximation of your dream of Provence. **Pros:** beautiful breakfast terrace with views; lovely full-service spa; perfectly located for touring Ménerbes and the Luberon. **Cons:** far from nightlife; some rooms on the smaller side; a car is essential. [$] *Rooms from: €421* ✉ *64 chemin des Peirelles* ☎ *04–90–72–30–20* 🌐 *labastidedemarie.com* 🛏 *16 rooms* 🍴 *No meals.*

Aix-en-Provence

82 km (51 miles) southeast of Avignon.

Longtime rival of edgier, more exotic Marseille, the lovely town of Aix-en-Provence (pronounced "*ex*") is gracious, cultivated, and made all the more cosmopolitan by the presence of some 40,000 university students. In keeping with its aristocratic heritage, Aix quietly exudes well-bred suavity and elegance—indeed, it is now one of the 10 richest townships in France. The influence and power it once had as the old capital of Provence—fine art, noble architecture, and graceful urban design—remain equally important to the city today. And, although it is true that Aix owns up to a few modern-day eyesores, the overall impression is one of beautifully preserved stone monuments, quietly sophisticated nightlife, leafy plane trees, and gently splashing fountains. With its thriving market, vibrant café life, spectacularly chic shops, and superlative music festival, it's one Provence town that really should not be missed.

Aix's artistic roots go back to the 15th century, when the town became a center of Renaissance arts and letters. A poet himself and patron of the arts, the king encouraged a veritable army of artists to flourish here. At the height of its political, judicial, and ecclesiastical power in the 17th and 18th centuries, Aix profited from a surge of private building, each *grand hôtel particulier* meant to outdo its neighbor. It was into this exalted elegance that artist Paul Cézanne (1839–1906) was born, though he drew much of his inspiration not from the city itself but from the raw countryside around it, often painting scenes of Montagne Ste-Victoire. A schoolmate of Cézanne's made equal inroads on modern society: the journalist and novelist Émile Zola (1840–1902) attended the Collège Bourbon with Cézanne and described their friendship as well as Aix itself in several of his works. You can sense something of the vibrancy that nurtured these two geniuses in the streets of modern Aix. The city's famous Festival d'Aix (International Opera Festival) has imported and created world-class opera productions as well as related concerts and recitals since 1948. Most of the performances take place in elegant, old Aix settings, and during this time the cafés, restaurants, and hotels spill over with the beau monde who've come to Aix especially for the July event.

GETTING HERE AND AROUND

Aix lies at a major crossroads of autoroutes: one coming in from Bordeaux and Toulouse, then leading up into the Alps toward Grenoble; the other a direct line from Lyons and Paris, and it's a quick half hour from Marseille. The Aix-en-Provence TGV station is 10 km (6 miles) west of the city and is served by regular shuttle buses. The old Aix train station is on the slow Marseille–Sisteron line, with trains arriving roughly every hour from Marseille St-Charles. The center of Aix is best explored by foot, but there is a municipal bus service that serves the entire town and the outlying suburbs. Most leave from La Rotonde in front of the tourism office.

VISITOR INFORMATION Aix-en-Provence Tourist Office ✉ *Les allées provençales, 300 av. Giuseppe Verdi, Aix-en-Provence* ☎ *04–42–16–11–61* ⊕ *www.aixen-provencetourism.com.*

Sights

Atelier Cézanne (*Cézanne's Studio*)
MUSEUM | Just north of the Vieille Ville loop you'll find Cézanne's studio. After the death of his mother forced the sale of the painter's beloved country retreat, Jas de Bouffan, he had this atelier built and some of his finest works, including *Les Grandes Baigneuses* (*The Large Bathers*), were created in the upstairs workspace. But what is most striking is the collection of simple objects that once featured prominently in his portraits and still lifes—redingote, bowler hat, ginger jar—all displayed as if awaiting his return. The atelier is behind an obscure garden gate on the left as you climb Avenue Paul-Cézanne. ✉ *9 av. Paul-Cézanne, Aix-en-Provence* ☎ *04–42–21–06–53* ⊕ *www.atelier-cezanne.com* ✉ *€7.*

Cathédrale St-Sauveur
RELIGIOUS SITE | Many eras of architectural history are clearly delineated and preserved here. The cathedral has a double nave—Romanesque and Gothic side by side—and a Merovingian (5th-century) **baptistery,** its colonnade mostly recovered from Roman temples built to honor pagan deities. The deep bath on the floor is a remnant of the total-immersion baptisms that used to occur here, marking the forsaking of one's old life (going down into the water) for a new life in Christ (rising up from the water). Shutters hide the ornate 16th-century carvings on the **portals,** opened by a guide on request. The guide can also lead you into the tranquil Romanesque **cloister** next door, with carved pillars and slender columns.

The extraordinary 15th-century *Triptyque du Buisson Ardent* (*Mary and the Burning Bush*) was painted by Nicolas Froment in the heat of inspiration following his travels in Italy and Flanders, and depicts the generous art patrons King René and Queen Jeanne kneeling on either side of the Virgin, who is poised above a burning bush. To avoid light damage, it's rarely opened for viewing; check with the tourist office beforehand. ✉ *Pl. des Martyrs de la Résistance, Aix-en-Provence* ☎ *04–42–23–45–65* ⊕ *www.cathedrale-aix.net.*

★ **Caumont Centre d'Art**
MUSEUM | Part of the Culturespaces network of museums and monuments, this arts center is a jewel in the organization's impressively laden crown and is one of Aix's top cultural attractions since opening in May 2015 after a lavish two-year, €12.6 million restoration. Given that the center is housed in the glorious Hôtel de Caumont, one of the city's most spectacular 18th-century mansions, it's no wonder that its period rooms are a joy to behold. It hosts two world-class art exhibitions per year in beautifully conceived exhibition spaces (the inaugural show was devoted to Venetian master Canaletto), and there are daily screenings of the film *Cézanne in the Aix Region* and a series of jazz and classical performances. The elegant gardens have been painstakingly restored to their original 18th-century layout, and visitors can enjoy a drink, light lunch, or dessert in the garden restaurant. The indoor Café Caumont is easily Aix's most elegant. ✉ *3 rue Joseph Cabassol, Aix-en-Provence* ☎ *04–42–20–70–01* ⊕ *www.caumont-centredart.com* ✉ *From €7.*

Cours Mirabeau
NEIGHBORHOOD | Shaded by a double row of tall plane trees, the Cours Mirabeau is one of the most beautiful avenues anywhere, designed so its width and length would be in perfect proportion with the height of the dignified 18th-century hôtels particuliers lining it. You can view this lovely assemblage from one of

the dozen or so cafés that spill onto the pavement. ✉ *Aix-en-Provence.*

Fontaine d'Eau Chaude (*Hot Water Fountain*)

FOUNTAIN | Deliciously thick with dripping moss, this 18th-century fountain is fed by Sextius's own thermal source. It seems representative of Aix at its artfully negligent best. In sunny Provence, Aix was famous for its shade and its fountains; apropos, James Pope-Hennessy, in his *Aspects of Provence,* compares living in Aix to being at the bottom of an aquarium, thanks to all the fountains' bubbling waters and the city's shady streets and boulevards. ✉ *Cours Mirabeau, Aix-en-Provence.*

La Rotonde

FOUNTAIN | If you've just arrived in Aix's center, this sculpture-fountain is a spectacular introduction to the town's rare mix of elegance and urban bustle. It's a towering mass of 19th-century attitude. That's Agriculture yearning toward Marseille, Art leaning toward Avignon, and Justice looking down on Cours Mirabeau. But don't study it too intently—you'll likely be sideswiped by a speeding Vespa. ✉ *Pl. de Gaulle, Aix-en-Provence.*

★ Musée Granet

MUSEUM | Once the École de Dessin (Art School) that granted Cézanne a second-place prize in 1856, the former priory of the Église St-Jean-de-Malte now showcases eight of Cézanne's paintings, as well as a nice collection of his watercolors and drawings. Also hanging in the galleries are 300 works by Bonnard, Picasso, Klee, Rubens, David, and Giacometti. ✉ *Pl. St-Jean-de-Malte, Aix-en-Provence* ☎ *04–42–52–88–32* ⊕ *www.museegranet-aixenprovence.fr* 🎟 *From €6* 🕙 *Closed Mon.*

★ Pavillon de Vendôme

HOUSE | This extravagant Baroque villa was built in 1665 as a country house for the Duke of Vendôme; its position just outside the city's inner circle allowed the duke to commute discreetly from his official home on Cours Mirabeau to this retreat, where his mistress, La Belle du Canet, was comfortably installed. The villa was expanded and heightened in the 18th century to draw attention to the classical orders—Ionic, Doric, and Corinthian—on parade in the row of neo-Grecian columns. Inside the cool, broad chambers you can find a collection of Provençal furniture and artwork. Note the curious two giant Atlantes that hold up the interior balcony. ✉ *32 rue Celony, Aix-en-Provence* ☎ *04–42–91–88–75* ⊕ *www.aixenprovence.fr* 🎟 *€4* 🕙 *Closed Tues.*

Site-Mémorial du Camp des Milles

HISTORIC SITE | Controversial up to its opening in 2012, this museum and memorial is France's only still-intact deportation camp, where 10,000 men, women, and children of 38 nationalities (2,000 of whom were eventually transferred to Auschwitz) were detained over a period of three years, before the structure was repurposed as an armaments factory. Direct contact with internment areas, including sleeping and dining quarters and hiding places, makes for a rare immediacy. Traces of the many artists and intellectuals who were detained here, including Surrealist artists Max Ernst and Hans Bellmer and novelist Lion Feuchtwanger, can be found in the many artworks displayed (all made here) and the graffiti still vibrantly intact on the walls. At the conclusion of the visit, museumgoers retrace the deportees' path to a railroad wagon parked near the main building, a sobering reminder of a terrible chapter in French history. ✉ *40 ch. de la Badesse, Aix-en-Provence* ☎ *04–42–39–17–11* ⊕ *www.campdesmilles.org* 🎟 *€10.*

Crammed with elegant shops, chic cafés, and 18th-century houses, Aix-en-Provence is one of France's most charming towns.

 Restaurants

La Fromagerie du Passage

$$ | FRENCH | You can't sample all of France's 600 types of cheese at La Fromagerie du Passage, but there's a decadent selection of 20 or so, all *fait à la masion* by Laurent and Hervé Mons,who won the prestigious Meilleurs Ouvriers (Best Craftsman of France) award for outstanding cheese maker. The waiters lyrically—and patiently—explain the region or texture of each cheese, and suggest a wine with the right composition to bring out the subtle (and not so subtle) flavors. **Known for:** quality handcrafted cheeses; copious cheese and charcuterie plates; delicious sandwiches to stay or go. $ *Average main: €19* ⊠ *Passage Agard, 55 cours Mirabeau, Aix-en-Provence* ☎ *04–42–22–90–00.*

★ Le Saint Estève

$$$$ | MODERN FRENCH | A short drive from Aix over scenic Route Cézanne, this elegant restaurant on the grounds of Les Lodges hotel has a spiffed-up menu showing new inspiration—and who wouldn't be inspired with these breathtaking views of Cézanne's beloved mountain? Michelin-starred chef Mathias Dandine's doesn't have far to look for the locally sourced products he favors, such as wild mushrooms for a luscious *velouté de cèpes* (wild mushroom soup) with ham and spicy Provençal olive oil, or sea bass with chanterelles and Szechuan pepper. **Known for:** stupendous views of Cezanne's mountain; best restaurant around Aix; lovely terrace. $ *Average main: €65* ⊠ *2500 rte. Cézanne, Le Tholonet* ☎ *04–42–27–10–14* ⊕ *www. leslodgessaintevictoire.com* ☉ *Closed Mon. Jan.–Mar.*

★ Mickaël Féval

$$$ | MODERN FRENCH | This is the kind of place where young cooks dream of working to learn the ropes, and Féval, quite young himself, has trained many a Michelin chef. After earning his fame in Paris, Favel opened this casual-elegant dining room, tucked away on a typically picturesque Aix side street, with a menu of dishes so masterful and flavorful that the restaurant soon became a local benchmark. **Known for:** gorgeous presentation; market-fresh dishes that change frequently; impeccable service. $ *Average main: €28* ✉ *11 Petite rue St-Jean* ☎ *04–42–93–29–60* ⊕ *www.mickaelfeval.fr* ⊘ *Closed Sun. and Mon.*

Hotels

Hôtel Cardinal

$ | HOTEL | In a graceful 18th-century house in the Quartier Mazarin, this eccentric and slightly threadbare inn is the antithesis of slick, which, coupled with the location, makes it a favorite among writers, artists, and musicians at festival time. **Pros:** the price for the location is excellent; rooms are clean and bright; central location. **Cons:** rooms can be noisy and hot in summer; bathroom decor is a throwback to the 1970s; some rooms have only handheld showers. $ *Rooms from: €80* ✉ *24 rue Cardinale, Aix-en-Provence* ☎ *04–42–38–32–30* ⊕ *www.hotel-cardinal-aix.com* ⊅ *35 rooms* ⊚ *No meals.*

Hôtel Cézanne

$$ | HOTEL | FAMILY | Three blocks from Cours Mirabeau and the train station, this smart, spiffy, and cozily stylish hotel is a very handy option. **Pros:** spacious rooms; Clarins bath products; in the heart of things. **Cons:** some rooms get street noise; no pool; breakfast room gets crowded. $ *Rooms from: €135* ✉ *40 av. Victor-Hugo, Aix-en-Provence* ☎ *04–42–91–11–11* ⊕ *www.hotelaix.com* ⊅ *55 rooms* ⊚ *No meals.*

★ Le Pigonnet

$$$$ | HOTEL | FAMILY | Cézanne painted Ste-Victoire from what is now the large flower-filled terrace of this enchanting abode, and you can easily imagine former guests Princess Caroline, Iggy Pop, and Clint Eastwood swanning their way through the magnificent, pool-adorned, topiary-accented garden or relaxing in the spacious, light-filled guest rooms. **Pros:** stunning garden setting; Nespresso machines in all rooms; in the center of the city. **Cons:** not all rooms have balconies; some bathrooms on the small side; breakfast not included in room price. $ *Rooms from: €225* ✉ *5 av. du Pigonnet, Aix-en-Provence* ☎ *04–42–59–02–90* ⊕ *www.hotelpigonnet.com* ⊅ *44 rooms* ⊚ *No meals.*

★ Les Lodges Sainte-Victoire

$$$$ | HOTEL | Set on a picture-perfect 10 acres of woods, olive groves, and vineyards, just outside Aix, with Cézanne-immortalized Mont Ste-Victoire as a backdrop, this hotel with a Michelin-starred restaurant raises the bar for lodging in the region. **Pros:** has one of the city's best restaurants; four swanky private villas; beautiful grounds and views. **Cons:** outside the city center; some first-floor rooms lack views; decor a little dark. $ *Rooms from: €345* ✉ *2250 rte. Cézanne, Le Tholonet* ☎ *04–42–24–80–40* ⊕ *www.leslodgessaintevictoire.com* ⊅ *39 rooms* ⊚ *No meals.*

Villa Gallici

$$$$ | HOTEL | Bathed in the lavenders, blues, ochers, and oranges of Aix, rooms here are adorned in the most gorgeous Souleiado and Rubelli fabrics, conjuring up the swank 19th-century Provence colonized by Parisian barons and dukes. **Pros:** rich fabrics and dashing interiors; beautiful garden spot; 15-minute walk to town and shops. **Cons:** meals are pricey; no elevator; some rooms could some modernization. $ *Rooms from: €500* ✉ *Av. de la Violette, Aix-en-Provence* ☎ *04–42–23–29–23* ⊕ *www.villagallici.com* ⊘ *Closed Jan.* ⊅ *22 rooms* ⊚ *No meals.*

Nightlife

To find out what's going on in town, pick up a copy of the events calendar *L'Agenda Cuturel* at the tourist office.

Pasino Grand

CASINOS | In between bouts at the roulette tables and slot machines of the Casino Aix-en-Provence, you can grab a bite at one of five restaurants or take in a floor show. ✉ *21 av. de l'Europe, Aix-en-Provence* ☎ *04–42–59–69–00* ⊕ *www.casinoaix.com.*

 Performing Arts

Festival d'Aix

FESTIVALS | In late June and July, opera and music lovers descend on Aix for the internationally acclaimed Festival d'Aix to see world-class opera productions in the courtyard of the Palais de l'Archevêché and more of the city's most beautiful venues. The repertoire is varied and often offbeat, featuring works like Britten's *Curlew River* and Bartók's *Bluebeard's Castle* as well as the usual Mozart, Puccini, and Verdi. Most of the singers, however, are not celebrities, but rather an elite group of students who spend the summer with the Academie Européenne de Musique, training and performing under the tutelage of stars like Robert Tear and Yo-Yo Ma. ✉ *Aix-en-Provence* ☎ *04–34–08–02–17* ⊕ *www.festival-aix.com.*

Le Ballet Preljocaj

DANCE | Angelin Preljocaj has created original ballets for the New York City Ballet and the Paris Opera Ballet, and his modern-dance troupe, Ballet Preljocaj, is based at the monolithic Pavillon Noir, designed by architect Rudy Ricciotti. The Pavillon hosts an annual series of contemporary ballet and modern dance performances featuring an international roster. The season runs September through May. There are also 6 pm rehearsals, free for the public. ✉ *530 av. Wolfgang Amadeus Mozart, Aix-en-Provence* ☎ *04–42–93–48–00* ⊕ *www.preljocaj.org.*

🛍 Shopping

In addition to its old-style markets and jewel-box candy shops, Aix is a modern shopping town—perhaps the best in Provence. The winding streets of the Vieille Ville above Cours Mirabeau—centered on Rue Clemenceau, Rue Marius Reinaud, Rue Espariat, Rue Aude, and Rue Maréchal Foch—have a head-turning parade of goods.

Béchard

FOOD/CANDY | The most picturesque shop specializing in calissons is the venerable bakery Béchard, founded in 1870. ✉ *12 cours Mirabeau, Aix-en-Provence.*

Santons Fouque

HOUSEHOLD ITEMS/FURNITURE | Aix's most celebrated *santon* (miniature statue) maker was established in 1936. ✉ *65 cours Gambetta, Aix-en-Provence* ☎ *04–42–26–33–38* ⊕ *www.santons-fouque.com.*

Weibel

FOOD/CANDY | An Aix institution since 1954, Maison Weibel is chock-full of sweets that look good enough to immortalize in a still life, let alone eat. Their version of the iconic Provençal calisson is hands down the best around. The shop also makes sublime gifts, packaged in lovely lavender boxes. ✉ *2 rue Chabrier, Aix-en-Provence* ☎ *04–42–23–33–21* ⊕ *www.maisonweibel.com.*

Marseille

31 km (19 miles) south of Aix-en-Provence, 188 km (117 miles) west of Nice, 772 km (483 miles) south of Paris.

Popular myths and a fishy reputation have led Marseille to be unfairly maligned as dingy urban sprawl plagued with impoverished immigrant neighborhoods and slightly louche politics. The city used to be given wide berth by travelers in search of a Provençal idyll. A huge mistake. Marseille, even its earliest history, has maintained its contradictions with a kind of fierce and independent pride. Yes, there are scary neighborhoods and some modern eyesores, but there is also tremendous beauty and culture. Cubist jumbles of white stone rise up over a picture-book seaport, bathed in light of blinding clarity, crowned by larger-than-life neo-Byzantine churches, and framed by massive fortifications; neighborhoods teem with multiethnic life; souklike African markets reek deliciously of spices and coffees; and the labyrinthine Old Town radiates pastel shades of saffron, marigold, and robin's-egg blue.

Called Massalia, this was the most important Continental shipping port in antiquity. The port flourished for some 500 years as a typical Greek city, enjoying the full flush of classical culture, its gods, its democratic political system, its sports and theater, and its naval prowess. Caesar changed all that, besieging the city in 49 BC and seizing most of its colonies. In 1214 Marseille was seized again, this time by Charles d'Anjou, and was later annexed to France by Henri IV in 1481, but it was not until Louis XIV took the throne that the biggest transformations of the port began. The Sun King pulled down the city walls in 1666 and expanded the port to the Rive Neuve (New Riverbank). The city was devastated by plague in 1720, losing more than half its population. By the time of the Revolution, Marseille was on the rebound once again, with industries of soap manufacturing and oil processing flourishing, encouraging a wave of immigration from Provence and Italy. With the opening of the Suez Canal in 1869, Marseille became the greatest boom-town in 19th-century Europe. With a large influx of immigrants from areas as exotic as Tangiers, the city quickly acquired the multicultural population it maintains to this day.

GETTING HERE AND AROUND

The main train station is Gare St-Charles on the TGV line, with frequent trains from Paris, the main coast route (Nice–Italy), and Arles. The gare routière is on Place Victor Hugo. This is the departure point for Cartreize buses into the Bouches du Rhône and Eurolines coaches between Marseille, Avignon, and Nice via Aix-en-Provence.

Marseille has a very good local bus, tram, and métro system (€1.50 per 90 mins), and the César ferry boat (immortalized in Pagnol's 1931 film *Marius*) crosses the Vieux Port every few minutes and is free of charge. Itineraries for wherever you want to go in the Bouches-du-Rhone can be found on ⊕ *www.lepilote.com*. ■TIP→ **Le Vélo is Marseille's citywide bicycle network. Grab a bike, take it to your destination, and then pick up another when you're ready to move on.** The first 30 minutes are free and a seven-day pass (⊕ *en.levelo-mpm.fr/how-it-works*) costs only €1.

VISITOR INFORMATION Marseille Tourist Office ✉ *11 la Canebière, La Canebière* ☎ *08–26–50–05–00 (€0.15 per min)* ⊕ *www.marseille-tourisme.com* Ⓜ *Vieux Port*.

Sights

Abbaye St-Victor

RELIGIOUS SITE | Founded in the 4th century by St-Cassien, who sailed into Marseille full of fresh ideas on monasticism that he acquired in Palestine and Egypt, this church grew to formidable proportions. With a Romanesque design, the structure would be as much at home in the Middle East as its founder was. The **crypt,** St-Cassien's original, is preserved beneath the medieval church, and in the evocative nooks and crannies you can find the 5th-century sarcophagus that allegedly holds the martyr's remains. Upstairs, a reliquary contains what's left of St-Victor, who was ground to death between millstones, probably by Romans. There's also a passage into tiny **catacombs** where early Christians worshipped St-Lazarus and Mary Magdalene, said to have washed ashore at Stes-Maries-de-la-Mer, in the Camargue. ✉ *3 rue de l'Abbaye, Rive Neuve* ☎ *04–96–11–22–60* ⊕ *www.saintvictor.net* Ⓜ *Vieux Port or Estrangin Préfecture.*

Cathédrale de la Nouvelle Major

RELIGIOUS SITE | This gargantuan, neo-Byzantine 19th-century fantasy was built under Napoléon III—but not before he'd ordered the partial destruction of the lovely 11th-century original, once a perfect example of the Provençal Romanesque style. You can view the flashy interior (think marble and rich red porphyry inlay) of the newer of the two churches; the medieval one is being restored. ✉ *Pl. de la Major, Le Panier* Ⓜ *Joliette.*

La Vieille Charité (*Center of the Old Charity*)

ARCHAEOLOGICAL SITE | At the top of the Panier district lies this superb ensemble of 17th- and 18th-century architecture designed as a hospice for the homeless by Marseillais artist-architects Pierre and Jean Puget. Even if you don't enter the museums, walk around the inner court, studying the retreating perspective of triple arcades and admiring the Baroque chapel with its novel egg-peaked dome. Of the complex's two museums, the larger is the **Musée d'Archéologie Méditerranéenne** (Museum of Mediterranean Archaeology), with a sizable collection of pottery and statuary from classical Mediterranean civilization, elementally labeled (for example, "pot"). There's also a display on the mysterious Celt-like Ligurians who first peopled the coast, cryptically presented with emphasis on the digs instead of the finds themselves. The best of the lot is the evocatively mounted Egyptian collection—the second-largest in France after the Louvre's. There are mummies, hieroglyphs, and gorgeous sarcophagi in a tomblike

Marseille City Pass

If you plan on visiting many of the museums in Marseille, buy a **City Pass** (€27 for 24 hours, €37 for 48 hours, €43 for 72 hours) at the tourism office or online. It covers the entry fee for all the museums in Marseille as well as public transit, a ride on the petit train, and free guided tour of the city.

setting. Upstairs, the **Musée d'Arts Africains, Océaniens, et Amérindiens** (Museum of African, Oceanic, and American Indian Art) creates a theatrical foil for the works' intrinsic drama: the spectacular masks and sculptures are mounted along a pure black wall, lighted indirectly, with labels across the aisle. ✉ *2 rue de la Charité, Le Panier* ☎ *04–91–14–58–80* ⊕ *www.vieille-charite-marseille.com* 🎫 *Exhibitions from €7* Ⓜ *Joliette.*

Le Panier

NEIGHBORHOOD | This is the heart of old Marseille, a maze of high-shuttered houses looming over narrow cobblestone streets, *montées* (stone stairways), and tiny squares. Long decayed and neglected, the quarter is a principal focus of the city's efforts at urban renewal. In the last few years an influx of "bobos" (bourgeois-bohemians) and artists have sparked the gentrification process, bringing charming B&Bs, chic boutiques, lively cafés, and artists' ateliers. Wander this picturesque neighborhood of pastel-painted town houses, steep stairways, and narrow streets at will, making sure to stroll along Rue du Panier, the Montée des Accoules, Rue du Petit-Puits, and Rue des Muettes. ✉ *Marseille* Ⓜ *Colbert Hôtel de Région.*

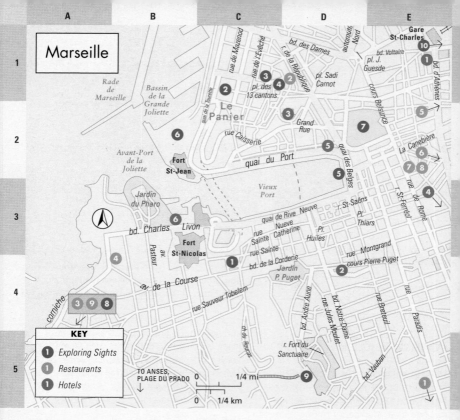

Marseille

Sights ▼

1 Abbaye St-Victor **C4**
2 Cathédrale de la
   Nouvelle Major **C1**
3 La Vieille Charité.........**C1**
4 Le Panier..................**C1**
5 Marché aux Poissons..**D2**
6 MuCEM **B2**
7 Musée d'Histoire de
   Marseille..................**D2**
8 Navette Maritime **A4**
9 Notre-Dame-
   de-la-Garde **D5**
10 Palais de
   Longchamp...............**E1**

Restaurants ▼

1 AM by Alexandre
   Mazzia **E5**
2 Chez Etienne **D1**
3 Chez Fonfon **A4**
4 Chez Michel **B4**
5 La Boîte à Sardine.......**E2**
6 La Cantinetta **E2**
7 La Mercerie **E2**
8 L'Épicerie Idéal..........**E2**
9 L'Epuisette **A4**

Hotels ▼

1 Alex Hotel **E1**
2 C2 Hotel..................**D4**
3 Intercontinental
   Marseille
   Hôtel Dieu **D2**
4 Mama Shelter............**E3**
5 Residence du
   Vieux Port................**D2**
6 Sofitel Vieux-Port........**B3**

Marché aux Poissons (*Fish Market*)

MARKET | Up and going by 8 am every day, this market—immortalized in Marcel Pagnot's *Fanny* (and Joshua Logan's sublime 1961 film adaptation)—puts on a vivid and aromatic show of waving fists, jostling chefs, and heaps of still-twitching fish from the night's catch. Hear the thick soup of the Marseillais accent as blue-clad fishermen and silk-clad matrons bicker over prices, and marvel at the rainbow of Mediterranean creatures swimming in plastic vats before you, each uglier than the last: the spiny-headed *rascasse* (scorpion fish), dog-nosed *grondin* (red gurnet), the monstrous *baudroie* or *lotte de mer* (monkfish), and the eel-like *congre*. "Bouillabaisse" as sold here is a mix of fish too tiny to sell otherwise; the only problem with coming for the early morning show is that you have to wait so long for your bouillabaisse lunch. ⊠ *Quai de la Fraternité, Vieux Port* Ⓜ *Vieux Port.*

MuCEM

MUSEUM | Made up of three sites designed by Rudy Ricciotti, MuCEM is all about new perspectives on Mediterranean cultures. Themes like "the invention of gods," "treasures of the spice route," or "at the bazaar of gender" are explored in Ricciotti's virtuosic J4 (named for the esplanade). ■ **TIP→ The museum's popular café, bistro, and restaurant (reservations required), overseen by star chef Gérald Passédat, are great for refreshment and taking in the views.** You can access the 12th-century Fort St-Jean, built by Louis XIV with guns pointing *toward* the city, in order to keep the feisty, rebellious Marseillais under his thumb. If you're not the queasy type, take a walk across the suspended footbridge over the sea; it provides spectacular photo ops and unique panoramas. On the other side, you can visit a Mediterranean garden and a folk-art collection. A third building—the Center for Conservation and Resources, near the St-Charles train station—holds the museum's permanent collection of paintings, prints, drawings, photographs, and objects. ⊠ *7 Promenade Robert Laffont, Vieux Port* ☎ *04–84–35–13–13* ⊕ *www.mucem.org* ⊠ *From €10* ⊙ *Closed Tues.* Ⓜ *Joliette.*

★ Musée d'Histoire de Marseille (*Marseille History Museum*)

MUSEUM | With the Port Antique in front, this modern, open-space museum illuminates Massalia's history with a treasure trove of archaeological finds and miniature models of the city as it appeared in various stages of history. Best by far is the presentation of Marseille's Classical halcyon days. There's a recovered wreck of a Roman cargo boat, its 3rd-century wood amazingly preserved, and the hull of a Greek boat dating to the 4th century BC. The model of the Greek city should be authentic—it's based on an eyewitness description by Aristotle. ⊠ *2 rue Henri Barbrusse, Vieux Port* ☎ *04–91–55–36–00* ⊕ *musee-histoire-de-marseille.marseille.fr* ⊠ *From €8* Ⓜ *Vieux-Port or Noailles.*

★ Navette Maritime

TRANSPORTATION SITE (AIRPORT/BUS/FERRY/TRAIN) | In keeping with the Vieux Port's substantially spiffed-up image, the Marseille regional transportation service now offers an efficient public ferry service, with hourly departures from the eastern side to Pointe Rouge (8 am–7 pm), L'Estaque (8:30 am–7:30 pm), and Les Goudes (8:50 am–7:50 pm). The nominal ticket charge (€5, available only on board) is well worth it for the fun and convenience of crossing the port by boat. ⊠ *Pl. des Huiles on Quai de Rive Neuve side and Hôtel de Ville on Quai du Port, Vieux Port* ⊕ *www.rtm.fr* ⊠ *€5 (free with métro pass)* Ⓜ *Vieux Port.*

Notre-Dame-de-la-Garde

RELIGIOUS SITE | Towering above the city and visible for miles around, this overscaled neo-Byzantine monument was erected in 1853 by Napoléon III. The interior is a Technicolor bonanza of red-and-beige stripes and glittering mosaics, and the gargantuan *Madonna and Child* on the steeple (almost 30 feet high) is covered in real gold leaf. While the panoply of ex-votos, mostly thanking the Virgin for deathbed interventions and shipwreck survivals, is a remarkable sight, most impressive are the views of the seaside city at your feet. ✉ *Rue Fort du Sanctuaire, off Bd. André Aune, Garde Hill* ☎ *04–91–13–40–80* 🌐 *www.notredamedelagarde.com* [M] *Estrangin Préfecture.*

Palais de Longchamp

CASTLE/PALACE | This extravagant and grandiose 19th-century palace, inaugurated in 1869, was built to celebrate the completion of an 84-km (52-mile) aqueduct bringing the water of the Durance river to the open sea. The massive, classical-style building crowns a hill and is splayed with impressive symmetrical grace around a series of fountains with a triumphal arch at its center and museums in either wing. In the **Musée des Beaux-Arts** (Fine Arts Museum) are 16th- and 17th-century paintings, including several by Rubens, as well as fine marble sculptures and drawings by the Marseille architect Pierre Puget. There's a delightful group of sculptures by caricaturist Honoré Daumier, and the collection of French 19th-century paintings, including Courbet, Ingres, and David, is strong. In the right wing of the palace is the **Muséum d'Histoire Naturelle** (Natural History Museum) with a collection of prehistoric and zoological artifacts, plus a large aquarium with fish from around the world. ✉ *Eastern end of bd. Longchamp, La Canebière* ☎ *04–91–14–59–30, 04–91–14–59–50* 🌐 *musee-des-beaux-arts.marseille.fr* 🎟 *Musée des Beaux-Arts €6* 🕘 *Closed Mon.* [M] *Longchamp.*

🍴 Restaurants

★ AM by Alexandre Mazzia

$$$$ | **FRENCH** | Architect, artist, creator—whatever you call him, one thing's for sure: you won't soon forget this master chef who was awarded a Michelin star within nine months of opening his own restaurant. With a background working in French, African, and Asian kitchens, his combinations are music to the mouth, like the charred satay tuna in tapioca speckled with bright green fish eggs, served with wasabi ice cream. **Known for:** exquisite small dishes; unusual pairings; far-flung influences. [$] *Average main: €140* ✉ *9 rue François Rocca, Prado* ☎ *04–91–24–83–63* 🌐 *www.alexandre-mazzia.com* 🕘 *Closed Sun. and Mon.*

Chez Etienne

$$ | **PIZZA** | A well-known hole-in-the-wall, this small pizzeria is filled daily with politicos and young professionals who have patronized this institution since when the famous late-chef Stéphane Cassero presided. Brace yourself for an epic meal, starting with a large anchovy pizza from the wood-burning oven, then dig into fried squid, eggplant gratin, and a slab of rare grilled beef all served with the background of laughter and rich Marseille patois. **Known for:** stupendous pizza; lots of local flavor; huge portions. [$] *Average main: €19* ✉ *43 rue de Lorette, Le Panier* 💳 *No credit cards* 🕘 *Closed Sun.* [M] *Colbert Hôtel de Région.*

Chez Fonfon

$$$$ | **SEAFOOD** | Tucked into the tiny fishing port of Vallon des Auffes, this local landmark has one of the loveliest settings in greater Marseille. A variety of fresh seafood, impeccably grilled, steamed, or roasted in salt crust, is served in two pretty dining rooms with picture windows overlooking the fishing boats that supply your dinner. **Known for:** bouillabaisse; fresh catch of the day; wonderful setting. [$] *Average main: €50* ✉ *140 rue du Vallon des Auffes, Vallon des Auffes* ☎ *04–91–52–14–38* 🌐 *www.chez-fonfon.com.*

Chez Michel

$$$$ | **BRASSERIE** | This beachside Michelin-starred brasserie near the Jardin du Pharo is considered the last word in bouillabaisse and draws a knowing local clientele willing to shell out a few extra

The heart of Marseille is its Vieux Port (Old Port), with its small boats and port-side cafés, while the city's soul is hilltop Notre-Dame-de-la-Garde.

euros (€75) for this authentic classic. Before dining, the fish are paraded by your table then ceremoniously filleted before being served with the classic accompaniments: a spicy rouille, buttery croutons. **Known for:** cozy atmosphere; small but excellent menu; bouillabaisse that's worth the splurge. [$] *Average main: €70* ✉ *6 rue des Catalans, Pharo* ☎ *04–91–52–30–63* 🌐 *www.restaurant-michel-13.fr* 🕒 *No dinner Sun.*

★ La Boîte à Sardine

$$ | SEAFOOD | Owner Fabien Rugi's passion for seafood may come off as gruff, but that's only because he wants his customers to appreciate his Mediterranean-inflected seafood dishes as much as he does. He puts his formidable energy into serving the freshest seafood, prepared *comme il faut*. **Known for:** daily catch; delicious local wines; convivial atmosphere. [$] *Average main: €22* ✉ *2 bd. de la Libération, La Canebière* ☎ *04–91–50–95–95* 🌐 *www.laboiteasardine.com* 🕒 *Closed Sun. and Mon. No dinner* [M] *Réformés Canebière.*

★ La Cantinetta

$ | ITALIAN | FAMILY | Ask any Marseille food enthusiast where they go for great Italian food and they're sure to send you to this legendary spot near the Cours Julien. It's not just the food but the lively ambience, flowing wine, and happy camaraderie as gorgeous plates of charcuterie topped with giant Parmesan shavings and fragrant bowls of steaming risotto, pasta, or line-caught fish of the day exit the kitchen, followed by a towering *tiramisu maison*. **Known for:** friendly atmosphere; abundant dishes; excellent wine list of Mediterranean favorites. [$] *Average main: €16* ✉ *24 cours Julien, Cours Julien* ☎ *04–91–48–10–48* 🌐 *www.restaurantlacantinetta.fr* 🕒 *Closed Sun.* [M] *Noailles.*

★ La Mercerie

$$$ | FRENCH | A stylishly high-low decor that joins distressed walls, minimalist lighting, and sleek designer chairs with a setting in Marseille's emerging Noailles neighborhood is your first clue that this neobistro and wine bar is Marseille's newest impossibly hip eatery. British chef Harry Cummins, lately of Paris's gastronomic mecca Frenchie, crafts a subtle, imaginative cuisine from local seasonal products that's both highly satisfying and sensitive to vegetarians and those with food allergies. **Known for:** culinary awards; all the rage among young foodies; healthy dining. $ *Average main: €25* ✉ *9 cours St-Louis, Noailles* ☎ *04–91–06–18–44* ⊕ *www.lamercerie-marseille.com* ⊗ *Closed Mon. and Tues.* Ⓜ *Noailles, Vieux-Port-Hôtel de Ville.*

★ L'Épicerie Idéal

$ | **FRENCH** | For a fresh, seasonal lunch, we can't get enough of this chic little outpost in the marché Noailles that is part restaurant, part gourmet grocer. Imaginative Mediterranean-inflected salads and light dishes are healthy and delicious, and pair well with a gourmet soda, Marseille microbrew, or a local rosé. **Known for:** great value; perfect for gourmet discoveries and gifts; fresh, seasonal dishes and salads. $ *Average main: €12* ✉ *11 rue d'Aubagne, Noailles* ☎ *09–80–39–99–41* ⊕ *www.epicerielideal.com* ⊗ *Closed Sun. and Mon.* Ⓜ *Noailles, Vieux-Port-Hôtel de Ville.*

L'Epuisette

$$$$ | **SEAFOOD** | Artfully set on a rocky, fingerlike jetty surrounded by the sea, this fine seafood restaurant offers gorgeous views of crashing surf on one side and the port of Vallon des Auffes on the other. Chef Guillaume Sourrieu has acquired a big reputation (and a Michelin star) for sophisticated cooking featuring the fresh catch of the day—Atlantic turbot in citrus rind with oxtail ravioli, and slow-cooked sea bass baked in a salt-butter crust and walnut oil are some top delights—matched with a superb wine list. **Known for:** stupendous seafood; lovely setting; good service. $ *Average main: €55* ✉ *158 rue du Vallon des Auffes, Pharo* ☎ *04–91–52–17–82* ⊕ *www.l-epuisette. com* ⊗ *Closed Sun. and Mon., and last 2 wks in Aug.*

Hotels

Alex Hotel

$ | **HOTEL** | This reasonably priced boutique hotel, across from St-Charles train station, is set in a beautiful historic building. **Pros:** great prices; convenient to the train station, and a 15-minute walk to the old port; some rooms have small balconies. **Cons:** nearby restaurants lacking; rooms lack character; not in the city center. $ *Rooms from: €85* ✉ *13–15 pl. des Marseillaises, St-Charles* ☎ *04–13–24–13–25* ⊕ *www.alex-hotel.fr* ⚑ *21 rooms* ⊘ *No meals* Ⓜ *Gare St-Charles.*

C2 Hotel

$$$$ | **HOTEL** | It took two years to transform this 19th-century home, previously occupied by a prominent Marseille family, into 20 beautifully designed accommodations. **Pros:** a few minutes from the port; impeccable service; intimate spa with steam room, Jacuzzi, and pool. **Cons:** extra charge for breakfast; some of the lighting in common areas is a bit too neon; rooms vary drastically in size. $ *Rooms from: €269* ✉ *48 rue Roux de Brignoles, St-Charles* ☎ *04–95–05–13–13* ⊕ *www.c2-hotel.com* ⚑ *20 rooms* ⊘ *No meals* Ⓜ *Estrangin Préfecture.*

★ Intercontinental Marseille Hôtel Dieu

$$$$ | **HOTEL** | Housed in Marseille's majestic 18th-century Hôtel Dieu, a beloved landmark built according to plans by Jacques Hardouin-Mansart, architect to Louis XIV, this place has been transformed into a gleaming palace—and it's worth a stop even if you don't stay here (enjoy a drink on the sprawling terrace bar, with gorgeous views of the old port). **Pros:** a one-stop luxury spot; splendid views from open-air bar; rates include breakfast. **Cons:** only a fifth of rooms have a terrace; such indulgence does have a price; snob appeal. $ *Rooms from: €229* ✉ *1 pl. Daviel, Vieux Port* ☎ *04–13–42–42–42* ⊕ *www.ihg.com/intercontinental/hotels/ us/en/marseille/mrsha/hoteldetail* ⚑ *195 rooms* ⊘ *Free breakfast* Ⓜ *Vieux Port.*

Mama Shelter

$ | HOTEL | Manufacturing hip is this urban chain hotel's claim to fame (no wonder: it's the brainchild of designer Philippe Starck). **Pros:** buffet breakfasts can't be beat; friendly service; cool vibe. **Cons:** not always a bargain; not to everyone's taste; iffy neighborhood. $ *Rooms from: €89* ✉ *64 rue de la Loubière, Cours Julien* ☎ *04–84–35–20–00* ⊕ *www.mamashelter.com* ⤴ *127 rooms* ❚⊘❙ *No meals* Ⓜ *Baille or Notre Dame du Mont.*

★ Residence du Vieux Port

$$$ | HOTEL | FAMILY | The flat glass-and-concrete facade of this postwar structure grants all the port-facing rooms here broad views of the Vieux Port all the way to Notre-Dame-de-la-Garde. **Pros:** great price for this ideal location; superb views of the Vieux Port; cheerful decor and service. **Cons:** terrace views are partially obstructed by concrete railings; breakfast not included in price unless chosen when booking; some bathrooms cozy. $ *Rooms from: €200* ✉ *18 quai du Port, Vieux Port* ☎ *04–91–91–91–22* ⊕ *www.hotel-residence-marseille.com* ⤴ *51 rooms* ❚⊘❙ *No meals* Ⓜ *Vieux Port.*

★ Sofitel Vieux-Port

$$$ | HOTEL | FAMILY | Its plum location next to the beautiful Palais de Pharo and park and its legendary service already raised this five-star luxury hotel to a great deal more than standard issue, but the recent addition of a rooftop terrace with some of the city's best views puts it right up there with the top hotels in the city. **Pros:** exemplary service; stupendous views; valet parking. **Cons:** pool can be crowded in summer; some rooms on the small side; not an intimate hotel. $ *Rooms from: €210* ✉ *36 bd. Charles Livon, Pharo* ☎ *04–91–15–59–00* ⊕ *www.sofitel.com* ⤴ *137 rooms* ❚⊘❙ *No meals.*

⧩ Nightlife

With a population of nearly 860,000, Marseille is a big city by French standards, with all the nightlife that entails. Arm yourself with the monthly *In Situ* (a free guide to music, theater, and galleries) or *Sortir* (a weekly about film, art, and concerts in southern Provence). They're both in French.

La Caravelle

MUSIC CLUBS | Restaurant by day, bluesy jazz club and tapas bar by night, La Caravelle hearkens back to prewar jazz clubs, but without the smoke. There are great views over the port and live jazz two nights a week. ✉ *Hotel Belle Vue, 34 quai du Port, Vieux Port* ☎ *04–91–90–36–64* ⊕ *www.lacaravelle-marseille.com* Ⓜ *Vieux Port.*

Red Lion

BARS/PUBS | This bar is a mecca for English speakers, who pour onto the sidewalk, beer in hand, pub style. There's live music, DJs on the weekend, and a lounge for the die-hard rugby and soccer fans who can't go without watching a game. ✉ *231 av. Pierre Mendès France, Vieux Port* ☎ *04–91–25–17–17* ⊕ *www.pub-redlion.com.*

Performing Arts

Opéra Municipal de Marseille

CONCERTS | Operas and orchestral concerts are held at the Opéra Municipal. ✉ *2 rue Molière, Vieux Port* ☎ *04–91–55–11–10* ⊕ *opera.marseille.fr* Ⓜ *Vieux Port.*

🛍 Shopping

Savon de Marseille (Marseille soap) is a household standard in France, often sold as a satisfyingly crude and hefty block in odorless olive-oil green. But its chichi offspring are dainty pastel guest soaps in almond, lemon, vanilla, and other scents. You can never have too many Provençal gifts to take home, so peruse the market in the Old Port on weekdays in July and August and Thursday and Friday in June and the first half of September.

★ Chez Laurette

CLOTHING | Ex-fashion designer Laure Traverso (Marc Jacobs, Paul & Joe) escaped the Paris treadmill to open her own wildly creative concept store that spotlights all things French, sustainable and ethical, design-conscious, and just plain cool. Discoveries abound—look for chic emerging fashion labels, beautiful leather and straw bags, shoes, belts, avant-garde jewelry, lingerie, handmade home furnishings, organic cosmetics made in Provence, and a grocery corner featuring such local delicacies as microbrew beers, chocolates, and teas. ⊠ *16 rue Edmond Rostand* ☎ *04–88–04–31–70* ⊕ *chez-laurette.com.*

Four des Navettes

FOOD/CANDY | This famous bakery, up the street from Notre-Dame-de-la-Garde, has made orange-spice, shuttle-shape *navettes* in the same oven since it opened in 1781. These cookies are modeled on the little boat that, it is said, carried Lazarus and the Three Marys (Mary Magdalene, Mary Salome, and Mary Jacobe) to the nearby shore. ⊠ *136 rue Sainte, Pharo* ☎ *04–91–33–32–12* ⊕ *www.fourdesnavettes.com* Ⓜ *Vieux Port.*

La Maison du Pastis

FOOD/CANDY | Specializing in pastis, anisette, and absinthe, this smart little shop offers a dizzying range, but to really savor these unique delights, sign up (in advance) for one of the 90-minute tastings. ⊠ *108 quai du Port, Vieux Port* ☎ *04–91–90–86–77* ⊕ *www.lamaisondu-pastis.com* Ⓜ *Vieux Port.*

★ Maison Empereur

LOCAL SPECIALTIES | If Made in France sounds good to you, this 190-year-old Marseille institution is your dream come true. A treasure trove of all things French, from housewares, linens, knives and kitchenware, tableware, and hardware to huge cotton scarves, towels, timeless French perfumes, espadrilles, classic toys, and the real Savon de Marseille. The main store is home to all of the above, but there's also a clothing shop across the street (8 rue des Recolettes) with irresistible items for women, men, and kids, including wool or sheepskin slippers, rakish straw hats, cashmere capes and caps, chunky wool sweaters, and classic French cotton work shirts. ⊠ *4 rue des Récolettes* ☎ *04–91–54–02–29* ⊕ *empereur.fr.*

Marianne Cat

CLOTHING | A curated selection of sophisticated, superchic European-designed clothes, shoes, scarves, jewelry, and accessories for women is displayed in a soaring 18th-century space. ⊠ *53 rue Grignan, Belsunce* ☎ *04–91–55–05–25* Ⓜ *Estrangin Préfecture.*

Savonnerie Marseillaise Licorne

PERFUME/COSMETICS | One of Marseille's oldest traditional manufacturers sells fragrant savon in blocks, ovals, or fanciful shapes. This soap maker uses the highest olive oil content possible (72%) in the soaps, and only natural essential oils from Provence for the fragrances. Call ahead for a guided tour (in English) of this atmospheric factory—a great way to see the whole process done on traditional machines. ⊠ *34 cours Julien, Cours Julien* ☎ *04–96–12–00–91* ⊕ *www.savon-de-marseille-licorne.com* Ⓜ *Notre Dame du Mont.*

Cassis

30 km (19 miles) southeast of Marseille.

Surrounded by vineyards, flanked by monumental cliffs, guarded by the ruins of a medieval castle, and nestled around a picture-perfect fishing port, Cassis is the prettiest coastal town in Provence. Best known for its delicate white wines and wild Calanques, it is a quiet fishing

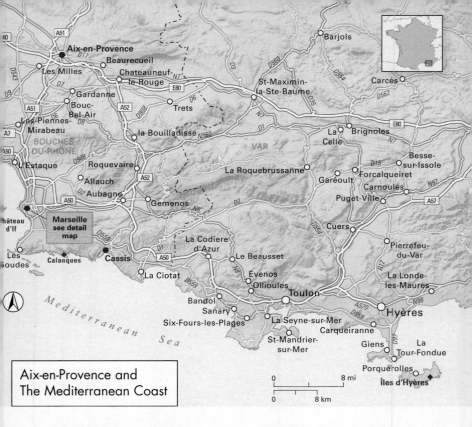

village out of season and inundated with sun worshippers in the summer. The pastel houses at rakish angles framing the port and harbor attracted early-20th-century artists including Dufy and Matisse. Even the mild rash of parking-garage architecture in the outer neighborhoods can't spoil the effect of unadulterated charm.

Stylish without being too recherché, Cassis's picture-perfect harbor provides shelter to numerous pleasure boaters, who restock their galleys at its market, replenish their St-James nautical duds in its boutiques, and relax with a bottle of local wine and a platter of sea urchins in one of its numerous waterfront cafés.

GETTING HERE AND AROUND

By car, leave the A50 from Marseille or Toulon and take Exit 8 for Cassis. The D559 from Marseille to Cassis is dramatically beautiful, continuing along the coast to Toulon, but it might be too curvy for motion-sickness sufferers.

Hourly trains between Marseille and Toulon stop at Cassis, but the station is about 3 km (2 miles) from the center. From the station, there is a local shuttle to the town center that runs at least once an hour. There is also the M06 Marseille–Cassis bus, which takes an hour.

TOURS

Icard Maritime

BOAT TOURS | Boats make round-trips several times a day to the Calanques de Cassis from Marseille's Quai de la Fraternité (Quai des Belges). This company offers a 3½-hour round-trip. ⊠ *1 quai Marcel Pagnol, Marseille* ⊕ *www.visite-des-calanques.com* 🕿 *From €30.*

From Cassis be sure to take an excursion boat to the Calanques, the rocky finger-coves washed by emerald and blue waters.

La Visite des Calanques

BOAT TOURS | This company offers several boat tours of the Calanques from the unmistakable red and yellow kiosk at Quay St-Pierre, not far from the tourist office. A 45-minute, three-calanques tour runs every 45 minutes 10–4:30, February through April, October and November, and every 30 minutes 9:30–6, May through September. Longer explorations last from just over an hour to nearly two hours and cover up to nine scenic inlets. Tickets must be purchased (at the kiosk) at least 30 minutes in advance, or you can call and reserve by phone, which is your safest option in busy July and August. ✉ *Quai St-Pierre, Cassis* ☎ *04–42–01–03–31* ⊕ *www.lavisitedes-calanques.com* ✉ *From €16.*

VISITOR INFORMATION Cassis Tourist Office ✉ *Quai des Moulins, Cassis* ☎ *08–92–39–01–03* ⊕ *www.ot-cassis.com.*

 ## Sights

Calanques

BODY OF WATER | Touring the Calanques, whose fjordlike finger bays probe the rocky coastline, is a must. Either take a sightseeing cruise in a glass-bottom boat that dips into each Calanque in turn (tickets, sold at the eastern end of the port, are €16–€27, depending on how many Calanques you see) or hike across the cliff tops, clambering down the steep sides to these barely accessible retreats. Or do both, going in by boat and hiking back; make arrangements at the port. Of the Calanques closest to Cassis, **Port Miou** is the least attractive. It is also the only one fully accessible by car. It was a *pierre de Cassis* (Cassis stone) quarry until 1982 when the Calanques became protected sites, and now has an active leisure and fishing port. **Calanque Port Pin** is prettier, with wind-twisted pines growing at angles from white-rock cliffs. But with its tiny beach and jagged cliffs looming overhead, covered with gnarled pine and scrub and its rock spur known to climbers as the "finger of God," **Calanque En Vau** is a small piece of paradise.

Restaurants

★ La Villa Madie

$$$$ | **FRENCH** | Chef Dimitri Droisneau may profess his cuisine to be humble, but his two–Michelin star restaurant (earned within a year of opening) merits a change out of your beachwear (closed-toe shoes are required). Droisneau and his wife, Marielle, run the restaurant and offer standouts like delicately grilled Mediterranean rouget with almonds and fennel and drizzled lightly with an urchin-and-saffron sauce. **Known for:** a top choice in the region; brilliant seafood dishes; exquisite Citron (lemon pie)—a must-have. [$] *Average main: €75* ✉ *Av. de Revestrel-anse de Corton, Cassis* ☎ *04–96–18–00–00* 🌐 *www.lavillamadie.com* 🕒 *Closed Tues. and Wed., and Jan.–mid-Feb.*

Le Chaudron

$$$ | **BISTRO** | Just off Cassis's picturesque port, locals and visitors alike flock to this off-the-beaten-tourist path and welcoming bistro and terrace serving classic Provençal meals on one of the town's charming backstreets. This being Cassis, fish is a mainstay on the menu; start with gratin of mussels followed by roasted John Dory with Provençal vegetables, or spicy fish soup, all to be savored with the local Cassis wines. **Known for:** top-notch bistro fare with a Mediterranean twist; fresh catch of the day; family-run since 1970. [$] *Average main: €27* ✉ *4 rue Adolphe Thiers, Cassis* ☎ *04–42–01–74–18* 🕒 *Closed Tues. and mid-Dec.–Mar. No lunch.*

Hotels

★ Les Roches Blanches

$$$$ | **HOTEL** | Featuring views of the port and the Cap Canaille, both from the best rooms and from the panoramic dining room, this exquisite cliff-side villa underwent a two-year total makeover, shedding its Art Deco–style decor and reopening in 2018 with a spiffy contemporary look. **Pros:** sweeping vistas are captivating; service is quick and friendly; most rooms have balconies. **Cons:** hard to find (use your GPS); breakfast is expensive; in-room dining could be better. [$] *Rooms from: €323* ✉ *Rte. des Calanques, Cassis* ☎ *04–42–01–09–30* 🌐 *www.roches-blanches-cassis.com* 🕒 *Closed Nov.–Mar.* 🛏 *24 rooms* 🍴 *No meals.*

Îles d'Hyères

32 km (20 miles) off coast south of Hyères.

Strung across the Bay of Hyères and spanning some 32 km (20 miles) is an archipelago of islands reminiscent of a set for a pirate movie. In fact, they have been featured in several, thanks not only to their wild and rocky coastline but also their real pirate history. In the 16th century the islands were seeded with convicts meant to work the land; they promptly ran amok, ambushing and sacking passing ships heading for Toulon. Today the pirates are long gone, replaced by a thriving local population and tourists.

The islands consist of three main bodies: Levant, Port-Cros, and Porquerolles. Eight percent of **Levant** is military property and is kept strictly guarded with barbed-wire fences. The remaining area, Héliopolis, is a nudist colony, where you're welcome only if you want to participate, as opposed to simply being curious. **Port-Cros** is a magnificent national park with no cars, no smoking, and no dogs. You can hike on pine-scented trails with spectacular views, or follow the underwater path, snorkeling or diving with aquatic life representative of the Mediterranean. **Porquerolles** (pronounced "pork-uh- *rohl*") is the largest and most popular escape from the modern world. The village of Porquerolles was originally used as a retirement colony for Napoleonic officers (the Fort du Petit-Langoustier and the Fort Ste-Agathe, although no longer active, still loom imposingly over the marina), which explains its remarkable resemblance to a military outpost. At the turn of the 20th century a Belgian engineer named François-Joseph Fournier made a killing in the Panama Canal, then bought Porquerolles at auction as a gift for his new bride. It was only in 1970 that France nationalized the island, leaving Fournier's widow with a quarter of her original inheritance; her granddaughter now helps run the luxurious Mas du Langoustier. Off-season it's a castaway idyll of pine forests, sandy beaches, and plunging cliffs over a rocky coastline. Inland, its preserved pine forests and orchards of olives and figs are crisscrossed with dirt roads to be explored on foot or, if you prefer, on bikes rented from one of the numerous rental outfits in both the port and village. In high season (April through October), day-trippers pour off the ferries, running for the beaches and soap boutiques, and T-shirt shops appear out of the woodwork to cater to vacationers' whims.

GETTING HERE AND AROUND
To get to the islands, follow the narrow Giens Peninsula to La Tour–Fondue at its tip. Ferries run from La Tour–Fondu in Giens (every 30 minutes in summer, every 60–90 minutes in winter; €19.50 round-trip) for the 20-minute trip to Porquerolles, and from Hyères at Hyères Plages to Port-Cros and Levant (€28.10–€31.50 round-trip). You can also get to all three islands from Port-de-Miramar or Le Lavandou (35- to 60-minute crossing, €31.50 round-trip).

 Hotels

Mas du Langoustier
$$$$ | HOTEL | A fabled forgetaway, the Langoustier comes with a lobster-orange building, pink bougainvillea, a choice of California modern– or old Provençal–style guest rooms, and a secluded location at the westernmost point of the Ile de Porquerolles. **Pros:** a bastion of taste; can "upgrade" to dinner at L'Olivier; beach nearby and on-site pool. **Cons:** a hike to get here; no rooms have a sea view; the property's Michelin-star restaurant closed. $ *Rooms from: €500* ✉ *Pointe du Langoustier, 3 km (2 miles) from harbor, Ile de Porquerolles* ☎ *04–94–58–30–09* ⊕ *www.langoustier.com* ⊗ *Closed Oct.–Apr.* ↪ *49 rooms* ❍ *Free Breakfast.*

THE FRENCH RIVIERA

Updated by
Nancy Heslin

👁 Sights	🍽 Restaurants	🛏 Hotels	🛍 Shopping	🍸 Nightlife
★★★★☆	★★★★★	★★★★★	★★★☆☆	★★★★☆

WELCOME TO THE FRENCH RIVIERA

TOP REASONS TO GO

★ **Picasso and Company:** Because artists have long loved the Côte d'Azur, it's blessed with superb art museums, including the Fondation Maeght in St-Paul and the Musée Picasso in Antibes.

★ **St-Tropez:** Brave the world's most outlandish fishing port in high summer, but don't forget the sunglasses and sunblock.

★ **Cannes:** Get your film fix during the glitzy Cannes International Film Festival, or put yourself in the picture by taking a selfie on the Allée des Étoiles (Stars' Walk).

★ **Èze:** An island in the sky, Èze has some of the most breathtaking views this side of a NASA space capsule.

★ **Nice:** With its bonbon-color palaces, blue chair-lined promenade, and time-stained Old Town, this is one of France's most colorful cities.

1 St-Tropez. One of the most lively (and glitzy) stretches of the Riviera.

2 Fréjus. A rare unspoiled town on the coast.

3 St-Raphaël. A sprawling resort city with a rich port history.

4 Mandelieu-La-Napoule. Dual centers of golf and sailing in the region.

5 Cannes. A ritzy resort home to a famous film festival.

6 Mougins. A sleek suburb where Picasso spent his final days.

7 Grasse. The capital of the French perfume industry.

8 Vallauris. An urban village where Picasso spent some time.

9 Antibes. A charming town that lured many artists, including Picasso and Monet.

10 Cap d'Antibes. A stretch of the coast that has long hosted the rich and famous.

11 Juan-les-Pins. A resort town that bloomed in the Jazz Age.

12 St-Paul-de-Vence. A medieval village that's now home to world's best art museum/hotel/restaurant, La Colombe d'Or.

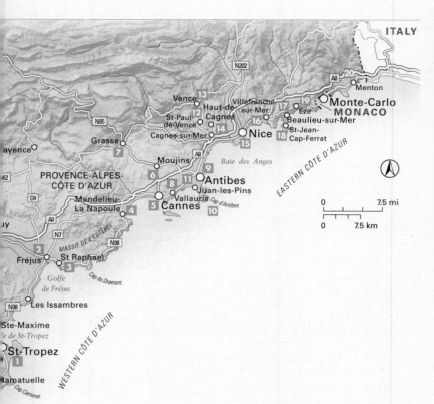

13 Vence. A historic market town with a staggering number of tourist-friendly shops and galleries.

14 Haut-de-Cagnes. A gorgeous village long home to artists like Renoir.

15 Nice. The Riviera's biggest city with plenty of Provençal charm.

16 Villefranche-Sur-Mer. A port town known for its restorative vibe.

17 Beaulieu-Sur-Mer. An old-fashioned resort town most popular in the 19th century.

18 St-Jean-Cap-Ferrat. One of the Riviera's most exclusive resort towns.

19 Èze. Perched on the edge of a cliff and widely considered the region's most gorgeous town.

20 Menton. The least pretentious resort town on the Riviera.

You may build castles in Spain or picture yourself on a South Sea island, but when it comes to serious speculation about how to spend that first $10 million and slip easily into the life of the idle rich, most people head for the French Riviera.

This is where the azure waters and indigo sky begin, where balustraded white villas edge the blue horizon, the evening air is perfumed with jasmine, and parasol pines are silhouetted against sunsets of ripe apricot. As emblematic as the sheet-music cover for a Jazz Age tune, the French Riviera seems to epitomize happiness, a state of being the world pursues with a vengeance.

But the Jazz Age dream confronts modern reality: on the hills that undulate along the blue water, every cliff bristles with cubes of hot-pink cement and balconies of ironwork, each skewed to catch a glimpse of the sea and the sun. Like a rosy rash, these crawl and spread, outnumbering the trees and blocking each other's views. But the Côte d'Azur (or Azure Coast) has always been exceedingly popular, starting with the ancient Greeks, who were drawn eastward from Marseille to market their goods to the natives. From the 18th-century English aristocrats who claimed the coast as one vast spa, to the 19th-century Russian nobles who transformed Nice into a tropical St. Petersburg, to the 20th-century American tycoons who cast themselves as romantic sheiks, the beckoning coast became a blank slate for their whims. Like the modern vacationers who followed, they all left their mark—villas, shrines, Moroccan-fantasy castles—as temples to the sensual pleasures of the sun and the sultry sea breezes. Artists,

too, made the French Riviera their own, as museumgoers who have studied the sunny legacy of Picasso, Renoir, Matisse, and Chagall will attest.

Today's admirers can take this all in, along with the Riviera's textbook points of interest: self-indulgent St-Tropez; the Belle Époque aura of Cannes; the towns made famous by Picasso—Antibes, Vallauris, Mougins; the urban charms of Nice; and a number of spots where the per capita population of billionaires must be among the highest on the planet, including Cap d'Antibes, St-Jean-Cap-Ferrat, and Cap d'Ail.

But with just a little luck and a bus ride or two, you can find towns and villages far from the madding crowd, especially if you head to the low-lying mountains known as the *arriére-pays* (backcountry). Here, medieval stone villages cap rocky hills and play out scenes of Provençal life, with games of *boules*, slowly savored drinks of pastis, and very little mobile phone coverage. Some of them—Èze, St-Paul, Vence—may have become virtual Provençal theme parks but even so you'll probably find a gorgeous and deserted Riviera alleyway hidden in one of their cobblestone mazes.

GETTING ORIENTED

The French Riviera can supply visitors with everything their hearts desire (and their wallet can stand). Home to sophisticated resorts beloved by billionaires, remote hill villages colonized by artists, Mediterranean beaches, and magnificent views, the Côte d'Azur (to use the French name) stretches from Marseille to Menton. Thrust out like two gigantic arms, divided by the Valley of the Var at Nice, the peaks of the Alpes-Maritimes throw their massive protection, east and west, the length of the favored coast all the way from St-Tropez to the Italian frontier.

MAJOR REGIONS

The Western French Riviera. Put on the map by Brigitte Bardot, St-Tropez remains one of France's flashiest vacation spots, small and laid-back. Conspicuous consumption characterizes the celluloid city of Cannes when its May film fest turns it into Oscar-goes-to-the-Mediterranean, but the Louis Vuitton set enjoys this city year-round. More modest resorts—such as Fréjus, St-Raphaël, and Mandelieu-La-Napoule—offer a more affordable Riviera experience. Grasse is well-known for its perfumes, while Mougins and Vallauris were two places Picasso spent some time. For the utmost in Riviera charm, head up the coast to Antibes: once Picasso's home, it has a harbor and an Old Town so dreamy you'll be reaching for your paintbrush. Further on, jazzy Juan-les-Pins straddles the peninsula of Cap d'Antibes

The Hill Towns. The hills that back the Côte d'Azur are often called the *arrière-pays,* or backcountry. This particular wedge of backcountry—behind the coast between Cannes and Antibes—has a character all its own: deeply, unself-consciously Provençal, with undulating fields of lavender watched over by villages perched on golden stone. Many of these villages look as if they do not belong to the last century—but they do, since they played the muse to some of modern art's most famous exemplars, notably Pablo Picasso and Henri Matisse. High in the hills overlooking Nice are the medieval walled villages of St-Paul-de-Vence, Vence, and Haut-de-Cagnes,

invaded by waves of artists in the 20th century. Today, you can hardly turn around without bumping into a Calder mobile, and top sights include the famous inn La Colombe d'Or, Matisse's sublime Chapelle du Rosaire, and the Fondation Maeght—probably the best museum this side of the Louvre.

Nice. Walking along the seaside *promenade des Anglais* is one of the iconic Riviera experiences. Add in top-notch museums, a charming old quarter, scads of ethnic restaurants, a world-class Carnaval, and the 30-acre promenade du Paillon in the city center and you'll see why Nice is one of France's most rewarding cities.

The Eastern French Riviera. With the mistral-proof Alps and Pre-Alps playing bodyguard against inland winds, this part of the Riviera is the most renowned and glamorous stretch of coastline in Europe. The 24-karat sun shines most brightly on the glamorous ports of Villefranche-sur-Mer, Beaulieu-Sur-Mer, and St-Jean-Cap-Ferrat. Crowded with sunseekers and billionaires, the Riviera still reveals quiet corners with heart-stopping views of sea, sun, and mountains—all within one memorable frame. If you want to kiss the sky, head up to the charming, mountaintop village of Èze. To the east lies Menton, an enchanting Italianate resort where winters are so mild that lemon trees bloom in January.

Planner

When to Go

Unless you enjoy jacked-up prices, traffic jams, and sardine-style beach crowds, avoid the coast like the plague in July and August. Many of the better restaurants simply shut down to escape the coconut-oil crew, and the Estérel—the rocky hillside that overlooks the

Mediterranean—is closed to hikers during this flash-fire season. Cannes books up early for the film festival in May, so aim for another month (April, June, September, or October). Between Cannes and Menton, the Côte d'Azur's gentle microclimate usually provides moderate winters; it's protected by the Estérel from the mistral wind that razors through places like St-Raphaël.

Although the area is famous for having more than 340 days of sunshine per year, locals will say winter (November–early March) is cold, rainy, and miserable; in recent years, official snow days—complete with surging sea waves and road closures—have even hit parts of the coast at the end of February. This is a sign that Nice's Carnaval is around the corner.

Planning Your Time

If you're settling into one town and making day trips, it's best to divide your time by visiting west and then east of Nice. Parallel roads along the corniches provide access into towns with different personalities, and the A8 main *autoroute* makes motoring from Monaco to St-Raphaël a breeze (just keep spare change handy, as there's a toll to use different parts of it—€4.60 between Cannes and Nice, for example). The coastal train is equally efficient when employees are not on strike. Tear yourself away from the coastal *plages* (beaches) at some point to visit the perched villages that this region is famed for, via Route Napoléon (N98), the D995, or the corniche roads, and plan on at least one overnight stop.

Getting Here and Around

The less budget-conscious can consider buzzing around by helicopter (there are heliports in Nice, Cannes-Mandelieu, St-Tropez, and some of the hill towns) or by speedboat (providing service to

all resort towns), but affordable transport along the Riviera translates to the train, the bus, or a rental car. Trains access major coastal areas, and most of the *gares* (train stations) are in town centers. Note that only a handful of hill towns have train stations, and St-Tropez is not on the rail line. The bus network between towns is fantastic, and a helpful website ⊕ *www.ceparou06.fr* allows you to calculate your route anywhere in the Alpes-Maritimes region. Renting a car is a good option, and the network of roads here is well marked and divided nicely into slow and very curvy (Bord de Mer Coast Road), faster and curvy (N98), and fast and almost straight (A8).

AIR TRAVEL

Nice, the main point of entry for the French Riviera, is home to France's second-largest airport—the Aéroport Nice-Côte d'Azur. Located 7 km (4 miles) southwest of the city center, it's linked to Nice by the No. 98 and No. 99 Lignes d'Azur buses (☎ 08–10–06–10–06 ⊕ *www.lignesdazur.com*), which loop to the bus and train station respectively (€6). Nice's Line 2 tramway (€1.50; tickets must be purchased before boarding) services both airport terminals and runs to the port of Nice. Nice Airport Xpress (☎ 08–00–06–01–06 ⊕ *www.rca.tm.fr*) also provides regular airport shuttle service to Nice, Cannes, Antibes, and Menton (€11–€22). Although Nice airport taxis now have flat-rate fares, it's still an expensive option (Nice center €32; Monaco €90; Cannes €80), especially compared to Uber.

CONTACT Aéroport Nice-Côte d'Azur (*NCE*) ☎ 08–20–42–33–33 (*€0.12 per min*) ⊕ *en. nice.aeroport.fr.*

BOAT TRAVEL

The Côte d'Azur is one of the most beautiful coastlines in the world, and there are several companies that allow you to savor its scenery from the water. April through October, shuttle boats operated by Les Bateaux Verts make the trip between

St-Tropez and Ste-Maxime in 15 minutes (€13.90 round-trip). Trans Côte d'Azur vessels, departing from Nice and Cannes, go to Corniche de l'Estérel (€50 round-trip), and St-Tropez (€67 round-trip); note that some routes are only available from May to early October.

CONTACTS Les Bateaux Verts ☎ *04–94–49–29–39* ⊕ *www.bateauxverts.com.* **Trans Côte d'Azur** ☎ *04–92–00–42–30* ⊕ *www.trans-cote-azur.com.*

BUS TRAVEL

Trains are quickest if you're traveling along the coast, but to reach backcountry spots not on the rail line—such as St-Paul-de-Vence and Vence—buses fill the gap. Lignes d'Azur runs to 24 communes in the Alpes-Maritimes for the bargain price of €1.50 (an exception is the Nice airport bus, which costs €6). The Envibus line, which originates in Antibes, covers that city before heading into the hills; going west to Cannes or east to Nice, for instance, you jump on Bus No. 200 (€1.50). From St-Tropez's station on Avenue du Général de Gaulle, VarLib buses travel to and from St-Raphaël, the town with the nearest railway station (1½ hrs, €3). In high season, traffic can lead to two-plus-hour bus rides, so if it may be wiser to take a Bateaux Verts shuttle boat between the two ports. Bus schedules are available at tourist offices and at the local *gare routière* (bus station).

CONTACTS Envibus ☎ *04–89–87–72–00* ⊕ *www.envibus.fr.* **Lignes d'Azur** ☎ *08–10–06–10–06* ⊕ *www.lignesdazur. com.* **VarLib** ☎ *09–70–83–03–80* ⊕ *www. varlib.fr.*

■ TIP→ **You must hail buses; don't presume the driver sees you. Drivers give change and hand you a ticket, which you must get stamped (composté) in the ticket validator and keep as proof of payment, as inspectors often board buses to check.**

CAR TRAVEL

The best way to explore the secondary sights in this region is by car. Driving allows you the freedom to zip along A8 between the coastal resorts of St-Raphaël and Menton, and lets you enjoy the views provided by the three corniches that trace the shoreline from Nice to the Italian border. The scenic N98 follows the coast more closely, connecting Mediterranean towns in between, but it can be slow. If you're coming from Paris, the main southbound artery is A6/A7, known as the Autoroute du Soleil; it passes through Provence and joins the eastbound A8 at Aix-en-Provence.

TRAIN TRAVEL

Nice is the major rail crossroads for trains arriving from Paris, other northern cities, and from Italy, too. To reach Nice from Paris (with stops along the coast), you can take the TGV, though it only maintains high speeds to Valence.

You can easily move along the coast between Cannes, Nice, and Ventimiglia on the slick double-decker Côte d'Azur line, a dramatic and tourist-pleasing branch of the SNCF, with more than 40 trains a day. This line is also called the Marseille–Vintimille (Ventimiglia, in Italy). Some of its main stops from Nice are Antibes (30 mins), Cannes (40 mins), and Menton (30 mins); others include Villefranche-sur-Mer, Beaulieu, and Èze-sur-Mer.

For the western parts of the French Riviera, head to St-Raphaël, where the rail route begins its scenic crawl along the coast. There's no rail access to St-Tropez; St-Raphaël is the nearest stop.

■ TIP→ **"Tarifs prem" are the cheapest train fares available from SNCF on a limited number of TGV tickets purchased 90 days before travel date, but there is no exchange. "Loisir" fares are flexible and offer peace of mind for the spontaneous traveler.**

CONTACTS SNCF ☎ *3635 (€0.40 per min)* ⊕ *www.sncf.com.* **TGV** ☎ *3635* ⊕ *en.oui. sncf.*

Restaurants

Even in tiny villages some haute-cuisine places can be as dressy as those in Monaco—if not more so—but restaurants on the Côte d'Azur are generally quite relaxed. At lunchtime, a decent T-shirt and shorts are fine in all but the fanciest spots; bathing suits, however, should be kept for the beach. Nighttime wear is casual, too—just be aware that for after-dinner drinks, many clubs and discos draw the line at running shoes. Food plays a crucial role in the south of France, and some of the best eateries aren't so easy to access; make sure to include taxi money in your budget to reach the more remote restaurants, or plan on renting a car. Try to visit in truffle, lavender, or olive season.

Hotels

It's up in the hills above the coast that you'll find the charm you expect from France, both in sophisticated hotels with gastronomic restaurants and in friendly mom-and-pop *auberges* (inns); the farther north you drive, the lower the prices. Of course, certain areas of the Riviera book up faster than others, but all hit overload from June to September. It's essential to reserve lodgings in advance: up to half a year for the summer season is not unheard of—indeed, it's much appreciated. Festivals and good weather will also affect your chances. If you arrive without a reservation, try Airbnb or the tourist information centers, which can usually be of help. *Restaurant and hotel reviews have been shortened. For full information, visit Fodors.com.*

What It Costs in Euros

	$	$$	$$$	$$$$
RESTAURANTS				
	under €18	€18–€24	€25–€32	over €32
HOTELS				
	under €125	€125–€225	€226–€350	over €350

Visitor Information

For information on travel around St-Tropez, contact the Tourisme du Var. For Marseille to Cannes over to Menton, contact the Comité Regional du Tourisme de Provence-Alpes-Côte d'Azur.

CONTACTS Comité Regional du Tourisme de Provence-Alpes-Côte d'Azur ☎ *04–91–56–47–00* ⊕ *www.tourismepaca.fr/en.* **Tourisme du Var (L'Agence de Développement Touristique)** ✉ ☎ *04–94–18–59–60* ⊕ *www.visitvar.fr.*

St-Tropez

73 km (45 miles) southwest of Cannes, 106 km (66 miles) southwest of Nice.

At first glance, it really doesn't look all that impressive. There's a pretty port with cafés charging €5 for a cup of coffee and a photogenic old town in sugar-almond hues, but there are many prettier in the hills nearby. There are sandy beaches, rare enough on the Riviera, and old-fashioned squares with plane trees and pétanque players, but these are a dime a dozen throughout Provence. So what made St-Tropez an internationally known locale? Two words: Brigitte Bardot. When this *pulpeuse* (voluptuous) actress showed up in St-Tropez on the arm of Roger Vadim in 1956 to film *And God Created Woman*, the heads of the world snapped around. Neither the gentle descriptions of writer Guy de Maupassant (1850–93), nor the watercolor tones of Impressionist Paul Signac (1863–1935), nor the stream of painters who followed (including Matisse and Bonnard) could focus the world's attention on this seaside hamlet as did this one sensual woman in a scarf, Ray-Bans, and capris.

Anything associated with the distant past seems almost absurd in St-Tropez. Still, the place has a history that predates the invention of the string bikini, and people have been finding reasons to come here since AD 68, when a Roman soldier from Pisa named Torpes was beheaded for professing his Christian faith in front of Emperor Nero, transforming this spot into a place of pilgrimage. Along medieval streets lined with walled gardens and little squares set with dripping fountains, you can discover historic delights like the Chapelle de la Misericorde, topped by its wrought-iron campanile, and Rue Allard, lined with picturesque houses such as the Maison du Maure.

GETTING HERE AND AROUND
Keep in mind that getting here can be hellish. Out on a limb, scorned by any train route, you can only get to St-Trop by car, bus, or boat (from nearby ports like St-Raphaël). Driving can test anyone's mettle, thanks to the crowds, the narrow roads, and the parking situation: you have the main Parking du Port lot (opposite the bus station on Avenue du Général de Gaulle, with shuttle bus into town mid-March through October) or the Parc des Lices (beneath the Place des Lices) in the center of town. If you decide to rent a car, take the N98 coast road, the longest route but also the prettiest, with great picnic stops along the way.

A train–bus connection can be made if you're leaving from Nice center: take the train (direction St-Raphaël) from the Gare SNCF Nice Centre-Ville station (€12.80 one way); from St-Raphaël, there's the daily Bus No. 7601 service with VarLib (€3 one way). Make sure you get to St-Raphaël's bus station early or you'll be elbowed out of a seat by aggressive

bronzed ladies and forced to stand the whole way. Travel time from St-Raphaël to St-Tropez is 1½ hours. The other option is to take a 2½-hour boat from the Nice harbor with Trans Côte d'Azur, which has daily trips June through September and costs €67 round-trip (from Cannes, it's only 75 minutes and €52 round-trip).

VISITOR INFORMATION St-Tropez Tourist Office ⊠ *Quai Jean Jaurès, St-Tropez* ☎ *04–94–97–45–21* ⊕ *www.sainttropez-tourisme.com.*

 Sights

Citadelle
MILITARY SITE | Head up Rue de la Citadelle to these 16th-century ramparts, which stand in a lovely hilltop park offering a fantastic view of the town and the sea. Amid today's bikini-clad sun worshippers it's hard to imagine St-Tropez as a military outpost, but inside the Citadelle's dungeon the modern **Musée de l'Histoire Maritime Tropézienne** (St-Tropez Maritime Museum) resides a stirring homage to those who served the nation. ⊠ *Rue de la Citadelle, St-Tropez* ☎ *04–94–97–59–43* 🖆 *€3, includes museum entry.*

La Maison des Papillons
MUSEUM | FAMILY | A block west of Rue Clémenceau, in a pretty house at the end of a typically Tropezien lane, the butterfly museum is a delight for children (and their parents). Sweetly aflutter, the 35,000 specimens can be toured by appointment with the collector, Dany Lartigue. ⊠ *17 rue Étienne Berny, St-Tropez* ☎ *04–94–97–63–45* 🖆 *€2* ⊙ *Closed Feb.–Apr. and Thurs. and Fri. May, June, and Sept.–Nov.*

Musée de l'Annonciade (*Annunciation Museum*)
MUSEUM | The legacy of the artists who loved St-Tropez—including Signac, Matisse, Braque, Dufy, Vuillard, and Rouault—has been carefully preserved in this extraordinary museum, housed in a 14th-century chapel just inland from

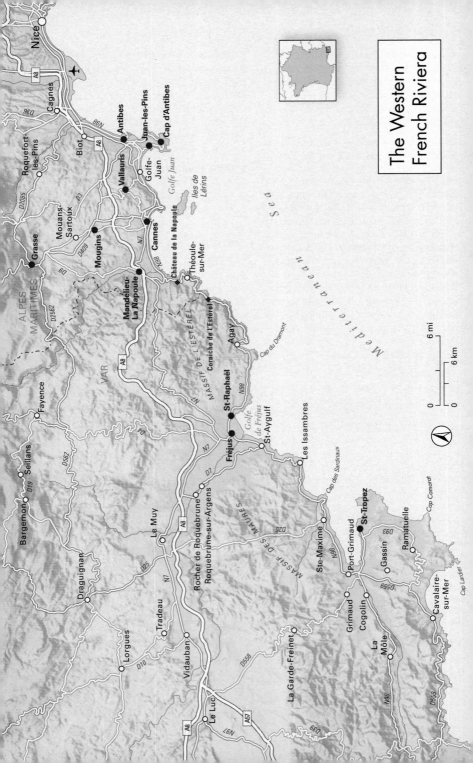

The Western
French Riviera

the southwest corner of the Vieux Port. Cutting-edge temporary exhibitions featuring local talent and up-and-coming international artists keep visitors on their toes, while works by established artists from Impressionism to Expressionism line the walls. ⊠ *2 pl. Georges Grammont, St-Tropez* ☎ *04–94–17–84–10* 🖾 *€6* 🕑 *Closed Nov. and Mon.*

Place des Lices

PLAZA | Enjoy a time-out in the social center of the Old Town, where a symmetrical forest of plane trees provides shade to rows of cafés and restaurants, skateboarders, children, and grandfatherly pétanque players. Also called Place Carnot, the square becomes a moveable feast—for both eyes and palate—on market days (Tuesday and Saturday), while at night, a café seat is as coveted as a quayside seat during the day. Just as Deborah Kerr and David Niven once did in *Bonjour Tristesse,* watch the boules players under the glow of hundreds of electric bulbs. Heading back to the Vieux Port area, take in the boutiques lining Rues Sibilli, Clemenceau, and Gambetta to help accessorize your evening look— you never know when that photographer from *Elle* will be snapping away at the *trendoisie.* ⊠ *Av. Foch and Bd. Vasserot, St-Tropez.*

Quartier de la Ponche

HISTORIC SITE | Walk along Quai Suffern where the statue of the Bailli de Suffren, an 18th-century customs official, stands guard, and continue past the quayside streets lined with famous cafés to the Môle Jean Réveille, the harbor wall, where, if the wind isn't too strong, you can walk out for a good view of Ste-Maxime across the sparkling bay, the hills of Estérel, and, on a clear day, the distant Alps. Retrace your steps along the digue to the 15th-century **Tour du Portalet** and head onward to the old fishermen's quarter, the Quartier de la Ponche, just east of Quai Jean Jaurès. Here you can find the **Port des Pécheurs** (Fishermen's

Port), on whose beach Bardot did a star turn in *And God Created Woman.* Twisting, narrow streets, designed to break the impact of the mistral, open to tiny squares with fountains. Complete with gulf-side harbor, St-Tropez's Old Town maze of backstreets and old ramparts is daubed in shades of gold, pink, ocher, and sky-blue. Trellised jasmine and wrought-iron birdcages hang from the shuttered windows, and many of the tiny streets dead-end at the sea. The main drag here, Rue de la Ponche, leads into Place l'Hôtel de Ville, landmarked by a *mairie* (town hall) marked out in typical Tropezienne hues of pink and green. Head up Rue Commandant Guichard to the Baroque **Église de St-Tropez** to pay your respects to the bust and barque of St-Torpes, every day but May 17, when they are carried aloft in the Bravade parade honoring the town's namesake saint. ⊠ *St-Tropez.*

Vieux Port

NEIGHBORHOOD | Bordered by Quai de l'Épi, Quai Bouchard, Quai Peri, Quai Suffren, and Quai Jean Jaurès, Vieux Port is a place for strolling and looking over the shoulders of artists painting their versions of the view on easels set up along the water's edge. Meanwhile, folding director's chairs at the famous port-side cafés Le Gorille (named for its late, exceptionally hirsute manager), Café de Paris, and Sénéquier—all well placed for observing the cast of St-Tropez's living theater play out their colorful roles. ⊠ *St-Tropez.*

Beaches

Nikki Beach

BEACH—SIGHT | Off the Route des Plages is this most notorious of all the beaches famous for A-list debauches and a regular clientele of movie megastars and wannabes. But Nikki Beach isn't actually on the beach, but rather steps from the beach with a pool and restaurant. If you want to mingle with

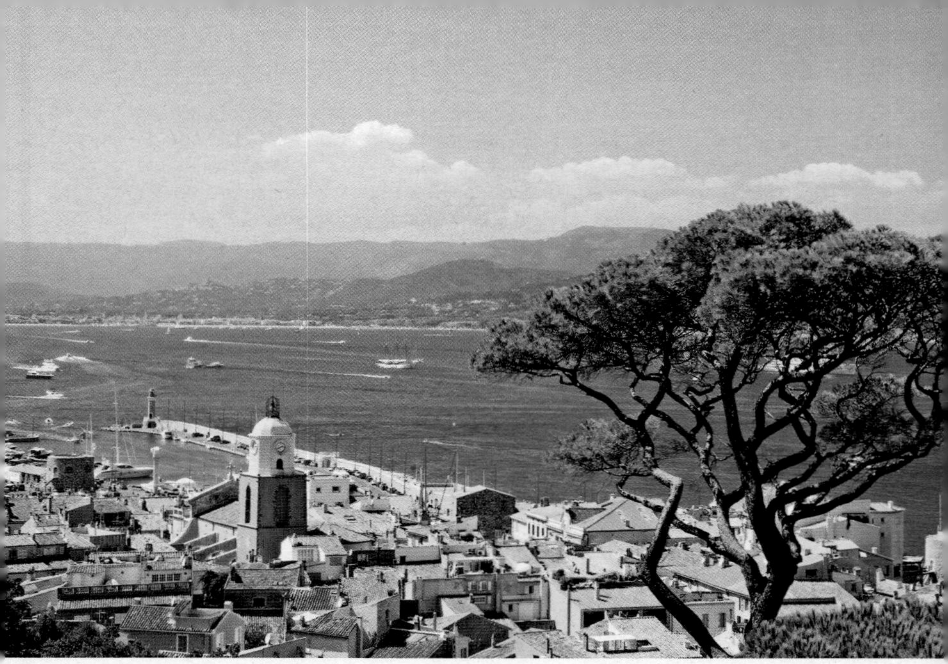

St-Tropez is absolutely gorgeous, but be aware that this is a playground for the rich, with prices to match.

the famous, rent an Opium bed (€100 for maximum three people), but you may want to avoid the poolside where champagne showers spare no one. There is also a VIP Bed Ponton by the Sea for up to four people; its typically €120, but this is St-Tropez so the price may vary depending on the DJ. **Amenities:** food and drink; parking (fee and no fee); showers; toilets. **Best for:** partiers. ✉ *Rte. de l'Épi, Ramatuelle* ☎ *04–94–79–82–04* 🌐 *saint-tropez.nikkibeach.com* 🕒 *Closed mid-Sept.–mid-Apr.*

Plage des Graniers

BEACH—SIGHT | The closest beach to the town of St-Tropez, at the southern base of the Citadelle and past the cemetery, Graniers beach is easily accessible by foot (it's part of the sentier du littoral) and the most family-friendly. At the east end, you can rent loungers (€22 plus €7 for an umbrella) from the restaurant. There are no toilets or showers. **Amenities:** parking (no fee). **Best for:** swimming. ✉ *Ch. des Graniers, St-Tropez.*

Plage des Salins

BEACH—SIGHT | Situated between Cap des Salins and Point du Capon, this 600-meter public white sand beach is the gateway to a stretch of Pampelonne beach, although it's more exposed to the wind and the sea can quickly become rough. It's lined by huge umbrella pine trees, and you can rent loungers from the beach's private section. To the left by coastal path is a quieter cove. **Amenities:** parking (no fee); showers; toilets. **Best for:** swimming. ✉ *Rte. des Salins, St-Tropez.*

🍴 Restaurants

Basilic Burger

$ | **FRENCH** | **FAMILY** | Not every lunch in St-Tropez requires a Platinum AmEx for payment. Basilic Burger serves up tasty gourmet burgers, bagels, and copious salads at more than affordable prices. Just €15 gets you a meal and dessert; the kids' menu is only €10. **Known for:** reasonable prices; vegan burgers; late hours (until 10 pm) in July and August. [$] *Average main: €15* ✉ *Pl. des Remparts,*

St-Tropez ☎ 04–94–97–29–09 ⊗ Closed Nov.–Mar. ⊟ No credit cards.

Dior des Lices

$$$ | FRENCH | What could be more fashionable than tucking into exquisite cuisine by three–Michelin star chef Arnaud Donckele in an enchanting sheltered garden designed by Peter Wirtz at the House of Dior? Dior des Lices elegantly serves a full menu of breakfast, lunch, dinner, and snacks, with a range of reasonable prices compared to the Vague d'Or, chef Donckele's full-time gig across town. **Known for:** huge dessert menu, including famed D'Choux; comparatively reasonable prices; garden vibe. Ⓢ Average main: €26 ⊠ 13 rue François Sibilli, St-Tropez ☎ 04–98–12–67–65 ⊗ Closed mid-Oct.–May.

Le Sporting

$$ | BRASSERIE | FAMILY | You'll have to brace yourself for lively conversations at nearby tables and children not behaving as French children are reputed to; however, pizza, pasta, burgers, and lamb chops are served in generous portions and at reasonable prices, every day, all year long. The fixtures are nothing fancy—red awning, metal chairs, and typical café tables—but at least there's a place in St-Tropez that feels a little home. **Known for:** noisy crowds; typical American fare; low-key vibe. Ⓢ Average main: €24 ⊠ 42 pl. des Lices, St-Tropez ☎ 04–94–97–00–65.

Hotels

Hôtel B. Lodge

$$ | HOTEL | All of the small, delicately contemporary rooms (now all equipped with air-conditioning) of this attractively priced, four-story charmer overlook the Citadelle's green park, some from tiny balconies. **Pros:** very good value for location; breakfast and Wi-Fi included; excellent service. **Cons:** four-night minimum stay in July and August; only two available parking spots; small rooms. Ⓢ Rooms

from: €200 ⊠ 12 rue de l'Aïoli, St-Tropez ☎ 04–94–97–06–57 ⊕ www.hotel-b-lodge.com ⊗ Closed Jan. and early Feb. ⇝ 13 rooms ⦿| Free Breakfast.

⭐ Hôtel de Paris Saint-Tropez

$$$$ | HOTEL | The first thing you'll notice when you walk into the lobby of this five-star, service-friendly urban hotel, spread over an entire block near the port, is space—a novelty for this tiny fishing port—and second you'll see a rooftop pool suspended 15 meters in the air, with its glass floor peering down at you. **Pros:** perfectly located; unique rooftop bar and pool with fab 360-degree views; excellent service. **Cons:** some rooms are small; few poolside loungers; breakfast €35 per person. Ⓢ Rooms from: €450 ⊠ 1 Traverse de la Gendarmerie, St-Tropez ☎ 04–83–09–60–00 ⊕ www.hoteldeparis-sainttropez.com ⊗ Closed Nov.–Feb. ⇝ 90 rooms ⦿| No meals.

Le Byblos

$$$$ | HOTEL | Forget five stars: this toy Mediterranean village, grouped around courtyards landscaped with palms, olive trees, and lavender has "Palace" classification and access to the exclusive Byblos Beach Ramatuellea. **Pros:** exquisite service; best buffet breakfast includes 3-, 4- or 5-minute hard boiled egg; beach access with seaside restaurant. **Cons:** minimum four-night stay in July and August; some rooms can be noisy in summer; can be hard to get beach loungers. Ⓢ Rooms from: €955 ⊠ Av. Paul-Signac, St-Tropez ☎ 04–94–56–68–00 ⊕ www.byblos.com ⊗ Closed late Oct.–mid-Apr. ⇝ 90 rooms ⦿| No meals.

⭐ Lou Cagnard

$$ | HOTEL | Set inside a lovely garden courtyard, this pretty little villa hotel is owned by an enthusiastic young couple, who have fixed it up room by room and provided amenities including satellite TV and free Wi-Fi. **Pros:** fantastic value for your money (try Room 17); walking distance to everything; free parking. **Cons:** a few of the older rooms share a

bathroom, but at much reduced rates; seven-night minimum June–September; strict cancellation policy. $ *Rooms from: €160* ✉ *18 av. Paul-Roussel, St-Tropez* ☎ *04–94–97–04–24* ⊕ *www.hotel-loucagnard.com* ⊙ *Closed Nov.–Mar.* ⇩ *18 rooms* ⦿ *No meals.*

Nightlife

Les Caves du Roy

DANCE CLUBS | Costing the devil and often jammed to the scuppers, this disco in the Byblos Hotel is *the* place to see and be seen. When you hear the theme from *Star Wars,* take comfort while you sip your €26 glass of water that someone other than yourself has just spent €25,000 on a Methuselah of champagne. There's a horrific door policy during high season—don't worry, it's really not you. It's open every night in July and August, and weekends only the rest of the year. ✉ *Av. Paul-Signac, St-Tropez* ⊕ *www. lescavesduroy.com.*

VIP Room

DANCE CLUBS | So notorious is the VIP Room for drawing flashy, gilded youths with deep pockets that it spawned a VIP Room Cannes expressly for those needing a dose during the film festival before this location opens nightly from mid-June to mid-September. ✉ *Residence du Nouveau Port, St-Tropez.*

Performing Arts

Les Nuits du Château de la Moutte

CONCERTS | Every August, exceptional classical music concerts are given in the formidable gardens of the Château de la Moutte. You can book tickets (€60) online or by phone. ✉ *Château de la Moutte, St-Tropez* ☎ *04–94–96–96–94 for info* ⊕ *lesnuitsduchateaudelamoutte.com.*

 Shopping

There is something about St-Tropez that makes shopping simply irresistible— unlike Cannes, you'll be welcomed into the stores no matter what you look like or what you're wearing. Where else will you find Vilebrequin 24-carat-gold-embroidered Golden Turtle swim trunks from €6,200? **Rue Sibilli,** behind Quai Suffren, is lined with all kinds of trendy boutiques, many carrying those all-important sunglasses.

La Vieille Mer

ANTIQUES/COLLECTIBLES | You probably will do more looking than buying here (unless you have a very large suitcase) but the Old Sea's owner, Walter Wolkowicz, will put you in a time machine exploring navigational tools, lamps, and antique accoutrements of nautical yesteryear at his 100% marine shop. It's open April–October, daily 10–1 and 5–midnight. ✉ *11 pl. de l'Ormeau, St-Tropez* ☎ *06–74–07–91–46* ⊕ *www.lavieillemer.fr.*

Le Dépot

CLOTHING | If you prefer traditional luxe, Le Dépot stocks castoffs by Chanel, Prada, Hermès, Vuitton, Gucci, and so forth. ✉ *6 bd. Louis-Blanc, St-Tropez* ☎ *04–94–97–80–10* ⊕ *www.ledepot-saint-tropez.com.*

Place des Lices

OUTDOOR/FLEA/GREEN MARKETS | The aorta of the village, connecting with Rue Gambetta and Rue Allard, this congregational square overflows with produce and regional foods, as well as clothing and *brocantes* (secondhand items), every Tuesday and Saturday morning. The last weekend in October is the "Grande Braderie," a four-day giant sidewalk sale across the entire town. ✉ *St-Tropez.*

Rondini

SHOES/LUGGAGE/LEATHER GOODS | You wear those strappy flip-flops back home, but are they the real *sandales Tropeziennes*? Here's your chance to pick up the genuine, handmade article at Rondini,

St-Tropez's original cobbler, launched in 1927. You can also have two or more pairs delivered within 10 days for less than €15. ⊠ *18–18 bis rue Clemenceau, St-Tropez* ☎ *04–94–97–19–55* ⊕ *www. rondini.fr.*

Fréjus

37 km (23 miles) northeast of St-Tropez.

Turn your back on modern times—the gargantuan, pink, holiday high-rises that crowd the Fréjus-St-Raphaël waterfront—and head uphill to Fréjus-Centre, with its maze of narrow streets lined with butcher shops, patisseries, and neighborhood stores barely touched by the cult of the lavender sachet. Unspoiled as it is, you'll still find yourself in a hot spot offering free Wi-Fi. In July and August, the crowds roll in for the sandy beaches by day, and the seaside markets by night (daily 8 pm–2 am) as well as for fireworks (Les nuits de Port-Fréjus) on Monday at 10:30 pm. Stick around in September for the Giant Omelette festival.

But don't be fooled: Fréjus (pronounced "fray- *zhooss*") has the honor of having some of the most important historic monuments on the coast. Founded in 49 BC by Julius Caesar himself and named Forum Julii, this quiet town was once a thriving Roman shipbuilding port with 40,000 citizens. In its heyday, Roman Fréjus had a theater, baths, and an enormous aqueduct that brought water all the way from Mons in the mountains, 45 km (28 miles) north of town. Today you can see the remains: a series of detached arches that follow the main Avenue du Quinzième Corps (leading up to the Old Town). ■TIP→ **The Fréjus Pass (€4.60) is valid for seven days and gives you access to various historical landmarks and museums in the city, including those listed here, and can be purchased directly on-site.**

The direct Varlib 3003 bus to Fréjus from the Nice–Côte d'Azur airport takes about an hour and costs €20. By car, you are only 35 minutes from the airport on the A8 highway (Exit 38, Fréjus/St-Raphaël). You can follow the DN7 for a more scenic drive, but it takes a lot more time, particularly with summer traffic. Train travelers will pay €12.40 for the 60-minute journey from the Nice St-Augustin station, a five-minute walk from the airport.

VISITOR INFORMATION Fréjus Tourist Office ⊠ *Le Florus II, 249 rue Jean-Jaurès, Fréjus* ☎ *04–94–51–83–83* ⊕ *www.frejus. fr.*

 Sights

Arènes

ARCHAEOLOGICAL SITE | The Arènes (often called the Amphithéâtre) is still used for concerts and bullfights, and can still seat up to 5,000. Back down on the coast, a big French naval base occupies the spot where ancient Roman galleys once set out to defeat Cleopatra and Mark Antony at the Battle of Actium. ⊠ *Rue Henri Vadon, Fréjus* ☎ *04–94–51–34–31* 🎟 *€2* 🕑 *Closed Mon. year-round and Sun. Oct.–Mar.*

Chapelle Cocteau (*La Chapelle Notre-Dame de Jérusalem*)

RELIGIOUS SITE | This eccentric chapel was the last designed by Jean Cocteau as part of an artists' colony that never happened. It's an octagon built around a glass atrium and is embellished with stained glass, frescoes depicting the mythology of the first Crusades, and a tongue-in-cheek painting of the apostles above the front door that boasts the famous faces of Coco Chanel, Jean Marais, and poet Max Jacob. ⊠ *Av. Nicolaï, La Tour de la Mare, Fréjus* ✛ *5 km (3 miles) north of Fréjus on the RN7* ☎ *04–94–53–27–06* 🎟 *€2* 🕑 *Closed Mon. year-round and Sun. Oct.–Mar.*

Groupe Épiscopal

RELIGIOUS SITE | Fréjus is graced with one of the most impressive religious monuments in Provence: the Groupe Épiscopal is made up of an early Gothic **cathedral,** a 5th-century Roman-style **baptistery,** and an early Gothic **cloister,** its gallery painted in sepia and earth tones with a phantasmagoric assortment of animals and biblical characters. Off the entrance and gift shop is a small museum of finds from Roman Fréjus, including a complete mosaic and a sculpture of a two-headed Hermès. ⊠ *48 rue de Fleury, Fréjus* ☎ *04–94–51–26–30* ✉ *Cathedral free; cloister, museum, and baptistery €6* ⊗ *Closed Mon. year-round and Sun. Oct.–May.*

Plage de la République

BEACHES | This large, public sand beach, just east of the port and capitainerie is close to a restaurant where you can rent a lounger. Get here early in the summer to claim your towel space close to the sea; you'll be able to spot the tourists from the locals by the bottoms-only beach wear. **Amenities:** lifeguards; parking (fee); showers; toilets. **Best for:** sunrise; swimming. ⊠ *Bd. Alger, Fréjus.*

Théâtre Romain

ARCHAEOLOGICAL SITE | Northeast of Old Town and near the Porte de Rome is the Roman theater (circa 1st century); its remaining rows of arches are mostly intact and much of its stage, including the orchestra and substructures, are still visible at its center. Today the site is known as the Philippe Léotard Theatre and hosts Les Nuits Auréliennes every July. ⊠ *Av. du Théâtre Romain, Fréjus* ✉ *Free* ⊗ *Closed Mon. year-round and Sun. Oct.–May.*

St-Raphaël

38 km (24 miles) northeast of St-Tropez.

Right next door to Fréjus, with almost no division between, spreads St-Raphaël, a sprawling resort city with a busy downtown anchored by a casino and a Vieille Ville that may not the most picturesque, although you will stumble across Palladian and Belle Époque villas circa 18th and 19th centuries (the tourist office provides a map). It's also a major sailing center, has five golf courses nearby, and draws the weary and indulgent to its seawater-based thalassotherapy. Along with Fréjus, it serves as a rail crossroads, the two being the closest stops to St-Tropez. The port has a rich history: Napoléon landed at St-Raphaël on his triumphant return from Egypt in 1799; it was also from here in 1814 that he cast off in disgrace for Elba. And it was here, too, that the Allied forces landed in their August 1944 offensive against the Germans, known as the Champagne Campaign.

GETTING HERE AND AROUND
Take the Nice airport bus from either terminal; it's €20 for the 75-minute journey. If you take a taxi, it'll be between €145–€192. The TGV Paris–St-Raphaël (4 hrs 45 mins, €118) runs throughout the year and there are numerous trains arriving from Nice and Cannes. St-Raphaël is the western terminus of the TER line that runs along the Riviera. To get to towns farther west, you have to take a bus from just behind the train station. If you want a day trip to St-Tropez, April–October, there's a one-hour ferry ride (€15 one way) or a taxi for at least €100. From St-Raphaël's bus station on Avenue Victor-Hugo, next to the train station, Bus No. 7601 links up with St-Tropez (via Grimaud and Ste-Maxime; 1½ hrs, €3), some towns in the Haut Var, and selected stops along the coastal Corniche de l'Estérel. There are daily buses to Fréjus (€3), or you can take a taxi for about €20. Popular ferries

The marina in the resort city of St-Raphaël is dominated by a casino and the Notre-Dame de la Victoire Basilica.

leave from St-Raphaël's Vieux Port for St-Tropez, the Îles-de-Léerins, and the Calanques de l'Estérel.

VISITOR INFORMATION St-Raphaël Tourist Office ⊠ *99 quai Albert 1er, St-Raphaël* ☎ *04–94–19–52–52* ⊕ *www.saint-rapha-el.com.*

 ## Sights

Musée Archéologique Marin (*Marine Archaeology Museum*)
MUSEUM | On the same quiet square as St-Pierre, shaded by an old olive tree, this intimate museum offers a quirky diversion. Its few rooms contain a concise and fascinating collection of ancient amphorae gleaned from the shoals offshore, where centuries' worth of shipwrecks have accumulated; by studying this chronological progression of jars and the accompanying sketches, you can visualize the coast as it was in its heyday as a Greek and Roman shipping center. The science of exploring these shipwrecks was relatively new when

French divers began probing the depths; the underwater Leicas from the 1930s and the early scuba gear from the '50s on display are as fascinating as the spoils they helped to unearth. Upstairs, a few objects—jewelry, spearheads, pottery shards, and skulls—illustrate the Neolithic and Paleolithic eras and remind you of the dense population of Celto-Ligurians who claimed this region long before the Greeks and Phoenicians. A few of their dolmens and menhirs are still visible on the Estérel. ■TIP→ **You can use QR codes throughout the museum as a guide; iPads and iPods can be borrowed from reception.** ⊠ *Rue des Templiers, St-Raphaël* ☎ *04–94–19–25–75* ⊕ *www.musee-saintraphael.com* 🎟 *Free* ⊙ *Closed Sun. and Mon.*

 ## Restaurants

Le Bouchon Provençal
$$$ | FRENCH | *Trés sympa* in decor and ambience, this Lyonnaise-influenced restaurant is a three-minute walk from

the main strip to St-Raphaël's Vieille Ville. It's famous for its traditional *terroir* cuisine; think cod crumble in a creamy chorizo sauce, lobster-tail stew, and their specialties: five-fish bouillabaisse on Wednesday and the *aioli façon Pastorel,* a famous mayonnaise dip, on Friday. **Known for:** excellent-value dinner menu; traditional Provençal food with a dash of Lyon; terrace dining in nice weather. [$] *Average main: €26* ✉ *45 rue de la République, St-Raphaël* ☎ *04–94–53–89–18* ⏲ *Closed Sun., Mon., and 3 wks in Jan.*

Les Voiles Saint-Raphael

$$$ | **FRENCH** | Welcome to Les Voiles, a beach restaurant just east of the city center, where a three-course prix-fixe meal will set you back only €32. Diners can also order dishes like grilled entrecôte or white cod and risotto with coconut milk à la carte. **Known for:** beautiful views; express lunch menu only €16; Michelin Bib Gourmand for best table at low prices. [$] *Average main: €28* ✉ *Port Santa Lucia, St-Raphaël* ☎ *04–94–40–39–15* ⏲ *Closed 3 wks in Jan.* 💳 *No credit cards.*

Hotels

Hôtel Thimothée

$ | **B&B/INN** | This attractive 19th-century villa offers comfortable, well-priced rooms (the two on the top floor have poster-perfect sea views, worth the extra €30) as well as a lovely garden, where grand palms and pines shade the walk leading to a pretty little swimming pool, making it all seem more than a two-star establishment. **Pros:** familial atmosphere and gentle hospitality; clean rooms and modern bathrooms; free parking and Wi-Fi. **Cons:** beach and waterfront cafés are a 20-minute walk away; standard rooms are on the small side; breakfast is extra. [$] *Rooms from: €90* ✉ *375 bd. Christian-Lafon, St-Raphaël* ☎ *04–94–40–49–49* 🌐 *www.hotel-thimothee.com* 💳 *No credit cards* 🛏 *12 rooms* 🍴 *No meals.*

Mandelieu–La Napoule

32 km (20 miles) northeast of St-Raphaël.

La Napoule is a small, old-fashioned port village; Mandelieu the big-fish resort town that devoured it. You can visit Mandelieu for a golf-and-sailing retreat—the town is replete with sporting facilities and hosts a bevy of events, including sailing regattas, windsurfing contests, and golf championships (there are two major golf courses in Mandelieu right in the center of town, by the sea). A yacht-crammed harbor sits under the shadow of some high-rise resort hotels. La Napoule, on the other hand, offers the requisite quaintness, ideal for a port-side stroll, casual meal, beach siesta, or visit to its peculiar castle. Unless you're here for the sun and surf, however, these twinned towns mostly serve as a home base for outings to Cannes, Antibes, and the Estérel. In fact, the easternmost beach in Mandelieu dovetails with the first beach of its glamorous neighbor, Cannes.

GETTING HERE AND AROUND

From Terminal 1 or 2 at Nice airport, take the A8 to Exit 40 (about 30 minutes) or the 35-minute airport bus (direction St-Raphaël, €20). The closest train station is in Cannes, and you can either take a taxi (about €30 to the city center during the day) or catch Bus No. 22 from Cannes train station, departing frequently throughout the day, for €1.50. It sets you down at "Plage de la Raguette", just 250 meters west of the château.

VISITOR INFORMATION Mandelieu–La Napoule Tourist Office ✉ *806 av. de Cannes, Mandelieu-la-Napoule* ☎ *04–93–93–64–64* 🌐 *www.ot-mandelieu.fr.*

Sights

Château de la Napoule

CASTLE/PALACE | Looming over the sea at Pointe des Pendus (Hanged Man's Point), the Château de la Napoule is a spectacularly bizarre hybrid of Romanesque, Gothic, Moroccan, and Hollywood cooked up by the eccentric American sculptor Henry Clews (1876–1937). Working with his architect wife, Clews transformed the 14th-century bastion into something that suited his personal expectations and then filled the place with his own fantastical sculptures. The couple reside in their tombs in the tower crypt, its windows left slightly ajar to permit their souls to escape and allow them to "return at eventide as sprites and dance upon the windowsill." Today the château's foundation hosts visiting writers and artists, who set to work surrounded by Clews's gargoyle-ish sculptures. ✉ *Av. Henry Clews, Mandelieu-la-Napoule* ☎ *04–93–49–95–05* 🌐 *www.chateau-lanapoule.com* 🎫 *From €4.*

Restaurants

Le Boucanier

$$$ | **SEAFOOD** | Several years ago, former French pro soccer player Wilfried Gohel teamed up with Eric Chaumier, president of the regional retailers union, and took over this popular waterfront favorite. They could have just banked on the wraparound views of the marina and château to bring in the dinner crowds, but instead they refined the menu to include grilled fillet of bass with smoked salt petals or salmon marinated with pure malt whisky and sautéed with matcha tea velouté sauce. **Known for:** seafood galore; incredible views; vegan and pasta options. [$] *Average main: €26* ✉ *Port de La Napoule, 273 av. Henry Clews, Mandelieu-la-Napoule* ☎ *04–93–49–80–51* 🌐 *www.boucanier.fr* 🕒 *Closed Mon. Oct–Mar. No dinner Sun.*

L'Oasis

$$$$ | **MODERN FRENCH** | A culinary landmark for more than 60 years, executive chef Alain Montigny, Meilleur Ouvrier de France, has incorporated Art Deco decor that's both more intimate and more cultural, and that ties in to his high-end cuisine (so high end in fact that the set-lunch menu starts at €69 and comes with pre-dessert). The sea and earth options may not appeal to everyone (think pigeon, sweetbread, and red mullet) but the starters will win over the crowds; the scrambled eggs and caviar and oasis truffle are a delight. **Known for:** legendary eatery; extraordinary service; Mediterranean-inspired dishes. [$] *Average main: €80* ✉ *6 rue Jean Honoré Carle, Mandelieu-la-Napoule* ☎ *04–93–49–95–52* 🌐 *www.oasisetoile-mandelieu.fr* 🕒 *Closed Sun.–Tues.*

Activities

Centre Nautique Municipal

BOATING | Small sailboats and windsurfers can be rented from Centre Nautique Municipal, next to the restaurant La Plage. It's open daily year-round. ✉ *Av. du Général de Gaulle, Mandelieu-la-Napoule* ☎ *04–92–97–07–70* 🌐 *www.mandelieu.fr.*

Golf Club de Cannes-Mandelieu

GOLF | Grand Duke Michael of Russia founded the Riviera's first golf course in 1891, known familiarly as the Old Course, and it's been played by all of Europe's royals. Officially it's the International Golf Club Cannes-Mandelieu and has two courses, which are the most visually stunning courses in the south of France. The 18-hole course is shaded by old pine trees and features a ferry across the Slagne River from Hole 2 to 3 and again from Hole 12 to 13. ✉ *Rte. du Golf, Mandelieu-la-Napoule* ☎ *04–92–97–32–00* 🌐 *www.golfoldcourse.com* 🎫 *18-hole course: €90 (€65 after 2 pm, €55 after 4 pm). 9-hole course: €50* 🏌 *18 holes, 6287 yards, par 71; 9 holes, 2316 yards, par 33.*

Cannes

73 km (45 miles) northeast of St-Tropez, 33 km (20 miles) southwest of Nice.

Cannes is pampered with the luxurious year-round climate that has made it one of the most popular resorts in Europe. Settled first by the Ligurians and then dubbed Cannoïs by the Romans (after the cane that waved in its marshes), Cannes was an important sentinel site for the monks who established themselves on Île St-Honorat in the Middle Ages. Its bay served as nothing more than a fishing port until 1834, when an English aristocrat, Lord Brougham, fell in love with the site during an emergency stopover with a sick daughter. He had a home built here and returned every winter for a sun cure—a ritual quickly picked up by his peers. Between the popularity of Le Train Blue transporting wealthy passengers from Calais, and the introduction in 1936 of France's first paid holidays, Cannes became the destination, a tasteful and expensive breeding ground for the upper upscale.

Cannes has been further glamorized by the ongoing success of its annual film festival, as famous as—and, in the trade, more respected than—Hollywood's Academy Awards. About the closest many of us will get to feeling like a film star is a stroll here along La Croisette, the iconic promenade that gracefully curves the wave-washed sand coastline, peppered with chic restaurants and prestigious private beaches. This is precisely the sort of place for which the French invented the verb *flâner* (to dawdle, saunter): strewn with palm trees and poseurs, its fancy boutiques and status-symbol grand hotels—including the Carlton, the legendary backdrop to Grace Kelly in *To Catch a Thief*—all vying for the custom of the Louis Vuitton set. And the city takes their role as a tourist destination seriously, especially when it comes to

common incivilities: €180 fine for flicking a cigarette butt; €375 for honking too much; and €450 for not cleaning up dog poop.

GETTING HERE AND AROUND

Cannes has one central train station, the completely modernized Gare SNCF. All major trains pass through here—check out the SNCF website for times and prices—but many of the trains run the Mandelieu–Ventimiglia route, and the Italian Thello train now offers Cannes-Milan routes (5 hrs 15 minutes, from €15). You can also take the TGV directly from Paris (5 hrs). Cannes's main bus hub is in front of the l'Hôtel-de-Ville by the port and serves all coastal destinations.

Within Cannes, use Palm Bus (€1.50). For excursions out of the city, Lignes d'Azur runs routes from in front of the train station, including Bus No. 200 to Nice (€1.50, 1½ hrs), which stops at every town en route. Their bargain-basement fares are a steal (be patient, you may not get a seat), but keep in mind that between Cannes and Nice, it's much faster to take the train. The Zou 210 Express bus is a direct airport shuttle (50 mins, €22).

VISITOR INFORMATION Cannes Tourist Office ⊠ *1 bd. de la Croisette, Cannes* ☎ *04–92–99–84–22* ⊕ *www.cannes-destination.com.*

Sights

La Croisette

NEIGHBORHOOD | Head to this famous waterfront promenade—which runs for 1.6 km (1 mile) from its western terminus by the Palais des Festivals—and allow the *esprit de Cannes* to take over. Stroll among the palm trees and flowers and crowds of poseurs (fur coats in tropical weather, mobile phones on Rollerblades, and sunglasses at night). Continue east past the broad expanse of private beaches, glamorous shops, and luxurious

hotels. A two-year renovation of the Croisette will finish March 2020, and in the meantime, there may be a few disruptions as they widen the beaches, improve seaside concessions (particularly the Bijou and Pointe Croisette areas), and do construction work on the Town Hall. ⊠ *Bd. de Croisette, Cannes.*

Le Suquet

NEIGHBORHOOD | Climb up Rue St-Antoine into the picturesque Vieille Ville neighborhood known as Le Suquet, on the site of the original Roman castrum. Shops proffer Provençal goods, and the atmospheric cafés provide a place to catch your breath; the pretty pastel shutters, Gothic stonework, and narrow passageways are lovely distractions. In July, the "Nuits Musicales du Suquet" concerts mesmerize in front of Notre-Dame church, while Le Suquet des Arts provides three days of art in the streets at the end of August. ⊠ *Rue St-Antoine, Cannes.*

Malmaison

MUSEUM | If you need a culture fix, check out the modern art and photography exhibitions held at the Malmaison, a 19th-century mansion that was once part of the Grand Hotel. ⊠ *47 bd. La Croisette, La Croisette* ☎ *04–97–06–44–90* ⊡ *Admission varies* ⊗ *Closed weekends.*

Musée de la Castre

MUSEUM | The hill is topped by an 11th-century château, housing the Musée de la Castre, with its mismatched collection of weaponry, ethnic artifacts, and ceramics amassed by a 19th-century aristocrat. The imposing four-sided **Tour du Suquet** (Suquet Tower) and its 109 steps were built in 1385 as a lookout against Saracen-led invasions. You can book your tickets in advance online at ⊕ *www. cannesticket.com.* ⊠ *Pl. de la Castre, Le Suquet* ☎ *04–93–38–55–26* ⊡ *€6* ⊗ *Closed Mon. Sept.–June.*

Palais des Festivals

ARTS VENUE | Pick up a map at the tourist office in the Palais des Festivals; the building sets the scene for the famous Festival International du Film, otherwise known as the Cannes Film Festival. As you leave the information center, follow the Palais to your right to see the 24 red-carpeted stairs that A-listers ascend every year. Set into the surrounding pavement, the **Chemin des Étoiles** (Stars' Walk) enshrines some 300 autographed hand imprints—including those of Depardieu, Streep, and Stallone (the clay imprints are sent to a potter in—where else?—Vallauris, before being cast in metal in Rhône). From October to April, a cultural season offers music, theater, dance, and comedy at the Paiais for surprisingly reasonable prices. ⊠ *Bd. de la Croisette, Cannes* ⊕ *www.palaisdesfestivals.com.*

Rue d'Antibes

MARKET | Two blocks behind La Croisette lies this high-end shopping street. At its western end is **Rue Meynadier,** packed tight with trendy clothing boutiques and fine-food shops. Not far away is the covered **Marché Forville,** the scene of the animated morning food market. **Rue Houche,** behind Rue d'Antibes and down from Galleries Lafayette, has lots of boutiques and cafés. ⊠ *Cannes.*

Vieux Port (*Old Port*)

MARINA | Sparkling at the foot of Le Suquet, this narrow, well-protected port harbors a fascinating lineup of luxury yachts and slick little pleasure boats that creak and bob beside weathered-blue fishing barques. From the east corner, off La Pantiéro at Quai Laubeuf, you can catch a cruise to the Îles de Lérins. The port, as well as Quai St-Pierre (which runs alongside and hosts a plethora of restaurants), has emerged from its tattered and tired midlife crisis to become a smartly dressed, more energized version of its former self. ⊠ *Cannes.*

Restaurants

Astoux et Cie Brun

$$$ | SEAFOOD | A beacon to all fish lovers since 1953, Astoux et Cie Brun deserves its reputation for impeccably fresh *fruits de mer*. Well-trained staff negotiate cramped quarters to lay down heaping seafood platters, shrimp casseroles, and piles of oysters shucked to order. Open 365 days a year, it is noisy, cheerful, and always busy (so don't expect rapid service). **Known for:** legendary address; cheerful atmosphere; big crowds so arrive early or be prepared for long lines and slow service. $ *Average main: €30* ⊠ *27 rue Félix Faure, La Croisette* ☎ *04–93–39–21–87* ⊕ *www.chezastoux. com.*

★ La Villa Archange

$$$$ | FRENCH | You wouldn't expect to find a restaurant with two Michelin stars set in such a residential background, 10 minutes by car from La Croisette, but Bruno Oger promises you an unforgettable evening in this très cozy spot surrounded by centennial trees and gardens. Yes, it's pricey, but concentrate on the selection (prix-fixe menus from €72 to €350, or à la carte), which features dishes such as No. 2 oysters with mint cucumber and Petrossian caviar or sea bass with lemongrass. **Known for:** impeccable service; wonderful pairings by sommelier; nine-course Inspiration Menu that costs €500 with wine. $ *Average main: €100* ⊠ *15 bis rue Notre-Dame des Anges, Le Cannet* ☎ *04–92–18–18–28* ⊕ *bruno-oger. com* ⊙ *Closed Sun. and Mon. No lunch Tues.–Thurs.*

L'Affable

$$$$ | FRENCH | When chef Battaglia decided to set up shop in Cannes, gastronomes were delighted—and the chef does not disappoint—so much so that it's not uncommon for tourists to eat here more than once during their stay in Cannes. The sea bass is fantastic, the roast beef succulent, and the curry prawns impossibly fragrant. **Known for:** signature Grand Marnier soufflé; hustle-and-bustle vibe; reservations essential. $ *Average main: €44* ⊠ *5 rue Lafontaine, La Croisette* ☎ *04–93–68–02– 09* ⊕ *www.restaurant-laffable.fr* ⊙ *Closed Sun. and Aug. No lunch Sat.*

★ Le Park 45

$$$$ | FRENCH | In the chic, 1960s-retro Grand Hotel Cannes, this modern spot with sleek plate-glass windows overlooking the garden and sea is the showcase for chef Hervé Busson. He continues to put on a real show: picture dishes like Menton lemon risotto, local pumpkin and basil, or roast duckling with crisp foie gras and Provençal honey. **Known for:** spectacularly colorful decor; beautiful presentation; pricey set menus (but affordable lunch menu). $ *Average main: €55* ⊠ *45 bd. de la Croisette, Cannes* ☎ *04–93–38–15–45* ⊕ *www.grand-hotel-cannes.com.*

Le Roof

$$$$ | FRENCH | Occupying the fifth floor of a former post office, this trendy rooftop restaurant formerly known as Sea Sens has had an awakening, but not to worry, the fabulous views over Le Suquet are still there and so is chef Arnaud Tabarec. The whole setting oozes intimacy, with starters, desserts, and even mains ordered to share (but not the veal confit with mashed potatoes and gravy); organic eggs have their own section on the menu. **Known for:** finger foods and mains for sharing; magical rooftop ambience; excellent value. $ *Average main: €34* ⊠ *1 rue Notre-Dame, Cannes* ☎ *04–63–36– 05–05* ⊕ *www.fiveseashotel.com.*

Table 22

$$$$ | FRENCH | In a city where style often wins out over substance, food lovers treasure this Suquet address, run by former chef and maître d' Noël Mantel, who, among other top-notch jobs, worked with Ducasse at Louis XV in Monaco. The contemporary setting

continues to harmonize with his exquisitely detailed Mediterranean cuisine such as the Italian risotto with veal sauce asparagus and Alba white truffles. **Known for:** affordable seasonal prix-fixe menus; intimate setting; excellent and varied wine selection. $ *Average main: €39* ✉ *22 rue St-Antoine, Cannes* ☎ *04–93–39–13–10* ⊕ *www.restaurantmantel.com.*

 # Hotels

Five Seas Hotel
$$$$ | HOTEL | Housed in the town's old post office, steps from the Palais des Festivals, Five Seas has a stylish interior that evokes voyages to the Far East: decent-size rooms dressed in red fabrics blend with exquisite dark-wood furniture against all-white linens and bathroom fixtures, while amenities are plentiful—a rooftop pool, personal shoppers, jogging routes, yacht charters, and dog sitters are all at your fingertips. **Pros:** good size-rooms; free minibar for nonalcoholic drinks; rooftop restaurant with panoramic views. **Cons:** who needs a scale in the bathroom when on holiday in France?; can be tricky to find when driving; all this luxury comes with a hefty price tag. $ *Rooms from: €380* ✉ *1 rue Notre-Dame, Cannes* ☎ *04–63–36–05–05* ⊕ *www.fiveseashotel.com/en* ⇗ *45 rooms* ⦿ *No meals.*

★ Grand Hotel Cannes
$$$$ | HOTEL | A two-minute walk from the Palais, this 11-story, white-brick number with an amazing hotel garden fronting the Croisette is a fun and relaxing place to stay, with rooms that are spacious, modern, and designed to have the eyes flow toward the sea view. **Pros:** quieter than some other Croisette properties because it sits back from the road; excellent service; lots of free tech stuff including in-room Netflix and Drigme smartphone. **Cons:** beach is not exclusive to hotel so gets crowded; extras can add up (€25 parking); rooms feel a little

dated. $ *Rooms from: €350* ✉ *45 bd. de la Croisette, Cannes* ☎ *04–93–38–15–45* ⊕ *www.grand-hotel-cannes.com* ⦿ *Closed mid-Dec.–Jan.* ⇗ *75 rooms* ⦿ *No meals.*

Hotel Colette
$$ | HOTEL | Facing the train station, this boutique hotel is suspiciously affordable considering its proximity to the beach, particularly when you book in advance for rooms in the off-season (mid-October–June). **Pros:** steps away from Palais des Festivals; interior courtyard a bonus; L'Occitane toiletries provided. **Cons:** €15 for breakfast; no parking at hotel; Wi-Fi isn't great. $ *Rooms from: €135* ✉ *5 pl. de la Gare, Cannes* ☎ *04–93–39–01–17* ⊕ *www.hotelcolette.com* ⇗ *45 rooms* ⦿ *No meals.*

Hôtel de Provence
$$ | HOTEL | This affordable choice has a fabulous location, and its very gracious owners, Julie and Jerry Duburcq (who speak English), go the extra distance to ensure guests have the service and experience of a much-higher-caliber modern hotel. **Pros:** all-day continental breakfast for €9.80; five-minute walk from Cannes center; lower rates if prepaid. **Cons:** only 10 parking places (€19 per night); smallish rooms; no spa but partners with Institut Aurélie beauty center. $ *Rooms from: €169* ✉ *9 rue Molière, Cannes* ☎ *04–93–38–44–35* ⊕ *www.hotel-de-provence.com* ⦿ *Closed mid-Jan.–mid-Feb.* ⇗ *36 rooms* ⦿ *No meals.*

InterContinental Carlton Cannes
$$$$ | HOTEL | Used by Hitchcock as a suitably glamorous frame for Grace Kelly in *To Catch a Thief,* this neoclassical landmark built in 1911, with is gleaming facade, staked out the best position early on, sitting right on the sidewalk of La Croisette, radiating symmetrically from its figurehead waterfront site—the better for you to be seen on the popular brasserie's terrace. **Pros:** sense of history; five-star service; legendary bar and terrace.

Cons: some rooms are lackluster so opt for sea views; daily valet parking €45; strict 2 pm check-in and noon check-out times. [$] *Rooms from: €375* ✉ *58 bd. de la Croisette, Cannes* ☎ *04–93–06–40–06* 🌐 *www.carlton-cannes.com* 🛏 *382 rooms* 🍴 *Free Breakfast.*

Le Cavendish Boutique Hotel

$$ | **HOTEL** | Lovingly restored by friendly owners Christine and Guy Welter, the giddily opulent former residence of Lord Cavendish and a listed Belle Époque building is a true delight, playing up both a contemporary style of "wintergarden" greens and "incensed" reds, and 19th-century elegance. **Pros:** close to Palais des Festival and beach; complimentary drinks and snacks each evening; the only Cannes hotel that serves breakfast until the last guest has eaten. **Cons:** hotel is on busiest street in Cannes, so ask for a room in the back; not open year-round; parking €25 per day. [$] *Rooms from: €140* ✉ *11 bd. Carnot, Cannes* ☎ *04–97–06–26–00* 🌐 *www.cavendish-cannes.com* 🕒 *Closed mid-Dec.–mid-Mar.* 🛏 *34 rooms* 🍴 *Free Breakfast.*

Nightlife

Casino Barrière

CASINOS | The famous Casino Barrière on La Croisette—open 10 am to 3 am (until 4 am on weekends and until 5 am during summer)—is said to draw more crowds to its slot machines than any other casino in France. ✉ *Palais des Festivals, 1 La Croisette, Cannes* ☎ *04–92–98–78–00* 🌐 *www.lucienbarriere.com.*

Le Bâoli

DANCE CLUBS | The biggest player on the Cannes nightlife scene, Le Bâoli attracts the likes of Kim and Kanye, Channing Tatum, Jude Law, and oh, some 3,000 other revelers. It's usually packed until dawn even outside of festival time. If staying up past 10 is not your scene, head to Cloud Nine, the 360-degree panoramic rooftop bar, for sunset cocktails. ✉ *Port Canto, Bd. de la Croisette, La Croisette* ☎ *04–93–43–03–43* 🌐 *www.lebaoli.com.*

Performing Arts

Cannes International Film Festival

FESTIVALS | The Riviera's cultural calendar is splashy and star-studded, and never more so than during the Cannes International Film Festival in May. The film screenings are not open to the public, so unless you have a pass, your stargazing will be on the streets or in restaurants (though if you hang around the back exits of the big hotels around 7 pm, you may bump into a few celebs on their way to the red carpet). *Cinéma de la Plage* shows Cannes Classics and Out of Competition films free at Macé beach at 9:30 pm. In addition, Cannes Cinéphiles (🌐 *www.cannes-cinema.com*) gives 4,000 film buffs a chance to view Official Selections; you can apply online starting in February. ✉ *Cannes* 🌐 *www.festival-cannes.com.*

Shopping

Whether you're window-shopping or splurging on that little Kim Jones number in the Dior window, you'll find some of the best shopping outside Paris along Boulevard de la Croisette and its offspring: Rue Amouretti, Rue des Serbes, and Rue des Belges, all perpendicular to the waterfront. Rue d'Antibes is the town's main shopping drag, home base to every kind of clothing and shoe shop, as well as mouthwatering candy, fabric, and home-design stores. Rue Meynadier mixes trendy young clothes with high-end food specialties.

Activities

Most of the beaches along La Croisette are owned by hotels and restaurants, and they rent out chaise loungers, mats, and umbrellas to the public and to hotel guests (who also have to pay). Public beaches are between the color-coordinated private beach umbrellas and offer simple open showers and basic toilets. Keep in mind that the city's beach development project will continue through 2020 and could create a few minor inconveniences for your desired tan lines.

Mougins

8 km (5 miles) north of Cannes.

Passing through Mougins, a popular residential community convenient to Cannes, Nice, and the big Sophia-Antipolis business park, you may perceive little more than sleek, upscale suburban sprawl. But in 1961 Picasso found more to admire and settled into a farmhouse that became a mecca for artists and art lovers—he died there in 1973. Over the decades, others of note also colonized the town, including Jean Cocteau, Man Ray, Fernand Léger, and Christian Dior. Despite overbuilding today, Mougins claims extraordinary (yet distant) views over the coast and an Old Town (which is a *zone piétonne,* or pedestrian zone), on a hilltop above the fray, that has retained a pretty, ultragentrified charm. You'll see a few off-duty celebrities here and any number of wealthy Parisians who have chosen to buy a Riviera pied-à-terre here. Where they go, noted chefs follow, and Mougins is now a byword in gourmet circles. If you're not coming here specifically for the food, the town also has plenty of galleries and a handful of expensive cafés with pleasant terraces.

GETTING HERE AND AROUND
Getting to Mougins by public transportation is time-consuming. Bus Nos. 600 and 630 from Cannes stop in Mougins; from there it's a 15-minute walk up the hill to the Vieux Village. If you don't have time to burn, opt for a taxi (around €35 from Cannes or around €80 from the Nice airport). From Nice, the train to Cannes costs €7.20 one way. If you continue on the train to Mouans-Sartoux (60 mins, €9.30), you can take Bus No. 26 to the village.

VISITOR INFORMATION Mougins Tourist Office ✉ *39 pl. des Patriotes, Mougins* ☎ *04–92–92–14–00* ⊕ *www.mougins-tourisme.fr.*

 ## Sights

Les Étoiles de Mougins

FESTIVAL | Every other year, this festival transforms the medieval village of Mougins into a vast "open-air theater of gastronomy" as it pays tribute to Roger Vergé, one of the all-time greatest figures in contemporary French cooking. Since it first started in 2006, hundreds of the world's best chefs have converged to share their passion with demonstrations, workshops, and tastings. Now the festival hopes to increase its presence abroad in countries like Japan and Russia by taking a road tour every other year. In 2019, it kicks off in Pietra Santa, Italy, before returning to Mougins in 2020. ✉ *Vieux Village, Mougins* ☎ *04–92–92–14–00* 🖱 *From €5.*

★ Musée d'Art Classique de Mougins

MUSEUM | This hidden gem "highlights the dialogue between the old and the new" with Roman, Greek, and Egyptian art rubbing shoulders with pieces by Picasso, Matisse, Cézanne, Warhol, and Dalí. Expect to come across a sarcophagus alongside a Cocteau or a Hirst sculpture next to an ancient bust. Spread over four floors, the museum also houses antique jewelry and the world's largest armory collection. Check their website for special events, like Soirée Beaujolais and late-night openings. ⊠ *32 rue Commandeur, Mougins* ☎ *04–93–90–00–91* ⊕ *www.mouginsmusee.com* ☜ *€14.*

Notre-Dame-de-Vie

HOUSE | You can find Picasso's final home, where he lived for 12 years until 1973, by following the D35 south of Mougins 2 km (1 mile) to the ancient ecclesiastical site of Notre-Dame-de-Vie. From his room, he could see the 13th-century belltower and arcaded chapel, a pretty ensemble once immortalized in a painting by Winston Churchill. The **chapel,** listed as a historical monument since 1927, is said to date back to 1655. Approached through an allée of ancient cypresses, the former priory house Picasso shared with his wife, Jacqueline, overlooks the broad bowl of the countryside (now blighted with modern construction). Unfortunately, his residence was bought by a private investor and is now closed to the public. ⊠ *Ch. de la Chapelle, Mougins* ☜ *Free.*

🍴 Restaurants

Paloma

$$$$ | **FRENCH** | Young Nicolas Decherchi earned his first Michelin star only one year after opening Paloma, set in the serenity of a Provençal farmhouse and complete with distant views (in this case, of the sea and the Îles de Lérins off Cannes). The service is flawless, from the valet to the sommelier, and the food combines time-honored southern cooking techniques with a hefty dollop of imagination—think Limousin smoked veal rib cooked on a barbecue, glazed with bone marrow and fresh thyme, truffled half-cooked artichokes, and confit marrow. **Known for:** gorgeous interior; bread service with pyramids of butter; cotton candy foie gras. $ *Average main: €80* ⊠ *47 av. du Moulin de la Croix, Mougins* ☎ *04–92–28–10–73* ⊕ *www.restaurant-paloma-mougins.com* ☉ *Closed*

Sun. and Mon., 1 wk in Feb., and 1 wk after film festival.

🛏 Hotels

Le Mas Candille

$$$$ | **HOTEL** | Nestled in an 8-acre private park, this 19th-century *mas* (farmhouse) has been cleverly transformed into an ultraluxurious hotel with antique wallpapers, "reissued" vintage furniture, and many other high-gloss touches that make the place *Elle Decor*–worthy. **Pros:** three pools and gardens; Michelin-starred restaurant on-site; parking and Wi-Fi included in price. **Cons:** tricky to find; need to pay extra to avoid rooms facing parking lot; €24 cheeseburger at poolside La Pergola. $ *Rooms from: €358* ⊠ *Bd. Clément-Rebuffel, Mougins* ☎ *04–92–28–43–43* ⊕ *www.lemascandille.com* ☉ *Closed most of Jan.* ☜ *45 rooms* ¶ *Free Breakfast.*

Grasse

10 km (6 miles) northwest of Mougins.

High on a plateau over the coast, this busy modern town is usually given a wide berth by anyone who isn't interested in its most prized industry, perfume. But its unusual art museum features works of the 18th-century artist Fragonard, while the famed perfume museum and the picturesque backstreets of its very Mediterranean Vieille Ville round out a pleasant day trip from the coast. You can't visit the laboratories where the great blends of Chanel, Dior, and Guerlain are produced, but to accommodate the crowds who come here wanting to know more, Grasse has three functioning perfume factories that create simple blends and demonstrate production techniques for free. The skills linked to cultivating flowers and blending fragrances in Grasse are so prestigious that they've been added to the UNESCO list of protected treasures.

GETTING HERE AND AROUND

The train from Nice takes just over an hour (€10.40), but it's only 30 minutes from Cannes (€4.60). Alternatively, Bus No. 500 from Nice has daily service to Grasse, and Bus No. 610 comes from Cannes; both cost €1.50. Once here, you can get around aboard Le Petit Train de Grasse for a 35-minute circuit (€6.50) of the town, including Place aux Aires, Vieille Ville, and the Cathedral. It departs daily except for Sunday, 11–6 from the Cours Honoré Cresp, April through October (and by reservation the rest of the year).

VISITOR INFORMATION Grasse Tourist Office ⊠ *Pl. de la Buanderie, Grasse* ☎ *04–93–36–66–66* ⊕ *www.tourisme. paysdegrasse.fr/en.*

Sights

Fragonard

FACTORY | Built in 1782, this perfume factory is open to the public daily for free guided tours, and has the best boutique: look for the brioche-scented candle—your home will have the wonderful scent of a French *boulangerie*. Sign up for a Do-it-Yourself Perfume (DIYP) workshop for a more specialized memento of your visit. ⊠ *20 bd. Fragonard, Grasse* ☎ *04–93–36–44–65* ⊕ *www.fragonard. com* ☞ *Free.*

Galimard

FACTORY | Tracing its pedigree back to 1747, Galimard is one of the world's oldest perfume houses. Today its factory is open to visitors 365 days a year, where for €53 you can create and name your own perfume in a two-hour workshop. They're held Monday through Saturday at 10, 2, and 4 in Galimard's Studio des Fragrances, around the corner at 5 route de Pegomas; for those with more time, try the Haute Couture workshops with a decadent champagne break. ⊠ *73 rte. de Cannes, Grasse* ☎ *04–93–09–20–00* ⊕ *www.galimard.com* ☞ *Free.*

Molinard

FACTORY | Established in 1849, Molinard offers an extensive tour that includes visits to the Soap Factory, the Distillery (witness "the nose" at work concocting new fragrances), and the Cream Room, where the packaging team hand-labels each bottle or pump. For €30—and without a reservation—you can create your perfume in a few basic steps (20 minutes). ⊠ *60 bd. Victor Hugo, Grasse* ☎ *04–93–36–01–62* ⊕ *www.molinard. com* ☞ *Free.*

Musée d'Art et d'Histoire de Provence

(*Museum of the Art and History of Provence*)

MUSEUM | Just down from the Fragonard perfumery and open every day, the Musée d'Art et d'Histoire de Provence has a large collection of faïence from the region, including works from the famous pottery towns of Moustiers, Biot, and Vallauris. ⊠ *2 rue Mirabeau, Grasse* ☎ *04–93–36–80–20* ⊕ *www.museesde-grasse.com* ☞ *€2.*

Musée International de la Parfumerie

(*International Museum of Perfume*)

MUSEUM | This is one of the more sleekly spectacular museums along the coast. Housed in a soaring structure of steel, glass, and teak, the museum traces the 3,000-year history of perfume making; highlights include a fascinating collection of 4,000 antique perfume bottles. In the rooftop greenhouse you can breathe in the heady smells of different herbs and flowers, while the expert and amusing guide crushes delicate petals under your nose to better release the scents. ⊠ *2 bd. du Jeu de Ballon, Grasse* ☎ *04–97–05–58–00* ⊕ *www.museesdegrasse. com* ☞ *€4, includes entry to Villa Musée Fragonard.*

Vieille Ville (*Old Town*)

NEIGHBORHOOD | Go down the steps to Rue Mirabeau and lose yourself in the dense labyrinth of the Vieille Ville, where steep, narrow streets, austere facades,

discreet gardens, and random flights of stairs are thrown into shadow by shuttered houses five and six stories tall ✉ *Grasse.*

Villa Musée Fragonard
MUSEUM | This museum headlines the work of Grasse's own Jean-Honoré Fragonard (1732–1806), one of the great French "chocolate-box" artists of his day (these artists were known for their maudlin style that stemmed from the type of artwork found on boxes of chocolate). The lovely villa contains a collection of Fragonard's drawings, engravings, and paintings; also on display are works by his son Alexandre-Evariste and his grandson, Théophile. ✉ *23 bd. Fragonard, Grasse* ☎ *04–93–36–93–10* 🌐 *www.fragonard.com/parfums_grasse/GB/fragonard/grasse/fragonard_costa_museum.cfm* 🎫 *€2, includes entry to Museum of the Art and History of Provence.*

Hotels

La Bastide Saint-Antoine
$$$$ | **HOTEL** | This ocher mansion, once the home of an industrialist who hosted the Kennedys and the Rolling Stones, is now the domain of celebrated chef Jacques Chibois, who welcomes you with old stone walls, shaded walkways, an enormous pool, and guest rooms that glossily mix Louis Seize, Provençal, and high-tech delights. **Pros:** a bastion of culinary excellence; Malongo coffee machine and organic tea in each room; choice of Provençal or modern decor. **Cons:** deposit of 50% of the total stay is charged at time of booking; breakfast not included so look for online specials; restaurant is expensive. [$] *Rooms from: €350* ✉ *48 av. Henri-Dunant, Grasse* ☎ *04–93–70–94–94* 🌐 *www.jacques-chibois.com* 🛏 *16 rooms* 🍴 *No meals.*

Vallauris

6 km (4 miles) northeast of Cannes.

This ancient village in the low hills above the coast, dominated by a blocky Renaissance château, owes its four-square street plan to a form of medieval urban renewal. Ravaged and eventually wiped out by waves of the plague in the 14th century, the village was rebuilt by 70 Genovese families imported by the Abbaye de Lérins in the 16th century to repopulate the abandoned site. They brought with them a taste for Roman planning—hence the grid format in the Old Town—but more importantly, a knack for pottery making. Their skills and the fine clay of Vallauris were a perfect marriage, and the village thrived as a pottery center for hundreds of years. In the late 1940s Picasso found inspiration in the malleable soil and settled here, giving the flagging industry new life. Sadly, the town has developed a more shady reputation (so keep your hands on your purse) despite Saudi's King Salman owning a 1930s villa where Churchill and Hollywood celebs stayed, running along 1 km (½ mile) of Vallauris's beachfront.

GETTING HERE AND AROUND

The SNCF Golfe–Juan train station is in Place Pierre Sémard in the center of Vallauris–Golfe–Juan. Tickets cost €5.90 one way from Nice and €2.10 from Cannes. Bus No. 8, part of the Envibus network, runs between the Golfe–Juan train station and Vallauris about every 15 minutes (45 mins on Sunday). Bus No. 200, connecting Nice and Cannes, stops in Golfe–Juan and runs about every 15 minutes. Tickets cost €1.50. There's also the Zou No. 250, a daily airport express bus (55 mins, €11) that stops in Antibes, Juan-les-Pins with Vallauris as its final destination.

Sights

Musée National Picasso

MUSEUM | In the late 1940s Picasso settled here in a simple stone house, "le château de Vallauris"—the former priory of the Abbaye de Lérins and one of the rare Renaissance buildings in the region—creating pottery art from the malleable local clay with a single-minded passion. But he returned to painting in 1952 to create one of his masterworks in the château's Romanesque chapel, the vast multipanel oil-on-wood composition called *La Guerre et la Paix* (*War and Peace*). Today the chapel is part of the Musée National Picasso, where several of Picasso's ceramic pieces are displayed. ⊠ *Pl. de la Libération, Vallauris* ☏ *04–93–64–71–83* ⊕ *www.musees-nationaux-alpesmaritimes.fr/picasso* ⊠ *€6* ⊙ *Closed Tues. Sept.–June.*

Antibes

11 km (7 miles) east of Cannes, 15 km (9 miles) southeast of Nice.

Named Antipolis—meaning across from (*anti*) the city (*polis*)—by the Greeks, who founded it in the 4th century BC, Antibes flourished under the Romans' aristocratic rule, with an amphitheater, aqueducts, and baths. The early Christians established their bishopric here, the site of the region's cathedral until the 13th century. It was in the Middle Ages that the kings of France began fortifying this key port town, an effort that culminated in the recognizable star-shape ramparts designed by Vauban. The young general Napoléon once headed this stronghold, living with his family in a humble house in the Old Town; his mother washed their clothes in a stream. There's still a *lavoir* (public laundry fountain) in the Old Town where locals, not unlike Signora Bonaparte, rinse their clothes and hang them like garlands over the narrow streets.

With its broad stone ramparts scalloping in and out over the waves and backed by blunt medieval towers, it's easy to understand why Antibes (pronounced "Awn- *teeb*") inspired Picasso to paint on a panoramic scale. Stroll Promenade Amiral-de-Grasse along the crest of Vauban's sea walls, and watch the sleek yachts purring out to sea. Even more intoxicating, just off the waterfront, is the souklike maze of old streets, its market filled with fresh fish and goat cheese, wild herbs, and exotic spices. This is **Vieil Antibes,** with a nearly Italianate feel, perhaps no great surprise considering that Antibes' great fort marked the border between Italy and France right up to the 19th century.

Monet fell in love with the town, and his most famous paintings show the fortified Vieil Antibes against the sea. He arrived in January 1888 and expected to stay only a few days; three months later, he had shipped off 39 canvases to be exhibited in Paris at the gallery of Vincent van Gogh's brother. The Antibes that Monet knew has become a hub for the yachting community, particularly popular with Brits, which is why you'll hear so much (maybe too much) English when you're walking around. Port Vauban, one of the most attractive ports in Europe, is one of the few marinas offering long-term berthing contracts in the region for yachts up to 550 feet. Still, to see Antibes as Monet—and Picasso, Cross, Boudin, and Harpignies—once did, head to the tourist office for a guided tour on the Painters' Trail; other themes include old town, gourmet Antibes, and a guided hike along the Sentier du Littoral.

GETTING HERE AND AROUND

Antibes has one central train station, the Gare SNCF, which is at the far end of town but still within walking distance of the Vieille Ville and only a block or so from the beach. Local trains are frequent, coming from Nice (26 mins,

€4.80), Juan-les-Pins, Biot, Cannes (10 mins, €3.10), and almost all other coastal towns.

There are high-speed TGVs (Trains à Grand Vitesse) to Antibes. Bus service, available at Antibes' Gare Routière (✉ *1 pl. Guynemer*) is supplied by Envibus (☎ *04–89–87–72–00* ⊕ *www.envibus. fr*). For local routes or to get to Cannes, Nice, Cagnes-sur-Mer, Juan-les-Pins, take the Lignes d'Azur No. 200 (☎ *08–10–06– 10–06* ⊕ *www.lignedazur.com*), which runs every 15 minutes and costs €1.50.

VISITOR INFORMATION Antibes Tourist Office ✉ *42 av. Robert Soleau, Antibes* ☎ *04–22–10–60–10* ⊕ *www.antibesjuan- lespins.com.*

Sights

★ **Commune Libre du Safranier** (*Free Commune of Safranier*)

NEIGHBORHOOD | A few blocks south of the Château Grimaldi, aka the Picasso Museum, is the Commune Libre du Safranier, a magical little neighborhood with a character (and mayor) all its own, even though it's technically part of Antibes. Not far off the seaside promenade, Rue de la Touraque is the main street to get here, and you can amble around Place du Safranier, where tiny houses hang heavy with flowers and vines, and neighbors carry on conversations from window to window across the stone-stepped Rue du Bas-Castelet. ✉ *Rue du Safranier, Rue du Bas-Castelet, Antibes.*

Eglise de l'Immaculée-Conception
(*Cathédrale Notre-Dame*)

RELIGIOUS SITE | This sanctuary served as the region's cathedral until the bishopric was transferred to Grasse in 1244. The church's 18th-century facade, a marvelously Latin mix of classical symmetry and fantasy, has been restored in stunning shades of ocher and cream. Its stout medieval watchtower was built in the 11th century with stones "mined" from Roman structures. Inside is a Baroque

altarpiece painted by the Niçois artist Louis Bréa in 1515. ✉ *Rue du St-Esprit, Antibes.*

Musée Archéologique (*Archaeology Museum*)

MILITARY SITE | Promenade Amiral-de-Grasse—a marvelous spot for pondering the mountains and tides—leads directly to the Bastion St-André, a squat Vauban fortress that now houses the Musée Archéologique. In its glory days this 17th-century stronghold sheltered a garrison; the bread oven is still visible in the vaulted central hall. The museum collection focuses on Antibes's classical history, displaying amphorae and sculptures found in local digs as well as in shipwrecks from the harbor. ✉ *Bastion St-André, Av. Général-Maizières, Antibes* ☎ *04–22–10–60–10* 💳 *€3* ⊙ *Closed Sun. and Mon.*

Musée Picasso

MUSEUM | Rising high over the water, this museum is set in the stunning medieval Château Grimaldi. As rulers of Monaco, the Grimaldi family lived here until the revolution; this fine old castle, however, was little more than a monument until its curator offered use of its chambers to Picasso in 1946, when that extraordinary genius was enjoying a period of intense creative energy. The result was a bounty of exhilarating paintings, ceramics, and lithographs inspired by the sea and by Greek mythology—all very Mediterranean. The château, which became the museum in 1966, houses some 245 works by the artist (but not all are on display), as well as pieces by Miró, Calder, and Léger; the first floor displays more than 100 paintings by Russian-born artist Nicholas de Staël. Even those who are not great Picasso fans should enjoy his vast paintings on wood, canvas, paper, and walls, alive with nymphs, fauns, and centaurs. ✉ *Château Grimaldi, Pl. Marie-jol, Antibes* ☎ *04–92–90–54–20* 💳 *€8* ⊙ *Closed Mon.*

Along with its time-burnished alleys and cul-de-sacs, Antibes is packed with little squares that offer the perfect chance to chill out and get to know the locals.

Restaurants

★ Le Figuier de Saint-Esprit

$$$$ | FRENCH | Christian Morrisset's Michelin-starred restaurant is named after the 40-year-old fig tree that, along with a canopy of vines, gorgeously shades the private courtyard. Typical of the chef's style, which focuses on local ingredients, the menu includes a saddle of lamb from the Alpilles cooked in a crust of Vallauris clay with gnocchi and truffles, zucchini, eggplant, and thyme jus. **Known for:** excellent French cuisine; magical courtyard; local, big labels, and organic wines. $ *Average main: €45* ⊠ *14 rue Saint-Esprit, Antibes* ☎ *04–93–34–50–12* ⊕ *www.christian-morisset.fr* ⊗ *Closed 1 wk in Feb., late June, 3 wks in Nov., Tues. yr-round, and Wed. Nov.–.Apr. No lunch Mon. and Wed. May–Oct.*

Taverne le Safranier

$$ | FRENCH | Part of a tiny Old Town enclave determined to resist the press of tourism, this casual tavern is headquarters for the tables scattered across the sunny terrace on Place Safranier. Install yourself at one, and tuck into dishes like zucchini beignet, Saint Jacques and lobster cassoulet, thick handmade ravioli, or whole *dorade,* a delicate Mediterranean fish unceremoniously split, fried, and garnished with lemon. **Known for:** nautical decor; gorgeous terrace setting; homemade blackboard specials. $ *Average main: €23* ⊠ *1 pl. Safranier, Antibes* ☎ *04–93–34–80–50* ⊗ *Closed Mon. and Jan.*

🛏 Hotels

Le Mas Djoliba

$$ | HOTEL | FAMILY | Tucked into a residential neighborhood on the crest between Antibes and Juan-les-Pins, this cool, cozy inn feels like the private home it once was, surrounded by greenery and well protected from traffic noise. **Pros:** peaceful neighborhood yet only seven-minute walk to beach; tea and coffee in the rooms; top-floor family suite with terrace and views of Cap d'Antibes.

Cons: car park is free but closes at 10 pm; breakfast costs extra; 30% deposit required. $ *Rooms from: €170* ⊠ *29 av. de Provence, Antibes* ☎ *04–93–34–02–48* ⊕ *www.hotel-djoliba.com* ⊗ *Closed Nov.– mid-Mar.* 🛏 *13 rooms* ❌ *No meals.*

 Nightlife

Blue Lady Pub

BARS/PUBS | Next to the legendary Geoffrey's British food shop, this pub is frequented by French and foreigners alike (and their kids and dogs). It's a great little spot to collect your thoughts over a drink after a long day, or to hear some live music. The Blue Lady has daytime appeal, too. Beginning at 7:30 am you can grab a latte, a smoothie, or even an English breakfast (there are newspapers on deck). If you stick around for lunch, you can order homemade burgers, potpies, and fresh salads (the kitchen closes at 3 pm). Friendly service and free Wi-Fi are bonuses, but note it's closed on Sunday. ⊠ *La Galerie du Port, Rue Lacan, Antibes* ☎ *04–93–34–41–00* ⊕ *www. blueladypub.com.*

La Siesta

DANCE CLUBS | This is an enormous summertime entertainment center and the largest beach club in France—some 15,000 revelers pack in every Friday and Saturday, May through early September. The casino has 195 slot machines, English roulette, and blackjack tables, a bistro, and a terrace overlooking the sea. ⊠ *Rte. du Bord de Mer, Antibes* ☎ *04–93–33–31–31* ⊕ *www.joa-casino. com.*

Cap d'Antibes

2 km (1 mile) south of Antibes.

For the most part, this fabled 4-mile-long peninsula has been carved up into luxurious estates perched high above the water and shaded by thick, tall pines.

Since the 19th century, its wild greenery and isolation have drawn a glittering assortment of aristocrats, artists, literati, and the merely fabulously wealthy. Among those claiming the prestigious Cap d'Antibes address over the years are: Guy de Maupassant, Anatole France, Claude Monet, the Duke and Duchess of Windsor, the Greek shipping tycoon Stavros Niarchos, and the cream of the Lost Generation, including Ernest Hemingway, Dorothy Parker, Gertrude Stein, and F. Scott Fitzgerald. Now the focal point is the famous Hotel Eden Roc, which is packed with stars during the Cannes Film Festival (not surprisingly, as movie studios always pick up the tab for their favorite celebs). Reserve a table for lunch here during the festival and be literally surrounded by celebrities to-ing and fro-ing to the pool. Just play it cool, though: keep your sunglasses on at all times and resist the urge to take photos.

GETTING HERE AND AROUND
Envibus No. 2 (€1.50) connects Cap d'Antibes to downtown Antibes, with a stop at Eden Roc.

 Sights

Jardin Thuret (*Thuret Garden*)

GARDEN | To fully experience the Riviera's heady hothouse exoticism, visit the glorious Jardin Thuret, established by botanist Gustave Thuret in 1856 as a testing ground for subtropical plants and trees. Thuret was responsible for the introduction of the palm tree, forever changing the profile of the French Riviera. On his death the property was left to the Ministry of Agriculture, which continues to dabble in the introduction of exotic species. Download a discovery map in English from the website to make the most of a weekday visit. ⊠ *90 ch. Raymond, Antibes* ✛ *From Port Gallice, head up Chemin du Croûton, turn right on Bd. du Cap, then right again on Chemin Raymond* ☎ *04–97–21–25–00*

Vauban's Fort Carré and the seawalls he designed guard Antibes's harbor, home to some of the most envy-inducing yachts in the world.

🌐 *www6.sophia.inra.fr/jardin_thuret*
🎫 *Free* 🕐 *Closed weekends.*

★ **Le Sentier du Littoral** (*Sentier Tire-poil*)
TRAIL | Bordering the Cap's zillion-dollar hotels and over-the-top estates runs one of the most spectacular footpaths in the world. Nicknamed the Sentier "Tire-poil" (because the wind is so strong it "ruffles the hair"), the circuit was recently extended, bringing it "full circle" around the gardens at Eilenroc over to l'Anse de l'Argent Faux. It now stretches about 5 km (3 miles) along the outermost tip of the peninsula. The Sentier du Littoral begins gently enough at the pretty Plage de la Garoupe (where Cole Porter and Gerald Murphy used to hang out), with a paved walkway and dazzling views over the Baie de la Garoupe and the faraway Alps. Round the far end of the cap, however, and the paved promenade soon gives way to a boulder-studded pathway that picks its way along 50-foot cliffs, dizzying switchbacks, and thundering breakers. (Signs read, "*Attention Mort*" [Beware: Death], reminding you this path can be very dangerous in stormy weather.) Continue along the new portion of the path to the cove l'Anse de l'Argent Faux, where you can stop and catch your breath before heading up to entrance of Eilen Roc. Then follow Avenue Beaumont impasse tangent until it touches the Cap's main road RD2559. On sunny days, with exhilarating winds and spectacular breakers, you'll have company, although for most stretches all signs of civilization completely disappear except for a yacht or two. The walk takes about two hours to complete, but it may prove to be two of the more unforgettable hours of your trip (especially if you tackle it at sunset). By the way, if you come across locked gates blocking your route it's because storm warnings have been issued and you are not allowed to enter. ■ **TIP→ From the station in town take Bus No. 2 to Fontaine stop. To return, follow the Plage de la Garoupe until Boulevard de la Garoupe, where you'll make a left to reconnect with the bus.** ✉ *Antibes.*

Phare de la Garoupe (*Garoupe Lighthouse*)
LIGHTHOUSE | You can sample a little of what draws famous people to this part of the world by walking up Chemin de Calvaire from the Plage de la Salis in Antibes—a distance of about 1 km (½ mile) via a challenging pathway—and taking in the extraordinary views from the hill surmounted by this old *phare* (lighthouse). By 2021, you'll be able to climb to the top. Next to it, the 16th-century double chapel of **Notre-Dame-de-la-Garoupe** contains ex-votos and statues of the Virgin, all in memory of and for the protection of sailors. **TIP→ Reward your trek with a drink or a meal at the Bistrot du Curé next door.** ✉ *Chemin de Calvaire, Antibes* ☎ *04–22–10–60–10.*

★ **Villa Eilenroc**
HOUSE | Le Sentier du Littoral passes along the beach at the Villa Eilenroc, designed by Charles Garnier, who created the Paris Opéra—which should give you some idea of its style. It commands the tip of the peninsula from a grand and glamorous garden. Over the last decade an ecomuseum was completed and a scented garden created at the entrance to the rose garden. On Wednesday, September through June, visitors are allowed to wander through the reception salons, which retain the Louis Seize-Trianon feel of the noble facade. The Winter Salon still has its *1,001 Nights* ceiling mural painted by Jean Dunand, the famed Art Deco designer; display cases are filled with memorabilia donated by Caroline Groult-Flaubert (Antibes resident and goddaughter of the great author); and the boudoir has *boiseries* (decorative wood features) from the Marquis de Sévigné's Paris mansion. As you leave, be sure to detour to La Rosaerie, the rose garden of the estate—in the distance you can spot the white portico of the Château de la Cröe, another legendary villa (now reputedly owned by a syndicate of Russian billionaires). It has a host of big names attached to it—singer Helene Beaumont built it; and King Leopold II of Belgium, King Farouk of Egypt, Aristotle Onassis, and Greta Garbo all rented here. ✉ *460 av. L.D. Beaumont, at the peninsula's tip, about 4 km (2½ miles) from Garoupe Bay, Antibes* ☎ *04–93–67–74–33* 🌐 *www.antibesjuanlespins.com* 🎫 *€2.*

🍴 Restaurants

Restaurant de Bacon
$$$$ | **SEAFOOD** | Since 1948, under the careful watch of the Sordello brothers, Restaurant de Bacon has been the ultimate spot for seafood on the French Riviera. Now run by the next generation, the restaurant still has the catch of the day right out of the sea and a dreamy terrace over the Baie des Anges, with views of the Antibes ramparts to justify the extravagant prices. **Known for:** €125 bouillabaisse prepared at table; splendid views; lots of great seafood options, but not much for nonfish lovers. [$] *Average main: €85* ✉ *664 bd. de Bacon, Antibes* ☎ *04–93–61–50–02* 🌐 *www.restaurant-debacon.com* 🕑 *Closed Mon. and Nov.–Feb. No lunch Tues.*

🛏 Hotels

Hôtel du Cap–Eden Roc
$$$$ | **HOTEL** | **FAMILY** | In demand by celebrities from De Niro to Madonna, this extravagantly expensive hotel looking out on 22 acres of immaculate gardens bordered by rocky shoreline has long catered to the world's fantasy of a subtropical idyll on the French Riviera and yet remains *the* place to stay. **Pros:** hands down one of the world's best hotels; fascinating glimpse into 20th century history; breakfast included in price. **Cons:** if you're not a celebrity, tip big to keep the staff interested; massage at the organic spa may be relaxing until you see the price; formal dress required for dinner in restaurant and bars. [$] *Rooms from: €970* ✉ *Bd. J.F. Kennedy, Antibes* ☎ *04–93–61–39–01* 🌐 *www.*

hotel-du-cap-eden-roc.com ⏲ *Closed mid-Oct.–mid-Apr.* 🛏 *118 rooms* 🍴 *Free Breakfast.*

Activities

Plage de la Garoupe

BEACHES | Thanks to the perfect oval bay of La Garoupe, the finest, softest sand on the Riviera, magnificent views that stretch out to Antibes, and relatively calm waters, this northeast-facing beach is a real jewel—and the first in the country to impose a "No Selfie" zone. Getting the Gucci-clad spillover from the Hotel du Cap-Eden Roc, the high-end beach clubs here open onto the sand. Wannabeseens head to the private Joseph Plage at one end of the beach, where you can rent loungers (€26), while the quieter folk stick to the public middle section. For the weak-walleted, there are also two snack bars (if you dare to be seen at one). **Amenities:** parking (no fee); showers; toilets. **Best for**: swimming. ✉ *Chemin de la Garoupe, Antibes.*

Juan-les-Pins

5 km (3 miles) southwest of Antibes.

From Old Antibes you can jump on a bus over the hill to Juan-les-Pins, the jazzy younger-sister resort town that, along with Antibes, bracelets the wrist of the Cap d'Antibes. This stretch of beach was "discovered" by the Jazz Age jet set, who adopted it with a vengeance; F. Scott and Zelda Fitzgerald lived in a seaside villa here in the early 1920s, dividing their idylls between what is now the Hôtel Belle Rives and the mansions on the Cap d'Antibes. Here they experimented with the newfangled fad of water-skiing, still practiced from the docks of the Belle Rives today. Ladies with bobbed hair and beach pajamas exposed lily-white skin to the sun, browning themselves like peasants and flaunting bare, tanned arms. American industrialists had swimming pools introduced to the seaside, and the last of the leisure class, weary of stateside bathtub gin, wallowed in Europe's alcoholic delights. Nowadays, the scene along Juan's waterfront is something to behold, with thousands of international sunseekers flowing up and down the promenade or lying flank to flank on its endless stretch of sand, but the town is simply not as glamorous as its history.

GETTING HERE AND AROUND

Regional rail service connects Juan-les-Pins to Nice (30 mins, €5.20), Cannes (€2.70), and other coastal towns; from the train station, Envibus No. 15 (€1.50) loops through town, stopping at the public beach. Juan-les-Pins can also be reached from either Nice or Cannes via Lignes d'Azur Bus No. 200 (75 mins, €1.50).

VISITOR INFORMATION Juan-les-Pins Tourist Office ✉ *60 chemin des Sables, Juan-les-Pins* ☎ *04–22–10–60–01* 🌐 *www.antibesjuanlespins.com.*

Hotels

Hotel des Mimosas

$ | **HOTEL** | In an enclosed hilltop garden studded with tall palms, mimosas, and tropical greenery, this is the sort of place where only the quiet buzzing of cicadas interrupts silent nights. **Pros:** lovely garden, pool, and grounds; easy 10-minute walk to train station; free parking. **Cons:** some rooms are small; free Wi-Fi but signal can be weak; decor feels dated. [$] *Rooms from: €100* ✉ *Rue Pauline, Juan-les-Pins* ☎ *04–93–61–04–16* 🌐 *www.hotelmimosas.com* 💳 *No credit cards* ⏲ *Closed Oct.–Apr.* 🛏 *34 rooms* 🍴 *No meals.*

★ **Les Belles Rives**

$$$ | **HOTEL** | Lovingly restored to 1930s glamour, this fabled landmark proves that what's old is new again, as France's stylish young set make this endearingly *neoclassique* place with lovely Art Deco

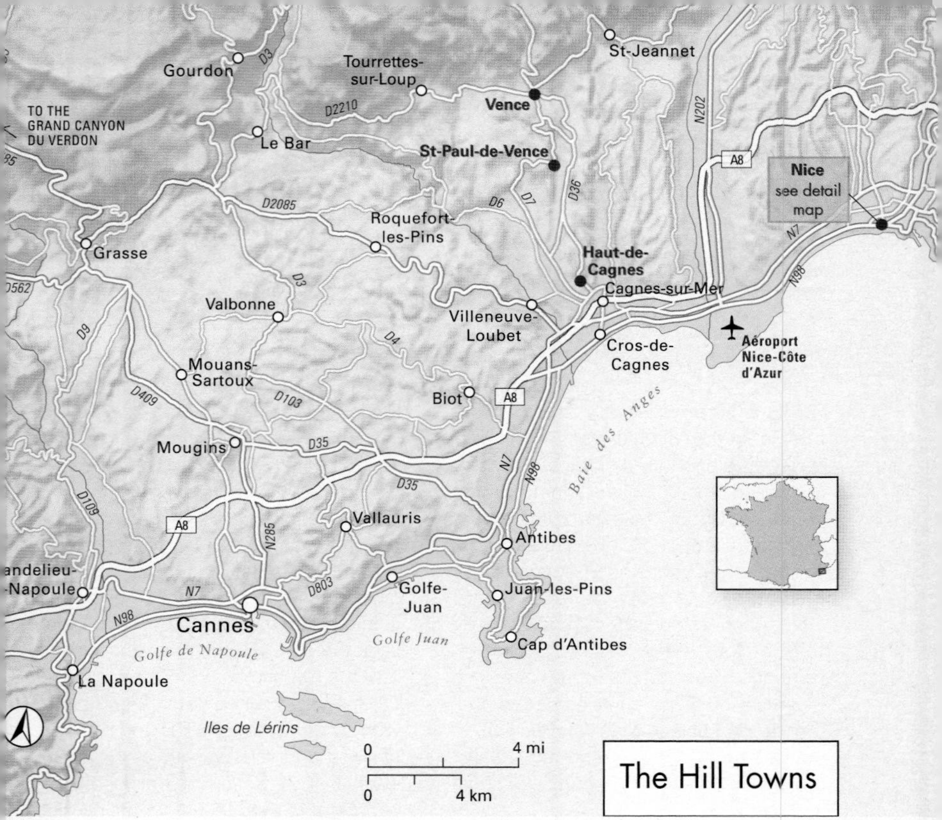

accommodations one of their latest favorites. **Pros:** views are quite spectacular, but ask for a room with a frontal (not lateral) sea view; lots of water sports; reduced rates for early-bird bookings. **Cons:** everything at beach costs extra (loungers, towels, umbrella); some rooms are on the small side; thin walls. [$] *Rooms from: €315* ✉ *33 bd. Édouard Baudoin, Juan-les-Pins* ☎ *04–93–61–02–79* 🌐 *www.bellesrives.com* 🕒 *Closed Jan.–early Mar.* 🛏 *42 rooms* 🍴 *No meals.*

Nightlife

Eden Casino (*Casino Partouche Juan-les-Pins*)

CASINOS | The glassed-in complex of the Eden Casino houses slot machines, roulette and blackjack tables, and a panoramic beach restaurant. Texas Hold 'Em Poker is played every night. Players park for free. The casino is open until 4 am (5 am in summer). ✉ *17 bd. Baudoin, Juan-les-Pins* ☎ *04–92–93–71–71* 🌐 *www.casinojuanlespins.com.*

Performing Arts

Festival International Jazz à Juan

FESTIVALS | Every July the world-renowned Jazz à Juan festival stages a stellar lineup in a romantic venue under ancient pines. Launched in 1960, this festival hosted the European debut performances of such stars as Miles Davis and Ray Charles. More recently, it spawned the fringier Jazz Off, with 200 musicians and free street concerts, as well as the Jazz Club at Les Ambassadeurs beach, where you can enjoy a drink with live music (headliners have been known to pop in for impromptu concerts here).

Book online or buy tickets directly from the tourist office in Antibes or Juan-les-Pins. ☒ *Juan-les-Pins* ☎ *04–22–10–60–01 ticket information* ⊕ *www.jazzajuan.com.*

St-Paul-de-Vence

18 km (11 miles) northwest of Nice.

The medieval village of St-Paul-de-Vence can be seen from afar, standing out like its companion, Vence, against the skyline. In the Middle Ages St-Paul-de-Vence was basically a city-state, and it controlled its own political destiny for centuries. But by the early 20th century it had faded to oblivion, overshadowed by the growth of Vence and Cagnes—until it was rediscovered in the 1920s when a few penniless artists began paying for their drinks at the local auberge with paintings. Those artists turned out to be Signac, Modigliani, and Bonnard, who met at the **Auberge de la Colombe d'Or,** now a sumptuous inn, where the walls are still covered with their ink sketches and daubs.

The most commercially developed of Provence's hilltop villages, St-Paul-de-Vence is a magical place. Artists are still drawn to its light, its pure air, its wraparound views, and its honey-color stone walls, soothingly cool on a hot Provençal afternoon. Get here early in the day to get a jump on the cars and tour buses, which can clog the main D36 highway by noon, or plan to stay overnight. If you're here on a Wednesday, there's a local farmers' market from 9 am until 2 pm selling everything from fruit and vegetables to cheese and jams at Place de Gaulle.

GETTING HERE AND AROUND

It's only 15 minutes from the coast by car; take the Cagnes-sur-Mer highway to Exit 47 or 48 (depending on the direction you're coming from) and look for signs on the RD 436 to La Collle sur Loup/Vence. St-Paul-de-Vence is between the two.

There's no train station, but you can get off at Cagnes-sur-Mer and take Bus No. 400 (15 mins, €1.50), which departs directly from Nice or Cannes.

VISITOR INFORMATION St-Paul-de-Vence Tourist Office ☒ *2 rue Grande, St-Paul-de-Vence* ☎ *04–93–32–86–95* ⊕ *www. saint-pauldevence.com.*

 ## Sights

Fondation Maeght

MUSEUM | Many people come to St-Paul-de-Vence just to visit the Fondation Maeght, founded in 1964 by art dealer Aimé Maeght. High above the medieval town, the small modern art museum attracts 100,000 visitors a year. It's an extraordinary marriage of the arc-and-plane architecture of Josep Sert; the looming sculptures of Miró, Moore, and Giacometti; the mural mosaics of Chagall; and the humbling hilltop setting, complete with pines, vines, and flowing planes of water. On display is an intriguing and ever-varying parade—one of the most important in Europe—of works by modern masters, including Chagall's wise and funny late-life masterpiece *La Vie* (*Life*). On the extensive grounds, fountains and impressive vistas help to beguile even those who aren't into modern art. Café F, should you need time to reflect, is open year-round. Contact the tourist office for a private guided visit in English (€7 plus admission). ☒ *623 ch. des Gardettes, St-Paul-de-Vence* ☎ *04–93–32–81–63* ⊕ *www.fondation-maeght.com* ☒ *€16.*

Restaurants

★ La Colombe d'Or

$$$$ | FRENCH | It might be a bit overpriced for such simple fare, but where else in the world could you dine under a Picasso, on a terrace beside a ceramic Léger mural, or next to a pool where an idyllic garden comes complete with a Calder sculpture? The quirky but unpretentious Provençal menu has hardly changed over

30 years—its famous hors d'oeuvres de la Colombe (basket of crudité and hunks of charcuterie), the salmon quenelles, the Sisteron lamb, and the Grand Marnier soufflé flambé are still as acclaimed as ever. **Known for:** dining amid priceless, museum-level artwork; lunch spot for celebs during Cannes Film Fesival; long-standing menu that hasn't missed a beat in years. $ *Average main: €40* ⊠ *Pl. Général-de-Gaulle, St-Paul-de-Vence* ☎ *04–93–32–80–02* ⊕ *www.la-colombe-dor.com* ⊘ *Closed Nov.–Christmas.*

 Hotels

⭐ **La Colombe d'Or**

$$$ | B&B/INN | Often called the most beautiful inn in France, "the golden dove" occupies a rose-stone Renaissance mansion just outside the walls of St-Paul-de-Vence, and is so perfect overall that some contend you haven't really been to the French Riviera until you've stayed or dined here. **Pros:** original art, including works by Picasso and Rodin; gem of a hotel oozing charm and class in a laid-back vibe; gorgeous decor in rooms. **Cons:** some rooms in the adjoining villa have blocked views; menu selection often outshone by the art; hard to get a reservation. $ *Rooms from: €250* ⊠ *Pl. Général-de-Gaulle, St-Paul-de-Vence* ☎ *04–93–32–80–02* ⊕ *www.la-colombe-dor.com* ⊘ *Closed Nov.–Christmas* ⇌ *25 rooms* ⦿❘ *Free Breakfast.*

Vence

4 km (2½ miles) north of St-Paul-de-Vence.

Encased behind stone walls inside a thriving modern market town, the historic part of Vence dates to the 15th century. Although its backstreets and alleys have been colonized by crafts stores and "art galleries," the town remains conscious of its history—plaques guide you through the age-old *portes* (gates) and around atmospheric little squares, like Place du Peyra. The area is especially lively on Tuesday when a Provençal market sets up near the cathedral. Every morning there's a local produce and flower market at Place du Grand Jardin, where you can also discover antiques and secondhand books on Wednesday and a food and clothing market on Friday.

GETTING HERE AND AROUND
As with St-Paul-de-Vence, take the Cagnes-sur-Mer highway to Exit 47 or 48 (depending on the direction you're coming from) and look for signs on the RD 436 to La Colle sur Loup/Vence. St-Paul-de-Vence is between the two.

There's no train station, but you can get off at Cagnes-sur-Mer and take Bus No. 400 bus (15 mins, €1.50), which departs directly from Nice or Cannes.

VISITOR INFORMATION Vence Tourist Office ⊠ *Villa Alexandrine, Pl. du Grand Jardin, 36 rue du 8 Mai 1945, Vence* ☎ *04–93–58–06–38* ⊕ *www.vence-tourisme.com.*

 Sights

Cathédrale de la Nativité de la Vierge (*Cathedral of the Birth of the Virgin*) **RELIGIOUS SITE |** In the center of the Vieille Ville, the Cathédrale de la Nativité de la Vierge was built on the Romans' military drilling field in the 11th and 12th centuries and is a hybrid of Romanesque and Baroque styles. The cathedral has been expanded and altered many times over the centuries. Note the rostrum added in 1499—its choir stalls are carved with particularly vibrant and amusing scenes of daily life in the Middle Ages. In the baptistery is a ceramic mosaic of Moses in the bulrushes by Chagall. ⊠ *Pl. Godeau, Vence* ⊑ *Free.*

⭐ **Chapelle du Rosaire** (*Chapel of the Rosary*)

RELIGIOUS SITE | On the outskirts of "new" Vence, toward St-Jeannet, is the Chapelle du Rosaire, better known to the world-at-large as the Matisse Chapel. The artist decorated it with beguiling simplicity and clarity between 1947 and 1951 as his gift to nuns who had nursed him through illness. It reflects the reductivist style of the era: walls, floor, and ceiling are gleaming white, and the small stained-glass windows are cool greens and blues. "Despite its imperfections I think it is my masterpiece … the result of a lifetime devoted to the search for truth," wrote Matisse, who designed and dedicated the chapel when he was in his 80s and nearly blind. ✉ *466 av. Henri-Matisse, Vence* ☎ *04–93–58–03–26* 💶 *€7* 🕐 *Closed Sun. and Mon.*

 Restaurants

Les Bacchanales

$$$$ | **FRENCH** | Michelin-starred chef Christophe Dufau's weekly changing menu puts an inventive spin on traditional local ingredients; the suckling pig with onion, fresh walnut, and pumpkin is a must when it's available. Meals are served in a sun-filled, beautifully decorated garden villa, a mere 10 minutes by foot from Vence. **Known for:** perfect combination of innovative and French cooking; garden setting a few steps from Matisse Chapel; cheese courses. 💲 *Average main: €75* ✉ *247 av. de Provence, Vence* ☎ *04–93–24–19–19* 🌐 *www.les-bacchanales.com* 🕐 *Closed Tues., Wed., and Dec. No lunch Thurs.*

 Hotels

Château du Domaine St. Martin

$$$$ | **HOTEL** | Occupying the site of an ancient Knights Templar fortress and set amid acres of greenery designed by Jean Mus, this hilltop domain has 180-degree panoramic views, a noteworthy restaurant, and a helicopter pad. **Pros:** spectacular views matched by flawless service; recognized biodiversity refuge that supports Bird Protection charity and provides nesting boxes; superb Michelin-starred restaurant on-site. **Cons:** steep restaurant prices (€31 for an asparagus starter); nothing really within walking distance; expensive rates. 💲 *Rooms from: €670* ✉ *2490 av. des Templiers, Vence* ☎ *04–93–58–02–02* 🌐 *www.chateau-st-martin.com* 🕐 *Closed mid-Oct.–mid-Apr.* 🛏 *46 rooms* 🍽 *Free Breakfast.*

L'Auberge des Seigneurs et du Lion d'Or

$ | **B&B/INN** | Dating to the 17th century and the only hotel set within Vence's old walls, this former stagecoach inn has an ambience *à la François Premier* and the owners go out of their way to make your stay memorable. **Pros:** lovely family atmosphere; fresh flowers and fruit in rooms; affordable breakfast (€12). **Cons:** front rooms are noisy (especially in summer) while quieter back rooms lack views; no air-conditioning; village parking can be tricky. 💲 *Rooms from: €90* ✉ *Pl. du Frêne, Vence* ☎ *04–93–58–04–24* 🌐 *www.auberge-seigneurs.fr* 🕐 *Closed mid-Dec.–mid-Jan.* 🛏 *6 rooms* 🍽 *Free Breakfast.*

🎭 Performing Arts

Nuits du Sud

FESTIVALS | Since 1997, world-music lovers have taken over Place du Grand Jardin in Vence in mid-July for four weeks, with up to 9,000 revelers a night gyrating to various beats. Even if you don't want to buy concert tickets, come for the atmosphere and share a picnic—the music will find you no matter where you are. ✉ *39 rue de 8 Mai 1945, Vence* ☎ *04–93–58–40–17* 🌐 *www.nuitsdusud.com.*

Haut-de-Cagnes

6 km (4 miles) south of St-Paul-de-Vence.

Could this be the most beautiful village in southern France? Part-time residents Renoir, Soutine, Modigliani, and Simone de Beauvoir are a few who thought so. Although from the N7 you may be tempted to give wide berth to the seaside town of Cagnes-sur-Mer—with its congested sprawl of freeway overpasses, numerous tourist-oriented stores, beachfront pizzerias, and the train station—follow the brown signs inland for the "Bourg Médiéval" and the steep road will lead you up into one of the most heavenly perched villages on the Riviera. Even Alice, of Wonderland fame, would adore this steeply cobbled Vieille Ville, honeycombed as it is with tiny piazzas, return-to-your-starting-point-twice alleys, and winding streets that abruptly change to stairways. Many of the pretty residences are dollhouse-size (especially the hobbit houses on Rue Passebon) and most date to the 14th and 15th centuries.

GETTING HERE AND AROUND

Frequent daily trains from Nice or Cannes stop at Cagnes-sur-Mer (get off at Cros-de-Cagnes if you're heading to the beach) from where you take a navette to Haut-de-Cagnes. Bus No. 44 runs throughout the day seven days a week. The Lignes d'Azur Bus No. 200 (€1.50) also stops in Cagnes-sur Mer (which has several beachfront cafés, like Art Beach, open year-round). By car from Paris or Provence on the A8 highway take Exit 47 (Villeneuve–Loubet/Cagnes-sur-Mer); if coming from the east (Monaco, Nice), look for Exit 48 (Cagnes-sur-Mer).

VISITOR INFORMATION **Cagnes-sur-Mer Tourist Office** ✉ *6 bd. Maréchal Juin, Cagnes-sur-Mer* ☎ *04–93–20–61–64* ⊕ *www.cagnes-tourisme.com.*

◉ Sights

Château-Museé Grimaldi

CASTLE/PALACE | Crowning Haut-de-Cagnes is the fat, crenellated Château-Musee. Built in 1310 by the Grimaldis (yes, Prince Albert of Monaco's family) and reinforced over the centuries, this imposing fortress lords over the coastline, banners flying from its square watchtower. You are welcomed inside by a grand balustraded stairway and triangular Renaissance courtyard with a triple row of classical arcades infinitely more graceful than the exterior. Beyond lie vaulted medieval chambers, a vast Renaissance fireplace, and a splendid 17th-century trompe-l'oeil fresco of the fall of Phaëthon from his sun chariot. The château also contains three highly specialized museums: the **Musée de l'Olivier** (Olive Tree Museum), an introduction to the history and cultivation of this Provençal mainstay; the obscure and eccentric **Collection Suzy-Solidor,** a group of portraits of the cabaret chanteuse painted by her artist friends, including Cocteau and Dufy; and the **Musée d'Art Moderne Méditerranéen** (Mediterranean Museum of Modern Art), which contains paintings by some of the 20th-century devotees of the Côte d'Azur, including Chagall, Cocteau, and Dufy. If you've climbed this far, continue to the **tower** and look over the coastline views in the same way that the guards once watched for Saracens. ✉ *Pl. du Château, Haut-de-Cagnes* ☎ *04–92–02–47–35* ⊕ *Closed Tues.* 💶 *From €4.*

Musée Renoir

MUSEUM | After staying up and down the coast, Auguste Renoir (1841–1919) settled into a house in Les Collettes, just east of the Vieille Ville, which is now the Musée Renoir. He passed the last 12 years of his life here, painting the landscape around him, working in bronze, and rolling his wheelchair through the

Our vote for France's most beautiful *village perché*, Haut-de-Cagnes is an enchanting place filled with tiny piazzas, winding alleys, and staircase streets.

luxuriant garden tiered with roses, citrus groves, and spectacular olive trees. You can view this sweet and melancholic villa as it has been preserved by Renoir's children, and admire 15 of his last paintings and 30 sculptures. Although up a steep hill, Les Collettes is a 10-minute walk from Place du Général-du-Gaulle in central Cagnes-Ville (or take the free No. 45 shuttle). ✉ *Chemin des Collettes, Cagnes-sur-Mer* ☎ *04–93–20–61–07* 🎟 *From €6* ⏱ *Closed Tues.*

Hotels

★ Château Le Cagnard

$$$ | HOTEL | There is no better way to experience Old Haut-de-Cagnes's grand castle views than to stay in this acclaimed 13th-century manor, now completely renovated and affiliated with Small Luxury Hotels, perched on the ramparts of the Grimaldi fortress. **Pros:** free shuttle bus to Cagnes-sur-Mer; high-quality linens and heated bathroom floors; gorgeous setting ideal for romance. **Cons:** not much to do in village; breakfast

€25; village parking expensive. $ *Rooms from: €230* ✉ *54 rue Sous Barri, Cagnes-sur-Mer* ☎ *04–93–20–73–22* ⊕ *www. lecagnard.com* ⏱ *Closed Jan.–early Feb.* 🛏 *28 rooms* ⏇ *No meals.*

Nice

15 km (9 miles) northwest of Antibes, 23 km (14 miles) southwest of Monaco.

France's fifth-largest city strikes an engaging balance between historic Provençal grace, port-town exotica, urban energy, and high culture. You could easily spend your entire vacation here, attuned to Nice's quirks, its rhythms, its very multicultural population, and its Mediterranean tides. The high point of the year falls in mid-February, when the city hosts one of the world's most spectacular Carnaval celebrations (⊕ *www. nicecarnaval.com*). But at any time of year you can appreciate the 10-km-long (6-mile-long) waterfront, paralleled by the fabled promenade des Anglais and lined by gorgeous grand hotels.

Back in the 4th century BC, Greeks founded a market-port here and named it Nikaia. Celts and Romans followed—as did Saracen invaders; by the Middle Ages, however, Nice had developed into an important port and was ready to flex its muscles. In 1388, under Louis d'Anjou, Nice, along with the hill towns behind, effectively seceded from the county of Provence and allied itself with Savoie as the Comté de Nice (Nice County). Thus began a relationship that lasted some 500 years, adding a rich Italian flavor to the city's culture, architecture, and dialect.

Nice, of course, has continued to evolve. In the 19th century it emerged as a tourist destination when first the English, and then the Russian nobility, discovered its extraordinary climate and superb waterfront position. Now it's being transformed into the "the Green City of the Mediterranean." For proof, witness the 30-acre Promenade de Paillon Park in the middle of town or the east-west T2 tramline that uses a power supply of rechargeable Ecopack supercapacitors—so no ugly overhead wires.

GETTING HERE AND AROUND

TGV trains can link Paris to Nice in 5½ hours. Air travelers can reach town from the airport using the T2 tramway (☎ 08–10–06–10–06 ⊕ tramway.nice.fr), which stops at both terminals and takes you to the port. Tickets are €1.50 and need to be purchased before boarding and validated in the tram. You can also take Bus No. 98 or No. 99 (€6) from the airport into the city. The No. 98 stops along the promenade and at the port; get off at the J.C. Bermond stop for connections to buses up and down the Riviera. The No. 99 turns off the promenade just before the Hôtel Negresco and goes to the main train station; from there you can access all major coastal locales by rail.

To get around the city, you can use the tram or bus operated by Lignes d'Azur. For the tram, you'll need to purchase your ticket prior to boarding, but with the bus, you can buy directly from the driver. Tickets are €1.50, €10 for a multipass, €5/24-hour or €15/week. Alternately, you can rent a Vélo Bleu bike (☎ 04–93–72–06–06 ⊕ www.velobleu.org) at any of 175 stations for €1 a day or €5 a week; sign up online in advance (you'll need your mobile phone with you to activate once in Nice) or use your credit card at the city's main docking stations.

VISITOR INFORMATION Nice Tourist Office ✉ 5 promenade des Anglais, Nice ☎ 04–92–14–46–14 ⊕ www.nicetourism.com.

Sights

Framed by the "château"—really a rocky promontory—and Cours Saleya, the Old Town of Nice is its strongest drawing point and, should you only be passing through, the best place to capture the city's historic feeling. Its grid of narrow streets, darkened by houses five and six stories high with bright splashes of laundry fluttering overhead and jewel-box Baroque churches on every other corner, creates a magic that seems utterly removed from the Côte d'Azur fast lane.

Nice takes on a completely different character west of Cours Saleya, with broad city blocks, vast neoclassical hotels and apartment houses, and a series of inviting parks dense with palm trees, greenery, and splashing fountains. From the Jardin Albert Ier, once the delta of the Paillon River, the famous Promenade des Anglais stretches the length of the city's waterfront.

Once the site of the powerful Roman settlement Cemenelum, the hilltop neighborhood of Cimiez—4 km (2½ miles) north of Cours Saleya—is Nice's most luxurious quarter (use Bus No. 15

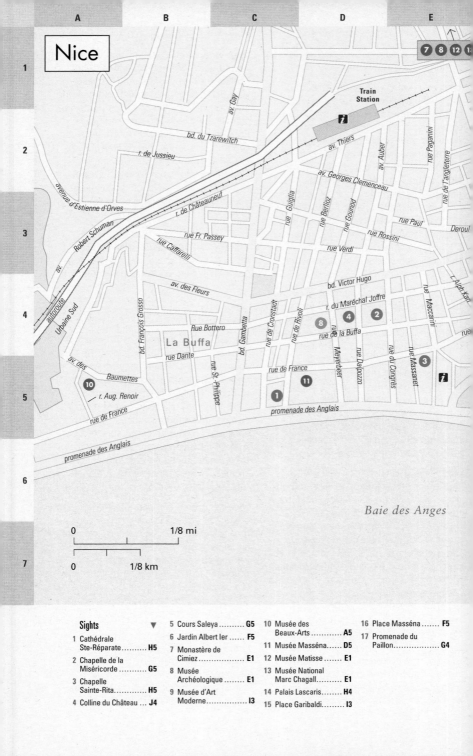

Nice

Sights ▼

1 Cathédrale Ste-Réparate **H5**
2 Chapelle de la Miséricorde **G5**
3 Chapelle Sainte-Rita **H5**
4 Colline du Château ... **J4**
5 Cours Saleya **G5**
6 Jardin Albert Ier **F5**
7 Monastère de Cimiez **E1**
8 Musée Archéologique **E1**
9 Musée d'Art Moderne **I3**
10 Musée des Beaux-Arts **A5**
11 Musée Masséna **D5**
12 Musée Matisse **E1**
13 Musée National Marc Chagall **E1**
14 Palais Lascaris **H4**
15 Place Garibaldi **I3**
16 Place Masséna **F5**
17 Promenade du Paillon **G4**

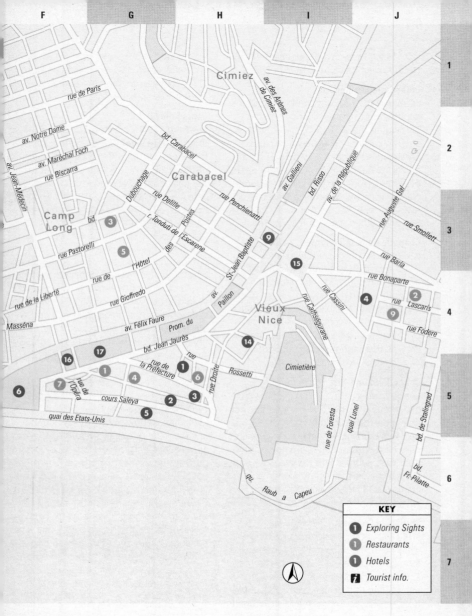

KEY

- ① Exploring Sights
- ① Restaurants
- ① Hotels
- 🛈 Tourist info.

from Place Masséna or Avenue Jean-Médecin to visit its sights).

Cathédrale Ste-Réparate

RELIGIOUS SITE | An ensemble of columns, cupolas, and symmetrical ornaments dominates the Vieille Ville, flanked by an 18th-century bell tower and glossy ceramic-tile dome. The cathedral's interior, completely restored to a bright palette of ocher, golds, and rusts, has elaborate plasterwork and decorative frescoes on every surface. ⊠ *3 pl. Rossetti, Old Town* ⊕ *www.cathedrale-nice.fr* ۞ *Closed Mon.*

Chapelle de la Miséricorde

RELIGIOUS SITE | A superbly balanced *pièce-montée* (wedding cake) of half-domes and cupolas, this chapel is decorated within an inch of its life with frescoes, faux marble, gilt, and crystal chandeliers. A magnificent altarpiece by Renaissance painter Ludivico Brea crowns the ensemble. ⊠ *7 cours Saleya, Old Town* ۞ *Closed July and Aug.*

Chapelle Sainte-Rita (*Église de l'Annonciation*)

RELIGIOUS SITE | This 17th-century Carmelite chapel, officially known as the Église de l'Annonciation, is a classic example of pure Niçoise Baroque, from its sculpted door to its extravagant marble work and the florid symmetry of its arches and cupolas. ⊠ *1 rue de la Poissonerie, Old Town* ⊕ *www.sainte-rita.net.*

Colline du Château (*Château Hill*)

CITY PARK | FAMILY | Although nothing remains of the once-massive medieval stronghold but a few ruins left after its 1706 dismantling, the name *château* still applies to this high plateaulike park, from which you can take in extraordinary views of the Baie des Anges, the length of Promenade des Anglais, and the red-ocher roofs of the Old Town. Children can let off steam at the playground, while you enjoy a picnic with panoramic views and a bit of shade. You can take the 213 steps up to it, or the free elevator next to the Hotel Suisse; alternatively, ascend the

hill slower from the port side, near Place Garibaldi, which is a more gentle climb. ⊠ *Promenade des Anglais, east end, Centre Ville* ⊠ *Free.*

Cours Saleya

NEIGHBORHOOD | This long pedestrian thoroughfare—half street, half square—is the nerve center of Old Nice, the heart of the Vieille Ville, and the stage set for the daily dramas of marketplace and café life. Framed with 18th-century houses and shaded by plane trees, the narrow square bursts into a show of color Tuesday through Sunday until 1 pm, when flower-market vendors roll armloads of mimosas, roses, and orange blossoms into *cornets* (paper cones) and thrust them into the arms of shoppers, who then awkwardly continue forward to discover a mix of local farmers and stallholders selling produce (try the fresh figs), spices, olives, and little gift soaps. Arrive early, especially in summer, to avoid being at the mercy of the crowd's general movement (and a target for the rampant pickpockets). On Monday mornings, antiques and *brocantes* (collectibles) draw avid vintage hounds and from June to September, there's also an artisanal craft market selling jewelry, pottery, purses, and paintings. At the east end of Cours Saleya, you'll find an imposing yellow stone building at Place Charles Félix, where Matisse lived on the third and then fourth floor from 1921 to 1938. Today, there's no plaque that bears his name, only a broken shutter of his workshop to serve as a commemoration. Its future remains uncertain, but for many Niçois, this building is a part of Nice's heritage. ⊠ *Cours Saleya, Old Town.*

Jardin Albert Ier (*Albert I Garden*)

GARDEN | Along Promenade des Anglais, this luxurious garden stands over the delta of the River Paillon, underground since 1882. Every kind of flower and palm tree grows here, thrown into exotic relief by night illumination. Home base for many city festivals with its Théâtre de Verdure and also Ciné Prom in the summer (screenings of box office hits at 7:30 pm), the garden is the starting point for Nice's Promenade du Paillon. ⊠ *2–16 av. de Verdun, New Town* 🚊 *Free.*

Monastère de Cimiez

RELIGIOUS SITE | This fully functioning monastery is worth the pilgrimage. You can find a lovely **garden,** replanted along the lines of the original 16th-century layout; the **Musée Franciscain,** a didactic museum tracing the history of the Franciscan order; and a 15th-century **church** containing three works of remarkable power and elegance by Bréa. ⊠ *Pl. du Monastère, Cimiez* 🕾 *04–93–81–00–04* 🚊 *Free* ⊘ *Museum closed Tues.*

Musée Archéologique (*Archaeology Museum*)

MUSEUM | This museum, next to the Musée Matisse, has a dense collection of objects extracted from digs around the Roman city of Cemenelum, which flourished from the 1st to the 5th century. Among the fascinating ruins are an amphitheater, frigidarium, gymnasium, baths, and sewage trenches, some dating back to the 3rd century. ■ **TIP→ It's best to avoid midday visits on warm days.** ⊠ *160 av. des Arènes-de-Cimiez, Cimiez* 🕾 *04–93–81–59–57* ⊕ *www.musee-archeologique-nice.org* 🚊 *€6* ⊘ *Closed Tues.*

Musée d'Art Moderne

MUSEUM | The assertive contemporary architecture of the Modern Art Museum makes a bold statement regarding Nice's presence in the modern world. The collection inside focuses intently and thoroughly on works from the late 1950s onward, but pride of place is given to sculptor Nikki de St-Phalle's recent donation of more than 170 exceptional pieces. The rooftop terrace, sprinkled with minimalist sculptures, has stunning views over the city. Guided tours in English are given by reservation Wednesday at 4 pm. ⊠ *Promenade des Arts, Nice* 🕾 *04–97–13–42–01* ⊕ *www.mamac-nice.org* 🚊 *From €10* ⊘ *Closed Mon.*

Musée des Beaux-Arts (*Jules-Chéret Fine Arts Museum*)

MUSEUM | Originally built for a member of Nice's Old Russian community, the Princess Kotschoubey, this Italianate mansion is a Belle Époque wedding cake, replete with one of the grandest staircases on the coast. After the *richissime* American James Thompson took over and the last glittering ball was held here, the villa was bought by the municipality as a museum in the 1920s. Unfortunately, many of the period features were sold; but in its place are paintings by Degas, Boudin, Monet, Sisley, Dufy, and Jules Chéret, whose posters of winking *damselles* distill all the *joie* of the Belle Époque. From the Hôtel Negresco area the museum is about a 15-minute walk up a gentle hill. ⊠ *33 av. des Baumettes, New Town* 🕾 *04–92–15–28–28* ⊕ *www.musee-beaux-arts-nice.org* 🚊 *€10* ⊘ *Closed Mon.*

Musée Masséna (*Masséna Palace*)

CASTLE/PALACE | This spectacular Belle Époque villa houses the **Musée d'Art et d'Histoire** (Museum of Art and History), where familiar paintings from French, Italian, and Dutch masters line the walls. A visit to the palace gardens, a park set with towering palm trees, a marble bust of the handsome General Masséna, and backdropped by the ornate trim of the Hôtel Negresco, is a delight; this is one of Nice's most imposing oases. ⊠ *65 rue de France, New Town* 🕾 *04–93–91–19–10* 🚊 *€6* ⊘ *Closed Tues.*

★ Musée Matisse

MUSEUM | In the 1960s, the city of Nice bought this lovely, light-bathed 17th-century villa, surrounded by the ruins of Roman civilization, and restored it to house a large collection of Henri Matisse's works. Matisse settled along Nice's waterfront in 1917, seeking a sun

Like the Rio of France, Nice is lined with a gigantic crescent beach whose prime spot, Promenade des Anglais, is home to many palace-hotels.

cure after a bout with pneumonia, and remained here until his death in 1954. During his years on the French Riviera, Matisse maintained intense friendships and artistic liaisons with Renoir, who lived in Cagnes, and with Picasso, who lived in Mougins and Antibes. He eventually moved up to the rarefied isolation of Cimiez and took an apartment in the Hôtel Regina (now an apartment building, just across from the museum), where he lived out the rest of his life. Matisse walked often in the parklands around the Roman remains and was buried in an olive grove outside the Cimiez cemetery. The collection of artworks includes several pieces the artist donated to the city before his death; the rest were donated by his family. In every medium and context—paintings, gouache cutouts, engravings, and book illustrations—the collection represents the evolution of his art, from Cézanne-like still lifes to exuberant dancing paper dolls. Even the furniture and accessories speak of Matisse, from the Chinese vases to the bold-printed fabrics with which he

surrounded himself. A series of black-and-white photographs captures the artist at work, revealing telling details. Note that you can't get into the museum with a backpack or travel bag. ⊠ *164 av. des Arènes-de-Cimiez, Cimiez* ☎ *04–93–81–08–08* ⊕ *www.musee-matisse-nice.org* ⊠ *€10* ⊘ *Closed Tues.*

Musée National Marc Chagall (*Marc Chagall Museum of Biblical Themes*)
MUSEUM | Inaugurated in 1973, this museum has one of the finest permanent collections of Chagall's (1887–1985) late works. Superbly displayed, 17 vast canvases depict biblical themes, each in emphatic, joyous colors. Chamber music and classical concert series also take place here, though admission fees may apply. Bus Nos. 15 and 22 stop at the museum. ⊠ *Av. du Dr-Ménard, Cimiez* ☎ *04–93–53–87–20* ⊕ *www.musee-chagall.fr* ⊠ *From €8* ⊘ *Closed Tues.*

Palais Lascaris
CASTLE/PALACE | The aristocratic Lascaris Palace was built in 1648 for Jean-Baptiste Lascaris-Vintimille, *marechal* to the Duke

of Savoy. The magnificent vaulted staircase, with its massive stone balustrade and niches filled with classical gods, is surpassed in grandeur only by the Flemish tapestries (after Rubens) and the extraordinary trompe-l'oeil fresco depicting the fall of Phaëthon. With a little luck, you'll be in time for one of the many classical concerts performed here. ⊠ *15 rue Droite, Old Town* ☏ *04–93–62–72–40* 🔖 *€10* ⊘ *Closed Tues*.

Place Garibaldi

PLAZA | Encircled by grand vaulted arcades stuccoed in rich yellow, the broad pentagon of this square could have been airlifted out of Turin. In the center, the shrinelike fountain sculpture of Garibaldi seems to be surveying you as you stroll under the very attractive arcades and lounge in the surrounding cafés. An antiques market takes over the square on the third Saturday of every month (8–5), but if antiques are your thing, you're in the right place because the *place* is the start (or end) of La Promenade des 100 Antiquaires du Port de Nice, which runs down to the port. ⊠ *Old Town.*

Place Masséna

PLAZA | As Cours Saleya is the heart of the Vieille Ville, so this impressive and broad square is the heart of the entire city. It's framed by early-17th-century, Italian-style arcaded buildings, their facades stuccoed in rich red ocher. This enticing space hosts an event at least once a month, from Carnaval to the Christmas market; Promenade du Paillon runs through it. ⊠ *Pl. Masséna, Centre Ville.*

Promenade de Paillon

CITY PARK | Running parallel behind the Old Town, from the Museum of Modern Art to the Théâtre de Verdure, is Nice's emerald jewel: the Promenade de Paillon, a €40 million, 30-acre park. Inaugurated in 2013, it serves as a playground for kids, a refuge for adults (who take advantage of the free Wi-Fi), and a venue for many of the city's one-off events, like April Fool's Day (in French, Poisson

d'Avril, or "Fish Day"). No matter when you arrive, there's plenty to photograph here. ⊠ *Promenade de Paillon, Centre Ville.*

 Restaurants

Attimi

$ | ITALIAN | Specializing in salads, pizzas, and pastas—prepared on the spot from local produce—this place offers a refreshing, light alternative to all those heavy French dishes. But Attimi is as hot as the lasagna Bolognese it serves, so you'll need to reserve or eat early. **Known for:** thin-crust pizza; terrace seating with great people-watching; line to get a table, but worth it. $ *Average main: €16* ⊠ *10 pl. Masséna, Centre Ville* ☏ *04–93–62–00–22* ⊕ *www.attimi.fr.*

★ Chez Pipo Socca

$ | FRENCH | There are plenty of places where you can sample *socca* in the Old Town, but if you want to understand why so much fuss is made in Nice over this chickpea pancake, this out-of-the-way café behind the Port is the place to go. As is normal for making this recipe, a batter of chickpea flour, water, olive oil, and salt is baked in giant copper tins in a wood-fired oven, but here, the cook expertly scrapes the surface of the nearly-cooked dough with a metal spatula so that it comes out extra-crispy. **Known for:** authentic Niçois food; long lines (come at 5:30 when it opens for the shortest wait); cash-only policy. $ *Average main: €7* ⊠ *13 rue Bavastro, Port Nice* ☏ *04–93–55–88–82* ⊕ *www.chezpipo.fr* ⊘ *Closed Mon. and Tues. July and Aug.*

Flaveur

$$$$ | MODERN FRENCH | One of only two two-Michelin-starred restaurants in Nice, Flaveur is run by a young trio (two chefs and a maître d') with a haute cuisine background and is perpetually packed—which means you should book at least a week ahead for dinner and several days ahead for lunch. The key to the trio's success is the heart that goes into their cooking: the limited menu changes often, and the chefs like to experiment with historical recipes such as *petits farcis* (stuffed vegetables) from a 19th-century cookbook. **Known for:** modern interiors; creative fish dishes; hand-cut steak tartare with chickpea fries. $ *Average main: €60* ✉ *25 rue Gubernatis, New Town* ☎ *04–93–62–53–95* ⊕ *www.flaveur. net* ⊗ *Closed Sun., Mon., and last 2 wks in Aug. No lunch Sat.*

La Merenda
$$$ | FRENCH | The back-to-bistro boom climaxed here when Dominique Le Stanc retired his crown at the Negresco to take over this tiny, unpretentious landmark of Provençal cuisine. Now he works in the miniature open kitchen creating ultimate versions of stuffed sardines, tagliatelle with pistou, slow-simmered *daubes* (beef stews), and the quintessential stockfish (the local lutefisk), while his wife whisks the dishes into the dining room. **Known for:** typical French bistrot; amazing food for the price; cash-only policy. $ *Average main: €27* ✉ *4 rue Raoul Bosio, Old Town* ☎ *No phone* ▭ *No credit cards* ⊗ *Closed weekends and 1st 2 wks in Aug.*

La Part des Anges
$$ | FRENCH | This wine shop with some 300 labels and a few tables and chairs at the back is really about *vins naturels*—unfiltered, unsulfured wines made by small producers from hand-harvested grapes—but the often-simple food served here also happens to be excellent. Whether you choose a charcuterie or cheese plate or one of the handful of hot dishes (like spaghetti with razor clams or octopus cooked in red wine), you can expect it to be generous and fresh. **Known for:** natural and organic wines; informative staff; perfect spot to sample wine and cheese. $ *Average main: €18* ✉ *17 rue Gubernatis, New Town* ☎ *04–93–62–69–80* ⊕ *www.la-part-des-anges-nice.fr* ⊗ *Closed Sun.*

★ Le Bistrot d'Antoine
$$ | BISTRO | You won't find any "concept" cooking here, just pure French bistro fare at its finest—beef salad with anchovy dressing, butter risotto with truffles, sliced leg of lamb, and traditional pork casserole. Leave room for the day's dessert, such as the wonderfully warm peach-and-frangipane tart. **Known for:** hands down Nice's best restaurant; eye-poppingly good food; reservations usually necessary. $ *Average main: €19* ✉ *27 rue de la Préfecture, Old Town* ☎ *04–93–85–29–57* ⊗ *Closed Sun. and Mon., 3 wks in Aug., 10 days at Christmas, and at Easter.*

Le Bistro Gourmand
$$$$ | BISTRO | Steps from the Hotel Beau Rivage and with an outdoor terrace, the focus here is on the preservation of French cuisine, courtesy of chef David Vaqué. The sommelier amazingly seems to know your order before you do; a decent bottle will set you back around €55. **Known for:** six-course Legend Menu for only €85; famous soufflé; online reservations only. $ *Average main: €35* ✉ *3 rue Desboutin, Old Town* ☎ *04–92–14–55–55* ⊕ *www.lebistrogourmand.fr* ⊗ *Closed Sun.*

★ Le Canon
$$ | FRENCH | Walking into this small bistrot, you can tell that this is the French dining experience people travel to Provence for, thanks to a handwritten menu on a board, wine bottles as far as the eye can see, and a low-key assemblage of chairs and tables that look like they came out of a 1970s-era attic. Owner Sébastien Perinetti and chef Elmahdi Mobarik source the freshest hyperlocal produce to bring you a parade of taste sensations, all seductively priced. **Known for:** organic food and natural wine; changing menu influenced by local suppliers; reservations in advance necessary. $ *Average main: €24* ✉ *23 rue Meyerbeer, New Town* ☎ *04–96–79–09–24* ⊗ *Closed weekends* ▭ *No credit cards.*

Restaurant Jan

$$$$ | **FRENCH** | South African Jan Hendrik's resume includes a stint as food contributor to the international *ELLE* magazine and two years as the head chef on a luxury yacht in Monaco before opening this exquisite restaurant. Within two years he was awarded a Michelin star, and those hard-to-get reservations for a taste of his menu—veal cheeks, potato dauphine, potato puree, trumpet mushrooms, foie gras, and lavender mayonnaise—became next to impossible. **Known for:** homemade bread and ice cream; intimate setting; reservations can only be made online. [$] *Average main: €55* ✉ *12 rue Lascaris, Port Nice* ☎ *04–97–19–32–23* 🌐 *www.restaurant-jan.com* 🕒 *Closed Sun., Mon., and 2 wks in late Nov. No lunch Sat.–Thurs.*

Hotels

★ Hôtel Negresco

$$$ | **HOTEL** | This white-stucco slice of old-fashioned Riviera extravagance accommodates well-heeled guests in elegant, uniquely decorated (and sometimes quirky) rooms replete with swagged drapes and fine antiques (plus a few unfortunate "with it" touches like those plastic-glitter bathtubs)—everyone should experience one night here. **Pros:** with 6,000 works of art it's like staying in a museum; attention and service from the moment you arrive; best bar on the Riviera. **Cons:** breakfast is expensive (€30); some rooms have more history than comfort; decor not for everyone. [$] *Rooms from: €330* ✉ *37 promenade des Anglais, Promenade* ☎ *04–93–16–64–00* 🌐 *www.hotel-negresco-nice.com* 🛏 *125 rooms* 🍴 *No meals.*

Nice Garden Hotel

$ | **HOTEL** | It's hard to believe that this little gem of a hotel, with its own courtyard garden, is smack in the middle of Nice, next to the pedestrian shopping streets and a five-minute walk from the Old Town. **Pros:** delicious breakfast with homemade jam in the garden; extremely helpful owner; short walking distance to everything. **Cons:** parking is down the street at public garage; not a modern hotel; rooms are smallish. [$] *Rooms from: €120* ✉ *11 rue du Congrès, New Town* ☎ *04–93–87–35–62* 🌐 *www.nicegardenhotel.com* 🛏 *9 rooms* 🍴 *No meals.*

Solara

$ | **HOTEL** | One block from the beach and two from Place Masséna, this tiny budget hotel perches on the fourth and fifth floors, high above the main shopping street. **Pros:** fabulous location near the beach; top-floor terraces overlooking pedestrian street; soundproof windows. **Cons:** rooms on the small size; tricky to find by car; public areas seem a bit run-down. [$] *Rooms from: €105* ✉ *7 rue de France, New Town* ☎ *04–93–88–09–96* 🌐 *www.hotelsolara.com* 🛏 *12 rooms* 🍴 *No meals.*

Windsor

$$ | **HOTEL** | This is a memorably eccentric hotel—most of its white-on-white rooms either have frescoes of mythological themes or are works of artists' whimsy—but the real draw at this otherworldly place is its astonishing city-center garden, a tropical oasis of lemon, magnolia, and palm trees, only outdone by the excellent service—and you're still only three blocks from the beach. **Pros:** private pool and garden in heart of city; a good base to explore Nice; good dining options on-site and nearby. **Cons:** artist-inspired interior design isn't for everyone (look online before booking!); street rooms can be noisy; ultraviolet elevator is cool the first time but annoying by the end of the week. [$] *Rooms from: €144* ✉ *11 rue Dalpozzo, New Town* ☎ *04–93–88–59–35* 🌐 *www.hotelwindsornice.com* 🕒 *Restaurant closed Sun.* 🛏 *57 rooms* 🍴 *Free Breakfast.*

Nightlife

Nice was the first city in France to obtain the "Gay Comfort" international label, awarded by the IGLTA (International Gay and Lesbian Travel Association). The LGBT community here tends to congregate around Le Petit Marais Niçois, the area between Place Garibaldi and the port, and especially along Rue Bonaparte (like Malabar Station at No. 10). The area has experienced a revival in recent years, due mostly to a hip nightlife scene with bars and restaurants. Additionally, the Pink Parade takes place every July and the In&Out Festival in April.

★ Bar Le Relais

BARS/PUBS | If you're all dressed up and have just won big, invest in a drink in the intimate walnut-and-velour Bar Le Relais in the iconic Hôtel Negresco. It's worth the price (€17 for a glass of red wine, or €6 for Evian) just to get a peek at the washrooms. ⊠ *37 promenade des Anglais, Promenade* ☎ *04–93–16–64–00* ⊕ *www.hotel-negresco-nice.com.*

Casino du Palais de la Méditerranée

CASINOS | In the 1920s, the swanky Palais de la Méditerranée drew performers like Charlie Chaplin and Edith Piaf; however, the establishment lost its glory and was demolished in 1990, save for the facade you see today. Reopened with hotel service in 2004, the contemporary version has 180 slot machines, plus 38 electric roulette tables and one blackjack table, plus a Texas Hold 'Em Poker table. ⊠ *15 promenade des Anglais, Promenade* ☎ *04–92–14–68–00 for show reservations* ⊕ *www.casinomediterranee.com.*

Glam

DANCE CLUBS | The city's most colorful LBGT club has DJs who compel you to dance to the best mixes around. It's open to all clubbers in the know, with only one criterion: be cool. ⊠ *6 rue Eugène Emmanuel, Centre Ville* ☎ *04–93–87–29–67.*

High Club

DANCE CLUBS | Nice was a sleepy city until High came along (just ask the neighbors). Right across from the sea, its three designated floors have something for everyone: a massive dance floor with legendary DJs; Studio 47, a tribute to the 1980s and for those on the other side of 25; and the LGBT SkyHigh. Expect to pay a €20 cover and another €120 for a table (four people/one bottle); a VIP magnum will set you back €400. Don't show up unless you're here to be seen. Doors open at 11:45 pm, and it's hopping until 6 am. ⊠ *45 promenade des Angais, New Town* ⊕ *www.highclub.fr.*

Moon Bar

BARS/PUBS | Don't forget your camera when heading up to this panoramic bar on the seventh floor of the Aston La Scala Hotel. The views of old Nice and the new Promenade du Paillon across to the airport are spectacular, and drink prices are more than reasonable. In summer the bar moves to the rooftop, where there's a pool (for guests) and a 360-degree view. Note that there are 23 steps from the hotel lobby to the bar's elevator. ⊠ *12 av. Felix Faure, Centre Ville* ☎ *04–93–17–53–00* ⊕ *www.hotel-aston.com.*

Performing Arts

Acropolis

CONCERTS | Classical music, ballet performances, traditional French pop concerts, and even dog shows take place at Nice's convention center, the Acropolis. ⊠ *Palais des Congrès, Esplanade John F. Kennedy, Nice* ☎ *04–93–92–83–00* ⊕ *www.nice-acropolis.com.*

Nice Jazz Festival

FESTIVALS | For five days in July, the Nice Jazz Festival and Jazz Off draw performers from around the world to Place Masséna and Théâtre de Verdure. Tickets cost €39 per show and can be purchased online or at Place Masséna. ⊠ *Pl.*

No wonder Matisse lived on the top floor of the golden yellow building seen here at the end of Cours Saleya in Nice—this marketplace is one of the most colorful in France.

Masséna and Théâtre de Verdure, Nice ☎ *08–92–68–36–22* ⊕ *www.nicejazzfestival.fr.*

Opéra de Nice

DANCE | A half block west of Cours Saleya stands a flamboyant Italian-style theater designed by Charles Garnier, architect of the Paris Opéra. It's home today to the Opéra de Nice, with a permanent chorus, orchestra, and ballet corps. The season runs mid-November through June, and tickets cost €10–€100. ✉ *4 rue St-François-de-Paule, Old Town* ☎ *04–92–17–40–79* ⊕ *www.opera-nice.org.*

🛍 Shopping

Nice's main shopping street, **Avenue Jean-Médecin,** runs inland from Place Masséna; all needs and most tastes are catered to in its big department stores (Galeries Lafayette, Monoprix, and the split-level Étoile mall). Line 1 of the tramway has made this mini Champs-Elysées all the more accessible, so expect crowds on Saturday (the majority of

shops are still closed on Sunday). Luxury boutiques, such as Emporio Armani and Chanel, line Rue du Paradis (Louis Vuitton is at the end of the street on Avenue de Suède), while Tiffany's and Cartier can be found along Avenue de Verdun. Rue de France and the Old Town have more affordable offerings from independent shops.

Alziari

FOOD/CANDY | Tiny Alziari sells olive oil by the gallon in the famous blue and yellow cans with old-fashioned labels. ✉ *14 rue St-François-de-Paule, Old Town* ⊕ *www.alziari.com.fr.*

Confiserie Florian du Vieux Nice

FOOD/CANDY | Open every day except Christmas, this spot is a good source for crystallized fruit (a Nice specialty). It's located on the west side of the port. ✉ *14 quai Papacino, Old Town* ⊕ *www.confiserieflorian.com.*

La Promenade des 100 Antiquaires

ANTIQUES/COLLECTIBLES | France's third largest *regroupment* of antiques collectors forms a triangle from Place Garibaldi to the port (Quai Papacino) and along Rue Catherine Ségruane at the bottom of the château. Rue Antoine Gautier and Rue Emmanuel Philibert are worth discovering as is Les Puces de Nice, which has 30 stalls under one roof in Quai Lunel, and Place Garibaldi hosts a morning antiques market on the third Saturday of the month. ⊠ *Old Town* ⊕ *www. nice-antic.com.*

Mademoiselle

CLOTHING | You have to hand it to the French: they even do secondhand fashion right. Steps away from the Hôtel Negresco, Mademoiselle has quickly become a must-stop shop in Nice. Chanel, Dior, Louis Vuitton, Hermès—you name it, the gang's all here, at least in vintage terms. You'll find lots of luxury-brand clothes, shoes, bags, and belts to rummage through—all of it excellently priced and gorgeously displayed by owner Sephora Louis. ⊠ *41 rue de France, New Town.*

Maison Auer

FOOD/CANDY | Open Tuesday through Saturday, the venerable Henri Auer has been selling chocolate and crystallized fruit since 1820. ⊠ *7 rue St-François de Paule, Old Town* ⊕ *www.maison-auer.com.*

Star Dog Boutique

PETS | For the jet-set pet, Star Dog Boutique has iPawds (a plush toy with FaceBark, DogTube, and Bark Street Journal apps), Doggle sunglasses, and Oh My Dog! cologne to get Fido's tail wagging. ⊠ *40 rue de France, New Town* ☎ *04–97–03–27–40* ⊕ *www.jophicote-dazur.com.*

 Activities

Beau Rivage

BEACH—SIGHT | Across from Cours Saleya, Beau Rivage Plage—which claims to be the Riviera's largest private beach—has a split personality. On the Zen side, topless sunseekers can rent a cushy lounge chair with umbrella for €25; on the scene-y Trend side, bathers can enjoy cocktails and tapas. The beach itself is stony, so water shoes are advisable. If there are jellyfish sightings, you'll see a written warning of "*méduse*" on a beach board; ditto for strong winds. Steps from Beau Rivage on the Prom, you'll find Nice's own Statue of Liberty (look carefully, as she's only 4½-feet tall). **Amenities:** food and drink; showers; toilets. **Best for:** sunset; swimming. ⊠ *107 quai des États-Unis, Nice* ☎ *04–92–00–46–80* ⊕ *www. plagenicebeaurivage.com.*

Castel Plage

BEACHES | At the east end of the promenade, near Hotel Suisse, there is both a large public beach and a private one, where the water is calm and clear (you can rent a lounger at the latter for about €24, with umbrella). The public beach is composed of large stones, which are more comfortable to walk on than pebbles. Jellyfish are also less of a problem in this corner due to the currents, and lifeguards at the neighboring beach are on duty mid-June–mid-September. **Amenities:** showers. **Best for:** snorkeling; sunrise; sunset; swimming. ⊠ *8 quai des États-Unis, Nice.*

Villefranche-sur-Mer

10 km (6 miles) east of Nice.

The character of Villefranche was subtly shaped by the artists and authors who gathered at the Hôtel Welcome. Among them were Diaghilev and Stravinsky, taking a break from the Ballet Russe in Monaco; Somerset Maugham and Evelyn Waugh; and, above all, Jean Cocteau, who came here to recover from the excesses of Paris life. Luckily, this pretty port retains a restorative vibe—despite being flanked by the big city of Nice and the assertive wealth of Monaco. The streets of the Vieille Ville tilt downhill just as they did in the 13th century; and whether it's just the force of gravity, or

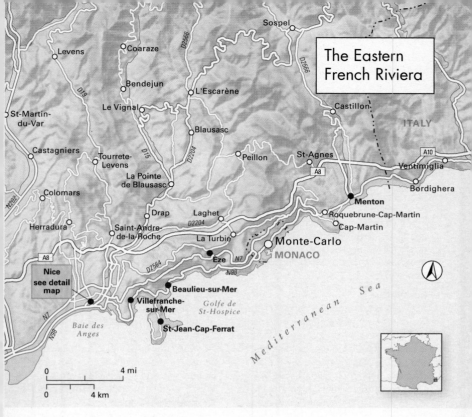

The Eastern French Riviera

the fact that it remains so picturesque, the deep harbor here continues to attract visitors. Set in the caldera of a volcano, it was once filled with yachts belonging to royals and assorted Greek tycoons. Today you're more likely to spot cruise ships, whose passengers take over the town's tiny streets, but genuine fishermen still skim up to its docks in weathered-blue barques. Guided tours of the village (sometimes in English) depart every Friday morning from April to October at 10 from the tourist office (€5). Just remember to wear flat shoes—there are lots of cobblestone streets and stairs to climb.

GETTING HERE AND AROUND
Villefranche is a major stop on the Marseilles–Ventimiglia coastal train route, with more than 40 arrivals every day from Nice (6 mins). Buses connect with Nice

and Monaco via Lignes d'Azur No. 100 or from Nice, Nos. 80, 81, or 84 (€1.50). Most street parking is paid during the day (9–7, €1.10 per hour) and can be tricky to find, but there are three paid parking lots (up to €1.80 per hour).

VISITOR INFORMATION Villefranche-sur-Mer Tourist Office ⊠ *Jardin François Binon, Villefranche-sur-Mer* ☎ *04–93–01–73–68* ⊕ *www.tourisme-villefranche-sur-mer. com.*

 ## Sights

Chapelle St-Pierre
RELIGIOUS SITE | So enamored was Jean Cocteau of this painterly fishing port that he decorated the 14th-century Chapelle St-Pierre with images from the life of St. Peter and dedicated it to the village's fishermen. ⊠ *Quai de l'Amiral Courbet,*

Villefranche-sur-Mer ☎ *04–93–76–90–70* 🎟 *€3* 🕒 *Closed Mon., Tues., and mid-Nov.–mid. Dec.*

Citadelle St-Elme

MILITARY SITE | Restored to perfect condition, the stalwart 16th-century Citadelle St-Elme anchors the harbor with its broad, sloping stone walls. Beyond its drawbridge lie the city's administrative offices and a group of minor gallery-museums, with a scattering of works by Picasso and Miró. Whether you stop into these private collections (all free of charge), you're welcome to stroll around the inner grounds and circle the imposing exterior. ✉ *Harbor, Villefranche-sur-Mer* 🎟 *Free.*

Rue Obscure

NEIGHBORHOOD | Running parallel to the waterfront, the extraordinary 14th-century Rue Obscure ("Dark Street") is entirely covered by vaulted arcades; it sheltered the people of Villefranche when the Germans fired their parting shots—an artillery bombardment—near the end of World War II. ✉ *Villefranche-sur-Mer.*

🍴 Restaurants

La Mère Germaine

$$$$ | **FRENCH** | This is a place to linger over warm lobster salad or sole meunière in butter with almonds while watching the world go by; the food is tasty, but the fabulous setting of this veritable institution is reflected in the prices (and service can fall on the rude side). The seaside restaurant opened in 1938, and proprietor Germaine Halap soon became a second mother to American naval officers and sailors who came into port. **Known for:** legendary local eatery for lovers of fresh seafood; setting right next to the sea; place in U.S. Navy history. [$] *Average main: €55* ✉ *Quai Corbert, Villefranche-sur-Mer* ☎ *04–93–01–71–39* 🌐 *www.meregermaine.com* 🕒 *Closed late Nov.–Christmas.*

★ **Le Serre**

$ | **FRENCH** | It might look like just another pizzeria, but Le Serre is a family-run restaurant where everything from the pizzas to the local specialties is prepared with care. The warm welcome ensures that the restaurant attracts plenty of locals who have learned to tread carefully around tourist traps. **Known for:** classic Provençal beef-and-wine stew with herbs; lively atmosphere; local hangout. [$] *Average main: €17* ✉ *16 rue de May, Villefranche-sur-Mer* ☎ *04–93–76–79–91* 🕒 *Closed mid-Nov.–Dec.*

🛏 Hotels

★ **Hôtel Welcome**

$$$ | **HOTEL** | Somerset Maugham holed up in one of the tiny crow's-nest rooms at the top, Jean Cocteau lived here while writing *Orphée,* and Elizabeth Taylor and Richard Burton used to tie one on in the bar (now nicely renovated) at this waterfront landmark—which remains a comfortable and noteworthy retreat. **Pros:** excellent English-speaking service; artistic heritage makes for a nostalgic trip into the Roaring '20s; paddleboard and kayak rentals. **Cons:** style, especially on the top floor, is overtly nautical in flavor; some rooms are oddly shaped—narrow and long—so they feel smaller; expensive parking in summer. [$] *Rooms from: €235* ✉ *3 quai Amiral Courbet, Villefranche-sur-Mer* ☎ *04–93–76–27–62* 🌐 *www.welcomehotel.com* 🕒 *Closed mid-Nov.–Christmas* 🛏 *35 rooms* 🍴 *Free Breakfast.*

Beaulieu-sur-Mer

4 km (2½ miles) east of Villefranche.

With its back pressed hard against the cliffs of the corniche and sheltered between the peninsulas of Cap Ferrat and Cap Roux, this once-grand resort basks in a tropical microclimate that earned its central neighborhood the

name "Petite Afrique." The town was the pet of 19th-century society, and its grand hotels welcomed Empress Eugénie, the Prince of Wales, and Russian nobles.

GETTING HERE AND AROUND
With frequent arrivals and departures, Beaulieu is a main stop on the Marseille–Ventimiglia coastal train line. From Beaulieu's train station the hourly Bus No. 81 (€1.50) connects with neighboring St-Jean-Cap-Ferrat. Bus No. 100 takes you to and from Nice/Monaco, while No. 84 goes to Nice via Villefranche.

VISITOR INFORMATION Beaulieu Tourist Office ✉ *Pl. Georges Clemenceau, Beaulieu-sur-Mer* ☎ *04–93–01–02–21* ⊕ *www.otbeaulieusurmer.com.*

Sights

★ **Villa Kerylos**
HOUSE | One manifestation of Beaulieu's Belle Époque excess is the eye-popping Villa Kerylos, a 1902 mansion built in the style of classical Greece (to be exact, of the villas that existed on the island of Delos in the 2nd century BC). It was the dream house of amateur archaeologist Théodore Reinach, who hailed from a wealthy German family, helped the French in their excavations at Delphi, and became an authority on ancient Greek music. He commissioned an Italian architect from Nice, Emmanuel Pontremoli, to surround him with Grecian delights: cool Carrara marble, rare fruitwoods, and a dining salon where guests reclined to eat *à la grecque*. It's one of the most unusual houses in the south of France. Organized through the tourist office, tours in English (€5) depart every Thursday at 9:30. Note that a combination ticket allows you to also visit Villa Ephrussi del Rothschild in St-Jean-Cap-Ferrat within the same week. ✉ *Impasse Gustave-Eiffel, Beaulieu-sur-Mer* ☎ *04–93–01–01–44* ⊕ *www.villa-kerylos.fr* 🎫 *€12.*

St-Jean-Cap-Ferrat

2 km (1 mile) south of Beaulieu.

One of the most exclusive addresses in the world, the peninsula of Cap Ferrat is moored by the luxuriously sited pleasure port of St-Jean; from its port-side walkways and crescent of beach you can look over the sparkling blue harbor to the graceful green bulk of the corniches. Yachts purr in and out of port, and their passengers scuttle into cafés for take-out drinks to enjoy on their private decks. On shore, the billionaires come and go, and trade gossip while residents of Cap Ferrat fiercely protect it from curious tourists; its grand old villas are hidden for the most part in the depths of tropical gardens. You can nonetheless try to catch peeks of them from the **Coastline Promenade.** Or just concentrate on shopping: Wednesday evenings in July and August there's a night market (7–11) at the Théâtre de la Mer.

GETTING HERE AND AROUND
The humor is not lost that a bus fare of €1.50 brings you to one of the most exclusive pieces of land on the planet; Bus No. 81 accesses the cape from Nice.

VISITOR INFORMATION St-Jean-Cap-Ferrat Tourist Office ✉ *5 and 59 av. Denis Semeria, St-Jean-Cap-Ferrat* ☎ *04–93–76–08–90* ⊕ *www.saintjeancapferrat-tourisme.fr.*

Sights

Coastline Promenade
PROMENADE | While Cap Ferrat's villas are sequestered for the most part in the depths of tropical gardens, you can nonetheless walk its entire coastline promenade if you strike out from the port; from the restaurant Capitaine Cook, cut right up Avenue des Fossés, turn right on Avenue Vignon, and follow Chemin de la Carrière. The 11-km (7-mile) walk passes through rich tropical flora

and, on the west side, follows white cliffs buffeted by waves. When you've traced the full outline of the peninsula, veer up Chemin du Roy past the fabulous gardens of the **Villa des Cèdres,** owned by King Leopold II of Belgium at the turn of the last century. The king owned several opulent estates along the French Riviera, undoubtedly paid for by his enslavement of the Belgian Congo. Past the gardens, you can reach the **Plage de Passable,** from which you cut back across the peninsula's wrist. A shorter loop takes you from town out to the **Pointe de St-Hospice,** much of the walk shaded by wind-twisted pines. From the port, climb Avenue Jean Mermoz to Place Paloma and follow the path closest to the waterfront. At the point are an 18th-century prison tower, a 19th-century chapel, and unobstructed views of Cap Martin. Two other footpath maps can be found at the Tourist Office at 59 avenue Denis-Séméria; the shorter loop takes you from town out to the Pointe de St-Hospice, much of the walk shaded by wind-twisted pines. From the port, climb Avenue Jean Mermoz to Place Paloma and follow the path closest to the waterfront or the Promenade Maurice Rouvier, which runs along the eastern edge of the peninsula. You'll stumble on reasonably priced cafés, pizzerias, and ice-cream parlors on the promenade of the Plage de St-Jean. The best swimming in the region is a bit farther south, past the port, at Plage Paloma. Keep trekking around the wooded area, where a beautiful path (*sentier pédestre*) leads along the outermost edge of Cap Ferrat. Other than the occasional yacht, all traces of civilization disappear, and the water is a dizzying blue. ✉ *St-Jean-Cap-Ferrat.*

Villa Ephrussi de Rothschild

GARDEN | Between the port and the mainland, the floridly beautiful Villa Ephrussi de Rothschild bears witness to the wealth and worldly flair of the baroness who had it built. Constructed in 1905 in neo-Venetian style (its flamingo-pink facade was thought not to be in the best of taste by the local gentry), the house was baptized "Île-de-France" in homage to the Baroness Béatrice de Rothschild's favorite ocean liner. In keeping with that theme, her staff used to wear sailing costumes and her ship travel kit is on view in her bedroom. Precious artworks, tapestries, and furniture adorn the salons—in typical Rothschildian fashion, each is given over to a different 18th-century "époque." Upstairs are the private apartments of Madame la Baronne, which can only be seen on a guided tour offered around noon. The grounds are landscaped with no fewer than seven gardens and topped off with a Temple of Diana. Be sure to allow yourself time to wander here, as this is one of the few places on the coast where you'll be allowed to experience the lavish pleasures characteristic of the Belle Époque Côte d'Azur. Tea and light lunches, served in a glassed-in porch overlooking the grounds and spectacular coastline, encourage you to linger. ✉ *Av. Ephrussi, St-Jean-Cap-Ferrat* ☎ *04–93–01–33–09* 🌐 *www.villa-ephrussi.com* 🎫 *€15.*

🍴 Restaurants

Le Pancha du Sloop

$$ | **SEAFOOD** | Catering to the yachting crowd, this established port-side restaurant has outdoor tables surrounding a tiny "garden" of potted palms. The focus remains fish, of course: *soupe de poisson* (fish soup), St-Pierre (John Dory) steamed with asparagus, and roasted whole sea bass. **Known for:** long-running port-side eatery; views of boats and yachts; good value for Cap Ferrat. [$] *Average main: €23* ✉ *Port de St-Jean-Cap-Ferrat, St-Jean-Cap-Ferrat* ☎ *04–93–01–48–63* ⏲ *Closed Tues. and Wed.*

🛏 Hotels

Brise Marine

$$ | **HOTEL** | With a Provençal-yellow facade, blue shutters, a balustraded sea terrace, and pretty pastel guest rooms, Brise Marine fulfills most desires for that perfect, picturesque Cap Ferrat hotel. **Pros:** views, views, views; excellent value for location; short walking distance to beach. **Cons:** some rooms are small; parking €16; nighttime quiet interrupted by gently breaking waves. $ *Rooms from: €206* ⊠ *58 av. Jean Mermoz, St-Jean-Cap-Ferrat* ☎ *04–93–76–04–36* ⊕ *www.hotel-brisemarine.com* ☼ *Closed Nov.–Feb.* ➟ *16 rooms* ⦿ *No meals.*

★ Grand-Hôtel du Cap-Ferrat, A Four Seasons Hotel

$$$$ | **HOTEL** | **FAMILY** | Just this side of paradise, this extravagantly expensive hotel has always been the exclusive playground for Hollywood's elite; now, managed by Four Seasons, it is *the* standard for discreet Cap-Ferrat moneyed luxury. **Pros:** epitome of wealth and luxury; every detail is well thought out and promptly attended to; fantastic restaurant and spa. **Cons:** forget it if you're on a budget (breakfast alone is €45); three-night minimum in July and August, two-night in June and September; can feel snooty. $ *Rooms from: €675* ⊠ *71 bd. du Charles du Gaulle, St-Jean-Cap-Ferrat* ☎ *04–93–76–50–50* ⊕ *www.fourseasons.com/capferrat* ☼ *Closed Dec.–Mar.* ➟ *74 rooms* ⦿ *No meals.*

Royal Riviera

$$$$ | **HOTEL** | Completely revamped by Parisian designer guru Grace Leo Andrieu, this former *residence hôtelière* for British aristocrats now invites visitors on an intimate voyage into neo-Hellenic style, complete with an admiring wink at the nearby Villa Kerylos. **Pros:** excellent service and concierge; gorgeous property with gym and spa; heated outdoor pool. **Cons:** some small rooms facing railroad; €38 breakfast; website difficult to navigate. $ *Rooms from: €395* ⊠ *3 av. Jean Monnet, St-Jean-Cap-Ferrat* ☎ *04–93–76–31–00* ⊕ *www.royal-riviera.com/en* ☼ *Closed mid-Nov.–Jan.* ➟ *94 rooms* ⦿ *No meals.*

Èze

2 km (1 mile) east of Beaulieu, 12 km (7 miles) east of Nice.

Medieval and magnificent, towering like an eagle's nest above the coast and crowned with ramparts and the ruins of a medieval château, Èze (pronounced "*ehz*") is unfortunately the most accessible of all the perched villages. So even during off-season its streets flood with tourists, some not-so-fresh from the beach, and it was one of the first towns to post pictorial warnings that say, in effect, "No Shoes, No Shirt, No Service." It is, nonetheless, the most spectacularly sited; its streets are steep and, in places, only for the flamboyantly fit; its time-stained stone houses huddle together in storybook fashion. No wonder U2 frontman Bono and guitarist The Edge have beachside villas here.

GETTING HERE AND AROUND

By car, you should arrive using the Moyenne Corniche, which deposits you near the gateway to Èze Village; Bus Nos. 112 and 82 from Nice also use this road, but No. 100 (to Monaco) goes by the sea while No. 116 heads up the Grande Corniche from Nice (€1.50 each). By train, you'll arrive at the station in Èze-sur-Mer, where a daily navette shuttle bus (No 83; €1.50) takes you up to hilltop Èze, a trip that, with its 1,001 switchbacks up the steep mountainside, takes a full 15 minutes (keep this in mind if you're hiring a taxi to "rush" you down to the train station). Or you could walk from the train station up the Nietzsche Path to the village (90 minutes at least): high heels are not allowed, and the trek isn't advised in the dark.

VISITOR INFORMATION Èze Tourist Office ⊠ *Pl. du Général de Gaulle, Èze* ☎ *04–93–41–26–00* ⊕ *www.eze-tourisme.com.*

The "eagle's-nest" village of the Riviera, Èze perches 1,300 feet above the sea; travelers never fail to marvel at the dramatic setting.

Sights

Jardin Exotique

GARDEN | Set 1,310 feet above sea level, the Jardin Exotique is one of the Riviera's most visited sites. Full of rare succulents and Jean-Philippe Richard sculptures, the botanical garden is also blessed with superlative views: from this crest-top locale you can pan all the way from Italy to St-Tropez (on a clear day, you can even see Corsica). Just a few feet from the entrance, take a time-out lunch at the Nid d'Aigle, an inexpensive eatery featuring focaccias and salads, quaintly set on stone levels rising up around a tall tree. ✉ *20 rue du Château, Èze* ☎ *04–93–41–10–30* 🌐 *www.jardinexotique-eze.fr* 🎟 *€6.*

Restaurants

Cap Estel–La Table de Patrick Raingeard

$$$$ | **FRENCH** | For over 50 years celebs have holidayed and dined at Cap Estel along Èze's *bord de mer,* enjoying its private 5-acre peninsula with all-encompassing views of the Med. Chef Patrick Raingeard's Michelin-star cuisine is worthy of the setting. **Known for:** great brunch; paradisical views; produce from the hotel's garden. [$] *Average main: €62* ✉ *1312 av. Raymond-Poincaré, Charbonnières-les-Bains* ☎ *04–93–76–29–29* 🌐 *www.capestel.com* 🕒 *Closed Jan.–Mar.*

Hotels

★ **Château de la Chèvre d'Or**

$$$$ | **HOTEL** | The "Château of the Golden Goat" is actually an entire stretch of the village, streets and all, bordered by gardens that hang from the mountainside in nearly Babylonian style; in addition to divine accommodations, it delivers some of the most breathtaking Mediterranean views—at a price. **Pros:** insane views; fabulous infinity pool; faultless service. **Cons:** cobblestone walking involved to reach hotel; no elevator; some en suites are on different levels. [$] *Rooms from: €430* ✉ *Rue du Barri, Èze* ☎ *04–92–10–66–66* 🌐 *www.chevredor.com* 🕒 *Closed mid-Nov.–Feb.* 🛏 *40 rooms* 🍴 *No meals.*

Menton

14 km (9 miles) east of Èze, 9 km (5½ miles) east of Monaco.

Modesty makes Menton—the most Mediterranean and least pretentious of the French Riviera resorts—all the more alluring. Rubbing shoulders with the Italian border, the town owes its balmy climate to the protective curve of the Ligurian shore. Its picturesque harbor skyline seems to beg artists to immortalize it, while its Cubist skew of terra-cotta roofs and yellow-ocher houses, Baroque arabesques capping the church facades, and ceramic tiles glistening on their steeples all evoke the villages of the Italian coast. Menton acquaints you with its rich architectural heritage by offering regular *visites du patrimoine* (heritage tours) to its villas, museums, and gardens; tours start at €6. Details are available at the tourist office.

GETTING HERE AND AROUND

Trains run all day from Nice and Monaco. There are a couple of bus options: Lignes d'Azur No. 100 from Menton to Nice (1 hr, €1.50) or the No. 110 airport express (stopping at Monte-Carlo Casino) is an hour and costs €22 one way. To get to Monaco via Roquebrune it's Zest Ligne No. 21, or if passing through Beausoleil, take Bus No. 18 (also €1.50).

VISITOR INFORMATION Menton Tourist Office ✉ *Le Palais de l'Europe, 8 av. Boyer, Menton* ☎ *04–92–41–76–76* ⊕ *www.tourisme-menton.fr.*

Sights

Basilique St-Michel

RELIGIOUS SITE | This majestic basilica dominates the skyline of Menton. Beyond the beautifully proportioned facade—a 19th-century addition—the richly frescoed nave and chapels contain several works by Genovese artists plus a splendid 17th-century organ. Volunteers man the doors here, so you may have to wait for the church to open before visiting. The parvis plays host to concerts during the Menton music festival every August. ✉ *Parvis St-Michel, 22 rue St-Michel, Menton* ⊗ *Closed weekends.*

Chapelle de l'Immaculée-Conception

RELIGIOUS SITE | Just above the main church, the smaller Chapelle de l'Immaculée-Conception answers St-Michel's grand gesture with its own pure Baroque beauty. The sanctuary, dating to 1687, is typically closed to the public; however, you can try and slip in to see the graceful trompe-l'oeil over the altar and the ornate gilt lanterns early penitents carried in processions. ✉ *Pl. de la Conception, Menton.*

Marché Couvert (*Covered Market*)

MARKET | Between the lively pedestrian Rue St-Michel and the waterfront, the marvelous Marché Couvert (Les Halles) sums up Menton style with its Belle Époque facade decorated in jewel-tone ceramics. It's equally appealing inside, with merchants selling chewy bread and mountains of cheese, oils, fruit, and Italian delicacies daily (on Saturday, clothing is also sold). Be sure to try *barbbajuans*, the local dish of fried vegetables and rice. ✉ *Quai de Monléon, Menton.*

Serre de la Madone

GARDEN | With a temperate microclimate created by its southeastern and sunny exposure, Menton attracted a great share of wealthy horticultural hobbyists, including Major Lawrence Johnston, a gentleman gardener best known for his Cotswolds wonderland, Hidcote Manor. He wound up buying a choice estate in Gorbio—one of the loveliest of all perched seaside villages, 10 km (6 miles) west of Menton—and spent the 1920s and 1930s making the Serre de la Madone a masterpiece. Johnston brought back exotica from his many trips to South Africa, Mexico, and China, and planted them in a series of terraces, accented by little pools, vistas, and stone steps. While most of his creeping plumbago, pink belladona, and night-flowering cacti are now gone, his garden has been reopened by the municipality. If you don't have a car, you can reach it from Menton via Bus No. 7. ✉ *74 rte. de Gorbio, Menton* ☎ *04–93–57–73–90* 🎟 *€8* 🕓 *Closed Mon.*

Val Rahmeh Botanical Garden

GARDEN | Green-thumbers will want to visit Menton's Val Rahmeh Botanical Garden—especially in the fall when the hibiscus and brugmansias are in bloom. Planted by Maybud Campbell in the 1910s and much prized by connoisseurs, it's bursting with rare ornamentals and subtropical plants, and adorned with water-lily pools and fountains. The tourist office can also give you directions to other gorgeous gardens around Menton, including the Fontana Rosa, the Villa Maria Serena, and the Villa Les Colombières. ✉ *Av. St-Jacques, Menton* ☎ *04–92–10–97–10* 🎟 *€7* 🕓 *Closed Tues.*

🍴 Restaurants

★ Mirazur

$$$$ | **MODERN FRENCH** | Chef Mauro Colagreco learned his craft in Latin America before acquiring a solid French base with the likes of Bernard Loiseau in Burgundy and both Alain Passard and Alain Ducasse in Paris, and now is at the helm at Mirazur, an innovative restaurant on the border of France and Italy that's earned three Michelin stars. He is a perfect example of the wave of young chefs whose style has been dubbed *la jeune cuisine*; for Colagreco, the plate is a palette, and each ingredient has its precise place and significance. **Known for:** avant-garde French cuisine by an Argentinian-Italian chef; one of the top restaurants in the entire world; beautiful views. [$] *Average main: €160* ✉ *30 av. Aristide Briand, Menton* ☎ *04–92–41–86–86* 🌐 *www.mirazur.fr* 🕓 *Closed Mon., Jan.–early Mar., and last week of Dec. No lunch Tues. and Wed. Mar.–May and Sept.–Dec.*

🛏 Hotels

Hôtel Lemon

$ | **HOTEL** | Subtropical gardens and 19th-century architecture are two of Menton's main attractions, and this hotel a few minutes' walk from the train station gives you a taste of both and at prices rarely seen along the Riviera. **Pros:** plenty of charm at rock-bottom prices; a few blocks from the sea; rooms are basic but tasteful. **Cons:** parking can be difficult; street can be noisy; no air-conditioning. [$] *Rooms from: €64* ✉ *10 rue Albert 1er, Menton* ☎ *04–93–28–63–63* 🌐 *www.hotel-lemon.com* 💳 *No credit cards* 🔑 *18 rooms* 🍽 *No meals.*

Chapter 14

MONACO

Updated by
Nancy Heslin

◉ Sights	🍴 Restaurants	🛏 Hotels	👜 Shopping	🍸 Nightlife
★★★☆☆	★★★☆☆	★★★☆☆	★★★★☆	★★★☆☆

WELCOME TO MONACO

TOP REASONS TO GO

★ **Monte Carlo:** Even if you aren't a gambler, the gold leaf and over-the-top rococo in the casino are definitely worth a long look.

★ **Grace Kelly:** Follow in Grace Kelly's footsteps with a visit to the Palais Princier, the official residence of the "royal" family, including the actress's grandson, heir apparent Prince Jacques.

★ **Parks:** Yes, Virginia, you can afford to visit Monte Carlo—that is, if you head to its magnificent Jardin Exotique de Monaco.

★ **Underwater museum:** One of the world's best ocean-ography museums, the Musée Océanographique is an architectural masterpiece in its own right.

★ **Beaches:** Monaco's chic waterfront is well known for its private clubs and people-watching.

Monaco covers just 473 acres and would fit comfortably inside New York's Central Park. (That said, it also reaches a height of 528 feet, so bring some walking shoes.) Despite its compact nature, everybody drives here, whether from the Palais Princier perched on the Rock down to the port or up to Casino Gardens at the eastern tip.

1 Monaco. The principality's sensational position on a broad peninsula that bulges into the Mediterranean seduces billionaires and A-listers, as well as those who just want to see how the 1% live. One out of every three people is a millionaire here, with the microstate boasting the world's most expensive property to buy ($1 million per 16 square miles) and to rent (up to $220,000 a month).

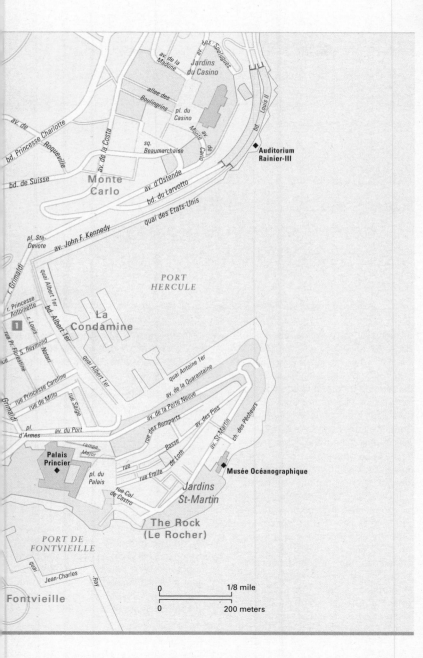

This compact fairy-tale Mediterranean destination is one of the most sought-after addresses in the world—but even a million dollars won't buy you much here. Overshadowed by the seven ultramodern glass buildings in Casino Square, known as One Monte-Carlo, you have to look hard to find the Belle Époque grace of yesteryear. But if you head inside the town's great 1864 landmark Hôtel de Paris or attend the opera at Salle Garnier, you may still be able to conjure up Monaco's elegant past.

Reigning monarch Prince Albert II traces his ancestry back to the Grimaldi dynasty, when Franceso Grimaldi was expelled from Genoa and in 1297 seized the fortified medieval town known today as Le Rocher (the Rock). Except for a short break under Napoléon, the Grimaldis have been here ever since, which makes them the oldest reigning family in Europe. In the 1850s, a Grimaldi named Charles III saw that the Rock needed revenue, but not wanting to impose additional taxes on his subjects, he contracted with a company to open a gambling facility. The first spin of the roulette wheel in Monaco was on December 14, 1856. With the 1868 introduction of the railroad, the threadbare principality became an elegant watering hole for European society. Profits were so great that Charles eventually abolished all direct taxes; in exchange for this tax-free living, Monégasque citizens have never been allowed inside the casino, as all revenues must be generated from foreigners.

Prince Rainier III, who reigned 1949–2005, worked hard to regain Monaco's glitz and glamour post–World War II occupation and is credited for developing tourism and the financial sector. He married 26-year-old Hollywood legend Grace Kelly in 1956, helping to introduce America to Monaco's "royal" family (as there is no king or queen, the Grimaldis are not officially considered a royal family). They had three children: Caroline, Albert (the current reigning price), and Stephanie, who was a passenger in her mother's Rover when it plummeted 120 feet off a cliff in nearby La Turbie. Some 100 million people watched Grace Kelly's funeral on September 18, 1982.

The principality is divided into eight quarters. To the west, bordering Cap d'Ail, is the newest area, Fontvieille, with its rose garden, soccer stadium, and tempting marina-side restaurants. Look up from here and you can see old Monaco-Ville (or Le Rocher), a medieval town perched on the Rock, topped by the palace, the government's national council, the world-class Oceanographic Museum, and the cathedral where Grace Kelly is buried. On the other side is the port-facing La Condamine, which offers a smorgasbord of eateries and pedestrian shopping streets, and connects the Rock to Monte-Carlo, home to Casino Square, the Metropole shopping center, and the illustrious Hotel de Paris. To the east, Larvotto is all about the beach, restaurants, and bars—including places where you can spend €28 for a glass of water. Currently, Larvotto is also where Monaco's €2 billion land reclamation is underway, and to create the 6-hectare neighborhood by 2026, the government has closed the beach for two years starting September 2019. The Exotic Garden district, behind Fontvieille, includes the magical gardens, Villa Paloma art museum, the Museum of Prehistoric Anthropology, and Princess Antoinette Park, where you can play outdoor badminton and minigolf. La Rousse and Les Moneghetti are Monaco's other, more residential neighborhoods.

As you might expect, even the most modest hotels cost more here than in nearby Nice or Menton, and dining is expensive. For the frugal, Monaco is the ultimate day trip by train. The Princess Grace Rose Garden in Fontvieille and the Monte-Carlo Japanese Garden are free to stroll around from sunrise to sunset. Pick up some fresh edibles at La Condamine daily market at the Place d'Armes to savor at the public rose garden or look for the daily happy hour at Stars 'n' Bars in the port. You don't have to be a member of the Yacht Club to eat port side at the Société Nautique, Monaco's rowing club, where the food is as impressive as the views. Art lovers can visit the luminous Opera Galery, next to the Hermitage, for free. At the very least, make use of the free public toilets everywhere.

If lunch is not in the budget, splurge at one of the trendy local cafés to catch a glimpse of the working class (yes, really). With a population of 38,000, every day 55,000 employees make the commute to Monaco.

Planner

When to Go

Even Monégasques escape the swelter of July and August, and the beaches are at their best in June or September. To avoid the shiploads of travelers during high season, visit in the fall or winter. The temperatures may not be as sizzling, but you'll still get color from reflecting diamonds.

FESTIVALS

Monte-Carlo Sporting Summer Festival
MUSIC | Where else but Monaco can you see Lady Gaga and Tony Bennett, Elton John, Rod Stewart, or Duran Duran at a sit-down dinner venue for 700 people? Since 1974, the Monte-Carlo Sporting Summer Festival has been held at Le Sporting, a summer-only entertainment complex on the waterfront with a roof that opens up to the stars, perhaps justifying the €200 ticket (or the €1,000 Red Cross Gala)—although the celebrities are also part of the draw. ☎ 377/98–06–41–59 ⊕ en.sportingsummerfestival.com.

Printemps des Arts
FESTIVALS | Monte Carlo's monthlong spring arts festival, Printemps des Arts, brings together the world's top ballet, operatic, symphonic, and chamber-music performers at venues across Monaco—the Opéra de Monte-Carlo, Oceanographic Museum, Grimaldi Forum, St-Charles Church, and Auditorium Rainier III.

☎ *377/98–06–28–28* ⊕ *www.printemps-desarts.com.*

Getting Here and Around

If you're flying into the Nice airport, a taxi to Monaco costs a flat fee of €90 (there's no Uber in Monaco). Or you can save time with Monancair's seven-minute helicopter transfer, starting from around €140 one way (includes door-to-door shuttle service and luggage check). A less glamorous but more affordable option is the Nice Airport-Menton 110 bus, which stops in Monaco (45 mins, €22 one way).

From Nice, Monaco is serviced by regular trains along the Cannes–Ventimiglia line; from Nice Ville, the main station, the journey costs €3.90 one way and takes 20 minutes. By bus, the Lignes d'Azur Bus No. 100 departs from the Port in Nice, but can be very crowded in high season. You can pay the €1.50 fare on board.

Monaco is a relatively easy place to navigate on foot, especially if you take advantage of its 78 public elevators, 35 escalators, and 8 travelators. But if you're looking for an insider's view, native Jean-Marc Ferrié at Monaco Rando (⊕ *www. monaco-rando.com*) gives guided walking tours in English, from the secrets of the Rock and the Grand Prix Circuit to the four-hour Via Alpina with stunning overviews of the principality. Prices run €15–€50 per person.

BUS TRAVEL

Compagnie des Autobus de Monaco operates a bus line that threads the avenues of Monaco. Purchase your ticket on board for €2, or save €0.50 a ticket by buying in advance from a ticket machine or online (a 24-hour ticket costs €5.50). The company also operates both the Bateaux Bus, a solar electric boat from Quai des États-Unis to the casino—it runs daily 8–8 and costs €1.50—and Les Vélos Electriques de Monaco, where you can sign up for unlimited use of one of 105 electric bikes for a nominal subscription fee of €15.

BUS INFORMATION Compagnie des Autobus de Monaco ☎ *377/97–70–22–22* ⊕ *www.cam.mc.*

Restaurants

With nine Michelin stars, there is no shortage of lavish dining in the principality, so wear something presentable and don't forget your wallet.

Hotels

Hotel prices skyrocket during the Monaco Grand Prix, so reserve as far ahead as possible. That goes for festivals like the Printemps des Arts as well. No matter the time, however, hotels cost more here than in nearby Nice or Menton. For the cost-conscious, Monaco is the ultimate day trip by train.

Restaurant and hotel reviews have been shortened. For full information, visit Fodors.com. Restaurant prices are the average cost of a main course at dinner or, if dinner is not served, at lunch. Hotel prices are the lowest cost of a standard double room in high season.

What It Costs in Euros			
$	$$	$$$	$$$$
RESTAURANTS			
under €18	€18–€24	€25–€32	over €32
HOTELS			
under €125	€125–€225	€226–€350	over €350

Visitor Information

CONTACTS Monaco Tourist Office ✉ *2 bd. des Moulins, Monte Carlo* ☎ *377/92–16–61–66* ⊕ *www.visitmonaco.com.*

👁 Sights

Casino Monte-Carlo

CASINO—SIGHT | Place du Casino is the center of Monte Carlo and a must-see, even if you don't like to bet. Into the gold-leaf splendor of the 1863 casino, the hopeful descend from tour buses to tempt fate beneath the gilt-edge rococo ceiling—and some spend much more than planned here, as did the French actress Sarah Bernhardt, who lost once 100,000 francs. Jackets are required after 8 pm in the private back rooms, which open at 4 pm. Bring your passport (under-18s not admitted) and note the €17 admission to get into any of the period gaming rooms (open from 2 pm). For €17, you can also visit the casino in the off-hours (daily 10–1) for access to all rooms. ✉ Pl. du Casino, Monte Carlo ☎ 377/98–06–21–21 ⊕ www.casinomontecarlo.com.

Collection des Voitures Anciennes (Collection of Vintage Cars)

MUSEUM | FAMILY | The car collection of the Prince of Monaco is an impressive assemblage of vintage cars, with everything from a De Dion Bouton to a Lamborghini Countach. All were owned by Prince Rainier, with a few models courtesy of his son, Prince Albert, including the Lexus from the princely wedding in 2011. ✉ 5 Terrasses de Fontvieille ☎ 377/92–05–28–56 ☎ From €8.

Jardin Exotique de Monaco (Tropical Garden)

GARDEN | More than a thousand varieties of cacti and succulents cling to a sheer rock face at Monaco's magnificent Tropical Garden, a brisk half-hour walk west from the palace. The garden traces its roots to days when Monaco's near-tropical climate nurtured unheard-of exotica, amazing visitors from the northlands as much as any zoo. The plants are of less interest today, especially to Americans familiar with southwestern flora. The views over the Rock and coastline, however, are spectacular. Also on the grounds, or actually under them by descending 300 steps, are the **Grottes de l'Observatoire**—spectacular grottoes and caves adrip with stalagmites and spotlit with fairy lights. The **Musée d'Anthropologie** showcases two rooms: "Albert I" covers general prehistory, while "Ranier III" unearths regional Paleolithic discoveries. And a rarity for Monaco, all three attractions are included in one ticket. ✉ 62 bd. du Jardin Exotique ⊕ www.jardin-exotique.mc ☎ €8.

⭐ Le Tigre Yoga Club and Spa

SPA/BEAUTY | Most visitors to Monaco don't know the Monte Carlo Beach Club exists; because it's located so far east it's technically in France. Built in 1929, it features an eye-popping, Olympic-size heated seawater pool overlooking a private beach—and now the ultraluxurious setting is also home to the Parisian concept Le Tigre Yoga Club and Spa, open seven days a week and, most importantly, open to non-club members. Amid the salty sea and pine trees (and Michelin-star organic restaurant Elsa), daily outdoor group yoga, meditation, and Pilates classes take place on the pontoon. Inside, three exquisitely designed cabanas make up the 80-square-meter Le Tigre Spa, where its deep-tissue signature massage combines Ayurvedic, lomi-lomi, yogic, and Californian techniques to produce a surprisingly energizing yet overall relaxing result (60 minutes; €185). Parking is free (otherwise, take the No. 5 or 6 Larvotto bus and walk 10 minutes) and, if you're lucky, renting a lounger at the Beach Club may round off your well-being experience like a true jet-setter. ✉ Monte Carlo Beach Club, Av. Princess Grace ☎ 377/98–06–51–05 ⊕ www.tigre-yoga.com/en/capsule/le-tigre-monte-carlo 🕑 Closed mid-Nov.–mid-Mar.

Les Thermes Marins de Monte-Carlo (Sea Baths of Monte-Carlo)

HOT SPRINGS | Added to the city in the 1990s, this seawater-therapy treatment

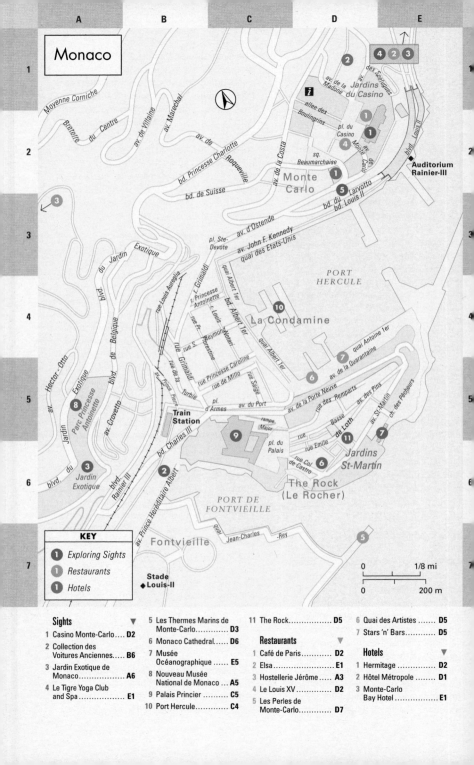

Monaco

KEY
- ① Exploring Sights
- ① Restaurants
- ① Hotels

Moyenne Corniche
Bretella du Centre
av. de Villaine
av. Maréchal
av. de
bd. Princesse Charlotte
Roqueville
bd. de Suisse
av. de la Costa

av. de la Madone
des Spélugues
Jardins du Casino
allée des Boulingrins
pl. du Casino
av. du Monte Carlo
blvd. Louis II
sq. Beaumarchaise

Monte Carlo

bd. du Larvotto
bd. Louis II

♦ **Auditorium Rainier-III**

av. d'Ostende
pl. Ste-Dévôte
av. John F. Kennedy
quai des Etats-Unis

du Jardin Exotique

PORT HERCULE

blvd Exotique
blvd. de Belgique
r. Grimaldi
r. Princesse Antoinette
r. Louis Aureglia
av. Hector – Otto
bd. Albert 1er
La Condamine
quai Albert 1er

rue S. Raymond
rue Plati
rue P. Forestine

av. Crovetto
rue de la Turbie
rue Princesse Caroline
rue de Millo
rue Saige

quai Antoine 1er
av. de la Quarantaine

Parc Princesse Antoinette

Jardin du blvd.

Jardin Exotique

blvd. Rainier III
bd. Charles III
av. Prince Pierre
Train Station
pl. d'Armes
av. du Port
rampe Major
av. de la Porte Neuve
rue des Remparts
av. des Pins
ch. des Pêcheurs
av. St-Martin
Bassé de Loth

Jardins St-Martin

av. Prince Héréditaire Albert
pl. du Palais
rue Emile
rue Col de Castro

The Rock (Le Rocher)

PORT DE FONTVIEILLE

quai Jean-Charles-Rey

Fontvieille

♦ **Stade Louis-II**

0 ——— 1/8 mi
0 ——— 200 m

Sights ▼
1 Casino Monte-Carlo.... **D2**
2 Collection des Voitures Anciennes..... **B6**
3 Jardin Exotique de Monaco................. **A6**
4 Le Tigre Yoga Club and Spa................. **E1**
5 Les Thermes Marins de Monte-Carlo............. **D3**
6 Monaco Cathedral...... **D6**
7 Musée Océanographique **E5**
8 Nouveau Musée National de Monaco..... **A5**
9 Palais Princier **C5**
10 Port Hercule.............. **C4**
11 The Rock................. **D5**

Restaurants ▼
1 Café de Paris............ **D2**
2 Elsa....................... **E1**
3 Hostellerie Jérôme..... **A3**
4 Le Louis XV **D2**
5 Les Perles de Monte-Carlo............. **D7**
6 Quai des Artistes **D5**
7 Stars 'n' Bars............ **D5**

Hotels ▼
1 Hermitage **D2**
2 Hôtel Métropole **D1**
3 Monte-Carlo Bay Hotel **E1**

center stretches along the port's upper side between the landmark Hôtel de Paris and its sister, the Hermitage, and can be accessed directly from either hotel. Within its sleek, 6,600-square-meter multilevel complex, you can pursue every creature comfort, from underwater massage and seaweed body wraps to a 90-minute Prairie Platinum Ultimate Youth Treatment for €330. This is also the only spot in Europe offering cryotherapy, a treatment where you spend a couple of minutes in two cold chambers at -60°C and then-110°C, which is said to help with jet lag, sleep disorders, and antiaging. You'll definitely want to indulge in the outdoor hot tub afterward and enjoy an elegant spa lunch at L'Hirondelle as you thaw. ✉ 2 av. de Monte-Carlo ☎ 377/98–06–69–00 ⊕ www.thermesmarinsmontecarlo.com.

Monaco Cathedral

RELIGIOUS SITE | Follow the crowds down the last remaining streets of medieval Monaco to the 19th-century Cathédrale de l'Immaculée-Conception, which contains the tomb of Princess Grace and Prince Rainier III, as well as a magnificent altarpiece, painted in 1500 by Louis Bréa. From September to June, the Monaco's Boys Choir (Les Petits Chanteurs) provide the music for Sunday mass at 10:30 am. ✉ Av. St-Martin ☎ 377/93–30–87–70 ⊕ www.cathedrale.mc.

★ Musée Océanographique (Oceanography Museum)

MUSEUM | FAMILY | Perched dramatically on a cliff, this museum is a splendid Edwardian structure, built under Prince Albert I to house specimens collected on amateur explorations, including Jacques Cousteau–led missions from 1957 to 1988. The main floor exhibits the Whale Room, with skeletons and taxidermy of enormous sea creatures, early submarines and diving gear dating to the Middle Ages, and a few interactive science displays. The main draw is the blockbuster **aquarium,** a vast complex of backlighted tanks containing more than 6,000 species of fish, crab, and sharks in pools running 100–450,000 liters. ✉ Av. St-Martin ☎ 377/93–15–36–00 ⊕ www. oceano.mc/en ✉ From €14.

Nouveau Musée National de Monaco

MUSEUM | Monaco's national museum is actually divided into two separate buildings at opposite ends of town. One of the surviving buildings from the Belle Époque, Villa Sauber, with its rose garden, is in the Larvotto Beach area (take the elevator down from Place des Moulins). The Villa Paloma (next door to the Jardin Exotique) was recently restored with fabulous stained-glass windows. The museums are open to the public only during exhibitions so check the website for more information. ✉ Villa Sauber, 17 av. Princesse Grace ☎ 377/98–98–91–26 ⊕ www.nmnm.mc ✉ €6.

Palais Princier

CASTLE/PALACE | The famous Rock, crowned by the palace where the royal family resides, stands west of Monte Carlo. An audio guide leading you through this sumptuous chunk of history, first built in the 13th century and expanded and enhanced over the centuries, reveals an extravagance of 16th- and 17th-century frescoes, as well as tapestries, gilt furniture, and paintings on a grand scale. Note that the **Relève de la Garde** (Changing of the Guard) is held outside the front entrance of the palace most days promptly at 11:55 am. Les Grands Appartements are open to the public from early April through October, and you can buy a joint ticket with the Musée Océanographique. Beginning in mid-July, a summer concert series can be enjoyed at 9:30 pm in the palace's esteemed courtyard. Tickets can be purchased through the Orchestre Philharmonique de Monte-Carlo (⊕ www.opmc.com). ✉ Pl. du Palais ☎ 377/93–25–18–31 ⊕ www.palais.mc ✉ From €8 ⊗ Closed mid-Oct.–Apr.

Monaco's Belle Époque opulence is epitomized by its famed Casino Monte-Carlo, which is just as visually stunning at night.

Port Hercule

MARINA | It's a blissful hike down from Monte Carlo to the port along Boulevard Albert Ier, where pleasure boats of every shape flash white and blue. You can catch a glimpse of the spectacular yachting club, one of the world's most prestigious and a staple in the local social circuit, where performers like Elton John and Duran Duran have played. It's along here that they erect the stands for fans of the Grand Prix, while the far corner of the port is where the Institut Océanographique launches research boats to study aquatic life in the Mediterranean, as its late director Jacques Cousteau did for some 30 years. You can also access the seawall from here, and get some great shots of the Rock.

The Rock

NEIGHBORHOOD | On the broad plateau known as Le Rocher, or the Rock, the majority of Monaco's touristic sights are concentrated with tidy, self-conscious charm. This is the medieval heart of Monaco, and where its cathedral, palace, and Musée Océanographique can be found, along with the delightful St- Martin Gardens, the country's first public garden (opened since 1816). Only vehicles with Monaco license plates can drive through the gate, so you can either climb up the 42 long steps of the Rampe Majeur from Place d'Armes, behind the right corner of the port, or approach it by elevator from the seafront at the port's farthest end.

Beaches

Larvotto Beach

BEACHES | FAMILY | The pebbly Larvotto Beach just off Avenue Princess Grace, said to be one of the world's most costly streets to live on, is the only free public beach in Monaco, and it has the added bonus of being protected by jellyfish nets. Note that extensive renovations of the beach are currently in the works; it closed completely in October 2019, with plans to reopen July and August 2020. It will be closed again from September 2020 to June 2021. The complete reopening of the beach and shops is scheduled for the summer season 2021. All developments are scheduled to be completed in early 2022. Since construction plans can change, it's always best to confirm if the beach is open before you go. **Amenities:** lifeguards; showers; toilets; water sports. **Best for:** sunrise, sunset. ✉ *Av. Princesse Grace.*

Plage Mala

BEACHES | This lovely stretch of sandy, shaded land is easily one of the most stylish of the Riviera beaches, and despite its proximity to Monaco—half an hour by foot—Plage Mala's public area never gets crowded. Another upside is that the coves under the impressive cliffs produce the best area for snorkeling along the coast. Nearby are private beach restaurants where you can rent loungers. The 3.5-km (2.2-mile) Mala footpath that stretches to Plage Marquet in Fontvieille in Monaco is relatively easy to walk, with the most challenging leg being the access to Mala beach itself with more than 100 steps. Walking to Monte Carlo generally takes less than an hour; however, avoid the path during stormy conditions. **Amenities:** lifeguard; showers. **Best for:** snorkeling; swimming; walking. ✉ *Av. Raymond Gramaglia, Cap-d'Ail.*

🍴 Restaurants

Café de Paris

$$$$ | **BRASSERIE** | The landmark Belle Époque "Brasserie 1900"—better known as Café de Paris—offers the usual classics (shellfish, steak tartare, matchstick frites, and fish boned tableside). Supercilious, superpro waiters fawn gracefully over titled preeners, jet-setters, and tourists alike. **Known for:** ultimate spot for people-watching while you eat; Sunday lunch menu; late hours until 2 am. Ⓢ *Average main: €36* ✉ *Pl. du Casino* ☎ *377/98–06–76–23* ⊕ *www.casinocafedeparis.com.*

Elsa

$$$$ | **FRENCH** | Paoli Sari is not the first chef to earn a cherished Michelin star, but he is the first to be awarded the honor for an all-organic restaurant, located at the Monte Carlo Beach Club. The Venetian-born chef uses the produce of a dozen local growers from within 150 km, and the seafood on his menu comes from small inshore fishermen. **Known for:** Michelin-starred food in a refreshing setting; everything, including the cola, is organic; away from the Monaco crowds. Ⓢ *Average main: €62* ✉ *Monte-Carlo Beach, Av. Princesse Grace, Roquebrune-Cap-Martin* ☎ *377/98–06–50–05* ⊕ *www.montecarlosbm.com/en/restaurant-monaco/elsa* ⊗ *Closed Nov.–early Mar.* 🎩 *Jacket required.*

Hostellerie Jérôme

$$$$ | **FRENCH** | Prince Albert's country home, Roc Angel, is about 10 km (6 miles) behind Monaco in La Turbie, so it's no wonder a top-notch dinner restaurant (read: expensive, expensive, expensive) with a 30,000-bottle wine cave that picked up France's Best Wine List Award in a gastronomic restaurant is situated here as well. Chef Bruno Cirino's scampi Mediterranean in an almond crust with dates or roasted local white figs, sugared black olives, and buffalo milk sherbet have become signature dishes for a reason. **Known for:** outstanding French wine selection; exquisite dishes; experience of two-Michelin-star dining. Ⓢ *Average main: €55* ✉ *20 rte. Comte de Cessole* ☎ *04–92–41–51–51* ⊗ *Closed Sun., Mon., and mid-Nov.–mid-Feb. No lunch.*

★ Le Louis XV

$$$$ | **FRENCH** | In Monaco, cosmetic surgery extends even to buildings, and no better example can be seen than at Alain Ducasse's flagship restaurant, the three-Michelin-star Le Louis XV at the Hôtel de Paris. Opulence is all part of the Ducasse experience, which goes beyond his overhauled menu—a return to the Riviera's art de vivre and simplicity,

like the Provence garden vegetables cooked with black truffle or baked locally caught fish, tomatoes, and olives from Nice. **Known for:** meal of a lifetime from a celebrity chef; selection of 350,000 bottles of wine; gorgeous decor. $ *Average main: €100* ⊠ *Hôtel de Paris, Pl. du Casino* ☎ *377/98–06–88–64* ⊕ *www. alain-ducasse.com* ☉ *No lunch Wed. and Thurs. No dinner Wed. Sept.–June* 🏛 *Jacket required.*

Les Perles de Monte-Carlo

$$$ | SEAFOOD | Tucked away at the far end of the Fontvieille Port, with spectacular views of the Monaco Cathedral and oceanography museum suspended on the Rock above, Clooney and Pitt have been rumored to come here for a *dégustation* (tasting) at the few unpretentious wooden tables and chairs. Whether they were dining next to a prince, a model, or an ordinary local—it wouldn't matter to the owners, two marine biologists who grew up in Brittany—to them, everyone is made to eat the freshest of shellfish, crustaceans, and fish. **Known for:** hands down best seafood (and most affordable meal) in Monaco; unique location akin to eating on a yacht; small space so reservations necessary. $ *Average main: €25* ⊠ *47 Quai Jean Charles Rey* ☎ *377/97–77–84–31* ⊕ *www.perlesdemontecarlo. com* ☉ *Closed Sun. No dinner Sat., Mon., and Tues.* ▬ *No credit cards.*

Quai des Artistes

$$$ | FRENCH | Packing well-heeled diners shoulder to shoulder at banquettes lined up for maximum people-watching, this warehouse-scale neo–Art Deco bistro on the port packs in the chicest of chic Monégasque residents. Rich brasserie classics (lamb shank on the bone, potato puree with rosemary, and spicy gravy) are counterbalanced with high-flavor international experiments (salmon served sushi-rare with warm potatoes, pickled ginger, and wasabi sauce). **Known for:** boisterous ambience; palatial views from the terrace; French brasserie classics

with a twist. $ *Average main: €32* ⊠ *4 quai Antoine Ier* ☎ *377/97–97–97–77* ⊕ *www.quaidesartistes.com.*

★ Stars'n'Bars

$$ | AMERICAN | FAMILY | This American-style port-side bar–restaurant–entertainment center is almost like the Monégasque version of the Hard Rock Café, but super eco-friendly and owned by a childhood friend of the prince (the singer Prince, coincidentally, once played a secret concert here). Sports memorabilia and photos hang on the wall, while fat and juicy burgers, barbecue baby back ribs, vegan nachos, pecan pie, real iced tea in thick glasses, and (gasp!) pitchers of ice water make it the heart of Monaco's expat community. **Known for:** no-waste policy: option to order without sides, fries, or buns and pay less; vegan, gluten-free, and allergy friendly; delicious American cuisine. $ *Average main: €20* ⊠ *6 quai Antoine Ier* ⊕ *www.starsnbars. com.*

Hotels

Hermitage

$$$$ | HOTEL | FAMILY | They've all been here—kings, queens, Pavarotti in jeans—among the riot of frescoes and plaster flourishes embellished with gleaming brass in this landmark yet relatively low-profile 1900 hotel set back a block from the casino scene. **Pros:** unrivaled meals and views in Michelin-starred Vistamar; best lobby bar in Monaco; free access to Thermes Marins wellness center. **Cons:** expensive, of course; can be noisy; easy to get lost. $ *Rooms from: €676* ⊠ *Sq. Beaumarchais* ☎ *377/98–06–86–83* ⊕ *www.hotelhermitagemontecarlo.com* ➷ *278 rooms* ⚭ *No meals.*

★ Hôtel Métropole

$$$$ | HOTEL | This Belle Époque hotel, set on land that once belonged to Pope Leon XIII, has pulled out all the stops in its decor—famed Paris designer Jacques

Garcia has given the rooms his signature hyper-aristocratic look, and the late Karl Lagerfield was the architect behind the Odyssey pool and lounge; it also has the unique distinction of housing two Michelin-starred restaurants. **Pros:** flawless and attentive service; free newspapers and Hermès products; one of the best spas in Europe. **Cons:** expensive; parking extra; check-in from 3 pm only. $ *Rooms from: €587* ⊠ *4 av. de la Madone* ☎ *377/93–15–15–15* ⊕ *www.metropole.com* ⊲ *190 rooms* |○| *Free Breakfast.*

Monte-Carlo Bay Hotel

$$$$ | **HOTEL** | Perched on a 10-acre peninsula, with 75% of its rooms offering sea views, this highly acclaimed luxury resort—which immodestly bills itself as "a natural Eden reinvented"—seeks to evoke the Côte d'Azur's 1920s heyday with its neoclassical columns and arches, exotic gardens, lagoon swimming pool, casino, and concert hall. **Pros:** one of two proper beach resorts in Monaco; close to nightlife and restaurants; free access to Monte Carlo Casino. **Cons:** breakfast extra; free Wi-Fi only for maximum two devices; might seem a little too over-the-top, even for Monaco. $ *Rooms from: €575* ⊠ *40 av. Princesse Grace* ☎ *377/98–06–20–00* ⊕ *www.montecarlobay.com* ⊲ *356 rooms* |○| *No meals.*

Nightlife

CASINOS

Casino de Monte-Carlo

CASINOS | The bastion and landmark of Monte Carlo gambling is, of course, the gorgeously ornate Casino de Monte-Carlo. The main gambling hall is the Salle Européene (European Room), where you can play roulette and Texas Hold 'Em, while the slot machines stand apart in the Salle des Amériques, which all open at 2 pm and have a €17 admission fee. Bring your passport, as you have to be at least 18 to enter. ⊠ *Pl. du Casino* ☎ *377/98–06–23–00* ⊕ *www.casinomontecarlo.com.*

Sun Casino

CASINOS | Described as the "most American" of all the casinos in the principality thanks to a more extensive range of gaming tables, the Sun Casino is part of the Fairmont Monte-Carlo. While you can't hit the tables until 5 pm (4 pm on weekends), slot machines open daily at 2 pm and entry is free (you must be over 18 and snappily dressed). Don't be surprised to cross paths with women's poker champion Isabelle Mercier, a true fan of Sun Casino. ⊠ *12 av. des Spélugues* ☎ *377/98–06–12–12* ⊕ *www.montecarlosuncasino.com.*

DANCE CLUBS

Jimmyz

DANCE CLUBS | Dominating the club scene, Jimmyz boasts an edgy reputation that reaches far beyond Monaco. This legendary disco at Sporting Monte-Carlo is not for lightweights: the year-round partying is as serious as the need to be seen, so if surgically enhanced faces and body parts or paying €28 for a water upset you, then stay at your hotel. Note that the club doesn't even open until 11:30 pm. ⊠ *Sporting Monte-Carlo, Av. Princesse Grace* ☎ *377/98–06–70–68* ⊕ *fr.jimmyz-montecarlo.com.*

 ## Performing Arts

OPERA

Opéra de Monte-Carlo

ARTS VENUE | In the true spirit of the town, it seems that the Salle Garnier Opera House, with its 18-ton gilt-bronze chandelier and extravagant frescoes, is part of the casino complex. The designer, Charles Garnier, also built the Paris Opéra, and American-born Princess Alice, married to Prince Albert I, is also credited with making the opera a cultural destination. On display are some of the coast's most significant performances of dance, opera, and orchestral music. ⊠ *Pl. du Casino* ☎ *377/98–06–28–28* ⊕ *www.opera.mc.*

📥 Shopping

Shopping in Monaco will be pricey, but it can also be a lot of fun. The Promenade Princess Charlene, located behind Casino Square in the One Monte-Carlo complex, is the heart of the most high-end shopping street in all the Riviera. Some 60 luxury boutiques line the promenade and Avenue des Beaux-Arts, including brands like Cartier, Louis Vuitton, Prada, and Chanel, as well as Akris, the princess's go-to label. You can find the same haute couture at the very casual secondhand shop Queen's Bee at Place de la Crémaillère, run by stylist Katie Holmes (no, not of Tom Cruise fame).

The only couture made in Monaco is by fashion designer Isabell Kristensen, who was Princess Charlene's maid of honor and designed her bridal gown. Isabell's ultrafeminine gowns and cocktail dresses can been seen in her boutique on the Rock (18 rue Princesse Marie de Lorraine). Pick up a bottle of her Monaco perfume (€65), a celestial scent made for Albert and Charlene's wedding.

Another made-in-Monaco product can be found at the atelier l'Orangerie (9 rue de la Turbie). The delicious orange liqueur—a perfect cocktail when mixed with prosecco—was created by Irish-Italian Philip Culazzo who discovered a way to use the bitter oranges produced by Monaco's 600 trees.

🏃 Activities

AUTO RACING
Grand Prix de Monaco

AUTO RACING | When the film stars depart, the auto racing begins: the Grand Prix de Monaco takes place the last Sunday of the Cannes Film Festival in May. To watch live, it's €10,000 per person to stand on a balcony overlooking the course. If that's more than you want to spend but you still want to watch action on the same track, pick up tickets for the Thursday practice and qualifying rounds (€80 for Place du Casino seats) or drive the course for free when it opens that same night at 7:30 pm. Tickets for the Historic Grand Prix of Monaco, which takes place two weeks earlier on the same track every other year, run €25–€65. On alternate years, you can see the Formula E, the electric-car racing series. ☎ *377/93–25–47–78* ⊕ *www.formula1.com.*

Chapter 15

CORSICA

15

Updated by
Sean Hillen

Sights ★★☆☆☆   Restaurants ★★☆☆☆   Hotels ★★☆☆☆   Shopping ★★☆☆☆   Nightlife ★☆☆☆☆

WELCOME TO CORSICA

TOP REASONS TO GO

★ **Hiking:** From a stroll in the countryside to an overnight hike in the mountains, Corsica offers more than 100 peaks and scenic trails, including the famous 201-km (125-mile) GR20 trek across the island.

★ **Water adventures:** Warm and crystal waters are ideal for snorkeling, diving, boating, and windsurfing.

★ **Rich cuisine:** Blending French specialties with Italian cuisine, Corsica tempts the palate with the rich flavors of honey, chestnuts, wine, and brocciu cheese.

★ **Coastal drives:** These curvy mountain roads, skirted by turquoise waters, are not to be missed.

★ **Cultural exploration:** Dotting the island are chapels, towers, and more than 350 villages framed by fields of grazing goats and sheep. Corsica's cultural treasures, preserved through centuries of tradition, find expression in the island's art, music, food, and festivals.

The northern half of the island (Haute Corse) is generally wilder than the southern half (Corse du Sud), which is hotter and more barren. Southern Corsica's archaeological site at Filitosa, the towering rippling rock of Col de Bavella, its majestic Laricio pine forest, and the ancient town of Bonifacio all rank indisputably among the island's finest treasures. One of the prettiest drives is the tour around the northward-pointing finger of Cap Corse. Don't hesitate to drive into the interior highlands, which also represent the true Corsica; if you spend too much time at sea level you'll be missing the remote villages and dramatic heights for which the island is famous.

1 Ajaccio. The French administrative capital of the region.

2 Porticcio. An upscale resort town.

3 Bonifacio. An ancient fortressed town.

4 Porto-Vecchio. A charming town defined by cobblestone streets and a lively marina.

5 Corte. The center of Corsica, culturally and historically.

6 Porto and Calanches di Piana. Red rock formations that are one of the island's best natural wonders.

7 Calvi. A little taste of the Riviera in Corsica.

8 Pigna. A village centered on traditional Corsican arts and crafts.

9 Bastia. A Baroque coastal town with a strong Italian flavor.

CAP CORSE

D80

D60

Nonza

Erbalunga

Santa-Maria-di-Lota

Bastia

Patrimonio

Saint-Florent

Furiani

L'Ile-Rousse

Losari

D81

D62

Biguglia

Algajola

Pigna

N1197

Sorio

Murato

N193

Calvi

Cateri

N197

Lama

N197

8

Suare

D151

Calenzana

Ponte Leccia

Morosaglia

La Porta

7

N197

Haut-Asco

D81

Asco

N147

D71

N193

Monte Cinto

Castirla

Piedicroce

D71

Cervione

Albertacce

Corscia

Soveria

Valle-d'Alesani

D84

Osani

D81

Corte

5

HAUTE

CORSE

Alistro

Porto–Les
Calanches

Ota

6

Lugo

Piana

N198

Cargèse

D81

D70

Víco

Vivario

N200

Aleria

Sagone

CORSE
DU SUD

N193

Ghisoni

Tiuccia

Tavera

Accìani

D81

Carbuccia

D69

Mignataja

N193

Bastelica

Palneca

Travo

Ajaccio

Chisa

1

Bastelicaccia

Grosseto

Zìcavo

Solenzara

Porticcio

2

Zàvaco

D268

N196

D69

Verghia

Col de Bavella

Favone

Bicchisano

Casalabriva

Zérubia

Zonza

N198

Marmontaja

Filitosa

Pinarellu

Capiniellu

Sainte-Lucie-
de-Tallano

Sartène

4

Porto-
Vecchio

Tizzano

N196

Sotta

Precojo

Pianottoli-
Caldarello

Chiova-d'Asino

Bonifacio

3

Ile Cavallo

0   10 mi

0   10 km

"The best way to know Corsica," according to Napoléon, "is to be born there." Not everyone has had his luck, so chances are you'll be arriving on the overnight ferry from Marseille or flying in from Paris or Rome to discover "the Isle of Beauty." This vertical, chalky, granite world of its own, rising in the Mediterranean between Provence and Tuscany, remains France's very own Wild West: a powerful natural setting and, literally, a breath of fresh air.

Corsica's strategic location 168 km (105 miles) south of Monaco and 81 km (50 miles) west of Italy made it a prize hotly contested by a succession of Mediterranean powers, notably Genoa, Pisa, and France. Their vestiges remain: the city-state of Genoa ruled Corsica for more than 200 years, leaving impressive citadels, churches, bridges, and nearly 100 medieval watchtowers around the island's coastline. The Italian influence is also apparent in village architecture and in the Corsican language: a combination of Italian, Tuscan dialect, and Latin.

Corsica gives an impression of immensity, seeming far larger than its 215-km (133-mile) length and 81-km (50-mile) width, partly because its rugged, mountainous terrain makes for very slow traveling and partly because the landscape and the culture vary greatly from one microregion to another. Much of the terrain of Corsica that is not wooded or cultivated is covered with a dense thicket of undergrowth, which, along with chestnut trees, makes up the *maquis,* a variety of wild and aromatic plants including lavender, myrtle, and heather, which gives Corsica one of its sobriquets: "the perfumed isle."

MAJOR REGIONS

Corse du Sud. Southern Corsica prides itself on its picturesque coastline, ancient hilltop villages, fortified cities, prehistoric sites, and breathtaking natural wonders. The regional capital of Ajaccio, Napoléon's birthplace, remains the island's modern commercial hub. Famous for its dramatic white limestone cliff-top setting, historic Bonaficio is the stunning backdrop to the postcard-perfect marine reserve surrounding the Lavezzi Islands—a UNESCO World Heritage Site. Porticcio and Porto-Vecchio are other gems of the region.

Haute Corse. Haute Corse (Upper Corsica) is the northeastern end of the island and is, indeed, higher in mean altitude than Corse du Sud, topped by the 8,876-foot Monte Cinto. Most Corsica enthusiasts agree that Haute Corse is the island's finest trove of highland forests, remote villages, hidden cultural gems, vineyards, beaches, and alpine lakes and streams. In the center of Haute Corse is the city of Corte, Corsica's historic heart. To the east is the forested region of La Castagnic-cia, named for its *châtaigniers* (chest-nut trees), one of Corsica's treasures, especially in the fall, when fallen leaves and chestnuts blanket the ground. The forest's tiny roadways go through villages with stunning Baroque churches and houses still roofed in traditional blue-gray slate. The north is also renowned as an important wine-producing region, where some of the finest vineyards benefit from the area's fertile soil and perfect tem-peratures. Important towns here include Calvi, Pigna, and Bastia.

Planner

When to Go

The best time to visit Corsica is fall or spring, when the weather is cool. Most Corsican culinary specialties are at their best between October and June. Try to avoid July and August, when mostly French and Italian vacationers fill hotels, crowd beaches, and jam roads. Prices soar and the Corsican temperament is at its most volatile. In winter the island has the best weather in France, but a majority of the hotels and restaurants are closed.

Travelers enjoying Corsica's laid-back vibe might be surprised to hear that it has the highest homicide rate per capita in France. Organized crime is the reason, and a spate of bombings and shootings has not helped improve the island's reputation. The good news is that none of the violence has targeted visitors, and the government of France is so confident that things are under control that it allowed the Tour de France to pass through the island for the first time in 2013.

Getting Here and Around

AIR TRAVEL

Air Corsica has regular year-round and summer routes to the four airports in Corsica (Ajaccio, Bastia, Calvi, and Figari) from several national and international airports such as Paris-Orly and Par-is-Charles de Gaulle, Marseille, Nice, Lyon, Toulon, Toulouse, Clermont-Ferrand, Bordeaux, Nantes, Brussels Charleroi, and London-Stansted. Some of the flights are sold by Air France but partly operated by Air Corsica.

Corsica has four major airports: Ajaccio Napoléon Bonaparte, Bastia-Poretta, Fig-ari-Sud Corse, and Calvi Sainte Catherine. The airports at Ajaccio and Bastia run regular shuttle-bus services to and from town. Taxis are also available in front of the terminals. Expect to pay around €25–€30 to go from Napoléon Bonaparte Airport to Ajaccio city; €42–€58 from Poretta Airport to Bastia city. At Figari Sud Corse, during summer months, a bus meets all incoming flights and will take passengers as far as Bonifacio and Porto-Vecchio for about €9.

CONTACTS **Ajaccio Napoléon Bonaparte Airport** (*AJA*) ✉ *N193, Ajaccio* ☎ *04–95–23–56–56*. **Bastia–Poretta Airport** (*BIA*) ✉ *D507, Bastia* ☎ *04–95–54–54–54* ⊕ *www.bastia.aeroport.fr.* **Calvi Sainte Catherine Airport** (*CLY*) ✉ *D81, 8 km (5 miles) southeast of Calvi, Calvi* ☎ *04–95–65–88–88*. **Figari–Sud Corse Airport** (*FSC*) ✉ *D322, 3 km (2 miles) northwest of Fig-ari, Figari* ☎ *04–95–71–10–10* ⊕ *www.2a. cci.fr/contact_figari_airport.html.*

BOAT AND FERRY TRAVEL

Regular car ferries run from Marseille, Nice, and Toulon to Ajaccio and Bastia. These crossings take 5–13 hours, with sleeping cabins available, and are operated by Corsica Ferries, Corsica Linea, and La Meridionale. The high-speed ferry from Nice to Bastia takes about five to seven hours and is operated by Corsica Ferries and Moby Lines. Connections from the Italian mainland are run by Corsica Ferries and Moby Lines. Sardinia can be reached by ferry from Propriano, Bonifacio, Porto Vecchio, and Ajaccio on Corsica Ferries, Corsica Linea, La Meridionale, Blu Navy, and Moby Lines.

CONTACTS Blu Navy ☎ 39/0565–26–97–10 ⊕ blunavytraghetti.com/en. **Corsica Ferries** ✉ Le Palais de la Mer, Av. Pascal Lota BP 275, Bastia ☎ 08–25–09–50–95 ⊕ www.corsica-ferries.fr. **Corsica Linea** ✉ 3 quai de l'Herminier, Ajaccio ☎ 33–82–58–88–088 for reservations (€0.15 per min) ⊕ www.corsicalinea.com. **La Méridionale** ✉ Port de Commerce, Bd. Sampiero, Ajaccio ☎ 09–70–83–20–20 ⊕ www.lameridionale.fr. **Moby Lines** ✉ Quai Sott, Portigliola, Bonifacio ☎ 49–61–11–40–20 ⊕ www.mobylines.com.

CAR TRAVEL

Although driving is undoubtedly the best way to explore the island's scenic stretches, note that winding, mountainous roads, uneven surfaces, and microclimates with fog or precipitation can actually double or triple your expected travel time. A good map is essential. Drive defensively: you'll find that others on the road tend to move at terrifying speeds, even when the road curves. Night driving, especially in the mountains, is not recommended, because many areas are poorly lighted.

CRUISE TRAVEL

Ships dock in Ajaccio port, a short walk from the town of Ajaccio. Cafés and shops can be found immediately outside the port gates.

Renting a car allows you to explore several towns and surrounding attractions during your stay on the island. Be aware that travel times may be longer than map distances suggest, because the mountain roads can be narrow and winding.

TRAIN TRAVEL

The main line of Corsica's simple rail network runs from Ajaccio, in the west, to Corte, in the central valley, then divides at Ponte Leccia. From here one line continues to L'Ile Rousse and Calvi, in the north, and the other to Bastia, in the northeast. Another service runs four times daily between Ajaccio and Bastia.

CONTACTS SNCF ☎ 08–92–35–35–35 ⊕ www.sncf.com/en.

Restaurants

Corsican cuisine has been called a "winter cuisine," better between October and May, when game like *sanglier* (wild boar) are well represented on all menus. The Corsican maquis supports some of Europe's wildest flora and fauna, ranging from free-range pigs to woodcock and pigeon, while chestnuts are a Corsican staple not to miss—whether in pastries, *pulenta,* or even in local beer. Cheeses, especially the characteristic *brocciu* fresh variety, are omnipresent upland delicacies.

Hotels

Corsica's *fermes-auberges* (farmhouse-inns) have had a healthy dose of restoration, and tastefully designed hotels are still being built. During the peak season (July through mid-September) prices are significantly higher, and some hotels insist that charges for breakfast and dinner be tacked onto the price. The best seaside hotels are priced only marginally lower than on the Riviera, but lodgings in the interior villages remain substantially cheaper. *Restaurant and hotel reviews have been shortened. For full information, visit Fodors.com.*

What It Costs in Euros			
$	$$	$$$	$$$$
RESTAURANTS			
under €18	€18–€24	€25–€32	over €32
HOTELS			
under €106	€106–€145	€146–€215	over €215

Visitor Information

The Agence du Tourisme de la Corse can provide practical and in-depth information about the whole island. The Parc Naturel Régional de la Corse, Corsica's wildlife and natural-resource management authority, controlling well over a third of the island, can provide trail maps, booklets, and a wide variety of information.

CONTACTS Agence du Tourisme de la Corse ⊠ *3 bd. du Roi Jérôme, BP 21, Ajaccio* ☎ *04–95–51–53–03* ⊕ *www.visit-corsica. com.*

Tours

BOAT TOURS
Colombo Line Cruises
Most of Corsica's spectacular scenery is best viewed from the water. This company organizes daylong glass-bottom-boat tours. ⊠ *Quai Landry, Ajaccio* ☎ *04–95–65–32–10* ⊕ *www.colombo-line.com.*

Nave Va Promenades en Mer
In Ajaccio, Nave Va Promenades en Mer organizes daily trips to the stunning Iles Sanguinaires. ⊠ *SARL NAVE VA, Promenades en Mer, 1 passage poggiolo, Ajaccio* ☎ *04–95–51–31–31* ⊕ *www. naveva.com.*

BUS TOURS
Ollandini Voyages
This company arranges whole- and half-day bus tours of the island, leaving from Ajaccio. ⊠ *1 rue Paul Colonna d'Istria, CS 10304, Ajaccio* ☎ *04–95–23–92–91* ⊕ *www.groupencorse.com.*

Ajaccio

50 mins by plane, 5–10 hrs by ferry from Marseille, Nice, or Toulon.

Considered Corsica's primary commercial and cultural hub, the largest city and regional capital of Ajaccio is on the west coast of the island, approximately 351 km (218 miles) southeast of Marseille. Founded in 1492, vestiges of ancient Corsica in this *ville impériale* revolve around the city's most famous son, Napoléon Bonaparte, whose family home—now the national museum Maison Bonaparte—pays tribute to the emperor's historical influence.

Remnants from what was originally a 12th-century Genoese colony are still visible around the Old Town near the imposing citadel and watchtower. Perfect for exploring, the luminous seaside city surrounded by snowcapped mountains and pretty beaches offers numerous sites, eateries, side streets, and a popular harbor, where sailboats and fishing vessels moor in the picturesque Tino Rossi port lined with well-established restaurants and cafés serving fresh local fare.

GETTING HERE AND AROUND
Flights into Aéroport d'Ajaccio Napoléon Bonaparte arrive regularly. To travel the short distance into the city center, take a shuttle bus to the main Gare Routière station that operates Monday to Saturday (€4.50). Alternatively, a taxi (€25) will take approximately 20 minutes. Ferries from Nice, Toulon, and Marseilles connect directly to Ajaccio and operate up to eight

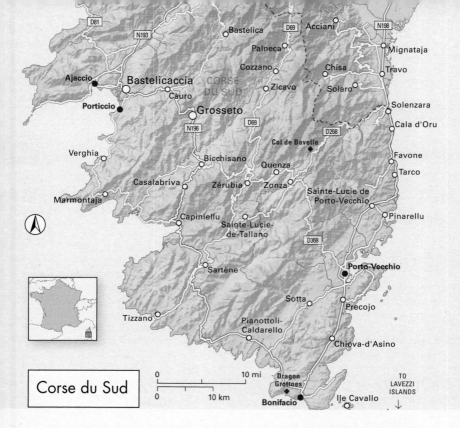

Corse du Sud

```
0              10 mi
0         10 km
```

times daily. The average ferry crossing time is six hours.

VISITOR INFORMATION Office de Tourisme d'Ajaccio ⊠ *3 bd. du Roi Jérôme* ☎ *04–95–51–53–03* ⊕ *www.ajaccio-tourisme.com.*

⊙ Sights

Cathédrale Notre-Dame de L'Assomption

RELIGIOUS SITE | The 16th-century Baroque cathedral where Napoléon was baptized sits at the end of Rue St-Charles. The interior is covered with trompe-l'oeil frescoes, and the high altar, from a church in Lucca, Italy, was donated by Napoléon's sister Eliza after he made her princess of Tuscany. Eugène Delacroix's *The Triumph of Religion* hangs above the Virgin of the Sacred Heart marble altar from the 17th century. ⊠ *Rue St-Charles,*

BP 80152 ☎ *04–95–21–07–67* ⊕ *www. cathedrale-ajaccio.fr* 🎟 *Free.*

Chapelle Impériale

RELIGIOUS SITE | In the south wing of the Palais Fesch, the neo-Renaissance-style Imperial Chapel was built in 1857 by Napoléon's nephew, Napoléon III, to accommodate the tombs of the Bonaparte family (Napoléon Bonaparte himself is buried in the Hôtel des Invalides in Paris). The Coptic crucifix over the altar was taken from Egypt during the general's 1798 campaign. The somber chapel, which is officially classified as a historical monument, is constructed from the white calcified stone of St-Florent and worth a visit to view its neoclassical cupola and ecclesiastical iconography. ⊠ *50–52 rue Cardinal Fesch* ☎ *04–95–21–48–17* ⊕ *www.ajaccio.fr/La-Chapelle-Imperiale_a353.html* 🎟 *€2.*

La Cuisine Sauvage

Authentic Corsican fare is based on free-range livestock, game (especially *sanglier*, or wild boar), herbs, and wild mushrooms best found between October and May in the villages of the mountainous interior. *Civets* (meaty stews) headline menus, as do the many versions of the prototypical, hearty Corsican soup (*soupe paysanne, soupe corse*, or *soupe de montagne*) made from herbs and vegetables simmered for hours with a ham bone. Seafood dishes available on the coast include *aziminu*, a rich bouillabaisse.

Excellent *charcuterie* (pork products) include *lonzu* (shoulder), *coppa* (fillet), and *figatelli* (liver sausage), along with *prizuttu* (ham). Corsica's most emblematic cheese is really not a cheese at all: *brocciu* (pronounced "broach"), similar to ricotta, is used in omelets, *fiadone* (cheesecake), *fritelli* (chestnut-flour doughnuts), and as stuffing for trout or rabbit. Cheeses from Corsica's microregions include *bastelicaccia*, a soft, creamy sheep cheese, and the harder and sharper *sartenais*. Many of the most powerful cheeses are simply designated as *brebis* (sheep) or *chèvre* (goat).

Chestnuts and chestnut flour, major players in Corsican gastronomy, are found in *castagna* (Corsican for chestnut), a cake; *panetta*, a kind of bread; *canistrelli*, dry cookies; beignets; *pulenta*, a doughy bread; and *Pietra*, chestnut beer. Corsica's best wines include the Arenas, Orenga de Gaffory, and Gentile cellars from the Patrimonio vineyards; Domaine Peraldi, Clos de Capitoro, or Clos Alzeto, from Ajaccio; Fiumicicoli, from Sartène; or Domaine de Torracia, from Porto-Vecchio.

Hôtel de Ville (*Town Hall*)
GOVERNMENT BUILDING | Ajaccio's town hall houses the Empire-style grand Salon napoléonien, which is hung with portraits of a long line of Bonapartes. Also here are a fine bust of Letizia, Napoléon's formidable mother, a bronze death mask of the emperor himself, and a frescoed ceiling depicting Napoléon's meteoric rise. ⊠ *Av. Antoine Serafini* ☎ *04–95–51–52–53* ⊕ *www.ajaccio.fr/Salon-Napoleonien_a50.html* ✆ *€3* ⊙ *Closed weekends in winter.*

L'Oratoire Saint Jean Baptiste
RELIGIOUS SITE | At the intersection of Rue du Roi-de-Rome and Rue St-Charles, you can visit the *confrérie,* or religious brotherhood, of St-Jean Baptiste. On June 24, the patron saint is honored with a solemn mass conducted by the city's bishop and a Corsican music concert. ⊠ *Rue du Roi-de-Rome* ☎ *04–95–22–27–38* ⊕ *www.petit-patrimoine.com/fiche-petit-patrimoine.php?id_pp=2A004_5* ✆ *Free.*

★ Maison Bonaparte (*Bonaparte House*)
BUILDING | One of four national historic museums dedicated to Napoléon, the multilevel house where the emperor was born on August 15, 1769, contains memorabilia and paintings of the extended Bonaparte family. History aficionados can tour bedrooms, dining rooms, and salons where Charles and Letitzia Bonaparte raised their eight children. Period furnishings and antiques in Corsican and Empire styles are scattered about and pay tribute to the family's bourgeois upbringing. Head downstairs to see the cellars and granite oil-pressing mill acquired by Napoléon III in 1860, which depict the importance of rural industry for the Bonaparte's income. Visit the trapdoor room and find the opening next to the door through which Napoléon

The birth of an empire: Napoléon's birthplace and childhood home are on display in Ajaccio.

allegedly escaped in 1799. The building itself changed hands multiple times through Bonaparte heirs until 1923, when it was donated to the state of France by Prince Victor, elder son of Prince Jérôme Napoléon. ⊠ *Rue St-Charles* ☎ *04–95–21–43–89* ⊕ *www.musees-na-tionaux-malmaison.fr/musee-maisonbon-aparte* ☞ *€7* ☉ *Closed Mon.*

Marché Central
MARKET | FAMILY | For an authentic view of daily Corsican life, tour this wonderful open-air food market brimming with gastronomic delights. There is an array of local cheeses, charcuterie, breads, pastries, olives, condiments, and aromatic meats for sale. Traditional indulgences like chestnut-infused beignets can be savored in an atmosphere guaranteed to be lively and local. ■**TIP**→ **Bring your euros—cash is the preferred method of payment.** ⊠ *Pl. Foch* ☉ *Closed Mon.*

★ Musée des Beaux-Arts–Palais Fesch
MUSEUM | FAMILY | This internationally recognized museum houses one of the most important collections from the

Napoleonic era; it's undoubtedly one of the most significant displays in France of ancient Italian masterpieces spanning the 14th to 20th centuries. There are nearly 18,000 items, all part of an astounding inventory that belonged to Napoléon's uncle, Cardinal Fesch. Thanks to his nephew's military conquests, the cardinal was able to amass (steal, some would say) many celebrated old-master paintings, the most famous of which are now in Paris's Louvre. The museum's beautiful vaulted corridors showcase 700 paintings, portraits, still lifes, and sculptures from the First and Second Empire from the French school. Don't miss the new gallery with engravings and drawings depicting historic Corsica. The building itself, constructed by the cardinal as the Institute of Arts and Sciences, dates back to 1837. ⊠ *50–52 rue Cardinal Fesch* ☎ *04–95–26–26–26* ⊕ *www.musee-fes-ch.com* ☞ *€8.*

Place Maréchal-Foch
PLAZA | Surrounded by a row of stately palm trees, Place Maréchal-Foch is

easily recognizable by its fountain of four Corsican granite lions encircling a commanding statue of Napoléon, the work of sculptor Jérôme Maglioli. Popular as a spot to people-watch on a sunny day, this triangle is surrounded by cafés and opens up to the Ajaccio port. ✉ *Pl. Marechal Foch.*

🍴 Restaurants

Le Cabanon Bleu

$$ | SEAFOOD | About a mile outside Ajaccio, this restaurant provides wonderful views across Ajaccio Bay from its attractive terrace at the edge of the sea. Given its location, it's no surprise that Le Cabanon Bleu specializes in fresh fish and seafood dishes such as grilled langoustine and tuna, but grilled lamb and beef are also on the menu. **Known for:** John Dory in creamy aioli sauce; fresh seafood platters; lobster. [$] *Average main: €20* ✉ *65 cours Lucien Bonaparte* ✣ *Next door to Hotel Les Mouettes, off main coast road* ☎ *04–95–51–02–15* 🌐 *www.cabanonbleu.com.*

Le Week End

$$$ | MEDITERRANEAN | FAMILY | At this eatery about 10 minutes from downtown Ajaccio, white rattan furniture and blue tablecloths are overshadowed by a spectacular ocean view and fine seafood menu, which has featured everything from lobster to octopus. Family-run since 1956, this restaurant flourishes with secret recipes handed down from generations. **Known for:** Corsican-cured ham; tuna spring rolls; rockfish soup. [$] *Average main: €30* ✉ *Rte. des Iles Sanguinaires* ☎ *04–95–52–01–39* 🌐 *www.hotel-le-weekend.com/en.*

20123

$$$$ | FRENCH | This popular establishment is known for its traditional cuisine, fresh daily catches, and in-season game specials. The rustic interior has a starry sky above, antique lanterns, and a stone fountain, where guests pour their own water into ceramic jugs. **Known for:** civet de sanglier (wild boar stew) casserole with cheesy polenta; exquisite cheese platter with homemade fig confiture; fresh-baked loaves of wheat bread. [$] *Average main: €35* ✉ *2 rue Roi-de-Rome* ☎ *04–95–21–50–05* 🌐 *www.20123.fr.*

🛏 Hotels

Hotel Kalliste

$$ | B&B/INN | The central location is the main draw of this simple hotel near the port. **Pros:** superb view from outdoor pool; pet-friendly; convenient location near train station. **Cons:** small rooms with few amenities; no elevator; Wi-Fi speed varies. [$] *Rooms from: €115* ✉ *51 cours Napoleon* ☎ *04–95–51–34–45* 🌐 *www.hotel-kalliste-ajaccio.com* 🔑 *45 rooms* 🍽 *Free Breakfast.*

Hôtel San Carlu

$$ | HOTEL | On the edge of the Old Town, overlooking the ramparts and sea, this friendly hotel with comfortable rooms is an ideal base for exploring Ajaccio. **Pros:** faces 12th-century citadel and ramparts; 164 feet from beach and port; near cafés and restaurants. **Cons:** 20-minute uphill walk from airport bus drop-off; rooms are on the small side and need an update; expensive breakfast. [$] *Rooms from: €120* ✉ *8 bd. Danielle Casanova* ☎ *04–95–21–13–84* 🌐 *www.hotel-sancarlu.com* 🔑 *39 rooms* 🍽 *Free Breakfast.*

La Dolce Vita

$$$$ | HOTEL | FAMILY | Spread out over whitewashed terraces at the edge of the Golfe d'Ajaccio, this hotel is more known for its restaurant, which ranks as one of the island's better establishments for stylish interpretations of traditional Corsican dishes. **Pros:** swimming pool overlooks the sea; restaurant deck offers island views; peaceful location outside town between rocky coves and sandy beaches. **Cons:** no elevators; bus needed to get into town; not many restaurants nearby. [$] *Rooms from: €220* ✉ *Rte.*

des Iles Sanguinaires, 9 km (5 miles) from center of town ☎ *04–95–52–42–42* 🌐 *www.hotel-dolcevita.com* 🕒 *Closed mid-Nov.–early Apr.* 🛏 *32 rooms* 🍴 *Free Breakfast.*

Les Mouettes Hotel Demeure

$$$ | **HOTEL** | With a charming garden overlooking the glistening waters of the bay, this four-star hotel offers great views of the picturesque town of Porticcio. **Pros:** heated saltwater pool and private beach; spa facilities; pine and palm-lined terrace. **Cons:** French-only TV channels; restricted parking; 25-minute walk from Old City. [$] *Rooms from: €195* ✉ *9 cours Lucien Bonaparte* ☎ *04–95–50–40–40* 🌐 *www.hotellesmouettes.fr* 🕒 *Closed early Nov.–late Mar.* 🛏 *28 rooms* 🍴 *Free Breakfast* 💳 *No credit cards.*

Palazzu u Domu

$$$ | **B&B/INN** | Steps away from the house where Napoléon was born, this clean and comfortable lodging with seasonal patio restaurant once served as the ancestral residence of Duke Charles-Andre Pozzo di Borgo of the notable Ajaccio family. **Pros:** located in historic center, next to Casa Buonaparte, the former aristocrat's home; delicious homemade Corsican specialties—canistrons and canistrellis; charming garden terrace. **Cons:** inconsistent Wi-Fi service; parking not included and it can be a bit of a schlep from car to hotel; narrow balconies. [$] *Rooms from: €189* ✉ *17 rue Bonaparte* ☎ *04–95–50–00–20* 🌐 *www.palazzu-domu.com* 🛏 *42 rooms* 🍴 *Free Breakfast.*

Nightlife

La Place

DANCE CLUBS | A well-known *boîte du nuit* (nightclub), La Place draws both young clubbers and older locals looking for a good, loud time. Dance away the hours to techno and house music. ✉ *Pl. du Diamant* ☎ *06–18–86–74–30.*

Performing Arts

Carnival d'Ajaccio

CULTURAL FESTIVALS | Scheduled in early summer, the festive Carnival of Ajaccio is when townspeople in colorful disguises parade in the *cité imperiale.* As part of the 250th anniversary of the birth of Napoleon, the year 2019 had many events, including the Carnaval, dedicated to the emperor. ✉ *Av. Marechal Moncey Résidence Palmiers* ☎ *04–95–51–53–20* 🌐 *www.ajaccio.fr/Ajaccio-lance-Napoleon-2019-une-annee-dediee-a-l-Empereur_a7784.html.*

Fêtes Napoléoniennes

FESTIVALS | **FAMILY** | Held August 13–15, the Fêtes Napoléoniennes is one of the island's major festivals. It culminates with fireworks, historical reconstructions, and parades to celebrate the Little Corporal's birthday on August 15. For 2019 the city launched a program entitled "Napoleon 2019" to celebrate the 250 years since Napoleon's birth. ✉ *Office de Tourisme d'Ajaccio, 3 bd. du Roi Jerome, BP 21* ☎ *04–95–51–53–20.*

La Madunnuccia

(*Feast of Our Lady of Mercy*)

FESTIVALS | Started in 1656, La Madunnuccia is a true Ajaccian tradition spotlighting the Procession de la Madunnuccia (Procession of the Madonna). A large Mass is held March 18 at the cathedral, followed by a citywide tour of the famous statue. ✉ *Cathedrale d'Ajaccio, Rue Forcioli Conti* ☎ *04–95–51–52–53* 🌐 *www.ajaccio.fr/Les-fetes-tradionnelles-et-religieuses-Ajacciennes_a20.html.*

Shopping

Art'Insula

GIFTS/SOUVENIRS | A large selection of leather, pottery, and beautiful jewelry crafted by local artisans is available at Art'Insula. For the gourmand, there's an assortment of honeys, vinegars, and liqueurs. ✉ *57 rue Fesch* ☎ *04–95–50–54–67* ⊕ *www.artisula.com.*

Casa Napoléon

FOOD/CANDY | This well-stocked boutique sells organic jams, olives oils, wines, and traditional dishes. It belongs to Charles Antona, who's been in business for more than 30 years. ✉ *3 rue Fesch* ☎ *04–95–21–47–88* ⊕ *www.casanapoleon.com.*

Les Pierres de Corse

JEWELRY/ACCESSORIES | The "Oeil de Sainte Lucie," the small plate that closes a mollusk's shell, can be found here in pendants, rings, earrings, and bracelets. Natural Corsican stones are also showcased at this friendly corner boutique. ✉ *23 rue Fesch* ☎ *04–95–10–45–57* ⊕ *www.lespierresdecorse.com.*

Paese Nostru

CERAMICS/GLASSWARE | Corsican crafts of all kinds are for sale in this tiny souvenir shop. Of special interest is the cutlery, hand-forged with wrought-iron and wooden handles. ✉ *29 rue Fesch* ☎ *04–95–51–05–07.*

U Stazzu

FOOD/CANDY | Known for its high-quality cheese and wine, this award-winning shop offers some of the best hams on the island, including the waist-busting Coppa and Lonzu. Tasting is encouraged. ✉ *1 rue Bonaparte* ☎ *04–95–51–10–80.*

U Tilaghju

CERAMICS/GLASSWARE | Near the cathedral, this art studio and boutique holds an impressive collection of hand-painted silk, ceramics, paintings, and woodwork. ✉ *12 rue Forcioli Conti* ☎ *04–95–51–21–40.*

Activities

BOATING AND SAILING

Societé Nautique d'Ajaccio

SAILING | **FAMILY** | Perfect for children and those passionate about sailing, the Nautical Society of Ajaccio was founded in 1867. It specializes in training young skippers, but adults are also welcome. ✉ *Fossés de la Citadelle, Port Tino Rossi* ☎ *04–95–21–40–43* ⊕ *www.snajaccio.fr.*

Porticcio

17 km (11 miles) south of Ajaccio.

Between the sea and mountain, this upscale resort town a short scenic drive from the capital benefits from unforgettable views and a palette of nautical activities perfect for the clear, calm waters of the Ajaccio Gulf. It's an oasis, dotted with a number of luxury resorts, notable for its beaches, verdant countryside, and ancient Tower of Capitello.

GETTING HERE AND AROUND

Découvertes Naturelle and other companies shuttle passengers between Ajaccio and Porticcio throughout the summer season (€5 one way, €8 round-trip). Buses leave Ajaccio's Gare Routière and stop at Porticcio Mare e Monti Sud and Mare a Mare Centre (€3 one way). The 19-km (11-mile) drive by taxi (€28) or car takes approximately 30–40 minutes from downtown Ajaccio.

TOURS

Découvertes Naturelle

TOUR—SIGHT | **FAMILY** | Discover the stunning landscape with boat excursions from Ajaccio, Porticcio, and Propriano offered by Découvertes Naturelle. The company also runs shuttles between Ajaccio and Porticcio costing €5 each way. ✉ *1 rue Emmanuel Arene, Ajaccio* ☎ *06–03–13–46–80 for tours departing Ajaccio, 06–69–29–14–71 for tours departing Porticcio* ⊕ *www.promenades-en-mer.org.*

VISITOR INFORMATION Office Municipal de Tourisme de Porticcio ✉ *Les Echoppes, BP 125* ☎ *04–95–25–10–09* ⊕ *www.porticcio-corsica.com.*

Restaurants

La Carte Postale

$$$$ | MEDITERRANEAN | Inside the Sofitel Golfe d'Ajaccio, La Carte Postale presents a sedate ambience with floor-to-ceiling pillars, candlelit tables, and a pianist tickling the ivories. The kitchen incorporates Corsican flavors into contemporary cuisine. **Known for:** roasted swordfish with lime; prawn brochettes in satay sauce; wraparound windows offering terrific views of the coastline. $ *Average main: €40* ⊠ *Sofitel Golfe d'Ajaccio Thalassa Sea & Spa, Domaine de la Pointe, Golfe d'Ajaccio* ☎ *04–95–29–40–40* ⊕ *sofitel. accorhotels.com/gb/hotel-0587-sofitel-golfe-d-ajaccio-thalassa-sea-spa/index. shtml.*

Hotels

★ Le Maquis

$$$$ | HOTEL | FAMILY | One of the island's finest *hôtels de charme,* this graceful, ivy-covered Genoese-style retreat rambles down through terraced gardens to a private beach overlooking the Golfe d'Ajaccio. **Pros:** exceptional restaurant with terrace; its own beach with naturally protected cove; a massage and treatment room. **Cons:** near airport, so there is some airplane noise; no gym; nonheated outdoor pool (but heated one inside). $ *Rooms from: €520* ⊠ *Bd. Marie-Jeanne Bozzi* ✛ *19 km (12 miles) south of Ajacio* ☎ *04–95–25–05–55* ⊕ *www. lemaquis.com* ⊙ *Closed Jan.–Feb. 14* ⊅ *25 rooms* ⦵ *No meals.*

Sofitel Golfe d'Ajaccio Thalassa Sea & Spa Hotel

$$$$ | RESORT | Located just 15 minutes from Ajaccio airport, the Sofitel Golfe d'Ajaccio Thalassa Sea & Spa has a French Riviera theme and the sea is the highlight of a stay here—leave your door ajar, and the rhythmic ebb and flow of the sea over rocks outside your bedroom provides a perfect accompaniment to sleep. **Pros:** comprehensive thalassotherapy (seawater) facilities; faces Ajaccio Bay and the Sanguinaires Islands; outdoor seawater pool open all year. **Cons:** beach is small and rocky; nearby airport traffic noise; pricey breakfast. $ *Rooms from: €368* ⊠ *Sofitel Golfe d'Ajaccio Thalassa Sea & Spa, Domaine de la Pointe, Golfe d'Ajaccio* ☎ *04–95–29–40–40* ⊕ *sofitel. accorhotels.com/gb/hotel-0587-sofitel-golfe-d-ajaccio-thalassa-sea-spa/index. shtml* ⊙ *Closed Jan.–mid-Feb.* ⊅ *98 rooms* ⦵ *No meals.*

Activities

Institut de Thalassothérapie

FITNESS/HEALTH CLUBS | Part of the Sofitel Golfe d'Ajaccio, the Institut de Thalassothérapie (Institute of Thalassotherapy) is a 30-minute drive from the capital. Notable for its seawater cures, hydrotherapies, and restorative massages and scrubs, the institute is the perfect place to unwind after a long day of sightseeing and sunbathing. ⊠ *Sofitel Golfe d'Ajaccio Thalassa Sea & Spa, Domaine de la Pointe, Golfe d'Ajaccio, Ajaccio* ☎ *04–95–29–40–40* ⊕ *www.thalassa.com/gb/spa-hotel/0587-golfe-ajaccio-sofitel.html.*

Bonifacio

110 km (68 miles) southeast of Porticcio.

The ancient fortress town of Bonifacio occupies a spectacular cliff-top aerie above a harbor carved from limestone cliffs. It's 13 km (8 miles) from Sardinia, and the local speech is heavily influenced by the accent and idiom of that nearby Italian island. Established in the 12th century as Genoa's first Corsican stronghold, Bonifacio remained Genoese through centuries of battles and sieges. As you wander the narrow streets of the Haute Ville (Upper Village), inside the walls of the citadel, think of Homer's *Odyssey.* It's here, in the harbor, that scholars place the catastrophic encounter (Chapter X) between Ulysses's fleet and the Laestrygonians, who hurled lethal boulders down from the cliffs.

GETTING HERE AND AROUND
Bonifacio is approximately 20 km (12 miles) south of Figari airport (Figari-Sud Corse), with transfers by taxi (€45) or seasonal shuttle bus (€10). In summer months, expect congested streets in and around Bonifacio, delaying journey times.

VISITOR INFORMATION Office Municipal de Tourisme Bonifacio ⊠ 2 rue Fred Scamaroni ☎ 04–95–73–11–88 ⊕ www. bonifacio.fr.

 Sights

Bastion de l'Étendard (Bastion of the Standard)
HISTORIC SITE | From Place d'Armes at the city gate, enter the 13th-century Bastion de l'Étendard, where you can still see the system of weights and levers used to raise the drawbridge. The former garrison, the last remaining part of the original fortress, houses life-size dioramas of the bombardment of the bastion in the 16th-century Franco-Turkish war. Climb the steep steps for an incredible panoramic view of the white-chalk cliffs along the coastline. ⊠ Av. Charles de Gaulle ☎ 04–95–73–11–88 ⊕ www.bonifacio.fr/ site-historique-bastion-de-letendard.html ☑ €3 ⊗ Closed Dec.–Mar.

Dragon Grottoes
NATURE SITE | FAMILY | Boats from Bonifacio bring you to see the blue Dragon Grottoes, a spectacular geological site. Tours typically venture to Venus's Bath, sea caves at Sdragonatto and St-Angoine, and the Lavezzi Islands. Boats set out every 15 minutes during July and August. ⊠ Bonifacio ⊕ www.bonifacio.fr/visite-decouverte/ grottes-marines-millenaires.

Eglise Sainte Marie Majeure
RELIGIOUS SITE | The oldest structure in the city, the 12th-century church with buttresses attaching it to surrounding

houses is located in the center of the citadel's maze of cobblestone streets. Inside the Pisan-Genoese church, look for the 3rd-century white-marble Roman sarcophagus and the Renaissance baptismal font. Walk around the back to see the loggia built above a huge cistern that stored water for use in times of siege. The 14th-century bell tower rises 82 feet. ⊠ Rue du St-Sacrement ☎ 04–95–73–00–15 ⊕ www.bonifacio-mairie.fr/ patrimoine-culture/monuments.

🍴 Restaurants

La Bodega
$$$ | MEDITERRANEAN | This small and cozy restaurant with friendly service offers typical Corsican lunch and dinner dishes. There is inside seating for 18 as well as dining on the terrace for 10. **Known for:** eggplant lasagne with half-sweet, half-salted goat cheese; Corsica tasting plate; grilled sea bream with regional spices. Ⓢ Average main: €25 ⊠ 1 av. de la Carotola ☎ 06–73–75–94–70 ⊗ Closed Sun. and mid-Oct.–mid-Mar.

L'A Cheda
$$$ | MEDITERRANEAN | FAMILY | Just two minutes from the port of Bonifacio, this stylish restaurant takes pride of place in the center of the Acheda Lodge de Charme. Diverse dishes range from John Dory fish and parsnip with saffron from Cozzano to ravioli of vegetables, as well catch of the day with hazelnut. **Known for:** candied pork's cheek with fried foie gras; organic Corsican veal tataki; poultry from Bonifacio with chestnuts. Ⓢ Average main: €30 ⊠ Cavallo Morto ☎ 04–95–73–02–83 ⊕ www.restaurant-bonifacio. com/en.

Le Voilier
$$$ | SEAFOOD | FAMILY | With their warm welcome and attentive service, chef Jean Paul Bartoli and his wife make this year-round restaurant at the port a popular dining spot. The couple serves carefully selected and prepared seafood,

including seared tuna steaks and a mixed dish of octopus, cuttlefish, and squid, along with fine Corsican sausage and traditional cuisine from soups to *fiadone* (cheesecake). **Known for:** mullet stuffed with sea urchin tongues; sweetbread with scampi; bigorre pig with spices and honey. $ *Average main: €30* ⊠ *81 quai Jerome Comparetti* ☎ *04–95–73–07–06* ⊕ *www.restaurant-levoilier-bonifacio. com.*

Hotels

Hôtel le Genovese

$$$$ | B&B/INN | Set on an attractive location, this intimate boutique hotel is built into the ramparts of the upper town's citadel. **Pros:** many sites for panoramic viewing over harbor and Old Town of Bonifacio; excellent Wi-Fi; central location. **Cons:** restaurant cannot accommodate people with reduced mobility; parking in its adjacent lot is restricted (use second parking area behind); breakfast not included. $ *Rooms from: €295* ⊠ *Haute Ville, Pl. de l'Europe, Haute Ville* ☎ *04–95–73–12–34* ⊕ *www.hotel-genovese. com* ⌁ *15 rooms* ❍ *No meals.*

Nightlife

B'52

DANCE CLUBS | For an evening of clubbing, head to this popular nightspot filled with the rich but not necessarily famous during summer. During off-season, the club is a weekend haunt for young locals who enjoy DJ theme nights. ⊠ *35 quai Comparetti* ☎ *06–32–82–18–69* ⊕ *www. b52bonifacio.com.*

Activities

KITEBOARDING

Corsica Kiteboarding

WATER SPORTS | This well-known *école de kite* offers lessons and equipment rental for beginners to advanced levels. Experienced trainers choose the best

and safest spots according to weather conditions, including the long beaches of Balistra and Piantarella. ⊠ *Golfe de Ventilegne* ☎ *06–75–01–50–04* ⊕ *www. corsica-kiteboarding.com.*

WATER SPORTS

Club de Voile de Bonifacio

KAYAKING | FAMILY | On one of the most beautiful spots of Corsica, Club de Voile offers lessons and equipment rental for catamaran sailing, kayaking, and windsurfing. Reserve in advance, especially during high season. ⊠ *Plage de Piantarella* ☎ *06–83–17–37–17* ⊕ *www. ecole-windsurf.com.*

Porto Vecchio

29 km (18 miles) north of Bonifacio, 140 km (87 miles) southeast of Ajaccio.

With a compact Old Town of cobblestone streets lined with charming buildings, a modern marina teeming with yachts, and white-sand beaches lapped by turquoise water, Porto Vecchio is most attractive. Place de République, the main square, is filled with lively restaurants and cafés, as is the neighboring Cours Napoléon. There are more along the harbor area, where you can purchase tickets for boat trips to Bonifacio or the nature preserve on the Lavezzi Islands. Walking the Old Town is easy with the tourist office's free map of historic sights, including well-maintained fortresses. For great views, walk along the top of the ancient wall, especially near the the Porte Genoise Gate.

GETTING HERE AND AROUND

Porto Vecchio is reached by air and sea. Figari Sud Corse Airport, 24 km (15 miles) south of Porto Vecchio, receives flights from Paris, Marseille, and Nice, as well as other European cities in high season. Buses connect Porto Vecchio to Figari airport for around €10. Taxi fares from Porto Vecchio to the airport are around €50. In season, buses also go from Porto Vecchio to different area beaches and

Palombaggia Beach

Driving north from Bonifacio, head east off the N198 on a long, winding road to reach **Palombaggia**, the most famous beach on Corsica. Considered one the best beaches in Europe for its shallow crystal waters and umbrella pine backdrop, this pristine 3-km (2-mile) stretch of white sand rivals even the Caribbean as the perfect family vacation spot. Diversified terrain and powdery beaches continue to extend nearly 16 km (10 miles) up to **Porto Vecchio**, one of the richest regions in Corsica that attracts the world's most famous jet-setters and their glimmering yachts each summer. Considered the island's "St-Tropez," it boasts a large marina and historical Old Town with cobblestone streets lined with cafés, restaurants, and boutiques. On Sunday morning, merchants gather at the center's Place du Monument, where they sell local produce, meat, and cheese. As the island's main exporter of cork and tangerines, Porto Vecchio backs onto Corsica's largest cork-oak forest, **L'Ospédale.** An excursion across the forest on D368, climbing 49 km (30 miles) to the mountain pass of **Col de Bavella,** is one of the island's best tours. Take the flat, straight road (N198) up the east coast only if you have a boat leaving Bastia in two hours.

connect with ferries that head to Marseille and Toulon in France and Civitavecchia, Italy.

VISITOR INFORMATION Office Municipal de Tourisme Porto Vecchio ✉ *Rue Marechal Leclerc, Porto Vecchio* ☎ *04–95–70–09–58* 🌐 *www.ot-portovecchio.com.*

Sights

Col de Bavella

TRAIL | There's no better place to enjoy this region's raw, beautiful scenery than Col de Bavella, a mass of towering, rippling rock formations shaped like a huge church organ. Numerous walks here cater to people of all fitness levels. There's a small information point at the parking lot that describes options. A three- to four-hour circuit to the Trou de la Bombe—an 26-foot hole in the rock—is a popular choice. Other activities include rock climbing and canyoning. ✉ *D268, Zonza* 🌐 *www.ot-portovecchio.com/sud-corse/en/1-134/in-the-mountains.html.*

Restaurants

La Table de Cala Rossa

$$$$ | **MEDITERRANEAN** | This restaurant within Hotel Calarossa serves Corsican dishes with fresh aromatic products from its own garden. A three-course menu with two options for each course changes daily and ranges from squares of piglet roasted in their own skin with Asian spices to lightly grilled scallops in a soup of pumpkin with hazelnut oil. **Known for:** regional wine; pigeon cooked with Corsican fig leaves; pear and chocolate dessert with sesame seed. [$] *Average main: €49* ✉ *Grand Hotel de Cala Rossa, Cala Rossa, Porto Vecchio* ☎ *04–95–71–61–51* 🌐 *www.hotel-calarossa.com/en/la-table* 🕒 *Closed Nov.–late Apr.*

Les Jardins de la Paresse

$$ | **ECLECTIC** | Shaded by tangerine trees and ivy trellises, tables at this eatery are spread among three terraces that overlook the harbor. The mixed grill with shrimp and swordfish is delicious, as is the paella with chicken and seafood. **Known for:** garden ambience; romantic

Haute Corse

setting under the orange trees, bougain-
villea, and ivy; good food. $ *Average
main: €20 ⊠ 18 rue de la Porte Genoise,
Porto Vecchio* ☎ *04–95–24–21–57* ⊕ *jar-
dinsdelaparesse.com* ⊘ *Closed Oct.–Apr.*

 Hotels

★ Grand Hotel de Cala Rossa

$$$$ | HOTEL | Protected by thick foliage
in a peaceful bay of the Gulf of Porto-Vecchio, the Grand Hotel Calla Rossa
emanates the feel of a tropical retreat.
Pros: private sandy beach; gourmet restaurant; extensive gardens. **Cons:** need a
car to get around; sauna and steam room
area quite small; not all rooms have a
sea view. $ *Rooms from: €747* ⊠ *Rte. de
Cala Rossa, Porto Vecchio* ☎ *04–95–71–
61–51* ⊕ *www.hotel-calarossa.com/en*
⊘ *Closed Nov.–Apr.* ⇄ *42 rooms* ⦿ *Free
Breakfast.*

Le Roi Theodore

$$$$ | HOTEL | This hotel, just 3 km (2
miles) from Old Town, is tranquil despite
its setting and is creatively constructed,
with each room facing inward toward a
large courtyard and infinity pool. **Pros:**
three swimming pools, two outdoor;
spacious, bright rooms; cozy well-
stocked library. **Cons:** some elements
need refurbishing; massage services bit
pricey; along a busy road in an industrial
area. $ *Rooms from: €289* ⊠ *Av. de
Bastia, Porto Vecchio* ☎ *04–95–70–14–94*
⊕ *www.roi-theodore.com/en* ⊘ *Closed
mid-Oct.–early Apr.* ⇄ *53 rooms* ⦿ *Free
Breakfast.*

Corte

82 km (51 miles) northeast of Ajaccio.

Set amid spectacular cliffs and gorges at the confluence of the Tavignano, Restonica, and Orta Rivers, Corte is the spiritual heart and soul of Corsica. Capital of Pasquale Paoli's government from 1755 to 1769, it was also where Paoli established the Corsican University in 1765. Closed by the victorious French in 1769, the university, always a symbol of Corsican identity, was reopened in 1981. To reach the upper town and the 15th-century château overlooking the rivers, walk up the cobblestone ramp from Place Pasquale-Paoli. Stop in lovely Place Gaffori at one of the cafés or restaurants. Note the bullet-pocked house where the Corsican hero Gian Pietro Gaffori and his wife, Faustina, held off the Genoese in 1750.

GETTING HERE AND AROUND

Public transport is quite poor in Corsica, so to access stunning views of interior Corsica, your best bet is to rent a car or take a local minibus. The shortest distance to Corte is from Bastia. Count on at least an hour to negotiate the 68-km (42-mile) drive. From Ajaccio, a distance of 82 km (51 miles) will take at least 90 minutes.

The Corsican train called the *trinighellu* is infrequent and slow, and the journey from Ajaccio to Corte takes about one hour and 40 minutes; from Bastia, it's 90 minutes. A main bus line connects Bastia to Corte (90 mins).

VISITOR INFORMATION Office de Tourisme Corte ⊠ *La Citadelle* ☎ *04–95–46–26–70* ⊕ *www.corte-tourisme.com.*

Sights

Citadelle

MILITARY SITE | FAMILY | One of six island fortifications of its kind, the Citadelle, a Vauban-style fortress (1769–78), is built around the original 15th-century bastion at the highest point of the cliff, with the river below. In 1769, after the defeat of Ponte Novu, Corsica came under French rule. Count de Vaux, who held Corte, undertook the construction of the citadel's second reconstruction to strengthen the defense system of the city. The building contains the **Musée de la Corse** (Corsica Museum), dedicated to the island's history and ethnography. ⊠ *Rue de Donjon* ☎ *04–95–45–25–45* ⊕ *www.musee-corse.com* ⊒ *€6* ⊘ *Closed Dec. 31–Jan. 14.*

Gorges de la Restonica (*Restonica Gorges*)

CANYON | FAMILY | Put on your hiking boots—the Gorges de la Restonica make a spectacular day tour, 10 km (6 miles) southwest of Corte. At the top of the Restonica Valley, leave your car in the parking area. A two-hour climb will take you to Lac de Mélo, a trout-filled mountain lake 6,528 feet above sea level. Another hour up is the usually snow-bordered Lac de Capitello. Information on trails is available from the Parc Naturel Régional. Light meals are served in the stone shepherds' huts at the Bergeries de Grotelle. ⊠ *Off D623* ☎ *04–95–51–79–00* ⊕ *www.pnr.corsica.*

La Scala di Santa Regina

SCENIC DRIVE | The Stairway of the Holy Queen is one of Corsica's most spectacular roads—and one of the most difficult to navigate, especially in winter. About 20 km (12 miles) northwest of Corte, it traces the twisty path of the Golo River, which has carved its way through layers of red granite, forming dramatic gorges and waterfalls. Follow the road to the Col de Verghio (Verghio Pass) for superb views of Tafunatu, the legendary perforated mountain, and Monte Cinto. On the way up you'll pass through the Valdo Niello Forest, Corsica's most important woodlands, filled with pines and beeches. As you descend from the Verghio Pass through the Forêt d'Aitone (Aitone Forest), note how well manicured it is—the pigs, goats, and sheep running rampant through the tall Laricio pines keep it this way. As you pass the village of Evisa, with its orange roofs, look across the impressive Gorges de Spelunca (Spelunca Gorge) to see the hill village of Ota. A small road on the right will take you across the gorge, where there's an ancient Genoese-built bridge. ✉ *D84* 🌐 *www.visit-corsica.com.*

Palais National (*National Palace*)
CASTLE/PALACE | The Palais National, just outside the citadel and above Place Gaffori, is the ancient residence of Genoa's representatives in Corsica and was the seat of the Corsican parliament from 1755 to 1769, where Paoli set up his government for independent Corsica. Today it is part of Corte University. ✉ *3 rue du Palais National* ☎ *04–95–45–00–97* 🌐 *upalazzu.universita.corsica.*

Quartier de Chiostra
NEIGHBORHOOD | **FAMILY** | Leave the Haute Ville and go through the tiny alleys of the Quartier de Chiostra. Follow the cobblestone path (as you look down) to the right from the Belvédère, bearing right and across at the **Chapelle St-Théophile.** Coming into the tiny square on your left, don't miss the open stone staircase on the opposite wall, or the prehistoric fertility goddess carved into the wall to the left. Farther downhill you will rejoin the ramp leading into place Pasquale-Paoli. ✉ *Haute Ville* 🌐 *www.visit-corsica.com.*

🍴 Restaurants

L'Annexe
$$ | **ITALIAN** | This quaint eatery's modern decor (including funky artwork on the walls), ambient music, and young staff dressed in jeans and black T-shirts make it a hip spot. Popular with the locals are the brick-oven pizzas, grilled hamburgers, and gourmet salads. **Known for:** warm goat cheese salads; trout dishes; shrimp linguine. [$] *Average main: €20* ✉ *1 Rampe Ste-Croix* ☎ *04–95–38–37–59.*

Le 24 Restaurant
$$$ | **MODERN FRENCH** | Rough-hewn archways, stone walls, and atmospheric lighting give this chic restaurant a cavernous feel. The chalkboard menu, brought to each table, features shrimp tempura, seafood pasta, and sautéed dorado, among other favorites. **Known for:** filet mignon, topped with foie gras; live music evenings; chocolate soufflé and homemade sorbet. [$] *Average main: €30* ✉ *24 cours Paoli* ☎ *04–95–46–02–90.*

🛏 Hotels

Duc de Padoue Hotel
$$ | **B&B/INN** | Named for the faithful general in Napoléon's army, this 19th-century hotel is located on the town's quietest square. **Pros:** quiet location; helpful staff; clean rooms. **Cons:** no parking; not all rooms have views; no amenities. [$] *Rooms from: €118* ✉ *2 pl. Padoue* ☎ *04–95–46–01–37* 🌐 *www.ducdepadoue.com* ⏲ *Closed Jan.–Apr.* 🛏 *11 rooms* 🍴 *Free Breakfast.*

Hôtel Dominique Colonna
$$$$ | **B&B/INN** | This modern hotel is full of delightful surprises, including sliding doors leading directly out to breakfast nooks beside a stream. **Pros:** incredible breakfast; enchanting location; gracious staff. **Cons:** hard mattresses; no shade at the pool; a bit outside town. [$] *Rooms from: €230* ✉ *Vallee de la Restonica, BP 83* ☎ *04–95–45–25–65* 🌐 *www.dominique-colonna.com* ⏲ *Closed Nov. 5–Apr. 8* 🛏 *29 rooms* 🍴 *Free Breakfast.*

Porto and Calanches di Piana

5 km (3 miles) west of Ota, 74 km (45 miles) south of Calvi.

Set between the small resort town of Porto and petite, historic 18th-century village of Piana, the dramatic red-rock formations rising nearly 1,000 feet high on the western coast are set against the crystalline **Golfe de Porto** (Gulf of Porto). The massive pink-granite mountains rise and fall dramatically, with strange rock shapes plunging into the blue waters. The region is best seen at dusk, when the jagged landscape transforms into a luminescent glow of red as the sun sets. Porto itself is built around a small port that has a boardwalk lined with touristy restaurants and hotels. A short hike from here will bring you to a 16th-century Genoese tower that overlooks the bay. Boat excursions leave daily for the **Réserve Naturel de Scandola** on the Cape Girolata Peninsula that protects indigenous wildlife in its extraordinary waters, inlets, and caves. Designated UNESCO World Heritage Sites, both the reserve and rock formation region draw crowds of tourists during summer months.

GETTING HERE AND AROUND
From Calvi, head south on N197 to D81. Follow D81 along the coast for 73 km (45 miles) until you reach Porto; the drive takes 90 minutes. From Porto, follow D81 southeast for 6 km (3 miles) to view the famous Calanches di Piana.

Book an afternoon boat ride to capture the most impressive views of the rugged precipices. Excursions tour coastal caves and cove. Tickets cost around €25 per person.

VISITOR INFORMATION Tourism Office Piana ✉ *Hôtel de Ville, Pl. de la Mairie, Piana* ☎ *09–66–92–84–42* ⊕ *www. otpiana.com.*

Calvi

85 km (53 miles) north of Piana, 164 km (100 miles) north of Ajaccio, 112 km (70 miles) west of Bastia.

Corsica's slice of the Riviera, Calvi has been described as "an oasis of pleasure on an otherwise austere island." Today Calvi sees a summertime invasion of tourists, drawn to the 6-km (4-mile) stretch of sandy white beach, impressive citadel overlooking the Old Town, and lively restaurants. Calvi is a city for strolling, whether in search of bars, picturesque coastline views, or simply a bit of retail therapy.

GETTING HERE AND AROUND
From Bastia, follow D81 until you cross St-Florent. Continue on D81 past St-Florent for 52 km (32 miles), then go right onto N197. Follow the N197 for 40 km (24 miles) to reach Calvi. The drive will take approximately 2½ hours. Trains arrive from the main cities. Coach buses and boats are also available to access and tour the popular resort promontory.

VISITOR INFORMATION Office de Tourisme Calvi ✉ *Port de Plaisance, Chemin de la Plage* ☎ *04–95–65–16–67* ⊕ *www. balagne-corsica.com/calvi-ile-rousse-corse.html.*

Sights

Cathédrale St-Jean-Baptiste
BUILDING | The austere facade of the 13th-century Cathedral of John the Baptist is worth a visit to see its alabaster Renaissance baptismal font decorated with angel heads and rows of pews where the city's chaste upper-class women used to pray. ✉ *Pl. d'Armes* ☎ *04–95–65–16–67* ⊕ *www.balagne-corsica.com/cathedrale-saint-jean-baptiste-de-calvi.html.*

Citadelle

BUILDING | **FAMILY** | This Genoese citadel is perched on a rocky promontory at the tip of the bay. An inscription above the drawbridge—"*Civitas calvi semper fidelis*" (The citizens of Calvi are always faithful)—reflects the town's unswerving allegiance to Genoa. At the welcome center, just inside the gates, you can watch the video on the city's history, book an English-language guided tour, or follow the self-guided walking tour. ✉ *Rte. de la Citadelle* ☎ *04–95–65–16–67* 🌐 *balagne-corsica.com/decouvrir-la-balagne/calvi* 🎫 *€7 audio guide.*

🍴 Restaurants

Emile's

$$$ | **FRENCH** | With an open terrace offering panoramic views of the port of Calvi, this elegant restaurant offers a wide range of dishes from lobster ravioli to roasted rack of lamb. Divided into "The Sea" and "The Countryside" the menus vary in price and range; there is also a signature menu. **Known for:** fish tartare with calamansi vinegar and red fruits coulis; squid ratatouille in a lemongrass broth; homemade sherbet. [$] *Average main: €25* ✉ *45 Quai Adolphe Landry* ☎ *04–95–65–09–60* 🌐 *www.restaurant-emiles.com.*

La Palmeraie

$$$$ | **MEDITERRANEAN** | Formerly an 18th-century manor house and grounds, this stylish restaurant in a beautiful conservatory at La Signoria Hotel is cheese heaven, stocking 40 different Corsican varieties. Dinner highlights include a starter of pressed duck foie gras with local figs and sautéed veal with wild mushrooms. **Known for:** Corsican sweetbread chestnuts and hazelnuts; deer and gooseberries; chestnut soufflé. [$] *Average main: €47* ✉ *Rte. de la Foret de Bonifato* ☎ *04–95–65–93–00* 🌐 *www.hotel-la-signoria.com.*

La Table by La Villa

$$$$ | **MEDITERRANEAN** | Within the five-star Hôtel La Villa perched high amid rambling hills overlooking the ocher-color Old Citadel, La Table by La Villa offers such memorable dining highlights as varied as *oeuf mollet frit* (poached eggs with celery, mushrooms, and black truffles); carpaccio of John Dory and spider crab with fennel, fresh coriander, and shiso leaves; and braised pigeon breast with confit of pigeon leg, porcini mushrooms, and dried fruits. **Known for:** monkfish and pineapple with avocado and coriander; candied cod; veal dishes. [$] *Average main: €45* ✉ *Chemin Notre Dame de la Serra* ☎ *04–95–65–83–60* 🌐 *www.hotel-lavilla.com* 🕒 *Closed Oct. 9–Apr. 28.*

🛏 Hotels

Calvi Mariana Hotel

$$$ | **B&B/INN** | On a hillside overlooking Calvi Bay, this five-star hotel stands just minutes from downtown. **Pros:** free access to sauna and hammam; wide range of spa treatments (including in-room); pool on roof level with mountain view. **Cons:** restricted gym (though nice garden view); located at busy crossroads; steep approach walk to hotel. [$] *Rooms from: €155* ✉ *Av. Santa Maria* ☎ *04–95–65–31–38* 🌐 *www.hotel-mariana.com* 🛏 *54 rooms* 🍴 *Free Breakfast.*

Hotel La Signoria

$$$$ | **HOTEL** | Set amid acres of beautifully landscaped grounds, this luxury property sits in the shadow of mountains near Bonifato Valley. **Pros:** Michelin-star restaurant; guests can use a private beach; spa with natural products. **Cons:** transport needed to reach Calvi and beach; beach deck chairs and towels cost extra; expensive bar drinks. [$] *Rooms from: €570* ✉ *Rte. de la Forêt de Bonifato, 5 km (3 miles) from Calvi* ☎ *04–95–65–93–00* 🌐 *www.hotel-la-signoria.com* 🕒 *Closed Jan.–mid-Apr.* 🛏 *26 rooms* 🍴 *No meals.*

Hotel Le Magnolia

$$$ | B&B/INN | In this pretty 19th-century former mansion between the church and the market in downtown Calvi, cozy rooms are named after French literary figures. **Pros:** central location; tranquil garden; wild boar stew with myrtle. **Cons:** no access by car; some rooms can be very small; old-fashioned decor. $ *Rooms from: €160* ✉ *Rue Alsace Lorraine* ☎ *04–95–65–19–16* ⊕ *www.hotel-le-magnolia.com* ⊟ *No credit cards* ⊘ *Closed Nov.–Apr.* ⬘ *10 rooms* ⦿ *Free Breakfast.*

★ La Villa Hotel & Spa

$$$$ | HOTEL | FAMILY | This hotel sits on a manicured hill with marvelous views of the town and citadel and feels like a private Mediterranean villa. **Pros:** spectacular views; outstanding restaurant; two swimming pools. **Cons:** wasps can be an irritating problem; tough uphill walk back from Calvi; hotel shuttle stops at 8 pm. $ *Rooms from: €575* ✉ *Chemin de Notre-Dame de la Serra* ☎ *04–95–65–10–10* ⊕ *www.hotel-lavilla.com* ⊘ *Closed Oct. 5–Apr. 25* ⬘ *55 rooms* ⦿ *Free Breakfast.*

Nightlife

L'Eden Port

BARS/PUBS | A popular nightspot, this centrally located disco offers expensive drinks, electronic music, and enthusiastic crowds. A good place for sushi or aperitifs on the terrace. ✉ *Port de Plaisance, Quai Adolphe Landry* ☎ *04–95–60–57–44.*

Pigna

25 km (15 miles) northeast of Calvi.

The village of Pigna is dedicated to bringing back traditional Corsican music and crafts. Here you can listen to folk songs in cafés, visit workshops, and buy handmade musical instruments. During the first half of July, the Casa Musicale hosts a Festivoce featuring international vocal groups.

GETTING HERE AND AROUND

From Calvi, follow N197 toward L'Ile Rousse, take a right on D71 at Curso and left onto D151 in Casaposa. Continue on D151 until you reach Pigna.

Hotels

Casa Musicale

$ | B&B/INN | This enchanting rustic mansion has traditional home-style cuisine and music of all kinds—including authentic Corsican polyphonic chanting—and a commanding view of the coast. **Pros:** most rooms overlook Algajola Bay; relaxed bohemian ambience; close to Pigna, theme village. **Cons:** narrow road access; often postdinner noise; luggage must be transported few hundred meters over pavement. $ *Rooms from: €90* ✉ *Plaza de l'Eglise* ☎ *04–95–61–77– 31* ⊕ *www.casa-musicale.org* ⬘ *9 rooms* ⦿ *Free Breakfast.*

Shopping

Casa di l'Artigiani

CRAFTS | Created to showcase local artisans, Casa di l'Artigiani is the perfect place to find handmade crafts, from traditionally forged knives, leather items, and musical instruments, to hand-knit sweaters. There are also locally produced culinary treasures like olive oils, jams, honeys, and *canistrelli* biscuits. ✉ *Rte. des Artisans* ☎ *04–95–61–76–57* ⊕ *www.routedesartisans.fr/nos-coups-de-coeur/casa-di-lartigiani.*

Bastia

170 km (105 miles) north of Bonifacio, 153 km (95 miles) northeast of Ajaccio.

Notably more Italianate than the French-influenced Ajaccio, Bastia is quintessentially Corsican. The Baroque

A microcosm of mountains, beaches, fishing ports, wilderness, Corsica is the purest strain of proto-Mediterranean culture.

coastal town has a historic center that retains the timeless, salty flavor of an ancient Mediterranean port. Its name is derived from the word "bastion," in reference to the fortress the Genoese built here in the 14th century as a stronghold against rebellious islanders. The Terra Vecchia (Old Town) is best explored on foot. Start at the wide, palm-filled Place St-Nicolas, bordered on one side by docked ships looming large in the port and on the other by two blocks of popular cafés along Boulevard Général-de-Gaulle.

GETTING HERE AND AROUND

You can reach Bastia by air or sea. Flights arrive regularly from main cities in Europe at the Aéroport de Bastia-Poretta situated in Lucciana, southeast of the city. From here, Autobus Bastiais shuttle bus lines run from 6:30 am to 10 pm (depending on season) to downtown in 40 minutes for €9. Expect to pay €30–€45 for a taxi.

Ferries cross from France (Nice, Toulon, Marseilles) and Italy (Livorno, Genova, Verde Ligure). The average crossing time is around five hours. Train services link Bastia to Ajaccio and Calvi. The station is only a short distance from Bastia's ferry port, on Rond-point Maréchal Leclerc.

VISITOR INFORMATION Office de Tourisme Bastia ⊠ *Pl. St-Nicolas* ☎ *04–95–54–20–40* ⊕ *www.bastia-tourisme.com.*

 Sights

Cathédrale Ste-Marie

RELIGIOUS SITE | FAMILY | A network of cobbled alleyways rambles across the citadel to the 15th-century Cathédrale Ste-Marie, one of the town's prettiest churches. Inside, classic Baroque style abounds in an explosion of gilt decoration. Numerous works of art from the 18th and 19th centuries, forged metalwork, sculptures, and statues that were generous gifts from the bishops of Mariana, residents of the cathedral from 1600 to 1622, are showcased. ⊠ *12 rue Notre-Dame* ☎ *04–95–54–20–40* ⊕ *www.bastia-tourisme.com/bastia/la-cathedrale-sainte-marie.*

Chapelle Ste-Croix (*Chapel of the Holy Cross*)
RELIGIOUS SITE | The sumptuous rococo style of the Chapelle Ste-Croix, behind the cathedral, makes it look more like a theater than a church. The chapel owes its name to a blackened oak crucifix, dubbed "Christ of the Miracles," discovered by fishermen at sea in 1428 and venerated to this day by Bastia's fishing community. The most ancient church of the town, this chapel has officially been classified as a historic monument since 1931. ✉ *4 rue de l'Evêché* ☎ *04–95–32–91–66* 🌐 *www.bastia.corsica/fr/batiments/oratoire-de-la-confrerie-de-sainte-croix-596.html.*

Église de la Conception (*Church of the Conception*)
RELIGIOUS SITE | The 16th-century Église de la Conception occupies a cobblestone square. Step inside the Baroque portal to admire the church's ornate 18th-century interior, requiring a bright day to see much detail as interior lighting is quite dim. The walls are covered with wood carvings, gold, marble, and velvet fabric. Check out the altar's interpretation of the *Assumption* by Murillo, whose original version sits in Madrid's El Prado Museum. ✉ *Rue Napoléon* ☎ *04–95–32–91–66* 🌐 *www.bastia.corsica/fr/batiments/oratoire-de-la-confrerie-de-l-immaculee-conception-597.html.*

Musée de Bastia
MUSEUM | The vaulted, colonnaded galleries of the Palais des Nobles Douzes house the Musée de Bastia. Don't miss the *Casablanca,* a French submarine used by the Resistance, with swastikas on the turret representing downed Nazi aircraft. The building itself has been undergoing modifications since the 18th century, when it was used as the meeting place for rural commune leaders. ✉ *Pl. du Donjon and Cours Favale, La Citadelle* ☎ *04–95–31–09–12* 🌐 *www.bastia-tourisme.com/que-faire/musee-de-bastia* 🎫 *From €5.*

Terra Nova (*New Town*)
NEIGHBORHOOD | **FAMILY** | The city's more modern quarter is well worth a promenade. Climb the Escalier Romieu steps beside the leafy Jardins Romieu for a sweeping view of the Italian islands of Capraia, Elba, and Montecristo. ✉ *Citadelle* 🌐 *www.bastia-tourisme.com/bastia/le-jardin-romieu.*

Vieux Port (*Old Port*)
MARINA | The picturesque Vieux Port, along Quai des Martyrs de la Libération, is dominated by the hilltop citadel. Take a stroll along the harbor, which is lined with excellent seafood restaurants. You can still find many bright red-and-blue fishing boats with tangles of old nets and lines. ✉ *Quai des Martyrs de la Libération* ☎ *04–95–54–20–40 tourism office* 🌐 *www.bastia-tourisme.com/bastia/le-vieux-port-de-bastia.*

🍴 Restaurants

Brasserie L'Imperial
$$ | **BRASSERIE** | Located on the Place St-Nicolas in the heart of Bastia, opposite the port, this restaurant with a shady terrace and impressive wood frontage is a perfect place to people-watch and bask in its brewery-like atmosphere. Thin-crust pizzas and salads are a bargain; for something more substantial, try the risotto with shrimp, beef fillet with foie gras, or wok-sautéed salmon with fresh vegetables. **Known for:** warm goat cheese salad; crispy prawns with Thai sauce; seafood spaghetti. [$] *Average main: €20* ✉ *11 bd. Général De Gaulle* ☎ *04–95–31–04–42.*

Chez Huguette
$$$ | **SEAFOOD** | Specializing in fish and seafood, including a succulent bouillabaisse, oysters, clams, and prawns, Chez Huguette is located in the old port of Bastia. It also serves meat dishes such as veal and beef. **Known for:** gourmet salad with duck and foie gras; mussels with assorted herbs; octopus in a piquant tomato sauce. [$] *Average main: €30* ✉ *4*

rue de la Marine ☎ *04–95–31–37–60* ⊕ *www.chezhuguette.fr* ▭ *No credit cards.*

La Fabrica

$$ | BISTRO | Polished wood floor, vintage furnishings, stone-brick walls, and vaulted arch ceiling make this popular restaurant well worth visiting simply for its atmospheric ambience not to mention its fine food. Hearty diverse dishes range from delicious Black Angus steaks to creamy risottos. **Known for:** pizza with truffle; veal chops; melted Camembert in a bread bowl. **$** *Average main: €20* ⊠ *1 bd. du Général Giraud,* ☎ *04–95–58–32–95* ⊕ *www.la-fabrica-bastia.com.*

 ## Hotels

Hôtel Castel Brando

$$$ | HOTEL | More a walled château than a medieval fortress, Hôtel Castel Brando sits across from the harbor town of Erbalunga. **Pros:** two swimming pools; vaulted ceiling lounge and library; fine patio and gardens decorated with olive and palm trees. **Cons:** 15 minutes from Bastia; restaurant service could be improved; limited menu. **$** *Rooms from: €200* ⊠ *Brando, Erbalunga* ☎ *04–95–30–10–30* ⊕ *www.castelbrando.com* ⊗ *Closed early Nov.–mid-Mar.* ⇆ *43 rooms* ❖❖ *Free Breakfast.*

Hotel Posta Vecchia

$ | HOTEL | At the end of a quiet promenade near the water's edge, this former post office turned hotel lies close to Place St-Nicolas and the Citadelle. **Pros:** central location—waterfront and downtown; spic-and-span rooms; pet-friendly. **Cons:** needs some renovations and better air-conditioning; small rooms, including bathrooms; no parking. **$** *Rooms from: €75* ⊠ *Quai des Martyrs-de-la-Libération, 8 rue Posta Vecchia* ☎ *04–95–32–32–38* ⊕ *www.postavecchia-bastia.com* ⊗ *Closed mid-Dec.–early Jan.* ⇆ *60 rooms* ❖❖ *Free Breakfast.*

 ## Nightlife

L'Alba

PIANO BARS/LOUNGES | Between the Vieux Port and Place St-Nicolas, L'Alba is a trendy lounge that occasionally hosts cabaret and floor shows. ⊠ *22 quai des Martyrs-de-la-Libération* ☎ *06–83–59–42–97.*

Performing Arts

One of Corsica's major carnivals, the **Fête du Christ Noir** (Feast of the Black Christ), dedicated to Bastia's most important religious icon, is on May 3. In early June the streets of Calvi become a musical haven with the **Annual Festival of Jazz,** while Calvi on the Rocks keeps it hopping in early July. The **Fête de St-Jean,** on Midsummer's Eve (June 23), means concerts in all of Bastia's Baroque spaces. All of Corsica celebrates Bastille Day (French Independence) on July 14. A **Film Festival of Mediterranean Cultures** is held every November. An **International Music Festival** is in early December.

Shopping

Domaine Mavela

GIFTS/SOUVENIRS | Jean Claude Venturini and his sons developed this distillery to turn the main fruits of the island into brandy and liqueur from fruits such as myrtle, lemons, chestnuts, pear, and raspberry. The distillery also produce the P & M Whiskey. ⊠ *U Licettu, Aléria Distillerie, Aléria* ☎ *04–95–56–60–30* ⊕ *www.domaine-mavela.com/en.*

Marché Traditionnel

OUTDOOR/FLEA/GREEN MARKETS | In front of the town hall, meander through myriad stalls selling everything from local cheeses to charcuterie, oils, and other fine Corsican gastronomic products every weekend. ⊠ *4 rue Cardinal Viale Prélat* ⊕ *www.bastia-tourisme.com/bastia/la-place-du-marche.*

Chapter 16

TOULOUSE AND THE LANGUEDOC

16

Updated by
Diane Vadino

WELCOME TO TOULOUSE AND THE LANGUEDOC

TOP REASONS TO GO

★ **Art towns:** Captivating Collioure, the main town of the Vermilion Coast, was where Matisse and Derain went crazy with color and created the Fauvist art movement in the early 20th century.

★ **Fairy-tale Carcassonne:** Complete with towers, turrets, and battlements, Carcassonne's fortified upper town is a UNESCO World Heritage Site that feels like a medieval theme park.

★ **Tumultuous Toulouse:** With rosy roofs and red-brick mansions, the "Pink City" is a place where high culture is an evening at an outdoor café.

★ **Albi's Toulouse-Lautrec:** Presided over by the fortresslike Cathédrale Ste-Cécile, Albi honors its most famous native son, Toulouse-Lautrec, with the largest museum of his works.

★ **Historic abbey:** At an altitude of nearly 3,600 feet, the picture-postcard medieval Abbaye St-Martin du Canigou enjoys a perch that (literally) takes your breath away.

1 Toulouse. The modern gateway to the south and France's fourth-largest city.

2 Albi. The charming hometown of famed artist Henri de Toulouse-Lautrec.

3 Cordes-Sur-Ciel. A storybook hilltop village.

4 Carcassonne. Perhaps the best preserved medieval town in all of France.

5 Perpignan. The main hub of Roussillon.

6 Prades. A market town that makes a good base for the region.

7 Vernet-les-Bains. A spa town that's home to Abbaye St-Martin due Canigou.

8 Céret. The birthplace of Cubism.

9 Collioure. The Vermilion Coast fishing village that attracted the likes of Matisse and Derain.

10 Narbonne. An important town for Roman history.

11 Béziers. The center of the Languedoc wine region.

12 Montpellier. The lively capital of the Loungedoc region.

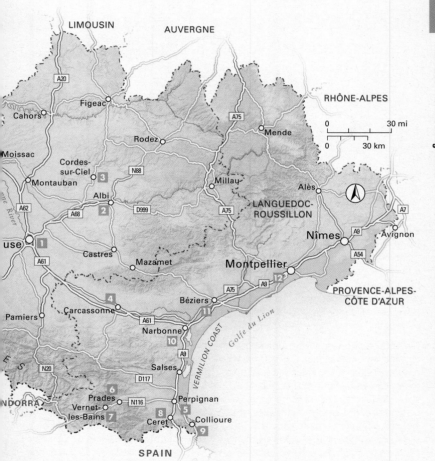

LIMOUSIN

AUVERGNE

RHÔNE-ALPES

A20

Figeac

Cahors

Moissac

A75

Mende

Rodez

Cordes-
sur-Ciel   N88   Millau

Montauban

Albi   D999   A75

A62   A68   LANGUEDOC-
                                                         ROUSSILLON

A61   Castres   Mazamet   Alès

use   Nîmes

                                                                 Montpellier

A61   Carcassonne   Béziers

Pamiers

FR
S   N20   Narbonne

ANDORRA   Prades   N116   Perpignan

Vernet-
les-Bains   Ceret   Collioure

SPAIN

0   30 mi
0   30 km

A7

Avignon

A9

A54

A75   A9

PROVENCE-ALPES-
CÔTE D'AZUR

VERMILION COAST   Golfe du Lion

D117   Salses

A9

0 1

0 2

0 3

0 4

0 5

0 6

0 7

0 8

0 9

0 10

0 11

0 12

Like the most celebrated dish of this area, cassoulet, the southwestern region of France is made up of diverse ingredients. Just as it would be a gross oversimplification to refer to cassoulet merely as a mixture of baked beans, southwestern France is much more than just Toulouse, the peaks of the Pyrénées, and the fairy-tale ramparts of Carcassonne.

For here you'll also find, like so many raisins sweetening up a spicy stew, the pretty seaside town of Collioure, the famed Côte Vermeille (where Matisse, Picasso, and Braque first vacationed to paint), and Albi, a hilltop town that honors its hometown hero, Toulouse-Lautrec, with a great museum. But in most cases, every traveler heading to this area begins with the regional gateway: "La Ville Rose," so called for Toulouse's redbrick buildings.

Big enough to be France's fourth-largest city and yet with the look and vibe of a gorgeous small town, Toulouse is all that more famous regional capitals would like to have remained, or to become. The cultural hub of this corner of France, the city has a vibrancy that derives from its large student population and lively music scene, plus a rich heritage of sculpture and architectural gems. Snaking along the banks of the Garonne as it meanders north and west from the Catalan Pyrénées on its way to the Atlantic, romantic Toulouse has a Spanish sensuality unique in all of Gaul. The city began as the ancient capital of the province called Languedoc, so christened when it became royal property in 1270, *langue d'oc* meaning the country where the word *oc* replaced the *oui* of northeastern France for "yes."

If you head out in any direction from Toulouse you'll enjoy a feast for the eyes. Albi, with its Toulouse-Lautrec legacy, is a star attraction, while Céret is the gateway to a fabled "open-air museum" prized by artists and poets, the Côte Vermeille. The Vermilion Coast is centered on Collioure, the lovely fishing village where Matisse, Derain, and the Fauvists—the "wild beasts" of the early-20th-century art world—threw out the pretty pastel rule book, drawing inspiration instead from the savage tones found in Mother Nature hereabouts. When you see picturesque Collioure's stunning Mediterranean setting, you can understand why Matisse went color mad. Sheer heaven for painters, the town's magic did not go unnoticed, and it soon drew vacationers by the boatload, who quickly discovered that everything around here seems to be asking to be immortalized on canvas: the Mediterranean, smooth and opalescent at dawn; villagers dancing sardanas to the music of the raucous and ancient woodwind *flaviolés* and *tenorés*; and the flood of golden light so peculiar to the Mediterranean.

MAJOR REGIONS

Toulouse. Now the center of Europe's high-tech aerospace industry (Airbus is made here), the city sees itself as the modern gateway to the south. Happily, Toulouse's new forward-looking attitude hasn't infringed on the well-preserved *centre ville* (city center), a veritable museum of mansions, where the brick-paved streets make you feel as if you're in a small town and aerospace engineers own Renaissance houses.

Albi and the Gers. Some 75 km (47 miles) northeast of Toulouse, Albi sits on the Tarn River and was once a major center of the Cathars, a medieval Christian sect; the huge Cathédrale Ste-Cécile was a symbol of the Roman Catholic Church's victory over these heretics. Art lovers make a pilgrimage to the famed Musée Toulouse-Lautrec. West from Albi, along the river, the land opens up to the rural Gers *département,* home of the heady brandy, Armagnac, and heart of the former dukedom of Gascony. Studded with châteaux—from simple medieval fortresses to ambitious classical residences—and with tiny, isolated village jewels like Cordes-sur-Ciel, the Gers is an easy place to fall in love with, or in.

Languedoc-Roussillon. One of the most diverse backdrops in France, Languedoc-Roussillon skirts the Mediterranean coast southward toward Spain where the Pyrénées plunge dramatically into the sea. The southern half of the region, Roussillon and its main city Perpignan, was long dominated by Spanish Catalonia's House of Aragon—which explains why the area is also known as French Catalonia. Historically rooted in agricultural pursuits, Roussillon's varied landscape allows for citrus and cherry trees, while the snowcapped Pic du Canigó towers over palm trees in the valley. Olive groves and vineyards thrive on arid hillsides inland and earthy cheeses come from herds in the bordering high mountains. Included in the region are famous sights like Carcassonne's La Cité—the largest medieval town extant—and *le littoral Languedocien* (the Languedoc coast), where France's "second Riviera" draws both artists and sun worshippers to Collioure and other towns along the Côte Vermeille (Vermilion Coast). Immortalized by Matisse and Picasso, the Côte Vermeille attracts droves of European sun worshippers (plus aspiring painters) to its craggy shoreline. Heading northward, Languedoc begins around the ancient Roman capital of Narbonne and extends to the region's hub, the elegant city of Montpellier. Other smaller villages include Prades, Vernet-les-Bains, Céret, and the wine-focused Béziers.

Planner

When to Go

You can expect pleasantly warm weather as early as April and as late as October, but be prepared for rainstorms and/or heat waves at almost any time. The weather is especially unpredictable in the Pyrénées: a few passing clouds can rapidly turn into a full-blown storm. Needless to say, during July and August towns high on tourist lists—like Albi, Carcassonne, and Collioure—are packed, so perhaps opt for April and May, which are delightful months on the Côte Vermeille and also the time when the Pyrenean flowers are at their best. June and September (grape-picking season, or *vendange*) are equally good for both inland and coastal areas. As October draws near, the chilly winds of winter begin to blow and frenzied mushroom hunters ferret amid the chestnut and pine trees. Olive harvesters set to work in November.

No matter the season, there's plenty here to occupy those who love the outdoors, whether it be scaling lofty peaks, skiing sun-dappled snowfields, or hiking the Grandes Randonnées (GRs), particularly the 140-mile GR-70, which follows Robert Louis Stevenson's 1878 trek through the region.

Planning Your Time

Getting to know this vast region would take several weeks, or even years. But it's possible to sample all of its finest offerings in nine days, if that's all the time you have. Begin by practicing your "olé's" in Spanish-soul Toulouse; after two days and two nights in this vibrant city, veer west to the Gers département to spend Day 3 in Albi and discover the masterworks of Toulouse-Lautrec at his famous museum here, including a self-portrait, made at the age of 16, that speaks to his prodigious talents. On Day 4, continue some 112 km (70 miles) south to once-upon-a-timefied Carcassonne to introduce your kids to the Puss-in-Boots fantasy of this castellated wonder. After a night filled with medieval history and glamour, travel southeast on Day 5 to the Vermilion Coast. It's time to pack your crayons for a trip to Matisse Country and head to the Roussillon's coastal town of Collioure to channel the spirits of the famous Fauve painters. Spend all of Day 6 here. Then on Day 7, drive north past Perpignan, the historic hub city of the Roussillon, and head to marvelous Montpellier. After your seventh night, enjoy Day 8 by touring this city's fascinating Vieille Ville (Old Town), steeped in culture, history, and young blood (a famous university is based here). Add on a Day 9 to chill out before returning to reality.

Getting Here and Around

AIR TRAVEL

Flying here is easy because the region has four airports—Toulouse-Blagnac being the largest. They're served by major airlines, like Air France (⊕ www.air-france.com), as well as budget carriers, including easyJet, Hop!, and Ryanair.

AIRPORT INFORMATION Aéroport Montpellier-Méditerranée ☎ 08–25–83–00–03 ⊕ www.montpellier.aeroport.fr. **Aéroport Sud de France-Carcassonne** ☎ 08–20–67–34–11 ⊕ www.aeroport-carcassonne.com. **Aéroport Sud de France-Perpignan** ☎ 04–68–52–60–70 ⊕ www.aeroport-perpignan.com. **Aéroport Toulouse-Blagnac** ☎ 08–25–38–00–00 ⊕ www.toulouse.aeroport.fr.

BUS TRAVEL

Many public and private bus companies thread through the Occitanie, including Cars Teissiers from Carcassonne and Herault Transport from Montpellier. It's wise to check with the pertinent local tourist office regarding your best options, as bus stops and schedules can be confusing even for native commuters. Generally speaking, Toulouse's bus routes run to and from Albi and Carcassonne; Albi connects with Cordes-sur-Ciel, while Montpellier connects with Narbonne. From Perpignan, the liO's extensive network of buses links almost all towns and villages in the department for €1. Note that if you are coming from Spain, operators including FlixBus, Ouibus, and Eurolines run cross-border buses to Perpignan.

BUS INFORMATION Cars Teissiers ☎ 04–68–25–85–45 ⊕ www.teissier.fr. **Herault Transport** ☎ 04–34–88–89–99 ⊕ www.herault-transport.fr. **liO Buses** ☎ ⊕ www.laregion.fr/-lio-service-public-occitanie-transports.

CAR TRAVEL

The fastest route from Paris to Toulouse, 677 km (406 miles) south, is via Limoges on A20, then A62; the journey time is about six hours. If you choose to head south over the Pyrénées to Barcelona, the Tunnel du Puymorens (€6.90) saves half an hour of switchbacks between Hospitalet and Porta; but in good weather—and with time to spare—the drive over the Puymorens Pass is spectacular. Plan on taking three hours between Toulouse and Font-Romeu and another two-and-a-half to Barcelona. The fastest route from Toulouse to Barcelona is the under four-hour, 391-km (235-mile) drive via Carcassonne and Perpignan on A61 and A9, which becomes AP-7 at Le Perthus. A62/A61 slices through the region on its way through Carcassonne to the coast at Narbonne, where A9 heads south to Perpignan. At Toulouse, where A62 becomes A61, various highways fan out in all directions. A9 (called La Languedocienne and La Catalane) is the main highway artery that connects Montpellier with the Spanish border to the south and Nîmes to the north.

TRAIN TRAVEL

At least 10 high-speed TGVs per day leave Paris's Gare Montparnasse and Gare Austerlitz bound for Toulouse, including an overnight train; depending on which one you choose, the journey can take four to seven hours. There are also 14 daily departures from Paris to Narbonne and 11 to Perpignan. Most of these trips take five to six hours, but if you get a TGV from the Gare de Lyon you can be in Narbonne in 4½ hours. A TGV line from Paris also serves Montpellier 18 times a day, departing from the Gare de Lyon. A new TGV station, Montpellier Sud de France, handles trains for Paris, Barcelona, and Madrid. The regional TER rail network provides regular service to many towns, though not all. Buses complete the network where rails don't go. Within Occitanie, Toulouse is the biggest hub, with a major line linking Carcassonne (45 mins), Narbonne (80 mins, change here for Perpignan), and Montpellier (2 hrs); trains link up with Albi (1 hr), too. Toulouse trains also connect with Biarritz

(4 hrs 15 mins), Pau (2 hrs 15 mins), and Bordeaux (2 hrs). In Languedoc-Roussillon, Montpellier connects with Carcassonne (90 mins), Perpignan (90 mins), and other towns. From Perpignan, take one of the dozen daily trains to Collioure (20 mins). All TER trains in the region offer a limited number of seats to any town for only €1; tickets must be purchased in advance online (⊕ www.ter. sncf.com/occitanie).

TRAIN INFORMATION Gare SNCF Carcassonne ⊠ 1 av. Marechal Joffre, Carcassonne ☎ 3635. **Gare SNCF Montpellier Sud de France** ⊠ Rue de la Fontaine de la Banquière, Montpellier ☎ 3635. **Gare SNCF Montpellier Saint-Roch** ⊠ Pl. Auguste Gibert, Montpellier ☎ 3635. **Gare SNCF Narbonne** ⊠ 1 bd. Frédéric Mistral, Narbonne ☎ 3635. **Gare SNCF Perpignan** ⊠ 1 Pl. Salvador Dali, Perpignan ☎ 3635. **Gare SNCF Toulouse-Matabiau** ⊠ 64 bd. Pierre Semard, Toulouse ☎ 3635. **SNCF** ☎ 3635 ⊕ www.oui.sncf. **TGV** ☎ 3635 ⊕ www. tgv.com.

Restaurants

As a rule, the closer you get to the Mediterranean coast, the later you dine and the more you pay for your seafood platter and bottle of iced rosé. The farther you travel from the coast, the higher the altitude, the more rustic the setting, and the more reasonable the prices will be. During the scorching summer months in sleepy mountain villages, lunches are light, interminable, and *bien arrosé* (with lots of wine). Here you can also find that small personal restaurant where the chickens roasting on spits above the open fire have first names and the cheese comes from the hippie couple down the road who arrived here in the 1960s and love their mountains, their goats, and the universe in general.

Hotels

Hotels range from Mediterranean modern to medieval baronial to Pyrenean chalet, and most are small and cozy rather than luxurious and sophisticated. Toulouse has the usual range of big-city hotels, for which you need to make reservations well in advance if you plan to visit in spring or fall. Look for *gîtes d'étape* (hikers' way stations) and *chambres d'hôtes* (bed-and-breakfasts), which offer excellent value, a chance to meet local and international travelers, and, perhaps, to sample life on a farm, as well as the delights of *cuisine du terroir* (country cooking). As for off-season—if there is such a thing, since chic Parisians often arrive in November in their SUVs with a hunger for the authentic—call ahead and double-check when hotels close for their annual hibernation. This usually starts sometime in winter, either before, or right after, the Christmas holidays. *Restaurant and hotel reviews have been shortened. For full information, visit Fodors.com.*

What It Costs in Euros			
$	$$	$$$	$$$$
RESTAURANTS			
under €18	€18–€24	€25–€32	over €32
HOTELS			
under €125	€125–€225	€226–€350	over €350

Visitor Information

The Occitanie region includes both the former administrative regions of the Midi-Pyrénées and the Languedoc-Roussillon. The single tourism bureau maintains two offices, one in Montpellier, the other in Toulouse.

Other handy websites for this region are ⊕ *www.audetourisme.com*, ⊕ *www. tourisme-pyreneesorientales.com*, and ⊕ *www.tourisme-tarn.com*.

CONTACTS Comité Régional du Tourisme Occitanie - Montpellier ✉ *417 rue Samuel Morse, Montpellier* ☎ *04–67–22–98–09* ⊕ *www.tourisme-occitanie.com*. **Comité Régional du Tourisme Occitanie - Toulouse** ✉ *15 rue Rivals, Toulouse* ☎ *05–61–13–55–55* ⊕ *www.tourisme-occitanie.com*.

Toulouse

Ebullient Toulouse is the capital of the Occitanie region and the fourth-largest city in France. Just 100 km (60 miles) from the border with Spain, Toulouse is in many ways closer in flavor to southern European Spanish than to northern European French. Weathered redbrick buildings line sidewalks, giving the city its nickname, "La Ville Rose" (the Pink City). Downtown, the sidewalks pulse late into the night with tourists, technicians from the giant Airbus aerospace complex, and—since this is the country's second-largest university center—loads of students. Despite Toulouse's bustling, high-tech attitude, its well-preserved *centre ville*—the brick-paved streets between the Garonne River and the Canal du Midi—retains the feel of a small town, where food, Beaujolais nouveau, and the latest rugby victory are the primary concerns. So be prepared to savor the city's Mediterranean pace, southern friendliness, and youthful spirit.

Toulouse was founded in the 4th century BC and quickly became an important part of Roman Gaul. In turn, it was made into a Visigothic and Carolingian capital before becoming a separate county in 843. Ruling from this Pyrenean hub, the counts of Toulouse held sovereignty over nearly all of the Languedoc and maintained a brilliant court known for its fine troubadours and literature. In the early 13th century, Toulouse was attacked and plundered by troops representing an alliance between the northern French nobility and the papacy, ostensibly to wipe out the Albigensian heresy (Catharism), but more realistically as an expansionist move against the power of Occitania, the French southwest. The counts toppled, but Toulouse experienced a cultural and economic rebirth thanks to the *woad* (blue dye) trade, and, consequently, wealthy merchants' homes constitute a major portion of Toulouse's architectural heritage.

You can learn more about the city's past and present by sampling a wide range of guided tours (€7–€15) with topics focusing on the city's monuments, the history of the Cathars in the city, and its cathedral; sign up online at ⊕ *www.toulouse-tourisme.com/visites-guidees*. The office also sells Pass Tourisme passes, valid for 24, 48, or 72 hours (€18, €28, or €35), that admit you to 30 tourist sites free or at a reduced rate and give you free transport on the tram, bus, métro, and airport shuttle. For a personalized introduction to the city, contact Toulouse Greeters; the complimentary program can link you up with a local volunteer who'll show you around (⊕ *www.toulousegreeters.fr*).

GETTING HERE AND AROUND

Aéroport Toulouse-Blagnac is served by a range of airlines, including Air France and easyJet; a shuttle (⊕ *www.tisseo.fr*) runs every 16 minutes weekdays and every 20 minutes weekends between 5:40 am and 12:10 am from the airport to Toulouse's railway and bus stations on Boulevard Pierre Sémard (€8). If you're coming by train, there are at least 10 high-speed TGVs a day from Paris; travel time for direct service is about 4 hours 30 minutes (from €43). There are now two daily TGVs from Barcelona, too; they take 3 hours 30 minutes (from €60). Toulouse is also a regional rail hub, so train links to other locales within the region are widely available.

The main square of Toulouse's centre ville, Place du Capitole, is a 15-minute walk from the train station but only a few blocks away from the city's other focal points—Place Wilson, Place Esquirol, and the Basilique St-Sernin. (If you've driven into town, there's a huge parking garage beneath Place du Capitole, too; it's possible to prebook a space online.) Within Toulouse, the public transit system (⊕ *www.tisseo.fr*) includes a métro, which conveniently connects the Gare Matabiau with Place du Capitole and Place Esquirol, as well as a tram line and an efficient bus network. If you're interested in getting to know Toulouse's cycle-friendly side, you can rent bikes at conveniently placed VéloToulouse stations; be sure to drop into La Maison du Vélo (⊕ *www.maisonduvelotoulouse.com*) by the train station for information about cyclotourism in and around the city.

VISITOR INFORMATION Toulouse Tourist Office ✉ *Donjon du Capitole* ☎ *08–92–18–01–80* ⊕ *www.toulouse-tourisme.com*.

 Sights

The area between the boulevards and the Garonne forms the historic nucleus of Toulouse. Originally part of Roman Gaul and later the capital for the Visigoths and then the Carolingians, Toulouse was one of the artistic and literary centers of Europe by AD 1000. Although defeated by the lords of northern France in the 13th century, it quickly reemerged as a cultural and commercial power and has remained so ever since. Religious and civil structures bear witness to this illustrious past, even as the city's booming student life mirrors a dynamic present. This is the heart of Toulouse, with Place du Capitole at its center.

South of Rue de Metz you'll discover the Cathédral St-Étienne, the antiques district along Rue Perchepinte, and town houses and palaces on Rue Ninau, Rue Ozenne, and Rue de la Dalbade—all among the top sights in Toulouse.

★ Basilique St-Sernin

RELIGIOUS SITE | Toulouse's most famous landmark and the world's largest Romanesque church once belonged to a Benedictine abbey, built in the 11th century to house pilgrims on their way to Santiago de Compostela in Spain. Inside, the aesthetic high point is the magnificent central apse, begun in 1080, glittering with gilded ceiling frescoes, which date to the 19th century. When illuminated at night, St-Sernin's five-tier octagonal tower glows red against the sky. Not all the tiers are the same: the first three, with their rounded windows, are Romanesque; the upper two, with pointed Gothic windows, were added around 1300. The ancient crypt contains the relics and reliquaries of 128 saints, but the most famous item on view is a thorn that legend says is from the Crown of Thorns. ⊠ *Pl. St-Sernin* ☎ *05–61–21– 80–45* ⊕ *www.basilique-saint-sernin.fr* ⊠ *Basilica free, crypt €3* ⊗ *Closed during Sun. Mass.*

Capitole/Hôtel de Ville (*Capitol/Town Hall*)

GOVERNMENT BUILDING | The 18th-century Capitole is home to the Hôtel de Ville and the city's highly regarded opera company. Halfway up the **Grand Escalier** (Grand Staircase) hangs a large painting of the Jeux Floraux, the "floral games" organized by a literary society created in 1324 to promote the local Occitanian language, Langue d'Oc. The festival continues to this day: poets give public readings here each May, and the best are awarded silver- and gold-plated violets, one of the emblems of Toulouse. At the top of the stairs is the **Salle Gervaise,** a hall adorned with a series of paintings inspired by the themes of love and marriage. The mural at the far end of the room portrays the Isle of Cythères, where Venus received her lovers, alluding to a French euphemism for getting married: *embarquer pour Cythères* (to

embark for Cythères). More giant paintings in the **Salle Henri-Martin,** named for the artist (1860–1943), show the passing seasons set against the eternal Garonne. Look for Jean Jaurès (1859–1914), one of France's greatest socialist martyrs, in *Les Rêveurs* (*The Dreamers*); he's wearing a boater-style hat and a beige coat. At the far left end of the elegant **Salle des Illustres** (Hall of the Illustrious) is a large painting of a fortress under siege, portraying the women of Toulouse slaying Simon de Montfort, leader of the Albigensian crusade against the Cathars, during the siege of Toulouse in 1218. ⊠ *Pl. du Capitole* ☎ *05–61–22–34–12* ⊠ *Free.*

Cathédrale St-Étienne

RELIGIOUS SITE | The cathedral was erected in stages between the 13th and the 17th century, though the nave and choir languished unfinished because of a lack of funds. A fine collection of 16th- and 17th-century tapestries traces the life of St-Stephen. In front of the cathedral is the city's oldest fountain, dating from the 16th century. ⊠ *Pl. St-Étienne* ☎ *05–61–52–03–82.*

Chapelle des Carmélites

RELIGIOUS SITE | All that remains of the Carmelite convent that once stood here is its chapel, begun in 1622 by King Louis XIII and Anne of Austria. Look up to admire the remarkable painted vaulted ceiling. ⊠ *1 rue de Périgord* ☎ *05–34–44– 92–05* ⊠ *Free* ⊗ *Closed Mon. and Tues.*

Château d'Eau

MUSEUM | This 19th-century water tower at the far end of the Pont Neuf, originally used to store water and build water pressure, is now the oldest public institution in France dedicated to photographic exhibits. It was built in 1822, the same year Nicéphore Nièpce created the first permanent photographic images. ⊠ *1 pl. Laganne* ☎ *05–61–77–09–40* ⊕ *www. galeriechateaudeau.org* ⊠ *€4* ⊗ *Closed Mon.*

Ensemble Conventuel des Jacobins

ARTS VENUE | An extraordinary structure built in the 1230s for the Dominicans (renamed Jacobins in 1216 for their Parisian base in Rue St-Jacques), this church is dominated by a single row of seven columns running the length of the nave. The easternmost column (on the far right) is one of the finest examples of palm-tree vaulting ever erected, the much-celebrated Palmier des Jacobins, a major masterpiece of Gothic art. Fanning out overhead, its 22 ribs support the entire apse. The original refectory site is used for temporary art exhibitions, dance performances, and community events. The cloister is one of the city's aesthetic and acoustical gems, and in summer hosts piano and early music concerts. ✉ Pl. des Jacobins ☎ 05–61–22–23–82 ⊕ www.jacobins.toulouse.fr ✉ Church free; cloister €5 June–Sept., €4 Oct.–May ⊗ Closed Mon.

Hôtel d'Arnault Brucelles

HOUSE | One of the tallest and best of Toulouse's 49 towers can be seen at this 16th-century mansion. ✉ 19 rue des Changes.

Hôtel d'Assézat

MUSEUM | The city's most elegant mansion was built in 1555 by Toulouse's top Renaissance architect, Nicolas Bachelier. Notable for its arcades and ornately carved doorways, the Hôtel d'Assézat is now home to **Fondation Bemberg,** which has an exceptional collection of paintings by artists ranging from Tiepolo to Toulouse-Lautrec, Monet, and Bonnard. ✉ Pl. Assézat ☎ 05–61–12–06–89 ⊕ www.fondation-bemberg.fr ✉ €10 ⊗ Closed Mon.

Hôtel d'Astorg et St-Germain

HOUSE | This 16th-century mansion is notable for its lovely Romanesque wooden stairways and galleries and for its top-floor mirande, or wooden balcony. ✉ 16 rue des Changes.

Hôtel de Bernuy

HOUSE | Now part of a school, this mansion, around the corner from the Ensemble Conventuel des Jacobins, was built for Jean de Bernuy in the 16th century, the period when Toulouse was at its most prosperous. De Bernuy made his fortune exporting woad, the dark-blue dye that brought unprecedented wealth to the city; his success is reflected in the use of stone (a costly material in this region of brick) and by the octagonal stair tower. ■TIP➔ **You can visit this mansion on one of the many themed city tours (€10); the Grands Monuments de Toulouse program includes a stop here.** ✉ 1 rue Gambetta.

Hôtel de Clary

HOUSE | One of the finest mansions on Rue de la Dalbade is also known as the Hôtel de Pierre because of its unusually solid pierre (stone) construction, which was considered a sign of great wealth at the time. The ornately sculpted facade was designed by Nicolas Bachelier in the 16th century. ✉ 25 rue de la Dalbade.

Hôtel Delpech

HOUSE | Look for the 17th-century biblical inscriptions carved in Latin in the stone under the windows. ✉ 20 rue des Changes.

Hôtel du Vieux Raisin

HOUSE | Officially the Hôtel Beringuier Maynier, this building was dubbed the Vieux Raisin (Old Grape) after the early name of the street and even earlier inn. Built in the 15th and 16th centuries, the mansion has an octagonal tower, male and female figures on the facade, and allegorical sculptures of the three stages of life—infancy, maturity, and old age—over the windows to the left. ✉ 36 rue de Languedoc.

Marché Victor Hugo (Victor Hugo Market)

MARKET | This hangarlike indoor market, where you're sure to find the ingredients for almost any French recipe, is always a refreshing stop. Consider eating lunch

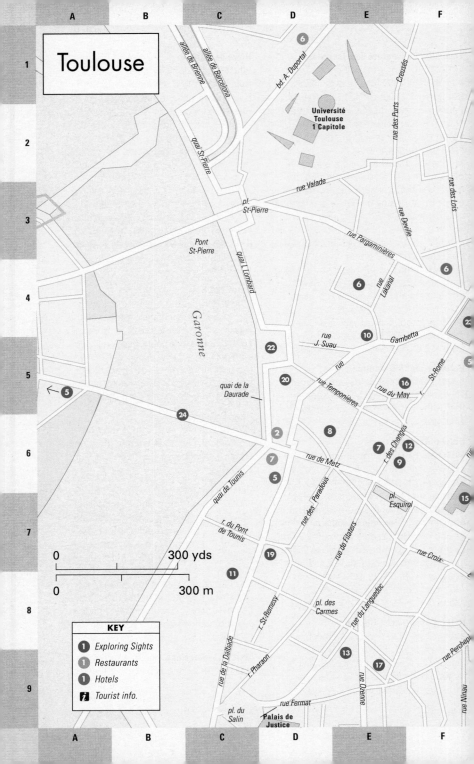

Sights ▼

1. Basilique St-Sernin **G2**
2. Capitole/ Hôtel de Ville **G4**
3. Cathédrale St-Étienne **G8**
4. Chapelle des Carmélites **G3**
5. Château d'Eau.......... **A5**
6. Ensemble Conventuel des Jacobins **E4**
7. Hôtel d'Arnault Brucelles **E6**
8. Hôtel d'Assézat **D6**
9. Hôtel d'Astorg et St-Germain **E6**
10. Hôtel de Bernuy.......... **E5**
11. Hôtel de Clary **C8**
12. Hôtel Delpech............ **F6**
13. Hôtel du Vieux Raisin **E9**
14. Marché Victor Hugo.............. **H4**
15. Musée des Augustins................. **F7**
16. Musée du Vieux Toulouse **F5**
17. Musée Paul Dupuy **E9**
18. Musée St-Raymond **G2**
19. Notre-Dame de la Dalbade **D7**
20. Notre-Dame de la Daurade **D5**
21. Notre-Dame du Taur ... **G4**
22. Place de la Daurade.... **D5**
23. Place du Capitole **F4**
24. Pont Neuf............... **B6**

Restaurants ▼

1. J Bistrot de l'Étoile **I8**
2. Brasserie Flo "Les Beaux Arts" **D6**
3. Chez Emile.............. **G6**
4. Huguette................ **H5**
5. Jardins de l'Opéra....... **F5**
6. Michel Sarran........... **D1**
7. Py-r...................... **D6**

Hotels ▼

1. Grand Hôtel de l'Opéra................ **G5**
2. Grand Hôtel d'Orléans **I3**
3. Hôtel Albert I **H4**
4. Hôtel Royal Wilson **I6**
5. Le Boutique Hôtel Garonne........... **D6**
6. Le Grand Balcon......... **F4**

at one of the five upstairs restaurants; **Chez Attila,** just to the left at the top of the stairs, is among the best. ✉ *Pl. Victor Hugo* ☎ *05–61–22–76–92* ⊕ *www.marche-victor-hugo.fr* ⊗ *Closed Mon.*

Musée des Augustins (*Augustinian Museum, Musée des Beaux-Arts*)

MUSEUM | One of Europe's finest collections of Romanesque sculpture can be seen inside the sacristy, chapter house, and cloisters of a former Augustinian convent. Built around the same time as the Louvre, the medieval Mediterranean-Gothic architectural complex is vast, and, like the Louvre, it contains many treasures from Napoléon's conquests. ✉ *21 rue de Metz* ☎ *05–61–22–21–82* ⊕ *www.augustins.org* ⊠ *€4* ⊗ *Closed Tues.*

Musée du Vieux Toulouse (*Museum of Old Toulouse*)

MUSEUM | This museum is worthwhile for the building itself as much as for its collection of Toulouse memorabilia, paintings, sculptures, and documents. Be sure to note the ground-floor fireplace and wooden ceiling. ✉ *7 rue du May* ☎ *05–62–27–11–50* ⊕ *toulousainsdetoulouse.fr* ⊠ *€4* ⊗ *Closed Sun. and Nov.–mid-Apr.*

Musée Paul Dupuy

MUSEUM | This museum, dedicated to medieval applied arts, is housed in the Hôtel Pierre Besson, a 17th-century mansion. ✉ *13 rue de la Pleau* ☎ *05–31–22–95–40* ⊕ *www.ampdupuy.fr* ⊠ *€5* ⊗ *Closed Mon.*

Musée St-Raymond

MUSEUM | The city's archaeological museum, next to the Basilica of St-Sernin, has an extensive collection of imperial Roman busts, as well as ancient coins, vases, and jewelry. It's second only to the Louvre in the richness of its sculptures and Gallo-Roman vestiges. ✉ *1 ter pl. St-Sernin* ☎ *05–61–22–31–44* ⊕ *www.saintraymond.toulouse.fr* ⊠ *€5* ⊗ *Closed Mon.*

Notre-Dame de la Dalbade

RELIGIOUS SITE | Originally called Sancta Maria de Ecclesia Alba in Langue d'Oc and Ste-Marie de l'Église Blanche in French (*alba* and *blanche* both meaning "white"), the name of this church evolved into "de Albata" and later "Dalbade." Ironically, one of its outstanding features today is the colorful 19th-century ceramic tympanum over the Renaissance door. ✉ *Rue de la Dalbade* ☎ *05–61–25–58–05.*

Notre-Dame de la Daurade

RELIGIOUS SITE | The 18th-century Notre-Dame de la Daurade overlooks the Garonne. The church's name—derived from *doré* (gilt)—refers to the golden reflection given off by mosaics decorating the 5th-century temple to the Virgin Mary that once stood on this site. It's also known as Notre-Dame la Noire, a nod to the church's "Black Virgin," a figure of devout worship and dressed in special finery by designers, including Christian Lacroix. ✉ *1 pl. de la Daurade* ☎ *05–61–21–38–32.*

Notre-Dame du Taur

RELIGIOUS SITE | Built on the spot where St-Saturnin (or Sernin), the martyred bishop of Toulouse, was dragged to his death in AD 250 by a rampaging bull, this church is famous for its *cloche-mur,* or wall tower. The wall looks like an extension of the facade and has inspired many similar versions throughout the region. ✉ *12 rue du Taur* ☎ *05–61–21–80–45* ⊕ *basilique-saint-sernin.fr/site/paroisse-catholique/decouvrir-nos-3-eglises/notre-dame-du-taur/notre-dame-du-taur* ⊠ *Closed Sun.*

Place de la Daurade

PLAZA | Set beside the river, Place de la Daurade ranks among the city's nicest squares. The corner of the quay offers a romantic view of the Garonne, the Hôtel Dieu on the other bank, and the pretty Pont Neuf. A stop at Café des Artistes is almost obligatory. ✉ *Toulouse.*

Seat of the municipal government, Place du Capitole is an elegant square that's often transformed into an open market.

Place du Capitole

PLAZA | Lined with shops and cafés, this vast, open square in the city center is a good spot to get your bearings, soak up some sun, or peruse the outdoor markets held here weekly. A parking garage is conveniently underneath. ✉ *Toulouse.*

Pont Neuf (*New Bridge*)

BRIDGE/TUNNEL | Despite its name, the graceful span of the Pont Neuf is hardly new: it opened to traffic in 1632. Remains of the old bridge—one arch and the lighter-color outline on the brick wall of the **Hôtel-Dieu** (hospital)—are visible across the river. The 16th-century hospital was used for pilgrims on their way to Santiago de Compostela. Just over the bridge, on a clear day in winter, the snowcapped peaks of the Pyrénées can often be seen in the distance. ✉ *Toulouse.*

🍴 Restaurants

Bistrot de l'Étoile

$$$ | **BISTRO** | Don't let the dismal backstreet exterior put you off: Bistrot de l'Étoile is a delightfully retro 1960s pub that promises fast service and a great choice of dishes on the blackboard menu. The homemade desserts are great, too. **Known for:** excellent grilled meats, cooked over fire at restaurant's center; warm staff; fun decor. [$] *Average main: €25* ✉ *6 rue de l'Étoile* ☎ *05–61–63–13–43* 🌐 *www.bistrotdeletoile.fr* 🕓 *Closed Sun., 3 wks in Aug., and 1 wk in May. No lunch Sat.*

Brasserie Flo "Les Beaux Arts"

$$$ | **BRASSERIE** | Overlooking the Pont Neuf, this elegant brasserie is idyllic at sunset, as artists Ingres and Matisse—who were regulars—knew all too well. Watch the colors change over the Garonne from a sidewalk table while enjoying seafood sauerkraut with champagne or wild sea bass with salmon tartare. **Known for:** late-night closing

Eating Well in Southwest France

Dining in France's southwest is a rougher, heartier, and more rustic version of classic Mediterranean cooking—the peppers are sliced thick, the garlic and olive oil used with a heavier hand, the herbs crushed and served au naturel.

Expect *cuisine du marché* (market-based cooking), savory seasonal dishes based on the culinary trinity of the south—garlic, onion, and tomato—straight from the village market.

Garlic and goose fat are generously used in traditional recipes. Be sure to try some of the renowned foie gras and *confit de canard* (preserved duck). The most famous regional dish is cassoulet, a succulent white-bean stew with *confit d'oie* (preserved goose), duck, lamb, or a mixture of all three.

Keep your eyes open for festive *cargolades*—Catalan for huge communal barbecues starting off with thousands of buttery-garlic snails roasted on open grills and eaten with your fingers, followed by cured bacon and lamb cutlets and vats (and vats) of local wine. In the Roussillon and along the Mediterranean coast from Collioure up through Perpignan to Narbonne, the prevalent Catalan cuisine features olive-oil-based cooking and sauces like the classic aioli. When you're on the coast, it's fish, of course, often cooked over a wood fire.

(11:30 pm) on weekends; killer views from the quayside windows; beautiful Belle Époque–influenced dining room. $ *Average main: €31* ⊠ *1 quai de la Daurade* ☎ *05–61–21–12–12* ⊕ *www.brasserielesbeauxarts.fr.*

Chez Emile
$$$$ | FRENCH | With a great location, this is the place to savor regional specialties like cassoulet. The locals love it, which speaks volumes here in the heart of cassoulet country. **Known for:** good-value "menu du jour" at lunch; cassoulet available to-go; lovely terrace. $ *Average main: €33* ⊠ *13 pl. St-Georges* ☎ *05–61–21–05–56* ⊕ *www.restaurant-emile.com* ⊙ *Closed Sun., Mon., and 2 wks at Christmas.*

Huguette
$$ | FRENCH | This bustling bistro has been serving locally sourced regional dishes for a quarter of a century—way before farm-to-table was a thing. The house specialties include dishes like cod and cassoulet. **Known for:** wild boar in season; quick, unpretentious service; reservations recommended. $ *Average main: €18* ⊠ *15 bis pl. Wilson* ☎ *05–61–23–07–17* ⊕ *www.lebonvivre.com.*

Jardins de l'Opéra
$$$$ | FRENCH | Stéphane Tournié's elegant restaurant next to the Grand Hôtel de l'Opéra is a perennial favorite. Inspired by the seasons, the food is gastronomical local fare with added nouvelle and Gasscon touches. **Known for:** extravagant "menu confiance" with optional wine pairing; over-the-top interiors; gluten-free options. $ *Average main: €40* ⊠ *1 pl. du Capitole* ☎ *05–61–23–07–76* ⊕ *www.lesjardinsdelopera.com* ⊙ *Closed Sun., Mon., and 1st wk of Jan.*

★ Michel Sarran
$$$$ | MODERN FRENCH | The postnouvelle haven for what is arguably Toulouse's finest dining departs radically from the traditional stick-to-your-ribs cuisine of southwest France, instead favoring Mediterranean formulas suited to the rhythms and reasons of modern living. Delicacies

like foie gras soup with Belon oysters or wild salmon in green curry sauce prove that chef Michel Sarran's two Michelin stars are well deserved. **Known for:** the best fine dining in the city; expert balance of sophistication and warmth; highly flavorful but light food. $ *Average main: €60* ✉ *21 bd. Armand Duportal* ☎ *05–61–12–32–32* ⊕ *www.michel-sarran.com* ⊙ *Closed weekends, Aug., and 2 wks at Christmas. No lunch Wed.*

Py-r

$$$$ | **FRENCH FUSION** | Chef Pierre Lambinon won a Michelin star at age of 30 for his fantastic restaurant (pronounced "Pierre") in this former 16th-century fish market. The €78 six-course tasting menu is a must. **Known for:** beautiful, creative presentation; charming interiors with vaulted ceilings; central location next to Pont Neuf. $ *Average main: €50* ✉ *19 descente de la Halle aux Poissons* ☎ *05–61–25–51–52* ⊕ *www.py-r.com* ▬ *No credit cards* ⊙ *Closed weekends. No lunch Mon.*

 Hotels

Grand Hôtel de l'Opéra

$$ | **HOTEL** | Little wonder the likes of Deneuve, Pavarotti, and Aznavour favored this downtown doyen: its keynote grandeur is obvious the moment you step into the lobby, complete with soaring columns, Second Empire bergères, and sofas of blue tasseled velvet. **Pros:** ideally situated on main square; within five minutes of the train station; tranquil atmosphere. **Cons:** splendor and a certain reserved professionalism rank higher than intimacy; busy outside location; breakfast not included. $ *Rooms from: €160* ✉ *1 pl. du Capitole* ☎ *05–61–21–82–66* ⊕ *www.grand-hotel-opera.com* ⇗ *50 rooms* ⦿| *No meals.*

Grand Hôtel d'Orléans

$ | **HOTEL** | Although it's in a slightly sketchy neighborhood, this picturesque former stagecoach relay station—built in

1867—still retains a certain 19th-century charm and is home to a good restaurant. **Pros:** fine restaurant; close to train and bus stations; good value. **Cons:** surrounding neighborhood is a little dicey; rooms on the small size; basic amenities. $ *Rooms from: €90* ✉ *72 rue Bayard* ☎ *05–61–62–98–47* ⊕ *www.grand-hotel-orleans.fr* ⇗ *54 rooms* ⦿| *No meals.*

Hôtel Albert I

$ | **HOTEL** | The building may seem undistinguished, but its bright and cheerful guest rooms are spacious (especially the older ones with giant fireplaces), and the location is central to everything; it's the personable owner, however, who really sets this hotel apart. **Pros:** ideal location; warm and helpful service; lovely decor. **Cons:** parking can be arranged but the lot is difficult to find; some rooms are small; breakfast not included. $ *Rooms from: €110* ✉ *8 rue Rivals* ☎ *05–61–21–17–91* ⊕ *www.hotel-albert1.com* ⇗ *47 rooms* ⦿| *No meals.*

Hôtel Royal Wilson

$ | **HOTEL** | With a quiet city-center location across from the Théâtre National, this two-star hotel—one of the best deals in Toulouse—attracts theater professionals, business travelers, and garden-variety tourists. **Pros:** great central location; good value; rooms on the spacious side. **Cons:** some bathrooms don't have wall-mounted showerheads; slightly random design sensibility; breakfast not included. $ *Rooms from: €80* ✉ *6 rue Labéda* ☎ *05–61–12–41–41* ⊕ *www.hotelroyal-wilson-toulouse.com* ⇗ *27 rooms* ⦿| *No meals.*

Le Boutique Hôtel Garonne

$$ | **HOTEL** | In the thick of the most Toulousain part of town, next to the Pont Neuf and the former fish market (although somewhat far from the city center), this is a small but hyperstylish spot with contemporary perks—like gourmet takeout delivered to your room on request. **Pros:** hip design; chic bohemian neighborhood with eclectic shops and

restaurants nearby; helpful staff. **Cons:** a hike to the city center; lobby and rooms feel a bit small; best amenities come at extra charge. [$] *Rooms from: €180* ✉ *22 descente de la Halle aux Poissons* ☎ *05–34–31–94–80* 🌐 *www.leboutique-hotelgaronne.com* 🛏 *14 rooms* 🍴 *No meals.*

Le Grand Balcon

$ | **HOTEL** | You can dream in the clouds with Toulouse's famous aviators in this 1930s hotel tucked into a corner of Place du Capitole—popular with pioneering pilots back in the glory days, it's been playfully retrofitted with a smart design that pays homage to Toulouse's high-flying heritage. **Pros:** A-plus location next to Place du Capitole; stylish design; congenial staff. **Cons:** lower-level rooms get street noise; no on-site parking; some rooms feel small. [$] *Rooms from: €110* ✉ *8–10 rue Romiguières* ☎ *05–34–25–44–09* 🌐 *www.grandbalconhotel.com* 🛏 *47 rooms* 🍴 *No meals.*

🍸 Nightlife

Bar Basque

BARS/PUBS | You'll find Bar Basque among the many watering holes around Place St-Pierre. It turns into a dance party after 11. ✉ *7 pl. St-Pierre* ☎ *05–61–21–55–64.*

Chez Ton Ton

BARS/PUBS | A somewhat raucous crowd is drawn to this very popular Place St-Pierre dive. ✉ *16 pl. St-Pierre* ☎ *05–61–21–89–54* 🌐 *www.pastisomaitre.com.*

Cosmopolitain

MUSIC CLUBS | You can dine, sip, or dance until 2 am at this industrial-chic restaurant, wine bar, and cocktail lounge combo. ✉ *1 rue des 3 Journées* ☎ *05–61–29–89–33* 🌐 *cosmopolitain-toulouse.fr.*

La Bonita

MUSIC CLUBS | Brazilian guitarists perform at La Bonita, a festive *restaurant musical.* ✉ *112 Grand-Rue St-Michel* ☎ *05–62–26–36–45* 🌐 *www.labonita.fr.*

L'Atelier de l'Echarpe

WINE BARS—NIGHTLIFE | Good food, fine wine, classic cocktails, and a retro-cool aesthetic make this spot popular among young (but not university young) Toulousains. ✉ *8 rue de l'Echarpe* ☎ *05–34–30–93–35* 🌐 *latelierdelecharpe.fr.*

Le Bijou

MUSIC CLUBS | If you don't mind a short bus ride across the Garonne, take Line 12 to the front of a small concert hall and restaurant filled with an eclectic, all-ages crowd; most are regulars who come for the great bistro menu and a musical lineup featuring top Toulouse acts, including jazz groups who once played at the famous (now closed) Mandala. ✉ *123 av. de Muret* ☎ *05–61–42–95–07* 🌐 *www.le-bijou.net.*

Le Taquin

MUSIC CLUBS | Le Mandala reigned as the best jazz space in Toulouse for decades, only to close its doors in 2014. It's now been reborn as Le Taquin, with a lauded and eclectic program of five-nights-a-week live music. ✉ *23 rue des Amidonniers* ☎ *05–61–21–80–84* 🌐 *www.le-taquin.fr.*

Melting Pot

BARS/PUBS | This pub lives up to its name, with young people from around the world crowding the bar. ✉ *26 bd. de Strasbourg* ☎ *05–61–62–82–98.*

No. 5 Wine Bar

WINE BARS—NIGHTLIFE | At this stylish wine bar, epicureans can choose from 500 wines by the glass and more than 4,000 bottles—or settle in for a full meal, offering dishes with wine pairings. ✉ *5 rue de la Bourse* ☎ *05–61–38–44–51* 🌐 *www.n5winebar.com.*

Père Louis

WINE BARS—NIGHTLIFE | Begin your night on the town at Père Louis, an old-fashioned winery (and restaurant), with barrels used as tables. ✉ *45 rue des Tourneurs* ☎ *05–61–21–33–45.*

Performing Arts

Toulouse is jammed with small, independent concert halls and theaters, most of them covered in the mini-mag *Clutch,* which can be found in any hotel lobby. As for cultural highlights, so many opera singers perform at the Théâtre du Capitole and the Halle aux Grains that the city is known as the *capitale du bel canto.* Opera season lasts from October until late May, with occasional summer presentations as well. A wide variety of dance companies also perform in Toulouse: the Ballet du Capitole stages classical ballets, while Ballet-Théâtre Joseph Russillo and Compagnie Jean-Marc Matos put on modern-dance performances. The Centre National Choréographique de Toulouse, in the St-Cyprien quarter, welcomes international companies each year.

Halle Aux Grains

ARTS CENTERS | Home of L'Orchestre du Capitole, the hexagonal Halle Aux Grains ranks among the best music auditoriums in Europe. ✉ *Pl. Dupuy* ☎ *05–61–63–13–13* ⊕ *www.onct.toulouse.fr.*

Shopping

Toulouse is a chic design center for clothing and artifacts of all kinds. Rue St-Rome, Rue Croix Baragnon, Rue des Changes, and Rue d'Alsace-Lorraine are all good shopping streets. For artful vintage finds look for the word *friperie* on storefronts along Rue Peyrolières.

Albi

75 km (47 miles) northeast of Toulouse.

Toulouse-Lautrec's native Albi is a busy, beautifully preserved provincial market town. In its heyday Albi was a major center for the Cathars, members of a dualistic and ascetic religious movement critical of the hierarchical and worldly ways of the Catholic Church.

GETTING HERE AND AROUND
About 18 trains daily (1 hr, €15) run between Toulouse and Albi's main station on Place Stalingrad (in a somewhat isolated part of town). Buses also make the trip from Toulouse (1½ hrs, €13) and adjoining towns to the Albi bus station on Place Jean Jaurès.

VISITOR INFORMATION Albi Tourist Office ✉ *42 rue Mariès* ☎ *05–63–36–36–00* ⊕ *www.albi-tourisme.fr.*

Sights

★ Cathédrale Ste-Cécile

RELIGIOUS SITE | One of the most unusual and dazzling churches in France, the huge Cathédrale Ste-Cécile (also known as Cathedrale d'Albi), with its intimidating clifflike walls, resembles a cross between a castle and an ocean liner. It was constructed as a symbol of the Church's return to power after the 13th-century crusade that wiped out the Cathars. The interior is an astonishingly ornate contrast to the massive austerity of the outer walls. Maestro Donnelli and a team of 16th-century Italian artists (most of the Emilian school) covered every possible surface with religious scenes and brightly colored patterns—it remains the largest group of Italian Renaissance paintings in any French church. On the west wall you can find one of the most splendid organs in the world, built in 1734 and outfitted with 3,500 pipes, which loom over a celebrated fresco of the Last Judgment. ✉ *Pl. Ste-Cécile* ☎ *05–63–43–23–43* 🎟 *€6.*

Cloître St-Salvi

RELIGIOUS SITE | From the central square and parking area in front of the Palais de la Berbie, walk to the 11th- to 15th-century college and Cloître de St-Salvy. ✉ *Rue Maries* ☎ *05–63–43–23–43.*

Maison du Vieil Albi (*Old Albi House*)
HOUSE | Take a look at Albi's finest restored traditional house, the Maison du Vieil Albi. ✉ *Corner of Rue de la Croix-Blanche and Puech-Bérenguer* ☎ *05–63–54–96–38* 🎫 *€2.*

Maison Natale de Toulouse-Lautrec (*Hôtel du Bosc*)
HOUSE | Real fans of Toulouse-Lautrec may want to snap a photo of his birthplace, the Maison Natale de Toulouse-Lautrec, which remains a private residence. ✉ *14 rue Henri de Toulouse-Lautrec.*

★ **Musée Toulouse-Lautrec**
MUSEUM | In a garden designed by the renowned André Le Nôtre, creator of the "green geometries" at Versailles, the landmark **Palais de la Berbie** (Berbie Palace), between the cathedral and the Pont Vieux (Old Bridge), is the setting for this exceptional museum. Built in 1265 as a residence for Albi's archbishops, the fortresslike structure was transformed in 1922 into a museum to honor Albi's most celebrated son, Belle Époque painter Henri de Toulouse-Lautrec (1864–1901). Toulouse-Lautrec left Albi for Paris in 1882 and soon became famous for his colorful, tumultuous evocations of the lifestyle of bohemian glamour found in and around Montmartre. Son of a wealthy and aristocratic family (Lautrec is a village not far from Toulouse), the young Henri suffered from a genetic bone deficiency and broke both legs as a child, which stunted his growth. But it was the artist's fascination with the decadent side of life that led him to an early grave at the age of 37. The museum's collection of artworks—more than a thousand, representing the world's largest Toulouse-Lautrec corpus—has been deftly organized into theme rooms, including galleries devoted to some of his greatest portraits and scenes from Paris's *maisons closées* (brothels), with paintings stylishly hung amid the palace's brick ogival arches. There are other masterworks here, including paintings by Georges de la Tour and Francesco Guardi. ✉ *Palais de la Berbie, Off Pl. Ste-Cécile* 🌐 *www.museetoulouselautrec.net* 🎫 *€8, gardens free* 🕒 *Closed Tues. Oct.–Mar.*

Place du Vigan
PLAZA | Rue de l'Hôtel de Ville, two streets west of the Maison Natale, leads past the Mairie (City Hall), with its hanging globes of flowers, to Albi's main square, Place du Vigan. Take a break in one of the two main cafés, Le Pontié or Le Vigan. ✉ *Pl. du Vigan.*

🍴 Restaurants

Le Jardin des Quatre Saisons
$ | **FRENCH** | A good-value menu and superb fish dishes are the reasons for this restaurant's excellent reputation. Chef-owner Georges Bermond's house specialties—which change seasonally—include pot-au-feu of the sea. **Known for:** excellent value; seasonal specialties like suprême de sandre, a freshwater fish cooked in wine; old-fashioned atmosphere. [$] *Average main: €17* ✉ *5 rue de la Pompe* ☎ *05–63–60–77–76* 🌐 *www.le-jardin-des-quatre-saisons.com* 💳 *No credit cards* 🕒 *Closed Mon. No dinner Sun. and Thurs.*

🛏 Hotels

★ **Alchimy**
$$ | **HOTEL** | At Albi's smallest hotel, everything feels built to last, perhaps because local artisans (rather than cheap imported labor) were used for the overhaul of this previously derelict estate. **Pros:** hip, young vibe; perfectly located for exploring on foot; comfortable extras abound. **Cons:** no real lobby besides the chic brasserie or outdoor patio lounge; only 10 rooms, so be sure to reserve in advance; breakfast not included. [$] *Rooms from: €179* ✉ *10–12 pl. du Palais* ☎ *05–63–76–18–18* 🌐 *alchimyalbi.fr* 🔑 *10 rooms* 🍽 *No meals.*

Albi honors native son Toulouse-Lautrec with a museum crammed with his masterpieces, including *Salon in the rue des Moulins.*

Hostellerie St-Antoine

$ | **HOTEL** | Founded in 1734, this eminently comfortable hotel in the center of town is one of the oldest in France and has been run by the same family for five generations (note the Toulouse-Lautrec sketches given to the owner's great-grandfather, a friend of the painter). **Pros:** slightly off the beaten path in a quiet area; friendly staff; interesting history. **Cons:** breakfast is very expensive; overall, doesn't quite live up to its four-star rating; some rooms on the small side. [$] *Rooms from: €85* ✉ *17 rue St-Antoine* ☎ *05–63–54–04–04* 🌐 *www.hotel-saint-antoine-albi.com* 🕓 *Closed Nov.–Apr.* 🛏 *44 rooms* 🍴 *No meals.*

Hôtel Chiffre

$ | **HOTEL** | A former stagecoach inn, this centrally located town house has fairly lackluster rooms and a hearty restaurant all overlooking a cozy garden. **Pros:** tasty restaurant; historic ambience; good value. **Cons:** foyer and rooms are sparsely decorated; some beds need to be replaced; restaurant closed weekends. [$] *Rooms from: €78* ✉ *50 rue Séré-de-Rivières* ☎ *05–63–48–58–48* 🌐 *www.hotelchiffre.com* 🕓 *Closed mid-Dec.–mid-Jan.* 🛏 *39 rooms* 🍴 *No meals.*

Shopping

Albi has many produce markets: one takes place Tuesday to Sunday in the market halls near the cathedral; another is held on Tuesday and Saturday mornings at Place Fernand Pelloutier. An all-organic market runs Tuesday afternoons at Place Fernand Pelloutier. Around **Place Ste-Cécile** are numerous clothing, book, music, and antiques shops.

Alby Foie Gras

FOOD/CANDY | The finest foie gras in town is found at Alby Foie Gras. ✉ *29 rue Mariès* ☎ *05–63–38–21–33* 🌐 *alby-foiegras.com.*

Flea and Antiques Market

OUTDOOR/FLEA/GREEN MARKETS | A Saturday-morning flea and antiques market is held in the Halle du Castelviel. ✉ *Pl. du Castelviel.*

Crusading Cathars

Scorched by the southern heat, the dusty ruins high atop cliffs in southern Languedoc were once the refuges of the Cathars, the notoriously ascetic religious group persecuted out of existence by the Catholic Church in the 12th and 13th centuries. The Cathars inhabited an area ranging from present-day Germany all the way to the Atlantic Ocean. Adherents to this dualistic doctrine of material abnegation and spiritual revelation abstained from fleshly pleasures in all forms, forgoing procreation and the consumption of animal products. In some cases, they even committed suicide by starvation; diminishing the amount of flesh in the world was the ultimate way to foil the forces of evil. However, not thrilled by a religion that did not "go forth and multiply" (and that saw no need to pay taxes to the Church), Pope Innocent III launched the Albigensian Crusade (Albi was one of the major Cathar strongholds), and Pope Gregory IX rounded up the stragglers during a period of inquisition starting in 1233. All these forces had been given scandalously free rein by the French court, which allowed dukes and counts from northern France to build *bastides* (fortified medieval towns built along a strict grid plan) through the area to entrap the peasantry.

The counts were more than happy to oblige the pope with a little hounding, an inquisition or two, and some burnings at the stake. Entire towns were judged to be guilty of heresy and inhabitants by the dozens were thrown to their deaths from high town walls. The persecuted "pure" soon took refuge in the Pyrénées Mountains, where they survived for 100 years. Now all that remains of this unhappy sect are their former hideouts, with tour groups visiting the vacant stone staircases and roofless chapels of haunted places like Peyrepertuse and Quéribus. For more information, log on to ⊕ *www.cathar. info* or go hiking with medievalist Ingrid Sparbier (⊕ *www.guide-sud-france.com*).

Michel Belin (*Chocolatier Michel Belin*) **FOOD/CANDY** | Michel Belin's chocolate delights are deservedly famous. ✉ *4 rue Dr-Camboulives, on Pl. du Vigan* ☎ *05–63–54–18–46.*

Cordes-sur-Ciel

25 km (15½ miles) northwest of Albi, 80 km (50 miles) northeast of Toulouse.

A must-stop for many travelers, the picture-book hilltop town of Cordes-sur-Ciel appears to hover in midair when mists steal up from the Cérou Valley below, hence the name—*sur-ciel* means "in the sky/heaven." It was established in 1222 by Count Raymond VII of Toulouse as a redoubt after the Occitan wars waged against the region's Cathars; and its conical hill is riddled with caves that served as granaries during times of siege. Today you may find Cordes-sur-Ciel besieged by summertime tourists, who come to admire well-preserved buildings (like the 14th-century St-Michel church) and to peruse plentiful shops and markets. The town is particularly busy during the annual Fêtes Médiévales du Grand Fauconnier (⊕ *www.medievale-cordes.fr*) in mid-July—a two-day blowout, replete with an artisan fair and costumed Bal Médiéval.

GETTING HERE AND AROUND

Tarnbus makes the 30-minute trip from Albi to the bottom of Cordes at least five times daily (€2). If you're driving, note that traffic is banned in the upper town in summer, and parking nearby is virtually impossible.

VISITOR INFORMATION Cordes-sur-Ciel Tourist Office ✉ *38-42 Grand-Rue Raimond VII* ☎ *05–63–56–00–52* 🌐 *www.cordessurciel.fr.*

Sights

Grand-rue Raymond VII

NEIGHBORHOOD | When peace arrived in the late Middle Ages, the town prospered and many rich residents built pink-sandstone Gothic-style houses—a sizable number of which still line the main street, Grand-rue Raymond VII. Today, many are occupied by painters, sculptors, weavers, leatherworkers, and even creators of illuminated manuscripts, whose ateliers and stores lure the summer crowds. ✉ *Grand-rue Raymond VII.*

Musée Charles-Portal

MUSEUM | The small museum has relics from the town's medieval past, plus items uncovered during excavations of the 372-foot-deep Cordes Well. ✉ *1 rue St-Michel* ☎ *09–72–87–07–95* 🌐 *museecharlesportal.fr* 🎟 *€3* 🕓 *Closed Nov.–mid-Apr.; Mon.–Thurs. in Sept., Oct., Apr., and May; and Tues. June–Aug.*

Musée Les Arts du Sucre et du Chocolat

MUSEUM | For proof that life is indeed sweet in Cordes-sur-Ciel, visit this two-room museum dedicated to sugar and chocolate. It showcases the confectionery creations of noted chef Yves Thuriès. ✉ *33 Grand-Rue Raimond VII* ☎ *05–63–56–02–40* 🌐 *www.yvesthuries.com/info/musee-des-arts-et-du-sucre-14* 🎟 *€6.*

Hotels

Hôtel Raymond VII

$ | **HOTEL** | **FAMILY** | At the very top of the village, tucked away from the pedestrian-busy streets, sits this small, family-owned hotel with magical views of the countryside. **Pros:** located in the heart of the village; attentive host; spectacular sunrises from top of the village. **Cons:** difficult to reach by car in the midst of tourist season; parking is a hassle, especially in July and August; a bit of a climb with luggage if walking. [$] *Rooms from: €95* ✉ *19 Grand-rue Raymond VII* ☎ *05–63–60–02–80, 06–75–04–62–68 mobile* 🌐 *www.raymond7.fr* 🛏 *8 rooms* 🍴 *No meals.*

L'Hostellerie du Vieux Cordes

$ | **HOTEL** | One of famed chocolatier Yves Thuriès's lovely Cordes hotels, this 13th-century house, built around a spectacular courtyard dotted with tiny tables and shaded by a magnificent 300-year-old wisteria, has stylishly decorated guest rooms and a fine on-site eatery. **Pros:** some rooms have views of the valley (book well in advance); excellent on-site restaurant; interesting history. **Cons:** cramped Room 4 should be avoided; uphill hike to the hotel from parking area; breakfast is extra. [$] *Rooms from: €75* ✉ *21 rue St-Michel* ☎ *05–63–53–79–20* 🌐 *www.hotelcordes.fr* 🕓 *Closed Jan.–mid-Feb.* 🛏 *19 rooms* 🍴 *No meals.*

Carcassonne

88 km (55 miles) southeast of Toulouse, 105 km (65 miles) south of Albi.

Poised atop a hill overlooking lush green countryside and the Aude River, Carcassonne's fortified upper town, known as La Cité, looks lifted from the pages of a storybook—literally, perhaps, as its circle of towers and battlements is said to be the setting for Charles Perrault's classic tale *Puss in Boots*. With its turrets and

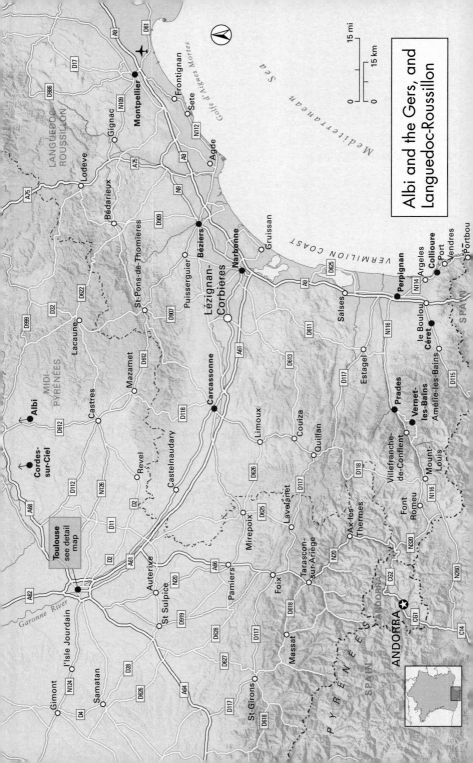

Albi and the Gers, and Languedoc-Roussillon

LANGUEDOC-
ROUSSILLON

MIDI-
PYRÉNÉES

Mediterranean Sea

Golfe d'Aigues-Mortes

VERMILION COAST

SPAIN

PYRÉNÉES

SPAIN

ANDORRA

Garonne River

Montpellier

Frontignan

Sete

Agde

Gignac

Lodeve

Bédarieux

St-Pons-de-Thomières

Puisserguier

Béziers

Narbonne

Gruissan

Lézignan-
Corbières

Carcassonne

Salses

Perpignan

Argeles

Collioure

Port
Vendres

Portbou

le Boulou

Céret

Amélie-les-Bains

Prades

Vernet-
les-Bains

Estagel

Couiza

Quillan

Limoux

Villefranche-
de-Conflent

Mount-
Louis

Font
Romeu

Lacaune

Mazamet

Castres

Albi

Cordes-
sur-Ciel

Revel

Castelnaudary

Toulouse
see detail
map

Auterive

St Sulpice

l'Isle Jourdain

Gimont

Samatan

St-Girons

Massat

Pamiers

Mirepoix

Lavelanet

Foix

Tarascon-
sur-Ariège

Ax-les-
Thermes

0   15 mi

0   15 km

N109

D61

D17

D986

A9

N112

A75

N9

A75

D909

D622

D32

D989

D612

D907

D118

A61

D613

D611

D117

D117

N116

N114

D625

D115

A9

N116

D118

N320

CG2

CG1

C14

N260

D112

N126

D2

D11

D2

A61

A66

N20

D919

D618

D117

D627

D626

D28

D4

N124

A62

A64

D618

D625

D626

A68

D612

castellated walls, it appeals to children and those with a penchant for the Middle Ages. The lower, newer part of the city is the Ville Basse, where you'll find the train station and a smattering of sights (most notably the Musée des Beaux-Arts).

GETTING HERE AND AROUND

Ryanair operates regular flights from London, Dublin, and several other European cities; a €6 airport shuttle transports passengers to the rail station (on Avenue du Maréchal Joffre, beside the Canal du Midi), stopping at La Cité en route. Arriving by boat or barge via the historic canal is a romantic alternative, but trains are more reliable—there are a dozen per day from Narbonne and 15 from Toulouse alone; from the station you can take a cab, hop a *navette* shuttle, or make the 30-minute walk up to La Cité. Bus service is available, too (a trip from Toulouse takes 80 minutes and costs €7 and up on carriers like Flixbus). If you're driving, be advised that unless you're staying at a hotel in La Cité, you are not allowed to enter it with your vehicle. Paid parking is available in a lot across the road from the drawbridge.

VISITOR INFORMATION Carcassonne Tourist Office ⊠ *28 rue de Verdun* ☎ *04–68–10–24–30* ⊕ *www.tourisme-carcassonne.com.*

◉ Sights

Château Comtal
CASTLE/PALACE | The 12th-century château is the last inner bastion of Carcassonne. It has a drawbridge and a museum, the **Musée Lapidaire,** where medieval stone sculptures unearthed in the area are on display. ⊠ *La Cité* ☎ *04–68–11–70–70* ⊕ *www.carcassonne.monuments-nationaux.fr* ⊠ *€9.*

★ La Cité de Carcassonne
HISTORIC SITE | FAMILY | La Cité de Carcassonne is the original fortified part of the town, often first glimpsed as a fairy-tale-like castle floating on a distant hilltop when approaching by car. Legend has it that Charlemagne laid siege to the original settlement here early in the 9th century, only to be outdone by one Dame Carcas—a clever woman who boldly fed the last of the city's wheat to a pig in full view of the would-be conqueror. Thinking this indicated endless food supplies (and an endless siege), Charlemagne promptly decamped, and the exuberant townsfolk named their city after her. During the 13th century, Louis IX (St-Louis) and his son Philip the Fair strengthened Carcassonne's fortifications—so much so that the town came to be considered inviolable by marauding armies and was duly nicknamed "the virgin of Languedoc."

A town that can never be taken in battle is often abandoned, however, and for centuries thereafter Carcassonne remained under a Sleeping Beauty spell. It was only awakened during the 19th-century craze for chivalry and the Gothic style, when, in 1835, the historic-monument inspector (and poet) Prosper Mérimée arrived. He was so appalled by the dilapidated state of the walls that he commissioned the architect, painter, and historian Viollet-le-Duc (who found his greatest fame restoring Paris's Notre-Dame) to undertake repairs. Today the 1844 renovation is considered almost as much a work of art as the medieval town itself. No matter if La Cité is more Viollet than authentic; it still remains one of the most romantic sights in France.

There's no mistaking the fact that 21st-century tourism has taken over this UNESCO World Heritage Site. La Cité's streets are lined with souvenir shops, crafts boutiques, restaurants, and tiny "museums" (a Cathars Museum, a Hat Museum), all out to make a buck and rarely worth that. But you should still plan on spending at least a couple of hours exploring the walls and peering over the battlements across sun-drenched plains toward the distant Pyrénées. Staying overnight within the ancient walls lets you savor the timeless atmosphere after the daytime hordes are gone. ✉ *La Cité* 🌐 *www.remparts-carcassonne.fr.*

Musée des Beaux-Arts (*Fine Arts Museum*)
MUSEUM | The real draw in the Ville Basse (newer, lower portion of Carcassonne), this museum houses a nice collection of porcelain, 17th- and 18th-century Flemish paintings, and works by local artists—including some stirring battle scenes by Jacques Gamelin (1738–1803). ✉ *1 rue de Verdun, Ville Basse* ☎ *04–68–77–73–70* 🎫 *Free* 🕓 *Closed Sun. and Mon. Oct.–mid-June (except 1st Sun. of the month).*

Carcassonne's Medieval Festival

Carcassonne usually goes medieval in mid-August with Les Médiévales (🌐 *www.carcassonne-tourisme.com*), a festival of troubadour song, rich costumes, and jousting performances (some years the event isn't held; check with the tourist office). And don't forget the spectacular Bastille Day (July 14) fireworks over La Cité.

🍴 Restaurants

Bloc G
$$ | **MODERN FRENCH** | Just outside the upper city walls, this all-white urbanesque restaurant and wine bar, run by three food-and-design-savvy sisters, offers a reality check after the touristic, turreted streets of La Cité. The blackboard menu highlights experimental touches to classic dishes (like sautéed foie gras in a Thai broth) and helps attract a sophisticated, casual clientele. **Known for:** experimental approach to classic dishes; huge rooms in the upstairs inn; classy atmosphere. [$] *Average main: €21* ✉ *112 rue Barbacane* ☎ *04–68–47–58–20* 🌐 *www.bloc-g.com* 🕓 *Closed Sun. and Mon. in winter.*

Le Puits du Tresor
$$$$ | **MODERN FRENCH** | At the foot of the famous Cathar castle of Lastours, this Michelin-starred treat comes as something of a surprise. Headed by the talented Jean-Marc Boyer, the restaurant serves inventive and artistic meals based on local ingredients. **Known for:** lovely settling in an old textile factory above the Orbiel River; highly seasonal cuisine; high prices. [$] *Average main: €67* ✉ *Rte. des Châteaux, Lastours, 12 km (8 miles) north of Carcassonne* ☎ *04–68–77–50–24* 🌐 *www.lepuitsdutresor.fr* 🕓 *Closed Mon., Tues., and Mar.*

Sire de Cabaret
$ | **FRENCH** | Nestled beneath the château of Roquefère, an unspoiled *village fleuri* in the Cabardés region of the Montagne Noire, this regional favorite dishes up amazing steaks and bottomless plates of homemade pâté and charcuterie. Cooked over wood fires, many of the meat-centered dishes are accompanied by mushrooms picked from nearby mountains by the genial chef. **Known for:** covetable terrace seating overlooking the oak-cloaked hills; plenty of rustic charm; utterly picturesque surroundings. [$] *Average main: €17* ✉ *Roquefère, 25 km (11 miles) north of Carcassonne, off D9* ☎ *04–68–26–31–89* 🌐 *www.auberge-sire-decabaret.fr* 🕓 *Closed Jan.–mid-Feb.; Mon.–Wed. mid-Feb.–Easter, Nov., and Dec.; and Wed. Easter–Oct. No dinner Sun.*

🛏 Hotels

Château La Villatade
$ | **B&B/INN** | On a sprawling wine estate, far from Carcassonne's madding crowd, this serene retreat is owned by ever-hospitable hosts who happily share their best vintages and fine countryside lifestyle with guests. **Pros:** real French living amid vineyards; natural swimming pool; charming rustic decor. **Cons:** somewhat

Carcassonne's historic ramparts give off a gorgeous glow at night.

isolated; no on-site restaurant; car is essential. [$] *Rooms from: €95* ✉ *15 km (10 miles) north of Carcassonne, Sallèles-d'Aude* ☎ *04–68–77–57–51* 🌐 *www.villatade.com* 💳 *No credit cards* 🛏 *5 rooms* 🍴 *No meals.*

Domaine d'Auriac

$$ | **HOTEL** | Minutes away from Carcassonne, this seriously elegant 19th-century manor has one of the best restaurants in the region, and the entire building oozes grace and old-world charm; rooms vary in size, with the largest of them offering views over a magnificent park and vineyards. **Pros:** excellent 18-hole golf course; stately interiors; excellent restaurant. **Cons:** a few miles from Carcassonne's center; classic French luxury may grate on guests seeking a low-key ambience; breakfast not included. [$] *Rooms from: €170* ✉ *Rte. de St-Hilaire, 4 km (2½ miles) southwest of Carcassonne* ☎ *04–68–25–72–22* 🌐 *www.domaine-d-auriac.com* 🕒 *Closed Jan., 2nd wk of Feb., and 2nd wk of Nov.* 🛏 *24 rooms* 🍴 *No meals.*

★ **Hôtel de la Cité**

$$$ | **HOTEL** | Enjoying the finest location within the walls of the old city, this ivy-covered former Episcopal palace provides a high level of creature comfort, which the ascetic Cathars would most definitely have deprived themselves of. **Pros:** no better location in Carcassonne; vintage luxury; garden-side pool. **Cons:** must coordinate parking behind the city walls in advance; pool is small; some guests might prefer something a little more down-to-earth. [$] *Rooms from: €285* ✉ *Pl. August-Pierre Pont, La Cité* ☎ *04–68–71–98–71* 🌐 *www.hoteldelacite.com* 🛏 *60 rooms* 🍴 *No meals.*

Hôtel Montségur

$ | **HOTEL** | With its central lower city location, this hotel isn't only handy to Carcassonne's shops, restaurants, and nightlife; it also has special touches that belie the sweet prices here—many guest rooms feature Louis XV and Louis XVI furniture, some of it genuine. **Pros:** the Faugras family has been in the hospitality business for over a century, so they know how to take care of their guests; convenient location; gorgeous, historical decor. **Cons:** lends itself to street noise; may be disappointing to those wishing to sleep inside the walls of La Cité; not all rooms have the same level of decor. [$] *Rooms from: €97* ✉ *1 av. Bunau Varilla* ☎ *04-68-25-31-41* 🌐 *www.hotelmontsegur.com* 🕒 *Closed Dec. 22–Feb. 1* 🛏 *18 rooms* 🍴 *No meals.*

Performing Arts

Festival de Carcassonne

FESTIVALS | Carcassonne hosts a major arts festival in July that includes world-class dance, theater, and circus performances. Music concerts feature musicians like Pharrell Williams, Indochine, James Blunt, and Lana Del Rey. There's also an "OFF Festival" lineup that showcases emerging artists on 12 different stages offering 80 shows free of charge. ✉ *Carcassonne* ☎ *04-68-11-59-15* 🌐 *www.festivaldecarcassonne.fr.*

Perpignan

118 km (71 miles) southeast of Carcassonne, 27 km (17 miles) northwest of Collioure.

Salvador Dalí once called Perpignan's train station "the center of the world." That may not be true, but the city certainly is the capital hub of Roussillon. Perpignan tends to echo its surrounding agricultural landscape, rough around the edges and full of yet-unrealized potential that attracts a kind of bold spirit. Scratch the surface of Perpignan and you'll find Roma music, deep Catalan pride, loud Spanish influences, and the occasional classic crêpe. It's just as varied as the region's dynamic winemakers, who might hail from the Loire Valley or South Africa. Center of the world? Could be.

GETTING HERE AND AROUND

Ryanair flies daily to Aéroport Sud de France-Perpignan from London and Brussels, while planes operated by HOP! arrive from Paris; Bus Line 7 operates between the airport and Place Catalonia, where you can transfer to Line 2 to reach the train station at the end of Avenue du Général de Gaulle, or it's a 10-minute walk. If you're arriving from Paris by rail, the TGV takes about five hours and costs €65 and up. Plenty of trains connect Perpignan with Montpellier (2 hrs, €27) and Narbonne (45 mins, €12), as well as many other communities. Bus links operate out of a terminal on Boulevard St-Assicle, next to the TGV station.

VISITOR INFORMATION Perpignan Tourist Office ✉ *Pl. de la Loge* ☎ *04-68-66-30-30* 🌐 *www.perpignantourisme.com.*

Sights

Cathédrale St-Jean

RELIGIOUS SITE | Note the frilly wrought-iron campanile and dramatic medieval crucifix on the Cathédrale St-Jean. ✉ *Pl. Gambetta.*

Le Castillet

MUSEUM | Perpignan's alluring town center is lined with rosemary bushes and landmarked by a medieval monument, the 14th-century Castillet, with its tall, crenellated twin towers. Originally this hulking brick building was the main gate to the city; later it was used as a prison. Now the **Casa Pairal,** a museum devoted to Catalan art and traditions, is housed here. ✉ *Pl. de Verdun* ☎ *04-68-35-42-05* 🎟 *€2* 🕒 *Closed Mon.*

Palais des Rois de Majorque (*Kings of Majorca Palace*)

CASTLE/PALACE | The Spanish influence is evident in Perpignan's leading monument, the fortified Palais des Rois de Majorque, begun in the 13th century by Jacques II of Majorca. Highlights here are the majestic **Cour d'Honneur** (Courtyard of Honor), the two-tier Flamboyant Gothic chapel of **Ste-Croix Marie-Madelene,** and the **Grande Salle** (Great Hall), with its monumental fireplaces. ✉ *Rue des Archers* ☎ *04–68–34–64–93* 🎟 *€4.*

Petite Rue des Fabriques d'En Nabot

NEIGHBORHOOD | To see some interesting medieval buildings, walk along the Petite Rue des Fabriques d'En Nabot—near Le Castillet—to the adjacent Place de la Loge, the town's nerve center. ✉ *Perpignan.*

Promenade des Plantanes

CITY PARK | Across Boulevard Wilson from Le Castillet, this is a cheerful place to stroll among flowers, plane trees, and fountains. ✉ *Perpignan.*

Restaurants

Crêperie du Théâtre

$ | **FRENCH** | Walk past the pubs and bars on this narrow alley for the best crêperie in Perpignan. Owned by a young couple from Brittany, it prepares authentic buckwheat crêpes with a modern twist. **Known for:** tasty buckwheat galettes (suitable for gluten-free travelers); organic and seasonal ingredients; outdoor tables great for lounging. [$] *Average main: €7* ✉ *12 rue du Théâtre* ☎ *04–68–34–29–06* 🌐 *www.creperie-du-theatre.fr* 💳 *No credit cards* 🕓 *Closed Sun., Mon., and 10 days in Jan.*

★ **Garriane**

$$$$ | **INTERNATIONAL** | Foodies appreciate Garriane's direct approach to eating and drinking well. Here a plain-Jane decor and a dim neighborhood spectacularly contrast with immaculate plates presented by the Aussie-bred chef (who incidentally shook up Perpignan's sleepy food scene with a strictly seasonal menu emphasizing local produce boldly prepared for an exotic outcome). **Known for:** nine-course degustation menu that's the best meal in Perpignan; affordable lunch menu; booking ahead a must. [$] *Average main: €37* ✉ *15 rue Valette* ☎ *04–68–67–07–44* 🕓 *Closed Sun.–Tues. No lunch Wed. and Sat.*

Le France

$ | **BISTRO** | Occupying a 15th-century former stock market with exposed beams and arcades, this café-restaurant in the center of Perpignan is a perfect place to enjoy an easy meal under the umbrellas as you watch the world go by. Options include scallop salad, foie gras with green beans and raisins, and grilled duck breast with apples. **Known for:** wide-ranging menu from veal's head to tapas; open late until 11 pm on weekends; solid prices. [$] *Average main: €15* ✉ *1 pl. de la Loge* ☎ *04–68–51–61–71.*

Hotels

★ **Casa 9**

$$ | **HOTEL** | Among the orchards and vineyards in the countryside surrounding Perpignan sits Casa 9, a 15th-century *mas* (farm) with a barn that's been converted into lavish lodgings. **Pros:** all rooms look onto a patio or garden; property shaded by lush palms and 100-year old trees; stylish interiors. **Cons:** no on-site restaurant; a car is essential; breakfast not included. [$] *Rooms from: €135* ✉ *Mas Petit, Rte. de Corbère, 17 km (10½ miles) west of Perpignan* ☎ *07–78–80–54–35* 🌐 *www.casa9hotel.fr* 🕓 *Closed Jan.* 🛏 *9 rooms* 🍴 *No meals.*

Château la Tour Apollinaire

$$ | **B&B/INN** | This Belle Époque château turned postmodern B&B was once the mayor's residence and surrounded by sprawling vineyards. **Pros:** great location; lovely grounds with pool and gardens; walking distance to city center. **Cons:** larger suites cost way more; breakfast is tasty but extra; no on-site restaurant. [$] *Rooms from: €190* ✉ *15 rue Guillaume Apollinaire* ☎ *04–68–92–43–02* 🌐 *www.latourapollinaire.com* 🛏 *7 suites* 🍴 *No meals.*

La Villa Duflot

$ | **HOTEL** | In a large park filled with olive and cypress trees, this hotel-restaurant complex prepares some of the best meals in one of the calmest settings just outside the city center. **Pros:** restaurant is a local favorite; trees screen the property from the road; lovely wellness area/spa. **Cons:** located in a commercial zone on the outskirts of town; though very comfortable, rooms and lobby lack originality; infrequent bus service from city center. [$] *Rooms from: €120* ✉ *Rond Point Albert Donnezan* ☎ *04–68–56–67–67* 🌐 *www.villa-duflot.com* 🛏 *52 rooms* 🍴 *No meals.*

Shopping

Rue des Marchands, near Le Castillet, is filled with chic shops.

Sant Vicens Céramiques

CERAMICS/GLASSWARE | Excellent local ceramics can be found at this picturesque crafts center. Crowds flock here over Christmas to see the tiny—and extremely detailed—Nativity scenes made with ceramic figurines called *santons.* ✉ *40 rue Sant Vicens, off D22 east of town center* ☎ *04–68–50–02–18* 🌐 *www.santvicens.fr.*

Prades

45 km (27 miles) west of Perpignan.

It may be easy to bypass Prades en route to the region's high peaks, but to do so would mean missing out on this authentic market town. Farmers, artists, vendors, and loyal shoppers descend from the tiny surrounding villages each Tuesday to sustain the vibrant stalls. Serenely positioned at the foot of the imposing north face of Mont Canigou, Prades is also a great jumping-off spot for mountain excursions.

Olive Oil in Roussillon

Historically, Roussillon was France's leader in olive-oil production—that is, until the crippling winter of 1956 persuaded growers to abandon their trees for more lucrative crops. But the biblical fruit regained popularity with the Mediterranean diet buzz. Visit **Domaine Les Fonts,** about 14 km (8½ miles) west of Perpignan, for a tasting and olive-grove tour with producers Carmen and Didier Lamirand (☎ *04–68–92–82–05* 🌐 *www.olivesbiolesfonts.fr*).

GETTING HERE AND AROUND

To reach Prades, take a regional train or liO public bus from Perpignan (€1 each). From Prades, the Abbaye de St-Michel de Cuxa is a straightforward 25-minute walk; pick up a map of "Le Tour de l'Abbaye de St-Michel de Cuxa" from the tourist office and follow the easy trail through the woods.

VISITOR INFORMATION Prades Tourist Office ✉ *10 pl. de la Republique* ☎ *04–68–05–41–02* 🌐 *www.tourisme-canigou.com.*

Sights

Abbaye de St-Michel de Cuxa

RELIGIOUS SITE | One of the gems of the Pyrénées, this medieval abbey's sturdy, crenellated bell tower is visible from afar. The remains of its cloisters are divine in every sense of the word—if they seem familiar, it may be because you've seen the missing pieces in New York City's Cloisters museum. A hauntingly simple, six-voice Gregorian vespers service held (somewhat sporadically) at 7 pm in the monastery is medieval in tone and texture; next door, the 10th-century pre-Romanesque church (France's largest) has superb acoustics that make it an unforgettable concert venue. ✉ *3 km (2 miles) south of Prades on D27* ☎ *04–68–96–15–35* 🌐 *abbaye-cuxa.com* 🎫 *€6* 🕒 *Closed 2 wks late Jan.*

Festival Pablo Casals

FESTIVAL | World-renowned Catalan cellist Pablo Casals, who took refuge in Prades during the Spanish Civil War, gave his name to the international music festival based here each year from late July to mid-August. Concerts are also held in other churches and sacred places in villages in the surrounding hills. ✉ *Prades* ☎ *04–68–96–33–07* 🌐 *www.prades-festival-casals.com.*

Restaurants

★ El Taller

$$ | MODERN FRENCH | Run by four entrepreneurial friends just down the road from the famous Abbaye de St-Michel de Cuxa, this hip bistro serves fine locally sourced fare in large portions, like pork tenderloin in *corriollette* (fairy-ring mushroom) sauce. Like the food, the setting is stylish: its sleek glass-walled building and steel-framed terrace were constructed by the village specifically to house this Bistrot de Pays (a government-subsidized network of village restaurants promoting commerce in rural areas). **Known for:** reliably great meals; location in a picturesque village at the base of Mont Canigou; convenient stop after visiting the Abbaye de St-Michel de Cuxa. [$] *Average main: €24* ✉ *5 km (3 miles) south of Prades, Taurinya* ☎ *04–68–05–63–35* 🌐 *bar-restaurant-el-taller.weebly.com* 🕒 *Closed Wed., 2 wks in Jan., and Mon. and Tues. Nov.–Apr. No dinner Sun. in Nov.–Apr.*

Les Loges du Jardin d'Aymeric

$$$$ | FRENCH | In a quiet mountain village just outside Prades, this semisecret gourmand restaurant serves classic five-course meals that locals swear by. The ambience is refined yet relaxed, and the market-inspired menu changes seasonally. **Known for:** excellent value weekday lunch menu; more extravagant tasting menu at dinner; local favorite. [$] *Average main: €38* ✉ *7 rue du Canigou, 8 km (5 miles) south of Prades* ☎ *04–68–96–08–72* 🌐 *www.logesaymeric.com* 🕒 *Closed Jan. No dinner Mon. and Sun. Sept.–June.*

Hotels

★ Le Château de Riell

$$ | HOTEL | An eccentric late-19th-century castle that blends baroque style and English elements, this Relais & Châteaux property welcomes guests who want to enjoy its tranquil mountain setting or soak in the healing waters of Molitg-les-Bains. **Pros:** rooftop swimming pool; spectacular views of Mont Canigou; superb restaurant. **Cons:** though a bus connects Molitg to Prades, a car is more practical; odd accents may be a bit much for some; restaurant closed Tuesday except in summer. [$] *Rooms from: €220* ✉ *9 km (5½ miles) north of Prades, Molitg-les-Bains* ☎ *04–68–05–04–40* 🌐 *www.chateauderiell.com* 🕒 *Closed mid-Nov.–Mar.* 🛏 *17 rooms* 🍴 *No meals.*

L'Orri de Planès

$ | B&B/INN | FAMILY | At the base of the Cirque du Cambre d'Aze (an extra-impressive glacially formed peak) is an immaculately restored stone farmhouse turned eco-lodge that combines comfort and design. **Pros:** refreshingly modern ambience; high-tech solar design; on the GR10 trans-Pyrénées footpath. **Cons:** eco means room temps may not meet luxury standards; not much to do if you're not into hiking; room quality varies. [$] *Rooms from: €80* ✉ *Orri de Planès, Cases del Mitg* ☎ *04–68–04–29–47, 06–22–32–25–32 mobile* 🌐 *www.orrideplanes.com* 🕒 *Closed Nov.–Apr. and weekdays May and Oct.* 🛏 *9 rooms, 4 yurts, 1 bunkhouse* 🍴 *Free Breakfast* 💳 *No credit cards.*

Maison 225

$ | **B&B/INN** | Don't let the bland street-front facade of this late 1800s town house deter you—inside, the renovated interior mixes stately original attributes with contemporary edges, and natural light spills in from the quiet gardens and terrace with front-row views of snow-capped Mont Canigou. **Pros:** attentive hosts; casual yet cultivated service; swimming pool with mountain views. **Cons:** breakfast is included but tables are shared; rooms book up fast; only one room has an outdoor terrace. $ *Rooms from: €70* ✉ *225 av. du General de Gaulle* ☎ *04–68–05–52–79, 06–42–91–79–21 mobile* ⊕ *www.225prades.com* ▭ *No credit cards* ⟿ *4 rooms* ⏹ *Free Breakfast.*

Vernet-les-Bains

12 km (7 miles) southwest of Prades, 55 km (34 miles) west of Perpignan.

Many notables—including English writer Rudyard Kipling—have come to take the cure at this long-established spa town, which is dwarfed by imposing Mont Canigou.

GETTING HERE AND AROUND
Take a direct liO bus (Line 240, €1) from Perpignan to Vernet-les-Bains. To access the Abbaye St-Martin du Canigou, stay on the same bus to the end of the line at Casteil, and then be prepared to proceed on foot.

VISITOR INFORMATION Vernet-les-Bains Tourist Office ✉ *Maison du Patrimoine, 2 rue de la Chapelle* ☎ *04–68–05–41–02* ⊕ *www.vernet-les-bains.fr.*

 Sights

⭐ **Abbaye St-Martin du Canigou**

RELIGIOUS SITE | Visitors tackling a steep, mile-long climb from the parking area, come to make a pilgrimage—esthetic or spiritual—to this celebrated medieval abbey. It's one of the most photographed in Europe thanks to its sky-kissing location atop a triangular promontory at an altitude of nearly 3,600 feet. St-Martin du Canigou's breathtaking mountain setting was due, in part, to an effort to escape the threat of marauding Saracens from the Middle East. Constructed in 1009 by Count Guifré of Cerdagne, then damaged by an earthquake in 1428 and abandoned in 1783, the abbey was diligently (perhaps too diligently) restored by the Bishop of Perpignan early in the 20th century. The oldest parts are the cloisters and the two churches, of which the lower church, dedicated to Notre-Dame-sous-Terre, is the most ancient. Rising above is a stocky, fortified bell tower. ■**TIP**➔ **Masses are sung daily—Easter Mass is especially joyous and moving—but the Abbey can only be visited by guided tour, offered five times daily; reservations are not needed unless traveling as a group of 15 or more.** ✉ *Casteil, 2 km (1 mile) south of Vernet-les-Bains* ☎ *04–68–05–50–03* ⊕ *www.stmartinducanigou.org* ✆ *€6* ⏱ *Closed Jan., and Mon. Oct.–May.*

Céret

68 km (41 miles) southeast of Prades, 35 km (21 miles) west of Collioure, 31 km (19 miles) southwest of Perpignan.

The "Barbizon of Cubism," Céret achieved immortality when leading artists found the small Catalan town irresistible at the beginning of the 20th century. Here in this medieval enclave set on the banks of the Tech River, Picasso and Gris developed a vigorous new way of visualizing that would result in the fragmented forms of Cubism, a thousand years removed from the Romanesque sculptures of the Roussillon chapels and cloisters. The town famously grows the first and finest crop of cherries in France.

GETTING HERE AND AROUND

Buses to Céret (40 mins, €1) leave from Perpignan's Gare Routiére, next to the train station.

VISITOR INFORMATION Céret Tourist Office ✉ *5 rue St-Ferréol* ☎ *04–68–87–00–53* 🌐 *www.vallespir-tourisme.fr.*

Sights

★ **Musée d'Art Moderne** (*Modern Art Museum*)

MUSEUM | Some of the town landscapes captured in paintings by Picasso, Gris, Dufy, Braque, Chagall, Masson, and others are on view in this fine museum. ✉ *8 bd. Maréchal-Joffre* ☎ *04–68–87–27–76* 🌐 *www.musee-ceret.com* 🎫 *€10* 🕒 *Closed Mon. Oct.–June.*

Vieux Céret (*Old Céret*)

NEIGHBORHOOD | Place Picasso is the heart of Old Céret, and the sardana dancers and *castellers* (human tower troops) who perform here are evidence of the pride locals take in their Catalan heritage. While in this pretty quarter, stroll around **Place de la Fontaine des Neuf Jets** (Nine Fountains Square). Drop into the church, wander out to the lovely fortified **Porte de France** gateway, then leave the historic town center and head toward the single-arched medieval **Pont du Diable** (the Devil's Bridge) on the perimeter of town, said to have been built by the devil himself in a single night. ✉ *Céret.*

Restaurants

★ **Percherons**

$$ | **CATALAN** | When a young Catalan native returned home from the pull of the Paris restaurant scene and partnered with a friend to open Percherons, Picasso's Céret finally got a restaurant worthy of a detour beyond art history. The prix-fixe dégustation menu (with two appetizers, two mains, a cheese course, and dessert) calls on Catalan basics like suckling pig from Spanish Catalonia's Emporda, Vallespir tomatoes from the French side, and aged goat cheese from the frontier-forming Alberes mountains. **Known for:** most dynamic wine collection in Céret; lovely, tucked-away courtyard; old-school vibe with vintage tiling, a zinc bar, solid oak tables, and moleskin benches. [$] *Average main: €20* ✉ *7 rue de la République, Vernet-les-Bains* ☎ *04–11–64–41–12* 🕒 *Closed Tues.*

Hotels

Les Arcades

$ | **HOTEL** | This comfortable, well-priced spot in mid-Céret looks and feels exactly the way an inn ensconced in the heart of a provincial French town should, and having the world-class collection of paintings of the Musée d'Art Moderne just next door further elevates it as a desirable place to stay. **Pros:** family-run business with great customer service; superior art in the public areas; very convenient on-site parking garage. **Cons:** some rooms are small; walls are thin; drab room decor. [$] *Rooms from: €65* ✉ *1 pl. Picasso* ☎ *04–68–87–12–30* 🌐 *hotelarcadesceret.fr* 🛏 *30 rooms* 🍴 *No meals.*

Collioure

35 km (21 miles) east of Céret, 27 km (17 miles) southeast of Perpignan.

The fishing village where famed painters Henri Matisse, André Derain, and the Fauvists committed chromatic mayhem in the early 20th century, Collioure is still the jewel of the Vermilion Coast. A town of espadrille merchants, anchovy packers, and lateen-rigged fishing boats in the shadow of a 13th-century Château Royal, it is now as much a magnet for travelers (beware the crowds in July and August) as it once was and remains a lure for artists.

Matisse set up shop here in the summer of 1905 and was soon inspired by the

As color-splashed as a Matisse or Braque painting, Collioure's harbor once inspired those masters and continues to seduce today's artists.

colors of the town's terra-cotta roofs. André Derain, Henri Martin, and Georges Braque—who were dubbed "Fauves" for their "savage" approach to color and form (*fauve* means "wild beast")—quickly followed. To discover tomorrow's Matisses and Derains, head to the streets behind the Place du 18-Juin and to the old Le Mouré neighborhood, beneath Fort Miradou—the studios here are filled with contemporary artists at work; or visit the streets behind the Vieux Port to find former fishermen's quarters now occupied by smart boutiques and restaurants. Other dining delights await on the café-terraces overlooking the main beach and the fashionable Rue Camille Pelletan by the harbor, where you can feast on Collioure's tender, practically boneless anchovies and the fine Banyuls and Collioure AOC wines coming from the impeccably cultivated vineyards surrounding the town. Although nearby villages are apparently only rich in quaintness, Collioure is surprisingly prosperous, thanks to the cultivation of *primeurs,* early ripening fruit and vegetables, shipped to the markets of northern France.

GETTING HERE AND AROUND
About a dozen daily trains from Perpignan (20 mins, €6.30) pull into Collioure's rail station at the end of Avenue Aristide Maillol. All seats on the liO's Line 400 buses making the 25-minute trip between Perpignan to Collioure (and most other area towns) are €1.

VISITOR INFORMATION Collioure Tourist Office ⊠ *Pl. du 18-Juin* ☎ *04–68–82–15–47* ⊕ *www.collioure.com.*

Sights

Château Royal
CASTLE/PALACE | A slender jetty divides the Boramar Beach, beneath Notre-Dame-des-Anges, from the small landing area at the foot of the Château Royal. The castle served as the summer residence of the kings of Majorca from 1276 to 1344 and was remodeled by Vauban 500 years later. ⊠ *Collioure* ☎ *04–68–82–06–43* 💰 *€4.*

Chemin du Fauvisme

HISTORIC SITE | Composed of narrow, cobbled streets and pretty houses, Collioure today is a living museum, as evidenced by the Chemin du Fauvisme (Fauvist Way), a pedestrian trail winding through town with 20 points where you can compare reproductions of noted Fauvist canvases with the actual scenes that were depicted in them. The information center, behind the Plage Boramar, has an excellent map. Viewfinder picture frames let you see how delightfully little of what the artists once admired has changed in the ensuing century. To the north, the rocky Îlot St-Vincent juts out into the sea, a modern lighthouse at its tip, and inland the Albères mountain range rises to connect the Pyrénées with the Mediterranean. The town harbor is a painting unto itself, framed by a 13th-century castle and a 17th-century church fortified with a tower. ✉ *Collioure.*

Musée d'Art Moderne Fonds Péské

MUSEUM | No Matissses hold pride of place at the town's Musée d'Art Moderne Fonds Péské, but the collection of 180 works deftly sums up the influence the painter had on this *cité des peintures* (city of artists). Works by Cocteau, Valtat, and others are impressively housed in a picturesque, ivy-shrouded villa on a beautiful hillside site. ✉ *Rte. de Porte-Vendres* ☎ *04–68–82–10–19* 🎫 *€3* ⏲ *Closed Tues. Oct.–May.*

Notre-Dame-des-Anges

RELIGIOUS SITE | At the end of Boulevard du Boramar is the 17th-century church of Notre-Dame-des-Anges. It has exuberantly carved, gilded churrigueresque altarpieces by celebrated Catalan master Joseph Sunyer and a pink-dome bell tower that doubled as the original lighthouse. ✉ *Pl. de l'Église.*

🍴 Restaurants

Le 5eme Péché

$$ | **FRENCH FUSION** | On one of Collioure's quieter cobblestoned streets you'll find Le 5eme Péché, where the clean-lined decor seems in synch with Japanese owner-chef Iijima Masashi's simple yet innovative dishes like tempura shrimp with chestnut cream and apple crisps. With only 18 seats and an open kitchen plan, you'll feel like you know him personally by the time your meal is done. **Known for:** inventive menu of French-Japanese fusion dishes; small space so reservations necessary; limited menu (finicky eaters, beware). [$] *Average main: €22* ✉ *18 rue de la Fraternité* ☎ *04–68–98–09–76* 🌐 *www.le5peche.com.*

🛏 Hotels

Casa Païral

$$ | **HOTEL** | This idyllic, palm-shaded 19th-century town house surrounded by a leafy garden feels like an oasis in often-tumultuous Collioure. **Pros:** in the center of Collioure; very helpful staff; close to the water. **Cons:** closed in winter; rooms vary in terms of size and decor; breakfast not included. [$] *Rooms from: €141* ✉ *Impasse des Palmiers* ☎ *04–68–82–05–81* 🌐 *www.hotel-casa-pairal.com* ⏲ *Closed Dec. and Jan.* 🛏 *27 rooms* 🍴 *No meals.*

Les Templiers

$ | **HOTEL** | Matisse, Maillol, Dalí, Picasso, and Dufy used to hang out here, and the current owner, the granddaughter of René Pous (the driving force behind Collioure's art colony), is proud to show off the 2,500-plus original works hanging from every nook and cranny of this celebrated inn and restaurant—universally considered the "soul" of Collioure. **Pros:** in the center of town; short walk to beaches, shops, and restaurants; excellent artwork and decor throughout. **Cons:** on a pedestrian alley, so no access for cars; noisy during the hustle and bustle of August; breakfast not included. [$] *Rooms from: €93* ✉ *12 quai de l'Amirauté* ☎ *04–68–98–31–10* 🌐 *www.hotel-templiers.com* 🕓 *Closed Jan. and last wk of Nov.* 🛏 *45 rooms* 🍴 *No meals.*

★ **Relais des Trois Mas**

$$ | **HOTEL** | With a perfect perch overlooking the harbor from the cliffs south of town, this hotel enjoys vistas that are priceless—which is the main reason why staying here is pricey. **Pros:** breathtaking views of Collioure; beach access and a small pool; fine restaurant. **Cons:** some standard rooms are very small; lodgings are basic for the price; no lobby, sitting area, or bar. [$] *Rooms from: €170* ✉ *Rte. de Port-Vendres* ☎ *04–68–82–05–07* 🌐 *www.relaisdes3mas.com* 🕓 *Closed mid-Nov.–early Feb.* 🛏 *24 rooms* 🍴 *No meals.*

Narbonne

61 km (38 miles) north of Perpignan, 60 km (37 miles) east of Carcassonne, 94 km (58 miles) south of Montpellier.

In Roman times, bustling, industrial Narbonne was the second-largest town in Gaul (after Lyon) and an important port, though today little remains of its Roman past, except an impressive underground warehouse (*horreum* in Latin) once used to store the wines and goods shipped through its harbor. Until the sea receded during the Middle Ages, Narbonne prospered. Today, the city center would be considered sleepy in comparison, but it has an elegant feel in tune with Montpellier's classy shops.

GETTING HERE AND AROUND

There are 14 daily departures from Paris to Narbonne, and TGVs leaving the Gare de Lyon can cover the distance in 4½ hours (€99). Narbonne is also an important rail junction for the region, with frequent trains departing for Perpignan (45 mins, €12.40), Montpellier (1 hr, €17.10), Carcassonne (30 mins, €11.80), and Toulouse (1½ hrs, €26.50). The train station is on Boulevard Frédéric Mistral, north of the city center and adjacent to the Gare Routière (bus station) at 1 Avenue Maréchal Foch.

VISITOR INFORMATION Narbonne Tourist Office ✉ *31 rue Jean Jaurès* ☎ *04–68–65–15–60* 🌐 *www.narbonne-tourisme.com.*

Sights

Cathédrale St-Just-et-St-Pasteur

RELIGIOUS SITE | The town's former wealth is evinced by the 14th-century Cathédrale St-Just-et-St-Pasteur—its vaulting rises 133 feet from the floor, making it the tallest cathedral in southern France. Only Beauvais and Amiens (both in Picardy) are taller, and, as at Beauvais, the nave here was never completed. The "Creation" tapestry is the cathedral's finest treasure. Enter from the back side (Rue Gustave Fabre) for an especially impressive look at the unfinished nave and insight into the construction process. ✉ *Rue Armand-Gauthier.*

Palais des Archevêques (*Archbishops' Palace*)

MUSEUM | Richly sculpted cloisters link the cathedral to the former Palais des Archevêques, home to collections covering archaeology, art, and history. Note the Donjon Gilles-Aycelin and its late-13th-century keep; climb the 162 steps to the top for a view over the town and surrounding region. ✉ *Pl. de l'Hôtel de Ville* ☎ *04–68–90–31–34* 🎟 *From €6* 🕓 *Closed Tues. Oct.–May.*

Hotels

★ **Château L'Hospitalet**

$$ | **HOTEL** | A stay at this sprawling family-owned wine estate, located between Narbonne's city center and its beaches, is like a course in the art of Mediterranean living complete with surrounding vineyards, sea breezes, an immense

wine-tasting cellar, organic kitchen garden, and resident artist studios. **Pros:** a good sampling of wine, art, and lifestyle; close to beaches and town; visiting artists and workshops. **Cons:** guest rooms lack character; property has a somewhat commercial undertone; breakfast not included. $ Rooms from: €145 ⊠ Rte. de Narbonne Plage ☎ 04–68–45–28–50 ⊕ www.chateau-hospitalet.com ⊙ Closed 3 wks in Jan. ⇥ 38 rooms ⦿ No meals.

Hôtel La Résidence

$ | HOTEL | One block from the Canal de la Robine and another block from Place Salengro and the cathedral, Hôtel La Résidence has housed French arts icons like singer Georges Brassens and actor Michel Serrault; the 19th-century building is itself charming, and rooms combine old-fashioned warmth with modern comforts. **Pros:** centrally located for shops, restaurants, and museums; friendly service; historic building. **Cons:** three-spot parking area can be difficult to navigate and can fill up; though on a quiet street, some rooms get street noise; breakfast not included. $ Rooms from: €105 ⊠ 6 rue 1er Mai ☎ 04–68–32–19–41 ⊕ www.hotel-laresidence-narbonne.fr ⇥ 26 rooms ⦿ No meals.

Le Relais du Val d'Orbieu

$ | HOTEL | This pretty spot west of town is a viable solution to Narbonne's scarcity of good hotels—rooms are grouped around a courtyard and most are reached through covered arcades. **Pros:** pretty countryside setting; well situated for wine-tasting excursions; decent on-site restaurant. **Cons:** no air-conditioning means hot in summer; although comfortable, rooms could use an update; not all rooms have nice views. $ Rooms from: €120 ⊠ D24, 14 km (8 miles) west of Narbonne, Ornaisons ☎ 04–68–27–10–27 ⊕ www.relaisduvaldorbieu.com ⇥ 20 rooms ⦿ Free Breakfast.

Béziers

25 km (12 miles) northeast of Narbonne, 65 km (33 miles) southwest of Montpellier.

Béziers—centerpiece of the Canal du Midi and the Languedoc's *capital du vin* (crowds flock in for tastings during the October wine harvest festival)—owes its reputation to the genius of native son and royal salt-tax collector Pierre-Paul Riquet. That's his statue presiding over the Allées Paul Riquet. He was a visionary at a time when roads were in deplorable shape and grain was transported on the backs of mules, yet he died a pauper in 1680, a year before the canal into which he sank his fortune was completed (it was begun by the ancient Romans), revolutionizing commerce in the south of France. Few would have predicted much of a future for Béziers in July 1209, after Simon de Montfort, leader of the crusade against the Cathars, scored his first major victory here, massacring thousands. Today the Canal du Midi hosts mainly pleasure cruisers, and Béziers serenely overlooks the distant Mediterranean and the foothills of the Cévennes Mountains. Mid-August sees the four-day *féria*—a festival with roots in Spain and replete with gory bullfighting (you've been warned).

GETTING HERE AND AROUND

There are frequent daily trains to Béziers from Perpignan (1 hr, €16.50) and Montpellier (44 mins, €15.50). Buses also run from Montpellier five times a day (2 hrs, €1.60).

VISITOR INFORMATION Béziers Tourist Office ⊠ Pl. du Forum ☎ 04–99–41–36–36 ⊕ www.beziers-in-mediterranee.com.

Sights

Ancienne Cathédrale St-Nazaire

RELIGIOUS SITE | Rebuilt over several centuries after the sack of Béziers, the cathedral's western facade resembles a fortress for good reason—it served as a warning to would-be invaders. Note the medieval wall along Rue de Juiverie, which formed the limit between the cathedral precincts and the Jewish quarter. Inside the cathedral, look for the magnificent 17th-century walnut organ and the frescoes representing the lives of St-Stephen and others. ⊠ *Plan des Albigeois* ☎ *04–67–28–22–89.*

Église de la Madeleine

RELIGIOUS SITE | The heavily restored church, with its distinctive octagonal tower, was the place where the infamous 1209 massacre began. Some 7,000 townspeople, who had sought refuge from Simon de Montfort inside the church, were burned alive before he turned his attention to sacking the town. The event is known as *le grand mazel* (the great bonfire). ⊠ *Off Rue de la République.*

Halles (*Market Hall*)

MARKET | The late-19th-century Halles in Béziers mirrors the style of the architect Baltard, who built the original Les Halles in Paris. This is a particularly beautiful example, with large stone cabbages gracing the entrance like urns. ⊠ *Entrances on Rue Paul Riquet and Pl. Pierre Sémard* ☎ *04–67–49–25–45* ☉ *Closed Mon.*

Jardin des Évêques (*Bishops' Garden*)

GARDEN | Adjoining the cathedral are a 14th-century cloister and the Jardin des Évêques, a terraced garden descending to the banks of the Orb. The views from here, which take in Béziers's five bridges, are magnificent. ⊠ *Plan des Albigeois.*

Hotels

★ Château les Carrasses

$$$ | HOTEL | FAMILY | Enveloped by vineyards, olive trees, lavender, and sunshine, this opulent 19th-century domain lets you experience regal living without the royal stuffiness—self-catering kitchens encourage guests to settle into the gracious

scene. **Pros:** all rooms have kitchens and some have private pools; complimentary bikes available; 10-acre grounds. **Cons:** pricey for the area; skeletal service between mealtimes; breakfast not included. ⓢ *Rooms from: €255* ⊠ *Château les Carrasses, Rte. de Capestang, 20 km (12½ miles) west of Béziers* ☎ *04–67–93–12–33, 04–67–00–00–67 restaurant* ⊕ *www.lescarrasses.com* ☉ *Closed last wk Dec. and 2 wks late Feb.* ⇥ *28 suites* ☒ *No meals.*

Activities

Daylong excursions on the Canal du Midi include passage over the canal bridge spanning the Orb and through the nine locks.

Les Bâteaux du Soleil

TOUR—SPORTS | Cruise companies working the Canal de Midi can have extensive routes—some go as far as the Mediterranean resort town of Agde, 21 km (14 miles) away. Les Bâteaux du Soleil offers a wide range of excursions; the Agde trip is six hours total. ⊠ *Ecluses de Fonseronnes* ☎ *04–67–94–08–79* ⊕ *www. bateaux-du-soleil.fr* ☒ *From €29.*

Montpellier

140 km (87 miles) northeast of Perpignan, 42 km (26 miles) southwest of Nîmes.

The vibrant capital of the Languedoc-Roussillon region, Montpellier (pronounced "monh-pell- *yay*") has been a center of commerce and learning since the Middle Ages, when it was both a crossroads for pilgrims on their way to Santiago de Compostela, in Spain, and an active shipping center trading in spices from the East. Along with exotic luxuries, Montpellier imported Renaissance learning, and its university—founded in the 13th century—has nurtured a steady influx of ideas through the centuries.

Although the port silted up by the 16th century, the city never became a backwater. A student population of some 80,000 keeps things lively, especially on Place de la Comédie; and, as a center of commerce and conferences, Montpellier keeps its focus on the future. An imaginative urban planning program has streamlined the 17th-century Vieille Ville, and monumental perspectives dwarf passersby on the Promenade du Peyrou. An even more utopian venture in urban planning is the Antigone district, a vast, harmonious, 100-acre complex designed in 1984 by Barcelona architect Ricardo Bofill.

GETTING HERE AND AROUND

Air France, easyJet, and Ryanair all serve the Aéroport Montpellier-Méditerranée, southeast of the city; from the airport, you can reach Montpellier via shuttle (€2.60). Multiple TGV rail options will get you here from Paris's Gare de Lyon in 3 hours (about €96). Regional TER rail lines connect the city with destinations like Narbonne (1 hr, €17.70), Toulouse (2 hrs, €25), Carcassonne (90 mins, €27.30), and Perpignan (90 mins, €27.80); there are also direct trains as far afield as Avignon, Nice, and Marseille. If you're trying to get to the sea, hail Bus No. 131 (which passes hourly for Palavas), or take No. 32 to Villeneuve-lès-Maguelone, where you can get one of the city's free Vélomagg' bicycles to pedal the rest of the way.

Montpellier's historic center, with its labyrinth of stone paths and alleys leading from courtyard to courtyard, is well suited to walkers. Hotels, restaurants, and sights can all be reached on foot from Place de la Comédie; however, the city also has a comprehensive public transit system—TAM (⊕ www.tam-voyages.com)—which includes brightly painted tram cars. The Gare Routière bus and tram stations are by the train terminal on Rue Jules Ferry. If you like to cycle, TAM also operates the Vélomagg' bike rental program, with 56 automated stations accessible around the clock.

VISITOR INFORMATION Montpellier
Tourist Office ✉ 30 Pl. de la Comédie ☎ 04–67–60–60–60 ⊕ www.montpellier-france.com.

TOURS

Montpellier Tourist Office

TOUR—SIGHT | English-language walking tours organized by the Montpellier Tourist Office depart on Saturday from the tourism office (€11, reserve online or at the office). If you prefer to explore independently, borrow a free audio guide from the tourism office for a tour of nearby sights. You can also purchase a City Card, good for 24, 48, or 72 hours (€13.50, €19.80, or €25.20), which provides you with free public transport, plus free entry into one tourist site and reduced admission at the others. Other theme tours (food and wine, bicycle, history, and art) can also be reserved online. ✉ Pl. de la Comédie ☎ 04–67–60–60–60 ⊕ www.montpellier-tourisme.fr.

Tourist Train

TOUR—SIGHT | Mid-February through October, a small tourist train with broadcast commentary leaves from Place de la Comédie daily at 11, noon, 2, 3, and 4 (extra runs are added in high season). Tickets cost €8. ✉ Montpellier ☎ 04–67–66–24–38 for info ⊕ www.petittrainmontpellier.fr.

Sights

Antigone

NEIGHBORHOOD | At the far-east end of the city loop, Montpellier seems to transform itself into a futuristic metropolis designed in one smooth, low-slung postmodern style. This is the Antigone district, the result of city planners' efforts (and local industries' commitment) to pull Montpellier up out of its economic doldrums. It worked. This ideal neighborhood, designed by the Catalan architect Ricardo Bofill, covers 100-plus acres with

Both the Three Graces fountain and the Opéra Comédie theater anchor Place de la Comédie, the social and cultural hub of Montpellier.

plazas, esplanades, shops, restaurants, and low-income housing constructed out of stone-color, prestressed concrete. Don't miss Place du Nombre d'Or—symmetrically composed of curves—and the long vista that stretches down a mall of cypress trees to the glass-fronted Hôtel de Region. ⊠ *Montpellier.*

Arc de Triomphe

BUILDING | Looming majestically over the peripheral highway that loops around the city center, this enormous arch is the centerpiece of the Peyrou. Designed by d'Aviler in 1689, it was finished by Giral in 1776. Together, the noble scale of these harmonious stone constructions and the sweeping perspectives they frame make for an inspiring stroll through this upscale stretch of town. At the end of the park is the historic **Château d'Eau,** a Corinthian temple and the terminal for **les Arceaux,** an 18th-century aqueduct; on a clear day the view from here is spectacular, taking in the Cévennes Mountains, the sea, and an ocean of red-tile roofs (it's worth coming back at night to see the entire promenade illuminated). ⊠ *Montpellier.*

Cathédrale St-Pierre

RELIGIOUS SITE | After taking in the broad vistas of the Promenade de Peyrou, cross over into the Vieille Ville and wander its maze of narrow streets full of pretty shops and intimate restaurants. At the northern edge of the Vieille Ville, visit this imposing cathedral. Its fantastical 14th-century entry porch alone warrants the detour: two cone-top towers—some five stories high—flank the main portal and support a groin-vaulted shelter. The interior, despite 18th-century reconstruction, maintains the formal simplicity of its 14th-century origins. ⊠ *Pl. St-Pierre.*

Faculté de Médecine

COLLEGE | Peek into this noble institution on Rue de l'École de Médecine, next door to Cathédrale St-Pierre. Founded in the 13th century and infused with generations of international learning (especially Arab and Jewish scholarship), it is one of France's most respected medical schools and Europe's oldest active one. ⊠ *Rue de l'École de Médecine* ⊕ *www.umontpellier.fr/universite/composantes/faculte-de-medecine.*

Jardin des Plantes

GARDEN | Boulevard Henri IV runs north from the Promenade du Peyrou to France's oldest botanical garden, which was planted on order of Henri IV in 1593. An exceptional range of plants, flowers, and trees grows here. ⊠ *Bd. Henri IV* ☎ 04–34–43–36–20 ⊕ *www.umontpellier.fr/patrimoine/jardin-des-plantes* 🎫 *Free* ♡ *Closed Mon.*

Musée Fabre

MUSEUM | From crowd-packed Place de la Comédie, Boulevard Sarrail leads north past the shady Esplanade Charles de Gaulle to this rich, renowned art museum. The building—combining a 17th-century *hôtel,* a vast Victorian wing with superb natural light, and a remnant of a Baroque Jesuit college—is a mixed bag of architectural styles. The collection inside is surprisingly big, thanks to the museum's namesake, a Montpellier native. François-Xavier Fabre, a student of the great 18th-century French artist David, established roots in Italy and acquired a formidable collection of masterworks—which he then donated to his hometown, supervising the development of this fine museum. Among his gifts were the *Mariage Mystique de Sainte Catherine,* by Veronese, and Poussin's coquettish *Venus et Adonis.* Later contributions include a superb group of 17th-century Flemish works (Rubens, Steen), a collection of 19th-century French canvases (Géricault, Delacroix, Corot, Millet) that inspired Gauguin and Van Gogh, and a growing group of 20th-century acquisitions that buttress a legacy of paintings by early Impressionist Frédéric Bazille. ⊠ *39 bd. Bonne Nouvelle* ☎ 04–67–14–83–00 ⊕ *museefabre.montpellier3m.fr* 🎫 *€8* ♡ *Closed Mon.*

Place de la Comédie

PLAZA | The number of bistros and brasseries increases as you leave the Vieille Ville to cross Place des Martyrs, and if you veer right down Rue de la Loge, you emerge onto the festive gathering spot known as Place de la Comédie. Anchored by the neoclassical 19th-century **Opéra-Comédie,** this broad square is a beehive of leisurely activity, a cross between Barcelona's Ramblas and a Roman *passeggiata* (afternoon stroll, en masse). Eateries and entertainment venues draw crowds, but the real pleasure is getting here and seeing who came before, wearing what, and with whom. ⊠ *Montpellier.*

Promenade du Peyrou

PROMENADE | Montpellier's grandest avenue was built at the end of the 17th century and dedicated to Louis XIV. ⊠ *Montpellier.*

🍴 Restaurants

Cellier Morel (*La Maison de la Lozère*)
$$$$ | MODERN FRENCH | Dine under a medieval vaulted ceiling or in a shaded courtyard at Cellier Morel, arguably the finest restaurant in Montpellier's historic center. Regional specialties are served in haute-cuisine fashion starting with an amuse bouche and ending with a house-made *douceur* (sweet). **Known for:** Montpellier's top table; signature aligot (a mass of potatoes, garlic, and cheese from the Lozère region); region's best bottles on the wine list. $ *Average main: €45* ⊠ *27 rue de l'Aiguillerie* ☎ 04–67–66–46–36 ♡ *Closed Sun. No lunch Mon. and Wed.*

Chistera

$$$ | MODERN FRENCH | Expect to eat well at this pub-restaurant hidden on a backstreet near Place de la Comèdie. The restaurant side is a fashionable steak house *á la francaise,* where cuts of duck and beef are grilled over a wood fire and artfully served. **Known for:** elegant and

upscale sports spot owned by a rugby star; expansive beer list; nice regional selection of wines. $ *Average main: €25* ⊠ *2 bis rue d'Obilion* ☎ *04–67–55–39–51* ☉ *Closed Sun.*

Le Chat Perché

$$$ | FRENCH | This eatery is a popular choice, especially when sunny weather encourages taking a seat on the terrace, overlooking the square below. The cuisine varies with the seasons, the markets, and the humor of the chef, but everything is homemade and reasonably priced. **Known for:** warm bistro ambience; carefully curated regional wine list; traditional dishes served with flair. $ *Average main: €26* ⊠ *Pl. de la Chapelle Neuve, 10 rue college Duvergier* ☎ *04–67–60–88–59* ☉ *Closed Sun. No lunch.*

 # Hotels

★ Baudon de Mauny

$$ | B&B/INN | The finest rooms in Montpellier (and quite possibly the whole region) can be found at this chic guesthouse on one of the historic district's nicest streets. **Pros:** gorgeous architectural design; extra-spacious rooms; flawless service. **Cons:** no on-site parking; several flights of stairs; expensive for the area. $ *Rooms from: €220* ⊠ *1 rue de la Carbonnerie* ☎ *04–67–02–21–77* ⊕ *www. baudondemauny.com* ⇆ *9 rooms* ⦿ *No meals.*

Domaine de Verchant

$$$ | HOTEL | This 14th-century wine-producing estate is now a posh retreat, where stylish rooms are intended for serious comfort and relaxation; walls are encased in old stone, and the decor is supplied by Italian designers. **Pros:** tranquility in the countryside; close to Mediterranean beaches; fine on-site dining. **Cons:** no elevator; far from town center; quite pricey. $ *Rooms from: €290* ⊠ *1 bd. Philippe Lamour, 9 km (5½ miles) northeast of Montpellier, Castelnau le Lez* ☎ *04–67–07–26–00* ⊕ *www. domainedeverchant.com* ⇆ *26 rooms* ⦿ *No meals.*

Le Guilhem

$ | HOTEL | On the same quiet backstreet as the restaurant Le Petit Jardin, this *hôtel de charme* is actually a series of 16th-century houses rebuilt from ruins, replete with an extraordinary old garden. **Pros:** location close to Cathedrale St-Pierre, Jardin des Plantes, and Promenade du Peyrou; on a quiet street; historic ambience. **Cons:** it's a long walk from Place de la Comédie; lacks character; some rooms are very small. $ *Rooms from: €86* ⊠ *18 rue Jean-Jacques-Rousseau* ☎ *04–67–52–90–90* ⊕ *www.leguilhem.com* ⇆ *35 rooms* ⦿ *No meals.*

Les 4 Etoiles

$$ | B&B/INN | In the owner's family for five generations, this 1930s manor features four stylish guest rooms; comfortably equipped with large beds, crisp linens, and grand walk-in showers, they exemplify modern design while still maintaining original features like colorful antique cement tiles and big French windows. **Pros:** personalized service; communal kitchen available; tranquility in the city. **Cons:** 10-minute walk from city center; only four rooms so books up quickly; only serves breakfast so on your own for other meals. $ *Rooms from: €125* ⊠ *3 rue Delmas* ☎ *04–67–02–47–69* ⊕ *www.les4etoiles.com* ⇆ *4 rooms* ⦿ *Free Breakfast.*

THE BASQUE COUNTRY, GASCONY, AND HAUTES-PYRÉNÉES

Updated by
Nick Inman

👁 Sights	🍴 Restaurants	🛏 Hotels	🛍 Shopping	🍸 Nightlife
★★☆☆☆	★★★☆☆	★★☆☆☆	★★☆☆☆	★☆☆☆☆

WELCOME TO THE BASQUE COUNTRY, GASCONY, AND HAUTES-PYRÉNÉES

TOP REASONS TO GO

★ **Biarritz:** This former fishing village has been trumped by a glitzy Second Empire aura, but you won't find the bathing beauties and high rollers complaining.

★ **Basque villages:** The camera-ready villages of Ainhoa, Sare, and St-Jean-de-Luz show off quirky, colorful, and asymmetrical Basque architecture.

★ **Michel Guérard's Les Prés d'Eugénie:** The co-father (with Paul Bocuse) of nouvelle cuisine still creates glorious meals in tucked-away Eugénie-les-Bains.

★ **Gavarnie:** Victor Hugo called the 1,400-foot-high waterfall here "the greatest architect's greatest work."

★ **Pau:** With views of the Pyrénées, Pau is the historic capital of Béarn—and regal monuments recall its royal past as the birthplace of King Henri IV.

1 Bayonne. A graceful French provincial city.

2 Biarritz. The region's imperial beach domain.

3 St-Jean-de-Luz. A vibrant fishing port.

4 Sare. A cozy village with Basque houses and pelota games aplenty.

5 Ainhoa. A charming village set amid picturesque hills.

6 St-Jean-Pied-de-Port. A fortified town known for colorful architecture and flower-festooned balconies.

7 Eugénie-les-Bains. The co-birthplace of nouvelle cuisine (along with Lyon) thanks to Michel Guérard.

8 Pau. The most culturally vibrant city in Gascony and the gateway to the Pyrénées.

9 Lourdes. A town famed for its healing holy waters.

10 Cauterets. A thermal spa town home to the area's best hot springs.

11 Gavarnie. A natural mountain amphitheater that has long attracted travelers, including Victor Hugo.

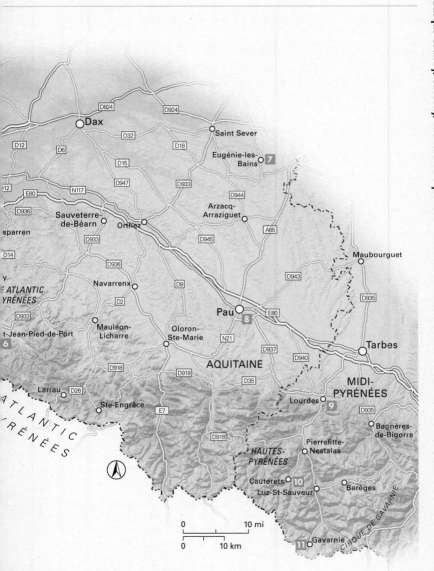

Several years back, a mayor in the province of Soule welcomed a group of travelers with the following announcements: the Basque Country is the most beautiful place in the world; the Basque people are very likely direct descendants of Adam and Eve via the lost city of Atlantis; his own ancestors fought in the Crusades; and Christopher Columbus was almost certainly a Basque. There, in brief, was a composite picture of the pride, dignity, and humor of the Basques.

And if Columbus was not a Basque (a claim very much in doubt), at least historians know that whalers from the regional village of St-Jean-de-Luz sailed as far as America in their three-mast ships, and that Juan Sebastián Elkano, from the Spanish Basque village of Getaria, commanded the completion of Magellan's voyage around the world after Magellan's 1521 death in the Philippines. The distinctive culture—from berets and pelota matches to Basque cooking—of this little "country" has cast its spell over the corners of the Earth.

The most popular gateway to the entire region is Biarritz, the "king" of France's Atlantic coast resorts, whose refinements once attracted the crowned heads of Europe. It was Empress Eugénie who gave Biarritz its coming-out party, transforming it, in the era of Napoléon III, from a simple bourgeois town into an international glitterati favorite. Today, after a round of sightseeing, you can still enjoy the Second Empire trimmings from a perch at the roulette table in the town's casino. Then work on your suntan at Biarritz's famous beach or, a few miles away, really bask under the Basque sun at the picturesque port of St-Jean-de-Luz. As for the entire Pays Basque (Basque Country), it's happily compact: the ocher sands along the Bay of Biscay are less than an hour from the emerald hills of St-Jean-Pied-de-Port in the Basque Pyrénées.

Heading eastward toward the towering peaks of the central Pyrenean cordillera lies the Béarn region, with its splendid capital city of Pau, while northward lies a must-detour for lovers of the good life: Eugénie-les-Bains, where you can savor every morsel of a Michel Guérard

feast at one (or all!) of his magnificently stylish restaurants and hotels. East
through the Aubisque Pass, at the
Béarn's eastern limit, is the heart of the
Hautes-Pyrénées, where the mountains
of Vignemale and Balaïtous compete with
the Cirque de Gavarnie, the world's most
spectacular natural amphitheater, centered on a 1,400-foot waterfall. Whether
you finish up with a vertiginous Pyrenean
hike or choose to pay your respects
to the religious shrine at Lourdes, this
region will lift your spirits.

GETTING ORIENTED

This is the southwesternmost corner of
France's sprawling "Southwest." The rolling hills of the Basque provinces stretch
from the Atlantic beaches of glittering
Biarritz to the first Pyrenean heights: the
hills and highlands of Gascony around
the city of Pau. These are mere stepping-stones compared to the peaks of
the Hautes-Pyrénées, which lie to the
east and sit in the center of the towering
barrier historically separating the Iberian
Peninsula from continental Europe.

MAJOR REGIONS

The Basque Coast. La Côte Basque—a
world unto itself with its own language,
sports, and folklore—occupies France's
southwest corner along the Spanish
border. Inland, the area is laced with
rivers: the Bidasoa River border with
Spain marks the southern edge of the
region, and the Adour River, on its northern edge, separates the Basque Country
from neighboring Les Landes. The Nive
River flows through the heart of the
verdant Basque littoral to join the Adour
at Bayonne, and the smaller Nivelle River
flows into the Bay of Biscay at St-Jean-
de-Luz. Bayonne, Biarritz, and St-Jean-de-
Luz are the main towns along the coast,
all less than 40 km (25 miles) from the
first peak of the Pyrénées.

The Atlantic Pyrénées and Gascony. The
Atlantic Pyrénées extend eastward from
the ocean to the Col du Pourtalet, and

encompass the inland uplands of the
Basque Country as well as the mountains
and valleys of the neighboring region of
the Béarn. The Atlantic Pyrénées's first
major height is at La Rhune (2,969 feet),
known as the Balcon du Côte Basque
(Balcony of the Basque Coast). The
highest Basque peak is at Orhi (6,617
feet); the Béarn's highest is Pic d'Anie
(8,510 feet). Beneath these heights are
a series of immaculate villages—including Sare and Ainhoa—that serve as
picturesque stepping-stones leading to
St-Jean-Pied-de-Port.

This journey ends in Pau, in the Béarn
region, far from the Pays Basque. The
Béarn is akin in temperament to the
larger region that enfolds it, Gascony.
Gascony may not be as rich as some
regions of France, but it is certainly rich
in scenery and lore. Its proud and touchy
temperament is typified in literature by
the character d'Artagnan in Dumas's
The Three Musketeers, and in history
by the lords of the château of Pau. An
inscription over the château's entrance—
"*Touchez-y, si tu l'oses*" (Touch this if
you dare)—was left by the golden-haired
Gaston Phoebus (1331–91), 11th count of
Foix and viscount of Béarn, a volatile arts
lover with a nasty temper who murdered
his brother and his only son. To the north
the hills of Gascony morph into those of
the Landes region, where a charming valley shelters the spa and culinary paradise
of Eugenie-les-Bains.

The Hautes-Pyrénées. East of the Béarn is
the aptly named region of the Hautes-
Pyrénées (High Pyrenees), which
contains the highest and most spectacular natural wonders in the cordillera: the
legendary Cirque de Gavarnie (a natural
mountain amphitheater), the Vignemale
(the highest summit in southern France
at 10,833 feet), and the craggy gateway
of the Brèche de Roland. The valleys here
all run north to south, reducing east–
west travel to a slow, meandering pace.
Adjoining valleys are connected by roads

that snake over bleak mountain passes used by the route planners of the Tour de France. The world-famous shrine town of Lourdes, in the foothills, makes an excellent low-altitude base for exploring the heights.

Planner

When to Go

The Basque Country is known for its wet climate, but when the skies clear the hillsides are so green and the air so clean that the weather gods are immediately forgiven. Late fall and winter are generally rainier than early autumn or late spring. The Pyrenean heights such as Brèche de Roland and Gavarnie, on the other hand, may only be approached safely in midsummer. Treacherous ice and snow plaques can be present even in mid-June, and summer blizzards remain a risk. Climate change may be shrinking glaciers and extending the safety period in the high Pyrénées, but freak conditions—the reverse side of the same coin—may be creating even more unpredictable and dangerous weather patterns. Beach weather is from May through September, and sometimes lasts until mid-October's été de la St-Martin (Indian summer). Skiing conditions are reliable from December through March and, on occasion, into April.

Planning Your Time

Traveling west to east, with the sun behind you as the shadows lengthen, is the best way to approach this part of the Pyrénées. Bayonne is the natural starting point, at the mouth of the Atlantic Pyrenean watershed, with the Basque Museum as an instructive primer for the culture of the villages you are about to go through. Biarritz and St-Jean-de-Luz offer opportunities for beach time and

glamour. The picturesque villages of Sare and Ainhoa guide you into the mountains and valleys, threaded by rivers flowing into the Nive. St-Jean-Pied-de-Port is a Pyrenean hub from which Eugénie-les-Bains is a short detour before continuing east to Pau, the Hautes-Pyrénées, and their crowning glory, Gavarnie.

Wherever you head, take your time: this region's proximity to Spain comes to life in its architecture, in the expressive Midi accent, which turns the word demain (tomorrow) into "demaing," and the slow-paced lifestyle.

Getting Here and Around

A car is best for getting around the Basque Coast and the Pyrénées. The mountain roads are good, albeit slow—60–70 kph (37–43 mph) on average. But the A64 highway from Bayonne to Pau is fast and has spectacular views of the Pyrénées. Train and bus connections will get you from Bayonne to Biarritz and up to St-Jean-Pied-de-Port easily; moving east, Pau and Lourdes are readily accessible as well. Public transportation to less pivotal destinations, however, can entail much waiting and loss of valuable time.

AIR TRAVEL

Air France (⊕ www.airfrance.com) serves the Aéroport de Biarritz-Anglet-Bayonne with six direct daily flights from Paris; easyJet (⊕ www.easyjet.com) also operates one flight per day from the capital, and Ryanair (⊕ www.ryanair.com) offers a London link three times per week. Once you arrive, Chronoplus buses will take you to train stations in Biarritz (10 mins) or Bayonne (30 mins) for €1. Air France lands another six direct daily flights from Paris at the Aéroport Pau-Pyrénées; the airport is also connected to Lyon by HOP! (⊕ www.hop.com) and to Marseille by Twinjet (⊕ www.twinjet.fr). You'll pay €1 for the half-hour ride from the airport into town.

CONTACTS Aéroport de Biarritz Pays Basque ☎ *05–59–43–83–83* ⊕ *www.biarritz.aeroport.fr.* **Aéroport Pau-Pyrénées** ☎ *05–59–33–33–00* ⊕ *www.pau.aeroport.fr.*

BUS TRAVEL

Numerous private bus companies are consolidated into regional bus networks. Key ones include Transports-64 (covering the Pyrénées-Atlantiques department from Lourdes to the coast), Chronoplus (covering the Bayonne-Anglet-Biarritz greater metropolitan area), and R.D.T. L. (covering the Landes department). Where the regional network buses don't go, the trusty SNCF national bus lines occasionally do (⊕ *www.oui.sncf*). Local tourist offices and train stations can provide you with schedules and network maps. When traveling by bus in summer, beware of peak-hour traffic on roads, which can mean both delays and fewer seats on buses.

BUS INFORMATION Chronoplus ☎ *05–59–52–59–52* ⊕ *www.chronoplus.eu.* **R.D.T.L. Buses** ✉ *Bayonne* ☎ *05–58–05–66–00* ⊕ *www.rdtl.fr.* **Transports-64** ☎ *08–00–64–24–64* ⊕ *www.transports64.fr.*

CAR TRAVEL

The A64 connects Pau and Bayonne in less than an hour, and the A63 runs up and down the Atlantic coast. The N134-E7 connects Bordeaux, Pau, and Spain via the Col de Somport and Jaca. The D918 along the Nive River from St-Jean-de-Luz to St-Jean-Pied-de-Port is a pretty drive, continuing on (as the D918, D919, and D933) through the Béarn countryside to Pau. Roads are often slow and tortuous in the more mountainous areas, but valley and riverside roads are generally quite smooth and fast.

TRAIN TRAVEL

High-speed TGV Inoui trains link Paris to Bayonne (5 hrs), to Biarritz (5 hrs 15 mins), and to Pau (5 hrs 34 mins). Biarritz has trains connecting with Bayonne, Bordeaux, St-Jean-de-Luz, and many other destinations. Bayonne and Toulouse are connected by SNCF trains via Pau, Tarbes, and Lourdes. Bayonne also has links to other popular locales (like St-Jean-de-Luz). Hendaye is connected to Bayonne and to San Sebastián via the famous *topo* (mole) train, so called for the number of tunnels it passes through.

TRAIN INFORMATION Bayonne ✉ *Pl. Pereire, Bayonne* ⊕ *www.gares-sncf. com.* **Biarritz** ✉ *18 allée Moura, Biarritz* ⊕ *www.gares-sncf.com.* **SNCF** ☎ *3635 (€0.40 per min)* ⊕ *www.oui.sncf.* **TGV Inoui** ⊕ *www.oui.sncf.*

Restaurants

Dining in the regions of the Basque Country is invariably a feast, whether it's seafood, local lamb, or the famous migratory *palombes* (wood pigeons). Dishes to keep in mind include *ttoro* (hake stew), *pipérade* (tomatoes and green peppers cooked in olive oil, and often scrambled eggs), *bakalao al pil-pil* (cod cooked in oil—"al pil-pil" refers to the bubbling sound the fish makes as it creates its own sauce), *marmitako* (tuna and potato stew), and *zikiro* (roast lamb). Home of the eponymous *sauce béarnaise,* Béarn is also famous for its *garbure,* a thick vegetable soup with *confit de canard* (preserved duck) and *fèves* (broad beans).

Civets (stews) made with *isard* (wild goat) or wild boar are other specialties. La Bigorre and the Hautes-Pyrénées are equally dedicated to garbure, though they may call their version *soupe paysanne bigourdane* (Bigorran peasant soup) to distinguish it from that of their neighbors. The Basque Coast's traditional fresh seafood is unsurpassable every day of the week except Monday, the fleet having stayed in port on Sunday. The inland Basque Country and upland Béarn are famous for game in fall and winter and lamb in spring. In the Hautes-Pyrénées, the higher altitude makes power dining attractive and thick bean soups and wild-boar stews come into their own.

Hotels

From palatial beachside splendor in Biarritz to simple mountain auberges in the Basque country and Pyrenean refuges in the Hautes-Pyrénées, the gamut of lodging in southwest France is conveniently broad. Be sure to book summertime accommodations on the Basque Coast well in advance, particularly for August. In the Hautes-Pyrénées, Lourdes presents the greatest challenge. Pilgrims pack the place between Easter and All Saint's Day (November 1), with August 15 being especially busy, so make reservations as far ahead as possible. *Restaurant and hotel reviews have been shortened. For full information, visit Fodors.com.*

What It Costs in Euros			
$	$$	$$$	$$$$
RESTAURANTS			
under €16	€16–€24	€25–€32	over €32
HOTELS			
under €125	€125–€225	€226–€350	over €350

Visitor Information

The Atlantic and Hautes-Pyrénées region has three main tourist offices. For Biarritz and France's Big Sur in the southwest corner of the country, contact the Comité Régional du Tourisme d'Aquitaine. For Pau and the Basque and Béarnaise Pyrénées, contact the Comité Départemental du Tourisme Béarn Pays Basque in Pau. For Gavarnie and the Hautes-Pyrénées contact the Hautes-Pyrénées Tourisme office in Tarbes. ⇨ *For specific local tourist offices, see the town entries in this chapter.*

CONTACTS Comité Départemental du Tourisme Béarn Pays Basque ⊠ *12 bd. Hauterive, Pau* ☎ *05–59–30–01–30* ⊕ *www.tourisme64.com.* **Comité Departmentale du Tourisme des Landes** ⊠ *Av. Aristide Briand, Mont-de-Marsan, Eugénie-les-Bains* ☎ *05–58–06–89–89* ⊕ *www.tourismelandes.com.* **Tourisme Hautes-Pyrénées** ⊠ *11 rue Gaston Manent, BP 9502, Tarbes* ☎ *05–62–56–70–00* ⊕ *www.tourisme-hautes-pyrenees.com.*

Bayonne

184 km (114 miles) south of Bordeaux, 295 km (183 miles) west of Toulouse.

Located at the confluence of the Adour and Nive Rivers, Bayonne was a Roman *castrum* (fort) in the 4th century and an English colony from 1151 to 1451; today it is the proud capital of the Pays Basque. Even though its port is spread out along an estuary some 5 km (3 miles) inland from the sea, two rivers and five bridges lend this small city a definite maritime feel. From the elegant 18th-century homes along Rue des Prébendés to the 17th-century ramparts and the market stalls of Place des Halles, it is a city worth wandering.

GETTING HERE AND AROUND

Air France, Ryanair, and easyJet planes land at the Aéroport de Biarritz Pays Basque; a shuttle bus runs from there to the central train station (30 mins, €1). Four daily TGV Inoui trains connect Bayonne and Paris (5 hrs, €80). Train connections from Bayonne include St-Jean-de-Luz (28 mins, €6), St-Jean-Pied-de-Port (1 hr 26 mins, €10.10), Pau (1 hr 33 mins, €18.60), Lourdes (1 hr 44 mins, €24.60), Bordeaux (1 hr 39 mins, €33), and Toulouse (3 hrs 21 mins, €49). Frequent daily trains also make the short jaunt to Biarritz (8 mins, €2.90). The Chronoplus bus network connects Bayonne with towns on the French Basque Coast, notably Biarritz (15 mins, €1) and Anglet (20 mins, €1).

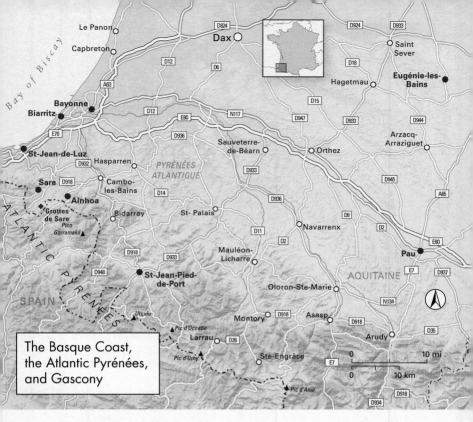

The Basque Coast,
the Atlantic Pyrénées,
and Gascony

Sights

Cathédrale

RELIGIOUS SITE | Built mainly in the 13th
century, the Cathédrale (called both
Ste-Marie and Notre-Dame) is one
of France's southernmost examples
of Gothic architecture. Its 13th- to
14th-century cloisters are among its
best features. ⊠ *Pl. Mr Vansteenberghe*
☎ *05–59–59–17–82* ⊕ *www.cathe-
drale-bayonne.fr* 🎟 *Free.*

Musée Basque

MUSEUM | The handsomely designed and
appointed Musée Basque on the right
bank of the Nive offers an ethnographic history of the Basque Country and
culture. ⊠ *37 quai des Corsaires* ☎ *05–
59–59–08–98* ⊕ *www.musee-basque.
com* 🎟 *€8* ⊘ *Closed Mon. Sept.–June.*

 Restaurants

Bayonnais

$$ | BISTRO | Next to the Musée Basque,
with a dining terrace over the River Nive
just short of its confluence with the
Adour, this unassuming and unpretentious local favorite serves honest Basque
cuisine in a traditional setting. The
agneau de lait (suckling lamb) and *chip-
irons en persillade* (cuttlefish in chopped
parsley and garlic) are classics. **Known for:**
river views; central location close to the
sights; traditional Basque dishes. $ *Aver-
age main: €20* ⊠ *38 quai des Corsaires*
☎ *05–59–25–61–19* ⊘ *Closed Sun. and
Mon. Sept.–mid-July.*

L'Auberge du Cheval Blanc

$$$ | FRENCH | Run by the Tellechea family since 1715, this former stagecoach inn in the Petit Bayonne quarter serves a combination of *cuisine du terroir* (home-style regional cooking) and original recipes in contemporary surroundings. Michelin-starred chef Jean-Claude Tellechea showcases fresh fish as well as upland specialties from the Basque hills, sometimes joining the two in dishes such as the *merlu rôti aux oignons et jus de volaille* (hake roasted in onions with essence of poultry). **Known for:** Basque wines; some of the best fine dining in the area; celebrated chef. $ *Average main: €30* ✉ *68 rue Bourgneuf* ☎ *05–59–59–01–33* ⊕ *www.cheval-blanc-bayonne.com* ⏲ *Closed Mon. No lunch Sat. No dinner Sun.*

 ## Hotels

Le Grand Hôtel

$ | HOTEL | Just down the street from the Château-Vieux, this reasonably priced Mercure property offers an old-world feel in a great location. **Pros:** prime location; triple and quad rooms good for families; helpful staff. **Cons:** pricey breakfast; vintage elevator not everyone's cup of tea; somewhat impersonal atmosphere. $ *Rooms from: €84* ✉ *21 rue Thiers* ☎ *05–59–59–62–00* ⊕ *www.legrandhotel-bayonne.com* ⤶ *54 rooms* �“❘ *No meals.*

 ## Shopping

Atelier du Chocolat de Bayonne

FOOD/CANDY | FAMILY | Fancy chocolates are a specialty of the Basque Country, and you can sample some at this store that is also a workshop. Before you decide which kind to take home, take a tour (€6) to watch chocolates being made by the chefs and try some samples. ✉ *7 allée de Gibéléou* ☎ *05–59–55–70–23* ⊕ *www.atelierduchocolat.fr.*

Biarritz

8 km (5 miles) south of Bayonne, 190 km (118 miles) southwest of Bordeaux, 50 km (31 miles) north of San Sebastián, Spain.

Biarritz may no longer lay claim to the title "the resort of kings and the king of resorts," but there's no shortage of deluxe hotel rooms or bow-tied gamblers ambling over to the casino. The city first rose to prominence when rich and royal Carlist exiles from Spain set up shop here in 1838. Unable to visit San Sebastián—just across the border on the Basque Coast—they sought a summer watering spot as close as possible to their old stomping ground. Among the exiles was Eugénie de Montijo, destined to become empress of France. As a child, she vacationed here with her family, fell in love with the place, and then set about building her own palace once she married Napoléon III. During the 14 summers she spent here, half the crowned heads of Europe (including Queen Victoria and Edward VII) were guests in Eugénie's villa: a gigantic wedding-cake edifice, now the Hôtel du Palais, on Biarritz's main seaside promenade. Whether you consider the bombastic architectural legacies of that era an eyesore or an eyeful, the builders at least had the courage of their convictions. If you want to rediscover yesteryear Biarritz, start by exploring the narrow streets around the cozy 16th-century church of St-Martin.

GETTING HERE AND AROUND

The Aéroport de Biarritz Pays Basque receives flights from Air France, Ryanair, and easyJet; a shuttle bus from the airport takes 10 minutes and costs €1. TGV Inoui trains connect Paris and Biarritz six times daily (5 hrs 15 mins, €75). Biarritz's train station has rail connections with St-Jean-de-Luz (12 mins, €3.50), Bordeaux (1 hr, €33.80), and many other places, including San Sebastián, Spain, via Hendaye (1 hr 20 mins, €25). Multiple trains also arrive daily from Bayonne (8 mins, €2.90) and Pau (1 hr 50 mins, €26). The station is 3 km (2 miles) southeast of the city core, so catch Bus No. 2 to reach the centrally located Hôtel de Ville, near the main beach. Chronoplus buses serve the Biarritz-Anglet-Bayonne area (€1); Transports-64 buses travel regularly to and from other Basque towns, including St-Jean-de-Luz.

VISITOR INFORMATION Biarritz Tourist Office ✉ *1 sq. d'Ixelles* ☎ *05–59–22–37–10* 🌐 *www.tourisme.biarritz.fr.*

Sights

Église Orthodoxe Russe

RELIGIOUS SITE | Eugénie and her Carlist compatriots weren't the only exiled royals to arrive in Biarritz. White Russians found refuge, too, turning the city into their Yalta-by-the-Atlantic. Witness the Église Orthodoxe Russe, a Byzantine-style church they built adjacent to the Grand Plage in the early 1890s. ✉ *8 rue de l'Impératrice* ☎ *05–59–24–16–74* 🌐 *www.eglise-orthodoxe-biarritz.com* 🕓 *Closed weekdays.*

La Chapelle Impériale

RELIGIOUS SITE | If you wish to pay your respects to the Empress Eugénie, visit La Chapelle Impériale, which she had built in 1864 to venerate a figure of a Mexican Black Virgin from Guadalupe (and perhaps to expiate her sins for furthering her husband's tragic folly of putting Emperor Maximilian and Empress Carlotta on the "throne" of Mexico). The style is a charming hybrid of Roman-Byzantine and Hispano-Mauresque. ✉ *Rue des Cents Gardes* ☎ *05–59–22–37–10* 🕓 *Closed Sun.*

La Grande Plage

BEACH—SIGHT | Biarritz's urban beaches are understandably popular—particularly the fine, sandy strands of La Grande Plage and the neighboring Plage Miramar, both set amid craggy natural beauty. A walk along the seaside promenade gives a view of the foaming breakers that beat constantly upon the sands, giving the name Côte d'Argent (Silver Coast) to this part of France's Basque Coast. As you drink in that view, try to imagine the gilded days when the fashionable set used to stroll here in Worth gowns and picture hats. ✉ *Biarritz.*

Place Ste-Eugénie

PLAZA | During Biarritz's original heyday, the elite often retired to the terraced restaurants of festive Place Ste-Eugénie, still considered the social center of town. ✉ *Pl. Ste-Eugénie.*

Restaurants

Chez Albert

$$$ | SEAFOOD | The Port des Pêcheurs (Fishing Port) provides a tantalizing glimpse of old Biarritz, plus some tantalizing dining options. Water views and salty harborside aromas make Chez Albert's hearty fish and seafood offerings all the more irresistible. **Known for:** big crowds, especially in summer, so get there early; delicious seafood; beautiful ocean views from terrace. [$] *Average main: €25* ✉ *51 bis allée Port des Pêcheurs* ☎ *05–59–24–43–84* 🌐 *www.chezalbert.fr* 🕓 *Closed Dec., Jan., and Wed.*

Hotels

Château de Brindos

$$$ | HOTEL | Take Jazz Age glamour, Renaissance stonework, the most luxe of guest rooms, and add fine dining, and you have this Pays Basque Xanadu—a large, rambling, white-stone manor topped with a Spanish belvedere tower set 4 km (2½ miles) east of Biarritz in Anglet. **Pros:** flawless performance by staff; excellent dining; ultimate comfort. **Cons:** fitness facilities limited; addictively grande luxe; far from the city's sights. [$] *Rooms from: €246* ✉ *1 allée du Château, Anglet* ☎ *05–59–23–89–80* 🌐 *www.chateaudebrindos.com* 🕓 *Closed 2 wks*

What is Basque Culture?

While the Basque Country's future as an independent nation-state has yet to be determined, the quirky, fascinating culture of the Basque people is not restricted by any borders. Experience it for yourself in the food, history, and sport.

Origins of Basque

Stretching across the Pyrénées from Bayonne in France to Bilbao in Spain, the New Hampshire--size Basque region retains a distinct culture, neither expressly French nor Spanish, fiercely guarded by its 3 million inhabitants. Fables stubbornly connect them with Adam and Eve, Noah's Ark, and the lost city of Atlantis, but a leading genealogical theory points to common bloodlines with the Celts. The most tenable theory is that the Basques are descended from aboriginal Iberian people who successfully defended their unique cultural identity from the influences of Roman and Moorish domination.

It was only in 1876 that Sabino Arana—a virulent anti-Spanish fanatic—proposed the ideal of a "pure" Basque independent state. That dream was crushed by Franco's dictatorial reign (1939--75), during which many Spanish Basques emigrated to France, and was immortalized in Pablo Picasso's *Guernica*. This famous painting, which depicts the catastrophic Nazi bombing of the Basque town of Gernika, stands not only as a searing indictment of all wars but as a reminder of history's brutal assault upon Basque identity.

Basque Cooking

An old saying has it that every soccer team needs a Basque goaltender and every restaurant a Basque chef. Traditional Basque cuisine combines the fresh fish of the Atlantic and upland vegetables, beef, and lamb with a love of sauces that is rare south of the Pyrénées. Today, the *nueva cocina vasca* (new Basque cooking) movement has made Basque food less rustic and much more nouvelle. And now that *pintxos* (the Basque equivalent of tapas) have become the rage from Barcelona to New York City, Basque cuisine is being championed by foodies everywhere. Even superchef Michel Guérard up in Eugénie-les-Bains has, though not himself a Basque, influenced and been influenced by the master cookery of the Pays Basque.

Popular Basque dishes include *angulas,* baby eels cooked in olive oil and garlic with a few slices of guindilla pepper; *bacalao al pil-pil,* cod cooked at a low temperature in an emulsion of olive oil and fish juices, making a unique pinging sound when it sizzles; *besugo,* or sea bream, a traditional Christmas dish enjoyed with *sagardo,* the signature Basque apple cider; *marmitako,* tuna stew with potatoes and pimientos; *ttoro,* peppery Basque bouillabaisse; and *txuletas de buey,* ox steaks marinated in parsley and garlic and cooked over coals.

Basque Sports

Over the centuries, the rugged physical environment of the Basque hills and the rough Cantabrian sea traditionally made physical prowess and bravery valued attributes. Since Basque mythology often involved feats of strength, it's easy to see why today's Basques are such rabid sports fans.

A Basque village without a *frontón* (a pelota court) is as unimaginable as an American town without a baseball diamond. "The fastest game in the world," pelota is called *jai-alai* in Basque (and translated officially as "merry festival"). With rubber balls flung from hooked wicker gloves at speeds up to 150 mph—the impact of the ball is like a machine-gun bullet— jai-alai is mesmerizing. Whether singles or doubles, the object is to angle the ball along or off of the side wall so that it cannot be returned. Betting is very much part of the game, and courtside wagers are brokered by bet makers as play proceeds. While pelota is the word for "ball," it also refers to the game.

Herrikirolak (rural sports) are based on farming and seafaring. Stone lifters heft weights up to 700 pounds and *aizkolari* (axe men) chop wood in various contests while a gizon proba (man trial) pits three-man teams moving weighted sleds. *Estropadak* are whaleboat rowers who compete in spectacular regattas, culminating in the September competition off La Concha beach in San Sebastián, Spain. *Sokatira* is tug-of-war, and *segalariak* is a scything competition. Other events include oxcart lifting, milk-can carrying, and ram fights.

Speaking Basque

Although the Basque people speak French north of the border and Spanish south of the border, they consider Euskera their first language and identify themselves as the Euskaldunak (the "Basque speakers"). Euskera remains one of the great enigmas of linguistic scholarship. Theories connect it with everything from Sanskrit to Japanese to Finnish. What is certain is where Euskera did *not* come from, namely the Indo-European family of languages that includes the Germanic, Italic, and Hellenic language groups. Currently used by about a million people in northern Spain and southwestern France, Euskera sounds like a consonant-ridden version of Spanish, with its five pure vowels, rolled "r," and palatal "n" and "l." Basque has survived two millennia of cultural and political pressure and is the only remaining language that was spoken in south-western Europe before the Roman conquest.

Biarritz's main beach, the Grande Plage, is the town's focal point, especially for those who don't have money to lose in the resort casinos.

in Feb. and Mar. ➡ 29 rooms ⦿ No meals.

Hôtel du Palais

$$$$ | HOTEL | Set on the beach, this majestic, colonnaded redbrick hotel with an immense driveway, lawns, and a grand semicircular dining room still exudes an opulent, aristocratic air, no doubt imparted by Empress Eugénie who built it in 1855 as her Biarritz palace. **Pros:** historic grounds; gastronomical nirvana; perfect location. **Cons:** staff obsessed with hotel rules; slightly stuffy; magisterially expensive. ⓢ Rooms from: €525 ✉ 1 av. de l'Impératrice ☎ 05–59–41–64–00 ⊕ www.hotel-du-palais.com ➡ 139 rooms ⦿ No meals.

La Ferme de Biarritz

$ | B&B/INN | For those in search of rustic and affordable quarters near swank Biarritz, this beautifully restored 17th-century farmhouse offers the best of both worlds—particularly delightful are the guest rooms' antique furnishings, which might have been used by Empress Eugénie herself. **Pros:** near the beach; cute dormer rooms with antique furniture; breakfast in the garden or in front of the fire. **Cons:** small rooms; no restaurant; one-week minimum stay in summer. ⓢ Rooms from: €80 ✉ 15 rue Harcet ☎ 05–59–23–40–27 ⊕ www.fermedebiarritz.com ▬ No credit cards ⊙ Closed Jan. ➡ 7 rooms ⦿ No meals.

Maïtagaria

$ | HOTEL | This typical Basque town house 400 yards from the beach is a handy and comfortable family operation that makes you feel more like a guest in a private home than a hotel patron. **Pros:** good price and location; intimate yet friendly; leafy garden. **Cons:** somewhat cramped quarters; limited soundproofing (and thus privacy); decor and furniture somewhat unexciting. ⓢ Rooms from: €65 ✉ 34 av. Carnot ☎ 05–59–24–26–65 ⊕ www.hotel-maitagaria.com ⊙ Closed 3 wks around Christmas ➡ 15 rooms ⦿ No meals.

Windsor

$ | HOTEL | Built in the 1920s, close to the casino and overlooking the Grand Plage, this service-oriented hotel has crisp, contemporary accommodations with light walls and linens offset by bright splashes of color; rooms with sea views cost about twice as much as the larger ones facing the inner courtyard and street. **Pros:** central beachfront location; excellent restaurant; expert service. **Cons:** sea views cost double; street rooms get some noise; can be lines for the elevator. $ *Rooms from: €109* ⊠ *11 av. Edouard VII* ☎ *05–59–24–08–52* ⊕ *www.hotelwindsorbiarritz.com* ⤳ *48 rooms* ⦿ *No meals.*

▼ Nightlife

Casino de Biarritz

CASINOS | At the glitzy Casino de Biarritz you can play the slots and blackjack or just chill while channeling your inner James Bond. It's open daily from 9 am until 4 am. ⊠ *1 av. Edouard-VII* ☎ *05–59–22–77–77* ⊕ *www.lucienbarriere.com/fr/casino/biarritz/accueil.html.*

Le Carré Coast

MUSIC CLUBS | Sip cocktails while listening to soul, jazz, and house music in a glamorous setting close to the surf. ⊠ *7 bd. de Général de Gaulle* ☎ *05–59–24–64–64.*

Le Caveau

DANCE CLUBS | There's guaranteed action every night at Le Caveau—a legendary Biarritz dance club. ⊠ *4 rue Gambetta* ☎ *05–59–24–16–17* ⊕ *www.caveau-biarritz.com.*

Le Playboy

BARS/PUBS | In the summer, the surfing crowd fills Le Playboy. ⊠ *15 pl. Georges Clémenceau* ☎ *05–59–24–38–46.*

Newquay

BARS/PUBS | This midtown Irish pub is popular with surfers. ⊠ *20 pl. Georges Clemenceau* ☎ *05–59–22–19–90.*

⚡ Performing Arts

Le Temps d'Aimer

FESTIVALS | In September (or occasionally October), the three-week Le Temps d'Aimer festival presents dance performances, from classical to hip-hop, in a range of venues throughout the city. They're often held at the Théâtre Gare du Midi, a renovated railway station. Troupes such as the Ballets Biarritz, Les Ballets de Monte-Carlo, and leading *étoiles* from other companies take to the stage in an ambitious schedule of events, with admission generally starting at about €20. ⊠ *Biarritz* ⊕ *www.letempsdaimer.com.*

🏃 Activities

Biarritz Athletic Club

LOCAL SPORTS | Instruction in every type of Basque pelota—including *main nue* (bare-handed), *pala* (paddle), *chistera* (with a basketlike racquet), and *cesta punta* (another game played with the same curved basket)—is available at the Biarritz Athletic Club. It also organizes the Biarritz Masters Jai-Alai tournament in July, as well as Golden Glove boxing competitions. ⊠ *Parc des Sports d'Aguilera, Fronton Euskal Jai* ☎ *05–59–23–91–09* ⊕ *www.cesta-punta.com.*

Golf de Biarritz Le Phare

GOLF | Greens fees at the 18-hole, par-69 Golf de Biarritz Le Phare course start at €78 in the height of summer. ⊠ *2 av. Edith-Cavell* ☎ *05–59–03–71–80* ⊕ *www.golfbiarritz.com.*

Parc des Sports d'Aguilera

LOCAL SPORTS | This stadium is the fiefdom of the champion rugby club Biarritz Olympique. Call for information or check the website for scheduled matches. ⊠ *Biarritz* ☎ *05–59–01–64–60* ⊕ *www.bo-pb.com.*

Surfing in Biarritz

For wave action in Europe's hot-cool surfing center, head to the coast north of Biarritz and the towns of Anglet and Hossegor. La Barre beach doubles as the hangout for dedicated surfers who live out of their vans. On the southern end (by the Anglet-Biarritz border) are surf shops, snack bars, and one boulangerie. These give the main beach drag, Chambre d'Amour, a decidedly California flair. If you're coming by train, get off in Bayonne or Biarritz and transfer to a Chronoplus bus bound for Anglet. The main tourist office (⊠ *1 av. de la Chambre d'Amour* ☎ *05–59–03–77–01* ⊕ *www.anglet-tourisme.com*) is closed off-season. Hossegor, 20 km (12 miles) north of Bayonne, hosts the Rip Curl Pro and the ASO Junior Surf Tour Championships every August as well as the ASP World Tour competition in September.

St-Jean-de-Luz

23 km (16 miles) southwest of Bayonne, 54 km (32 miles) northwest of St-Jean-Pied-de-Port.

Back in 1660, Louis XIV chose this tiny fishing village as the place to marry the Infanta Maria Teresa of Spain. Ever since, travelers have journeyed here to enjoy the unique charms of St-Jean. Along the coast between Biarritz and the Spanish border, it remains memorable for its colorful harbor, old streets, curious church, and elegant beach. Its iconic port shares a harbor with its sister town Ciboure, on the other side of the Nivelle River. The glorious days of whaling and cod fishing are long gone, but some historic multihue houses around the docks are evocative enough.

GETTING HERE AND AROUND

Frequent train service is available from Biarritz (12 mins, €3.50) and Bayonne (23 mins, €6). Regional Transports-64 buses also arrive at Place Maréchal Foch by the tourist office. Though slower than the train and only slightly less expensive, buses give you more beach-town options.

VISITOR INFORMATION St-Jean-de-Luz
Tourist Office ⊠ *Pl. Foch* ☎ *05–59–26–03–16* ⊕ *www.saint-jean-de-luz.com*.

⊙ Sights

Église St-Jean-Baptiste
RELIGIOUS SITE | The marriage of the Sun King and the Infanta took place in 1660 in the church of St-Jean-Baptiste. The marriage tied the knot, so to speak, on the Pyrénées Treaty signed by French chief minister Mazarin on November 7, 1659, ending Spanish hegemony in Europe. Note the church's unusual wooden galleries lining the walls, creating a theaterlike effect. Fittingly, St-Jean-Baptiste hosts a "Musique en Côte Basque" festival of early and Baroque music during the first two weeks of September. ⊠ *Pl. des Corsaires.*

Maison Louis-XIV
HOUSE | Take a tour of the twin-tower Maison Louis-XIV. Built as the Château Lohobiague, it housed the French king during his nuptials and is austerely decorated in 17th-century Basque fashion. ⊠ *Pl. Louis XIV* ☎ *05–59–26–27–58* ⊕ *www.maison-louis-xiv.fr* ⊠ *€7* ⊙ *Closed Tues., and Nov.–Easter.*

Place Louis-XIV
PLAZA | Tree-lined Place Louis-XIV, alongside the Hôtel de Ville, with its dainty statue of Louis XIV on horseback, is the hub of the town. In summer, concerts are offered on the square, as well as the famous "Toro de Fuego" festival, which

honors the bull with a parade and a papier-mâché beast. ✉ *St-Jean-de-Luz.*

🍴 Restaurants

Chez Pablo

$$ | **SEAFOOD** | The catch of the day determines the offerings here. Long tables covered with red-and-white tablecloths, benches, and plaster walls give off a casual vibe, but the dishes are often excellent. **Known for:** informal atmosphere; rotating menu of seafood classics; takeaway food. [$] *Average main: €17* ✉ *5 rue Mlle. Etcheto* ☎ *05–59–26–37–81* 🌐 *www.restaurant-chez-pablo.com* 🕒 *Closed Wed.*

Txalupa

$$ | **SEAFOOD** | The name is Basque for "skiff" or "small boat," and you feel like you're in one when you are this close to the bay—yachts and fishing vessels go about their business just a few yards away. The mixed seafood platter here is legendary, and daily nonstop service from noon to midnight makes it a hard meal to miss. **Known for:** excellent seafood; good draft beer; late night hours. [$] *Average main: €22* ✉ *Pl. Louis-XIV* ☎ *05–59–51–85–51.*

🛏 Hotels

Le Grand Hôtel

$$$$ | **HOTEL** | Built in the 1920s and traditionally considered to be St-Jean-de-Luz's premier hotel, Le Grand offers ocean views, intimacy, plus a general sense of being where the action is. **Pros:** great views; lots of comfort; close to all the action. **Cons:** expensive; not very relaxing unless your pockets are *très* deep; slightly self-absorbed staff. [$] *Rooms from: €355* ✉ *43 bd. Thiers* ☎ *05–59–26–35–36* 🌐 *www.luzgrandhotel.fr* 🔑 *52 rooms* 🍽 *No meals.*

Sare

14 km (8 miles) southeast of St-Jean-de-Luz, 9 km (5½ miles) west of Ainhoa.

The much-prized and picturesque village of Sare, described by author Pierre Loti in his *Ramuntxo* as a virtually autonomous Eden, is built around a large *fronton*, or backboard, where a pelota game rages around the clock; not surprisingly, the Hôtel de Ville offers a permanent exhibition on Pelote Basque. Sare was a busy smuggling hub throughout the 19th century, but today's visitors are drawn by lovely sights, not illicit activities. Chief among them are a collection of wood-beam and whitewashed Basque houses, and the late-Romanesque church with its triple-decker interior. There are also more than a dozen tiny chapels sprinkled around Sare that were built as ex-votos by seamen who survived Atlantic storms.

GETTING HERE AND AROUND

Buses leaving from the train station in St-Jean-de-Luz travel to Sare (30 mins, €2) and neighboring villages.

VISITOR INFORMATION Sare Tourist Office ✉ *Mairie* ☎ *05–59–54–20–14* 🌐 *www.sare.fr.*

👁 Sights

Église Saint-Martin de Sare

RELIGIOUS SITE | One of the Labourd province's prettiest churches, Église St-Martin de Sare was built in the 16th century and enlarged in the 17th with a triple-decker set of galleries. Parish priest Pierre Axular ranks among the great early authors in the Basque language. His tomb is under the bell tower with an epitaph by Prince Bonaparte: "Every hour wounds; the last sends you to your tomb." ✉ *Le Bourg* 🎟 *€8.*

Grottes de Sare

CAVE | Follow the Sare Valley up to the panoramic Col de Lizarrieta and the Grottes de Sare. Just outside these huge

Hiking the Pyrénées

Supping on hearty regional cuisine makes perfect sense after a day of hiking the Pyrénées, which are best explored on foot. Day trips to La Rhune overlooking Biarritz and the Basque Coast and the walk up to Biriatou from the beach at Hendaye are great ways to get to know the countryside. Hiking the Pyrénées end to end is a 43-day trip. The GR (Grande Randonnée) 10, a trail signed by discreet red-and-white paint markings, runs from the Atlantic at Hendaye to Banyuls-sur-Mer on the Mediterranean, through villages and mountains, with refuges along the way.

The HRP (Haute Randonnée Pyrénéenne, or High Pyrenean Hike) follows terrain in France and Spain irrespective of borders. Local trails are well indicated, with blue or yellow markings. Some classic walks in the Pyrénées include the Iparla Ridge walk between Bidarrai and St-Étienne-de-Baïgorry, the Santiago de Compostela Trail's dramatic St-Jean-Pied-de-Port to Roncesvalles walk over the Pyrénées, and the Holçarté Gorge walk between Larrau and Ste-Engrâce. Get trail maps at local tourist offices.

caves, you can learn about the Basque region's culture and millennia-long history at the **Musée Ethnographique** (Ethnographic Museum); then take a multilingual guided tour that leads 1 km (½ mile) underground to see a subterranean son-et-lumière show. ⊠ *Sare* ☎ *05–59–54–21–88* ⊕ *www.grottesdesare.fr* 🎫 *€9*.

Musée du Gâteau Basque
MUSEUM | This sweet museum traces the evolution of the most famous of all Basque pastries; call ahead for a schedule of workshops and baking classes. ⊠ *Maison Haranea, Quartier Lehenbiscay* ☎ *06–71–58–06–69* ⊕ *www.legateaubasque.com* 🎫 *€9* ☉ *Closed weekends, Nov.–Apr., and Mon. Apr.– June, Sept., and Oct.*

Ortillopitz
HOUSE | Take a guided tour of Ortillopitz, a vintage Basque country manor. Its typical architecture and traditional furnishings give a glimpse into 17th-century farm life. The rural vistas are especially lovely. ⊠ *Sare* ☎ *05–59–85–91–92* ⊕ *www.ortillopitz.com* 🎫 *€10* ☉ *Closed weekends.*

★ **Petit Train de la Rhune**
SCENIC DRIVE | FAMILY | Not much on the Petit Train has changed since its inaugural voyage to the peak of La Rhune on June 30, 1924. Today, passengers still ride in the original varnished cars made of pine and chestnut from Pyrenean forests at the less-than-dizzying speed of 8 kph (5 mph); and, as they ascend, present-day passengers are just as enthralled by the incredible views of the Bay of Biscay and the grassy Basque farmlands below. You can board this high-climbing cogwheel train (one of only three in France) at the Col de St-Ignace, 3½ km (2¼ miles) west of Sare. ⊠ *West of Sare on the D4* ☎ *05–59–54–20–26* ⊕ *www.rhune.com* 🎫 *€19*.

🛏 Hotels

Baratxartea
$ | B&B/INN | This little inn, located 1 km (½ mile) from the center of Sare in one of the town's prettiest and most ancient *quartiers,* is a beauty—a 16th-century town house complete with exposed wood-beam framework. **Pros:** upland

location 20 minutes from beach; personalized family service; restaurant serves tasty regional dishes. **Cons:** rooms can get hot in August; open windows in farm country attract insects; basic, no-frills accommodations. [$] *Rooms from: €63* ✉ *Quartier Ihalar* ☎ *05–59–54–20–48* 🌐 *www.hotel-baratxartea.com* 🕒 *Closed mid-Nov.–mid-Mar.* 🛏 *22 rooms* 🍴 *No meals.*

Ainhoa

9 km (5½ miles) east of Sare, 31 km (19 miles) northwest of St-Jean-Pied-de-Port.

The Basque village of Ainhoa, officially selected by the national tourist ministry as one of the prettiest in France, is a showcase for the Labourd region. Established in the 13th century, its little streets are lined with lovely 16th- to 18th-century houses featuring whitewashed walls, flower-filled balconies, brightly painted shutters, and carved master beams.

GETTING HERE AND AROUND

Exploring Ainhoa on foot is a pleasure, but you'll need your own wheels to get here.

VISITOR INFORMATION Ainhoa Tourist Office ✉ *Karrika* ☎ *05–59–29–93–99* 🌐 *www.ainhoa-tourisme.com.*

Sights

Notre-Dame de l'Assomption

RELIGIOUS SITE | The village's most noteworthy building is the Romanesque church of Notre-Dame de l'Assomption. Founded in the 13th century by Premonstratensian monks, it has a traditional Basque three-tier wooden interior with carved railings and ancient oak stairs; women sat on the ground floor, while men occupied the first balcony, and the choir sang in the loft above. ✉ *Ainhoa.*

Hotels

★ Ithurria

$$ | **HOTEL** | A registered historic monument, this 17th-century Basque-style building was once a staging post on the fabled pilgrims' route to Santiago de Compostela, and today it still makes a fitting resting spot if you're doing a modern version of the pilgrimage or just need a stopover on your way deeper into the mountains. **Pros:** country charm; pretty grounds and pool; cheery family service. **Cons:** no elevator; some room decor undistinguished; closed all winter. [$] *Rooms from: €130* ✉ *Rue Principale* ☎ *05–59–29–92–11* 🌐 *www.ithurria.com* 🕒 *Closed Nov.–Apr.* 🛏 *28 rooms* 🍴 *No meals.*

Oppoca

$ | **B&B/INN** | This 17th-century *relais,* or stagecoach relay station, on Ainhoa's main square and pelota court is one of the loveliest Basque houses in town, with small but adequate guest rooms. **Pros:** helpful service; superb fare; historic site. **Cons:** cramped spaces in some rooms; center of town can be noisy on weekends and holiday eves; limited menu options for vegetarians. [$] *Rooms from: €89* ✉ *Pl. du Fronton* ☎ *05–59–29–90–72* 🌐 *www.oppoca.com* 🕒 *Closed mid-Jan.–mid-Feb.* 🛏 *10 rooms* 🍴 *No meals.*

Ostapé

$$ | **HOTEL** | Alain Ducasse may no longer be here, but his taste and touch are palpable in the style, the ultracontemporary equipment and accoutrements, and, especially, in the regional Basque cuisine with international accents at this 100-acre park around a 17th-century farmhouse. **Pros:** top comfort in wild setting; refined cuisine; impeccable service. **Cons:** a tad too tame for true mountaineers; idle and isolated if you're not a hiker; upmarket atmosphere can be off-putting. [$] *Rooms from: €180* ✉ *Chahatoa, 3 km (1½ miles) west of Bidarrai* ☎ *05–59–37–91–91* 🌐 *www.ostape.com* 🕒 *Closed Nov. 15–Apr. 2* 🛏 *22 suites* 🍴 *Free Breakfast.*

St-Jean-Pied-de-Port

31 km (19 miles) southeast of Ainhoa.

St-Jean-Pied-de-Port, a fortified town on the Nive River, got its name from its position at the foot (*pied*) of the mountain pass (*port*) of Roncevaux (Roncesvalles). The pass was the setting for *La Chanson de Roland* (*The Song of Roland*), the anonymous 11th-century epic poem considered the true beginning of French literature; and the town itself remains a major stop for pilgrims en route to Santiago de Compostela. After a tour through the quiet villages of the Béarn countryside, it feels like a frenzied metropolis—even in winter. In summer, the bustling center is filled to the gills, and the tone is something between exciting and unbearable.

GETTING HERE AND AROUND

SNCF trains between Bayonne and St-Jean-Pied-de-Port depart six times daily in each direction (1 hr 26 mins, €10.10).

VISITOR INFORMATION St-Jean-Pied-de-Port Tourist Office ✉ *14 pl. Charles-de-Gaulle* ☎ *05–59–37–03–57* 🌐 *www.saintjeanpieddeport-paysbasque-tourisme.com.*

Sights

Notre-Dame-du-Bout-du-Pont (*Our Lady of the End of the Bridge*)
RELIGIOUS SITE | Walk into the old section of St-Jean-Pied-de-Port through the Porte de France, just behind and to the left of the tourist office; climb the steps on the left up to the walkway circling the ramparts, and stroll around to the stone stairway down to the Rue de l'Église. The church of Notre-Dame-du-Bout-du-Pont, known for its magnificent Gothic Rayonnant doorway, is at the bottom of this cobbled street. Built in the 12th century and designated a church in the 13th century, it is a characteristically Basque three-tier structure. ✉ *Rue de l'Église.*

Pont Notre-Dame (*Notre-Dame Bridge*)
BRIDGE/TUNNEL | From the Pont Notre-Dame you can watch the wild trout in the Nive (also an Atlantic salmon stream) as they pluck mayflies off the surface. Note that fishing is forbidden in town. Upstream, along the left bank, is another wooden bridge. Cross it and then walk around and back through town, returning to the left bank on the main road. ✉ *St-Jean-Pied-de-Port.*

Rue de la Citadelle
MILITARY SITE | Several sights of interest line Rue de la Citadelle, including the **Maison Arcanzola** (Arcanzola House), at No. 32 (1510); the **Maison des Évêques** (Bishops' House), at No. 39; and the famous **Prison des Évêques** (Bishops' Prison), next door to it. Continuing up you'll reach the **Citadelle** itself—a classic Vauban fortress built between 1625 and 1627, now occupied by a school. The views from the top, complete with maps identifying the surrounding heights and valleys, are panoramic. ✉ *Rue de la Citadelle.*

Restaurants

★ **Les Pyrénées**
$$$$ | **FRENCH** | A former stagecoach inn on the route to Santiago de Compostela now houses the best restaurant in the Pyrénées. Created by renowned master chef Firmin Arrambide, it is now run by his son and daughter, Philippe and Sandrine, and the haute cuisine is still characterized by refined interpretations of Pays Basque cooking with a focus on Pyrenean delicacies. **Known for:** regional mountain cuisine; famed gâteau Basque for dessert; trout from the Nive and local wood pigeon. [$] *Average main: €44* ✉ *19 pl. Charles-de-Gaulle* ☎ *05–59–37–01–01* 🌐 *www.hotel-les-pyrenees.com* 🕒 *Closed Mon. and early Jan.–early Feb.*

Hotels

Central Hôtel

$ | **HOTEL** | This family-run hotel and restaurant over the Nive is a vintage venue (note the 200-year-old oak staircase)—it's also the best value in town. **Pros:** central location, as suggested by the name; personal family service; river sounds and views. **Cons:** creaky bedsprings; can be hot in midsummer; village life starts early and you're at the heart of it. $ Rooms from: €85 ✉ 1 pl. Charles-de-Gaulle ☎ 05–59–37–00–22 ⏱ Closed Dec.–Mar. ➥ 13 rooms ❍❍ No meals.

Eugénie-les-Bains

151 km (94 miles) northeast of St-Jean-Pied-de-Port, 56 km (35 miles) north of Pau.

Empress Eugénie popularized the region's thermal baths at the end of the 19th century, and in return the villagers named this town after her. Then, in 1973, Michel and Christine Guérard made the village world famous by putting together one of France's most fashionable thermal retreats, which became one of the birthplaces of nouvelle cuisine, thanks to the great talents of chef Michel. Their empire now includes restaurants serving four types of cuisine (*minceur, gourmand, terroir,* and *tartines*), four places to stay, a cooking school, and a spa.

GETTING HERE AND AROUND
Neither buses nor trains serve Eugénie-les-Bains. If you haven't rented a car, contact the local tourist office for a list of taxi companies; the fare from Pau (an hour away) is about €100.

VISITOR INFORMATION Eugénie-les-Bains Tourist Office ✉ Pl. Gaston Larrieu ☎ 05–58–51–13–16 ⊕ www.tourisme-aire-eugenie.fr.

Sights

Thermes d'Eugénie-les-Bains

HOT SPRINGS | This therapeutic *station thermale* is certified by the French Ministry of Health to treat digestive, urinary, and metabolic problems, as well as rheumatism. Three-week "cures" are prescribed by doctors and covered by national health insurance. But foreign visitors can sign up for weight-loss retreats or simply enjoy a restorative stint in healing baths filled with 39°C (102°F) water that comes from nearly 1,300 feet below the surface. ✉ Eugénie-les-Bains ☎ 05–58–05–06–06 ⊕ www.chainethermale.fr.

Restaurants

Le Café "Mère Poule"

$ | **FRENCH** | **FAMILY** | If you want something quick and casual that still bears the stamp of Michel Guérard, try this latest addition to his culinary empire, an elegant café with a terrace on the main street. It specializes in *croq'poules*, a special version of the French staple, the croque monsieur. **Known for:** informal way to get the Michel Guérard experience; central location; outdoor terrace tables. $ Average main: €13 ✉ Les Prés d'Eugénie ☎ 05–58–03–83–83 ⊕ lespresdeugenie.com.

Hotels

La Maison Rose

$$ | **HOTEL** | A (relatively) low-cost, low-calorie alternative to famed Les Prés d'Eugénie, Michel and Christine Guérard's "Pink House" spa beckons with a renovated, superstylish 18th-century farmhouse adorned with old paintings, rustic antiques, and Pays Basque handicrafts. **Pros:** surprisingly easy on the wallet; a sybaritically simple spa approach; superb dining without being stuffy. **Cons:** might be too health-conscious for some; no room service; the decor can

The Hautes-Pyrénées have some of the best hiking trails in Europe, especially those found on the way to the Cirque de Gavarnie.

be overwhelming rather than homely. $ *Rooms from: €160* ⊠ *Rue René Vielle* ☎ *05–58–05–06–07* ⊕ *lespresdeugenie. com* ⤳ *30 rooms* ⦿ *No meals.*

Le Logis des Grives

$$$$ | **B&B/INN** | With four superb suites for the lucky first-comers, the Guérards' delightfully re-created old coaching inn, set at one end of their Prés d'Eugénie fiefdom, is meant to be a more rustic alternative to their main flagship. **Pros:** the rusticity is more relaxing than the full-on Guérard treatment; finest country cooking in the land a few yards away; wonderful decor. **Cons:** isolated from village life; only for those on an elite budget; food might be a bit too adventurous for some. $ *Rooms from: €600* ⊠ *Rue René Vielle* ☎ *05–58–05–06–07* ⊕ *lespresdeugenie.com* ⊘ *Closed Jan. 4– Feb. 12* ⤳ *4 suites* ⦿ *No meals.*

★ Les Prés d'Eugénie

$$$$ | **HOTEL** | Ever since Michel Guérard's restaurant fired the first shots of the nouvelle revolution in the late 1970s, the excellence of this suave culinary landmark has been a given (so much so that breakfast here outdoes dinner at most other places); hence a visit to Les Prés d'Eugénie remains an important notch on any gourmand's belt. **Pros:** magical cuisine; intelligent and attentive service; range of recreational options. **Cons:** very expensive; nouvelle cuisine might not be to everyone's tastes; the atmosphere isn't relaxing for everyone. $ *Rooms from: €360* ⊠ *Rue René Vielle* ☎ *05–58–05–06–07, 05–58–05–05–05 for restaurant reservations* ⊕ *lespresdeugenie.com* ⤳ *38 rooms* ⦿ *No meals.*

Pau

56 km (35 miles) south of Eugénie-les-Bains, 106 km (63 miles) southeast of Bayonne and Biarritz, 41 km (27 miles) northwest of Lourdes.

The stunning views, mild climate, and elegance of Pau—the historic capital of Béarn, a state annexed to France in 1620—make it a lovely place to visit and a convenient gateway to the Pyrénées. The birthplace of King Henri IV, Pau was "discovered" in 1815 by British officers returning from the Peninsular War in Spain, and it soon became a prominent winter resort town. Fifty years later English-speaking inhabitants made up one-third of Pau's population, many of them believing in the medicinal benefits of mountain air (later shifting their loyalties to Biarritz for the sea air). While here, the Brits not only introduced fox hunting and popularized tea drinking—they started the Pont-Long Steeplechase (still one of the most challenging in Europe) in 1841, and created France's first golf course in 1856.

GETTING HERE AND AROUND

The Pau-Pyrénées airport, 12 km (7 miles) north of town, receives daily flights from Paris, Lyon, and other points; a shuttle bus into Pau runs hourly from 6:40 am to 7:10 pm (30 mins, €1.50). The TGV Inoui connects Pau and Paris with four trains daily (5 hrs 25 mins, €80). Overnight sleeper trains from Paris run via Bayonne or Toulouse (11 hrs, €110). Trains connect with Biarritz five times daily (1½ hrs, €21). You can also take the train to Lourdes (58 mins, €8.30), Bayonne (1 hr 18 mins, €23), and Toulouse (3 hrs 46 mins, €34.20). To reach the center of Pau from the train station on Avenue Gaston-Lacoste, cross the street and take the funicular up the hill to Place Royale. If you prefer the bus, Transports-64 connects Pau with Bayonne.

VISITOR INFORMATION Pau Tourist Office
✉ *Pl. Royale* ☎ *05–59–27–27–08* 🌐 *www.tourismepau.com.*

Sights

Musée des Beaux-Arts

MUSEUM | For some man-made splendors, head to the Musée des Beaux-Arts and ogle works by El Greco, Degas, Sorolla, and Rodin. ✉ *Rue Mathieu-Lalanne* ☎ *05–59–27–33–02* 🎫 *€5* 🕒 *Closed Tues.*

★ Musée National du Château de Pau

CASTLE/PALACE | Pau's regal past is commemorated at its Musée National du Château de Pau, begun in the 14th century by Gaston Phoebus, the flamboyant count of Béarn. The building was transformed into a Renaissance palace in the 16th century by Marguerite d'Angoulême, sister of François I. A woman of diverse gifts, she wrote pastorals, many performed in the château's sumptuous gardens. Her bawdy *Heptameron*—written at age 60—furnishes as much sly merriment today as it did when read by her doting kingly brother. Marguerite's grandson, the future king of France Henri IV, was born in the château in 1553. Exhibits connected to Henri's life and times are displayed regularly, along with portraits of the most significant of his alleged 57 lovers and mistresses. His cradle, a giant turtle shell, is on exhibit in his bedroom, one of the sumptuous, tapestry-lined royal apartments. ✉ *Rue du Château* ☎ *05–59–82–38–00* 🌐 *www.chateau-pau.fr* 🎫 *€7.*

Sentiers du Roy

TRAIL | The "King's Path" is a marked trail just below Boulevard des Pyrénées. At the top, near the Boulevard Aragon, look for the map identifying the main peaks of the Pyrenees in the distance. ✉ *Pau.*

Restaurants

Henri IV

$$ | **FRENCH** | On a quiet pedestrian street near the château, this dining room with its open fire is a cozy find for a cold, wet winter night, and the terrace is a shady place to cool off in summer. Traditional Béarn dishes here include *magret de canard* (duck breast) cooked over coals, and *cuisses de grenouille* (frogs' legs) sautéed dry and crispy in parsley and garlic. **Known for:** central location handy for a break during sightseeing; traditional regional dishes; cozy atmosphere. [$] *Average main: €22* ✉ *18 rue Henri IV*

☎ *05–59–27–54–43* ⏲ *Closed Tues. and Wed.*

L'Isle au Jasmin

$ | CAFÉ | This informal café close to the château has bamboo decor inside and comfortable chairs outside so you can sit along the boulevard. The owner roasts and grinds the coffee beans herself, and there is also a wide selection of teas, ice creams, and homemade cakes available. **Known for:** charming café and tearoom; outdoor dining; macarons and other tasty pastries. [$] *Average main: €6* ✉ *28 bd. des Pyrénées* ☎ *09–84–04–01–03* 💳 *No credit cards.*

Hotels

Hôtel de Gramont

$ | HOTEL | This 17th-century stagecoach stop is a convenient base that's frequented by a mixed bag of travelers seeking respectable lodgings at reasonable prices. **Pros:** a short walk from the Château de Pau and overlooking the oldest part of town; relaxing and unpretentious; easy on the wallet. **Cons:** breakfast (extra charge) is to be avoided; small rooms; old-fashioned atmosphere not to everyone's tastes. [$] *Rooms from: €64* ✉ *3 pl. de Gramont* ☎ *05–59–27–84–04* 🌐 *www.hotelgramont.com* 💳 *No credit cards* 🛏 *35 rooms* 🍴 *No meals.*

Hôtel Parc Beaumont

$$ | HOTEL | If you're craving New World efficiency and unquestionable comfort, this place has definite appeal. **Pros:** plush rooms and polished service; contemporary style; air-conditioning and heated pool. **Cons:** longish walk to the historic center of town; comfort takes precedence over charm; resolutely modern architecture makes it feel a little impersonal. [$] *Rooms from: €160* ✉ *1 av. Edouard VII* ☎ *05–59–11–84–00* 🌐 *www.hotel-parc-beaumont.com* 🛏 *80 rooms* 🍴 *No meals.*

★ **Hôtel Villa Navarre**

$$ | HOTEL | In the 1800s Pau became home to a colony of elite British expats (including famed climber Henry Russell), who were drawn here by the mountains and climate; evidence of that era remains at Villa Navarre: built in the second half of the 19th century, it's the only English manor in Pau open to overnight guests and one of only two hotels in town with views of the High Pyrénées. **Pros:** views of the Pyrénées; beautiful gardens; well-preserved English heritage. **Cons:** a very long walk to town; caters to business travelers (like most of Pau's hotels); not the place if you are looking for full French immersion. [$] *Rooms from: €197* ✉ *59 rue Trespoey* ☎ *05–59–14–65–65* 🌐 *www.villanavarre.fr* 🛏 *30 rooms* 🍴 *No meals.*

Nightlife

Casino

CASINOS | The streets around Pau's imposing château are sprinkled with cozy pubs and dining spots, although the casino in the Palais Beaumont, at the other end of the Boulevard des Pyrénées, offers racier entertainment. ✉ *Parc Beaumont* ☎ *05–59–27–06–92* 🌐 *pau.groupetranchant.com.*

Shopping

Au Parapluie des Pyrénées

GIFTS/SOUVENIRS | This is the only shop in France where the large umbrellas still used by Basque and Bearnais shepherds are handmade to specially withstand sun, rain, and the force of the wind. If cared for properly, one of these umbrellas should last you a lifetime. ✉ *12 rue Montpensier* ☎ *05–59–27–53–66* 🌐 *www.parapluiedeberger.com.*

Lourdes

41 km (27 miles) southeast of Pau, 30 km (19 miles) north of Cauterets.

The mountain town of Lourdes is arguably the most famous Catholic pilgrimage site in the world, but its origins are decidedly humble and its renown relatively recent. In February 1858, a 14-year-old miller's daughter named Bernadette Soubirous claimed she saw the Virgin Mary in the Grotte de Massabielle (in all, she had 18 visions). Bernadette dug in the grotto, releasing a gush of water from a spot where no spring had flowed before. From then on, pilgrims thronged the Massabielle rock for the water's supposed healing powers. Today, around 6 million visitors come each year from every corner of the globe—not all of them are Christian, but most are bound by their common hope for a miracle cure.

GETTING HERE AND AROUND

With direct rail service from Pau (28 mins, €8.30), Bayonne (1 hr 52 mins, €24), and Toulouse (2 hrs 4 mins, €30.10), Lourdes's train station on Avenue de la Gare is one of the busiest in the country. In fact, so many pilgrim trains arrive between Easter and All Saint's Day (November 1) that the station has a separate entrance to accommodate them, and dedicated local buses shuttle passengers to the grotto every 20 minutes. Transports-64 and SNCF-run buses also serve the area.

VISITOR INFORMATION Lourdes Tourist Office ⊠ *Pl. Peyramale* ☎ *05–62–42–77–40* ⊕ *www.lourdes-infotourisme.com.*

Sights

Basilique Souterraine St-Pie X

RELIGIOUS SITE | Lourdes celebrated the centenary of Bernadette Soubirous's visions by building the world's largest underground church, the Basilique Souterraine St-Pie X, with space for 20,000 people—more than the town's permanent population. The Basilique Supérieure (1871), tall and white, hulks nearby. ⊠ *Lourdes.*

Cachot

HISTORIC SITE | The cachot, a tiny room where, in extreme poverty, Bernadette and her family took refuge in 1856, can be visited. ⊠ *15 rue des Petits-Fossés* ☎ *05–62–94–51–30* ⊠ *Free.*

Grotte de Massabielle

RELIGIOUS SITE | Lourdes wouldn't even be on the map if it weren't for this deep grotto near the Gave de Pau where 14-year-old Bernadette Soubirous first claimed to see visions of the Virgin Mary in 1858. Church authorities initially reacted with skepticism: it took four years for the miracle to be authenticated by Rome and a sanctuary erected over the grotto. But in 1864 the first organized procession was held. Now there are six official annual pilgrimages between Easter and All Saints' Day, the most important being on August 15. In fall and winter there are far fewer visitors, but that will be a plus for those in search of peace and tranquility. ⊠ *Lourdes.*

Moulin de Boly (*Boly Mill*)

HISTORIC SITE | Across the river is the Moulin de Boly, where Bernadette was born on January 7, 1844. ⊠ *12 rue Bernadette-Soubirous* ⊠ *Free.*

★ Musée Pyrénéen

CASTLE/PALACE | The château on the hill above town is reached from the ticket office by escalator or by a flight of 131 steps. Once a prison, the castle now contains the Musée Pyrénéen, a provincial museum devoted to the popular customs, arts, and history of the Pyrénées. There are splendid views over the rooftops of Lourdes and the sanctuary area. ⊠ *25 rue du Fort* ☎ *05–62–42–37–37* ⊕ *www.chateaufort-lourdes.fr* ⊠ *€8.*

Musée Sainte-Bernadette

RELIGIOUS SITE | Bernadette's life story is chronicled through mementos and more

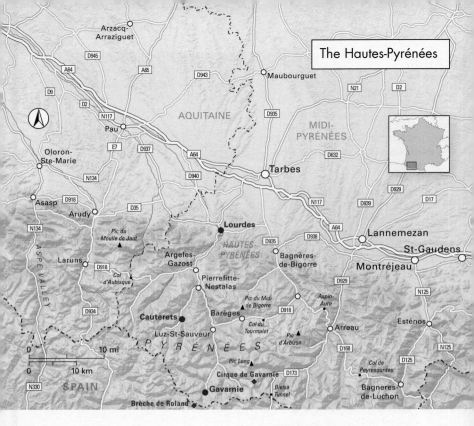

The Hautes-Pyrénées

at the museum that bears her name; information about the construction of the nearby sanctuaries is also provided. ✉ Bd. Rémi Sempé ☎ 05–62–42–78–78 ⊕ www.lourdes-france.com ✉ Free ⏱ Closed Nov.–mid-Mar.

Restaurants

Le Chalet de Biscaye

$$ | FRENCH | Outstanding seafood is on the menu at this restaurant a little bit outside of Lourdes on the way to the lake. Game and wild mushrooms are also available, depending on the season. **Known for:** relaxing location beyond the bustle of central Lourdes; fish and seafood cuisine; exquisite presentation of dishes. $ Average main: €16 ✉ 26 rte. du Lac ☎ 05–62–94–12–26 ⊕ www.chalet-de-biscaye.fr.

Hotels

Grand Hôtel Gallia et Londres

$$ | HOTEL | A feel of traditional France in the Louis XVI furniture and the general ambience of the place makes the pretty Gallia, not far from the sanctuaries and the grotto, something of a retreat within a retreat. **Pros:** traditional French hotel; near the sanctuaries; maintains a certain dignity in the midst of the prevailing commercial vibe of Lourdes. **Cons:** closed during the winter; breakfast is extra; in the busiest part of town. $ Rooms from: €150 ✉ 26 av. B. Soubirous ☎ 05–62–94–35–44 ⊕ www.hotelsvinuales.com ⏱ Closed Nov.–Apr. 20 ↻ 85 rooms ❌ No meals.

★ **Grand Hôtel Moderne**
$ | **HOTEL** | After braving the pilgrim-packed streets, this hotel—built in 1896 by one of Bernadette's nephews—may seem like the answer to your prayers; after all, it promises comfortable rooms, attentive service, and an excellent restaurant right in the center of everything. **Pros:** premier location across from the Grotto; warm service; good restaurant. **Cons:** attracts large groups; driving into the heart of town is tricky; the front door opens straight on to the town's busiest streets. [$] *Rooms from: €125* ✉ *21 av. Bernadette Soubirous* ☎ *05–62–94–12–32* 🌐 *www.grandhotelmoderne.com* 🛏 *111 rooms* 🍴 *No meals.*

Cauterets

30 km (19 miles) south of Lourdes, 30 km (19 miles) north of Gavarnie.

Cauterets—which derives from the word for hot springs in the local *bigourdan* dialect—is a spa resort town set high in the Pyrénées. It has been revered since Roman times for thermal baths thought to cure maladies ranging from back pain to infertility. Novelist Victor Hugo (1802–85) frequented here, and Lady Aurore Dudevant—better known as the writer George Sand (1804–76)—is said to have discovered her feminism here. Other famous visitors include Chateaubriand, Sarah Bernhardt, King Edward VII of England, and Spain's King Alfonso XIII.

GETTING HERE AND AROUND

Unless you're coming to Cauterets from a hiking path, only one road leads into town. SNCF buses travel to and from Lourdes on it up to seven times a day (1 hr, €8.30).

VISITOR INFORMATION Cauterets Tourist Office ✉ *Pl. Foch* ☎ *05–62–92–50–50* 🌐 *www.cauterets.com.*

Sights

Les Bains du Rocher
HOT SPRINGS | The naturally heated sulfur water here was particularly popular among 19th-century aristocrats who arrived in Cauterets to "take the cure." Today, it's still used to alleviate rheumatism and respiratory maladies (three-week treatments can even be covered by national health insurance). In keeping with modern trends, however, the *station thermale* now caters to guests who simply want to indulge as well. Les Bains du Rocher has a genuine spa aesthetic, and offers massages, facials, aqua-gym sessions, and, of course, soaks in hot healing pools both inside and outside. ✉ *Av. du Dr. Domer* ☎ *05–62–92–14–20* 🌐 *www.bains-rocher.fr.*

Gavarnie

30 km (19 miles) south of Cauterets.

Geologists point to the natural wonder that is the Cirque de Gavarnie as one of the world's most formidable examples of the effects of glacial erosion; the cliffs were worn away by the advancing and retreating ice sheets of the Pleistocene epoch. Seeing it, one can understand its irresistible appeal for mountain climbers—appropriately, the village has a statue honoring one of the first of them, Count Russell.

GETTING HERE AND AROUND

Conseil Général and SNCF buses from Lourdes will take you as far as Luz-St-Sauveur (50 mins, €9); you can cover the last 20 km (12 miles) by taxi or, from June to September, connect to another bus that travels onward to Gavarnie (30 mins, €2).

VISITOR INFORMATION Gavarnie Tourist Office ✉ *Pl. de la Bergère, in center of village* ☎ *05–62–92–49–10* 🌐 *www.gavarnie.com.*

Sights

★ Brèche de Roland

VIEWPOINT | One dramatic sight is 12 km (7 miles) west of the village of Gavarnie. Take D923 up to the Col des Tentes, where you can park and walk five hours up to the Brèche de Roland Glacier (you cross it during the last two hours of the hike). For a taste of mountain life, have lunch high up at the Club Alpin Français's **Refuge la Brèche de Roland–Sarradets**. This is a serious climb, only feasible from mid-June to mid-September, for which you need (at least) good hiking shoes and sound physical conditioning. Crampons and ice axes can be rented in Gavarnie. ✉ *Gavarnie.*

★ Cirque de Gavarnie

NATURE SITE | A spectacular natural amphitheater, the Cirque de Gavarnie has been dubbed the "Colosseum of Nature" and inspired many writers, including Victor Hugo. At its foot is the village of Gavarnie, a good base for exploring the mountains in the region. Thanks to glacial erosion, the Cirque is a Cinerama wall of peaks and a daunting challenge to mountaineers. Horses and donkeys, rented in the village, are the traditional way to reach the head of the valley (though walking is preferable). When the upper snows melt, numerous streams tumble down from the cliffs to form spectacular waterfalls; the greatest of them, the **Grande Cascade**, drops nearly 1,400 feet. ✉ *Gavarnie.*

🍽 Restaurants

★ Hôtel du Cirque

$ | **FRENCH** | With its legendary views of the Cirque de Gavarnie, this spot, which opened at the head of the valley in 1848, is well worth the one-hour hike up from the village. Despite its name, the hôtel is a restaurant, but not just any old one: the garbure here is as delicious as the view is grand; the eighth-generation owner claims his recipe, using water from the Cirque and *cocos de Tarbes,* or *haricots tarbais* (Tarbes broad beans), is unique. **Known for:** unique recipe for garbure; setting in a magnificent mountain village; requiring a hike to get there. $ *Average main: €15* ✉ *1-hr walk above village of Gavarnie* ☎ *05–62–92–48–02* *Closed Nov.–May.*

🛏 Hotels

Hôtel Vignemale

$$ | **HOTEL** | Built in 1902, this spacious châteaulike hotel has an imposing granite facade with steep rooflines reflecting the towering Hautes-Pyrénées to the south; sunny guest rooms with floor-to-ceiling windows overlook the rushing Gave de Gavarnie, and the breakfast terrace out front is an ideal place to start a day in the mountains. **Pros:** rushing water music provided by the stream; a tranquil sense of space; historic mountaineer's haven. **Cons:** small balconies; decor somewhat dated; bathrooms not as splendid as the facade might suggest. $ *Rooms from: €160* ✉ *Chemin du Cirque* ☎ *05–62–92–40–00* ⊕ *www.hotel-vignemale.com* *Closed mid-Oct.–mid-May* 🛏 *10 rooms* 🍽 *Free Breakfast.*

Chapter 18

BORDEAUX AND THE WINE COUNTRY

18

Updated by
Nick Inman

Sights	Restaurants	Hotels	Shopping	Nightlife
★★★☆☆	★★☆☆☆	★★★☆☆	★★☆☆☆	★★☆☆☆

WELCOME TO BORDEAUX AND THE WINE COUNTRY

TOP REASONS TO GO

★ **La Route de Médoc:** With eight *appellations* (districts) in this small area alone, and names like Rothschild, Latour, and Margaux on its bottles, the route will fulfill your biggest wine expectations.

★ **Bordeaux:** Eighteenth-century wine merchants endowed this city with an almost regal elegance—for proof, see their gracious mansions and the city's sublime squares.

★ **The Rothschild legacy:** Although the family's Château Lafite is often locked, oenophiles will be welcomed with open arms at Château Mouton Rothschild's visitor center and museum.

★ **St-Émilion:** With its 13th-century ramparts, cobblestone streets, and rock-hewn hermitage, this hilltop town presides over one of the region's richest wine districts.

★ **Bordeaux bacchanal:** Wine-theme festivals—most notably the Fête du Vin extravaganza, held in Bordeaux's biggest square at the end of June—keep corks popping.

Along with Burgundy and Champagne, Bordeaux is one of the great wine regions of France. As the capital of the Gironde *département* and of the historic province of Aquitaine, the city of Bordeaux is both the commercial and cultural center of southwest France and an important transportation hub. It is smack-dab in the middle of one of the finest wine-growing areas in the world: Sauternes lies to the south, flat and dusty Médoc to the northwest, and Pomerol and St-Émilion to the east.

1 Bordeaux. One of the world's great wine cities and home to the acclaimed La Cité du Vin, a museum dedicated entirely to wine making.

2 Margaux. One of the world's oldest wine appellations.

3 Pauillac. Home to three of Bordeaux's celebrated grands crus wines.

4 St-Émilion. A charming town surrounded by celebrated vineyards.

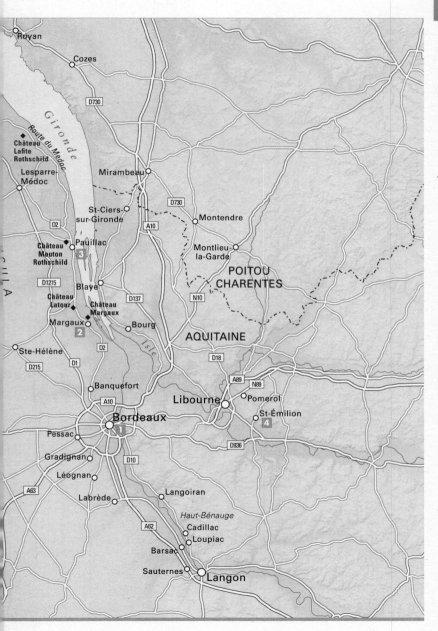

VISITING THE VINEYARDS

Touring a region with more than 1,555 square km (600 square miles) of wine-growing country, 5,000 châteaux, and 100,000 vineyards producing around 70 million gallons of wine annually, you'll find it hard to resist sampling Bordeaux's liquid bounty—but where to start?

The best bet is to head north for the Route de Médoc (also called the Route des Châteaux or the Route des Grands-Crus), armed with maps and pointers from Bordeaux's helpful Office of Tourism (the *tourisme de viticole* desk is the place for this)—it's at 12 cours du XXX-Juillet in the city center of Bordeaux. Or check out the "Wine Tours" section of the official Bordeaux tourism website (⊕ *www.bordeaux-tourisme.com*) before you travel. A map is essential, as signage is poor and many "châteaux" are small manors hidden in the hills. Three main wine regions surround the city: Médoc to the northwest, St-Émilion to the east, and Graves-Sauternes to the south. Each boasts big-name vineyards, but remember that Baron Philippe de Rothschild, owner of Mouton Rothschild, drank *vin ordinaire* at most meals.

BY APPOINTMENT ONLY

If you're planning on visiting any of the famous growers (or some of the lesser known ones for that matter), make sure to contact them ahead of time to arrange a *dégustation* (wine tasting)—many of the labels are "by appointment only" because they're too small to have full-time guides. Even the famous Château Mouton Rothschild—visited by thousands—requires reservations, at least a week in advance for a regular tour and several weeks for a tour that includes the cellars. Conveniently, you can create your agenda online by booking your visits through the tourism office's website—it also supplies you with a printable map for your personalized itinerary.

VINEYARD TOURS

The staff at Bordeaux's tourism office is very helpful, and because many vineyards are inaccessible without a car or bike, the easiest way to reach those of the Route de Médoc and Gironde is to join one of the theme bus tours it sponsors.

Here's the scoop: these tours depart from (and return to) the Office de Tourisme at 12 cours XXX-Juillet. In the off-season, same-day reservations can be had; in high season, make them in advance. There are daylong trips and also half-day versions (the latter usually run from 1:30 to 6:30 in the afternoon).

In high season there's a tour every day; otherwise a few run per week. Most tours stop at two châteaux only—for instance, in the Médoc, you can visit the Château Palmer (Troisième Cru Classé) and the Château Lanessan (Cru Bourgeois)—but there are so many diverse tours that you could go on a different one each day for a week and not see the same domains. Tours are

offered in several languages, including English, and usually a bus holds 50 participants.

You can view information regarding each tour (including availability) at ⊕ www.bordeaux-tourisme.com; then book your choice online.

STAYING THE NIGHT

Want to play vigneron (vintner) for a night? Some great vineyards welcome guests. The 14th-century estate of Château Smith Haut Lafitte (☎ 05–57–83–11–22 ⊕ www.smith-haut-lafitte.com) houses the very successful Les Sources de Caudalie hotel as well as a spa offering wine-based treatments (☎ 05–57–83–83–83 ⊕ www.sources-caudalie.com).

Wine king Bernard Magrez has rooms available at his 17th-century Château Fombrauge, and others at Château Pape Clément and Château la Tour Carnet. All can be booked through his big Luxury Wine Tourism company (☎ 05–57–26–38–38 ⊕ www.luxury-winetourism.fr).

When travelers arrive here, Bordeaux's countryside enchants them without their quite knowing why: what the French call *la douceur de vivre* (the sweetness of living) may have something to do with it.

To the east, extending their lush green rows to the rising sun, the renowned vineyards of the Route de Médoc entice visitors to discover magical medieval wine towns like St-Émilion. To the north, the Atlantic coast offers elite enclaves with white-sand beaches. In between is the metropolis of Bordeaux, replete with 18th-century landmarks, 20-year-old college students, and one impressive museum dedicated entirely to wine. Some complain that Bordeaux is like Paris without the good stuff, but if you're a wine lover it's still the doorway to paradise. And things are on the move in Bordeaux these days; it's consistently voted one of the top French cities for young people to live in.

From the grandest *premiers grands crus*—the Lafite-Rothschilds, the Margaux—to the modest *supérieur* in your picnic basket, Bordeaux wines command respect around the world. So much so that oenophiles by the thousands come here to pay homage: to gaze at the noble symmetries of estate châteaux, whose rows of green-and-black vineyards radiate in every direction; to lower a nose deep into a well-swirled glass, inhaling the heady vapors of oak and almond and leather; and, finally, to reverently pack a few bloodline labels into a trunk or a suitcase for home.

The history, economy, and culture of Bordeaux have always been linked to the production and marketing of wine. The birth of the first Bordeaux winery is said to have occurred between AD 37 and 68, when the Romans called this land Burdigala. By the Middle Ages, a steady flow of Bordeaux wines was headed to England, where it's still dubbed "claret," after *clairet,* a light red version from earlier days. During these centuries the region was also put on the tourist radar because it had become a major stop on the fabled Santiago de Compostela pilgrimage road. With all these allurements, it's no wonder the English fought for it so determinedly throughout the Hundred Years' War. This coveted corner of France became home to Eleanor of Aquitaine, and when she left her first husband, France's Louis VII, to marry Henry II of Normandy (later king of England), both she and the land came under English rule. Henry Plantagenet was, after all, a great-grandson of William the Conqueror, and the Franco-English ambiguity of the age exploded in a war that defined much of modern France and changed its face forever. Southwestern France was the stage upon which much of the war was conducted—hence the region's many castles and no end of sturdy churches dedicated to the noble families' cause.

What they sought, the world still seeks. The wines of Bordeaux set the standard against which other wines are measured, and to truly savor them you should drink them on-site—from the mouthful of golden Graves that eases the oysters down to the syrupy sip of Sauternes that civilizes the smooth gaminess of the foie gras to the last glass of Médoc paired with the salt-marsh lamb that leads to pulling the cork on a Pauillac—because there is the cheese tray yet to come. With a smorgasbord of 57 wine appellations to choose from, the revitalized city of Bordeaux, and the wine country that surrounds it with a veritable army of varieties, the entire region is intoxicating.

MAJOR REGIONS

Bordeaux. Dominated geographically by the nearby Atlantic Ocean and historically by great wine merchants and shippers, Bordeaux has long ranked among France's largest cities. There is considerable, if concentrated, affluence, which hides behind 18th-century facades. Showing off may not be a regional trait but, happily, the city fathers left a bevy of cultural riches to discover, including the spectacular Place de la Bourse, the Grand Théâtre, and the Musée des Beaux-Arts.

The Médoc. Northwest of Bordeaux, this triangulated peninsula extends from the Gironde estuary to the Atlantic coast. Dutch engineers drained its marshy landscape in the 18th century to expose the gravelly soil that is excellent for growing grapes, and today the Médoc is home to several of the *grands crus classés,* including Château Margaux, Château Latour, Château Lafite Rothschild, and Château Mouton Rothschild. Wines from the Médoc are made predominantly from the Cabernet Sauvignon grape, and can taste dry, even austere, when young. The better ones often need 15–25 years before "opening up" to reveal their full spectrum of complex flavors. Public buses run here but stops are sometimes in the middle of nowhere—a car, bike, or guided tour may be the best option.

St-Émilion. On the right bank of the Dordogne, this region was put on the map by two great wine districts—St-Émilion and Pomerol. Crowds head here because the town of St-Émilion looks as delicious as its wines taste: a UNESCO World Heritage Site, this open-air museum was constructed out of a limestone plateau honeycombed with vast caves and passageways, the source for the golden stonework of its 19th-century houses and steep streets. During summer, the small town is often swamped with visitors, so plan your parking and hotels carefully.

Planner

When to Go

Southwestern France can have bad storms even during the summer because of the nearby Atlantic. Happily, inclement weather doesn't hang around for long. The French usually vacation within their own national borders, so that means mid-July to the end of August is when you'll have company—lots of it—especially in the more famous destinations. Spring and fall are the best times to visit, when there aren't as many tourists and the weather is still pleasant. The *vendanges* (grape harvests) usually begin about mid-September in the Bordeaux region (though you can't visit the wineries at this time), and two weeks later in the Cognac region, to the north.

Planning Your Time

How do you find the best vineyards (also referred to as *crus, clos,* and *domaines*) if you're based in Bordeaux? Easy—just head in any direction. The city is at the hub of a patchwork of vineyards: the Médoc peninsula to the northwest; Bourg and Blaye across the estuary; St-Émilion inland to the east; then, as you wheel around clockwise, Entre-Deux-Mers, Sauternes, and Graves.

The nearest vineyard to Bordeaux itself is one of the best: Haut-Brion, on the western outskirts of the city, and one of the five châteaux to be officially recognized as a *premier cru,* or first growth. There are only five premiers crus in all, and Haut-Brion is the only one not in the Médoc (Château Mouton Rothschild, Château Margaux, Château Latour, and Château Lafite Rothschild complete the list). The Médoc is subdivided into various appellations, or wine-growing districts, with their own specific characteristics and taste. Pauillac and Margaux host premiers crus; St-Julien and St-Estèphe possess many domaines of almost equal quality, followed by Listrac and Moulis; wines not quite so good are classed as Haut-Médoc or, as you move farther north, Médoc, pure and simple.

The Médoc wine region begins at the meeting point of the Dordogne and Garonne Rivers, just north of the city. The D2 (aka the Route des Châteaux) cuts northwest through the majority of the wine country along the Gironde all the way to Talais, and the D1215 farther west runs through the other side of the region, entering appellations like Listrac and Moulis.

Eastward lies the Libournais and St-Émilion regions, with Libourne being the main transportation hub if you're heading to the stunning Vieille Ville (Old Town) of St-Émilion, which deserves at least a day, if not two. The surrounding vineyards see the Merlot grape in control, and wines here often have more immediate appeal than those of the Médoc. There are several small appellations apart from St-Émilion itself, the most famous being Pomerol, whose Château Pétrus is the world's most expensive wine. South of St-Émilion is the region known as Entre-Deux-Mers ("between two seas"—actually two rivers, the Dordogne and Garonne), whose dry white wine is particularly flavorful. This region is famed for its sweet wines, including the world's best, which hail from legendary Sauternes.

Getting Here and Around

Bordeaux is one of France's main transportation hubs. However, once you get out into the surrounding Gironde—the "Wine Country"—you may find its seven regions (divided according to geography and the types of wine produced) difficult to reach without a car. Public buses run frequently through the countryside, but they don't necessarily stop in convenient places. The Conseil Général's comprehensive TransGironde website outlines your options in English. If you have access to a car, you'll find life much easier, particularly if you purchase a Michelin map; Map No. 234 covers a large portion of the southwest. Another option is to go on a bus tour organized by the Bordeaux tourism office.

AIR TRAVEL

Daily flights on Air France (⊕ *www. airfrance.com*) link Bordeaux and Paris; the Bordeaux airport is also served by several budget carriers—including easy-Jet (⊕ *www.easyjet.com*).

AIRPORT INFORMATION Aéroport de Bordeaux-Mérignac ☎ *05–56–34–50–50* ⊕ *www.bordeaux.aeroport.fr.*

BUS TRAVEL

The Conseil Général's TransGironde network of buses covers towns in the wine country and beach areas not well served by rail. The main Gare Routière (bus terminal) in Bordeaux is on Allées de Chartres (by Esplanade des Quinconces), near the Garonne River and Stalingrad Square.

CONTACTS TransGironde ☎ *09–74–50–00– 33* ⊕ *www.transgironde.fr.*

CAR TRAVEL

As the capital of southwest France, Bordeaux has superb highway links with Paris, Spain, and even the Mediterranean (the A62 expressway via Toulouse links up with the A61 to Narbonne). The A10 is the Paris–Bordeaux expressway, and the A63 south brings you past Bayonne. The A20 south is the main route from Paris to just before Cahors, but it's an hour quicker to go south on the A10 through Tours and Poitiers.

TRAIN TRAVEL

The superfast TGV Atlantique service links Paris's Gare Montparnasse to Bordeaux, 585 km (364 miles) away, in 3½ hours. Trains link Bordeaux to Lyon (6½ hrs) and Nice (9 hrs) via Marseille as well. At least a half dozen trains leave Bordeaux most days bound for St-Émilion, arriving 37 minutes later. If you're heading north to Pauillac (75 mins), there are also at least half a dozen trains daily from Bordeaux.

CONTACTS Gare de Bordeaux St-Jean ⊠ *Rue Charles Domercq, Bordeaux* ☎ *3635.* **SNCF** ☎ *3635 (€0.40 per min)* ⊕ *www.sncf.fr.* **TGV Inoui** ⊕ *www.tgv. com.*

Restaurants

Although countryside Médoc eateries are few, the city of Bordeaux is jammed with restaurants, especially around Place du Parlement; plus it has many cafés (notably in the Quartier St-Pierre) and bars (Place de la Victoire and Cours de la Somme). Not surprisingly, the wines of the region are often used as a base for regional food specialties. Lamprey, a good local fish, is often served in a red wine sauce as *lamproie à la Bordelaise*; and sturgeon is cooked in a white wine sauce, as *esturgeon à la Libournaise* (Libourne style). As for meat, the lamb from Pauillac and the beef from Bazas and Aquitaine are rightly famous, as is

the wood pigeon (*palombe*). And Bordeaux has spectacular desserts, such as *fanchonnette Bordelaise* (puff pastry in custard covered with meringue), *cannelé de Bordeaux* (small cakes, made in fluted molds, that can only be found here), and the famed macarons from St-Émilion, invented there by the town's Ursuline nuns in the 17th century.

Hotels

Countryside hotels can be gorgeous— not to mention convenient for touring the region's famed vineyards—but basing yourself in Bordeaux city is definitely worth considering, because pickings for rural inns can be slim in summer months and nonexistent in winter, when most of them close. And don't fret about missing the vineyards. Many of the city hotels can create tours for you. *Restaurant and hotel reviews have been shortened. For full information, visit Fodors.com.*

What It Costs in Euros			
$	$$	$$$	$$$$
RESTAURANTS			
under €16	€16–€24	€25–€32	over €32
HOTELS			
under €125	€125–€225	€226–€350	over €350

Visitor Information

The Office de Tourisme in Bordeaux is the first place to head for further information on local and regional sights, including wine tours and tastings; a round-the-clock phone service in English is available. The office also organizes coach tours of the surrounding vineyards every day in high season and nearly every Wednesday and weekends in the off-season. In addition to the main office (at 12 cours du XXX-Juillet), there are branches at the Gare de Bordeaux train station and the airport.

CONTACT Office of Tourism of Bordeaux
✉ *12 cours du XXX-Juillet, Bordeaux* ☎ *05–56–00–66–00* ⊕ *www.bordeaux-tourisme.com.*

Bordeaux

Bordeaux as a whole, rather than any particular points within it, is what you'll want to visit in order to understand why Victor Hugo described it as Versailles plus Antwerp, and why the painter Francisco de Goya, when exiled from his native Spain, chose it as his last home (he died here in 1828). The capital of southwest France and the region's largest city, Bordeaux remains synonymous with the wine trade: wine shippers have long maintained their headquarters along the banks of the Garonne, while buyers from around the world arrive for the huge biennial Vinexpo show (held in odd-number years).

Bordeaux is, admittedly, a less exuberant city than many others in France, but lively and stylish elements are making a dent in its conservative veneer. The cleaned-up riverfront is said by some, after a bottle or two, to exude an elegance reminiscent of St. Petersburg, and that aura of 18th-century élan also permeates the historic downtown sector—"le vieux Bordeaux"—where fine shops invite exploration. To the south of the city center are old docklands undergoing renewal—one train station has now been transformed into a big multiplex movie theater—but the area is still a bit shady. To get a feel for the historic port of Bordeaux, take the 90-minute boat trip that leaves Quai Louis-XVIII every weekday afternoon, or the regular passenger ferry that plies the Garonne between Quai Richelieu and the Pont d'Aquitaine in summer. A nice time

to stroll around the city center is the first Sunday of the month, when it's pedestrian-only and vehicles are banned.

GETTING HERE AND AROUND
Served by both national airlines and budget carriers, the Aéroport de Bordeaux-Mérignac is 10 km (7 miles) west of Bordeaux; the airport's 30'Direct shuttle bus loops between it and the city center every 45 minutes (€8 one way). You can also come by rail from Paris, with high-speed TGVs making the 3½-hour trip at least 16 times a day; the train deposits you at one of the country's major hubs, the Gare de Bordeaux St-Jean, about 3 km (2 miles) from downtown. Tramline C will take you from the train station to the city center for €1.70 (⊕ *www.infotbc.com/en*). The TransGironde network of regional buses goes farther afield in the Gironde, and even to other nearby départements.

 Sights

CAPC Musée d'Art Contemporain (*Contemporary Art Center*)
MUSEUM | Just north of the Esplanade des Quinconces (a sprawling square), this two-story museum is imaginatively housed in a converted 19th-century spice warehouse—the Entrepôt Lainé. Many expositions here showcase cutting-edge artists who invariably festoon the huge expanse of the square with hanging ropes, ladders, and large video screens. ✉ *7 rue Ferrère* ☎ *05–56–00–81–50* ⊕ *www.capc-bordeaux.fr* 🎫 *€7* ⊙ *Closed Mon.*

Cathédrale St-André
RELIGIOUS SITE | This may not be one of France's finer Gothic cathedrals, but the intricate 14th-century chancel makes an interesting contrast with the earlier nave. Excellent stone carvings adorn the facade of the hefty edifice. You can also climb the 15th-century, 160-foot **Tour Pey-Berland** for a stunning view of the

Red Gold: The Wines of Bordeaux

Everyone in Bordeaux celebrated the 2000 vintage as the "crop of the century," a wine that comes along once in a lifetime. But bringing everything down to earth are some new sour grapes: the increasingly loud whispers that Bordeaux may be "over." In this world of nouvelle cuisine and uncellared wines, some critics feel the world has moved away from pricey, rich, red wines and more people are opting for younger choices from other lands. Be that as it may, if you have any aspirations to being a wine connoisseur, Bordeaux will always remain the bedrock of French viticulture.

It has been considered so ever since the credentials of Bordeaux wines were traditionally established in 1787. That year, Thomas Jefferson went down to the region from Paris and splurged on bottles of 1784 Château d'Yquem and Château Margaux, for prices that were, he reported, "indeed dear." Jefferson knew his wines: in 1855, both Yquem and Margaux were officially classified among Bordeaux's top five. And two centuries later, some of his very bottles (the authenticity of their provenance has since been disputed, as well as documented in the controversial book *The Billionaire's Vinegar*) fetched upward of $50,000 when offered in a high-flying auction in New York City.

As it turns out, Bordeaux's reputation dates to the Middle Ages. From 1152 to 1453, along with much of what is now western France, Bordeaux belonged to England. The light red wine then produced was known as *clairet*, the origin of the word "claret." Today no other part of France has such a concentration of top-class vineyards.

The versatile Bordeaux region yields sweet and dry whites and fruity or full-bodied reds from a huge domain extending on either side of the Gironde (Blaye and Bourg to the north, Médoc and Graves to the south) and inland along the Garonne (Sauternes) and Dordogne (St-Émilion, Fronsac, Pomerol) or in between these two rivers (Entre-Deux-Mers).

At the top of the government-supervised scale—which includes, in descending order, Appellation d'Origine Protégée (AOP, previously known as AOC), Indication Géographique Protégée (IGP, formerly known as Vins de Pays), and Vin de France—are the fabled vintages of Bordeaux, leading off with Margaux. Sadly, the vineyards of Margaux are among the ugliest in France, lost amid the flat, dusty plains of the Médoc.

Other towns better represent Bordeaux's wine country. St-Émilion, with its cascading cobbled streets, is more beautiful; and even humble Sauternes is more interesting, though nothing in the latter would suggest the mind-boggling wealth lurking amid the picturesque vine-laden slopes and hollows. The village has a wineshop where bottles gather dust on rickety shelves, next to handwritten price tags demanding small fortunes.

Making Sauternes is a tricky business. Autumn mists steal up the valleys to promote *Botrytis cinerea*, a fungus known as *pourriture noble* or "noble rot," which sucks moisture out of the grapes, leaving a high proportion of sugar. Sauternes's liquid gold is harvested in *vendanges* beginning in September and lasting to December.

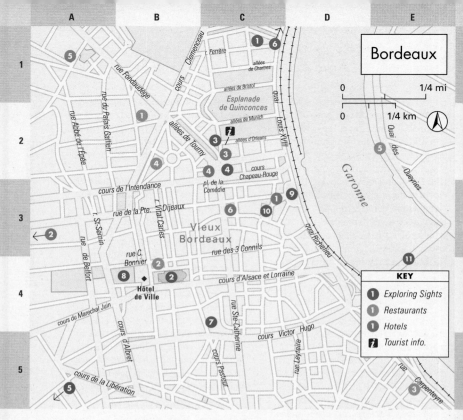

Bordeaux

KEY

- 1 Exploring Sights
- 1 Restaurants
- 1 Hotels
- 🛈 Tourist info.

Sights ▼	Restaurants ▼	Hotels ▼
1 CAPC Muséed'Art Contemporain **C1**	1 Baud et Millet **B2**	1 Acanthe Hotel............ **C3**
2 Cathédrale St-André ... **B4**	2 Café Français **B4**	2 Burdigala **A3**
3 École du Vinde Bordeaux **C2**	3 La Tupina **E5**	3 Des Quatre Sœurs....... **C2**
4 Grand Théâtre............ **C2**	4 Le Chapon-Fin.......... **B2**	4 Grand Hôtel de Bordeaux & Spa **C2**
5 Haut-Brion............... **A5**	5 L'Estacade **E2**	5 La Maison Bord'eaux................. **A1**
6 La Cité du Vin............ **C1**		6 Quality Hôtel Bordeaux Centre......... **C3**
7 Musée d'Aquitaine **C4**		
8 Musée des Beaux-Arts **B4**		
9 Place de la Bourse **D3**		
10 Place du Parlement **C3**		
11 Pont de Pierre............ **E4**		

city. ✉ *Pl. Pey-Berland* ☎ *05–56–81–26–25* 🎟 *Tower €6* 🕐 *Tower closed Mon. Oct.–May.*

École du Vin de Bordeaux

WINERY/DISTILLERY | On tree-lined Cours du XXX-Juillet, not far from the banks of the Garonne and the main artery of the Esplanade des Quinconces, you'll find the École du Vin. Run by the CIVB (Conseil Interprofessionnel des Vins de Bordeaux, which oversees the Bordeaux wine trade), this school offers two-hour wine appreciation workshops (€32) as well as intensive programs and summer courses for professionals. The on-site Bar à Vin is a good place to sample reds (like Pauillac or St-Émilion), dry whites (like an Entre-Deux-Mers, Graves, or Côtes de Blaye), and sweet whites (like Sauternes or Loupiac). This can be particularly useful when trying to decide which of the 57 wine appellations to focus on during your trip. ✉ *1 cours du XXX-Juillet* ☎ *05–56–00–22–66* ⊕ *www.ecoleduvin-debordeaux.com* 🕐 *Closed Sun.*

Grand Théâtre

ARTS VENUE | One block south of the École du Vin is the city's leading 18th-century monument: the Grand Théâtre, designed by Victor Louis and built between 1773 and 1780. It's the pride of the city, with an elegant exterior ringed by graceful Corinthian columns and a dazzling foyer with a two-winged staircase and a cupola. The theater hall has a frescoed ceiling with a shimmering chandelier composed of 14,000 Bohemian crystals. Contact the Bordeaux tourist office to learn about guided tours. ✉ *Pl. de la Comédie* ☎ *05–56–00–85–95* ⊕ *www.opera-bordeaux.com.*

Haut-Brion

WINERY/DISTILLERY | One of the region's most famous wine-producing châteaux is actually within the city limits: follow N250 southwest from central Bordeaux for 3 km (2 miles) to the district of

Bordeaux's Wine Festival

The four-day Fête du Vin (Wine Festival) at the end of June sees glass-clinking merriment along the banks of the Garonne. The city's grandest square gets packed with workshops, booths, and thousands of wine lovers. Check ⊕ *www. bordeaux-fete-le-vin.com* for all the heady details.

Pessac, home to Haut-Brion, producer of the only non-Médoc wine to be ranked a premier cru (the most elite wine classification). It's claimed that the very buildings surrounding the vineyards create their own microclimate, protecting the precious grapes and allowing them to ripen earlier. The white château looks out over the celebrated pebbly soil. The wines produced at **La Mission–Haut Brion (Domaine Clarence Dillon)**, across the road, are almost as sought-after. ✉ *135 av. Jean-Jaurès, Pessac* ☎ *05–56–00–29–30* ⊕ *www.haut-brion.com* 🎟 *Free 1-hr visits with tasting, weekdays by appointment* 🕐 *Closed mid-July–mid-Aug.*

★ La Cité du Vin

MUSEUM | FAMILY | The exterior of this contemporary building is inspired by the way wine swirls when it is poured into a glass; inside, you'll find an interactive museum highlighting the world of wine and wine making. Every aspect of the history, culture, and manufacture of wine is explored through a range of interactive exhibits that are explained via an audio guide. The visit concludes with a wine tasting on the panoramic terrace at the top of the building. ✉ *1 Esplanade de Pontac* ☎ *05–56–16–20–20* ⊕ *www. laciteduvin.com.*

At the end of June, Bordeaux becomes one big party thanks to the four-day Fête du Vin (Wine Festival).

Musée d'Aquitaine

MUSEUM | Two blocks south of the Cathédrale St-André, this excellent museum takes you on a trip through Bordeaux's history, with emphasis on Roman, medieval, Renaissance, colonial, and 20th-century daily life. The detailed prehistoric section almost saves you a trip to Lascaux II, which is reproduced here in part. ⌧ *20 cours Pasteur* ☎ *05–56–01–51–00* ⊕ *www.musee-aquit-aine-bordeaux.fr* ⌧ *€5* ☾ *Closed Mon.*

Musée des Beaux-Arts

MUSEUM | Bordeaux was one of 15 French cities chosen by Napoléon to showcase his war-acquired works (most notably from Italy) along with bits of existing royal art, so this museum has a fetching collection. Expanded to include pieces from the 15th century to the present, it now displays important paintings by Paolo Veronese (*St-Dorothy*), Camille Corot (*Bath of Diana*), and Odilon Redon (*Apollo's Chariot*), plus sculptures by Auguste Rodin. Located near the Cathédrale St-André and ornate Hôtel de Ville, the

Musée des Beaux-Arts is flanked by tidy gardens. ⌧ *20 cours d'Albret* ☎ *05–56–10–20–56* ⊕ *www.musba-bordeaux.fr* ⌧ *€5* ☾ *Closed Tues.*

Place de la Bourse

PLAZA | The centerpiece of the left bank is this open square built in 1729–33. Ringed with large-windowed buildings, it was beautifully designed by the era's most esteemed architect, Jacques Gabriel, father of Jacques-Ange Gabriel (who went on to remodel Paris's Place de la Concorde). Across the road from the square, just beside the river is the Miroir d'Eau (Mirror of Water), a large rectangle of shallow water that reflects the sky and periodically comes to life as a fountain. ⌧ *Bordeaux.*

Place du Parlement

PLAZA | A few blocks southeast of Place de la Bourse, Place du Parlement is also ringed by elegant 18th-century structures and packed with lively outdoor cafés. ⌧ *Bordeaux.*

Pont de Pierre

BRIDGE/TUNNEL | For a view of the picturesque quayside, stroll across the Garonne on this bridge, built on the orders of Napoléon between 1810 and 1821, and until 1965 the only bridge across the river. ✉ *Bordeaux.*

🍴 Restaurants

Baud et Millet

$$$ | **FRENCH** | With a cellar full of *fromage*—and a vast wine stock that you peruse in lieu of a list—Baud et Millet is a good place to get acquainted with some of the 246 different French cheeses that Charles de Gaulle famously blamed for making this such a complex, and thus difficult, country to govern. Order from the cheese buffet and serve yourself from the downstairs cellar, or start with a cherry-tomato-and-Roquefort clafoutis, then move on to Camembert flambéed in Calvados. **Known for:** fantastic diverse list of cheeses; excellent wines; need to buzz door to gain entry. [$] *Average main: €25* ✉ *19 rue Huguerie* ☎ *05–56–79–05–77* 🕒 *Closed Sun.*

Café Français

$$$ | **BRASSERIE** | Situated on a *grande place* in the Vieille Ville, with cathedral views and a traditional menu of solid sustenance, this venerable bistro attracts those looking for an all-day mixture of café and restaurant. It's the quintessential spot for people-watching over a coffee or meal. **Known for:** central location beside the cathedral; gorgeous views over Place Pey-Berland; terrace tables for people watching. [$] *Average main: €25* ✉ *5–6 pl. Pey-Berland* ☎ *05–56–52–96–69.*

La Tupina

$$$ | **FRENCH** | Under the eye of flamboyant owner Jean-Pierre Xiradakis, *cuisine de terroir* is served up at this classic restaurant on one of Bordeaux's oldest streets. Like the room itself, the menu aspires to *nostalgie,* and it succeeds. **Known for:** olde world atmosphere; products for sale in the épicerie next-door; classic southwestern French cuisine. [$] *Average main: €31* ✉ *6 rue Porte-de-la-Monnaie* ☎ *05–56–91–56–37* 🌐 *www.latupina.com.*

★ Le Chapon-Fin

$$$$ | **FRENCH** | Some say you haven't really been to Bordeaux if you haven't been to Le Chapon-Fin—an epicurean indulgence, housed in one of Bordeaux's most historically esteemed establishments, where guests once included wealthy wine merchants, elite transatlantic travelers, and cultural icons such as Sarah Bernhardt and Toulouse-Lautrec. Founded in 1825, this was one of the first 33 restaurants crowned by Michelin in 1933. **Known for:** gorgeous rococo grotto dining room; prestigious history, including a kingly, 500-year-old dish of whole jackrabbit cut into pieces and then cooked for days in fine wine thickened with blood and liver; superb wine list. [$] *Average main: €38* ✉ *5 rue Montesquieu* ☎ *05–56–79–10–10* 🌐 *www.chapon-fin.com* 🕒 *Closed Sun., Mon., and Aug.*

L'Estacade

$$$ | **MODERN FRENCH** | *Le tout Bordeaux* comes to this trendy glass-encased restaurant, which hangs spectacularly over the Garonne River, for its privileged views of Bordeaux proper and the 18th-century Place de la Bourse on the opposite bank. The cuisine is creative but not edgy (imagine sesame-and-soy-marinated veal, or mullet tartare with cream and fish eggs), while the wine list focuses on young Bordeaux. **Known for:** river views by day, city views by night; contemporary, sleek atmosphere; quiet location away from the bustle of the city center. [$] *Average main: €29* ✉ *Quai de Queyries* ☎ *05–57–54–02–50* 🌐 *www.estacade-restaurant.com.*

Bordeaux doesn't have many grand châteaux-hotels, but the Grand Barrail Château Hôtel & Spa is a winner.

Hotels

Acanthe Hotel

$ | **HOTEL** | Just steps from Place de la Bourse, this budget hotel is an extremely convenient choice if you're looking for something less than grand; rooms have double-paned windows, environmentally friendly wall paint, and freshened bathrooms—top-floor rooms also have views over the neighboring rooftops. **Pros:** genial staff; breakfast (extra charge) includes an organic option; surprisingly inexpensive. **Cons:** some rooms feel a bit claustrophobic; gets a lot of street noise; not all rooms have air-conditioners. $ *Rooms from: €84* ✉ *12 rue St-Remi* ☎ *05–56–81–66–58* ⊕ *www.acanthe-ho-tel-bordeaux.com* ⇗ *20 rooms* ▮⊙▮ *No meals.*

Burdigala

$$$ | **HOTEL** | The modern exterior may be bland, but the interior of this five-star M Gallery Collection hotel dispels any risk of dullness. **Pros:** soundproof rooms; short walk to Gambetta Square; good restaurant and bar. **Cons:** if you want old-world charm, this is not the place; room styles vary; reception can be slightly snooty. $ *Rooms from: €230* ✉ *115 rue Georges-Bonnac* ☎ *05–56–90–16–16* ⊕ *www.burdigala.com* ⇗ *83 rooms* ▮⊙▮ *No meals.*

Des Quatre Sœurs

$ | **HOTEL** | In an elegant 1840 town house near the Grand Théâtre, this hotel has sober, but well-kept rooms of varying sizes, all with air-conditioning. **Pros:** only a few steps from the tourist office; friendly staff; beautiful building with a cool history. **Cons:** central location outshines all other amenities; dull furnishings; not recommended for a lengthy stay. $ *Rooms from: €105* ✉ *6 cours du XXX-Juillet* ☎ *05–57–81–19–20* ⊕ *www.hotel-bordeaux-4soeurs.com* ⇗ *34 rooms* ▮⊙▮ *No meals.*

Grand Hôtel de Bordeaux & Spa

$$$$ | **HOTEL** | Festooned in luxury fabrics and 18th-century furnishings, this posh extravaganza, designed by France's über-chic Jacque Garcia, put Bordeaux back

on the world scene with its veritable army of restaurants and bars, along with a swanky Roman bath–inspired spa—all just steps from the city's Golden Triangle shopping district. **Pros:** marble bathrooms and loads of in-room amenities; deluxe service; superb central location. **Cons:** some rooms lack natural light; superior rooms are small (but executive rooms let you sprawl out); formal atmosphere not great for relaxing. $ *Rooms from: €395 ⊠ 2–5 pl. de la Comédie ☎ 05–57–30–44–44 ⊕ www.ghbordeaux.com ⤶ 126 rooms* ⦿ *No meals.*

La Maison Bord'eaux

$$ | HOTEL | Northwest of the city center, the street-front door of this inconspicuous boutique hotel opens onto a quiet courtyard that once served as a relay stable for carriages and today provides a welcome respite for modern travelers seeking urban tranquility. **Pros:** nicely situated to enjoy both city center and a quiet retreat; chic lounge and dining room; tasteful minimalist decoration. **Cons:** modern style may not ring every traveler's bells; rather spartan room decor; some say rates don't match amenities. $ *Rooms from: €145 ⊠ 113 rue Dr. Albert Barraud ☎ 05–56–44–00–45 ⊕ www. lamaisonbordeaux.com* ⦿ *Closed early Jan.* ⤶ *14 rooms* ⦿ *No meals.*

Quality Hôtel Bordeaux Centre

$$ | HOTEL | At the heart of Bordeaux's pedestrian center, this fully modernized hotel—in a 19th-century building in the old part of town—has compact, deep-tone rooms, and a helpful reception staff. **Pros:** convenient location for sightseeing and shopping; functional rooms; facilities include use of nearby fitness center. **Cons:** somewhat generic furnishings; parking is five minutes away; more efficient than comfortable. $ *Rooms from: €145 ⊠ 27 rue du Parlement-Ste-Catherine ☎ 05–56–81–95–12 ⊕ www.quality-hotelbordeauxcentre.com* ⤶ *84 rooms* ⦿ *No meals.*

🍸 Nightlife

Aux Quatre Coins du Vin

WINE BARS—NIGHTLIFE | This sleek wine and tapas bar has dispensing machines that allow you to taste as many wines as you want in a single sitting. ⊠ *8 rue de la Devise* ☎ *05–57–34–37–29.*

Café des Moines

MUSIC CLUBS | To discover the local band scene, check out Café des Moines, but don't wait too late because the live music in this pub ends before midnight. ⊠ *12 rue des Menuts* ☎ *05–56–92–01–61 ⊕ www.cafedesmoines33.com.*

Café Utopia

CAFES—NIGHTLIFE | Housed in an old church, Utopia is a unique art-house movie theater with original architecture still visible in certain cinema rooms. You can drink and dine at the casual canteen inside. ⊠ *5 pl. Camille-Jullian* ☎ *05–56–52–00–03 ⊕ www.cinemas-utopia.org/ bordeaux.*

l'Apollo

BARS/PUBS | Named after Harlem's Apollo Theater, this casual, friendly pub comes to life around aperitif hour. Once the night gets going, prepare for some serious funk and soul music. ⊠ *19 pl. Fernand-Lafargue* ☎ *05–56–01–25–05 ⊕ www.apollobar.fr.*

🎭 Performing Arts

Grand Théâtre

THEATER | Arguably one of the most beautiful historic theaters in Europe, the Grand Théâtre puts on performances of French plays and, occasionally, operas. The venue (which can be visited on guided tours) is an 18th-century showpiece studded with marble muses. ⊠ *Pl. de la Comédie* ☎ *05–56–00–85–95 ⊕ www. opera-bordeaux.com.*

Shopping

Between the cathedral and the Grand Théâtre are numerous pedestrian streets (Rue Ste-Catherine being the biggest), where stylish stores and clothing boutiques abound. Bordeaux may favor understatement, but there's no lack of elegance in and around its Golden Triangle shopping district.

Bear in mind that the *soldes* (sales) start in France at the height of summer, especially just before the Bastille (July 14) weekend.

Baillardran

FOOD/CANDY | With nine stores in Bordeaux alone, Baillardran is going to be hard to walk by without at least looking in its windows at those indigenous sweet delights, *cannelés de Bordeaux*. Much like a Doric column in miniature, the small indented, caramelized cakes, made with vanilla and a dash of rum, are a delicious regional specialty. ✉ *55 cours de l'Intendance* ☎ *05–56–52–92–64* ⊕ *www. baillardran.com*.

Fromagerie Deruelle

FOOD/CANDY | For a grand selection of cheeses—along with raw milk, smoked-sea-salt butter, bulk honey, and all things creamy and tasty—stop in at Elodie Deruelle's shop, Fromagerie Deruelle. ✉ *66 rue du Pas-St-Georges* ☎ *05–57–83–04–15*.

Grand Déballage de Brocante

OUTDOOR/FLEA/GREEN MARKETS | Within the shadow of the church of St-Michel, a few blocks south of the Pont de Pierre and just off the river, one of the country's largest flea markets operates every second Sunday during the months of March, June, September, and December—all day long. Year-round, a weekly Sunday flea market is also held here, which is just the ticket if you're looking for real bargains away from the storefronts or need a nice excuse to explore the historic St-Michel quarter. ✉ *Pl. St-Michel*.

Jean d'Alos Fromager-Affineur

FOOD/CANDY | For an exceptional selection of cheeses, go to Jean d'Alos Fromager-Affineur. ✉ *4 rue Montesquieu* ☎ *05–56–44–29–66*.

Krazy Kat

BOOKS/STATIONERY | To experience the French fascination for comic books, take a peek in this bookstore, where you'll find Tintin alive and well. The café in back is a nice place to get a feel for the *bande dessinée* (comic book) scene. ✉ *10 rue de la Merci* ☎ *05–56–52–16–60* ⊕ *www. canalbd.net/krazy-kat*.

La Fabrique Pains et Bricoles

FOOD/CANDY | Want Bordeaux's best bread to go with your cheese? Get in line. Apparently, the word's out about La Fabrique Pains et Bricoles because the queue is out the door at this fine bakery—and that's always a good sign. ✉ *47 rue du Pas-St-Georges* ☎ *05–56–44–84–26*.

Vinothèque

WINE/SPIRITS | Next to the tourist information office, Vinothèque sells top-ranked Bordeaux wines. ✉ *8 cours du XXX-Juillet* ☎ *05–57–10–41–41* ⊕ *www. vinotheque-bordeaux.com*.

Margaux

30 km (18½ miles) north of Bordeaux.

Margaux is home to the eponymous appellation that landed more châteaux in the original wine classification of 1855 than any other in Bordeaux. The appellation was a favorite of Thomas Jefferson, who supposedly ordered several cases of the 1784 Château Margaux during a visit to the region. But the unexciting village of Margaux itself still wouldn't be much without the famed terroir that surrounds it.

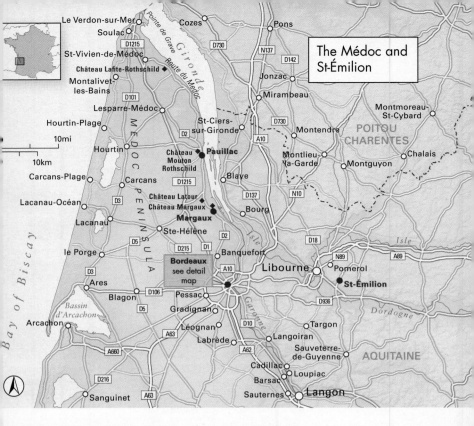

The Médoc and St-Émilion

10mi

10km

Bordeaux
see detail
map

Bay of Biscay

GETTING HERE AND AROUND

TransGironde buses connect Bordeaux with Margaux (90 mins, €2.60) three times a day. The more expensive TER train (€7.70) runs roughly every hour and gets you here in 55 minutes.

 Sights

Château Lascombes

WINERY/DISTILLERY | This classically elegant 17th-century château is actually a facade for a sleek and modern operation. Historically considered an underperformer according to its second grand cru classification, Château Lascombes welcomes novices, wine lovers, and professionals to take a free guided tour of the vineyards and cellars followed by a tasting (by appointment only). ⊠ Margaux ☎ 05–57–88–70–66 ⊕ www.chateau-lascombes.com.

Château Margaux

CASTLE/PALACE | Housed in a magnificent neoclassical building from 1810, Château Margaux is recognized as a producer of premiers crus, and its wine ranks with Graves's Haut-Brion as one of Bordeaux's five finest reds. As with most of the top Bordeaux châteaux, visits and tastings are by appointment only. While there's no charge for these, appointments are reserved for serious seekers accompanied by professionals in the trade. ⊠ Margaux ☎ 05–57–88–83–83 ⊕ www.chateau-margaux.com.

Château Palmer

WINERY/DISTILLERY | It is said that in some years the wines of Château Palmer (classified as a third cru) can rival those of neighboring Château Margaux (a premier cru). Now operating according to a biodynamic philosophy, it accepts visitors at no charge on weekdays by appointment. ✉ *Margaux* ☎ *05–57–88–72–72* 🌐 *www.chateau-palmer.com.*

Hotels

Villa St. Simon

$ | **B&B/INN** | A 15-minute ferry ride across the other side of the Garonne estuary takes you to the pretty waterfront town of Blaye, where this welcoming hotel is located. **Pros:** town is home to an UNESCO-designated citadel; quality on-site bistro; personalized service with wine experts. **Cons:** not the place for chichi châteaux seekers; must cross river to access Médoc vineyards; might be too old-fashioned for some. [$] *Rooms from: €100* ✉ *8 cours du Generale De Gaulle, Blaye* ☎ *05–57–42–99–66* 🌐 *villastsimon.com* 🛏 *12 rooms* 🍴 *No meals.*

Pauillac

90 km (56 miles) north of Bordeaux.

Pauillac lays claim to three of the five Bordeaux grands crus—Lafite Rothschild, Latour, and Mouton Rothschild. It's said that Pauillac wines are textbook Bordeaux in style, with the ability to age and evolve for decades. But if the posh prices of these top reds aren't for you, ask about bike rentals at the town's tourist office and pedal off to visit any of the slightly less expensive wineries nearby. Pauillac is the prettiest of all the towns and villages in the Médoc, so just strolling the riverfront or lingering at a waterside restaurant has its own rewards.

GETTING HERE AND AROUND

If you're heading north, you'll have to make your way to or through Pauillac. TransGironde runs buses from Bordeaux three times a day (2 hrs, €2.70). TER trains cost extra (€11.20), but they're faster (1 hr 15 mins) and more frequent; at least 12 from Bordeaux arrive daily at the Gare de Pauillac on 2 bis place Verdun.

VISITOR INFORMATION Pauillac Tourist Office ✉ *La Verrerie* ☎ *05–56–59–03–08* 🌐 *www.pauillac-medoc.com.*

Sights

Château Lafite Rothschild

WINERY/DISTILLERY | Lafite Rothschild is among the most resonant names in the wine world. Even by the giddy standards of the Médoc, Lafite—owned by the Rothschild family since 1868 and a recorded producer since 1234—is a temple of wine making at its most memorable. Prices may be sky-high, but no one fortunate enough to sample one of the classic vintages will forget the experience in a hurry. Too bad you can't visit the family château on the grounds—its rooms are the defining examples of *le style Rothschild,* one of the most opulent styles of 19th-century interior decoration. ✉ *Pauillac* ☎ *05–56–59–26–83* 🌐 *www.lafite.com* 🎟 *Free* 🕒 *Closed Sun. and Aug.–Oct.*

Château Latour

WINERY/DISTILLERY | Tastings and tours at the renowned Château Latour are typically free, but very selective—you have to be a serious taster, accompanied by a guide or professional in the wine trade, and you will be expected to make a purchase. Reservations are also required, and these must sometimes be made a month in advance. ✉ *St-Lambert* ☎ *05–56–73–19–80* 🌐 *www.chateau-latour.com.*

★ Château Mouton Rothschild

WINERY/DISTILLERY | Most of the great vineyards in this area are strictly private, although owners are usually receptive to inquiries from bona fide wine connoisseurs. One, however, has long boasted a welcoming visitor center: Mouton Rothschild, whose eponymous wine was brought to perfection in the 1930s by that flamboyant figure Baron Philippe de

Cobblestoned St-Émilion is filled with medieval beauty.

Rothschild. Wine fans flock here for visits lasting from 1 hour, 45 minutes to 2½ hours. Depending on the tour, your visit might include a trip to the cellars, the *chai* (wine warehouse), and the museum, including a display of wine labels. There, is of course, a wine tasting at the end. Prices depend on the length of the tour and the wines sampled. Visits are by appointment only; be sure to reserve at least two weeks in advance. ✉ *Le Pouyalet* ☎ *05–56–73–21–29* 🌐 *www.chateau-mouton-rothschild.com* 🎫 *From €50* 🕒 *Closed weekends.*

Hotels

Château Cordeillan-Bages

$$ | **HOTEL** | Though the clean-lined, contemporary interior of this 17th-century, stone-faced, wine-producing mansion may not speak to everyone, the vines growing right up to the property, the luxury rooms, the sommelier's dream of a wine cellar (with over 200 different champagnes alone), and the celebrated restaurant are definite inducements. **Pros:** lovely marble building; tranquil location; expert wine-tasting and discovery courses offered. **Cons:** very modern decor not to everyone's taste; remote with airport 45 km (27 miles) away—but you could ask to use the château's helipad; even the "premium" rooms are not cheap. [$] *Rooms from: €213* ✉ *Rte. des Châteaux, 1½ km (1 mile) south of town* ☎ *05–56–59–24–24* 🌐 *www.cordeillan-bages.com* 🕒 *Closed late Dec.–mid-Mar.* 🛏 *28 rooms* 🍴 *No meals.*

France & Angleterre

$ | **HOTEL** | Occupying a low-slung, 19th-century building that overlooks the quaint waterfront and Gironde estuary, this low-key spot is a convenient choice if you wish to explore Pauillac's winding streets. **Pros:** central location; estuary views; good food in restaurant. **Cons:** small, generic rooms; budget furnishings; not rich in facilities. [$] *Rooms from: €77* ✉ *3 quai Albert-Pichon* ☎ *05–56–59–01–20* 🌐 *www.hoteldefrance-angleterre.com* 🕒 *Closed mid-Dec.–mid-Jan.* 🛏 *48 rooms* 🍴 *No meals.*

St-Émilion

74 km (41 miles) southeast of Pauillac, 35 km (22 miles) east of Bordeaux.

Suddenly the sun-fired flatlands of Pomerol break into hills and send you tumbling into St-Émilion. This jewel of a town has old buildings of golden stone, ruined town walls, well-kept ramparts offering magical views, and a church hewn into a cliff. Sloping vineyards invade from all sides, and thousands of tourists invade down the middle, many thirsting for the red wine and macarons that bear the town's name. The medieval streets, delightfully cobbled (though often very steep), are filled with craft shops, bakeries, cafés, restaurants, and—of course—wine stores (St-Émilion reaches maturity earlier than other Bordeaux reds and is often better value for the money than Médoc or Graves). For the best export prices try Ets Martin (⊠ *25 rue Guadet* ⊕ *www.etsmartin.com*), or climb the stairs to the *crémant* (sparkling wine) specialist and its *bar à bulles* ("bubbles bar") Les Cordaliers (⊕ *www.lescordeliers.com*), where you can buy a glass or bottle of Bordeaux's bubbly to sip in a lovely courtyard beneath 13th-century cloister ruins. Note that the town's Office de Tourisme organizes tours of the pretty local vineyards, as well as assorted wine-theme classes and workshops. It also rents bikes (€18 per day) if you'd prefer to explore the surrounding area independently.

GETTING HERE AND AROUND

Direct TER trains from Bordeaux depart at least a dozen times daily during the week and six times daily on weekends and holidays (37 mins, €9.50). It will cost you €2.70 if you opt to take a TransGironde bus from Bordeaux to St-Émilion, with a total travel time of about an hour. Alternatively, you can take a bus to Libourne and from there take a taxi to St-Émilion.

VISITOR INFORMATION St-Émilion Tourist Office ⊠ *Pl. des Cremeaux* ☎ *05–57–55–28–28* ⊕ *www.saint-emilion-tourisme.com.*

Sights

Château Angelus

WINERY/DISTILLERY | Named for the prayer-signaling church bells that can be heard from its vineyards, this fabled château is a premier grand cru property. ⊠ *St-Émilion* ☎ *05–57–24–71–39* ⊕ *www.angelus.com.*

Château Ausone

WINERY/DISTILLERY | Just south of the town walls, Château Ausone is an estate that is ranked with Château Angelus as a producer of St-Émilion's finest wines. ⊠ *St-Émilion* ☎ *05–57–24–24–57* ⊕ *chateau-ausone.fr.*

Château du Roi (*King's Castle*)

CASTLE/PALACE | A stroll along the 13th-century ramparts takes you to the Château du Roi. To this day nobody knows whether it was Henry III of England or King Louis VIII of France who chose the site and ordered its building. ⊠ *St-Émilion.*

Église Monolithe (*Monolithic Church*)

RELIGIOUS SITE | One of Europe's largest underground churches, the Église Monolithe was hewn out of the rock face between the 9th and 12th centuries by monks faithful to the memory of St-Émilion, an 8th-century hermit and miracle worker. Its spiretop *clocher* (bell tower) rises out of the bedrock, dominating the center of town. The church may only be visited on a guided tour reserved online. The visit includes the catacombs and the underground cell of St-Émilion. ⊠ *Pl. du Marché* 🎫 *€9.*

Place du Marché

PLAZA | From the castle ramparts, cobbled steps lead down to Place du Marché, a leafy square where cafés remain open late into the balmy summer night—just be prepared for the inflated prices they charge. ⊠ *St-Émilion.*

 Restaurants

Chai Pascal

$ | **BISTRO** | This cozy yet stylish restaurant and wine bar is popular with locals in the wine trade. The menu is limited, but made fresh and very good value compared to the generally elevated prices of St-Émilion. **Known for:** local cuisine including hearty stews; excellent value; intellectual vibe. $ *Average main: €15* ⊠ *37 rue Guadet* ☎ *05–57–24–52–45* ⊕ *www.chai-pascal.com* ⊗ *Closed Sun. Nov.–June. No dinner Mon.*

Chez Germaine

$$ | **BRASSERIE** | Family cooking and regional dishes are the focus at this central St-Émilion eatery, which serves lunch only. The upstairs dining room and the terrace are both pleasant places to enjoy reasonably priced set menus. **Known for:** grilled meats and fish; almond macarons for dessert; outdoor seating. $ *Average main: €16* ⊠ *13 pl. du Clocher* ☎ *05–57–74–49–34* ⊗ *Closed mid Nov.– mid Feb. No dinner.*

Hotels

Auberge de la Commanderie

$ | **HOTEL** | Close to the ramparts, this 19th-century hotel has a gorgeous, white-shuttered facade that blends in beautifully with St-Émilion's stonework. **Pros:** lovely location inside the village; some rooms overlook the garden; charming decor. **Cons:** some rooms are small and simply equipped; mod color scheme may be too bold for some tastes; you have to pay for parking: €15/night. $ *Rooms from: €95* ⊠ *2 rue Porte Brunet* ☎ *05–57–24–70–19* ⊕ *www.aubergedela-commanderie.com* ⊗ *Closed mid-Dec.– mid-Feb.* ⌨ *17 rooms* ⦿| *No meals.*

Château Lamothe du Prince Noir

$$ | **B&B/INN** | Magically set on a circular moat, fitted out with a storybook turret, and covered in an ambuscade of ivy, this manor house is one of the most charming options to be found between St-Émilion and Bordeaux—it's also one of the oldest estates: Edward, Prince of Wales (aka the "Black Prince"), reputedly set up shop here in the 14th century. **Pros:** very tranquil; all bedrooms are south-facing with lots of light; generous breakfast. **Cons:** no restaurant—you'll have to go out for dinner; ornate embellishments can seem overdone; long way from St-Émilion proper. $ *Rooms from: €195* ⊠ *6 rte. du Stade, 25 km (16 miles) west of St-Émilion, 20 km (12 miles) northeast of Bordeaux, St-Sulpice-et-Cameyrac* ☎ *05– 56–44–91–21* ⊕ *www.lechateaulamothe. com* ⌨ *5 suites* ⦿| *Free Breakfast.*

★ Grand Barrail Château Hôtel & Spa

$$$ | **HOTEL** | Presiding over the picturesque vineyards encircling St-Émilion, this fairy-tale Belle Époque château has gorgeous guest rooms that are at once classic and contemporary (for the full storybook experience, ask for one in the main 19th-century building rather than the modern luxury annex). **Pros:** expansive vineyard views; special spa packages; golf and hot-air-balloon rides nearby. **Cons:** pricey; fairy-tale ambience borders on unoriginal; breakfast not included. $ *Rooms from: €320* ⊠ *Rte. de Libourne, 4 km (2½ miles) northwest of St-Émilion on D243* ☎ *05–57–55–37–00* ⊕ *www.grand-barrail.com* ⌨ *46 rooms* ⦿| *No meals.*

Le Relais de Franc Mayne

$$ | **HOTEL** | Once a relay station for weary travelers on an ancient Gallo-Roman path, this grand cru classé property has a choice of comfortable guest rooms, including a unique tree house with a beautiful view over the vineyards. **Pros:** walking or biking distance to town through classic vineyards; natural swimming pool; fascinating focus on wine. **Cons:** no restaurant; definitely rural and distant from nightlife; no service after 7 pm until the following morning. ⓢ *Rooms from: €195* ✉ *14 la Gomerie* ☎ *05–57–24–62–61* ⊕ *www.relaisfranc-mayne.com* ⊙ *Closed mid-Nov.–Mar.* ⇌ *5 rooms* ⓞⓛ *Free Breakfast.*

★ L'Hostellerie de Plaisance

$$$$ | **HOTEL** | Flaunting a unique interior design masterminded by Alberto Pinto and an elite location in the upper part of town, just across the way from the famous Église Monolithe, this stunning Italianate mansion has long been considered the top hotel in St-Émilion. **Pros:** superb style; ideally located in St-Émilion proper; gorgeous rooftop views. **Cons:** some rooms are small; extremely pricey; parking somewhat distant from the hotel. ⓢ *Rooms from: €390* ✉ *3 pl. du Clocher* ☎ *05–57–55–07–55* ⊕ *www.hostelleriedeplaisance.com* ⊙ *Closed mid-Dec.–mid-Feb.* ⇌ *21 rooms* ⓞⓛ *No meals.*

Chapter 19

THE DORDOGNE

Updated by
Jennifer Ladonne

⊙ Sights   🍴 Restaurants   🛏 Hotels   🛍 Shopping   🍸 Nightlife

★★★☆☆   ★★★★☆   ★★☆☆☆   ★★☆☆☆   ★☆☆☆☆

WELCOME TO THE DORDOGNE

TOP REASONS TO GO

★ **Fantastic food:** Périgord truffles, foie gras, walnuts, plums, and myriad species of mushroom jostle for attention on restaurant menus here—and the goose-liver pâté is as good as it gets.

★ **Very ancient art:** Lascaux is like the Louvre of Paleolithic art, and millions have witnessed prehistory writ large on its spectacularly painted cave walls.

★ **Religious Rocamadour:** Climb toward heaven up the towering cliff to Place St-Amadour's seven chapels and you might be transported to a better place.

★ **Sarlat's Cité Médiévale:** Feast your eyes on Sarlat's honey-color houses and 16th-century streets, and then just feast at the hundred or so wine and foie gras shops.

★ **Versailles in the sky:** A dizzying 400 feet above the Dordogne River, the Jardin de Marqueyssac is a glorious garden with a 3-km (2-mile) maze of topiaries, parterres, and hedges.

Just northeast of Bordeaux, the region of Périgord is famed for its prehistoric art, truffle-rich cuisine, and once-upon-a-time villages. The best of these delights are found in the beloved *département* (province) called the Dordogne. Part of the Aquitaine region, this living postcard is threaded by the Dordogne River, which, after its descent from the mountainous Massif Central, weaves westward past prehistoric sites like Lascaux. Astounding, too, are the medieval cliff-hewn villages like Rocamadour—provided that you manage to peer through the crowds in high season.

1 Bergerac. The region's main transportation hub.

2 Monbazillac. A hilltop wine village with a stunning castle.

3 Monpazier. A beautiful fortified village.

4 Biron. Home to a massive hilltop château.

5 Cahors. A great base for exploring the Lot River Valley.

6 St-Corq-Lapopie. A beautiful village perched atop the Lot River.

7 Rocamadour. A medieval village set over a dramatic cliff.

8 Le Roque-Gageac. A cliff-facing village.

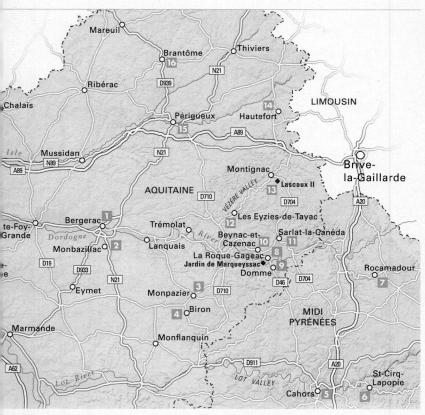

9 Domme. Home to a prehistoric grotto.

10 Beynac-et-Cazenac. Home to a storybook castle.

11 Sarlat-la-Canéda. A regional center famed for its half-timber medieval vibe.

12 Les Eyzies-de-Tayac. The entryway to the prehistoric capital of France.

13 Lascaux. The famous caves that are one of the world's first works of art.

14 Hautefort. A town with a spectacular castle.

15 Périgueaux. A bustling little city.

16 Brantôme. A small town that was once the site of a secluded monastery.

Want to smile happily ever after? Linger in a fantasyland full of castles, clifftop châteaux, and storybook villages? Join the club. Since the 1990s the Dordogne region has ranked among the hottest destinations in France. Formerly one of those off-the-beaten-path areas, it's now in danger of getting four-starred, boutiqued, and postcarded to death, but scratch the surface and you can still find one of the most authentic and appealing regions of rural France.

What's more—and unlike the Loire Valley, for example, where attractions are often far apart—you can discover romantic riverside château after château with each kilometer traveled. Factor in four troglodyte villages, numerous natural *gouffres* (chasms), the sky-kissing village of Rocamadour, and some of the most famous prehistoric sights in the world, and you can see why all these attractions have not gone unnoticed: in July and August even the smallest village is often packed with sightseers.

The Dordogne *département* (province) is in the Aquitaine region of southwest France, where oak and chestnut forests crowd in on about 1,200 châteaux, most from the 13th and 14th centuries. The area is marked by rich, luxuriant valleys, through which flow clear-water rivers such as the Dordogne, Isle, Dronne, Vézére, and Lot. Separating the valleys are rugged plateaus of granite and limestone, sharp outcroppings of rock,

and steep, sheer cliffs. Offering a nice contrast to the region's rugged physiognomy and *nature sauvage* (wilderness) are hyper-picturesque villages such as La Roque-Gageac, wedged between rocky cliffs and the Dordogne River.

The region is centered on Sarlat, and its impeccably restored medieval buildings make it a great place to use as a base, except in high season when crowds are dense. The area around Sarlat is honeycombed with dozens of *grottes* (caves) filled with Paleolithic drawings, etchings, and carvings. Just north of Sarlat is Lascaux, a painted cave that is like the "Louvre" of Cro-Magnon man (early modern Europeans) and the region's most notable prehistoric sight. In modern times the area's caves gained additional historic significance when members of the French Resistance came here during World War II to hide themselves and their cache of weapons from the Nazis.

In the Middle Ages this region was under Merovingian rule, a Frankish dynasty. From the 9th century the first group of French kings ruled the region; it was subsequently divided up by the dukes of Aquitaine, who blended Roman law with Visigothic laws. The region later came under English rule, and was returned to the French crown around 1370. The crown complicated matters further by giving the area to the Spanish house of Bourbon in 1574, which meant Henry of Navarre inherited it—but in 1589 Henry became Henri IV, king of France, so the region returned to the French crown once again. Well, history is repeating itself, at least from an English perspective, as over the last several decades the British have moved back here in droves. They see the Dordogne as the quintessential French escape—and now the rest of the world is following in their footsteps.

MAJOR REGIONS

Western Dordogne. The western part of the Dordogne is rife with castles, like those at Monbazillac and Biron; and lands cultivated by peasant farmers for centuries ring *bastide* towns, such as Monpazier, which were once heavily fortified. Heading southeast, the Lot Valley—a 50-km (31-mile) gorge punctuated by medieval villages—is anchored by the lively town of Cahors. Nearby St-Cirq-Lapopie is like a Renaissance-era time machine, while Rocamadour's sky-touching Cité Religieuse is one of France's most famous pilgrimage shrines.

Eastern Périgord. You'll have a tough time figuring out which sector of the Dordogne is the most beautiful, but many give the prize to the Périgord Noir. Immerse yourself in the past at Sarlat-la-Canéda, a regional capital so beautifully preserved that film crews flock here for its 16th- and 17th-century turrets and towers. Nearby are the riverside village of La Roque–Gageac and the hilltop castle at Beynac. To the north is the Vézère

Valley, the prehistoric capital of France, home to fabled Lascaux. Beyond lies the thriving little city of Périgueux. For three centuries during the Middle Ages, this entire region was a battlefield in the wars between the French and the English. Of the châteaux dotting the area, those at Hautefort and Beynac are among the most spectacular.

Planner

When to Go

The Dordogne has a temperate climate, but it's not Provence. Because this is France's third-largest département, local differences abound—winds blow in from the Atlantic along the western borders, and varying topographic and continental weather conditions affect the eastern and northern areas. Sarlat, in the southeast, tends to get a lot more winter sun than other locales. As you move westward toward the Atlantic conditions get foggier, cloudier, and colder; however, in summer the southwestern Dordogne is sunnier than the rest of the region. All in all, spring and autumn are the best times to visit since there aren't as many tourists around, and the weather is still pleasant.

Planning Your Time

From a practical perspective, staying in Sarlat or thereabouts would be your best plan if you want to really appreciate this diverse region. Not only is the historic town a worthwhile destination in its own right, it's also near the top sights: Lascaux and Les Eyzies de Tayac lie to the north; Beynac-et-Cazenac, La Roque-Gageac, and Domme are immediately south; Rocamadour is a little farther to the southeast. Sarlat is also just off the A20 highway, which brings you south to Cahors and north to the regional airport in Brive La Gaillarde (the Bergerac airport to the west is a bit farther afield).

After getting yourself situated, you can explore the camera-ready villages, imposing châteaux, and captivating caves that sprinkle this part of France like so much historical and cultural confetti. If you prefer solitude and unspoiled scenery you won't have any trouble finding them in the vast, sparsely populated countryside. All you have to do is head for the hills—literally. Wherever you go, just be sure to leave plenty of time for dining. The Dordogne's edible delights (foie gras and truffles chief among them) are as famous as the region's varied sights.

Visiting the Prehistoric Wonders

Perhaps the Dordogne's most famous sights are its prehistoric caves and grottos, with the legendary Lascaux topping the list. It's been closed to the public since 1963, but many others are open for viewing. Lascaux IV—a near-perfect replica—can accept up to 2,000 visitors a day; on the other hand, the Grotte des Combarelles takes only 40 in total and no more than six on any given tour, thereby guaranteeing an intimate look.

Either because demand far outstrips supply, or because tickets are so limited, it's recommended that you call or email to prebook tickets whenever possible. For places like Lascaux IV, reserve as far ahead as you can (up to a year), especially in summer and the French school vacations, which happen four times a year for two weeks at the end of October, December, February, and April. For less popular sights, a couple of days should suffice. Alternately, you can try signing up for a day-of tour first thing in the morning.

The main tourist offices in the region, such as the one at Les Eyzies-de-Tayac,

have the lowdown on all the caves and prehistoric sights in the area. If you can't secure tickets in advance, it's worth stopping by the cave of your choice even if the office says they are sold out, as space often opens up. Be forewarned: you might get signed onto a tour that starts in a couple of hours, leaving you with time to kill, so have a game plan handy for other places to visit nearby.

Getting Here and Around

AIR TRAVEL
The closest major airport is in Bordeaux, 88 km (55 miles) west of Bergerac, but the Dordogne has regional airports in Bergerac itself as well as in Brive La Gaillarde. The former, Aéroport de Bergerac-Périgord-Dordogne, receives regular flights from Paris Orly, operated by Twin Jet, plus two dozen flights per week from the United Kingdom, operated by budget carriers Flybe and Ryanair. Ryanair also lands farther east at Aéroport de Brive–Vallée de la Dordogne, as does the low-cost airline HOP!, thereby providing links with Paris and select other European cities.

AIRPORT INFORMATION Aéroport de Bergerac-Périgord-Dordogne ⊠ *Rte. d'Agen, Bergerac* ☎ *05–53–22–25–25* ⊕ *www.bergerac.aeroport.fr.* **Aéroport de Bordeaux-Mérignac** ☎ *05–56–34–50–50* ⊕ *www.bordeaux.aeroport.fr.* **Aéroport de Brive–Vallée de la Dordogne** ☎ *05–55–22–40–00* ⊕ *www.aeroport-brive-vallee-dordogne.com.*

BIKE TRAVEL
The Dordogne is prime biking territory. In particular, the hour-long ride between Rocamadour and the Gouffre de Padirac might just be one of your fondest experiences in France; and let's not forget daylong bike trips through the neighboring Célé Valley and the 35-km (22-mile) trip to the prehistoric Grotte du Pech Merle outside the town of Cabrerets. Happily, there are plenty of *cyclotourisme*

operators who rent bikes in assorted styles and sizes. Electric bicycles are increasingly available, too.

CONTACTS Bike Bus ☎ *05–53–31–10–61* ⊕ *www.bike-bus.com.* **Liberty Cycle** ✉ *1 av. du Périgord, Sarlat-la-Canéda* ☎ *078–1–84–78–79* ⊕ *liberty-cycle.com.*

BOAT TRAVEL

One popular way to see the Dordogne's landscape is by canoe or kayak. Rental depots spring up frequently along the rivers of the region, especially near campgrounds. The curving and winding Vézère River is a very boat-friendly stretch, while the valley of the Lot River is famous for its dreamy dawn mists. Single-person boats go for about €10–€20 an hour, double that for two-person boats. Some rental companies will take you by car to a departure point upstream, and some will even provide tents and waterproof casings for overnight trips. For more information, pick up boating brochures at any tourist office in the region.

BUS TRAVEL

The regional bus operator in the Dordogne is CFTA. It connects the main towns with 14 bus lines, operated by eight different outfits. The maximum fare is €2, and there are reduced rates if you buy 10 passes (€14), so traveling by bus in the Dorgdogne could save you a lot of money. For urban transport in Périgueux use Peribus; in Bergerac use CAB (Communauté d'Agglomération Bergeracoise).

BUS INFORMATION CAB (*Communauté d'Agglomération Bergeracoise*) ☎ *05–53–63–96–97* ⊕ *www.la-cab.fr.* **CFTA** ✉ *Gare Routière, 19 rue Denis-Papin, Périgueux* ☎ *05–53–08–43–13* ⊕ *www.cftaco.fr.* **Peribus** ✉ *22 cours Montaigne, Périgueux* ☎ *05–53–53–30–37* ⊕ *peribus.agglo-perigueux.fr.*

CAR TRAVEL

The Dordogne has a surplus of memorable sights, many of them off the beaten path; the public transport system here, however, is limited. So you'll want a car

to maximize touring opportunities and minimize frustration. The A20 is the main route for motorists, extending from Paris almost all the way to Cahors. It connects with the N21 at Limoges, which brings you down into Périgueux and Bergerac. A89 links Bordeaux to Périgueux and D936 runs along the Dordogne Valley from Libourne to Bergerac continuing as D660 toward Sarlat.

TRAIN TRAVEL

The superfast TGV Atlantique service links Paris's Gare Montparnasse to Bordeaux—the major rail hub in this part of France—covering 585 km (365 miles) in 3 hours 30 minutes. From Bordeaux, 15 trains daily run to Bergerac (1 hr 23 mins), at least a dozen serve Périgueux (1 hr 30 mins), and another six go to Sarlat (2 hrs 45 mins). If you're bound for Cahors, in the southern Dordogne, you can get there direct from Paris's Gare d'Austerlitz in just more than five hours.

TRAIN INFORMATION SNCF ☎ *3635* (*€0.40 per min*) ⊕ *www.sncf.com.*

Restaurants

If you're traveling in the Dordogne between October and March, it's essential to call restaurants ahead of time to avoid disappointment, as some shut down for the slow season. Closing times, too, can be variable. When you do snag your table, scan the menu for listings of dishes "à la périgourdine," which usually means you're about to enjoy truffles or foie gras, or perhaps even both.

Hotels

Advance booking is recommended in the highly popular Dordogne, where hotels fill up quickly, particularly in midsummer. Many country or small-town hotels expect you to have at least one dinner with them, and if you have two meals a day with your lodging and stay several nights, you can save money. Prices off-season (October–May) often drop as much as 20%, but note that some hotels close from the end of October through March. *Restaurant and hotel reviews have been shortened. For full information, visit Fodors.com.*

What It Costs in Euros			
$	$$	$$$	$$$$
RESTAURANTS			
under €18	€18–€24	€25–€32	over €32
HOTELS			
under €106	€106–€145	€146–€215	over €215

Visitor Information

The main tourist office for the region, the Comité Départemental du Tourisme de la Dordogne, is in Périgueux. Its multilingual website is a great resource (to access English info, simply click the Union Jack icon). Specific areas—including Périgord Noir and the Lot Valley—also have their own helpful websites, as do many of the local tourist offices (⇨ *listed under town names below*). Note that in the small villages many tourist offices have unusual opening hours.

CONTACTS Comité Départemental du Tourisme de la Dordogne ✉ *25 rue Wilson, Périgueux* ☎ *05–53–35–50–24* ⊕ *www.dordogne-perigord-tourisme.fr.* **Comité Départemental du Tourisme de Lot-et-Garonne** ✉ *271 rue de Péchabout* ☎ *05–53–66–14–14* ⊕ *www.tourisme-lotetgaronne.com.* **Les Offices de Tourisme du Périgord Noir** ✉ *3 rue de Tourny, Sarlat-la-Canéda* ☎ *05–53–31–45–45* ⊕ *www.perigordnoir.com.* **Tourisme dans le Lot** ☎ *05–65–35–07–09* ⊕ *www.tourisme-lot.com.*

Bergerac

57 km (36 miles) east of St-Émilion, 112 km (70 miles) east of Bordeaux.

In case you made the connection, yes, this is the Bergerac of Cyrano de Bergerac fame—but not exactly. The real satirist and playwright Cyrano (1619–55), who inspired Edmond Rostand's long-nose swashbuckler, was born in Paris and never set foot anywhere near here. That hasn't prevented his legend from being preempted by the town fathers, who erected an exceedingly ugly statue of Cyrano and plastered his schnoz all over Bergerac's promotional materials. Frankly, they needn't have bothered. The town's gorgeous old half-timber houses, narrow alleys, riverside setting, and gastronomic specialties are more than enough to attract tourists from Bordeaux or Sarlat. If you're only coming for the day, try to arrive on Wednesday or Saturday, when colorful farmers' markets are held (the latter being the larger of the two).

GETTING HERE AND AROUND
About 5 km (8 miles) south of town, the Aéroport Bergerac-Dordogne-Périgord is served by budget carriers that fly passengers in from Paris (Orly), London (Stansted), and a handful of other cities. There is no airport shuttle yet, so you have to take a taxi (☎ *05–53–23–32–32*) into the town center. Fifteen trains daily link Bergerac with Bordeaux (1 hr 23 mins) and Sarlat (1 hr 20 mins); regular buses from Périgueux (1 hr 35 mins) also pull in at the train station on Avenue du 108e. Within Bergerac, the CAB urban bus service will help you get around (€1.10).

VISITOR INFORMATION Bergerac Tourist Office ✉ *97 rue Neuve d'Argenson* ☎ *05–53–57–03–11* ⊕ *www.pays-bergerac-tourisme.com.*

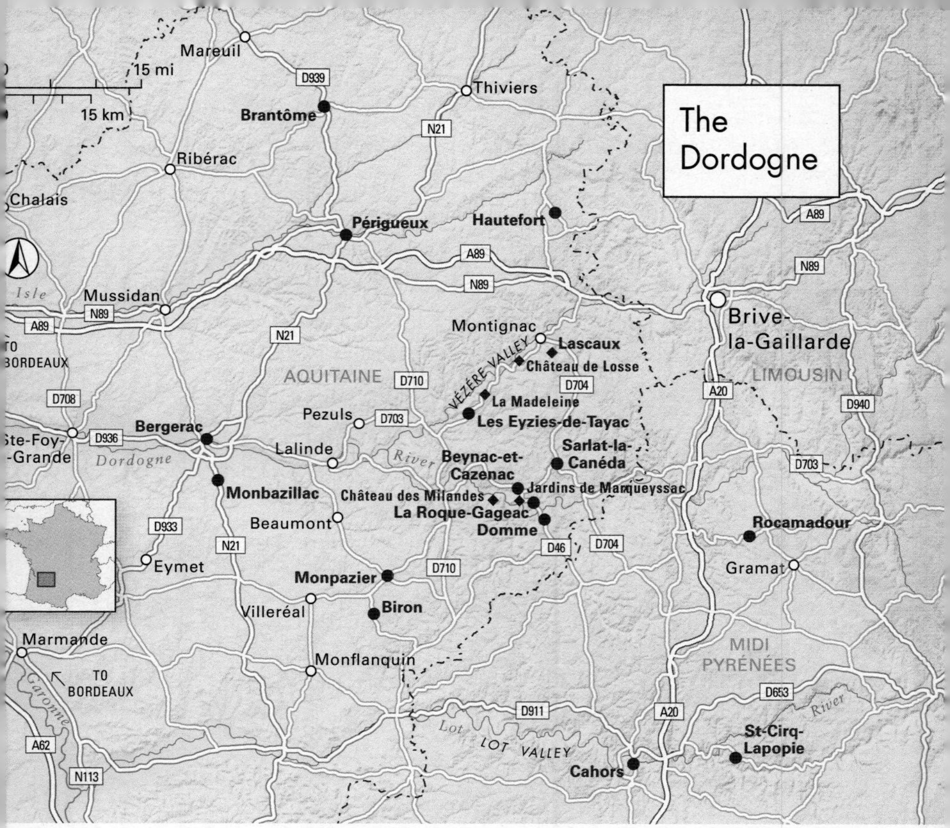

Sights

Cloître des Récollets

WINERY/DISTILLERY | This former convent is now in the wine business, and its stone-and-brick buildings, dating from the 12th to the 15th century, include galleries, a large vaulted cellar, and a cloister where the **Maison des Vins** (Wine Center) provides information on—and samples of—local vintages of sweet whites and fruity young reds. ✉ *1 rue des Récollets* ☎ *05–53–63–57–55* 🎟 *€5* 🕒 *Closed Jan.*

Périgord Gabarres

TOUR—SIGHT | From Easter to October, you can cruise along the Dordogne in an old wooden sailboat operated by Périgord Gabarres; trips cost €9.50–€12. ✉ *Bergerac* ☎ *05–53–24–58–80* 🌐 *www.gabarres.fr* 🕒 *Closed Nov.–Mar.*

Restaurants

★ Le Vin'Quatre

$$ | **MODERN FRENCH** | If the tantalizing list of daily specials on the blackboard isn't temptation enough, tables full of happy diners should clue you in that this is Bergerac's top bistro. Though modern in decor and presentation, the menu is steeped in classic French gastronomy, favoring fresh local meats and produce, but with a flair for the exotic: roasted cod with squash puree and Madras curry risotto, or crispy slow-roasted pork shoulder caramelized in tamarind sauce and served with cola-nut-spiced mashed potatoes. **Known for:** frequently changing seasonal menu; impeccable service; a top address in town. [$] *Average main: €24* ✉ *14 rue St-Clar* 🌐 *levinquatre.fr.*

L'Imparfait

$ | FRENCH FUSION | In the heart of old Bergerac, this restaurant is full of character with beamed ceilings, openwork stone, brick walls, large lamps, and cane-back chairs. The lunch and dinner menus, which change with the seasons, are good values, considering you can start with such delights as warm oysters with saffron or a skewer of langoustine with honey and rosemary, and then move on, perhaps, to ravioli in a citron sauce. **Known for:** excellent price-to-quality ratio; pleasant rustic atmosphere; elegant presentation. *$ Average main: €16* ☒ *8–10 rue des Fontaines* ☎ *05–53–57–47–92* ⊕ *imparfait.com.*

Hotels

Bordeaux

$ | HOTEL | Although it's been in business since 1855 and has occasionally played host to some famous guests (Francis Bacon and François Mitterrand among them), the Bordeaux of today has contemporary furnishings and simple, tidy rooms—the best of which look out on the garden courtyard. **Pros:** good location close to the market, the Old Town, and the train station; good value; secure, inexpensive parking. **Cons:** rooms are a little too understated; rooms and grounds in need of some updating; no coffee or tea-making facilities in rooms. *$ Rooms from: €90* ☒ *38 pl. Gambetta* ☎ *05–53–57–12–83* ⊕ *www.hotel-bordeaux-bergerac.com* ↪ *40 rooms* ⦿ *No meals.*

Château les Merles

$$$ | HOTEL | A nice way to experience the lovely rolling countryside just outside Bergerac, this handsome château offers everything you need for a relaxing visit, including a large pool, fine dining, golf, and charming paths for lovely walks. **Pros:** exceedingly helpful and friendly staff; very good restaurant with local specialties; close to many sites. **Cons:** some stairs for top-floor access; some rooms in need of updating; pool not heated.

$ Rooms from: €190 ☒ *3 chemin des Merles, 15 km (9 miles) east of Bergerac, just off D660* ☎ *05–53–63–13–42* ⊕ *www.lesmerles.com* ↪ *15 rooms* ⦿ *No meals.*

Monbazillac

6 km (4 miles) south of Bergerac.

The hilltop village of Monbazillac provides spectacular views of the sweet-wine–producing vineyards tumbling toward the Dordogne River.

GETTING HERE AND AROUND

CAB buses on the Bergerac–Bouniagues route travel to Monbazillac three times a day—but the 6-km (4-mile) journey takes 40 minutes, so you're better off driving.

Sights

Château de Monbazillac

CASTLE/PALACE | The storybook corner towers of the beautifully proportioned, 16th-century, gray-stone château pay tribute to the fortress tradition of the Middle Ages, but the large windows and sloping roofs reveal a Renaissance influence. Regional furniture and an ornate early-17th-century bedchamber enliven the interior. A wine tasting is included to tempt you into buying a case or two of the famous but expensive bottles. ☒ *Le Bourg* ☎ *05–53–63–65–00* ⊕ *www.chateau-monbazillac.com* 🎫 *€8, includes wine tasting* ⊘ *Closed Jan.*

🍴 Restaurants

La Tour des Vents

$$$ | MODERN FRENCH | This welcoming Michelin-starred dining room is the region's best bet for an excellent gourmet meal. Add exceptional prices on the prix-fixe menus (€41 for three courses at lunch, €51 for a four-course dinner) and beautiful panoramic views from both inside and out and it's well worth making

Eating and Drinking in the Dordogne

The Dordogne—or as the French like to call it, the Périgord—is considered by those in the know to have one of the best regional cuisines in the country. The rich resources of the Périgord are legendary: forests and fields are alive with wild game feasting on the nuts and leaves of chestnut, walnut, and oak trees, which encourages the growth of rare mushrooms and coveted truffles. Few regions in France can boast such a wide selection of local meats (particularly the famed Dordogne foie gras and equally famous pork, duck, and goose dishes); cheeses like Cabécou, Cujassous, Dubjac, Thieviers, and Échougnac; and distinctive wines, liqueurs, and brandies.

Foie Gras

The region has numerous farms with advertisements for foie gras everywhere you go, in shop windows and on road signs, portraying plump geese and ducks happily meandering toward you. At any food shop, you'll find containers of fresh and frozen foie gras, and it is an ever-present restaurant offering, prepared *pôelé* (panfried, usually accompanied by a sweet side), in a terrine (pâté), or otherwise added to your salads and main courses.

Regional Specialties

Many well-known French meat dishes are named after surrounding villages and towns. Don't miss steak *à la Sarladaise* (stuffed with pâté de foie gras) or chicken *à la mode de Sorges* (stuffed with a mixture of chicken liver, mustard, bacon, and herbs). And for a sure dose of truffles, try any dish with *sauce Périgueux* or *à la périgourdine* in its name.

Truffles

Between November and March, the region's black gold—a fungus called *tuber melanosporum*—is unearthed and sold for exorbitant prices. Found at the roots of oak trees by trained dogs and pigs, truffles contribute to the local economy, and to the region's celebrated cuisine. Their earthy perfume and delicate flavor have inspired countless dishes prepared by home cooks and restaurant chefs alike.

Walnuts

The importance of *noix* (walnuts) in the Dordogne—and the rest of this country—cannot be overstated, because the walnut is *the* nut here. The French make walnut oil for cooking and drizzling on salads, incorporate walnut meat into savory and sweet dishes, and even make alcoholic beverages infused with walnut flavor. In fact, the aperitif of choice in the Dordogne is a sweet dark wine made from green walnuts picked in summer.

Wine and Liquor

If you are dining on the region's fabulous bounty, the best accompaniment is a local wine, liqueur, or brandy. Bergerac is known for its white wines made from Sémillon and Sauvignon Blanc grapes, and for its reds made from Merlot, Cabernet Sauvignon, and Cabernet Franc varieties. The area also produces excellent white dessert wines from the Sémillon grape. The *fait maison*, or homemade, liqueurs are made from many fruits, including plum, quince, and black currant. Fruit is also favored here for distilling brandies, with some of the best known made from cherries, grapes, pears, and plums.

a detour. **Known for:** outstanding service; beautiful views over valley to Bergerac; stellar presentation. $ *Average main: €26* ✉ *Moulin de Malfourat* ☎ *05–53–58–30–10* ⊕ *www.tourdesvents.com* ⊘ *Closed Mon. and Tues.*

Monpazier

45 km (28 miles) southeast of Bergerac.

Built in ocher-color stone by English king Edward I in 1284 to protect the southern flank of his French possessions, Monpazier, on the tiny Dropt River, ranks among "Les Plus Beaux Villages de France" (the most beautiful villages of France). With three of its original six stone gateways still standing, it is also one of the country's best-preserved *bastide* (fortified) communities.

GETTING HERE AND AROUND
Monpazier is a drive-to destination.

VISITOR INFORMATION Monpazier Tourist Office ✉ *Pl. des Cornières* ☎ *05–53–22–68–59* ⊕ *www.pays-bergerac-tourisme.com.*

◉ Sights

Église Saint-Dominique
RELIGIOUS SITE | This austerely beautiful medieval church dates back to 1284 and the founding of Monpazier, but it was extensively rebuilt in 1450. A new bell, still in use today, was added in 1476. The gorgeous Gothic-style wooden choir stalls were added in 1506. ✉ *Pl. des Cornières* ⊕ *www. fondation-patrimoine.org/les-projets/eglise-saint-dominique-a-monpazier.*

Maison du Chapître (*Chapter House*)
HOUSE | Opposite the church, this chapter house is the finest medieval building in town. Once used as a barn for storing grain, its wood-beam roof is constructed of chestnut to repel insects. ✉ *39 rue Notre-Dame.*

Hotels

★ Hôtel Edward 1er
$$$ | **HOTEL** | One of the many advantages of this small but stately historic château-hotel is its setting between the town and the lovely Dordogne countryside. **Pros:** fully equipped for people with disabilities; close to both town and countryside; excellent restaurant on the premises. **Cons:** some rooms have better views than others; no spa; books up quickly in high season. $ *Rooms from: €147* ✉ *5 rue Saint-Pierre* ☎ *05–53–22–44–00* ⊕ *www.hoteledward1er.com* ⇴ *17 rooms* ❙◎❙ *Free Breakfast.*

Biron

8 km (5 miles) south of Monpazier.

Dominated by the graceful Château de Biron, this time-burnished town offers a glimpse of life in the past lane.

GETTING HERE AND AROUND
You'll want your own wheels to reach Biron.

◉ Sights

★ Château de Biron
CASTLE/PALACE | Stop in Biron to see its massive hilltop castle, the highlights of which include a keep, square tower, and chapel, dating from the Renaissance, and monumental staircases. In addition to the period apartments and the kitchen, with its huge stone-slab floor, there's a gigantic dungeon, complete with a collection of scarifying torture instruments. The classical buildings were completed in 1760. The Gontaut-Biron family—whose ancestors invented great typefaces centuries ago—has lived here for 14 generations. The château has been undergoing renovations on a room-by-room basis since 2013, but these interfere only minimally with the viewing. It's well worth renting an audio guide (€3) to get a

detailed history, plus specifics about the architecture and decor. ⊠ *Biron* ☎ *05–53–63–13–39* ⊕ *www.chateau-biron.fr* 🖃 *€9* ⊘ *Closed Jan.*

Cahors

60 km (38 miles) southeast of Monpazier.

Just an hour north of Toulouse (southwestern France's main city), Cahors makes a fine base for exploring the Lot River valley. Less touristy and populated than most of the Dordogne, this valley has a subtler charm. The clustered towns lining the eponymous river and smaller waterways that cut through the dry, vineyard-covered plateau have a magical, abandoned feel. After visiting them, Cahors (the area's largest community) offers a pleasant change of pace—especially if you're an oenophile. Once an opulent Gallo-Roman town, it's famous for *vin de Cahors,* a tannic red known to the ancients as "black wine." Caesar is said to have taken a supply with him when he returned to Rome; another booster was the local bishop, who went on to become Pope John XXII—in the 14th century he made his hometown libation the communion wine of the Avignon church. Malbec is the most common grape used here; there's also a sizable amount of Merlot in the region, with other vintners specializing in the local Jurançon Noir grape. Many small estates offer tastings, and the town tourist office on Place François-Mitterrand can direct you to some of the more notable vineyards, including the Domaine de Lagrezette (in Caillac) and the Domaine de St-Didier (in Parnac).

GETTING HERE AND AROUND

Multiple direct trains per day from Paris's Gare d'Austerlitz pull into the Cahors station on Place Jouinot Gambetta (5 hrs 10 mins, €65). As in the rest of the Dordogne, buses serving regional routes can be erratic, but they cost only €2 a trip.

VISITOR INFORMATION Cahors Tourist Office ⊠ *Pl. François-Mitterrand* ☎ *05–65–53–20–65* ⊕ *www.tourisme-cahors.com.*

◉ Sights

Cathédrale St-Étienne

RELIGIOUS SITE | The fortresslike cathedral is in Byzantine style, and its cloisters connect to the courtyard of the archdeaconry, awash with Renaissance decoration and thronged with townsfolk who come to view art exhibits. ⊠ *Off Rue du Maréchal-Joffre.*

★ La Villa Cahors Malbec

WINERY/DISTILLERY | For an introduction to Cahors wine, this is the place. Though Cahors may not be as familiar as Bordeaux or Bourgogne, the local appellation is well-known and loved in France. Made from the inky black Malbec grape, this is a robust wine, bold and full-bodied and perfect for pairing with the local delicacies: walnuts, truffles, Rocamadour cheese, and foie gras. Adjacent to the Cahors tourist office, La Villa Cahors and chic Malbec Lounge provide visitors the opportunity to explore, taste, and learn about the local wines in an ever-changing series of tastings, courses, and evening events. ⊠ *Pl. François-Mitterrand* ☎ *05–65–53–20–65* ⊕ *www.tourisme-cahors.fr.*

★ Pont Valentré

BRIDGE/TUNNEL | The town's finest sight is this 14th-century bridge, its three elegant towers constituting a spellbinding feat of medieval engineering. ⊠ *Cahors.*

◉ Restaurants

★ Le Balandre

$$$ | **FRENCH** | Family run for three generations, this handsome Art Deco restaurant, set in the 1920's-era Hôtel Terminus, is an excellent example of French gastronomic cuisine with deep local roots. Dishes—house-made duck foie gras in a gelée of red peppercorns with pineapple chutney; roasted duck breast in caviar butter with grilled leeks and mussels; roasted squab with smoked walnut, asparagus, and artichoke mousseline—are paired with local wines and provide a primer in classic Périgord cooking. **Known for:** regional specialties; service perfect in every way; superb wine list featuring local appellations. [$] *Average main: €27* ✉ *Hôtel Terminus, 5 av. Charles de Freycinet* ☎ *05–65–53–32–00* 🌐 *www.balandre.com.*

★ **L'Ô à la Bouche**
$$ | **MODERN FRENCH** | This contemporary, centrally located restaurant draws gastronomes from near and far with its top-notch seasonal menu. Jean-François Dive's creative market-driven cuisine features artfully presented dishes with a knack for highlighting the natural goodness of vegetables—scallops simmered in celery and endive with chestnut puree and cèpe oil, or poached foie gras with a truffle-infused consommé of Jerusalem artichoke and fennel. The elegant, contemporary dining room is tranquil and relaxing, and the large outdoor terrace offers pleasant views of the square. **Known for:** elegant dining in a chic setting; unbelievable price-to-quality ratio; gorgeous presentation. [$] *Average main: €19* ✉ *56 allées Fénelon* ☎ *05–65–35–65–69* 🌐 *www.loalabouche-restaurant.com* 🕒 *Closed Sun. and Mon.*

🛏 Hotels

★ **Château de Mercuès**
$$$$ | **HOTEL** | Set on a rocky spur just outside town, the former home of the count-bishops of Cahors has older rooms in baronial splendor (ask for one of these), as well as unappealing modern ones (which tend to attract midges); others have a mix of French Moderne and medievalesque furniture that can be jarring, but the ambitious restaurant and great views make up for a lot of sins. **Pros:** unbeatable views; great pool; beautiful, romantic setting. **Cons:** eclectic furnishings may not be to some tastes; spotty air-conditioning; no spa. [$] *Rooms from: €380* ✉ *8 km (5 miles) northwest of Cahors on road to Villeneuve-sur-Lot, Mercuès* ☎ *05–65–20–00–01* 🌐 *www.chateaudemercues.com* 🕒 *Closed Nov.–Mar.* 🔑 *30 rooms* 🍴 *No meals.*

St-Cirq-Lapopie

32 km (20 miles) east of Cahors.

Poised on the edge of a cliff 330 feet up, sublime St-Cirq (pronounced "san- *seer*") looks as though it could slide right into the Lot River. With its steep paths and alleyways among flower-filled balconies, it deserves its reputation as one of the most beautiful villages in France. Pretty boutiques, artisan workshops, and tempting eateries invite lingering. But if you feel energetic, the tourist office will direct you to the mostly ruined 13th-century château—it's a stiff walk away along a path that starts near the Hôtel de Ville. Morning hikes in the misty gorges of the valley are beyond breathtaking.

GETTING HERE AND AROUND

If you're driving, there's plenty of parking up a steep winding hill above the town. Otherwise, the easiest way to access St-Cirq-Lapopie is by taking the Figeac-bound bus from Cahors's train station (20 mins); St-Cirq is a 25-minute hike from where the bus drops you. From the Tour de Faure bus stop, go back to the D181 (sign reads "St-Cirq 2 km"), cross the bridge, and walk uphill—it's a haul, but worth the effort.

VISITOR INFORMATION St-Cirq-Lapopie Tourist Office ✉ *Pl. du Sombral* ☎ *05–65–31–31–31* 🌐 *www.saint-cirqlapopie.com.*

👁 Sights

Croisières de St-Cirq-Lapopie
TOUR—SIGHT | This cruise line offers popular 75-minute boat rides on a picture-perfect 8-km (5-mile) stretch

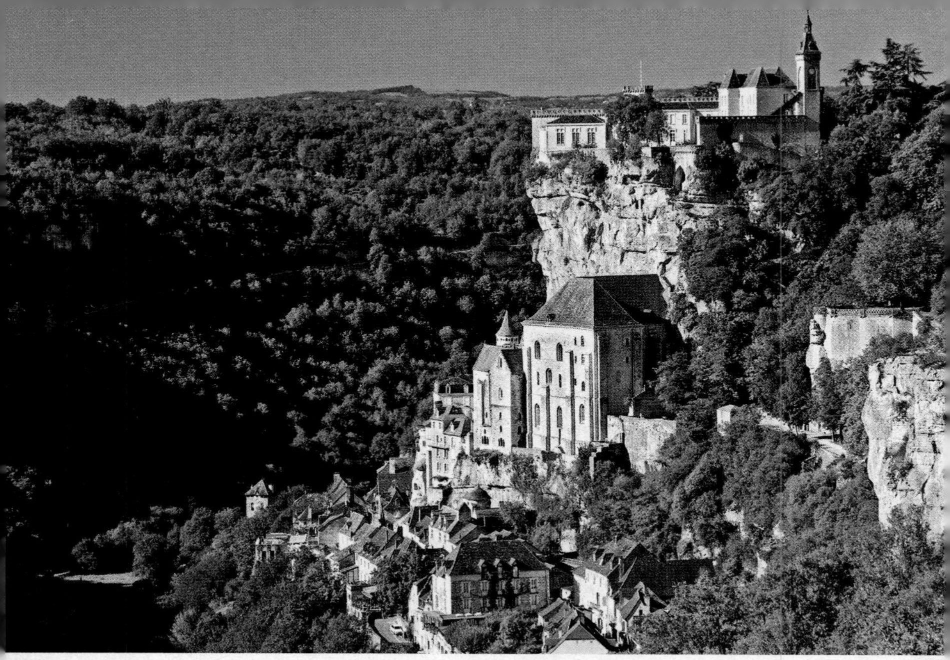

Draped on a cliff 1,500 feet over the Alzou River gorge, Rocamadour is one of the most dazzling towns of the Dordogne.

of the Lot River that meanders below St-Cirq-Lapopie past dramatic cliffs, grottoes, and forest. Adventurous types can rent smaller vessels (€60 for two hours for a five-person boat; €150 per day) to explore river and grottoes on their own. ✉ *St-Cirq-Lapopie* ☎ *05–65–31–72–25* 🌐 *croisieres-saint-cirq-lapopie.com.*

Grotte du Pech Merle

ARCHAEOLOGICAL SITE | Discovered in 1922, the Grotte du Pech Merle displays 4,000 square feet of prehistoric drawings and carvings. Particularly known for its peculiar polka-dot horses, impressions of the human hand, and footprints, this is the most impressive "real" Cro-Magnon cave that is open to the public in France. The admission charge includes a 20-minute film, an hour-long tour, and a visit to the adjacent museum. Tickets are at a premium, with a daily limit of 700 visitors, so for peak summer days book at least one week in advance. If you like cycling, it's lovely to arrive by bike from St-Cirq-Lapopie. ✉ *10 km (6 miles) north of St-Cirq-Lapopie* ☎ *05–65–31–27–05* 🌐 *www.pechmerle.com* 🎫 *€14* 🕓 *Closed Nov.–Mar.*

🛏 Hotels

L'Auberge du Sombral

$ | **B&B/INN** | If location and views are your top priorities, then this old auberge poised on a quaint cobbled square in the center of town is just the place. **Pros:** unbeatable location; good value; charming, historic setting. **Cons:** things could be spiffed up a bit; more rustic than luxurious; somewhat no-frills. [$] *Rooms from: €85* ✉ *St-Cirq-Lapopie* ☎ *05–65–31–26–08* 🌐 *www.lesombral.com* 🕓 *Closed Nov. 15–Mar.* 🔑 *8 rooms* 🍴 *No meals.*

Rocamadour

72 km (45 miles) north of St-Cirq.

A medieval village that seems to defy the laws of gravity, Rocamadour surges out of a cliff 1,500 feet above the Alzou River gorge—an awe-inspiring sight that makes this one of the most visited tourist spots in France. Rocamadour got its name after the 1,000-year-old body of St-Amadour was discovered "quite whole" in 1166. Legend has it that Amadour was actually a publican named Zacheus, who entertained Jesus in his home and, after the crucifixion, came to Gaul, eventually establishing a private chapel in the cliff here. In any case, his saintly remains soon began working miracles, and the sanctuary that housed them began attracting pilgrims who'd ascend the 216 steps to the church on their knees. Making the climb on foot is a sufficient reminder of the medieval penchant for agonizing penance; today two elevators lift weary souls. Unfortunately, the summer influx of a million tourists can itself be agonizing.

GETTING HERE AND AROUND
Brive–Vallée de la Dordogne—the nearest airport, 54 km (34 miles) north of Rocamadour—receives regular flights from Paris and select other European cities. Trains run from Toulouse (about 3 hrs 30 mins, €35) and Brive (40 mins, €9.50); keep in mind, however, that the Rocamadour–Padirac station is 4 km (3 miles) outside the village. Walking takes about an hour, biking 15 minutes, or you can call Taxi Pat (☎ 06–86–18–71–55). Motorists should note that cars are not allowed in Rocamadour; you must park in the lot below it.

VISITOR INFORMATION Rocamadour Tourist Office ⊠ *Maison du Tourisme* ☎ *05–65–33–22–00* ⊕ *www.vallee-dordogne.com.*

Sights

★ Cité Religieuse
RELIGIOUS SITE | The Basse Ville's Rue Piétonne, the main pedestrian street, is crammed with crêperies, tea salons, and hundreds of tourists, many of whom are heading heavenward by taking the **Grand Escalier** (staircase) or elevator (€2.80)

from Place de la Carreta up to the Cité Religieuse, set halfway up the cliff. If you walk, pause at the landing 141 steps up to admire the fort. Once up, you can see tiny Place St-Amadour and its seven chapels: the basilica of **St-Sauveur** opposite the staircase; the **St-Amadour crypt** beneath the basilica; the chapel of **Notre-Dame,** with its statue of the Black Madonna, to the left; the chapels of **John the Baptist, St-Blaise,** and **Ste-Anne** to the right; and the Romanesque chapel of **St-Michel** built into an overhanging cliff. St-Michel's two 12th-century frescoes—depicting the Annunciation and the Visitation—have survived in superb condition. ⊠ *Rocamadour.*

Hôtel de Ville
HISTORIC SITE | The town is split into four levels joined by steep steps. The lowest level is occupied by the village of Rocamadour itself, and mainly accessed through the centuries-old Porte du Figuier (Fig Tree Gate). Past this portal, the **Cité Médiévale,** also known as the **Basse Ville,** though in parts grotesquely touristy, is full of beautifully restored structures, such as the 15th-century **Hôtel de Ville,** near the Porte Salmon, which houses the **tourist office** and an excellent collection of tapestries. If you enter from the top of the town, the **Château** and vertiginous **Ramparts** (€2, coins only) offer tremendous views well loved by bird-watchers for the many birds of prey that circle the cliffs. The picturesque ruins of 14th-century **Hospitalet St. Jean,** with vestiges dating as far back as the 11th century, also offer wonderful views. ⊠ *Rocamadour* ☎ *05–65–33–22–00* ⊕ *www.vallee-dordogne.com* 💰 *€2.*

🛏 Hotels

★ Château de la Treyne
$$$$ | HOTEL | Certainly the most spectacular château-hotel in the Dordogne, this Relais & Châteaux outpost sits amid Baroque gardens perched over the Dordogne River. **Pros:** sparklingly renovated; modern amenities like Jacuzzis and

minibars; impeccable service. **Cons:** restaurant is pricey; rooms with mind-blowing views are not cheap; decor old-fashioned in some rooms. $ *Rooms from: €250* ✉ *15 km (9 miles) northwest of Rocamadour, Lacave* ☎ *05–65–27–60–60* ⊕ *www.chateaudelatreyne.com* ⊗ *Closed Jan.–mid-Mar.* ⇆ *17 rooms* ¶◎¶ *No meals.*

Hôtel Beau Site Notre Dame
$$ | HOTEL | Set in a handsome 19th-century stone mansion smack-dab in the center of bustling Rocamadour, this hotel has charm to spare and a very good gastronomic restaurant. **Pros:** parking is free; marvelous views of the town and surrounding countryside; excellent location in town. **Cons:** no bathrobes or slippers; water pressure lacking in some rooms; attention to detail lacking. $ *Rooms from: €135* ✉ *Cité Médiévale* ☎ *05–65–33–63–08* ⊕ *www.beausite-rocamadour.com* ⇆ *30 rooms* ¶◎¶ *No meals.*

Hôtel Les Esclargies
$ | HOTEL | FAMILY | This contemporary hotel is only a 10- to 15-minute walk from Rocamadour's major sites but feels a world apart from the tourist-clogged town. **Pros:** free parking; exceptional prices; welcoming service. **Cons:** breakfast not included in price; not right in town; spare accommodations. $ *Rooms from: €105* ✉ *L'Hospitalet, Rte. de Payrac* ☎ *05–65–38–73–23* ⊕ *www.esclargies.com* ⇆ *16 rooms* ¶◎¶ *No meals.*

★ Manoir de Malagorse
$$$ | B&B/INN | Using local materials and furnishings, Anna and Abel (a Franco-British husband-and-wife team) have spent more than a dozen years gracefully restoring the 19th-century stone farm buildings on their 10-acre parcel of quietude; in the process, they've brought this refined, family-friendly manor into the 21st century—soothing earth tones set the scene, with light oak floors matching the sand-colored stone walls, which in turn match the blond house dogs. **Pros:** hosts know great food and wine but keep it simple; lovely breakfast included;

idyllic setting. **Cons:** reservations essential for July and August; somewhat remote; forces you to relax. $ *Rooms from: €175* ✉ *26 km (16 miles) northwest of Rocamadour, Cuzance* ☎ *06–89–33–54–45* ⊕ *www.manoir-de-malagorse.fr* ⊗ *Closed Nov.–Mar.* ⇆ *7 rooms* ¶◎¶ *Free Breakfast.*

La Roque-Gageac

55 km (36 miles) west of Rocamadour, 10 km (6 miles) southwest of Sarlat.

Across the Dordogne from Domme, in the direction of Beynac, one of the best-restored villages in the valley is huddled romantically beneath a cliff. Crafts shops line its narrow streets, dominated by the outlines of the 19th-century mock-medieval Château de Malartrie and the Manoir de Tarde, with its cylindrical turret. If you leave the main road and climb one of the steep cobblestone paths, you can check out the medieval houses on their natural perches and even hike up the mountain for a magnificently photogenic view down to the village.

GETTING HERE
No buses serve La Roque-Gageac, so you'll have to come by car.

 ## Hotels

★ Les Hauts de Gageac
$$ | B&B/INN | Your hosts at this welcoming "chambre d'hôtes" (basically a charming B&B, set in an 18th-century stone farmhouse, go the extra mile to make an already delightful place completely enchanting. **Pros:** convenient to the town and principal sites in the area; beautifully situated in the countryside; well-being packages include yoga. **Cons:** only three rooms; must book well ahead in high season; no on-site restaurant. $ *Rooms from: €130* ✉ *La Roque-Gageac* ☎ *05–53–31–28–76* ⊕ *www.leshautsde-gageac.fr* ⇆ *3 rooms* ¶◎¶ *Free breakfast.*

Domme

5 km (3 miles) southeast of La Roque-Gageac.

Stunning views aside, the cliff-top village of Domme offers a hefty dose of history. Some of its fortified walls and doors, dating back to 1280, are still standing; and the Porte des Tours still harbors graffiti from the Knights Templar, who were imprisoned here from 1306 to 1318 awaiting trial. Most visitors, however, come to see something much older—Domme's renowned grotto.

GETTING HERE AND AROUND

Like La Roque-Gageac, Domme isn't covered by public transit; hence a car is required.

VISITOR INFORMATION Domme Tourist Office ✉ *Pl. de la Halle* ☎ *05–53–31–71–00.*

Sights

Grotte de Domme

ARCHAEOLOGICAL SITE | Beneath the fortified city lies the largest natural cave in the Périgord Noir. There are no wall drawings, but the 500-yard-long illuminated galleries are lined with impressive stalactites. The view of the countryside upon exiting the dark cave is stellar. Bison and rhinoceros bones have been discovered in the cave, and you can see them just as they were found. ✉ *Pl. de la Halle, entrance opposite City Hall* ☎ *05–53–31–71–00* 🎟 *€9.*

Hotels

Esplanade

$ | HOTEL | Make sure your room overlooks the Dordogne—the expansive view is what really makes this hotel special. **Pros:** the views are hotel's best asset; good restaurant and lovely terrace; clean rooms. **Cons:** rooms could use an upgrade; customer service lacking; dinner portions are on the small side. [$] *Rooms from: €100* ✉ *Rue du Pont-Carrat* ☎ *05–53–28–31–41, 05–53–28–49–92* 🌐 *www.esplanade-perigord.com* 🕓 *Closed mid-Nov.–mid-Feb.* 🛏 *25 rooms* 🍴 *Free Breakfast.*

Beynac-et-Cazenac

11 km (7 miles) northwest of La Roque-Gageac.

One of the most picturesque sights in the Dordogne is the medieval castle that sits atop the wonderfully restored town of Beynac.

GETTING HERE AND AROUND

You'll want a car to reach Beynac and its châteaux-dotted environs.

VISITOR INFORMATION Beynac-et-Cazenac Tourist Office ✉ *La Balme* ☎ *05–53–29–43–08* 🌐 *www.sarlat-tourisme.com/beynac-et-cazenac.*

Sights

Castelnaud

CASTLE/PALACE | With a fabulous mountaintop setting, the now-ruined castle of Castelnaud, containing a large collection of medieval arms, is just upstream from Beynac across the Dordogne. Make sure to give yourself at least an hour to visit. In summer the castle comes to life with demonstrations, reenactments, and opportunities to try out some of the medieval weapons yourself. ✉ *Beynac-et-Cazenac* ☎ *05–53–31–30–00* 🌐 *www.castelnaud.com* 🎟 *€10.*

Château de Beynac

CASTLE/PALACE | Perched above a sheer cliff face beside an abrupt bend in the Dordogne River, the muscular 13th-century Château de Beynac has unforgettable views from its battlements. Thanks to its camera-ready qualities, it frequently doubles as a film set. During the Hundred Years' War, this castle often faced off with forces massed directly across the way at the fort of Castelnaud. ⊠ *Beynac-et-Cazenac* ☎ *05–53–29–50–40* ⊕ *chateau-beynac.com* 🖃 *€8.*

Château des Milandes

CASTLE/PALACE | Five kilometers (3 miles) from Castelnaud, the turreted Château des Milandes was built around 1489 in Renaissance style, and has lovely terraces and gardens. It was once owned by the American-born cabaret star of Roaring '20s Paris, Josephine Baker, and it was here that she housed her "rainbow family"—a large group of adopted children from many countries. An on-site museum is devoted to her memory. Falconry displays (April–October) are another attraction. From here D53 (via Belvès) leads southwest to Monpazier. ⊠ *Beynac-et-Cazenac* ☎ *05–53–59–31–21* ⊕ *www.milandes.com* 🖃 *€11* ☉ *Closed mid-Nov.–late Mar.*

★ Jardins de Marqueyssac

GARDEN | For Périgord Noir at its most enchanting, head to the heavenly heights of this hilltop garden in Vézac, just south of Beynac. Founded in 1682, its design—including a parterre of topiaries—was greatly influenced by André le Nôtre, the "green geometer" of Versailles. Shaded paths bordered by 150,000 hand-pruned boxwoods are graced with breathtaking viewpoints, rock gardens, waterfalls, and verdant glades. From the belvedere 400 feet above the river, there's an exceptional view of the Dordogne Valley. For a unique and romantic perspective, the garden stays open until midnight under candlelight each Thursday in July and August. You can drink in panoramic views from the terrace of the tea salon, from March to mid-November. ⊠ *Belvédère de la Dordogne, 3 km (2 miles) south of Beynac-et-Cazenac, Vézac* ☎ *05–53–31–36–36* ⊕ *www.marqueyssac.com* 🖃 *€10.*

Sarlat-la-Canéda

10 km (6 miles) northeast of Beynac, 74 km (46 miles) east of Bergerac.

Tucked among hills adorned with corn and wheat, Sarlat-la-Canéda (or simply Sarlat) is a well-preserved medieval town that has managed to retain some of its true character, despite the hordes of visitors. The end of the Hundred Years' War in 1453 led to the construction of beautiful urban buildings in the Dordogne, and Sarlat was especially favored: when the English handed the region back to the French king, he rewarded loyal townspeople here with royal privileges. Before long, a new merchant class sprang up, building sublime stone mansions in the latest French Renaissance style. To do justice to Sarlat, meander through its Cité Médiévale in the late afternoon or early evening, aided by the tourist office's walking map. ■ TIP→ The tourist office also organizes English-language walking tours that give you an in-depth look at the town's architecture; they depart every Thursday at 11 am from mid-May to mid-October (€11). As the capital of the Périgord Noir, Sarlat-la-Canéda makes an ideal base for exploring the area, including the many nearby perched villages and caves.

GETTING HERE AND AROUND

Regular flights from Paris, London, and Amsterdam land at Brive–Vallée de la Dordogne, 51 km (32 miles) northeast of Sarlat. Trains make the trip from Paris in six hours, with a change in Souillac. Fifteen trains daily link Bergerac with Sarlat. Multiple trains per day also arrive from Les Eyzies and Périgueux, with connections in Le Buisson, or direct from Bordeaux. Note that the station is 1½ km (1 mile) northeast of Sarlat's center. Buses connect the town to Périgueux and other area communities.

VISITOR INFORMATION Sarlat-la-Canéda Tourist Office ⊠ *3 rue Tourny* ☎ *05–53–31–45–45* ⊕ *www.sarlat-tourisme.com.*

19

The Dordogne SARLAT-LA-CANÉDA

Did You Know?

Sarlat's tourist office has seasonal walking tours that enable you to fully savor the town's golden-stone splendor—heading out from Rue Tourny, these walks include charming nooks wanderers might otherwise miss.

Sights

Cathédrale St-Sacerdos

RELIGIOUS SITE | The elaborate turreted tower of the Cathédrale St-Sacerdos, begun in the 12th century, is the oldest part of the building and, along with the choir, all that remains of the original Romanesque structure. ⊠ *Pl. du Peyrou.*

Eco-Musée de la Noix

MUSEUM | If you're nuts about nuts, Sarlat is your town—the Périgord is the second-biggest producer of walnuts in France, and those from the Sarladais region are prized. The nuts are sold in the markets in October and November and walnut wood (often preferred here to oak) is used to make beautiful furniture. Visit the Eco-Musée de la Noix, just south of Sarlat in Castelnaud-la-Chapelle, to learn more. ⊠ *La Ferme de Vielcroze, 12 km (7 miles) southwest of Sarlat via D57, Castelnaud-la-Chapelle* ☎ *05–53–59–69–63* ⊕ *ecomuseedelanoix.fr* ⊡ *€5* ⊘ *Closed Nov.–Mar.*

Jardin des Enfers

GARDEN | The sloping garden behind the cathedral, the Jardin des Enfers, contains a strange, conical tower known as the Lanterne des Morts (Lantern of the Dead), which was occasionally used as a funeral chapel. ⊠ *Pl. du Peyrou.*

Place du Peyrou

NEIGHBORHOOD | Sarlat's Cité Médiévale has many beautiful photo ops. Of particular note is Rue de la Liberté, which leads to Place du Peyrou, anchored on one corner by the steep-gabled Renaissance house where writer-orator Étienne de la Boétie (1530–63) was born. ⊠ *Sarlat-la-Canéda.*

Rue des Consuls

NEIGHBORHOOD | The church of Ste-Marie points the way to Sarlat's most interesting street, Rue des Consuls. Among its medieval buildings are the Hôtel Plamon, with broad windows that resemble those of a Gothic church, and, opposite, the 15th-century Hôtel de Vassal. ⊠ *Sarlat-la-Canéda.*

Rue Montaigne

NEIGHBORHOOD | Running the length of the Enfer gardens is Rue Montaigne, where the great 16th-century philosopher Michel de Montaigne once lived. Some of the half-timber houses that line it cast a fairy-tale spell. Rue d'Albusse (adjoining the garden behind the cathedral) and Rue de la Salamandre are narrow, twisty streets that head to Place de la Liberté and the 18th-century Hôtel de Ville. ⊠ *Sarlat-la-Canéda.*

Ste-Marie

MARKET | Opposite the town hall and overlooking Place du Marché aux Oies, the deconsecrated Gothic church of Ste-Marie was redesigned by star architect Jean Nouvel to become the town's covered food hall. Open daily until 8 pm from April through November (every day but Thursday other months), it overflows with everything you'll need for a gourmet picnic or mouthwatering memento. Try to come on Saturday when a farmers' market winds all the way here from the entrance to the evocative Cité Médiévale. All the (liverless) ducks and geese on sale are proof of the local addiction to foie gras; and you'll have the opportunity to stock up on homemade confiture, everything walnut—pastry, oil, liqueur—plus truffles galore. ⊠ *Pl. du Marché aux Oies.*

Hotels

Hostellerie La Couleuvrine

$ | HOTEL | Sarlat is not overly blessed with beautiful historic hotels, so this one stands out—literally—thanks to its massive crenellated tower (an imposing structure that held off besieging forces during the Wars of Religion) and an interior that includes a magically medieval restaurant. **Pros:** excellent prices; vegan-friendly restaurant; some rooms have private terraces. **Cons:** a few blocks east of the Cité Médiévale; quality of food can vary widely; no spa or pool. $ *Rooms from: €97* ✉ *1 pl. de la Bouquerie* ☎ *05–53–59–27–80* ∰ *www.la-couleuvrine.com* ⏳ *28 rooms* ❑ *No meals.*

Hôtel La Hoirie

$ | HOTEL | This charming hotel, set in a 13th-century stone manor about a mile outside Sarlat, has emerged as a top choice in the area and a great way to avoid Sarlat's high-season madness. **Pros:** friendly, attentive service; great price; excellent restaurant. **Cons:** no indoor lounge; pool not heated; a walk into town. $ *Rooms from: €105* ✉ *Rue Jacques Anquetil* ☎ *05–53–59–05–62* ∰ *www.lahoirie.com* ⏳ *19 rooms* ❑ *No meals.*

★ La Villa des Consuls

$ | HOTEL | FAMILY | On a meandering cobbled street in the heart of Sarlat's Cité Médiévale, La Villa des Consuls lets you bed down in either four guest rooms or nine self-service apartments; some are on two floors, and all boast soaring beamed ceilings, modern bathrooms, plus charming views over the Old City's rooftops. **Pros:** exemplary service; extremely reasonable rates; clean, quiet, air-conditioned rooms. **Cons:** staircases in duplex rooms aren't for everyone; breakfasts basic; no in-hotel restaurant. $ *Rooms from: €102* ✉ *3 rue Jean-Jacques Rousseau* ☎ *05–53–31–90–05* ∰ *www.villaconsuls.fr* ⏳ *13 rooms* ❑ *No meals.*

★ Plaza Madeleine

$$ | HOTEL | Constructed in the 19th century, this elegant stone building, just north of the Old Town, has been extensively renovated by owners Monsieur and Madame Florent and in the process, welcome extras—including a pool, Turkish bath, and spa—have been added. **Pros:** spacious lounge to relax in; nice outdoor terrace; cozy billiards room and bar. **Cons:** very hard to find parking nearby; artwork not to all tastes; some rooms on the

Movie-Making in Sarlat

Among French cities, only Nice and Paris have had more movies shot on site than Sarlat. Many of the 45-plus films that have used it as a backdrop are historical epics, but others—most notably Lasse Hallstrom's *Chocolat* (2000) with Johnny Depp and Juliette Binoche—highlight Sarlat's romantic side. The town even has its own annual film festival; each November, stars, producers, and film technicians arrive to host an informational get-together for 500 students (∰ *www.festivaldufilmde-sarlat.com*).

small side. $ *Rooms from: €145* ✉ *1 pl. de la Petite-Rigaudie* ☎ *05–53–59–10–41* ∰ *www.plaza-madeleine.com* ⏳ *39 rooms* ❑ *No meals.*

Les Eyzies-de-Tayac

21 km (13 miles) northwest of Sarlat.

Sitting comfortably under a limestone cliff, Les Eyzies is the doorway to the prehistoric capital of France and a gem for archaeologists. In 1868 skeletal remains of Cro-Magnon man (European early modern humans)—along with artifacts related to their culture—were first found in Les Eyzies. Today a number of excavated caves and grottoes, many with drawings by early man and some with interesting cave formations, are open for public viewing. The tourist office can give you the lowdown on all of them; it also sells tickets for most sites, and you should reserve here because a surprising number of tours sell out in advance.

GETTING HERE AND AROUND

Five trains arrive from Sarlat daily (€10.10); the trip can take anywhere from 50 minutes to 2 hours 30 minutes.

VISITOR INFORMATION Eyzies-de-Tayac Tourist Office ✉ *19 rue de la Préhistoire, Les Eyzies-de-Tayac-Sireuil* 🕾 *05–53–06–97–05* ⊕ *www.lascaux-dordogne.com/en.*

Sights

★ Grotte de Combarelles

CAVE | Want an up-close look at Cro-Magnon cave drawings? Those at les Combarelles are considered among the best in the world. Although traces of pigments have been found, the colors have long since vanished, leaving the sinuous graven outlines of woolly mammoths, cave bears, lions, and astonishingly lifelike reindeer. There are well over 600 drawings all told, and seeing them is an almost mystical experience, especially since only 40 people are admitted per day. ■**TIP→ Hour-long tours are available in English at 11:15; guides on other tours may speak English, but it's the luck of the draw.** ⚠ **This is not a spot for the claustrophobic**—the winding 1,000-foot long cavern is 6½ feet tall and, at most, 3 feet wide. ✉ *1 km (½ mile) from Les Eyzies-de-Tayac, Les Eyzies-de-Tayac-Sireuil* 🕾 *05–53–06–86–00* ⊕ *eyzies.monuments-nationaux.fr* 🎫 *€10* ⊘ *Closed Sat.*

Grotte du Grand-Roc

CAVE | Amid the dimness of the Grotte du Grand-Roc you can view weirdly shaped crystalline stalactites and stalagmites. At the nearby **Abri Préhistorique de Laugerie,** you can visit caves that were once home to prehistoric man. ✉ *Av. de Laugerie, Les Eyzies-de-Tayac-Sireuil* 🕾 *05–53–06–92–70* ⊕ *www.grotte-grand-roc.fr* 🎫 *€8* ⊘ *Closed Jan.*

★ Grotte-Font-de-Gaume

CAVE | Font-de-Gaume is the last French cave with polychrome paintings that remains open to the public. Though discovered in the late 1800s, it wasn't until the early 20th century that the importance of the artwork (dating back to around 17,000 BC) was recognized by archaeologists. Astonishingly graceful animal figures, many at eye level, include woolly mammoths, horses, reindeer, rhinos, and more. The cave's masterpiece is a grouping of five large superimposed bison in vivid color that was uncovered in 1966 during a routine cleaning. Like similar representations in Lascaux, the sophisticated shading techniques used for their bellies and thighs create a stunning impression of dimensionality and movement. ■**TIP→ Guided tours run every 40 minutes, but only 80 visitors are admitted each day—down from 160 in 2012.** The cave is destined to close, so see it while you can. ✉ *1 km (½ mile) from Les Eyzies-de-Tayac, Les Eyzies-de-Tayac-Sireuil* 🕾 *05–53–06–86–00* ⊕ *eyzies.monuments-nationaux.fr* 🎫 *€10.*

La Madeleine

ARCHAEOLOGICAL SITE | As you head north from Les Eyzies-de-Tayac toward Lascaux, stop off near the village of Tursac to discover the mysterious troglodyte "lost village" of La Madeleine, found hidden in the Valley of Vézère at the foot of a ruined castle. The site was abandoned in the 1920s, but it has a picturesque, eye-catching cliff-face chapel that was constructed during the Middle Ages as well as an interesting history. Geologists and anthropologists will especially enjoy learning about the village's backstory, including the prehistoric settlement that was here. Download a guide about the site or take a guided tour—call ahead for English tours. There also are weekly summer workshops for children. ✉ *7 km (4 miles) north of Les Eyzies-de-Tayac, Les Eyzies-de-Tayac-Sireuil* 🕾 *05–53–46–36–88* ⊕ *www.la-madeleine-perigord.com* 🎫 *€7* ⊘ *Closed Dec.–Feb.*

Musée National de Préhistoire (*National Museum of Prehistory*)

MUSEUM | To truly enhance your understanding of the paintings at Lascaux and other caves in the Dordogne, visit the Musée National de Préhistoire. Its renowned collection of prehistoric artifacts—including primitive sculpture, furniture, and tools—attracts large crowds. You can also get ideas at the museum about which excavation sites to visit in the region. ✉ *1 rue du Musée, Les Eyzies-de-Tayac-Sireuil* ☎ *05–53–06–45–65* 🌐 *musee-prehistoire-eyzies.fr* 🎟 *€6* 🕒 *Closed Tues. in June and Sept.–May.*

Pole International de la Prehistoire (*Prehistory Welcome Center*)
INFO CENTER | This well-equipped welcome center provides a solid introduction to the region's important prehistoric sites. Its exhibits, slide shows, and time lines (all free of charge) help you wrap your brain around the immensity of the archaeological riches in the Dordogne. ✉ *30 rue du Moulin, Les Eyzies-de-Tayac-Sireuil* ☎ *05–53–06–06–97* 🌐 *www.pole-prehistoire.com* 🎟 *Free.*

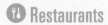

🍴 Restaurants

★ L'Auberge de Layotte
$$ | **FRENCH** | A scenic 10-minute drive from the Grotte du Grand-Roc, this proudly authentic restaurant deep in the Périgord countryside is the perfect finale to a day of exploring. Guests are whisked to a long table to feast on seasonal dishes, many hunted or foraged from the chef's property. **Known for:** one-of-a-kind in France; foraged wild ingredients; copious servings. [$] *Average main: €18* ✉ *Tursac* ☎ *05–53–06–95–91* 🌐 *www.aubergelayotte.com* 🕒 *Closed Jan. and Feb.*

🛏 Hotels

★ Le Vieux Logis
$$$ | **HOTEL** | Built around the most gorgeous dining room in the Dordogne, this vine-clad manor house in Trémolat is one of the region's top hotels. **Pros:** breathtaking grounds; Le Bistrot de la Place offers a value version of the restaurant's delectable food; rooms bright and cheerful. **Cons:** swimming pool is small; dining is expensive; no spa. [$] *Rooms from: €215* ✉ *24 km (15 miles) west of Les Eyzies, Le Bourg* ☎ *05–53–22–80–06* 🌐 *www.vieux-logis.com* 🛏 *23 rooms* 🍽 *No meals.*

Lascaux

27 km (17 miles) northeast of Les Eyzies.

Named a UNESCO World Heritage Site in 1979, Lascaux is one of the world's great galleries of Paleolithic art, a mysterious remnant that scientists still debate the meaning of. Although the actual cave has been closed to the public for more than 50 years, Lascaux IV—a near-perfect replica that replaced Lascaux II in 2017, part of a whole new and sophisticated complex, the Lascaux International Center for Cave Art—is an awe-inspiring must-visit. Nearby, the Château de Losse puts a different spin on this area's rich history.

GETTING HERE AND AROUND

Lascaux IV is best reached by car. If you're driving from Sarlat, head toward Montignac, 26 km (16 miles) north on route D704; the cave is 1 km (½ mile) south of Montignac. If you're relying on public transport, Sarlat has early buses to Montignac (at 7 and 9 am), leaving from Place de la Petite Rigandie.

VISITOR INFORMATION Lascaux Tourist Office ✉ *Pl. Bertrand-de-Born* ☎ *05–53–51–82–60* 🌐 *www.lascaux-dordogne.com.*

👁 Sights

Château de Losse
CASTLE/PALACE | **FAMILY** | There are more grandiose castles in France, but few can offer a more intimate a look at how 16th-century nobles lived than the Château de Losse. Built in 1576 on the site of the family's original

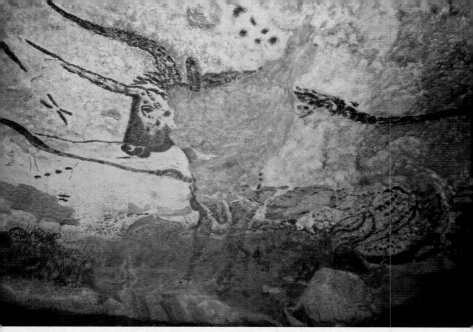

The Raphaels, Leonardos, and Picassos of prehistoric art are on view in the amazing caves of Lascaux IV.

11th-century stronghold, the graceful Renaissance-style structure retains the furnishings, artwork, and other authentic trappings of daily life during the Wars of Religion. The beautiful wooded grounds and formal gardens overlooking the Vézère River make for a lovely stroll, and a charming café with a grassy terrace is the perfect place for a gourmet lunch. ■ TIP➔ **Although tours of the interior are offered in French only, a detailed text in English is provided.** ✉ *8 km (5 miles) southwest of Montignac-Lascaux, Thonac* ☎ *05–53–50–80–08* ⊕ *www. chateaudelosse.com* 🎫 *€10* ⊙ *Closed Sat., and Oct.–Apr.*

★ **Lascaux Cave** (*Lascaux Caves*)
CAVE | In 1940, four school children looking for their dog discovered hundreds of wall paintings in this cave just south of Montignac. The paintings of horses, cows, black bulls, and unicorn on the cave walls were determined to be thousands of years old, thus the cave became famous and attracted throngs of visitors to the site. Over time, the original Lascaux cave paintings began to deteriorate due to the carbon dioxide exhaled by thousands of visitors. To make the mysterious paintings accessible to the general public, the French authorities spent 12 years perfecting a facsimile, duplicating every aspect of two of its main caverns to create Lascaux II. In 2017, Lascaux IV, the most complete replica to date, opened within a sophisticated new complex—the International Center for Cave Art—that incorporates the latest technologies, including virtual reality, 3-D cinema, and digital tablets, for a totally immersive experience. Painted in black, purple, red, and yellow, the powerful images of stags, bison, and oxen are brought to life by the curve of the stone walls under flickering "torchlight," and even the precise humidity and muffled sound. Unlike other caves marked with authentic prehistoric art, Lascaux IV is completely geared toward visitors and literally takes you back in time from the point of view of the original discoverers, archaeologists, and prehistorians. There are several ticketing options, which can

include the Parc du Thot, Le Grand Roc Cave, and the Laugerie-Basse Rock, or Lascaux IV. This is one of the most visited sites in the Dordogne and in summer tickets are at a premium. ■ **TIP→ Tickets sell out quickly, especially in summer; so reserve tickets online up to a day before your visit or at the center on the day of your visit, and arrive early.** ⊠ *Rte. de la Grotte de Lascaux* ☎ *05–53–05–65–60* ⊕ *www. lascaux.fr* ⊠ *€20* ⊙ *Closed Jan.*

Hotels

Manoir d'Hautegente

$$ | RENTAL | Originally a forge, this old, ivy-covered edifice occupies a pastoral nook by the Coly River—a lovely vista to enjoy from your guest room or the impressive restaurant and less expensive bistro. **Pros:** cozy family feel; close to Sarlat; gorgeous setting and gardens. **Cons:** bathrooms need updating; rooms suffer somewhat from an attack of French Moderne style; some rooms could do with an update. $ *Rooms from: €115* ⊠ *12 km (7 miles) east of Lascaux, Coly* ☎ *05–53–51–68–03* ⊕ *www.manoir-hautegente. com* ⊙ *Closed mid-Oct.–Apr.* ⇥ *17 rooms* ⫶ No meals.

Hautefort

25 km (15½ miles) north of Lascaux.

The reason to come to Hautefort is its castle, which presents a forbiddingly arrogant face to the world.

GETTING HERE AND AROUND
Weekdays, CFTA's Bus No. 9 from Périgueux makes two round-trips per day (1 hr, €2); otherwise, you'll have to come by car.

VISITOR INFORMATION Hautefort Tourist Office ⊠ *Pl. Marquis Jacques François de Hautefort* ☎ *05–53–50–40–27* ⊕ *www. ot-hautefort.com.*

 ## Sights

Château de Hautefort

CASTLE/PALACE | The silhouette of the Château de Hautefort bristles with high roofs, domes, chimneys, and cupolas. The square-line Renaissance left wing clashes with the muscular, round towers of the right wing, and the only surviving section of the original medieval castle—the gateway and drawbridge—plays referee in the middle. Adorning the inside are 17th-century furniture and tapestries. ⊠ *Hautefort* ☎ *05–53–50–51–23* ⊕ *www. chateau-hautefort.com* ⊠ *€10* ⊙ *Closed mid-Nov.–Feb.*

Périgueux

46 km (27 miles) west of Hautefort, 120 km (75 miles) northeast of Bordeaux.

For anyone tired of bucolic delights, even a short visit to the region's capital can provide a restorative urban fix. Since Périgueux is the commercial center of the Périgord, the shops here are stylish and sophisticated—some consider them the best reason for visiting this thriving little city. Specialty-food purveyors proliferate (pâtés are the chief export), as do fashionable clothing boutiques—and don't forget Périgueux's appetite-inducing open-air markets.

GETTING HERE AND AROUND
Air travelers from Paris and London can fly into Bergerac, 48 km (29 miles) south, or Brive–Vallée de la Dordogne, 81 km (50 miles) west. By rail, you can get from Paris's Gare d'Austerlitz to Périgueux's train station on Rue Denis Papin in five hours, with a connection in Bordeaux (€75.80). CFTA buses link the gare routiere (also on Rue Denis Papin) with Brantôme, Hautefort, and Bergerac for €2 per trip. Peribus provides public transit within Périgueux itself (€1.25).

VISITOR INFORMATION Périgueux Tourist Office ⊠ *26 pl. Francheville* ☎ *05–53–53–10–63* ⊕ *www.tourisme-perigueux.fr.*

👁 Sights

Cathédrale St-Front

RELIGIOUS SITE | Périgueux's history reaches back more than 2,000 years, yet the community is best known for this odd-looking church, which was associated with the routes to Santiago de Compostela. Finished in 1173 and fancifully restored in the 19th century, Cathédrale St-Front seems like it might be on loan from Istanbul, given its shallow-scale domes and the elongated conical cupolas sprouting from the rooflike baby minarets. You may be struck by similarities between it and the Byzantine-style Sacré-Coeur in Paris; that's no coincidence—architect Paul Abadie (1812–84) had a hand in the design of both. ■TIP➜ **After a mandatory visit to the cathedral, you can make for the cluster of tiny pedestrian-only streets that run through the heart of Périgueux.** ⊠ *Périgueux.*

Farmers' Markets

MARKET | A farmers' market is open daily on Place du Coderc from 8 am to 12:30 pm; on Wednesday and Saturday bigger versions spill over the square to the front of the Hôtel de Ville (Town Hall). If you love your *gras* (fat) as much as the locals do, you'll also want to witness one of the many *marchés au gras* that run on Wednesday and Saturday, November through March. The Saturday morning *marché aux truffes* (truffle market)—held December through February on Place St-Louis—is tempting, too. ⊠ *Périgueux* ⊕ *perigueux.fr.*

Sorges Truffle Ecomuseum

MUSEUM | This museum is open year-round, but if it's truffles you're after, take a guided tour of the newly renovated museum, followed by the truffle groves in Sorges, a picturesque village northeast of Périgueux. Organized by the Sorges Truffle Museum (L'écomusée de la Truffe), the hour-long outings run every Tuesday and Thursday in July and August, beginning at 2:30 for the museum and 3:30 for the hiking trail. ⊠ *Le Bourg, 20 km (12½ miles) northeast of Périgueux via N21, Sorges* ☎ *05–53–46–71–43* ⊕ *www.guide-du-perigord.com/en/tourism/tasting/perigord-products/truffles/sorges-129/the-truffle-ecomuseum-3538.html* 🖃 *€5.*

🍴 Restaurants

⭐ L'Essentiel

$$ | FRENCH | Picturesquely set in the old town, near the cathedral, this chic Michelin-starred restaurant is a big draw for foodies from near and far. Though unanimously lauded as one of the area's best restaurants, L'Essentiel won't give you an ounce of attitude, just excellent, market-fresh cuisine emphasizing the local delicacies—truffles, asparagus, duck, foie gras, chestnuts, and more—served with a smile. **Known for:** service; inventive pairings; tranquil atmosphere. 💲*Average main: €24* ⊠ *8 rue de la Clarté* ☎ *05–53–35–15–15* ⊕ *www.restaurant-perigueux.com* 🕑 *Closed Sun. and Mon. and from mid-Feb.–mid-Mar.*

Un Parfum de Gourmandise

$$$ | FRENCH | Outside the city center, but well worth the detour, Un Parfum de Gourmandise is where natives go for inventive seasonal cuisine. This tiny eatery, which won its first Michelin star in 2019, makes excellent use of the local bounty and has a flair for introducing surprising ingredients: think guinea fowl with tonka-bean-flecked endive or roasted veal with hazelnut oil and sweet potatoes perfumed with bitter orange. **Known for:** its Michelin star; meticulous presentation; good price-to-quality ratio. 💲*Average main: €28* ⊠ *67 cours St-Georges* ☎ *05–53–53–46–33* ⊕ *www.unparfumdegourmandise.com* 🕑 *Closed Mon. and Tues. No dinner Sun.*

Brantôme

27 km (17 miles) north of Périgueux.

When the reclusive monks of the abbey of Brantôme decided the inhabitants of the village were getting too inquisitive, they dug a canal between themselves and their nosy neighbors, setting the *brantômois* adrift on an island in the middle of the River Dronne. How happy for them—or at least for us. Brantôme has been unable to outgrow its small-town status and remains one of the prettiest villages in France. Today it touts itself as the "Venice of Périgord." Enjoy a walk along the river or through the old, narrow streets. The meandering river follows you wherever you stroll. Cafés and small shops abound.

GETTING HERE AND AROUND

If you don't have your own car, CFTA's Bus No. 1A makes a single weekday circuit between Périgueux and Brantôme (45 mins, €2).

VISITOR INFORMATION Brantôme Tourist Office ✉ *Abbaye de Brantôme, 2 rue Puyjoli de Meyjounissas* ☎ *05–53–05–80–63* ⊕ *www.perigord-dronne-belle.fr.*

Sights

Abbaye Bénédictine

RELIGIOUS SITE | Possibly founded by Charlemagne in the 8th century, Abbaye Bénédictine has none of its original buildings left, but its bell tower has been hanging on since the 11th century (the secret of its success is that it's attached to the cliff rather than the abbey, and thus it withstood waves of invaders). Fifth-century hermits carved out much of the abbey, and some rooms have sculpted reliefs of the Last Judgment. Also here is a small museum devoted to the 19th-century painter Fernand-Desmoulin. At night the abbey is romantically floodlighted. ✉ *Bd. Charlemagne* ☎ *05–53–05–80–63* 🎟 *€6* ⏱ *Closed Jan.–mid-Feb.*

Hotels

Le Moulin de l'Abbaye

$$$$ | **HOTEL** | In a storybook setting in the heart of Brantôme, this ivy-covered, turquoise-shuttered stone building looks directly over the placid waters of the Dronne, making this the ideal place to sample the watery charms of this little town (and taste its delights, thanks to the newly Michelin-starred restaurant here). **Pros:** proximity to several good restaurants in the area; beautiful setting; renovated rooms. **Cons:** expensive; management can be quite indifferent; old-fashioned charm lost in the renovations. ⓢ *Rooms from: €225* ✉ *1 rte. des Bourdeilles* ☎ *05–53–05–80–22* ⊕ *www.moulinabbaye.com* 🛏 *20 rooms* ⦿ *No meals.*

★ Le Moulin du Roc

$$$ | **HOTEL** | There is very little about this hotel set in an old farmhouse and walnut-oil mill that doesn't charm, enchant, or delight, from its situation on the Dronne River to its Michelin-starred gastronomic restaurant. **Pros:** some rooms have terraces overlooking the river; electric car at guests' disposal; exquisite grounds. **Cons:** out-of-hotel dining a five-minute drive away; breakfast included only with certain deals; 3 miles from Brantôme. ⓢ *Rooms from: €189* ✉ *Av. Eugène le Roy* ☎ *05–53–02–86–00* ⊕ *www.moulinduroc.com* 🛏 *15 rooms* ⦿ *No meals.*

★ Les Jardins de Brantôme

$$ | **HOTEL** | **FAMILY** | Although it's within easy walking distance of the town, this intimate spot is pleasantly removed from the hustle and bustle of the main tourist center. **Pros:** attentive hosts; tranquil, tasteful setting; close to the town center. **Cons:** pool is on the small side; smallish parking spaces; not all rooms have terraces. ⓢ *Rooms from: €145* ✉ *33 rue de Mareuil* ☎ *05–53–05–88–16* ⊕ *lesjardinsdebrantome.com* ⏱ *Closed mid-Dec.–mid-Jan.* 🛏 *7 rooms* ⦿ *No meals.*

Index

Photo Credits

Front Cover: Pakin Songmor [Description: Beautiful nature of Calanques on the azure coast of France.] **Back cover, from left to right:** Rrrainbow/Shutterstock. abadesign/Shutterstock. Dominik Michalek/Shutterstock. **Spine:** Ron van Elst/Shutterstock. **Interior, from left to right:** Lane Clark, Fodors.com member (1). OT Colmar (2). **Chapter 1: Experience France:** ayane/shutterstock (8). Pierre Carton/Office de Tourisme Pays Basque (10). karamysh/Shutterstock (11). Salome-Abrial/Office de Tourisme Vallée de Chamonix (11). Antoine Collas pour/Toinou1375 (12). JFFotografie/Shutterstock (12). L. Recouvrot/Normandie Tourisme (12). cynoclub/Shutterstock (12). P. Berthé/CMN Paris (13). Takashi Images/Shutterstock (13). canadastock/Shutterstock (14). Sophie Duboscq/Bordeaux Tourisme (14).Joe Sohm/Dreamstime (14). TAITCAVES (14). Jim Prod/OTMSMN (15). Nikolai Korzhov/Dreamstime (15). DAN COURTICE/Semitour Périgord (16). Daniel Thierry/Paris Tourist Office (16). Letot Ludovic (17). Amélie Dupont/Paris Tourist Office (18). NICOLAS VILLION/Lyon Tourisme et Congrès (18). C. Mouton (18). C. Mouton (18). Eva Bocek/Shutterstock (19). Veran/Ville de Nice (19). Romrodphoto/Shutterstock (20). Sophie Spiteri/Office de Tourisme Aix en Provence (20). Alain DOIRE/Bourgogne-Franche-Comté Tourisme (20). LAMOUREUX Alexandre/Tourisme Bretagne (20). Daniel Schoenen/Strasbourg Tourist Office (21). gianliguori/iStockphoto (21). norikko/Shutterstock (26). wanessa-p/iStockphoto (26). wmaster890/istockphoto (26). Oxana Medvedeva/iStockphoto (27). Sergey Fatin/Shutterstock (27). 5PH/iStockphoto (28). Olexander Kozak/Dreamstime (28). margouillat photo/Shutterstock (28). LuckyBusiness/iStockphoto (29). Ekaterina79/Dreamstime (29). Courtesy_Parfums Galimard (30). Anna_Pustynnikova/Shutterstock (31). Paris Tourist Office/Fabian Charaffi/Renzo Piano et Richard Roger (32). Fondation du Camp des Milles – Mémoire et Éducation. (32). Andres Serrano (32). 2009 Musée du Louvre/Stéphane Olivier (32). Paris Tourist Office/Sarah Sergent (33). HUANG Zheng/Shutterstock (33). HUANG Zheng/Shutterstock (33). Dmytro Surkov/Dreamstime (33). mLeonid Andronov/Shutterstock (34). Kirk Fisher/Shutterstock (34). Arndale/Shutterstock (34). Iam_Autumnshine/Shutterstock (35). Krisztian Juhasz/Shutterstock (35). Isogood_patrick/Shutterstock (36). RnDmS/shutterstock (36). Nellmac/iStockphoto (36). EQRoy/Shutterstock (36). tbralnina/istockphoto (36). DaLiu/Shutterstock (37). Southtownboy Studio/Shutterstock (37). Valery Egorov/Shutterstock (37). illpaxphotomatic/shutterstock (37). Boris Stroujko/Shutterstock (37). **Chapter 3: Paris:** Luciano Mortula/iStockphoto (67). Manel Subirats/iStockphoto (78). Directphoto.org/Alamy (81). fabio chironi (93). Fischer/Bilderberg (104-105). Public Domain (105). Rough Guides/Alamy (106). Peter Horree/Alamy (107). Public Domain (107). INTERFOTO Pressebildagentur/Alamy (107).m Public Domain (107). PCL/Alamy (108). THE BRIDGEMAN ART LIBRARY (109). Iegge/Alamy (109). Public Domain (109). Too Labra (109). Steve Vidler/SuperStock (110). Public Domain (111). Hideo Kurihara/Alamy (111). Public Domain (111). Public Domain (111). Walter Bibikow/agefotostock (122). Kevin George/Alamy (125). KavalenkavaVolha/istock (132). PicsFactory/iStockphoto (135). Look/Alamy (138). P. Narayan/agefotostock (156). Aliaksandrkazlou/Dreamstime (160). **Chapter 4: Side Trips from Paris:** Wojtek Buss (171). AM Corporation/Alamy (182-183). Jason Cosburn/Shutterstock (184). Public Domain (184). Michael Booth/Alamy (184). Michael Booth/Alamy (184). Elias H. Debbas II/Shutterstock (184). Public Domain (185). Jens Preshaw (185). The Print Collector/Alamy (185). Tommaso di Girolamo (186). Mike Booth/Alamy (186). michel mory/iStockphoto (186). Hemis /Alamy (187). Jason Cosburn/Shutterstock (188). Public Domain (188). Visual Arts Library (London)/Alamy (188). Guy Thouvenin/agefotostock (188). Public Domain (189). Guy Thouvenin/agefotostock (189). Jose Ignacio Soto/Shutterstock (195). ShutterbugBill, Fodors.com member (198). bobyfume/wikipedia.org (209). Jean-Luc Bohin/agefotostock (212). **Chapter 5: The Loire Valley:** Kevin Galvin (217). vittorio sciosia/agefotostock (229). Travel Pix Collection/agefotostock (236-237). Edyta Pawlowska/Shutterstock (245). Steve Vidler/SuperStock (251). **Chapter 6: Normandy:** San Rostro (257). JTB Photo/agefotostock (267). Renaud Visage/agefotostock (277). Matz Sjoberg/agefotostock (281). S Tauqueur/agefotostock (292). iStockphoto (293). impact productions/Alamy (294). Visual Arts Library (London)/Alamy (295). Martin Florin Emmanuel/Alamy (295). Wojtek Buss/agefotostock (295). Sylvain Grandadam/agefotostock (295). **Chapter 7: Brittany:** danilo donadoni (297). GUIZIOU Franck/agefotostock (302). MATTES Ren /agefotostock (309). Guy Thouvenin/agefotostock (319). Christophe Boisvieux/agefotostock (324). clu/iStockphoto (330). Elena Elisseeva/iStockphoto (332). **Chapter 8: Champagne Country:** Doug Pearson (337). Michel de Nijs/iStockphoto (347). Sylvain Grandadam/agefotostock (355). Yann Guichaoua/agefotostock (359). **Chapter 9: Alsace-Lorraine:** SGM (363). David Hughes/agefotostock (368). Kevin O´Hara/agefotostock (376). Mary Jane Glauber, Fodors.com member (382). ARCO/G Lenz/agefotostock (386). RIEGER Bertrand (394). BODY

Photo Credits

Philippe/agefotostock (398-399). **Chapter 10: Burgundy:** Sylvain Grandadam/agefotostock (403). RIEGER Bertrand/agefotostock (408).RIEGER Bertrand/agefotostock (414). Clay McLachlan/IPN (419). Ernst Fretz/iStockphoto (420). Alain DOIRE - CRT Bourgogne (420). lynnlin/Shutterstock (422). Tomasz Parys/iStockphoto (432). Steve Vidler/SuperStock (439). Austrophoto/agefotostock (441). R. Matina/agefotostock (445). **Chapter 11: Lyon and the Alps:** AJ Kersten, Fodors.com member (447). MOIRENC Camille/agefotostock (460). Saillet Erick/agefotostock (465). CHICUREL Arnaud/agefotostock (470). von Essen hotels (476). GUIZIOU Franck/agefotostock (479). Lazar Mihai-Bogdan/Shutterstock (488). Lazar Mihai-Bogdan/Shutterstock (490). Walter Bibikow/agefotostock (493). nikolpetr/shutterstock (498). **Chapter 12: Provence:** Sylvain Grandadam/agefotostock (501). Guillaume Piolle/wikipedia.org (504). anjči/Flickr (505). Andy Hawkins/Flickr (505). Mike Tumchewics, Fodors.com member (513). Zyankarlo/Shutterstock (517). JTB Photo/agefotostock (520). JTB Photo / age fotostock (524). JACQUES Pierre/agefotostock (530). Minerva Bloom, Fodors.com member (539). Renaud Visage/age fotostock (543). Chad Ehlers/age fotostock (543). David Barnes/agefotostock (544). Bruno Morandi/age fotostock (545). David Buffington/age fotostock (545). Plus Pix/age fotostock (546). Susan Jones/age fotostock (546). Plus Pix/age fotostock (547). Doug Scott/age fotostock (548). Doug Scott/age fotostock (549). SGM/age fotostock (549). David Hughes/Shutterstock (549). Peter Adams/agefotostock (551). MOIRENC Camille/agefotostock (555). Brasil2/iStockphoto (563). Johan Sjolander/iStockphoto (568). **Chapter 13: The French Riviera:** mkinct, Fodors.com member (571). Priamo Melo/iStockphoto (582). trabantos/shutterstock (587). Alan Copson/agefotostock (591). GARDEL Bertrand/agefotostock (602). MOIRENC Camille/agefotostock (604). Renaud d'Avout d'Auerstaedt/wikipedia.org (612). Raga Jose Fuste/agefotostock (618). Richard Anson/agefotostock (623). Giancarlo Liguori/Shutterstock (630). **Chapter 14: Monaco:** Ostill/shutterstock (633). MONTE-CARLO Société des Bains de Mer (642). **Chapter 15: Corsica:** Boris Buschardt/iStockphoto (647). Christophe Boisvieux/Alamy (656). Oleksiy Drachenko/Shutterstock (670). **Chapter 16: Toulouse and the Languedoc:** Javier Larrea/agefotostock (673). FELIX Alain/agefotostock (687). wikipedia.org (693). seeyourworld, Fodors.com member (699). Christian Musat/iStockphoto (706). Jose Antonio Moreno/agefotostock (712). **Chapter 17: The Basque Country, Gascony, and Hautes-Pyrénées:** Josu Altzelai/agefotostock (715). Gonzalo Azumendi/agefotostock (728). GUIZIOU Franck/agefotostock (736). **Chapter 18: Bordeaux and the Wine Country:** J.D. Dallet/agefotostock (743). Benjamin Zingg/wikipedia.org (746). Benjamin Zingg/wikipedia.org (747). Benjamin Zingg/wikipedia.org (747). The BORDEAUX WINE FESTIVAL /Jean Bernard NADEAU (756). Fabrice RAMBERT (758). t56gf, Fodors.com member (763). **Chapter 19: The Dordogne:** P. Narayan/agefotostock (767). Peter Garbet/iStockphoto (781). BODY Philippe/agefotostock (786). CINTRACT Romain/agefotostock (791). **About Our Writers:** All photos are courtesy of the writers except for the following: Lyn Parry, courtesy of Brett Jones.

*Every effort has been made to trace the copyright holders, and we apologize in advance for any accidental errors. We would be happy to apply the corrections in the following edition of this publication.

Notes

Notes

Notes

Notes

Notes

Notes

Fodor's ESSENTIAL FRANCE

Publisher: Stephen Horowitz, *General Manager*

Editorial: Douglas Stallings, *Editorial Director*; Jacinta O'Halloran, Amanda Sadlowski, *Senior Editors*; Kayla Becker, Alexis Kelly, Teddy Minford, Rachael Roth, *Editors*

Design: Tina Malaney, *Director of Design and Production*; Jessica Gonzalez, *Graphic Designer*; Mariana Tabares, *Design & Production Intern*

Production: Jennifer DePrima, *Editorial Production Manager*; Carrie Parker, *Senior Production Editor*; Elyse Rozelle, *Production Editor*; Jackson Pranica, *Editorial Production Assistant*

Maps: Rebecca Baer, *Senior Map Editor*; David Lindroth, Mark Stroud (Moon Street Cartography), *Cartographers*

Photography: Viviane Teles, *Senior Photo Editor*; Namrata Aggarwal, Ashok Kumar, Carl Yu, *Photo Editors*; Rebecca Rimmer, *Photo Intern*

Business & Operations: Chuck Hoover, *Chief Marketing Officer*; Robert Ames, *Group General Manager*; Tara McCrillis, *Director of Publishing Operations*; Victor Bernal, *Business Analyst*

Public Relations and Marketing: Joe Ewaskiw, *Senior Director Communications & Public Relations*; Esther Su, *Senior Marketing Manager*

Fodors.com: Jeremy Tarr, *Editorial Director*; Rachael Levitt, *Managing Editor*

Technology: Jon Atkinson, *Director of Technology*; Rudresh Teotia, *Lead Developer*; Jacob Ashpis, *Content Operations Manager*

Writers: Linda Hervieux, Nancy Heslin, Sean Hillen, Nick Inman, Jennifer Ladonne, Lyn Parry, Virginia Power, Diane Vadino, Jack Vermee

Editors: Amanda Sadlowski, Debbie Harmsen

Production Editor: Elyse Rozelle

2nd Edition

ISBN 978–1–64097–186–8

ISSN 2472–5633

Library of Congress Control Number 2019938467

All details in this book are based on information supplied to us at press time. Always confirm information when it matters, especially if you're making a detour to visit a specific place. Fodor's expressly disclaims any liability, loss, or risk, personal or otherwise, that is incurred as a consequence of the use of any of the contents of this book.

SPECIAL SALES

This book is available at special discounts for bulk purchases for sales promotions or premiums. For more information, e-mail SpecialMarkets@fodors.com.

PRINTED IN THE UNITED STATES OF AMERICA

10 9 8 7 6 5 4 3 2 1

Since swapping Canada for the Côte d'Azur in 2001, **Nancy Heslin** has distinguished herself as a "go-to" expert in the region, from Marseille to Monaco to St-Tropez. She currently serves as Editor-in-Chief of Forbes Monaco and ÖTILLÖ Swimrun Life, and regularly contributes to Women's Running US and various airline magazines. Nancy became a French citizen in 2010; she works her baguette butt off swimming and running along the French Riviera. For this edition, she updated the Experience, Travel Smart, French Riviera, and Monaco chapters.

 Writer **Sean Hillen** updated the Corsica chapter for this edition.

Writer **Nick Inman** updated the Basque Country and Bordeaux chapters this edtion.

 When writer-editor **Jennifer Ladonne** decided it was time to leave her longtime home of Manhattan, there was only one place to go: Paris. Her insatiable curiosity—which earned her a reputation in New York for knowing just the right place to go for just the right anything—has found the perfect home in the inexhaustible streets of Paris. An avid cook and wine lover, she's a frequent contributor on wine, culture, and travel and a monthly columnist for the magazine *France Today*. For this book she updated the Side Trips from Paris, Loire Valley, Brittany, Lyon, and the Alps, Provence, and Dordogne chapters as well as contributed to the Paris chapter.

 British travel writer and editor **Lyn Parry** has lived in France for almost 20 years. In Britain her Masters in Hotel and Catering Management, together with a stint in a luxury four-star hotel, gave her a taste for fine French food and wine. After working for the wine trade in London her nose led her to Bordeaux. Since then she has lived near Paris, and latterly in the Rhône Valley. For this edition of France, she updated the Alsace-Lorraine, Burgundy, and Champagne Country chapters.

Writer **Diane Vadino** updated the Normandy and Toulouse and the Languedoc chapters this edition.

Updating our Paris chapter was our team of writers from *Fodor's Paris 2020*: **Jennifer Ladonne**, **Linda Hervieux**, **Virginia Power**, and **Jack Vermee**.

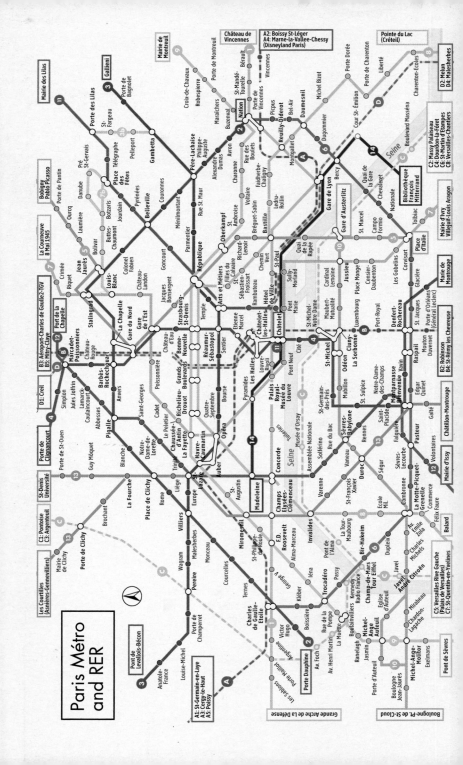

Paris Métro and RER